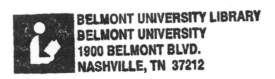

International Directory of

COMPANY
HISTORIES

International Directory of
COMPANY HISTORIES

VOLUME 26

Editor
Jay P. Pederson

ST. JAMES PRESS

AN IMPRINT OF THE GALE GROUP

DETROIT • SAN FRANCISCO • LONDON
BOSTON • WOODBRIDGE, CT

STAFF

Jay P. Pederson, *Editor*

Miranda H. Ferrara, *Project Manager*

Joann Cerrito, Nicolet V. Elert, Kristin Hart, Laura S. Kryhoski,
Margaret Mazurkiewicz, Michael J. Tyrkus, *Contributing Editors*

Peter M. Gareffa, *Managing Editor, St. James Press*

Library of Congress Catalog Number: 89-190943

British Library Cataloguing in Publication Data

International directory of company histories. Vol. 26
I. Jay P. Pederson
338.7409

ISBN 1-55862-385-X

Printed in the United States of America
Published simultaneously in the United Kingdom

St. James Press is an imprint of The Gale Group

Cover photograph: The New York Federal Reserve Building, New York, New York
(courtesy Federal Reserve Bank of New York)

10 9 8 7 6 5 4 3 2 1

CONTENTS _____

Company Histories

PREFACE

The St. James Press series *The International Directory of Company Histories (IDCH)* is intended for reference use by students, business people, librarians, historians, economists, investors, job candidates, and others who seek to learn more about the historical development of the world's most important companies. To date, *IDCH* has covered over 3,600 companies in 26 volumes.

Inclusion Criteria

Most companies chosen for inclusion in *IDCH* have achieved a minimum of US$50 million in annual sales and are leading influences in their industries or geographical locations. Companies may be publicly held, private, or nonprofit. State-owned companies that are important in their industries and that may operate much like public or private companies also are included. Wholly owned subsidiaries and divisions are profiled if they meet the requirements for inclusion. Entries on companies that have had major changes since they were last profiled may be selected for updating.

The *IDCH* series highlights 10% private and nonprofit companies, and features updated entries on approximately 40 companies per volume.

Entry Format

Each entry begins with the company's legal name, the address of its headquarters, its telephone, toll-free, and fax numbers, and its web site. A statement of public, private, state, or parent ownership follows. A company with a legal name in both English and the language of its headquarters country is listed by the English name, with the native-language name in parentheses.

The company's founding or earliest incorporation date, the number of employees, and the most recent sales figures available follow. Sales figures are given in local currencies with equivalents in U.S. dollars. For some private companies, sales figures are estimates. The entry lists the exchanges on which a company's stock is traded and its ticker symbol, as well as the company's principal Standard Industrial Classification codes.

Entries generally contain a *Company Perspectives* box which provides a short summary of the company's mission, goals, and ideals, a list of *Principal Subsidiaries, Principal Divisions, Principal Operating Units,* and articles for *Further Reading.*

American spelling is used throughout *IDCH,* and the word 'billion' is used in its U.S. sense of one thousand million.

Sources

Entries have been compiled from publicly accessible sources both in print and on the Internet such as general and academic periodicals, books, annual reports, and material supplied by the companies themselves.

Cumulative Indexes

IDCH contains two indexes: the **Index to Companies**, which provides an alphabetical index to companies discussed in the text as well as companies profiled, and the **Index to Industries**, which allows researchers to locate companies by their principal industry. Both indexes are cumulative and specific instructions for using them are found immediately preceding each index.

Suggestions Welcome

Comments and suggestions from users of *IDCH* on any aspect of the product as well as suggestions for companies to be included or updated are cordially invited. Please write:

The Editor
International Directory of Company Histories
St. James Press
27500 Drake Rd.
Farmington Hills, Michigan 48331-3535

ABBREVIATIONS FOR FORMS OF COMPANY INCORPORATION

A.B.	Aktiebolaget (Sweden)
A.G.	Aktiengesellschaft (Germany, Switzerland)
A.S.	Atieselskab (Denmark)
A.S.	Aksjeselskap (Denmark, Norway)
A.Ş.	Anomin Şirket (Turkey)
B.V.	Besloten Vennootschap met beperkte, Aansprakelijkheid (The Netherlands)
Co.	Company (United Kingdom, United States)
Corp.	Corporation (United States)
G.I.E.	Groupement d'Intérêt Economique (France)
GmbH	Gesellschaft mit beschränkter Haftung (Germany)
H.B.	Handelsbolaget (Sweden)
Inc.	Incorporated (United States)
KGaA	Kommanditgesellschaft auf Aktien (Germany)
K.K.	Kabushiki Kaisha (Japan)
LLC	Limited Liability Company (Middle East)
Ltd.	Limited (Canada, Japan, United Kingdom, United States)
N.V.	Naamloze Vennootschap (The Netherlands)
OY	Osakeyhtiöt (Finland)
PLC	Public Limited Company (United Kingdom)
PTY.	Proprietary (Australia, Hong Kong, South Africa)
S.A.	Société Anonyme (Belgium, France, Switzerland)
SpA	Società per Azioni (Italy)

ABBREVIATIONS FOR CURRENCY

DA	Algerian dinar	M$	Malaysian ringgit
A$	Australian dollar	Dfl	Netherlands florin
Sch	Austrian schilling	Nfl	Netherlands florin
BFr	Belgian franc	NZ$	New Zealand dollar
Cr	Brazilian cruzado	N	Nigerian naira
C$	Canadian dollar	NKr	Norwegian krone
RMB	Chinese renminbi	RO	Omani rial
DKr	Danish krone	P	Philippine peso
E£	Egyptian pound	Esc	Portuguese escudo
Fmk	Finnish markka	SRls	Saudi Arabian riyal
FFr	French franc	S$	Singapore dollar
DM	German mark	R	South African rand
HK$	Hong Kong dollar	W	South Korean won
HUF	Hungarian forint	Pta	Spanish peseta
Rs	Indian rupee	SKr	Swedish krona
Rp	Indonesian rupiah	SFr	Swiss franc
IR£	Irish pound	NT$	Taiwanese dollar
L	Italian lira	B	Thai baht
¥	Japanese yen	£	United Kingdom pound
W	Korean won	$	United States dollar
KD	Kuwaiti dinar	B	Venezuelan bolivar
LuxFr	Luxembourgian franc	K	Zambian kwacha

International Directory of

COMPANY
HISTORIES

AAF-McQuay Incorporated

111 S. Calvert Street, Suite 2800
Baltimore, Maryland 21202
U.S.A.
(410) 528-2755
Fax: (410) 528-2797
Web site: http://www.mcquay.com

Wholly Owned Subsidiary of Hong Leong Group
Incorporated: 1982 as SnyderGeneral Corp.
Employees: 5,000
Sales: $900 million (1997 est.)
SICs: 3585 Refrigeration & Heating Equipment

A leading manufacturer of air conditioning and air filtration equipment, AAF-McQuay Incorporated comprises two separate operating companies, AAF International and McQuay International. AAF-McQuay operated as SnyderGeneral Corp. until 1994, when the company was acquired by Hong Leong Group Malaysia. SnyderGeneral was subsequently renamed and divided into two companies. AAF International ranked as the world's largest manufacturer and marketer of air filtration products and systems, with operations in 19 countries. Based in Louisville, Kentucky, AAF International represented the vestige of Snyder-General's 1988 acquisition of American Air Filter. McQuay International, an outgrowth of SnyderGeneral's 1984 acquisition of McQuay Inc., was based in Minneapolis. The company designed, manufactured, marketed, and serviced heating, ventilating, and air conditioning (HVAC) equipment for commercial, industrial, and institutional installations. Both companies were operated internationally under the auspices of O.Y.L. Industries Berhad, which was part of Hong Leong Group Malaysia. O.Y.L. Industries was a multinational corporation principally involved in the manufacture, sale, and service of residential and light commercial air conditioning units and systems.

Early 1980s Spinoff

The idea that turned Richard W. Snyder into a multimillionaire within a matter of months occurred to him on January 15, 1981. Snyder, a Kansas City native who earned a B.A. from Indiana University and an M.B.A in finance from the University of Detroit, was at home reading an article in a business journal when the inspiration hit him. At the time, he was in his early 40s, earning a six-figure annual salary as president of Singer Co.'s Climate Control division, a heating and air conditioning business. For more than a decade he had dreamed of owning his own manufacturing company in the heating, ventilating, air conditioning, and refrigeration (HVAC/R) business, but after three failed attempts to buy a small company during the 1970s, he had resigned himself to the fact that, in his words, "I was destined to be a big-company guy for the rest of my career." His career took a decided turn, however, when he read an article about Singer in a business journal. The article speculated that Singer was desirous of exiting the air conditioning business to focus on its aerospace divisions.

At the time Snyder was reading the article, his division was performing poorly. Demand for Climate Control's products, which was heavily dependent on new construction activity, was down 30 to 40 percent. Interest rates were rising to 21 percent, stifling growth, and Climate Control's sales growth rate was lagging behind the rate of inflation. Further, the division did not contribute much in the way of profits, generating a modest pretax profit of 2.5 percent. Against this bleak backdrop, Snyder envisioned an entrepreneurial opportunity. "I thought," he explained to *Forbes* in July 1986, "why shouldn't they [Singer] sell it [Climate Control] to me?" Despite the anemic state of the division, Snyder believed there was hope for the future, that if properly managed, an air-conditioning business was bound to recover once interest rates fell and construction activity increased. "I saw the opportunity to take costs out of the business," he remarked. "Some people thought I was loony."

Without telling Singer, Snyder began to hatch a strategy to acquire the Climate Control division. He drew up a business plan and spent the next seven months trying to secure the financing to make Singer an offer. He worked tirelessly, conducting secret talks with 94 banks and numerous venture capital companies before he gained the financial backing to approach Singer for the first time. He revealed his plan to his employers with a fair bit of trepidation. "They [Singer executives] were a

---

Company Perspectives:

McQuay International is a world leader in the manufacture, sales and service of heating, ventilating and air conditioning equipment principally for the commercial, industrial and institutional markets.

Dedicated to providing innovative, quality products and services that make our customers' lives easier and more comfortable, McQuay has evolved into an international leader in the air conditioning industry with tens of thousands of prestigious installations worldwide.

little bit shocked,'' he later explained. ''They would have been justified in firing me on the spot.'' Climate Control had a book value of $54 million, but during negotiations Snyder persuaded Singer to sell the division to him for $27.5 million. He borrowed $25.5 million from banks, contributed $300,000 of his own money, and raised $1.7 million from venture capital funds. In April 1982 the deal was official, making Snyder the owner of the $120-million-in sales, newly named SnyderGeneral Corp.

After giving his enterprise a new name, Snyder set to work on less cosmetic changes, searching feverishly to cut costs. ''In large corporations like Singer,'' he said, ''there's a built-in bureaucracy. I thought that if we operated on a lean and mean basis, we could do very well.'' Snyder stripped away several layers of management, streamlined distribution, and cut interest expenses 55 percent by accelerating inventory turnover and removing 20 days from accounts receivable. Perhaps more importantly, Snyder instilled a new managerial spirit within the company, imbuing his staff with the same sense of entrepreneurism that had driven him to acquire Climate Control. Although this was achieved in part by ''cheerleading,'' as he called it, Snyder also motivated his management team with more tangible rewards, offering productivity incentives with executive bonuses worth up to 100 percent of annual salary.

The more efficient, more responsive, more motivated SnyderGeneral quickly took on a new luster. Sales climbed energetically, rising at an average of 20 percent during the first several years, and the company was generating ample profits, earning sufficient money to begin reducing its debt. Within nine months the company had paid more than half ($14 million) of its bank debt. By early 1984 Snyder had bought out the venture capitalists who had helped raise the cash to buy the company. Industry observers looked on in amazement, as Snyder resurrected a floundering business. One competitor offered high praise, noting, ''Snyder has lured people away from very reputable, well-run firms by appealing to their entrepreneurial spirit. He's built a solid distribution network, a very energy-efficient product line, and increased his market share.''

1980s Acquisitions

Once Snyder had reduced the company's debt, he began expanding its operations aggressively. He embarked on the acquisition trail, aiming to broaden the company's HVAC/R interests to reduce the cyclicality of its business. In 1984 he completed three acquisitions that diversified SnyderGeneral's business beyond residential heating and air conditioning and into the other two major markets: commercial and refrigeration. The first two acquisitions were Atlantic Richfield's ARCO Comfort Products Co. and the Halstead & Mitchell division of Halstead Industries. Next, Snyder's biggest move occurred. He executed a friendly takeover of $230-million-in-sales McQuay Inc., a publicly traded company with a strong presence in commercial air conditioning. McQuay ranked as one of the industry's giants, with a line of commercial and industrial air conditioners it marketed domestically and overseas. Its inclusion within SnyderGeneral's operations leapfrogged Snyder's company to the number three position in the United States, so that it trailed only Trane Co. and Carrier Corp., each owned by massive multinational parent companies. With the addition of the three acquisitions, SnyderGeneral stood positioned in the HVAC/R industry's three major markets, something Snyder had purposefully pursued. ''Each market peaks at a different time,'' he explained with satisfaction, ''so when one is down, the others are up.''

With everything coming together as designed, SnyderGeneral competed during the mid-1980s as a fast-growing, industry heavyweight. By 1985 annual sales had increased from $120 million four years earlier to $520 million. The company's average annual sales growth of 20 percent was nearly three times the industry average and far more than the 12 percent growth rate Snyder had projected in his business plan in 1981. Snyder, meanwhile, had amassed a fortune, increasing his original investment a hundredfold in three years. Before he purchased Climate Control, Snyder's net worth was estimated at $750,000. By 1985 he was worth an estimated $300 million. ''I'm loving it,'' Snyder gushed. ''I still have to pinch myself sometimes when I go out into the plants and realize this is all mine.''

Snyder stayed on the acquisition hunt during the latter half of the 1980s, purchasing a handful of new companies that added depth and breadth to his company. Among the acquisitions completed were two companies in 1986: the Barry Blower division of Marley-Wylain Co. and Wesper Co., a subsidiary of Paris, France-based Acova S.A. The absorption of Wesper, combined with the addition of McQuay two years earlier, gave SnyderGeneral a sizable presence in the European market, where a substantial percentage of the company's sales would be derived in the years ahead. A presence in Europe also helped Snyder mitigate the company's exposure to market fluctuations because historically the European construction market ran countercyclically to the U.S. construction market. On the heels of these acquisitions, Snyder set a lofty goal in 1987, announcing SnyderGeneral would be a $1 billion company by 1991.

Recessive 1990s Lead to Ownership Change

Snyder nearly met his sales goal by the appointed year, but as sales approached $1 billion in 1991, economic conditions promised to shackle the company's leaping financial growth. SnyderGeneral by this point derived nearly one-third of its sales from Europe, where the company employed 2,000 people in a dozen production facilities. Much of the company's international expansion had come from its 1988 acquisition of American Air Filter (AAF), an air filtration equipment manufacturer with 27 production facilities and sales coming from more than

100 countries. Despite the addition of AAF and Snyder's efforts to insulate the company from capricious economic cycles, economic conditions during the early 1990s hobbled SnyderGeneral's strideful progress. The early years of the decade were pocked by a global economic recession, creating a business environment in which scores of businesses of all types suffered, SnyderGeneral included. For the first time since it was formed in 1984, the company's commercial products group recorded a decline in sales, a ten percent drop that was mirrored by a 21 percent decline in nonresidential construction. As he had been in the early 1980s, Snyder was optimistic that the economic downturn would lead to a sharp recovery. His optimism was fueled by the fall of communism in the Soviet Union, which opened markets behind the Iron Curtain, and by the formation of a unified European market. Increasingly, it seemed, international markets would serve as SnyderGeneral's prime area for growth. Indeed, over the course of the next several years, the international flavor of SnyderGeneral's operations would intensify significantly, ultimately forging an inseparable bond with the country of Malaysia.

A turning point of unprecedented importance in the history of SnyderGeneral occurred in 1994. In a transaction estimated to be between $400 million and $500 million, SnyderGeneral was sold to Hong Leong Group Malaysia, comprising O.Y.L. Industries Berhad, a manufacturer of residential and light commercial HVAC equipment and hundreds of other investors. Concluded in May 1994, the deal ended Snyder's relationship with SnyderGeneral and precipitated sweeping changes. While Snyder diverted his attention to Energyline Systems, a company he started in 1988, the company he left behind was renamed and split in two. In June 1994 SnyderGeneral was renamed AAF-McQuay Incorporated and divided into two major companies, AAF International and McQuay International. Operated internationally under the stewardship of O.Y.L. Industries, the two companies were each given their own chief executive officer and separate headquarters. Based in Louisville, Kentucky, AAF International ranked as the world's largest manufacturer and marketer of air filtration products and systems. The company's products, manufactured in 19 countries, included commercial, industrial, and residential air filters, as well as air pollution control products, machinery filtration, and acoustical systems. To the north, McQuay International designed, manufactured, marketed, and serviced all the HVAC systems and products

formerly undertaken by SnyderGeneral. Based in Minneapolis, McQuay International sold its products under various brand names, including Wesper, JennFan, Barry Blower, and AAF (commercial and institutional HVAC equipment).

As affiliates of Hong Leong Malaysia, AAF International and McQuay International were supported by the massive financial might of the Malaysian conglomerate. With interests in banking and financial services, property investment and development, and in a wide assortment of industrial and consumer products, Hong Leong Malaysia enjoyed a diversified presence in hundreds of international markets. The extensive global reach of the conglomerate was expected to aid the development of AAF International and McQuay International in foreign markets. As each company prepared for the late 1990s, the future held the answer to the question of whether the rampant growth of the 1980s could be replicated in the 21st century.

Principal Subsidiaries

McQuay International; AAF International.

Further Reading

"AAF-McQuay Picks Tambornino, Boehrs to Head Two Companies," *Air Conditioning, Heating & Refrigeration News,* June 13, 1994, p. 1.
Field, Alan M., "Cool Millions," *Forbes,* July 14, 1986, p. 86.
Mahoney, Thomas A., "Dick Snyder Finds New Worlds to Conquer," *Air Conditioning, Heating & Refrigeration News,* April 25, 1994, p. 14.
——, "SnyderGeneral President Says: 'Capitalism Will Fuel a 20-Year Expansion,'" *Air Conditioning, Heating & Refrigeration News,* December 23, 1991, p. 11.
Miller, Mike, "Global Strategy, Products, and Leveraging: A Visit with the New McQuay International," *Air Conditioning, Heating & Refrigeration News,* January 30, 1995, p. 12.
——, "Marketing Takes Top Priority at McQuay International," *Air Conditioning, Heating & Refrigeration News,* October 6, 1997, p. 12.
Miller, William H., "Hot Performer in a Cool Industry," *Industry Week,* October 19, 1987, p. 40.
"SnyderGeneral Is Sold to Malaysian Investors," *Air Conditioning, Heating & Refrigeration News,* April 11, 1994, p. 1.

—Jeffrey L. Covell

ABC Carpet & Home Co. Inc.

888 Broadway
New York, New York 10003-1204
U.S.A.
(212) 473-3000
Fax: (212) 228-1763
Web site: http://www.abchome.com

Private Company
Founded: 1897
Employees: 750
Sales: $125 million (1997 est.)
SICs: 5713 Floor Covering Stores; 5719 Miscellaneous Home Furnishing Stores

ABC Carpet & Home Co. Inc.'s eight-story building in Manhattan's Flatiron district, with nearly eight acres of selling space, is the largest rug and carpet store in the world, attracting about a million visitors each year. The company's array of products include not only carpets and rugs but also antiques, furniture, textiles, gifts and accessories, and bed and bath items. Because of its inventive displays and eclectic offerings, ABC has been called ''Disneyland for rich adults.''

Discount Rug Dealer: 1897–1983

ABC Carpet & Home traces its beginning to 1897, when Sam Weinrib, an Austrian immigrant, loaded a cart with used carpeting and linoleum and pushed it through Manhattan's Lower East Side. His son Max opened a store under the (since demolished) Third Avenue rapid-transit elevated tracks at East 29th Street, and Max's son Jerry, who started selling carpets and rugs in 1947, moved the discount establishment to two floors on 881 Broadway, at East 19th Street, in 1961. This location put ABC at the right place at the right time when the neighborhood—once known as Ladies' Mile for its late 19th-century department and specialty stores—returned to fashion at the beginning of the 1980s.

Weinrib already had broadened his company's range in 1979 by buying Schumacher's area rugs (''every mistake they ever bought,'' he later said). That purchase added more than 500,000 square feet of rugs to the company's stock, and there was not enough room in ABC's quarters to house them. In 1980 Weinrib rented the basement and first floor of what had been the quarters of the century-old former W&J Sloane department store, directly across the street at 888 Broadway. The following year he exercised an option to buy the building. In order to fill the seven-story structure, ABC branched out in 1983 from floor coverings into the broader field of home furnishings. At some point the company also filled adjoining 880 Broadway, which was the original Sloane store.

Chic Home Furnishings Emporium: 1983–95

The ensuing transformation of ABC Carpet into a chic home furnishings emporium is credited to Weinrib's daughter Paulette and her husband, Evan Cole. At this time, many established suppliers would not sell to ABC because of its reputation for discounting, but in the mid-1980s Paulette Cole began stocking the store with antiques and accessories she bought on her travels. Soon she had won a reputation as a trendspotter who sagaciously anticipated the growing importance of home life to aging baby boomers. Evan Cole was described as an astute businessman and brilliant negotiator. By 1993 half of ABC's sales were coming from home furnishings—half of that being furniture—and nearly half of this merchandise was exclusive to the store. ''Our customer is the $100,000 family that comes here to buy quality but save money,'' Evan Cole said that year.

Rugs and carpets continued, of course, to be a staple of the store. By 1988 ABC Carpet was the nation's largest single-store floor coverings operation, with annual sales of $60 million. The floor coverings division was broken down into carpets and area rugs, with the ratio, once roughly equal, now about 75 percent rugs and 25 percent carpets. A 100,000-square-foot warehouse in the Bronx held inventory valued at $3 million. Buying in volume and directly importing many products, ABC was able to offer floor coverings for as little as $5 a square yard, yet its customers included Katharine Hepburn, Meryl Streep, Diana Ross, Peggy Lee, and Keith Richards. A company executive explained, "Everybody is interested in good value. Even people who have tons of money want a good deal."

ABC Carpet & Home began selling furniture in 1988, starting with antiques and reproductions. A year or so later, the company added high-end lines of domestic manufacturers, and in 1992 furniture sales came to about $25 million, or about one-quarter of total store sales. But Evan Cole made no secret of his scorn for what he called the "how-many-suites-are-you-buying" mentality of many furniture producers. "Our furniture business is a collecting business, it's a piece business," he told a reporter in 1993. "People are not decorating, they're collecting. We don't even sell the same chairs with a dining table these days."

Prominent among domestic suppliers of ABC's furniture in 1993 were Baker, Kindel, Hickory Chair, and John Widdicomb. Shoppers were buying traditional shapes with what Cole called "a high face—finishes, painted looks, unique effects, satin-woods, ormolu detailing—instead of flat mahogany." A key element for sales, he said, was the store's ability to deliver 90 percent of its furniture at once. As another ABC executive explained, "It's an old cliché, but everybody in New York wants something yesterday."

ABC Carpet & Home's stylish home accessories and antiques were, in 1993, arranged in vignette rooms that varied from cozy, crowded Victorian settings to a contemporary one filled with natural, undyed cloths. Topical sections such as "White Trash Fifties" and "The Fairy Kingdom" cross-sold various kinds of eclectic merchandise, including not only table-cloths, lamps, and overstuffed chairs but even cookie jars.

ABC Carpet & Home added another 100,000 square feet of selling space during 1993–94 and a number of leased departments, including in-store boutiques by Ralph Lauren and Estée Lauder's Origins and an area for state-of-the-art consumer electronics (to entertain the men while their wives shopped in other departments, according to Evan Cole). The main floor (or "parlor") of the main store, formerly stocked with rugs, was now filled with a wide range of merchandise the company had bought from an old English department store. Furniture, formerly on two floors, was given a third as well.

The space expansion included roughly 50,000 square feet added to the carpet-and-rug store at 881 Broadway, enabling the design-rug department to move across the street from the main floor of 888 Broadway. This new three-level floor covering gallery included several new custom services, including hardwood flooring and vinyl and ceramic tile. Personal shoppers were made available to help customers select furniture, accessories, and fabrics to coordinate with their area rugs. Decorative handmade rugs and Orientals remained in their loft space on the sixth floor of the main 888 Broadway store. ABC also acquired Absolutely Rugs, a retail store based in Boca Raton, Florida, in 1993.

Top selling rugs at this time, according to Weinrib, were flatweaves, including kilins, dhurries, chainstitch rugs, and needlepoints. Natural looks and colors, such as sisals in beige and off-white, also were selling well. Top suppliers included Karastan, Nourisan, Pande Cameron, and Whitney. The best-selling size was $9' \times 12'$. ABC Carpet & Home hung samples in this size rather than the usual industry practice of showing $4' \times 6'$ or $6' \times 9'$ samples. As for carpets, the store had always skipped expensive showroom decoration because the costs would simply be passed on to the consumer, preferring to roll out carpets on the floor rather than show samples.

The second floor decorative home collection established in the main store in 1994 contained what management believed to be one of the world's largest collections of home fabrics in one location. It held about 1,000 bolts of fabric on the selling floor and about 4,000 hanging samples, plus endless varieties of tassels, ropes, and trims, and a huge array of decorative hardware. Racks were organized by fabric type and color. Customers could buy fabric alone or order it made into a variety of textile products, including draperies, slipcovers, spreads, and pillows. The floor also included bedroom displays, huge armoires used as display cases, and muslin-covered sofas and chairs in popular silhouettes to help shoppers choose their own upholstery. Three skilled artisans cut and sewed in a large open workroom in one corner of the floor.

By 1995 ABC Carpet & Home was pulling in out-of-towners beguiled by the company's eclectic selection of merchandise, and these visitors were not necessarily from the suburbs; Los Angeles was its biggest market outside Manhattan. "Browsing through ABC's cluttered floors is akin to shopping in your grandmother's attic," one reporter wrote. "Much of the charm is that the merchandise does not look as if it is for sale. Chandeliers of Venetian glass drip from exposed pipes. Silk pillows are tossed willy-nilly across velvet sofas. Tall, antique secretaries are littered with tiny picture frames, pretty boxes, stationery, perhaps an old ink well. Outrageously priced Italian bedding is thrown across beds as if someone incredibly chic had just arisen from them." The National Retail Federation had cited ABC in 1994 as Small Retailer of the Year.

By this time the Coles were giving most of their attention to creating new departments. They planned to subdivide and relocate established departments in order to accommodate a larger modern-furniture section, specialty goods, gourmet kitchen wares, and a bookstore specializing in interior design and Eastern philosophy. "Paulette's into the spiritual thing right now," her husband explained. Accessories, comprising about 10 percent of the entire business, remained especially dear to her heart. Grouped casually on tables, tossed over counters, and stuffed in baskets and armoires, they did not look as if they were for sale, but each item had a price tag. "We really believe accessories are like little spokespeople—they're the soul of the store," she told a reporter. Interviewed by another reporter, she said, "We've created a bit of romantic fantasy and warmth in what is sometimes considered a cold, unfriendly city."

A visit in 1995 to ABC Carpet & Home's main building began with the 27-window display, filled with fanciful and varied offerings. The first floor included fragrances; decorative and antique accessories, including pillows and throws; stationery and books; and "Spirit East" (including tatami mats and "meditation cushions"), "Things for Men," (including canes, sailboat models, and antique pocket watches), and "ABC Baby." The lower mezzanine was divided into Moroccan, Indian Teak, Indonesian, Stone Statuary, South American, and Pine imported furniture, while the upper mezzanine housed art deco and 20th-century modern furniture and a section for Herman Miller.

The second floor included tapestries, curtains, draperies, trimmings, custom upholstery, and hanging fabric samples. The third floor included bedding and bath, two Ralph Lauren shops, and lighting and fixtures. The fourth and fifth floors carried furniture, upholstery, formal reproductions and antiques (including an eight-foot folk art birdhouse), and another Ralph Lauren section. The top floor, a loft with 25-foot ceilings, held decorative handmade rugs, among them antique Aubussons from France, and Oriental carpets.

Expansion to Other Sites: 1996–98

In 1996 ABC Carpet & Home opened a cafe in a dormer display space in the back of the first floor of the main building. Presided over by the chef at former mayor Edward Koch's official residence, the breakfast to dinner menu was contemporary American, with bagels and muffins, pancakes, salads, sandwiches, and simple entrees, all for less than $10. Evan Cole said he planned to add a food shop and housewares department before the end of the year.

The year 1996 also brought other innovations. On Memorial Day weekend, ABC Carpet & Home held its first "On the Road" promotion in a Morristown, New Jersey, armory, offering a combined clearance sale and special price purchases. It featured 2,000 pieces of furniture, 2,000 rugs, and 20,000 sheets. In July the road show moved to the fashionable Hamptons on Long Island, and two further such events were being lined up for later in the year. ABC also launched a 60,000-square-foot outlet store in Delray Beach, Florida, with "no white Florida furniture," according to Evan Cole. The company decorated this white, cinder-block building with a 330-foot trompe l'oeil mural of the façade of 888 Broadway. In December the company formed HomeBrand, a joint venture with Trade-Am founded to sell home furnishings to retailers.

With the expansion completed in 1994, ABC Carpet & Home had more than 350,000 square feet of selling space, including three floors at 881 Broadway holding 35,000 rugs and thousands of broadlooms. It opened another 50,000-square-foot store, entitled ABC Home on the Road, in 1997 in The Source, an enclosed mall in Westbury, Long Island. In addition, the company maintained 200,000 square feet of warehouse space and a factory store outlet in the Bronx. In 1998 ABC opened ABC Carpet at Harrods, an 8,000-square-foot area on the third floor of the famed London department store, offering more than 20,000 handmade rugs.

Further Reading

"ABC Carpet & Home Takes Store on the Road," *HFN/Home Furnishings News,* September 15, 1997, p. 4.

Buchholz, Barbara B., "New York Institution's Success Speaks Volumes About Its Approach to Selling Home Furnishings," *Chicago Tribune,* October 1, 1995, Sec. 15, pp. 1, 8.

Griffin, Linda Gillan, "Fantasy Shopping for Home Easy As ABC in the Big Apple," *Houston Chronicle,* December 28, 1995, p. 2F.

Hall, Linda, "Home Team," *New York,* October 9, 1995, pp. 73–77.

Hamlin, Suzanne, "Knowing the ABCs of Carpet & Home," *HFD/Home Furnishings Daily,* August 8, 1994, p. 24.

——, "More Stores Add Menus to Shoppers' Choices," *New York Times,* March 27, 1996, p.. C7.

Herlihy, Janet, "Spotlight on ABC Carpet & Home," *Carpet & Rug Industry,* July/August 1997, pp. 14–16.

Iovine, Julie V., "On 3rd Floor at Harrods: ABC Carpet," *New York Times,* August 13, 1998, Sec. 3, p. 12.

Naughton, Julie, "ABC Carpet in Florida Foray," *HFD/Home Furnishings Daily,* July 19, 1993, p. 28.

Rigg, Cynthia, "As Easy As ABC," *Crain's New York Business,* July 19–25, 1993, pp. 1, 38.

Sloan, Carole, "ABC Expansion to Boost Furniture," *Furniture Today,* July 26, 1993, pp. 1, 36.

——, "ABC Launching 2 New Divisions," *Furniture Today,* May 27, 1996, pp. 1, 94.

Strom, Stephanie, "Is It the Next New York Miracle?" *New York Times,* January 30, 1995, pp. D1, D6.

Wright, Heather, "ABC Carpet: Big, Bright and Brash," *HFD/Home Furnishings Daily,* July 11, 1988, p. 60.

Wyman, Lissa, "ABC to XYZ of Selling Fabric," *HFN/Home Furnishings News,* September 18, 1995, p. 28.

——, "Globetrotting at Home Brand," *HFN/Home Furnishings News,* December 9, 1996, p. 70.

—Robert Halasz

VOLVO

AB Volvo

S-405 08
Göteborg
Sweden
(31) 59 00 00
Fax: (31) 54 57 72
Web site: http://www.volvo.com

Public Company
Incorporated: 1926 as a subsidiary of AB Svenska
    Kullagerfabriken (SKF)
Employees: 70,330
Sales: US$23.23 billion (1997)
Stock Exchanges: Stockholm London Düsseldorf
    Frankfurt Hamburg Oslo Paris NASDAQ Brussels
    Antwerpen Tokyo Zürich Basel Geneva
Ticker Symbol: VOLVY (NASDAQ)
SICs: 3711 Motor Vehicles & Car Bodies; 3531
    Construction Machinery; 3519 Internal Combustion
    Engines, Not Elsewhere Classified; 3724 Aircraft
    Engines & Engine Parts

AB Volvo is Sweden's largest industrial company and its last independent automobile manufacturer. Renowned for its practical, high-quality trucks and automobiles, Volvo was trying in the late 1990s to shift its image from ''safe but boring'' to ''safe and exciting.'' The company was also struggling in its efforts to remain independent in face of widespread consolidation in the industry.

Early History

Volvo began as a subsidiary of Svenska Kullagerfabriken (SKF), a large Swedish industrial company. In 1924, Scania Vabis ceased production of what had been Sweden's only domestically built automobile to concentrate on more profitable trucks. A year later, with the encouragement of the Swedish Association of Engineers and Architects, SKF began a confidential study of the feasibility of manufacturing its own car. Assar Gabrielsson and Gustav Larson started the project. Ga-

brielsson, who had represented SKF in France and the United States, was a ball bearing salesperson who had closely studied American automobiles. Larson was an engineer with substantial experience in Britain, having worked for the English company White & Poppe.

SKF named the secret project Volvo—Latin for ''I roll''—a dormant product name the company had introduced in 1915 for a line of ball bearings. Independently incorporated, hence the title *aktiebolaget,* or ''AB,'' the venture itself was only informally associated with SKF. The primary owners were Larson and Gabrielsson.

After agonizing over dozens of designs, the two partners settled on a simple model that would negotiate Swedish roads, with their snow, mud, steep hills, and millions of potholes, especially well. The original design, a car called the GL, or ''Larson,'' was assembled at an abandoned SKF ball bearing factory at Hisingen, near Göteborg, from parts ordered out of various supplier catalogs from throughout Europe and the United States.

The first production model, an ÖV4, later called the ''Jakob,'' rolled out of the factory on April 14, 1927. To the horror of all involved, it was discovered that the differential had been misconnected, resulting in a car that had three gears in reverse and only one gear for forward motion. The mistake took only ten minutes to correct and Volvo survived the comical episode.

With 60 workers turning out five cars a week, the company proceeded with plans to manufacture a truck. The first truck model, introduced in 1928, was, in fact, from a design that predated the GL by four months. Volvo trucks, equipped with in-line six-cylinder engines, became extremely popular. Whereas auto sales remained slow and their profits only marginal, the truck models consistently sold out. Profits from truck sales financed the operation for the next 20 years.

Volvo's cars and trucks were extremely sturdy and, by many measures, better assembled than American and other European models. In what was the most effective advertising of the day, Volvo models won several speed and endurance tests, racing across Sweden and speeding from Moscow to Leningrad, and later winning contests in Monte Carlo and Argentina. However, because both Larson and Gabrielsson detested automobile contests, Volvo refused to sponsor racers.

Volvo introduced a six-cylinder model, the PV651, in 1929, which proved highly successful with the lucrative taxicab market, and a larger version was soon planned. The following year, with the introduction of several new models and strong sales, Volvo purchased a controlling interest in its engine manufacturer, Pentaverken, located in Skövde. The company also purchased the Hisingen plant from SKF.

Challenges During the Great Depression and World War II

As the economy ground to a halt from the effects of the Great Depression, car sales fell into a slump. General Motors (GM), which had a Chevrolet plant in Stockholm at the time, attacked Volvo for being, in effect, ''kit made.'' The company conducted a quick study that revealed that its cars were about 90 percent domestic content. Thus, it hit back at GM, advertising its products as ''the *Swedish* cars.''

Such competition kept Volvo on the alert, constantly studying other manufacturers. In 1935 it brought out a revolutionary new design: the PV36 Carioca, a streamlined art deco model, named for a popular South American dance. Later that year, the company took full control of Pentaverken and floated its first share issue on the Stockholm exchange.

While the company was introducing variations on the PV36, growing hostilities in Europe began to interrupt fuel supplies. In response, Volvo developed a means of manufacturing a combustible gas from charcoal in 1939. However, by this time the government was prohibiting the operation of private cars. Despite the lack of crucial foreign components, Volvo continued production of cars and trucks, though mostly for military use. The company pressed on with new civilian designs in anticipation of the end of the war. Meanwhile, in 1942, Volvo took control of Svenska Flygmotor, a precision engineering company, and Köpings Mekaniska Verkstad, a gear and gearbox manufacturer.

In 1944 Volvo began taking orders for its long-awaited new model, the PV444—priced at SEK4800, the same as the 1927 ÖV4—although actual production had to wait until the end of the war the following summer. By then, however, an engineering strike crippled production, and gasoline was still under strict ration. Plans to introduce another model, the PV60, were similarly delayed in 1946 when a sheet metal supplier could not be lined up.

By 1947 these problems were alleviated, and production began, albeit slowly. Volvo now had a domestic competitor, Scania, which resumed automobile manufacturing after the war

as a unit of SAAB, an aircraft manufacturer. By 1948, car sales exceeded truck and bus sales for the first time, and by 1950, Volvo employed 6,000 people and had turned out more than 100,000 vehicles, including 20,000 for export.

The 1950s and 1960s: New Models and Markets

Gustav Larson retired from active involvement with Volvo in 1952 but continued to serve the company as an advisor. The following year, the company introduced the Duett, the first of many family estate cars designed for work and leisure. In 1954 Volvo had built a new truck factory in Göteborg, increasing annual production capacity to 15,000 vehicles, and had introduced fuel injection systems and turbochargers on its diesel engines.

In 1955 Volvo rolled out a small convertible with a plastic body and puncture proof tires called the Sport. Sales languished, however, and production was halted after only 67 had been produced. Volvo had better luck the next year with the Amazon, a welded frame sedan that borrowed heavily from other European models of the day. Later that year, Assar Gabrielsson also retired. He was succeeded by Gunnar Engellau, the head of Volvo Flygmotor.

Engellau took Volvo's helm at the height of the Suez Canal Crisis when all shipping, including oil, was refused passage. The resulting oil shortage in Sweden caused a severe drop in automobile sales. Engellau gambled that the crisis would be resolved within months, and he began laying plans for a major expansion, deciding to boldly go after export markets, especially the huge American market. Engellau was correct, and when the crisis subsided, Volvo was ready to meet the demand for new cars.

By 1959, with more than 15,000 employees, Volvo broke ground on a massive new production facility at Torslanda, near Hisingen. The following year, the company introduced a new sports car, the P1800. The car was prominently featured in the British television series ''The Saint.'' In fact, the car was even driven in private life by the star of the series, Roger Moore.

As other models in the product line were improved with ergonomically designed seats and new safety features—including the introduction of three-point safety belts as standard equipment in 1959—Volvo offered a revolutionary five-year engine guarantee that included coverage for damage resulting from accidents. The Swedish insurance industry, with government backing, sued Volvo for infringing on its business but, after four years of litigation, lost.

In 1963, Volvo opened a plant in Halifax, Nova Scotia, for the assembly of cars for the North American market. The initial 1956 introduction of the PV444 in the United States had been met with indifference, as most Americans still favored large, stylish vehicles such as the Buick Roadmaster. But despite its plain appearance, the PV444 was extremely well built. Subsequent models, such as the PV544, featured larger engines and windows and many new accessories. Furthermore, the company began sponsoring auto races.

The Torslanda plant, with an annual production capacity of 200,000 vehicles, opened in 1964. However, the Swedish government's decision not to join the European Economic Community stood to lock out Volvo sales on the continent due to import duties. In response, the company established an assembly plant at Ghent, Belgium, where Volvo cars would be exempt from import taxes. During this time, Volvo continued to improve its truck lines, rolling out its most powerful rig, the L495 Titan. This was followed by the tilt-cab L4571 Raske-Tiptop.

In 1966, the year before Sweden switched to right-lane driving, Volvo hit the market with a highly practical new sedan, the Volvo 144. Fitted with state-of-the-art safety features, including new safety belts and a new braking system, the 144 won Sweden's Car of the Year award. This model and its variations were especially popular in the United States, where—despite strong competition from Ford's new Mustang—the car sold for $2,995. As sales jumped by 70 percent in Britain, Volvo established another assembly plant in 1968, this one in Malaysia. Meanwhile, in Sweden, Volvo's new Amazon model was leading sales. In 1969 Volvo purchased Svenska Stålpressnings AB, which had supplied car bodies to Volvo since 1927. The following year, plans were laid for a new research and development division, the Volvo Technical Centre, which Volvo funded with between four and five percent of its sales. The VTC, as it was called, began testing hundreds of new safety features that quickly established Volvo as the world leader in automobile safety.

Joint Ventures and Merger Talks in the 1970s

In 1971 Gunnar Engellau retired and was succeeded by Pehr G. Gyllenhammar. Also that year, Volvo employees gained board representation. As part of a ten-year plan to maintain its feverish growth rates of the 1960s, Volvo attempted several industrial associations. The first of these occurred in 1972, when the company acquired a 33 percent interest in the Dutch auto manufacturer DAF. The company then forged links with Renault and Peugeot. While this substantially increased Volvo's production capacity within the European community, the company still regarded the United States as its largest market, bigger even than Sweden.

While auto sales were hurt severely by the oil crisis of 1973–74, its inflationary effects quickly tied up consumers' funds. This only hastened Volvo's need to find new growth markets. During this time, Volvo introduced two new models: the 265 and the DAF-built 66. In 1975 Volvo assumed greater control of DAF's auto business and changed the name of the company to Volvo Car B.V.

In 1977, Volvo proposed a merger with its Swedish rival SAAB-Scania. While the combination would produce one of Europe's largest industrial operations, effectively locking up the domestic market, SAAB did not share Volvo's enthusiasm for the deal and allowed the matter to be dropped entirely. Volvo next turned to Norway, where it had hoped to establish a relationship with the state oil industry and therefore tie Volvo sales to the rising fortunes of the North Sea oil business. But Volvo shareholders rejected the ill-conceived proposal even before the Norwegians had a chance to say no.

Meanwhile, Volvo restructured its operations, converting the car operation into a separate subsidiary. In 1979, with production at an all-time peak, Volvo turned out its four millionth car. It also established a closer relationship with Renault, combining research and product development and selling the French car maker a 9.9 percent interest in Volvo Car Corpora-

tion. Volvo's sales began to rise at this point, causing an increase in share values that sustained a new share issue, followed by two more in 1981 and 1982.

Stronger Sales in the 1980s

Volvo owed much of its strength to its reputation for quality, its 1980 introduction of the first turbocharged auto, the 240, and modifications to the popular 340. Furthermore, in 1982, a top-of-the-line sedan known as the Volvo 760 was introduced and became a symbol for Volvo quality and safety. The 240, the 340, and the 760 designs represented the ideal range for the market.

In 1981 the Dutch government exercised its option to repurchase a majority in Volvo Car B.V., increasing its interest to 70 percent and thereby reducing Volvo's to 30 percent. During this time, Volvo continued its elaborate and expensive experiments with light components and new safety options. Many of these, tried on a series of testbed vehicles, found their way into new variations of the 300 and 700 series cars.

By 1985, Roger Holtback was promoted to head of the Volvo Car Corporation, and Håkan Frisinger was named president of AB Volvo. Under Frisinger's leadership, the company began planning a new production facility in Uddevalla, 80 kilometers northwest of Göteborg. In addition, the Dutch subsidiary introduced a new 400 series compact car.

Catalytic converters, which the company began installing in 1976, became standard on most European models in 1986. New child safety options were also incorporated into Volvo designs as were a variety of electronic sensors and controls.

Volvo's sales were extremely strong during the mid-1980s, due primarily to a devaluation in the Swedish krona. Output continued to rise until 1988, when production targets were ruined by a three-week strike. A few months later, the Uddevalla plant went on line, allowing the company to renovate the Torslanda facility, but too late to make up for lost time.

The Early 1990s: Struggling to Survive

By 1990, Sweden's currency had rebounded, causing export sales to slow. The squeeze was too much for many Swedish companies to bear. In fact, in an effort to stay alive, SAAB concluded a deal with General Motors in which GM gained effective control of the company. Volvo responded by entering into a complex agreement with Renault to share the increasingly high costs of research and product development. As part of a wider reorganization, marketing responsibilities were transferred from regional sales offices back to Göteborg. Dissatisfied with these events, Holtback resigned in protest and was replaced by Björn Ahlström, head of North American operations.

Volvo concluded a deal with Mitsubishi in 1991 in which the Japanese manufacturer would take a one-third interest in the Dutch facility, allowing Mitsubishi to manufacture parts for cars it intended to assemble in Europe. The deal outraged many, including some at Renault, which resented Mitsubishi's attempts to enter the French market. The alliances also indicated that Volvo management believed it could not survive on its own.

In 1990 and 1991, Volvo introduced two new models, the 940/960 and the five-cylinder 850, which had taken more than seven years to develop. The company had spent $2 billion to modernize its plants and develop the new models. The company once again swept a series of quality and safety awards for its automobiles, and the high marks it received from automotive critics and government agencies had a considerable effect on sales. Those able to purchase one chose a Volvo because they believed it to be the safest car available. This fact was not lost upon Volvo's marketing department. In the United States, where there were millions of young, upwardly mobile families, Volvo's reputation for safety was made the primary message of ad campaigns. As a result, the boxy Volvo gained an almost unshakable reputation for being the car of choice among America's "yuppies."

As economic downturns plagued Sweden, the government was faced with the precariousness of several of the country's lines of business and the possible loss of its automobile industry. To bolster the position of Swedish enterprises, the government introduced reforms to labor policies that had previously prevented Volvo and other companies from enforcing stricter absenteeism policies. This, combined with costcutting measures and the rationalization of the product line—dropping such models as the 760—helped to shore up Volvo's position. Nevertheless, the company faced difficult times.

In 1992 Volvo reported a loss of $469 million. Although sales rose by more than $1.6 billion the following year, the company still suffered a loss of $416 million. Hoping to strengthen itself by increasing its connections with Renault, the company worked on a merger in 1993. At the last minute, Volvo board members voted down the deal when they realized their CEO Pehr Gyllenhammar had agreed to a provision giving the French government the right to increase their ownership of the merged company beyond the 65 percent already in the contract. Gyllenhammar resigned, and Soren Gyll took over as chief executive officer.

Gyll pointed Volvo in a new direction: The company would go it alone and refocus on its vehicle and engine manufacturing. The Swedish government had divested Procordia in 1993, and BCP, the consumer products group, became a subsidiary of the Volvo Group. By the end of 1994 Volvo had sold this subsidiary and within a couple years had sold its pharmaceutical interests, a financial brokerage, and its food and brewing businesses. Proceeds from these sales returned Volvo to profitability, reduced the company's debt from $2 billion to $100 million, and enabled the company to buy out its joint ventures with Clark and General Motors.

Part of Gyll's plan for Volvo was sculpting a new image and market niche. With baby boomers aging, the demographics did not favor the safe, reliable cars bought by families with children. In 1986, at the height of its appeal in the United States, Volvo had sold more than 111,000 cars. By 1995, the company was selling fewer than 88,000 cars in the United States. Volvo decided to move into a more upscale market, with sporty and luxury models that would appeal to empty-nest boomers. The strategy met with a mixed response from analysts, some who felt Volvo needed the new racier image to compete and others who claimed consumers were confused by the apparent contradiction between "safety" and "excitement."

In 1997 Gyll suddenly stepped down from the CEO position and was replaced by Leif Johansson. A veteran of the Swedish appliance manufacturer Electrolux, Johansson continued Volvo on its course toward selling more upscale cars. Although Volvo had already introduced more stylish sedans and wagons redesigned from the old 850s, in 1997 it began selling the C70 coupe and convertible. Its price placed it in direct competition with other luxury coupes, like Mercedes' CLK. To foster its new image, Volvo described the C70 in advertisements as the car that "will move you in ways Volvo never has."

Volvo brought in $95 million in 1997 with the sale of its 11 percent interest in Renault. The following year the company divested its remaining shares in Pharmacia & Upjohn. Also in 1998 Volvo added to its racier fleet of cars with the S80, a luxury sedan. Although Volvo had maintained its independence while numerous other small automakers were being swallowed by larger rivals, analysts were skeptical that Volvo could last on its own. In fact, rumors were circulating in 1998 of a merger between Volvo and Volkswagen.

Principal Subsidiaries

BCP Group; Forsakringsaktiebolaget Volvia; AB O Annerstedt; Volvo Aero Support Corporation; Volvo Bus Corporation; Volvo Car Corporation; Volvo Truck Corporation; Volvo Cars Intercontinental AB; Volvo Data Corporation; Volvo Aero Corporation; Volvo Group Finance Sweden AB; Volvo Group Insurance Forsakring; Volvo Parts Corp.; AB Volvo Penta; Volvo Transport Corporation; AB Volvo Technological Development; Volvo Cars of North America, Inc. (U.S.A.); Volvo Penta of the Americas, Inc. (U.S.A.); VL Bus Asia (Pte) Ltd. (Singapore); Steyr Bus Gesmbh (Austria); Volvo Australia Pty. Ltd.; Oy Volvo-Auto Ab (Finland); Volvo Automobiles France S.A.; Volvo Bus Limited (U.K.).

Principal Divisions

Volvo Car; Volvo Truck; Volvo Bus; Volvo Marine and Industrial Engines; Volvo Aircraft Engines; Volvo Construction Equipment.

Further Reading

Berman, Phyllis, "Stretching the Platform," *Forbes,* December 19, 1994, pp. 197–200.

Holstein, William J., "Volvo Can't Play It Safe," *U.S. News & World Report,* July 27, 1998, pp. 40–42.

Lindh, Björn-Eric, *Volvo: Cars from the '20s to the '90s,* (commissioned by Volvo), Förlagshuset Norden AB, 1990.

Olsson, Christer, *Volvo: Sixty Years of Truckmaking,* (commissioned by Volvo), Förlagshuset Norden AB, 1990.

Osterland, Andrew, "Volvo: Swedish for Undervalued," *Financial World,* January 2, 1996, p. 20.

Taylor, Alex, "Too Slow for the Fast Lane? Volvo and Saab," *Fortune,* July 21, 1997, pp. 68–73.

"Volvo Searching Hard for Relief," *New York Times,* June 12, 1991.

"Volvo's U.S. Chief Quits in Response to Reorganization," *Wall Street Journal,* October 1, 1990.

—John Simley
—updated by Susan Windisch Brown

AMERICAN PRINTING HOUSE
FOR THE BLIND, INC.

American Printing House for the Blind

1839 Frankfort Avenue
P.O. Box 6085
Louisville, Kentucky 40206-0085
U.S.A.
(502) 895-2405
(800) 223-1839
Fax: (502) 899-2274
Web site: http://www.aph.org

Nonprofit Company
Incorporated: 1858
Employees: 500
Sales: $16.4 million (1997)
SICs: 2732 Book Printing

The American Printing House for the Blind (APH) is the oldest company in the United States manufacturing products for blind and visually impaired people. It is also the world's largest such company. APH is nonprofit, and operates by means of donations and an annual appropriation from the U.S. Congress, mandated in 1879. APH collected over $6 million in federal funds in 1998. The company is the official supplier of educational materials for blind students at the pre-college level. APH makes braille, large-type, and electronic textbooks as well as educational guides to help students learn braille. It also provides learning materials for preschool children. Besides making books and texts for students, the company also provides an array of services for visually impaired people of any age. The company is a leading distributor of computer software that makes computers accessible to the blind. It provides voice-activation software, which allows computers to respond to voice commands and to speak to blind users. APH also provides talking software that can be used as texts in classrooms.

APH also operates a recording studio to produce hundreds of talking books each year. APH puts out a recorded version of *Newsweek* and *Reader's Digest*. Its recorded magazines are made available to visually impaired consumers at the same time the print version hits the newsstands. The recording studio also produces talking books for the National Library Service for the Blind and Visually Handicapped, covering a wide assortment of fiction and nonfiction.

The company also manufactures or distributes a variety of tools needed by blind people, such as braille slates, special reading lamps, and tactile rulers, as well as paper used by braille writers and special notebooks for storing braille materials.

Early History

The American Printing House for the Blind began as the project of a blind Kentuckian, Morrison Heady. In 1854 Heady commenced collecting donations in order to print a raised letter version of Milton's *Paradise Lost*. Two years later, Heady inspired a blind man in Mississippi, Dempsey B. Sherrod, to try to raise funds in his state. Sherrod's idea was that a national publishing house for raised print books should be established. The enterprising Sherrod convinced the Mississippi legislature to set aside funds for such a publishing house in 1857. For reasons that are not quite clear, the Mississippian selected Louisville, Kentucky, as the site for the new venture. So with the help of the Mississippi legislature, the American Printing House for the Blind was incorporated in Louisville in 1858. Kentucky's general assembly passed an act establishing the company, and a space for it was set aside in the basement of the Kentucky Institution for the Education of the Blind. It was not until 1860 that APH collected its first funds, an appropriation of $1,000 each from Kentucky and Mississippi. The company used the money to buy an embossing press, but with the advent of the Civil War, APH's funding vanished, and the press did not become active until 1866. The first book APH printed was a raised-letter book called *Fables and Tales for Children*.

The big boost to the fledgling press came when the U.S. Congress passed an act in 1879 that provided an annual subsidy to APH. The Act to Promote the Education of the Blind selected the firm to receive funds to make embossed books and other materials for blind students. Congress established a perpetual trust fund of $250,000 to be invested in U.S. bonds, and $10,000 was to be spent annually on the manufacture of books and other materials for the blind. The books and materials were to be distributed free of charge to students at state residential schools for the blind. In 1906 the provision was changed to allow for a simple grant of $10,000 annually. This amount went up through the years, to $40,000 in 1919, then to $75,000 in 1927, and on up until 1962, when APH was allowed to ask for the amount it needed, with no ceiling.

With more money, and more students needing services each year, APH grew rapidly. In only a few years the company was too big for the cramped basement of the Kentucky Institution for the Education of the Blind, and it needed to raze its own building. Its federal funds could not be used for that purpose, but APH was able to get money from the state of Kentucky. APH's trustees bought land adjacent to the old site in 1882, and by 1883 the new building was completed. The company produced more books each year. In 1894, its catalog of publications was 15 pages long, but ten years later the catalog had stretched to 100 pages.

Early 20th Century

Though Congress raised the APH appropriation frequently, the cost of printing books for the blind was inordinately expensive. Braille books (or books embossed in other tactile systems) had to be printed on special heavy paper. The books were printed from brass plates, and these too were expensive. Some figures from 1922 show the enormous difference in price between braille and ink books: $.85 for *Pilgrim's Progress* in ink, versus $21.15 for braille, $1.75 for *Huckleberry Finn* in ink, compared to $31.10 in braille. Adding to the cost was the size and weight of braille editions: Dickens's *David Copperfield* in a 1920s braille edition took up six volumes and weighed 32 pounds. APH was receiving $50,000 a year in the early 1920s, but this came out to only $7 per pupil enrolled in a state school for the blind. No funds were available to make books for adult readers. In 1922 a famous advocate for the blind, M. C. Migel, appealed to President Harding for funds to print braille books for the 450 or so veterans blinded in World War I. Migel's emotional appeal brought $100,000 out of the Veteran's Bureau. APH contracted to print the veterans' books, though its mandate up until then had been only to produce books for school children. However, as the largest braille publisher in the country, it was the only company that could handle the large Veteran's Bureau order.

During the 1920s and 1930s, improvements were made in the braille printing process, eventually bringing down the cost of braille book production. APH had turned out books in five different kinds of type in its beginning years. These early printing systems, such as New York Point and Boston Line Type, had their impassioned advocates, but as braille presses and type-writers improved, braille became the preeminent system in use in America by the mid-1920s. The American Printing House was a leader in bringing superior European braille printing tactics to the United States. APH superintendent E. E. Bramlette was a member of a consulting group that toured braille presses in England, France, Germany, and Austria in 1924. The European presses used the interpoint system, where braille characters were printed on both sides of the page. This saved paper and other production costs. But APH's Bramlette was at first against switching over to the new system, because it would increase labor costs. Bramlette feared that the increased costs would not offset the savings. APH did not endorse interpoint printing until another U.S. braille press began to take away orders from it, because it could produce books more cheaply using interpoint. This competition finally swayed APH, and by the end of the 1920s, the company was producing two-sided braille pages at a lower production cost than it had achieved before.

A notable landmark of the 1920s was APH's publication of a braille edition of *Reader's Digest*. Other news magazines written especially for the blind, such as the *Braille Mirror*, had been available to blind readers earlier. This, however, was the first general news magazine to be translated into braille. The idea for producing a braille news magazine originated with APH's superintendent Bramlette. He chose *Reader's Digest* because it covered diverse topics, both news and literary. The magazine's publisher was enthusiastic, agreeing to forego a royalty fee for the material. After a successful national fundraising campaign, the first braille edition of *Reader's Digest* came out in September 1928. The magazine soon reached over 15,000 blind readers around the world.

The Pratt-Smoot Act of 1931 gave further impetus to the American Printing House's activities. This bill provided a federal appropriation to the Library of Congress to purchase and publish books for the blind. APH, already established as the largest braille publisher in the United States, thus was given contracts to produce more books, especially books for adult readers. APH expanded in other ways, too, in the 1930s. Under the direction of a new superintendent, A. C. Ellis, APH established its own machine shop to manufacture equipment and apparatus needed by the blind. APH machinists designed and built new arithmetic slates, writing frames, and special devices for notating music. In 1936, APH built its own recording studio to record talking books. In 1939, APH extended its publication of *Reader's Digest* to include a recorded version. APH made monthly recordings of *Reader's Digest* on long-playing record discs, and distributed them to the 27 regional libraries for the blind. APH raised the money for this venture with the help of the Reader's Digest Fund for the Blind, which had thousands of donors in 50 countries. The recorded *Reader's Digest* was accepted gratefully by the many people who had gone blind late in life and never learned to read braille.

World War II and After

APH grew rapidly in the 1930s. Staff had grown to more than 80 people, and the company's building had grown too small. American Printing House looked for a new space, but was unable to buy a new building. Instead it leased additional space and set up a fund to pay for remodeling the old building. Nonetheless, all the new products the company had begun in the

1930s were jeopardized when the United States entered World War II. Most of the materials APH used to manufacture braille books, talking books, and the various mechanical apparatus for the blind were on the list of materials critical to the war effort, and so the company had great difficulty getting the supplies it needed. In addition, many employees left, either to join the military or to work in defense-related jobs, which paid better than APH could. The Printing House made do with a smaller staff, who kept the presses going by working longer hours.

After the war was over, business resumed at APH. APH expanded its production of educational aids in the 1950s, making new classroom items such as plastic relief maps and globes. The Printing House also expanded its output of braille magazines. By 1952, it was printing and distributing over 50 different magazines in braille. It also made recorded versions of other magazines. In 1959, the company came out with a talking version of *Newsweek*. With the help of a special fund from the magazine, APH put out *Newsweek* on cassette tape every week.

In the 1960s, APH embarked on some ambitious projects. One was the publication of the *World Book* encyclopedia in braille, called the largest braille project ever undertaken. As in the cases of *Reader's Digest* and *Newsweek*, the publisher of *World Book* was excited about the project and helped raise money for it through a charitable foundation. This, the Field Foundation and Field Educational Enterprises Inc., gave APH $115,000 to pay for the brass printing plates and for the printing and binding of the first 250 copies. It eventually took two years to produce the encyclopedia, which ran to 145 volumes.

APH also began to investigate computer technology in the 1960s. In 1964, IBM donated a computer valued at $2 million to the Printing House. It was used to automate the composition of braille textbooks. This was the beginning of many computer-aided projects at APH.

Staff grew as APH took on more projects. The company built an addition to its administration building in 1970, and planned to expand its manufacturing facilities as well. In addition to braille and recorded books, APH put out many books and educational materials in large type. By 1972, the Printing House was manufacturing around 45,000 copies of large type books annually, comprising close to 500 different titles. That year, the company updated its recording facilities. Instead of LP records, APH started putting its recorded books and magazines on flexible discs and on cassette tapes.

Technological Upgrades in 1980s and 1990s

One of the high points of APH in the 1960s was its publishing of the *World Book* encyclopedia in braille. In 1981, the American Printing House brought out a new edition of the encyclopedia, this time on cassette tape. The recorded encyclopedia took up 219 tapes, each containing six hours of material. A similarly ambitious project was the 1984 publication of the first voice-indexed dictionary for the blind. APH put out the *Concise Heritage Dictionary* on 55 cassette tapes, working with a division of the Library of Congress. Besides these large recording projects, APH made advances in braille publication in the 1980s. By that time, computer technology had made braille production much easier. Almost all aspects of the translation of braille books was done on computer at APH, allowing the Printing House to reduce its staff.

APH's computers were also set to work compiling a database of material for visually impaired people. The Printing House had collected a card file on resources for the blind beginning in 1958. In the 1980s, the card file was automated, and became known as Central Automated Resource List, or CARL. CARL gave access to some 40,000 records. CARL was updated in 1993 to include databases from hundreds of other agencies, and it was renamed CARL ET AL. The data base indexed approximately 120,000 titles, and was available to individuals, school systems, libraries, and educators across the United States and Canada. CARL ET AL underwent more changes in the 1990s. In 1996 APH changed the database's name to Louis, for Louis Braille, and the system became available on the Internet with a speech accessible interface. This meant that any visually impaired computer user with the right hook-up could have immediate access to Louis's records, and APH was able to provide free telecommunications software to users.

APH made some managerial changes in the late 1990s, reorganizing its business office in 1997. The company also joined the Center for Quality Management that year, a nonprofit consortium of companies dedicated to employing the latest and best management practices. In the same vein, APH received assistance from the Toyota Corporation to improve the productivity of its manufacturing facilities. The number of officially registered blind students rose to over 56,000 in 1997, and APH had a growing pool of people needing its resources. The Printing House had many plans to serve its clients better, including investigating new developments in electronic media and working on a National Geographic world atlas for the blind.

Further Reading

History of the American Printing House for the Blind, Louisville, Ky.: American Printing House for the Blind, 1998.

Koestler, Frances A., *The Unseen Minority: A Social History of Blindness in the America*, New York: David McKay Company, Inc., 1976.

—A. Woodward

America Online, Inc.

22000 AOL Way
Dulles, Virginia 20166
U.S.A.
(703) 448-8700
(800) 827-6364
Fax: (703) 265-2039
Web site: http://www.aol.com

Public Company
Incorporated: 1985 as Quantum Computer Services,
   Inc.
Employees: 7,371
Sales: $42.6 billion (1998)
Stock Exchanges: New York
Ticker Symbol: AOL
SICs: 7375 Information Retrieval Services; 7379
   Computer Services, Not Elsewhere Classified

America Online, Inc. is the largest provider of branded information services that are delivered to customers' personal computers (PCs) over phone lines. The company's America Online service and CompuServe service, acquired in 1998, include a wide variety of electronic mail facilities, bulletin boards, conferences, and classes, as well as software, games, and online shopping. America Online's trademark has been easy-to-use, visually oriented services that make the online environment accessible and not intimidating to ordinary customers. America Online got its start in the mid-1980s as an adjunct offering for owners of one type of personal computer and expanded by branching out to other brands. In the 1990s, America Online's offerings were restructured and updated for more current operating systems, and, after the institution of an aggressive marketing drive, the company's customer base skyrocketed. Initially a niche-based product, America Online later expanded through agreements with a wide variety of computer manufacturers and media companies, considerably broadening its offerings and its reach.

Company Origins

America Online was founded by Stephen M. Case, a marketer who worked in the consumer division of PepsiCo Inc. In 1982, Case became intrigued by the possibilities of interacting with other personal computer owners through electronic telecommunications. At the time, there were small networks available for use, including the sharing of news and other data, but they were extremely difficult and cumbersome to use and, as a consequence, were mainly employed by computer buffs or other specialists in the field. Case reasoned that the demand for online computer communication would be much greater if it was easier for people to use.

In 1985, Case got an opportunity to put some of his ideas into practice when he formed Quantum Computer Services, Inc., in partnership with Commodore International, Ltd., a leading manufacturer of personal computers, and Control Video. Using $2 million in venture capital, Case created an exclusive online service for owners of Commodore computers. The deal worked well for both partners. Commodore had an added selling point for its products, and Quantum had a ready-made pool of customers for its service. Named "Q-Link," the service consisted of a few rudimentary bulletin boards, to which users gained access from their personal computers via a telephone modem.

Within two years, the Q-Link concept had proven its merit. Quantum's revenues had reached $9 million by 1987, and the company had started to turn a profit. With the Commodore Q-Link service as a model, Quantum then branched out to offer programs to owners of computers made by other companies. First, the company set up an alliance with the Tandy Corporation, which manufactured IBM-compatible computers. In November 1988, online services for owners of IBM-compatible PCs were introduced. Later, Quantum also began offering services to owners of Apple computers. This service began in September 1989, after a dispute with Apple about whether its name would include the designation "Apple." As personal computers became cheaper and more plentiful and as new, more powerful software and modems were developed, Quantum's subscriber base grew quickly and the company boomed.

In October 1989, Quantum introduced a new nationwide network for computer owners under the name "America Online." Two years later, the company changed its name to that of its main offering. At the same time, the company began to reorganize its operations, consolidating the services it offered to owners of different computers and focusing its efforts on the IBM-compatible and Macintosh market.

In addition, America Online undertook an ambitious marketing campaign to increase the number of its subscribers. Each customer who signed up for the America Online service was charged $7.95 a month for the first two hours spent on the network, and then ten cents a minute after that. In mid-1991, the company expanded its pool of possible subscribers when it introduced services for IBM-compatible computers using DOS operating systems.

Strategic Alliances in the Early 1990s

As part of its push to expand its subscriber base, America Online devised a number of creative ways to attract new users. In keeping with a policy of growth through strategic alliances, America Online entered into a joint venture with the Tribune Company, the owner of the *Chicago Tribune,* in an effort to ease its move into the Midwestern market. America Online created a news and information service designed especially for Chicago by making use of materials from the local daily paper. The product was a success, as thousands of Chicago residents began logging on to the service to exchange opinions on local politics, team sports, and other issues. In addition, America Online gained further capitalization from the deal, as the Tribune Company bought a 9.5 percent stake in the company for $5 million.

In another such arrangement, America Online teamed up with a group called SeniorNet, an organization formed to encourage senior citizens to use computers. With its 5,000 members, SeniorNet provided a new source of customers for America Online, which paid the group a premium for every new member who signed on. In return, America Online offered specialized programming to attract seniors, instituting special news and bulletin services covering topics of interest to them, such as healthcare.

Case described America Online's strategy as being focused on exploiting niches, such as those formed by the senior citizens group. Rather than trying to enroll the general population, as some larger network services did, America Online turned a profit catering to smaller special groups. "We see ourselves as a series of specialized magazines catering to specific interests," he told *Business Week* in 1992.

In May 1992, America Online capitalized on its history of solid growth when it sold stock to the public for the first time. The company's offering was greeted with enthusiasm, and its stock price rose sharply. At the end of June 1992, America Online reported its fifth annual profit in its last six years of operation. The company's revenues had reached $26.6 million, yielding profits of $3.5 million, a stark contrast to the persistent red ink generated by its larger competitors in the online services field. Continued growth and profitability appeared likely, as America Online's subscriber base grew rapidly, increasing by nearly 50 percent every 12 months.

At the end of 1992, America Online announced another important strategic alliance when Apple Computer Inc. signed a licensing and development agreement with America Online to use its technology in Apple's own future information services. The company was to earn $15 million from the agreement over five years. In addition, Apple contracted to pay for America Online's conversion of its technology for use on Apple machines. The two companies announced that they intended to improve the America Online technology and develop it into an industrywide standard for online information services. This joint venture lent weight and authority to America Online's efforts to expand its market share beyond the 10 percent it then held.

In January 1993, America Online expanded its offerings further, introducing an online service designed especially for the Windows operating system. As users of IBM-compatible computers moved in droves to the new, easier operating system, America Online saw an opportunity to convert them to its own graphically based online environment. The America Online Windows service featured the company's trademark high-quality graphics and ease of access and quickly became the most popular new product America Online had ever marketed.

America Online formed another corporate alliance when it reached an agreement with the Sprint Corporation, a long-distance telephone company, in April 1993. In return for discounts on the telephone usage that America Online needed to send its service out to users, America Online gave Sprint a large package of stock options.

Rebuffs Microsoft

By the spring of 1993, America Online's success had attracted the interest of another innovator in the computer industry, Paul G. Allen, a cofounder of Microsoft Corporation. When Allen's stock holdings in the company began to approach 25 percent of America Online's outstanding shares, the company's board of directors moved to prevent him from threatening America Online's independence by adopting a secret shareholders' rights plan that would go into effect if any one party's holdings in the company topped one quarter. In response, Allen filed documents with the Securities and Exchange Commission indicating his interest in acquiring America Online. He also stated that he might seek a seat on the company's board of directors and reported that he had refused to sign a statement proposed by America Online promising that he would not involve himself any further in the company's affairs.

Case and other America Online executives were concerned that any one overwhelming alliance would limit America Online's ability to maneuver and negotiate with other companies. "We've built this company by establishing strategic alliances with a wide range of companies, and we believe it's the best strategy for the company to remain independent," he told the *Wall Street Journal.* On May 11, 1993, Allen met with America Online executives and proposed that America Online and his other high-tech ventures work together to develop software for use in multimedia formats. This overture was initially rebuffed by America Online. Ultimately, Allen withdrew from his attempt to increase his involvement in America Online, as the two parties worked out an agreement to collaborate on some future endeavors.

The fruits of another America Online alliance were unveiled in June 1993, when Casio, Inc., and the Tandy Corporation, two computer manufacturers, introduced the "Zoomer," the first in a new generation of products called personal digital assistants. This device incorporated software developed by America Online to offer electronic communications, such as fax, electronic mail, and access to other online services. The company believed that devices of this sort would open the interactive services market to a much broader segment of the population. Consequently, it agreed to work with Apple on its hand-held Newton product and with Sharp on its Personal Digital Assistant.

Booming Subscriptions in 1993

By the end of June 1993, America Online's annual revenues topped $40 million, an increase of 50 percent over the previous year. In addition, the company's subscriber base surpassed 300,000, an increase of more than 60 percent. Not surprisingly, these gains made America Online the country's fastest-growing commercial online services company. By September, America Online's consumer base had grown even more, as an additional 50,000 customers logged on, pushing subscriber growth to 80 percent.

As America Online's subscriber base grew exponentially, the company began to move away from its early emphasis on niche marketing—the strategy that had provided its initial growth and profitability—toward a stress on a broader array of services that would appeal to its new, broader selection of customers. As part of this effort, the company took a number of steps. It announced that it would offer access to the Internet, a consortium of smaller governmental and academic computer networks that was run as a cooperative. In this way, America Online hoped to tap into the popularity of the Internet, with over 10 million users in more than 50 different countries. The Internet was known as a difficult online environment to master, but America Online hoped to simplify its use by offering its customers access to the network through its own software.

In addition to its Internet venture, America Online also embarked upon a series of alliances with media companies. The service added features from the Knight-Ridder newspaper chain, *Time, Omni,* the *Atlantic,* and the *New Republic,* among other magazines, and from the cable network CNN. America

Online also joined a branch of the Disney entertainment conglomerate called Disney Adventures.

Along with its expanded offerings, America Online instituted an aggressive marketing program to insure that its subscriber base would continue to grow at a healthy rate. The company started selling membership kits at bookstores and computer supply stores and also began to have starter disks bound into selected computer trade magazines. In addition, America Online continued to pre-install its software in many computers, making it particularly easy for new computer buyers to join the online community. Manufacturers incorporating America Online software into their products included IBM, Apple, Compaq, AST, Tandy, NEC, and Compudyne. Finally, in an effort to make its service appear more economical, America Online revised its pricing structure, lowering some costs. Although this move would have a negative impact on the company's revenues, America Online believed that this would be offset by the fact that more people would sign up and those who were already signed up would keep paying for the service longer.

By October 1993, America Online's campaign to increase its subscriber base and enhance its market share had pushed its number of users past 400,000, as its blistering pace of growth continued. The size of the company's customer core had more than doubled in the previous 12 months. In the same month the company reported that quarterly revenues had also doubled in the year before. In addition, the company's web of media linkages became more complex, as it brought online National Public Radio, the San Jose *Mercury News,* and a number of publications produced by Matra Hachette, the world's largest magazine company. In November 1993, America Online sponsored an "interactive event" with Christian evangelist Billy Graham. At a prearranged time, America Online users could send messages to Graham through their computer and receive general or, possibly, personal messages in return.

At the start of December 1993, America Online took another step to maintain its position on the cutting edge of information technology when it announced that it would participate in California with three other companies in delivering its interactive service to customers through a cable network, instead of through a telephone line hooked up to a modem. Cable delivery paved the way for fuller integration of video and sound into the multimedia mix of text and graphics already provided through personal computer-based services. In this way, America Online hoped to position itself to survive and thrive in a changing information services market and mitigate the danger that advances in technology would leave its offerings behind, or that huge information, communications, and computing behemoths, such as AT&T and Microsoft, would move into a revolutionized marketplace and squeeze smaller competitors such as America Online out of business. To this end, the company also announced plans to work with General Instrument, a manufacturer of cable television equipment, to develop services for interactive television.

In addition to these futuristic plans, America Online continued to strengthen its position by adding subscribers, whose number had passed the half-million mark by the end of 1993, and by adding media partners, including Rodale Press, a health and fitness magazine publisher, a reinvented online *Saturday*

Review, and the *New York Times.* In the area of hardware alliances, America Online added Dell and US Robotics to the list of manufacturers that incorporated America Online products into their own.

By the end of January 1994, America Online's subscriber base had topped 600,000 members, and quarterly revenues had grown by 130 percent, as the company's customer base continued to skyrocket. "The unprecedented demand for America Online has caught us by surprise," Case announced in a company press release. "Our focus now is on expanding our infrastructure." As part of that process, America Online cemented its second agreement with a major television network when it added NBC Online to its offerings. In addition, at the end of January 1994, the company announced a further use of the network's interactive capabilities when it joined with Shopper's Express to provide a grocery and pharmacy ordering and home delivery service.

The company's subscriber base grew rapidly throughout 1994, soon exceeding a million subscribers. The same year, American Online acquired Redgate Communications, a multimedia developer, and Booklink Technologies, an Internet browser software developer. Strategic alliances continued to play a prominent role in America Online's growth. To gain access to the European market, the company joined forces in 1995 with the media conglomerate Bertelsmann to offer online services. Within two years, the partnership had more than 800,000 subscribers in Europe. That same year, an alliance with Intuit, maker of the popular financial software Quicken, brought electronic banking services to America Online users.

Facing increased competition from direct Internet providers, America Online sought to add value to its Internet access. In 1995 the company bought WAIS and Medior, two Internet-related businesses, to help AOL subscribers publish their own Web pages. By 1996, however, America Online was still losing customers to direct Internet providers. To stem the tide of canceled subscriptions, America Online began providing Internet access for a flat rate.

Struggling with Rapid Growth in the Mid-1990s

New subscribers, however, more than made up for those lost to direct Internet providers. Aggressive marketing brought in hordes of new subscribers. A major marketing tactic employed by America Online was to send out millions of free trials of AOL on diskettes, bundled with products as various as magazines, boxes of cereal, and Blockbuster video rentals. By the end of 1995, America Online could boast 4.6 million members, more than quadruple its subscriber base from a year before. However, the marketing costs and the rapid expansion in infrastructure required by so many new subscribers ate every dime of profit. Although America Online had reported a few scattered profitable quarters, it could only do so by treating its marketing expenses as capital costs. Although not illegal, the practice was heavily criticized, and America Online changed its accounting methods in 1996. As a result, the company took a $385 million write-off that year.

Rapid growth had other drawbacks as well. In December 1996 America Online changed its subscription fees from a per-hour access charge to a flat monthly rate with unlimited access. The resulting boom in online usage by its subscribers not only left many customers unable to access the system, it also resulted in the system overloading and crashing several times. Facing lawsuits from several states, America Online was forced by regulators in 1997 to offer refunds. Despite the refunds, the debacle left customers, content providers, and advertisers all distrustful of the online service's reliability.

The company attacked the traffic problem by building up its infrastructure. To accommodate almost three million new subscribers in 1997, America Online had to invest $700 million in its access network and in customer service. Although the company cut back on marketing (reducing the cost of attracting a new subscriber from $375 in 1996 to $90 in 1998), the shift in funds was not enough. Cost-cutting, including employee layoffs, played a significant role, but generating revenue from advertisers and retailers was the real savior. America Online worked out lucrative deals with retailers who wanted access to AOL's subscribers. For example, Preview Travel paid $30 million to be the exclusive travel agent on AOL, and Barnes & Noble struck a similar deal for $40 million. Although advertising took off more slowly, it still proved an important source of income for America Online. The brokerage firms E*Trade and DLJdirect both paid almost $500,000 in 1998 for ad space on AOL's personal finance channel. Revenues from advertising and commerce were 93 percent higher in the last quarter of 1997 than they were in the same quarter in 1996.

As profitable quarters accumulated, America Online's stock rose in value, reaching $80 a share and then splitting two for one in 1998, the fifth time since 1994. The company still struggled with customer service problems, however. System outages and e-mail problems occurred occasionally, and some customers complained about the proliferation of pop-up advertisements and distracting banners.

America Online began an aggressive program of acquisitions in 1998. In February AOL acquired CompuServe's 2.6 million subscriber base, its content operations, and $175 million in cash through the sale of Compuserve's transmission network to telecommunications provider WorldCom. Because CompuServe focused on more sophisticated online users, including small businesses and professionals, America Online decided not to merge the service into its existing offerings. The company established separate divisions, AOL Interactive Services and CompuServe Interactive Services, which together controlled over 60 percent of the market. In June of the same year, the company purchased ICQ, the largest Internet chat service in the world.

But in November, America Online announced an agreement for its biggest purchase yet, and one that could transform the company into a serious rival of industry giant Microsoft. The $4.2 billion deal to buy Netscape Communications would give America Online the expertise of a highly influential Internet access provider and its respected software tools. In addition, America Online brought in Sun Microsystems, maker of high-end workstations and the programming language Java, as a supporter of the merger. Sun agreed to license the AOL/Netscape software for three years for $350 million, and AOL agreed to buy server computers from Sun worth $500 million. According to the *Economist,* the combination held a great deal of promise: "The strategy looks impeccable. AOL has shown a capacity for re-inventing itself that has dumbfounded rivals and skeptics alike. Sun is a genuine technology heavyweight; together, the two companies certainly have the ability to make more of Netscape's assets than Netscape could have done on its own. But it will not be easy.''

Principal Subsidiaries

The Imagination Network; Redgate Communications Corp.; CompuServe Interactive Services, Inc.

Principal Divisions

AOL Interactive Services; AOL Studios; AOL International.

Further Reading

Eng, Paul M., ''America Online Is Hooked Up for Growth,'' *Business Week,* June 21, 1993.

Gunther, Marc, ''The Internet Is Mr. Case's Neighborhood,'' *Fortune,* March 30, 1998, pp. 68–77.

''Internet Riders,'' *Economist,* November 28, 1998, pp. 63–64.

Miller, Michael W., ''Tycoon Is Tapping into Online Service,'' *Wall Street Journal,* May 24, 1993.

Ramo, Joshua Cooper, John Greenwald, and Michael Krantz, ''How AOL Lost the Battles but Won the War,'' *Time,* September 22, 1997, pp. 46–54.

Schwartz, Evan I., ''For America Online, Nothing Is As Nice As a Niche,'' *Business Week,* September 14, 1992.

—Elizabeth Rourke
—updated by Susan Windisch Brown

Arcadis NV

Utrechtseweg 68
P.O. Box 33
6800 LE Arnhem
The Netherlands
(31) 26 3778911
Fax: (31) 26 3515235
Web site: http://www.arcadis.nl

Public Company
Incorporated: 1888 as Nederlandsche Heidemaatschappij
    [Heidemij]
Employees: 6,471
Sales: NLG 1.27 billion (US$647.9 million) (1997)
Stock Exchanges: Amsterdam NASDAQ
Ticker Symbol: ARCAF
SICs: 8711 Engineering Services

Arcadis NV is an internationally operating engineering consulting and project firm with an emphasis on environmental and infrastructure fields. Known as Heidemij (pronounced as "hy-de-my") before changing to the more pronounceable Arcadis in 1998, this Netherlands-based company is one of the largest engineering consultants, with some 7,000 employees and projects in more than 100 countries. Arcadis's chief areas of competence include waste management; soil, groundwater; air quality, and geo-technical information services; infrastructure activities, including public utilities development and implementation; urban and rural development projects, and real estate consulting.

While the Netherlands represents a large percentage of the company's annual sales—as much as 47 percent in the late 1990s—the United States, through U.S. subsidiary Geraghty & Miller, represents an increasing proportion of annual revenues, at 24 percent of the company's sales. The rest of Europe, particularly Germany, France, Belgium, and Spain, add 22 percent of company sales. The company has also been building its presence in the Asian and South American markets, which combined to form just seven percent of total sales in 1997. The nature of Arcadis's market focus means that the company's principal clients typically are local, regional, and national governments. In the 1990s, however, Arcadis has been looking more and more to the private market for expanding its client base.

In the five years between 1992 and 1997, Arcadis more than tripled its sales, reaching NLG 1.27 billion (US$647.9 million) in 1998, for a net profit of NLG 43.2 million (US$22.4 million). A chief source of revenue growth has been the company's steady acquisition drive, including the August 1998 acquisition of Mainz, Germany-based Grebner GmbH. That acquisition gives Arcadis a position as one of the top five engineering consulting firms in Germany.

Nonprofit in the 1880s

Dutch farmers of the second half of the 19th century were hit by a grain crisis, as cheaper imports from the Americas and Russia cut the price of wheat by half. Unable to support themselves, farmers were abandoning the farmlands for the urban centers. Although the crisis would later prove beneficial—many farmers began searching for more profitable crops, turning to potatoes, sugar beets, or to dairy products, and in this way expanded the country's production—its immediate impact raised concern among the country's notables. The Markenwet of 1886, which liberalized public lands for private ownership, inspired the formation of a new association, the Nederlandsche Heidenmaatschappij, later known as Heidemij. The "heide" referred to the Netherlands' vast tracts of undeveloped marshland, particularly in the country's eastern provinces. Heidemij, formed on January 5, 1888, was to be a nonprofit organization with a dual purpose: to reclaim and promote the development of the Dutch soil and to provide work opportunities as a means to prevent the depopulation of the provinces.

Heidemij's initial activity revolved chiefly around the giving of advice and instruction for the reclaiming of marshlands, the reforesting of fields, irrigation, and other agricultural activities.

Through Heidemij, the Dutch farmer was encouraged to seek out and adopt technological advantages that would enable increasing yields at lower cost. Before long, Heidemij also became involved in building and maintaining the country's all-important system of dikes as well as in the burgeoning fisheries market. By the turn of the century, Heidemij had transformed itself from a consulting association to an organization committed to all phases of various projects, including the sale of supplies, tools, and other equipment. The association had grown from a benevolent association of notables to a quasi-governmental organization with a near-monopolistic grip on its market.

This market continued to expand in the early years of the 20th century, as Heidemij added to its areas of competence, moving into road design and construction, fruit production, and the digging and maintenance of the Dutch canal system. The association also was active in education, operating schools and courses in its specialized areas. In the 1920s Heidemij became involved in one of its more important roles, that of overseeing much of the country's *ruilverkaveling* (roughly, "exchanging parcels")—in a country known for conquering the ocean, it was perhaps inevitable that the Dutch would next turn to reconquering the land. Ruilverkaveling involved redividing land to make it productive, while also improving its connection to the country's canal system. Although its origins were primarily agrarian, the concept of ruilverkaveling later would expand to involve a more general concept of land use policy.

Ruilverkaveling became especially important with the economic crisis years of the late 1920s and 1930s. As part of the country's public works program, ruilverkaveling was used increasingly for fending off unemployment; by the early 1930s Heidemij, operating as the government's principal arm in this area, was overseeing as many as 70,000 workers in the country's fields, forests, dikes, and waterways, as well as at the municipal levels. In this way, Heidemij oversaw, for example, the building of many or most of the nation's public swimming pools. By then Heidemij long had been identified closely with the Dutch government at the local, regional, and national levels; these bodies would remain Heidemij's main, even sole, client, and Heidemij would consider itself an unofficial branch of the civil service.

This close association with the government would lead to Heidemij's involvement with the Nazi occupation government during World War II, including the establishment of work camps, which later would be accused of operating slave labor and concentration camps. In 1998 Heidemij, now known as Arcadis, admitted to its actions during the war and agreed to pay restitution to some of its victims.

Postwar Transformation

Heidemij would remain a nonprofit organization until 1972. Yet, in the postwar years, the association had already begun adopting a more businesslike approach, while searching for new areas to operate. In this Heidemij had little choice. In the early 1950s the Dutch government moved to end its longstanding work creation programs. Heidemij also was facing the end of its involvement in other public areas. In the mid-1950s Heidemij's educational activities were being called into question, and by the mid-1960s pressure had mounted to the extent that the association was forced to end its longtime control over many of the country's principal agricultural training academies. Having for so long relied on the government for its revenues, Heidemij had to learn to seek work in the private domain. The association charted a new course for its interests, broadening its primarily environmental focus to include infrastructure projects, such as urban planning, traffic control, and recreation.

These new areas could not be enough for the company to maintain its revenues as well as its large payroll, in which salaries continued to be adjusted according to the same scale as government civil servants. Heidemij needed to look elsewhere for work. In keeping with the association's "good works" principles, Heidemij found its new market overseas in the developing countries, especially the Netherlands' former and soon-to-be former colonies. Heidemij's foreign activities began in 1952, with cooperation on a project in Syria. To limit the financial risks for the association, its Third World operations were brought under a separately operating firm, Imlo, and its daughters Ilaco (consulting) and Lareco (project operations). The move into developing countries also provided the association, tainted as a wartime collaborator, the opportunity to improve its public name. Indeed, the association was awarded the right to add the appellation *Koninglijke* (Royal) to its name.

By the 1960s the association had been confronted with growing competition from the private sector, and Heidemij was forced to adapt. After decades of more or less decentralized operations, according to the variety of its activities or to their regional location, Heidemij was forced to reorganize and move in a more consolidated, centralized direction. Meanwhile, the modern organization was being burdened by its own past successes. Its identity remained closely linked to the government—with many Dutch continuing to believe that Heidemij itself was a Dutch government institution—while its sphere of operations remained rooted, in the popular view, to its former solely agrarian activities, even though such activities now represented only a small part of the association's business. By the end of the 1960s the association chose to undergo a transformation, and it prepared to make the leap from a nonprofit association to a full-fledged, for-profit company.

Surviving the 1980s

The first step toward becoming a company called for uncoupling the nonprofit association from its revenue-generating activities. Upon a decision taken in 1969, Heidemij was reorganized into four operating companies: Heidemij Nederland, responsible for consulting and project operations, especially for government projects; Adviesbure Arnhem, grouping the association's engineering consulting services; Imlo, which continued its foreign market activities, and would be regrouped as Euroconsult in the early 1970s; and Lareco, which had changed its focus from the developing countries to focus on Dutch public works projects. These four companies remained grouped under the nonprofit parent association Koninglijke Nederlands Heidemaatschappij (KnHM). In 1972, however, Heidemij Nederland was transformed into the full-fledged holding and operating company NV Heidemaatschappij Beheer, group the Adviesbureau Arnhem and Imlo as subsidiaries. KNHM became the company's sole shareholder; its revenues, which continued to be earmarked for nonprofit activities, now came solely from Heidemij's profits.

The early 1970s seemed to hold the same promise of the sustained economic growth that the Netherlands—and most of Western Europe—had experienced in the decades following World War II. The new Heidemij prepared to reap those benefits, determining on an ambitious expansion and diversification program, including a series of acquisitions of more than 20 businesses, many of which had already been losing money, between 1970 and 1973. Financing for this expansion came primarily from banks. The acquisitions brought the company into such new directions as the lumber industry, as well as areas of engineering and architecture, with which the company had no experience. Meanwhile, the company's many new and existing operations remained only loosely connected, even as the company attempted to consolidate its holdings during the second half of the decade. As such, Heidemij was in poor position to weather the economic crisis of the 1970s, brought on by the Oil Embargo of 1973. The wind had been taken out of the European—and world—economy's sales.

By the beginning of the 1980s Heidemij was losing money rapidly. While its core activities had continued to be profitable, its diversified activities had been wholly unprofitable, dragging the company's balance sheet into the red. By mid-1982 the banks that had supported Heidemij's expansion effort now began to pressure the company to declare bankruptcy on its unprofitable activities and turn its profitable core over to its financiers. This move would have meant the end of Heidemij. Instead, the company chose another reorganization method, a so-called *sterfhuisconstructie* (literally, mortuary construction), in which the ailing parts of the company were spun off, while the healthy part of the company was declared bankrupt. This allowed Heidemij's core activities to be bought up by Heidemij itself, under the Stichting Lovinklaan, an organization formed to represent Heidemij employees, while eliminating its failing businesses. The rescued Heidemij was freed from its creditors' claims (which would take more than 15 years to bring to resolution). Reorganized as Heidemij Holding, the company was restructured into independent operations, notably splitting its consulting, project management, and foreign operations into separate units. This construction was further refined in 1987, as Heidemij slowly rebuilt itself around its core competencies. By the company's 100th anniversary in 1988, revenues had grown to NLG 334.2 million (approximately US$150 million), with profits of NLG 8.2 million.

Renewed Expansion for the 1990s

At the time of Heidemij's 1970s expansion drive, part of the company's management had insisted that the company cling to its core activities and seek expansion through international growth. In the 1990s Heidemij would do just that, calling for more than half of its revenues to come from international activities by the end of the decade. Once again, Heidemij went on an acquisition drive, adding companies that would bring Heidemij into position to compete in the coming open European market. At the same time Heidemij also began seeking entry into the vast North American market, notably via a partnership with—and in 1993 the acquisition of—publicly held Geraghty & Miller Inc. of Plainview, New York. That acquisition helped raise Heidemij's 1993 revenues to NLG 816 million, almost double the revenues of the year before. The Geraghty & Miller acquisition, for some $130 million, also brought Heidemij onto its first stock exchange, with a listing on the NASDAQ.

With its new acquisition drive, Heidemij sought out not only new international markets, but also complementary competencies, by which the company could extend its consulting and project design and management activities. Whereas government institutions would remain of necessity the company's primary clientele, international expansion also enabled the company to attract a growing number of private sector corporations. One such company was General Motors, which turned to Heidemij not only for support of its U.S. operations, but also much of its European operations.

By late 1997 the company had grown to revenues of more than NLG 1.2 billion (US$600 million), with subsidiaries not only in the Netherlands, but throughout Europe, including Germany, France, Belgium, the United Kingdom, Spain, Russia, and Ukraine, and with a growing presence in Asia, Africa, and Latin America as well. The increasing cooperation and consolidation among the company's many subsidiaries and the resulting confusion arising from so many different names—as well as the inability of much of the world to pronounce the name Heidemij—led the company to change its name in 1998 to Arcadis, from the mythical Arcadis, said to be the most beautiful place on Earth. In this way Arcadis also signaled its intention to continue building as one of the major players in the worldwide environmental and infrastructure engineering markets.

Principal Subsidiaries

Arcadis Heidemij Advies BV; Arcadis IMD BV; Dynamicon BV; Inspectrum BV; ILIS International Land Information Services CV; KLM Aerocarto BV; Tukkers Milieu-onderzoek BV; Arcadis Bouw/Infra BV; V.o.f. Stationseiland; V.o.f. SAT; Arcadis Heidemij Realisatie BV; Copijn Utrecht Holding BV; Arcadis Heidemij Realisatie Lelystad BV; Serasea BV; Kafi BV; Boonstoppel Invorderings-en Advieskantoor BV; Fiscal Control BV; Involon BV; Arcadis Geraghty & Miller, Inc. (U.S.A.); JSA Environmental (U.S.A.); Arcadis Grabowsky & Poort Caribbean NV (Curacao); Eurolatina (El Salvador); Ilaco Suriname NV (Surinam); Arcadis Geotecnica (Chile);

Geotecnicos Peru S.A. (Peru); Copijn België Boomchirurgen BVBA (Belgium); Gedas NV (Belgium); Enviras (Belgium); Starke Diekstra NV (Belgium); Antea SA (France); CFG SA (France); Arcadis ASAL Ingenieure GmbH (Germany); Arcadis Trischler & Partner (Germany); Gebr. Becker Sportanlagenbau GmbH (Germany); Arcadis Ekokonrem Spólka z o.o. (Poland); Grupo EP/Eptisa (Spain); Arcadis Geraghty & Miller International, Inc. (U.K.); Arcadis Euroconsult; BMB Management Consulting for Development BV; Darwish Consulting Engineers (Egypt); Grabowsky & Poort Consulting Engineers (Kenya); EurAsia Consult (Kazakhstan); Euroconsult Pakistan; Arcadis Konsult (Russia); Recon (Russia); Ukron (Ukraine).

Further Reading

"Frans Luttmer of Heidemij: Cleaning Up," *Institutional Investor,* March 1996, p. 23.

Meijer, Harry, "Bedrijf zit nu in infrastructuur en milieu in plaats van eikels en kastanjes," *NRC Handelsblad,* September 25, 1995, p. 16.

Reina, Peter, "Dutch Firm Faces Ups and Downs of International Growth," *Engineering News-Record,* May 29, 1995, p. 34.

Van de Geijn, Louis, "Expansie Heidemij 'nog lang niet aan een eind," *De Gelderlander,* May 2, 1995, p. 1.

Zweers, Louis, "In het belang van ons eigen land en volk: Heidemij," *Trouw,* January 31, 1998, p. 5.

—M. L. Cohen

Ashworth, Inc.

2791 Loker Avenue West
Carlsbad, California 92008
U.S.A.
(760) 438-6610
(800) 627-4274
Fax: (760) 438-6657
Web site: http://www.ashworthinc.com

Public Company
Incorporated: 1987 as Charter Golf, Inc.
Employees: 574
Sales: $89.1 million (1997)
Stock Exchanges: NASDAQ
Ticker Symbol: ASHW
SICs: 2321 Men's & Boy's Shirts; 2325 Men's & Boy's
    Trousers & Slacks; 2329 Men's & Boy's Clothing

Ashworth, Inc. is a leading producer of golf apparel and sportswear. An innovative company, Ashworth revolutionized the golf apparel industry in both fashion and function. The company changed golf style from polyester and hard collars to cotton and twill. Originally producing only men's fashions, Ashworth has grown to design comfortable styles for women and young men. Its variety of products is distributed worldwide at country clubs, pro shops, and upscale department and specialty stores.

Starting Out As Charter Golf, Inc. in 1987

Ashworth was created through the partnership of Gerald Montiel, the entrepreneur, and John Ashworth, the golf fanatic. In 1984, after selling a small chain of craft stores that he had started, Montiel decided to open a chain of sporting goods stores. While at a golf tournament in Albuquerque, New Mexico, he met Ashworth, who was caddying for a friend on the pro tour. Just getting the sporting goods chain off the ground, Montiel offered Ashworth a job as a golf apparel and equipment

buyer for his new stores. Within two years, with Montiel's wife having divorced him and the two partners now sharing a condo in Denver, the sporting goods chain was liquidated and the two began planning their next business, a chain of golf driving ranges.

The idea to produce golf clothes came up while they were driving down the California coast looking for possible range locations. Ashworth thought that golf needed something better than the current styles of polyester pants and hard collars. The company was started even though neither one of them knew anything about the clothing business. Montiel began raising money to get the company on its feet, while Ashworth began developing the designs.

Working out of a dingy office in Los Angeles's garment district and starting to lose money, Montiel decided to take the company public. Despite not having generated any revenue or product yet, Montiel was able to sell the idea to Grady and Hatch, a New York-based underwriter. They had agreed to sell 42 percent of Charter Golf for $1.2 million, but had to cancel the deal because of the October 1987 stock market crash. Undaunted by the setback, Montiel started to sell the shares himself. Selling 20 percent of Charter at 75 cents per share, he was able to raise $685,000 by March 1988. With Montiel raising capital, Ashworth went to work and convinced a local manufacturer to provide 200 all-cotton sample shirts, which Ashworth sold to golf shop buyers he knew in southern California.

By the end of its first year Charter Golf had sold $374,000 worth of its Ashworth line of shirts, pants, and shorts, but had lost $324,000. Knowing good publicity was required for the company to be successful, the partners needed to find a big name to promote the line. Ashworth turned to a friend on the PGA Tour and consequently signed golfer Fred Couples to an endorsement deal, paying him in Charter Golf stock rather than cash.

Charter Golf Begins to Grow in 1989

As the comfort and style of their clothing began to catch on, Charter Golf's sales for fiscal 1989 were $2.14 million compared to the previous year's $374,000. Needing more room for

---

Company Perspectives:

Ashworth revolutionized golf apparel 10 years ago and has been acknowledged as "the" leader in golf apparel. The Ashworth brand is built on a solid foundation that cannot easily be replicated by the competition.

Over the past ten years, the Company has taken the steps necessary to ensure that the Ashworth label represents the soul of the greatest game on the planet. We have accomplished this through our innovative designs, product quality, controlled distribution and strong representation on the PGA Tour. By continuing to create novel product and by providing the highest customer service to our accounts Ashworth will continue to keep the lead into the 21st century.

---

distribution, Charter Golf relocated from its Oceanside facility to a new 14,000-square-foot headquarters in Carlsbad, California. With another PGA Tour Player, John Cook, added to its list of endorsers, the company continued to grow, increasing its market to 2,300 pro shops and resorts.

Charter Golf reached the NASDAQ board in 1990 under the symbol CGOL. The company marked its first profitable quarter, reporting earnings of $32,000 on sales of $972,000. The increased sales prompted Ashworth to be named the fastest-growing line of golf shirts in America by *Golf Pro Merchandiser* magazine. Also in 1990, Scott Verplank and Mark Wiebe joined Couples and Cook as company endorsers. Expecting more growth in 1991, Charter Golf moved into a new 35,000-square-foot facility in Carlsbad.

Charter Golf had created its success by following one simple motto: Keep it simple, and two years ahead of everyone else. They managed to appeal to the younger generation of golfers by making comfortable golf clothes. By early 1991, accounts had to grown to 3,000, with products sold in 41 percent of resorts around the country. That total was dramatically up from 16 percent the year before.

By late 1991, the company had grown to 3,500 accounts, with about 2,800 of those being golf course pro shops. Now looking to foreign markets, deals were signed to distribute Ashworth apparel in European and Japanese markets. The company entered into a multi-year agreement with Nissho Iwai, a major Japanese trading company, to market products in Japan. They expected these new markets to represent eight to ten percent of total sales volume by the next year.

Charter Golf's success was even shared by the professionals who endorsed their product. Fred Couples had the PGA Tour's lowest stroke average in 1991 and was named the PGA player of the year by *Golf World* magazine. He had another great year in 1992, winning the Masters and being named PGA player of the year for the second year running. Dave Stockton, the captain of the U.S. Ryder Cup team, also began wearing Ashworth, becoming the first player on the Senior Tour to wear the brand.

In 1992, a survey by *Golf Pro Merchandiser* again named Charter Golf's Ashworth line as the fastest-growing line in the country and number one in customer preference. Buoyed by its success, Charter Golf had another public offering in February 1992, selling 1.5 million shares at a price of $7.25 per share. With new capital and increasing orders, the company opened a new 42,000-square-foot distribution center next to its corporate headquarters. The new facility had four times more storage space than the previous one and could support sales volumes of $125 million.

Frequently customizing its Ashworth line to put the country club or course logo on the apparel, Charter Golf was now selling to about 3,200 of the nations 11,500 pro shops and resorts, with the average shop bringing in $8,351 in merchandise in 1992. They continued to expand in Europe and Japan as well, selling to more than 15 countries. Foreign accounts made up seven percent of 1992 sales, while the new women's line accounted for 12 percent of total sales.

Introducing New Product Lines in 1993

Now selling products all over the world, Charter announced in 1993 that it would introduce a new clothing line. The new line differed from the Ashworth line in that it was to be sold in department and specialty stores, rather than the traditional golf pro shops. The new line, sold under the fictional name Harry Logan, had its own designs and had a sales force separate from the Ashworth line. The company hired CBS sports announcer Jim Nantz as the spokesman for the new line. Adding more products to the mix, the company also entered into the hat business, trying to catch a piece of the $100 million annual sales.

Charter Golf Becomes Ashworth, Inc.

In 1994, Charter Golf officially adopted the name of its premier clothing line and became known as Ashworth, Inc. While the name changed, the sales figures did not. Its continued strength in the golf industry had Ashworth repeatedly ranked as one of the top 50 fastest-growing companies by several national magazines. The number of golf shops carrying the line increased to 4,100, with average sales per shop jumping to $9,607.

Strengthened by the company's success and his own achievements, Fred Couples entered into a lifetime contract to represent the company. The contract gave him a combination of cash and stock options, making him the company's largest stockholder. Ashworth also announced that Couples would endorse the company's new line of shoes, scheduled for release in 1995. Other Ashworth golfers had successful years in 1994 as well. Ernie Els won the U.S. Open and was ranked number three on the Sony World Golf Rankings, while Dave Stockton continued winning on the PGA Senior Tour.

Growing Pains in 1995

Despite numerous growing pains in 1995, the company still managed to have its eighth straight year of growth. Ashworth's products were being sold in over 30 countries around the world, with the international division representing 24 percent of total business. The Harry Logan line, which was now in over 500 specialty and department stores, saw sales increase to $4.41 million. In addition, Ashworth opened ten factory stores to sell prior season and irregular merchandise.

The company did have some troubles in 1995. Ashworth announced in May 1995 that it was going to discontinue its womens and childrens lines. Citing that the womens and childrens lines were poor uses of the company's expenses and resources, Ashworth returned its focus to its line of mens products. Also, the company ran into some problems as it tried to upgrade its computer and information systems. The process took longer than expected and caused delays in shipping as the company was running on one system while starting the other. At the end of 1995, Rick Werschkul left his position as president and CEO of the company leaving Chairman and cofounder Gerald Montiel to take over his duties for the company.

Despite the troubles in 1995, Ashworth was again ranked the fastest-growing, number one brand of golfwear in America. Ashworth had expanded its product mix to now include apparel (shirts, pants, sweaters, shorts, vests), accessories (watches, socks, boxers), shoes, weather gear, and hats.

Changes Begin at Ashworth in 1996

In December 1996, Randy Herrel, Sr., became president and CEO after a successful stint in the same position at Quicksilver, the country's largest surfwear manufacturer. Herrel brought a no-nonsense attitude with him to Ashworth. During his six years at Quicksilver, sales had risen from $90 million to $190 million and earnings per share from a nickel to $1.65. He knew Ashworth needed considerable retooling, but he also saw cause for hope, and parallels between his old company and his new one. While Ashworth's operations, customer service, and management required repair, the company was still an industry leader.

Ashworth announced in 1996 that it would launch a new golf label for 1997 and would be making all levels of merchandise available for pro shop and department store accounts. Each of its three types of merchandise were clearly defined by style and geared for certain demographics. The new line, Golfman, targeted 16- to 25-year-olds, and included T-shirts, shorts, graphic prints, and some denim. The Ashworth core line continued to target golfers age 25 to 45, with solid, printed, and jacquard knit tops and twill bottoms. The Harry Logan line moved to focus on 45- to 65-year-olds, evolving into a more formal collection of sportswear, sport coats, fine-gauge knits, merino wool, and cashmere pieces.

As a way to improve sales even further in pro shops and department stores, Ashworth developed the concept of the Golfman Shop. The Golfman Shop was a merchandising system that integrated the Ashworth product line into one self-contained marketing unit. Set up in the retail stores, the Shop readily adapted to changing inventory levels and new product development, while displaying a variety of Ashworth merchandise.

Ashworth also opened its own store in June 1997. The Ashworth Studio, located in at South Coast Plaza in Costa Mesa, California, offered a full line of golf apparel, weather-gear, and hats, plus home and office furniture, luggage, and bathing accessories.

At the end of 1997, the Darrel Survey, a consumer survey conducted with golfers across America, named Ashworth the number one brand in golf. With a 10.4 percent market share, Ashworth became the first brand to surpass a 10 percent market share in golf since 1985. The survey showed that the company maintained the most popular brand with golfers under 30 years old, as well as showed that its product was worn by 25 percent of the best golfers (0–5 handicap) in the United States.

Goal Set for 1998

The company continued to look for ways to improve in 1998 and especially wanted to expand the core business into existing retail operations, both by improving designs and being more aggressive with the Golfman Shop program. Ashworth also wanted to gain new distribution into pro shop accounts and upscale department stores, expanding on its already existing 4,500 accounts. Finally, the company wanted to continue to be a product-driven and innovative company, strengthening the Ashworth image for fashion and function.

To expand its core business, Ashworth relaunched its women's line for spring 1998. The company had not manufactured a women's line since 1993, when it discontinued the line because of poor sales. This time the company set up a design staff and customer service staff to focus on its women's division. Projected volumes for the women's line were at least $5 million, with pro shops accounting for up to 90 percent of sales.

Ashworth also launched its AGCo label in 1998. The label, targeted at the young golfer, was sold in pro shops and resorts, but was expected to earn higher sales from department and specialty stores. The line consisted of knits, wovens, pants, shorts, fleece items, jackets, wind shirts, sweaters, and hats. Prices for the new AGCo line were set to be competitive with other manufacturers.

The company looked to strategic alliances with golf properties to increase its distribution. Ashworth developed three-year strategic alliances with two major golf property management firms, Club Corporation of America (CCA) and Troon Golf. Working to add other management firms, they anticipated the company would have three-year alliances with over 300 of the premier volume-producing properties in the United States. The Golfman Shop program would be used in each case to secure at least 20 percent of the properties' floor space. The company added 20 Golfman shops in early 1998, bringing the total to 220.

Ashworth also continued to be an innovative company. Using the latest developments in fiber and garment technology, Ashworth established itself as the first golf apparel company to create an entire line of technical clothing. Its Weather Systems line featured knit-solar protection fabric, moisture-removing performance knits, and new lightweight, waterproof, breathable clothing.

The Future of Ashworth

Co-founder Gerald Montiel announced he would retire from Ashworth on December 31, 1998. He planned to remain a stockholder in the company and looked forward to watching the company continue to grow. With 550 Golfman Shops in place and product placements increasing, the company presumably would have no problem keeping Montiel happy.

Principal Subsidiaries

Ashworth Canada; Ashworth UK, Ltd.; Ashworth, Inc., et Cie (Luxembourg); Ashworth International, Inc. (U.S. Virgin Islands); Ashworth Store (I-X), Inc.

Further Reading

"Ashworth Takes Another Swing at Women's," *Women's Wear Daily,* August 13, 1998, p. 7.

"Ashworth Pulls Plug on Women's, Kids' Lines," Golf Pro, June 1995, p. 8.

"Corporate Profiles 1993: Charter Golf Inc.," *San Diego Daily Transcript,* January 11, 1993, p. 3.

"Corporate Profiles 1995: Ashworth Performance Sets Record, But Expenses Rising," *San Diego Daily Transcript,* January 23, 1994, p. 7.

Cropper, Carol, "A Stock-for-Name Deal," *Forbes,* October 11, 1993, pp. 118–20.

"The Golfman Cometh," *Golf Pro,* October 1996, p. 9.

"Gunning for Young Guns," *Golf Pro,* March 1998, p. 6.

Kragen, Pam, "Carlsbad, Calif.-Based Ashworth Looks to Links for Success," *North County Times,* March 10, 1997.

Kramer, Scott, "Ashworth Answers," *Golf Pro,* February 1996, pp. 39–41.

McClain, Timothy, "Ashworth's Golf Apparel Remains Hot As Expenses Eat into Company Bottom Line," *San Diego Daily Transcript,* December 22, 1994, p. 7.

——, "No Recession at Charter Golf As Sales Hit Record," *San Diego Daily Transcript,* December 13, 1991, p. 1.

Neumeier, Shelley, "Charter Golf," *Fortune,* April 20, 1998, p. 125.

—Robert Alan Passage

Barr Laboratories, Inc.

2 Quaker Road
Pomona, New York 10970
U.S.A.
(914) 362-1100
(800) BARRLAB; (800) 227-7522
Fax: (914) 362-2774
Web site: http://www.barrlabs.com

Public Company
Incorporated: 1970 as Barr Laboratories, Inc.
Employees: 467
Sales: $377.3 million (1998)
Stock Exchanges: New York
Ticker Symbol: BRL
SICs: 2834 Pharmaceutical Preparations

A fast-growing generic drug company, Barr Laboratories, Inc. develops, manufactures, and markets generic and proprietary pharmaceuticals. The heart of the company and its original focus was on the generic side, a fast-growing segment of the general pharmaceutical industry in which Barr was one of the early pioneers. The company earned notoriety during the late 1980s, when its founder testified before a congressional committee about bribes between generic drug producers and U.S. Food & Drug Administration officials. Barr began to realize phenomenal financial growth during the 1990s, when the U.S. generic pharmaceutical industry grew from a $4-billion-a-year business to an $11-billion-a-year business. By targeting drugs it considered to be covered by weak patents, Barr scored major successes, such as the right to distribute the cancer drug tamoxifen citrate, which accounted for roughly 75 percent of the company's sales during most of the 1990s. During the late 1990s the company's product line was focused on several therapeutic categories, including anti-infectives, cardiovascular agents, hormonal agents, analgesics, oncology, and psychotherapeutic products. At manufacturing facilities in New York, New Jersey, and Virginia, Barr produced more than 60 drug products, including proprietary pharmaceuticals, which the company began manufacturing in 1998.

Industry and Company Origins

Barr was founded in 1970 as a generic pharmaceutical concern based in New York. At the time of the company's formation, the generic drug industry was in its infancy, having first gained legitimacy as a business during the mid-1960s. The catalyst for the industry's emergence was the Drug Efficacy Study Implementation (DESI) program conducted by the National Research Council of the National Academy of Sciences in 1962, which evaluated all drugs that had been approved for use prior to 1962. The DESI evaluation reviewed more than 3,000 products, determining which products were effective and which were ineffective. Those products that gained the DESI stamp of approval paved the way for a new breed of drug makers: generic manufacturers. With a list of products deemed effective by the National Research Council, generic drug companies could manufacture a product according to the prescribed chemical formula and mark the product without additional study, eliminating the need for the costly and time-consuming biostudies conducted by proprietary drug makers. Barr, founded by Edwin A. Cohen and a partner, became one of the early contenders in the generic drug industry when it introduced its first product in 1972.

Initially, Barr concentrated on making antibiotic products, manufacturing generic drugs primarily for other pharmaceutical companies, such as Lederle Standard Products. For more than a decade Barr remained a small enterprise without the ability to realize much financial growth. The restraints on the company's growth stemmed from the immaturity of its industry, which had sprung to life in the wake of the DESI program but retained its fledgling characteristics until the mid-1980s. The turning point in the generic drug industry's evolution occurred when the Drug Price Competition and Patent Restoration Act was promulgated in 1984. Also referred to as the Waxman-Hatch Act, the legislation allowed the production of generic versions of all pharmaceutical products approved after 1962, provided the generic manufacturer could prove the generic version was equivalent to the branded version. The ruling ignited the generic drug industry's growth, ushering in a new era of frenetic expansion and signaling what observers regarded as the beginning of the modern generic pharmaceutical industry. In the first year following the approval of the Waxman-Hatch Act, more than

Company Perspectives:

The people of Barr Laboratories are focused on being first-to-market with quality, off-patent pharmaceuticals in specific therapeutic categories that generate sustainable profitability. Our confidence in our ability to achieve success is based on the skill and dedication of our employees and their commitment to excellence in science, manufacturing and customer satisfaction.

1,000 applications for new generic drugs were received by the U.S. Food & Drug Administration (FDA), as scores of new generic producers scurried to secure the decisive rights to be the first to market generic equivalents of branded pharmaceuticals. For an industry long held in check, however, the forces that unleashed its potential nearly caused its ruin. Scandal, bribery, and a litany of criminal accusations followed the passage of the Waxman-Hatch Act, staining the image of generic drug producers and the FDA. At the center of the maelstrom of controversy were Barr and its founder, Edwin Cohen.

Crime and Punishment in the Late 1980s

Much of a generic drug producer's success depended on being "first to market," a race that began with the submission of detailed information to the FDA concerning the bioequivalence of a generic alternative, that is, providing proof that the generic drug had the same therapeutic effects as the branded version. Once FDA approval was obtained, a generic producer could introduce its generic alternative into the market, but in the wake of the Waxman-Hatch Act many began to question the FDA approval process, particularly Cohen. Cohen approached the FDA in 1987 and 1988, accusing the agency of favoring his competitors, complaining that other generic producers were securing approval while his applications languished on the desks of FDA officials. Part of Cohen's frustration stemmed from Barr's attempts to market its generic version of erythromycin estolate, an antibiotic. Barr submitted an application for the antibiotic in January 1987 and a short time later the FDA agreed that the company's drug was bioequivalent, but numerous delays followed. By the end of 1987 Cohen still had not received approval for the antibiotic, so he complained to the FDA. By the end of 1988 approval still had not arrived, prompting Cohen to voice his complaints again. The FDA never responded to Cohen's accusations, but in mid-1989 Cohen found someone who would listen. In May 1989 the House Subcommittee on Oversight asked Cohen to testify against the FDA during its investigation of the generic drug industry.

Cohen testified before the congressional committee that FDA officials were accepting bribes from generic drug producers to quicken the approval process. Because of the committee's nearly three-year investigation, more than 40 FDA employees and company executives pleaded guilty to or were convicted of fraud or corruption charges. Of the 52 generic drug producers examined during the investigation, only five, including Barr, were not implicated in the scandal. Although Cohen had helped expose rampant corruption, his triumph did not benefit Barr—if any-

thing, it exacerbated relations with the FDA. By early 1990 Barr still had not received approval for its generic version of erythromycin estolate. Cohen believed the delays were retribution for his testimony in front of the congressional subcommittee and his complaints against the FDA, so he filed a lawsuit against the agency. The antibiotic at last was granted approval in October 1990, nearly four years after the application was submitted, but the end of the long wait did not mark the end of Barr's problems with the FDA. After failing to force Barr to suspend manufacturing and distribution pending the resolution of certain regulatory disputes, the FDA put Barr on its "alert list" of pharmaceutical manufacturers who did not conform to FDA standards. Barr filed another lawsuit in April 1992, contending that its inclusion on the alert list was preventing the company from winning approval on roughly 90 new drugs. Two months later the FDA dropped Barr from its alert list.

There was ample cause for Cohen and other Barr officials to eliminate any impediments to new product introduction as the 1990s began. At stake were billions of dollars of business, business to be won by those generic producers who could identify prime pharmaceutical drugs to produce and then move expeditiously through the FDA approval process. Between 1991 and 1996, patents were to expire on a host of prescription drugs whose aggregate value was estimated at $10 billion in sales. At the time this potentially lucrative five-year period was set to begin, the U.S. generic drug industry was a $4-billion-a-year business and Barr was a $70-million-in-sales company; both were poised for prolific growth. Barr's first major victory during this period was its challenge on the patent for tamoxifen citrate, a breast cancer treatment that became the financial foundation upon which the company rested. Tamoxifen, which Barr distributed but did not produce, accounted for three-quarters of the company's sales during the 1990s and represented an early sign of the company's willingness to dispute the patents of large drug companies. As Barr moved forward during the generic drug industry's decade of opportunity, it focused on drugs that were hard to copy in order to reduce competition and, more notoriously, it earned a reputation for challenging what it considered weak patents. Aggressive and persistent, Barr displayed no reluctance to avoid fiercely contested legal disputes, even on the heels of its fractious battle with the FDA.

Energetic Growth During the 1990s

Beginning in 1993 Barr recorded a five-year period during which annual sales increased an average of 35 percent per year. Much of this growth rested on the shoulders of tamoxifen, which contributed roughly 75 percent of the company's total sales during the period, but the financial success also was attributable to Barr's progress with other drugs, progress achieved after butting heads with some of the country's biggest drug makers. To lead the company forward during this volatile period was Bruce L. Downey, who became Barr's president, chief operating officer, and a member of the company's board of directors in January 1993. Cohen relinquished his title of chief executive officer in early 1994 and was replaced by Downey in February 1994. In Downey, Barr gained a leader well equipped to handle the litigious future it faced. A former partner in the law firm of Winston & Strawn, Downey had served as the lead attorney during Barr's legal battle with the

FDA, which would serve him well as Barr pursued its strategy of challenging the patents of larger drug companies.

After smoothing over relations with the FDA in 1995, Barr earned FDA approval to sell a generic version of the AIDS drug AZT. Before the company could market its product, however, it had to win court approval to overturn existing patents, held by Glaxo Wellcome. The legal battle over Barr's generic AZT was just one of several ongoing patent challenges that Downey directed during the middle and late 1990s, including the company's 1996 challenge of the patent held by Eli Lilly for Prozac, which collected $6 million in sales daily. Meanwhile, as Barr contested various patents in the courtroom, its success outside the courtroom was resounding. Financially, the company had suffered during its long dispute with the FDA, entering the 1990s with $70 million in annual sales and watching that total drop to $58 million by 1993. From 1993 forward, however, sales climbed robustly, swelling to $109 million in 1994, $199 million in 1995, and $232 million by 1996. With managed care organizations growing in number and prominence amid escalating health care costs, generic drugs were becoming more sought after than ever before. Evidence of this rise in demand was illustrated at Barr in 1996 when the company purchased a 65,000-square-foot manufacturing facility in Forest, Virginia, to complement its existing facilities in Pomona, New York, and Northvale, New Jersey.

Downey led the company's charge against DuPont Merck Pharmaceutical Co., which petitioned the FDA in September 1996 for a stay of action against Barr's warfarin sodium, an anti-coagulation agent that was the generic equivalent of DuPont Merck's Coumadin. DuPont Merck fought a state-by-state battle to prohibit the distribution of Barr's generic version of Coumadin, trying to keep the $500 million in sales it collected from Coumadin to itself. Barr received FDA approval in March 1997 and began shipping its warfarin sodium tablets in July 1997, accumulating $15 million in sales during the first month, as DuPont Merck's attempts to stop distribution continued into 1998.

Thanks to its encouraging sales growth, Barr entered 1997 ranked as one of the top ten generic drug makers in the country. Its role as an industry whistle-blower had weakened its stock performance during the late 1980s and early 1990s, but by the late 1990s the company was drawing praise from Wall Street. One stock analyst noted: "Not every company can do well if the industry is doing well. Barr is a major turnaround company in the industry. They went through some tough times, but have since turned around ... Barr is getting a reputation of being aggressive in litigation and patent challenging. Barr is willing to take on Goliath."

Taking on larger pharmaceutical companies continued to be a major focus of the company's strategy as it competed in the late 1990s, but in 1997 it added another facet to its operations by launching a proprietary pharmaceutical development program. Research and development spending increased as a result, jumping 54 percent in 1997 to $10.4 million and another 40 percent in 1998 to $19 million. "R&D [research and development] spending is the future," Downey declared, "and the last

thing we'd cut. It leads to the most earnings and in the fastest way." Less than 18 months after launching its proprietary development program, Barr introduced its first product, a contraceptive codeveloped with Gynetics, Inc. Approved by the FDA in September 1998, the product was the PREVEN Emergency Contraceptive Kit, which contained an information booklet, a pregnancy test, and four high-dosage birth control pills. According to the partnership agreement between the two companies, Barr manufactured the pills and Gynetics marketed the product, billing it as a postcoital "morning-after" product to be taken within 72 hours of intercourse, the first FDA-approved product specifically designed for such use.

Aside from celebrating its first success in proprietary drug development, Barr officials could point to other favorable developments that suggested a bright future for the company. Financially, Barr was performing admirably, registering a 68 percent increase in net earnings in 1998 to $32.7 million and a 33 percent increase in revenues to $377.3 million, more than six times the total collected five years earlier. With a number of potentially lucrative generic products expected to be introduced once approval was granted, Barr's generic business was as strong as ever, while its new proprietary business, which had four proprietary products in various stages of development in late 1998, provided a promising avenue for future growth. Downey was overjoyed by Barr's success, declaring, "By all measures, 1998 represents the most successful year in our company's history." As Downey prepared for the century ahead, his hope for a succession of record-setting years appeared well-founded, as Barr exited the 1990s in full stride.

Further Reading

Barr Laboratories, Inc., "History," http://www.barrlabs.com/barr1.html.

Barr Laboratories, Inc., "History of the Generic Drug Industry," http://www.barrlabs.com/drugpast.html.

"Barr Laboratories, Inc.," *Insiders' Chronicle,* June 1, 1992, p. 3.

"Barr Laboratories Reports Record Fiscal 1998 EPS of $1.45 Revenues Climb to $377 Million; Net Earnings Jump to $32.7 Million," *PR Newswire,* August 20, 1998, p. 82.

"Barr's First Proprietary Product Receives FDA Approval; Contraceptive Product Co-Developed with Gynetics, Inc.," *PR Newswire,* September 2, 1998, p. 9.

Carrell, Steve, "Firestorm Erupting over Generic Warfarin Release," *Drug Topics,* November 4, 1996, p. 35.

Fleming, Harris, Jr., "Warfarin Vs. Coumadin: Managed Care Joins Battle," *Drug Topics,* November 3, 1997, p. 63.

"Generic Drug Battle Wins Round on List," *Chemical Marketing Reporter,* June 22, 1992, p. 3.

"Indiana Becomes Latest Battleground over a Lucrative Anti-Coagulant Product," *Knight-Ridder/Tribune Business News,* January 20, 1998, p. 12.

Lavelle, Louis, "FDA Approves New Jersey Firm's Morning-After Birth Control Pill," *Knight-Ridder/Tribune Business News,* September 4, 1998, p. 2.

Malone, Bridget, "Generic Drug Firm Offers 'No-Frills' Alternative," *Knight-Ridder/Tribune Business News,* January 2, 1997, p. 10.

Sawaya, Zina, "Getting Even," *Forbes,* April 29, 1991, p. 92.

Zoeller, Janice, "Barr Reissues Warfarin Materials," *American Druggist,* October 1997, p. 24.

—Jeffrey L. Covell

BHC Communications, Inc.

767 Fifth Avenue
New York, New York 10153
U.S.A.
(212) 421-0200
Fax: (212) 935-8462

Public Subsidiary of Chris-Craft Industries, Inc.
Incorporated: 1977 as BHC, Inc.
Employees: 1,181
Sales: $443.5 million (1997)
Stock Exchanges: American
Ticker Symbol: BHC
SICs: 4833 Television Broadcasting Stations

BHC Communications, Inc. was, in 1997, operating nine television stations in the United States, including stations in the New York City and Los Angeles metropolitan areas. Five of these stations were being operated by one or the other of two wholly owned subsidiaries; the other four were being run by United Television, Inc., a majority-owned subsidiary. BHC Communications also jointly owned, with Viacom, Inc., United Paramount Network, which was providing programming to 178 television stations in early 1998. BHC was 79 percent-owned by Chris-Craft Industries, Inc. at this time.

Growing Chris-Craft Subsidiary: 1977–90

Herbert J. Siegel, described as a consummate dealmaker with an affinity for entertainment properties, acquired Chris-Craft at the end of 1967. Among the properties held by this diversified company were two television stations: KCOP in Los Angeles and KPTV in Portland, Oregon. In 1977 these stations were placed in a new Chris-Craft subsidiary, BHC (which apparently was an acronym for ''broadcasting holding company'') Inc. Chris-Craft Television, Inc. was a subsidiary of BHC, while KCOP Television, Inc. and Oregon Television, Inc. were subsidiaries of Chris-Craft Television. During fiscal 1978 (the year ended August 31, 1978) television accounted for about $30.1 million of parent Chris-Craft's revenues and $9.4 million in

operating income, a profit margin typical of the highly lucrative television broadcasting field.

In the same year BHC was incorporated Siegel obtained, in Chris-Craft's name, a minority interest in 20th Century-Fox Film Co. Four years later he sold this interest, which had grown to about 22 percent, to Marvin Davis and Marc Rich for $140 million in cash and 19 percent of United Television, Inc., a Fox subsidiary. Founded in 1956 to operate station KMSP-TV in Minneapolis, United Television in 1975 acquired KTVX, an ABC affiliate in Salt Lake City, and KMOL-TV, an NBC affiliate in San Antonio. BHC became the fourth largest television broadcast company not owned by a network in 1983, when its stake in United Television reached 50.1 percent of the common stock. Also that year, United Television purchased an ultra-high-frequency (UHF) station in San Francisco. The six television stations had combined revenue of $115 million and operating income of $39.1 million in fiscal 1983.

Chris-Craft, early in 1984, acquired convertible preferred stock valued at more than $200 million from entertainment giant Warner Communications, Inc. in exchange for a 42.5 percent stake in BHC taken by Warner. The cross-ownership agreement, which gave Chris-Craft 19 percent of the voting power in Warner, was sought by Warner to prevent a takeover by Rupert Murdoch's News Corporation Limited. It also made sense to Siegel because, he told a reporter, ''They make feature films and have a large film library. We have mostly independent television stations and the cost of programming is going up.'' Investor Mario Gabelli hailed the deal, saying ''Siegel sold the stations at retail price, and he bought Warner's stock wholesale.'' Eventually Chris-Craft upped its voting stake in Warner to 29 percent.

BHC continued to thrive under the autonomous management characteristic of Chris-Craft's divisions, although operating income declined slightly in the 1980s after reaching a peak of $38.8 million in fiscal 1984. In (calendar year) 1988 it was $30.7 million on record operating revenues of $230.6 million. In late 1985 United Television launched a second UHF station, KUTP, in Phoenix.

Time Inc. acquired control of Warner (which then became Time Warner Inc.) in 1989–90. For its shares in Warner BHC received cash, some of the shares of its own stock previously held by Warner, and convertible preferred stock in Time Warner. Payment, in all, was valued at $2.3 billion, almost a sixfold pretax gain over a six-year period. Following this settlement, BHC was reincorporated as BHC Communications, Inc. and recapitalized into two classes of stock in an arrangement that gave Chris-Craft almost the entire voting power.

Awash in Cash: 1990–95

The distribution of other BHC shares by Time Warner to other Warner stockholders turned BHC Communications into a public company, although it remained a majority owned Chris-Craft subsidiary with the same headquarters in New York City as Chris-Craft and the same chairman and president, Siegel. Part of BHC Communications' windfall was used to retire its debt and buy back about 10 percent of its (virtually nonvoting) Class A shares. The remainder—about $1.3 billion at the end of 1990—remained in BHC's coffers. By early 1993 this sum had grown to $1.6 billion. One of the company's most enthusiastic shareholders was Gabelli, who, along with his funds, now held 21 percent of the Class A shares of common stock.

Although Siegel showed no interest in using BHC's cache to negotiate another megadeal, in 1992 the company purchased, for $313 million, Pinelands, Inc., holder of WWOR, a television station based in Secaucus, New Jersey. WWOR was one of only six over-the-air VHF television stations broadcasting in the metropolitan New York City area—the nation's largest. Although it ranked last of the six in viewer ratings, acquisition of the station anchored BHC Communications at the eastern end of the continent. Moreover, WWOR was a superstation being beamed to other parts of the nation by cable operators. At the end of 1996, however, AEC Corp., which was providing the satellite feed outside of the New York area, pulled the plug on the station. This action, which affected some 12.5 million cable subscribers nationwide, came shortly after Tele-Communications Inc., the largest cable operator, decided to drop WWOR from many of its cable systems.

At the other end of the continent, KCOP was the leading independent television station in Los Angeles. Founded in 1948 and purchased by Chris-Craft in 1960 for $5 million, KCOP began beaming the Los Angeles Marathon race at its inception in 1985 and later covered the local premieres of such stage shows as "Miss Saigon," "Tommy," and "Sunset Boulevard." The station, in 1994, was doing well both in daytime and primetime with first-run syndicated programs aimed at young adults, such as "The Ricki Lake Show" and "Star Trek: Deep Space Nine." In the fall of that year KCOP introduced a 2½-hour block of original, syndicated late-night programming aimed at young adults.

Operating revenues for BHC Communications and its subsidiaries increased from $278.1 million in 1990 to $447.5 million in 1994. Operating income fell from $25.7 million in 1990 to only $517,000 in the recession year of 1991 but increased to $22.4 million in 1992, $79.3 million in 1993, following the acquisition of WWOR, and $113 million in 1994. Because of sales of Time Warner securities, net income was much higher—

as high as $481.2 million in 1990 and $224.3 million in 1993. The BHC/United stations formed, in 1995, United Sales Enterprises, a firm designed to sell national spot advertising time for all eight.

Forming United Paramount Network: 1995–98

In January 1995 BHC Communications launched United Paramount Network, the nation's sixth television network. Among the 100-odd stations to receive UPN's original two nights per week, two hours per night primetime programming were the six stations owned by BHC or its subsidiaries that were not network affiliated and nine of the 11 owned by Viacom's Paramount Television Group, which acted as the network's producer. Since research had targeted men aged 18 to 49 as the audience most willing to channel surf, looking for new programs, UPN introduced "Star Trek: Voyager" to show on Monday nights. Buyers of advertising time for "Voyager" were required to buy time on the other four UPN shows as well.

"Star Trek: Voyager" was a hit, but the other original UPN shows were poorly received. They were replaced by several urban-theme situation comedies, most notably "Moesha." In March 1996 UPN added a third night of two-hour programming in primetime and by the end of the year had 152 affiliates in markets covering about 92 percent of all television households in the United States. It also had added a two-hour Sunday slot for children's shows. By the end of 1997 UPN was being carried by 178 affiliates in markets covering 90 percent of all U.S. households and had added two hours of previously exhibited movies on Saturday afternoons. UPN was being watched by an average of five percent of all television viewers during the fall 1996 season.

The agreement with Viacom provided that Chris-Craft would finance the first two years of UPN and allow Viacom an option to buy a half-share in the network before December 15, 1996, by paying half its losses. Viacom did so in early December of that year, purchasing half the network for about $160 million. As part of the deal, Viacom agreed to sell UPN "Star Trek: Voyager" rather than syndicate the series.

UPN was not expected to become profitable in the near future because of heavy start-up and expansion costs and intense competition from other fledgling networks such as WB. Nevertheless, BHC and Paramount considered their investment in the network vital because they were finding it hard to compete against more powerful station groups for quality programming. UPN's net revenues grew from $30.4 million in 1995 to $90 million in 1997. Operating expenses grew proportionately, however, and the network's net loss increased from $133.8 million in 1995 to $170.2 million in 1997.

After reaching a peak in 1994, BHC Communications' operating revenues fell slightly for each of the next three years. Operating income peaked at $118.6 million in 1995, then fell in the next two years. The figures for 1997 were $443.5 million and $101.3 million, respectively. Net income, $92.9 million in 1994, fell sharply the next two years as BHC absorbed all of UPN's losses. In 1997 the company benefited from sharing UPN's loss with Viacom and collecting $153.9 million for Viacom's half-share in the joint venture. Net income was

$131.2 million for the year. The company had no long-term debt. Its stock, which traded between $48 and $54 a share in 1989, reached a high of $145 in 1998.

In 1997 BHC Communications' Chris-Craft Television subsidiary owned KCOP and KPTV, the Los Angeles and Portland stations. The Pinelands subsidiary owned WWOR, the New York-area station. The other six stations were owned by United Television. These included KMSP (Minneapolis/St. Paul), KTVX (Salt Lake City), KMOL (San Antonio), and the UHF stations KBHK (San Francisco) and KUTP (Phoenix). In January 1998 United Television acquired a third UHF station in Baltimore for $80 million, changed its call letters to WUTB, and made the station a UPN affiliate. United, in October 1997, agreed to purchase WRBW, a UHF station and UPN affiliate in Orlando, Florida, for $60 million and possible further considerations. This acquisition was subject to approval by the Federal Communications Commission and other conditions.

Herbert Siegel's son William became president of BHC Communications in 1996, and Herbert's son John became chairman of United Television. Herbert Siegel remained chairman and chief executive officer of BHC, however. He showed no inclination to spend the company's hoard of cash and marketable securities, whose value totaled $1.4 billion at the end of March 1998, on new acquisitions. In a 1997 telephone interview, he conceded, "In hindsight, cash has not been king. Stocks have been king. . . . Obviously, we should have bought the Vanguard 500" with the proceeds from the 1989 sale of BHC's Warner Communications stock to Time Warner. Still, he concluded, "you can't look back at the deals you didn't do." Siegel had little need to second-guess his performance as chief of BHC Communications. At the end of February 1998 Chris-Craft Industries owned 79 percent of the company's Class A stock and all of the Class B stock, representing 97 percent of the voting power.

Principal Subsidiaries

Chris-Craft Television, Inc. (and its subsidiaries, BHC Network Partner, Inc., BHC Network Partner II, Inc., BHC Network Partner III, Inc., KCOP Television, Inc., and Oregon Television, Inc.); Pinelands, Inc.; United Television, Inc. (58.8%; and its subsidiaries, UTV of Baltimore, Inc.; UTV of San Antonio, Inc.; UTV of San Francisco, Inc.; United Television Sales, Inc.).

Further Reading

"The Chris-Craft Connection," *Financial World,* December 1–15, 1982, pp. 43–44.

Fabrikant, Geraldine, "As Chris-Craft Idles, Deals Are Elusive," *New York Times,* August 4, 1997, pp. D1, D8.

Hofmeister, Sallie, "Looking for an Outlet, Viacom to Buy Half of UPN," *Los Angeles Times,* December 5, 1996, pp. D1, D4.

Jones, Alex S., "Chris-Craft's Feisty Chairman—He's Relishing the Intense Battle Over Warner," *New York Times,* January 23, 1984, Sec. 3, pp. 6–7.

Lane, Randall, "Something for Nothing," *Forbes,* February 1, 1993, p. 120.

Littleton, Cynthia, "In It for the Long Run," *Broadcasting & Cable,* March 31, 1997, p. 91.

Mannes, George, "Time Warner Marches On with Stock Buyout," *Broadcasting,* August 28, 1989, pp. 51–52.

McClellan, Steve, "United, BHC Come Together in United Sales," *Broadcasting & Cable,* March 20, 1995, p. 48.

McConville, Jim, "N.Y.'s WWOR Loses Super Status," *Broadcasting & Cable,* January 16, 1997, p. 118.

Mirabella, Alan, "Can WWOR Cash In on Trash TV?" *Crain's New York Business,* March 15, 1993, pp. 3, 25.

Sandler, Linda, "BHC Communications' Stock Offers a Chance to Ride on the Coattails of Chris-Craft's Siegel," *Wall Street Journal,* December 28, 1989, p. C2.

"A Savvy Investor Livens Up the Warner Fight," *Business Week,* January 23, 1984, p. 108.

Sharkey, Betsy, "Anxious Parents Await the Birth of a TV Network," *New York Times,* January 15, 1995, Sec. 2, pp. 1, 34.

Weinstein, Steve, "KCOP Takes a 'Risky' Path in Late-Night TV," and "Channel 13 Struggles to Redo the News," *Los Angeles Times,* September 7, 1994, pp. F1, F9.

—Robert Halasz

Billing Concepts®

Billing Concepts Corp.

7411 John Smith Drive, Suite 200
San Antonio, Texas 78229-4898
U.S.A.
(210) 949-7000
Fax: (210) 949-7014
Web site: http://www.billingconcepts.com

Public Company
Incorporated: 1985 as U.S. Long Distance Corp.
Employees: 530
Sales: $122.84 million (1997)
Stock Exchanges: NASDAQ
Ticker Symbol: BILL
SICs: 7374 Data Processing & Preparation; 7389
Business Services, Not Elsewhere Classified

Billing Concepts Corp. (BIC) is one of the largest third-party providers of billing clearinghouse and information services to the telecommunications industry. In addition to processing call records, the company provides a wide range of other services, including billing inquiry, data processing, tax filings, accounting services, and an advance funding program for a client's accounts receivables. BIC also offers custom convergent billing solutions through its Modular Business Applications (MBA) software. MBA supports billing for multiple services, such as local, long distance, cellular, personal communications systems (PCS), paging, Internet, cable/satellite TV, gas, and electricity—all included on one bill. BIC has more than 400 customers, including direct-dial, long distance telephone companies; providers of operator and information services; suppliers of telecommunications equipment; and gas and electric utilities. BIC claims 67 percent of the annual $200 million market for billing done via local-exchange carriers. The company offers its products and services through four separate lines of business: Local Exchange Carrier (LEC) Billing; Direct Billing; Software Licensing and Developing; and Back-Office Services. BIC has billing and collection agreements with more than 1,300 local telephone companies that have access lines into approximately 95 percent of the

United States, Canada, and Puerto Rico. Under its former name, U.S. Long Distance Corp., in 1993 and 1995 BIC was named one of the 100 fastest-growing companies in America by *Fortune* and *Inc.* magazines. BIC ranked 13th in *Equities* April 1997 list of "America's Most Profitable Companies." The company was listed in a May 1997 *Business Week* article titled "1997 Hot Growth Companies" and was ranked 30th out of 10,000 publicly traded corporations. In July 1997 BIC also was named to *Standard & Poor's SmallCap 600 Index*. At the beginning of fiscal 1997 the company's stock price was $22.25. By the end of that fiscal year, stock sold for $35 a share, representing a 57 percent increase in shareholder value.

Deregulation of Telecommunications: 1984–96

The 1984 breakup of American Telephone & Telegraph (AT&T) and of the Bell System revolutionized the operation of the telecommunications industry. Local telephone companies that made up the Regional Bell Operating Companies (also known as the Baby Bells) had to provide billing and collections on a nondiscriminatory basis to all carriers that supplied telecommunication services to their end-user customers. Only the largest long distance carriers, such as AT&T, MCI Telecommunications Corporation, and Sprint Incorporated, could afford the cost of agreements with local telephone companies for direct billing. Several entrepreneurs recognized an opportunity for establishing companies that would enter into these billing and collection agreements to aggregate telephone-call records for local exchange carriers and long distance carriers.

Furthermore, with the 1986 advent of technology that allowed zero-plus dialing (ZPD), customers could use an automated credit card for long distance calls or use the prefix 1 before a telephone number to make zero-minus calls (collect, third-party billing, operator-assisted calling card, or person-to-person calls). These calls were routed away from AT&T to a competitive long distance services provider. Typically, the billing information resided with the billed person's local telephone company. In order to bill for ZPD and zero-minus calls, a long distance services provider either had to obtain billing and collection agreements with LECs or use the services of third-party clearinghouses.

Company Perspectives:

Billing Concepts Corp. will continue to build BIC, leveraging our expertise and resources with three key goals in mind: satisfy the needs and expectations of our customers; explore new opportunities in the telecommunications industry and beyond; and build increased value for our shareholders.

The Telecommunications Act of 1996 dramatically changed the ground rules for competition and regulation in virtually all sectors of the communications industry. After promulgation of the 1984 antitrust consent decree that dismantled the Bell System, major strides had been made in relaxing federal regulation and in ensuring fair competition in the long distance telephone market. But emerging technology for telecommunications led to conflicting interpretations of the Communication Act of 1934 that had prevailed for 62 years. With the Telecommunications Act, Congress set a course that clearly adopted competition as the basic charter for all telecommunications markets for the next five years. The Telecommunications Act cleared market-entry barriers for entrepreneurs and other small businesses in the provision and ownership of telecommunications services.

Roots of Billing Concepts Corp.: 1985–95

While the telecommunications industry was taking shape, in 1985 Parris H. Holmes, Jr., invested $50,000 to start a small pay-phone business in his Houston garage. However, Holmes was not comfortable with the Texas regulatory environment for billing services and he switched into the long distance business by founding a company named U.S. Long Distance Corp., later known as USLD Communications Corp. According to Don Sheron's 1997 article in the *San Antonio Express News,* "from 1986–87 Holmes raised $9.2 million from people who had known him for a long time." Within a few years USLD acquired 11 companies.

Among these acquisitions was the 1988 purchase of Zero Plus Dialing, Inc., which brought with it a portfolio of billing and collection agreements with several local telephone companies. Using these agreements, USLD billed and collected from the local telephone companies for its own operator services. Billing and collection agreements were subsequently made with additional LECs, including GTE and the Baby Bells. Furthermore, USLD marketed its billing and collection services to LECs, arguing that outsourcing the administration of these operations would save time and money. The company also began to offer its third-party clearinghouse services to other operator services that did not have proprietary agreements with the local telephone companies.

By 1989 USLD was a $200,000-a-year business. The company continued its rapid expansion through the early 1990s, especially through the profitable operations of US Billing, Inc. and Enhanced Services Billing, Inc.—companies acquired in 1993 and 1994, respectively. However, the disparate functions of these subsidiaries raised concerns among clients and industry analysts. Was USLD a telecommunications company or a billing company, and was the financial data acquired through billing operations available for USLD to use against its competitors? To allay concerns, USLD separated its business into two groups that functioned independently of each other: The Billing Group and The Telecommunications Group.

Meanwhile, USLD improved its information management services with the 1990 development of a comprehensive information management system capable of processing, tracing, recording, and accounting for telephone-call transactions. USLD was also the first third-party billing clearinghouse to offer an advance funding program for its customers' accounts receivable. In 1992 the company began to offer LEC billing services to providers of direct-dial long distance services. From 1993 to 1995 the company offered enhanced clearinghouse billing and information management services to other businesses, including providers of telecommunications equipment and information, as well as other providers of nonregulated communication services and products (for example, 900 access pay-per-call transactions, cellular long distance services, paging services, voicemail services, and equipment for Caller ID and other telecommunications applications). The billing of nonregulated telecommunication products and services became a significant factor in the successful evolution of USLD's business. Revenues grew steadily reaching $33.16 million in 1992, $46.46 million in 1993, $57.75 million in 1994, and $80.85 million in 1995.

Two New Public Companies Emerge: 1996–97

By 1996, USLD's two Groups (Billing and Telecommunications) operated profitably in their respective markets. According to Sheron in the *San Antonio Express News,* Parris Holmes later commented that the Groups "simply outgrew the marriage. This was just a healthy growth situation." On July 10, 1996, USLD's board of directors approved the spinoff of the commercial billing clearinghouse and information management services into a public company. The Billing Group Business became Billing Information Concepts Corp., and on February 27, 1998, was renamed Billing Concepts Corp. (BIC). The Telecommunications Business Group remained the focus of the new USLD, later renamed USLD Communications Corp. (USLD), which in 1998 was acquired as a subsidiary by Qwest Communications International, the nation's fourth largest long distance provider.

Holmes remained Chairman/CEO of USLD until June 1997. "I felt like the separation process had been completed," said Holmes in a December 1997 interview with Diane Mayoros in the *Wall Street Corporate Reporter.* "It was a natural progression to move on to focus my time and energy" as chairman and CEO of Billing Concepts.

Positioning for Continuous Growth: 1996–97

Holmes focused on getting a head start for building the information infrastructure of the 21st century by tapping into the opportunities opened up by the Telecommunications Act, which allowed local, long distance, and cable service providers to enter each other's markets. BIC also strengthened its presence in billing services through the June 1997 acquisition of Computer Resources Management, Inc., a company that developed software systems for the direct billing of telecommunication services and was already performing billing for the utility industry. As a single-source, direct-billing solution (also referred to as convergent billing or one-stop billing) for long distance and cellular calls, PCS, paging, cable and satellite television, Internet, and utilities, Computer Resources Management software aggregated all bills on one invoice. In September this new acquisition was reorganized into Billing Concepts as a subsidiary called Billing Concepts Systems, Inc. (BCS); it offered software licensing, equipment sales, service-bureau billing, custom programming, and other ancillary services. Since Billing Concepts Systems was a Premier Business Partner of IBM, the acquisition also brought BIC an alliance that allowed for immediate expansion of its technological resources.

BIC relocated 528 employees to new headquarters, added three industry professionals to its senior management team, and doubled its technical staff. The company defined its products and services as four separate lines of business: Local Exchange Carrier Billing, Direct Billing, Software Licensing and Developing, and Back-Office Services. LEC Billing, the company's core product, consisted of three distinct divisions: U.S. Billing, Inc., Zero Plus Dialing, Inc., and Enhanced Services Billing, Inc.

U.S. Billing was BIC's fastest-growing division and accounted for more than half of the company's annual revenue. The division served carriers of direct-dial, long distance companies. This service consisted of billing ''1 + '' long distance telephone calls to individual residential customers and small commercial accounts. The growing volume of these telephone calls soon placed long distance carriers in the position of having to increase their collection rates if they billed through the local telephone companies. U.S. Billing offered these carriers a more effective way to bill and receive payment from residential customers.

Zero Plus Dialing was devoted exclusively to billing and information management services for operator-assisted calls (known as zero-plus/zero-minus calls), such as third-party calls, collect calls, and credit card calls. Zero Plus's customers included private-pay telephone owners, hotels, universities, airports, and prisons. This service was BIC's original form of LEC billing and drove the development of the systems and infrastructure used by all of the company's LEC billing services. Enhanced Services Billing, founded in 1994, billed local telephone companies for nonregulated and enhanced telecommunications services. These businesses included providers of telecommunications equipment and Internet providers; paging and voicemail services; cellular and PCS long distance services; caller ID and premium pay-per-call services (900-prefixed calls), such as weather, sports, and information services. Enhanced Services Billing's profit margins were significantly higher than those of BIC's other core products because fees could be based on a percentage of revenue rather than charged to each processed record.

At the request of its customers, BIC spent the last months of 1996 and the greater part of 1997 developing invoice-ready billing, a product that gave BIC's customers—long distance companies and providers of operator-assisted services—the ability to prepare a customized bill statement. This product was more than a generic statement on which BIC's customers could place their name; it allowed them to personalize the statement with their name, their logo, and/or marketing messages. BIC was the first company, outside of the ''big three'' AT&T, MCI, and Sprint, to market this product. The first invoice-ready bill was produced in October 1997.

For many of its LEC customers, BIC processed the tax records associated with telephone-call records and other transactions and files, as well as certain federal excise, state, and local telecommunications-related tax returns covering these records and transactions. The company submitted over 1,800 tax returns each month on behalf of its customers and provided customer service to end-users inquiring about calls for which they were billed.

BIC's 1997 acquisition of Billing Concepts Systems (BCS) gave it a head start to bundle services in a direct billing environment. As early as 1988 the subsidiary company had developed billing and customer care solutions. When the Telecommunications Act of 1996 allowed providers of local, long distance, and cable services to enter each other's markets, BCS positioned itself to become a competitive player in the market as a one-stop supplier of convergent telecommunications products and services. BCS developed state-of-the-art billing software, dubbed Modular Business Applications (MBA), to provide a single-source, direct-billing solution that allowed billing for multiple products such as local, long distance, cellular, PCS, paging, cable/satellite TV, Internet, and even utilities. The convergent-billing platform had the capability to produce a ''universal bill'' whereby multiple services and products could be billed directly to the end-user on one consolidated billing statement. MBA was offered as a service-bureau (back office) or in-house software solution utilizing the IBM AS/400 as the operational platform. BCS was ready for the not-too-distant future when long distance carriers would enter the $100 billion local markets, and when LECs would enter the $80 billion long distance markets.

In addition to billing services, BIC offered customer service, accounting services and reports, data processing, tax filings, and an advance funding program. The customer service center handled over 30,000 calls per day during fiscal 1997. As many as nine taxes could accrue for each long distance call. Each quarter, BIC's tax department prepared over 5,000 tax returns on behalf of its customers. Furthermore the company, predominantly with its own cash, funded a program that proved to be very valuable to customers who could not afford to wait the typical 60-day billing cycle to receive their payments from the local telephone companies. After qualification for this advance funding program, participants were advanced up to 80 percent of their receivables within five days of submitting their call records. When Billing Concepts received payment from the LECs for these call records, the company submitted the balance to customers, less its fees and incurred interest. BIC maintained a $50 million revolving line of credit to fund any growth in this program.

At the end of fiscal 1997, BIC revenues of $122.84 million and net income of $21.86 million were up 18 percent and 22 percent, respectively, from the revenues and net income of 1996.

Toward the 21st Century

On January 30, 1998, BIC distributed a one-for-one stock dividend to its shareholders of record. During the third quarter, actions by the FCC and the Regional Bell Operating Companies on "slamming and cramming" issues led to a temporary interruption in the revenue growth of BIC's business. "Slamming" refers to the unauthorized switching of consumers' long distance provider and "cramming" refers to the practice of billing consumers for unauthorized charges, such as the Universal Service Charge, a new federal tax added to phone bills to fund library and school access to the Internet.

However, for the first nine months of fiscal 1998, BIC reported that total revenues increased 37.4 percent to $119.7 million from $87.1 million during the comparable period of fiscal 1997. Chairman/CEO Holmes said that BIC was conducting its billing business "in a manner consistent with what the FCC was to publish in its upcoming 'Best Billing Practices' document." Furthermore, seven major industry analysts went on record as supporting BIC's strong position in its specialized niche and its ability to maintain a revenue growth rate of at least 25 percent annually over the next several years.

"BIC's energies," Holmes emphasized, "are being focused on competitive local exchange carriers and telecommunication carriers who are diversifying their product and service offerings. . . . Our competitive advantage is time-to-market and a highly marketable convergent billing solution. . . . We remain focused on our long-term goals and are excited about our opportunities."

BIC continued to seize opportunities for expansion by providing add-on services to both new and existing customers and by acquiring new business. For instance, during the second quarter of 1998, BIC announced that Intermedia Communications, a provider of integrated telecommunications solutions, chose BCS's Modular Billing Application to replace a number of its billing systems. Another significant event occurred when LCI International Telecommunications Corp., a subsidiary of Qwest Communications and one of the nation's fastest-growing major telecommunication companies, signed a multiyear agreement for BIC to provide billing services for customers of LCI's operator-assisted services while LCI provided long distance and 800 services for BIC's customers. During the third quarter, BIC signed 26 new accounts and received renewal of 18 contracts. BCS also continued to add new business by selling three in-house systems and signing two service-bureau agreements.

Then in July 1998, WinStar Communications, Inc. chose BCS to consolidate its multiple billing platforms onto the MBA system, thereby receiving a complete solution set to support WinStar's long distance, local resale, calling card, and enhanced services for retail and wholesale customers. In August of the same year, Philadelphia-based Eagle Communications, entered into a five-year contract for BIC's entire suite of product offerings, which included MBA, BIC's customer service and billing software, and back-office support. Also in August, BIC signed an agreement to acquire 22 percent of the capital stock of Princeton Telecommunications Corporation (PTC), a private company specializing in electronic-bill publishing over the Internet and advanced payment solutions. According to Chairman/CEO Holmes, "this association with PTC is a key to our on-going strategy to grow our solution set. Consumers are rapidly embracing the ability to pay their bills over the Internet and this phenomenon is causing vendors to publish their bills electronically. . . . Instead of developing these services, we will deliver them through PTC." He went on to say that this way of sharing billing strategies "will not only enhance our investment in PTC, but will catapult Billing Concepts into the emerging Internet market."

As the 20th century drew to a close, Billing Concepts Corp. was well positioned to move into the 21st century as a significant player in the multibillion-dollar telecommunications and billing markets.

Principal Subsidiaries

Billing Concepts Systems, Inc.; Enhanced Services Billing, Inc.; U.S. Billing, Inc.; Zero Plus Dialing, Inc.

Further Reading

Ashton, Douglas C., and Connie Fang, "Cramming & Slamming Hits the Clearinghouses," *Equity Research Department,* Jefferies & Company, Inc., June 9, 1998, pp. 1–3.

"BILL: Conference Call Confirms Earlier Analysis, No Change in Outlook," *Equity Research Department,* Robert W. Baird & Co. Incorporated, June 11, 1998, pp. 1–4.

Bolen, Robert V. "Reducing Estimates Due to Moratorium on New Services by Bells; BCS Remains Strong," *Equity Research Department,* J.C. Bradford & Co., June 9, 1998, pp. 1–2.

Cullen, Lisa Reilly, "How You Can Make Money in Telecommunications Without Getting Tangled in Turf Wars," *Money,* April 1988, pp. 60–62.

Grozovsky, Ilia, "Billing Concepts Pre-Announces Quarter Below Expectations; Estimates Reduced; Maintain Hold Rating," *Research Notes,* Furman Selz LLC, June 12, 1998, pp. 1–3.

Johnson, Robert M., and Joseph P. Beaulieu, "BILL Has a Strong Position in a Specialized Niche—Reiterate Buy," *Research Notes,* ABN AMRO Incorporated, June 23, 1998, pp. 1–3.

Mayores, Diane, "Market Will Explode: Interview with Parris H. Holmes," *Wall Street Corporate Reporter,* December 8–14, 1997.

Mensheha, Mark, "Billing Firm Lines Up Credit Package," *San Antonio Business Journal,* January 31, 1997, pp. 1–2.

Much, Marilyn, "The New America," *Investor's Business Daily,* November 17, 1997, p. 1.

Picchi, B., and M. Logani, "Billing Concepts: Redux—Slamming Revisited; Lower 1999 EPS to Be Safe," *Document #0610Bill,* A-Lehman Brothers, Inc., June 10, 1998, pp. 1–3.

Sheron, Don, "Billing Concepts Corp. Proves It Can Stand Alone: USLD Spinoff Carves a $1.2 Billion Niche," *San Antonio Express News,* August 17, 1997, pp. 1H, 5H.

Weiss, Sebastian, "Corpus [Christi] Gains Call Center Due to Tight Labor Market Here," *San Antonio Business Journal,* May 15, 1998, p. 5.

—Gloria A. Lemieux

Boart Longyear Company

2340 West 1700 South
Salt Lake City, Utah 84104
U.S.A.
(801) 972-6430
Fax: (801) 977-3374
Web site: http://www.boartlongyear.com

Private Company
Incorporated: 1911 as E.J. Longyear Company
Employees: 8,000
Sales: $600 million (1997 est.)
SICs: 3532 Mining Machinery; 3569 General Industrial
   Machine, Not Elsewhere Classified

Boart Longyear Company is a major provider of diamond drill bits and related drilling parts and services for the mining, construction, and environmental industries. The company's experts in contract drilling have helped many exploration companies find deposits of copper, gold, silver, and other metals. The company's geotechnical services include soil and rock sampling that help construction companies prepare for their work. From humble roots in Minneapolis and South Africa, Boart Longyear has grown to become a significant international firm with most of its revenues coming from foreign contracts.

Company Origins in the Late 19th Century

Company founder Edmund J. Longyear was born on November 6, 1864 in Grass Lake, Michigan. In 1888 he graduated as a mining engineer from the first class of the Michigan School of Mines. In 1890 Longyear drilled the first diamond drill hole on the famous Mesabi Iron Range in northern Minnesota. Years later the Iron Range Historical Society placed a historic marker at the site of Longyear's first diamond drilling.

Edmund Longyear contracted to help other firms drill on the Mesabi Range, the major source of iron ore for the giant steel mills of Andrew Carnegie and the American steel industry. Longyear endured difficult conditions, living in tents before boom towns were built. He worked with Russians, Slavs, Germans, Italians, and other miners from different nations.

Meanwhile, in 1903 Longyear and John E. Hodge organized a partnership called Longyear and Hodge to operate their business ventures, which included shaft sinking, contract drilling, mineral ventures, and related consulting work, outside of Minnesota. That partnership and Longyear's drill contracting business merged in 1911, when the E.J. Longyear Company was incorporated under the laws of Delaware. At that point Hodge moved from Marquette to the company headquarters in Minneapolis.

The company's first price list in 1912 featured 19 drill models with capabilities from 750 to 5,000 feet. These drills were powered mainly by steam engines, which later would be replaced by internal combustion engines developed in the 1920s.

Expansion in the Early 20th Century

Longyear expanded early in the United States and overseas. From 1912 to 1916 the company drilled for copper in Cuba, the firm's first international project. In 1914 Longyear began setting up the first of six drills to help the Phelps Dodge Corporation find copper in Arizona. The company in 1919 began a 15-month project in Yunnan Province, China, and by the 1920s about half of the firm's work was outside the continental United States.

In 1915 Edmund Longyear sent his head geologist Hugh Roberts to oversee diamond drilling in Ontario, Canada. As the result of this work, Roberts designed a new form of technology called a core splitter, which divided cores into three to five inch lengths for better analysis. Eventually other drilling firms used Roberts's core splitter as standard equipment.

During America's post-World War I depression of 1920–21, Longyear's business declined. Its annual sales slumped from a high of $550,000 in 1916 to only $220,000 in 1921. The following year the Consolidated Coal Company hired Longyear to sink three shafts in the coal fields of Appalachia. Water in one shaft and a strike by Longyear workers caused Longyear to lose $100,000 on that contract, but Robert D. Longyear, who became president of the firm in 1924, learned to avoid lump-sum contracts from that experience.

| **Company Perspectives:** |

The Boart Longyear Group is a leading manufacturer and supplier of tools, equipment and contracting services for the international exploration, mining, construction, quarrying, geotechnical, environmental and industrial markets.

Robert Longyear, the only one of founder Edmund Longyear's six children to continue in the family business, had learned firsthand from his father about the drilling and mining business. He attended Williams College, served in the Corps of Engineers during World War I, earned his M.S. degree in geology from the University of Wisconsin, and continued his geological studies with postgraduate education at Stanford and the University of Minnesota. This combination of formal training with hands-on experience prepared him to be the second-generation leader of Longyear for over 40 years.

As the business climate improved in the roaring 1920s, Longyear prospered. Sales increased steadily from 1925 to 1929. In 1928 the company moved its headquarters from modest Minneapolis offices to the 17th floor of the new 30-floor Foshay Tower. Longyear in 1929 sold almost $1.5 million worth of drilling equipment and contract services and the following year the company formed its first foreign subsidiary in Canada.

In 1929 the company signed its first contract for work in Africa, sending equipment and a crew of 58 to northern Rhodesia to provide drilling for copper ores. Longyear's men lived in adobe and grass huts and faced the hazards of malaria during the rainy season, but in spite of the rough conditions work was completed just before Christmas 1930.

Surviving the Great Depression and the Boart Connection

Meanwhile, the stock market crashed in October 1929 and the Great Depression hit the nation with full force. E.J. Longyear Company barely survived those trying times. The firm's sales fell to a historic low of just $79,500 in 1933.

One interesting project during the 1930s was drilling for core samples for the proposed Golden Gate Bridge in San Francisco. Enduring storms and deep water, Longyear workers obtained their samples for the bridge, which was completed in 1937.

A major change in diamond drilling technology began in the 1930s. Since the 1890s, Longyear and other firms relied on natural Brazilian diamonds called carbonados or "carbons." Then in the 1930s some drillmakers began using industrial quality diamonds called "boarts" (or bortz) mined in Africa. Smaller than carbons, boarts usually were a fraction of a carat and generally were imperfect crystals in a variety of shapes and colors.

In 1936 South Africa's Anglo American Corporation created Boart Products South Africa (Pty) Limited, later renamed Boart International, to create markets for their accumulated stores of boarts built up during the Depression. Boart Products developed the first mechanically set diamond drill bits, which some firms began using instead of the hand-set bits using carbons. That pioneering technology was used successfully for the first time in Zambia for copper exploration.

Longyear in 1938 bought its first mechanically set bits from the R.S. McClintock Company of Spokane, Washington. Eventually all Longyear contract drilling relied on the mechanically set bits. In addition, Longyear began selling McClintock bits to American and foreign customers.

The 1940s Through the 1970s

In the 1940s and 1950s Don Davidson directed mineral ventures ranging from gold explorations in Canada and lead-zinc efforts in New York State to gold ventures in Cripple Creek, Colorado. One of Davidson's most ambitious efforts was undertaken in the Tintic Mining District near Eureka, Utah, a historic mining area that had produced hundreds of millions of dollars of lead, zinc, and silver since 1869. In the 1940s Davidson formed a joint venture with Kennecott Copper and Calumet and Hecla Copper Company. This experimental drilling effort attempted to get through gravel and lava flows to reach underlying mineral deposits, but the project was eventually abandoned.

Don Davidson continued his consulting work in the 1950s. In 1952 he served on the President's Materials Policy Commission to look into possible shortages of raw materials in the postwar period. The same year he began a 30-month contract to survey parts of Angola and Mozambique, two African nations then still under Portuguese rule. By 1955 Davidson, along with other Longyear and Portuguese geologists, produced a major geological study of areas never before accurately surveyed and mapped.

In 1949 Longyear began a close relationship with Christensen Diamond Products (CDP). Following a joint operation that filled a large Brazilian order for diamond bits, the two firms worked out an arrangement in which they pooled their diamond purchases from the Central Selling Organization. Christensen agreed to manage the joint diamond inventory and to set all Longyear bits to Longyear specifications. Longyear sold those bits under its own name, while Christensen was free to sell its own bits in competition with Longyear.

Frank and George Christensen of CDP worked closely with Vince Burnhart of Longyear. The two firms jointly developed projects in Japan (Nippon Longyear subsidiary), France, Canada (Canadian Longyear subsidiary), Mexico (Longyear de Mexico subsidiary), the Netherlands (Longyear Nederland subsidiary), Australia (Longyear Australia subsidiary), Germany, the Philippines, and Costa Rica (Longyear Centroamericana, S.A. subsidiary) between 1953 and 1970. Business continued to boom into the 1970s with new operations in New Zealand, Brazil, and Chile.

To promote its business in France and French-speaking African nations, in 1953 Longyear created a subsidiary called Longyear France. Four years later it formed Longyear International based in The Hague. Longyear Germany was created in

1963 in response to oil exploration opportunities in the North Sea. In 1968 the office in The Hague was closed. Its staff and functions were moved to Etten-Leur, where a manufacturing plant was opened.

International conflicts sometimes prevented Longyear and other firms from doing business. Starting in 1960, Longyear, Christensen Diamond Products, and Larson & Toubro formed Christensen Longyear India Limited to make diamond drill bits in India. Following the 1964 border war between India and China and other political changes, the joint venture ended in 1973.

Meanwhile, Longyear expanded its Canadian business. Formed in 1931 with just six workers, Canadian Longyear by the end of 1967 employed over 400 and its annual sales reached $10 million. By the late 1960s the firm's North Bay manufacturing plant had become too small to accommodate the company's growing Canadian operations, and in 1970 a major expansion was completed. In that year Canadian Longyear sales grew to $15 million.

Such growth, both in the United States and overseas, was fueled by new technology. In 1958 two Longyear employees patented a new drilling innovation called Wireline that helped the firm remain competitive and proved to be a major contribution to the drilling industry. Previously, drillers obtained core samples by withdrawing a long pipe after drilling had occurred. Wireline permitted cores to be withdrawn without removing the pipe, which made drilling more efficient, protected drill holes from erosion, and prevented damage to drill bits.

Longyear began a series of important management and ownership changes in the 1950s. Robert Longyear considered taking the firm public, but eventually decided against the move. In 1958 he retired, marking the end to the Longyear family's direct running of the company. In 1960 Longyear named Vince Burnhart as its new president. Then in 1964 Longyear sold 25 percent of its family-owned stock to FACTS, a Luxembourg-based holding company owned jointly by Boart International and Christensen Diamond Products Company. Three years later FACTS exercised its option to purchase another 25 percent of Longyear's family stock. The Longyear family retained 30 percent of the company's stock, with the remaining 20 percent owned by employees.

By 1965 Longyear's annual sales had reached $15 million, so the company bought more land in Minneapolis and persuaded the city government to vacate Erie Street to accommodate its expansion. In 1969 Longyear opened its new office building and an enlarged manufacturing plant. For the first time in its history, the company's headquarters and its U.S. production were located at one site. Longyear sales reached $40 million in 1970.

Robert Longyear died in 1970, and Vince Burnhart died the year after. Following these losses the board of directors appointed John Hoffmeister as president and chairman of the board of the company. Meanwhile, ownership of Longyear was still not finalized. FACTS was dissolved when Boart bought out CDP's interest. Then on July 31, 1974 Boart International, headquartered in Johannesburg, South Africa, purchased all outstanding shares of Longyear, becoming the company's sole owner.

Although Longyear's name remained the same, the Boart purchase resulted in a new corporate culture, according to *Longyear: The Mesabi and Beyond*. Previously, Longyear emphasized its Minnesota roots and American operations, with foreign subsidiaries seen as branches of the main company. Under Boart influence, "The new idea was that of a group of companies scattered over the world; the U.S. company one of the group. The Corporate Headquarters, which happened to be in Minneapolis, was increasingly thought of as separate from U.S. operations, a distinction non-existent under the old guard."

New ownership also brought new management. By 1976 Longyear President/Chairman John Hoffmeister had retired. Peter Bremmer became the new president in 1975. In 1976 Hilton Davies, Boart International's managing director, became Longyear's board chairman.

Meanwhile, Longyear acquired new technology from a competitor. In 1975 the Chicago Pneumatic Tool Company decided to end its production of diamond drills. Longyear purchased the right to make and sell Chicago Pneumatic's small CP-65 compressed air drill designed for underground use. Longyear also made spare parts for the hundreds of CP-65s already in use.

In the late 1970s Longyear benefited from the availability of small synthetic diamonds, the hardest substance on earth. By scattering these small particles uniformly throughout the matrix, Longyear made impregnated diamond bits, which allowed deeper and faster drilling. Longyear Canada first sold the new bits in 1979 and by 1980 was the major bit supplier in Canada. Longyear in 1979 built a new plant in Salt Lake City to produce both the impregnated bits and the older surface set bits. Other diamond bit facilities were purchased overseas.

In the 1960s and 1970s Longyear began to diversify into areas beyond its traditional mineral exploration drilling. The company began using diamond bits for drilling and sawing concrete in the construction industry. In 1977 Longyear purchased rights to make concrete saws from the Drillistics Company. The firm's Salt Lake City plant began making diamond saw blades in the early 1980s.

From 1957 to 1978 Longyear drilled 432 holes in northeastern Minnesota to explore for copper, nickel, and other minerals. This Minnamax Project, the longest in the company's history in Minnesota, resulted in a permanent collection of split-core samples less than 15 miles from Edmund Longyear's 1890 drill site on the Mesabi Range.

Crisis in the 1980s

In 1979 Longyear exceeded $100 million in annual sales for the first time. The worldwide mineral exploration boom continued, and the company added its Longyear Iberica subsidiary in Spain in 1980. By 1981 company sales reached almost $200 million.

In the mid-1980s, however, metals prices collapsed and the good times for the mining industry ended. Longyear's business decreased by over 50 percent, and the company ceased its operations in Japan and Brazil. Facing decreased worldwide demand for minerals, Longyear in 1985 closed its historic Minneapolis plant and made its North Bay, Ontario plant its main production site. In 1988 the company moved its headquarters to Salt Lake City, where the company already operated a contracting office and a diamond bit plant. Utah's right-to-work law helped Longyear save on its labor costs, and its new headquarters were closer to the nation's mining areas in the West.

Meanwhile, the company stepped up its diversification program. In 1983 Longyear acquired Lang Exploratory Drilling based in Utah and in 1984 purchased Cushion Cut, a firm with 25 years experience making and using diamond tools to saw concrete in runways and highways. In 1986 Longyear acquired three more companies: Morissette, an underground and surface diamond drilling firm; Brainard-Kilman, a maker of civil engineering devices, such as well monitoring and test equipment; and Chemgrout. Longyear acquired Slope Indicator Company, the nation's largest producer of geotechnical instruments and Northern Air Supply in 1988, followed by the Campbell Pacific Division in 1989 and WTD Environmental Drilling in 1990.

In the 1980s Longyear sold more than $1 million worth of equipment to help the renovation and seismic upgrading of the historic Salt Lake City-County Building built in the 1890s. The firm has contributed to other construction-related projects, such as restoring parts of the Panama Canal and earthquake studies of Egypt's famous Aswan Dam.

Developments in the 1990s

In the 1990s the Longyear Company continued its historic drilling activities and continued to find new applications. More American firms found Longyear's environmental testing services and products useful because of increased government regulations. For example, new gasoline stations called on Longyear to install four federally mandated wells to monitor storage tank leakage that might pollute underground water sources. Longyear products helped save many lives in 1994. Company instruments detected an imminent earthquake at London's Heathrow Airport, which allowed three subways under the airport to be evacuated before they collapsed.

On January 2, 1995, the Longyear Company changed its name to the Boart Longyear Company and adopted a new logo and colors. However, management and ownership remained the same; Hilton Davies continued as the board chairman and Michael H. Moore, as president.

Most of Boart Longyear's employees and revenues in the mid-1990s came from international operations. Operations in the United States employed about 1,000 people and accounted for about $130 million in sales, a relatively small part of the firm's 8,000 employees and over $600 million in annual revenues worldwide. With diverse products and services and decades of international experience, the Boart Longyear Company seemed well prepared to enter the new century.

Principal Subsidiaries

Slope Indicator Company; Chemgrout.

Principal Divisions

Cushion Cut; Lang Exploratory Drilling.

Further Reading

Longyear, Edmund J., and Walter R. Eastman, *Longyear: The Mesabi and Beyond,* Gilbert, Minn.: Iron Range Historical Society, 1984.

Pine, Carol, "Around the World with Longyear," *Northliner,* January–February 1977, pp. 30–33.

Swinton, Heidi, *Longyear: The First 100 Years,* Minneapolis: Longyear Company, 1990.

Walden, David, "Boart Longyear Company," in *Centennial Utah: The Beehive State on the Eve of the Twenty-First Century,* edited by G. Wesley Johnson and Marian Ashby Johnson, Encino, Calif.: Cherbo Publishing Group, 1995, pp. 112–13,.

—David M. Walden

BROWN

Brown Printing Company

2300 Brown Avenue
P.O. Box 1549
Waseca, Minnesota 56093-0517
U.S.A.
(507) 835-2410
Fax: (507) 835-0238
Web site: http://www.brownprinting.com

Wholly Owned Subsidiary of Bertelsmann/Gruner +
*   Jahr,*
Founded: 1957
Employees: 2,600
Sales: $396 million (1998 est.)
SICs: 2721 Periodicals; 2741 Miscellaneous Publishing

Brown Printing Company, headquartered in rural Minnesota, is a nationally recognized producer of business, trade, and consumer special interest publications. In-house services include conventional/digital pre-press, platemaking, bindery, distribution services (label/ink jet), and desktop publishing. The company is owned by Bertelsmann/Gruner + Jahr Company, the third largest communications conglomerate in the world, behind Disney and Time Warner.

Small-Town Entrepreneur to Regional Printer 1950s–70s

Wayne (Bumps) Brown established Brown Printing Company in his hometown of Waseca, Minnesota, a small community about 80 miles south of the Twin Cities. Waseca was the site of a number of prior Brown family entrepreneurial ventures. Wayne's father, Donald Brown, was editor and owner of the *Waseca Daily Journal.* His mother, Bell Brown, owned the Corner Lunch. His grandfather Walter Brown was proprietor of Brown's Dry Goods located in Waseca and Rochester, Minnesota.

In 1957, Wayne Brown sold his interest in the family newspaper, bought the commercial printing end of the business, and began producing catalogs and publications on flatbed letter-presses. Brown and his team of printing artisans increased the speed of production with a switch to a four-color, heatset, web offset printing later in the decade. In 1964, Brown Printing Company began construction on a new facility also located in Waseca.

In 1969, Bemis Company, Inc., a Minneapolis-based manufacturer of packaging products with $300 million in sales, purchased Brown Printing. Wayne Brown retained his position as company president of the wholly owned subsidiary. At the time of the sale Brown Printing's annual sales were over $7 million.

While the existing facility was expanded numerous times, and an ink production division was added in 1972, Brown Printing remained a single-plant company until 1978. The company expanded outside of Waseca for the first time when it opened a second web offset printing plant in East Greenville, Pennsylvania.

The East Greenville Printing Plant served the regional magazines and news weeklies located in the mid-Atlantic states. To satisfy customer demand, another eastern subsidiary began operation the next year. The Franklin, Kentucky, rotogravure plant was among the most modern in the nation when it opened in 1979. The gravure facility gave Brown Printing the ability to reproduce the high quality pictures desired by the publication and long-run catalog markets.

Sale to International Concern Sets Tone for the 1980s and 1990s

In 1979, Bemis sold Brown Printing to a subsidiary of Hamburg, West Germany-based, Gruner & Jahr AG & Co., a publishing and printing firm. Bemis received $45 million for Brown Printing, which embodied the largest part of their graphics business line.

In 1986, Brown Printing's parent company, Bertelsmann, became the second largest publisher of books in the United States thanks to the procurement of Doubleday & Co. The worldwide communications giant also owned American-based Bantam Books. Bertelsmann, which had annual sales of more than $3.8 billion in 1985, also gained sole ownership of RCA

Company Perspectives:

Customer service, high-quality printing and state-of-the-art technology are taken very seriously at Brown Printing Company. Each day, highly skilled and dedicated employees strive to make our customers' experience with Brown satisfactory in every way.

This strong commitment to quality, service and technology has truly benefited our customers over the years and has elevated Brown's reputation as one of America's most prominent full-service printers of magazines, catalogs and inserts.

As the printing and publishing industry continues evolving, you can always count on Brown to be there with innovative solutions and technology to meet today's demands.

Corporation's record business, the third largest among U.S. record makers, in 1986.

Brown Printing, notable in its own right, ranked 28th in the nation among printing companies, according to *Printing Impressions* magazine's 1987 list of the 500 largest U.S. printing companies with estimated sales of $300 million. According to a January 1988 *Minneapolis/St. Paul CityBusiness* article, some of the largest specialty printers in the country were located in Minnesota: 15 Minnesota companies in all made the top 500 list.

Brown Printing expanded to the West Coast in 1987. The California operation included the Riverside County Publishing Company (Riverside) and First Western Graphics (San Leandro). With the addition, Brown Printing had proximity to major population centers on both coasts and in middle America. Two years later, Brown established a PrepSAT division which encompassed the electronic pre-press operations. State-of-the-art equipment furnished Brown with new methods to process customers' images and words in preparation for printing.

The 1980s held challenges for many industries; the printing business was no exception. Increased competition and rapidly changing technology put pressure on even established printing companies. High-speed presses, according to a June 1989 *Minneapolis/St. Paul CityBusiness* article by Nora Leven, "crank out more pieces per hour than did the previous generation of presses." Subsequently, the industry was capable of producing more product than the market demanded. The over-capacity led to falling prices. Brown Printing responded by improving operation efficiencies and retiring outdated equipment a step ahead of the competition, but the company's growth slowed.

Brown Printing broadened its reach with the creation of the Alliance List Services Division in 1991 to serve high-volume customers. The purchase of CMP Printing Co., Thorofare, New Jersey—a subsidiary of New York-based CMP Publishing Co.—in 1993, added seven new titles, including *Computer Reseller News* and *Electronic Buyers News*, to Brown Printing's cache of magazines: high-profile national publications, such as *Time*, *Sports Illustrated*, and *People*, were among those already printed at Brown's East Greenville, Pennsylvania, plant.

"It's much easier for the large printers like Brown to buy an existing business than to try to take business away from the competitors," said Kelvin Johnson, president of the St. Paul-based Printing Industry of Minnesota Inc., in a January 1993 *CityBusiness* article by Betsy Weinberger. Brown Printing's total annual revenue exceeded $400 million. The company was the eighth largest catalog printer and fourth largest publications printer in the nation. As a whole, the U.S. commercial printing industry generated about $85 billion a year in sales.

Through affiliate company BGJ Enterprises, Inc., Brown Printing purchased Graftek Press, Inc., a subsidiary of Connecticut-based Devon Group, Inc., in July 1997. Graftek, which had annual sales of about $60 million, specialized in printing, binding, and fulfillment services to magazine, catalog, and commercial clients.

"The acquisition of Graftek and its subsidiaries fits perfectly with Brown Printing's long-term strategy of further building upon its dominant position in the trade/business, consumer special interest magazine and catalog markets," said Brown Printing President and CEO Dan L. Nitz in a July 1997 news release.

The 40-year-old company printed more than 280 magazine titles for publishers and more than 250 catalogs for direct marketers. Brown Printing had manufacturing facilities in seven U.S. locations and employed more than 3,800 people. In its Waseca facility alone, the company used over 400 rolls of paper a day. The rolls averaged about 1,800 pounds and were about 10 miles long. More than 95 percent of the five million pounds of ink used at the plant a year was produced by the company's Ink Division.

Brown Printing added to its holdings a few months later with the acquisition of Tulsa, Oklahoma-based PennWell Printing Company. The trade and business publication printer had spun off PennWell Publishing Company in the early 1980s. Well-established, Brown Printing's new acquisition printed more than 100 magazine titles for 70 different publishers. The 1997 purchases of PennWell Printing and Graftek Press boosted Brown Printing into the number one spot among U.S. trade and business publications printers.

While building on the trade and business publications aspects of the company, Brown Printing dropped out of the gravure printing with the sale of the Franklin Printing Plant in Kentucky. The division printed circulars for local and national retailers. The advertising business, which used electronic media as well as printed media to sell its message, was subject to more volatility than the business publications arena. Minnesota-based print industry consultant Gershom Wu speculated, in an October 1997 *Minneapolis/St. Paul CityBusiness* article by Jennifer Ehrlich, that Brown Printing "is probably trying to go for a more conservative path now."

Looking Toward the Future

The $120 million sale of the Franklin Division to Boston-based Quebecor Printing USA, the second largest commercial printer in the United States, and a subsidiary of Montreal, Canada-based Quebecor Printing Inc., was representative of the direction the industry was heading. Just as Brown Printing facilitated growth by acquisition so did its even larger competitors. ''As technological advances continue to fuel consolidation in the print industry nationwide, Quebecor has embarked on an aggressive acquisition strategy to beat out the competition by sheer size,'' wrote Ehrlich. Quebecor Printing Inc. had 115 plants in Canada, the United States, Europe, Asia, and Latin America. Brown Printing had exited a facet of the printing business in which Quebecor held a dominant position.

Brown's own parent company, Bertelsmann, advanced its U.S. holdings in 1998 with the acquisition of Random House and boosted its share of the U.S. book market from six to ten percent. The giant media company held book, magazine, broadcasting, digital pay-TV, and online service concerns. Brown Printing was able to supplement its own in-house offerings through its union with Bertelsmann/Gruner + Jahr: web site and CD-ROM development, as well as custom publishing services offered by various divisions of the parent company, complemented Brown's core printing business line.

Brown Printing had long prided itself on its commitment to both customer service and leading edge technology. The company continued to uphold both those traditions in 1998. The Minnesota-based company, with an eye to changing customer demographics, opened a sales office in suburban Tampa in 1998 in order to better serve the rapidly-growing southeastern region. Ongoing equipment upgrades within Brown Printing's facilities provided customers with the most up-to-date and widest variety of options available in the industry from formatting to binding.

Brown Printing was among the first, worldwide, to install computer-to-plate (CTP) technology, which allowed customers to move their materials through the entire printing process in digital form. Data could be transferred directly from computer to printing plate eliminating film and chemical waste as well as cutting turnaround time. Instead of waiting for films and proofs customers inspected the printing job on their own computer screens. The conversion from mechanical to electronic printing was viewed as the wave of the future, and Brown Printing was at the forefront.

The combination of market know-how and financial strength positioned Brown Printing well in terms of retaining existing customers and bringing on new ones in the future. The company headed toward the 21st century quite secure in its position as one of America's leading producers of business, trade, and consumer special interest publications.

Further Reading

''Bemis Co. Agrees to Acquire Brown Printing,'' *Minneapolis Tribune*, May 15, 1969, p. 15.

''Bemis Co. Agrees to Sell Subsidiary Brown Printing Co.,'' *Minneapolis Tribune*, June 15, 1979.

''Brown Printing Company,'' *Corporate Report Fact Book 1998*, Minneapolis: Corporate Report, 1998, pp. 668–69.

''Brown Printing Company: 40th Anniversary,'' Waseca, Minn.: Brown Printing Company, 1997.

''Brown Printing Will Enlarge Plant at Waseca,'' *Minneapolis Star*, March 4, 1972.

''Brown Signs Purchase Agreement for Graftek Press, Inc., July 22, 1997 (press release).

Ehrlich, Jennifer, ''Brown Sells Division to Quebecor for $120 Million,'' *Minneapolis/St. Paul CityBusiness*, October 24, 1997, pp. 1, 48.

''German Firm Agrees to Buy Random House,'' *Star Tribune* (Minneapolis), March 24, 1998, p. 1D.

Hahn, Shannon, ''Largest Minnesota Printing Companies: Top 25 List,'' *Minneapolis/St. Paul CityBusiness*, September 11, 1998, p. 24.

Leven, Nora, ''Overcapacity Plagues State's Printing Industry,'' *Minneapolis/St. Paul CityBusiness*, June 26, 1989, p. 22.

Meryhew, Richard, ''Campus Closing Teaches Waseca a Hard Lesson,'' *Star Tribune* (Minneapolis), February 7, 1992, p. 1A.

Rosengren, John, ''Printers Adopt Digital Imaging,'' *Minneapolis/St. Paul CityBusiness*, September 11, 1998, pp. 27–28.

Weinberger, Betsy, ''Brown Printing Turns East to Buy Printer of Biz Pubs,'' *Minneapolis/St. Paul CityBusiness*, January 8–14, 1993, p. 4.

''West German Firm to Purchase Doubleday,'' *Star Tribune* (Minneapolis), September 27, 1986, p. 7B.

Ylinen, Jerry, ''Minnesota Among Leaders in Printing Industry,'' *Minneapolis/St. Paul CityBusiness*, January 25, 1988, pp. 12–13.

—Kathleen Peippo

Bruno's, Inc.

Bruno's, Inc.

800 Lakeshore Parkway
P.O. Box 2486
Birmingham, Alabama 35201-2486
U.S.A.
(205) 940-9400
Fax: (205) 940-9568
Web site: http://www.brunos.com

Public Company
Incorporated: 1959
Employees: 25,000
Sales: $2.9 billion (1997)
Stock Exchanges: NASDAQ
Ticker Symbol: BRNOQ
SICs: 5411 Grocery Stores; 5912 Drug Stores &
    Proprietary Stores

Bruno's, Inc., 82 percent-owned by Kohlberg Kravis Roberts & Co., operates some of the largest supermarket chains in the southeastern United States. Once one of the nation's most successful supermarket companies, Bruno's was struggling under Chapter 11 bankruptcy protection in 1998. The corporation operated more than 200 stores, including a variety of retail food stores, pharmacies, and combination food and drug stores in Alabama, Georgia, Florida, Mississippi, and Tennessee. Located in urban and rural settings, these stores comprised Food World, Bruno's Food and Pharmacy, FoodMax, and Food Fair. For years the company had operated dozens of stores under the Piggly Wiggly name but had terminated its franchise agreement allowing it to use the name in 1997.

Early History

In 1932 during the Great Depression, Joseph Bruno, the son of Sicilian immigrants, opened his first grocery, an 800-square-foot corner store in Birmingham, Alabama. Using his parent's savings for an initial investment of $600, Joe would achieve the kind of success that young immigrants still dream of. Joe's cash-only policy enabled him to keep prices low, and customers came from all over Birmingham to the first Bruno's store. As they became old enough to work, Joe's three brothers, Anthony, Angelo, and Lee, joined the business. In 1935 the family opened a second store. By April 1, 1959, when the company was incorporated in Alabama as Bruno's, Inc., all four Bruno sons were well established in the business. The company had a firm foundation of 10 stores that year.

A decade later Bruno's began its strategy of opening different chains to target different markets. In 1968 the company opened its first Big B Discount Drug Store, a chain that would grow steadily over the next dozen years. Bruno's Food Stores had also been expanding, reaching a total of 29 stores throughout Alabama by 1970. The following year the family took their business public, although they retained 30 percent of the shares and held on to the management of the company.

In 1972 Bruno's launched its Food World chain. The stores were designed as discount supermarkets, and Bruno's kept prices low with many innovative strategies that would later be widely imitated. More than 40,000 square feet in area, the stores were essentially warehouses that displayed shelves of food in manufacturers' cartons. Their economical store design and no-frills service encouraged high sales volume and low overhead. Food World was the first chain in the region to forgo periodic sales on selected merchandise in favor of everyday low prices.

Expansion in the 1980s

After the success of the Food World chain, Bruno's refined its marketing strategy in the 1980s, more closely targeting different market segments. First, Bruno's divested its Big B Discount Drug Stores in 1980 by offering all stock in the subsidiary to the public. In 1983 the company remodeled its Bruno's Food Stores and renamed the chain Bruno's Food and Pharmacy. Aiming for a higher-end market, these stores stocked gourmet items from the United States and overseas and boasted larger-than-average departments for produce, meat, seafood, deli items, and baked goods. With about 50,000 square feet per store, Bruno's Food and Pharmacy featured one-stop shopping, in-store banks, and specialty items. The combination food and drug stores were committed to customer service, with such amenities as bag boys carrying groceries to customers' cars. The same year Bruno's opened its first Bruno's Finer Foods, and in 1985 it launched its Food Fair chain. Food Fair stores, at only approximately 30,000 square feet, were designed as conventional neighborhood stores with personal service and promotional pricing.

Bruno's also expanded through acquisitions in the 1980s. In 1985 the company bought the Birmingham, Alabama, chain Megamarket. Bruno's changed the new stores' name, adding them to its FoodMax chain, another "Value Format" supermarket chain with warehouse-like facilities in the 50,000 to 60,000 square foot range. Bruno's moved into Tennessee in 1987 with the purchase of the Steven's Supermarket chain in Nashville. The company also bought seven BiLo supermarkets in 1988, which moved the company into Georgia.

Also in 1988, Bruno's acquired PWS Holding Corp., which held Piggly Wiggly Southern, Inc. This purchase helped Bruno's achieve a substantial expansion in northern Georgia and Florida. The acquisition of 58 Piggly Wiggly stores was Bruno's first major competitive purchase. The price was 2.49 million shares of Bruno's common stock. Bruno's retained some of Piggly Wiggly's management, naming the former Piggly Wiggly Southern president, William White, executive vice-president of Bruno's for merchandising and operations. Piggly Wiggly stores were conventional supermarkets typically 28,000 square feet in size. They offered store specials, double manufacturers' coupons, and weekly selected merchandise specials.

In September 1987 Angelo Bruno, cofounder and then chair, signed a joint venture agreement with Kmart. Considered a bold move for Bruno's, the idea was to build hypermarkets of approximately 200,000 square feet all over the country. The hypermarkets would combine groceries and general merchandise, selling everything from vegetables to clothing and featuring up to 50 checkout stands. Such shopping centers already existed in Europe, and this was not the first time hypermarkets would open in the United States. However, this venture represented the first partnership between a grocery chain with the food expertise of Bruno's and a general retailer with expertise in merchandise sales. The management of Bruno's felt that the new sales could boost growth, even in the traditionally slow grocery trade. Three American Fare hypermarkets owned jointly by Kmart and Bruno's opened between 1989 and 1991 in Atlanta, Georgia; Charlotte, North Carolina; and Jackson, Mississippi.

In the late 1980s Bruno's had a reputation in the industry for aggressive, effective management and practices. For instance, it bought most of its food directly from manufacturers rather than from wholesalers. When manufacturers wanted their products sold at Bruno's stores, they made presentations directly to a committee of Bruno's managers, many of whom were part of the Bruno family. If the committee decided to buy the products, they usually bought large quantities and qualified for the largest volume discounts. That way, Bruno's could save money and pass the savings on to their customers. In addition, Bruno's store managers were compensated according to how much money their stores made. This put pressure on them to keep inventories moving, but most Bruno's managers were happy to

hustle, especially knowing they could earn as much as $80,000 in a good year. Many of these managers started at Bruno's while they were still in high school and stayed, and this loyalty served the company well.

Always on the lookout for new technology to improve operations in its stores, in the early 1990s Bruno's installed minicomputers connected to the Birmingham mainframe computer in its stores. These computers were used primarily to improve direct store buying and delivery. The system also enabled stores to monitor customer traffic in order to adjust labor needs. They also used the computers to keep track of store employees' attendance and working hours. The warehouse was also highly computerized. Food arrived from manufacturers and was priced, inventoried, and loaded onto Bruno's trucks for delivery to stores. The shipments, arrivals, pricing, and deliveries were also tracked on computer.

A tremendous test to Bruno's organization came in a tragic accident on December 11, 1991, when six Bruno's executives and three others were killed in a crash of the corporate jet shortly after takeoff in Rome, Georgia. The executives, including cofounders Angelo Bruno and his brother Lee Bruno, were on their annual Christmas visit to all of their stores when the crash occurred. Also killed were Sam Vacarella, the senior vice-president for merchandising; Edward Hyde, vice-president for store operations; Randolph Page, a vice-president for personnel; Karl Mollica, produce director; and Mary Faust, an advertising account executive working with Bruno's. The accident took an emotional toll on the family business and required much shifting of personnel. Angelo's son Ronald Bruno, who had been groomed to run the company and who had already been designated president and chief executive officer, was elected to the chair. In August 1992 Bruno's, Inc. bought 3.6 million shares of common stock from the estates of Angelo and Lee Bruno.

Bruno's entered the 1990s in the top 40 of some 270 food stores ranked by sales volume. National competition consisted of such chains as American Stores, Kroger, Safeway, Winn-Dixie, and Jewel, whereas Food Lion, Albertson's, and Giant Food competed with Bruno's mainly in the southeast region. Many of Bruno's competitors in Georgia suffered after Bruno's 1988 acquisition of Piggly Wiggly. But Bruno's continued to keep watch over its competition as Warehouse clubs and Wal-Mart supercenters began to pose a challenge to Bruno's in several of its larger markets.

Problems in the 1990s

Bruno's, like many food retailers and supermarket operators, suffered during the recession of the late 1980s and early 1990s. Some store sales were slow while consumer spending plummeted. Food prices went down, and consumers were spending less money on food. In addition, competition from Wal-Mart and supermarket chains Winn-Dixie and Publix intensified in the 1990s. In 1992 alone Wal-Mart opened three Supercenters in Birmingham and Publix elbowed into Bruno's territory in Atlanta. Profits for Bruno's, which had more than quadrupled in the last decade, fell 37 percent in 1992. Combined with the loss of the company's leadership in the 1991 plane crash, the lowered profits fed doubts about the company's future on Wall Street. The stock price plummeted from a high of

$21 a share in 1991, coming to rest around $12 in 1993. With 256 stores and $2.7 billion in sales in 1992, Bruno's still had a firm foundation on which to rebuild its growth.

Two major changes hurt Bruno's bottom line in 1992 but promised savings in the future. In June 1992 Bruno's announced an end to its joint venture with Kmart. Kmart assumed full ownership of the hypermarkets, taking over Bruno's 49 percent interest in the Atlanta and Charlotte stores and its 51 percent interest in the Jackson store. Bruno's management noted, "We felt it was time to eliminate our loss from the American Fare stores and focus our full attention on our primary store concerns." The company took a charge of $.13 a share, or $10.8 million, for the fiscal year ending in June 1992. Although the one-time charge contributed to the company's lowered profits in 1992, the sale would eliminate the company's $3.5 million annual loss from the joint venture.

Also during fiscal 1992, Bruno's finalized plans to consolidate the Piggly Wiggly division offices from Vidalia, Georgia, to a unit in the Birmingham corporate office. According to Ronald Bruno, savings from the closed Vidalia division offices would be in the vicinity of $5 million. The offices were officially closed in 1992, but the distribution center in Vidalia remained. Bruno's planned to use the facility as a jumping-off point for new operations in that geographic area.

Sales and earnings remained stagnant throughout 1993 and 1994, and despite a reorganization eliminating several layers of management, Bruno's share price continued to fall. Fluctuating between $7 and $10 a share, the low stock price made Bruno's ripe for a takeover. Rumors of a buyout were circulating in 1994, and the following year Kohlberg Kravis Roberts & Co. (KKR) approached Bruno's with an offer to acquire the company for $12.50 a share. The Bruno family held 24 percent of the company in 1995, and Ronald Bruno still ran the company as chief executive officer. Bruno's agreed to the $1 billion offer, which would give KKR 97 percent of the company. Although during negotiations there was talk of Ronald Bruno remaining as chairman of the board for at least three years, he stepped down soon after the buyout. KKR finished the acquisition in 1995, making its subsidiary Crimson Associates L.P. the official owner of the stock.

Optimism was high after the KKR takeover. KKR had made resounding successes of two other grocery chains, Safeway and Stop & Shop, and hoped to do the same for Bruno's. One of the first changes initiated by KKR was moving from every day low pricing at the Bruno's Food and Pharmacy stores to high-low pricing. For example, Bruno's began featuring buy-one-get-one-free offers. In 1996 the company cut costs by closing its distribution center in Georgia and closing or selling 47 under-performing stores.

These efforts did little to slow Bruno's fall: Sales stayed flat at around $2.9 billion, but earnings fell from $33 million in 1995 to a loss of $71 million in 1996. In 1997 KKR brought in Jack Demme, who had helped make a success of supermarket chain Homeland Stores, as president, CEO, and chairman of the board. The same year, Bruno's did not renew the franchise agreement that gave it the use of the Piggly Wiggly name.

Losses for 1997 came in around $50 million, and debt had skyrocketed to approximately $1 billion. Early in 1998 Bruno's filed for Chapter 11 bankruptcy protection. KKR, which owned 82 percent of Bruno's at the time, stood to lose the $250 million it had put up in the 1995 leveraged buyout.

Principal Subsidiaries

PWS Holding Corporation.

Further Reading

"Brokers Hail Bruno's, Winn-Dixie," *Frozen Food Age,* July 1996, p. 14.

"Bruno's After the Crash," *Forbes,* July 6, 1992.

"Bruno's Agrees to Be Acquired by KKR for $12.50 Per Share," *Corporate Growth Report,* May 1, 1995, p. 7820.

"Bruno's Could Protest Too Much," *Business Week,* September 26, 1994, p. 112.

"Bruno's Leaves American Fare Venture with Kmart," *New York Times,* June 11, 1992.

Donegan, Priscilla, "Merchandising the Store," *Progressive Grocer,* August, 1987.

"Getting Hyper," *Forbes,* January 11, 1988.

Grossman, Laurie M., and Martha Brannigan, "Six Bruno's Officials and Three Others Die in Jet Crash During Goodwill Tour," *Wall Street Journal,* December 12, 1991.

Kindel, Stephen, "Bruno's: On the Mend, Slowly," *Financial World,* March 30, 1993, pp. 20–22.

——, "Rebel Sell," *Financial World,* January 9, 1990.

Setton, Dolly, "Sorry About That," *Forbes,* March 9, 1998, p. 130.

Smothers, Ronald, "Crash of Private Plane in Georgia Kills 9," *New York Times,* December 12, 1991.

—Fran Shonfeld Sherman
—updated by Susan Windisch Brown

Cabela's Inc.

One Cabela Drive
Sidney, Nebraska 69160
U.S.A.
(308) 234-5555
(800) 237-4444
Fax: (308) 254-6745
Web site: http://www.cabelas.com

Private Company
Incorporated: 1965
Employees: 2,000
Sales: $450 million (1998 est.)
SICs: 5961 Catalog & Mail-Order Houses; 3949 Sporting
    & Athletic Goods, Not Elsewhere Classified

A Midwest catalog and retail operator, Cabela's Inc. derives roughly 90 percent of its revenue from its mail-order business, selling fishing, camping, and hunting equipment, footwear, and apparel through its catalogs. Cabela's operated four retail stores that served as showcases for merchandise found in its catalogs. The stores were located in Kearney and Sidney, Nebraska, Prairie du Chien, Wisconsin, and Owatonna, Minnesota, the company's flagship store. During the late 1990s, the company produced nearly 60 million catalogs a year, mailing them to customers in the United States, Canada, and 120 foreign countries. Roughly 90 percent of Cabela's customers were male, generally between the ages of 35 and 60, residing in suburban and rural communities. Two brothers, Dick and Jim Cabela, owned the company.

Early 1960s Origins

Cabela's historical roots stretched back to quintessential, home-born beginnings. In 1961, Dick Cabela placed a classified advertisement in a Casper, Wyoming newspaper. He had purchased a collection of fishing flies at a furniture show in Chicago, taken the flies back to his home in Chappell, Nebraska, and thought placing a classified advertisement in a small newspaper would be the best way to make a profit from his modest investment. Cabela's advertisement read: "12 hand-tied flies for $1." Unwittingly, Cabela had taken the first step toward creating a half-billion-dollar business, a flourishing mail-order enterprise that would become known as Cabela's, but his intentions at the start were decidedly less ambitious. Orders from the Casper, Wyoming advertisement were filled by Dick and his wife Mary, who worked in their home in Chappell, seated around the kitchen table. As orders for the flies increased, Dick Cabela purchased other outdoor recreational items and mailed a mimeographed list of other products available. For the Cabelas, direct-mail marketing worked quick wonders. The couple's inventory grew rapidly as more and more customers placed orders from the mimeographed lists. By 1962, the growth of their inventory required the establishment of a warehouse. Although the kitchen table still served as the business office, there was now another component to the couple's operations—a small backyard shed that served as their warehouse.

During the first several years of their business, the Cabelas fueled greater demand by continually expanding their mimeographed list of products until it developed into a mimeographed catalogue of merchandise. As the business expanded, its growth created the need for the trappings of a conventional business, but the evolution of the business away from its kitchen-table roots occurred in measured steps. By the fall of 1962, the Cabelas realized their homebound business required greater support, both in terms of personnel and proper facilities. Initially, they had relied on temporary typists to help with catalogue preparation, mailing, and labeling; but not long after devoting their backyard shed to warehouse space, Dick and Mary Cabela knew their business required full-time attention and full-time employees. Dick Cabela convinced his younger brother Jim to join the enterprise in 1963, but neither Jim, Mary, nor Dick received any compensation during the first several years. All the profits were directed toward increasing mailing activities, purchasing a greater selection of merchandise, and paying for bigger facilities. In 1964, after three years of using a kitchen table as their primary office space, the Cabela brothers moved the company's operations into the basement of their father's furniture store in Chappell. By the following year, the business had grown large enough to warrant incorporation and another move to larger facilities. The business was moved

Company Perspectives:

The backbone of our business lies in our mail-order catalogs. Together, our Spring and Fall catalogs contain our entire line of 90,000 products. In addition, we mail sales and special merchandise catalogs throughout the year. Our customers worldwide know they can rely on our dedicated service and our 100% Satisfaction Guarantee every time. Order with confidence from Cabela's, the World's Foremost Outfitter.

across the street into a former U.S. Department of Agriculture building, and then two years later into the American Legion Hall in Chappell. At the Chappell Legion Hall, which housed the company's warehousing operations and its offices, a small retail display was showcased in the corner of one floor. Although a negligible contributor to the company's financial stature, the retail product display in the American Legion Hall was a precursor to Cabela's grandiose foray into the retail side of the business more than 20 years later.

One year after moving into the Chappell Legion Hall, the Cabela brothers packed up the business and moved again, venturing out of Chappell for the first time. A search for larger quarters had revealed a vacant John Deere building near downtown Sidney, Nebraska. The building, which comprised four stories and 50,000 square feet of space, had been donated to a local hospital as a tax write-off, but the hospital wanted to sell the building before it incurred property taxes. Because of the hospital's predicament, the Cabelas were able to acquire the building at a sharply reduced price, purchasing it in September 1968. The business was moved to the old John Deere building in 1969, and for the first time in its history, the Cabela enterprise occupied a facility that was larger than the company's needs. At first, only one floor—the first floor—of the building was used. Upstairs, above the warehousing, packing, shipping, and retail operations located on the first floor, Cabela employees used a portion of one floor as an archery range, but eventually the needs of the company required the space occupied by the archery range. Gradually, as the 1970s progressed, Cabela's moved up into the empty floors, ultimately occupying the entire building.

By the mid-1980s, more than a decade of steady growth had stretched the company to the physical limits of the building in Sidney, forcing the Cabela brothers to search again for facilities that could accommodate their business's growing needs. The need for more space sprang from the company's ever-growing mail-order operations. As it had from the start, Cabela's produced its catalog on its own, a rarity among direct-mail businesses. The company's employees performed all the work involved in producing the catalog, including the copywriting, typesetting, photography, and merchandising. Aside from the in-house catalog operations, the company also performed all its own warehousing, packing, and shipping duties, as well as staffing its own telemarketing operations, all of which required additional space. In 1986, the Cabela brothers fulfilled their need by acquiring a former Rockwell International plant in

Kearney, Nebraska. Into this building, the Cabelas moved their telemarketing operations, which became a source of employment for the community's college students. With a steady supply of college students to operate the telephone lines, Cabela's ran its telemarketing operations 24 hours a day. The Kearney facility also became the home of Cabela's second retail store, a facet of the company's business that attracted nearly all of the attention directed at Cabela's during the 1990s.

Retail a Highlight During the 1990s

During the 1990s, Cabela's opened several new retail stores that managed to transcend the allure of even the most popular retail businesses to become something far more captivating. Cabela's retail stores, all situated in the Midwest, became tourist destinations, attracting weekend crowds that exceeded the population of the communities in which they were located. The stores were massive, intricately and abundantly outfitted with displays that reflected the company's outdoor sporting merchandise. Not surprisingly, when these stores opened to voluminous crowds, the business press focused their attention on the sprawling retail outlets, but at the heart of Cabela's was its mail-order business. Catalog sales propelled the company forward, not the revenue generated by its retail stores. The retail side of the company's business was developed to support the mail-order business, serving the same purpose during the 1990s as it had at its origin in 1967. The difference was in the scale of the company's retail efforts; the difference between a small retail display tucked in a corner of the Chappell Legion Hall in 1967 and the 75,000-square-foot to 150,000-square-foot stores that debuted during the 1990s. The leap in scale between these two eras was in proportion to the enormous growth of Cabela's catalog business, which had grown from a one-line classified advertisement into an operation that mailed millions of catalogs both domestically and abroad each year.

Despite the fact that Cabela's retail stores contributed a small percentage to the company's overall sales, the artistically designed stores were hard to ignore. The first retail store to epitomize Cabela's retail efforts during the 1990s was opened in July 1991, one year after work had begun on the new store. Located on the southern edge of Sidney, the store was situated on a 45-acre plot that included a 450-vehicle parking lot, with a separate lot for semi-trucks and recreational vehicles, a 3½-acre pond, and a 16-foot tall, bronze sculpture of two bull elk in fighting pose. Inside the store, which measured 75,000 square feet, a 27-foot-tall replica mountain towered at the opposite end of the entryway, decorated with 40 game mounts of North American wildlife in a recreated habitat display. There were also four, 2,000-gallon aquariums stocked with trout, panfish, gamefish, and predator fish; a gun library, featuring a broad collection of firearms; and a travel center, where customers could plan trips to take them across the globe. The merchandise in the store mirrored the product mix found in the company's catalogs, with apparel taking up roughly 50 percent of the retail space, footwear accounting for 30 percent, and the rest of the floor and shelf space filled with hard goods, such as hunting, fishing, and camping equipment.

By all measures, the store was a resounding success, located on the outskirts of a community of 6,000 people, yet capable of attracting more than one million customers a year. Away from the grandeur of the Sidney store, however, the real work of the company was conducted in Kearney, where Cabela's "800 Service Center" was located. In two large rooms, 150 operators stood by the telephones 24 hours a day, seven days a week, receiving an average of two million calls a year during the early 1990s. During peak holiday periods, the 800 center's telephone staff doubled, occasionally taking as many as 35,000 telephone orders in a single 24-hour period. To house and ship the orders generated from the 800 center and to stock the retail stores in Sidney and Kearney, massive distribution centers were needed. At roughly the same time Cabela's was involved in designing and constructing its new Sidney store, the company acquired three buildings on the former Sioux Ordinance Depot grounds in Sidney for warehouse space. In 1992, another five buildings situated at the same location were acquired, making Cabela's warehouse space in Sidney equal to more than ten football fields. The company's distribution capabilities were further enhanced with the construction of a facility in Prairie du Chien, Wisconsin. The 600,000-square-foot distribution center in Prairie du Chien was completed in 1996, positioning the company to better serve its upper Midwestern customers.

Late 1990s Expansion

Physical expansion, both in terms of Cabela's retail business and in the number of facilities that supported its catalog operations, characterized the company's progress during the late 1990s. After more than 35 years of operating in Nebraska, the company had two retail stores in its home state, the massive warehouse in Sidney, its main telemarketing operation in Kearney, which was supported by an additional telemarketing operation in Grand Island, and a customer-service center in North Platte. During the late 1990s, the company's most notable activity took place outside the state of Nebraska, following up on its move into Wisconsin with the Prairie du Chien distribution facility. The one exception was the establishment of a new headquarters in Sidney in January 1998. The company moved out of its original Sidney headquarters building and into a new 120,000-square-foot, two-story building adjacent to the Sidney store. Meanwhile, as employees settled into their new offices in Sidney, the company was preparing for the opening of its largest retail store to date. The store, located in Owatonna, Minnesota, opened in April 1998, by far eclipsing the standard set by the Sidney store seven years earlier. The Owatonna store was twice the size of its Sidney counterpart, comprising 150,000 square feet of space. Half of the retail square footage was devoted to outdoor apparel, including 60 different patterns of camouflage, with the balance divided between footwear and hard goods, nearly identical to the product mix in the company's catalogs. The Owatonna store, a 45-minute drive south

from Minneapolis, also contained the eye-catching features and habitat displays found in the Sidney store. Inside, the company built a 35-foot replica mountain, complete with running streams and waterfalls, two dioramas featuring African wildlife, a live-bait shop, a firearms and archery training center, and three aquariums with a combined capacity of 54,000 gallons. Outside the store, there was room for roughly 800 vehicles, including a parking lot for buses and semi-truck trailer rigs, as well as two two-acre ponds. Like the store in Sidney, the Owatonna store was an immediate success, attracting 120,000 customers during its grand opening weekend.

Despite the legions of customers drawn to the Owatonna store, overall retail sales only accounted for between nine and 12 percent of Cabela's total sales during the late 1990s. The balance was generated from catalog sales, which approached $500 million. The company mailed 28 editions of its catalog each year, sending nearly 60 million catalogs to customers in the United States, Canada, and 120 foreign countries. Looking ahead, Cabela's was intent on expanding its retail presence as a strategy to bolster catalog sales. The company was scouting five potential locations for retail stores in late 1998, anticipating its future stores to measure between 75,000 and 80,000 square feet. In October 1998, Cabela's opened its fourth retail store next to its distribution center in Prairie du Chien. A 40,000-square-foot store, the Prairie du Chien outlet was opened to meet the overflow of customers flocking to the flagship Owatonna store. With yet another successful catalog showcase added to its operations, Cabela's prepared for additional retail grand openings in the coming decade, its self-touted claim as the "World's Foremost Outfitter" held secure by a vast and flourishing mail-order business.

Further Reading

Brumback, Nancy, "Cabela's, the Mail Animal, Is Pushing the Retail Envelope," *Daily News Record,* July 27, 1998, p. 6.

"Cabela's Catalog Showroom Set for October Opening in Prairie du Chien, Wis.," *PR Newswire,* August 26, 1998, p. 8.

"Cabela's—Unending Progress and Growth Since 1961," Sidney, Neb.: Cabela's Inc., 1998, 7 p.

Gribble, Roger A., "Cabela's Sporting-Goods Mail-Order Center Good News for Platteville, Wis.," *Knight-Ridder/Tribune Business News,* June 22, 1996, p. 6.

Grier, Bob, "Cabela's: A Store with a Story," *NEBRASKAland Magazine,* August 1993, p. 8.

McCartney, Jim, "Giant Sporting Goods Stores Opens 40 Miles from Minnesota's Twin Cities," *Knight-Ridder/Tribune Business News,* April 3, 1998, p. 4.

—Jeffrey L. Covell

Camelot Music, Inc.

8000 Freedom Ave. NW
North Canton, Ohio
U.S.A.
(330) 494-2282
(800) 226-3568
Fax: (330) 494-0394
Web site: http://www.camelotmusic.com

Private Company
Incorporated: 1956 as Stark Record and Tape Service
Employees: 5,950
Sales: $400.4 million (1998 est.)
SICs: 5735 Record & Prerecorded Tape Stores

Camelot Music, Inc. is the third largest music retailer in the United States, with nearly 500 stores in 37 states and Puerto Rico. In the mid-1990s, following increased competition for sales from powerful non-music chains like Best Buy and Borders, and a general music business sales slump, Camelot entered bankruptcy protection, emerging in just over a year with renewed strength and plans to go public. The company, while still fighting for survival in a much-changed music retailing marketplace, is showing its determination to survive, creating an innovative web site as a means of marketing its products in cyberspace, and buying up additional chains of stores to extend its geographic reach.

Beginnings

Camelot Music was founded by Paul David in Massillon, Ohio, in 1956 as the Stark Record and Tape Service, a rack jobber which stocked LP and 45 rpm records in drug, specialty, variety, and grocery stores in the mid-Ohio area. A rack jobber operates by placing racks of products in stores, maintaining and stocking the displays, and paying the store for the space. David, one of 13 children born to Lebanese immigrants, was working as a sales representative for his brother's business when he noticed that a grocery store was selling used 45 rpm records. Taking note of the fact that they were not selling new LPs

and 45s, he soon started his own business supplying racks of records to grocery and drug stores, later expanding his accounts to include large discounters like Woolworth, Kresge, and W.T. Grant. David's timing was perfect, as record sales were just beginning to take off in conjunction with the huge popularity of Elvis Presley and other Rock 'n Roll artists in the mid-1950s, with Motown and The Beatles just around the corner in the 1960s.

In 1965 the company opened its first retail store, in Canton, Ohio, adding a location at a Canton shopping mall a few months later. Camelot Music, as it was now known, concentrated on opening mall-based stores over the next few years, with a total of over a hundred by 1980. In addition to its own outlets, the company began to operate music departments in leased spaces inside large discount stores. Other, freestanding locations were opened as well. By the end of the 1980s Camelot Music had nearly 300 stores, including several new, giant-sized "Superstores," in addition to its standard outlets. The company's operation of leased spaces in discount stores, meanwhile, had fallen out of favor, and was phased out by 1990.

Over the years, a number of changes had taken place in the music business, and Camelot adapted to meet the demands of the marketplace. Vinyl LP and 45 rpm records, always subject to warping and scratching, were being supplanted by the less fragile cassette tape and compact disc formats by the late 1980s, with Camelot removing 45s from most of its stores in 1988, and LPs several years later. By 1988, cassettes accounted for about half of the company's sales, with compact discs making up a quarter of the total and LPs just five percent. Videotapes, added during the 1980s, had already grown to encompass a larger share than vinyl records, and were the source of some 10 percent of the company's sales. Other goods sold at Camelot stores included blank audio- and videotapes and music-related accessory products.

The 1990s: Further Expansion; Sale to Investcorp

Camelot had continually been expanding its number of locations and geographic reach, and in the early 1990s intensified these efforts, buying groups of stores from other chains,

Company Perspectives:

Since its founding in 1956, Camelot Music, Inc. has developed into one of the most well-regarded specialty retailers in the United States. Today, Camelot ranks as one of the top five retailers in the music industry, both in sales volume and number of stores. During the last decade, Camelot has been one of the most productive mall-based music chains in the industry due to its leading production per square foot of retail space.

such as California-based Rainbow Records in 1990, and Philadelphia-headquartered Record World in 1992. In the latter case, Camelot teamed up with a United Kingdom-owned chain called Wee Three to buy part of the bankrupt company's holdings, with Camelot ending up with six stores and the inventory from several more. By mid-1993 the company owned more than 360 stores, and its annual sales topped $420 million. Keeping up with the times, Camelot remodeled a store in its home base of Canton to look sleek and futuristic, with banks of video screens, neon signs, specially lighted display systems, and a "New & Hot" bestseller area at the front of the store. The record industry's decision around this time to yield to public pressure and abandon the "longbox" cardboard CD display package also forced the company to redesign its methods of stocking and displaying products chainwide.

In late 1993, founder and majority owner Paul David decided to sell his interest in Camelot, partly owing to his view that the record business was heading toward a slump. The buyer was Investcorp, a Bahrain-based holding company which owned a number of different businesses including Gucci, Tiffany & Co., and Sak's Fifth Avenue. Investcorp was also expecting the music business to experience hard times, but was banking on major player Camelot to absorb floundering competitors' stores in the aftermath. Following the sale of Camelot, David turned the position of Chief Executive Officer over to Chief Operating Officer James Bonk, a 25-year company veteran. David was quoted as saying that he had chosen Investcorp over several other buyers because of the company's pledge to let Camelot retain the same management personnel and headquarters location. Following the buyout, the company was run in much the same manner as before, with additional new stores opening or being acquired. By January 1994, 16 Hastings Music and Books and three Cavages Music stores had been added. Investcorp's leveraged buyout had left Camelot with a large amount of debt, however, and this would weigh heavily on the company during the next several years.

The music retailing business was undergoing significant change at this time. Several different types of stores which traditionally had not sold music began to add and aggressively market it as a means of drawing in customers for their main lines of products. These included such large bookstore chains as Borders, discount superstores Kmart and Wal-Mart, and discount appliance chains Best Buy and Circuit City. The latter were particularly threatening to music retailers like Camelot, as they tended to sell recordings at significant discounts, and focus

heavily on the bestselling CDs and tapes. All of this shifted business away from traditional music retailers. A Recording Industry Association of America study showed that record stores' share of the market had dropped from 70 percent in 1990 to just 52 percent five years later. In addition to this significant shift, sales of music recordings industrywide were falling off, as the baby boomers who had been "upgrading" from records to CDs finished that process, and the novelty of the new CD format, which had fueled a string of spectacular sales years, began to wear off.

1996: Bankruptcy and Reorganization

By early 1996, Camelot was experiencing financial difficulties. The company, with almost 390 stores, $400 million in annual sales, and 3,500 employees, announced in March that it would lay off 170 people and close 18 stores. In addition, as many as 80 other outlets were under review, with an estimated 20 to 30 more stores likely to close. Attempts were also being made to renegotiate leases at malls where some stores were close to the edge of failure. All of this could not keep the company above water, however, and in August Camelot filed for Chapter 11 bankruptcy protection. Under this form of bankruptcy, the company was allowed to continue operating while it reorganized and tried to pay off creditors. The company's debt was pegged at $476.7 million, with assets of $511.6 million. The largest part of the debt, some $300 million, was attributed to obligations from the leveraged buyout by Investcorp. A loan of $35 million was obtained from Chase Manhattan Bank to continue operating. CEO Bonk announced that the company would concentrate on its most profitable core group of stores, and intended to "become a leaner, stronger music retail specialist, committed to serving its customers and competing aggressively in the years to come." By this time the company had closed an additional 18 stores, and was expecting as many as 40 more to be shuttered. Other music chains had also gone into bankruptcy, including Nationwide, Peaches, Wherehouse, and Kemp Mills Music. National sales leader Musicland had suffered from losses and company restructuring, and many independent music retailers had gone out of business entirely.

One of the company's first efforts to get back on its feet came in November 1996, when it announced the creation of a World Wide Web site called CD Genie. The new site was set up to allow users to listen to 30 second sound bites from several hundred current releases and order discs online. Within a year the amount of sound clips was slated to be greatly expanded. Other services offered on the site included listings of store locations and music gift-giving advice. Prices were the same as in Camelot's retail stores, plus shipping charges, but customers were offered free subscriptions to *Rolling Stone* or *Spin* magazines after making a small number of purchases. The site's purpose was partially to compete with the growing phalanx of online compact disc retailers such as CD Now, but also was intended to help enhance sales at the company's struggling retail outlets.

Just over a year after filing for bankruptcy, Camelot filed a Joint Plan of Reorganization in U.S. Bankruptcy Court, which proposed eliminating the company's debt by converting it into equity for reorganization—in effect making the company's creditors its owners. This would also eliminate Investcorp's stake in the company. The plan was approved by Camelot's creditors and the bankruptcy court judge in December 1997, and the next month the company was allowed to emerge from court protection. In the 16 months since it had declared bankruptcy, the chain had closed a total of 88 stores, dropping in size to 307.

Free from court supervision, Camelot immediately began expanding again, announcing the acquisition of the 153 store chain The Wall, based in Philadelphia. That company's mid-Atlantic region, mall-based stores complemented Camelot's existing geographic distribution. In July 1998, Camelot merged with Spec's Music, which consisted of 41 stores primarily located in Florida. This put Camelot's total holdings up to nearly 500 stores, with outlets in 37 states and Puerto Rico. Later in 1998, the company began making plans to go public, with stock expected to be offered on the NASDAQ exchange.

Camelot Music, after years of steady growth that were derailed by market turbulence and a leveraged buyout in the mid-1990s, appeared to be getting back on track as the decade drew to a close. With major changes in music retailing still facing it, the company was reacting by launching a web site and acquiring chains of stores in complementary locations, as well as by focusing on its traditional strengths. Camelot's experienced management team, and the survival of its brush with bankruptcy (which a number of competitors had not managed), were clear signs that it was likely to remain in the game for some time to come.

Further Reading

Albright, Mark, "Camelot Music to Buy Spec's," *St. Petersburg Times*, June 5, 1998, p. 1E.

"Camelot's New Look: Retailer Prepares for Jewel-Box Conversion," *Chain Store Age Executive with Shopping Center Age*, July 1, 1993, p. 68.

Flint, Troy, "Camelot Music May Exit Bankruptcy By Year-End," *Plain Dealer, Cleveland, Ohio*, October 9, 1997, p. 1C.

——, "Camelot Music Plans to Go Public," *Plain Dealer, Cleveland, Ohio*, April 22, 1998, p. 1C.

Johnson, Terrence L., "Camelot Offers Net Sound Bites," *Plain Dealer, Cleveland, Ohio*, December 10, 1996, p. 6C.

Meckler, Laura, "Paul David's American Dream Began in Massillon: Camelot Music Chief Among WHS Honorees," *Repository—Canton, Ohio*, April 20, 1993.

Pritchard, Edd, "Camelot Files for Protection in Bankruptcy," *Repository—Canton, Ohio*, August 10, 1996, p. A1.

——, "Camelot Music on the Cutting Edge of Business," *Repository—Canton, Ohio*, March 29, 1996, p. B7.

——, "Riding Out Rough Times," *Repository—Canton, Ohio*, April 22, 1996, p. B1.

Sabath, Donald, "Stacking Up the Profits—Camelot Music Picks a Hit in Music Distribution," *Plain Dealer, Cleveland, Ohio*, August 24, 1993, p. 1F.

Semmler, Edward, "Camelot Joins Stable of Names: Buyer Owns Tiffany, Gucci," *Repository—Canton, Ohio*, October 5, 1993, p. 1.

Takiff, Jonathan, "CDs, Cassettes Are Signaling Demise of Vinyl Records," *Chicago Tribune*, September 16, 1988, p. 72.

Tebben, Gerald, "Local Firm's Web Site Playin' the Hits Online," *Columbus Dispatch*, December 11, 1996, p. H1.

Yerak, Becky, "Camelot Files for Bankruptcy—Fierce Competition Hurting North Canton Music Retailer," *Plain Dealer, Cleveland, Ohio*, August 10, 1996, p. 1C.

——, "Camelot Music Lays Off 170, Shuts 18 Stores—Competition Makes More Cuts Possible," *Plain Dealer, Cleveland, Ohio*, March 29, 1996, p. 1C.

—Frank Uhle

Campbell Soup Company

Campbell Place
Camden, New Jersey 08103-1799
U.S.A.
(609) 342-4800
(800) 909-SOUP; (800) 909-7687
Fax: (609) 342-3878
Web site: http://www.campbellsoup.com

Public Company
Incorporated: 1922
Employees: 24,256
Sales: $6.70 billion (1998)
Stock Exchanges: New York Philadelphia London Swiss
Ticker Symbol: CPB
SICs: 2015 Poultry Slaughtering & Processing; 2032
Canned Specialties; 2034 Dried & Dehydrated Fruits,
Vegetables & Soup Mixes; 2035 Pickled Fruits &
Vegetables, Salad Dressings, Vegetable Sauces &
Seasonings; 2051 Bread, Cake & Related Products;
2052 Cookies & Crackers; 2066 Chocolate & Cocoa
Products; 2096 Potato Chips, Corn Chips & Similar
Snacks; 2099 Food Preparations, Not Elsewhere
Classified

Campbell Soup Company is the number one maker of soups in the United States and is also a leading manufacturer of other food products. Campbell divides its operations into three areas: soups and sauces, biscuits and confectionery, and a foodservice unit. The first of these includes the flagship soup line, Prego spaghetti sauce, Franco-American pastas and gravies, Pace Mexican foods, Swanson broths, and V8 beverages. The second comprises three main businesses—Pepperidge Farm (which itself includes the Milano and Goldfish brands), Godiva Chocolatier, and Australia-based Arnotts. The foodservice unit is responsible for distributing products—such as Campbell's Restaurant Soups, Pace Tabletop picante sauce, and Campbell's Specialty Kitchens entrees—to the foodservice and home meal replacement markets. Campbell Soup Company generates about 72 percent of its sales in the United States, 13 percent in Europe, nine percent in Australia and the Asia-Pacific region, and six percent in other countries.

Early History

The roots of the Campbell Soup Company can be traced back to 1860, when Abraham Anderson opened a small canning factory in Camden, New Jersey. In 1869 Philadelphia produce merchant Joseph Campbell became Anderson's partner, forming Anderson and Campbell. The company canned vegetables, mince meat, jams and jellies, and a variety of soups. In 1876 Anderson and Campbell dissolved their partnership and Campbell bought Anderson's share of the business, changing its name to Joseph Campbell Preserve Company. In 1882 a partnership was formed between Campbell's son-in-law, Walter S. Spackman; Campbell's nephew, Joseph S. Campbell; and Arthur Dorrance, Spackman's personal friend who brought a cash infusion to the partnership. At this time the company was renamed Joseph Campbell Preserving Company. The senior Campbell maintained daily involvement in the company until his death in 1900.

In 1896 the company built a large factory in Camden and expanded its product line to include prepared meats, sauces, canned fruits, ketchup, and plum pudding. The next year Arthur Dorrance hired his nephew John Thompson Dorrance, a chemical engineer and organic chemist. By 1899 John Dorrance had successfully developed a method of canning condensed soup. This innovation helped Campbell outstrip its two soup-canning competitors. While others were still shipping heavy, uncondensed soup, Campbell was able to ship and sell its product at one-third the cost. As the company began increasing the variety of soups it offered, it began canning less produce. John Dorrance became director of the company in 1900 and soon after the company was renamed the Joseph Campbell Company.

Campbell's soup began finding its way into American kitchens at a time when the prepared-food industry was growing rapidly yet was still small. By 1904 the company sold 16 million cans of soup a year. Boasting 21 varieties of soup by 1905, Campbell began to eye a bigger market; in 1911 Campbell began selling its products in California, thus becoming one of the first companies to serve the entire nation.

In 1910 Dorrance was made general manager of the company, and in 1914 he became president. Dorrance focused on soup and discontinued the marginal line of ketchups, preserves, and jams. In 1915 Dorrance became sole owner of Campbell when he bought out his uncle, Arthur Dorrance.

In 1912 Campbell began growing its own produce in an effort to standardize quality. This program was the first of an ongoing series of efforts Campbell made to grow what it processed. At that time, during the eight summer weeks in which tomatoes were harvested, the Campbell plant devoted its entire effort to the production of tomato soup and tomato juice. During World War I almost half of Campbell's sales were from these two products.

Incorporated in 1922

In 1921 Campbell acquired the Franco-American Food Company, and the next year the company was incorporated as the Campbell Soup Company. In 1923 Arthur C. Dorrance, John Dorrance's brother, became Campbell's general manager. In 1929 Arthur C. Dorrance was made a director and vice-president of the board of directors. When John Dorrance died in 1930, Arthur C. Dorrance was elected president.

Throughout this period Campbell continued to grow. In 1929 the company opened a second major facility in Chicago. In the early 1930s Campbell opened Campbell Soup Company Ltd., in Canada, as well as Campbell's Soups Ltd., in Great Britain. In 1936 Campbell began making its own cans and in 1939 its agricultural research department was formed. In 1942 sales topped $100 million for the first time. In 1946 Arthur C. Dorrance died and James McGowen, Jr., became president. The following year Campbell began growing its own mushrooms in Prince Crossing, Illinois.

Acquired Swanson in 1955

Despite this growth, Campbell was slow to diversify. In 1948 the company acquired V-8 juice, but its first major purchase was not made until 1955, when it bought the Omaha, Nebraska-based C.A. Swanson & Sons, producers of the first complete-meal frozen entrees called TV dinners.

In the midst of this growth, W.B. Murphy was elected president, following McGowan's retirement in 1953. In 1954 Campbell took its stock public and, in 1957, the company formed an international division to oversee its foreign concerns.

In 1958 sales exceeded $500 million for the first time and Campbell established Campbell's Soups, S.p.A. in Italy. This venture was followed, in 1959, by the opening of subsidiaries in Mexico and Australia.

Several Acquisitions Marked the 1960s

Throughout the 1960s Campbell was conservatively managed and quite successful. In that decade the company opened two mushroom growing facilities and 11 new plants on three continents. In the 1960s Campbell's growth—which underwent a slight shift in emphasis—began to include regular acquisitions in addition to internal expansion. In 1961 Campbell acquired Pepperidge Farm, a maker of quality baked goods, and a similar Belgian company, Biscuits Delacre. In 1965 Campbell created a foodservice division and, in 1966, began marketing EfficienC, its own brand of foodservice products through that division. Also in 1966 Campbell formed Godiva Chocolatier to distribute the Belgian-made chocolates in the United States. In 1974 the company completed a purchase of the European Godiva company and became its sole owner. Campbell created Champion Valley Farms, a pet food concern, in 1969.

During the 1970s the company's slow but steady growth continued. Campbell, which had built its fortune on Dorrance's invention of condensed soup, introduced the first Chunky brand of ready-to-serve soups. This became a highly successful enterprise. In 1971, for the first time, Campbell's sales topped $1 billion. In 1972 Murphy retired and was replaced as president by Harold A. Shaub. Also that year, Swanson introduced Hungry Man meals, a line of frozen dinners with larger-than-average portions.

Diversified in the 1970s and 1980s

In 1973 Campbell acquired Pietro's Pizza Parlors, a chain based in the Pacific Northwest. This led, in 1974, to the formation of a restaurant division, and heralded Campbell's intention to add more restaurants to its growing list of subsidiaries.

In 1978 Campbell purchased Vlasic Foods, a Michigan-based producer of pickles and similar condiments, for approximately $35 million in capital stock. This acquisition gave Campbell the lead over archrival H.J. Heinz in the pickle-packing business. Campbell added seven small European food producing companies and three domestic operations in 1979. That same year sales topped $2 billion for the first time. In 1978 Campbell made a brief and unsuccessful foray into the Brazilian soup market.

The diversification movement started by Shaub in the early 1970s prepared the company for long-term growth. Campbell's debt remained low and the company's new products and acquisitions provided it with popular brand names in a variety of food industry sectors. Campbell realized that the key to growth in this mature market was diversification. Shaub changed a long-standing policy on new product development requiring a profit within the first year. His most notable innovation, however, was his decentralization of marketing for major product lines.

To sustain these growth-oriented policies, Campbell broke its tradition of relying on internally generated funds to finance its efforts. In June 1980 the company entered the debt market with a $100 million ten-year offering. As a cautious food producer, Campbell's earnings have always been healthy, but Shaub hoped to increase both sales and profits margins. A key reason for Shaub's determination to allow Campbell to diversify was the recognition that the market for many of these products had matured and growth had slowed.

In 1980 R. Gorden McGovern succeeded Shaub as president and Campbell made two acquisitions—Swift-Armour S.A. Argentina and a small American poultry processing plant used by Swanson for its frozen chicken dinners. Campbell's efforts in Argentina were not entirely fruitful, with much of the difficulty related to currency-transaction adjustments. Also in 1980 Campbell acquired additional bakery, pasta, and pickle operations.

In 1981 McGovern reorganized Campbell's management structure, dividing the company into two new divisions— Campbell U.S.A. and Campbell International—and about 50 business groups. This new structure was meant to foster entrepreneurship and heighten management's sensitivity to consumer opinion, long a weakness at Campbell. The company acquired Snow King Frozen Foods, a large producer of uncooked frozen specialty meats, and introduced the wildly successful Prego spaghetti sauce nationally in 1981. In 1982 Campbell acquired Mrs. Paul's Kitchens, a processor of frozen prepared seafood and vegetables. Several of the company's subsidiaries also made major purchases. Vlasic Foods acquired Win Schuler Foods, a specialty foods producer, and Pepperidge Farm completed the purchase of an apple juice processor, Costa Apple Products, with markets primarily on the East Coast. Also in 1982, Juice Bowl Products, a fruit juice processor, was acquired.

A variety of other acquisitions in the early 1980s added Annabelle's, a restaurant chain; Triangle Manufacturing, a manufacturer of physical fitness and sports-medicine products; a fresh produce distributor; a Puerto Rican canning company; and an Italian manufacturer of premium biscuits.

Marketing Emphasis Began in the 1980s

McGovern further increased emphasis on marketing and new product development in an effort to shift the company away from its production-oriented focus. McGovern also introduced Total Systems, a worker-oriented system designed to increase quality and efficiency that was similar to the successful worker management strategies employed by many Japanese companies.

One of McGovern's primary concerns was turning Campbell into a ''market-sensitive food company.'' After McGovern publicly referred to some of the company's Swanson TV dinner line as ''junk food'' in 1982, Campbell initiated Project Fix in an effort to upgrade food quality and improve packaging of its older products. As McGovern told *Business Week* in 1983, one of the most important facets of his makeover was making the company ''somebody who is looking after [consumers'] well-being.'' The 1983 Triangle Manufacturing purchase and 1982 formation of a health and fitness unit were both designed to meet that goal. Campbell's involvement in frozen fish, juices, and produce were also part of the new market sensitivity urged by McGovern.

In addition, Campbell attempted to market products regionally and according to age group. The central marketing system was broken into 20 regions to allow tailoring of advertising and marketing to fit each region's peculiar demographics. For instance, the company sold spicier nacho cheese soup in Texas than in the rest of the country. The company also aimed its national brands at regional audiences, with spots featuring local celebrities and locally arranged promotions. Campbell, which reached half the nation's homes just by sponsoring the television show ''Lassie'' in the 1950s, spent 15 percent of its advertising budget in regional efforts in 1983. That figure was expected eventually to reach 50 percent.

McGovern increased Campbell's sales and earnings significantly in his first few years. His encouragement of new product development and line extensions may have been overzealous. The company introduced frozen entrees to compete with Stouffer's, dried soups to challenge Lipton, and name-brand produce such as Farm Fresh mushrooms and tomatoes, complemented by exotic varieties of mushrooms, refrigerated salads and pasta sauces, and juices. In all, Campbell introduced 334 new products in the first half of the 1980s. This included several costly mistakes, such as the 1984 failure of Pepperidge Farm's Star Wars cookies, which did not fit the brand's high-quality image. Yet spurred on by successes such as Le Menu frozen dinners, McGovern concentrated on marketing and new product development. In 1985, however, the company decided to cut back on new product gambles and McGovern reevaluated his goals and returned the company's focus to product quality and efficiency.

Throughout this period, during which it became increasingly clear that McGovern's plan was destined to fail, acquisitions and group formations continued, but at a pace reminiscent of the old Campbell. The company purchased a Belgian food producer and 20 percent of Arnotts Ltd., an Australian biscuit manufacturer, in 1985. In 1986 the company bought two more American food companies and established Campbell Enterprises to oversee non-grocery products. Meanwhile new products were gradually but steadily introduced.

In 1984 John T. Dorrance, Jr., the son of condensed soup's inventor, retired as chairman of the board and became director of the board's executive committee. He was succeeded as chairman by William S. Cashel, Jr. Dorrance and other members of his family, however, still controlled 58 percent of Campbell's stock and showed no interest in selling, keeping the company safe from takeover.

By 1987 McGovern began selling off some of Campbell's less successful ventures. In 1987 the company sold its disappointing pet food, Triangle physical fitness, and Juice Works beverage businesses. In 1988 the Pietro's pizza and Annabelle's restaurants were also sold, taking Campbell out of the restaurant business entirely.

However, Campbell also bought several smaller companies in 1987 and 1988 that were more compatible with its traditional lines of business. These included a French cookie maker, the Open Pit barbecue sauce line, an American olive producer, and Campbell's largest acquisition to date, Freshbake Foods Group PLC, a British producer of frozen foods. Also in 1988, Robert J. Vlasic, whose Vlasic Foods Campbell had purchased in 1978, became chairman of Campbell.

Campbell's management crisis was exacerbated by the death, in April 1989, of John Dorrance. Dorrance's 31 percent of the company's stock was split between his three children, who demonstrated an interest in preserving family control of the company. The remaining 27 percent of the family-owned stock was split among other members of the clan, some of whom (representing about 17.4 percent of the company's stock) expressed a desire to sell Campbell. Chairman Vlasic, however, had loaded the board with family members loyal to the company (six of the 15 board members were family members, including John Dorrance's three children), so a proxy battle never materialized.

McGovern—who failed in an attempt to merge the company with Quaker Oats in 1989—left Campbell that same year. His final attempt to recoup Campbell's losses, a $343 million restructuring program, earned him little praise. Although sales had doubled during his term, profits had dropped 90 percent as a result of his aggressive capital commitments. From 1988 to 1990 alone, earnings fell from $274.1 million to $4.4 million.

Back to Basics in the 1990s

In January 1990 David W. Johnson was elected president and CEO. Johnson came to Campbell from Gerber Products Company, where he had been successful in streamlining that company's operations. Johnson employed a back-to-basics strategy that called for drastic restructuring. The new CEO oversaw the divestment of whole businesses, including mushroom farms, a salmon processing plant, the refrigerated salads line, and cookie maker Lazzaroni. By June 1991, Johnson had closed or sold 20 plants worldwide, reduced the company's 51,700 person workforce by 15.5 percent, and pulled unprofitable lines from store shelves. While Johnson purported to support marketing, he also cut Campbell's advertising budget.

Johnson was most interested in promoting the company's core product, soup. Even into the early 1990s, Campbell soups had 66 percent, or $1.6 billion, of the $2.6 billion U.S. soup market, which contributed almost half of the conglomerate's $570 million operating profits.

In anticipation of the North American Free Trade Agreement, Johnson also supervised the merging of Campbell's Canadian operations, some Mexican companies, and the U.S. businesses into one division called Campbell North America. Late in 1991, Campbell also focused on the impending European Community's single market, which promised 344 million consumers (50 percent more than the United States) and had potential for future growth. The cookie subsidiary of Campbell Soup, Campbell Biscuits Europe, got a head start on the market in February 1990, when it reorganized its European corporate structure, consolidated marketing, and standardized packaging.

By the end of 1991, some indicators showed that Johnson's efforts had paid off: Campbell's earnings through the first three quarters of 1991 had risen 33 percent, making the company's profits the second fastest-growing in the food industry. But some analysts warned that the profits came at the expense of core brand promotion, which was cut in 1991. The growth in earnings were not based on sales increases, which only rose 1.9 percent during the same period.

Johnson was given an overall good rating in the quick turnaround at Campbell. In 1992 the company made bolder goals, with a vision expressed as "Campbell Brands Preferred Around the World." The plan made further preparations for the European Community's single market and expanded those efforts around the world. The company was reorganized into three multinational divisions: Campbell North and South America grouped Campbell's Swift-Armour subsidiary in Argentina with the previously organized North American group; Campbell Biscuit and Bakery united Pepperidge Farm in North America with Delacre in Europe and Australia's leading biscuit company, Arnotts Ltd. (of which Campbell by then owned 58 percent); Campbell Europe/Asia was a growth-oriented division that comprised the company's "greatest opportunity and challenge," according to the 1992 annual report.

In 1993 Vlasic retired as chairman, with Johnson taking on this additional title. Also, Bennett Dorrance, a grandson of condensed soup inventor John Dorrance, was named vice-chairman of Campbell Soup. Bennett Dorrance represented the Dorrance family's interests on the board of directors and took an active role, particularly in tying executive pay to performance and putting oversight practices into place. The family's power was soon diminished somewhat, after Bennett's brother, John T. Dorrance III, sold most of his stake in the company by late 1996, leaving the family in control of 44 percent of the stock. No attempts at a takeover—hostile or otherwise—were immediately evident, however.

Johnson continued to restructure Campbell as the decade continued. The company recorded a $300 million restructuring charge in 1993 in relation to the divestment of several underperforming units. That year also saw the launch of a new soup campaign using the slogan "Never Underestimate the Power of Soup." The Mrs. Paul's frozen seafood line was sold to Pillsbury Co.'s Van de Kamp's unit in 1996. Altogether, Johnson dumped $500 million worth of noncore, underperforming assets from 1990 through 1996.

Simultaneously Johnson led Campbell Soup in a more aggressive overseas push and sought out compatible acquisitions. In addition to a big push into the Mexican soup market, the company in 1993 began selling V8 vegetable juice in Europe and established a joint venture with Nakano Vinegar Co. Ltd. to market Campbell's soups in Japan. In January 1995 Campbell completed the largest acquisition in its long history, paying $1.1 billion for Pace Foods Ltd., the leading maker of Mexican sauces (picante and salsa) with 1994 sales of more than $200 million. Later in 1995, the company picked up Greenfield Healthy Foods, the number one maker of fat-free brownies and cookies for the health and convenience store markets, and Fresh Start Bakeries, a supplier of baked goods to fast-food restaurants. The latter, however, was sold in 1998.

Campbell Soup continued its overseas push with the 1996 purchases of Homepride, the leading cooking sauce brand in the United Kingdom, and the Cheong Chan soup and sauce business in Asia; and the 1997 acquisition of Erasco Group, the leading seller of canned soup in Germany, from Grand Metropolitan PLC for $210 million. Also in 1997 Arnotts acquired the Sydney, Australia-based Kettle Chip Company. Campbell then the following year spent about $290 million to purchase the remainder of Arnotts, making it a wholly owned subsidiary. Campbell also extended its soup business in Europe through the $180 million acquisition of the Liebig soup business of France. Even with all of these foreign maneuvers, Campbell was far from a goal Johnson had set in 1993 of increasing overseas operations to 50 percent of sales by 2000. The figure had stood at 28 percent in 1993 and had risen to 31 percent in 1994, but by 1998 was back at 28 percent.

Despite the lack of progress toward this goal, Johnson had succeeded in improving Campbell Soup's profitability thanks to his aggressive restructuring efforts. The company's net profit margin stood at 10.4 percent for 1996, compared to five percent for 1988 and 6.5 percent for 1991. But Johnson was not finished with his tinkering. Campbell recorded restructuring charges of $204 million in 1997 and $262 million in 1998 related to plant closures and the divestment of nonstrategic businesses. Jettisoned in 1997 were the Marie's salad dressing and dip unit, the company's Argentinean beef operations, and its German chilled foods business, Beeck-Feinkost GmbH.

After the installation of Dale F. Morrison as president and CEO (with Johnson remaining chairman), Campbell Soup made its most dramatic divestment yet. In March 1998 the company completed the spinoff of its Specialty Foods segment, which included seven noncore businesses. The $1.5 billion spinoff created a new public company, Vlasic Foods International Inc., which included Vlasic pickles, Swanson frozen foods, Swift Armour meats in Argentina, Open Pit barbecue sauce, U.K. canned foodmaker Stratford Upon Avon, Gourmet Specialty Foods of Germany, and a fresh mushroom business in the United States. This move left Campbell Soup with three main core business segments: soups and sauces, biscuits and confectionery, and foodservice. The 1998 dealmaking was not quite over, however, as Campbell sold Delacre, its European biscuit business, to United Biscuit (Holdings) PLC for $125 million in cash in June—leaving Pepperidge Farm and Arnotts as its mainstays in biscuits and crackers. In June the company sold its can-making assets to Stamford, Connecticut-based Silgan Holdings Inc. for $123 million. In August Campbell completed the purchase of Fortun Foods, maker of Stockpot soup, the market leader in premium refrigerated soups, a rapidly growing segment of the foodservice sector.

According to *Business Week,* Morrison warned employees in the fall of 1997, "We are driving the incredibly shrinking company." Reduced to a much more manageable core of leading brands, Campbell faced a number of challenges. In addition to the slower than expected growth in international sales, Campbell's canned soup sales in the United States were on the decline, leading to the implementation in 1998 of the largest advertising campaign in company history, which centered around a new slogan, "Good For The Body, Good For The Soul."

Principal Subsidiaries

Campbell Finance Corp.; Campbell Foodservice Company; Campbell Investment Company; Campbell Sales Company; CSC Brands, Inc.; Godiva Chocolatier, Inc.; Joseph Campbell Company; Pepperidge Farm, Incorporated; PF Brands, Inc.; Stockpot Inc.; Arnotts Limited (Australia); Campbell's Australasia Pty. Limited (Australia); Campbell Foods Belgium N.V.; Campbell Soup Company Ltd—Les Soupes Campbell Ltee (Canada); Campbell France S.A.S.; Erasco GmbH (Germany); Campbell's de Mexico, S.A. de C.V.; Campbell's U.K. Limited

Further Reading

Barrett, Amy, "Campbell Soup: Hail to the Chef," *Financial World,* June 11, 1991, pp. 52–54.

——, "Souping Up Campbell's," *Business Week,* November 3, 1997, pp. 70, 72.

Berman, Phyllis, and Alexandra Alger, "Reclaiming the Patrimony," *Forbes,* March 14, 1994, p. 50.

"Campbell: Now It's M-M-Global," *Business Week,* March 15, 1993, pp. 52–54.

Collins, Douglas, *America's Favorite Food: The Story of Campbell Soup Company,* New York: Abrams, 1994.

Donlon, J.P., "Top Spoon Stirs It Up," *Chief Executive,* November 1996, pp. 44–47.

Dwyer, Steve, "Red Alert: The Soup's Back On," *Prepared Foods,* September 1997, pp. 14–16, 18, 21, 23.

"From Soup to Nuts and Back to Soup," *Business Week,* November 5, 1990, pp. 114, 116.

Glosserman, Brad, "Campbell Soup Works for Spill Over Effect," *Japan Times Weekly International Edition,* May 11–May 17, 1992, p. 17.

Grant, Linda, "Stirring It Up at Campbell," *Fortune,* May 13, 1996, pp. 80.

Hays, Constance L., "Will Goldfish Tactics Help Campbell's Soups?," *New York Times,* October 18, 1998, sec. 3, p. 4.

A History, Camden, N.J.: Campbell Soup Company, 1988.

Mastrull, Diane, "Campbell and Pace Recipe: A Mixing of Disparate Cultures," *Philadelphia Business Journal,* February 17, 1995, pp. 1, 27, 28.

Nulty, Peter, "The National Business Hall of Fame," *Fortune,* March 11, 1991, pp. 98–103.

O'Connell, Vanessa, "Campbell Decides Its IQ Health Meals May Be Ahead of the Curve for Foods," *Wall Street Journal,* April 27, 1998, p. B8.

——, "Changing Tastes Dent Campbell's Canned-Soup Sales," *Wall Street Journal,* April 28, 1998, pp. B1, B25.

——, "How Campbell Saw a Breakthrough Menu Turn into Leftovers," *Wall Street Journal,* October 6, 1998, pp. A1, A12.

Pehanich, Mike, "Brand Power," *Prepared Foods,* Mid-April 1993, pp. 38–40, 42.

Saporito, Bill, "Campbell Soup Gets Piping Hot," *Fortune,* September 9, 1991, pp. 142–48.

"Seizing the Dark Day," *Business Week,* January 13, 1992, pp. 26–28.

Sim, Mary B., *History of Commercial Canning in New Jersey,* Trenton, N.J.: New Jersey Agricultural Society, 1951.

Weber, Joseph, "Campbell Is Bubbling, but for How Long?," *Business Week,* June 17, 1991, pp. 56–57.

——, "What's Not Cookin' at Campbell's," *Business Week,* September 23, 1996, p. 40.

Wentz, Laurel, "Europe: How Smart Marketers Cash In," *Advertising Age,* December 2, 1991, pp. S-1, S-9.

Wimp, Marilyn, "Campbell Spins Off Frozen Food, Pickles," *Philadelphia Business Journal,* March 27, 1998, p. 20.

—April Dougal Gasbarre
—updated by David E. Salamie

Carey International, Inc.

4530 Wisconsin Avenue, NW
Washington, D.C. 20016
U.S.A.
(202) 895-1200
Fax: (202) 895-1201
Web site: http://www.careyint.com

Public Company
Incorporated: 1920 as Grand Central Cadillac Renting
   Corp.
Employees: 689
Operating Revenues: $86.37 million (1997)
Stock Exchanges: NASDAQ
Ticker Symbol: CARY
SICs: 4119 Local Passenger Transportation, Not
   Elsewhere Classified

The world's largest chauffeured vehicle service company, Carey International, Inc. operates through a worldwide network of company-owned and operated companies, licensees, and affiliates. As of August 1998, Carey served 420 cities in 65 countries on six continents, providing 7,500 chauffeured sedans, limousines, vans, and minibuses for such transportation needs as airport pickups and dropoffs, business meetings and conventions, and multi-city travel to special events. About 80 percent of Carey's business is from corporate customers, with the rest from government and leisure travelers. The company estimates it provides more than 22,000 trips a day for its clients.

From Haircuts to Touring Cars: 1921–68

In 1921, New York businessman J.P. Carey acquired a limousine service with six Packard touring cars to serve wealthy travelers arriving at Grand Central Station. Carey, a barber, had emigrated to New York in the early 1900s. He opened a barbershop at Grand Central Station, and eventually had 50 barbers working for him. Over the years he expanded his Grand Central Station operations to include a laundry, shoe store, and haberdashery, before opening the limo service. All three of the Carey sons, John, Edwin, and J. Paul worked in the family businesses, and J.P. eventually created a transportation company for each of them.

J. Paul was put in charge of the Grand Central Cadillac Renting Corp., which later became known as the Carey Cadillac Touring Company. In 1935 Carey opened one of the first Hertz franchises, putting son Edwin in charge of the self-drive operation. During the depression of the 1930s, Carey Cadillac added regularly scheduled service to the area's only airport, in Newark, New Jersey, first with touring cars and then with buses. When LaGuardia Airport opened, Carey served it as well. In 1939 the airport service was spun off into a separate company, operating under the name Carey Transportation and headed by son John.

From its earliest days, Carey prided itself on its customer service and innovation. A favorite company story related how a Carey mechanic created the first air-conditioned chauffeured vehicle to ease the King of Sweden's asthma condition. The mechanic put a block of ice in the trunk of the touring car and hooked up a fan to blow over it into the back seat.

By the late 1960s, Carey Cadillac was the only one of the transportation companies still in the family; Edwin Carey had joined Hertz when it began buying its franchises in the 1950s, eventually becoming Hertz president, and Greyhound Corporation had bought Carey Transportation, the airport bus company. The third generation of Careys wanted to expand the limousine service beyond New York, and three Carey cousins formed Carey Chauffeur Driven Systems, licensing the Carey name to local operators. Carey Cadillac became the new company's first licensee. Others soon followed as the company began augmenting its fleet of limousines with sedans for the corporate market.

National Executive Service Founded in the 1960s

As Carey was moving outside of New York, several former United Airlines employees were establishing a limousine service in San Francisco. Dan Dailey and his partners had worked as customer service and sales employees at United, serving executive and top corporate accounts. They found that the existing limo services in the Bay Area catered to top corporate executives such as board chairmen and company presidents, but no one was serving the middle and upper levels of corporate management.

After conducting a market research study, they created National Executive Service (NES) with eight cars. Within 15 months, NES had 25 cars and customers in other cities requesting similar radio-equipped, chauffeur-driven sedans. By developing a plan to serve management clients with a sedan and limo service built on what was then a sophisticated communication network, NES attracted investment money, enabling it to acquire established operations in Seattle, Detroit, Boston, and Chicago.

Merger: 1969–79

As Carey Cadillac and National Executive Services explored growth opportunities, they found each other. At the end of 1969, the two companies merged on a 50–50 basis, becoming Carey Corporation, a 13-city operation that did business as Carey Limousine. Dan Dailey was named president of the merged company and Vincent Wolfington, a major NES investor, became chairman of the board. The Carey family continued to own and run the New York operation as a licensee.

The new company operated on a franchise system, charging initial and monthly licensing fees for the use of the Carey name, for reservation and billing services, and for marketing activities. Over the years, the company added affiliates to its network as well, developing relationships and joint ventures with companies in smaller cities where there was no Carey presence. The company also began developing partnerships with various corporate entities. One of its first airline programs was created during the 1970s with American Airlines. VIP flyers who belonged to the American Admirals Club had access to a direct telephone line to the local Carey office from each Admirals Club at an airport. By the late 1970s, the company's network served more than 100 cities in the United States, and management decided to expand overseas.

Going International: 1979–86

To reflect this new global strategy, in 1979 Dailey and Wolfington incorporated the company as Carey International, Inc. The company also acquired certain rights to the "Carey" name and moved into Europe, establishing licensees and affiliates. Within four years Carey had more than tripled the size of its network, and by 1984 travelers could book a Carey vehicle in over 390 cities in 60 countries. To make that booking as easy as possible, Carey began developing its one-stop reservation center, which included a computerized reservation system and access to the rates in each of the cities where the company provided service.

Nearly 80 percent of Carey's business came from chauffeuring traveling executives and mid-level managers, but itineraries included more than just trips to and from airports or business meetings. A 1984 column in the *Arkansas Democrat-Gazette* announced that readers could call Carey's 800 number to arrange a three-day trip through Normandy, the Champagne country, or the Loire Valley for around $1,600, with a chauffeur who doubled as a licensed, English-speaking guide.

Carey-Owned and Operated Companies: 1987–89

In 1987 Carey expanded from being solely a holding company and reservation system through the purchase of the company's licensees in New York, Washington, D.C., and Los Angeles. The new subsidiaries essentially gave Carey control of chauffeur-driven services in three of the largest U.S. limousine markets. The company raised the money for these acquisitions through a private financing agreement.

The subsidiaries continued to operate as separate companies that were managed locally with access to Carey's corporate infrastructure for marketing and sales, quality service, customer satisfaction, technology, accounting, and budgeting. Unlike some chauffeured transportation companies, Carey stressed entrepreneurship among its chauffeurs, converting them from salaried employees to independent operators. Carey owned the brand, but the drivers owned and maintained their vehicles. This strategy met two objectives according to Carey: independent operators were more productive, efficient, and service-oriented, and the company saved money on labor and capital costs, allowing it to focus resources on its infrastructure services.

Under the typical 10-year agreement, an independent operator paid Carey a fee ranging from $30,000 to $45,000 (depending on the local market), which the company financed at an annual interest of nine to 12 percent. The individual also agreed to purchase their vehicle and pay all of the vehicle's maintenance and operating expenses, including gasoline. In return, the company agreed to bill and collect all revenues and remit 60–67 percent of those revenues to the operator. If the driver failed to meet Carey's standards of service, the company could terminate the agreement.

Acquisitions: 1990–97

The 1990s saw Carey seriously and successfully begin implementing an acquisition strategy as it moved to consolidate a highly fragmented industry. From 1991 through 1997, the company bought 19 chauffeured vehicle companies, including four of its own licensees.

As the company expanded, an important factor in its operations was its quality assurance system. Based on a 250-point checklist, the system evaluated everything from how quickly a telephone was answered to the use of the proper logo on business cards. Every chauffeur had to satisfy strict standards as defined in a list of 40 items that ranged from such crucial factors as on-time arrival and knowledge of destinations to more minor criteria such as chauffeur attire, courtesy, and the age and condition of a car. This verification system made it possible for Carey to state that all of the company's sedans offered cellular phones and all of its limousines came equipped with televisions and VCRs. All employees received initial and follow-up training, coordinated by a central training department, and the company held two meetings a year internationally and two domestically for management and licensees.

Beginning in 1993, the company invested heavily in developing its proprietary central reservations and billing system, Carey International Reservation System (CIRS). Linked to major reservations systems used by the travel and tourism industry, CIRS allowed customers to make their chauffeured transportation arrangements in multiple cities with one phone call. It also enabled those making travel arrangements for others (over 300,000 travel agents, corporate travel departments, and government offices) to organize Carey transportation in conjunction with other travel plans.

By the end of 1997, CIRS provided more than 27,000 screens of information, including services available in each city, customer profiles, airport greeting capabilities, and over 200,000 rates in both U.S. and foreign currencies. The system also made it possible for Carey to provide its clients centralized billing in many currencies for transportation provided in several different countries, as well as for multi-city use of Carey services.

The company bought its first European operations in 1996, acquiring Camelot Barthropp Ltd. and Europcar Chauffeur Drive U.K. International, both based in London and with offices throughout the United Kingdom. Camelot, a former Carey affiliate, had a fleet of 70 cars; Europcar Chauffeur had about 25. Carey opened its second worldwide reservation center, linked to its U.S. center, at the Camelot headquarters. In the first three months of the year, Carey moved aggressively into Eastern Europe, setting up affiliates in Bulgaria, Croatia, Romania, and Belorussia; into the Middle East with new affiliates in Qatar and the United Arab Emirates; and into Kenya and South Africa.

By the end of the year, the first of Carey's 10-year agreements with its independent operators began expiring. Carey introduced a new 15-year agreement, with fees of $45,000 to $75,000, financed by the company at an annual interest rate of 15.75 percent. In the company's 1997 annual report Carey claimed that the typical independent operator earned, after expenses, two to four times the average annual wage of an employee driver.

Carey went public in May 1997, selling 2.9 million shares and raising over $30 million. The company used the money to pay off debt and to finance a portion of the $17.1 million paid by the company for the June acquisition of Manhattan International Limousine Network Ltd. and an affiliate. Long Island-based Manhattan Limousine, with a worldwide network of more than 300 affiliates, had revenues of approximately $18.4 million in 1996. This acquisition gave Carey greater power in the largest chauffeured vehicle service market in the world, the New York metropolitan area.

Before 1997 was over, Carey bought three more companies: Commonwealth Limousine Services, Ltd., based in Los Angeles, with 1996 revenues of $1.7 million; Indy Connection, an 11-year-old Indianapolis firm with annual revenues of $6.8 million; and TWW Plc, established in 1961 and serving the London metropolitan area, with annual revenues of about $2 million. The same year, Carey added three new domestic licensees and signed an agreement with Virgin Atlantic Airways to serve its Upper Class passengers, a contractual arrangement similar to ones the company had with JAL, British Airways, Air France, Aer Lingus, and other carriers. Carey also maintained service partnerships with major hotel chains and credit card companies.

Further Acquisitions in the Late 1990s

In March 1998, Carey moved into the Boston area as an operator, acquiring Custom Transportation Services, Inc., with revenues of approximately $5 million. A month later, Carey bought certain assets of A and A Limousine Renting, Inc., which had been its Boston licensee since 1970. A and A had annual revenues of approximately $3.7 million. Also in April, Carey purchased certain assets of American VIP Limousine, Inc., a Miami-based company with annual revenues of about $1.2 million. Carey paid some $5.5 million in cash and notes and over 900,000 shares of stock for these six companies.

Expanding through acquisitions was one of Carey's key strategic objectives. With over 9,600 companies in the highly fragmented chauffeured vehicle industry, consolidation was an obvious means to grow. Carey, with about two percent of the market, anticipated strengthening its presence in its existing markets and moving into new cities in North America and Europe by buying current licensees as well as other companies. Carey also planned to expand operations in Africa, Asia, and South America by developing alliances with companies in major cities on those continents. In July 1998, Carey announced it was in acquisition talks with 63 companies representing $420 million in annual revenue, and in August, purchased American Limousine Corp., the largest limo service in Chicago.

In addition to acquisitions, the company's strategy included increasing its share of the international market, which by the end of fiscal 1997 was generating $9.9 million for Carey, expanding its licensee network, and converting salaried drivers to independent operators. Ultimately, according to Steven Ginsberg in a 1997 *Washington Post* article, Carey hoped "to control the market in the largest U.S. and international cities, to compete in second-tier cities such as Baltimore and to have a presence in smaller cities."

Most of Carey's revenues came from the companies it owned and operated in Boston, Chicago, Indianapolis, London,

Los Angeles, New York, Philadelphia, San Francisco, South Florida, and Washington, D.C. In fiscal 1997, these companies accounted for over 81 percent of Carey's net revenues, up from 76 percent the year before. While some of these companies, such as American Limousine and Indy Connection, were competitors when Carey bought them, others, including companies in Boston, London, and Washington, D.C., grew as Carey licensees before being purchased. Carey indicated it would continue to help its licensees grow, through marketing and sales efforts, and then acquire those that fit its strategic plans. Many licensees were previously affiliates, meeting the company's quality standards and paying Carey a commission for all referred business, but not licensed to use the Carey name and not paying license fees.

The only public company in the industry, Carey International grew dramatically from the 13-city operation created by the merger in 1969. During those three decades the global economy and the resulting increase in business travel changed a chauffeur-driven limousine from an executive perk to a business necessity. Carey not only recognized but encouraged that shift, developing its global reservation system and offering one-stop shopping for chauffeur services for any need; Carey services ranged from airport pickup and transportation to meetings, to getting people to and from special events such as Presidential Inaugurations, the Super Bowl, or international financial conferences, to weekend sightseeing or multi-city "road shows." With more than 75,000 companies using its services, by the late 1990s Carey was the leader in the industry.

Principal Subsidiaries

Carey Services, Inc.; Herzog Cadillac Rental Service NY, Inc.; Carey Limousine SF, Inc.; Carey UK Limited; Carey Limousine L.A., Ltd.; Carey Limousine Indiana, Inc.; Carey Limousine DC, Ltd; Carey Limousine Florida, Inc.; International Limousine Network Ltd.; Manhattan International Limousine Network Ltd.; Squire Limousine, Inc.; American Limousine Corp.

Further Reading

"BancAmerica Robertson Stephens Conference," CNBC/Dow Jones—Business Video, Interactive Desktop Video, LLC, June 16, 1998.

"Carey Says It Is in Talks to Acquire 63 Companies," *New York Times,* June 26, 1998, p. D3.

"Driven to Success," *Travel Agent,* August 19, 1996, p. 48.

Foster, Sam, "Carey International, Inc.," *Venture Capital Journal,* July 1, 1997.

"The French Chateau County by Limo? What Better Combination?" *Arkansas Democrat-Gazette,* December 9, 1984.

Ginsberg, Steven, "Carey International's Limousines Traveling the Globe," *Washington Post,* July 7, 1997, p. F12.

Lazarus, George, "Chicago Limo Deal May Trigger Others," *Chicago Tribune,* August 21, 1998, p. 3.

McCormick, Susan, "Carey Financing Lets Limo Firms Expand System," *Travel Weekly,* September 21, 1987, p. B17.

Woods, Lynn, "Carey Purchases Two U.K. Limousine Companies," *Business Travel News,* April 8, 1996, p. 9.

—Ellen D. Wernick

The Charles Schwab Corporation

101 Montgomery Street
San Francisco, California 94104
U.S.A.
(415) 627-7000
Fax: (415) 627-8538
Web site: http://www.schwab.com

Public Company
Incorporated: 1974 as Charles Schwab & Co., Inc.
Employees: 12,700
Operating Revenues: $2.30 billion (1997)
Stock Exchanges: New York Boston Cincinnati Midwest
    Pacific Philadelphia
Ticker Symbol: SCH
SICs: 6211 Security Brokers & Dealers; 6282 Investment
    Advice; 6719 Holding Companies, Not Elsewhere
    Classified

The Charles Schwab Corporation, through its operating subsidiary Charles Schwab & Co., Inc., is the largest discount stock broker in the United States, and the largest provider of online brokerage services. A pioneer in the area of no-transaction fee mutual funds, the company is one of the three largest managers of mutual funds, alongside Fidelity and Vanguard. Expanding at a dizzying pace, Charles Schwab is one of the nation's fastest-growing financial services firms.

Pioneer Discount Broker

Charles Schwab, the company's founder, had received an M.B.A. degree from Stanford University and had been working for a small California investment advisor when, in 1971, he founded his own company, First Commander Corp. He and two partners created a stock mutual fund that soon had $20 million in assets. They ran into trouble with securities regulators, however, when it was learned that they had failed to register the fund. This error temporarily forced Schwab out of business, but he soon reopened a small money-management firm, Charles

Schwab & Co., Inc., in San Francisco, which he incorporated in 1974.

On May 1, 1975, the U.S. Congress deregulated the stock brokerage industry by taking away the power of the New York Stock Exchange to determine the commission rates charged by its members. This opened the door to discount brokers, who took orders to buy and sell securities, but did not offer advice or do research the way larger, established brokers such as Merrill Lynch did. This presented an opportunity to win individual investors well enough versed in the stock market not to need the advice offered by established brokers. Schwab quickly took advantage of deregulation, opening a small San Francisco brokerage, financed primarily with borrowed money, and buying a seat on the New York Stock Exchange.

The new discount brokers, whose commissions might be only 30 percent of the rates before deregulation, were scorned by the old-line brokerages. During his first few years as a discount broker, Schwab had to contend with bad publicity generated by the older firms, some of whom threatened to break their leases if landlords allowed Schwab to rent offices in the same building.

Schwab fought back by buying newspaper ads featuring his photograph and asking customers to contact him personally, helping to build the firm's credibility. Possibly the most important early decision made by Schwab was to open branch offices around the United States. He reasoned that even investors not needing advice would prefer doing business through a local office instead of a toll-free telephone number. The move won customers and helped differentiate Schwab from the large number of discount firms appearing after deregulation.

Over the next few years Schwab did several things to pull away from the pack. The company offered innovative new services including the ability to place orders 24 hours a day. It bought advanced computer systems to deal quickly with huge volumes of orders and continued its heavy advertising, seeking to project an upscale image. Top executives were given expensive foreign cars, and an interior design staff was commissioned to help showcase certain new branches. Some industry analysts maintain that with these measures Schwab helped bring discount brokering into the mainstream of financial institutions.

Acquired by BankAmerica in 1983

The firm's rapid expansion was costly, however. Partly as a result of high operating costs and partly because sales were dependent on the sentiments of small investors, profits were erratic. Schwab sometimes turned to employees and larger customers to raise money for further expansion. By 1980 Schwab was by far the largest discounter in the country. That year, to fund further growth, Schwab decided to take the company public. The offering was called off, however, when some problems caused by the attempted conversion to a new computer system proved an embarrassment to the company. Raising sufficient capital in private became more difficult, partly because of the erratic earnings. Finally, in 1983, Schwab arranged for San Francisco's BankAmerica Corporation to acquire the company for $55 million in BankAmerica stock. BankAmerica also agreed to supply Schwab with capital. The bank loaned Schwab $50 million over the next three years, but Schwab remained one of the most highly leveraged brokerages.

The sale to BankAmerica may have provided needed capital, but it also fettered the company with banking regulations. Schwab wanted to offer new, proprietary lines of investments including Charles Schwab mutual funds. However, federal law at the time forbid banks and their subsidiaries from underwriting such securities. Although Schwab initially sought to challenge the law, as its wording contained some ambiguities, BankAmerica did not want to irritate banking regulators. Tensions between Schwab and its parent were further exacerbated when BankAmerica's stock price began falling, making Schwab's stake in the corporation worth less.

Schwab introduced the Mutual Fund Marketplace in 1984 with an initial investment of $5 million. The Marketplace allowed customers to invest in 250 separate mutual funds and switch between them using Schwab as the bookkeeper. All of a customer's mutual fund accounts were put on a single monthly statement. The company's profile was further raised in 1984 when Schwab's book *How to Be Your Own Stockbroker* was published. In it Schwab presented himself as a populist fighting against Wall Street stockbrokers in the name of the average investor. He contended that there is an inherent conflict of interest when a firm owns stock in inventory, writes favorable research recommendations on those stocks, and has commissioned salespeople sell those stocks to the public. At the same time, Schwab's company was moving into elegant new headquarters in downtown San Francisco.

In 1985 Schwab had 90 branches and 1.2 million customers, generating $202 million in revenue. Though it was far larger than its leading discount competitors, it was small compared with the largest retail brokerages, which had over 300 branches. The firm was growing in other ways, however. It offered personal computer software, called the Equalizer, that allowed investors to place orders via computer as well as to call up stock information and obtain research reports.

Buyback and Public Offering in 1987

In 1987 Charles Schwab and a group of investors bought the company back from BankAmerica for $280 million. Seven weeks later, he announced plans to take the company public. The buyback had resulted in a debt of $200 million, and the public offering was partly designed to eliminate some of this debt. It was also intended to raise money for further expansion. Schwab wanted to increase the number of branches to 120, including offices in Europe. The September 1987 IPO created a new holding company, The Charles Schwab Corporation, with Charles Schwab & Co., Inc. as its principal operating subsidiary.

The discount brokerage business had grown intensely competitive. Discounters handled a significant amount of retail equity trades by 1987, but hundreds of firms had entered the field, including banks, savings and loans, and mutual fund companies. Since Schwab was clearly the player to beat in discounting, competitors' advertisements specifically offered rates lower than Schwab's. Nevertheless, at this time Schwab had 1.6 million customers, about five times as many as its nearest competitor, Quick & Reilly Group. In 1987 the firm had sales of $465 million and profits of $26 million, twice the industry's average profit margin. To achieve this success, Schwab was spending about $15 million a year on advertising.

Schwab was already doing well with its expanded product line. Mutual Fund Marketplace had attracted $1.07 billion in client assets by year-end 1986. The company was also offering Individual Retirement Accounts, certificates of deposit, money-market accounts, and Schwab One cash-management accounts. Despite these successes, Schwab was badly hurt by the stock market crash of October 1987. By mid-1988, trading volume had fallen to about 10,400 trades a day, a 40 percent drop from the months before the crash. Schwab cut costs to maintain profitability, reducing managerial salaries anywhere from five to 20 percent and laying off employees. Charles Schwab cut his own pay by 20 percent for six months and put branch expansion plans on hold. The firm also raised its trading commission by ten percent, so that it needed only 8,000 trades a day to break even, down from 12,000 trades. Even with the cost-cutting, the firm's 1988 earnings plummeted 70 percent to $7.4 million on sales of $392 million.

Rapid Expansion

By 1989 Schwab was expanding again. The company bought Chicago-based Rose & Co. for $34 million from Chase Manhattan; as the fifth largest discount broker in the United States, Rose & Co. brought Schwab 200,000 new customers at a cost of about $70 each. With the purchase, Schwab controlled about 40 percent of the discount market, though discounters made only eight percent of all retail commissions. Over the long run, Schwab realized its best strategy was to win customers from the full-service brokers. To help create more independent stock investors, it pioneered a service called TeleBroker that let customers place stock orders and get price quotes from any touchtone telephone 24 hours a day. It also released a new version of the Equalizer. The software had already sold 30,000 copies at $169 each since its introduction.

Individual investors returned to the stock market in 1989, and the firm's income surged to $553 million, with profits of $18.9 million. Income was further helped by an increase in client assets, from $16.8 billion in 1987 to $25 billion in early 1990. Commissions accounted for 70 percent of revenue, down from 85 percent in 1987.

Throughout the 1980s, Schwab updated its Mutual Fund Marketplace to allow customers to switch their investments from fund to fund by telephone. Customers paid a commission ranging from .6 percent to .08 percent, with a minimum fee of $29. Analysts were generally positive, pointing out that the amount of interest lost from having a check in the mail would pay for most of the service's commission fees. In 1991 Schwab entered a new and lucrative market with the acquisition of Mayer & Schweitzer, an over-the-counter stock market maker.

Meanwhile Schwab was opening branch offices at a furious pace—17 in 1992 alone—and doubling the amount of money it spent on advertising. Schwab's aggressive stance helped raise its share of the discount market to 46 percent as the company attracted more than 40,000 new accounts a month. In 1992 Schwab acquired its first corporate jet, spending $12 million on a model with enough fuel capacity to reach London, where it was opening its first European branch. These additional costs helped drag down third-quarter earnings in 1992 when stock trading temporarily tapered off. The dip was a reminder that the company was still highly dependent on commissions and caused its stock to drop 20 percent.

Schwab cut advertising by 20 percent and took other steps to slow cost increases. The company converted a greater share of new branch offices into bare-bones operations with only one broker. Schwab already paid its 2,500 brokers less than other discounters, an average of $31,000 a year, compared with $50,000 at Fidelity Brokerage Services and $36,000 at Quick & Reilly.

OneSource Introduced in 1992, Leading to Explosive Growth

The firm also continued searching for ways to become less dependent on commissions. The introduction in July 1992 of the Mutual Fund OneSource—a program allowing investors to trade mutual funds (more than 200 in all) from eight outside fund companies, without paying any transaction fees—attracted more than $500 million in assets within two months and over $4 billion by July 1993; it was thus the most successful first-year pilot of any new service in Schwab's history. The fund companies paid Schwab a small percentage fee—typically 0.25 to 0.35 percent—of the fund assets held in Schwab accounts.

During 1992 Schwab customers opened 560,000 new accounts at its 175 branch offices, while assets in customer accounts grew 38 percent to $65.6 billion. Revenue soared to $909 million, with record profits of $81 million. As a result of these successes, Schwab opened 20 more branch offices in 1993, opened an office in London (its first in Europe), and introduced several proprietary mutual funds, including Schwab International Index Fund and Schwab Small-Cap Index Fund.

As the 1990s continued, the OneSource program became wildly successful. By 1997 investors could choose among more than 1,400 mutual funds and had poured $80 billion into the funds through the program. OneSource—aided by the long bull market—helped Schwab grow at an amazing rate in the 1990s. From 1992 through 1997, revenues increased at a 25 percent compounded annual rate, while customer assets increased 40 percent per year, from $65.6 billion to $353.7 billion. Also fueling this growth was the emergence of Internet trading as Schwab rapidly gained the number one position among online brokerage services. By May 1997 the firm claimed 700,000 of the 1.5 million active, online brokerage accounts in the United States. It also moved into the top five among all U.S. brokerages.

Schwab's explosive growth, which saw customer accounts increase from 2.0 million in 1992 to 4.8 million in 1997, was accompanied by several technological snafus, prompting some company clients to conclude that Schwab was growing too fast. For instance, in the summer of 1997 two computer-related outages temporarily left thousands of Schwab clients without access to their accounts. In addition, some clients were mistakenly sent the statements of other clients. Schwab officials contended that these were isolated incidents and not indicative of out-of-control growth.

The company also had to contend with the aging of the baby boom generation, the members of which were somewhat belatedly planning for retirement. Schwab set up a retirement plan services unit offering 401(k) and other retirement plans. Aging investors also tended to want more advice before deciding where to put their money. In response, Schwab bolstered its ability to deliver investment advice to clients, developing written investment kits; providing access to a wide range of research reports, earnings forecasts, and news stories on its web site; and offering the opportunity to meet in person with representatives at company branches. Another new and highly sought-after service added by Schwab in 1997 was access to initial public offerings at the offering price. The firm entered into alliances with Credit Suisse First Boston Corporation, J.P. Morgan & Co., and Hambrecht & Quist Group to gain access to IPOs led by these companies.

On January 1, 1998, David S. Pottruck became president and co-CEO of Charles Schwab Corporation, with Charles Schwab remaining chairman and sharing the co-CEO title. This unusual arrangement seemed to indicate that Pottruck, age 49 at the time, was in line to succeed the 60-year-old Schwab, though the company founder had made no retirement plans. Just a month or so earlier, Timothy F. McCarthy was named president and chief operating officer of Charles Schwab & Co., giving him day-to-day responsibility for the management of the brokerage unit, with Pottruck controlling overall administration, finance, technology, and corporate strategy.

It was this new management team that would have to contend with what would likely be an increasingly volatile stock market in the early 21st century. Also, the shift to more trading on the Internet—where fees were lower—was cutting into Schwab's bread-and-butter commissions. It was reported in September 1998 that the company, which already offered services in Hong Kong and the United Kingdom, was considering entering the Japanese market, among other international expansion possibilities.

Principal Subsidiaries

Schwab Holdings, Inc.; Charles Schwab & Co., Inc.; Charles Schwab Investment Management, Inc.; The Charles Schwab Trust Company; Mayer & Schweitzer, Inc.; Charles Schwab Europe (U.K.).

Further Reading

Bianco, Anthony, "Schwab Vs. Les Quick," *Business Week,* May 12, 1986.

Ferguson, Tim W., "Do It Yourself: Charles Schwab Has Riden the Bull Market to a Splendid Present, but Its Future Is in Boomer Retirements," *Forbes,* April 22, 1996, p. 70.

Heins, John, "After Cost Cuts, What?," *Forbes,* May 1, 1989.

——, "How Now, Chuck Schwab?," *Forbes,* June 15, 1987.

Laderman, Jeffrey M., "Remaking Schwab," *Business Week,* May 25, 1998, pp. 122–24, 127–29.

McGeehan, Patrick, "Charles Schwab's Pottruck Will Share Title of CEO with Company's Founder," *Wall Street Journal,* December 2, 1997, p. B5.

——, "Schwab's Offer of Rivals' Research Meets a Quick End," *Wall Street Journal,* January 19, 1998, pp. C1, C19.

McGough, Robert, "Schwab's Swelling Girth Holds Sway in the Fund Field," *Wall Street Journal,* November 9, 1993, pp. C1, C21.

Mitchell, Russell, "The Schwab Revolution," *Business Week,* December 19, 1994, pp. 88–91, 94–95, 98.

Oliver, Suzanne L., "One-Stop Shopping," *Forbes,* November 11, 1991.

Pare, Terence P., "How Schwab Wins Investors," *Fortune,* June 1, 1992, p. 52.

Raghavan, Anita, "Schwab's Series of Misfires Puts Firm on the Defensive," *Wall Street Journal,* February 24, 1998, pp. C1, C27.

Raghavan, Anita, and Patrick McGeehan, "Schwab Again Plans to Offer Stock Research," *Wall Street Journal,* July 8, 1998, pp. C1, C15.

Schifrin, Matthew, "Cyber-Schwab: As Retail Brokerage Moves On-line, Charles Schwab Has Grabbed Nearly Half the Market," *Forbes,* May 5, 1997, p. 42.

Shao, Maria, "Suddenly the Envy of the Street Is Schwab?," *Business Week,* March 19, 1990.

Siconolfi, Michael, "Schwab's Profit Stumbles Amid Rise in Expenses Coupled with Less Trading," *Wall Street Journal,* September 29, 1992.

—Scott M. Lewis
—updated by David E. Salamie

Christensen Boyles Corporation

4446 West 1730 South
Salt Lake City, Utah 84104
U.S.A.
(801) 974-5544
Fax: (801) 972-6769
Web site: http://www.christensenproducts.com

Wholly Owned Subsidiary of Layne Christensen Company
Incorporated: 1895 as Boyles Bros. Drilling Company
Employees: 900
Sales: $120 million (1997 est.)
SICs: 1081 Metal Mining Services; 6719 Holding
   Companies, Not Elsewhere Classified

Christensen Boyles Corporation (CBC) operates as a leading holding company overseeing 19 internationally integrated companies or divisions that make diamond drilling products, distribute related products made by other firms, and provide contract services for a variety of customers in the mining, geotechnical, and environmental industries. With over 100 years of experience, CBC has a reputation for quality products and services, operations that span the globe, and innovative joint operations with related firms.

Origin of Boyles Bros. Drilling Operations

Elmore and Page Boyles were born in Monona, Iowa, in humble circumstances. The two brothers worked on farms and saved a little, then in 1886, at ages 22 and 19, they moved to southern Arizona. For five years they worked for the Silver King Mining Company. In 1891 they moved to Spokane, Washington, where Elmore worked in the feed business and Page worked for the recently completed Northern Pacific Railway.

In the midst of a nationwide depression, in 1895 the brothers used their savings to start the Boyles Bros. Drilling Company in Spokane. They purchased their first diamond drill, using carbonados or black diamonds found in Brazil, and gained their first contract with the Hecla Mining Company in Republic,

Washington. The firm's main customer before 1905 was the Granby Consolidated Mining, Smelting and Power Company, which owned about 700 acres of mining claims in southeastern British Columbia. In these early days Boyles Bros. drilled mainly in search of copper deposits.

Early Changes at Boyles Bros.

Elmore eventually became the president/general manager of Boyles Bros., while Page functioned as the firm's field superintendent. The firm expanded its operations in the western United States, Canada, and Alaska. By 1914 Boyles Bros. operated many of the over 30 kinds of diamond drills then available in the industry.

In 1917, just before the United States entered World War I, Page Boyles died. That same year, because of low copper prices in the United States and increased operations in British Columbia, Elmore Boyles moved the firm's headquarters from Spokane to Vancouver, British Columbia. By that time Charles and Fred Pettersson, two brothers who had emigrated from Sweden and then changed their last name to Lindhe, and L.L. Jessen controlled most of the firm's business. Up until this time Boyles Bros. had bought its diamond drills from other companies, mainly Sullivan Machinery or Longyear, but under Jessen's direction the firm began manufacturing its own drills. In the 1920s gasoline-powered diamond drills began replacing the earlier steam-powered drills.

By the late 1920s, Boyles Bros. had become Canada's leading diamond drilling company, although the firm also had operations in the United States and South America. In 1928 Elmore Boyles died, and the second-generation leaders Fred Lindhe and L.L. Jessen took over ownership of the company.

Boyles Bros., now incorporated in Canada, opened a division in Utah to provide drilling services for the Utah Copper Company. After gaining some government public works contracts during the Great Depression, by 1935 Boyles Bros. recovered sufficiently to move out of its rented Salt Lake City offices at the corner of 300 South and Main Street to a building owned by the firm on 1300 South. In 1935 Charles Lindhe, who had left

Boyles Bros. in 1922 to start Continental Drilling Company in Los Angeles, returned to Utah and bought Boyles Bros.

Expansion in the 1940s

In 1942 Boyles Bros. was reorganized with Charles Lindhe, Harold L. Baker, Arthur F. Goldsworthy, and Robert T. Goldsworthy each having 25 percent ownership. On January 31, 1948, those four plus Grant H. Bagley incorporated Boyles Bros. Drilling Company under the laws of Utah. The company listed Lindhe as president and Robert Goldsworthy as vicepresident.

Originally Boyles Bros. concentrated on hard rock drilling for mineral exploration in the western United States, British Columbia, and Alaska. In 1945 the company expanded into civil construction by providing cement and chemical grouting and monitoring wells; drilling for rock bolts, ground anchors, and drain holes; and instrumentation for the building of dams, highways, and tunnels.

Origins of Christensen Diamond Products

During World War II two unrelated friends with the same last name started a new company. Frank and George Christensen met while playing professional football for the Detroit Lions. By the early 1940s Frank ran a machinery shop that made mostly mining equipment and had a good working relationship with Boyles Bros. George meanwhile had worked for Koebel Diamond Tools, which marketed diamond tools to Detroit-area car makers. With two friends, George approached Koebel about manufacturing diamond tools, but Koebel turned down the offer. Nevertheless, in 1943 George started Christensen Diamond tools in 1943, but he lacked a supply of diamonds. George contacted a representative of South Africa's Boart International to supply his firm with natural diamonds called boarts, then called Frank Christensen to merge their two businesses. In 1944 the two partners created a new corporation called Christensen Diamond Products (CDP).

In 1949 CDP began a joint venture with the Longyear Company in which CDP agreed to manage a joint diamond inventory and to set Longyear's diamond bits according to that firm's requirements. While Longyear used its name to sell these bits, Christensen at the same time competed with Longyear by selling its own diamond bits. The two firms ran joint business operations in Asia, Australia, South America, Europe, and Canada between 1953 and 1970.

By the early 1950s Christensen Diamond Products in Salt Lake City had expanded to produce diamond drill bits for both mining and oil companies. While mining firms had used diamond drill bits for about 60 years, the oil industry at this time understood little about using such technology. To meet the needs of the oil industry, CDP created sales/services offices in

Denver; Houston; Bismarck, North Dakota; Midland, Texas; and Lafayette, Louisiana, while manufacturing plants were started in Oklahoma City; Shreveport, Louisiana; and Hobbs, New Mexico.

CDP in 1954 organized Christensen Diamond Products Company, France (CDPF). In a rented Paris building, CDPF began manufacturing diamond drill bits and core barrels. In 1961 CDP designed and made the diamond bit, core barrel, and recovery equipment used to drill the ocean floor for the first time in history. This successful drilling 2.3 miles below the Pacific resulted in other drillings through the Moho, the discontinuity between the earth's crust and mantle.

In 1958 the Longyear Company had developed a new drilling technique called Wireline. Previously core drillers had obtained their samples by withdrawing long pipes after drilling was completed. Wireline allowed cores to be withdrawn without removing the pipe, thus making drilling much more efficient, and many companies adopted this technology. In 1967 Boyles Bros. improved the wireline system by developing its new Quad-Latch system for latching and retrieving wireline inner barrels. Impressed with this new technology, Christensen replaced its own "C" (for Christensen) Series Barrels with the "B" (Boyles) Series Barrels.

Boyles Bros. and Christensen Operations in Latin America

Boyles Bros. in 1961, under President Robert Goldsworthy, negotiated an agreement with the Chilean government to start drilling operations in Chile. With a five-year tax freeze and five years of duty-free imports, the deal "was the best agreement the Chilean government had ever given a foreign company," according to a CBC history. By January 1962 the firm had shipped its first equipment to Chile under contract with Acero del Pacifico, and other contracts soon followed. By 1963 Boyles Bros. played a key role in Chile's mining industry, which supplied about 80 percent of that nation's foreign exchange.

Also in 1963 Boyles Bros. received a huge contract from the American Smelting and Refining Company (ASARCO) in northern Peru. Completed in 1965, that project earned Boyles Bros. about $3 million. An ASARCO subsidiary subsequently awarded Boyles another large contract for drilling in copper reserves south of Lima. To handle these operations, Boyles created a subsidiary called Boyles Bros. Sucursal del Peru, later changed to Boyles Bros. Diamantina S.A. That subsidiary built its headquarters in Lima, but political unrest in the 1970s interfered with its successful operation.

In 1970 the communist government in Chile under Allende undertook the nationalization of the country's mining and drilling industry, leading Boyles Bros. to sell its equipment to the government and to leave Chile. At the same time, Christensen stayed in the country and sold its diamond bits to the government-run drilling business. When Allende was deposed in the 1973 military coup led by General Augusto Pinochet, Christensen was well-positioned to take advantage of that nation's economic recovery.

Mergers in the 1970s and 1980s

In 1970 Christensen purchased a 50 percent interest in Boyles Bros. and then in 1975 acquired the company outright. According to company literature, "It was a perfect marriage between manufacturer [CDP] and contractor [Boyles Bros.]. Christensen provided the world's leading drilling company with the best diamond bits and related equipment available. Boyles provided their observations of what design modifications and new instrumentation were needed, and a hands-on testing environment."

In 1977 the Norton Company, an abrasive products manufacturer based in Worcester, Massachusetts, purchased Christensen, Inc., including the Boyles Bros. operations. Many, including Norton executives, believed the energy crisis caused by the 1973 Arab oil embargo would result in coal becoming the energy source of the future. In an era of booming minerals exploration and mining, the 1977 merger allowed Boyles Bros. to gain much needed expansion capital, and the future looked bright.

By the early 1980s, however, oil prices had decreased and coal had lost its attraction. Copper prices also plummeted. Falling profits led Norton, as well as many other companies in the industry, to lay off many workers. Finally, in 1986 Norton decided to cut its losses and let Christensen and Boyles operate independently. Norton netted $8 million from this deal, which involved an eastern bank, Boston's Greylock Financial Partnership, and nine former Norton managers. The newly independent company, renamed Christensen Boyles Corporation (CBC), was launched in December 1986. CBC was led by Eric Despain, a 1973 accounting graduate of Brigham Young University, who had joined Norton during the boom of the early 1980s. When Despain became the president of the newly formed company in 1986, CBC employed only 500 workers, about half the number before the decline of the mining industry of the mid-1980s.

Under Despain's leadership CBC acquired other firms and increased its international presence. CBC purchased the Contract Drill Division of LaPorte, Indiana's Joy Technologies Inc., acquired a partnership interest in Norton Christensen de Mexico, and began Christensen Drilling Supplies, Ltd. in Canada. CBC also acquired 49 percent of Elgin Exploration, a Calgary, Canada-based firm which specialized in evaluating and monitoring construction projects. Elgin's instruments monitored highwalls, tailings dams, and embarkment slopes, and the company was well-respected in the hydroelectric, mining, and engineering fields. Elgin operations also included oil coring and exploration. With its origin in the Arctic, Elgin had a reputation for working in extreme environments with barges, tracked vehicles, or whatever it took to get the job done. CBC's international growth continued in 1988 when it helped start Technidrill, a sales company in Nice, France, that distributed CBC's products in Europe and Africa.

Using newly developed computerized technology, CBC provided clients with specialized services such as directional drilling, a technique that allowed holes to be drilled vertically, horizontally, or at any angle. CBC's directional drilling, offered through its Navi-Drill Division, could drill precisely placed holes for difficult applications such as sending telephone lines under rivers or electrical lines through dams.

In the 1980s companies like CBC gained new sales due to several new environmental protection laws passed by Congress in the 1970s. After the establishment of the Environmental Protection Agency in 1970, Congress passed the Clean Water Act in 1972 and the Safe Drinking Water Act of 1974, to be followed by the Resource Conservation and Recovery Act. CBC helped cities and companies meet these new federal guidelines by using its auger, rotary, and core drilling to take soil samples and monitor underground sources of water pollution.

Mergers and Projects in the 1990s

CBC in 1992 merged with the Acker Drill Company of Scranton, Pennsylvania, a firm that had started contract drilling in the Pennsylvania anthracite coal fields in 1917. Brothers Warren and William Acker had started the company, and the Acker family continued to run it at the time of the 1992 merger.

The acquisition of Acker occurred while both CBC and Acker were bidding on a project to provide multipurpose drills to help the Egyptian government repair the Aswan Dam. The merged firms combined their bids into a single bid chosen by the Egyptians. "It really tied the groups closer together, it really made us aware of what our capabilities are," said CBC's director of manufacturing, Bill Higgins, in the company's fall 1993 newsletter. While Christensen Boyles produced diamond bits for mining and civil construction industries, Acker served the geotechnical and environmental sectors. They also served complementary parts of the world: CBC in the United States, Canada, Europe, and Latin America; and Acker in Africa, Asia, Australia, and the Near East. CBC's plant in Salt Lake City covered 84,000 square feet, while the Acker facility in Scranton provided another 75,000 square feet.

With these various acquisitions in the late 1980s and early 1990s, Christensen Boyles Corporation could claim to be the "largest, best-equipped manufacturer of drilling equipment in the United States." It offered virtually every piece of drilling equipment and service, "from the top of the rig to the bottom of the hole," including smaller underground drills, drilling muds and fluids, well cleaning products, PVC pipe, augers, mobile or stationary surface drill rigs, pumps, core orientation, chemical and cement grouting, water wells, geophysical logging, and various development and consulting services.

CBC provided three kinds of diamond drill bits; surface set bits with rows of natural diamonds in the crown, impregnated bits made with tiny synthetic diamonds scattered throughout the crown, and polycrystalline diamond bits. Impregnated bits, which allowed hard rock drilling three to four times deeper than the older surface set bits, became popular in the late 1970s when competition between General Electric and DeBeers lowered prices for synthetic diamonds. The more expensive polycrystalline diamond bits were introduced in the 1980s for drilling mainly in relatively soft coals and shales, but by the early 1990s CBC's ChrisDril products featured improved polycrystalline bits that could penetrate soft to medium-hard substances.

CBC gained 40 percent of its sales from natural and synthetic diamond bits, while 60 percent came from other items such as drill rods, core barrels, and spare parts. President Eric Despain in an interview said that 1995 worldwide sales exceeded $120 million. The company employed an average of 600 workers in the United States although that figure could reach as high as 1,000 during the busy drilling season from May to October. CBC also employed 250 full-time nonseasonal workers in South America, 50 in Canada, and 15 in Europe.

In the mid-1990s CBC gained an interesting contract to aid the California state government in retrofitting the famous San Francisco Bay Bridge to prevent future seismic damage. Earlier, 114 retrofit highway bridges had survived the terrible 1994 earthquake in the Los Angeles area, while seven bridges not retrofitted collapsed. CBC worked closely with the California Department of Transportation to take core samples from near the bridge's foundations. Three specially designed CBC drill bits were used. In spite of bad weather and difficult drilling conditions, the project recovered 100 percent of the vital core samples.

In 1996 Christensen Boyles Corporation merged with Layne, Inc. based in Mission Woods, Kansas, to form the Layne Christensen Company. Layne had been founded in 1882 to provide water drilling and had later added drilling for minerals exploration. After the 1996 merger, Layne combined its mineral products manufacturing at the CBC plant in Salt Lake City, while Christensen Boyles' geotechnical and environmental activities were consolidated under Layne's plants and operations.

CBC's products proved their worth in 1998 when TEG Oceanographic Services used them to complete a drilling project in Hawaii. To prepare for a sewage plant pipeline extension, TEG used CBC's wireline coring technology to take samples from ten different locations at the mouth of Pearl Harbor. Also in 1998, the firm's reaming shells were used to reach record drilling depths. In Carlin, Nevada, Newmont Gold used one CBC shell to drill to over 20,000 feet, and the project supervisor said it could have gone even further.

These projects illustrated the diversity and innovation typical of Christensen Boyles's long history. The firm's drillers have worked in challenging situations and places, from the South Pole to the Gobi Desert, and clients have used CBC products for all kinds of purposes. This flexibility and reliability, combined with additional resources from the Layne merger, gave the firm's leaders confidence for future growth.

Principal Subsidiaries

Boyles Bros. Drilling Company; CBC Drilling; Chris-Well Products; Global Drilling Suppliers, Inc.; Elgin Exploration (Canada); Christensen Mining Products of Canada; Christensen Boyles International (Cayman Islands); Productos De Diamante Christensen (Mexico); Technidrill, Ltd. (Nice, France); Boytec S.A. (Panama City); Geotec (Lima, Peru); Boyles Bros. Diamantina. S.A. (Lima, Peru); Christensen De Chile (Santiago); Norton Chile (Santiago); Geotec Boyles Bros., S.A. (Santiago); American Hard Chrome (Chile).

Principal Divisions

Contracting Division; Christensen Mining Products Division; Acker Division.

Further Reading

Derdak, Thomas, "Layne Christensen Company," in *International Directory of Company Histories,* vol. 19, Detroit: St. James Press, 1998, pp. 245–47.

Walden, David, "Christensen Boyles Corporation," in *Centennial Utah: The Beehive State on the Eve of the Twenty-First Century,* edited by G. Wesley Johnson and Marian Ashby Johnson, Encino, Calif.: Cherbo Publishing Group, 1995, pp. 104–05.

Woody, Robert H., "Christensen Boyles Men Learned Survival Lesson Well," *Salt Lake Tribune,* n.d.

—David M. Walden

Chronimed Inc.

10900 Red Circle Drive
Minnetonka, Minnesota 55343
U.S.A.
(612) 979-3600
(800) 444-5951
Fax: (612) 979-3969
Web site: http://www.chronimed.com

Public Company
Incorporated: 1984
Employees: 330
Sales: $140.7 million (1998)
Stock Exchanges: NASDAQ
Ticker Symbol: CHMD
SICs: 8099 Health & Allied Services, Not Elsewhere
Classified; 5047 Medical & Hospital Equipment

Chronimed Inc. is a leading integrated healthcare company specializing in diagnostic products, specialty pharmacy services, and disease management for people with chronic health conditions. The company develops, manufactures, markets, and distributes pharmaceuticals and medical diagnostic products, and provides specialized patient management services for people with chronic conditions such as HIV/AIDS, diabetes, organ failure, and diseases treated with injectable medications. Chronimed works directly with patients, providers, and payors in a concerted effort to improve clinical and cost-of-care outcomes, and to enhance the quality of life for the chronically ill.

From Cranes to Chronic Diseases, 1970s–80s

Chronimed Inc. was founded by Maurice R. Taylor II in 1985, a year after Taylor took over the drug, supply, and marketing division of the International Diabetes Center. Taylor came from a varied background which included starting a crane manufacturing company, an international trading company, and a fast-foods products company. Taylor's position immediately before founding Chronimed was as executive vice-president and chief operating officer of Summit Gear, a manufacturer of precision instruments for the aerospace industry. His broad knowledge of manufacturing and distribution positioned him well to succeed in this new venture. Though his background in healthcare and chronic diseases was minimal, Maurice Taylor recognized the burgeoning need for information and products in this market and the inevitable growth of the industry. Taylor knew that he could bring to the company the medical expertise it would need. What he brought to the table was his unique ability to read the trends and shifts in consumer needs and carve out a vision for Chronimed's role in the emerging healthcare market.

Since the early 1970s, the International Diabetes Center had been acting as an advocate and clearinghouse for research and information used primarily by professionals in the care of chronic (Type I and Type II) diabetes. This gave them widespread recognition as a reliable source for medical information. In January 1986 Steven Crees joined Chronimed. His background was as a marketing representative with the Baxter Travenol Corporation, a healthcare products distributing company. He brought to Chronimed added marketing expertise specifically in the healthcare arena.

Under Taylor's leadership, now assisted by Steven Crees, Chronimed broadened the emphasis of making diabetes information available to the growing number of professionals and patients as well.

From the start, business was brisk for Taylor and Crees. Even though diabetes had been around for several thousand years, insulin was only discovered in 1922. Moreover, insulin was not systematically manufactured until 1978, when advances in the field of biotechnology made it possible. By the time Chronimed emerged, the new treatment of diabetes was spreading fast. Other advances in medical science were making organ transplantation more and more possible. Successes were still scattered, yet there was a very hopeful attitude among professionals, and researchers were making great strides forward. New antiviral drugs were being developed as transplants became more and more a reality. Add to this the emergence of

HIV/AIDS. The first cases of this new virus were reported in patients in New York and San Francisco in June 1981. By 1983, medical scientists announced they had isolated what they now called the HIV virus. There was evidence that this new disease was growing to epidemic proportions and there was a serious outcry for funding and research to meet the challenge. As the 1990s approached, the demand for information, drugs, and supply gave the impetus for Chronimed to broaden its strategy to include other chronic diseases.

Organ Transplant Specialty Pharmacies

In 1990, the company opened an organ transplant specialty pharmacy to serve patients who had undergone solid organ and bone marrow transplants. The company realized the unique nature of the organ transplant patient who is faced with intensive, high-cost drug therapies that could continue over a long period of time. It became clear that the traditional drug distribution systems in existence at the time may not be able to serve these chronic patients adequately due to the precise monitoring and personal tailoring required in the scheduling and administering of drugs to transplant recipients. Chronimed's specialty pharmacies continued to grow, becoming an important aspect of their work in later years.

The 1990s: Accelerated Growth

The early 1990s saw remarkable, steady growth for Chronimed as market demands for their products and services compounded year after year. Nearing the end of the decade, the company reported nearly a 45 percent growth rate overall in all their business units.

The company began serving HIV/AIDS patients through its mail-order pharmacy in 1994. Also by that time, materials on chronic diseases had been translated into 12 foreign languages and the company was considered the largest publisher of chronic-disease literature in the world. In this year, Chronimed also began its Orphan Medical Division to develop pharmaceuticals for the treatment of rare diseases. Through this division the company began distributing Cystadane for patients with the rare disorder called Homocystinuria. They also became the exclusive distributor of Cystagon, a drug used for Nephropathic Cystinosis, another rare genetic disorder.

In 1995, Chronimed extended its distribution channels to begin working with large insurers. After a very successful pilot program, Prudential Insurance Company started offering

Chronimed pharmaceuticals through its nationwide HMOs. In February of that same year Norman A. Cocke came to Chronimed as senior vice-president and chief financial officer and secretary of the board of directors. Cocke came from a background in computer information systems The following year Patrick L. Taffe joined the Chronimed management team as vice-president of information systems, a position he formerly had with MedPower Systems. The combined expertise of Cocke and Taffe proved to be a valuable asset as the company upgraded its internal information handling and storage systems and took steps to meet the market demands for information and resources.

Chronimed acquired the assets of StatScript Management Services and its nine specialty pharmacies in July 1996. StatScript was providing drug therapy services primarily to the HIV/AIDS market. This gave Chronimed a major presence in the HIV/AIDS marketplace from which to expand. The company quickly moved to expand drug therapies in existing outlets resulting in increased patient intake and vigorously open new pharmacies. By the fall of 1998, there were 24 StatScript Specialty Pharmacies in operation. Supervising this expansion was Perry L. Anderson, formerly vice-president at StatScript, who came to Chronimed as the divisional vice-president of StatScript Pharmacy. Dr. Henry Blissenbach joined the Chronimed team as president and COO in May 1997 from a background in management with Diversified Pharmaceutical Services, Inc. His leadership helped continue the momentum and further establish Chronimed as a leader in the healthcare industry.

Chronimed, the Publisher

Over time the publishing division of the company continued to grow as well. By 1998, it published or distributed more than 80 books and educational pamphlets for patients, families, and caregivers of patients with chronic diseases. The range of topics included nutrition, stress management, and the physical, psychological, and sociological needs of patients with chronic conditions. Chronimed continued its main goal of helping chronically ill people and their families to better care for themselves. Through its commitment, Chronimed had become one of the largest publishers of diabetes-related materials in the United States.

By its 13th year of operation, Chronimed had organized its business into three main segments: Diagnostic Products, Specialty Pharmacy Services, and Disease Management. To build and energize its employees and strengthen overall leadership, the company added a human resources person and increased the number of board members to seven.

Diagnostic Products

A major National Institute of Health study in 1993 concluded that frequent monitoring of blood glucose levels and more frequent insulin injections along with a regimen of diet and exercise could reduce complications of diabetes, such as blindness, loss of nerve sensation, and amputation, by as much as 60 percent. The study also reported that about 16 million Americans at that time had diabetes, yet only about five million had been diagnosed correctly. Chronimed took very seriously the relationship between proper diagnostics and disease management. Its diagnostic tools were designed for use in both the institutional setting by long-term care facilities, clinics, and hospitals and by customers themselves. They expanded their diagnostic products in 1998 with the acquisition of Dia-Screen, a medical diagnostics products maker. The Dia-Screen brand also brought to Chronimed a test strip for leukocytes and specific gravity bringing the number of reagent strips it carried to 14. The use of a single test strip was then able to give the physician 10 different clinical markers in a patient's urine. Already in use was its Supreme II blood glucose monitor system which provided long term care facilities a way to monitor more than one patient at a time. The same year, it also introduced a new meter that used electrochemical biosensor technology to measure blood glucose called the Assure Blood Glucose Monitoring System. The new system proved to be more accurate than existing glucose meters and was easier and more convenient for patients to use. The company also extended its distribution channels into Mexico, Germany, and Brazil, bringing the total number of outlets to 11 countries with goal being to be in 30 countries covering all continents by the end of 1999.

In November 1998, under contract with Cell Robotics, Chronimed began marketing the Lasette extraction device to diabetics, a nearly painless tool to extract capillary blood for testing glucose levels. The Lasette was designed to use a laser beam to penetrate the skin to obtain a capillary blood sample, instead of the traditional lancets that tear the skin. Use of the Lasette also eliminated accidental needle sticks, reduced cross contamination, and eliminated residual pain. The company also had begun exploring HIV genotyping and phenotyping of DNA to help in the battle against AIDS and the development of more effective antiretroviral drugs.

Specialty Pharmacy Services

By 1998, through it specialty pharmacy services, Chronimed was distributing over 2,700 prescription drugs, 10 percent of which were immunosuppressive drugs for the prevention of organ and marrow rejection. The company was dedicated to serving patients with the following needs: Diabetes, HIV/AIDS, Multiple Sclerosis, Hemophilia, Growth Hormone Deficiency, Infertility, Hepatitis B and C, Oncology, and Organ Transplants. Patients with chronic diseases were increasingly requiring very personalized programs of drug therapy, so the company included in its protocol ways to monitor compliance with patient regimen established by the patient's whole healthcare team. Through this, Chronimed became a leader in developing a strong network of healthcare agencies and coordinating the services of physicians, nursing services, payors like HMOs, and major health insurers. Specific programs were set up just for patients requiring injectable medications for chronic diseases, solid organ and bone marrow transplant recipients, and a Diabetes Care System tailored to the diabetics needs.

The company became known for its ability to handle large volumes of patients and produce consistent, personal outcomes at a lower cost. To support the massive volume of transactions efficiently, the company combined state-of-the-art scanning and filing computer technology for forms and records handling. They also adopted the use of an intranet, web-based system to coordinate billings between multiple payors, reducing costs and saving time. At that time, Chronimed was one of the few companies that had ventured into this technology.

Disease Management

In the area of disease management, Chronimed truly became a leader. Patients with chronic disease must learn to live with a long-term, life-altering or life-threatening condition. By its commitment to the patient's total care and ability to work together with the entire healthcare team, Chronimed set itself above the competition. This gave rise to the third business segment of Chronimed, that of disease management. In June 1998, the company acquired Clinical Partners, Inc., a provider of medical case management to HIV/AIDS patients. This brought the whole aspect of data analysis, case management, and clinical protocol to Chronimed. The company hired highly distinguished clinicians in the field of HIV/AIDS to develop its guidelines and supervise its follow-through. The case management protocols were implemented through its growing number of StatScript Pharmacies and also through its well established direct mail-order channel. The company realized that the management of drug therapies for this disease was most critical. In 1998, surveys found that nearly 26 percent of HIV patients admitted to failing to take their medications properly. With the chronic patient in need of ongoing drug therapy, the pharmacy was the logical place to manage the care for the patient.

A Company Above the Rest

There was a steady increase in the number of Chronimed employees, with the number reaching 330 by 1998. In that year alone, employee growth increased 13.8 percent from the previous year. Company representatives were located throughout the country, working closely with distributors and networking with healthcare teams to provide the best possible care to patients and customers. To do this most effectively, all employees received extensive training and competency testing.

Revenue growth for Chronimed was no less spectacular. In 1997 and 1998, Chronimed was listed as one of "America's Top 100 Fastest-Growing Companies" by *Fortune* magazine. In 1998, growth was announced at 20.1 percent with total revenues amounting to $140.7 million. Projected revenue for fiscal 1999 was $196 million, which was up 39 percent from the previous year.

Integrated Healthcare

For the future, Chronimed saw itself becoming an increasingly vital partner with those committed to the improved health of chronic persons. It planned to further increase its distribution of prescription drugs and proprietary medical products by increasing the number of patients served through its programs, and by increasing sales of proprietary and licensed products to new patients and institutions. Through the year 2002, the company anticipated a 55–70 percent increase in the demand for early intervention (HIV) oral medication therapy alone! Chronimed also plans to apply its successful disease management model to other selected chronic conditions in the future. With the expansion of its leadership team in late 1998, the company has a strong infrastructure, well-positioned for cost containment and improved outcomes into the next millennium.

Principal Divisions

Specialty Pharmacy Services; Diagnostic Products; Disease Management Services.

Further Reading

"America's Fastest-Growing Companies: The Top 100," *Fortune,* September 29, 1997.

Andberg, Ernest W., "Research Report: Chronimed, Inc.," *RJ Steichen & Co.,* October 28, 1998, pp. 1–3.

"Cell Robotics Announces Third Quarter 1998 Financial Results," *PR Newswire,* November 10, 1998.

"Chronimed Names Steve Russek Senior Vice-President of Disease Management," *PR Newswire,* November 30, 1998.

Fleming, Harris, Jr., "Drug Topics: Attack on AIDS," *Drug Topics Magazine,* July 6, 1998, p. 1.

Miller, Ken, M.D. "Institutional Research: Chronimed, Inc.," *Hambrecht & Quist LLC,* October 26, 1998, pp. 4–6.

Mullich, Joe, "Curing Those Piles-of-Paper Blues," *PCWeek,* June 29, 1997.

"TransMedia Drops Lawsuit Against Cell Robotics," *PR Newswire,* December 12, 1998, p. 1.

—J. D. Fromm

CMP Media Inc.

600 Community Drive
Manhasset, New York 11030
U.S.A.
(516) 562-5000
Fax: (516) 562-7830
Web site: http://www.cmp.com

Public Company
Incorporated: 1971 as CMP Publications Inc.
Employees: 1,775
Sales: $473.9 million (1997)
Stock Exchanges: NASDAQ
Ticker Symbol: CMPX
SICs: 2721 Periodicals, Publishing; 7389 Business
    Services, Not Elsewhere Classified; 8732 Commercial
    Economic, Sociological & Educational Research

When CMP Media Inc. became a public company in 1997, it had enjoyed 26 years of uninterrupted sales growth, 22 years of profitability, and six consecutive years of rising operating income. After such steady growth, the company controlled the largest market share in U.S. high-technology ad pages. Its core business consisted of several print publications that served three key segments across the technology spectrum: the builders, sellers, and users of technology.

CMP's two controlled-circulation titles, *EE Times* and *Electronic Buyers' News,* became the top two titles in the original equipment manufacturer (OEM) sector and formed the company's OEM Group. These publications provided business and technology news to manufacturers, managers, engineers, designers, and purchasers of electronic systems and components, including computers, telecommunications equipment, semiconductors, software, peripherals, and related products.

Three periodicals—*Computer Reseller News, VARBusiness,* and *Computer Retail Week*—made up the Channel Group. They reached a wide range of technology resellers, including distributors, value-added resellers (VARs), retailers, systems integra-

tors, dealers, consultants, computer superstores, mass merchandisers, warehouse clubs, consumer electronics retailers, and mail-order sellers. *Computer Reseller News* became the largest technology trade publication in the United States in terms of ad pages.

Several CMP periodicals served the needs of technology users and buyers, including *InformationWeek, Network Computing, InternetWeek,* and *Windows Magazine.* Audiences for these periodicals included end users of information systems, computer systems, personal computers, software, the Internet, and related products and services. Their readers included information systems executives, network communications and departmental applications managers, and Internet and intranet managers. In May 1998 CMP acquired *Data Communications, LAN Times, tele.com,* and *Byte,* from The McGraw-Hill Companies. Publication of *Byte* was suspended with the June 1998 issue. These periodicals served other technology buyers and became part of CMP's new Business Computing and Communications Group, a portfolio of publications that would reach the full spectrum of business information technology (IT) buyers.

In addition to its print publications, CMP Media offered a comprehensive menu of Internet sites through CMPnet. CMP Media was the fist media company to establish Internet sites for all of its publications in 1994 with the launch of TechWeb. In 1997 the company launched CMPnet (www.cmpnet.com) to provide a single point of access to all of CMP's Internet products, services, and utilities.

CMP Media was also active in conducting industry conferences and special events, custom publishing, research, software testing, and database marketing.

Company Origins with
Electronic Buyers' News, *1971*

Founded as CMP Publications Inc., the company's first publication, *Electronic Buyers' News,* was launched in 1971. The magazine targeted procurement managers, purchasing and financial professionals, and corporate executives in the electronic industry. Its editorial focus was to help its readers manage the risk of making product and sourcing decisions on a timely basis.

The periodical was created by Gerard (Gerry) and Lilo Leeds, who produced the first issues out of their home in Great Neck, New York, on Long Island. They soon moved to offices in Manhasset, New York.

In 1972 a second publication, *EE Times,* was introduced for engineers and technical managers in the electronics industry. A weekly, *EE Times* covered business and technology news, analyzed key industry trends and developments, and included opinions from government and industry leaders.

New Publications Launched in the Mid-1980s

In 1982 *Computer Reseller News,* the company's first periodical aimed specifically at information technology sellers, was launched. The weekly's broad editorial coverage was aimed at all resellers, including dealers, distributors, value-added retailers (VARs), and value-added distributors (VADs). In addition to industry news, the publication included a wide range of product reviews, industry analyses, and training and development opportunities, among other topics.

Two additional audiences were targeted with the launch of *CommunicationsWeek* and *Business Travel News* in 1982. *CommunicationsWeek* was the first CMP periodical aimed at end-users of technology. *Business Travel News* was the company's first travel publication. It was begun by Michael Leeds, son of CMP's founders, who had just joined the company. After publishing *Business Travel News* for ten successful years, CMP sold its travel publishing unit to Miller Freeman to focus on the exploding technology market. *CommunicationsWeek* was relaunched in 1997 as *InternetWeek* to focus on buyers and end users of Internet-related technology.

A second publication for technology buyers, *InformationWeek,* was launched in 1985. In 1987 CMP started up a second publication for sellers of information technology called *VARBusiness,* which targeted value-added resellers (VARs).

Michael Leeds Takes Over Day-to-Day Operations in 1988

In 1988 Michael Leeds, the eldest son of the founders, took over day-to-day operations of the company. While continuing to serve on CMP's board of directors, Gerry and Lilo Leeds turned their attention to the nonprofit sector. They founded the nonprofit Institute for Community Development in 1990, which addressed the needs of students at risk of dropping out of school. By 1996 the Institute was providing aid for 1,000 students in school districts on Long Island and in New York City.

Under Michael Leeds's leadership CMP's revenues tripled between 1988 and 1996. He was also responsible for CMP's aggressive development of Internet products and services. In 1994 the company launched TechWeb, which put all of its print products online. Subsequently, CMP developed online products that were distinct from the company's print publications, and in 1997 CMP expanded its Web presence with the debut of CMPnet, a hub for all of the company's online products and services.

Sales Growth and New Publications in the Early 1990s

By 1992 CMP's revenues had grown to $218.2 million with income from operations amounting to $7.4 million. The company had successfully launched *Computer Retail Week* and *Network Computing* in 1990, and in 1991 CMP acquired *Windows Magazine* which was relaunched in 1992. In 1991 the first InformationWeek Conference was held as the company began diversifying into conferences and special events for the IT industry.

In 1992 CMP also began to develop a global brand under the leadership of Daniel Leeds, Michael Leeds's younger brother, who was named president of CMP's international business operations. Over the next several years publishing bases were established in Germany, France, and the United Kingdom. The company began serving IT markets outside the United States by establishing wholly owned and joint-venture publications serving the builders, sellers, and users of IT.

Established an Internet Presence in the Mid-1990s

In the fall of 1994 CMP established web sites for all of its publications at its TechWeb site. During the year the company opened a satellite office in Jericho, New York, for some of its publications and purchased the name "NetGuide" from a book packager. *NetGuide Magazine* was launched in December 1994 with a circulation of 200,000. A monthly, *NetGuide Magazine* was a consumer publication aimed at users of the Internet and online services. By the end of 1996 the magazine's circulation had grown by 63 percent, including a 32.2 percent increase in 1996. Its January 1997 ad revenues were up 76 percent over the same period in the previous year. Ad pages increased by 44.4 percent during 1996, making *NetGuide Magazine* the fastest-growing consumer technology publication tracked by the *Computer Publishing and Advertising Report.*

CMP's revenues for 1995 reached $382 million, with *Computer Reseller News,* CMP's top magazine for advertising revenue, grossing an estimated $90 million in ad revenue. The periodical's strong sales had helped support CMP's expansion into magazines with a broader audience base. CMP was developing a reputation for being ahead of its competitors; the company launched *Windows* before Ziff-Davis's *Windows Sources;* the consumer-oriented *HomePC* was started in 1994 before *Family PC* hit the market; and *Network Computing* came out before its competitor *Corporate Computing*. However, publishing consumer titles cost more than trade magazines aimed at professionals, and CMP was forced to suspend production of the money-losing *Interactive Age* in August 1995 after less than a year of publication.

Name Changed to CMP Media Inc. in 1996

During 1996 CMP Publications Inc. changed its name to CMP Media Inc. in order to emphasize the company's presence in the Internet and electronic media markets. However, not all of CMP's ventures in this area would be successful, and rapidly changing conditions resulted in many shifts in direction. CMP's TechWeb site, which contained online versions of the company's periodicals, was one of the most popular computer sites with $4.5 million in 1996 advertising revenues from 144 advertisers. Less successful was the company's consumer publication *NetGuide*—in spite of increased circulation and ad revenues—and the related Internet site Netguide Live.

NetGuide Live was introduced in August 1996, after CMP spent about $10 million developing the site, according to one source. At the beginning, about 200 people were employed on the project, including about 100 freelance writers working at home. However, with the site producing little advertising revenue, two rounds of layoffs in 1996 reduced NetGuide Live's staff to 64 employees. Editor-in-chief Dan Ruby left in September 1996, and with the staff relocated to different offices, NetGuide Live underwent a redesign to make it more accessible.

With many web sites failing, the troubled NetGuide Live was a familiar story among web publishers attempting to make money off of the Internet. In addition to searching the web, NetGuide Live listed live chat events each day, highlighted new sites, had lessons to improve Internet usage, and provided capsule reviews and ratings of more than 50,000 web sites. Explaining NetGuide Live's problems, Ruby said in *Newsday* that NetGuide Live "tried to throw too much stuff into one product and it made it hard to be clear what we were or what we were best at. A lot of Web producers made similar mistakes."

In February 1997 *NetGuide Magazine* acquired *Online Access,* which was launched in 1986 and became the computer industry's first Internet publication. *Online Access*'s paid subscriber base would be added to *NetGuide'* s, further boosting the fast-growing publication's circulation. Just prior to its 1997 initial public offering (IPO), CMP announced it would stop publishing *NetGuide* with the August 1997 issue. Observers speculated that closing the magazine would improve CMP's financial performance, even though *NetGuide*'s advertising revenue for the first five months of 1997 was up 76.6 percent over the previous year to $7 million, and the number of ad pages had increased 39 percent. *NetGuide*'s circulation was 352,875, of which 285,608 was paid. The magazine had gone through four editors since its inception in 1994. Explaining the decision to stop publication, CMP said the closing "reflects rapid change in the market during the last two years." The company noted that the desktop and Internet markets had converged, "eliminating the need for a stand-alone monthly magazine exclusively targeting the Internet buyer."

Initial Public Offering in 1997

When CMP announced it was going public in 1997, it was the third largest computer magazine publisher behind Ziff-Davis Publishing and IDG (International Data Group). In its filing CMP revealed that the company's leading publications in terms of advertising revenue were its trade periodicals, while its consumer publications were not attracting as much advertising revenue and its Internet services were losing money.

On July 25, 1997, the first shares of CMP were offered to the public on the NASDAQ. The IPO was completed by July 30 and resulted in net proceeds to the company of approximately $84.7 million. Some 5.5 million shares of Class A common stock were sold at an offering price of $22 per share, of which 4.2 million were sold by the company and 1.25 million were sold by stockholders.

Upon completion of the IPO, Gerard and Lilo Leeds provided a gift of 200,000 shares of the new stock worth $4.4 million at the offering price to CMP employees, including some 400 editorial employees and 675 sales employees as well as a number of retirees. The amount of stock each employee received was based on length of service, with a five-year employee receiving 160 shares worth about $4,600. In addition, the Leeds gave $26 million in stock to charitable foundations.

Two classes of stock with different voting rights were created, and restrictions were placed on stock owned by the Leeds family in an attempt to maintain control and prevent an unwanted takeover. Class A Stock, which was sold to the public, had one vote per share, while Class B Stock, which was held by the Leeds family, had ten votes per share.

As the number three publisher in the fast-growing computer and electronics-related magazine publishing field, CMP quickly attracted the interest of analysts. The stock rose $2.88 on its first day of trading, and one analyst commented, "CMP deserves a premium (over shares of) traditional publishers because they're operating in a faster growing segment. New technology creates a need for new publications." Among technology-related companies, CMP was one of the few public companies that showed a profit.

Record Revenues and Profits in 1997

CMP achieved record revenues and profits in 1997. Sales rose 13.3 percent to $473.9 million, and adjusted net income increased to $19.8 million from $16.1 million the previous year. Operating income reached $39.3 million, up from $28.8 million in 1996. For the past five years, CMP's revenues had grown at a compounded annual rate of more than 16 percent, while adjusted operating income grew by 42 percent.

From 1993 to 1997 CMP Media was the only one of the top five technology media companies to increase its advertising pages every year. It was also the only one of the top five technology print publishers to hold a larger market share in 1997 (24.6 percent) than in 1993 (20.9 percent). CMP accounted for more than half of the entire growth of advertising pages in the U.S. technology publishing sector from 1993 to 1997. In 1997 it held the number one market share position in U.S. high-tech ad pages, with more than 40,000 ad pages.

During 1997 CMP continued to pursue its strategy for international growth by launching *Computer Reseller News* in France, acquiring two titles in the United Kingdom, and acquiring full ownership of the U.K. version of *InformationWeek.* In Germany, the company launched *InformationWeek* with its German joint-venture partner and acquired a 50 percent interest in three German networking publications. The company began to expand its reach by aggressively licensing its domestic editorial content, design, and titles to more than 25 foreign publishers with distribution in more than 60 countries. As part of its international growth strategy, CMP Media acquired a major international advertising representative firm and changed its name to CMP Worldwide Media Networks in 1996. By 1997 it represented 80 of the world's leading overseas high-technology publications, of which 40 percent were CMP-branded titles.

Internet-related revenues tripled in 1997, although this figure still represented only about five percent of the company's revenues in that year. In July 1997 the company launched CMPnet, which provided users with access to all of the company's Internet products, services, and utilities. CMPnet became the exclusive provider of computing and Internet content for Infoseek as well as the premier content provider for America Online's Computing Channel and Microsoft's IE4 Active Desktop Channel. It was also the first technology channel selected by PointCast Inc.

CMPnet sites included TechWeb, which provided daily news updates, expert analysis, hardware and software reports, and other features for corporate information-technology decision makers. TechWeb also contained the archives for all of CMP's publications. Another site, EDTN (Electronics Design, Technology, and News Network), was a joint-venture interactive Internet service that provided design information and other decision-support tools to electronics engineers. ChannelWEB was a subscription-only site that provided users with a customized news feed from CMP's channel publications. It included areas where vendors and resellers could exchange information, receive channel research, and learn more about industry issues, products, and technologies. In addition, there were several other technology-related sites that were part of CMPnet.

In addition to recognition as a rapidly growing company, CMP was also receiving kudos for being a good company to work for. It was named to *Fortune* magazine's first annual list of the "Best 100 Companies to Work For" in the United States. For the sixth time, *Working Mother* magazine named CMP one of the "Best 100 Companies for Working Mothers." The company had a nationally recognized child care center and provided an environment that allowed women to reach key management positions.

In April 1998 CMP Media sold *HomePC* to Imagine Media, Inc. With more than 500,000 readers monthly, *HomePC* was the largest PC consumer magazine in the United States. *HomePC* was a good fit for Imagine Media, which published several consumer-oriented computer periodicals such as *boot, MacAddict,* and *PC Gamer.* Publication of *HomePC* would be interrupted briefly and resume in September 1998. The sale of *HomePC* was part of CMP's strategy to focus on the business market rather than the consumer market. In 1997 *HomePC*'s ad pages had slipped by 9.3 percent, although advertising revenues

grew by a comparable percentage to $34.2 million. Begun in 1994, *HomePC* started with a circulation of 200,000 and grew to 500,000 by the time of its sale to Imagine Media.

CMP Media quickly added more publications by acquiring several computer and communications periodicals from the McGraw-Hill Companies in May 1998 for $28.6 million. These publications included *Data Communications, LAN Times, tele.com, Byte,* as well as an independent testing laboratory called NSTL (formerly National Software Testing Labs) which CMP planned to use to provide product and systems testing independently of its publishing operations. As part of the acquisition agreement, CMP Media and McGraw-Hill would have an ongoing relationship that would include cosponsoring technology conferences with McGraw-Hill's *Business Week* magazine. At the time of the acquisition, Michael Leeds said, "The addition of The McGraw-Hill Companies' titles to our own will enable us to offer our customers unparalleled access to every audience within the business computing market."

The McGraw-Hill acquisitions added an estimated 200,000 unduplicated qualified subscribers to CMP's base, which would now total 844,000 unduplicated qualified readers. *Data Communications, LAN Times,* and *tele.com* all served technology users, complementing CMP's *InternetWeek, InformationWeek,* and *Windows Magazine* in that segment. All of these publications would be included in CMP's new Business Computing and Communications Group, a portfolio of publications that would reach the full spectrum of business information technology buyers. CMP's new Business Computing and Communications Group was headed up by Jeffrey L. Strief, a CMP executive vice-president.

The end of an era for CMP came with the cessation of publication of *Byte* in June 1998. Founded in 1975, *Byte* was one of the most well-known names in computer publishing. Its readers were serious computer users, and the magazine dealt with a wide range of computer-related topics. At the time publication was suspended, the acquisition from McGraw-Hill was not fully completed, and neither McGraw-Hill nor CMP Media would take responsibility for shutting down the magazine, according to the *Boston Globe.* However, the periodical's advertising revenue had been declining for several years. CMP held out the possibility of relaunching the periodical at a later date.

CMP Media was now the number one publisher in the business computing and communications market with 1.22 million qualified subscribers—of which more than 900,000 were unduplicated—receiving its controlled circulation publications. In addition, there were 800,000 readers who subscribed to or purchased single copies of *Windows Magazine,* resulting in a total of more than two million professionals in information technology that advertisers could reach via CMP publications.

Layoffs and Lower Earnings, 1998

In July 1998 CMP Media laid off 50 people and announced it would not fill 35 vacant positions, thus reducing its workforce by 4.5 percent to 1,775 positions worldwide. In making the announcement, CMP noted that computer magazine advertising had softened in recent months. Among the factors contributing to fewer advertising pages were instability in the Asian markets, declining personal computer prices, and product delays. These factors also contributed to a decline in CMP's second quarter net income for 1998.

In the second half of 1998 CMP announced it would launch *CRN Enterprise Partner,* a newspaper supplement for systems integrators who work primarily with *Fortune* 1000 companies and other large organizations. *CRN Enterprise Partner* would join *Computer Reseller News* and related publications in CMP's Channel Group, whose publications were aimed at sellers of technology. Other CMP Channel Group products and services included the Channel Information Services research and consulting unit; ChannelWEB, the resellers-only virtual community; the CMP Channel Advocate Program; Channel Custom Publishing; and the XChange conference series.

Another new product launch was announced in August, with CMP partnering with the Education News and Entertainment Network (ENEN) to produce *Electronics Industry News.* The audio-based daily news service dedicated to the electronics industry, would be available over the Internet at either the ENEN web site or at RealNetwork's daily briefing web site.

As 1998 drew to a close CMP remained positioned to take advantage of changing trends and to reach new audiences and new markets in the IT industry. The company's expansion plans included acquisitions and new launches in the print arena as well as growth in international business. The company planned to expand its global presence through independent launches, joint ventures, and licensing of its flagship publications in different countries. CMP also strengthened its commitment to producing industry conferences and special events with the April 1998 acquisition of Kingbird Media Group LLC, which had produced IT conferences and events for 15 years.

CMP expected to achieve growth in Internet-related revenues by moving CMPnet and its subscription Internet ser-vices—ChannelWEB and EDTN—toward profitability. One source predicted that online media spending would reach $4.3 billion by the year 2000. The projected growth of Internet commerce was expected to result in more business for the company, and CMP Media established its TechShopper site on CMPnet to take advantage of this trend.

Principal Operating Units

OEM Group; Channel Group; Business Computing and Communications Group; International Group; CMPnet; NSTL.

Further Reading

Berkowitz, Harry, "CMP Media Decides to Go Public," *Newsday,* May 10, 1997, p. A25.

Bray, Hiawatha, "Byte Magazine Will Suspend Publication After June Issue," *Boston Globe,* May 29, 1998, p. D4.

"CMP Media Falls 31% After 3rd-qtr. Profit Warning," *Bloomberg News,* September 3, 1998.

Feigenbaum, Randi, and Pradnya Joshi, "Magazine's Name Changes As CMP Spiffs Up for IPO," *Newsday,* June 24, 1997, p. A36.

Messina, Judith, "CMP's New IPO Zooms in Its First Trading Day," *Crain's New York Business,* July 28, 1997, p.4.

Sanger, Elizabeth, "CMP Lays Off 50, Cites Drop in Ads and Revenue," *Newsday,* July 14, 1998, p. A37.

——, "CMP Media Shares the Wealth, Employees Get Stock in IPO—and Stake in LI Company's Success," *Newsday,* September 22, 1997, p. C18.

——, "CMP Sells HomePC to Imagine Media," *Newsday,* April 7, 1998, p. A54.

——, "CMP to Close 'Net Magazine," *Newsday,* June 13, 1997, p. A63.

——, "CMP's Bumpy Ride in Cyberspace," *Newsday,* January 27, 1997, p. C6.

——, "Riding the Next Wave," *Newsday,* June 24, 1996, p. C1.

—David Bianco

COCKERILL ⑤ SAMBRE

Cockerill Sambre Group

Chaussée de la Hulpe 187
B-1170 Brussels
Belgium
(2) 679 92 11
Fax: (2) 660 36 40
Web site: http://www.cockerillsambregroup.com

Majority State-Owned Company
Incorporated: 1981 as S.A. Cockerill Sambre
Employees: 26,545
Sales: BFr 210.32 billion (US$5.67 billion) (1997)
Stock Exchanges: Brussels Paris Luxembourg
Ticker Symbol: COC
SICs: 3312 Steel Works & Blast Furnaces; 3316 Cold
Rolled Steel Sheet, Strip & Bars; 3317 Steel Pipe &
Tubes; 3325 Steel Foundries, Not Elsewhere
Classified; 3441 Fabricated Structural Metal

One of the largest industrial groups in Belgium, the Cockerill Sambre Group is a medium-sized integrated steel-making concern. The group has three core activities: integrated steel manufacturing, particularly coated steel sheets; steel distribution, operating primarily in France and the Netherlands in addition to Belgium; and manufacturing of steel-based products for the construction industry. The group is also involved in several noncore areas, with these activities stemming from the historical development of the group and from a program of diversification embarked upon in the early 1990s. These include mechanical engineering and various services operations.

Cockerill Sambre entered 1998 as a majority state-owned company, 79 percent-owned by the regional government of Wallonia (the French-speaking southern half of Belgium)—the remainder was publicly traded. In October 1998 French steel-making giant Usinor S.A. reached an agreement with the government to acquire a 75 percent stake in Cockerill Sambre, with the government retaining 25 percent.

The Cockerill Sambre Group of the late 20th century resulted from the 1981 merger of the two major iron and steel groupings of the Walloon region of Belgium. From its beginnings, the Cockerill Group had been based at Seraing on the River Meuse a few miles upstream from Liège, while the company Hainaut-Sambre was based at the town of Charleroi, some 65 miles east of Liège on the banks of the River Sambre. The Sambre flows into the Meuse and provides a geographical link between these two regions, formerly rich in coal. In both areas, iron and steel production dates back before the 18th century, based on the coal mines of the areas, but the majority of the companies that have been absorbed gradually into the group were originally founded between 1800 and 1838.

Liège Region Roots

The key figure of the Liège region was an Englishman, John Cockerill, whose name the group still bears to this day. His father, William, was an English engineer who had emigrated and established a successful textile machinery manufacturing firm at Verviers, 15 miles from Liège. In 1814 John Cockerill acquired from King William of Orange the old chateau at Seraing, formerly the summer residence of the prince-bishops of Liège. This has remained the registered office of Cockerill Sambre, and still houses the mechanical engineering division. The new factory opened in 1817, at first producing steam engines for spinning mills and winding and pumping engines for collieries. As coal was available on site, the company decided to produce the metal it required as well. The company was the first in Europe to erect a coke-fired blast furnace, which began production in 1826. By 1847 there were six blast furnaces in use. The state of Belgium was not created until 1830, following a revolutionary episode which necessitated the closure of the works at Seraing for a time. When production resumed, the company produced some of the first locomotives for the Belgian State Railways.

When John Cockerill died in 1840, the financial crisis that followed resulted in the winding up of the company. But it was soon reconstituted as a limited company in 1842, and production began to revive in earnest the following year. By 1845 good progress was being made, and Cockerill engines obtained a

81

Grand Medal at the 1851 Great Exhibition in London. All kinds of heavy machinery were produced during this period: ships, including ironclad gunboats for Russia and cross-channel mailboats for the Dover-Ostend route; tunnelling machines; bridges; and various plants for steel works. In 1866 a new director-general, Eugene Sadoine, initiated the development of adjacent coal mines at Colard, and acquired two-fifths of the neighboring Esperance coal mines as well as iron mines in Spain. A new steel works was opened in 1883, accompanied by much modernization of the existing works. The social requirements of the workers were not neglected, there being workmen's houses, refectories, schools for both adults and children, a 250-bed hospital, a dispensary, and an orphanage with more than 100 places. During the International Exhibition held in Liège in 1905, the (British) Institution of Mechanical Engineers held its annual convention in the town, during which various visits were arranged for the members, including one to the Cockerill works. They were to see "large gas engines, steam turbines, blast-furnaces, steel works, collieries, etc." The party of British engineers also visited the Société d'Ougrée-Marihaye, to see another steel works which exactly 50 years later, in 1955, was to become part of the Cockerill company. The origins of the company Ougrée-Marihaye, which was established in 1835, lie in an iron foundry established at the beginning of the 19th century in the commune of Ougrée, between Seraing and the town of Liège itself, and the coal mines of Marihaye which had existed since 1778. This company occupied an important place in the Belgian iron and steel industry right up until the 1955 merger.

The other key company from the Liège area was Esperance-Longdoz. Its origins can be traced back to the Dothée family, which was already trading in ironmongery, copper ware, zinc objects and utensils, sheet metal, and hardware during the early 18th century. Esperance-Longdoz was formed in 1836, based on coal mines at Esperance, near Seraing, and with the involvement of John Cockerill. The first blast furnace opened there in 1838, followed in 1846 by a tin-plate works in the Longdoz district of Liège. The company was involved in joint ventures with Cockerill to exploit mineral rights, and became a major coke producer of this period. Esperance-Longdoz proved to be one of the most dynamic companies in the history of the group, surviving as a separate entity for 135 years until one of the penultimate mergers in 1970; as late as 1963 a brand new steelworks was built by Esperance-Longdoz on a greenfield site at Chertal, to the north of Liège.

Charleroi Region Roots

The 18th-century companies of the Liège region are only half of the story, and it is necessary to follow the rivers Meuse and Sambre upstream to Charleroi and examine the group's industrial antecedents. Most of the local companies there remained part of the Hainaut-Sambre side of the group until the formation of Cockerill Sambre in 1981, with the interesting exception of the Forges de la Providence. This company was founded in 1838 with the help of another Englishman, Thomas Bonehill, who had also been introducing industrial innovations to the Europeans. His successor, Alphonse Halbou, rose to fame by patenting the rolled I-section girder—often known today as the RSJ—in 1849, which accelerated the construction of high-

rise buildings, undertaken first in Paris and eventually throughout Europe. Forges de la Providence remained separate until 1966, when it was merged with Cockerill-Ougrée in Liège, forming Cockerill-Ougrée-Providence. At this time, Forges de la Providence was a major steel producer based at Marchienne-au-Pont in Charleroi, but also owned two factories in France along with six other important French subsidiaries. By a twist of fate, rationalizations during the late 1970s led to the disposal of the Providence works to the Charleroi-based Thy-Marcinelle et Monceau (TMM) group. This could be said to have restored the geographic balance, but too late, as TMM itself—which first became Thy-Marcinelle et Providence—was to become part of Hainaut-Sambre in 1980, and so by 1981 found itself back with its old parent Cockerill, following the final merger which created Cockerill Sambre. As for the other Charleroi companies, TMM had been formed in 1966 from the merger of Thy-Marcinelle and Acieries et Miniéres de la Sambre. The origins of TMM include the forge of Thy-le-Chateau, which had existed as early as 1763, and Marcinelle, on the south bank at Charleroi. During the 17th and 18th centuries the whole region between the Sambre and the Meuse was known for its ironmasters, and it was one of these, Ferdinand Puissant, who had enlisted the services of Thomas Bonehill at Forges de la Providence. A Frenchman, Albert Goffart, had established his blast furnace in the nearby town of Monceau-sur-Sambre in 1836.

The other main grouping of firms in the surrounding area became the Hainaut-Sambre company in 1955, Hainaut being the name of the province in which Charleroi is situated. The two companies involved in the first merger were the Usines Métallurgiques de Hainaut, founded in 1829, and Sambre-et-Moselle, founded in 1835. The merger between Hainaut-Sambre and Thy-Marcinelle et Providence took place in 1979, not long after the transfer of Providence to TMM by Cockerill.

Mergers, 1955–81, Created Cockerill Sambre

A chronological perspective provides a clearer overview of the complexities of all these mergers and regroupings. Beginning with the rise of the 19th-century companies, there were, to start with, four principal companies in each of the two regions of Liège and Charleroi. The first significant mergers did not take place until 1955, following reorganization plans initiated after the formation of the European Commission for Coal and Steel in 1952. These resulted in the formation of Hainaut-Sambre in the Charleroi region, and Cockerill-Ougrée at Liège. Another ten years passed before the mid-1960s witnessed two further rationalizations: the incorporation of Providence to form Cockerill-Ougrée-Providence at Liège, and the coming together of some of the earliest Charleroi-based companies to form Thy-Marcinelle et Monceau.

During this period the other important Liège steelmaker, Esperance-Longdoz, had constructed a modern steel complex at Chertal to the north of the town, opened in 1963 to replace its works on sites nearer the town. These had become surrounded by other developments and were consequently suffering from a shortage of space in which to expand and introduce the wider strip mills which had become necessary in order to remain competitive in the market. At the end of the 1960s, a government committee formed to study the problems of the Belgian metallurgical industries decided that further concentration was necessary in this region in order to maintain the competitiveness of the industry nationally, reduce overproduction, improve efficiency, and target investment and subsidies. Problems were also due to the rise in the price of oil at this time, as the industry had become increasingly reliant on this form of energy following the decline in coal production. The two companies therefore decided to effect a complete merger, following a one-year period of joint management beginning in July 1979. This led to the formation in June 1970 of Cockerill-Ougrée-Providence et Esperance-Longdoz. It was logical at that time for the new group to dispose of the Providence works—which were in Charleroi, not Liège—to the TMM company at Charleroi. For the next ten years, the company was known simply as Cockerill, appearing to renew the link with the years 1817 to 1955.

The early 1970s saw increasing steel production in Belgium, peaking in 1974, when there were nine major steelworks in operation. This resulted in overproduction, as the market was becoming saturated, and meant that drastic measures had to be taken. By 1979 both production and the number of plants had been halved, with reductions in the workforce continuing up until 1985, by which time employment in the industry had fallen to half its 1975 level. The Charleroi region, which had not benefited from the concentration effected in Liège ten years earlier, was now obliged to undergo its own rationalization, with the absorption of Thy-Marcinelle et Providence—formerly TMM—by Hainaut-Sambre in 1980. However, this step was not enough to stabilize the industry, and the government, which had already taken a 50 percent stake in the industry in 1978, now decided that complete integration of the metallurgical industries of the two regions under one management was necessary. There were also the wider problems of Belgian industry connected with the difficulties between the French-speaking Wallonia region, which includes Charleroi and Liège, and the Flemish-speaking northern regions. The two complexes were united with 80 percent state ownership (by the government of Wallonia), on June 26, 1981.

Gandois Plan, 1980s

The union took place in the depths of an economic recession, and the newly organized group of Cockerill Sambre began by posting massive losses. The European Economic Community was insisting that large government subsidies to the industry were unfair and had to be reduced substantially. A new center-right government introduced economic austerity measures and commissioned a report on the steel industry. This proposed further reductions in capacity, including plant closures at Cockerill Sambre—one at Charleroi and one at Liège—and more job losses. Each region was to be allotted a specialty. The restructuring plan, known as the "Gandois report," after the present chairman of Cockerill Sambre, was implemented in 1984. Production of steel was stabilized at around 1975 levels, concentrated on only three plants, and the workforce was reduced to 15,000, with the hope of even more reductions. It was also agreed that Arbed S.A., the Luxembourg state steel producer, would reduce its rolled steel capacity in exchange for the securing of orders from Cockerill.

The number of blast furnaces operating in Wallonia declined from their peak of 30 during the postwar period up to 1963: only a third of these were in use by the late 1970s, and by 1988 only four remained at Cockerill Sambre.

Within a few years of the implementation of the Gandois plan, the success of the measures had become evident, with the company being given a new lease of life, and diversification into other steel-based products taking place. The mid-1980s were a relatively stable period, culminating in further internal rationalizations, such as the decision to specialize in thin flat products on the steel production side; the development of new products such as coated steel roof tiles by the French-based construction products division; and concentration on heavy engineering in the mechanical engineering division. In 1990 came the acquisition of a majority holding in Ymos A.G., a major German manufacturer of metal and plastic parts for automobiles. Other diversification moves included ventures into financial and data processing services as well as environmental management services.

1990s Struggles Led to Sale of Majority Stake to Usinor

In the early 1990s, the entire European steel industry, largely state-owned at the time, was in crisis. International competition, most notably from Japanese and Korean steelmakers, kept prices chronically depressed. Only a US$8.5 billion 1993 bailout from the European Union saved the industry. Privatization, restructuring, and consolidation were the watchwords of the decade, and mergers created three dominating European steel giants: Arbed of Luxembourg, Usinor of France, and Thyssen-Krupp Stahl AG of Germany.

Cockerill Sambre posted losses of BFr 1.39 billion in 1992 and BFr 6.5 billion in 1993 before recovering somewhat in 1994, when it recorded net income of BFr 807 million. In early 1995 Cockerill paid DM 150 million (US$100 million) for a 60 percent stake in GmbH EKO Stahl, which had run the largest steel plant in East Germany prior to German reunification.

In September 1996 the still struggling Cockerill said that it would seek an alliance with another European steelmaker. The company also announced the launch of the "Horizon 2000" plan, a restructuring aimed at significantly reducing costs at one of Europe's most inefficient steelmakers by the turn of the century. To implement the plan, the company expected to cut more than 2,200 jobs from its 10,000-person workforce in Belgium. In late 1996 merger discussions with privately owned Belgian steelmaker Usines Gustave Boël led nowhere. For fiscal 1996, Cockerill posted a net loss of BFr 8.97 billion, including exceptional costs of BFr 7.7 billion related to "Horizon 2000."

In 1997, while still seeking out potential partners, Cockerill Sambre reached the decision to focus its operations on three core areas: integrated steelmaking, steel distribution, and the manufacture of steel-based construction products. The company subsequently exited from the manufacture of automotive components with the 1997 disposal of Ymos. By the beginning of 1998 Cockerill had largely divested its environmental management services sector.

In early 1998 the company and the government of Wallonia, which owned almost 79 percent of Cockerill Sambre at the time, began studying possible alliances. Two main partners soon emerged: Usinor and Thyssen-Krupp Stahl. The latter, however, dropped out of the bidding soon after it was named one of the two finalists. In mid-October 1998 Usinor agreed to acquire a 75 percent stake in Cockerill for about BFr 36 billion (US$1.1 billion), a move that would make the French company one of the three largest steelmakers in the world (along with Nippon Steel Co. of Japan and South Korea's Pohang Iron & Steel Co.). Under the agreement, Usinor would acquire 54 percent of Cockerill from the Wallonian government as well as the 21 percent held publicly. The government would retain a 25 percent ''blocking'' minority, with veto power over major strategic decisions concerning the Cockerill workforce for five years. Another condition of the agreement was that Cockerill would have to acquire the 40 percent of EKO Stahl it did not already own. Usinor agreed to invest BFr 30 billion (US$890 million) in Cockerill over a five-year period. Francis Mer, president of Usinor, was slated to serve as president of Cockerill Sambre following the deal's completion.

Principal Subsidiaries

Integrated Steel: S.A. Beautor (France; 99.24%); S.A. Société Carolorégienne de Cokéfaction (CARCOKE) (78.1%); S.A. Société Carolorégienne de Laminage (CARLAM) (75.31%); S.A. Cockerill Sambre Tailored Blanks; S.A. Tôleries Delloye-Matthieu (TDM) (99.6%); GmbH EKO Stahl (Germany; 60%); S.C.R.L. Eurogal; GmbH Steelinter Deutschland (Germany); S.R.L. Steelinter Italia (Italy; 94.19%); Steelinter (UK) Ltd; SàRL Galvalange (Luxembourg; 50%); S.C. Segal (33.33%). Distribution: S.A. Disteel; S.A. Distell Cold; GmbH EKO Feinblechhandel (Germany); GmbH EKO Handelsunion (Germany); A.B. Eurinter Svenska (Sweden); S.A. Laminoirs de Longtain (99.99%); S.A. Mosacier; S.A. Société Belge d'Oxycougape (OXYBEL) (74.93%); S.A. Profilsteel; mbH SRW-SPS Verwaltungsgesellschaft (Germany); GmbH SPS Südband Stahl-Service-Center (Germany); Groupe PUM dont Groupe Jean D'Huart (France); Groupe Dikema & Chabot (Netherlands); Fratelli Canessa (Italy; 51%); Groupe Dikema Stäl (Norway); ASK McGowan (U.K.; 65.5%). Construction: GmbH EKO Bauteile (Germany); GmbH Polydach Dachsysteme (Germany); Groupe Haironville (France); S.A. Metal Profil Belgium; S.A. Monopanel (France); S.A. Panneaux Frigorifiques Français (France); GmbH Haironville Deutsch-

land (Germany); GmbH Haironville Profilvertrieb (Germany); GmbH Haironville Austria; A.S. Haironville Danmark (Denmark); A.S. Haironville Norge (Norway); A.B. Haironville Sverige (Sweden); Tac Metal Forming Ltd (U.K.); S.A. Europerfil (Spain; 50%); S.A. Haironville Portugal (70%); s.r.o. Haironville Bohemia (Czech Republic; 98%); Haironville Polska (Poland). Mechanical Engineering: S.A. Cockerill Mechanical Industries (CMI); S.A. Cockerill Forges and Ringmill (CFR); S.A. Espace Mobile International (EMI); S.A. Heurbel. Services: S.A. Société d'Opérations Maritimes et Fluviales (SOMEF); S.A. Société de Service et d'Ingénierie en Informatique, Bureautique et Télématique (IBT); S.C. Recherche et Développement du Groupe Cockerill Sambre (RD-CS) (99%); S.A. Cockerill Sambre Finances et Services (CSFS).

Principal Divisions

Integrated Steel Division; Distribution Division; Construction Division; Mechanical Engineering Division; Services Division.

Further Reading

Buckley, Neil, ''Cockerill Sambre in the Red,'' *Financial Times,* March 27, 1997, p. 34.
——, ''Marriage Crosses Borders,'' *Financial Times,* November 3, 1998, p. FTS5.
du Bois, Martin, ''Usinor SA to Acquire a 75% Stake in Cockerill,'' *Wall Street Journal,* October 15, 1998, p. A17.
Pasleau, Suzy, *John Cockerill: Itineraire d'un geant industriel,* Alleur-Liège, Belgium: Editions du Perron, 1992, p. 207.
Smith, Michael, ''Usinor to Acquire Majority Stake in Cockerill,'' *Financial Times,* October 15, 1998, p. 30.
Tett, Gillian, ''Decline Steepens at Cockerill Sambre,'' *Financial Times,* April 15, 1994, p. 27.
Willem, Leon, *450 Ans D'Espérance: La S.A. Métallurgique D'Esperance-Longdoz de 1519 a 1969,* Alleur-Liège, Belgium: Editions du Perron, 1990.
Zwick, Steve, ''Steelmakers Swarm to Cockerill,'' *American Metal Market,* June 11, 1998, p. 1.

—Peter W. Miller
—updated by David E. Salamie

Commercial Financial Services, Inc.

2448 East 81st Street, 55th Floor
Tulsa, Oklahoma 74137-4248
U.S.A.
(918) 488-9119
Fax: (918) 488-1809
Web site: http://www.cfs-inc.com

Private Company
Incorporated: 1986
Employees: 3,000
Sales: $954.75 million (1997)
SICs: 7322 Adjustment & Collection Services

Commercial Financial Services, Inc. (CFS) is the leading collector of nonperforming loans in the United States. At the beginning of 1998 its loan portfolio totalled $9 billion, and the company was working with its customers to collect on some four million debts. Since its founding in 1986 CFS grew by acquiring portfolios of bad debts from failed financial institutions through the Federal Deposit Insurance Corporation and the Resolution Trust Corporation. The company also acquired nonperforming loans from healthy banks and either attempted to collect them or to restructure them and sell them back to the banks. It developed a unique marketable security based on pools of loans to finance much of its growth. In a September 1997 profile, *Inc.* magazine estimated CFS founder William R. Bartmann's net worth to be in the range of $2.4 to $3.5 billion.

Founded in 1986 to Purchase Bad Debts

Commercial Financial Services, Inc. (CFS) was founded in Muskogee, Oklahoma, in 1986 by William R. Bartmann, his wife Kathryn, and business partner Jay L. Jones. At the time, Bartmann was $1 million in debt following the failure of his Muskogee oil pipe manufacturing business, Hawkeye Pipe. Jones had been Hawkeye's chief operating officer.

CFS was established to purchase bad debts and similar nonproductive assets from banks and other financial institutions. It was literally a new industry that was made possible by the high rate of bank failures. At first, most of the firm's acquisitions came through the Federal Deposit Insurance Corporation (FDIC) from defunct or foundering banks. According to founder Bartmann, "In 1986, the FDIC was inundated with closings and just did not have the ability to service the sheer volume of it all." Bartmann noted that most of the businesses coming in to purchase nonproductive assets were out-of-state concerns that simply turned around and resold them for a higher price, rather than try to collect or service the outstanding debt. Bartmann's plan was to service the debt and work out a payment plan with the debtors.

In addition to bank closings, the economic downturn of the mid-1980s had created a pool of unemployed but highly qualified workers. Bartmann and partner Jay L. Jones decided they would take care of the FDIC's overflow, compete with outsiders, and hire displaced personnel. CFS became a full-service debt management company with a staff of appraisers, certified public accountants (CPAs), attorneys, account managers, and energy and real estate professionals.

The company acquired the first package offered by the Tulsa office of the FDIC in 1986 by submitting the winning bid for a portfolio of charged-off loans. To fulfill the contract, CFS had to obtain a hard-to-get $13,000 loan from American Bank of Muskogee, the same bank that held Bartmann's $1 million debt. After successfully collecting $64,000 on the first package of loans, CFS was able to borrow more money to acquire more bad debts. CFS began by acquiring loans that were charged off by banks. Later, it moved into acquiring distressed loans which had not yet been charged off by a financial institution. While distressed loans cost more than charged-off loans, CFS found that it got a better return servicing them. CFS acquired loans in packages, or portfolios, from the FDIC. One large portfolio it acquired had 480 loans.

By 1989 CFS had 71 employees in its Muskogee headquarters and branch office in Houston, Texas. The company would acquire a variety of loans, classified assets, charge-offs, and other assets and service them itself. It would work with each debtholder to restructure the loans by lowering the interest rate, monthly payment, or principal balance as needed. Describing

---

Company Perspectives:

We are innovators, enthusiasts—and our business is simple. We buy non-performing loans, those which banks have given up on. Then we turn these "bad" loans into cash by helping those who owe us money develop a workable payment plan. With CFS, everyone truly wins. Financial institutions turn charge-offs into cash for immediate reinvestment. Our investors see a safe and attractive return. Good people pay off debt and restore their credit. And we earn a profit in the process.

CFS's customers, Bartmann said, "Their lifestyles were induced by an artificially inflated economy, and when the economy started shrinking they got caught in the middle."

Unlike banks and savings and loan institutions, CFS was operating in an unregulated business environment. CFS could service the loans it purchased in any way that the company chose and could carry debts that a regulated financial institution would not be allowed to carry. It was this flexibility that was one of CFS's key strengths. In its first three years CFS acquired more than $100 million in loans. By 1989 CFS was servicing 6,700 loans with a face value of about $75 million. About 90 percent of CFS's purchases were through the FDIC in Oklahoma and Texas. The rest were direct acquisitions from banks. With the rate of bank failures declining in 1989 and 1990, CFS became more aggressive in soliciting nonperforming or underperforming assets directly from banks instead of going through the FDIC. Another source of income for CFS came from the sale of restructured loans back to banks. Once the loans were restructured they often carried a higher yield, making them attractive to banks once again.

Another area that CFS expanded into was total asset purchase and assumption agreements (TAPAs) with banks. Under regulations in effect at the time, a rescuing bank would have to take all of the assets of a failing bank instead of simply plucking the best assets. To reduce the risk for the rescuing bank, CFS would work with it as a joint venture partner and take the less desirable assets, leaving the more desirable assets for the rescuing bank. As a result, the FDIC would be more likely to get a higher bid to handle the failed bank.

Several subsidiaries were established to handle other functions. These included Commercial Financial Collections, Inc., a collection agency for retail merchants; Commercial Financial Information, Inc., a full-service credit bureau; Asset Marketing Inc., which packaged and marketed loan portfolios to financial institutions nationwide; and Commercial Computer Corporation, which designed and sold software and hardware.

Additional opportunities were provided by the shakeout in the savings and loan (S&L) industry in the late 1980s and early 1990s. A new government agency, the Resolution Trust Corporation (RTC), was established in 1989 to dispose of the assets of insolvent savings and loan institutions and CFS was placed on the RTC's bidder list. In 1990 CFS signed its first contract with the RTC, originating out of the RTC office in Eagan, Minnesota.

Downsizing and New Headquarters in the Early 1990s

At the end of 1989 CFS reduced its staff of 70 employees and auctioned off nearly all of the 10,000 loans it had acquired, keeping only some 280 loans. The company, reduced to only 17 employees, moved its headquarters from Muskogee to Tulsa in September 1991. It also obtained a $1 million line of credit from a local bank. At the time of the move, CFS owned 616 loans with a book value of $4.5 million, an estimated collection value of $1.6 million, and a market value of $480,000. Revenues for 1991 were $1.4 million.

In 1992, CFS made a groundbreaking arrangement with the RTC's San Antonio, Texas office to help the government agency liquidate millions of dollars in uncollected judgments and loan charge-offs from nine S&Ls in Texas. Under the agreement, CFS would package the RTC's uncollected accounts and sell them to asset management companies. CFS would receive 27 percent of the total sale price of the assets. The contract between the RTC and CFS, known as the Miscellaneous Asset Servicing and Disposition Agreement (MASDA), was the first such arrangement in the country and would serve as a template for similar contracts in the future.

An RTC spokesperson noted that these particular types of assets—uncollected judgments and loan charge-offs—were "the very dregs of this whole liquidation activity." Typically, these assets had already been worked on by a variety of groups before they were sold. The uncollected judgments often involved loans for which the collateral had already been sold to satisfy the loan, or for which the existing collateral was less than the loan value. Consequently, CFS was assuming considerable risk in acquiring these types of loans.

The RTC contract covered 2,481 assets from nine S&Ls in Texas and had a book value of $197 million. CFS's role was to evaluate the assets, sell them at an RTC-approved price, and attempt to collect payments up to the time of the sale. CFS also processed any payments that were made and did all the reporting and bookkeeping on the assets until they were sold. A similar contract, developed by the RTC's Tulsa office, had approximately $150 million worth of charge-offs and judgments that the agency had inherited by taking over 30 failed S&Ls in Oklahoma and Arkansas.

A National Leader in the Acquisition of Nonperforming Loans in the Mid-1990s

CFS's growth was tied to available financing, and as new methods of financing became available in the 1990s the company began to grow to its full potential. CFS had started with a $13,000 loan in 1986, then obtained a $1 million line of credit in 1991. In 1993 the company repaid a $20 million loan at 32 percent interest within 11 months, convincing its lender to advance CFS $40 million at 18 percent. By 1994 CFS was working with an $80 million revolving line of credit from investment bank J.P. Morgan and Company Inc. For the year, CFS planned to turn over its line of credit about 2.5 times, spending $200 million buying and selling nonperforming loans.

By 1994 CFS had grown to 182 employees and expected to hire another 125 by the end of the year. Approximately 100 employees worked in Tulsa, with the rest working at offices located in Oklahoma City, Dallas, and Phoenix. Many of the company's employees were high-ranking officials from the finance industry who had been laid off by banks and S&Ls because of failures or mergers. Others were former employees of the FDIC, helping the company better understand how the FDIC worked.

The company's loan portfolio had grown to 15,533 loans with a book value of $217 million, an estimated collection value of $30 million, and a market value of $3.3 million. Some analysts considered CFS to be among the top three firms in its industry, and others ranked it number one. The company appeared on *Inc.* magazine's list of the fastest-growing private companies in the United States. As the banking industry became generally healthier in the mid-1990s, CFS began working with financially sound banks to purchase their bad loans and help them sell their nonperforming assets instead of acquiring most of its loans from failed institutions.

Securitizations As a New Source of Working Capital, 1995

A new source of working capital for CFS came from securitizing its loans. After contacting several banks, CFS convinced BancOne Capital Corporation, a subsidiary of Bank One N.A. in Columbus, Ohio, to take loans that CFS owned and combine them into a pool called a securitization. BancOne would then sell the pool of loans in the form of securities to public or institutional investors, with CFS using the proceeds as working capital. According to Bartmann and *Tulsa World,* a deal involving this type of innovative security had never been done before.

On May 31, 1995, CFS completed its first securitization with BancOne, pooling some 14,000 nonperforming and restructured consumer loans and selling them in two groups for a combined total of $80 million. The loans were purchased by insurance companies SunAmerica Corporate Finance and Teachers Insurance and Annuity Association (TIAA). In spite of the fact that the loans were nonperforming, Standard & Poor's Corporation gave the marketable securities an "A" rating and created a new category for the unique securities called "loan collector." The security was like a bond, and SunAmerica and TIAA would receive back their principal plus interest. Meanwhile, CFS would try to collect on the debts.

Upon selling the securitizations, CFS realized an immediate profit of $25 million, since it had originally purchased the loans for $55 million. If CFS successfully collected all of the loans, it would receive an estimated $130 million, of which approximately $117 million would have to be paid back as principal and interest to SunAmerican and TIAA. That gave CFS the potential for another $13 million profit. CFS also received a monthly $500,000 servicing fee that was taken off the top of the collections before any principal or interest had to be paid. Collections went so well that CFS collected five months' worth of debts in two months.

For 1996, CFS planned to make similar offerings every six months, then accelerate them to every four months in 1997. For every $100 million securitization, some 15,000 to 20,000 loans

would have to be pooled. Bartmann expected no problems finding loans to be pooled, noting that collecting on bad loans was a $100 billion industry. He estimated that after seven such deals, CFS could be self-financing and would no longer have to rely on its line of credit with J.P. Morgan.

Expansion in the Mid-1990s

By April 1996 CFS had 400 employees in Tulsa and Oklahoma City. The company planned to double that number by the end of the year and to hire an additional 700 employees in 1997. The average compensation package per employee was $40,000. Most of the new workers would be account executives with financial and collection experience. This huge staffing increase was necessary to handle the company's growing loan portfolio, which by this time had exceeded $380 million. CFS also received $33 million from the state of Oklahoma under the state's Quality Jobs Act, which provided funds to growing companies out of new state revenues generated by increased employment.

With this new prosperity CFS was able to increase its community involvement. The company announced in April 1996 that it would donate $1 million for college scholarships and economic development, with $250,000 going toward programs of state and local chambers of commerce and $750,000 for 30 scholarships of $5,000 each over the next five years. The scholarships would be given to financially needy students who planned to attend universities in Oklahoma. Students who received scholarships would also be given employment opportunities during the summer while they were in college and full-time jobs once they graduated.

After successfully selling four securitizations for a total of $291.3 million, CFS committed to additional office space in CityPlex Towers in June 1996. The company signed a lease for an additional 18 floors in the Tulsa, Oklahoma building in which it already occupied 10 floors. With CFS planning to add 2,300 new jobs by the end of 1997, new employees were being hired at the rate of 45 to 50 per week. Approximately 1,200 new jobs were created between April 1996 and April 1997.

During the year CFS received several awards and recognitions, including the Franklin E. Bernsen Oklahoma Venture of the Year Award and recognition as a Blue Chip Enterprise by the six-year-old Blue Chip Enterprise Initiative program, a national program that acknowledged businesses for their creative use of resources. In addition, CFS was ranked 31st on *Inc.* magazine's list of the fastest-growing privately held companies. The ranking was based on performance from 1991 to 1995, during which time CFS sales grew from $1.4 million to more than $65.9 million, an increase of 4,445 percent. In 1996 CFS also began exploring opportunities in Europe and entered into discussions with an unnamed European bank to open offices in each of the 12 European Community (EC) nations.

During 1997 the company practically doubled its loan portfolio, from $4.7 billion in January to around $9 billion in November, and employed more than 3,000 people. Fueling CFS's rapid growth was the size of the debt collection market. By late 1997 delinquent credit card debt in the United States amounted to nearly $5 billion, and outstanding U.S. consumer debt had reached about $1.1 trillion and was expected to grow at an 11 percent rate annually. CFS also faced little competition, because banks were selling more delinquent loans than ever before, finding that it was cheaper to unload these loans than to try to collect them.

Bartmann was often quoted as saying that a lot of employers liked to say that their employees were their most important asset, but that CFS was putting its money where its mouth was. A range of employee benefits helped the company keep turnover lower than industry averages. Perhaps one of the most outstanding benefits was a March 1997 Caribbean cruise for all of CFS's employees and guests, some 2,275 people in all, which the company paid for. Previous company trips included an excursion to Las Vegas and a train ride to a Kansas City Royals baseball game. In 1998 the company reserved 4,000 rooms at Disney World in Orlando, Florida. Other benefits included onsite child care and full health insurance benefits, which helped CFS make *Working Mother* magazine's list of the best companies to work for in 1998. In 1996 CFS offered a 200 percent match on contributions to the company's 401(k) plan, and an annual profit-sharing bonus in 1996 resulted in an average check worth three weeks' salary.

In mid-1997 collection work involved 1,200 front-line account officers calling to collect debts for eight hours a day. While daily quotas had to be met, the company had a maximum 50-hour work week rule that it enforced to keep workers from working too many hours. The company was receiving 500 to 600 job applicants weekly, of which only 50 to 60 were hired. Following a rigorous screening, new hires had to complete a seven-week training course called CFS University, with about 15 percent dropping out. Employees could be terminated for not meeting their collection quotas as well as for any infractions of the Fair Debt Collections Practices Act. Bartmann was proud of the fact that no CFS employee had ever been cited for any violation of that law.

International Expansion, 1997–98

In November 1997 CFS hired Richard Langstaff to head CFS International Ltd., with headquarters in London, England. Langstaff came to CFS from Beutsche Morgan Grenfell of London, where he was director and global department head responsible for asset securitization. Plans called for the European operation to employ between 500 and 1,000 people within 18 months, with half expected to come from existing staffs in Tulsa and Oklahoma City. The rest would be hired in Europe, but would receive their training in Tulsa. CFS said it would invest between $5 million and $10 million in its European operations. Bartmann's logic was that as a market leader, CFS would eventually consume all the market share available in the United States. "In anticipation of reaching that cap level, we are now expanding into Europe to handle our future growth," he told *Tulsa World.*

In June 1997 CFS had announced plans to enter the lending business, and by May 1998 Bartmann announced that CFS was in the process of buying a savings and loan charter to enable it to extend credit in the form of credit cards or loans to debtors who had established a history of payment with the company. CFS had relationships with 3.6 million delinquent debt holders, and Bartmann planned to create a new company that would lend exclusively to these consumers. With the help of 20 large banks, CFS planned to offer lines of credit to its customers. CFS would operate the lending enterprise and start it with about $400 million in capitalization.

Bartmann viewed the lending operation as a natural extension of CFS's collection business. He told *Tulsa World,* "We were the first company to treat customers with respect and dignity." The lending company would help people with damaged credit restore their credit ratings. All they had to do was commit to making three consecutive payments to receive a credit card. Then, gradually, the rewards would be increased as the person began to make more consecutive payments. With 12 consecutive payments, CFS would help the customer obtain a new house.

As part of its strategy to start issuing credit cards, CFS led a campaign to loosen Oklahoma's state regulations on credit card fees. The company wanted more industry-friendly regulations so that it could begin issuing national credit cards from Oklahoma. However, CFS faced opposition from the state's largest association of bankers.

With a 12,277 percent increase in sales from 1993 to 1997, CFS was named Oklahoma's fastest-growing company in May 1998; it was also ranked number eight on *Inc.*'s 1997 list of fastest-growing private companies. CFS reported $954.75 million in revenue for 1997 and had about 3,000 employees. Net income was $182 million on collections of $954 million, a dramatic increase from 1996 net income of $79 million on collections of $274 million. During 1997 CFS had acquired bad debt with a $6 billion face value, typically paying from five cents to ten cents on the dollar. According to Bartmann, CFS usually collected from 28 cents to 32 cents on the dollar, compared to the collection industry average of 18 cents to 20 cents on the dollar.

Through May 1997, CFS had successfully floated 13 securitizations with about 60 institutional investors, making it unlikely that the company would ever need to go public to raise equity financing. As 1998 drew to a close, it appeared likely that CFS would enjoy another record year as it continued to expand its debt collection operations.

Principal Subsidiaries

Commercial Financial Collections, Inc.; Commercial Financial Information, Inc.; Asset Marketing Inc.; Commercial Computer Corporation.

Further Reading

Boyd, Danny M., "Debt Collection Company to Launch Lending Subsidiary," *Daily Oklahoman,* May 17, 1998, p. 1.
——, "Owner Proves Nice Companies Can Finish First," *Daily Oklahoman,* May 17, 1998, p. 2.
Busch, Melanie, "Tulsa Firm Plans 400 '96 Hires, 700 in '97," *Tulsa World,* April 10, 1996, p. E1.
Curtis, Bruce, "Problem Loans No Problem for Tulsa Company," *Tulsa World,* May 29, 1994, p. 1.
——, "Tulsa Company Finds Success Servicing Loans," *Tulsa Business Chronicle,* December 16, 1991, p. 1.
Erwin, Jane, "Opportunistic Financial Firm Prospers in Muskogee," *Tulsa World,* October 8, 1989, p. 1.

Hogan, Gypsy, "State's Top 50 Comes up Short," *Daily Oklahoman,* May 14, 1998, p. 15.

Kubina, Blythe, "CFS to Become Lender," *Tulsa World,* June 21, 1997, p. E1.

Robertson, Joe, "Bankers Wary of Credit Law Changes," *Tulsa World,* May 22, 1998, p. A1.

Robinson, Robin, "Tulsa Firm Packaging RTC 'Dregs,' " *Tulsa World,* March 29, 1992, p. 1.

Rutherford, Dan, "Celeb Status: Magazine Profiles CFS Billionaire Bartmann," *Tulsa World,* August 30, 1997, p. E1.

——, "CFS Gets $138 Million for Job Creation," *Tulsa World,* November 8, 1997, p. E1.

——, "CFS Hires Exec for Push into Europe," *Tulsa World,* November 15, 1997, p. E1.

——, "Commercial Financial Receives Round of Praise," *Tulsa World,* April 12, 1996, p. E1.

——, "Continued Growth Propels Commercial Financial Services into the Big Time," *Tulsa World,* November 23, 1997, p. E1.

——, "CityPlex Leases 18 Floors to CFS," *Tulsa World,* June 11, 1996, p. E1.

——, "Dream Employer Has Staffers Cruising," *Tulsa World,* March 15, 1997, p. E1.

——, "European Bank, CFS in Talks," *Tulsa World,* July 26, 1996, p. E1.

——, "The Good, the Bad, the Payoff; CFS Lures Workers Despite High Stress," *Tulsa World,* November 23, 1997, p. E1.

——, "Inc. 500 Includes Three Tulsa Companies," *Tulsa World,* October 18, 1996, p. E1.

——, "Ingenuity Brings Profits to Financial Services Firm," *Tulsa World,* July 18, 1995, p. 1.

——, "Let's Make a Deal," *Tulsa World,* June 22, 1997, p. E1.

——, "Quality Jobs Act Fuels CFS Tulsa Expansion," *Tulsa World,* April 11, 1996, p. E1.

Schafer, Shaun, "CFS Due National Award for Innovative Solution," *Tulsa World,* June 25, 1996, p. E2.

" 'Tis Season to Be Jolly, CFS Bonuses $5.2 Million," *Tulsa World,* December 10, 1997, p. E1.

Useen, Jerry, "The Richest Man You've Never Heard Of," *Inc.,* September 1997.

—David Bianco

Compaq Computer Corporation

20555 State Highway 249
Houston, Texas 77070
U.S.A.
(281) 370-0670
(800) 231-0900
Fax: (281) 374-1740
Web site: http://www.compaq.com

Public Company
Incorporated: 1982
Employees: 32,565
Sales: $24.58 billion (1997)
Stock Exchanges: New York
Ticker Symbol: CPQ
SICs: 3571 Electronic Computers; 3577 Computer
Peripheral Equipment, Not Elsewhere Classified; 7372
Prepackaged Software; 7373 Computer Integrated
Systems Design

Compaq Computer Corporation is the world's largest supplier of personal computers and, as a result of its acquisition of Digital Equipment Corporation in June 1998, is the second largest computer firm in the world (trailing only IBM). In addition to designing, developing, manufacturing, and marketing portables, laptops, desktops, workstations, and servers for businesses and consumers, the company also develops and markets computer hardware, software, solutions, and services. Compaq products are marketed in more than 100 countries worldwide.

Beginnings: Making IBM Clones

When International Business Machines Corporation (IBM) introduced its first personal computer (PC) in 1982, Compaq was among dozens of other companies entering the market with IBM clones—computers that look and perform like IBM PCs, and are often less expensive. Compaq set itself apart from other clone manufacturers by becoming an innovator itself, producing IBM-compatible PCs that were faster, superior in quality, and offered additional user features. Compaq's management team also set the company apart from others in the PC industry. Made up of seasoned professionals from Texas Instruments (TI) and IBM, the team's prior experience in the volatile computer industry gave Compaq the tools necessary to survive a period of phenomenal growth in 1983. Compaq's staff also had the technical and business grounding to establish new industry standards on its own—without following IBM.

Compaq's beginning was in the summer of 1981, when Joseph R. "Rod" Canion, James M. Harris, and William H. Murto, three senior managers from TI, decided to start their own company. They had not yet determined what their company would produce and market; managing a Mexican restaurant or manufacturing storage devices for minicomputers or beeping devices for finding misplaced items were among their original ideas. The entrepreneurs eventually decided to build a portable PC that met industry standards set by IBM. With only $1,000 each to invest in their company, Canion, Harris, and Murto approached Ben Rosen, president of Sevin-Rosen Partners, a high-technology venture capital firm in Houston. Rosen, who became Compaq's chairman, offered an initial investment of $2.5 million.

Compaq was established just after an era in which PC entrepreneurs had proliferated. The technological breakthrough of the microprocessor—an extraordinarily powerful semiconductor chip—enabled smaller computers to be built that were also faster, less expensive, and easier to use. Because this much less expensive microprocessor served to miniaturize computers, the demand for PCs increased, and development costs decreased significantly. As a result, many new PC companies were established. While these early companies were successful in technological leadership and often had a flair for marketing, deficiencies in inventory management and quality control eventually led many of them to fail. When Compaq arrived on the scene, venture capitalists were beginning to force many entrepreneurs to turn over control of their companies to more experienced management professionals. As Rosen—who had lost a $400,000 investment in another PC start-up—explained in *Management Today* in 1985, "In the early days, it was an area for flamboyant people ... who transformed their personalities into companies. Now the business requires a very different kind of manager. It has become a very unforgiving industry."

Company Perspectives:

Compaq has become one of the world's most successful companies and today leads the computer industry in market share performance and balance sheet strength. We've achieved this by consistently executing our strategic plans, delivering on our promises and striving to provide customers with the highest levels of innovation and flexibility at the lowest total cost of ownership. By continuing to do so, we believe that we will strengthen our capability to lead the future of computing.

Unlike most new PC companies, Compaq's management had the benefit of the experience of longtime professionals. Prior to joining Compaq, each of its original 20 employees had worked in the computer industry for 15 to 20 years. Their experience in management and engineering at such companies as TI and IBM—two pioneers in the industry—provided Compaq with a solid foundation. Compaq's management style was of the kind that was scorned by early iconoclastic PC entrepreneurs. Compaq made decisions by a consensus approach, which allowed every division of the company a say in product development. Compaq also instituted some traditional corporate mechanisms, such as tight fiscal controls and a forecasting system.

In 1983 Compaq's consensus management proved valuable. Canion, Compaq's chief executive officer, strongly supported the idea of producing a briefcase-size, or laptop, computer. The marketing research director, however, concluded that the market for such a computer did not exist. Canion relented, and Compaq waited while other companies, including Gavilan Computer Corporation and Data General Corporation, attempted to market such a product and failed. Meanwhile, Compaq shipped its first two products, the Compaq Portable and the Compaq Plus. These computers set the standard for portable—though larger than a briefcase—full-function PCs. In 1983 Compaq shipped more than 53,000 portable PCs throughout the United States and Canada. That year, the Compaq workforce grew from 100 to 600, and production increased from 200 machines in January to 9,000 in December. The company recorded $111.2 million in revenues, the most successful first year of sales for a U.S. company.

A key factor in Compaq's growth was a strong cooperative relationship with its dealers. With nearly 90 PCs on the market aimed at business professionals, shelf space was very competitive. Compaq did not have a direct sales force of its own, and thus did not compete with its authorized dealers. This arrangement gave dealers more incentive to carry Compaq computers. Compaq also motivated its authorized dealers through what was called ''Salespaq,'' whereby Compaq paid a percentage of the dealer's cost of advertising, sales training, or incentives.

Compaq's ability to develop, produce, and market new products in a very short time period was another key ingredient in its success. Once a product was approved, Compaq undertook all aspects of its development simultaneously: factories were built, marketing and distribution arrangements were made, and engineers refined the product design. The product cycle in the PC industry was typically 12 to 18 months; Compaq delivered in six to nine months. This fast turnaround in product development enabled Compaq to introduce the latest technology before its competitors. In 1984, for example, IBM announced a new version of its PC that experts felt would set back other PC manufacturers. Compaq pulled its resources from every branch of the company, and within six months introduced and shipped its DESKPRO line of desktop PCs. Fifteen months later IBM shipped its portable PC, which was two pounds heavier and offered fewer features than Compaq's portable model. From the first quarter of 1983 to the last quarter of 1984, Compaq's production increased from 2,200 computers to 48,000. Despite the 1984 industry shakeout, Compaq reported an increase in sales to over $500 million. In March 1985 Rosen's original investment of $2.5 million increased in value to $30 million.

The Late 1980s: New Products and Markets

Expediency in product development also led to a turning point in Compaq's history. In 1985 Intel, a leading manufacturer of microprocessors, wanted to market its powerful new microprocessor, the 80386, as soon as possible. Intel felt confident that a Compaq product based on the new microprocessor would see a quick entry into the market. Compaq and Intel worked together to correct defects in the 80386 microprocessor, and Intel redesigned many features of the chip to meet Compaq's standards. Their collaboration resulted in Compaq's 1987 introduction of the DESKPRO 386. Based on Intel's new chip, this new PC performed over three times faster than IBM's fastest PC, and nearly twice as fast as Compaq's closest competitor. It took IBM nine months to introduce a comparable machine using Intel's 80386. By then Compaq was developing a portable version of its new PC.

In 1986 Compaq became the first company to achieve *Fortune* 500 status in fewer than four years. From 1986 through 1989, Compaq's revenues increased fivefold to $3 billion, while other PC manufacturers—including Apple Computer and Sun Microsystems, the two top contenders—had setbacks. Much of this growth was due to Compaq's successful marketing efforts in Europe. Led by Eckhard Pfeiffer, former head of TI's European consumer electronics operation, Compaq began its European campaign in 1984, before most other U.S. vendors. In 1989 Compaq became the number two supplier of business PCs to the European market, achieving $1.3 billion in international sales. With the PC market in Europe growing about 33 percent faster than the U.S. market, Compaq had an edge on other PC manufacturers.

In November 1989 Compaq introduced the Compaq SYSTEMPRO personal computer and the Compaq DESKPRO 486. These PCs utilized a technology known as Extended Industry Standard Architecture (EISA), a hardware design that Compaq developed to challenge IBM's Microchannel hardware design for its PS/2 PCs. These technologies increased the speed of PCs, enabling them to perform such complex operations as networking and multitasking. An added advantage of EISA was its ability to attract customers accustomed to using more powerful minicomputers and mainframe computers. By incorporating EISA into its new products, Compaq began to set industry standards. While IBM was producing computers based on the Microchannel technology, many other manufacturers were using EISA technology. Initial sales of the SYSTEMPRO were slow but, as CEO Canion told a *Business Week* correspondent,

"We realized we were opening up a whole new market . . . . We knew it would take some time."

Company sales for 1990 reached $3.6 billion, with net income of $455 million, record figures for the eighth consecutive year. During that year, Compaq lengthened the list of countries in which it operated, opening new subsidiaries in Austria, Finland, and Hong Kong, and authorizing dealers in the former East Germany, Hungary, Yugoslavia, Argentina, Mexico, and Trinidad. International sales accounted for over half of Compaq's total revenue in 1990, eclipsing North American sales for the first time. Nine new products were introduced during that year. These included updated versions of the DESK-PRO 386 desktop PC and a high-performance notebook PC, the Compaq LTE 386s/20. By the end of 1990, Compaq had 3,872 authorized dealers throughout the world, over 2,000 of them in North America.

1991 Brings a Slump

However, Compaq slumped badly in 1991. For reasons ranging from economic recession and price competition to problems with the flow of distribution, Compaq's sales and earnings fell for the first time in the company's history. Once again, the DESKPRO 386 PC series was the bestseller, with desktop PCs accounting for close to three-fourths of Compaq's total revenue. In September 1991, a new line of Compaq computers was introduced that had a new feature known as "Intelligent Modularity." This system, the DESKPRO/M, enabled users to more readily upgrade key components as their needs and the available technology changed. This was possible by organizing components into five easy-to-access modules: memory, input/output, EISA/ISA expansion cards, processor, and video graphics controller. It was hoped that customers would prefer upgrading with ease to purchasing a new computer every time their needs increased.

Compaq was forced to alter its established distribution strategy somewhat in 1991. By that time eight of the company's ten most important dealer chains had merged into four. This led Compaq to gradually start authorizing computer consultants and discount chains to sell its products. Direct sales techniques of its own, such as a toll-free hotline, were stepped up as well.

In late 1991, a dramatic management shake-up took place. Following a gloomy board meeting at which a $70 million third-quarter loss was announced, company founder and CEO Canion was forced to resign. Pfeiffer, who had been promoted to executive vice-president and chief operating officer, was immediately named to replace Canion. A major reorganization of the corporate structure ensued. The company was realigned into desktop and systems divisions. As part of a 1,440-person staff reduction program, about 12 percent of the company's entire work force was laid off. In addition, five high-ranking executives left the organization, including senior vice-president of engineering James C. Harris, the last remaining company founder.

In June 1992 Compaq introduced an incredible total of 16 new products. The new machines were of several types, including the company's first low-cost desktop PCs (COMPAQ Pro-Linea), low-cost notebook PCs (Contura), and upgradeable desktop PCs with advanced graphics and audio capabilities. The same month, Compaq announced the initiation of a new Peripherals Division, a worldwide arm whose mission would be to develop printers and printer-related items. The division's initial line of products, including the August 1992 debut of the Compaq Pagem printer, launched Compaq into the rapidly growing market for network printers. The printer line was a failure, however, and was abandoned in 1993.

Presario Leads a Consumer Push in the Mid-1990s

Under the leadership of Eckhardt, Compaq also began a major push into the consumer and home office markets. This effort was centered around the Presario line of home computers launched in August 1993. The company's hottest new PC in company history, the Presario line included models selling for less than $1,500; Compaq sold more than 100,000 Presarios in the first 60 days after introduction, with sales fueled by a $12 million television advertising blitz, the company's first such campaign in three years. In 1993 alone, Compaq sold $500 million worth of Presarios. By aggressively pricing its PCs, Compaq placed itself in a better position from which to compete with manufacturers of lower-cost PC equipment, manufacturers that had helped put the brakes on Compaq's previously unchecked growth. By 1994 the company managed not only to fend off its low-price competitors, it also surpassed IBM as the number one seller of PCs worldwide.

Not content with its PC dominance, Compaq in the mid-1990s aimed to capture a much wider market. It had already introduced the Proliant server PCs as its entry into the market for servers (powerful computers used for corporate networks and Internet web sites). The company then went after the corporate mainframe and minicomputer market with the launch of the Armada mainframe-class server, the top-of-the-line model which sold for upwards of $100,000. On the lower-end server front, in 1994 Compaq launched the ProSignia VS server, which cost only about five to ten percent more than a desktop PC.

Also in 1994 Compaq revamped its logistics system in order to begin building its PCs to order from a huge stockpile of parts. Previously Compaq had estimated how many units of each product it wanted in its inventory and then had that number built. Under this build-to-inventory system the company risked making too many of a particular product and being stuck with excess, unwanted inventory, as well as not having enough of a particularly hot product on hand. With its build-to-order system Compaq would realize significant inventory and manufacturing cost savings.

Other Compaq initiatives of this period included moves into high-speed networking equipment and Internet services/products, as well as the October 1996 launch of a highly successful line of engineering workstations. The highly aggressive Compaq thereby realized astounding growth: revenues increased from $5.79 billion in 1992 to $20.01 billion in 1996; net income, which had peaked in 1990 at $577 million, registered at $988 million in 1994, $893 million in 1995, and $1.32 billion in 1996. Reflecting its wider range of products, Compaq generated about 15 percent of its revenues from the consumer PC market, 48 percent from corporate desktop PCs, and 35 percent from servers and workstations in 1997.

Acquisitions in the Late 1990s

In February 1997 Compaq released a $999 PC, the Presario 2000, in another aggressive, low-price move aimed at attracting the 60 percent of U.S. households without a PC. Later in 1997 the company made two significant acquisitions. In August Compaq acquired, through a stock-for-stock transaction valued at about $4 billion, Tandem Computers Incorporated, a leader in fail-safe high-end servers with annual sales of $2 billion and a sales force 4,000 strong. Compaq also spent $280 million for Microcom, Inc., a provider of devices for remote access to networks.

Moreover, Compaq had its eye on an even bigger deal. In June 1998 the company completed its $9.1 billion acquisition of Digital Equipment Corporation, the number four computer maker in the United States. Digital, which became a subsidiary of Compaq, was a leading maker of high-end workstations and servers, giving Compaq an even greater presence in those markets. Digital also brought to Compaq a 22,000-person service operation for large companies—computer services having been one of Compaq's weakest areas. The deal not only increased Compaq's annual revenues to more than $37 billion and vaulted the company into the number two position among all the computer firms in the world (behind only $78.5 million-in-revenues IBM), it also positioned Compaq as one of the world leaders in just about every computer sector. The company was number one worldwide in desktop computers, number three in portable computers, number three in workstations, number one in both PC servers (costing less than $25,000) and entry servers (less than $100,000), and number six in midrange servers ($100,000 to $1 million). In computer services, Compaq was suddenly number three, behind IBM and EDS.

Integrating the operations of Compaq and Digital was sure to be difficult and costly. Compaq took a $3.6 billion charge against earnings in 1998 related to the acquisition and announced plans to cut 15,000 Digital jobs and 2,000 at Compaq. Areas of overlap began to be addressed, such as the folding of Digital's PC production into that of Compaq and the scaling back of Compaq's network equipment unit. However, it would take some time before the full impact of this combination—at the time the largest merger in the relatively short history of computers—could be assessed.

Principal Subsidiaries

Digital Equipment Corporation; Microcom, Inc.; Tandem Computers Incorporated; Compaq Computer Australia Pty. Limited; Compaq Computer GesmbH (Austria); Compaq Computer N.V./S.A. (Belgium); Compaq Canada Inc.; Compaq Computer A/S (Denmark); Compaq Computer OY (Finland); Compaq Computer S.A.R.L. (France); Compaq Computer GmbH (Germany); Compaq Computer Hong Kong Limited; Compaq Computer S.p.A. (Italy); Compaq K.K. (Japan); Compaq Computer B.V. (Netherlands); Compaq Computer New Zealand Limited; Compaq Computer Norway A.S.; Compaq Computer Asia Pte. Ltd. (Singapore); Compaq Computer S.A. (Spain); Compaq Computer AB (Sweden); Compaq Computer AG (Switzerland); Compaq Computer Taiwan Limited; Compaq Computer Limited (U.K.).

Further Reading

Arnst, Catherine, et. al, "Compaq: How It Made Its Impressive Move Out of the Doldrums," *Business Week,* November 2, 1992, pp. 146 + .

Bank, David, and Leslie Cauley, "Microsoft, Compaq Make Net-Access Bet," *Wall Street Journal,* June 16, 1998, pp. A3, A8.

Burrows, Peter, "Compaq Stretches for the Crown," *Business Week,* July 11, 1994, pp. 140–42.

——, "Where Compaq's Kingdom Is Weak," *Business Week,* May 8, 1995, pp. 98, 102.

"Compaq's Compact," *Management Today,* May 1985.

Depke, Deidre A., "A Comeback at Compaq?," *Business Week,* September 23, 1991.

Gannes, Stuart, "America's Fastest-Growing Companies," *Fortune,* May 23, 1988.

Heller, Robert, "The Compaq Comeback," *Management Today,* December 1994, pp. 66–70.

Kirkpatrick, David, "Fast Times at Compaq," *Fortune,* April 1, 1996, pp. 120 + .

——, "The Revolution at Compaq Computer," *Fortune,* December 14, 1992, pp. 80 + .

Kotkin, Joel, "The Hottest Entrepreneur in America Is . . . the 'Smart Team' at Compaq Computer," *Inc.,* February 1986.

Loeb, Marshall, "Leadership Lost—and Regained," *Fortune,* April 17, 1995, pp. 217 + .

Losee, Stephanie, "How Compaq Keeps the Magic Going," *Fortune,* February 21, 1994, pp. 90 + .

McWilliams, Gary, "Compaq at the 'Crossroads,' " *Business Week,* July 22, 1996, pp. 70–72.

——, "Compaq-Digital: Let the Slimming Begin," *Business Week,* June 22, 1998, p. 44.

——, "Compaq: There's No End to Its Drive," *Business Week,* February 17, 1997, pp. 72, 74.

——, "Mimicking Dell, Compaq to Sell Its PCs Directly," *Wall Street Journal,* November 11, 1998, pp. B1, B4.

McWilliams, Gary, et. al., "Power Play: How the Compaq-Digital Deal Will Reshape the Entire World of Computers," *Business Week,* February 9, 1998, pp. 90–94, 96–97.

Nee, Eric, "Compaq Computer Corp.," *Forbes,* January 12, 1998, pp. 90 + .

Palmer, Jay, "Still Shining: Growth in PC Demand Abroad, Networking Make Compaq's Prospects Bright," *Barron's,* December 11, 1995, pp. 15–16.

Pitta, Julie, "Identity Crisis," *Forbes,* May 25, 1992.

Ramstad, Evan, "Compaq's CEO Takes Tricky Curves at High Speed," *Wall Street Journal,* January 5, 1998, p. B4.

Ramstad, Evan, and Jon G. Auerbach, "Compaq Buys Digital, an Unthinkable Event Just a Few Years Ago," *Wall Street Journal,* January 27, 1998, pp. A1, A14.

Uttal, Bro, "Compaq Bids for PC Leadership," *Fortune,* September 29, 1986.

Ward, Judy, "The Endless Wave: Eckhard Pfeiffer Has Turned Compaq Around—Only to Face New Competition," *Financial World,* July 4, 1995, pp. 32–35.

Webber, Alan M., "Consensus, Continuity, and Commonsense: An Interview with Compaq's Rod Canion," *Harvard Business Review,* July/August 1990.

Whiting, Rick, "Compaq Stays the Course," *Electronic Business,* October 20, 1989.

Zipper, Stuart, "Compaq—Life After Canion?," *Electronic News,* November 4, 1991.

—Lynn Hall and Robert R. Jacobson
—updated by David E. Salamie

Computer Learning Centers, Inc.

11350 Random Hills Rd., Ste. 240
Fairfax, Virginia 22030
U.S.A.
(703) 359-9333
Fax: (703) 359-8225
Web site: http://www.clcx.com

Public Company
Incorporated: 1987
Employees: 1,600
Sales: $97.0 million (1998)
Stock Exchanges: NASDAQ
Ticker Symbol: CLCX
SICs: 8200 Educational Services

Computer Learning Centers, Inc. (CLC) provides information technology and computer-related education and training to adults seeking entry-level jobs in information technology. CLC designs programs and courses to meet current information technology education needs, offering instruction in rapidly growing technologies such as client/server programming, databases, network engineering, information technology support, and computer systems. Through its accredited career programs, CLC offers associate degrees and non-degree diplomas in several primary areas of study, including business applications; electronics, systems and hardware; programming; networking; information technology support; and business applications with networking. CLC's Advantec Institute division offers customized ongoing training programs to corporate clients that focus on current and emerging technologies in information technology.

The Early Years—Acquisitions and Mergers

Located in Fairfax, Virginia, the original Computer Learning Centers was founded in 1967 and taught systems management, data entry, and computer operations to computer center operations personnel. Its first 20 years were ones of repeated acquisitions and mergers. In 1968, it acquired International Tabulation Institutes, a Los Angeles-based training school founded in 1957. In 1970, the company merged with the Washington School for Secretaries. Three years later, MCD Enterprises, a construction company located in Maryland, bought CLC and combined the Learning Center institutions with its own schools. In 1976 Airco, Inc., a business whose primary interests were in welding gases, medical products, and alloy production, acquired CLC from MCD.

By 1983, Airco had increased the number of CLC schools to 25. It was about that time that Airco merged with British Oxygen to form the $3 billion British Oxygen Group, whose core interests were in medical products and industrial gases. Then, in 1987, British Oxygen Group made the decision to divest six of the schools to Connecticut-based General Atlantic Partners. Reid Bechtle was retained by the new owners of CLC in 1991 to review the business for possible sale. Bechtle instead advised General Atlantic to invest in the fledgling information technology business and became the corporate chief executive officer and president of Computer Learning Centers in 1991. Charles L. Cosgrove, who came with Bechtle from Planning Research Corporation became vice-president and chief financial officer in 1992, while Harry H. Gaines became its chairman. The company, by this time, also had operations in the United Kingdom, where it was known as Comprehensive Learning Concepts.

Expansion in the Mid-1990s

Bechtle, Cosgrove, and Gaines proved good leaders for CLC in the highly fragmented post-secondary adult education and training market of the 1990s. The market for such programs and services was characterized by rapidly changing requirements, with no single institution or company holding a dominant share. CLC thus had to compete for students not just with other vocational and technical training schools, but also with degree-granting colleges and universities, and continuing education and commercial training programs. CLC met this challenge by designing a series of programs intended to meet the needs of adult learners pursuing information technology-related careers, offering programs which could be completed in as little as seven to 18 months; flexible class schedules; monthly start dates; and financial aid eligibility for qualified students.

Steady enrollment increases fueled the company's growth throughout the 1990s. In 1995, CLC had about $40 million in annual revenue and eight schools serving about 6,500 students in California, Illinois, Pennsylvania, and Virginia. Yet CLC was still a small fry when compared with companies such as National Educational Corporation, with $241 million in annual sales, and DeVry, with $228 million. (Other competitors included Sylvan Learning Systems, Apollo Group, and ITT Educational Services.) When the company went public on May 31, 1995, it sold 2.2 million shares of common stock and brought in net proceeds of about $14.9 million. This left it relatively debt free, although still with reported losses of $1.3 million from discontinued operations. After that point, CLC grew steadily, proving Chairman Gaines correct, when he said in 1995 that the market for information technology training was due to "explode."

By 1996, the *Washington Post* listed CLC among that paper's top-rated 100 companies with 1995 revenues of $46.1 million and profits of $1.9 million. The *Post* reported that CLC continued to increase enrollment, especially in its newer, associate degree programs, and had received approval from state regulators. In 1997, it had revenues of $64 million and profits of $5.6 million, and earnings per share at a little more than a dollar. The eight schools had grown to 19 schools, enrollment was up 32 percent over the previous year, and the company started a program of specialized courses geared to working adults, called the Advantec Institute. CLC was again featured by the *Post* as "one of the area's hottest stock performers" in 1996. In order to raise capital to open new facilities and expand programs, the company offered up 1.3 million shares in its second public offering in October 1996.

By 1998, CLC had 12,000 students at its 23 schools nationwide in the United States and three in Canada, up from about 8,500 in 1997, and $25 million in new computers and facilities. The company grossed $97 million in the fiscal year ending January 31 and netted $9.6 million. Stock prices reached a record almost $39 per share in March after adjusting for two stock splits, prompting traders to speculate that the company was in for an adjustment some time soon and leading critics to short sell four million shares of CLC stock. Bechtle, in an act of some bravado, taunted the "shorts" publicly, saying, "Every

dollar the stock goes up is $4 million [they] take out of their bank accounts," and continued CLC's acquisition spree. The company had acquired Boston Education Corporation, a privately held Boston, Massachusetts provider of information technology education and training, which served nearly 650 students, in late December 1997 and, in January 1998, Markerdowne Corporation, a privately held provider of information technology education and training based in Paramus, New Jersey, serving approximately 800 students a year. In March 1998, it closed the deal on Delta College, a Montreal, Quebec-based, privately held information technology training firm serving 800 students.

Legal and Regulatory Problems

Yet, while the company was reveling in its steady growth spurt in enrollment, stock prices, and earnings (more than 50 percent in its latest fiscal year), trouble was brewing on several CLC campuses. As early as 1991 through 1993, student default rates on federally financed student loans had reached "unacceptable" levels of 25 percent, according to the U.S. Department of Education, prompting this body to suspend CLC's eligibility from some of its Title IV programs from September 1996 until October 1997 when it showed a reduced student loan default rate.

In December 1997, 11 students at the company's Alexandria, Virginia campus filed complaints with the Virginia Council of Higher Education that CLC had misrepresented students' future career prospects. In March 1998, the attorney general of the state of Illinois sued CLC in a civil lawsuit and asked the judge to shut down operations on the school's Schaumburg campus, alleging that the company had violated seven provisions of the state's consumer fraud and private vocational school laws by misrepresenting course offerings and employment prospects to students at its Schaumburg school. CLC officials responded to the Illinois attorney general's allegations by signing an agreement which "affirms that there were legitimate grounds for certain students to voice complaints," but they denied any violation of state laws. A few months later, the company agreed to a settlement that entailed creating a program to promptly address student complaints; establishing a program to provide $95,000 worth of software to nonprofit institutions; and contributing $90,000 to the attorney general's consumer education fund. CLC also agreed to hire more faculty, install new computers, and revamp its student recruiting efforts. Finally, the company said that it would hire an independent arbitrator whose role would be to determine whether a student's restitution would be in the form of cash or free classes.

To complicate matters further, the Illinois State Board of Education (BOE) ordered the Schaumburg school to suspend marketing and to stop enrolling students on its campus. Thirty days later, the state lifted the Schaumburg suspension after CLC agreed to change its advertising, admissions, and student complaint procedures, and to tighten faculty qualifications—but not before a two-day sell-off by investors and speculators which slashed the company's share price by more than 49 percent. In the wake of these actions, seven lawsuits were filed in federal courts on behalf of stockholders who had lost money because of the dip in stock prices, accusing CLC executives of violating securities laws and making millions of dollars by short selling stock before it nosedived.

On the heels of the Illinois BOE's action, the U.S. Department of Education launched an investigation of CLC schools. In a public letter, officials of the DOE notified the company that it was tightening oversight of federal student aid programs and ordered the schools to produce the names of all students who had received federal aid in the past two years. This move carried potentially serious ramifications, since approximately 75 percent of CLC's revenue came from federal student loans. According to the *Washington Post*, the Federal Trade Commission, which has jurisdiction over the marketing practices of private career schools, also began gathering information on CLC's testing and recruiting of potential students and the quality of its classes. However, according to CLC, the FTC had never contacted them for an investigation.

Rebounding from Difficulty

Although these regulatory and legal problems cut into CLC's first-quarter 1998 profits by roughly 25 percent, in the wake of their settlement, stock prices once again climbed, back up to almost $29 in July 1998. However, the company's roller-coaster ride was not over yet. In that month, a private detective working for shareholders' plaintiff attorneys announced that he had found thousands of pages of discarded student records in a dumpster outside the Virginia campus. These pages allegedly included some of those sought by the DOE. Stock prices plunged one more time as a result. They turned upward again once Bechtle dismissed the importance of the discarded documents as "waste in the normal operations of our business," and two independent analysts dismissed the importance of the discarded documents as well. Still, the *Washington Post* reported in late August that there was an ongoing FTC investigation into the marketing of the school's computer courses and that this investigation had been expanded based on allegations that CLC threw out records just before the federal review began.

As the company headed into 1999, it sought to recover from its drop in earnings attributed to a sharp falloff in enrollment at campuses in the Washington and Chicago areas and the cost of settling the consumer fraud lawsuit filed by the state of Illinois. By August 1998, the Illinois settlement had cost CLC more then $300,000 in penalties and another $500,000 in legal fees and in lost student fees. More importantly, it had led to a situation in which CLC was having trouble attracting students. In that month, the company disclosed expected second quarter profits of only four to five cents a share rather than the 16 cents that analysts had earlier projected.

CLC predicted that its ability to rebound from its difficulties and meet its future operating and financial goals would depend upon its ability to shed its bad publicity and to implement a successful growth strategy which included the establishment of new learning centers in new locations; the development of new and/or the enhancement of existing programs; the expansion of the Advantec Institute; the improvement of student outcomes through academic services and job placement assistance; the increased availability of associate degree programs at its various centers; and the acquisition of assets and programs complementary to the company's actions. The company's objective overall at the end of 1998 was to strengthen and expand its position as one of the leading providers of information technology education and training programs for adults in the upcoming years.

Further Reading

Behr, Peter, "CLC's Profits up 50 Percent," *Washington Post,* March 13, 1998, p. F03.

"Class Action Commenced by Kaufman Malchman Kirby & Squire, LLP. and Futterman Howard Chtd.," *PR Newswire,* March 23, 1998.

Cullotta, Karen Ann, "Computer School Still Aims to Hire Ombudsman," *Chicago Tribune,* July 20, 1998, p. 1.

"Digest," *Washington Post,* June 3, 1995, p. C01.

Holt, Douglas, and Karen Cullotta Krause, "Tales, Charges of Fraud Plague Computer School; State Expands Probe of Sites in Schaumburg, Downtown," *Chicago Tribune,* May 21, 1998, p. 1.

Knight, Jerry, "CLC Settles Fraud Suit in Illinois," *Washington Post,* June 9, 1998, p. F03.

——, "Computer Learning Centers Faces Suit; Officials in Illinois Allege Fairfax-Based Vocational Chain Defrauded Students," *Washington Post,* March 11, 1998, p. C10.

——, "Computer Learning Faces Inspection; Student Loan Program in Va. Under Scrutiny," *Washington Post,* May 8, 1998, p. D01.

——, "Computer Learning Suffers Big Stock Hit," *Washington Post,* August 29, 1998, p. E03.

——, "An Education in Computer Learning Centers' Stock Flight," *Washington Post,* March 9, 1998, p. F07.

——, "Suit Says School Dumped Records Sought in Probe," *Washington Post,* August 13, 1998, p. E01.

——, "U.S. Probes Computer Learning Centers; Education Dept., FTC Seek Data," *Washington Post,* April 8, 1998, p. C11.

—Carrie Rothburd

Consumers Union

Consumers Union

101 Truman Avenue
Yonkers, New York 10703-1057
U.S.A.
(914) 378-2000
Fax: (914) 378-2900
Web site: http://www.consumerreports.org

Nonprofit Company
Incorporated: 1936
Employees: 455
Sales: $120 million (1997)
SICs: 2721 Periodicals; 2741 Miscellaneous Publishing;
8299 Schools & Educational Services, Not Elsewhere
Classified; 8999 Services, Not Elsewhere Classified;
8733 Noncommercial Research Organizations; 8734
Testing Laboratories

Consumers Union is the nonprofit organization that publishes the monthly magazine *Consumer Reports*, dedicated to providing consumers with information and advice on a wide range of consumer issues, including product safety, health care provision, financial services, and food production. Over the years, the *Consumer Reports* magazine has garnered an extensive and loyal following of approximately 20 million readers, largely due to its reputation for impartiality. Before each issue of the magazine is published, more than 100 experts work in 47 labs to test, analyze, evaluate, and rate the performance, safety, reliability, and value of products made by companies throughout the world. Consumers Union does not accept any fees for product samples, and refuses to grant permission for the commercial use of its name on any test results for a product it has evaluated. In addition to a national testing and research center in Yonkers, New York, and an auto testing facility in East Haddam, Connecticut, Consumers Union staffs advocacy offices in Washington, D.C.; Austin, Texas; and San Francisco for the purpose of testifying before state and federal regulatory agencies and filing lawsuits on behalf of consumers relating to product safety, housing, the environment, economic discrimination, and the telecommunications in-

dustry, just to name a few. Consumers Union has also established The Consumer Policy Institute, also located in Yonkers, New York, to conduct research and implement education programs in the areas of toxic air pollution, community right-to-know laws, pesticides, and biotechnology issues.

Early History

Consumers Union was the outgrowth of a book entitled *Your Money's Worth,* written by F. J. Schlink and Stuart Chase. When the book first appeared in 1927, it quickly became a bestseller, and it was easy enough to understand why. The book was the first of its kind to describe in detail the fraud and manipulation surrounding the manufacture of food, medicine, cosmetics, automobiles, and household appliances, and clearly showed how consumers were victims of dishonesty and misrepresentation that were common in the marketplace. The popularity of the book can be seen as an indication of the growth of the modern consumer movement within the United States during the 1920s. Authors like Upton Sinclair had already exposed the problems within the food industry, and President Herbert Hoover, himself an engineer, had encouraged the formation of groups such as the American Standards Association, and given more authority to the National Bureau of Standards to prescribe a standardization system for testing foods, textiles, and other products that the American government was likely to purchase.

Schlink, a former staff member of the National Bureau of Standards, employed its work and findings as a model for testing products that were used by consumers. After the publication of his book, Schlink utilized his men's club that he belonged to in White Plains, New York, and summarized the experiences the members of the club had with certain products. Assembling his findings into the *Consumer Club Commodity List,* he began to sell mimeographed copies of the listings for one dollar each. By 1929, Schlink had received such an enthusiastic response from the general public that he formed Consumers' Research, an organization incorporated as a not-for-profit consumer testing firm, the first such organization of its type in the world. Schlink opened an office in New York City and renamed his mimeographed list the *Consumers' Research Bulletin.* By 1933, there were over 42,000 subscribers.

Company Perspectives:

Test, Inform, Protect. Consumers Union, publisher of Consumer Reports, is a nonprofit [501(c)3] organization established in 1936 to provide consumers with information and advice on goods, services, health, and personal finance, and to initiate and cooperate with individual and group efforts to maintain and enhance the quality of life of consumers.

In 1933, Schlink decided to relocate his operation from New York City to the rural village of Washington, New Jersey. However, after a short period, the engineers and journalist that formed the core of his staff grew disenchanted with country life and the long hours and low pay Schlink had imposed. When employees asked for a raise, their request was summarily rejected. When three employees attempted to form a union within Consumers' Research, Schlink fired them. His action precipitated a strike, however, and the demand that the fired workers not only be reinstated but all employees given a raise. Schlink retaliated with strikebreakers and private detectives, refusing to either mediation or arbitration, and described the strikers as communists.

In February 1936, the strikers from Consumers' Research decided to form an organization of their own in New York City. Named Consumers Union, the new organization brought together journalists, engineers, academics, and scientists committed to testing products used by consumers. Arthur Kallet, an engineer and former director at Consumers' Research who joined the strikers against Schlink, was appointed the first director of the organization. By May of the same year, *Consumers Union Reports* appeared, with detailed articles evaluating and rating milk, soap, stockings, breakfast cereal, credit unions, and Alka-Seltzer. With little money and a circulation of only 4,000, the organization in its early reports was forced to concentrate on inexpensive items such as hot water bottles, radios, and fans. The reports were so successful, however, that by the end of 1936 circulation had increased dramatically to over 37,000 subscribers.

During the late 1930s, Consumers Union and its reports garnered a large amount of hostility from traditional magazine publishers. In fact, more than 60 publications refused to provide advertising space for Consumers Union since it had an explicit policy of criticizing products by name. In addition, during the late 1930s with the Depression still affecting most Americans, not many people were buying the reports since they were not buying large amounts of consumer products. Yet, despite these challenges the organization and its magazine continued to grow. By 1939, *Consumers Union Reports* numbered over 85,000 subscribers.

The advent of World War II changed everything. Since the focus of manufacturing was on the production of tanks, guns, airplanes, trucks, and military uniforms, rather than on radios, refrigerators, and automobiles, the staff at Consumers Union just did not have enough products to test and evaluate. When rationing was imposed, the staff at the organization found it even more difficult to procure items that it normally tested, such as shoes and soap. In 1942, Consumers Union changed the name of its magazine from *Consumers Union Reports* to *Consumer Reports* in order to indicate that it provided a service to all consumers, not just union members. Yet during the same year circulation dropped to half the level of 1939, and the main office in New York City was forced to cut its staff.

The Postwar Era

When the war ended in 1945, Consumers Union and its magazine was poised for rapid growth. After nearly five years of getting by on the necessities of life, people across America were ready to embark on a buying spree. Fortunately for Consumers Union, the American public turned to its magazine for advice on what to buy. In 1946, the circulation of *Consumer Reports* numbered 100,000, but had increased to 400,000 by 1950. In 1952, *Consumer Reports* published the first automobile frequency-of-repair table, in 1953 the magazine published the first of a series of articles and tables on the tar and nicotine content of cigarettes, and the dangers of smoking, and in 1954, *Consumer Reports* issued its first tests and ratings on color television sets. One of the most important turning points for Consumers Union also occurred in 1954 when the organization had become financially successful enough to expand and improve its laboratory and testing facilities. Consumers Union moved from New York City to Mt. Vernon, New York, in order to take advantage of larger space for its administrative office and laboratory facility.

Along with the move to a new location, Consumers Union decided not only to test and rate the quality of consumer products, but to advocate on behalf of consumer interests. Staff personnel and board members of the organization began to testify on a regular basis before federal and state committees on a wide range of issues, including watered ham, the price-fixing of drugs, and automobile safety. At the same time, due to the increased revenues from growing subscriptions, Consumers Union began to provide financial assistance to various other consumer groups such as the American Council on Consumer Interests and Ralph Nader's Center for Auto Safety. By the end of the 1950s, Consumers Union had grown large and influential enough to start building a world consumer movement, providing funding and advice to newly formed organizations such as the International Organization of Consumers Unions, and the British-based Consumer's Association. When the founding director, Arthur Kallet, retired in 1957 after 21 years of devoted service, Consumers Union had grown to become the largest and most influential organization promoting consumer interests.

Growth and Influence, 1960s–80s

Consumer Reports continued to enhance its reputation as an impartial judge of consumer products in the 1960s. In 1962, the magazine issued its first report on automobile insurance and discovered that reform was needed due to rates that varied by hundreds of dollars for the same level of insurance. In 1965, *Consumer Reports* rated the Toyota Corona particularly favorable for "long-distance driving." By 1975, the Corona was the number one import in the United States automobile market. After Ralph Nader published his famous book *Unsafe at Any Speed* in 1965, Consumers Union asked the author to serve as a board member for the organization, and dedicated itself to providing even more information on the cars and trucks made within the automobile industry.

During the decade of the 1970s, Consumers Union's influence as an advocate for consumer interests increased significantly. Due to the years of product ratings provided by *Consumer Reports,* the U.S. government established the National Commission on Product Safety. In 1972, Consumers Union opened an office in Washington, D.C., to impress government officials with its research and make them more aware of changes that were needed surrounding consumer issues. Regional offices were later opened in San Francisco, California, and Austin, Texas, for the same purpose. In 1974, *Consumer Reports* published a series on the extent of pollution in the waterways throughout America, with detailed recommendations for cleaning them up. The series was regarded so highly that it won the National Magazine Award, the first of three given to *Consumer Reports.*

In the 1980s, *Consumer Reports* initiated a television section, and also a magazine for children called *Penny Power.* In 1983, the magazine implemented a phone-in service for consumers to check automobile prices and the cost of repairs. Since the organization, especially under the earlier influence of Ralph Nader, continued to develop its methods for testing and rating automobiles, in 1986 the board of directors voted to purchase a drag strip in East Haddam, Connecticut, to renovate and construct a state-of-the-art evaluation facility for cars, trucks, and the growing market for recreational vehicles. Based on tests conducted at this facility, *Consumer Reports* discovered that the Suzuki Samurai easily rolled over, and rated it NOT ACCEPTABLE. By this time, the reputation and influence of *Consumer Reports* had become so great that sales of the Suzuki Samurai dropped precipitously.

The 1990s and Beyond

Having decided to transform the organization into a multimedia publisher, rather than stick with a single magazine, Consumers Union began to disseminate information in many forms, thus expanding its role of providing consumers with detailed evaluations and ratings of products. This expansion included a radio program, a newspaper column, television programming, online services, CD-ROM products, newsletters, *Consumer Reports* books, and *Consumers Union's Price Services* for cars, auto insurance, and household appliances.

In 1992, paid circulation for *Consumer Reports* reached two million; however, by the end of 1995, paid circulation had increased to approximately 4.7 million, placing the magazine in the top ten list for paid subscriptions. By the end of 1996, the publishing industry estimated that *Consumer Reports* had a total readership of over 18 million, including library subscribers and an estimated four readers per copy pass-along factor. One of the most popular magazines in America, *Consumer Reports* showed no sign of decreasing readership. Revenues for Consumers Union amounted to over $100 million at the end of fiscal 1995.

The influence of Consumers Union through its publications, especially *Consumer Reports,* has been vast and measurable. For instance, sales for a particular men's suit skyrocketed 50 percent after it was rated a BEST BUY in the magazine. At the same time, Consumers Union has influenced product improvement. The marketing war over the use of caffeine in soft drinks is just one example. What is less measurable, however, but equally as important, is the influence Consumers Union has had on empowering consumers. By providing impartial, unbiased, and accurate tests and ratings about particular products and services in the marketplace, Consumers Union has helped consumers make their way through a winding and sometimes convoluted road of misrepresentation and misleading product advertisement.

Further Reading

"Consumers Union Reports," *Consumers Union Publication,* May 1936.

"The Early Years Remembered," *Consumers Union Consumer Reports Publications,* 1996.

Horrigan, Jeremiah, "Consumer Reports: Tops in Testing," *Times Herald Record,* March 22, 1997, pp. 19–21.

Linn, Virginia, "Health Council Rates Magazines for Nutritional Value," *Atlanta Constitution,* April 16, 1998, p. 26.

Patton, Phil, "The Product Police," *Audacity,* Spring 1996, pp. 21–23.

Rouvalis, Cristina, "Consumer Reports Testers Give Products a Pounding," *Pittsburgh Post-Gazette,* July 27, 1998, pp. E1–E3.

Warne, Colston E., "Consumers Union's Contribution to the Consumer Movement," in *Consumer Activists: They Make A Difference,* edited by Erma Angevine, Mount Vernon, N.Y.: Consumers Union Foundation, 1982, pp. 85–110.

White, John R., "Who Are Those Guys at Consumer Reports?," *Boston Globe,* April 5, 1997, p. D1.

Woller, Barbara, "Consumer Champion," *Gannett Newspapers,* June 28, 1998, pp. 3A–3E.

—Thomas Derdak

CORT Business Services Corporation

4401 Fair Lakes Court
Fairfax, Virginia 22033
U.S.A.
(703) 968-8500
(800) 962-CORT; (800) 962-2678
Fax: (703) 968-8501
Web site: http://www.cort1.com

Public Company
Founded: 1972 as CORT Furniture Rental Corporation
Employees: 2,300
Sales: $287.21 million (1997)
Stock Exchanges: New York
Ticker Symbol: CBZ
SICs: 7359 Equipment Rental & Leasing, Not Elsewhere
    Classified

Calling itself "America's National Furniture Rental Company," CORT Business Services Corporation is the largest, and only national, company in the United States providing corporations and small businesses office furniture on a "rent-to-rent" basis (as opposed to the "rent-to-own" segment of the furniture rental business). The company also provides residential furniture and housewares for corporate apartments and individual employees and booth furnishings rentals for trade shows. CORT operates under the names CORT Furniture Rental (its wholly owned subsidiary), General Furniture Leasing, CORT Furniture Rental Clearance Center, CORT Housewares, CORT Trade Show Furnishings, CORT Special Projects, and Relocation Central. As of August 1998, the company's national network included 118 showrooms, 80 furniture clearance centers, and 74 distribution centers in 32 states and the District of Columbia.

Early History: 1972–87

During the 1960s, the Mohasco Corporation, then the maker of Mohawk Carpets and the largest carpet manufacturer in the country, was one of several companies that saw furniture as the core of a new retail home furnishings industry. In 1963 Mohasco began buying furniture makers, including Barcolo Manufacturing, the maker of the Barcolounger recliner; Stratford Corporation, which manufactured the Stratoliner recliner; Chromcraft; and Peters-Revington.

In 1972 Mohasco expanded its home furnishings activities with the purchase of five regional furniture rental companies, which it merged into CORT Furniture Rental. The acquisitions gave Mohasco an outlet for its excess manufacturing capacity. CORT provided furniture to people who needed furniture for a limited time—those moving into an area and taking a short-term apartment lease, newlyweds, and those recently separated.

The company offered basic furniture groups at its showrooms, with varying styles and prices. In 1977, for example, its least expensive package for a one-bedroom apartment cost $35 a month. The package included a bedroom set (dresser, single or double bed, mirror, nightstand, and lamp), a dining room set (table and four chairs), and furniture for a living room (couch, coffee table, chair, two end tables, and two lamps). Furniture for an efficiency apartment started at $20 a month. In addition to the monthly fee, the customer paid tax, an insurance fee, a refundable security deposit, and a $30 delivery fee. After a year's rental, CORT offered a purchase option on the entire package.

Residential rentals were CORT's primary business, but over the next several years both the furniture making and furniture renting divisions of Mohasco responded to a growing need for corporate furnishings—office chairs and desks, conference tables, cabinets, and credenzas. In the furniture rental business, a whole new segment was emerging.

Why would a business rent furniture rather than buy? The option was an obvious advantage for a business that was just getting started and could not afford a big cash outlay. In addition, there were tax advantages, with the monthly payments usually 100 percent tax deductible, as well as a single monthly accounting entry.

In 1987 Mohasco moved from upstate New York, where it had been located for more than 100 years, to Fairfax County, Virginia, in the suburbs of Washington, D.C., to be closer to its carpet and furniture plants in the South. CORT, which had five showrooms in the D.C. area, had had a regional office in Fairfax since the 1970s and had moved its headquarters there in 1980. That region, with a highly mobile population, government offices being reorganized, and new businesses opening, was an ideal location for a company meeting short-term furniture needs. CORT's revenue more than doubled between 1982 and 1986, reaching $84 million (11 percent of company sales). By 1987 CORT had revenues of $93 million, making it the fastest growing division in the corporation.

Leveraged Buyouts: 1988–93

CORT's success contributed to its parent's appeal as a takeover prospect. After almost going under in the early 1980s, Mohasco, with 1987 revenues of $807 million, was one of the healthiest furniture companies in the county. Its 1987 annual report announced that all three of its divisions—furniture rental, furniture manufacturing, and carpet manufacturing—had record sales. But in February 1988, Nortek Inc., a Rhode Island building and electrical supplies company, announced that it had acquired seven percent of Mohasco's shares and was considering a merger proposal. To avoid a takeover, Mohasco looked for a friendlier buyer, with 16 suitors eventually joining Nortek. In May, Mohasco announced that its best offer was a $455 million leveraged buyout by MHS Holding Corp., a company organized by Citicorp Venture Capital Ltd. and other investors. Mohasco management continued to run the company, which owed more than $300 million in long-term debt as a result of the buyout.

Less than a year later, Mohasco sold CORT for $150 million and Mohawk Carpet Corp. for $112 million to service that debt. In both instances, the buyers were management groups principally financed by Citicorp, making the big bank's venture capital arm both the seller and buyer in the transactions. This leveraged buyout left CORT burdened with debt and short of cash, and the next several years were difficult ones for the company. Led by CORT President Paul Arnold, who had been with CORT since Mohasco created it, management cut costs by closing some showrooms and curtailing growth. However, the company still suffered a loss of more than $6 million on revenues of $106.5 million for 1992.

Brighter Days: 1993–96

The situation improved in March 1993, when Citicorp Venture Capital incorporated New CORT Holdings Corporation, which acquired all of the stock of CORT Furniture Rental Corporation for about $82.2 million. Citicorp eased the interest rate burden and the sale provided management with money to grow. To accomplish that growth, the company established a strategy focused on four areas: 1) make selective acquisitions; 2) initiate operations in new markets and open showrooms and clearance centers in existing markets; 3) expand the corporate customer base; and 4) invest in the development of various products and services.

CORT quickly implemented its strategy, buying several small furniture rental companies. In purchasing smaller outfits where CORT already had a presence, the company usually made a lease portfolio acquisition, acquiring existing leases and rental furniture and retaining local sales personnel, but not buying showrooms, distribution centers, or clearance centers. In new markets, CORT might decide to buy the real estate as well as the leases.

In September 1993, CORT acquired one of its main competitors, Dallas-based General Furniture Leasing Co., which had 1992 revenues of $41.5 million. CORT ended the year with revenues of $128.6 million, a 21 percent increase over 1992 revenues. General Furniture accounted for approximately $13.4 million of the total.

The merger with General Furniture not only opened new market areas for CORT, it also provided a different format and cost structure, targeting smaller markets and offering lower-cost rentals. Because of that, CORT operated showrooms in those markets under the General Furniture Leasing trade name. A survey commissioned by the company found that the average 1994 income of an individual CORT Furniture Rental customer was approximately $73,000, compared with $47,000 for a General Furniture Leasing individual customer.

In 1995 the company reached agreement with the IRS over tax issues relating to its returns from 1989 through 1992. With that matter settled, New CORT Holdings Corporation went public, changing its name to CORT Business Services Corporation and selling slightly more than three million shares for an estimated $37.2 million. That year, CORT moved into Birmingham, Alabama, and Little Rock, Arkansas, and began offering interior design services and furniture for model homes in three large metropolitan areas.

The following year, CORT made a second stock offering, raising around $32 million. Citicorp Venture Capital recouped some of its investment, but remained the majority shareholder with 45 percent of the stock. The influx of cash from the stock sales enabled the company to cut its debt almost in half.

In 1996 the company began operations in Portland, Oregon, and St. Louis, Missouri, and made its second large acquisition, that of California-based Evans Rents, for $27 million. This move greatly strengthened the company's presence in the Los Angeles and San Francisco markets, where Evans rented high-margin office furniture and trade show furnishings. CORT also moved into New York, buying some assets of New York-based

AFRA Enterprises Inc. and Apartment Furniture Rental. Although both these companies rented primarily residential furniture, CORT viewed the purchases as a way to enter the New York corporate market.

Diversification: 1997 to the Present

About 80 percent of the company's rental revenues was from corporate customers. These ranged from huge corporations such as Warner Bros., MCI, and Exxon Company USA, to regional companies to small home-based businesses. Corporate rentals increased substantially as companies demanded more flexibility. They needed office furniture for work teams created for special projects, for training classes, and for consultants or employees on temporary assignments. Many of those consultants and employees, as well as employees relocating or changing jobs, also needed furnished apartments. In addition to serving the corporations themselves, CORT provided merchandise to apartment managers and to the employees themselves.

CORT's customers typically wanted high quality furniture to meet temporary needs, had established credit, paid on a monthly basis, and did not buy the rented articles. The company generally leased merchandise for three-, six-, and 12-month terms. Prices were set to recover the original cost of the furniture over a ten-month period, and new pieces were constantly being added to inventory. To control inventory levels, CORT sold the previously rented furniture through its CORT Furniture Rental Clearance Centers, with the merchandise selling, on average, three years after its original purchase.

During 1997, CORT began diversifying its product mix, offering its own package of kitchen and other housewares instead of depending on a third-party contractor as it had in the past. The housewares package was designed for corporate apartments or employees needing a completely furnished residence for a short period. It also established the Relocation Central web site for its customers.

CORT moved more deeply into the trade show furnishings business with the purchase of the stock of Levitt Investment Company and the McGregor Corporation and the assets of ALCO Trade Show Services. As a major player in this market segment, CORT served major trade show contractors and corporate exhibitors, renting desks, couches, tables, and other specialty furniture for conventions and trade shows. The three companies were integrated into a single division catering to the big convention cities such as Atlanta, Chicago, Dallas, Las Vegas, Los Angeles, New Orleans, Orlando, New York City, San Francisco, and Washington, D.C.

During 1997, CORT entered the Pittsburgh and Cleveland markets through acquisitions and changed the company's stock symbol to CBZ. When CORT went public, it took the CBS symbol, which was no longer in use after Westinghouse Electric Corp. bought the Columbia Broadcasting System. But when Westinghouse Electric changed its name to CBS Corp., it wanted the CBS ticker symbol. CORT agreed to relinquish the symbol for an undisclosed financial offer.

Since the beginning of 1993, CORT has developed into a national company through acquisitions and consolidation, including 15 small lease portfolio acquisitions and mergers with two larger regional rental companies. It also has expanded its products to include houseware packages and trade show furniture rentals. During 1998, CORT continued its acquisition strategy, buying Instant Interiors Corporation, a $12.5 million business operating in the Midwest. The "rent-to-rent" segment of the furniture rental industry, estimated to be a $750 million business, was highly fragmented. CORT, with 1997 revenues of nearly $287 million and a national network of showrooms and clearance centers, was clearly the "100-pound gorilla" of the industry.

Principal Subsidiaries

CORT Furniture Rental Corporation; Levitt Investment Company; McGregor Corporation.

Principal Operating Units

CORT Furniture Rental; General Furniture Leasing; CORT Furniture Rental Clearance Center; CORT Housewares; CORT Trade Show Furnishings; Special Projects; Relocation Central.

Further Reading

Boodman, Sandra G., "Leasing the Living Room Furniture," *Washington Post,* January 2, 1977, p. H1.

Brown, Warren, "Mohasco's Move to Fairfax Boosts County's Prestige," *Washington Post,* December 28, 1987, p. F3.

"CBS to Keep Eye Logo; Ticker Symbol Uncertain," *Media Daily,* February 5, 1997.

"CORT Business Services Announces Ticker Symbol Change," *PR Newswire,* August 13, 1997.

"CORT Completes Instant Interiors Acquisition," *PR Newswire,* August 18, 1998.

"Cort Goes Public," *Washington Times,* October 3, 1995, p. B6.

Gaulin, Jacqueline, "Cort Furniture Earnings Rebound," *Washington Times,* March 24, 1994, p. B12.

Hart, Charles, "Rent, Lease or Buy?," *Focus,* January 22, 1986, p. 94.

Hinden, Stan, "Comsat's Spinoff Strategy: That's Entertainment," *Washington Post,* October 30, 1995, p. F25.

Knight, Jerry, "A Stock Burst That Was a Quarter Century in the Making," *Washington Post,* October 20, 1997, p. F29.

Kopecki, Dawn, "Resale of Leased Furniture Cushions Cort's Bottom Line," *Washington Times,* November 10, 1997, p. D18.

Kramer, Elizabeth, "Renting Office Furniture Makes 'Cents' for Some," *Business First-Louisville,* June 3, 1985, p. 7B.

Levaux, Janet Purdy, "Suite Seats," *Investor's Business Daily,* November 11, 1996, p. A4.

Menninger, Bonar, "Buyout Eventually Cost Mohasco Two Divisions," *Capital District Business Review,* February 20, 1989, p. 13.

"Mohasco Receives Prepayment of Indebtedness from Cort Furniture," *PR Newswire,* January 19, 1990.

Much, Marilyn, "CORT Business Services Corp.," *Investor's Business Daily,* May 19, 1997, p. A4.

—Ellen D. Wernick

Crane & Co., Inc.

30 South St.
Dalton, Massachusetts 01226
U.S.A.
(413) 684-2600
Fax: (412) 684-0817
Web site: http://www.crane.com

Private Company
Founded: 1801
Employees: 1,400
Sales: $200 million (1997 est.)
SICs: 2678 Stationery Products; 2621 Paper Mills

Crane & Co., Inc. is a family-owned papermaker known for its high quality stationery and for making money—U.S. currency, that is. The company became the sole supplier of currency paper for the U.S. Treasury in 1879. It also produces business papers, including archival record paper and ledgers through its Weston Paper division; makes technical papers for architects, engineers, and artists; develops glass- and poly-fiber materials used in filters, insulation, and other applications; and, through its Excelsior Printing Co. division, provides engraving, design, and printing-related services.

Zenas Crane Founds a Company: 1801–45

In 1799, Zenas Crane chose the small, agricultural town of Dalton in western Massachusetts in which to build his paper mill, on the banks of the Housatonic River. Zenas was following in a family tradition.

His father, Stephen, a papermaker, had sold a special security-type paper to Paul Revere. Revere used that paper to print the first bank notes in the colonies, in December 1775, two years before Zenas was born.

Zenas learned the art and science of papermaking as a teenager, how to clean old rags, then beat them into pulp, from which the paper was made. Wanting his own mill, he looked

west, and found 14 acres near wood and water and a population that could supply both the rags and employees. It took him two years to raise the money for the land and a mill. But in 1801, Zenas and his two partners, Henry Wiswell and John Willard, were in business.

Local housewives provided the new mill with the rags needed to make paper. The company's first advertisement, reproduced in Wadsworth Pierce's history, urged "that every woman, who has the good of her country, and the interest of her own family at heart, will patronize them, by saving her rags, and sending them to their Manufactory, or to the nearest Storekeeper—for which the Subscribers will give a generous price." Most of the rags the housewives offered were of a tough, homemade linen that was difficult to reduce to pulp, but made a very high grade of paper. This happenstance, combined with Zenas Crane's own perfectionism, established the firm's tradition of uncompromising quality in its products. Early customers included publishers, storekeepers, banks (many of which printed their own money), and the government of Massachusetts.

In 1822, Zenas bought out his partners and became the sole owner. At the same time, machines were playing a more important role in the industry: a cylinder machine replaced hand molding, and then steam-heated drying cylinders were introduced. Zenas developed a machine to automatically remove the paper from the papermaking machines.

In 1842, Zenas turned management of the company over to two of his sons, Zenas Marshall Crane and James Brewer Crane. Two years later, Zenas Marshall developed a paper that significantly deterred the altering of banknotes. He was able to imbed silk threads vertically into the paper to indicate the note's denomination: one silk thread for a $1 bill, two for a $2 bill, and so on. The new paper meant that $1 bills could no longer become $10 bills with the addition of a "0." Banks quickly placed orders. In 1845, Zenas Crane died at the age of 68.

Second Generation of Cranes: 1845–64

One of the company's biggest problems—transportation—was significantly reduced during the mid-1880s when the Boston and Albany Railroad came to Dalton. Now the Cranes could

Company Perspectives:

Quality has been a consistent and principal objective throughout the history of this manufacturer of fine papers. Relations with employees, customers and suppliers have stressed this element above all others. This visible legacy is worthy of continuing pursuit by future generations.

send their paper by rail instead of transporting it over land to the Hudson River and then downstream. The railroad also opened new markets, particularly in the West, and the Crane brothers built a second mill. Production was increased with the introduction of the Fourdrinier machine, which automated the paper-making process.

In 1851, the Cranes became the owners of a woolen mill which had gone bankrupt (Zenas had held the mortgage). They turned it over to brother Seymour, who converted it into a papermaking mill, which operated under the name Crane & Wilson and produced nothing but fine writing paper. However, Seymour's operation went out of business before the end of the decade, as the country moved towards civil war.

Although the two Crane mills in Dalton continued to operate once the Civil War began, they lost all their Southern customers and much of the money owed to them. The Confederacy refused to pay creditors in the North. According to Pierce, however, several of the businesses paid their debt to Crane in full after the war.

New Uses for Paper

During the depression following President Lincoln's assassination, many Northern paper mills went bankrupt. In what could be considered an early marketing coup, Crane took a chance on a fashion fad and developed a new paper for men's collars. Men changed their collar every day, so the demand was great, and one of the company's two mills was kept busy making them. The new paper for the collars had to be stiff, fairly thick, and able to withstand damage from dirt and perspiration.

Although the rage for paper collars did not last long, its legacy within the Crane family was important. James Brewer Crane was granted patents in 1867 and 1868 for paper belts to drive machinery. He invented the belts in the process of developing the paper for the collars. The durability of these belts gradually won over the skeptics, as did the characteristic that they would not stretch or slip as did leather or rubber belts. James Brewer's sons continued to make the belts into the 1880s at their mill in Westfield, which they operated as Crane Brothers.

Crane Brothers also manufactured baskets and cans, washtubs, toboggans, even coffins, out of a plastic-like paper product called Linenoid. But they did not stop there. They used their paper to make light, graceful boats. The company's web site once included a description of a boat the brothers had at their mill in 1876: "It was about 15 feet long and three feet wide, yet so light that a couple of men could carry it with ease. The frame of the boat was made of wood and then covered with paper, about one-eighth to one-quarter-inch thick."

One of their customers used Crane Brothers paper to make domes, including one containing 1,000 pounds of paper for the observatory at Rensselaer Polytechnic Institute. The dome built in 1881 for the U.S. Military Academy, with 36 sections and using about 2,500 pounds of paper, survived until 1959 when the building was torn down.

Quality Stationery and Shell Wrappings: 1865–75

In 1865, Zenas Crane, Jr., son of Zenas Marshall and grandson of the company founder, was put in charge of the old Crane & Wilson facility, which was renamed the Bay State Mill. There, he restarted the manufacturing of writing papers. Three years later, he had paid off the $54,000 mortgage on the building.

When the mill was destroyed by fire, a common occurrence in the industry and for the Crane family, Zenas, Jr., went to Europe to study how papermakers there produced the tinted and colored stationery that was becoming tremendously popular in the United States. The social papers he made when he returned was so fine, the mill could not keep up with orders from customers including Tiffany in New York; Baily, Banks & Biddle in Philadelphia; Shreve, Crump & Low in Boston; and Marshall Field in Chicago. In 1886, Crane stationery was used for the invitations to the dedication of the Statue of Liberty.

Zenas's brother W. Murray Crane and cousin Frederick G. Crane joined him to form a partnership, Z. & W. M. Crane, to run the rebuilt Bay State mill. Murray was responsible for several Crane successes. In 1873, he helped develop a paper for the Winchester Arms Co. to be used as wrapping for the repeater shells of that company's new rifle. The specifications, according to Pierce, called for "a highly-combustible, strong-but-thin" paper that left "little or no ash."

Making Currency Papers: 1876–1900

Murray's biggest contribution to the company occurred in 1879, when he won for Crane the contract to make currency paper for the U.S. Treasury. With a bid of 38.9 cents a pound of paper, he beat out J. M. Wilcox & Co. of Philadelphia, which had been supplying the paper, as well as other big paper companies. Murray developed a new paper, based on his father's parallel silk thread security paper, to meet Treasury specifications, and the company bought another mill, renamed Government Mill, which made nothing but the currency paper. By the end of the century, Crane had tripled the life expectancy of one dollar bills and more than tripled the tonnage shipped to Washington, D.C.

However, the United States was not the only country the Crane's Dalton company made currency paper for. The American Bank Note Company was one of its biggest customers, supplying bank notes for 48 countries, as well as stock certificates, bonds, and checks. Pierce noted that "The Story of American Bank Note Company" (quoted from in *The First 175 Years of Crane Papermaking*) described how one of that company's early partnerships introduced a new term to the industry. The partnership used Crane paper to print bonds, and sent the company an order for "more of that bond paper," to use for its letterhead.

Crane's researchers and developers were busy during the last half of the 19th century, introducing a thick paper to replace the parchment or sheepskin used for diplomas and certificates and a special thin paper for Bibles. But even as Crane was finding new uses and customers for its fine rag paper, the paper industry discovered how to make paper with wood pulp, a much less expensive process than that needed for cotton and linen fiber. Although many papermakers switched, the Crane operations did not, continuing to develop and manufacture fine rag papers. However, the company now bought its cotton and linen directly from European and U.S. mills; housewives no longer supplied the rags.

The Third 50 Years: 1901–51

The company celebrated its 100th anniversary in 1901, with four paper mills and nearly 1,000 employees. Murray Crane was governor of Massachusetts and would go on to serve as senator from 1904 to 1913.

The company was shipping its paper all over the country, and in 1903, Crane sent a salesman over the Rockies for the first time. He soon found a new customer with a new challenge: drafting paper that was strong and transparent. The tracing paper the company developed became one of its largest, although lesser-known, product lines and the foundation for its specialty papers.

By 1922, there were five Crane mills, and the several partnerships that operated them incorporated as Crane & Co., Inc. Frederick G. Crane, the son of James Brewster and grandson of the founder, was named the new company's first president. When he died a year later, Murray's son, Winthrop Murray Crane, Jr., took over the position, holding it for 28 years, through the Great Depression, World War II, and the postwar period.

Crane & Co. did well during these years, and shared its success within the community of Dalton, establishing a scholarship fund for local high school graduates. One of the early changes under Winthrop had to do with the currency paper. In 1928, to foil counterfeiters, the company began scattering the red and blue silk threads throughout the bills rather than imbedding two lines of thread in each bill.

To keep going during the Depression, the company developed and produced cigarette paper, and in the process came up with a better carbon paper, which remained a major product line until computers reduced the need for carbon copies. In 1932, the company established its stationery division and opened a retail operation in Dalton. Employees of the new division cut the stock produced at the Bay State mill, cut and produced the envelopes and boxes, and hand-painted the colored borders on note cards and writing paper. A row of inspectors checked each piece of paper, discarding any sheet with the slightest flaw. Two years later, Crane & Co. bought Z. & W. M. Crane, which controlled the Bay State and Old Berkshire Mills, adding the Stationery Division to its operations.

During the war, Crane operated 24 hours a day, producing paper for currency, War Bonds, and finally, invasion money. The shortage of linen resulted in a new formula, reducing the amount of linen from 75 percent to 50 percent, and increasing the cotton content from 25 percent to 50 percent. The war also cut off Crane's access to European linen mills. To fill the need, the company used a linen byproduct from linseed oil mills in Minnesota.

Expansion and Modernization: 1951–89

In 1951, Bruce Crane assumed the presidency of Crane & Co. when Winthrop became chairman of the board, a new position. In the mid-1950s, the company began a major project to clean up the Housatonic River. Over the next 20 years, the company spent more than $1.5 million installing improvements including a pollution control system that sent most of the discharges from the mills to a central processing plant. "They were leaders in environmental pollution controls, very active very early on and very cooperative with the environmental program at the college," the chair of the local community college's Life Sciences Department told the *Los Angeles Times* in 1986.

Those expenditures were only a small portion of the some $35 million the company spent modernizing and expanding during Bruce Crane's presidency. In 1956, Crane bought Dalton's other paper manufacturer, the Byron Weston Company, the original supplier of paper for Social Security cards. In addition to ledgers, which it had been producing since 1863, Byron Weston products included diploma parchment, bond, and index papers, as well as archival record paper used by local governments. That same year, the formula for the currency stock changed again, increasing cotton to 75 percent in response to a new printing process that printed the money on dry paper.

In 1968, the company invested heavily in its research efforts to develop new products, building the $300,000 Crane-Weston Development Center. The following year, Crane & Co. expanded into printing and engraving with the purchase of the Excelsior Printing Company and Excelsior Process and Engraving, Inc., in Massachusetts, and, in 1970, of Standard Process & Engraving, Inc., in California.

The company introduced Craneglas in 1970, after ten years of research. This new paper product used glass and other manmade fibers instead of cotton, and could be used for insulation, filters, and food packaging. The company continued to develop what they called "nonwoven" products, and within 20 years Crane nonwoven papers were being used in applications ranging from pipewrap to airplane firewalls to circuit boards to cafeteria trays to vertical window blinds.

Benjamin J. Sullivan was elected president in 1975, the first person to hold that office who was not a member of the Crane family. However, his grandfather had worked for the company for some 50 years, as a paper machine tender at the Bay State Mill. That same year also saw the opening of the new $8.5 million Wahconah Mill to manufacture paper for U.S. currency. Wahconah was the first complete Crane paper mill built in the 20th century.

Ten years later, in 1985, Sullivan was named chairman and CEO, and Thomas White became president. The company's sales topped $100 million for the first time, with sales to the Treasury accounting for a quarter of that amount.

During the 1980s, Crane expanded its sales of currency paper directly to other governments so that by 1990 it had about a dozen foreign customers. Over the years, those clients included Mexico, Bolivia, and Taiwan. "They're typically the underdeveloped countries, because as one could logically assume, the more developed a country becomes, the more likely it would be to have its own manufacturing facilities as well as printing facilities," a Crane official stated in a 1990 article in *Boston Business Journal*.

Continuing to Innovate: 1990–95

The early part of the decade saw several innovations. Crane received a new patent for a method to deter counterfeiting by imbedding clear polyester threads in the paper which failed to show up when the paper was photocopied. The company also returned to its tradition of using clothing rags to make paper. It introduced Crest R, a paper composed of 30 percent recycled cotton such as old table cloths and 70 percent recovered cotton fiber. Then, in 1993, it developed a 100 percent denim paper made for Levi Strauss Inc. from recycled scraps of Levi blue jeans. The Levi company used the paper for letterhead, corporate checks, and envelopes. In addition to producing a distinctive and sturdy paper, the recycling process kept a large portion of Levi Strauss's over two million pounds of denim scraps out of landfills.

Continuing its creative reuse of materials, the following year Crane introduced its "Old Money" line of stationery, made from recycled U.S. dollar bills. Instead of trying to get the dark ink out of the bills, which would have caused a solid waste problem itself, Crane left the ink in, giving the paper the color of money. Each ream of Old Money contained nearly $15,000 worth of shredded bills.

1996 to the Present

In 1996, Congress increased its efforts to have the Treasury Department seek more competition for its currency contract. The first move was a reinterpretation of a 1988 law to mean that a bidder had to be 50 percent U.S.-owned, thus opening the door to foreign companies. The Department also posted a draft solicitation for the currency contract on the Internet, offering subsidies for start-up costs and equipment.

Crane and its Congressional representatives fought the effort over the next several years, and the subsidies were never approved. In 1998, the Government Accounting Office released a report concluding that Crane should face competition because the Treasury could not determine whether its prices were fair or not. "This has been a continuing and ongoing assault by inter-

national joint ventures to try and break through on this," Senator Edward M. Kennedy (D-Mass.) told the *Associated Press* in October 1998. In January, the government took bids from several companies in addition to Crane for the $400 million contract to supply currency paper through 2002, but by October it appeared that Crane would win that contract.

Crane & Co., with seventh-generation members of the family actively involved in the management of the company, had a history of responding innovatively to problems. As the century was coming to a close, the expanded competition for the lucrative currency contract, supported by government subsidies to help companies with start-up and equipment costs, certainly posed a threat to Crane, as did the possibility of a $1 coin. In the meantime, Crane's research and development activities explored possible markets for nonwoven materials and alternative fiber papers using flax and hemp in its ongoing efforts to create tree-free papers.

Principal Divisions

Weston Papers; Excelsior Printing Co.

Further Reading

Boye, Roger, "New Roadblocks Due for Counterfeiters," *Chicago Tribune*, March 17, 1991, p. C11.

Esper, George, "Crane Name Synonymous with Berkshire Hills Town Since 1801; Paper Mill's Good Neighbor Policy Pays Dividends of Respect, Affection," *Los Angeles Times*, October 12, 1986, p. 5.

Gaines, Judith, "Levis; Leftovers Get a New Lease on Life," *Boston Globe*, February 21, 1993, p. 34.

Gevirtz, Leslie, "Treasury Mulls Subsidies for Currency Contract," *Reuters Financial Service*, December 27, 1996.

Hower, Wendy, "Dalton Mills Making Money Making Money," *Boston Business Journal*, March 5, 1990, p. 6.

Killian, Linda, "Crane's Progress," *Forbes*, August 19, 1991, p. 44.

Knapp, Caroline, "The Buck Starts Here," *Boston Business*, September 1987, p. 18.

Pierce, Wadsworth R., *The First 175 Years of Crane Papermaking*, North Adams, Mass.: Excelsior Printing Company, 1977.

Puner, Janice, "Moving Stationery," *Greetings Magazine*, November 1994, p. 4.

"A Real Tiger in the Paper Trade," *Fortune*, March 28, 1988, p. 52.

Robinson, Melissa B., "Crane Gets Reprieve in Congressional Spending Bill," *Associated Press*, October 9, 1998.

"Significant Dates in the History of Crane & Co.," http://www.crane.com/about/ac_main/time.html.

Siwolop, Sana, "Fed Has Money to Burn," *New York Times*, May 28, 1995, pp. 3–8.

"When Paper Was the Medium of Invention," http://www.crane.com/about/ac_main/feature/html.

—Ellen D. Wernick

Cumberland Packing Corporation

2 Cumberland Street
Brooklyn, New York 11205
U.S.A.
(718) 858-4200
(800) 221-1763
Web site: http://www.sweetnlow.com

Private Company
Incorporated: 1947
Employees: 400
Sales: $100 million (1997 est.)
SICs: 2099 Food Preparations, Not Elsewhere Classified

Cumberland Packing Corporation is a relatively small, family-run business, yet it has been a major player in the artificial sweetener market for more than 50 years. Cumberland makes Sweet 'n Low, a saccharin-based sugar substitute. The brand was the first granular sugar substitute to be marketed nationally, and it controls about 30 percent of the table-top sugar substitute market. Over 30 million people use Sweet 'n Low each day, and the brand has wide recognition and customer loyalty, even as the sugar substitute market opened in the late 1990s to a slew of new products.

Early History

Cumberland Packing was founded by Benjamin Eisenstadt, a native of Brooklyn. He was from a poor family, but he nevertheless made it to St. John's University Law School, where he graduated at the top of his class in 1929. Despite his degree, Eisenstadt was unable to find employment as a lawyer during the Depression, and he worked instead at his father-in-law's food store. The thrifty Eisenstadt saved up enough money from his salary to buy a cafeteria in 1940, located just across from the Brooklyn Navy Yard. The cafeteria was called the Cumberland, and during the war years it did a thriving business. Sailors and shipyard workers packed the place around the clock. As soon as World War II ended, however, the ready supply of customers diminished and Eisenstadt decided to sell the Cum-

berland. Then, as fortune would have it, he changed his mind about selling the place and instead got the idea to buy a tea bag machine and pack tea. Apparently he had worked in that industry as a child, and he thought it might be profitable. Eisenstadt's wife, Betty, came up with the inspiration that would change the course of Cumberland Packing. Noticing a dirty sugar bowl in a restaurant, Mrs. Eisenstadt suggested to her husband that he begin packaging sugar. Thus, in 1947 Eisenstadt incorporated Cumberland Packing, and the company worked on contract to sugar distributors making single-serving sugar packets.

Benjamin's son Marvin, a chemist, joined the company in 1956. He induced the company to begin packaging soy sauce and catsup as well as sugar. In 1957 a local drug manufacturer approached Cumberland Packing, looking for someone to develop a granular sugar substitute. Because of Marvin's educational background, this was a project he could tackle. Up to that time, the sugar substitute saccharin had been available only as a pill or a liquid, and there was no sugar equivalent that dieters could pour into their coffee or sprinkle on their breakfast cereal. The Eisenstadts developed a granular powder using saccharin and cyclamates, and named it Sweet 'n Low, after Benjamin Eisenstadt's favorite Tennyson poem. With distinctive pink packaging and a claim of fewer than three calories per serving, Cumberland launched Sweet 'n Low in 1957.

The timing of Cumberland's introduction proved very lucky. Dieting soon became a craze, and the sugar substitute market picked up with the debut of diet sodas in 1962. Demand for Sweet 'n Low rose accordingly. A&P, one of the nation's leading grocery chains, contacted Cumberland and asked if it could distribute Sweet 'n Low nationally. Very quickly Cumberland's sugar substitute became the most popular brand of its type on the market.

Problems with Regulations in the 1960s and 1970s

Sweet 'n Low was a hit, a successful new product that swept to the top of a booming niche in the 1960s. However, the chemicals in Sweet 'n Low had not been thoroughly studied. Some testing had indicated that cyclamates might cause cancer or birth defects in chickens and rats, and in 1969 the Food and Drug Administration decided to run some more definitive tests on the chemical.

After just three weeks of testing, the Health, Education and Welfare Secretary abruptly declared a ban on cyclamate sweeteners. Preliminary results had shown the growth of cancerous tumors in rats, and consequently, cyclamates were deemed unsafe for humans. The ban was announced in late October, and all cyclamates were to be off the shelf by February 1.

This might well have been the end of Cumberland Packing and Sweet 'n Low. But Marvin Eisenstadt was able to use his chemical expertise and devise a new formula for Sweet 'n Low, made with saccharin but without the addition of cyclamates. As the ban loomed, the Eisenstadts went to their bank and borrowed $1 million. The company took all its old stock off shelves across the country and buried it in landfills. Then Cumberland supplied its distributors with its reformulated product. This quick action saved the company, and sales soon took off. High sugar prices in 1974 led to a sudden increase in sales that year. Over the next two years sales doubled, so that by 1976, Cumberland was bringing in around $40 million.

History almost repeated itself in 1977, when a study preliminarily linked saccharin with cancer in laboratory rats. The Food and Drug Administration acted quickly, and in March 1977 announced a ban on saccharin, due to take effect in three months. Faced with this new disaster, Marvin Eisenstadt figured the company would sell out its remaining stock and close. With a three-month supply on hand, the company should have lasted up until the ban kicked in. But consumers were apparently outraged at the coming loss of their diet product, and began hoarding Sweet 'n Low. Cumberland's three-month inventory sold out in just two days. The run on Sweet 'n Low was indicative of public sentiment, and Eisenstadt encouraged the public's outrage by taking to television commercials to inveigh against the FDA's tests. Eisenstadt used the airwaves to complain that researchers had fed laboratory rats the equivalent of 1,200 cans of soda a day. In an interview in *Forbes* in July 1977 he complained ''Those rats weren't *fed* saccharin; they were embryos in their mother's wombs, so they were literally bathed in it.'' Meanwhile, the company gloomily looked around for some other product to sell when the ban went through.

Congress was apparently impressed by the level of public support for saccharin, and it moved to block the FDA's ban from taking effect. The compromise solution was to require packagers to print a warning label on products containing saccharin, which advised that saccharin had caused cancer in animals and may cause cancer in humans. Eisenstadt continued to lobby against the saccharin warning, but Sweet 'n Low sold well even with the somber reminder printed on it.

Market Share in the 1980s

The warning label did not slow Sweet 'n Low's sales, and by 1980 the pink packets had an estimated 80 percent share of the nation's artificial sweetener market. As insurance, Cumberland diversified into other products around this time, introducing a salt substitute called Nu Salt, and Butter Buds, a powdered butter and margarine substitute made of corn syrup and restructured butterfat. By the early 1980s, the artificial sweetener market had grown to something close to $450 million a year, and Sweet 'n Low was firmly entrenched as a top player.

But Sweet 'n Low's market share began to fall in 1982, even as sales volume continued to rise by about five percent annually. The reason was the introduction of a formidable competitor, NutraSweet. NutraSweet was made from a different chemical, aspartame, and it was manufactured under patent by the G.D. Searle Company. Searle had actually approached Cumberland in 1972 with an offer to buy out the business. Searle wanted to use Cumberland to develop its aspartame product. The Eisenstadts refused to sell, and it took another ten years before Searle got NutraSweet to market. However, NutraSweet's debut was heralded with the aid of tens of millions in advertising dollars. Though aspartame was more expensive than saccharin, it was several hundred times sweeter, and soon it found its way into almost every diet soft drink recipe. With the introduction of NutraSweet and its sister, Equal, the whole artificial sweetener market expanded rapidly. Conversely, Sweet 'n Low's share of it began to shrink. From around 80 percent in 1980, Sweet 'n Low's market share fell to around 73 percent in 1983, and down to just over 66 percent in 1984.

Cumberland was not in peril, since its sales volume still grew, but it struggled to maintain its name recognition by licensing a Sweet 'n Low soda in 1984. Its butter substitute also sold well, first marketed directly to hospitals and dieticians, and later selling in supermarkets.

Changes in the 1990s

When NutraSweet hit the market in 1982, it was manufactured under an exclusive patent for its key ingredient, aspartame, and no other brands could use that chemical. The brand was bought by giant chemical company Monsanto, and Monsanto spent enormous sums backing its product. By the early 1990s, aspartame was an ingredient in more than 4,000 food and beverage products in the United States. In Europe, the aspartame patent expired in the late 1980s, and European competitors had been quick to put out lower-priced aspartame products. Monsanto protected its turf, and was said to have used price-gouging to convince European manufacturers to continue using its brand. The U.S. patent on NutraSweet was due to expire in 1992. In anticipation of this, Cumberland Packing began preparing to compete with its own new sweeteners.

Cumberland formed a partnership with the German chemical company Hoechst Celanese Corp., and marketed a new sweetener, called Sweet One. This was made with a new chemical, acesulfame-K. Sweet One sold in Europe as Sunette, and it had some key qualities that NutraSweet lacked: it was stable at high temperatures so could be used in baking and candy manufacturing. It also maintained its sweetness in sodas even over a long period of time. And unlike Sweet 'n Low, Sunette and Sweet One were not required to carry a warning label.

An interesting sidelight to Sweet One's marketing was that both Cumberland and another U.S. distributor, Stadt Corporation, were sued by NutraSweet's maker Monsanto for trademark violation. The issue was the color of the packaging. Sweet One came in pastel blue packets, very similar to the well-known color of NutraSweet's packaging. The U.S. Circuit Court of Appeals threw out Monsanto's case in November 1990, ruling that competitors were free to use similar packaging colors. Monsanto got the case into the Supreme Court the next year. Nonetheless, the highest court let stand the earlier ruling, and the copycat packaging was vindicated.

Nevertheless, Cumberland did not have the advertising dollars to back Sweet One in the United States. It turned to a new product in 1993, the year after the aspartame patent expired. Called Sweet 'n Low 2, Cumberland unveiled a new mixture of saccharin, aspartame, and Sunette, or acesulfame-K. Cumberland upped its advertising budget to boost the new product, which was to appeal to consumers who preferred the taste of aspartame. Oddly enough, NutraSweet also introduced a new product that year, an aspartame-saccharin blend aimed to draw in consumers who preferred the taste of saccharin. In other words, both companies launched brands that were meant to resemble the other's product, with echoes of the New Coke mentality. By late 1993, Cumberland had also introduced NatraTaste, a 100 percent aspartame sweetener. Sales for that year stood at $69.5 million, and the company's total market share fell to just under 30 percent.

Despite indications that many Americans were returning to that old standby sweetener, sugar, Sweet 'n Low continued to hold its own in the fracturing artificial sweetener market. Market share in the 1990s evidently stayed at between 25 and 30 percent, while sales dollars still increased. The company was dealt a blow from within in 1995, though, when a former vice-president of Cumberland pleaded guilty to funneling illegal campaign contributions to a variety of prominent politicians. The executive, Joseph Asaro, was well-connected politically. He had introduced Cumberland's president, Marvin Eisenstadt, to President Reagan and to former New York senator Alfonse D'Amato, and Asaro was apparently even on personal terms with the Pope. Asaro had masterminded a complex scheme of bundling money siphoned from Cumberland's contractors, and delivering huge sums to the campaigns of D'Amato, former senator Bob Dole, the Bush-Quayle presidential initiative, and others. These contributions violated federal election laws, and by fudging the books, Asaro also defrauded the Internal Revenue Service. Cumberland's president Eisenstadt claimed he had no knowledge of the scheme, and had been taken in by his slick vice-president. But Eisenstadt too pleaded guilty to signing a false tax return and to related charges. The company paid a $2 million fine. The purpose of the campaign donations had allegedly been to buy influence for the cause of saccharin, which was still under threat of an FDA ban. Mr. D'Amato had been strong in his opposition to the saccharin ban in the 1980s. In the aftermath of the guilty pleas, Cumberland instituted stricter financial controls and updated its computers to prevent anything similar from happening again.

By the late 1990s, Cumberland Packing Corporation was still holding its own in a market dominated by much bigger companies. Its market share was significant, though its advertising budget was much smaller than its competitors'. For example, Cumberland spent $2.4 million in 1996 to back Sweet 'n Low, whereas Monsanto poured over $16 million into advertising for its Equal brand that year. In addition, new sweeteners came on the market, the latest being Johnson & Johnson's sucralose. But Cumberland did not seem like it was ready to be knocked out of its niche. Despite its prominence in a market dominated by large chemical conglomerates, Cumberland remained a family-run business. Its employees made well above the average for unskilled labor in the New York area and received generous pensions, sick pay, and vacations. Still located in the Brooklyn neighborhood where the old Cumberland diner had been, the company consciously declined to modernize equipment if it meant sacrificing jobs for its workers. This rare spirit seemed to keep the company going despite many obstacles. Plans were to keep Cumberland in the family for a third generation, even after Marvin Eisenstadt retired.

Further Reading

Halbfinger, David M., ''Former Executives Guilty,'' *New York Times*, November 26, 1997, p. B6.

Hebel, Sarah, ''NutraSweet Keeps Aspartame Lead,'' *Advertising Age*, September 20, 1993, p. 12.

Hevesi, Dennis, ''Guilty Plea on Donations to Politicians,'' *New York Times*, April 13, 1995, p. B1.

Hwang, Suein L., ''Artificial Sweetener Makers Start Slugging,'' *Wall Street Journal*, November 5, 1992, p. B10.

''Justices Let Stand Ruling on Color Used in Packaging,'' *Wall Street Journal*, April 23, 1991, p. B10.

Mall, Elyse, ''A Look Back,'' *Your Company*, June/July 1998, p. 80.

Martin, Douglas, ''Nice 'n Easy at the Factory,'' *New York Times*, April 2, 1997, p. B1.

''Short 'n Sweet,'' *Forbes*, July 15, 1977, p. 80.

''Soured Sweets,'' *Newsweek*, October 27, 1969, p. 93.

''Sweet 'n Low Buffeted by Rival Aspartame,'' *New York Times*, May 27, 1985, pp. 33–34.

Warner, Fara, ''The Little Brand That Could,'' *Adweek's Marketing Week*, August 26, 1991, p. 16.

—A. Woodward

Daffy's Inc.

1 Daffy's Way
Secaucus, New Jersey 07094
U.S.A.
(201) 902-0800
Fax: (201) 902-9016
Web site: http://www.daffys.com

Private Company
Incorporated: 1961 as Daffy Dan's Bargaintown
Employees: 600
Sales: $114 million (1997 est.)
SICs: 5651 Family Clothing Stores

Daffy's Inc. is a discount retailer, based in the northeastern United States, of men's, women's, and children's apparel and accessories. Noted for cheap but often stylish clothing, it also was well known in the 1990s for its cheeky billboards and other outdoor print ads advising readers that they would be foolish to pay full price elsewhere.

Growing Retail Chain: 1961–94

Daffy's had its start in 1961, when Irving Shulman opened a small off-price clothing store named Daffy Dan's Bargaintown on a back street in Elizabeth, New Jersey. Shulman publicized his wares with zany promotional stunts that made him a local celebrity. He sold silver dollars for 88 cents, placed mannequins on the store's roof to attract the attention of passersby (who came into the store to warn that a woman was about to jump), and parked three leased Rolls-Royce limousines outside the store to illustrate his claim of "clothing bargains for millionaires." He also placed advertisements declaring, "99 out of 100 psychiatrists say Daffy Dan is O.K.; it's just his prices that are crazy."

There was, of course, method to this madness. Daffy's was still, in 1990, paying as much as 60 percent below regular wholesale price for its merchandise by purchasing goods that

manufacturers had been unable to sell to department and specialty stores. The manufacturer was happy to sell the overstock for what he could get since a new shopping season was, or soon would be, under way. Daffy's policy was to take delivery of purchased goods immediately and stock it in its stores within days. Most of its goods were domestic, but company buyers sometimes flew to Italy, France, or Spain to purchase clothing from suppliers' excess output. In a 1997 *New York* service article, Corky Pollan wrote that Daffy's had "cornered the market [for children's clothing] on the coveted European names that usually surface only in the kids' boutiques dotting upper Madison Avenue."

Neither of Shulman's two sons was interested in the business, but his daughter Marcia worked there on Saturdays and during the summer and went on buying trips with her father. She and her husband, Vance Wilson, joined the company in 1970. By the spring of 1987 Daffy Dan's—renamed Daffy's that year—had grown to a chain of five stores, 450 employees, and annual revenues of $35 million. Marcia Wilson, the prospective successor to her father, was then vice-president of operations and her husband was vice-president of real estate and development.

By this time Daffy's had gone from selling what Shulman called "shlock" to off-price but high-fashion merchandise. This was made possible because of a growing acceptance by suppliers of the role of the off-price apparel merchant, allowing such retailers access to better quality clothing. "With the department stores going in for price cutting," Vance Wilson told a reporter in 1990, "suppliers are seeing off-price retailers in a new light, maybe even as a necessity."

Competition from price-cutting department stores—and also from manufacturers themselves, who began opening their own outlet stores—did not seem to faze this retailer. By 1989 the number of Daffy's outlets had grown to nine, including its first in Manhattan, at Fifth Avenue and 18th Street, which became its flagship, with 34,000 square feet of space on three levels. This section of lower Fifth Avenue had been part of the city's main shopping district a century earlier and now was returning to vogue. The newer Daffy's stores were given more

Company Perspectives:

As other retailers seek ways to connect with their audience, Daffy's is recognized for its smart, highly creative and often head turning messages designed to keep it top-of-mind among consumers. Through advertising, both print and broadcast, window displays, in-store merchandising and special events, Daffy's appeals not only to the cost conscious consumer's sense of style and value but their sense of humor.

tasteful interiors, clearly with the intention of attracting a more upscale clientele.

Daffy's made an even bigger splash in 1990, when it opened a 15,000-square-foot store at Madison Avenue and East 44th Street, in the heart of Manhattan's shopping district for full-price conservative men's clothing and just across the street from Brooks Brothers' flagship store. But Shulman told a reporter, "We are not looking to compete directly with [traditional retailers], since we are off-price merchants. We would have gone there even if they weren't there because of the office buildings and affluent consumers right there or nearby." Shulman conceded that Daffy's offered "mostly self-service" rather than customer service but added, "Our goods are so cheap that a man who comes in for a white shirt will settle for a blue one."

Women's apparel, however, had the dominant role in Daffy's chain of outlets; even at the Madison Avenue store, women's accessories shared the main floor with menswear. A visit to the women's department—one flight down by escalator—turned up racks of Oscar de la Renta cashmere dresses for $99.99. Items such as a Randy Kemper silk jacket for $119.99 and Viewpoint's $29.99 swimsuits were further discounted by one-third at the cash register. Some goods had labels cut out at the option of the vendor. Vance Wilson said about 70 percent of the store's sales would be in women's apparel. By 1991 business was so good on Madison Avenue that he said the store needed more space.

Daffy's opened a store in the heart of Philadelphia, on Chestnut Street, in 1992, and a third Manhattan outlet in the World Trade Center in 1993, shortly after taking over the lease held by bankrupt Alexander's Inc. for $5.5 million. The following year Daffy's launched its fourth Manhattan store in the enclosed Herald Square Mall, at Broadway and West 34th Street. This outlet was described by Pollan as "the most stroller-friendly" of the chain in Manhattan, "bright, spacious, and super-organized."

New York shopping columnists were finding much to admire in Daffy's selection and prices during the middle to late 1990s. Lynn Yaeger spotted a navy blue wool Yves St. Laurent dress at the Fifth Avenue store for $69.99 and a silver-and-white-striped Cynthia Rowley T-shirt dress (with a "teensy hole" near the shoulder) for only $24.99. Besides "impossibly chic clothing for your youngest dependents" in the infant and

toddler departments, Pollan found well-stocked girls' and boys' departments, with most articles no more than $30. Dany Levy discovered a nice selection of lingerie, sports bras, leggings, and various Lycra-enhanced gear.

"In-Your-Face" Advertising: 1991–96

By 1995 Daffy's was attracting attention not so much for its price-friendly merchandise but for the "in-your-face" advertising campaigns disseminated by De Vito/Verdi (originally Follis DeVito Verdi), the irreverent agency that won the retailer's account in 1991. Daffy's had abandoned price-promotional advertising, even during the key Thanksgiving season, because although it resulted in a flurry of sales at some particular time, it did not lead to consistently strong sales every day of the week. Moreover, price-only promotions held down a retailer's profit margin and could cheapen its image. According to Ellis Verdi, his agency "worked to help the retailer build top-of-mind awareness to the point where their business thrived on no advertised discount or sale—only an increasing perception that this is a great place to shop every day."

Verdi went on to add that in taking "the inherently loud word 'Sale' out of the communication, it must be replaced with something just as attention-getting and even more memorable. . . . Our kind of advertising effectively tells people that they are out of their mind to shop elsewhere." Accordingly, Daffy's sunk money into outdoor billboards and posters putting down the full-price competition. One of these showed identical shirts side by side, but one, with a $20 price tag, was captioned "Shirt," while the other, with a $68 tag, was captioned "Bull-shirt." The copy for another read, "The suggested retail price of this shirt is $125." The arms of the depicted shirt formed an obscene gesture, while the next line of copy read, "We have a suggestion for whoever suggested it." An all-print ad read, "We believe people should be price conscious. They should remain conscious after they see the price."

Daffy's was reluctant to buy expensive television time, especially since its urban locations meant that it could reach a large number of people through outdoor advertising. A back-of-the-bus ad read, "Hey you, in the taxi. Nice shirt. You could have gotten it for less at Daffy's. But you're used to being taken for a ride." Another outdoor ad began, "When a clothing store has a sale on selected merchandise, why is it always merchandise you never select?" Daffy's billboards in front of many of New York City's most expensive stores during the Christmas season warned pedestrians to "watch your wallet in this neighborhood"—or to shop at Daffy's. Back-of-the-bus ads in Philadelphia proved so effective that Daffy's dropped its television spots in this market.

The copy for one of De Vito/Verdi's earliest ads for Daffy's read, "If you're paying over $100 for a dress shirt, may we suggest a jacket to go with it?" To the left of the copy was a photo of a straightjacket. Citing the ad for "indifference and contempt toward people with psychiatric symptoms," the Alliance for the Mentally Ill of New York State, joined by the Friends and Advocates of the Mentally Ill, petitioned New York City's Commission on Human Rights to treat it as a bias case. The commission referred the complaint to the American Association of Advertising Agencies, which concluded that De Vito/Verdi did not "knowingly" offend anyone and that words like "crazy" and "nuts" are stigmatizing but so prevalent in advertising that they would be difficult to remove.

Daffy's in 1996–97

By the fall of 1996 Daffy's had closed its store in the World Trade Center but had opened one on elegant East 57th Street. It was maintaining corporate headquarters in two buildings totaling 102,000 square feet in Secaucus, New Jersey, when, in 1996, the company purchased a 215,000-square-foot warehouse on 20 acres off the New Jersey Turnpike in neighboring North Bergen for about $9 million. It spent $6 million more on refurbishing the 42-year-old facility, which had been empty for nearly a decade, and before the end of 1997 reopened it as corporate headquarters, distribution center, and retail store. Daffy's had 12 other stores at the time: the four in Manhattan and the one in Philadelphia; New Jersey outlets in East Hanover, Elizabeth, Paramus, Secaucus, and Wayne; a store in Manhasset, Long Island; and one in Potomac Mills Mall, Virginia. Wilson said the company planned to double the size of the chain during the next five years.

Further Reading

Barmash, Isadore, "Daffy's Now on Madison Ave.'s Elite Retail Row," *New York Times,* May 28, 1990, p. 30.

Furman, Phyllis, "Moderately Priced Retailers Fight Downturn, Savvy National Chains," *Crain's New York Business,* January 7, 1991, p. 19.

Kanner, Bernice, "The Taste Police," *New York,* October 26, 1992, pp. 40–41.

Levy, Dany, "Marked-Down Town," *New York,* September 9, 1996, pp. 110–11.

Lockwood, Lisa, "Scoop," *Women's Wear Daily,* June 20, 1990, p. 12.

Pollan, Corky, "Cheap and Cheaper," *New York,* April 28, 1997, pp. 76–77.

"Succeeding in Family Businesses," *Nation's Business,* May 1987, p. 26.

Verdi, Ellis, "The Great Retailer Advertising Wars," *Chain Store Age,* September 1995, pp. 30–31.

——, "Mingling the Price Message with a Quality Image," *Discount Store News,* May 15, 1995, p. 71.

"A Warehouse Stays in Fashion," *New York Times,* September 28, 1997, Sec. 9, p. 1.

Yaeger, Lynn, "Hail to the Cheap," *Village Voice,* May 16, 1995, pp. 37–38.

—Robert Halasz

Deutsche Lufthansa Aktiengesellschaft

Von-Gablenz-Strasse 2-6
D-50679 Cologne
Germany
(49 221) 826-24 44
Fax: (49 221) 826-22 86
Web site: http://www.lufthansa.com

Public Company
Incorporated: 1926 as Deutsche Luft Hansa
    Aktiengesellschaft
Employees: 58,250
Sales: DM 23.15 billion (US$12.87 billion) (1997)
Stock Exchanges: Frankfurt
Ticker Symbol: DLAGY
SICs: 4512 Air Transportation, Scheduled; 4522 Air
    Transportation, Non-Scheduled; 4725 Tour Operators;
    4729 Arrangement of Passenger Transportation, Not
    Elsewhere Classified; 4789 Transportation Services,
    Not Elsewhere Classified

Deutsche Lufthansa Aktiengesellschaft (commonly referred to as Lufthansa) is the largest airline in Germany and one of the five largest airlines in the world. Its passenger business, run as the autonomous business unit Lufthansa German Airlines, is the flagship operation of the Lufthansa Group. More than 33 million passengers take Lufthansa flights each year, choosing among 25 destinations in Germany, 112 in Europe (excluding Germany), 11 in the Middle East, 72 in North America, seven in South America, 15 in Africa, and 36 in the Asia-Pacific region. Additionally, the May 1997-formed Star Alliance joined Lufthansa, Air Canada, Scandinavian Airlines System (SAS), Thai Airways International, United Airlines, Varig (of Brazil), Air New Zealand, and Ansett Australia in a cooperative venture serving more than 640 destinations in 108 countries. Lufthansa's young fleet includes a mix of Airbus models (A300, A310, A319, A320, A321, and A340) and Boeing 737s, 747s, and 757s.

The Lufthansa Group also includes Lufthansa CityLine, an all-jet regional airline; Condor Flugdienst, air charter service;

Lufthansa Cargo, air freight specialist; Lufthansa Technik, aircraft maintenance service; LSG Lufthansa Service, global catering arm; Lufthansa Systems, data processing; and Lufthansa Flight Training. Each of these units are wholly owned, autonomously operated subsidiaries of Deutsche Lufthansa.

Lufthansa's history parallels the development of aviation in Germany, dating back to a time when the first aviators were just beginning to fly. However, it was not established as a commercial airline in Germany until the 1920s.

Founded in the 1920s

After World War I the German government favored the development of a national airline system made up of a number of associated regional airlines. One of the largest airline companies, Deutscher Aero Lloyd, was incorporated in 1923 and centered its operations around Berlin's Temple Field. The following year Junkers Luftverkehr was founded. Junkers built airplanes in addition to operating an airline. Together the two companies dominated German aviation.

The two companies merged with all the other German aeronautic concerns in 1926 to form Deutsche Luft Hansa Aktiengesellschaft (the name "Hansa" was taken from the north-German Hanseatic trading league, which had contributed most of the airline's private capital). Luft Hansa was a government-private monopoly—the chosen instrument for all German air services. The company's logo was taken from Aero Lloyd and its blue and yellow colors were taken from Junkers. By May 1926 Luft Hansa served 57 domestic and 15 international airports.

In 1934, under the new name "Lufthansa," the company opened an airmail service between Stuttgart and Buenos Aires. As an instrument of state commerce and diplomacy Lufthansa flew to numerous destinations around the world including Beijing, New York, Cairo, Bangkok, and Tokyo. Regarded as an instrument of the state, Lufthansa increasingly came under the control of the ruling Nazi party. Lufthansa began service to destinations in the Soviet Union during 1940. These routes provided the German Luftwaffe (air force) with valuable strategic information used in Hitler's surprise invasion of the Soviet Union two years later. In 1941 the Luftwaffe assumed control of Lufthansa's airplanes and converted many of them for military

---

Company Perspectives:

The guiding principle of all our entrepreneurial activities is to enhance Lufthansa's market value on a lasting basis. We believe that the optimal conditions for achieving an attractive return on investment are created by achieving a balanced synthesis between the interests of shareholders, customers and employees.

---

use. As the war continued many Lufthansa employees were drafted into military service in support of the Luftwaffe; by the end of the war in 1945 many had lost their lives.

After the war Germany was occupied by the Soviet Union, the United States, France, and Britain. The Soviet-occupied zone later became the German Democratic Republic (East Germany), and the American, French, and British zones became the Federal Republic of Germany (West Germany). A general state of belligerency between the Soviet Union and the Western allies further divided East and West Germany. Under the conditions of the occupation both East and West Germany were forbidden to establish their own airline companies. British, French, and American airlines had a monopoly on air service in West Germany, while the Soviet airline Aeroflot assumed all air services in East Germany.

Lufthansa Reborn in the 1950s

By 1951 the reestablishment of a national airline for West Germany was proposed. The following year the West German government in Bonn set up a preparatory airline corporation, and then in 1953 Luftag was created. Hans Bongers, who joined Lufthansa in 1926, was reinstated as director of the national airline. Luftag began service with four Convair 340s, later joined by three DC-3s, and four Lockheed Constellations.

Luftag's airplanes were piloted by foreign airline personnel while former Lufthansa pilots were retrained in the United States. The Germans later flew as copilots until 1956 when all-German crews were assigned. In 1954 Luftag instituted its old name, Lufthansa, and in the following years reestablished its services to North and South America and the Middle East.

Lufthansa began flying Boeing 707 passenger jets on its international routes in 1961. The introduction of jets marked the beginning of an equipment rotation at Lufthansa. The older propeller-driven airplanes were slowly phased out and replaced by passenger jets. With this new equipment Lufthansa had firmly reestablished itself as one of the world's premier air carriers.

The expansion of Lufthansa continued with the reintroduction of services to Africa. The airline established service to Nigeria in 1962 and later that year began service to Johannesburg, South Africa. Despite the heavy investment required for the airline's expansion, Lufthansa was able to declare its first profitable year in 1964. Previously the airline had charged its losses to the federal government.

Lufthansa joined a maintenance pool called ATLAS in 1969. As a member of ATLAS, Lufthansa cooperated with Air France, Alitalia, Sabena, and Iberia in the repair and maintenance of aircraft and other equipment. Lufthansa's Hamburg facility was designated to perform repairs for the pool's B-747s, DC-10s, and A-300s.

The updating of equipment at Lufthansa continued over the next few years as the airline introduced Boeing's 737 for short distance shuttle routes, and a 747 jumbo jet for heavily traveled long distance services. In addition to the 747, Lufthansa purchased several McDonnell Douglas DC-10s. The new aircraft replaced the older propeller-driven airplanes, the last of which was removed from the fleet in 1971. During this period Lufthansa developed its air freight services with a fleet of 747s specially designated to haul cargo. The airline constructed automated freight handling facilities in a number of destinations across the world. Lufthansa recognized the importance of cargo services before most of its competition. The company established one of the most modern freight handling systems in the world. Cargo services became a major source of revenue for Lufthansa.

Survived Spate of Hijackings in the 1970s

Being a European airline Lufthansa was dangerously exposed to terrorist activities during the 1970s. Security was inadequate at many airports served by the company, which made it easy for terrorists to board and later commandeer an airplane. However, not one Lufthansa passenger lost his life despite numerous hijackings on the airline. The chairman of the company during the 1970s was Rolf Bebber and he must be credited for Lufthansa's success in ending the hijacking peacefully. He established a crisis management procedure which enlisted the diplomatic influence of the West German government. Through this procedure the company could respond quickly to terrorist demands in order to resolve a crisis. In addition, security at all Lufthansa airports was significantly upgraded.

The airline experienced considerable problems with German air traffic controllers who staged a ''go-slow'' from May to November 1973. Lufthansa estimated that it lost $71 million due to flight cancellations during that period. The controllers, who were civil servants, had been demonstrating their displeasure with working conditions in this manner since 1962. Lufthansa tried to persuade the federal government to change the status of the controllers in an effort to avoid future slowdowns but was unsuccessful.

Lufthansa received its first A-300 jetliner in 1976 from Airbus, the French-German-British-Spanish aircraft consortium. The A-300 was the first commercial aircraft to be built primarily by Germans in over 30 years. The German member of the Airbus group, Messerschmidt-Bölkow-Blohm (MBB), continued to contribute to the development of more advanced Airbus jetliners and Lufthansa continued to add them to its fleet. In 1983 the airline commissioned its first A-310 and later purchased the consortium's A-319, A-320, A-321, and A-340 jumbo jets.

MBB was particularly willing to involve Lufthansa in the Airbus projects. Since both companies were German they were encouraged by the Federal government to coordinate and serve each other's economic interests. As a result, Airbus was especially sensitive to Lufthansa's design requirements. Moreover, because Lufthansa was a highly respected modern air carrier, the jetliners built to its specifications were, in turn, more marketable to other airline companies.

In 1982, 80 percent of Lufthansa's stock was owned by the West German government. The board of directors, however, was appointed by Lufthansa's private investors. On June 22 of that year the board of directors narrowly elected a new chairman to succeed Herbert Culmann. Culmann was a popular chairman, but he retired two years early to save his company embarrassment over allegations of kickbacks to travel agents.

The new chairman was Heinz Ruhnau, a career bureaucrat with strong affiliations with the West German Social Democratic Party. His appointment generated an unusual amount of concern because many feared the ruling Social Democrats were attempting to politicize the airline. Ruhnau was an undersecretary in the Transport Ministry and a former chief assistant to the head of West Germany's largest trade union, IG Metall. He did not, however, have experience in private enterprise, and Lufthansa was being prepared for a further privatization of its stock. In 1985 the federal government held 74.31 percent of Lufthansa, 7.85 percent was held by government agencies, and the remaining 17.84 percent was held by private interests.

Ruhnau assumed his post on July 1, 1982, in a smooth transition of leadership. Ruhnau's immediate tasks were to improve Lufthansa's thin profit margin and win the support of the company's 30,000 skeptical employees. The company's performance in 1982 was impressive and resulted in its selection as airline of the year by the editors of *Air Transport World*.

A New Lufthansa Evolved During the 1990s

The early to mid-1990s was a period of enormous change in Europe, change that proved extremely challenging for Lufthansa. Most obvious was the 1990 reunification of Germany, a difficult process which nonetheless afforded Lufthansa the opportunity to fly to Berlin under its own colors for the first time since the Allied occupation. The period also featured steadily increasing competition which forced down ticket prices worldwide and cut into Lufthansa's market share. The company was particularly vulnerable because of its cumbersome bureaucracy and its relatively high-wage workforce, with the workers traditionally protected by the company's state-run status. Other forces reshaping the operating environment for Lufthansa included the gradual deregulation of the airline industry in Europe, the trend toward privatization sweeping the continent, and the planned economic integration of Europe during the 1990s. By the turn of the century, Lufthansa had made numerous changes in response to these challenges, emerging as a very different company.

Leading Lufthansa through most of the 1990s was Jürgen Weber, who became chairman in September 1991. The company was hemorrhaging at the time, amid fierce competition and the first decline in European air travel in history in 1991—with the Gulf War a major catalyst for the drop. For the first time since 1973, Lufthansa lost money, posting a net loss of DM 425.8 million in 1991, followed by another loss of DM 391.1 million in 1992. Starting in mid-1992 Weber began working

feverishly to bring the company's costs in line. By 1994 job cuts totaling 8,400 had been made, and Weber got workers to agree to an unprecedented one-year wage freeze in 1993. He also dumped unprofitable routes and cut some services, such as first class within Europe. US$1 billion in annual cost savings were realized through these efforts, leading Lufthansa back into the black by 1994, when it made DM 302 million.

Not everything went smoothly. A new low-cost domestic shuttle service, Lufthansa Express, was launched in 1992 but caused confusion among customers and was eventually scrapped. Meantime, Lufthansa faced a new and potentially formidable competitor in its home market when British Airways PLC in 1992 acquired a 49 percent interest in a Berlin-based carrier, newly dubbed Deutsche BA. The regional airline offered high-quality service to business travelers and competed directly with Lufthansa's regional airline, known as Lufthansa CityLine, which also catered to business travelers and which Lufthansa gained 100 percent control over in 1993. By the mid-1990s Deutsche BA had firmly established itself as Germany's number two scheduled airliner, with a market share of 14 percent.

By 1993 the German government still held 51.6 percent of Lufthansa. A rights issue soon reduced the stake to 35 percent, giving company workers less government protection. In July 1993 Weber began restructuring Lufthansa. With a vision of the company as a holding company for several separately operated units, he spun off Lufthansa Cargo as a stand-alone (but wholly owned) business, the largest specialized air cargo carrier in the world. In succeeding years, several additional operations were similarly spun off, creating Lufthansa Technik in the maintenance area, Lufthansa Systems in data processing, LSG Lufthansa Service in catering, and Lufthansa Flight Training. Lufthansa CityLine and air charter specialist Condor Flugdienst also operated autonomously. The culmination of this process came in April 1997 when Lufthansa's flagship scheduled passenger business was made independent as well, under the name Lufthansa German Airlines. Deutsche Lufthansa had thereby evolved into a holding company for what was referred to as the Lufthansa Group.

Another key goal of Weber's was to seek out international partnerships, as alliances became increasingly common and vital for survival in the 1990s. In October 1993 Lufthansa and United Airlines, the leading U.S. airliner, began a code-sharing arrangement, whereby a single flight number in a reservation system could involve a journey consisting of a Lufthansa leg and a United leg. This partnership eventually led to the May 1997 formation of the "Star Alliance," which initially involved Lufthansa, United, Air Canada, Scandinavian Airlines System (SAS), and Thai Airways International. The Star Alliance included not only code-sharing but also reciprocal frequent flyer programs, reciprocal lounge access agreements, and scheduling and pricing coordination efforts. In October 1997 the Brazilian airline Varig joined the alliance. In 1997 and 1998 Lufthansa also entered into separate bilateral partnerships with Singapore Airlines and All Nippon Airways of Japan. In May 1998 Air New Zealand and Ansett Australia agreed to join the Star Alliance during 1999. Regulators in Europe, however, were taking a close look at this and other alliances and were likely to require that changes be made before granting final regulatory approval.

In October 1997 Lufthansa was fully privatized with the sale of the government's remaining 37.5 percent stake in the airline, raising about DM 4.7 billion (US$2.77 billion). The company was now free of its government ties, operating within a new group structure, and considered one of the most profitable airlines in the world (net profits for 1997 were DM 834.7 million), an amazing turn of events from the depths of the early 1990s. With the airline industry fully open to competition throughout the European union, Lufthansa at the turn of the century was presented with new challenges—even greater competition—as well as additional opportunities. In the globally competitive industry environment, it seemed likely that the company's future depended heavily upon that of the Star Alliance.

Principal Subsidiaries

Passenger Business: Lauda Air Luftfahrt AG (Austria; 20%); Luxair Société Luxembourgeoise de Navigation Aérienne S.A. (Luxembourg; 13%); Günes Ekspres Havacilik A.S. (Sun Express) (Turkey; 40%); Condor Berlin GmbH. Cargo Business: DHL International Ltd. (Bermuda; 32.3%); Hinduja Lufthansa Cargo Holding B.V. (Netherlands; 40%); Airmail Center Frankfurt GmbH (40%). Technical Services: Aircraft Maintenance and Engineering Corp. (China; 40%); Lufthansa Airmotive Ireland Holdings Ltd. (90%); Lufthansa A.E.R.O. GmbH; Condor/Cargo Technik GmbH; Shannon Aerospace Ltd. (Ireland; 50%); Lufthansa Shannon Turbine Technologies Limited (Ireland; 90%); Lufthansa Technik Logistik GmbH. Information Technology Sales: Lufthansa AirPlus Servicekarten GmbH (48.8%); AMADEUS Global Travel Distribution S.A. (Spain; 29.2%); START Holding GmbH; Lufthansa City Center Reisebüropartner GmbH (50%); LIDO GmbH Lufthansa Aeronautical Services; Lufthansa Revenue Services GmbH. Catering: LSG Lufthansa Service Deutschland GmbH; LSG-Food & Nonfood Handel GmbH; LSG Lufthansa Service Europa/ Afrika GmbH; LSG Lufthansa Service Asia Ltd. (Hong Kong); LSG Lufthansa Service USA Corp.; Onex Food Service Inc. (U.S.A.; 23.49%). Handling Services: Lufthansa Airport- and Ground-Services GmbH; Berliner Lufthansa Airport Services GmbH (49%); AFC-Aviation Fuel Services GmbH; Lufthansa Engineering and Operational Services GmbH. Others: Delvag Luftfahrtversicherungs-AG; Lufthansa Gebäude Management GmbH (51%); Lufthansa Consulting GmbH; Lufthansa Technical Training GmbH; Lufthansa Leasing GmbH (49%); Lufthansa LOEWE Druck und Distribution GmbH (51%).

Principal Operating Units

Lufthansa German Airlines; Lufthansa Cargo AG; Lufthansa Technik AG; Lufthansa CityLine GmbH; LSG Lufthansa Service Holding AG; Condor Flugdienst GmbH; Lufthansa Systems GmbH; Lufthansa Flight Training GmbH; Lufthansa Commercial Holding GmbH.

Further Reading

"Airline of the Year: Lufthansa," *Air Transport World,* February 1995, pp. 39+.

Bowley, Graham, "Lufthansa Opens the Throttle," *Financial Times,* August 25, 1998, p. 21.

Braunburg, Rudolf, *Die Geschichte der Lufthansa: vom Doppeldecker zum Airbus,* Hamburg: Rasch und Rohring, 1991, p. 335.

Carey, Susan, "Lufthansa Jettisons Bureaucratic Baggage," *Wall Street Journal,* September 30, 1996, p. 36.

"Crash Marriage," *Economist,* October 9, 1993, pp. 75–76.

Davies, R.E.G., *Lufthansa: An Airline and Its Aircraft,* New York: Orion Books, 1989.

Fisher, Andrew, "Pilot for the Open Skies," *Financial Times,* April 1, 1997, p. 16.

French, Trevor, "Low Marks: The German Flag Carrier Lufthansa Is Grappling with Heavy Losses, Major Aircraft Investment Commitments, and a Deteriorating Home Economy," *Airline Business,* January 1993, pp. 54+.

Gill, Tom, "The Devil's in the Detail," *Airline Business,* September 1998, p. 2.

Grube, Lorri, "Network Dogfight," *Chief Executive,* January/February 1996, pp. 24–26, 28.

Hill, Leonard, "Banking on Acronyms," *Air Transport World,* November 1995, pp. 71–73.

——, " 'Leaner, Meaner' Lufthansa," *Air Transport World,* January 1992, pp. 82–84.

——, "Lufthansa's Bitter Pill," *Air Transport World,* July 1993, pp. 68–71.

Odell, Mark, "Germany's Perfect Union," *Airline Business,* September 1994, pp. 34+.

——, "Reid All About It," *Airline Business,* November 1997, pp. 24+.

Reed, Arthur, "Congestion, Competition Crimp Lufthansa's Growth," *Air Transport World,* July 1989, pp. 38+.

Reichlin, Igor, Andrea Rothman, and Stewart Toy, "Even Lufthansa Is Carrying Too Much Baggage," *Business Week,* September 7, 1992, p. 80.

Skapinker, Michael, and Bethan Hutton, "Lufthansa and United Extend Alliance to Japanese Airline," *Financial Times,* March 10, 1998, p. 6.

"State Ends Link with Lufthansa," *Financial Times,* October 14, 1997, p. 31.

Templeman, John, "A Crack Navigator—And Lufthansa Is On Course," *Business Week,* July 18, 1994, p. 78F.

——, "Just When Lufthansa Was Gaining Altitude . . .," *Business Week,* July 1, 1996, p. 44.

Wachtel, Joachim, *The Lufthansa Story,* Cologne: Lufthansa German Airlines, 1980, p. 135.

Whitaker, Richard, "In Transition," *Airline Business,* August 1991, pp. 58+.

——, "Lufthansa's Standard Bearer," *Airline Business,* November 1991, pp. 58+.

Woodruff, David, "Rivals Are Buzzing All Around Lufthansa," *Business Week,* March 3, 1997, p. 48.

—updated by David E. Salamie

ZTR® Mowers

Dixon Industries, Inc.

Airport Industrial Park
P.O. Box 1569
Coffeyville, Kansas 67337
U.S.A.
(316) 251-2000
(800) 264-6075
Fax: (316) 251-4117
Web site: http://www.dixon-ztr.com

Wholly Owned Subsidiary of Blount International, Inc.
Incorporated: 1973
Employees: 202
Sales: $45 million (1997 est.)
SICs: 3524 Lawn & Garden Equipment

A veteran in the outdoor power equipment industry, Dixon Industries, Inc. manufactures a full line of zero turning radius lawnmowers. Dixon's line of ZTR riding mowers captured consumer interest in the 1970s as the first zero turning radius mowers affordable to most homeowners. In 1990 Blount International, Inc. acquired the company. All of Dixon's operations were housed under one roof in Coffeyville, Kansas.

Origins

The Dixon family first established their business presence in Coffeyville, Kansas, in 1948 when W.O. Dixon expanded Dixon Manufacturing Company by establishing a production plant in the small, rural community. At the time of the expansion, W.O. Dixon operated a small machine shop in Wichita, Kansas, that did subcontract work primarily for Boeing, Beech, and Cessna. In 1951 Dixon sold his company to Continental Can Company and bought a cattle ranch near Grove, Oklahoma. Continental Can changed the name of the company to Olin-Dixon Inc. and for the next decade operated the enterprise, retaining Dixon's original business focus. In 1962 Continental Can decided to shutter its operations and approached Dixon, who had spent the previous 11 years tending his cattle and operating a pipeline equipment and supply company in Tulsa, Oklahoma, about buying his company

back. Dixon agreed to the proposal and several years later was joined by his son, K.O. Dixon.

After earning a degree in production management from the University of Oklahoma in 1960, K.O. Dixon had helped with the Dixon family ranch operations, but in 1967 he joined his father at Olin-Dixon as a plant manager. Father and son worked together until the aerospace industry dipped into one of its recessive cycles during the early 1970s, which prompted W.O. Dixon to seriously contemplate retirement. In 1972 the elder Dixon decided to complete the work for which he had contracted and then liquidate the company and retire. K.O. Dixon, after more than a decade of working in family-owned businesses, found himself without a job and without a clear idea of what he wanted to do, except for a vague desire to own his own business. His search for a job led to the formation of Dixon Industries and the affiliation of the Dixon family name to a novel breed of lawnmowers.

While sniffing about for job opportunities, K.O. Dixon heard about a company in Leavenworth, Kansas, that was willing to sell the patent for, and the assets to build, a zero turning radius riding lawnmower. During the early 1970s the concept of a zero turning radius lawnmower was not revolutionary. Several models were available commercially, made by manufacturers who used hydraulic transmissions to deliver power to the rear wheels, but all of the models available were very expensive and beyond the financial means of most homeowners. The concept Dixon heard about, however, could be made much more inexpensively than the zero turning radius mowers available at the time. The patents for the unique mechanical transmission for sale in Leavenworth allowed the steering to be controlled by the power wheels on the mower instead of the steering wheel. By delivering the power independently to each rear wheel, the operator could turn the mower around within its own dimension. Dixon was far from an expert in outdoor power equipment, but he was intrigued. "I didn't know anything about the lawn mower business," he recalled, "or even consumer products, but this unique concept seemed to have merits so I went to the auction."

The company in Leavenworth, Kramer Machine and Engineering Company, offered the patent and manufacturing assets at an auction in July 1973. Dixon made the trip, but to his

Company Perspectives:

From the time Dixon ZTR mowers were introduced 25 years ago, they have changed the industry. Zero Turning Radius mowers maneuver precisely around trees, bushes and obstacles. They have become known for cutting corners squarely, tracking contours cleanly and easy handling.

Both Dixon's patented ''Z'' Drive Transaxle and our Hydrostatic Drive deliver power to the drive wheels independently. A Dixon can turn in its own dimensions. So instead of making wide turns over cut sections and backing up, your time is spent productively, mowing uncut sections on every pass. You have control of speed and direction for efficiency that greatly reduces or even eliminates hand-trimming.

Over the years we have made many improvements and innovations in the ZTR line. For a residential mower, a larger estate mower or a commercial mower, your needs have been anticipated. And one thing remains constant: If you want a better mower, turn to Dixon!

chagrin he realized he lacked the finances even to make the opening bid. He returned home and forgot about the entrepreneurial opportunity until a Leavenworth bank telephoned and asked if he was still interested in the lawnmower idea. Dixon returned to Leavenworth and came back with his hands full, having struck a deal for the patent rights, the inventory, and the tooling to produce a new type of zero turn radius mower. ''I moved it all to Coffeyville and started from scratch,'' Dixon explained. Dixon Industries, Coffeyville's newest Dixon enterprise, went into production in 1974.

Dixon started with 25 employees who set to work in 1974 to introduce the first Dixon ZTR (zero turning radius) line of lawnmowers. During the first year production output reached 760 mowers, all powered by eight-horsepower engines and fitted with 42-inch blades. There was more to starting the company than simply gearing up production to feed demand, however. Dixon explained: ''We had a new company, a new product, and a new concept of mowing grass. That concept was we had a riding mower that had no steering wheel and could turn on a dime. It was a new idea that was unfamiliar to people. We had to do a lot of hands-on demonstration. It was a pioneering effort.'' To educate consumers and stimulate demand, the company started with the slogan, ''Cut your mowing in half,'' and relied heavily on the efforts of a small network of distributors and dealers to inform Midwest consumers about the benefits of a Dixon zero turning radius mower. Dixon's relationship with distributors and dealers was an important one, crucial to the company's success during its inaugural year of business, and no less so 25 years later. The distributors and dealers were the individuals who could use Dixon's marketing tools to the company's best advantage, serving as a network of salespeople able to communicate the novelty and efficacy of Dixon's unique riding mowers directly to the consumers.

Developing the optimum distribution and marketing system did not occur overnight. The process took time; it was at least

three years before Dixon could consider itself an established company with a sophisticated distribution system. By the company's second year of business, after it had moved into larger quarters, 820 mowers rolled off the production line, but the distribution of these mowers was fundamentally flawed. By this point, Dixon had nine distributors who covered a ten-state territory and placed the new line of ZTR mowers with local dealers, but the company used distributors who sold multiple lines of outdoor power equipment instead of selling Dixon products exclusively. As one of numerous product lines, Dixon ZTRs did not receive the undivided attention of either the distributor or the dealer, which meant consumers were not being persuaded as strongly as they could be to purchase ZTR mowers. Primarily, the reliance on such a system was a function of Dixon's relative anonymity in its industry during the company's early years. As awareness of the brand name and product increased, the company could then expect to cultivate distributors whose business could survive solely on the Dixon line.

The company's efforts at major industry trade shows helped accelerate the awareness of the ZTR line, providing well-attended venues where Dixon could showcase its marketing talents. In 1976, one example of the company's efforts to court dealers was its ''Mowdeo'' demonstrations, which dealers could use as a marketing tool to attract customers. The company also launched an aggressive direct mail program in an effort to broaden ZTR awareness, but perhaps nothing was more effective at extending the recognition of ZTR to a broad range of consumers than the introduction of a 30-inch model in 1977. With both a 42-inch and 30-inch model to market, Dixon was able to widen its geographic area of operation as its distributor network fanned out and led the way. Remarkably, the company extended distribution into Europe in 1977, three short years after the first ZTR was produced.

By the end of 1977 K.O. Dixon and his management team could rightly claim that they had established Dixon as a lasting player in the outdoor power equipment industry, having shouldered past the numerous difficulties that frequently hamper a start-up's maturation into an established company. Evidence of the company's success could be found in the steady rise in demand for its mowers, the growth of its distribution network, and in the interest other industry participants had in the burgeoning operations at Coffeyville. Dixon received several offers to produce private brand mowers for mass merchandisers, but despite the lure of the tremendous growth such an agreement could yield, K.O. Dixon refused to steer his company in a new direction. It was more important, he claimed, not to damage the company's relationship with its dealers and distributors, whose allegiance to Dixon was intrinsic to the company's future success. It was, he noted years later, ''a key decision, one we've never regretted and never changed.''

By the end of the 1978 selling season, unit sales were up to 3,200, a more than fourfold increase in a four-year span. The company's production payroll had tripled and its number of distributors had increased to 19, extending Dixon's operating territory to embrace a 24-state area. Dixon ZTRs were, by this point, the fastest-growing line of riding mowers in the United States, giving the company the confidence to project a growth rate that exceeded the growth of its industry as it entered the 1980s. Aside from steady growth of the company during the

1980s, the decade's most significant event occurred in 1986, when Dixon traded its independence for the greater resources and capital of a parent company.

Ownership Changes in 1986 and 1990

The 1986 acquisition of Dixon by Wichita-based Coleman Company testified to the strength of K.O. Dixon's company, but the transaction was most notable for its lack of effect on the operations in Coffeyville. Coleman sold a bevy of outdoor-related products, everything from campstoves to recreational powerboats to spas. K.O. Dixon's concern about the acquisition stemmed from the concern felt by his dealers and distributors, who looked at the way Coleman conducted its business and arrived at a logical conclusion. Coleman sold numerous products, including lanterns, campstoves, and coolers, through mass merchandisers, a business approach that would sound the death knell for Dixon's distributors and dealers if Coleman decided to operate its new acquisition in a similar fashion. But Coleman did operate several divisions that sold through dealer organizations, such as camping trailers, Skeeter and Mastercraft boats, and its line of spas, which assuaged some of the fears felt by Dixon's distributors and dealers, many of whom relied solely on Dixon products to survive. In the end, all concerns were swept aside, as the potentially divisive acquisition turned out to be a smooth, almost imperceptible, transition. K.O. Dixon remained in charge of the company, and business proceeded as it had prior to the change in ownership, without any changes made to the company's operation or its marketing channels.

Although brief, Dixon's relationship with Coleman proved to be a beneficial one. During the first three years of Coleman ownership, Dixon nearly doubled in size, but in 1989 Coleman's tenure of ownership came to a sudden end. The company was acquired by McAndrews and Forbes Co. in a leveraged buyout, and, as often happens after a takeover, several Coleman divisions were put up for sale. One of those divisions was Dixon, which now found itself thrust into an anxiety-ridden state of limbo. Unlike the deal that led to Coleman's acquisition of Dixon, K.O. Dixon had no control over whom the company's new owners might be, and without such control he could do little to assure Dixon distributors and dealers that they had a guaranteed future with the company. The concerns of 1986 arose again, but this time the situation was much more serious. For a year, the most difficult year in Dixon's history, the company remained on the auction block, scrutinized by competitors and investors, while K.O. Dixon and all those tied to the operations in Coffeyville awaited their fate. In early 1990 news of an interested buyer was announced and, to the relief of K.O. Dixon and all Dixon distributors and dealers, the news was good.

In April 1990 Dixon was acquired by Blount International, Inc., a Montgomery, Alabama-based construction and manufacturing conglomerate. Fortunately for Dixon, history repeated itself during the company's second ownership change in four years. Operation of the company remained the same as it had

during Coleman's ownership, K.O. Dixon remained in charge, and the company's marketing channels remained intact, with the same network of Dixon distributors and dealers selling the company's products. Dixon was organized into Blount's Outdoor Products Group, where it operated alongside three other companies (Oregon Cutting Systems, ICS, and Frederick Manufacturing Corporation).

Dixon in the 1990s

During the first half of the 1990s Blount exited the construction industry—its original business—and focused all of its efforts on its manufacturing companies, which were represented by three business segments: Outdoor Products Group, Industrial & Power Equipment Group, and Outdoor Sports Group. Operating within this multilayered structure, Dixon recorded one of the greatest growth surges in its history, doubling in size during the first half of the decade to eclipse $40 million in sales by 1995. Dixon's distribution methods had been well honed by this point in its history, having evolved away from reliance on distributors who carried multiple lines of outdoor power equipment and toward the preferred method of using direct dealers. Distributors who sold multiple lines of products were still used in sparsely populated areas where they could not survive on Dixon products alone, but 80 percent of Dixon mowers were distributed to direct dealers, who numbered more than 1,000 during the late 1990s. In addition, the company used three distributors who dealt with more than 200 dealers in the United States and Canada. Export distributors handled Dixon products in Europe, Australia, South Africa, New Zealand, and Israel.

On the heels of its rapid growth, Dixon expanded its operations by 39,000 square feet in 1995, giving the company a total of 161,000 square feet of space during the late 1990s. In March 1996 K.O. Dixon retired, but his departure and replacement occurred without disruption, eased by the promotion of a longtime employee named John P. Mowder, who joined Dixon in 1976. By the late 1990s Dixon was selling 15,500 mowers a year, ranging between 30-inch cut models and 60-inch cut models. The Dixon ZTR line was priced between $2,425 and $8,645 in 1998. Although the company's mainstay business was in residential mowers, it was achieving rapid progress during the latter half of the 1990s with mowers intended for commercial use. Nearly half of the company's product line in 1998 consisted of commercial mowers. Looking ahead, the company expected the 200,000th Dixon mower to roll off the production line in March 1999, and sales were projected to approach $80 million by 2002.

Further Reading

Blount International, Inc., "Outdoor Products Group," http://www. blount.com/Cutsytm.html.
"Changes & Continuity," *The Servicing Dealer*, October 1991, p. 22.
Huff, Roger, "Dixon's Idea Led to Coffeyville Industry," *Record: The Coffeyville Journal*, p. 1A.

—Jeffrey L. Covell

Domino Sugar Corporation

1114 Avenue of the Americas
New York, New York 10036-7783
U.S.A.
(212) 789-9700
Fax: (212) 789-9747
Web site: http://www.tate-lyle.co.uk

Wholly Owned Subsidiary of Tate & Lyle plc
Incorporated: 1891 as The American Sugar Refining
   Company
Employees: 330
Sales: $340 million (1997 est.)
SICs: 2062 Cane Sugar Refining

Domino Sugar Corporation is the leading sugar refining firm in the United States, and produces one of the world's most popular and well-known brands of sugar, namely, Domino sugar. One of the oldest companies started in the United States, with a rich historical background of continuous expansion and increasing sales, Domino Sugar Corporation has faced intense competition in the recent past. Although the company's market share is not threatened by competitors who produce refined sugar, such as C&H and Dixie Chrystals, the trend toward noncaloric artificial sweeteners has started to cut into the firm's profits. Moreover, as refined sugar comes under more scrutiny and attack from health food advocates, consumers have become more and more persuaded by negative press reports that a person's weight and general health are affected by eating refined sugar. When Tate & Lyle plc, the large British-owned and operated firm focusing on sugar production, cereal sweeteners, and starch processing, purchased Domino Sugar Company in 1988, Domino used an infusion of cash from its new parent company to undertake not only a comprehensive reorganization but to revitalize a public relations and marketing strategy in order to fight off the threat posed by the growing popularity of artificial sweeteners.

Early History

Domino Sugar Corporation traces its roots back to William Havemeyer, an enterprising English immigrant who had worked as a supervisor in a cane sugar refinery and arrived in New York in 1799. When his brother Frederick, a former sugar boiler, joined him three years later, the two young men saved their money from a baking business they operated together, and then established a sugar refinery on Vandam Street in 1807. The land on which the firm was situated had been leased from Trinity Church and, over the next few years, the Havemeyer brothers were able to purchase the land and expand their business. Named W. & F.C. Havemeyer Company, William and Frederick boiled and refined raw sugar cane in a small one-room building. Yet by 1816, the Havemeyer Company had expanded its operations to such an extent that it was able to produce nearly nine million pounds of sugar annually.

The business the Havemeyer brothers had established could not have started at a more opportune time. During his second voyage, Christopher Columbus brought sugarcane from the Canary Islands to the Caribbean, most probably the present nation of the Dominican Republic. The growing sugar trade in the Americas had a significant impact on the development of the colonies established by the British along the Atlantic coast, and one of the earliest sugar refineries was built in New York in 1689. At the time of the American Revolution against King George III and the armies of England in 1776, there already were numerous sugar refining businesses owned and operated by well-known New York entrepreneurs and families.

By the time the Havemeyer brothers opened their own business during the early part of the 19th century, New York was one of the leading centers in North America for sugar refining and production. Since the dawn of recorded history, all foods had been traditionally sweetened with the addition of either honey or molasses. Refined cane or beet sugar was considered a luxury, too difficult and time-consuming to produce and, consequently, much too expensive for the average American to purchase on a regular basis. When it was refined, the method involved boiling raw sugar in an open vessel, and then straining the product through blankets or cleansing it with bull's blood. Sold in large loaf or piece form, the product was laden with many impurities. However, as refined sugar became more popular, especially as a food staple, the process of sugar refining developed into a major business activity.

The Havemeyer brothers devoted themselves to improving and mechanizing the sugar refining process. At the forefront of modernization within the industry, the two men installed the most sophisticated technologies of the time to help expand their business. No longer boiling raw sugar in an open, cast-iron kettle, they instead used a vacuum pan; and rather than filtering the product with blankets or bull's blood, a new substance known as boneblack was used to clean the sugar. Finally, the Havemeyer brothers thought it most important to provide their customers with the highest quality product possible, so they tested the end product for its purity. With these technological advances in sugar refining, the Havemeyer Corporation grew steadily and, in 1828, the sons of Frederick and William, named Frederick C., Jr., and William F. Havemeyer, followed their fathers' footsteps and assumed management and control of the family firm.

The Late 19th and Early 20th Centuries

Handed down from brother to brother and from father to son, the W. & F.C. Havemeyer Company continued to expand its operations throughout the mid- and latter half of the 19th century. Realizing the need for quick and efficient transportation of the firm's product, the managing members of the family decided to relocate to a new site and build a state-of-the-art sugar refinery on the waterfront in Williamsburg, Brooklyn. When the facility burned to the ground in 1882, a new expanded factory was built on the same site. The rebuilt refinery stood 10 stories high, while its adjacent filter house was a huge building of 13 stories. By the 1890s, the company was producing 1,200 tons of sugar each day, and was widely regarded within the industry as operating the largest sugar refinery in the world. Confident of its future success, the managing family members decided to rename the company in order to reflect its growing reputation and position within the sugar industry. The newly chosen name was simple—the American Sugar Refining Company.

Always at the forefront of technological developments in sugar refining, the company grew larger and larger, forcing many smaller competitors out of business. In fact, by the mid-1890s the American Sugar Refining Company was providing almost 100 percent of the refined sugar purchased by consumers across the United States. Yet when Theodore ''Teddy'' Roosevelt became president of the country after the assassination of William McKinley in the year 1901, Roosevelt used his ''bully pulpit'' and the growing public sentiment against monopolies to enact legislation limiting the control of tobacco, sugar, petroleum, railroad, and steel manufacturing companies engaged in practices that eliminated competition within the marketplace. Suddenly, the prospect of future competition from other sugar refiners became imminent.

The astute leadership of Henry Havemeyer, however, sidestepped the problem. Henry came up with the idea of labeling the company's sugar products with a brand name, and thus Domino sugar was born when the name was applied to

sugar cubes that resembled dominoes. Having a trademark name assured the company of an increased awareness in the public eye, and the company continued to maintain a stranglehold on the sugar refining business in the United States. Proof of the brand name visibility and popularity of Domino sugar was evident when, in spite of being sued by the U.S. government for monopolistic practices within the sugar industry in 1907, the company's sugar products continued to sell best with American consumers.

By the beginning of World War I, however, there were over 100 sweeteners that customers could choose from as an alternative to Domino. The company's marketing strategy grew more aggressive as a result, focusing on convincing grocers to purchase its product in packages rather than ladling it to customers from a bulk container. Most importantly, the ladling of sugar from bulk containers kept customers in the dark about the brand of the sugar. Having convinced grocers to change their traditional method of selling sugar, Domino reaped the success of having greater brand name recognition and the demand that the nameless bulk sugar lacked. By the close of the 1920s, sales of Domino sugar had climbed to its highest level ever.

The 1930s and 1940s

Almost every individual and business was affected during the economic troubles of the 1930s that came to be described in the United States as the Great Depression, except perhaps for the fortunes of the American Sugar Refining Company. At the height of the Depression in 1932 and 1933, the company reported profits of over $5 million for both years. With over 5,000 men and women on its payroll, and five plants located in Boston, Brooklyn, Philadelphia, Baltimore, and New Orleans, the American Sugar Refining Company was regarded by most businessmen as one of the luckiest, and also one of the most well-managed companies in the United States. By the end of the 1930s, sugar consumption was at an all-time high, largely due to the perception that it was nutritious, good for one's health, and had become one of the staples in the American diet.

America's entry into World War II in December 1941 changed the good fortune of the company. The war disrupted the transportation of sugar cane from places such as Cuba and Central America to the company's refineries within the United States. In addition, some of the firm's cargo ships were conscripted by the U.S. Navy for use as war material and troop transports, thus reducing the amount of sugar cane the company was able to bring to its plants. The company's fortunes grew even worse in 1942, when the United States government imposed sugar rationing. From that time onward, until the end of the war in 1945, the American Sugar Refining Company barely made enough money to keep its administrative office and a few of its refineries in operation.

The Postwar Era and Prosperity

When the war ended, the American public's demand for consumer items exploded. For years the average citizen that lived through the war in the United States had gone without any luxuries and endured the time with the basic necessities of life. Now companies that manufactured such items as household appliances, automobiles, and electronic devices were overwhelmed by the public's demand for these products. New foodstuffs were also in great demand, such as soda in a bottle, a wide variety of candy and pastries, and sweeteners for baking and cooking. Of course, the mass production of soda in bottles and candy for the grocery and drugstore shelf required huge amounts of refined sugar. And the American Sugar Refining Company had the sugar cane fields, transportation system, and refineries to meet the ever-growing demand from manufacturers. By the end of the 1950s, the American Sugar Refining Company reported annual sales of over $180 million, and by 1964 annual sales had skyrocketed to $437 million.

In 1970, the board of directors at the company decided to change its name from the American Sugar Refining Company to Amstar Sugar Corporation in order to reflect the growing diversification of the firm into activities other than refining. None of these activities was more important that the firm's entry into the nutritive sweetener market. The company made a major commitment during the early 1970s to produce a new kind of corn syrup called high-fructose corn syrup. Part of this commitment involved a plant expansion at a facility in Dimmitt, Texas, at a cost of over $22 million. The expansion resulted in boosting capacity to produce high-fructose corn syrup to more than 300 million pounds annually. Since the company had been unable to meet the ever-increasing demand from food and drink manufacturers for this sweetener, the cost of the expansion was well worth it. Used in presweetened food and drink products such as cereals, candies, cakes, and soft drinks, the increased capacity for producing high-fructose corn syrup enabled the company to increase its sales to over $1 billion for the first time in its history.

During the 1980s, however, the use of refined sugar came under increasing hostile attack from food advocates and consumer groups. These groups argued that refined sugar was not as healthy as sugar substitutes and artificial sweeteners and, as a result of the negative publicity and increased competition from firms that produced non-caloric, artificial sweeteners, Amstar Sugar Corporation began to lose its market share and experience a loss of revenue. As the company continued to lose its market share, and suffered a continuing decline in revenue, Tate & Lyle plc purchased Amstar Sugar Corporation at a bargain price.

The 1990s and Beyond

As an operating subsidiary of Tate & Lyle, the firm renamed itself Domino Sugar Corporation in 1991, and began to reap the rewards of its rich parent company. During the mid-1990s, the company embarked on an intensive research and development program to develop non-sweet sugar for different food applications. For example, the company's development of such a product, which combined Lactisole, a sweetness inhibitor, with sucrose, enabled it to tone down the sweetness in sports drinks and energy boosting beverages. Another application involved using non-sweet sugar as a fat substitute for frostings, icings, and a variety of frozen desserts. By 1995, the company had received approval for 18 food applications for its non-sweet sugar, including use in low-oil salad dressings.

Under the direction of management at Tate & Lyle, the Domino Sugar Corporation has benefited from increased funding for research and development into artificial sweeteners, and has also modernized its attitude concerning the use of such ingredients in food production. Since sugar is an essential ingredient to the American food processing industry, and since the company has finally jumped into the artificial sweetener market with a splash, Domino Sugar Corporation will remain one of the most visible and enduring companies in American business.

Further Reading

"American Sugar Refining Corporation," *Fortune*, February 1933, pp. 59–65, 115.

"Amstar: Two Parts Sucrose, One Part Fructose and a Heap Of Money," *Financial World*, September 1, 1976, p. 23.

"A History of Domino Sugar Corporation in New York City: 1807 to the Present," New York: Domino Sugar Corporation, 1995.

Holleran, Joan, "Sweet Success," *Beverage Industry*, April 1996, pp. 50–51.

LaBell, Fran, "Sugar Sans Sweetness," *Prepared Foods*, May 1995, p. 123.

"Mixed Picture in the Sugar Group," *Financial World*, February 20, 1963, pp. 9–23.

"A Rose by Any Other Name," *Financial World*, October 1974, p. 28.

—Thomas Derdak

E.I. du Pont de Nemours & Company

1007 Market Street
Wilmington, Delaware 19898
U.S.A.
(302) 774-1000
(800) 441-7515
Fax: (302) 774-7321
Web site: http://www.dupont.com

Public Company
Incorporated: 1915
Employees: 98,000
Sales: $45 billion (1997)
Stock Exchanges: New York
Ticker Symbol: DD
SICs: 2911 Petroleum Refining; 2221 Broadwoven Fabric
     Mills—Manmade; 2819 Industrial Inorganic
     Chemicals, Not Elsewhere Classified; 2869 Industrial
     Organic Chemicals, Not Elsewhere Classified

E.I. du Pont de Nemours & Company is undoubtedly better known by consumers under the moniker DuPont, the oldest family name in American preindustrial wealth. Its reputation is synonymous with organic chemistry. Founded in 1802, the company began as a partnership in gunpowder and explosives. DuPont grew from a family business to a multinational conglomerate through the acquisition of competing companies and through the diversification of product lines. As of 1998 the company operated 30 petroleum refineries and natural gas processing plants through its Conoco subsidiary and 135 manufacturing and processing facilities throughout the world that produced chemicals, synthetic fibers, polymers, and biotech products for a number of different industries.

Company Founding

Founder Éleuthère Irenée du Pont de Nemours was born to French nobility. He studied with the chemist in charge of manufacturing the French government's gunpowder, Antoinne LaVoisier. The years of turmoil preceding the French Revolution caused him to immigrate to the United States in 1797. He chose to build his production facilities on a site on the Delaware's Brandywine River, which was central to all of the states at the time and provided sufficient water power to run the mills. Du Pont rapidly established a reputation for superior gunpowder. He died in 1834, leaving his sons Alfred and Henry to buy out French financiers and continue the business. His sons expanded the company's product line into the manufacture of smokeless powder, dynamite, and nitroglycerine.

One century after its founding, the gunpowder and explosives combine faced dissolution when senior partner Eugene du Pont died at the age of 62, after having served 42 years. With no new leadership, the surviving partners decided to sell the company to the highest bidder. Alfred I. du Pont, a distant relative of the founder, purchased the firm with the aid of his cousins. Alfred was intent on saving the family business. Although he had grown up working in gunpowder yards, he lacked the organizational skills needed to run the firm. His cousins Pierre S. du Pont and Thomas Coleman possessed the financial acumen and led the family company to unprecedented success. The purchase price was set at $12 million, but secret investigations by the cousins unveiled company assets conservatively valued at $24 million. The old partnership also held a great deal of undervalued shares in other companies, among them their direct competitors in the gunpowder business, Hazard and Laflin & Rand. Not having the initial capital for the purchase, the young cousins negotiated a leveraged buyout, giving them a 25 percent interest in the new corporation and four percent paid on $12 million over the next 30 years. Coleman was president, Pierre treasurer, and Alfred vice-president of E.I. du Pont de Nemours & Company. The only cash involved in the takeover was $8,500 in incorporation fees.

Sound management, luck, and hidden wealth resulted in the acquisition of 54 companies within three years. Pierre set out to dominate the industry through payoffs and by purchasing minority shareholders and vulnerable competitors. When the cousins first incorporated in 1902, the company controlled 36 percent of the U.S. powder market. By 1905 it held a 75 percent share of the market. DuPont alone supplied 56 percent of the

Company Perspectives:

Core Purpose: To be the world's most successful energy and chemistry-based company, dedicated to creating high quality, innovative materials that make people's lives better and easier.

People: Our goals can only be achieved through outstanding, committed, creative people. We will foster an environment that creates spirit, energy and a commitment to win—an environment in which our capable and diverse workforce sees personal growth and success being directly related to DuPont's success.

Value: Goals and strategies may change, but our values will remain constant. These values unite all of our businesses and are the foundation of our efforts to provide value to DuPont's stakeholders—our shareholders, our customers, our employees and society.

DuPont has a long tradition of innovation and discovery. We create value through science and technology, making a difference in people's lives, both today and in the future.

We are committed to safety and environmental stewardship—enhancing the quality of life of our employees and the communities in which we operate. Our goal is zero injuries, illnesses, incidents, waste and emissions.

We remain dedicated to the enduring values of integrity, high ethical standards and treating people fairly and with respect.

national production of explosives, with $60 million in estimated assets; it had become one of the nation's largest corporations.

A new method of operation was required to keep track of the rapidly growing organization. The cousins solicited the aid of Amory Haskell and Hamilton Barksdale, managers who had reorganized their dynamite business into an efficient organization. They remodeled the unwieldy company using elaborate family tree charts composed of levels of managers. The new structure revolutionized American business and gave birth to the modern corporation. The system of organization worked so well that Pierre bailed out the then struggling General Motors Corporation, buying 23 percent of the shares and applying the skills DuPont had perfected. (The Department of Justice later ordered DuPont to divest its General Motors holdings in 1951.)

A Gunpowder Monopoly by 1900

DuPont grew to command the entire explosives market. So dominant were they by 1907 that the U.S. government initiated antitrust proceedings against them. DuPont was deemed a gunpowder monopoly in 1912 and ordered to divest itself of a substantial portion of its business. In addition, early years of incorporation were fraught with tension between Alfred and his more practical cousins. Arguments ensued over the modernization of the Brandywine yards. Coleman and Pierre saw modernization as the only way to fully utilize the plant. The quarrel, along with other incidents, prompted Coleman and Pierre to take away Alfred's responsibilities in 1911. In effect, this left Alfred a vice-president in name only.

Modernization, diversification, good management, and a command of the market characterized DuPont's industrial era phase. The experiments of DuPont chemists with a product known as guncotton, an early form of nitroglycerine, led to the company's involvement in the textile business. The end of World War I proved the peacetime use of artificial fibers to be more profitable than explosives. In the 1920s DuPont acquired French rights for producing cellophane. DuPont made it moistureproof, transforming cellophane from a decorative wrap to a packaging material for food and other products. DuPont also produced the clothing fiber Rayon in the 1920s, and used a stronger version of the fiber for auto tire cord.

Developed Synthetics in the Mid-20th Century

DuPont gradually moved away from explosives and into synthetics. Their most important discovery, Nylon, was created in 1930 by a polymer research group headed by Wallace H. Carothers. The synthesis of nylon came from the hypothesis that polymeric substances were practically endless chains held together by ordinary chemical bonds. Long chain molecules could be built one step at a time by carrying out well-understood reactions between standard types of organic chemicals. Carothers chose one of nature's simplest reactions—alcohols reacting with acids to form esters. By reacting compounds with alcohol groups on each end with analogous acids, polyesters were produced. Super polymers were later formed when a molecular still was used to extract the water that was formed in the reaction. The excess water had created a chemical equilibrium that stopped reaction and limited chain growth. Experimentation with diamine-dibasic pairs produced a molten polyamide that could be drawn into filaments, cooled, and stretched to form very strong fibers. DuPont later marketed a 6–6 polymer, which was made from the inexpensive starting compound Benzene. The new fiber proved remarkably successful. It was employed as a material for undergarments, stockings, tire cord, auto parts, and brushes.

A large number of plastics and fibers followed. Products such as Neoprene (synthetic rubber), Lucite (a clear, tough plastic resin), and Teflon (a resin used in nonstick cookware) became commonplace, as did Orlon (a bulky acrylic fiber), Dacron polyester, and Mylar. DuPont quickly became known as the world's most proficient synthesizer. The range of textiles that they supplied reoriented the whole synthetic field.

Not every DuPont invention was a success, however. Corfam, a synthetic leather product, proved to be a disaster. Lammont du Pont Copeland, the last du Pont to head the company, invested millions of dollars into promoting Corfam in the 1960s. The product was not successful because, although the material lasted practically forever, it lacked the flexibility and breathability usually found in leather products. Lammont relinquished the chief executive post in 1967 and was succeeded by Charles B. McCoy, son of a DuPont executive. Irving Shapiro took the post in 1974. Shapiro had served DuPont well, acting as the principal lawyer negotiating the antitrust suit brought against DuPont and General Motors Corporation.

Shapiro led DuPont for six years during a period when the fibers industry stagnated from overcapacity. DuPont's stream of synthetic fiber discoveries had led it into a trap, for it left them content to exploit the fiber market without looking elsewhere for new products. The demand for fibers collapsed in the mid-1970s, causing a halt in the company's main business. Climbing raw material costs and declining demand combined to depress the market in 1979. The innovator of a new technology had been the last to recognize that the market it created was losing momentum. The collapse compelled DuPont to concentrate exclusively on repairing its old business, delaying actions to create a new base. DuPont's rebuilding efforts were also hindered by reducing its commitment to research and development. Continued reliance on fibers caused DuPont to be one of the worst hit chemical companies in the 1980 recession.

DuPont's continued attention to the fibers business, however, resulted in an important discovery in 1980. Kevlar was added to the company's assemblage of synthetic textiles. DuPont scientist Stephanie Kwolek discovered the solvent that unclumped the hard chains of molecules comprising an intractable polymer. The resultant revolutionary material proved to be light yet strong, possessing a tensile strength five times that of steel. Fabrics made of Kevlar were heat and puncture resistant. When laminated, Kevlar outstripped fiberglass. DuPont made the largest financial gamble in its history, investing $250 million in a Kevlar plant expansion. Applications for Kevlar ranged from heat resistant gloves, fire resistant clothing, and bullet resistant vests to cables and reinforcement belting in tires. Kevlar also proved successful in the fabrics industry: one half of the police force in the United States soon wore Kevlar vests. Kevlar's true success, however, depended on the price of its raw material—oil. Kevlar showed no threat of becoming a steel replacement, since the price of its production was considerably higher.

Diversification in the Early 1980s

DuPont reacted to the depressed market in textiles by arranging mergers and acquisitions of other companies in other industries. DuPont's takeover of the Conoco Oil company (the United States' number two petroleum firm) was the largest merger in history. Issues of antitrust were prevalent in negotiation for the merger, but in the end DuPont bought Conoco for $7.8 billion. DuPont merged with Conoco to protect itself from the rise in crude oil prices. As oil supplies dwindled, a supply of Conoco oil and coal as raw material for DuPont's chemicals provided a competitive advantage. Conoco's sites in Alberta, Canada, and off the north slope of Alaska provided large amounts of these resources. DuPont's only disadvantage in the Conoco takeover was the introduction of Edgar Bronfman, chairman of the Seagram Company, the world's largest liquor distiller, into a minority position in DuPont-Conoco. Conoco had been a major acquisition target for Seagram. The merger left Seagram with 20 percent of DuPont. Bronfman saw himself as a long-term investor in DuPont and desired an important voice in the company's direction. However, Seagram and DuPont arrived at an agreement whereby Seagram could not purchase more than 25 percent of DuPont stock until 1991.

Growth and greater financial security came to DuPont in 1980 when they bought Remington Arms, a manufacturer of sporting firearms and ammunition. The Remington Arms unit of DuPont made a number of multimillion-dollar contracts with the army to operate government-owned plants. DuPont also expanded its scope in the early 1980s with other major purchases. New England Nuclear Corporation, a leading manufac-

turer of radioactive chemicals for medical research and diagnosis, was acquired in April 1981, and Solid State Dielectrics, a supplier of dielectric materials used in the manufacture of multilayer capacitors, was acquired in April 1982.

DuPont management was determined to reduce the company's dependence on petrochemicals. It decided to take some risks in becoming a leader in the life sciences by delving into development and production of biomedical products and agricultural chemicals. In April 1982 DuPont purchased the agrichemicals division of SEPIC. In November the company acquired the production equipment and technology for the manufacture of spiral wound reverse osmosis desalting products. In March 1986 DuPont acquired Elit Circuits Inc., a producer of molded circuit interconnects.

In addition to mergers and acquisitions, DuPont became heavily involved in joint ventures. DuPont had agreements with P.D. Magnetics to develop, manufacture, and sell magnetic tape. It also became involved with PPG Industries to manufacture ethylene glycol. Aided by Olin Corporation, it planned to construct a chlor/alkali production facility. DuPont also forged extensive connections with Japanese industry. The 1980s united them with Sankyo Company (to develop, manufacture, and market pharmaceuticals), Idemitso Petrochemicals (to produce and market butanediol), Mitsubishi Gas Chemical Company, and Mitsubishi Rayon Company. Furthermore, DuPont established connections in Europe. They became partners with N.V. Phillips (to produce optical discs), EKA AB (to produce and market the Compozil chemical system for papermaking processes), and British Telecom (to develop and manufacture optoelectronic components).

In addition to stock chemicals and petrochemically based synthetic fibers, DuPont looked to the life sciences and other specialty businesses to produce earnings. Edward G. Jefferson, a chemist by training, succeeded Shapiro and directed the company into the biosciences and other specialty lines. DuPont supported these businesses with large amounts of capital investment and research and development expenditures. The company's fields of interest were genetic engineering, drugs and agricultural chemicals, electronics, and fibers and plastics.

DuPont had the kind of multinational marketing capability and resources to become a major influence in the life sciences. The company sought ways to restructure living cells to mass produce specific microorganisms in an attempt to manufacture commercial quantities of interferon, a human protein that was considered potentially useful in fighting viruses and cancer. DuPont claimed to be the first company to have purified fibroblast interferon, one of the three types of human interferon in the mid-1970s. DuPont developed a blood profile system, artificial blood, and a test for acquired immune deficiency syndrome (AIDS). They created drugs that control irregular heartbeats, aid rheumatoid arthritis pain, and were antinarcotic agents. In addition to new drugs, DuPont worked to develop new pesticides and herbicides. DuPont built a $450 million business as a major supplier to the electronics industry, providing sophisticated connectors and the dry film used in making printed circuits. DuPont also developed new high-performance plastics. The company's scientists developed a process called group transfer polymerization for solvent-based polymer acrylics, which was the first major polymerization process developed since the early 1950s.

In the early to mid-1980s DuPont had approximately 90 major businesses selling a wide range of products to different industries, including petroleum, textile, transportation, chemical construction, utility, healthcare, and agricultural industries. Business operations existed in more than 50 nations. DuPont had eight principle business segments: biomedical products; industrial and consumer products; fibers; polymer products; agricultural and industrial chemicals; petroleum exploration and production; petroleum refining, marketing and transportation; and coal. Total expenditure for research and development amounted to more than $1 billion in 1985, and over 6,000 scientists and engineers were engaged in research activities.

Refocusing on Core Businesses in the Late 1980s

However, by this time DuPont was bloated with the numerous businesses it had acquired over the years. Management decided to return to its former policy of focusing on areas of maximum profit. It began moving away from commodity production, instead concentrating on oil, healthcare, electronics, and specialty chemicals.

By 1987 the changes were paying off in some areas, as discretionary cash flow reached $4.5 billion. Biomedical products represented only four percent of sales, but the firm was moving into the large markets for cancer and AIDS testing and research. Breaking into its new markets was expensive, however. Earnings soared at rivals Rhone-Poulenc and Dow Chemical, which were less diversified. Meanwhile DuPont's pretax income climbed only 4.5 percent, to 3.8 billion in 1988, although sales climbed by eight percent. DuPont still had problems with quality control. In 1988 Ford Motor Co. gave DuPont's contract for mirror housings to General Electric because paint kept flaking off DuPont's plastic, according to an April 1989 *Business Week* article.

Edgar Smith Woolard, Jr., became president in 1989, backed by the Bronfman family. As part of his mission to raise the price of DuPont's stock and prevent a takeover, the firm bought back about eight percent of its outstanding stock. The electronics division had $1.8 billion in annual sales and had won business in films and imaging, though it was losing money in the highly competitive areas of fiber optics and optical disks. In addition, the pharmaceuticals business was still losing money. Investment in research and equipment had reached $1.8 billion since 1982, yet most of the drugs under development were years from the market. One area of clear success was DuPont's textile business. The $5.8 billion division was the firm's most profitable.

Seeking to raise public awareness of its fibers, DuPont started a consumer products catalogue featuring household items made from its products. The catalogue mentioned copyrighted fiber names like Lycra, Zytel, and Supplex as it advertised the clothes, sporting goods, and housewares. DuPont had reason to be interested in maintaining brand-name recognition in fibers. Lucre, a stretch polymer invented in 1959 and originally used for girdles, became a huge hit after being adopted for biking clothes and other exercise outfits during the early 1980s. By the end of the decade, Lucre clothing had become fashion-

able. Big name designers incorporated it into their wardrobes, and by 1990, Lucre profits topped $200 million a year. DuPont's patent on Lucre, the generic name of which is spandex, had long since expired, but DuPont had continued to improve the fabric and was its only major manufacturer. To make certain things stayed that way, the firm announced in 1990 that it would spend $500 million over three years to build or expand Lucre plants.

Another important area for DuPont was pollution control and cleanup. According to *Forbes* magazine, the firm was one of the country's biggest air polluters and was in the process of spending well over $1 billion on pollution control and cleanup. The firm's chlorofluorocarbon business was being replaced by chemicals less harmful to the ozone layer, at a cost of another $1 billion. DuPont also stood to make money, however, by creating safer herbicides and expanding into the growing recycling market. Partly because of these trends, DuPont's sales of agricultural chemicals tripled between 1985 and 1990, to $1.7 billion.

The Gulf War temporarily drove up oil prices and refinery margins, leading to profits of over $1 billion for Conoco in 1990. But a worldwide recession was hurting most of the rest of the company. Profits for 1991 fell to $1.4 billion on sales of $38.7 billion, down from sales of $40 billion in 1990. The firm's electronics products had garnered little prestige within the industry and had fallen well behind earlier projections. Consequently, DuPont began pulling back, beginning by selling an electronic connectors business with $400 million in annual sales. DuPont also took a step back from pharmaceuticals, putting that division into a joint venture with Merck & Co.

Although the company had been divesting businesses for a few years, it accelerated its efforts at streamlining in the early 1990s. With 133,000 employees and numerous management layers in 1991, DuPont was ready to cut back the bureaucracy. Chairman and CEO Edgar S. Woolard took several classic steps to restructure the company. The number of employees was reduced steadily in the early 1990s, to 97,000 in 1996, and several layers of vice-presidents and managers were eliminated. The remaining employees were given stock options for 600 shares each to encourage a sense of ownership and responsibility for the company. Executives were required to own shares more than equal to their annual salary. "Everyone is now connected to the company," John A. Krol, who became CEO in 1995, told *Forbes* in 1997. "They post the price of DuPont stock on watercoolers and safety signs around the company."

DuPont also continued to sharpen its focus on its core businesses of chemicals and fibers. The firm closed its declining Orlon division and in 1991 it sold half of Consolidation Coal Co. for over $1 billion to Germany's Rheinbraun A.G. In addition, Du Pont sold all of its medical products businesses. In 1993 the company also sold its acrylic business to ICI and in turn bought ICI's nylon business and later its worldwide polyester films, resins, and intermediates businesses. By acquiring the ICI polyester technology, DuPont could make plastic bottles, a growing market, for less than anyone else in the world. The company increased its marketing of synthetic fibers. DuPont looked for new uses for its popular spandex fabric Lycra, its high-performance fiber Tyvek (best-known for its use in Federal Express envelopes), and its synthetic Kevlar.

Record Profits in the Mid-1990s

After several years of declining profits (from $2.5 billion in 1989 to $0.6 billion in 1993), DuPont reaped the rewards from the restructuring years. The company reported a streak of record profits in the mid-1990s, beginning in 1994 with a net income of $2.7 billion and continuing through 1996 with a net income of $3.6 billion. The company's stock price enjoyed a corresponding rise: from a low around $15 a share in 1990 to a high of almost $50 in 1996.

Some of these earnings were used in 1995 to buy back the shares owned by Seagram since 1980. To raise money for a venture into showbusiness, Seagram sold its 24 percent stake in DuPont back to the company for $8.8 billion, a discount of 13 percent from the market value of the stock at the time.

Conoco played an important role in the rejuvenation of DuPont. In 1995 some analysts (and DuPont shareholders) were recommending DuPont sell off the subsidiary, which they felt was not even returning the cost of its capital. After scrutinizing the numbers, the DuPont management team decided to hold on to Conoco but reevaluate its decision in a year. In 1996 Conoco returned $860 million in net earnings and bought the support of DuPont's board. In 1997 Conoco acquired heavy oil reserves in Venezuela and a gas field in Texas, thus increasing its oil reserves by 50 percent.

Joint ventures continued to be an important strategy for DuPont in the mid- to late 1990s. From 12 joint ventures in 1990, DuPont had reached 37 by 1997. Among the most significant were its partnership with the Japanese chemical firm Asahi to market synthetic fibers in Asia, the 50–50 venture with Dow called DuPont Dow Elastomers, and the alliance with Pioneer Hi-Bred International to form Optimum Quality Grains.

DuPont reaffirmed its commitment to the life sciences as a core business in the late 1990s. Bioindustrial, pharmaceutical, and feed and food industries were seen as the new ground for the increasing integration of chemistry and biotechnology. As part of this push, in 1997 DuPont purchased Protein Technologies International, which developed soy-based products, from Ralston Purina for $1.5 billion. The following year the company agreed to buy Merck's 50 percent share in the joint venture DuPont Merck Pharmaceutical Company.

In 1998 DuPont announced its intention to divest Conoco, presumably as part of its effort to focus on core businesses. The divestment would begin with an initial public offering of as much as 20 percent of the energy subsidiary, from which

DuPont anticipated a return of up to $7.5 billion. With a second quarter decline in earnings in 1998 of 12 percent, the fall IPO was seen by analysts as a way to boost earnings and share price and further invest in DuPont's growing biotech business.

Principal Subsidiaries

Conoco Inc.; Marshall Labs Inc.; Carbide Biochemicals, Inc.; DuPont Canada Inc.; DuPont Asia Pacific Ltd.; Crosfield Electronics Limited; Conoco (U.K.) Ltd.; Conoco Norway, Inc.; Conoco Ireland Ltd.; Conoco Mineraloel Gmbh (Germany).

Principal Divisions

Consol; DuPont Agricultural Products; DuPont Automotive Products; DuPont Belle Plant; DuPont Biomedicals Department; DuPont Chambers Works; DuPont Chemicals; DuPont Electronics; DuPont Fabricated Products; DuPont Fibers; DuPont Imaging Systems; DuPont International; DuPont Materials & Logistics; DuPont Medical Products; DuPont NDT Systems; DuPont Pharmaceuticals; DuPont Photomasks; DuPont Polymer Products; DuPont Printing & Publishing; DuPont/Shell.

Further Reading

Chandler, Alfred D., Jr., and Stephen Salsbury, *Pierre S. du Pont and the Making of the Modern Corporation,* New York: Harper & Row, 1971.

Colby, Gerald, *du Pont Dynasty,* Secaucus, N.J.: Lyle Stuart, 1984.

Lenzer, Robert, and Carrie Shook, ''There Will Always Be a DuPont,'' *Forbes,* October 13, 1997, pp. 60–69.

Mosley, Leonard, *Blood Relations: The Rise and Fall of the du Ponts of Delaware,* New York: Atheneum, 1980.

Norman, James R., ''Turning Up the Heat at DuPont,'' *Forbes,* August 5, 1991.

Plishner, Emily S., ''The Dilemma: Will DuPont's New CEO Spin Off Conoco?,'' *Financial World,* December 5, 1995, pp. 34–37.

Scherreik, Susan, ''Analysts Are Standing by DuPont,'' *Money,* September 1998, p. 32.

Taylor, Graham D., and Patricia E. Sudnik, *DuPont and the International Chemical Industry,* Boston: Twayne, 1984.

Weber, Joseph, ''DuPont's Trailblazer Wants to Get Out of the Woods,'' *Business Week,* August 31, 1992.

——, ''DuPont's Version of a Maverick,'' *Business Week,* April 3, 1989.

Weiner, Steve, ''But Will They Ever Know Zytel from Lycra?,'' *Forbes,* June 26, 1989.

—Scott M. Lewis
—updated by Susan Windisch Brown

El Corte Inglés Group

Calle Hermosilla, 112
28009 Madrid
Spain
(91) 401 9200
Fax: (91) 402 5821
Web site: http://www.elcorteingles.es

Private Company
Incorporated: 1940 as El Corte Inglés, S.L.
Employees: 50,000
Sales: US$8.2 billion (1996 est.)
SICs: 5311 Department Stores; 5399 Variety Stores;
5411 Grocery Stores; 2731 Books: Publishing, or
Printing & Publishing; 4724 Travel Agencies; 4725
Tour Operators; 6311 Life Insurance; 6321 Accident
& Health Insurance; 6399 Insurance Carriers, Not
Elsewhere Classified; 7361 Computer Programming
Services

El Corte Inglés, S.A. is a private company that forms the core of the El Corte Inglés Group and was incorporated on January 2, 1952, from the limited liability company El Corte Inglés S.L., itself incorporated on June 28, 1940. The company runs Spain's largest chain of department stores, with about 55 stores under the Corte Inglés name, and the Hipercor hypermarket chain, through a subsidiary operation. It also operates, through additional subsidiaries, a wide range of services, including travel agencies, insurance, computer services, and the publication of university texts. El Corte Inglés is by far the largest privately held company in Spain, is the third largest company overall in that country (behind Telefónia and Repsol), and is the nation's largest retailer.

Entrepreneurial Origins

El Corte Inglés has become a model for the Spanish business world, owing to the efforts of its founder, Ramón Areces Rodriguez, and the firm's directors. The history of El Corte Inglés is closely linked with the life of Areces. Born in 1905 in Asturias, he emigrated to Cuba in 1919 aboard the ship *Alfonso XII,* following his brother, who had emigrated a few years earlier. With help from his uncle, César Rodriguez, Areces was able to find work in the department store El Encanto, owned by a Spanish family. At El Encanto he worked alongside José (Pepín) Fernández Rodriguez, his uncle's cousin, who would later become Areces's business rival in Spain.

El Encanto employed some of the retail management techniques that had been developed in the United States, based in particular on diversification and aggressiveness. Wishing to improve his understanding of business administration, Areces left Cuba in 1924 to go to New York and Montreal with César Rodriquez. For a year and a half he worked in a New York export firm, learning about international trade.

In 1928 at the age of 23, Areces returned to work in Cuba for six years before deciding to return to Spain to set up his own business. Spain was on the verge of civil war, but Areces launched directly into business nonetheless. He established himself in Madrid and invested his Cuban savings in the acquisition of a tailor's shop. This shop was strategically located in the center of Madrid, and had exits onto three streets, Preciados, Rompelanzas, and Carmen. Areces paid Pta 150,000 for the tailor's shop and changed everything except the store's name, El Corte Inglés.

The business started out with seven employees and was an immediate success, causing the company to expand quickly. In 1940, shortly after the end of the Spanish civil war, the business was moved to a location on Preciados Street, where Areces bought the department store El Aguila. The store would be converted, after several extensions, into the firm's first commercial shopping center. Areces's cousin, José Fernández, bought the original shop on Rompelanzas Street from him; it became the first store of the Galerías Preciados department store chain after it had been expanded several times.

On June 28, 1940, Ramón Areces Rodriguez formed El Corte Inglés, S.L., a limited liability company with a capital of Pta 1 million, with his younger brothers Luis and Celestino. In July 1949 the company formed Industrias y Confecciones, S.A.

(Induyco) as an independent company. It became a joint stock company in December 1955. Induyco was established to make clothes, as part of the founder's clear vision of vertical expansion and integration for El Corte Inglés. The aim of the new company was to ensure the supply of manufactured clothes to meet the demand at the shop in Preciados Street. This decision was made because during the civil war the Spanish clothing industry found itself facing great difficulties owing to the shortage of raw materials and capital to buy machinery and other basic items.

To ensure the company's continued development, it was changed into a joint-stock venture, being incorporated as El Corte Inglés, S.A. on January 2, 1952. At first Induyco manufactured clothes exclusively for El Corte Inglés, but later it began trading with clients outside the group. Induyco is not part of the El Corte Inglés Group, although El Corte Inglés S.A.'s president is also president of Induyco.

Ramón Areces Rodriguez did not have any children. He brought his 18-year-old nephew, Isidoro Alvarez, onto the staff of El Corte Inglés in 1953. Alvarez continued to study economics and business at the Complutense University, and in 1957 graduated with special distinction. Areces dedicated his time to training Alvarez. Alvarez was made a member of the board of directors of El Corte Inglés in 1959, having started in the company's warehouse and then worked in many of the firm's departments.

Ramón Areces Rodriguez's rival, Pepín Fernández, managing Galerías Preciados, had taken a great lead over him, with Galerías Preciados having a merchandise turnover 20 times greater than El Corte Inglés in 1960. Ramón Areces Rodriguez had to develop a strategy that would distinguish him from his competitor. He decided to change his shop's image to that of a store offering luxury goods. If Galerías Preciados worked on the principle of making huge sales of a wide range of products at cheap prices, El Corte Inglés would concentrate on offering personalized service and specialized articles. Areces's business strategy and his decision to start up business in Barcelona in 1962 were prompted by an external factor, a managerial crisis at Galerías Preciados, which affected that company's image and permitted Areces to achieve supremacy in the large department store sector.

Expansion and Diversification, 1965–89

The time from 1965 to 1975 was a boom period for El Corte Inglés. The opening of the El Corte Inglés department store in Barcelona was the first step in a policy of expansion that led to the opening of 20 shopping centers that were still open into the 1990s. This evolution was the result not only of the particular activities El Corte Inglés had developed in its department stores, but also of its strategy of vertical expansion and integration and its development of diversified services and activities.

In May 1966 El Corte Inglés shareholders formed the company Móstoles Industrial S.A. This company, with a capitalization of Pta 4 million, arose from the consolidation of the group's divisions dealing with window displays and wooden kitchen furniture. (Móstoles Industrial is not included in the El Corte Inglés Group.) In November 1969 the travel agency company

Viajes El Corte Inglés, S.A. was formed as a fully owned subsidiary of El Corte Inglés. With initial capital of Pta 5 million, it grew out of the company department that had previously organized staff vacations. At the beginning of the 1990s it was the second-largest of El Corte Inglés's subsidiaries by turnover, having established itself as the largest travel agency in Spain. Its turnover for the fiscal year 1990 was Pta 41.11 billion.

To help ensure the growth of the group, Induyco was strengthened by the creation of two additional companies, Confecciónes Teruel, S.A., incorporated in May 1975, and Industrias del Vestido, S.A., incorporated in June 1976. Both were set up as fully owned subsidiaries of El Corte Inglés. A further fully owned subsidiary, Construcción, Promociones e Instalaciones, S.A., was formed in May 1976 to meet the construction needs of the firms within the group.

The Ramón Areces Foundation was formed in 1976. Its purpose, apart from arranging a secure future for the company in the case of Ramón Areces Rodriguez's death, was to encourage scientific research, award grants, and support training programs, publications, and cultural activities in general. Its projects included the computerization of the Archivo de Indias in Seville, in collaboration with IBM and the Ministry of Culture, assisting with grants for overseas studies, and the support of organizations such as the Centro de Biología Molecular and the University of Navarra.

Hipercor, S.A., another of El Corte Inglés's fully owned subsidiaries, was founded in 1979 with a capital of Pta 1 million, which increased to Pta 1 billion the following year. Hipercor, operating in the hypermarket sector, based its strategy on combining the traditional hypermarket concept of low prices with the range of products and the customer care of a large department store. Hypermarkets typically combined grocery stores, nonfood retailing, and service businesses. The Hipercor centers covered a large surface area like a hypermarket. Within Tiendas Cortty, little shops gave the impression of independent franchise operations and sold products exclusive to El Corte Inglés under the Cortty trademark. Hipercor grew spectacularly during the 1980s. Its sales figure rose to Pta 121.77 billion in 1990, making it the group's largest subsidiary.

Induyco created two important new companies in the 1980s. Investrónica S.A. was incorporated in 1980 and was involved in the electronics and computer sector, in particular in the manufacture of microcomputers and hi-fi equipment and the design of software. The second, Invesgen S.A., was incorporated in 1985 and was geared toward the use of advanced technologies in biochemistry and genetics.

El Corte Inglés also created two new subsidiaries in the early 1980s. In 1982 it created Centro de Seguros, Correduría de Seguros, S.A., an insurance broker and assessor also offering family policies. In 1984, it created Videcor S.A., dedicated to the development of video clubs in El Corte Inglés's and Hipercor's shopping centers. Centro de Seguros developed successfully, collecting Pta 7.09 billion in premiums in 1990. Videcor ceased to exist as a public limited company in August 1988 and its activities were transferred to El Corte Inglés.

In 1983, branching out onto the international market, El Corte Inglés bought The Harris Company in the United States, which ran a chain of medium-sized stores in California and also owned various shopping centers.

In February 1988 Informática El Corte Inglés was formed to sell computer products and services to large firms and public institutions using computer centers and data processing. The subsidiary's turnover for the fiscal year 1990 was Pta 12.40 billion.

The year 1988 also saw the foundation of the publishing company Editorial Centro de Estudios Ramón Areces, S.A. Its aim was to become a publisher of texts for universities, and in particular of works needed for courses at the Ramón Areces Center for University Studies. In 1990 sales totaled Pta 295 million.

In December 1989 El Corte Inglés formed two insurance companies. The first, Seguros El Corte Inglés, Vida, Pensiones y Reaseguros S.A., covered life assurance and underwriting. The second, Seguros El Corte Inglés, Ramos Generales y Reaseguros S.A., covered accident, health, and travel insurance, as well as damages. El Corte Inglés had a 99.9 percent holding in these two companies; their accounts were separate from El Corte Inglés since their activities differed from those of other firms in the group.

El Corte Inglés also developed into a major competitor of the Spanish banks. It offered consumer credit in the manner of a bank or savings society. It held accounts for its employees, where they could cash or deposit their paychecks and take care of the expenses and purchases that they made within the company. El Corte Inglés introduced personal credit cards for its stores in 1967, and in 1991 it was the largest issuer of personal credit cards in Spain, with around 1.8 million in issue.

1989 Leadership Change

Ramón Areces Rodriguez died on July 30, 1989, leaving all his capital inheritance to the Ramón Areces Foundation. As a result, the foundation received Pta 36.5 billion. This effectively meant that the Ramón Areces Foundation controlled the business group, holding practically all the shares in the group's companies except for the insignificant number owned by the administrative board.

After Ramón Areces Rodriguez's death, the administrative board agreed unanimously to appoint Isidoro Alvarez as the new president of El Corte Inglés on August 1, 1989. Thus Alvarez took the position of patron and president for life of the Ramón Areces Foundation board of patrons.

Alvarez inherited a paternalistic style of management from Areces and rigorously followed the latter's stated principles of prudent investment, careful reinvestment of profits, and the avoidance of incurring unnecessary debts with banks. His initial aims were to compete successfully with the great retail multinationals, to increase the group's international ventures, and to raise profit margins. From his numerous trips and connections abroad he had an excellent knowledge of retailing outside of Spain. He was also intimately involved with Areces in El Corte Inglés's expansion, including the development of the Hipercor network and its expansion into new areas of business. In the fiscal year 1990, El Corte Inglés, S.A.'s sales rose to Pta 646.54

billion, representing an increase of 16.7 percent over the previous year.

Acquired Galerías in 1995

The most significant event of the 1990s for El Corte Inglés was its June 1995 acquisition of its great rival, Galerías Preciados. Galerías had fallen on hard times, having run up huge debts in the 1970s, then being taken over by its main creditor in 1977. Over the next 17 years, it had six different owners before applying for bankruptcy protection at the end of 1994. El Corte Inglés won the bidding for Galerías with an offer of Pta 30 billion (US$245 million), thereby adding the chain's 30 large department stores to its own 33. The purchase added an additional 13 cities to the company's market penetration, as well as giving it a total of 12 stores in Madrid and five in Barcelona. Acquiring Galerías also solidified El Corte Inglés's position as the top retailer in Spain and also propelled it to the number three position overall among all Spanish companies, trailing only telecommunications giant Telefónia and petrochemical concern Repsol.

El Corte Inglés spent another Pta 50 billion (US$410 million) to transform most of the Galerías units into Corte Inglés stores, reopening them in time for the Christmas buying season of 1995. Several of the acquired stores that were close to existing Corte Inglés stores were not converted, but were slated to be used in experimenting with new formats. Of particular interest were the development of "category killer" formats, the large specialty stores that were the hot retailing concept of the 1990s in the United States. As usual, El Corte Inglés was well aware of this trend and in August 1995 opened three new large format stores in Madrid: one selling records, videos, audio equipment, televisions, and musical instruments; one selling books; and one selling toys and video games.

In June 1997 El Corte Inglés entered into a 50–50 joint venture with Repsol to develop a chain of supermarket-style service stations. The stores were operated under the Supercor name and sold food, produce, and other supermarket products at service stations.

El Corte Inglés's 1983 expansion into the United States ran into difficulty in the 1990s when the Harris chain consistently lost money because of declining sales. In July 1998 Fresno, California-based Gottschalks Inc. reached an agreement with El Corte Inglés to acquire the assets of Harris. In return, El Corte Inglés gained a 20 percent stake in privately held Gottschalks, operator of 37 Gottschalks department stores and 22 Village East specialty stores in California, Nevada, Oregon, and Washington.

Principal Subsidiaries

Hipercor, S.A.; Viajes El Corte Inglés, S.A.; Informática El Corte Inglés, S.A.; Construcción, Promociones e Instalaciones, S.A.; Centro de Seguros, Correduría de Seguros, S.A.; Editorial Centro de Estudios Ramón Areces, S.A.

Further Reading

Areces, Ramón, "Discurso de investidura de Doctor Honoris Causa por la Universidad de Oviedo," 1987.

Bueno Campos, E., "El caso El Corte Inglés," in *Dirección estratégica de la empresa, Metodología, técnicas y casos,* Madrid: Ediciones Pirámide S.A., 1987.

Bueno Campos, E., and Morcillo, P., "El Corte Inglés-Hipercor," in *La dirreción eficiente,* Madrid: Ediciones Pirámide S.A., 1990.

Burns, Tom, "El Corte Inglés Buys Galerias," *Financial Times,* June 8, 1995, p. 32.

——, "Popular Landmarks," *Financial Times,* September 18, 1996, p. S4.

Celma, J., "El misterio de El Corte Inglés" in *Anuario de la Distribución,* 1990.

Cuartas, Javier, *Biografia de "El Corte Inglés,"* 2nd ed., Barcelona: Dictext, 1992, p. 806.

Cuervo, Alvaro, "Ramón Areces: empresa y cultura," *Revista de Económica,* No. 1, 1989.

Dauder, E., *Los empresarios,* Barcelona: Editorial Dopesa, 1974.

"El Corte Inglés. Una herencia bien aprovechada," *Actualidad Económica,* May 1991.

Westley, Ana, "Spanish Chain of Stores Wins Bankrupt Rival," *New York Times,* June 8, 1995, p. D8.

—Alejandro Molla Descals
—updated by David E. Salamie

Empi, Inc.

599 Cardigan Road
St. Paul, Minnesota 55126-4099
U.S.A.
(612) 415-9000
Fax: (612) 415-7447
Web site: http://www.empi.com

Public Company
Incorporated: 1977
Employees: 550
Sales: $73.5 million (1997)
Stock Exchanges: NASDAQ
Ticker Symbol: EMPI
SICs: 3841 Surgical & Medical Instruments; 3845
   Electromedical Equipment

Empi, Inc., one of the United States' largest medical device companies in rehabilitative therapy, develops, markets, and manufacturers electrotherapy, iontophoretic drug delivery, orthotic, and incontinence treatment products. The company, which began as a distributor of TENS (Transcutaneous Electrical Nerve Stimulation) devices, markets its products for both in-home and clinical use.

Man of Compassion Founds Empi in the 1970s

Empi, Inc. founder Donald D. Maurer did not begin his life with the dream of building a biotechnology business. ''Don Maurer, a gent with a dozen patents to cement his reputation as a guru of biomedical engineering, grew up in a remote corner of the Black Hills convinced that he was 'a real dumbbell,' '' wrote Dick Youngblood in a 1992 *Star Tribune* article. When Maurer left his impoverished life for a stint in the Navy, beginning in 1954, he found opportunity to spread his wings: training in electronics led to a college education and bachelor's degree in electric engineering and master's in biomedical engineering.

While working for Medtronic, Inc., a pacemaker and medical device manufacturer, Maurer and his engineering team developed the first wearable Transcutaneous Electrical Nerve Stimulator or TENS device. A TENS unit provided non-drug pain therapy via the introduction of low-voltage pulses of electricity to the pain site. Initially, the product was used to pre-screen patients for their tolerance to the implantable pain control devices Medtronic manufactured. But it was so effective Medtronic began selling it instead. Maurer also developed Neuromuscular Stimulation (NMS) products (later called Neuromuscular Electrical Stimulation or NMES) used to stimulate muscles for purposes of physical therapy.

In 1977, shortly after Medtronic rejected what Maurer believed to be a viable and sorely needed product, a device to cure female incontinence, he left Medtronic's neurological research division and established Empi, Inc. Through Empi, Maurer marketed a German-manufactured TENS unit. A sales manager handled the product while Maurer established an engineering program for Courage Center, a Twin Cities area rehabilitation services organization.

However, while Maurer fabricated devices such as adapted computer keyboards, the business was going under. A new investment group backed Maurer in designing his own TENS unit with the stipulation he would also run the company. A public stock offering funded production. Maurer took on the task of marketing his TENS device to clinics and built a reputation of being able to give relief to patients who had not been helped by other TENS products.

Nonetheless, Empi's first decade was marked by inconsistent earnings, with the company losing money until 1982 and then again in 1986. While the TENS and NMS market in general surged in the 1980s, the gains were accompanied by a period of price cutting. In addition, when sales volume dropped off, the battle for market share heightened and industry consolidation was on the horizon.

Shift in Tactics in Late 1980s; Payoff in Early 1990s

In 1988, Empi brought on Michael Connoy, an ex-sales and marketing executive with American Hospital Supply Corp., as president and chief operating officer. Connoy shifted the company away from the dealer-sales system it had in place to direct sales to clinics and therapists. Connoy also established a central distribution system for the $12 million company which freed the sales force from deliveries and product service. A move to bring manufacturing in-house cut costs. Empi also began marketing products, such as strength testing devices and athletic braces, for other companies.

Nevertheless, Empi entered the 1990s essentially a two-product company with TENS and NMS sales producing from 80 to 85 percent of sales. Twin Cities-based companies 3M, Medtronic, and Medical Devices, Inc., produced similar units. In an effort to expand its proprietary product line, Empi entered into a joint venture with giant medical products company C.R. Bard to develop and sell an incontinence product. The device stimulated the bladder control muscles by means of electric pulses and thus aided in strengthening them.

Meanwhile, the *New England Journal of Medicine (NEJM)* published an article which challenged the effectiveness of TENS on chronic back pain and put the squeeze on Empi's stock price. Maurer disputed the findings saying the study was flawed in terms of time and application. "Studies that followed patients for up to two years have reinforced our belief that TENS units are an effective, low-cost alternative to narcotic drug therapy and surgery for many pain sufferers," he said in a June 1990 *Star Tribune* article by Anthony Carideo. While Empi's revenues remained steady, analysts expressed concern over the potential impact of the study on Medicare and private insurance reimbursements for the use of the TENS units.

Empi received FDA approval in July 1991 for its female incontinence product—the C.R. Bard agreement had been dropped earlier when Maurer felt the larger company was taking too long to develop a proprietary electrode. Traditional treatment for involuntary loss of urine, which affected roughly nine million American women, included drugs, invasive surgeries, injectable products, and Kegel muscle control exercises. The Empi product stimulated the muscles controlling urinary flow by means of a tampon-like device attached to a pocket-sized microprocessor and treated urge, stress, and mixed incontinence.

The introduction of the incontinence device coupled with stabilized earnings helped Empi recover admirably from the TENS-related stock price drop: the company was the fourth biggest percentage gainer for the entire over-the-counter market in 1991. Stock price rose from $4 per share in the beginning of 1991 to $33.50 per share by year end. Net income for 1991 was $2 million on $22 million in revenues.

But Empi's TENS sales growth slowed due to cuts in Medicare reimbursements in the early 1990s. Furthermore, the University of Texas study published by *NEJM*, which said the pain relief TENS patients received was due to a placebo effect, added to the debate already in progress regarding the product. One theory maintained the electrical pulses produced by the TENS unit interfered with pain messages being transmitted to the brain. A second theory said TENS stimulated the release of naturally occurring pain blocking substances called endorphins. Empi claimed to be the technological leader and was the number two seller of TENS following Medtronic.

A broad-based rollout of the incontinence product, Innova, was slowed by Empi's nationwide study aimed at proving its effectiveness at a level above and beyond FDA standards. (The TENS technology was developed prior to the 1976 federal regulation requiring FDA approval of biomedical devices in terms of efficacy and safety.) Initial marketing targeted U.S. obstetricians, gynecologists, and urologists.

Empi brought out a non-invasive drug-delivery system called Dupel at the same time it introduced Innova. The device administered small molecule medications such as analgesics or anti-inflammatories through electrodes attached to the skin. Maurer improved on existing systems by adding a second electrode to increase speed of delivery, chemically buffering them to prevent injury to the skin. Dupel was marketed to physical therapists.

Expansion During the Mid-1990s

Empi landed on the *Forbes* list of America's 200 best small companies in November 1992. The same month, the company announced the acquisition of Medtronic's Nortech Division, the TENS unit Maurer helped start, for about $6 million in cash and warrants for shares, plus a contingent payment based on future sales. The $28 million business moved Empi's share of the U.S. electrical stimulation device market, including both pain relief and rehabilitation, up to about 30 percent, according to a November 1992 *Star Tribune* article by Steve Gross. The Nortech purchase was a boon to Empi's sales force and research and development budget, vastly improving their foothold in the important international TENS market, and pushing up sales, earnings, and ticker price. But about the same time as the sale, Aetna Insurance Company, Hartford, Connecticut, moved to restrict, but not eliminate, TENS reimbursements.

Thanks primarily to the Nortech purchase, Empi sales climbed to $66.4 million in 1993 compared with $33.4 million the previous year. Net income more than doubled, jumping to $9.3 million from 1992's $4 million. The purchase of Physical Health Devices, Inc., a Florida-based biofeedback company, broadened the rehabilitation and incontinence product line, and was part of Empi's ongoing diversification plan.

With sales and earnings gains back down to earth following the integration of Nortech, Empi's stock price fell off as well. The $1,200 incontinence product, so well received by Wall Street, had proven to be a "tough sell" to insurance companies and Medicare for reimbursement, according to a September 1993 *Forbes* article by Zina Moukheiber. The lion's share of female incontinence product spending continued to go to protective garments—a product which had come out of the closet through television ads featuring actress June Allyson.

Empi sought to gain product acceptance by establishing an education program which counseled women on incontinency options. The manufacturer's effort was met with skepticism by some doctors who saw it merely as a marketing tool for their product. Empi countered that the measure was necessary since many women were reluctant to approach doctors about the problem and, in turn, many doctors were unaware of all the options available for treating the malady. An additional factor hindering the new product was the uncertainty surrounding healthcare reform legislation: insurers were delaying reimbursement decision-making as they waited for a definitive move by the federal government.

Joseph E. Laptewicz, Jr., came on board as the new president and CEO in the second half of 1994. Maurer continued as chairman and chief scientific officer. Both revenue and net income for 1994 dropped off from 1993 levels. Empi attributed the downturn to a weakness in the core rehabilitation market, pricing pressures related to cost-containment efforts among third party payers, and investments in sales, clinical, and marketing programs. On the up side the company completed the long-delayed incontinence study and the development of a proprietary line of dynamic splints (range-of-motion orthoses).

In 1995, Empi cut the Innova price by about half and sold the incontinence education aspect of the business in order to concentrate fully on marketing the product. Non-core products, which included Empi's orthoses and iontophoreses system, as well as a cervical traction device manufactured by another company, grew to about one-third of sales in 1995, up from one-quarter a year earlier. During the year, Empi entered into an agreement to market Tennessee-based Rehab Med Equip, Inc.'s catalog line of more 200 rehabilitation products ranging from ice packs and whirlpool baths to orthotics. Both revenue and net income were up.

Empi experienced growth in all key business areas in 1996, especially in the incontinence and orthotics lines. The company continued to add new products through marketing agreements or expansion of proprietary lines. Public awareness and healthcare provider acceptance of the Innova incontinence product

also progressed in 1996. But Empi's Innova pelvic floor stimulator and biofeedback systems along with non-invasive treatment products by other manufacturers represented only a small part of the total incontinence market. The segment generated only $5 million in sales. In contrast, adult diaper products generated about $1 billion in sales, while $600 million was spent on surgery and another $50 million on drugs.

Prepared for the Future

In 1997, Donald Maurer retired as chairman of the board. The company he founded was once again named as one of *Forbes*'s 200 top small American companies thanks to an average five-year growth of 17 percent in sales, 15 percent in earnings, and 15 percent in return on equity. For the year, net income was $10.5 million on net sales of $73.5 million. The company continued to broaden its product line, while fighting to make gains with Medicare reimbursement for the incontinence products—an act vital to future growth.

In general, the outlook for incontinence products was strong. Millions of baby boomers were aging, and in response more and more manufacturers were entering the incontinence business. Medtronic, which had sold an implantable incontinence device in overseas markets since 1994, launched the product in the United States in 1998. It seemed the times had finally caught up with Maurer, who had begun the push for incontinence products some two decades earlier.

Further Reading

Abelson, Alan, "Technology Stocks: Have They Topped?," *Barron's*, January 30, 1995, p. 5.

Alexander, Steve, "Empi Disputes Article in Barron's," *Star Tribune* (Minneapolis), February 1, 1995, p. 3D.

——, "Laptewicz Finds New Career at Empi," *Star Tribune* (Minneapolis), September 19, 1994, p. 1D.

Carideo, Anthony, "Empi's Shareholders Have Been Undergoing Some Uncomfortable Hits," *Star Tribune* (Minneapolis), February 1, 1994, p. 2D.

——, "Empi's Strategy Eases Pain of Competition," *Star Tribune* (Minneapolis), April 30, 1990, p. 1D.

——, "Past 2 Weeks Have Been Troublesome Ones for Empi Chief Don Maurer," *Star Tribune* (Minneapolis), March 26, 1992, p. 2D.

——, "Questions About Empi Remain Despite Surge in Sales and Net Income," *Star Tribune* (Minneapolis), April 29, 1993, p. 2D.

——, "TENS Study Gave Jolt to St. Paul Firm's Stock," *Star Tribune* (Minneapolis), June 18, 1990, p. 1D.

"Corporate Capsule: Empi, Inc.," *Minneapolis/St. Paul CityBusiness*, March 24, 1995, p. 24.

"Empi, Inc.," *Corporate Report Fact Book 1998*, Minneapolis: Corporate Report, 1998, p. 270.

Feyder, Susan, "Malady of the Millennium," *Star Tribune* (Minneapolis), March 9, 1998, p. 1D.

Gross, Steve, "Empi Acquires Nortech Division of Medtronic for About $6 Million in Cash, Debt and Warrants," *Star Tribune* (Minneapolis), November 19, 1992, p. 1D.

Judge, Gillian, "Empi's Alternative Medicine," *Twin Cities Business Monthly*, February 1994, pp. 34, 36–37, 39.

Kennedy, Patrick, "Follow-Ups: Empi Adds by TENS," *Corporate Report Minnesota*, June 1993, p. 15.

Moukheiber, Zina, "Dopey Duck's Revenge," *Forbes*, September 27, 1993, pp. 80–81.

Nelson, Connie, "Problem Solver Is in the Right Place at Empi," *Star Tribune* (Minneapolis), December 12, 1988, p. 2D.

Nissen, Todd, ''An Industry in Declining Health,'' *Minneapolis/ St. Paul CityBusiness*, October 8–14, 1990, pp. 1, 26.

Peterson, Susan E., ''Honored by Forbes,'' *Star Tribune* (Minneapolis), October 27, 1992, p. 5D.

Royer, Mary-Paige, ''No Pain, No Gain,'' *Corporate Report Minnesota*, September 1992, pp. 51–54, 56.

Schafer, Lee, ''As the Cookie Crumbles: Empi Inc. (No.23),'' *Corporate Report Minnesota*, April 1995, pp. 49–50.

Scholl, Jaye, ''Painful Dispute: Does Empi Inc.'s TENS Technology Really Work?'' *Barron's*, June 12, 1993, p. 14.

Smith, Tom, ''Stat Man: Three Products to Watch,'' *Corporate Report Minnesota*, October 1991, p. 104.

Wascoe, Don, Jr., ''Cause of Incontinence, Not Just the Effects, Is Emphasized at New Clinic,'' *Star Tribune* (Minneapolis), July 28, 1994, p. 1B.

Youngblood, Dick, ''Black Hills Dreamer Builds Success Story,'' *Star Tribune* (Minneapolis), May 11, 1992, p. 2D.

—Kathleen Peippo

Equity Marketing, Inc.

131 South Rodeo Drive
Beverly Hills, California 90212
U.S.A.
(310) 887-4300
Fax: (310) 887-4400
Web site: http://www.emak.com

Public Company
Incorporated: 1983
Employees: 157
Sales: $146.51 million (1997)
Stock Exchanges: NASDAQ
Ticker Symbol: EMAK
SICs: 3944 Games, Toys & Children's Vehicles, Except
    Dolls & Bicycles; 3069 Fabricated Rubber Products,
    Not Elsewhere Classified; 3942 Dolls & Stuffed Toys

Equity Marketing, Inc. is a producer of toys and other products which are largely based on animated characters from motion pictures and television programs, as well as from the world of sports. Through its Equity Promotions division, the company produces licensed toys which are sold or given away by the company's customers in special promotional campaigns. The company's Equity Toys division manufactures toys that are sold by retailers, including such national chains as Toys "R" Us and Wal-Mart. Equity has relationships with major entertainment companies such as Disney, Twentieth Century Fox, and Universal Studios, as well as The Public Broadcasting System (PBS) and The National Association of Stock Car Auto Racing (NASCAR), to manufacture licensed products. Its clients include Burger King, Shell Oil, Pepperidge Farm, Coca-Cola/Latin America, Kellogg's/Latin America, and a number of others. Equity has shown steady annual growth since its founding, and continues to diversify its product line and customer base each year.

Beginnings

Equity Marketing's origins date to 1983, when it was created as a small division of a New York-based travel incentive firm,

Marketing Equities International, which promoted free trips for airlines. In 1984, Equity did its first premium promotion campaign for Arby's restaurants, and a year later was involved with a promotion involving Cabbage Patch characters for Coca-Cola. Two years later the company established a relationship with Burger King which would prove to be a key factor in Equity's success. The first Burger King promotional campaign, for the film *Thundercats,* shipped 13 million toys and was Equity's biggest success to date. Over the next several years other successful campaigns involved Looney Tunes characters manufactured for Arby's, a Burger King promotion using the television character Alf, and Indiana Jones premiums produced for Pepsi. The company was involved in all aspects of the promotional campaign, from looking for entertainment material to license, to executing the design, to consulting on the advertising and packaging. Manufacturing was contracted out.

Equity's business was built upon the synergy that existed between entertainment producers and retailers or restaurateurs. The latter would use the concept of giving away or selling toys depicting characters from popular films or television programs to bring customers through the door. They would promote such an offer through massive advertising campaigns, which would in turn benefit the entertainment product by helping create a "buzz" around the release of a movie or by providing added exposure to a particular television program. The campaign would also benefit the retail business or restaurant by increasing its market share and customer loyalty, and by convincing its customers that the business was giving them extra value for their money, offering special, collectible premiums not available anywhere else. The promotional products business was estimated to be worth $70 billion in the United States, with no particular company dominating the field.

In 1989, Equity was purchased from Marketing Equities by several investors, including senior executive Stephen Robeck. Within a year, the company had signed an exclusive agreement to use characters from "The Simpsons," the popular animated television series, and launched a highly successful Simpsons-based promotion for Burger King. In 1990, Don Kurz was hired into the company's management team, and a year later he and Robeck purchased Equity from the majority owner in a leveraged buyout, and began to run the company as co-CEOs. The

Company Perspectives:

The Company's operating philosophy is as follows: Service our customers with a passion, understanding that they are the basis for all our opportunities. Compete on the basis of superior quality in design and manufacturing at any given customer-determined price point. Provide a challenging, fun and rewarding work environment in order to attract and retain top personnel. Measure all major decisions as to their potential impact on long-term stockholder value. Operate ethically with respect to our customers, stockholders, employees and the communities in which we do business.

following year Equity's annual sales more than doubled, going from 1991's total of $15.3 million to more than $35 million. Equity's biggest customer at this point was Burger King, which accounted for close to 85 percent of sales. While this relationship had been an important factor in Equity's success, it also was potentially dangerous, were something to happen to Burger King or the two companies' compatibility. In any event, Equity continued to benefit from it, with a major "wrist watch self-liquidator" promotion in 1993 for Burger King based on the film *The Nightmare Before Christmas*. That same year, Equity opened an office in Hong Kong to coordinate the manufacture of its products, which was generally done in the Far East, and entered an agreement with Tycoon Enterprises, a Mexican licensing agent, to begin a joint marketing effort in that country.

1994: Initial Public Offering

Equity's first decade had followed a steady curve of upward growth, and co-CEOs Robeck and Kurz decided to take Equity public, with an offering of stock on the NASDAQ exchange in February 1994. The two CEOs retained ownership of some 60 percent of the stock between them. That same year, the company moved from New York to Beverly Hills, a strategic decision intended to provide a higher profile for Equity among the California-based film and television companies which were its greatest sources of product licenses. Indeed, the company soon reached an agreement with Warner Brothers to manufacture toys for overseas retail distribution, based on the perennially popular Looney Tunes cartoon characters. This was Equity's first venture into retail toy sales. Another big success in 1994 was a promotional campaign for Burger King based on the hit Disney movie *The Lion King*. Some 30 million toys were ordered, and the demand was so great that an additional 20 million were requested. The promotional toy business had smaller profit margins than retail sales, but it involved less risk for the company, with no worries about returns of unsold merchandise if the entertainment programming the products were tied to was a failure. After a decade in business, Equity had an established reputation for good product design, as well as for timely manufacturing, something extremely critical when products were being given away in conjunction with a national advertising campaign. In over 100 consecutive contracts, Equity had not missed a single deadline.

Because Equity management and stock market analysts had increasingly been concerned about the company's heavy dependence on Burger King, efforts were being made to boost sales to other customers. Business relationships were developed with a number of companies in Latin America, and sales to that region leapt from nothing in 1993 to $11 million a year later. Sales to Burger King decreased from 85 to 70 percent of total revenues during that time period, and Equity's co-CEOs declared a figure of less than 50 percent to be their goal for the future. The year 1995 saw Equity's success continue unabated, with the big promotion for Burger King being the Disney movie *Toy Story,* and new Latin American contracts including *Space Jam* toys for Kellogg's and *Power Ranger* figures for Coca-Cola. Annual sales hit a new high of $84 million.

1996: EPI Group Purchased

Equity made its first acquisition of another company in 1996, purchasing EPI Group Limited for approximately $2.9 million. EPI operated in much the same manner as Equity, with divisions devoted to both promotional products and toys. A major customer for EPI was Shell Oil, for whom EPI designed and supplied promotional products, in particular items tied to Shell's automobile racing endeavors. The company produced, for example, toy cars that were models of vehicles driven on the NASCAR and "Indy car" circuits, sponsored by Shell. These were typically made available as part of a special promotion at gas stations. EPI also manufactured toys for retail sale under the "Friends of . . ." (The Ocean, The Forest, etc.) name. This line of products was sold through museums, zoos, stores, and catalogs. The EPI purchase was touted by Equity's co-CEOs as representing "additional progress in our continuing effort to diversify our revenue base by broadening our customer and product mix." South of the border, Equity formed a new Mexican unit, to further enhance its presence in that country's developing promotional products market.

Equity also continued to prosper from its relationship with Burger King, being named that company's "Premiums Agency of Record." Other highlights from 1996 included a number of licensing deals for high-profile products, including toys based on the video series *The Land Before Time* and the film *The Lost World: Jurassic Park,* as well as PBS children's television series "Wishbone," "Kratt's Creatures," and "Go To Bed, Fred." A license to produce products based on the 1996 Olympics' official mascot "Izzy" yielded both promotional products made for Holiday Inn and a line of toys marketed by Equity's toy division. This type of deal was especially sweet for the company, since creating similar product lines for two markets enabled Equity to save money in some areas of design and manufacturing, and thus make a bigger profit from the license.

The year 1997 saw Equity continuing to expand its operations outside the United States, with sales to the Philippines, South Africa, and Korea, in addition to increases in the company's share of the market in South and Central America, although sales in the Far East were slow. Shell Oil gave the company its first contract to manufacture promotional products linked to a motion picture, the animated movie *Anastasia.* Equity let lapse its license to produce Looney Tunes toys, citing the high cost of the license as a factor. However, there were still many other choices of material, with new movie blockbusters continually on the horizon. Licensing deals were signed for both the forthcoming *Godzilla* movie and the sequel to the hit talking pig film *Babe,* both set for release in 1998. The company announced that it would be making a plush Babe toy which would cost about $40, and would be programmable, with the toy able to "remember" a child's name, and ask to be served breakfast or lunch, depending on the time of day. Because these licenses were signed months in advance of the appearance of the motion picture, announcements of forthcoming products were often intentionally vague, not mentioning the name of the film or even the movie studio involved. Equity's staff also was required to keep designs and contracts under wraps, in order to protect the secrecy of the various licensers and customers and remain ahead of the competition.

1998: Further Acquisitions; Godzilla Disappoints

The year 1997 was another banner one for Equity, and 1998 initially appeared to be just as bright, with three additional companies acquired in the first half of the year. In April, Corinthian Marketing, Inc. was purchased for approximately $8.7 million. Corinthian's main product line was the Headliners brand of collectible sports figurines. These were plastic toys that had oversized heads which depicted well-known athletes. A new division, Equity Sports, was formed to market Corinthian's products. Equity's established lines of toys licensed from NASCAR also were moved into the division. The acquisition gave Equity an opportunity to take advantage of the wider range of sports licenses held by Corinthian, and also to expand Corinthian's sports merchandising from that company's collectible toys to include the promotional products which were Equity's forte.

Equity also purchased a pair of companies in July, for a total outlay of about $15 million. These were U.S. Import and Promotions Co., Inc., of St. Augustine, Florida, and Contract Marketing, Inc., of West Boylston, Massachusetts. Both companies had already established a cooperative relationship in which they worked together to design, manufacture, and distribute promotional products. A major part of the companies' combined business was the manufacture of collectible toy trucks, generally distributed to motor fuel-related retailers, which complemented Equity's established toy car lines.

When the movie *Godzilla* was released in the spring of 1998, Equity had a number of products ready to capitalize on the expected blockbuster, but the film's reviews and grosses were poor, leaving retailers (and manufacturers) stuck with many unsold toys. When the full effect of the film's lack of business on its toy division was felt, Equity's stock price dropped almost 50 percent. As a result, the company announced it was taking steps to move away from being tied to the fortunes of such "event" movies, given their unpredictability. The company also ended its co-CEO setup, with Donald Kurz taking sole possession of that post and becoming chairman of the board, and Stephen Robeck stepping back to the position of consultant and board member.

Despite the *Godzilla* setback, Equity Marketing was still in a solid position overall, with its many licensing agreements, its established customer base, and its strong position in the still-young Central and South American markets. Its reputation for timeliness and value in the promotional products market was strong, and the company's annual revenues (and profits) had seen growth for many years running. As American cultural and sports icons became more and more global, and marketing efforts became more and more linked to popular entertainment, the demand for the company's products appeared certain to grow.

Principal Subsidiaries

Equity Marketing Hong Kong Ltd. (Hong Kong); Synergy Promotions SA de CV (Mexico; 65%).

Principal Divisions

Equity Toys; Equity Promotions; Equity Sports.

Further Reading

"Equity Marketing Shares Tumble in Wake of Gloomy Forecast," *Dow Jones Online News*, September 24, 1998.

"Equity Marketing—2: Excited About 'Go To Bed, Fred,' " *Dow Jones News Service*, February 14, 1997.

Grove, Chris, "Toying with Success (Equity Marketing, Inc.) (Company Profile)," *Los Angeles Business Journal*, September 9, 1996, p. 12.

King, Thomas R., "Equity Marketing's 'Toy Story' Tie-In Lifts Fourth Period Net," *Wall Street Journal*, February 16, 1996, p. A4B.

Kraul, Chris, "A Latin Play—Toy Exporter Shows State's Opportunity," *Los Angeles Times*, July 30, 1998, p. D2.

Maio, Patrick J., "The New America: Equity Marketing Inc.—Firm Finds Big Profit in Little Plastic Toys," *Investor's Business Daily*, December 15, 1995, p. A4.

——, "The New America: Equity Marketing Inc.—Toymaker Still Sold on Burger King Connection," *Investor's Business Daily*, July 5, 1996, p. A3.

Matzer, Marla, "Toy Maker Feels Crush of 'Godzilla' in Third Quarter," *Los Angeles Times*, September 25, 1998, p. D5.

Oestricher, Dwight, "Toy Maker Equity Marketing Sees Talking Pig Babe As Next Big Thing," *Dow Jones Online News*, February 11, 1998.

Rehak, Judith, "Equity Marketing's License to Sell (Nota Bene)," *Chief Executive (U.S.)*, November 1, 1995, p. 23.

Sundius, Ann, "One-On-One Interview with Equity Marketing (EMAK) President and CEO," *MSNBC Video*, October 30, 1997.

—Frank Uhle

Federal-Mogul Corporation

26555 Northwestern Highway
Southfield, Michigan 48034
U.S.A.
(248) 354 7700
Fax: (248) 354-8983
Web site: http://www.federal-mogul.com

Public Company
Incorporated: 1924
Employees: 56,000
Sales: $1.80 billion (1997)
Stock Exchanges: New York
Ticker Symbol: FMO
SICs: 2891 Adhesives & Sealants; 3053 Gaskets, Packing
    & Sealing Devices; 3452 Bolts, Nuts, Rivets, &
    Washers; 3562 Ball & Roller Bearings; 3592
    Carburetors, Pistons, Rings, Valves; 3714 Motor
    Vehicle Parts & Accessories

Federal-Mogul Corporation manufactures precision components for cars, trucks, and construction vehicles, marketing its products to original equipment manufacturers (OEMs) and aftermarket customers in the United States and around the world under brand names such as ''Federal-Mogul,'' ''Signal-Stat,'' and ''TRW.'' It also packages products for third-party private label brands. The company has about 20 manufacturing facilities in the United States and six other countries. Federal-Mogul sells its own products to major global automakers, including BMW, General Motors, and Nissan. It distributes about 150,000 auto parts to nearly 10,000 automotive aftermarket customers, primarily independent warehouse distributors, but also local parts suppliers and parts retailers.

The company rose to prominence through a series of expansions and acquisitions, which included the Bearing Company of America in 1953, the Bower Roller Bearing Company in 1955, and National Seal in 1956. In the early 1990s, Federal-Mogul sought to offset fluctuating demand in the OEM market by entering into aftermarket sales.

The Muzzy-Lyon Company & The Mogul Metal Company, 1899–1923

The history of Federal-Mogul may be traced to 1899, when J. Howard Muzzy and Edward F. Lyon, two mill supply vendors in Detroit, began searching for ways to produce better Babbitt metal. Babbitt metal, an alloy of tin, antimony, and copper, had been patented in 1839 by Isaac Babbitt as an anti-friction agent surrounding moving metallic locomotive parts. The use of Babbitt metal remained the principal means of preventing rotating metallic shafts from overheating and wearing out. However, the introduction of combustible engines early in the 20th century prompted a need for new, improved Babbitt metal.

Having developed an alternative formula for Babbitt metal, Muzzy and Lyon left secure jobs at J.T. Wing and Company, a vendor of mill and factory supplies and rubber goods, where their friendship and business acumen had gradually matured.

Determined to be their own bosses in the market they knew best, the two partners opened their first facility on Woodward Avenue in Detroit, Michigan, in 1900. During this time, the mill and factory supply business was highly competitive, and many producers offered shoddy merchandise at inexpensive prices. However, Muzzy and Lyon established a reputation for high-quality products and were able to reinvest most of their profits back into the business. They used aggressive and imaginative advertising, providing money-back guarantees and coupons good for prizes ranging from pocket rulers to firearms.

Whatever time Muzzy could spare from his primary responsibility of managing the financial and manufacturing end of the business he devoted to experimentation with Babbitt metals. Lyon, when not on the road selling company products, joined his partner in blending new formulas of tin, antimony, and lead. Their company soon garnered major orders from Clark Motor Company and the Sheffield Motor Company. As a result of the increased business, the partners formed a subsidiary company called the Mogul Metal Company.

Company Perspectives:

Federal-Mogul has over 250 locations, across 6 continents, in 24 countries, with 56,000 employees worldwide. Headquartered in Southfield, Michigan, Federal-Mogul is a $7 billion automotive parts manufacturer providing innovative solutions and systems to global customers in the automotive, light truck, heavy-duty, railroad, farm and industrial markets. A century of people serving customers through manufacturing mastery has made Federal-Mogul a global leader in the automotive industry. Recognized by our customers as the supplier of choice for powertrain systems, sealing systems, and general products of leading edge innovation and technology, Federal-Mogul is a dynamic, growth-oriented company dedicated to delighting customers.

During this time, the traditional method of making motor bearings was to pour molten Babbitt metal directly onto the motor block and to shape the metal to fit by hand. Mechanics replaced worn bearings by laboriously gouging out the old metal and then pouring in the new. When Sheffield's parent organization, the Fairbanks Morse Company, inquired as to whether die cast metals could be manufactured to form standard size bearings, Muzzy and Lyon began working on a method. They purchased a typecasting machine, and, by modifying it, they were able to make some of the new parts themselves, while commissioning various machine shops to produce the rest. The design and construction of Muzzy's and Lyon's new machine remained a secret, and while the partners had limited mechanical and engineering experience, the machine proved successful.

The potential of the die casting machine so impressed the partners that they decided to drop the mill supply business completely. The company would devote its entire resources to manufacturing and mechanizing automotive bearings and Babbitt metals. They sold their products under the brand names of ''Duro'' (made according to a purchased formula) and ''Mogul'' (their own formula developed by Muzzy and Lyon). Orders for their die cast bearings began to arrive, and, in 1910, an important order was placed for 10,000 connecting rod bearings for the massive Buick 10, one of the first cars to use parts produced by Mogul Metal. That year, the partners nearly lost a large order from the Hudson Motor Company, when they refused to compromise their secret processes by allowing Hudson engineers to inspect the plant.

Federal-Mogul Corporation, 1924–54

In 1923, Muzzy learned that Douglas-Dahlin, a large Kansas City-based parts distributor, stood in danger of bankruptcy while owing Mogul a large sum of money. S.C. Reynolds, vice-president of Federal Bearing and Bushing, which also stood to lose money, called Muzzy to discuss the situation, proposing a trip to Kansas City to protect their interests. When Muzzy and Reynolds began discussing their companies and assessing their relative strengths and weaknesses, they realized the advantages of a merger. The Federal Bearing employees were expert bronze foundrymen but lacked the capacity to produce Babbitt. Muzzy-

Lyon, on the other hand, operated a complete Babbitt foundry but purchased bronze on the market. The companies merged in 1924, taking the name Federal-Mogul Corporation. To protect its investments, Federal-Mogul took over the near-bankrupt Douglas-Dahlin Company, entering the parts distribution business.

In 1927, Federal-Mogul purchased U.S. Bearings Company, an Indiana distributor that resold replacement bearings. The following year, Federal-Mogul's involvement in the service business increased substantially with the acquisition of the Watkins Manufacturing Company of Wichita, Kansas. Following this major expansion, Federal-Mogul also purchased the Pacific Metal Bearing Company in San Francisco, primarily to supply its West Coast branches. In 1936, the corporation acquired the Indianapolis-based Superior Bearings Company, and, in 1937, the service division went international with the acquisition of the former Watkins Rebabbitting Limited, with Canadian locations in Toronto, Montreal, and Winnipeg. By 1939, Federal-Mogul was operating 53 service branches across the North American continent.

World War II led to further expansion. By 1941, Federal-Mogul had over 50 facilities devoted to military production, turning out millions of bearings, bushings, and seals for military applications. The company's marine division won highly competitive U.S. Navy tests for PT boat propellers and secured orders for over 24,000 Super Equi-poise wheels for every PT boat propeller used by all the Allied navies, including that of the Soviet Union. The marine division grew from a workforce of 50 in 1942 to nearly 1,000 by the end of the war. Moreover, from September 1939 to July 1945, the total area of Federal-Mogul plants increased nearly threefold, and annual sales were more than double the best prewar amounts.

Although postwar employee layoffs were necessary, the company continued to grow through acquisition. In 1953, Federal-Mogul merged with Bearings Company of America, marking the single largest acquisition in its history. The merger of the Bearings Company brought 610 new employees and approximately 121,000 square feet of manufacturing space into the organization.

Federal-Mogul-Bower Bearings, Inc., 1955–64

Even more significant growth occurred in 1955 when Federal-Mogul acquired the Bower Roller Bearing Company. Soon thereafter, the corporation announced its third major merger in as many years, when The National Motor Bearing Company (National Seal Division) joined the new Federal-Mogul-Bower Bearing Corporation in July 1956. At the time of the merger, National was one of the country's largest manufacturers of oil seals and a variety of other specialized parts ranging from grommets and gaskets to fiberglass ducts and railroad journal boxes. The acquisition earned the company its first listing among *Fortune* magazine's 500 largest American companies, ranking 350 with sales that exceeded $100 million that year. By the end of the 1950s, Federal-Mogul's service division had expanded from 58 to 96 branches, and the number of customers had doubled to over 10,000. The mergers and increased efficiency of the 1950s had increased annual sales to four times their 1949 level.

During the 1960s, the corporation's timely response to innovations in automobile production ultimately resulted in large dividends. One such development involved the steady expansion of foreign automobile manufacturers, facilitated by mass production technology and the development of the European Common Market. Observing a threat to American export sales, Federal-Mogul management began investing in foreign manufacturing operations and purchasing interests in various major European bearing firms. Domestic expansion also continued, and the firm began to focus on manufacturing parts for the highly sophisticated missile market. In 1964, Federal-Mogul opened a new oil seal facility that was publicized as the most highly mechanized plant of its kind in the world. The following year, the company purchased Steering Aluminum, a piston factory, and the Vellumoid Company, a manufacturer of gaskets and gasket materials.

Federal-Mogul Corporation . . . Again, 1965–90s

The company's name was changed back to Federal-Mogul Corporation in April 1965. One year later, Federal-Mogul's world headquarters officially relocated from its location in downtown Detroit to its present location in Southfield, Michigan, in July 1966.

The early 1970s marked a domestic expansion into the southern states. A highly automated new plant in Princeton, Kentucky, opened in late 1970, with 50,000 square feet devoted to producing super alloy metal powders. In 1971, a new plant in Virginia began manufacturing aluminum sleeve bearings, while another Federal-Mogul plant was introduced for the manufacture of bimetal bushings and bearings. The following year, an additional powdered metal parts plant was opened in Ripley, Tennessee, and, soon thereafter, a new 360,000-square-foot plant in Hamilton, Alabama, began producing tapered roller bearings ranging up to eight inches in diameter.

Economic recession in 1975 prompted management at Federal-Mogul to begin reassessing its long-term strategy. Although the company quickly recovered from the recession, recording its fourth consecutive year of record sales and earnings in 1979, management had found that the company's earnings were overly reliant on the fortunes of automotive OEMs. In the 1980s, chairperson and CEO Tom Russell placed increasing emphasis on a strategy of diversification, making acquisitions and entering into joint ventures to strengthen its manufacturing position. In July 1985, Federal-Mogul acquired the Mather Company, a manufacturer of high performance sealing products for the automotive and industrial markets and a leader in PTFE (Teflon) technology. In January 1986, the purchase of the Carter Automotive Company, Inc., a manufacturer and distributor of automotive fuel pumps and systems, and, in September of that year, the acquisition of Signal-Stat, a manufacturer, marketer, and distributor for lighting and safety components, further strengthened its position. In August 1989, Federal-Mogul completed a joint venture agreement with G. Bruss GmbH and Co. KG, a German manufacturer of seals and specialty molded products.

Dennis J. Gorley, who assumed Federal-Mogul's chief executive office upon Russell's 1989 retirement, accelerated his predecessor's diversification scheme. Gorley spearheaded Federal-Mogul's expansion into the automotive aftermarket, which promised higher profit margins and more stability than the OEM market. From 1989 to 1993, the firm continued to strengthen its operations through additional acquisitions, acquiring some of the best-known brands in automotive replacement parts and divesting itself of some peripheral OEM businesses. Principal acquisitions included: the vehicular lighting assets of R.E. Dietz and Co. in March 1990; German manufacturer of automotive and diesel engine bearings, Glyco AG in October 1990; Brown & Dureau (Australia) and Sealed Power Replacement. The company made its largest purchase ever in 1992, when it bought TRW Inc.'s automotive aftermarket business (AAB). The former TRW operations expanded Federal-Mogul's European and Japanese penetration and constituted nearly 20 percent of annual revenues in 1993.

During this period, Federal-Mogul worked to improve efficiency through automation, capital improvements, and staff reductions. The company adopted bar code technology for inventory control and invested in guided vehicles, hand-held scanners, and computers for its Jacksonville, Alabama, worldwide distribution center. These modernizations cut order fulfillment time from three days to one. Federal-Mogul also moved to transform its export operations into international enterprises. By 1993, 21 percent of the company's sales were generated by businesses outside the United States and Canada, while another 13 percent of annual revenues still came from exports.

The transition was not entirely smooth; Federal-Mogul recorded net losses in 1991 and 1992 totaling $87.4 million. However, when the company reported a $40.1 million profit for 1993, *Financial World* praised the company's "sound acquisition strategy, good cost controls, and participation in international markets." Noting that the company's stock had outperformed the Standard & Poor's 500 Index, CEO Gorley maintained that recent progress was "just the beginning," telling shareholders in the company's annual report that Federal-Mogul was "positioning itself as a company capable of sustained earnings growth." In March 1993, Federal-Mogul's lighting and electrical division was named one of the first General Motors Worldwide Suppliers of the Year for its excellence in quality, service, and price.

In September 1995, the company acquired Seal Technology Systems (STS), one of Europe's leading designers and manufacturers of a specialized range of seals and gaskets for the automotive sector and other industrial markets. Chrysler Corporation recognized the company for outstanding manufacturing plant performance in the areas of Quality, Delivery, and Warranty in May 1996, with its Gold Pentastar Award being given to Federal-Mogul's Blacksburg, Virginia engine bearing manufacturing facility. In November of that year, Dick Snell took the helm as chairman, CEO, and president of Federal-Mogul. Another accolade came in January 1997, when Federal-Mogul's engine bearings facility in Orleans, France, was honored with the first-ever Platinum Award for supplier excellence from the Rover Group, for winning the Gold Supplier Excellence Award three consecutive years. Concurrently, Federal-Mogul's STS division won the Rover Group's Silver Supplier Excellence Award for the second consecutive year.

Acquisition Spree, 1997–98

Beginning in October 1997, the company went on an acquisition spree, acquiring T&N PLC, one of the world's leading suppliers of high-technology automotive components, engineered products, and industrial materials.

In January 1998, Federal-Mogul acquired privately owned Fel-Pro Inc.—the premier automotive and industrial gasket manufacturer for the North American aftermarket and OE heavy-duty market, headquartered in Skokie, Illinois—and its subsidiaries. The acquisition of the venerable company (founded in Chicago in 1918 as Felt Products Manufacturing Company to manufacture Ford Model T car felt gaskets and washers) brought the Michigan giant capabilities in a broad variety of products, including custom and standard potting, encapsulation, and embedment compounds, resins, adhesives, sealants, epoxy and polyurethane compounds. The $720 million ($225 million common stock/$495 million cash) acquisition also brought 1,800 new employees to Federal-Mogul.

In March, Federal-Mogul strengthened its market position in Asia by increasing the company's ownership in KFM Bearing Co., Ltd., the leading manufacturer of engine bearings, bushings, and related parts for automotive and other applications in Korea, a joint venture formed that year with Kukje Special Metal Co., Ltd., from 30 percent to 87 percent. Also in March, the company expanded its engine bearing operations in Europe when it acquired Gdansk, Poland-based Bimet S.A., a manufacturer of engine bearings, bushings, and related products, bringing 600 employees and sales of $12 million to the company.

In October of that year, Federal-Mogul also acquired Tri-Way Machine Limited, a privately owned manufacturer of machines and machining systems serving the world metal-cutting industry, headquartered in Windsor, Ontario, Canada, and its subsidiary, J.I.S. Machining Ltd., a machiner of powertrain components. A second acquisition that month was Cooper Automotive, a business unit of Cooper Industries, Inc., whose principal products included brakes and friction, lighting, chassis parts, ignition, and wiper blades.

With over 250 locations across six continents, with 56,000 employees worldwide, and a century of business experience to its credit, Federal-Mogul reigned as a longtime leader in the automotive industry and yet promised to be a dynamic, growth-oriented company, with its eye on innovation well into the 21st century.

Principal Subsidiaries

BHW GmbH; Bimet SA; Carter Automotive Company, Inc.; Conaba S.A. de C.V. (51%); F-M Motorentiele Holding GmbH; Federal-Mogul Boliviana, S.A.; Federal-Mogul Bruss Scaling Systems (74%); Federal-Mogul Canada Investment Co.; Federal-Mogul Canada Ltd.; Federal-Mogul Cayman Investment Company Ltd.; Federal-Mogul Comercio International, S.A.; Federal-Mogul de Costa Rica, S.A.; Federal-Mogul de Guatemala, S.A.; Federal-Mogul de Venezuela C.A.; Federal-Mogul del Ecuador, S.A.; Federal-Mogul Distribuidora SAC (66%); Federal-Mogul Dominicana, S.A.; Federal-Mogul Funding Corp.; Federal-Mogul GmbH; Federal-Mogul Handelsgesellschaft MBH; Federal-Mogul Holding U.K., Ltd.; Federal-Mogul Japan KK; Federal-Mogul Ltd.; Federal-Mogul New Zealand Ltd.; Federal-Mogul Panama, S.A.; Federal-Mogul Pty. Ltd.; Federal-Mogul S.A. de C.V. (61%); Federal-Mogul S.A. (France); Federal-Mogul S.A. (Switzerland); Federal-Mogul SpA; Federal-Mogul Uruguay; Federal-Mogul Venture Corp.; Federal-Mogul World Trade Chile Ltda (99%); Federal-Mogul World Trade de Espana, S.A.; Federal-Mogul World Trade E.C.; Federal-Mogul World Trade Hong Kong, Ltd.; Federal-Mogul World Trade, Inc.; Federal-Mogul World Trade Ltd.; Federal-Mogul World Trade Pte. Ltd.; Federal-Mogul World Trade SDN BHD; Federal-Mogul World Wide, Inc.; Federal-Mogul Westwind Air Bearings Ltd. (89%); Fel-Pro Chemical Products L.P.; Fel-Pro Inc.; Fel-Pro Specialty Sealing Products L.P.; Femosa Mexico S.A. (90%); Glyco AG; Glyco Antriebstechnik GmbH; Glyco B.V.; Glyco do Brasil; Glyco KG; H. Minoli S.A.I.C. (59%); In-De-Co.; KFM Bearing Co. Ltd. (87%); Manufacturas Metalicas Linan S.A.; Mather Seal Co.; Metaltec, Inc.; Raimsa S.A. de C.V. (70%); Servicios Administrativos Industriales, S.A.; Servicios de Components Automotrices, S.A.; Subensambles Internacionales S.A. de C.V.; T&N PLC; Villa Fane Auto Supply, Inc.

Further Reading

"APS/Big A Auto Parts Challenge New Gasket Supplier to Speed Vendor Changeover," *Automotive Marketing*, November 1995, p. 108.

Bates, Chris, "Profile of a Successful Exporter, Fel-Pro, Inc.," *Business America*, June 28, 1982, p. 11.

Cowans, Deborah Shalowitz, "Fel-Pro Family-Friendly Benefits to Stay for Now Despite Sale," *Business Insurance*, January 19, 1998, p. 2.

——, "Investing in Employee Wellness: Companies See Big Returns from Offering Preventive Benefits," *Business Insurance*, March 11, 1996, p. 3.

Crown, Judith, "Family Ties Will Be Strained in Fel-Pro Deal," *Crain's Chicago Business*, December 1, 1997, p. 4.

"Elliot Lehman and Lewis Weinberg," *Industry Week*, October 27, 1980, p. 53.

Elstrom, Peter J.W., "Chaos Shattering Trade with Mideast," *Crain's Chicago Business*, January 21, 1991, p. 4.

"Employer Panel Shares Plan Experiences," *Employee Benefit Plan Review*, October 1991, p. 45.

"Employer's Family Benefits Attract Workers," *Employee Benefit Plan Review*, March 1992, p. 20.

"Federal-Mogul," *Rubber World*, February 1998, p. 8.

"Federal-Mogul Corp. Continues Its Buying Binge," *Ward's Auto World*, April 1998, p. 57.

"Federal-Mogul Finishes Purchase," *Wall Street Journal*, February 25, 1998, p. B6.

"Federal-Mogul Plans to Buy Fel-Pro for $720 Million," *New York Times*, January 13, 1998, p. C3.

"Federal-Mogul, Southfield, MI, Has Completed the Acquisition of Fel-Pro, a Privately-Owned Manufacturer Headquartered in Skokie, IL, for $720 Million," *Rubber World*, March 1998, p. 12.

"Federal-Mogul to Acquire Fel-Pro," *Industrial Distribution*, February 1998, p. 28.

Green, J. Howard, "Doing Well by Doing Good," *Time*, May 20, 1996, p. 42.

Hershey, Robert D., Jr., "Paradise Lost?: A Takeover of Workers' Dream Factory," *International Herald Tribune*, May 16, 1998, p. 19.

——, "Subjects Uneasy as a Benevolent Reign Ends," *New York Times*, June 7, 1998, p. B13.

Hogan, Brian J., "Pump Rotor Secured to Shaft by Anaerobic Adhesive; Bonding Permits Design Modifications That Simplify Pump Manufacture," *Design News*, September 23, 1985, p. 110.

McGeehan, Patrick, "Federal-Mogul Buys Fel-Pro for $720 Million," *Wall Street Journal, Europe*, February 25, 1998, p. 8.

Melcher, Richard, "Warm and Fuzzy, Meet Rough and Tumble; A Takeover Puts a Manufacturer's Generous Perks to the Test," *Business Week*, January 26, 1998, p. 38.

Panchapakesan, Meenakshi, "Federal-Mogul: Shifting Gears," *Financial World*, January 18, 1994, p. 24.

"Personnel," *Automotive News*, August 7, 1995, p. 25.

Puchalsky, Andrea, "Federal-Mogul Expected to Purchase Fel-Pro Inc.," *Wall Street Journal, Europe*, January 12, 1998, p. 3.

——, "Federal-Mogul Plans to Buy Fel-Pro Inc.," *Wall Street Journal*, January 12, 1998, p. A3.

——, "Federal-Mogul Sets Pact for Fel-Pro, a Car-Parts Maker," *Wall Street Journal*, January 13, 1998, p. A6.

Stone, Gene, et al, "Workstyle," *Inc.*, January 1986, p. 45.

Tait, Nikki, "Federal-Mogul Expands Further with $720M Buy," *Financial Times*, January 13, 1998, p. 26.

Zingraff, Mike, Jr., "Domestic Fel-Pro Claims Best Import Gaskets Coverage," *Motor Age*, September 1991, p. 78.

—updated by Daryl F. Mallett

Fortunoff Fine Jewelry and Silverware Inc.

70 Charles Lindbergh Boulevard
Uniondale, New York 11553
U.S.A.
(516) 832-9000
(800) 937-4376
Fax: (516) 832-9361
Web site: http://www.fortunoff.com

Private Company
Founded: 1922
Employees: 2,500
Sales: $375 million (1997 est.)
SICs: 5719 Miscellaneous Homefurnishings Stores; 5944
    Jewelry Stores

Fortunoff Fine Jewelry and Silverware Inc. provides customers in the New York City metropolitan area with jewelry and watches, silverware, tabletop and kitchenware items—including the world's largest selection of flatware—bedroom and bathroom items, outdoor furniture, and leather goods. During the 1990s its jewelry sales were consistently rated among the top 10 of any retailer in the United States. There were six stores in 1998, including one on Fifth Avenue in midtown Manhattan.

Discount Home Retailer: 1922–79

Fortunoff was founded in 1922 by Max and Clara Fortunoff under the elevated rapid-transit tracks in the East New York section of Brooklyn. The Russian-born Max Fortunoff, who had left school to join his father's wholesale pots-and-pans business, wanted to strike out on his own when he married. The couple at first stocked only pots and pans and other household articles in what was—and remained—a very poor neighborhood. They settled in an apartment behind the store and raised three children, all of whom took part in the business.

Fortunoff was later described as the first discount operation in the metropolitan New York area. The emphasis at the time was on a wholesale business—the store priced its goods at the wholesale level, or about 30 percent less than normal retail price. The original unit at Livonia Avenue grew over time to a sprawling complex of six or eight stores within a two-block area. According to one industry expert, "They probably furnished every house in Brooklyn and Queens in the 1940s, '50s, and '60s before they moved to Long Island." Sundays were particularly active, with pretzel vendors and other sidewalk hawkers offering their wares as lines of shoppers waited to enter the complex.

As East New York fell into urban decay, Fortunoff became plagued by increasing pilferage of goods. Management followed the practice of some larger retailers and installed dog patrols, but this provoked retaliatory attacks, and after a firebombing the complex was reduced to three units. By then the Fortunoff family had decided to seek a new, larger store in suburban Nassau County, Long Island. The 150,000-square-foot Westbury site where this store opened in 1964 was about three times the size that the Fortunoffs really wanted, but they decided to take the risk. By 1969 they had added another 50,000-square-foot level to the store. In 1972 Fortunoff announced it would more than double its Westbury space, to 440,000 square feet, making the store the second largest on Long Island.

Fortunoff's move to the suburbs was more than geographical. Its merchandise was upgraded with the addition of better-quality goods. Another unit was added in Valley Stream, Long Island. Annual volume for the chain was running at a $30 million level in 1969, with the Westbury store accounting for about 90 percent of the sales. The profit margin after taxes was estimated at two percent, or about $600,000.

Fortunoff opened a 4,000-square-foot store in a former townhouse on Manhattan's elegant East 57th Street in 1969, devoting two floors to jewelry and silverware, with the other two floors given over to offices and repair shops. The total enterprise was now composed of five autonomous divisions, each one a separate corporation run by a family member. The merchandise consisted of jewelry, silverware, furniture case goods, lawn and outdoor furniture, china, decorative accessories, and gifts. By 1977 Fortunoff also had opened a 12,000-square-foot store in a mall in Paramus, New Jersey.

Fortunoff was slow to take advantage of improvements in data processing. It did not install paper-tape-producing cash registers until 1969 and its first electronic cash registers until 1974. The latter units were connected to a minicomputer, and the following year Fortunoff was able to accept credit cards for the first time. Upgraded data processing also allowed the company to print various weekly and monthly merchandising reports.

Fortunoff in the 1980s

Fortunoff's sales were estimated at close to $100 million annually in 1979, when the company purchased a building at 681 Fifth Avenue, between 53rd and 54th streets in midtown Manhattan, for $5 million. Fortunoff opened a 20,000-square-foot unit here, building a new four-level Art Deco interior, and closed its smaller East 57th store. The Fifth Avenue outlet offered a full inventory of gold jewelry, diamonds, precious stones, sterling silver, silver plate, and flatware, but, unlike the Westbury store, did not stock costume or cheaper jewelry. Jewelry was accounting for about 60 percent of the firm's business.

Upscale jewelry dealers on Fifth Avenue such as Tiffany & Co. and Van Cleef & Arpels Inc. were not pleased to face competition in their bailiwick from a discounter like Fortunoff. In 1984 Fortunoff filed a federal antitrust suit against a Swiss watch distributor, accusing it of improperly refusing to supply Fortunoff with luxury watches. Also named was Tiffany, which Fortunoff charged conspired with this distributor to fix the prices of the watches and to deny them to any competing retailer that sold them at a discount. The distributing company conceded that it had stopped supplying Fortunoff with its products but said it had acted simply because the chain did not provide the right atmosphere for its high-priced goods. A company lawyer said, "We don't want our watches alongside barbecues and redwood outdoor furniture."

By 1987 Fortunoff had added stores in Wayne and Paramus, New Jersey. A Woodbridge, New Jersey, store opened in 1989. Outdoor furniture, including five-piece patio sets, chaise lounges, and charbroil barbecue grills, was an important draw at its suburban outlets, accounting for more than $20 million in annual sales. The chain was constantly promoting these items in circulars, newspaper ads, and catalogues, and by staging events such as face painting and putting ice sculptures on display.

Max Fortunoff was still chairman of the company when he died in 1987 at the age of 89. By then his only surviving child, Alan, was serving as president of the firm, having succeeded his sister, Marjorie, who assumed the presidency in 1957 and died

in 1983. Alan's wife, Helene, the secretary-treasurer of the company, was responsible for jewelry and had founded the company's fine-jewelry business in 1958 as an extension of the gift items being sold.

Home textiles was another profitable area for Fortunoff, accounting for $65 million in sales in 1989. One reason was the company's broad bed-and-bath assortment. The bedding ranged from top-of-the-line ensembles to items from makers considered more promotional and included a full range of juvenile bedding. The bath area included a towel department that one supplier said was the size of most retailers' total domestics department. The new Woodbridge store featured a bed-and-bath area with each category of merchandise seemingly occupying a separate wall, thereby allowing shoppers to easily see and choose from the large selection.

By the end of the 1980s Fortunoff had moved away from its reputation for discounting. Its success, according to one observer, rested not on price but on presentation, advertising, and customer service. The company devoted considerable effort to sales training and benefited from low employee turnover. It maintained its own in-house advertising and public relations staffs and used celebrities like Lauren Bacall to convey a prestige image. Another advantage was a large inventory that enabled customers to carry home the merchandise they had just bought.

Initiatives of the 1990s

Interviewed for the *New York Times* in 1989, Alan Fortunoff said the company had suffered large losses over a relatively short period because of sophisticated thievery by people with drug-abuse problems, aided by the proliferation of flea markets in the metropolitan area. He also said Long Island badly needed modern malls to offer goods and services in one enclosed, vertical, air-conditioned building. Fortunoff already had signed a letter of intent, in collaboration with a California-based developer, to build such a mall in Westbury. This 60-acre mall, to be called the Fortunoff Galleria, was to be built on the parking lot of the former Roosevelt Raceway and include department stores such as Nordstrom's and Neiman-Marcus as well as Fortunoff.

Proposals for a shopping mall at the Westbury site had circulated for many years and by 1978 involved several lawsuits and countersuits, $60 million in damage claims, and a dispute over leasing agreements between the proposed developer, Madison Square Garden Company Inc., and the two major retail concerns on Old Country Road, Fortunoff and Ohrbach's, which both were leasing space from the Garden and trying to block the development. A plan by the Westbury Properties Group in the 1980s to build a Y-shaped, enclosed mall south of Fortunoff and Ohrbach's and connect to both also failed.

Fortunoff's proposal, unveiled in 1990, fell victim to community opposition and a national recession. In 1991, however, he won approval for an indoor mall downscaled by about 40 percent, with two levels and enclosed atriums, and a Price Club to the west. Alan Fortunoff, who owned the 69 acre site, sold 30 acres to the Price Co. for more than $1 million an acre. Price Club Plaza, the 401,000-square-foot plaza whose centerpiece was a members only, warehouse style Price Club store, was completed in 1992.

Construction of the mall, which was renamed The Source and became Long Island's first new regional mall in nearly 25 years, did not begin until 1996. Fortunoff's partner was Simon DeBartolo Group Inc., the largest mall developer in North America. Built around off-price stores, themed restaurants, and specialty shops instead of department stores, the 522,000-square-foot Source opened in 1997 with half of its 75 tenants ready for business. Fortunoff, which modernized about two-thirds of its Westbury store, also connected it to the second level of the mall and opened separate outlets in The Source for baby furniture and watches on the concourse of the structure. By late 1997 The Source was drawing more than 100,000 cars a week.

Fortunoff began sponsoring home shopping on cable television in 1994, when it started offering, on a trial basis, programs displaying its upscale women's jewelry. The company signed an agreement with Cablevision Systems Corp. and its programming arm to offer a 30-minute "Direct Source" program four times a day, displaying merchandise ranging in price from $90 to $5,295. The program was available on Cablevision cable systems in New York City, Boston, New Jersey, and on Long Island. In 1997 Fortunoff and Long Island's Metropolitan Suburban Bus Authority applied for a federal radio license allowing "Radio Fortunoff" to air traffic information within a four-mile radius to help motorists avoid congestion.

The flagship Westbury store was attracting 60,000 shoppers weekly in 1995 and registering sales of $160 million annually. This store boasted the retail industry's highest sales of jewelry per square foot in 1995. Silverware also was an important part of the retailer's business, with virtually every pattern kept on display. The other five stores, in 1998, consisted of the Fifth Avenue store, outlets in Wayne and Woodbridge, New Jersey, and two in the Paramus Park Mall. Fortunoff was reported at that time to be looking in Suffolk County—the county east of Nassau—for a site to build a store as big as the Westbury outlet.

Further Reading

Barmash, Isadore, "Fortunoff Planning to Expand Store in Westbury, L.I.," *New York Times,* October 24, 1972, p. 67.
——, "Fortunoff's Going to Fifth Ave.," *New York Times,* November 27, 1979, p. 29.
——, "Fortunoff's Takes a Circle Route to Its New Manhattan Store," *New York Times,* September 28, 1969, p. 13.
"Battling for Luxury Watches," *New York Times,* June 5, 1984, p. D5.
Bernstein, James, "Channel 1 Shopping," *Newsday,* October 27, 1994, pp. A49–A50.
——, "Fortunoff to Open 2nd LI Store," *Newsday,* April 8, 1996, p. A69.
Bilello, Suzanne, "Ground Breaks for Galleria Mall Project," *Newsday,* May 14, 1992, pp. 47–48.
Cooper, Jeanne Dugan, "A Scaled-Down Mall," *Newsday,* September 29, 1991, p. 5.
Cuff, Daniel F., "Winning Over the Community for a Mall," *New York Times,* May 10, 1992, Sec. 3, p. 8.
Fleetwood, Selby, and Solomon, Barbara, "Fortunoff: A Well-Merited Mystique," *HFD/Home Furnishings Daily,* February 26, 1990, p. 38.
"Fortunoff Focuses on Basics of Retailing," *HFD/Home Furnishings Daily,* April 23, 1990, p. 10A.
Goldgaber, Arnold, "A Source for Retail on Long Island," *Chain Store Age,* September 1996, pp. 138, 140.
Hudson, Edward, "Max Fortunoff, 89, Is Dead; Headed Specialty Store Chain," *New York Times,* July 26, 1987, p. 26.
Kennedy, Shawn G., "Another Mall for Westbury?" *New York Times,* January 29, 1978, Sec. 21, pp. 1, 7.
Madore, James T., "Mall with a New Twist Set for Grand Opening," *Newsday,* September 4, 1997, pp. A55–A56.
——, "With FCC Approval, It's Radio Fortunoff," *Newsday,* November 30, 1997, p. A54.
"Marjorie Mayrock, 60, Fortunoff Chain's Head," *New York Times,* June 9, 1983, p. B12.
Mason-Draffen, Carrie, "Fortunoff Shifts Gears," *Newsday,* May 19, 1994, p. 51.
McIntosh, Claire, "Key People Making News in Diamonds," *Working Woman,* August 1989, p. 44.
Mitchell, Ellen, "Westbury Mall Plan Revived," *New York Times,* September 11, 1982, Sec. 21, p. 12.
Rather, John, "A Retailer Who Followed the Customers to the Suburbs," *New York Times,* July 22, 1989, Sec. 21, p. 2.
Sabia, Vince, "Fortunoff Merges POS and EFT in Mini-Based System," *Computerworld,* March 14, 1977, p. 51.
——, "A Jewel of a System," *Chain Store Age Executive,* January 1995, pp. 69–71.
"Shrewd Marketing Draws Traffic," *HFD/Home Furnishings Daily,* September 8, 1986, p. S10.
Slesin, Suzanne, "A Familiar Jewelry Emporium Arrives on 5th Ave.," *New York Times,* October 13, 1979, p. 46.

—Robert Halasz

GAGE

Gage Marketing Group

10000 Highway 55
Minneapolis, Minnesota 55441-6365
U.S.A.
(612) 595-3800
Fax: (612) 595-3871
Web site: http://www.gage.com

Private Company
Incorporated: 1991
Employees: 250
Sales: $70 million (1998 est.)
SICs: 8742 Management Consulting Services

Gage Marketing Group, a widely diversified marketing business, has provided services to roughly 75 percent of the *Fortune* 100. With consulting and communication expertise, in-store marketing and promotion, and travel services, the company is among the leading integrated marketing agencies in the United States.

Ties with Corporate Giant: 1960s–80s

Edwin C. (Skip) Gage III established Gage Marketing Group in 1991 following the return of his father-in-law, Curt Carlson, to the helm of Carlson Companies, Inc. Gage had been appointed CEO of the privately held, Minnesota-based company in 1989, during a period when Carlson was grappling with health problems.

Gage, who married Carlson's younger daughter, Barbara, in 1965, joined the company in 1968, leaving his position as account executive with Chicago-based Foote, Cone & Belding Advertising. Starting out as director of marketing, development, and research, Gage transformed a one-person office into a $50 million business by the mid-1970s through the acquisition and integration of direct marketing, promotion, and incentive operations. When Carlson moved into the travel business, Gage assumed responsibility for that area as well.

In 1980 Gage was named president of Carlson Marketing Group, Inc. Three years later he was appointed executive vice-president of the entire corporation and in 1984 succeeded Carlson as president.

In the mid-1980s the conglomerate, which began as the Gold Bond Stamp Company and then diversified into areas ranging from real estate to jewelry manufacturing, pared down its scope of operation to focus on hospitality, travel, and marketing. As chief operating officer, Gage drove the restructuring.

In 1988 the corporation reorganized. Carlson Holding Companies, Inc. was established as the parent company for the Carlson family concerns including Carlson Companies, which consisted of businesses such as T.G.I. Friday's restaurants, Radisson hotels, and Ask Mr. Foster travel agencies. Gage was named CEO in 1989, but his tenure proved to be short-lived.

Plans to expand the company's international travel holdings were hampered by the war in the Persian Gulf and an economic recession at home. Carlson Companies' profits fell off. Gage resigned as CEO and president when the 77-year-old Carlson—within a year after undergoing quadruple bypass surgery—took back control of daily operations of the $8 billion company.

No longer heir-apparent to the empire, Gage was named co-vice chair. He shared the newly created position with Carlson's older daughter, Marilyn Carlson Nelson, whose credentials included a degree in economics, experience as a security analyst with Paine Webber, board memberships with major corporations, and a major role in bringing the 1992 Super Bowl to the Minneapolis Metrodome. Nelson had been named senior vice-president of the holding company in 1989.

Setting a New Course: Early 1990s

Gage responded with an offer to buy Carlson Marketing Group; his father-in-law turned him down. Carlson did agree to sell four businesses—Promotion Management, Adistra, Carlson Lettershop, and Outdoor Travel, which according to a January 1992 *Star Tribune* article represented about 10 percent of Carlson Marketing Group's total revenues.

Company Perspectives:

To be the premier provider of integrated marketing services to our clients, measurably impacting their results through the delivery of superior strategic, developmental and executional marketing services.

"I built Carlson Marketing Group, and to a great extent the travel company. I made a major contribution to Carlson Companies and I really feel like this was the time for me to do my own thing and that's very difficult with Curt, because he likes people to do his thing. It was probably more the idea of doing my own thing, my own way, than necessarily being an entrepreneur. In a way, however, being in a family company, in a major job, is somewhat like being an entrepreneur in and of itself, because there is an ownership position, at least, through family," said Gage in a 1992 *Corporate Report Minnesota* interview with Lee Schafer.

Gage continued to serve on the Carlson board, and his family connection left open the possibility he might well return to the company one day. Wife Barbara and sister-in-law Marilyn stood in line to share their father's fortune which was estimated in a September 1991 *Fortune* article at $1.3 billion, making Carlson one of the nation's richest men.

The Carlson Company businesses Gage and his wife Barbara purchased formed the first leg of the integrated marketing business he envisioned building. The largest, Promotion Management, provided traditional fulfillment services such as the administration of rebate forms, samples, and gift items. They also dealt with coupons, catalog orders, and telemarketing. Michigan-based Adistra, founded in 1958 and purchased by Carlson in 1990, specialized in auto industry sales and incentive programs. A much smaller operation, Carlson Lettershop, offered printing and mailing services. Gage also bought another small Carlson business, Outdoor Travel, which arranged adventure vacations. In all, Gage Marketing Group employed about 1,500 people with about half in Minnesota and the rest in the Detroit area; El Paso, Texas; and Juarez, Mexico. Combined sales for the operations had been $65 million a year.

The promotional industry from which Gage Marketing drew the bulk of its revenues had experienced a drop in sales volume in the late 1980s, and sales volume was flat in the early days of the 1990s. A few large players dominated the field—Iowa-based Promotion Fulfillment Corp. was among the largest in the nation. In the light of a changing marketplace Gage planned to add two other divisions: one to develop market strategy and a second to implement advertising, promotion, and direct-mail plans.

A number of former Carlson company executives joined Gage in the new endeavor, and much of the established client base remained intact including Coca-Cola, Del Monte Foods, Ford Motor Co., General Mills, Kimberly-Clark, Mazda, Miller Brewing, and Northwest Airlines. During the first year of operation, the company acquired a California promotion agency and some small travel companies and established an in-store, point-of-purchase display company and an event marketing business.

Gage had positioned the business to become a full-service, integrated marketing company with services ranging from strategy to shelf placement. According to a 1993 *Star Tribune* article by Josephine Marcotty, Gage was the first to put marketing consulting, program development, program production, and program management all under one roof. Skeptics of integrated marketing questioned whether manufacturers would be willing to rely on one agency to perform for all the different aspects of their marketing plan.

Gage tried to purchase the Carlson Marketing division in 1993, but the unsolicited offer was refused. According to a May 1993 *Star Tribune* article by Sally Apgar, the departure of Gage and other executives left the division without a sense of direction. "Once the strongest component of Carlson companies, the Marketing Group was able to fuel much of the growth in other divisions. However, with the recession and changes in the marketing industry, the Marketing Group now trails the other two divisions in growth," wrote Apgar. The Carlson business specialized in employee and customer incentive strategies.

Established in Their Own Right: Mid-1990s

Advertising Age listed Gage Marketing Group as the largest promotion shop in the United States in 1993. Revenues for the privately held company climbed to about $80 million that year. According to a May 1994 *Twin Cities Business Monthly* article by Allison Campbell, the original business areas' sales were "relatively flat." The packaged goods industry had shifted away from promotions to everyday-low-pricing, and the auto industry was lagging.

Adistra looked for business opportunities outside the auto industry. New clients Taco Bell and Armstrong broadened their customer mix. Gage Marketing also capitalized on corporate downsizing: more and more companies were outsourcing functions once performed in-house. New York-based Publisher's Clearing House, for example, hired Minnesota-based Gage Marketing to perform customer-service work, a service made possible through the use of high-tech phone systems.

Gage Marketing Group's gross income rose 21.6 percent to $95.7 million in 1994. "One reason for that strong growth is Gage's strong database roots, which give the agency a crossover entree into direct marketing and direct response," wrote Kenneth Wylie in a 1995 *Advertising Age* article. Other technology-focused undertakings included: educational program, merchandising, and online promotion development for the National Hockey League and mail processing for the Atlanta Olympic Games. In November 1996 Gage purchased the computer print personalization business of Dynamark, a Minnesota-based company. In 1997 the company launched five new Internet marketing products aimed at lessening the risk for companies considering doing business on the web.

With agencies crossing over into each other's areas of expertise and creating a new industrial environment, Gage Marketing increasingly found itself ranked among traditional advertising agencies by the trade journals. In 1997 *Advertising Age* listed Gage Marketing 27th among the world's top 50 advertising organizations; Carlson Marketing Group ranked 18th.

Gage Marketing continued to hold the distinction as the nation's largest promotional marketing firm with 1996 sales of $128 million and 1,800 employees. In June 1997, the company announced its intent to purchase a neon sign and point-of-purchase display business from Minnesota-base Beryl Corp. The company, which generated $15 million in annual sales, elevated Gage's in-store operation to the largest among its business units.

Gage Marketing picked up a small German-based sales promotion office from Carlson Marketing earlier in the year, but according to a June 1997 *Star Tribune* article by Ann Merrill, the pace of acquisitions had been slower than Skip Gage had hoped due to an internal building effort. The company had plans to expand on the East Coast, complementing its already well-established presence in the Midwest and in the West.

Plans for the Future

Gage Marketing continued to fuel its other aspirations as well. "To help it reach its lofty goal of 20 percent annual growth, Gage Marketing is devoting much attention to the front-end businesses: strategic and developmental services that generally have higher margins," wrote Merrill. On this end of the business the company developed sales promotion, direct marketing, online marketing, and database marketing programs, plus sweepstakes and contests. Yet, the back-end businesses brought in 60 percent of Gage Marketing revenues. Printing for Ford, rebate redemption for Kraft General Foods and Procter & Gamble, and telemarketing for Reader's Digest were among the projects handled by those units.

Gage Marketing sold its back-end business operations to Atlanta-based AHL Services, Inc. in June 1998 for about $80 million. The consumer fulfillment, teleservices, trade support services, automotive marketing services, and the lettershop were to operate as a division of AHL under the name Gage Marketing Support Services and be managed by Skip Gage under a long-term consulting agreement. Gage, as one of the largest shareholders of AHL, would also serve on their board of directors. Gage Marketing Group would uphold its commitment to the concept of integrated marketing by continuing to offer back-end services, but now via its relationship with AHL.

According to a June 1998 Gage Marketing press release, the major factors leading to the partnership with AHL were the ongoing consolidation in the marketing support services industry which created "larger and more broadly positioned" competitors, and the need for capital investment, especially in technology, to remain on the cutting edge of the industry.

Gage Marketing Group continued to own and operate promotion and direct-marketing agencies in Minneapolis and California, the In-Store (point-of-purchase display) marketing and database marketing agencies in Minneapolis, as well as Gage Travel. The remaining Gage Marketing operations had sales in excess of $70 million and employed more than 250 people. Following the transaction, Gage Marketing ranked sixth among the largest promotion agencies in the United States.

Further Reading

Apgar, Sally, "Carlson Appoints Panel to Work on Marketing Group," *Star Tribune* (Minneapolis), May 15, 1993, p. 1D.

——, "Carlson Marketing Group Not for Sale," *Star Tribune* (Minneapolis), May 21, 1993, p. 1D.

Campbell, Allison, "Minding His Own Business," *Twin Cities Business Monthly*, May 1994, pp. 39–41.

Erdman, Andrew, "Billionaire Takes His Ball Back," *Fortune*, December 16, 1991, p. 137.

"Gage Marketing Group," *Corporate Report Fact Book 1998*, p. 567.

Geiger, Bob, "Kamstra '93 Billings Are Up 44% Over '92 to $36 Million," *Star Tribune* (Minneapolis), April 18, 1994, p. 2D.

Kennedy, Patrick, "Gage Gauges the Future," *Corporate Report Minnesota*, June 1993, p. 15.

Levy, Melissa, "AHL Services Will Buy Gage Marketing Fulfillment Unit," *Star Tribune* (Minneapolis), June 19, 1998, p. 1D.

Marcotty, Josephine, "Marketing Mission," *Star Tribune* (Minneapolis), February 5, 1993, p. 1D.

Merrill, Ann, "Carlson Marketing 18th in Industry Ranking," *Star Tribune* (Minneapolis), April 24, 1997, p. 3D.

——, "Ex-CEO at Carlson Starts Anew, Buys 3 Companies, "*Minneapolis/St. Paul CityBusiness*, January 13–19, 1992, pp. 1, 7.

——, "Gage Marketing Keeps Growing," *Star Tribune* (Minneapolis), June 20, 1997, p. 1D.

——, "Gage Marketing to Put NHL Online," *Star Tribune* (Minneapolis), April 28, 1995, p. 3D.

——, "Gage Selling Off Back-End Operations for Cash to Expand Marketing Empire," *Star Tribune* (Minneapolis), July 24, 1998, p. 3D.

Phelps, David, "Gage Announces Formation of His Marketing Firm," *Star Tribune* (Minneapolis), February 28, 1992, p. 5D.

Phelps, David, Tony Kennedy, and Sally Apgar, "Curt Carson Retakes Control of His Companies," *Star Tribune* (Minneapolis), November 8, 1991, p. 1A.

Rourke, Elizabeth, and David E. Salamie, "Carlson Companies, Inc.," *International Directory of Company Histories*, vol. 22, Detroit: St. James Press, 1998, pp. 125–29.

Schafer, Lee, "A Conversation with Skip Gage," *Corporate Report Minnesota*, July 1992, pp. 44–51.

Wiener, Jay, "Minnesota Business: Going for the Green," *Star Tribune* (Minneapolis), April 7, 1996, p. 4D.

Wylie, Kenneth, "Marketing Services: Agencies Morphing into What Marketers Need," *Advertising Age*, July 10, 1995, p. S1.

—Kathleen Peippo

Geffen Records Inc.

9130 Sunset Boulevard
Los Angeles, California 90069
U.S.A.
(310) 278-9010
Fax: (310) 858-7063
Web site: http://www.geffen.com

*Wholly Owned Subsidiary of Universal Music Group/
Seagram Ltd.*
Incorporated: 1980
Employees: 135
Sales: $505 million (1994 est.)
SICs: 3652 Phonograph Records & Prerecorded Audio
Tapes & Disks

Geffen Records Inc. is the second record label founded by David Geffen, the richest, most successful entertainment mogul of the 20th century and certainly one of the most controversial. A series of business deals highly favorable to Geffen left him with a personal fortune approaching $1 billion. The record labels he founded and has since sold are both identified with a legacy of highly respected popular music, produced by artists ranging from Bob Dylan to Peter Gabriel. David Geffen is also one of three founders of the entertainment enterprise Dreamworks SKG with partners Stephen Spielberg and Jeffrey Katzenberg.

Beginning in Brooklyn

Geffen's mother, Batya Volovskaya, was a Jewish emigré from the Soviet Union. She had fled the World War II pogroms of the Ukraine to Brooklyn, and later learned most of her family had been killed. As a seamstress, she was the breadwinner of the family. She is credited as the source of her younger son's drive and business savvy. Geffen's father, an intellectual dilettante, died when Geffen was 17.

As a child, Geffen dreamed of becoming an entertainment mogul. The life of Louis B. Mayer in particular inspired him.

Upon graduating from high school, Geffen promptly departed for Los Angeles. Then, after returning to New York, David Geffen forged UCLA graduation credentials to land a job in the mail room of the William Morris talent agency. His stint as a trainee there indoctrinated him in the pace and the lifestyle of the entertainment business.

Geffen eventually became an agent for the likes of Buffalo Springfield, Peter, Paul and Mary, and Janis Joplin, harbingers of an emerging musical scene. The hippie politics of the 1960s opened the way for folk rock, an infusion of rock and roll with the tradition, artistic aspirations, and populist leanings of newly revived American folk music.

Geffen took folk artist Laura Nyro under his wing, helping restore her career and confidence, and eventually left the Morris agency to become her full-time agent. The deal he engineered with Columbia on her behalf made him a millionaire at age 27.

Geffen returned to California and soon became known as an aggressive advocate for other acts. In 1969 he became a vice-president at Creative Management, the forerunner of ICM. Afterwards Geffen formally switched from the role of agent to manager in forming the Geffen-Roberts Company with Eliot Roberts. Geffen owned three-fourths of the partnership.

Asylum in the 1970s

Geffen founded Asylum Records, bankrolled by Atlantic Records, in 1970. It featured stars such as Joni Mitchell and Linda Ronstadt. Geffen announced Laura Nyro would be the first artist signed to the label, but she in fact surprised him by signing with Columbia Records. California songwriter Jackson Browne, whom Geffen had earlier tried to pitch to Atlantic, was first to record for Asylum.

In both the Geffen-Roberts management company and Asylum Records, Geffen allowed the artists unprecedented creative control. This proved attractive to some of the most-successful performers of the 1970s, including Ronstadt and the rock band the Eagles, who found their start on Asylum.

The Eagles worried about the conflicts of interest of Geffen-Roberts acting as both their manager and record company—essentially, both employee and employer—while at the same time controlling their publishing revenues. After parting company with Geffen, the Eagles achieved a dizzying level of success and eventually recovered their publishing rights through a lawsuit.

In 1972 Geffen sold the company to Warner Communications for $7 million, "the biggest number [he] could think of." He agreed to work for Warner for an additional five years. Asylum and Elektra were combined in 1973, the former taken out of the control of Atlantic Records, also a Warner subsidiary. Geffen was assigned to lead the label. He suggested all three labels be combined with Atlantic head Ahmet Ertegun and himself serving as co-chairmen. But the deal was scuttled by other wary Warner executives. Geffen would have a long relationship with Warner, eventually buying Jack Warner's estate.

Bob Dylan signed with Elektra/Asylum in 1973, where he had his first number one album, *Planet Waves*. The label failed to satisfy Dylan, however, and he soon returned to Columbia Records. This seemed to wound Geffen and he left to head Warner's film division for a brief, undistinguished time.

Warner Boss Steve Ross dismissed Geffen in 1976. At the same time, Geffen's doctors gave him a diagnosis of bladder cancer, prompting Geffen to leave L.A. and enter semi-retirement. He landed a teaching position at Yale University and became a devotee of Studio 54.

Revitalized in the 1980s

After being informed that he did not in fact have cancer, Geffen returned from his hiatus and persuaded Warner Brothers head Steve Ross to provide the start-up capital ($25 million) for a new label, Geffen Records, in return for a 50 percent share. Although Ross was known for lavishly rewarding his executives, this deal was surprisingly generous. Geffen also reserved overseas distribution rights, which he assigned to Warner archrival CBS Records for $17 million.

However, it was not an auspicious time to re-enter the music business. Industry sales had fallen for the first time since World War II. Favorable results eluded the ambitious start-up. John Lennon's career with Geffen was cut short by murder. Other high profile signings, Donna Summer and Elton John, failed to meet expectations. Geffen did manage to sign other respected artists who performed fairly well: Peter Gabriel, formerly with Genesis, and Joni Mitchell.

In 1982 Geffen wooed eccentric and unpredictable folk rock legend Neil Young, offering him the creative freedom he craved in the face of a more lucrative offer from RCA Records. However, by November of the next year Geffen sued Young for $3 million for breach of agreement, for not making "commercial" records. This suit and a $21 million countersuit were both eventually dropped.

Geffen fared better in his theatrical productions, such as the film that made Tom Cruise a star, *Risky Business*, as well as the play *Cats*. In 1984 he stepped out of his A&R role at Geffen Records. Perhaps due to his string of failures at picking success-ful talent, Geffen delegated this duty to others. John David Kaldoner, Gary Gersh, and John Zutaut each picked big winners for the company, such as Aerosmith, Nirvana, and Guns 'n Roses.

In 1984, upon renewing Geffen's contract with Warner, Ross conceded full ownership of the still floundering company to Geffen in exchange for Warner's right to distribute the company's records for five more years. Geffen Records lost money in 1984, 1985, and 1986. However in 1987, Geffen's music, film, and theater projects brought in $88 million in revenues and a profit of $19 million. Geffen Records alone garnered more $225 million in sales in 1989.

The Alternative 1990s

David Geffen reported that he wanted to catch the last end of the wave of consolidation in the music industry fueled by the decade's merger-mad atmosphere. After shopping Geffen Records around to Thorn EMI, which offered $750 million, and Time Warner, he sold it to MCA in March 1990 for stock worth $540 million. This stock appreciated to $710 million after MCA itself was acquired by Matsushita Electric Industrial Co. in November. The deal made Geffen a billionaire, or nearly one, by most estimates.

Geffen Records grossed $225 million in 1990, releasing 33 titles. In 1990, Geffen started its DGC imprint for new talent. The next year, Geffen Records changed distributors. It dropped WEA for Uni Distribution nationally and BMG abroad. David Geffen credited the change with improving the label's fortunes in the mid-1990s.

David Geffen stayed busy outside the music business, producing a film adaptation of *Interview with the Vampire,* based on Anne Rice's bestselling novel. In November 1992, while addressing the AIDS Project Los Angeles benefit, Geffen casually announced his homosexuality, attracting a new level of press attention both positive and negative.

The year 1994 began with three Geffen acts—Nirvana, Beck, and Counting Crows—occupying the top three slots of the Modern Rock charts. These three groups, and Nirvana in particular, helped usher in a whole new, darker "alternative" sound that would dominate rock sales for several years. At the time, Geffen reckoned that it cost $300,000 to record a debut album—equivalent to Asylum's entire budget in the 1970s.

The label prided itself on customizing its promotional approach to the particular needs of its various acts. Geffen used Minneapolis-based REP Co. to distribute certain recordings into smaller stores than those served by Uni. Geffen also struck up alliances with other labels such as Almo Sounds, recently created by Herb Alpert and Jerry Moss.

Geffen Records had a banner year in 1994, when its revenues were $505 million. Overseas sales accounted for $230 million. It released 33 titles in the United States. Twenty-eight of these reached the *Billboard* 200 chart in 1994, compared to only 18 in 1993. Twenty-four of the U.S. titles were also released overseas.

As Geffen's contract with Matsushita neared expiration, Geffen, Stephen Spielberg, and former Disney executive Jeffrey Katzenberg announced a new $3 billion entertainment venture, to be named DreamWorks SKG, in late 1994. After a slow start, the group finally proved itself with such acclaimed films as *Amistad* and *Saving Private Ryan* and would succeed in other media as well.

Geffen remained with MCA/Matsushita until April 1995, whereupon president and COO Ed Rosenblatt, responsible for operations since the label's founding, took over as chairman and CEO. After about a year Rosenblatt named Bill Bennett his successor as president.

Geffen Records would market SKG Records and Dreamworks records, as well as Almo. Another new label, Outpost Records, aligned with Geffen in 1995. In 1996 Geffen announced its Budget Gold Line, rereleases of older titles designed to appeal to such department store chains as Wal-Mart and Kmart; two years later it launched Delinquent Records specifically to release soundtrack albums.

A New World Order

Seagram Ltd. bought 80 percent of MCA from Matsushita for $5.7 billion in 1995, resulting in a new ultimate parent for Geffen Records. Both MCA and Geffen operated under the Universal Music Group. The labels soon announced a restructuring, with Geffen losing 20 employees.

Seagram's $10 billion acquisition of Dutch music giant Polygram N.V. in December 1998 hinted at massive layoffs to come for Geffen and its sister labels in the Universal Music Group and within Polygram. Twenty percent of the two companies' 15,500 employees were expected to lose their jobs. Seagram planned to consolidate U.S. operations of the combined company, unofficially dubbed "Unigram" at the time, into East Coast and West Coast groups, shedding 3,000 jobs in the process. Geffen Records was grouped with West Coast labels Interscope Records and A&M Records. Rosenblatt and other top executives were expected to depart. The label's talent roster was also reduced. After the merger the Universal Music Group stood as the largest music conglomerate in the world, controlling a third of the market with projected annual sales of $5 billion.

Further Reading

Farrand, J., Jr., and B. Witkowski, "Turning Rock into Gold," *New York Times Magazine,* December 8, 1991.
Goldstein, Patrick, "The Rolling Stone Interview: David Geffen," *Rolling Stone,* April 29, 1993.
Goodman, Fred, *The Mansion on the Hill: Dylan, Young, Geffen, Springsteen, and the Head-On Collision of Rock and Commerce,* New York: Times Books, 1997.
Morris, Chris, "Geffen's Rock Methodology Pays Off," *Billboard,* February 21, 1994, p. 10.
Rosen, Craig, "For Geffen's Rosenblatt, Intriguing Power Transfer," *Billboard,* April 22, 1995, p. 105.
——, "Geffen Records Enjoys Best Year," *Billboard,* January 21, 1995, pp. 1, 81.
Sandler, Adam, "Music Will Boot 3,000," *Variety,* December 11, 1998.
——, "U Music Group: New Giant of Tune Town," *Variety,* December 10, 1998.
Schwartz, John, Andrew Murr, and John Taliaferro, "Geffen Goes Platinum," *Newsweek,* December 10, 1990.
Turner, Richard, and Corie Brown, "Fishing Buddies," *Newsweek,* September 29, 1997.
Wade, Dorothy, and Justine Picardie, *Music Man: Ahmet Ertegun, Atlantic Records, and the Triumph of Rock 'n' Roll,* New York and London: Norton, 1990.
White, Edmund, "King David," *US,* April 1997.

—Frederick C. Ingram

GENTEX CORPORATION

A Smarter Vision™

Gentex Corporation

600 N. Centennial St.
Zeeland, Michigan 49464
U.S.A.
(616) 772-1800
(800) 444-GNTX; (800) 444-4689
Fax: (616) 772-7348
Web site: http://www.gentex.com

Public Company
Incorporated: 1974
Employees: 1400
Sales: $186.32 million (1997)
Stock Exchanges: NASDAQ
Ticker Symbol: GNTX
SICs: 3231 Glass Products, Made of Purchased Glass;
    3679 Electronic Components & Assemblies, Not
    Elsewhere Classified

Gentex Corporation is a recognized world leader in the manufacture of auto-dimming mirrors for the automobile industry. Its mirrors employ electrochromic technology, the process of reversibly darkening materials by applying electricity. Gentex's Automotive Products Group, which sells the mirrors to nearly every automobile manufacturer worldwide, accounts for 90 percent of the company's sales. The other 10 percent comes from the company's Fire Protection Products Group. Gentex's extensive line of commercial fire protection products includes a variety of smoke detectors and audible/visual signalling devices. Like the company's auto-dimming mirrors, its fire protection products employ photoelectric sensing devices with related electronic circuitry.

Gentex Corporation was founded in Zeeland, Michigan, by Fred Bauer in 1974 to make fire protection products. Bauer had launched Simicon Co., a manufacturer of electronic furnace-control units, in the late 1960s when he was 23 years old. When a *Fortune* 500 company bought Simicon in the early 1970s, Bauer used the capital to start Gentex.

The company began by making intrusion alarms and smoke detectors for mobile homes. It became known as a manufacturer of high-quality fire-protection products. The company's smoke detectors and signalling devices utilized electro-optics—photoelectric sensing devices combined with related electronic circuitry—which enabled the smoke detectors to "see" smoke and signal an alarm. The photoelectric fire detector was co-invented by Bauer. It is less prone to false alarms and quickly detects smoldering fires.

The company's expertise in electro-optics led to the solution of a problem that had been plaguing the automobile industry for 20 years: how to find a way to eliminate glare from rearview mirrors and make nighttime driving safer. The company's first automatically dimming rearview mirrors were electromechanical, or motorized.

Introduced World's First Automatically Dimming Mirror, 1982

In 1982 Gentex introduced the world's first electromechanical (motorized) dimming mirror. The technology for the motorized mirror was developed by a joint venture in which Bauer had participated. The company's first generation of glare-controlling rearview mirrors were used primarily on American luxury cars. They utilized a pair of electronic "eyes" to sense headlight glare. The electronic sensors were connected electronically to a small motor that adjusted the angle of the mirror for night driving. Gentex made about 1.1 million units of its first-generation mirrors between 1982 and 1991.

After becoming a public company in December 1981 to finance its motorized mirror production, Gentex did not show a profit until 1985. In 1983 it reported a net loss of $250,000 on sales of $2.6 million, followed by a net loss of $527,000 on sales of $5.3 million in 1984.

The following year, 1985, marked the company's first year of profitability, as it reported net income of $570,000 on sales of $9 million. It was the beginning of a fairly consistent record of sales and earnings growth. With the exception of a fallback in sales in 1990, sales increased steadily for the rest of the 1980s and 1990s. Net income peaked at $2.1 million in 1989, and after falling back in 1990 net income rose steadily through 1997. In 1987 mirrors accounted for nearly $9 million in sales, compared to about $5 million in sales generated by the company's fire protection products. To enhance its glass-working skills, Gentex acquired Zeeland-based Vanguard Glass Fabricators in 1986.

Introduced Second Generation of Auto-Dimming Mirrors, 1987

Sales of the motorized mirrors peaked in 1987 at 203,000 units. In the first half of 1988 sales of the motorized mirrors took a downturn. Company officials noted that the mirror's popularity had reached a plateau, and they expected lower sales as the automakers changed over to Gentex's new electrochromic mirrors for the 1988 model year. Some drivers had complained about the noise the motorized mirror made when it changed positions, and others found the movement distracting. Other factors influencing mirror sales included a lack of promotion of the option by the automobile manufacturers.

In 1987 Gentex's second generation of automatically dimming mirrors, called electrochromic mirrors, were introduced as an option on the 1988 Lincoln Continental and then on eight General Motors models in 1989. The electrochromic mirror, which Gentex developed in 1986, eliminated glare by automatically darkening when headlight glare was detected. The electrochromic mirrors were an improvement over the electromechanical mirrors, mainly because they dimmed to an infinite number of levels to eliminate glare while maintaining the driver's rear vision. They also remained stationary and did not move or make noise when adjusting to headlight glare. Gentex hoped that some automakers would make the electrochromic mirrors standard equipment on some models.

A company spokesperson told the *Grand Rapids Business Journal,* "The history of other successful options has been that they all start out very slowly as a specialized item on luxury cars, then they become standard equipment on certain luxury cars and an option for intermediately priced cars." Some of the automakers were including the mirrors as part of a "value package" of options that were sold at a discount to customers. As a stand-alone option, the electrochromic mirrors cost between $80 and $100.

The motorized mirror continued to be offered by car makers at about 20 percent less than the electrochromic mirror.

When Gentex first announced the electrochromic mirror in 1986, it was hailed as a technological breakthrough. Gentex officials noted that it was the first time a practical product had been made out of electrochromic technology, which had been around for about 40 years. The mirrors contained a thin gel sandwiched between two pieces of glass. When the gel is electrically charged, it darkens. When the electrical charge is turned off, the gel clears.

Research on the electrochromic mirror began in 1983, when Harlan Byker, a chemist at Battelle Laboratories, and his father, Gary Byker, visited Gentex. Harlan Byker told company officials he knew how to apply electrochromic technology to Gentex's motorized mirrors. Gentex decided to fund Byker's research on electrochromics at Battelle. Byker then joined Gentex to head its research and development team after he completed his research at Battelle.

As the interior electrochromic rearview mirrors became available on cars in 1988, Gentex expected its mirror sales to double to more than 400,000 units in 1989. The company forecast it would be making one million electrochromic mirrors a year by 1990, primarily for the automotive market. It also continued to produce the motorized mirrors.

In the fall of 1988 the company began constructing a $3.5 million, 70,000-square-foot addition to the former Vanguard Glass building for completion in fall 1989. The company had just completed a $1.5 million expansion at the Vanguard plant that had doubled its capacity to produce mirrors. The expansion was financed by industrial revenue bonds issued through the City of Zeeland.

Once the expansion was completed, the Vanguard plant would be devoted to mirror production. The company's original plant, located on Chicago Drive in Zeeland, would be used to manufacture the company's line of fire protection products. At the time, Gentex had about 230 employees and planned to add another 70 to 90 employees during 1989.

Sales for 1989 increased dramatically to $23.8 million, up from $14.7 million in 1988. During the year sales of the company's electrochromic rearview mirrors reached 234,000 units. Sales of the motorized mirrors were declining, and the product would be phased out after 1991. In 1989 the company also began to cultivate international markets. It entered into a distribution agreement with Tokyo-based Ichikoh Industries Ltd., whereby each company could distribute the other's products. Ichikoh would begin distributing Gentex's electrochromic mirrors to Japanese automakers and their transplants in the United States. Gentex could distribute Ichikoh's manually operated interior mirrors to American car manufacturers. No technology transfer was involved in the agreement. Gentex also issued 300,000 new shares of common stock, which were purchased by Ichikoh. The proceeds would be used to help fund the company's plant expansion.

"Mirror Wars" Began in May 1990

Noting Gentex's success with electrochromic mirrors in 1989, Donnelly Corporation, a mirror manufacturer based in nearby Holland, Michigan, announced that it would begin offering interior and exterior solution-phase electrochromic mirrors. Gentex was suspicious and after investigating further, believed that Donnelly's product was simply a copy of the Gentex mirror that was introduced in 1987. Gentex sued Donnelly in May 1990 for patent infringement, claiming that Donnelly's recent products were infringing on its patents for electrochromic mirrors. Gentex had chemical patents covering its gel technology, which produced the mirror-dimming effect, and an electronics patent on its mirror system, which combined exterior and interior mirrors. Gentex's position was that its mirror system patent protected the idea of bringing exterior and interior mirrors under one system, regardless of what technology was used in the mirrors.

Donnelly, aware that Gentex was going to sue, countersued on the same day but named a patent which Gentex had not included in its original suit. Donnelly countered that its products did not infringe on Gentex's patent, and that the patent covering gel technology was invalid and unenforceable. While Donnelly made both solid state and liquid-based electrochromic mirrors, the only Donnelly mirrors that were the subject of litigation were its liquid or gel-based mirrors. At the time Gentex was supplying electrochromic mirrors to Ford, General Motors, and Chrysler, and had recently won a contract with BMW in Germany. About 3.36 percent of new 1989 cars carried the optional mirrors.

In September 1990 Gentex and Donnelly announced they would settle their patent dispute by becoming partners. However, by November negotiations to form a partnership were in shambles, and the patent litigation initiated in May 1990 resumed in the U.S. District Court in Grand Rapids, Michigan.

Gentex continued to work on developing an exterior electrochromic mirror to complement its interior electrochromic rearview mirror. While the interior mirrors used ultraviolet radiation (UV) stabilizers, exterior mirrors were exposed to 1,000 times as much UV radiation and required more work. Gentex was able to develop electrochromic materials that were inherently more stable when subject to UV, and in 1991 Gentex introduced the world's first continuously variable exterior electrochromic mirror for the automobile industry.

Adopted Shareholder Rights Protection Plan, 1991

At its 1991 annual meeting, Gentex adopted a shareholder rights protection plan, or poison pill, to deter a potentially hostile takeover. Under the plan, whenever a shareholder acquired more than 15 percent of the company's outstanding shares, all other shareholders would receive an extra share for every share they already owned. That would reduce the 15 percent share to only 8.1 percent. At the time the plan was adopted, Gentex's largest shareholder was founder, chairman, and CEO Fred Bauer, who owned just over 11 percent of the outstanding shares. Bauer, along with other major shareholders, had formed a voting agreement in 1981 when the company went public. That agreement expired upon the adoption of the shareholder protection plan.

Gentex began using the trademark Night Vision Safety (NVS) to describe its electrochromic mirrors. During 1992

Gentex's automatically dimming NVS mirrors were used on more than 52 domestic and foreign models, including 15 new models that were added at the beginning of the 1993 model year in August 1992. In 1992 Gentex received the highest quality awards granted by domestic automakers: Ford's Total Quality Excellence (TQE), General Motors' Mark of Excellence, and Chrysler's Pentastar.

After sales of $21.2 million in 1990 and $26.9 million in 1991, Gentex achieved record sales of $45.1 million with net income of $5.1 million in 1992. It was the start of six consecutive years of record-setting sales as Gentex's electrochromic mirrors became more widely used by automobile manufacturers. By 1997 sales topped $186.3 million—nearly 200 percent more than 1992 sales—with mirrors accounting for 90 percent of the company's sales.

Foreign sales made a strong contribution toward 1992's increase in sales, as the company expanded into Germany, Japan, Italy, Mexico, Canada, Korea, and Brazil. Sales to non-domestic automakers increased from $513,000 in 1990 to $5.3 million in 1992.

The Fire Protection Products Group also posted strong sales for 1992, as the company introduced several new audible/visual signaling devices that were developed to meet the requirements of the Americans with Disabilities Act. These products included a strobe warning light for the hearing impaired, a four-inch primary evacuation horn, and a speaker evacuation device for public-use facilities. During 1992 employment at Gentex increased from 375 employees at the beginning of the year to 541 at year-end.

Began Adding Options to Mirrors, 1993

In 1993 Gentex introduced the NVS Compass Mirror, an interior electrochromic mirror that had a compass attached to it. The compass technology was developed and patented by Prince Corporation of Holland, Michigan, which later became Johnson Controls, Inc. The Compass Mirrors would be made available on 1994 luxury vehicles.

In an effort to increase sales of its mirrors in Japan, Gentex entered into a non-exclusive distribution agreement with Continental Far East, Inc. (CFE), whereby CFE would act as Gentex's sales agent in Japan. The agreement did not affect the distribution agreement already in place with Ichikoh, which had the exclusive rights to sell Gentex's mirrors to Nissan.

In September 1993 Gentex introduced the first convex mirror, which is used for the passenger-side exterior mirror in the United States, with full-range (gray scale) dimming. The convex mirrors used curved glass to increase the driver's field of view and helped eliminate blind spots. The addition of the exterior curved mirror enabled Gentex to offer a three-mirror electrochromic system with full-range dimming. The new system would debut on the 1995 BMW 700 series and was worth about $3 million in annual revenue to Gentex.

By 1993 Gentex had brought suits charging that Donnelly's products infringed on three other Gentex patents. During that time Donnelly developed alternative electrochromic solutions it contended did not infringe on Gentex patents, but in March

1993 the court found that three of the solutions did infringe and issued an injunction prohibiting further infringement. In April 1993 Gentex was awarded $2.2 million in damages by an eight-member jury that found that some of Donnelly's solutions did infringe on another Gentex patent. That award was followed by another injunction against Donnelly. In May 1993 Donnelly and Gentex settled some issues remaining from an earlier trial, and Donnelly paid Gentex $1.2 million as part of that settlement. In apparent retaliation, Donnelly brought another suit against Gentex for alleged infringement of four Donnelly patents, three of which concerned rearview mirrors with lights and one regarding rearview mirrors with a color-matched or dark seal. Gentex was granted a motion for summary judgment of invalidity on the lighted mirror patents in 1995, and in April 1996 the two companies reached a settlement of all remaining litigation between the two parties.

Continued to Introduce
New Mirror Products, 1996–98

In 1996 Gentex expanded its exterior mirror product line with the introduction of the world's first variable reflectance aspheric, or wide-angle, exterior mirror. By 1997 the company was making high-volume shipments of this difficult-to-manufacture product along with a new thin-glass exterior mirror introduced in 1997. In 1996 Gentex also introduced the first automatic-dimming rearview mirror with remote keyless entry. This patented invention utilized the electrically conductive coatings on the mirror glass and their electrical connections as the receiver for the radio frequency signal produced by the key fob. Integrating the two features made it possible for automakers to offer these two options to their customers cheaper than if they had been purchased from two separate sources.

Three significant new products were introduced in 1997–98: 1) a thin glass exterior electrochromic mirror, 2) an interior electrochromic mirror with compass and external-temperature displays, and 3) an interior electrochromic mirror with LED map lamps. The auto-dimming mirror with new map-lamp technology that utilized light emitting diodes (LEDs) would first appear on the 1998 ½ Intrigue, a new sedan by Oldsmobile. The Intrigue mirror would also feature the PathPoint Compass System by Johnson Controls. Among the new products in the works in 1998 was an electrochromic mirror with a cellular telephone in it, a product that was developed by Gentex and two other companies.

During the year the company made its first direct sales to Toyota when it began shipping its base automatic-dimming mirrors for Toyota's new mid-sized sport coupe, the Camry Solara, which went on sale in August 1998. It also marked the first time that a Gentex mirror would appear on a vehicle in the heart of the mid-sized, mid-priced segment of the market.

In other international developments, Gentex opened a sales and engineering office in Japan. The newly formed Gentex Japan, Inc., located in Nagoya, included sales and engineering operations that would serve Gentex's automotive customers in Japan and throughout the Asia/Pacific region. Gentex first entered the Japanese market in 1991, selling its mirrors through third parties.

In May 1998 Gentex also established a warehouse facility in Weinsberg, Germany, to provide logistics for local parts distribution. It was made necessary by the company's rapidly growing European business. Gentex planned to ship mirrors directly from its Zeeland facilities to the Weinsberg warehouse, where they would be packaged, labeled, sorted, and shipped to customers in Europe. At the same time, Gentex announced that its sales and engineering office in Neckarsulm, Germany, would be moving to the Weinsberg location. The company's most popular mirror in Europe was its exterior aspheric (wide angle) mirror.

In 1997, NVS unit shipments to offshore customers increased by 50 percent over 1996 levels and represented 32 percent of all units shipped in 1997. Approximately 20 percent of Gentex's revenues came from European customers, with about six percent from the Asia/Pacific region.

In May 1998 Gentex began offering NVS Mirrors directly to consumers. Previously, all of the company's mirrors had been sold to automakers, who then made them available on their models. Through an agreement with MITO Corporation of Elkhart, Indiana, Gentex would make its automatic dimming mirrors available to the automotive aftermarket. The base NVS mirror would sell for $99, while the premium version with a compass and temperature display sold for $249. MITO, a distributor of quality electronic products and accessories, would warehouse the mirrors and ship orders within 24 hours of receipt.

Gentex announced a two-for-one stock split at its annual meeting in 1998. It was the third time in five years that Gentex had issued a 100 percent common stock dividend. The company was in excellent financial shape. It had been free of long-term debt since 1992 and thus reported no interest expense. Net income had increased every year since 1990, reaching $35.2 million in 1997.

Awards and Recognition, 1997–98

In 1997 Fred Bauer received Michigan's Ernst & Young Master Entrepreneur of the Year Award. The award recognized individuals who have sustained management excellence over a substantial period of time. In 1998 Gentex was designated as a 1997 Supplier of the Year by General Motors. Gentex was one of 182 companies selected by General Motors for the award from its supplier base of more than 30,000 companies. Gentex also became the only company to win the *Automotive News* PACE Award three times. The 1998 award was given to Gentex for its auto-dimming aspheric mirror. The mirror solved two automotive safety issues: glare and blind spots. Gentex was also named to *Forbes* magazine's list of ''200 Best Small Companies in America,'' first in 1994 and then three years in a row from 1996 to 1998. Of all the companies on the list, Gentex was ranked 25th in profits in 1997 and 10th in profits in 1998.

With an excellent earnings record, a healthy balance sheet, and a dominant market share in auto-dimming automobile mirrors, Gentex was on track to enjoy substantial growth in the years ahead. Mirror shipments, which accounted for 90 percent of Gentex's revenues, were expected to reach five million units in 1998, and the company had the capacity to produce seven million mirrors annually. While Gentex mirrors were found on the majority of vehicles offering auto-dimming mirrors, that represented only six percent of the light vehicles produced annually in the world. Thus, the industry as well as Gentex had incredible room for growth.

Principal Subsidiaries

Gentex Japan Inc.; Gentex GmbH (Germany).

Principal Operating Units

Automotive Products Group; Fire Protection Products Group.

Further Reading

Calabrese, Dan, "Gentex Performance Reflects Expansion," *Grand Rapids Business Journal,* May 17, 1993, Sec. 2, p. 5.

"Entrepreneurs of the Year: Master Entrepreneur—Fred Bauer," *Crain's Detroit Business,* June 22, 1998, p. E4.

"Gentex Automatic-Dimming Mirrors Now Available to Automotive Aftermarket," company news release, May 28, 1998.

"Gentex Corporation Declares 100 Percent Stock Dividend," May 21, 1998 (press release).

"Gentex Debuts World's First Auto-Dimming Mirror with LED Map Lamps," May 26, 1998 (press release).

"Gentex Expands Internationally," May 12, 1998 (press release).

"Gentex Ranked 57th on *Forbes*' '200 Best Small Companies in America' List," October 21, 1998 (press release).

"Gentex Receives General Motors' Supplier of the Year Award," April 27, 1998 (press release).

"Gentex Wins 1998 PACE Award," February 23, 1998 (press release).

Hamblin, Connie, "Gentex Corp. Reflects on Success in 1992," *Holland Sentinel,* January 26, 1993.

——, "Gentex Forms Relationship with Japanese Sales Agent," *PR Newswire,* February 22, 1993.

——, "Gentex Seeks Preliminary Injunction Barring Donnelly from Selling and Marketing Electrochromic Mirrors," *PR Newswire,* September 3, 1992.

——, "Technology Breakthrough: Gentex Develops New Exterior Auto-Dimming Mirror for First Use on 1995 BMW 700 Series," *PR Newswire,* September 27, 1994.

Joyner, Tammy, "2 State Auto Mirror Makers Quit Fight, Become Partners," *Detroit News,* September 26, 1990, p. 1E.

Luymes, Robin, "Gentex, Donnelly Looking to Future," *Grand Rapids Business Journal,* October 1, 1990, p. 1.

——, "Gentex, Donnelly Square Off," *Grand Rapids Business Journal,* May 14, 1990, p. 1.

——, "Gentex Makes Move," *Grand Rapids Business Journal,* August 26, 1991, p. 1.

——, "Gentex Shooting for Improvement," *Grand Rapids Business Journal,* May 13, 1991, p. 1.

——, "Mirror Battles Reflect Change," *Grand Rapids Business Journal,* September 24, 1990, p. 1.

——, "Mirror Firms Show Mixed Results," *Grand Rapids Business Journal,* October 21, 1991, p. 6.

——, "Mirror Merger Nixed," *Grand Rapids Business Journal,* November 19, 1990, p. 1.

Turner, Mike, "Expansion to Meet Gentex's Future Growth," *Grand Rapids Business Journal,* September 12, 1988, p. 1.

——, "Gentex Breaks into Global Arena," *Grand Rapids Business Journal,* March 20, 1989, p. 5.

VanderVeen, Don, "Spin Doctors: Mirror Foes Claiming Win," *Grand Rapids Business Journal,* September 11, 1995, p. 1.

—David Bianco

GIB Group

111, rue Neuve
B-1000 Brussels
Belgium
(02) 729 21 11
Fax: (02) 729 20 96
Web site: http://www.gib.be

Public Company
Incorporated: 1974 as s.a. GB-Inno-BM n.v.
Employees: 54,180
Sales: BFr 217.88 billion (US$5.79 billion) (1997)
Stock Exchanges: Brussels
Ticker Symbol: GIB
SICs: 5211 Lumber & Other Building Materials Dealers;
5231 Paint, Glass & Wallpaper Stores; 5251
Hardware Stores; 5261 Retail Nurseries, Lawn &
Garden Supply Stores; 5311 Department Stores; 5411
Grocery Stores; 5531 Auto & Home Supply Stores;
5699 Miscellaneous Apparel & Accessory Stores;
5812 Eating Places; 5941 Sporting Goods & Bicycle
Shops; 5942 Book Stores; 5943 Stationery Stores;
6512 Operators of Nonresidential Buildings; 6552
Land Subdividers & Developers, Except Cemeteries;
6719 Offices of Holding Companies, Not Elsewhere
Classified

GIB Group, Belgium's top retailer, is active in four sectors: supermarkets and hypermarkets; do-it-yourself (DIY) home improvement and auto care stores; self-service and fast-food restaurants; and specialty retailing. A property division, GIB Immo, was formed in 1997 to manage the group's property interests. The group's parent company is GIB s.a. (formerly s.a. GB-Inno-BM n.v.).

GIB Group's supermarkets and hypermarkets operate under such diverse names as GB, with 58 stores trading under the name "Maxi GB," 88 as "Super GB," and three as "GB Express"; Bigg's Continent, with two stores; Unic, with 284 stores; Nopri, with 184 stores; and Globi, with 15 stores in Poland. The supermarket and hypermarket sector is by far the most important division for GIB Group, accounting for two-thirds of its total sales. Starting in early 1998 this sector was amalgamated into a single company called GB s.a., in which the French Promodès Group took a 27.5 percent stake.

The DIY sector accounts for almost 19 percent of GIB Group's total sales and seems to offer major growth potential both in Belgium and abroad. Within Belgium, Brico and Briko Depot, with their 100 outlets, are the undisputed leader in the country's DIY market. In addition, Auto 5 sells car accessories through its 48 outlets. DIY stores also are operated in France (37 Obi stores) and Portugal and Spain (19 Aki stores).

The success of fast-food restaurants is a phenomenon of our time, and GIB Group continues to expand in this high-growth market. The Quick fast-food chain includes 115 units in Belgium, Luxembourg, and The Netherlands, with 270 located in France. In addition, GIB Group operates the 63-unit Lunch Garden self-service restaurant chain and seven Crock'in sandwich bars. Restaurants account for about ten percent of GIB's overall sales.

The specialty sector of GIB Group includes department stores and some smaller retail chains. Inno, Belgium's only modern department store chain, operates 15 stores in major urban centers and shopping centers. GIB Group also operates 23 Disport sporting goods stores in Belgium and The Netherlands and 26 Club book and stationery shops in Belgium. About five percent of the group's revenues originate from its specialty sector.

GIB s.a.—from 1987, the name "GIB Group" has generally been used to refer to all of the activities of GIB s.a. (or s.a. GB-Inno-BM) and its subsidiaries—is the result of several mergers that took place in the 1960s and 1970s. In 1969, Innovation and Bon Marché, operating major department stores in Belgium, merged to form Inno-BM. Two years later Inno-BM also incorporated its subsidiary, Priba, which the two merged companies had set up jointly to operate variety stores. Finally, GB Enterprises merged with Inno-BM to form GB-Inno-BM on February 1, 1974.

Early History of Bon Marché

In 1861 François Vaxelaire, a 21-year-old native of the Vosges region of France, became manager of a small textile store, Au Bon Marché, at the rue Neuve in Brussels. During the following 30 years, Vaxelaire and his wife, Jeanne Claes, succeeded in expanding the company through the opening of new stores in Belgium and France. In 1894 upon the death of their mother, Raymond and Georges Vaxelaire joined their father as partners in the family business. Under their dynamic leadership, the company gradually was transformed into a full-fledged department store operator. A new department store, Au Bon Marché, was opened at the boulevard du Jardin Botanique in Brussels.

The company, from 1927 named Les Grands Magasins Au Bon Marché: Etablissements Vaxelaire-Claes, continued to grow with the founding of the Société Congolaise des Grands Magasins Au Bon Marché (Coboma) in 1928 and the Société Anonyme Belge des Immeubles Commerciaux in 1928, in 1933 renamed Société Anonyme Belge des Magasins Prisunic-Uniprix. Whereas the purpose of the first company was to enter the market of the then Belgian Congo, the goal of the second company was essentially a move to compete with variety stores, a new retail formula introduced by Sarma in 1928.

World War II and its aftermath—especially the Loi de Cadenas, or Padlock Law, which forbade the opening of new large diversified stores—slowed down the growth of the company considerably. The withdrawal of the Padlock Law in 1959 and the advent of the 1960s, however, resulted in a new wave of expansion with the opening of new department stores in Belgium's first shopping center.

Early History of GB Enterprises

In 1882 another Frenchman, Adolphe Kileman, opened his first store in Ghent, Belgium, under the name La Maison Universelle. He entrusted the running of this store to Mr. and Mrs. A. Martin. The year of his acquisition of the Grand Bazar du Bon Marché in Antwerp, 1885, is generally considered to be the founding date of the Grand Bazar d'Anvers, which would merge with Supermarchés GB in 1968 to become GB Enterprises. Kileman summoned Mr. and Mrs. Martin to Antwerp to run the newly acquired store, and in 1888 Mrs. Martin's sister and the latter's husband, Alfred Deslandes, were put in charge of the Ghent store.

World War I left the young company in a shambles. Upon his return from the French army in 1919, Auguste-Pierre Deslandes, nephew of Eugenie Martin—since 1890, a partner of Adolphe Kileman, and subsequently his heir—set up a new company, Les Grands Magasins d'Anvers Réunis S.A., with the aid of Émile Chaumont, an industrialist from Liège. The opening of new department stores in Antwerp in 1920 and in Ghent in 1921 were important events for the new company.

The Depression of the 1930s was almost fatal to Deslandes's company. Although the company had expanded its traditional range of merchandise through the introduction of novelties and had changed its name to the more stylish Galeries du Bon Marché, its financial situation deteriorated.

In 1932 Maurice Cauwe, previously employed by Innovation, was hired as administrative manager. After further difficult years and a reversion to the store's original and more popular name, Grand Bazar du Bon Marché, the new management was able to accomplish a gradual improvement over the period 1935–39. Despite World War II, the company was able to continue its expansion.

Cauwe was one of the first Belgian retailers to discover the United States and its modern distribution system. In 1956 he and Baron François Vaxelaire—son of Raymond Vaxelaire and later Cauwe's major negotiator in the merger of Inno-BM and GB Enterprises—attended a seminar held by the National Cash Register Company and led by Bernard Trujillo, in which they became acquainted with new retail formulas, such as shopping centers, supermarkets, and self-service discount department stores. Supermarkets and hypermarkets would become the keystones of GB Enterprises' fast growth during the 1960s.

The end of the Padlock Law in 1959 offered new opportunities for the company through the opening of a series of new department stores. Further growth was realized, however, with the introduction of supermarkets in 1958 and hypermarkets in 1961. Two separate companies were set up by the parent company: Supermarchés GB in 1960 and Super Bazars in 1961, in charge of the expansion process of a network of supermarkets and hypermarkets, respectively.

The opening of supermarkets and hypermarkets was pursued at a fast rate over the next ten years, partially in anticipation of the second Padlock Law. Soon the hypermarkets were joined by specialty stores such as Auto Centers in 1966, Garden Centers in 1968, and Brico Centers from 1973 onward. Initiatives to pursue expansion abroad were generally unsuccessful at the time. In 1967 Grand Bazar d'Anvers merged with Supermarchés GB to become GB Enterprises. A year later, Super Bazars also merged with GB Enterprises.

Early History of Innovation

In 1897 the third company, Bernheim-Meyer: A l'Innovation, established by Julien Bernheim and three brothers Meyer, all natives of the Alsace region, opened its first store in the rue Neuve in Brussels. The store proved highly successful, and additional stores were opened in Liège, Ghent, and Verviers.

After World War I the Tietz stores in Brussels, Bruges, and Antwerp, under sequester after the German defeat, were bought and gradually transformed into A l'Innovation department stores. Late in 1919 the company was renamed Les Grands Magasins à l'Innovation (Innovation).

In 1934 Priba, a subsidiary of Innovation, which had been set up in 1930 to develop a chain of variety stores, merged with Prisunic-Uniprix, a subsidiary of Au Bon Marché. For the first time a major link was established between two companies that would later participate in GIB Group. During the 1930s the variety stores did extremely well: by 1938 Sarma and Uniprix-Priba had become the first and the fourth largest retailers, respectively, in Belgium.

From 1959 onward, Innovation also pursued renewed growth through the opening of new department stores in several Belgian towns as well as in the Westland shopping center in Brussels. The great fire of May 22, 1967, in its Brussels department store, in which 251 people died, still casts a major shadow upon the success of Innovation in the 1960s. Growth also was pursued abroad through companies such as Inno-France, but with very little success. The time did not seem right yet for Belgian retailers to pursue expansion abroad.

Initiatives for cooperation or outright merger had been taken by several Belgian retail companies in the late 1920s, for example, by Émile Bernheim, but the first serious attempt at cooperation between Bon Marché and Grand Bazar d'Anvers did not happen until the early 1960s. The negotiations between the two department stores Innovation and Bon Marché were more fruitful, however. The companies decided to merge in October 1969 to form S.A. Innovation—Bon Marché N.V. (Inno-BM).

GB-Inno-BM Formed in 1974

New initiatives for cooperation were taken in the early 1970s between GB Enterprises, under Maurice Cauwe, and Inno-BM, under Émile Bernheim and François Vaxelaire. By the end of 1973 the two companies decided that the GB-Inno-BM merger would take place on February 1, 1974.

Maurice Cauwe became the first chairman of the new company, with Baron François Vaxelaire and Jacques Dopchie as managing directors. Upon Cauwe's retirement in 1977, Baron François Vaxelaire became chairman and Dopchie vice-chairman; both continued to act as managing directors.

The first two years after the merger were spent primarily in streamlining the organization and its operations and consolidating the selling and merchandising activities. Apart from the usual difficulties that follow any merger, the group was confronted with a series of problems arising from its economic and legal environment.

First, the Business Premises Act, the so-called second Padlock Law, made it virtually impossible to open new large stores or to enlarge existing ones. Expansion through the opening of supermarkets and hypermarkets all but stopped. Second, Belgium's small territory, already covered by an intensive distribution network, necessitated that further growth be pursued abroad. A third problem was related to the internal competition with which the department store division was confronted. In several major towns two or even three department stores, originally operated by GB-Inno-BM's constituent companies, fought for market share.

In the following years, GB-Inno-BM pursued expansion primarily through diversification. Important changes in structure were introduced to make this strategy possible. At the same time the group sought to rationalize its systems and to achieve economies of scale by integrating operations and merging production and service activities.

The department store division constituted a particular problem for the group. A special effort was made to assure its profitability, resulting in a "modularization" in the merchandising of the division, a revolutionary technique in department stores. Other measures included closing or modernizing older stores as well as opening new department stores in the newly developed shopping centers. In this context Fnac, the well-known French leisure goods retailer, was offered an opportunity to enter the Belgian market via the renovated Bon Marché store in the middle of Brussels (the New BM). GB-Inno-BM also decided to use the trade name Inno for all the department stores of the groups, with some minor exceptions. In 1975 GB-Inno-BM had already decided to close or convert the Priba variety stores as soon as possible, owing to reduced profitability and the need to reduce competition between the group's stores.

The strategy of diversification into new products and markets was maintained during the 1970s. Managers who were surplus to requirements after the merger were encouraged to study the opportunities for small specialty shops in Belgium. Benefiting from the growing success of the franchise formula in European retailing, this resulted in such new companies as Santal (perfumery shops, 1975), Club (books, stationery, and toys, 1975), and Sportland (sporting goods and sportswear, 1976). In 1982 the group acquired Christiaensen, the toys and games specialist.

In 1978 in response to an economic situation characterized by stagnation, inflation, and reduced consumer buying power, and in a further move to become even more diversified, GB-Inno-BM successfully introduced its own brand of goods (*produits blancs*) to offer consumers a low-cost alternative to branded goods. A diversification strategy also was actively pursued in 1979, where partnerships were established with other retailers abroad. Two activities stand out in this international expansion: DIY retailing and fast-food restaurants. New DIY ventures included Homebase in Great Britain (with Sainsbury), Somabri in France (with Casino), and Superdoe (with Vendex International) in The Netherlands. In the United States the group took a share in Scotty's, a DIY retailer in Florida, and in Handy Andy, a DIY chain in the Midwest. In the fast-food business the group established France Quick, a joint venture with Casino in France. GB-Inno-BM supplied the expertise and took a minority share in these new companies.

Operations Refined During the 1980s

In the 1980s the GB-Inno-BM merger had reached a certain level of maturity. After a very active period of diversification, the group concentrated on improvements and standardization of image, design, and equipment in its hypermarkets and super-markets, cost reductions, and better merchandising, ranges, and pricing.

In October 1982 GB-Inno-BM introduced its new hypermarket formula. The group's hypermarkets, whose image would be determined in large part by a permanent offer of discounts on products, became Maxi stores.

In an attempt to improve the performance of the unsuccessful GB Home-Stocks, established in 1974, IKEA-Belgium was set up as a 50–50 joint venture with IKEA, a furniture specialist, in 1983. In 1989, however, GIB Group withdrew from this sector.

After a thorough study of GB-Inno-BM by U.S. management consultants McKinsey, a restructuring plan was developed, focusing in particular on the decentralization of the group's commercial activities, and was gradually implemented during the next few years. The plan proved to be very effective in terms of sales, cash flow, and net profit.

In 1987 GB-Inno-BM took over the activities of Sarma-Nopri, a J.C. Penney subsidiary. After major reorganization and rationalization, a new company, Sarmag, began to operate 14 Sarma-Star hypermarkets, six department stores, and 26 Sarma Shop boutiques.

Starting in 1987, GB-Inno-BM or GIB Group also was the largest franchiser in Belgium. In addition to Unic, the leading chain of independent supermarkets in Belgium, it operated the Nopri chain of supermarkets, Nopri being the trade name for the former Sarma affiliates.

New Leadership Took Over in the Early 1990s

The favorable results of 1990, confirming the positive developments of the previous years, were overshadowed by the unexpected death of François Vaxelaire, chairman of GIB Group since 1977. Baron Vaxelaire was an early advocate of closer cooperation among major Belgian retailers. As managing director of Inno-BM, he carried out the negotiations with Maurice Cauwe that finally led to the merger of Inno-BM and GB Enterprises. Vaxelaire, as chairman essentially responsible for the internal activities, left behind a highly diversified and successful company.

On March 19, 1991, Pierre Schohier, a banker and—as a major shareholder of GIB Group—a member of the board of directors for many years, became the new chairman of GIB Group. A new executive structure, in which a clear distinction was made between the responsibilities of the board of directors and those of the executive board, was implemented in June 1991.

As he reached the age limit for senior executives, Jacques Dopchie, who for years had been primarily responsible for all operations and over the previous several years for the external relations and the international activities of GIB Group, relinquished his position as managing director on this occasion; he remained, however, an honorary vice-chairman of the board of directors. Also in 1991 the board of directors appointed Count Diego du Monçeau de Bergendal, already managing director, as

chairman of the executive board. Meanwhile, the group made its first foray into the territory of Eastern Europe, when it purchased a chain of four small supermarkets in Warsaw, Poland, in December 1991; GIB soon changed the chain's name to Globi.

Declining Profits Led to Restructuring Efforts in the Middle to Late 1990s

GIB's operating margin was a fairly respectable 2.17 percent in 1992, but the group's profitability suffered over the next several years, as the operating margin fell to a low of 1.39 percent in 1995 before recovering somewhat by 1997, when the figure was 1.55 percent. The group was hit hard by a recession in Belgium and also had to contend with increasing competition in both the food retailing and DIY markets.

Responding to these pressures, GIB Group cut costs and jettisoned unprofitable units. In its food retailing sector alone, staffing levels were cut from 30,075 employees in 1993 to 25,500 by 1997. These job cuts caused considerable labor unrest in Belgium. In an attempt to weaken the power of the labor unions with which it had to contend, GIB made significant alterations to its corporate structure, most notably transforming a number of divisions into full-fledged subsidiaries. In June 1993 a further step was taken with the Quick chain when it was floated on the Brussels stock exchange.

In the area of divestments, GIB Group began a retreat from the highly competitive U.S. DIY market in October 1995 when it sold its interest in the Handy Andy chain to the firm's management. In 1997 the group announced it would sell the Scotty's chain as well; the preceding year, GIB sold its 25 percent interest in Homebase to its partner, Sainsbury. This refocused the DYI unit entirely on continental Europe. Meanwhile, a new DYI warehouse concept, Briko Depot, was launched in May 1995.

In its restaurant sector, GIB in April 1996 converted its Resto GB restaurants into Lunch Garden cafeterias. In March 1994 the first Crock'in sandwich bar opened. GIB's specialty retailing sector was trimmed considerably in the mid-1990s, with the closure or sale of several chains: Sarma clothing stores, Fnac books/hi-fi/photographic shops, Christiaensen toy stores, and Pearle Vision Center optical shops in Belgium. This left only the Inno, Club, and Disport (sporting goods) chains.

As important as all of these events were, it was GIB's food retailing sector that saw the most dramatic changes. In October 1994 a new hypermarket concept was launched, initially called Bigg's, but eventually renamed Bigg's Continent. About a year later, GIB Group entered into an alliance with French retailer Promodès, in which the two companies agreed to combine their worldwide purchasing activities and to develop jointly the Bigg's concept, with Promodès taking a 20 percent interest in Bigg's. Another new concept, GB Express, consisted of a mini-supermarket designed for service station and railway station locations; it debuted in August 1997. That same year also marked the debut of a new Super GB Partner format. This concept was formulated for the purpose of consolidating the Unic and Nopri chains—which were entirely franchised—

under the GB banner, in the process achieving significant savings and benefits for the group and the franchisees.

In January 1998 GIB Group took another consolidating step when it brought all of its supermarket and hypermarkets businesses within a single new company called GB s.a. At the same time, GIB deepened its relationship with Promodès by selling the French group a 27.5 percent stake in GB for BFr 11 billion (US$292.5 million). In its combined form, GB had 630 stores in Belgium at the time of this deal and held 29 percent of the Belgian food retail market. The agreement between GIB and Promodès also anticipated that the partnership would become an equal one by 2003, sooner than that if a planned flotation of GB had not occurred by June 2001.

In February 1998 Roland Vaxelaire was named a managing director of the group's executive board, dividing the day-to-day management functions with Diego du Monçeau. Scohier remained chairman. It was this management team that would need to determine if GIB's years-long restructuring had gone far enough to turn the group's fortunes around.

Principal Subsidiaries

Aki Bricolage (Spain); Albi Restauration (France; 56.49%); Allinsure; Arilmart-RD (72.5%); Auto 5; Bascule-Rest (56.49%); Bayonne (France; 56.49%); Bel-Tex (72.5%); Bigg's (72.5%); Bigg's Continent Noord (72.5%); Brico Belgium; Brico International GEIE; Bricodis (Portugal); Bricogal (Portugal); Briko Depot; Briko Depot Noord; Cherbourg Rest (France; 56.49%); Club; Cotradis (72.5%); Crock'in; Disport International; Disport Luxembourg; Disport Partners; Distrirest; Ebam; Eufidis (Netherlands); Eufradis; Family Buffets; Filunic (72.5%); France Quick (56.49%); Fun Stores; GB International (Luxembourg); GB Retail Associates (72.5%); GB (72.5%); Gecotec; GIB Car Service (72.5%); GIB Consultant Services; GIB Coordination Center (99.85%); GIB Immo; GIB Management Services; GIB Toys; Globi (Poland; 47.6%); Grand Maine Restauration (France; 56.49%); Imodis; Inno; Jiceel (72.5%); La Rose d'Anjou (France; 56.49%); Lendit Kraainem (91.15%); Logimat (France; 56.49%); Logirest France (56.49%); Logirest Benelux (56.49%); Lunch Garden; Mabe (72.5%); Mantes est Restauration (France; 56.49%); Marseille Burel Restauration (France; 56.49%); Nausikaa (Netherlands; 56.49%); Negoce Pierre (France; 56.49%); New Motorest; Noprimmo; Obi (France); Outex (72.5%); Quick Coordination Center (56.49%); Quick Franchise Developpement (France; 56.49%); Quick Invest France (France; 56.49%); Quick Nederland (Netherlands; 56.49%); Quick Restaurants (56.49%); Ready (72.5%); Resto DM Jaude (France; 56.49%); Riom Rest (France; 56.49%); Rob (72.5%); Saboma (98.21%); Safe Insurance; Safe Reinsurance (Luxembourg); Sarma Shop; Sarmag; Societe Relais (72.5%); Sofira (France; 56.49%); Stigam (72.5%); Supertransport (72.5%); T.M.S.; Van Hemelrijck; Woippyrest (France; 56.49%).

Further Reading

Beenkens, A., *Historique du Grand Bazar d'Anvers: 1965–1968,* Antwerp: Imprimeries Générales Anversoises, 1972.

Brown-Humes, Christopher, ''Sainsbury Takes Full Control of Homebase,'' *Financial Times,* August 2, 1996, p. 18.

De Coster, P., *GB-INNO-BM—Het nederige begin en de groei,* Brussels: [n.p.], 1989.

Du Bois, Martin, ''GIB's CEO Has Work to Do As Retailer in Belgium Hits Another Rough Patch,'' *Wall Street Journal,* May 30, 1997, p. B5.

Knee, D., and Walters, D., *Strategy in Retailing: Theory and Application,* Oxford: Philip Allan Publishers, 1985.

Owen, David, ''Promodès Buys Stake in GIB Supermarkets,'' *Financial Times,* January 8, 1998, p. 30.

—Joseph V. Leunis
—updated by David E. Salamie

Golden Enterprises, Inc.

2101 Magnolia Avenue South, Suite 212
Birmingham, Alabama 35205
U.S.A.
(205) 326-6101
Fax: (205) 326-6148
Web site: http://www.goldenflake.com

Public Company
Incorporated: 1923 as Magic City Food Products
    Company
Employees: 1,440
Sales: $129.52 million (1997)
Stock Exchanges: NASDAQ
Ticker Symbol: GLDC
SICs: 2096 Potato Chips & Similar Snacks; 2099 Food
    Preparations, Not Elsewhere Classified

A leading snack food producer in the southeastern United States, Golden Enterprises, Inc. makes and distributes potato chips, corn chips, fried pork skins, tortilla chips, onion rings, and popcorn. Golden Enterprises served as the holding company for Golden Flake Snack Foods, its lone subsidiary. During the late 1990s, the company marketed its products in 12 Southeastern and Midwestern states spreading outward from its headquarters in Alabama. Production was conducted in Birmingham, Alabama; Nashville, Tennessee; and in Ocala, Florida. Despite the presence of much larger competitors such as Frito-Lay in its operating territory, Golden Enterprises enjoyed convincing success throughout its history as a regional favorite, attracting a loyal customer base drawn to the company's signature Golden Flake brand. Golden Enterprises also sold a line of cakes and cookies, dips, nuts, and dried meat products packaged by other manufacturers under the Golden Flake label. In 1998, former Chairman Sloan Bashinsky, whose family had managed the company since 1946, owned roughly 55 percent of Golden Enterprises.

Founded in the 1920s

Golden Enterprises began its business life in 1923, starting out in the basement of an old grocery store in Birmingham, Alabama.

The company, then known as Magic City Food Products Company, was founded by Mose Lischkoff and Frank Mosher, who adopted the nickname for Birmingham as the name for their entrepreneurial creation. The pair made and sold peanuts, peanut butter cracker sandwiches, and horseradish, but the principal product was potato chips—Golden Flake Potato Chips—so named because of their appearance. The snacks were all made by hand and sold to Birmingham residents living nearby, with the company's peanut butter cracker sandwiches proving to be the second most popular item after Golden Flake Potato Chips. At its start, the company was essentially hawking its homemade products to neighbors, but success came quick for Lischkoff and Mosher, despite the modest trappings of their business. Before the first year was over, the two owners were forced to hire two salesmen in order to keep pace with demand, as the business' signature Golden Flake Potato Chips quickly found a place in the hearts of Birmingham residents. The forging of this special relationship—the tie between the Deep South and Golden Flake Potato Chips—was an important one, because in the decades ahead, when the U.S. snack industry evolved into a $20 billion-a-year industry, the deep-seated awareness of the Golden Flake name would allow Golden Enterprises not only to survive, but to thrive. Massive food conglomerates would eventually saturate the Deep South with their products and hold sway as market share leaders, yet Golden Enterprises withstood the pressure and held steadfast to the number two position throughout its territory. This achievement was primarily due to the affection for the Golden Flake brand that began in 1923.

As Magic City's business burgeoned, more employees joined the payroll, including one employee who played a pivotal role within the company's history. Helen Friedman, better known at the time as the "Golden Flake Girl," joined Magic City not long after the company was started. Friedman did not remain an employee for long, however. With the help of her mother, Friedman bought out Lischkoff's interest in Magic City and in 1928 cemented her position at the company further by marrying the other co-owner, Mosher. The marriage did not last, however, and in the wake of Friedman's and Mosher's personal differences, ownership of Magic City was decided by the courts. Friedman gained full control over the company in the property settlement that concluded the divorce, putting the Golden Flake Girl in charge of the popular Golden Flake Potato Chips.

Company Perspectives:

Golden Flake: It's Where You Find the Flavor!

During Friedman's guardianship of the Golden Flake Brand, Magic City was transformed from a fledgling, basement-bound business into a flourishing, firmly established enterprise. Perhaps most impressive, Friedman fulfilled the difficult task of shaping Magic City into a genuine company during the most pernicious economic times of the 20th century, achieving meaningful strides during the decade-long Great Depression. Expanding while others businesses collapsed around her, Friedman built the foundation Magic City rested on during the 1930s, and by the time of her departure following the end of World War II, she left a substantially sized, profitable business, with annual sales hovering at approximately $750,000. Geographically, Friedman had extended the company outside of Birmingham and into other Alabama communities, establishing a network of 17 sales routes. Friedman's departure cleared the way for the Bashinsky family, who acquired Magic City in 1946. For the next half-century, the Bashinskys, through two generations, controlled the fortunes of the Golden Flake brand and its numerous products, developing the business into a multimillion-dollar snack foods enterprise.

1946: Bashinsky Ownership Begins

The Bashinskys acquired Magic City four years before annual sales reached the milestone mark of $1 million. Under their stewardship, annual revenues would increase a hundredfold, with nearly all of the credit for that achievement going to Sloan Y. Bashinsky. Bashinsky started working at Magic City shortly after his family had acquired the company and became one of the charter members of the board of directors, but the young Bashinsky did not enjoy any other advantages. He started at the bottom of Magic City's corporate ladder, working in production and traveling as a salesman before assuming greater responsibilities. His rise was quick, however, ending in 1956 when he bought the company from his father and uncle and assumed the duties of Magic City's president. A year later, he changed the name of the company to Golden Flake, Inc., adopting the name of the brand that had propelled sales for the previous 25 years. Bashinsky's next move was to relocate production to larger quarters. In 1958, the company began production at the Birmingham plant that would serve as a production site for the remainder of the century. Initially, before steady expansion of the plant would increase its production capacity exponentially, the Birmingham facility measured more than 45,000 square feet, resting on a five-acre plot.

Rapid Post-World War II Growth

Early during his tenure, Bashinsky demonstrated his desire to develop Golden Flake into a bigger company, a desire first evinced when he moved the company to a larger production facility shortly after assuming command. Five years after the move, he added to the company's might in a far more substantial way, completing Golden Flake's first major acquisition, which established the company's first operations outside Ala-

bama. In 1963, Bashinsky purchased a Nashville, Tennessee snack food producer and distributor named Don's Foods, Inc. The acquisition gave the company its second production facility, a 40,000-square-foot plant located in Nashville. Don's Foods was operated as a separate business until 1966, when Golden Flake was reincorporated as a Delaware corporation and the operations of the two companies were combined.

The acquisition of Don's Foods ushered in an era of expansion for Golden Flake that would see the company take on the characteristics of a modern corporation. Bashinsky had his sights set on not only steering the company into new markets but also into new business areas, businesses that had nothing in common with producing and distributing snack foods. To obtain the capital for Golden Flake's maturation into a more sophisticated corporation, Bashinsky took the company public in an initial offering of stock in 1968. At the time, there was a sweeping trend in corporate America toward diversification. Holding companies were being formed to serve as umbrella entities for entry into new business areas and to oversee the operation of a disparate collection of subsidiaries, as success in one area spawned forays into other areas far removed from a company's original business. In the general march toward far-flung diversification, Bashinsky did not stand aside as a spectator. He diversified with fervor, completing a series of acquisitions in 1971 that greatly expanded the scope of Golden Flake's operations, moving it well beyond snack foods. Bashinsky purchased Steel City Bolt & Screw, Inc., an advertising company named Nall & Associates, and diversified into real estate, insurance, and fastener production, developing a handful of subsidiaries to operate alongside Golden Flake. Although Bashinsky's diversification later proved to be unsuccessful, the basic objective of his plan—to accelerate the growth of the Golden Flake enterprise—was fulfilled. In the wake of the diversification begun in 1971, Golden Flake recorded a decade of robust financial and physical growth, demonstrating sufficient financial strength to draw the attention of the national business press to the bustling activity in Birmingham.

Shortly after the company moved to its new production facility in Birmingham, its sales began to increase at an encouraging pace, rising to roughly $3 million a year by the end of the 1950s. From this point forward, sales increased exponentially, doubling every five years for a 25-year period. Amid this energetic growth, Bashinsky altered the structure of the company to better conform to its increasing stature and to the numerous operating subsidiaries it had acquired in 1971. In 1977, a holding company was formed named Golden Enterprises, Inc. Concurrently, Golden Flake, Inc. changed its name to Golden Flake Snack Foods, Inc. and was organized as a wholly owned subsidiary of Golden Enterprises. Steel City Bolt & Screw and Nall & Associates also were organized as subsidiaries of the newly created Golden Enterprises, but assets of the real estate and insurance subsidiary were sold, divested from the company in September 1977, nine months after the formation of Golden Enterprise.

Although the diversification into real estate and insurance had proven to be a misstep, there could be little doubt about the prudence of Bashinsky's management of the company's mainstay business, its Golden Flake Snack Foods subsidiary. Sales reached $50 million by the end of the 1970s, and better yet, the company was exhibiting a profitability level that put it near the top of all snack food producers in the nation. Flush with success, Bashinsky began plotting a push into new markets during the early 1980s, hoping to build on the company's presence in Alabama, Mississippi, Tennessee, and Georgia and spread outward into Louisiana, Arkansas, Kentucky, and North and South Carolina. His biggest plans were for expansion into the lucrative markets in Florida, where he decided to build the company's third snack food production facility. The new plant, slated to be erected in Ocala, Florida, was part of an $18 million expansion program that tripled Golden Enterprise's corn procession capacity. At the time, the company derived 45 percent of its sales from potato chips, 30 percent from corn chips, and 15 percent from fried pork skins, but Bashinsky wanted to increase the percentage obtained from corn-based products because corn was less expensive and less vulnerable to weather than potatoes.

The new Ocala plant, measuring 100,000 square feet and resting on a 56-acre site, opened in 1984, serving as the hub for distribution throughout Florida. Sales by this point had reached the milestone mark of $100 million, a total collected from the company's 12-state operating territory, which was serviced by 800 company-owned trucks traveling 666 sales routes. Bashinsky, in his mid-60s, was at his peak, hailed by *Forbes* magazine as a ''junk-food king.'' Although Frito-Lay, which collected a numbing 40 percent of all salted snack food sales in the United States, ranked as the leading brand in all of Golden Enterprise's markets, the time-honored Golden Flake brand held steadfastly to the second position in all its markets except in recently explored Florida. In some ways, the company benefited from the presence of its much larger competition, carefully watching where the snack food giants succeeded and failed to determine the best path to pursue. When Frito-Lay introduced a new cheese chips brand dubbed O'Gradys in the mid-1980s, Bashinsky eyed the product introduction closely. ''We've been watching O'Gradys cheese chips for a year,'' he explained to a reporter. ''This month [May 1985] we'll introduce Au Gratin. Frito spent over $50 million researching O'Gradys. We didn't spend anything.''

The 1990s and Beyond

With sales topping $100 million and his company performing admirably, Bashinsky began to think about retirement and the important issue of his successor. His two sons had been trained as lawyers and expressed no interest in running a snack food business, so Bashinsky turned to a long-time employee named John S. Stein, who had joined Golden Enterprises during the 1960s. Stein was put in charge of the company's operating division, Golden Flake Snack Food, and from this vantagepoint he watched the company's eye-catching brilliance fade. After recording annual earnings growth of 16 percent between 1975 and 1985, the company's profits began to slip during the latter half of the 1980s. The costly push into Florida markets provoked a price war with Frito-Lay, owned by Pepsi-Cola Company, and Anheuser-Busch's Eagle Snacks, thrusting Golden Enterprises into the enviable position of having to battle head-on with multibillion-dollar adversaries. Sales growth became anemic and profits began to slide as a result, causing Golden Enterprises' earnings to fall from 73 cents a share in 1985 to 35 cents by 1991.

Despite having its 25-year period of remarkable growth shudder to a stop, Golden Enterprises operated during the 1990s as a solidly positioned and financially sound company. With Stein in charge as chief executive officer and chairman of the board, the company exuded many of the same strengths that had underpinned its success for decades. Golden Enterprises was debt-free and its Golden Flake brand benefited from the same awareness and loyalty that had enabled the company to thrive in the Deep South. The last remnants of the 1971 diversification were removed in 1995 when Golden Enterprises sold Steel City Bolt & Screw and Nall & Associates, leaving the company with only its Golden Flake Snack Foods subsidiary by the time it celebrated its 75th anniversary in 1998. Annual sales by this point hovered around $130 million after a decade of fluctuating results, while net income stood at a solid $3.7 million. As Golden Enterprises prepared for the 21st century, its past achievements provided a source of optimism for the future, fueled by the knowledge that its signature brand had earned the lasting affection of its Southern clientele.

Principal Subsidiaries

Golden Flake Snack Foods, Inc.

Further Reading

Behar, Richard, ''Copycat,'' *Forbes,* May 20, 1985, p. 126.
''The History of Golden Flake Snack Foods,'' http://www. goldenflake.com/gfhistory.html.
Willis, Clint, ''Here Are Five Stocks Under $10 That Promise 40% Growth,'' *Money,* May 1992, p. 77.

—Jeffrey L. Covell

Gold Kist Inc.

**244 Perimeter Center Parkway, Northeast
Atlanta, Georgia 30146
U.S.A.
(770) 393-5000
Fax: (770) 393-5262
Web site: http://www.goldkist.com**

Cooperative
Incorporated: 1936 as Georgia Cotton Producers
    Association
Employees: 16,000
Sales: $1.65 billion (1998)
SICs: 0251 Broiler, Fryer & Roaster Chickens; 0254
    Poultry Hatcheries; 0213 Hogs; 0762 Farm Manage-
    ment Services; 0921 Fish Hatcheries & Preserves

The second largest poultry processor in the United States, Gold Kist Inc. is an agricultural cooperative whose members control the common stock of the association. Gold Kist was founded as an instrument to aid cotton farmers in Georgia, giving them the means to control processing and marketing through the ownership of their own facilities. As the cooperative expanded outside of Georgia, it turned to other agricultural crops and activities and began offering marketing services for pecans, peanuts, livestock, grain, and catfish. During this diversification, much of which occurred during the 1950s, Gold Kist began providing poultry marketing services, the chief area of focus for the cooperative during the 1990s. By the end of the 1990s, Gold Kist was operating 12 poultry processing plants that processed roughly 14 million chickens per week in Georgia, Florida, North Carolina, and South Carolina. The cooperative's other operations include pork production, aquaculture research, and catfish breeding stock production, as well as joint venture projects involving pecan and peanut processing and marketing. Gold Kist serves approximately 31,000 farmer members in Alabama, Florida, Georgia, Mississippi, South Carolina, North Carolina, and Texas. Membership in Gold Kist is open to any person, firm, cooperative, or corporation involved in the production of farm commodities. The cooperative's products are sold domestically and abroad under private labels, store brands, and the Gold Kist Farms brand name.

Background of Founder

For nearly a half-century, D.W. Brooks represented the primary force in Gold Kist's development as an agricultural cooperative organization. A visionary and champion of farmers in the southeastern United States, Brooks served as an official advisor to five U.S. Presidents during his illustrious career, a career that began not long after he entered the University of Georgia in 1918. By the time he enrolled in the University of Georgia's School of Agriculture, Brooks had already displayed a powerful mind, skipping several grades of primary and secondary education. At the School of Agriculture in Athens, Georgia, the pattern repeated itself. Brooks was 19 years old when he completed the requirements for a B.S.A., finishing in just three years, and was still a teenager when he accepted an invitation to join the faculty. During his hours spent away from teaching, Brooks pursued a master's degree, concentrating on agricultural economics, which he approached with the passion of a zealot. He empathized with the impoverished state of Georgian cotton farmers and felt a driving need to improve their antiquated production methods and naive marketing systems. Said Brooks, ''My studies convinced me that farmers were not farming properly, they were not producing properly, and they were not marketing their products properly—and they never would do this as long as they tried to go it alone.'' For the rest of his life, Brooks would work tirelessly on the behalf of farmers, seeking to bring stability and prosperity to an occupation that had long been deprived of such qualities.

Brooks felt the greatest rewards could be achieved outside the classroom, although much of his work in the field was predicated on his studies and research at the University of Georgia. In 1921, he helped organize the first cooperative in north Georgia, devoting the summer months to the formation of the Georgia Cotton Growers Cooperative Association (GCGCA). Brooks resumed his teaching duties in the fall, but it soon became apparent that the GCGCA needed him to take on a more active role if the fledgling cooperative was to survive. In 1925, Brooks resigned his teaching post at the University of Georgia and was named supervisor of field operations throughout the greater Carrolton, Georgia area, where cotton farming was highly concentrated. Despite the day-to-day presence of Brooks, the GCGCA continued to suffer, its development not helped by the onset of the Great Depression. By 1933, it became clear to the GCGCA's leaders that the cooperative

Company Perspectives:

The Gold Kist mission is to contribute to the economic improvement of its farmer-owners by providing quality inputs and services at fair prices and by adding value to their products through efficient marketing to domestic and international customers. Relationships with all stakeholders will be guided by the highest ethical standards. All activities will reflect a commitment to environmental preservation and natural resources conservation.

could not survive, leaving them with two options: liquidate the cooperative or establish a completely new organization from a dismantled GCGCA. Clearly, the first experiment had failed, but for Brooks failure only served to instruct. "From 1925 to 1933 was an excellent training period for me," Brooks explained. "At least I had found out how a co-op ought not to be run, and had built up in my mind fully and completely the way it should be run."

The First Decades

Brooks quickly got a chance to put his theories to the test when he was selected to organize a new cooperative from the rubble of GCGCA. The reorganization that followed was thorough, so much so that Gold Kist did not trace its history back to the GCGCA but to the 1933 formation of the Georgia Cotton Producers Association, an organization that changed its name to the Cotton Producers Association (CPA) in 1943. Brooks assumed full control over CPA, running the co-op by day and speaking before small groups of farmers wherever they could be gathered by night. To interested yet hesitant farmers, Brooks preached the virtues of joining a cooperative and he railed against the old system that left farmers as the powerless victims of a host of agricultural intermediaries, the individuals and companies who transported, distributed, and processed the cotton—and pocketed most of the profits. "We've got to get on the profit side of agriculture," he declared. "Small farmers like us can no longer make the grade just by producing raw materials. To get on an equal footing with large corporate farms and other big businesses, we've got to pool our resources, buy—and later manufacture—our own supplies in wholesale quantities." Toward this end, Brooks started buying cotton warehouses and then fertilizer plants for CPA member farmers, acquiring the facilities at sharply reduced, Depression-era prices. In one illustrative deal, Brooks acquired a fertilizer plant that cost $100,000 to build, yet paid only $3,500. Brooks also created a sophisticated system for grading and weighing cotton, one that enabled cotton farmers to obtain optimum prices for their bales of cotton. Gradually, CPA gained momentum, but considering the pernicious economic conditions of the time, there was much to be done before the cooperative began to fully reflect the ideals of its founder. The emphasis during the 1930s was on survival; in the decades ahead, Brooks would have the opportunity to vertically integrate the cooperative further and diversify its activities into a range of agricultural fields.

Although CPA could not begin to focus on much beyond its own survival until after World War II, the cooperative did expand on the services it provided to farmers during the war years.

Gradually, farmers in the Southeast were beginning to turn away from cotton and toward other crops and activities, as cotton production moved westward. CPA, too, would begin to concentrate its efforts on other crops, but until the end of World War II the cooperative was engaged principally in providing cotton marketing services to its members. There were exceptions, however. The first farm supply store was opened in 1943, marking the starting point of what would develop into a network of Farmers Mutual Exchanges (FMX), which purchased supplies from CPA on a wholesale basis and distributed them to farmer members on a retail basis. The first store, which began with an inventory of 30 tons of feed and nothing else, led to the establishment of additional stores situated in CPA's expanding operating territory. By 1945, as CPA's membership expanded throughout much of Georgia and into Alabama and South Carolina, there were six FMX stores. Following the war, CPA began to diversify in earnest, beginning with a foray into poultry marketing services during the latter half of the 1940s and the establishment of a grain marketing operation in 1948. Organized to handle all types of grain grown in the Southeast, the grain marketing operations became more comprehensive in 1950, when CPA constructed a 300,000-bushel grain elevator in Waynesboro, Georgia. The diversification into poultry and grain touched off a period of ambitious expansion into a number of agricultural fields that began with a flourish in 1951.

Post-World War II Diversification

In 1951, grain marketing services became fully operational following the completion of the Waynesboro facility, as did the cooperative's poultry marketing services following the acquisition of CPA's first poultry processing plant, also in 1951. The move into poultry was extremely important, marking the starting point of a business that would serve as the cooperative's foundation at the end of the century. By the late 1990s, poultry would be to Gold Kist what cotton was to the cooperative during the 1930s, but in between cotton and poultry were a number of agricultural commodities that represented the breadth of CPA. These other agricultural fields became part of CPA's operations primarily during the 1950s. Cotton marketing activity reached its peak during the first half of the 1950s, then began to gradually diminish in succeeding years, finally disappearing altogether. In cotton's place came pecan marketing services, which CPA introduced in 1951. The following year, the cooperative began offering livestock marketing services. In 1956, by virtue of CPA's acquisition of Georgia Peanut Co., the cooperative established peanut marketing services and gained peanut storage facilities in Georgia, Florida, Alabama, Oklahoma, and Texas. The addition of these new agricultural fields into CPA's business scope pushed the cooperative's annual sales volume up from $35 million in 1950 to $140 million by the end of the decade. During the same period, the cooperative's profits exploded from $231,000 to a high of $2.4 million, giving Brooks the financial means to embark on the greatest facility expansion in the history of CPA. Aside from the remarkable increase in the cooperative's financial might and the physical growth it engendered, the diversification into other agricultural pursuits also had a symbolic importance, giving CPA its future name. During the 1950s, it was decided that the Gold Kist brand name, which first was used in the cooperative's pecan marketing operations, would be the name under which the poultry division would operate and under which a portion of the poultry would be sold. Although the official name change of the cooperative did not occur until the 1970s, from the

1950s forward the Gold Kist name began to take on growing prominence in the endeavors of CPA.

During the 1960s, expansion continued, but considerable attention was also paid to organizational and administrative change, a necessity after the feverish diversification and expansion of the 1950s. Although the decade represented a period of introspection and analysis, financial and geographic growth continued to push the cooperative forward, thanks in large part to the poultry division. The poultry division's sales volume increased from $35 million at the beginning of the 1960s to more than $114 million by 1968, which ranked poultry as the single most important facet of CPA's multifarious activities. For comparison, the cooperative's next greatest revenue-generating segment was peanut marketing services, which collected $67 million in 1968. Cotton, meanwhile, had dwindled in importance, generating $17 million in sales. Because of the increasing prominence of the cooperative's poultry division and the name it operated under, the 1960s marked the first time CPA began to identify itself as CPA/Gold Kist. The number of people exposed to the Gold Kist name was increasing substantially as well, broadened by the cooperative's rising export business. Although CPA had sales agents representing the cooperative in foreign markets before the 1960s, it did not place its first direct employee on foreign soil until 1965, when a sales office was established in Brussels to facilitate the export of poultry, cotton, grain, pecans, and peanuts in Europe.

The most memorable event during the 1960s for CPA members and employees was not the growth of poultry activities or increasing export business. Instead, the 1960s were remembered as the last decade CPA's founder influenced direct control over the cooperative. D.W. Brooks relinquished his post as general manager in 1968 and moved into the newly created position of chairman of the board. A second generation of leadership took control after Brooks's retirement from day-to-day management, led by C. Wesley Paris. Behind him, Brooks left a towering enterprise, with sales approaching $270 million and 180 plants in operation, sufficient to rank the cooperative 318th among *Fortune* magazine's 500 largest industrial firms. Although no longer directly guided by Brooks, Gold Kist continued to record remarkable growth during the 1970s. Annual sales climbed to $463 million by 1972, three times the total collected a decade earlier, and then doubled again in the next five years. In 1977, when Brooks stepped down from his position as chairman, sales eclipsed $1 billion. The small cooperative Brooks had started with less than $5,000, now held sway as a global agribusiness of mammoth proportions.

From the 1970s to the end of the century, Gold Kist concerned itself primarily with increasing the size of its poultry operations. Although the cooperative continued to develop other areas of its business, poultry was the compass point directing growth. A substantial amount of the progress achieved in poultry arrived via acquisitions, which eventually built Gold Kist into the second largest poultry processor in the United States. During the 1970s, the cooperative purchased several poultry facilities from Pillsbury Corporation in two transactions, one in 1971 and the other in 1972. These separate acquisitions gave Gold Kist two processing facilities, a feed mill, and a hatchery. In 1978, the cooperative purchased a poultry plant in Trussville, Alabama, from Purina Mills. In the 1980s, the growing stature of Gold Kist's poultry division prompted management to form a separate poultry company. Golden Poultry Company was formed to receive the assets from the 1981 acquisition of Swift Independent Packing Company, which had decided to exit the poultry business. Swift's poultry plant in Douglas, Georgia, became the first component of the newly created Golden Poultry Company. In 1986, shares of common stock in Golden Poultry Company were sold to the public in an initial public offering (IPO), but Gold Kist continued to hold sway over the company by retaining a controlling percentage of the shares. After the IPO, the Douglas plant was renovated and a new poultry facility was constructed in Sanford, North Carolina. In 1988, Golden Poultry Company's operations were expanded again when a processing plant, feed mill, and hatchery were constructed in Russellville, Alabama. After this two-decade-long expansion campaign, Gold Kist and its majority-owned subsidiary Golden Poultry Company entered the 1990s with the prominence of poultry set to become an even greater feature of the cooperative.

The 1990s and Beyond

By the 1990s, annual sales had passed $2 billion and Gold Kist stood as the only poultry processor that operated as a farmer-owned cooperative. The continual expansion of the cooperative's poultry operations from the first measured steps in the 1940s to the 1990s had created a formidably sized poultry processor that trailed only Tyson Foods in industry rankings. The transformation from a cotton-oriented cooperative to a poultry-oriented cooperative was made complete following a series of transactions late in the decade that left no question about the course of Gold Kist's future. In 1997, Gold Kist purchased the shares of Golden Poultry Company it did not already own and merged the company into its operations. In September 1998, nearly all the cooperative's cotton marketing assets were sold, leaving it with only a cotton warehouse in Georgia that was slated to be closed in 1999. Finally, in October 1998 Gold Kist completed a sale to Southern States Cooperative, Inc. that included the cooperative's 100 retail farm supply stores (the FMX units that debuted in 1943), Gold Kist's pet food and animal products division, and its fertilizer and chemicals division. In the aftermath of these divestitures, Gold Kist continued to provide peanut and pecan marketing services through joint venture partnerships, and operated pork production and catfish production facilities on its own, but the cooperative was primarily a poultry processor. As the cooperative prepared to enter the 21st century, its 12 poultry processing plants located in Georgia, Florida, North Carolina, and South Carolina led the way toward Gold Kist's future.

Principal Subsidiaries

AgraTech Seeds Inc.; Agvestments Inc.; AgraTrade Financing, Inc.; Luker Inc.; Gold Kist Foundation, Inc.

Further Reading

Dimsdale, Parks B., Jr., *A History of the Cotton Producers Association,* Atlanta: The Cotton Producers Association, 1970, 231 p.

Henry, David, "Capitalist in the Henhouse," *Forbes,* January 26, 1987, p. 37.

Martin, Harold H., *A Good Man . . . A Great Dream.* Atlanta: Gold Kist Inc., 1982, 196 p.

—Jeffrey L. Covell

The Golub Corporation

501 Duanesburg Road
Schenectady, New York 12306
U.S.A.
(518) 355-5000
Fax: (518) 355-0843
Web site: http://www.pricechopper.com

Private Company
Incorporated: 1932
Employees: 18,000
Sales: $1.60 billion (1997 est.)
SICs: 5141 Groceries, General Line; 5399 Miscellaneous
   General Merchandise Stores; 5411 Grocery Stores;
   5912 Drug Stores & Proprietary Stores

"Successful, innovative, and civic-minded" are terms that describe well The Golub Corporation of Schenectady, New York. Golub, parent company of Price Chopper Supermarkets, has been a leader in the retail grocery industry for over 60 years. From a single store in upstate New York in 1932, the company has grown to operate over 100 supermarkets, service stations, and convenience stores in five different states—and the growth has been near phenomenal. At fiscal year-end 1997, the corporation experienced a 16.36 percent increase in sales from the previous year with total sales in excess of $1.6 billion.

Small Change and a Million-Dollar Dream, 1900s

The earliest roots of the company date back to 1900 when Lewis Golub, a Russian immigrant, first arrived in this country. Like many immigrants, he had small change in his pocket but a very large dream in his heart. He quickly set out to build the dream, opening a wholesale grocery warehouse on Van Guysling Avenue in Schenectady in 1908. Lewis understood that even in hard times when money was short, people would need to eat. He saw this not only as a stable means of support for his own family, but also as a way to provide an important need within his community. From the very beginning, Lewis saw himself as indebted to the community which helped him get his start and always placed a high value on every employee and his or her needs.

Brothers William and Bernard

As with most family businesses, children grew up very much a part of making the business happen. Lewis's two sons, William and Bernard, helped out after school by hauling sacks and barrels of goods in the warehouse. Through their many hours pushing a broom, cleaning windows, and straightening shelves, the boys acquired both the knowledge of how to succeed as well as the commitment to the community that their father valued so highly. Upon the death of their father in 1930, William and Bernard joined with Joseph Grosberg in a partnership to continue operating the business. At this same time, the grocery industry as a whole was struggling. With the stock market crash and high unemployment, money was generally scarce and consumer spending weak. The new owners had to make some serious changes to revitalize their father's dream.

"Innovation = Success," 1930s

In November 1932, Bill and Bernard ("Ben") Golub embraced the entirely new concept of self-service retail merchandising. This was, in fact, an early development of what were later to be known as "supermarkets." The brothers broadened the product lines and purchased goods in very large quantities to reduce costs that they could then pass along to customers in the form of lower prices. The first store was located in Green Island, in northern New York, and was called the Public Service Market. The store went beyond the traditional grocery items to include fresh meat and produce, dry goods, clothing, and home appliances, all under the same roof. The success of the operation soon became very clear as the customer base grew rapidly. Within only a few months, two more stores opened, one on Broadway in Watervliet, New York, and the other on Eastern Parkway in Schenectady, New York. The third store which opened just around the corner from Central Park in Schenectady inspired the name of the newly established chain of stores, Central Market.

A Generation of Growing and Caring, 1940s–70s

Over the next four decades, The Golub Corporation continued to grow and succeed through its commitment to offer a wide variety of products and low prices. By the late 1950s there were Central Markets in operation throughout New York and into

Company Perspectives:

The Golub Corporation is committed to providing our customers with recognizable quality and value for the products and services offered, our Associates with challenging, culturally diverse, friendly, participative and rewarding environments free of harassment and intimidation, our community with people and resources to maintain and improve the quality of life, and our shareholders with a fair return on investments over the long term.

Massachusetts. New stores were being opened rapidly. By 1963, the company had opened seven more stores; four more opened in 1965. During this time, the corporation became a leader in the supermarket industry, taking chances on new ideas and encouraging creative approaches within the company. The company took seriously the participation of every employee in its operation, inviting their creativity. Service to the local community became a hallmark of Golub. Before corporate image became fashionable, Golub gave back to the community. One early example of this was providing free seeds and seedlings to 4H members and offering to buy back the best of the young farmers' crops. This program alone, begun in 1964, has helped over 2,000 youngsters to date.

Passing the Torch, 1972

In May 1972 the company mourned the death of Bernard Golub, then chairman of the board. He was known affectionately as "Mr. Ben" to all of his extended family within the corporation. Indeed he had left behind the tradition of his own father, that of innovation and caring. The business continued on in the hands of William Golub, known as "Mr. Bill," and the next 20 years saw the emergence of a new generation of Golubs to lead the company. Lewis Golub, Bernard's son, and Neil, William's son, had grown up in the business just as their fathers had and, as time would prove, they caught their fathers' passion and honored their legacy.

In 1972, the company adopted an "open 24 hours" policy to further its commitment to provide first-rate customer service. It also proved to enhance customer loyalty because of the great psychological impact of "always being there" for their customers. In 1973, the company began a companywide makeover and soon emerged with a renewed focus on providing goods at the lowest price under its new name: Price Chopper Discount Foods. The strategy was to become known as an everyday low price operator who did not rely on gimmicks to lure customers into its stores. The company added many more stores to its group as well during this time. In October 1992, William "Mr. Bill" Golub passed away, leaving his final mark on the company and completing the passing on of the torch to Lewis and Neil Golub.

Price Chopper—Food Online

By the fall of 1998, The Golub Corporation, under the name of Price Chopper, grew to over 100 retail outlets, including supermarkets, service stations, and convenience stores operating in five northeastern states. The newest of its stores ranged from 50,000 to 83,000 square feet in size and carried a blend of food and non-food items In addition to this, in many stores customers could also find a pharmacy, floral shop, video department, dry cleaning service, and a bank.

In addition to continuing its low prices, the company renewed its commitment to quality service and convenience, establishing a year-round hotline with cooks available to answer food-related questions from customers. Through this hotline, and the mouth-to-mouth advertising it provided, the company hoped to build its customer base and the loyalty of its existing customers.

Innovation has always been important at Price Chopper. The company started a "House Calls" service inviting customers to contact Price Chopper by toll-free phone, fax, or their own web site in order to get groceries delivered to their home or business for their family or party needs. Over 5,000 items including fresh meat and seafood, produce, and deli and bakery goods were made available through this service. In addition to "House Calls," Price Chopper developed "Ready Meals" and an "Online SOS" service to provide prepared food delivered at the customer's desired time and place. The menu was designed to offer a wide variety of meals highlighting local cuisine items ranging from "Rachael Ray's Blue Moon Burgers" to "Shrimp, Feta and Pasta Salad" combination meals.

To support its overall marketing efforts, Price Chopper established an industry-standard computer local area network (LAN) to work in conjunction with its point-of-sale (POS) system in each of its stores. This resulted in much faster and more efficient service to the customers and also cut the costs to Price Chopper to about half of what its former POS system cost them, reported Dave Daigler, technical maintenance supervisor of Golub Corporation. The state-of-the-art computer system also helped handle the technology demands of its online food ordering service. An "AdvantEdge Card" issued to customers offered automatic discounts at the checkout in addition to any manufacturer's coupons that the customers presented. The card also gave customers check-cashing privileges, automatic frequent-shopper additional discounts, and other perks.

Price Chopper: A Good Neighbor

By the late 1990s, under the leadership of Chairman and CEO Lewis Golub and President and COO Neil Golub, the company grew not only as a leader in the supermarket industry, but as a leader in its commitment to its employees, called "Associates," and the community. Associates of the company were considered active partners in the corporation and, by 1998, actually owned more than 44 percent of the company stock. The company provided the customary health and life insurance, retirement savings, and vacation benefits to associates but also offered educational reimbursements and many options for advancing with the company. Since 1932, the company has never recorded a single lost day due to labor disputes or strikes. In 1991, The Golub Corporation was recognized by New York's Capital District Personnel Association as one of the "10 Best Places to Work."

As a good corporate citizen, Golub/Price Chopper prided itself on the slogan "We're not just in your neighborhood. We're your neighbor." In 1998, company literature identified over 10,000 charitable and philanthropic organizations that benefited from its financial support. The programs it supported included drug abuse programs, support for senior citizen groups, providing Golub Foundation scholarships, and funds for research at St. Jude's Children's Research Hospital. Price Chopper helped start a hospice for the terminally ill and was for many years a major supporter of the Muscular Dystrophy Telethon which Neil Golub regularly cohosted. It provided significant support to the United Way with emphasis on youth and the elderly. Arts and athletics were regularly supported through major grants to the Albany and Schenectady Symphonies, the Saratoga Performing Arts Center, and the Knickerbockers Arena. In 1995 alone, hundreds of thousands of dollars were spent sponsoring free events and giving free and discounted tickets to those less fortunate who may have otherwise been unable to participate in these activities.

Successful and Independent, 1998 and Beyond

By 1998, Price Chopper found itself deeply involved in a food industry that was becoming increasingly complex and competitive. In the face of a growing number of grocery outlets consolidating and merging, The Golub Corporation renewed its commitment to remain an independent player. Officers of the company were very optimistic, citing that the most important reasons for its success in the past would pave the way for a successful future, that is, by innovative merchandising of its products and services and by continuously satisfying its customers.

Further Reading

Abrams, Geni, "Report of the New York State Credit Union League," April 24, 1996.

Amato-McCoy, Deena, "Price Chopper Rebates Build Loyalty," *Supermarket News,* March 3, 1997.
"Benchmarking and Best Practices: The Road to Success," *Grocery Marketing,* July 1996.
Bennet, Stephen, "Fast and Furious," *Progressive Grocer,* September 1995.
"Credit and Debit Fees Hold Steady Since Price Chopper Complaint," *Chain Store Age Executive with Shopping Center Age,* January 1996.
"The Do-It-Yourself Solution," *Grocery Marketing,* August 1995.
Fox, Bruce, "Price Chopper POS Moving from Unique to Standard (Point of Sale System)," *Chain Store Age Executive with Shopping Center Age,* July 1995.
Greco, Jo Ann, "Retailing's Rule Breakers," *Journal of Business Strategy,* March–April 1997.
Hammel, Frank, "On Time Arrivals," *Progressive Grocer,* September 1997.
Harper, Roseanne, "Price Chopper Stresses Services," *Supermarket News,* April 24, 1995.
Johnston, JoAnn, "Food Fight: Price Chopper Battles to Remain Successful and Independent," *Times-Union,* October 25, 1998.
Papiernik, Richard L., "Home-Meal Battle Warms Up," *Nation's Restaurant News,* December 15, 1997.
"Price Chopper Completes Wonder Deal," *Supermarket News,* January 29, 1996.
"Price Chopper Expands EAS Technology to 20 Stores," *Supermarket News,* February 2, 1998.
Raiola, Ralph, "Price Chopper Fights Fast Food Chains," *Supermarket News,* February 3, 1997.
"Report of the Vocational and Educational Services for Individual with Disabilities (VESID)," May 1998.
Robinson, Alan, "Price Chopper Scores with HMR," *Frozen Food Age,* January 1997.
Tosh, Mark, "Silver Bullet," *Progressive Grocer,* August 1, 1998.
Vaczek, David, "Renewing the Prescription," *Supermarket Pharmacy,* June 1995.

—J. D. Fromm

GoodMark Foods, Inc.

6131 Falls of Neuse Road
Raleigh, North Carolina 27609
U.S.A.
(919) 790-9940
Fax: (919) 790-6535
Web site: http://www.conagra.com

Wholly Owned Subsidiary of ConAgra, Inc.
Incorporated: 1970
Employees: 1,100
Sales: $178 million (1997 est.)
SICs: 2013 Sausages & Other Prepared Meats; 2096
    Potato Chips & Similar Snacks; 2099 Food
    Preparations, Not Elsewhere Classified

The world's largest producer of meat snacks, GoodMark Foods, Inc. makes Slim Jim dried meat sticks, Pemmican beef jerky, Penrose pickled sausage, and a line of baked grain snacks under the Andy Capp's label. GoodMark Foods produces its food products at a plant in Garner, North Carolina, which is supported by operations in California, Pennsylvania, Maryland, and the U.S. Virgin Islands. In 1998, the company was acquired by international food conglomerate ConAgra, Inc.

Origins of Predecessor

A half-century before the GoodMark Foods name first appeared, the company's signature product and its brand name emerged on the East Coast, introduced by a Philadelphia entrepreneur whose contribution to the world was the meat-stick snack Slim Jim. Adolph Levis made his living selling pickled cabbage, mushrooms, and tomatoes to delicatessens, a job that provided him with first-hand knowledge of which types of prepared foods consumers desired most. During his visits to one delicatessen after another, Levis noticed the sales of bologna and pepperoni rising steadily, an observation that sparked his entrepreneurial impulses and prompted him to ask a local meat company to make a small dried sausage. Once he had his product, Levis designed an emblem for its packaging, one reportedly inspired by his perception of the sausage as "elegant." He designed a man wearing a tuxedo to serve as the emblem for the product, complete with a top hat and a cane, and named him Slim Jim.

Initially, Levis sold his Slim Jim meat snacks to bars around the Philadelphia area. Later, he began distributing his all-beef snacks to convenience stores, accruing a small fortune from decades of Slim Jim sales. By the late 1960s, Levis was ready to retire. He sold his company, Cherry-Levis Co., which included Slim Jim, to the Minneapolis-based conglomerate General Mills in 1967. A General Mills employee at the time of the sale remembered Levis, recalling, "He made a great deal of money off it and decided to go to Florida and go to the tracks and enjoy life." Levis's association with his popular meat stick was over, but the history of Slim Jim was only beginning its second chapter.

At corporate headquarters in Minneapolis, there was one General Mills employee whose career took a pivotal turn the day Slim Jim became part of the massive food company. Ron E. Doggett, a rising executive at General Mills during the late 1960s and part of the executive team that recommended buying Levis's company, was to become Slim Jim's guardian for the next three decades. Described as a "soft-spoken son of a Minnesota farmer," Doggett had enlisted in the Korean War and used his GI Bill to put himself through Mankato State University, where he studied business. While still in school, Doggett made his first attempt as an entrepreneur, using the money he had saved while in the Armed Forces to develop a small shopping center in southern Minnesota. Within two years, the development project flopped, leading Doggett to pursue a less risky career path when his academic days were over. He graduated with a business degree from Mankato State in 1961 and went to work for General Mills as a controller.

1970 Formation of GoodMark Foods

When Levis sold his company to General Mills, Doggett was named vice-president of the new acquisition, which was renamed Slim Jim, Inc. Senior General Mills executives believed Slim Jim had greater market potential than its use as a bar snack, so the company began stocking Slim Jim in vending machines, grocery stores, and supermarkets. In 1970, General Mills acquired a Garner, North Carolina company named Jesse Jones Sausage Co., which was combined with Slim Jim, Inc. to form GoodMark Foods, Inc. The combination of the two companies moved Slim Jim's headquarters from what was described as a Philadelphia slum to the more pristine surroundings in Raleigh, North Carolina, where Doggett spent the next decade watching over the fortunes of the GoodMark Foods subsidiary.

By the end of the 1970s, GoodMark Foods was producing a variety of food products, everything from beef jerky to Jesse Jones sausage to potato Bugles. Financially, the company was doing well, collecting $50 million in sales a year and demonstrating consistent profitability. Doggett, however, was troubled by what he saw. Under General Mills' stewardship, the strength of GoodMark Foods' flagship Slim Jim brand was diminishing. In an effort to squeeze the maximum profits from the product, General Mills had reduced the amount of beef in an individual Slim Jim and used chicken, soy protein, and milk products in its place. Doggett, who served as vice-president of finance for GoodMark Foods by the end of the 1970s, was alarmed, remarking later, "we had lowered quality, increased price—and all the time our volume was going the wrong way." The situation worsened when General Mills decided at the beginning of the 1980s to pare back its extensive activities and refocus on cereals and baking goods. In October 1981, convinced that they had gleaned all the profits they could out of the company, General Mills put GoodMark Foods on the auction block. Doggett suddenly found himself facing a murky financial future.

In his mid-40s at the time General Mills announced its intended divestiture of GoodMark Foods, Doggett had three children nearing college age and was about to sign a new mortgage. Despite the threatening clouds gathering around him, Doggett went home the day he first heard about the sale and told his wife that he had happened upon "the chance of a lifetime." The opportunity, as Doggett saw it, was to buy GoodMark Foods from General Mills in a management buyout, but first came the prodigious task of securing the money to make an offer General Mills would accept. For six months, Doggett and three other General Mills vice-presidents struggled to borrow the money to make GoodMark Foods their own. General Mills agreed to $15 million in 1982 after Doggett had put up, according to a May 1997 *Business North Carolina* article, "my home, my cars, and my wheelbarrow," as collateral for loans. The completion of the transaction turned the page to the third chapter in the company's history, an era that saw Slim Jim flourish as it never had before.

1982 Spinoff

Doggett assumed the duties of president and chief operating officer for the newly independent GoodMark Foods, and quickly attempted to cure the ills Slim Jim had suffered under the latter years of General Mills' governance. First, the quality of the meat snacks was improved, making them more like the Slim Jim snacks Philadelphia bar patrons had enjoyed during the 1930s. The amount of soy and milk products was reduced, as was the amount of sodium nitrate. Having removed much of the "extenders" that made Slim Jim less expensive to produce,

Doggett and his associates next turned their attention to rethinking their marketing strategy. General Mills had concentrated on distributing Slim Jim primarily to supermarkets, but the new owners of the brand took a different stance and began distributing Slim Jim to convenience stores. A research and development department was formed as well, enabling the company to introduce four or five new products a year. Propelled by these new changes, sales at GoodMark Foods jumped from $68 million in 1982 to $82 million in 1985. At this point, Doggett and his team sold part of the company in a public offering, the proceeds from which testified to the growing optimism about GoodMark Foods' profitability and its future prospects. Three years after buying the entire company for $15 million, GoodMark Foods' owners realized $16 million for 39 percent of the company.

Infused with capital from the public offering, GoodMark Foods gained the financial resources to redouble its marketing efforts and increase its advertising budget. At first, the company missed the mark with its advertisements, projecting a wholesome family image and describing Slim Jim with the slogan, "Less Than a Meal and More Than a Snack." The multimillion-dollar advertising campaign launched in 1986 started paying big dividends when the company discovered its best customers were not families gathered around a kitchen table but teenage boys, who devoured six or seven Slim Jims at a time. The identification of its target customer was an important realization, one that would underpin the company's highly visible advertising efforts during the 1990s and add muscle to its dominant market position.

Cut free from the bureaucratic layers of management at General Mills, GoodMark Foods took on a new, vibrant luster during the 1980s, as the advantages of its independence continued to expose capabilities that were suppressed under the auspices of a giant parent company. The company possessed far greater ability to respond to changes in its market, giving it the agility to seize opportunities shortly after they were identified. When spicy food emerged as a trend in 1988, GoodMark Foods signed a licensing agreement with Louisiana's McIlhenny Co., maker of Tabasco sauce, to produce Tabasco-flavored Slim Jims. This flexibility extended to other products as well and spawned entirely new product lines, such as the company's foray into pork rinds. When Doggett learned that George Bush's favorite snack was pork rinds, he quickly located a producer of pork rinds, and then introduced Tabasco-flavored pork rinds two weeks before the 1988 Republican convention, emblazoning each bag with the slogan "They're Republickin' Good." GoodMark Foods exhausted its supply of 20,000 packages before the convention ended, and achieved an unexpected publicity coup when NBC's Tom Brokaw held up a bag of the pork rinds on national television.

Flush with success, Doggett sat atop a thriving enterprise by the end of the 1980s. The company controlled 44 percent of the meat snack market, which was a greater percentage than the next six competitors combined, and it had begun to broaden its product line, branching out into the cookie market through the 1988 acquisition of $8.5 million-in-sales Fleetwood Snacks. The focus on the company's other brands intensified during the early 1990s, although considerable attention continued to be paid to the mainstay Slim Jim brand, which was primarily responsible for GoodMark Foods' stalwart market share. During the early 1990s, Doggett increased the U.S. distribution of several brands, including Pemmican beef jerky, Jesse Jones sausage, and Penrose pickled pigs' feet. As the company sought to broaden its reach at home, it was also taking a greater interest in its international business, which generated slightly more than $5 million in sales in 1992 through the distribution of food products in Japan, Singapore, Hong Kong, and Taiwan. By 1993, GoodMark Foods was taking its first steps into China, Korea, and Canada and was beginning to research markets in Mexico and Europe. By continuing to branch out overseas, Doggett was hoping to collect between $10 million and $20 million in sales from foreign business by the mid-1990s.

High-Profile 1990s

As the company pushed overseas and promoted its other brands during the 1990s, its advertising efforts directed at the promotion of the Slim Jim brand took center stage. GoodMark Foods had made a tremendous leap from the "elegant" product Levis' had hawked and from the wholesome family image it briefly had tried to project. Once the company identified teenage boys as its target audience, it shaped its advertising around these customers. The brand assumed a rebellious, zany image, using professional wrestlers as the spokespeople for Slim Jims in advertisements that attacked authority figures and institutions teenage boys presumably disliked. The first such pitchman was the "Ultimate Warrior," replaced in 1992 by the bellicose "Randy 'Macho Man' Savage." The company spent roughly $10 million on advertising and marketing during the early 1990s to fund its boisterous and garish campaign and recorded successive annual sales gains of 20 percent as a result. By the mid-1990s, the company had doubled its advertising and marketing budget, widening its lead over other meat-snack producers who rarely, if ever, advertised. Along with sponsoring a car in Busch Grand National stock-car racing, the company's promotional efforts included signing on as a sponsor of ESPN and ESPN2's Summer X Games 1997, an event that embodied the image GoodMark Foods wanted to project.

By the mid-1990s, the Slim Jim brand was thoroughly revitalized, thriving after nearly 15 years under the beneficent control of Doggett. Accounting for half of GoodMark Foods' total sales, the meat snack was registering robust growth, with the only blemish occurring in 1996 when production failed to meet demand. Sales by 1996 had swelled to $178 million, nearly three times the total recorded when the company was spun off from General Mills. Internationally, the company had failed to reach its sales goal announced early in the decade, but it had begun to test market Slim Jims in British pubs. Doggett stuck to his goal of generating between $10 and $20 million from overseas business, something he hoped to achieve by the end of the decade, but as the company entered the late 1990s a momentous event diverted attention away from foreign shores and toward headquarters in Raleigh. A new era was set to begin, one that was similar in nature to the period preceding GoodMark Foods' independence.

In a deal valued at $216 million, GoodMark Foods announced it was being acquired by $24-billion-in-sales ConAgra, Inc., a diversified, global food company. The merger was completed in 1998, returning GoodMark Foods to the familiar role of operating under a much larger corporate umbrella. Slim Jim became one of 22 ConAgra brands with annual retail sales exceeding $100 million, but Doggett, at least publicly, did not seem to fear Slim Jim would suffer from the wide-ranging interests of a corporate parent. "I believe ConAgra offers GoodMark the best of both worlds," he said in an official announcement, "an entrepreneurial culture where our company can continue to thrive and grow, and the resources to support and enhance GoodMark's continued growth. In other words," he added, "we've found a good home for our people and GoodMark's future." Whether or not history would repeat itself and drain the Slim Jim brand of its strength, was a question to be answered in the 21st century.

Further Reading

"ConAgra, GoodMark Foods to Merge," *Nation's Restaurant News,* July 6, 1998, p. 87.

Duggan, Patrice, "'The Chance of a Lifetime,'" *Forbes,* April 17, 1989, p. 140.

Fusaro, Dave, "Slim Jims, Fat Profits," *Prepared Foods,* October 1995, p. 52.

"GoodMark Foods and ConAgra Have Definitive Agreement for GoodMark to Merge with ConAgra," *PR Newswire,* June 18, 1998, p. 6.

Gurley, Margot Lester, "Snack Attack," *Business North Carolina,* October 1993, p. 14.

McMillan, Alex Frew, "The Jerky Boys: Taking Aim at the Teen Scene, GoodMark Food Uses Savvy Marketing to Turn Its Premier Meat Snack into a Cash Cow," *Business North Carolina,* May 1997, p. 26.

"Slim Jim Joins the Games," *Supermarket News,* February 17, 1997, p. 14.

—Jeffrey L. Covell

Granite Rock Company

411 Walker Street
Post Office Box 50001
Watsonville, California 95077
U.S.A.
(408) 768-2000
Fax: (408) 768-2201
Web site: http://www.graniterock.com

Private Company
Incorporated: 1900
Employees: 500
Sales: $120 million (1997 est.)
SICs: 5032 1411 Dimension Stone; 1423 Crushed &
   Broken Granite; 3281 Cut Stone & Stone Products;
   1611 Highway & Street Construction

The largest U.S.-owned and -managed construction materials supplier in northern California, Granite Rock Company produces rock, sand, gravel aggregates, ready-mix concrete, asphalt, road treatments, and recycled road-base material. During the late 1990s, Granite Rock operated in a six-county area extending from San Francisco southward to Monterey, competing primarily against firms owned by multinational construction materials companies. The company also retailed building materials made by other manufacturers and operated a highway paving operation through a division named Pavex Construction Company.

Founded in 1900

Granite Rock's historical roots are embedded in a deposit of granite situated atop the San Andreas Fault, where 200 million years ago a mass of molten granite emerged from the depths of the earth and cooled, contracted, and cracked, providing the lifeblood for an enterprise that would flourish for a century. Although the company's founders did not discover their flagship source of granite, it was through their efforts that the quarry developed into the prodigious source it became. The deposit of granite that served as the backbone of Granite Rock was discovered in 1871, when civil engineers working to connect the coastal line of the Southern Pacific railroad found a granite field nine miles west of a small town named Watsonville, just south of Santa Cruz, California. The chance discovery proved to be fortuitous, providing railroad crews with excellent ballast to form railroad beds. Thirty years later, however, the quarry at Aromas was no longer able to support itself. It was at this juncture that the founders of Granite Rock pooled their cash and purchased the quarry.

The central figure behind Granite Rock's formative decades of operation was Arthur Roberts (A. R.) Wilson, born in San Francisco in 1866. Bright and ambitious, Wilson attended Massachusetts Institute of Technology, where he matriculated with a degree in engineering in 1890. Wilson returned to California shortly after his graduation and began his professional career in Oakland as a construction worker. During his stay in Oakland, Wilson served a term as Oakland City Civil Engineer and eventually managed a local quarry named Leona Heights Quarry. As Wilson earned recognition in the Bay Area, to his south a man named Warren Porter was preparing to make a move that would lure Wilson to Santa Cruz County. The son of a local banker named John T. Porter, Warren Porter counted himself as a lumberman, banker, and politician and was eager to add another occupation to his business card when his father's bank, the Pajaro Valley Bank, foreclosed on the Aromas quarry. Porter enlisted the help of Wilson and four other investors to help purchase and manage the small granite quarry, convinced that the property could be turned into a profitable enterprise. Wilson's interest was piqued as well, so he borrowed $10,000 and moved his wife and three small children south to Watsonville. On Valentine's Day, 1900, the partnership was incorporated as the Granite Rock Company.

At the start, Wilson and Porter employed 15 men who worked the quarry. Using sledgehammers, picks, shovels, and wheelbarrows, Granite Rock's small labor force worked ten hours a day shattering the slabs and boulders of granite into pieces six inches or less. The splintered granite was then loaded into horse-drawn wagons for shipment to the railroad line. The workers slept at the quarry bunkhouse, ate at the adjoining cookhouse, and were paid $1.75 per day, crushing roughly 12 tons of granite each between six o'clock in the morning and six o'clock in the evening. By 1903 there were nearly two dozen men working the quarry, each of whom must have been enormously relieved by the arrival of a steam-powered crusher, which reduced 20 tons of granite into two-and-a-half-inch pieces each hour.

The 1906 San Francisco earthquake laid ruin to the Bay Area, destroying city blocks, twisting train rails, and, in Santa Cruz County, wreaking havoc on the six-year-old Granite Rock Company. The new steam crushing plant was reduced to rubble by the earthquake, shutting down operations at the quarry, but Wilson was quick to respond to the calamity. A new crusher was procured and, in the aftermath of the widespread damage, a wealth of new business kept the crusher busy, and carried Granite Rock into new fields. Prior to 1906, the quarry's output was used primarily for railroad ballast. In the months following the earthquake, as crews set to work replacing twisted stretches of rail, the need for railroad ballast increased dramatically. The signal development stemming from the earthquake, however, was Granite Rock's entry into the construction business. Wilson joined the massive effort to rebuild those areas flattened by the earthquake by acting as a general building contractor, marking Granite Rock's debut as both a mining and construction firm.

Granite Rock's construction business in San Francisco and around the Monterey Bay area following the 1906 earthquake led the company into the street construction business during the ensuing decade. Against the backdrop of World War I, Granite Rock was awarded contracts to pave streets in Watsonville, Santa Cruz, and Salinas, as well as to construct a highway connecting Castroville and Moss Landing, a project known as the "Cauliflower Boulevard" and that employed a Salinas laborer named John Steinbeck.

The 1920s were years of definitive change for Granite Rock, predominated by leadership changes and the blossoming of the company into a multifaceted enterprise. Porter and Wilson continued to lead the company as the decade began, but in 1922 Porter fell victim to his ambitious and diverse business interests.

He suffered severe financial losses in a speculative investment with the Java Coconut Oil Company, causing his ownership stake in Granite Rock to be transferred to Java Coconut Oil. Wilson, on the other hand, was thriving as a businessman and Granite Rock stood as the chief beneficiary of his talents. In the same year, Porter made his troubled exit from the company and Wilson established the Granite Construction Company, of which he became president. Two years later, he broadened his interests further, forming Central Supply Company to distribute construction materials. As these new companies took shape, Wilson purchased the stock owned by Java Coconut Oil and became Granite Rock's majority shareholder and president.

The Great Depression and Granite Rock's Recovery

In 1929, while driving home from the Aromas quarry, Wilson suffered a heart attack and died, leading to the first change in leadership in the company's 30-year history. Wilson's wife, Anna, took over as president of the company, and her stepson, Jeff, assumed the duties of general manager. Ten days later, the Great Depression was touched off by the collapse of financial markets, leaving Granite Rock's new leaders to face the most difficult decade in the company's history. Granite Rock, like thousands of other businesses throughout the country, was hit hard by the debilitative economic conditions. The company was unable to offer regular employment as demand for rock and sand products disappeared. By 1936, Granite Rock's financial position had become precarious enough to warrant the sale of Granite Construction Company and several branches of Central Supply Company.

Robust financial times returned in the 1940s, sparked by the United States' entrance into World War II. At Granite Rock, bustling activity returned as the company supplied materials to build Fort Ord and Camp McQuaide, the Navy airstrip in Watsonville. Flush with business, the company expanded only a few short years after teetering on the brink of insolvency. A new plant was constructed at Asilomar in Pacific Grove, while at the quarry in Aromas excavation of the mining face was brought down 100 feet. At this lower level, which was even with the railroad tracks, a new primary crushing plant was erected, opening in 1946, and the company exited the 1940s with further expansion on the drawing boards.

During the 1950s, Granite Rock gained a number of new facilities, as construction activity recorded a two-decade-long increase fueled by the country's postwar economic rebirth. To meet the rising demand for rock and sand products, the company built wet processing and loading plants at the Aromas quarry and acquired new plants in Salinas, Felton, Santa Cruz, and Los Gatos. Central Supply Company, which had been stripped of some of its operations during the Great Depression, was moving in the opposite direction during the 1950s. The company purchased its first fleet of transit mixer trucks from Ford Motor Company. As physical expansion was underway, leadership changes at headquarters in Watsonville showed that Granite Rock was destined to be a family-run enterprise. Early in the decade, Jeff Wilson left the company and Anna Wilson retired, making room for the ascension of Mary Elizabeth Wilson Woolpert, A.R. and Anna Wilson's first child. Before the end of the decade, Mary Woolpert passed the reins of command to her husband, Bruce G. Woolpert, who would lead the company for the next three decades.

During the 1960s and 1970s, Granite Rock's expansion mirrored the booming growth of the Monterey and San Francisco Bay areas it served. During this period, Central Supply Company was merged into Granite Rock, forming a single entity responsible for production and sales, and new plants were opened in San Jose, Redwood City, Santa Cruz, Gilroy, Hollister, Salinas, and Seaside.

During the 1980s, the company's profits were funneled in a slightly different direction. Instead of using its financial resources to construct new facilities, the company spent capital on revamping its existing assets, namely the Aromas quarry. During the decade, Granite Rock initiated a complete modernization of its quarry in an effort to gain an edge over its competitors. A giant mobile primary crusher—the largest of its kind in the world—was designed and built, and conveyers were installed to carry rock from the crusher to a new wash plant and secondary crushers. In addition, a computer-controlled, automated track and railcar loading system was installed, providing the finishing touch on the newly christened A.R. Wilson Quarry. Although the state-of-the-art A.R. Wilson Quarry represented an important technological step forward for Granite Rock, there were more significant developments during the decade, developments that would shape the company for the future and underpin its success during the 1990s. Ironically, the 1980s would be remembered for Granite Rock's achievements away from the technological side of its business, and those achievements were won by the second generation of Woolpert management.

New Strategy Born in the 1980s

In the mid-1980s, Granite Rock, by all measures, looked to be in fine health. The company's financial standing was sound, the improvements to its quarry promising, and its share of the northern California market was on an upswing. When Bruce G. Woolpert's son Bruce W. Woolpert arrived, however, dramatic change took place immediately. Prior to joining the family business in 1986, Woolpert had distinguished himself both academically and professionally. He graduated from UCLA in 1974 with degrees in economics and mathematics and finished first in his class at Stanford Business School. Following his education, Woolpert joined Hewlett-Packard, where he eventually was put in charge of running a small software division. After eight years working for the computer company, Bruce Woolpert joined his brother Steve at Granite Rock and the brothers were named joint chief executive officers. Steve Woolpert assumed responsibility for land acquisition and long-range resource planning, and Bruce Woolpert took on the duties related to Granite Rock's daily operation.

"He had a lot of ideas when he came here," remembered a longtime company employee, recalling the arrival of Bruce Woolpert, ". . . scared us half to death because the company was successful." What Woolpert saw were meaningful changes in Granite Rock's industry that demanded immediate improvements to Granite Rock's way of doing business. When he arrived at the company, Woolpert found an organizational structure that was overly centralized. The company was hobbled by bureaucratic layers of command that slowed decision making and distanced company-customer relations. Ordering business cards, for example, required the approval of the vice-president. Taking this in, Woolpert looked outside Granite Rock and saw the dynamics of the company's industry quickly changing. Prior to the mid-1980s, the bulk of Granite Rock's competitors were similar in size and resources to Granite Rock, but during the mid-1980s multibillion-dollar multinational firms began to move in and acquire many of the smaller construction materials companies. "We realized," explained Woolpert, "that we couldn't compete with them in terms of dollars; we knew we had to win by doing things better." Within this context, Woolpert launched an exhaustive customer survey to narrow the gulf separating it from its customers and he implemented a personal development plan for Granite Rock's employees known as the Individual Personal Development Plan (IPDP).

The essence of the changes that occurred after the 1987 implementation of IPDP centered on shifting the company's focus from technology to the customer. Customers, according to the company's year-long survey, wanted faster, more precise, more flexible delivery service, which came to represent the cornerstone of Woolpert's changes. "Any time a customer asks us to do something—unless it's illegal or immoral—we will do it," he remarked. The company used Domino's Pizza as the standard from which to measure its delivery performance and instituted an automated loading system at its quarry that gave customers complete control over delivery times. As an integral part of its program to empower customers, the company spent considerable time and money empowering its employees so that they could better serve customers, and, accordingly, established Granite Rock University. The company spent more than ten times the industry average on training for its employees, enabling its employees to achieve their self-determined professional goals as established through IPDP.

Within a decade after Woolpert revamped a company that at first blush appeared to be suffering from no ills, the fruits of his work were readily discernible. Few could question the necessity of his actions. During the economically recessive early 1990s, which affected California severely, the company remained profitable, established a highway paving division named Pavex Construction, and nearly doubled its market share, a remarkable achievement considering the size of Granite Rock's new multinational competition. In fact, between 1987 and 1994, Granite Rock's market share increased 88 percent, despite a 43 percent decline in the California construction business. Further, in terms of revenue per employee, productivity at Granite Rock was 30 percent higher than the industry average. With the company's new way of doing business firmly in place by the late 1990s, Granite Rock's prospects were bright, as the company made its way through its second century of business, flourishing under the stewardship of A.R. Wilson's grandson.

Principal Divisions

Concrete & Building Materials; Road Materials; Truck Transportation Services; Aggregate Division & Rail Unloading Services; Transloadexpress Rail Unloading Service; Pavex Construction Company.

Further Reading

Anderson, Eric R., "A Tale of Two Companies," *Business Credit,* September 1993, p. 22.

Austin, Nancy K., "Where Employee Training Works," *Working Woman,* May 1993, p. 23.

Barrier, Michael, "Learning the Meaning of Measurement," *Nation's Business,* June 1994, p. 72.

Case, John, "The Change Masters," *Inc.,* March 1992, p. 58.

"Granite Rock Co.," *Business America,* November 2, 1992, p. 15.

Granite Rock Company, "Granite Rock Company History," http://www.graniterock.com.

Triplett, Tim, "Satisfaction Is Nothing They Take for Granite," *Marketing News,* May 9, 1994, p. 6.

Welles, Edward O., "How're We Doing? Granite Rock Co.'s Annual Report Card from Customers, and What's Done with the Grades," *Inc.,* May 1991, p. 80.

—Jeffrey L. Covell

Groupe Dassault Aviation SA

9, Rond-Point des Champs-Elyssees
Marcel Dassault
75008 Paris
France
(33) 1 47 41 7921
Fax: (33) 1 40 83 9938
Web site: http://www.dassault-aviation.fr

Public Company
Incorporated: 1911 as S.A. des Ateliers d'Aviation Louis
    Breguet
Employees: 12,044
Sales: FFr 21 billion (US$3.51 billion) (1997)
Stock Exchanges: Paris
Ticker Symbol: Dassault Aviation
SICs: 3721 Aircraft; 3724 Aircraft Engines & Engine
    Parts; 3728 Aircraft Parts & Equipment, Not
    Elsewhere Classified; 3669 Communications
    Equipment, Not Elsewhere Classified

One of France's most important developers and producers of military aircraft, including the famed Mirage series and 1990s-era Rafale, Groupe Dassault Aviation SA, with its Falcon series, is also the world-leading producer of executive class civil aircraft. Groupe Dassault Aviation also includes software development, through highly successful subsidiary Dassault Systèmes, and electronic communications products, through subsidiary Sogitec Industries. Long the only French company of its kind to have resisted government attempts to make it a completely nationalized industry, in 1995 Dassault Aviation signed a memorandum of agreement to merge its operations with the larger Aerospatiale. Pairing the private, profitable, debt-free Dassault Aviation with the chronically unprofitable state-owned Aerospatiale will present more than its share of challenges. Nonetheless, the French government's strong position in Dassault, with 45 percent of shares and a possible majority in voting rights, has overcome Dassault's resistance at giving up its long-cherished independence. The merger—performed in the face of heightened global competition for a vastly contracted military aircraft market—can be expected to occur as the century ends. Whether this will close an important chapter in France's aviation and economic history remains to be seen.

Aviation Pioneers

Dassault was founded by Marcel-Ferdinand Bloch who was born in Alsace on January 22, 1892. As a schoolboy in Paris Bloch viewed his first airplane, built by the Wright Brothers, making a low pass over the city and then circling the Eiffel Tower. As a young man, still fascinated with aviation, Bloch attended the Ecole Supérieure de l'Aéronautique, France's first school for aeronautical engineering. He established a factory in a converted garage, and convinced his father-in-law to finance his small aeronautical business. During World War I Bloch developed a variable pitch propeller for the Spad fighter which gave French pilots the ability to outmaneuver their German adversaries. The Spad propeller made a great deal of money for Bloch who, after the war, went into housing construction.

Bloch began to manufacture airplanes again in the early 1930s when French military contracts were once more available. But the complexion of French politics changed abruptly in 1936 when the Socialist-Communist ''Popular Front'' government of Léon Blum came to power. On January 1, 1937 Bloch's aircraft factories were nationalized by the Société Nationale de Constructions Aéronautiques de Sud-Ouest (S.N.C.A.S.O.), one of six state-controlled aeronautic factories. Bloch was retained as a civil servant and invested the compensation he received for his company in a variety of North American securities. After the Popular Front fell from power, Bloch founded a new aircraft company which later produced the highly successful Bloch 152 fighter.

After the Germans invaded France at the outset of World War II Marcel Bloch, a Jew, was asked to build aircraft for the German war effort as an ''honorary Aryan.'' Bloch refused to collaborate and was forced into hiding. He was later arrested in Lyon and jailed. Eight months before the war ended he was deported to the Buchenwald concentration camp where he remained until the area was liberated by American forces in May 1945.

Company Perspectives:

The real wealth of Dassault Aviation lies in the men and women working in the Company. Through them, it has acquired unrivaled experience in the fields of aeronautics and space and in their applications. These engineers, managers, technical staff, consultants and employees, help the Company to keep ahead and to retain its technical excellence in order to meet the challenges of the future.

Bloch converted to Roman Catholicism after the war and changed his last name to Dassault, the *nom de guerre* of his brother who was a member of the French resistance. Although an ''l'' was added, the name literally means ''on the attack.'' Marcel Dassault subsequently became an honored member of General de Gaulle's inner circle, but since his company had been destroyed by the war it was once again nationalized.

Post-World War II Renewals

Dassault recruited the most brilliant engineers from the best schools in France to work for a new company, Avions Marcel Dassault. Dassault's first project was the development of a small military liaison aircraft which was later manufactured for Air France under the name Languedoc. In 1951 the company began production of its Ouragan (Hurricane) jet fighter. When production of the Ouragan ended in 1953, the company had built 441 of the planes. In 1954 Dassault introduced its next jet, the Mystère. Designed as a subsonic fighter, the Mystère was the first European jet to break the sound barrier in level flight. The Mystère was followed by the Etendard attack jet. In 1953 Dassault acquired the manufacturing license for Armstrong Siddeley's Viper turbojet engine. The Viper was the intended power plant for Dassault's delta-wing Mirage fighter jet, which made its maiden flight in 1955.

Dassault had grown quickly in 10 years. Yet the company employed only a small workforce primarily comprised of engineers and designers. Most of the actual production of aircraft was subcontracted to the state-owned company Sud-Aviation. Doing so was an intentional policy of Marcel Dassault. Unlike Dassault, state-owned companies were better able to keep workers employed while demand for their products was low. As a private company, however, Dassault was free to continue developing new aircraft designs without worrying about laying off production workers. The company's engineers were less specialized than others; each was capable of designing an entire airplane. As a result, they could be moved easily from one project to the next, wherever they were needed most. In short, Dassault did not encounter the kinds of employment problems that plagued the state-operated companies.

In 1958 Marcel Dassault was elected a member of the French Parliament and represented the Beauvais region north of Paris. As a Gaullist deputy, Dassault continued to support the conservative political causes of his party. During this time France implemented a policy of independent military deterrence which culminated in the nation's 1966 decision to withdraw from the North Atlantic Treaty Organization. The defense of France was now solely the responsibility of the French military. Consequently, the demand for military equipment increased greatly, and the primary beneficiary was Avions Marcel Dassault.

Dassault owned factories in nine locations across France. The design facilities and primary factories were located at Saint-Cloud outside of Paris. The Bordeaux plant handled the final assembly of components manufactured by Sud-Aviation, while the other plants handled sub-assembly work and flight testing. The Martignas facility, however, later became primarily responsible for manufacturing missiles. Dassault also founded an electronics company in 1963 called l'Electronique Marcel Dassault. The electronics company, which was operated by Dassault's son Serge, provided his aircraft company with a variety of flight control and avionics devices.

Against the advice of several advisers, Marcel Dassault ordered the development of the Mystère into a small business jet. The civilian version of the Mystère was sold outside of France under the English name of Falcon (it was thought that this would increase its international marketability). The Mystère/Falcon later became one of the world's most popular private jets. In 1972 Dassault and Pan Am created an American subsidiary called the Falcon-jet Corporation for the sale and service of Falcon jets in the United States. Besides assisting Sud-Aviation in the development of the French-British Concorde SST at this time, Dassault also developed improved versions of its Mirage fighter jet. Regarded as the most successful European jet since Britain's Canberra bomber, the Mirage was sold to over a dozen foreign air forces.

In June 1967 Avions Marcel Dassault purchased a 62 percent majority interest in Breguet Aviation, the French partner in the Franco-British Jaguar jet project. Breguet was founded in 1911 by the French aviation pioneer Louis Breguet. The company was nationalized in 1936, but managed to regain a significant degree of independence three years later when it repurchased three of its former factories from the government.

During June of the same year, Egypt, Syria, and Jordan launched a surprise attack on Israel in what later became known as the Six Day War. Israel, however, was armed with Dassault's Mirage fighter jets which destroyed the Soviet-equipped Egyptian air force in three hours. The Mirages performed so well during the conflict that they were given much of the credit for the subsequent Israeli victory. President de Gaulle imposed an embargo on 50 additional Mirages bound for Israel. The embargo was lifted three years later by President Georges Pompidou, after it was learned that Israeli spies had acquired the plans for the Mirage and that modified versions were already being built in Israel. At approximately the same time, the French government also agreed to sell 110 Mirage fighters to Libya.

The French government, fully aware of the French aerospace industry's decreasing ability to compete internationally, campaigned for the rationalization (or merger) of several French aircraft manufacturers. The state-owned aircraft companies Sud-Aviation, Nord-Aviation, and Sereb (a missile manufacturer) were merged to form Aerospatiale in 1970. A year later, with the encouragement of the government, Breguet Aviation, a publicly traded company which was controlled by Marcel Dassault, merged with the larger, privately owned Avions Marcel Dassault. The new company, Avions Marcel Dassault-Breguet Aviation, operated 20 factories and accounted for 35 percent of all French aerospace production. Marcel Dassault's reason for merging his company with Breguet was that both companies could economize their operations by eliminating duplicated facilities and bureaus. Dassault also wanted to take advantage of Breguet's public stock listings in Paris and Brussels in order to raise capital. Dassault required a $280 million line of credit in order to develop a new 134-passenger commercial jetliner called the Mercure.

The Mercure was a twin-engine airliner very similar in appearance to the Boeing 737. In fact, the Mercure competed with the Boeing 737 for the same market. Only 10 Mercures had been sold by 1976, all of them to the French domestic airline Air Inter. The project was abandoned after the company failed to reach an agreement with McDonnell Douglas whereby the two companies would coproduce the subsequent Mercures.

Dassault-Breguet became involved in an unusual scandal during 1976 when the company's financial director, Hervé de Vathaire, disappeared with FFr 8 million from the company account. As the company accountant, de Vathaire was more familiar with the company's finances than anyone. He had become disillusioned a few months earlier after the death of his wife. He reportedly began assembling incriminating evidence against Dassault-Breguet, a photocopy of which fell into the hands of Jean Kay, a French right-wing "soldier of fortune" who became known for his flamboyant terrorist activities. Kay demanded FFr 8 million from de Vathaire for his copy of the dossier and threatened to turn the document over to news organizations if his demand was not met.

De Vathaire was introduced to Kay by his mistress Bernardette Roels, whose roommate was a friend of Kay's. Together with his mistress and Kay, de Vathaire went to Divone les Bains near the Swiss border. When French authorities began to search for de Vathaire, all three vanished. De Vathaire turned up a few weeks later in Corfu, and then returned to Paris where he surrendered to the police. In the meantime, an anonymous caller to a Paris television station announced that all 8 million francs had been turned over to Lebanese Christians for arms purchases. Marcel Dassault also confirmed that Kay had returned the document.

Details of the document's contents were published in *Le Point* in October. Among other things, Dassault was accused of diverting funds for his personal use and attempting to avoid payment of taxes. According to the allegations, Marcel Dassault used company funds to build a replica of King Louis XIV's Petit Trianon palace at Versailles. The disclosures led to tax evasion investigations of Marcel Dassault and severely damaged his political position.

In 1978 French Socialist and Communist politicians pledged to nationalize Dassault-Breguet if they were elected. Marcel Dassault, who owned 90 percent of the company and was believed to have been the wealthiest man in France, stood for all that leftist politicians opposed. The leftists charged that the French government was allowing Mirage fighters to be sold to anyone who had the money to purchase them. Dassault-

Breguet, they claimed, was only interested in making money by taking advantage of the ambitious military requirements of oil-rich and other third world nations. In answering these charges, Dassault maintained that these nations would purchase their arms from other manufacturers if they did not purchase them from Dassault and that its position as an arms supplier strengthened French political influence in the third world.

The following year leftists won enough seats in the national assembly to implement their nationalization policies. The government purchased a 21 percent share of Dassault-Breguet for $128.5 million. This included a special 33 percent voting interest which under French law enabled the government to exercise veto power over company decisions. When François Mitterand was elected president of France in 1981, the government increased its share in Dassault-Breguet to 46 percent, with a special 63 percent voting majority. The move was regarded by many as an act of spite against the 89-year-old Marcel Dassault who continued to be regarded as a political opponent.

The French arms industry broke into the newspaper headlines again in 1982 during the brief South Atlantic war between Britain and Argentina over the Falkland Islands. During the hostilities Argentina destroyed a number of British ships with Matra Exocet missiles launched from a Dassault-Breguet Super Etendard. A French embargo on additional arms for Argentina had little effect on the losses suffered by British forces, who successfully completed their invasion of the Falklands and achieved an Argentine surrender.

Nonetheless, Dassault-Breguet remained in excellent financial condition due to its continued marketing success with improved versions of the Mystère/Falcon and Mirage fighter. Generally, the company remained competitive because it avoided the costs involved in developing new aircraft from scratch. Instead, Dassault-Breguet continually improved existing aircraft, the designs of which had been thoroughly proven. This was Marcel Dassault's rationale for campaigning against French participation in the four-nation Eurofighter program led by British Aerospace and MBB. Without a government commitment to purchase, Dassault-Breguet developed an entirely French-built fighter jet called the Rafale, which was intended to serve as the basic instrument for the aerial defense of France.

Dassault-Breguet became involved in spacecraft engineering during 1985 when the French space agency Centre Nationale d'Etudes Spatiales assigned the company to lead the aeronautical development of the Hermes spaceplane as a subcontractor to Aérospatiale. The Hermes, similar in design to the American space shuttles, was expected to fly into space atop an Ariane 5 rocket in 1995. Despite its position in the Hermes program, Dassault-Breguet had no plans to establish a space division.

Shadow of Dassault in the 1990s

Marcel Dassault died on April 18, 1986, at the age of 94. His son Serge was placed in charge of the company. Dassault-Breguet remained through the 1990s France's most dynamic aeronautical manufacturer. In addition to the Super Etendard and Mirage and Falcon series, Dassault-Breguet was a partner with British Aerospace in the Jaguar fighter program, and with Dornier of West Germany in the Alpha jet program. The company also manufactured aircraft fuselages for Fokker of the Netherlands.

Serge Dassault would be roundly criticized as being a shadow of his powerful father; nonetheless, Serge Dassault would fight tenaciously to maintain the long-cherished independence of the family-controlled company, renamed Dassault Aviation in 1990. After the failure of the Mitterand government to nationalize the company in the early 1990s, the right-wing government led by family friend Jacques Chirac tried its hand at taming Dassault. In 1996, Chirac succeeded in winning an agreement to merge Dassault with Aerospatiale, but only after the larger state-owned aeronautics company would be privatized. The defeat of the rightists in 1997 and the installation of a Socialist government under Lionel Jospin did not relax the pressure on Dassault, however. The Socialists, wary of job losses, refused to privatize Aerospatiale, suggesting a derailment of the merger agreement. Nonetheless, the merger of Dassault into Aerospatiale was expected to be forced through, one way or another. In 1997, the government stepped up the pressure on Serge Dassault by turning over documents to a Belgian court investigating bribery and other charges against him. The move effectively ''imprisoned'' Dassault within French borders.

In the face of global competition against such giants as Lockheed-Martin, the restructuring of Dassault, Aerospatiale, and other important components—such as Matra, Snecma, and Thomson—of France's industrial military complex seemed inevitable in the late 1990s. Whether Serge Dassault and the Dassault family could be expected to maintain their grip on an important sector of France's aviation industry remained to be seen. Despite slowdowns in worldwide and French government aircraft purchases in the post-Cold War 1990s, and a corresponding drop in Dassault's revenues—from FFr 16.4 billion to FFr 13 billion in 1996—Dassault exhibited an impressive resiliency, maintaining its profitability and continuing the development of its aircraft. After the Rafale's debut in 1991, the company introduced new models of both this polyvalent aircraft and its Mirage predecessor; the company's civil aircraft, the Falcon, also saw its series expanded, as the company claimed 50 percent of the worldwide high-end executive jet market. In 1997, Dassault Aviation's revenues returned to a growth movement, reaching FFR 16 billion of the group's FFr 20 billion total sales.

Principal Subsidiaries

Génerale de Mécanique Aéronautique; La Compagnie de Gestion de Rechanges Aéronautiques (COGER); Sociedad de Coordinacion Aeronautica (Spain); Dassault Aéro Service; Dassault International (U.S.A.) Inc.; Dassault International (France); Falcon Jet Corporation (U.S.A.); Corse Composites Aéronautiques (with Aérospatiale and SNECMA); Dassault Systèmes (France).

Further Reading

Christienne, Charles, and Pierre Lissarrague, *A History of French Military Aviation,* translated by Frances Kianka, Washington, D.C.: Smithsonian Institution Press, 1986.
Fitchett, Joseph, ''Jospin's Cuts Take Aim at Dassault's Combat Plane,'' *International Herald Tribune*, August 13, 1997, p. 1.
Jannic, Hervé, ''Et si Dassault, loin de mourir, donnait plutôt l'exemple d'un ajustement à la crise?'' *L'Expansion*, April 2, 1992, p. 57.
Perry, Robert L., *A Dassault Dossier: Aircraft Acquisition in France,* Santa Monica, Calif.: Rand Memorandum No. R-1148-PR, September 1973.
Romeges, Jean, ''L'amorce d'un grand Meccano,'' *Le Point*, February 24, 1996, p. 56.

—updated by M. L. Cohen

GT Bicycles

2001 E. Dyer Road
Santa Ana, California 92705
U.S.A.
(714) 481-7100
Fax: (714) 481-7111
Web site: http://www.gtbicycles.com

Division of The Schwinn-GT Co.
Incorporated: 1979 as GT Bicycles, Inc.
Employees: 700
Sales: $200.0 million (1997)
SICs: 3751 Motorcycles, Bicycles & Parts; 5091 Sporting
& Recreational Goods; 5136 Men's & Boys' Clothing;
6719 Holding Companies, Not Elsewhere Classified

GT Bicycles is the nation's leading supplier of dirt-track racing, or bicycle motocross "BMX," bicycles and one of the nation's biggest sellers of adult mountain bikes, as well as over 4,500 different parts and accessories, ranging from bicycle frames and componentry to helmets, locks, and apparel through a distribution network.

Headquartered in Santa Ana, California, the company designs, manufactures, and markets some 143 mid- to premium-priced bicycle models, including 48 mountain, 73 juvenile BMX, and 22 road and specialty bicycle models sold under the company's brand names "Auburn," "Dynamo," "Dyno," "GT," "Powerlite," and "Robinson," ranging in price from $200 to $3,000.

A Decade from a Garage to a Giant, 1979–89

GT Bicycles was founded in 1979 by BMX racetrack operator Richard Long and engineer and former drag racer Gary Turner, who had been building customized bicycle frames in his garage in Santa Ana, California; the finished bikes were ridden by Turner's son in area races. Named GT after Turner's initials, the company was created to manufacture BMX bikes for boys. Their first products were chrome-moly steel frames, which made a bicycle light and sturdy, and designed to enhance per-

formance. By 1981, from a single bicycle shop in Anaheim, the company was selling complete BMX bicycles, and sales reached $4 million, with gross margins of nearly 70 percent due to the low overhead of manufacturing in Turner's garage.

In 1984, the company entered the fast-growing (and higher-priced than BMX) mountain bike industry, introducing its own line of mountain bicycles and going head-on against segment leader Cannondale, then a Pennsylvania-based manufacturer led by Joseph Montgomery.

The company acquired Riteway Distributor in 1987 and then proceeded to purchase three more distributors in the United States, to help market its products in the nearly $3 billion parts and accessories market. Revenues reached $41.2 million in 1989.

The 1990s

To compete with Cannondale's direct distribution network, complete with sales representatives, the company, from 1991–96, began shifting from outside distributors, spending nearly $20 million in that period on a nationwide distribution chain for bicycles and parts. President and cofounder Long began a continuous personal promotion campaign, going to weekend bike races to meet customers, dealers, the trade press, and vendors, and total revenue for 1991 reached $61 million. The following year revenues climbed to $93 million.

The company was incorporated in Delaware in August 1993 as GT Holdings, Inc. Two months later, the company acquired all of the outstanding common stock of GT Bicycles California, Inc. A line of road bicycles was introduced during that year, as well as a subsequent line of specialty bicycles, featuring cruisers and tandems.

Also during November of that year, the company's management led a leveraged buyout (LBO), purchasing the company for an undisclosed sum, and cofounder Turner departed from the management of the company, leaving Long alone at the helm. Though the leveraged buyout depressed net income, the company still remained in the black for the year, posting revenues of $123.8 million and a net income of $3 million. Competitor Huffy, meanwhile, posted a year-end 1993 loss of $4.9 million.

By the end of 1994, the U.S. bicycle market, which comprised only about 20 percent of the world market, began to stagnate, as sales dropped from 13 million to 12.5 million bicycles, well down from the all-time record of 15.2 million set in 1973. GT Bicycles accounted for over a million childrens bicycles in the United States from 1994 to 1997.

Despite the slump the company posted net income of $882,000 on total sales of $145.8 million, while its top competitors, Cannondale Corp. (by now relocated to Georgetown, Connecticut) and Miamisburg, Ohio-based Huffy Corp., posted a loss of $600,000 and a profit of $17.4 million, respectively.

Beginning in 1995, and over the next two years, sales of high-end bicycles, costing $600 and up, began bucking the generally slow bicycle market, with sales rising 10–15 percent in that period, according to analysts.

In July of that year, the company acquired the assets of a bicycle and accessory distributor for approximately $3.3 million in cash. The present name of the company was adopted the following month.

In October, the company completed its initial public offering, selling 4.7 million shares at $14 a share, bringing in approximately $65.8 million. Most of the money was used to repay Bain Funds of Boston and Jackson National Life Insurance Co. of Chicago, two of the key investors who financed part of the $66 million restructuring in 1993 following the management-led LBO. Montgomery Securities, Smith Barney Inc., and William Blair & Co. were the underwriters for the offering. In the company's first day as a public entity, stocks dropped $0.75 as the company issued a recall on nearly 8,000 bicycles built with potentially defective front forks.

By the end of 1995, the mountain bike fad had settled down a bit, and the segment dropped for the first time in a decade, down from $1.6 million to $1.5 million that year. Nevertheless, by December, GT had a development center in Colorado, distribution centers in four states, and was attributing approximately half of its income from its parts and juvenile BMX bikes sales and claimed some 40 percent of the youth-driven segments. Even though the company withdrew from the Chinese market, overseas sales were growing for the company as well. GT Bicycles posted a net income of $2.8 million on total sales of $168.9 million and, in 16 years of business, had never posted a loss.

Tragedy Strikes, 1996

By 1996, nearly 60 percent of the company's revenues were derived from the mountain bike segment, but Cannondale was still the segment leader, with their barn-manufactured, "100% American made," unique fat tire bicycles sweeping the market, making, in 1995, $13.5 million in operating profits on total revenues of $122 million compared to GT Bicycles' $8 million against sales of $169 million in the same period. Cannondale's success was partly attributable to the fact that its local manufacturing allowed it to quickly respond to market changes; most of GT Bicycles' mountain bikes and BMX bikes were being manufactured in Taiwan. But the company invested $750,000 that year to improve its manufacturing process. In April, the company purchased its first wholly owned and operated distribution center outside the United States, a distribution facility in Nancy, France. That year, the company was named the number one brand in Germany by readers of *Mountain Bike* magazine.

Just as things were looking up, cofounder Richard Long was killed in a motorcycle accident in July on his way to a mountain bike race in Big Bear, California, following a rigorous ten-day cross-country road show in which he was furiously trying to convince analysts and investors that the company was equal to Cannondale in the market. An article in the August 1996 issue of *Forbes* stated that "Only 46 years old, Long had been under intense pressure. In an interview a few weeks before his death, the founder of GT Bicycles showed dark shadows under his eyes and the drooping shoulders of a man wearied by the competitive struggle." The company's stock dropped approximately 10 percent at the news, but GT soldiered through the loss and subsequent hard blows.

Michael Haynes, who became the company's chief financial officer in 1989 and a member of the board of directors in 1993, replaced Long as interim president and CEO, and Geoffrey Rehnert, managing director of Bain Capital of Boston, GT's biggest shareholder, stepped in as chairman. GT Bicycles helped sponsor two athletes at the 1996 Summer Olympic Games in Atlanta, Georgia in the first-ever Olympic mountain bike event, where the U.S. Bicycle Team, riding the company's new Superbike (a $70,000 custom hand-crafted, ultralight, all-composite-framed racing bike that took two years to develop), brought home two silver medals. The company picked up a slight sales boost from the hours of international television exposure the games provided.

By the summer of 1996, the company's Riteway Products distribution subsidiary chain had accounts at approximately 4,000 of the estimated 6,800 independent dealers in the United States, an 80 percent market share which outpaced its biggest rivals, and had created a budding presence in countries such as France, Japan, and the United Kingdom. In July of that year, the company opened a 40,000-square-foot distribution center in Jacksonville, Florida's Westside Industrial Park in order to help GT better serve its customers in Florida, Georgia, Louisiana, North Carolina, and South Carolina. Also in July, the company acquired Caratti Sports, Ltd., its distributor in Bristol, England, for approximately $14 million, gaining direct access to more than 3,000 independent bicycle dealers in Britain.

In late 1996, GT Bicycles formed a partnership with Monrovia, California-based AeroVironment to create Charger Bicycles, LLC, which planned to produce and market an initial production run of approximately 2,500 units of an electric-assist bike called the "Charger," in which the design incorporated a

375-watt electric motor into a fully integrated bike and would feature the Impulse System, a human-power sensor enabling the bicycle to respond to the rider's efforts, enabling the bicycle to match or multiply the rider's physical effort. It retailed for $1,500.

GT Bicycles would go on to spend nearly $6 million on advertising throughout the year. Japan accounted for 25 percent of the company's business that year, and the company net income reached a record $11.6 million on total revenues of $208.4 million. Cannondale posted $146 million in total revenue.

Bouncing Back, 1997

By May 1997, retro-style bicycles were making a comeback. To compete with other industry leading models, such as Schwinn's Black Phantom (a single-speed remake of the same model from 1949—which cost $70–$90 then—complete with replicated fenders, horns, tires, chrome, colors, and coaster brakes, retailing at $3,000), Schwinn's Cruise Deluxe (with 1955 replicated frame, forged-steel stem, gas-tank-style center piece, rear rack, grips, pedals, chrome steel fenders, and white-wall tires, retailing at $480), and Huffy's Causeway (featuring classic looks, old-fashioned frame, seat, 26-inch chrome rims, and white-wall tires combined with a state-of-the-art six-speed shifting system, retailing at $140), the company released the Dyno Roadster Ltd. model (featuring a low-rider frame, heavy duty, shock-absorbing springer fork, oversized balloon fenders, white-wall tires, and rims with chrome-plated 10-gauge spokes, retailing at $490). The company also signed an agreement with American pop culture icon Harley-Davidson Motor Co. to build a limited edition of 1,000 numbered bicycles resembling Harley-Davidson motorcycles, complete with black frame, a 1950s-style chain guard, chrome accents, thick red-and-cream colored fenders, a motorcycle saddle, a simulated horn tank, and a Harley-Davidson insignia on the front, combined with a modern, quick-shifting, seven-speed internal drive train and custom suspension fork. Built at the company's Santa Ana, California headquarters, the bicycles retailed at approximately $2,300, were released for the Christmas market, and brought the company an estimated $2.3 million in new business. Montague's Backcountry mountain bike (featuring oversized tubing, flat handlebars, water bottle mounts, and an 18-speed gear system, weighing 30 pounds, folding in half for easy transport, and selling at $500) joined the ''old-timers'' at the top of the industry.

The bicycle industry saw some consolidation, with manufacturing giant Schwinn being acquired by Questor Partners. Also in 1997, the company's bicycles were prominently displayed in a new summer movie remake of *Leave It to Beaver*, Nike began selling GT-brand bicycle jerseys at its Niketown stores in the United States, and Coca-Cola purchased several thousand bicycles in a promotional giveaway it sponsored for its Fresca brand name drinks. By the end of the year, *Popular Science* magazine named the company's electric-assist bicycle ''the best new recreation product'' in 1997. The company's total revenue for 1997 was $216.2 million.

Hoping to broaden its exposure and market reach in March 1998, GT Bicycles, together with sponsors Pioneer and Honda,

spent nearly a half-million dollars to create a new television show called *Crank,* featuring riders on BMX racing bikes performing stunts, wild rides, and aerial feats to loud music, computer graphics, and flashing lights. The 19 episodes of the half-hour program debuted on The Fox Sports Network and focused on racing, freestyle riding, and other bicycle sports.

Early in 1998, the company entered into negotiations with Questor Partners to be acquired. In July, under the aegis of Schwinn, Questor acquired all of the stock and debt of GT Bicycles for a price of approximately $180 million. Following the acquisition, Cannondale remained the last publicly traded bicycle company in the United Sates.

Combined with Schwinn's brand-name recognition, GT Bicycle's innovation and history of profitability, the company was in a position to remain a leader in bicycle manufacture into the 21st century.

Further Reading

Beckert, Beverly, ''Mission Possible!: First to Market,'' *Industry Week*, July 17, 1995, p. 1A.

Furchgott, Roy, ''Rebel Without an Engine,'' *Business Week*, September 15, 1997, p. 8.

''GT Bicycles Inc.,'' *New York Times*, August 14, 1998, p. C5(N)/D5(L).

''GT Bicycles Inc.,'' *Wall Street Journal*, May 8, 1998, p. C16(W)/C28(E).

''GT Bicycles Inc. to Open Distribution Center in Jacksonville, Fla.,'' *Knight-Ridder/Tribune Business News*, May 24, 1996, p. 5240085.

Hardesty, Greg, ''Santa Fe-Based GT Bicycles Gets Cranking with Fox Sports Show,'' *Knight-Ridder/Tribune Business News*, March 26, 1998, p. 326B1001.

La Franco, Robert, ''The Battle of the Bikes,'' *Forbes*, August 26, 1996, p. 60.

Mouchard, Andre, ''GT Bicycles Founder Richard Long Killed in Motorcycle Crash,'' *Knight-Ridder/Tribune Business News*, July 16, 1996, p. 7160299.

——, ''GT Bicycles Hopes to Beat the Rap on Bike Makers,'' *Knight-Ridder/Tribune Business News*, December 8, 1995, p. 12080218.

——, ''Not-So-Smooth Sailing As GT Bicycles Raises $65.8 Million in Offering,'' *Knight-Ridder/Tribune Business News*, October 15, 1995, p. 10150226.

''*The Orange County Register*, Calif., Business Briefs Column,'' *Knight-Ridder/Tribune Business News*, March 13, 1998, p. 313B0949.

''*The Orange County Register*, Calif., Business Briefs Column,'' *Knight-Ridder/Tribune Business News*, August 15, 1995, p. 8150147.

Pargh, Andy, ''Pedal Back in Time with New Retro-Bikes,'' *Design News*, May 19, 1997, p. 134.

''Purchase of GT Bicycles for $80 Million Is Settled,'' *Wall Street Journal*, June 23, 1998, p. B4(W)/B4(E).

Rowe, Jeff, ''Santa Ana, Calif.-Based GT Bicycles to Make Harley Bike,'' *Knight-Ridder/Tribune Business News*, August 8, 1996, p. 8080088.

''Schwinn to Purchase GT Bicycles of California,'' *New York Times*, June 23, 1998, p. C4(N)/D4(L).

Teague, Paul E., ''Gold Rush!: Software, Sensors, Motors, and More Help Athletes Go for the Gold,'' *Design News*, June 24, 1996, p. 130.

—Daryl F. Mallett

Gwathmey Siegel & Associates Architects LLC

475 Tenth Avenue
New York, New York 10018
U.S.A.
(212) 947-1240
Fax: (212) 967-0890

Private Company
Incorporated: 1968 as Gwathmey, Henderson and Siegel, Architects
Employees: 80
Sales: $300 million (1997 est.)
SICs: 8712 Architectural Services

Gwathmey Siegel & Associates Architects LLC is one of the largest architectural firms in the United States. Founded in 1968, the firm designed nearly 200 projects in its first 25 years and received an assortment of some 80 honors and awards for its work in that time. Gwathmey Siegel served as the architect for the American Museum of the Moving Image, the Science, Industry and Business Library, and the addition to Frank Lloyd Wright's Guggenheim Museum, all in New York City. The firm is noted for its adherence to the principles of Modernism, especially the International Style of architecture embodied in the geometric designs of the French master Le Corbusier.

Establishing a Reputation: 1964–79

Charles Gwathmey—son of the painter Robert Gwathmey—and Robert Siegel became friends while studying at the High School of Music and Art in New York City. After becoming architects they were reunited as apprentices in the firm of Edward Larrabee Barnes. In 1964 Gwathmey designed his first house, the Miller residence on Fire Island, a popular beach resort off the southern shore of Long Island. He then took time off to learn in detail exactly how a house is built and subsequently erected much of the building himself.

Gwathmey's first major work was an ocean house and studio in Amagansett, Long Island, designed for his parents in 1965 in association with Richard Henderson and completed in 1967. This influential minimalist work, a composition of cubes, cylinders, and sharply slanted roofs clad in vertical cedar siding, established Gwathmey's career and led to a number of other residential commissions for him and Henderson. Soon eastern Long Island was dotted with similar vacation homes, many of them designed by the architects dubbed "The Five"— Gwathmey, Peter Eisenman, Michael Graves, John Hejduk, and Richard Meier—whom some critics lumped together as founders of a "New York School" based on Le Corbusier's principles of form, space, and volume after their work appeared together in a 1969 Museum of Modern Art exhibit.

In retrospect, however, it became clear that Gwathmey was no slavish follower of the austere Corbusian ideal. In his designs he emphasized diagonals as much as straight lines and complex interior volumes as much as overall form, and he left many of his houses with natural cedar siding instead of having them painted white, as Le Corbusier would have done. In their 1968 design for the Electric Circus, a New York City dance hall that was a sensation at the time, Gwathmey and Henderson filled the interior with an array of reflective and translucent materials that added glitter and an intentional visual ambiguity to their geometric contexts.

Gwathmey designed his first apartment in 1969 for actress Faye Dunaway in a building on Manhattan's Central Park West, "sculpting interior objects and playing them off against the rigid, pre-existing forms of the walls of the overall building," according to Paul Goldberger in his *New York Times* article "A Design for Orderly Living." Although the slate floors and cool white walls were typical of Gwathmey's aesthetic at the time, the apartment commissions that followed revealed a movement toward less austere, more sensuous forms by his willingness to employ lush carpets and fine woods. Since, for such projects, Gwathmey's control of the building shell was limited or nonexistent, he chose to explore the use of color as a substitute for three-dimensional manipulation.

When Siegel left Barnes to join the fledgling firm in 1968, it was renamed Gwathmey, Henderson and Siegel, Architects. After Henderson's departure in 1970, it became Gwathmey Siegel & Associates. With a reputation for being blunt as well as obsessive about detail, Gwathmey remained the chief designer. Calmer and more diplomatic, Siegel tended to oversee the firm's larger projects but, like Gwathmey, was involved in every design. So closely did the partners collaborate that they shared an office with a single common worktable in the firm's quarters, which were located in midtown Manhattan's Carnegie Hall building.

In 1973 a restaurateur named Pearl Wong asked Gwathmey Siegel to design new quarters for Pearl's, her restaurant on Manhattan's 48th Street. The long narrow dining room, with its quarter-arc ceiling and glass-block front, was widely praised and led to other restaurant commissions. These included Shezan, a Pakistani restaurant on West 58th Street, and the U.S. Steakhouse Co. in midtown Manhattan's Time-Life Building. Like the Electric Circus, Shezan was sensual, with soft lighting and mirrors and the materials employed including lush woods, polished aluminum ceiling tiles, and glass block. U.S. Steakhouse, by contrast, was so austere that one restaurant critic compared the ambience with that of a gymnasium. Management later hired another architect to add banners and new lighting and billed the restaurant as becoming "warmer, friendlier, more *gemutlich.*" Gwathmey Siegel's interior work also included a sleek revamping of five Vidal Sassoon hairdressing salons between 1974 and 1977.

Gwathmey Siegel continued to be in demand for residential commissions. One of its most successful was the Cogan house in East Hampton, Long Island, a rectangular Corbusian pavilion intersected with three projected ramps and a living area elevated to provide a view of the Atlantic Ocean. Completed in 1972, this work was followed by others more complex and larger in scale. They included the Kiselvetz house in Westhampton, Long Island, in 1977; the Weitz house in Quogue, Long Island, in 1978; the Taft residence in Cincinnati, also in 1978; and the deMenil residences in Houston and East Hampton in 1979. Gwathmey Siegel even designed a commercially successful "Tuxedo" tableware line in the early 1980s for Swid Powell.

Institutional Projects: 1973–96

Gwathmey Siegel completed its first large-scale design in 1973, for an 800-student dormitory for the State University of New York at Purchase. The firm followed up this project with other campus commissions. Its renovation of Princeton University's Whig Hall in the early 1970s lent a stark geometric order to the burned-out shell of the 1893 Greek Revival structure. Gwathmey Siegel also designed a 560-unit low-income residential community in Perinton, New York, completed in 1975. By the end of 1977 Gwathmey Siegel was engaged in designing two more major projects: the 1,000-unit Northgate apartment complex on Roosevelt Island (completed in 1980) and a Columbia University dormitory complex, both in New York City. The latter project, although substantially completed in 1981, was plagued by construction problems.

During the 1980s Gwathmey Siegel was hard at work designing structures for Eastern universities. These included an addition, completed in 1988, to Dartmouth University's gymnasium, the College of Architecture for the University of North Carolina at Charlotte, and two buildings at Cornell University, including one for its school of agriculture. For the latter structure, completed in 1989, Gwathmey Siegel expanded its range

of colors and materials to include an exterior in three shades of earth tones, with a metal barrel-vaulted roof and teak-framed windows. For the North Carolina building, the firm, aware that architecture students would be learning about design not only in, but also from, the structure, revealed as much about its workings as possible, employing a juxtaposition of materials for the exterior and enclosing the elevator in a glass cage to expose its machinery for study.

Later campus buildings designed by Gwathmey Siegel included a dining hall for Oberlin College (completed in 1991), a building for Hostos Community College in New York City (completed in 1992), a building for theater arts and fine arts at the State University of New York, Buffalo (completed in 1992), and a Jewish center at Duke University (completed in 1994). Werner Otto Hall, the new home for Harvard University's Busch-Reisinger Museum, was completed in 1991.

Gwathmey Siegel began work in 1981 on the American Museum of the Moving Image in New York City's borough of Queens. This renovation of a three-story industrial warehouse, not completed until 1988, was rendered in primary colors to relieve the gray uniformity of the neighborhood. In the same neighborhood, Long Island City, the firm drew up the plan for the transformation of two old concrete loft buildings into the International Design Center, completed in 1988.

Perhaps Gwathmey Siegel's most controversial undertaking was an addition to Frank Lloyd Wright's Guggenheim Museum on the upper stretch of Manhattan's Fifth Avenue. First proposed in 1984, the firm's plan called for an 11-story sea-green annex, including a 148-foot-long slab that would cantilever over the smaller rotunda of the main building. Unable to win city approval, the museum withdrew the proposal in 1987, and Gwathmey Siegel settled on a nine-story limestone structure separated from the main building by a sculpture garden. Litigation delayed construction for three more years, and the building was not completed until 1992. The firm also rehabilitated the original 1959 structure, including uncovering the original skylight by installing clear glass.

Gwathmey Siegel also designed the New York Public Library's new Science, Industry and Business Library, located in the former B. Altman department store on Manhattan's East 34th Street. Completed in 1996, this facility housed a collection of 1.2 million volumes and an electronic information center with some 100 workstations. A two-story atrium, intended for exhibition use, connected the two main public levels.

Corporate and Other High-Profile Clients: 1977–98

Gwathmey Siegel's engagement in corporate projects began in 1977 with the design of an AT&T Corp. office building in Parsippany, New Jersey. The following year the firm designed the Manhattan offices and showroom of Giorgio Armani Inc. It also designed IBM's office building and distribution center in Greensboro, North Carolina, completed in 1987. Gwathmey Siegel designed the interiors of a number of corporate headquarters in the 1980s. These included interiors for Lexecon, Inc. (1985–86), Georgetown Group, Inc. (1987–88), SBK Entertainment World, Inc. (1987–88), D'Arcy Masius Benton & Bowles, Inc. (1987–88), and The Capital Group (1991–92).

Gwathmey Siegel's biggest corporate project, and its first skyscraper, was the 1986–88 design of the Solomon Equities building, a strongly silhouetted 52-story structure in shimmering metal and glass completed in 1991 at 1585 Broadway, between 47th and 48th streets in midtown Manhattan. In praising the building, *New York Times* architecture critic Paul Goldberger wrote, "It isn't an East Hampton villa turned on its side. . . . Mr. Gwathmey and Mr. Siegel have given this building an exquisite sheathing of blue-green glass, white patterned glass, mirror glass, silver-gray aluminum panels and polished stainless steel. It's a kind of laundry list of modern elements, but here put together into a geometric pattern that manages to be neither flat nor dull. . . . What Mr. Gwathmey and Mr. Siegel have struggled to prove here is that it is possible to do in metal almost all the things that more traditional architecture does in masonry: offer richness, depth, texture and graphic complexity."

Corporate work remained an important part of Gwathmey Siegel's business in the 1990s, both for architecture and interiors. After AT&T sold its 35-story Manhattan flagship headquarters in the early 1990s to Sony Corp., the firm, armed with a $70 million budget, gutted the entire interior to accommodate an additional 1,000 employees in the 750,000-square-foot building. For the offices of EMI, a company on the leading edge of rock music, the firm chose cutting-edge materials like galvanized metal on the undulating ceiling, concrete pavers on the floor, and black glass for walls.

Walt Disney Productions Inc. was an important client for the firm in the early 1990s. Gwathmey Siegel designed the Disney World Convention Center (completed 1991) and the Disney World Golf Clubhouse (completed 1992). For Euro Disney, Gwathmey Siegel designed another golf clubhouse (completed 1992) with three distinct forms—a dome, a curved shed, and a barrel vault. During the mid-1990s Gwathmey Siegel designed Nanyang Polytechnic in Singapore, a 2.3-million-square-foot project sprawling over 75 acres, scheduled for completion in 1998.

Gwathmey Siegel's high-profile clients in the mid-1990s included movie director Steven Spielberg, for whom the firm was designing a Manhattan apartment as well as three additional structures at the East Hampton compound that it originally designed in 1985. For entertainment mogul David Geffen, the firm designed a New York apartment in the late 1970s and a three-story headquarters building in Beverly Hills that was completed in 1994. Gwathmey Siegel also designed the Malibu, California beachfront home and Utah wilderness home of Jeffrey Katzenberg, partner of Spielberg and Geffen in their joint Dreamworks company. In addition, Gwathmey was reported in 1995 to be commuting to Los Angeles to plan a new house for Hollywood superagent Ron Meyer and to renovate a house for actor Dustin Hoffman.

Before Gwathmey Siegel even drew up a blueprint for a residence, it required a client to participate in all aspects of the design process. Interviewed for *Harper's Bazaar* in 1995, Gwathmey explained, "Having people believe in the process is crucial, because the result is unknown; it's all speculative. A client is coming to you based maybe on what you've done for other people. There has to be a huge trust they are endowing you with that says, 'We don't know what we are going to get; it's millions of dollars of whatever it is, but we believe in it.' That's pretty wild. It's not like going to an auction and buying something that's already there. You're really investing in ideas." He added that the architect and the client must have "a mutual aspiration of making a great work of art together."

President Clinton was said to have been captivated by the beachfront Katzenberg home when he stayed there in 1997. He also stayed at Katzenberg's Utah house and Spielberg's East Hampton complex in 1998 and placed Gwathmey at his table at a White House dinner that year. Inevitably, therefore, there was speculation that Gwathmey Siegel would be commissioned to design the William J. Clinton Presidential Library in Little Rock. The three Dreamworks partners were friends of Clinton and were expected to play a role in giving and raising money to build and endow a $100 million complex to preserve the president's legacy. Also in 1998, the firm learned it had won the commission to build a new United States mission to the United Nations.

By 1993 Gwathmey Siegel had moved its quarters to a 15,000-square-foot warehouse loft on the West Side of midtown Manhattan. The firm had 14 associates that year and was employing 71 architects in its New York offices in 1996.

Further Reading

Abercrombie, Stanley, *Gwathmey Siegel*, New York: Watson-Guptill Publications, 1981.
Collins, Brad, and Kasprowicz, Diane, eds., *Gwathmey Siegel: Buildings and Projects, 1982–1992*, New York: Rizzoli, 1993.
Goldberger, Paul, "A Design for Orderly Living," *New York Times Magazine*, December 11, 1977, pp. 146–48, 163–67, 170.
——, "In Times Square, Dignity by Day, Glitter by Night," *New York Times*, February 10, 1991, Sec. 2, pp. 32, 34.
Goodman, Wendy, "Gwathmey on the Rise," *Harper's Bazaar*, July 1995, pp. 118–23, 136, 138.
Purdum, Todd S., "The Clintons Shop Architects," *New York Times*, August 13, 1998, pp. F1, F10.
Russell, Beverly, "Gwathmey Siegel at 25," *Interiors*, September 1993, pp. 55–83.
Taylor, John, "Born Again: The New Guggenheim," *New York*, June 1, 1992, pp. 30–33, 36–39.

—Robert Halasz

Hibbett Sporting Goods, Inc.

451 Industrial Lane
Birmingham, Alabama 35211
U.S.A.
(205) 942-4292
Fax: (205) 912-7290
Web site: http://www.hibbett.com

Public Company
Incorporated: 1945 as Dixie Supply Company, Inc.
Employees: 1,250
Sales: $113.56 million (1998)
Stock Exchanges: NASDAQ
Ticker Symbol: HIBB
SICs: 5941 Sporting Goods & Bicycle Shops

Hibbett Sporting Goods, Inc. is a leading operator of retail stores for a full line of sporting goods. Founded in 1945, the company targets small to mid-sized markets located mostly in the southeastern United States. In 1998 Hibbett had 159 stores located in 19 states. These stores consist of the company's flagship Hibbett Sports, Inc. stores; Sports & Co., Inc. superstores; and smaller-format Sports Additions, Inc. stores. The stores offer a broad assortment of quality athletic equipment, footwear, and apparel at competitive prices. They feature a core selection of brand-name merchandise for team and individual sports and localized apparel and accessories designed to appeal to customers within each market. About 90 percent of Hibbett's retail outlets are located in large enclosed malls, but the stores also operate profitably in strip-center locations. More than 80 percent of the company's stores are in county markets with a population of less than 250,000. Company subsidiary Hibbett Team Sales, Inc. specializes in customized athletic apparel, equipment, and footwear, selling directly to school, athletic, and youth associations in Alabama. Team Sales has its own warehouse and distribution center from which it manages its operations independently from those of the company's other divisions. When the company went public in 1996, Hibbett stock traded for $16 a share; in 1998, shares of Hibbett stock were in the $25 to $35 range.

Founding and Early Years

In 1945 Rufus Hibbett, a high-school coach and teacher in Florence, Alabama, founded Dixie Supply Company, a retailer of athletic, marine, and aviation equipment. When his two sons joined the business in 1952, Rufus changed the company's name to Hibbett & Sons and focused operating strategy on merchandise for team sports. In the mid-1960s, the company further refined its retail strategy and changed its name to Hibbett Sporting Goods, Inc.

In 1980 the Anderson family of Florence, Alabama, purchased Hibbett, invested in professional management and systems, and continued to expand the company's store base at a moderate pace. Hibbett's unique operating strategy was to target small to mid-sized markets ranging in population from 30,000 to 250,000. By focusing on markets of this size, the company achieved significant strategic advantages, including numerous expansion opportunities, comparatively low operating costs, and a more limited competitive environment than generally would have prevailed in larger markets. Hibbett was also able to establish greater customer and vendor recognition as the leading retailer of a full line of sporting goods in a local community. Furthermore, the company's regional focus enabled it to achieve significant cost benefits, including lower corporate expenses, reduced distribution costs, and increased economies of scale.

Rapid Expansion in the 1990s

By the early 1990s Hibbett's primary retail format was that of its flagship Hibbett Sports, Inc. stores: 5,000-square-foot stores located predominantly in enclosed malls. The company tailored this Hibbett Sports concept to the size, demographics, and competitive conditions of its small to mid-sized markets. Hibbett also established Sports Additions, Inc. stores, which were smaller units of 1,500 square feet. About 90 percent of the Sports Additions merchandise was footwear, with the remainder consisting of caps and limited apparel. These stores offered a broader assortment of athletic footwear, and emphasized a more fashionable footwear assortment than could be found in Hibbett Sports stores. All Sports Additions stores were located in the same malls as Hibbett Sports stores. By the end of fiscal 1993, Hibbett recorded combined sales of $32.03 million from

Company Perspectives:

Hibbett Sporting Goods, Inc.'s stores offer a high level of customer service and competitive prices for an extensive assortment of quality athletic equipment, footwear, and apparel for team and individual sports.

34 Hibbett Sports stores and four Sports Additions stores. By the end of fiscal 1994, company sales had grown to $40.12 million from the operation of 41 Hibbett Sports and eight Sports Additions stores. The company grew from 38 stores at the end of fiscal 1993 to 60 stores at the end of fiscal 1995.

According to the National Sporting Goods Association (NSGA), U.S. retail sales of sporting goods (including athletic footwear, apparel, and equipment) totaled approximately $36 billion in 1995. The market for sporting goods remained highly fragmented; large retailers of sporting goods competed for market share by using a variety of store sizes, including larger-format stores, called superstores. Although several retailers of sporting goods—namely, Foot Locker and Foot Action—were already present in most of Hibbett Sports' mall locations, the company believed that the Hibbett Sports store format could be adjusted effectively to a superstore format focused on a full line of quality sporting merchandise that included products for individual and team sports and a localized mix of apparel and accessories.

From a Private to a Public Company in 1996

In 1995 the Anderson family sold control of the company to Saunders Karp & Co., an investment firm. During the spring of the same year, Hibbett opened its first 25,000-square-foot superstore, dubbed Sports & Co., in Huntsville, Alabama. Athletic equipment and apparel represented a higher percentage of the overall merchandise mix at the Sports & Co. superstore than they did at Hibbett Sports stores. The superstore was designed to project the same atmosphere as that of Hibbett Sports stores, but on a larger scale. For example, the superstore included space for customer-participation areas, such as putting greens and basketball-hoop shoots. Periodically, the superstore featured special events with appearances by well-known athletes.

The need for expanded inventory and larger operating quarters led Hibbett to build a state-of-the-art office/warehouse in Birmingham's Oxmoor Industrial Park. In January 1996 the company relocated to this 130,000-square-foot center, which had significant expansion potential to support Hibbett's growth for the foreseeable future, and centralized the distribution process from its corporate headquarters located in the same building. The company saw strong distribution support for its stores as critical to its expansion strategy and central to maintaining a low-cost operating structure. Hibbett received substantially all of its merchandise at the Birmingham distribution center, where it maintained back stock of key products allocated and distributed to stores through an automatic replenishment program based on items sold during the prior week.

In October 1996 Hibbett completed an initial public offering (IPO) of its shares of common stock for $16 per share and

traded on the NASDAQ under the symbol HIBB. The company accelerated its rate of new store openings to take advantage of the growth opportunities in its target markets. Hibbett's clustered expansion program, which called for opening new stores within a two-hour driving radius of another company location, made for greater efficiency in distribution, marketing, and regional management. In evaluating potential markets, the company considered population, economic conditions, local competitive dynamics, and availability of suitable real estate. Although the core merchandise assortment tended to be similar for each Hibbett Sports store, the company recognized important local or regional differences by regularly offering products that reflected particular sporting activities in a particular community, local college, or professional sports team. Thus, Hibbett Stores was able to react quickly to emerging trends or special events, such as college or professional championships.

During fiscal 1996, sales from Hibbett's 67 stores increased 28.3 percent to $67.1 million. This gain was attributable to the opening of four Hibbett Sports stores and three Sports & Co. superstores. Hibbett's leading product categories, ranked according to sales, were athletic footwear, apparel, and sporting equipment. Although aggressive about expansion, Hibbett continued to emphasize the sale of quality brand-name merchandise at competitive prices. The breadth and depth of the company's merchandise selection generally exceeded that of local independent competitors. Among the brand names that Hibbett offered, the top 25 (based on sales) included: Adidas, Asics, Champion, Converse, Columbia, Dodger, Easton, Everlast, Fila, Louisville Slugger, K-Swiss, Mizuno, New Era, New Balance, Nike, Pro Line, Rawlings, Reebok, Rollerblade, Russell, Spalding, Starter, The Game, Umbro, and Wilson.

Because many of these branded products were highly technical and required considerable customer assistance, Hibbett coordinated with its vendors to educate the store-level sales staff about new products and trends. The merchandise staff analyzed current sporting goods trends by monitoring sales at competing stores; communicating with customers, store managers, and personnel; maintaining close relationships with the company's multiple vendors; and reviewing industry trade publications. The staff also worked closely with store personnel to assure availability of sufficient quantities of products at individual stores.

During 1997, the company further accelerated its store-opening rate by taking advantage of the growth opportunities in its target markets: Hibbett opened 21 Hibbett Sports stores and one Sports & Co. superstore, thereby making the company the operator of 77 stores at the end of fiscal 1997; sales peaked at $86.4 million. Hibbett's increase in sales was attributable to the opening of 22 new stores and to increased footwear sales. The company's largest vendor, Nike, represented approximately 40 percent of its total purchases. Based on its performance in the full-line sporting goods category, Hibbett received the Nike Retailer Excellence Award for the Southeast region for the ninth consecutive year.

Toward the 21st Century: 1998 and Beyond

Thirty years of profitable retailing in small to mid-sized markets validated Hibbett's adherence to the Hibbett Stores format for competing effectively against both the general and the specialty retailers in its industry. Compared to discounters and department stores that generally offered limited assortments of sporting goods, Hibbett carried a wide selection of branded products. Compared to national specialty retailers that typically focused on a single category, such as footwear, or on a specific activity, such as golf or tennis, Hibbett differentiated itself by its breadth of quality merchandise geared to local sporting and community interests. Although some competitors carried product lines and national brands similar to Hibbett's stores, Hibbett Sports stores were usually the primary retailers of a full line of sporting goods in their markets. In the company's 1998 annual report Hibbett President Michael J. Newsome commented that there were three options open to retailers in the sporting goods industry: "stand idly on the sidelines and let the world pass you by; 'slug it out' for incremental market share; or cater to a genuine need. We prefer the latter." The strength of Hibbett's niche, Newsome pointed out, was that the company "offers a full line of sporting goods with superior customer service. Concentration on smaller markets generally limits our competition to small, independent sporting goods operators and national footwear chains and allows us to better serve a broader customer base."

The company targeted special publicity opportunities in its markets to increase the effectiveness of its advertising budget. To further differentiate itself from national chain competitors, Hibbett preferred promotional spending in local media. Advertising in the sports pages of local newspapers served as the foundation of its promotional program; in 1997 the major portion of the company's publicity budget was spent in this way. Hibbett also used local radio, television, and outdoor billboards to reinforce name recognition and brand awareness in the community.

Hibbett's primary retail format and growth vehicle remained that of the Hibbett Sports 5,000-square-foot store located predominantly in enclosed malls. The company used relevant design, in-store atmosphere, and eye-catching signage to channel mall traffic into the stores. Hibbett's management information systems tracked different retail prices for the same item at different stores, thereby enabling more competitive pricing by location. Furthermore, the purchasing staff regularly reviewed and analyzed the company's point-of-sale computer system in order to make appropriate merchandise allocation and markdown decisions.

During 1998 Hibbett opened 31 Hibbett Sports stores and two Sports Additions stores; sales increased 31.4 percent to $113.6 million. The increase was due to the addition of 33 new stores, to larger sales for ladies' and children's footwear and apparel, and to higher equipment sales. Higher earnings also reflected lower store-operating and selling expenses as a percentage of sales due to improved leveraging of administrative costs. At the end of fiscal 1998, Hibbett operated 120 stores in 14 southeastern states. Hibbett expanded its geographic reach when it opened its first store in eastern Oklahoma and five stores in Arkansas, but the majority of the new stores were in states where Hibbett already operated. To keep pace with the company's rapid expansion, Hibbett continually evaluated and improved the capacity and effectiveness of its Birmingham distribution center. The addition of radio frequency technology reduced labor costs and increased accuracy. The installation of additional conveyors and of other equipment decreased processing time and improved inventory turns.

During the first six months of fiscal 1999, Hibbett surpassed all its previous records for increases in net income, net sales, and number of store openings. Net sales increased 25.3 percent to $65.86 million, compared with $52.56 million for the same period in fiscal 1998. Net income increased 33.2 percent to $3.2 million, compared with net income of $2.4 million for the first six months of fiscal 1998. During the first quarter, Hibbett opened a record 15 stores, making a total of 135 Hibbett stores operating in 16 southeastern states. During the second quarter, the company opened 20 additional stores, including 18 Hibbett Sports stores and two Sports Additions stores. Hibbett acquired two of the stores from W.C. Bradley Company and five of the stores from Olympia Sports. Five of the seven stores were converted to Hibbett Sports stores and two were converted to Sports Additions stores.

Commenting on these results, President Newsome said: "In light of the number of new store openings to date and a tremendous number of expansion opportunities, we have increased our goal for fiscal 1999 [from at least 42 to at least 48 new stores] and now expect to end the fiscal year with at least 168 stores. The acquisitions completed during the second quarter were opportunistic in nature and are an excellent fit to our existing store base." The new stores, including Hibbett's first stores in eastern Texas and southern Indiana, further expanded Hibbett's presence in several key markets in Alabama, Georgia, and Mississippi.

As the 21st century drew near, the company's strategy of targeting small to mid-size markets "For the Good Sport" (Hibbett's byline) prepared it for even more outstanding growth. The Hibbett Sports store format consistently produced a strong return on capital in the first year of operation and significant sales growth in the second and third years. New stores positioned within a two-hour driving distance of an existing store expanded Hibbett's store base while maintaining low costs for distribution of merchandise. Hibbett's plan for clustered expansion into over 500 potential markets identified for future Hibbett Sports stores, seemed an attainable goal.

Principal Subsidiaries

Hibbett Sports, Inc.; Hibbett Team Sales, Inc.; Sports Additions, Inc.; Sports & Co., Inc.

Further Reading

"Baseball Comes Out Swinging at Stores," *Daily News Record,* April 9, 1996, p. 1.
Evans, Chuck, "New Book Claims to Hold Keys to Retailing Secrets," *Birmingham Business Journal,* June 1, 1998.
Leand, Judy, "Masters of Invention," *SportStyle,* February 1995, pp. 88–89.
Milazzo, Don, "Hibbett to Relocate HQ and Warehouse to Oxmoor," *Birmingham Business Journal,* February 20, 1995, p. 6.
Parr, Karen, "Driving Ambition," *SportStyle,* July 1995, p. 62.
"Sporting Goods Executives Share Outlook at NSGA Show," *Discount Store News,* August 4, 1997.

—Gloria A. Lemieux

Holiday RV Superstores, Incorporated

Sand Lake Executive Park
7851 Greenbriar Parkway
Orlando, Florida 32819
U.S.A.
(407) 363-9211
Fax: (407) 363-2065
Web site: http://www.holidayrv.com

Public Company
Incorporated: 1978 as Holiday of Orlando, Inc.
Employees: 225
Sales: $68.0 million (1997)
Stock Exchanges: NASDAQ
Ticker Symbol: RVEE
SICs: 5561 Recreational Vehicle Dealers; 5551 Boat
   Dealers

Holiday RV Superstores, Incorporated is a multistore retail chain of dealerships for sales and service of recreational vehicles (RVs) and recreational boats. The company, founded by Newton C. Kindlund and his wife Joanne M., is the only public RV dealership in the United States and one of the two largest retailers of leisure-time vehicles. Holiday RV, through its eight sales and service retail centers located in California, Florida, Georgia, New Mexico, and South Carolina, represents 51 brands of RVs and 12 brands of boats. The company buys more than 78 percent of its RVs from Fleetwood Enterprises Inc., Thor Industries Inc., and Winnebago Industries. Holiday RV also sells new RVs and recreational boats purchased from other manufacturers, including Forest River, Inc.; Rexall Industries, Inc.; Bayliner Marine Corporation; and Sea Ray Boats, Inc. All the company's service centers maintain a full line of both new and used recreational vehicles and also function as full-service facilities for the repair of virtually any type of recreational vehicle. The Greer, South Carolina, and Las Cruces, New Mexico, centers sell and service boats, and the Atlanta center offers a limited line of boats. The majority of Holiday RV's sales are for travel trailers, including fifth-wheel trailers designed to be towed by another vehicle, and motorized self-

propelled units that are built on an automotive chassis. The company has more than 225,000 customers, of whom 82 percent are 35 years old or older and have an income ranging from $20,000 to $60,000. Holiday RV also exports new motorhomes and travel trailers to some 27 foreign countries.

The Early Years: 1964–87

Newton C. Kindlund began his career as an RV industry entrepreneur in the 1960s by working with companies that manufactured recreational vehicles. In 1964 the Recreational Vehicle Industry Association (RVIA) recruited him to open a regional office in Elkhart, Indiana. After a brief time with RVIA, Newton joined Indiana-based Holiday Rambler Corporation and worked in sales and marketing. In September 1977 Newton and his wife, Joanne, moved to Orlando to establish a Holiday Rambler dealership. This was one of the first factory-owned retail dealerships in the country, and it prospered. By June 1978, however, Holiday Rambler dealers nationwide forced the corporation to divest its ownership of the retail business. Newton and Joanne acquired the Orlando dealership on a leveraged buyout basis and, in July 1978, began to operate their own company, which they named Holiday of Orlando, Inc.

The business expanded rapidly; soon additional office space was needed. Since the Kindlunds spent almost all their time at the dealership and wanted to stay debt-free while building up the company, they moved into a double-wide mobile home that served as both office and home. Reinvesting their capital in the business proved to be a critical cornerstone of success. Sales grew slowly but consistently, and in 1984 Holiday of Orlando was able to acquire a second dealership in Tampa. By 1987 the Kindlunds had positioned Holiday of Orlando for an initial public offering (IPO) of stock. The name of the company was changed to Holiday RV Superstores, Incorporated, and the company was traded on the NASDAQ exchange.

The Public Company, a Hurricane, and a War: 1987–94

From its first year of operation, Holiday RV consistently operated at a profit, but in 1988—its first year as a public company—Holiday RV posted record sales of $32.65 million, an increase of 40.7 percent from the $23.2 million sales of the previous year. In contrast, the national recreational-vehicle industry grew at an annual rate of less than five percent during 1988. Earnings per share remained at 15 cents but overcame the 42.8 percent dilution factor of the IPO of 2.14 million shares to the public. Holiday RV continued its expansion, establishing the Fort Myers RV Center in Lee County, Florida—one of the fastest-growing regions in the country. Later that year the company founded the Jacksonville RV Center. Jacksonville, situated on the I-95 entrance corridor to the state of Florida, was one of the strongest Class A motorhome markets on the East Coast.

In 1981 the company had pioneered telemarketing in the RV industry; by the end of the next decade more than 60 percent of Holiday RV's winter business was carried out beyond its predominant Southern market. Additionally, the company expanded from two to five RV Centers in Orlando and Tampa and spent $660,000 to acquire the total assets of a 17-year-old RV Center, renamed Holiday Superstores of South Atlanta, Inc., in Forest Park, Georgia. Holiday RV expanded its product offering to 35 RV brands, up from 27 in 1987, and became the South's leading retailer of fifth-wheel vehicles and the industry's third largest RV retailer. Class A motorhomes continued to represent the majority of the company's dollar volume in sales revenues.

The economic lull of the early 1990s, the tightening of consumer spending, and war in the Persian Gulf impacted the recreational vehicle and leisure boat market; according to RVIA, there was a 27 percent drop in RV sales and a drop of 31 percent in marine sales. Holiday RV reduced operating costs, decreased major short-term expenditures, sharpened its retail focus, and moved into marine products by acquiring an existing dealership, Ledford's RV and Marine World, in Greer, South Carolina. Adherence to management principles and calculated risk paid off. Holiday RV outperformed industry sectors and increased its market share; 1990 sales and service revenues decreased less than one percent to $40.12 million from the fiscal 1989 sales of $40.42 million. The Greer acquisition contributed significantly to revenues, which otherwise would have dropped 19.5 percent.

The national economy remained soft and Holiday RV lost money in 1991. Increasingly, consumers opted for towable recreational vehicles (travel trailers and fifth-wheel travel trailers) that were "value-packaged" with standard options such as awnings, microwave ovens, and roof air-conditioning units. Since Holiday RV's primary historical market was in motorhomes, the company suffered from inventory imbalances and lower gross profit levels. Business picked up in 1992 when the storm clouds of Hurricane Andrew proved to have a silver lining for the company in an unprecedented demand for temporary housing. Holiday RV obtained the industry's largest single contract ($4.3 million) awarded by the Federal Emergency Management Agency (FEMA) to provide 400 Dutchmen Travel Trailers for relief from the devastation of the hurricane. The company, along with many other southeastern RV dealers, marketed self-contained travel trailers through temporary sale locations in Homestead, Florida. Taking into account sales to FEMA and sales made through the Homestead location, Holiday RV sold close to 620 units and returned to profitability. The Jacksonville dealership remained unprofitable, however, and was closed to eliminate a drain on the financial and human resources of the company.

In January 1994 Holiday RV became a coast-to-coast operation by acquiring Venture Out RV from Gulf Oil Corp. Venture Out RV was a 37-year-old California multistore retailer with stores in Bakersfield and Roseville (Sacramento). In the company's 1994 annual report, President, CEO, and Chairman Kindlund said that, although the year was disappointing from an earnings standpoint, the company had become truly "a national company with a much broader focus on expanding its future rate of growth." He noted that the company was becoming much better at meeting the needs of customers. For the first time in the company's history, sales of vehicles exceeded 2,000 units, up more than 35 percent over the last four years, and revenues had reached $53.21 million. There was reason to be optimistic about the future of the company. According to studies by the University of Michigan Survey Research Center and Louis Harris and Associates, the RV industry was nearing a potentially booming market in the next decade as baby boomers, younger and more affluent than their parents who were the traditional buyers of RVs, were approaching the over-45 age group targeted by Holiday RV.

Realizing Market Potential: 1995–96

Throughout fiscal 1995, Holiday RV's most successful year to date, the company maintained a strong financial position and high liquidity. Holiday RV's marketing plan took into account an anticipated upturn in new motorized vehicles at the expense of a downturn in new towable products and further diversified into high-line diesel motorhomes at the Tampa, Orlando, and Greer locations. By the end of April 1995, the company had reached record revenues of $39.5 million and had installed a state-of-the-art management information system. This system allowed all departments within the company and its various store locations to network online and maintain e-mail communication 24 hours a day. During the summer, marine sales were at record levels at the Greer location. At the exhibit of new 1996 models, the company won three Customer Service Index (CSI) awards for superior customer satisfaction, and a 1995 CSI rating indicated that 87 percent of Holiday RV customers would refer business to the company.

In September 1995 the company formed Holiday RV Superstores of New Mexico, Inc., after a $620,000 cash acquisition of Camptown RV, a 27-year-old RV retailer with stores in Albuquerque and Las Cruces, New Mexico. The new superstore fronted directly on Interstate 10 in Las Cruces and gave the company the opportunity to establish eight superstore locations on the strategic east/west "snow bird" (people who journey south for the winter) corridor. At the end of fiscal 1995—due in large part to expansion in California—Holiday RV's annual sales peaked at $70.03 million, an increase of 31.6 percent over 1994. Although industry unit sales of recreational vehicles decreased by 4.8 percent in 1995, Holiday RV sold a record 2,714 new or used recreational vehicles and boats during that year. The overall effect of improved operations driven by a national marketing campaign was a 100 percent increase in earnings per share, from 10 cents in 1994 to 20 cents in 1995. In 1995 Holiday RV completed a three-acre expansion that doubled the size of its superstore fronting directly on I-75 in Forest Park, Georgia.

It therefore came as no surprise that *RV News,* the RV industry's trade magazine, chose Newton C. Kindlund as "1995 RV Industry Executive of the Year." In an interview in the January 1996 issue of *RV News,* Newton spoke about the business principles that guided the molding of his unique, publicly held company and prepared it for success: "In this business there are four main expenses that you keep your eye on: . . . people, inventory, advertising, and facilities. We have been able to stay focused on disciplines in those areas, on how we control inventory, how we compensate people, how we do it consistently, how we set up the matrix of rewards, and how we handle advertising." He emphasized that developing systems and procedures based on these principles allowed the company to maintain control without removing power from "key people at the top." He also pointed to some of the future challenges for RV retailers including leasing programs to attract baby boomers, manufacturer-dealer franchise agreements that protected a dealer while helping him to be a professional businessman, consumer lending, and franchising. He further observed that "If we had franchising we would be doing a better job by knowing that we were building something more than a rebate check at the end of the quarter. We would be building some intangible net worth in the business."

The national drop-off in RV sales of 1995 became more pronounced in 1996. Management turnover, start-up costs, and minimal sales at the Las Cruces location contributed to profit losses for Holiday RV. Nevertheless, sales and service revenue increased 6.76 percent to $74.76 million in 1996. The company realized the need to fuel growth by building sales momentum on a store-by-store basis and took that goal as its special focus for 1996. Late in that year significant product innovations—such as wider bodies (102″ widths), diesels, and a slide-out feature that expanded living areas—increased sales of motorhomes. Also noteworthy was the growing demand for pre-owned RVs. In 1995 sales of pre-owned recreational vehicles had risen sharply in the western United States and in 1996 this consumer trend surfaced in the eastern part of the country as well. Unfortunately, while used inventory sales accounted for about 48 percent of unit sales in 1996, these vehicles produced only 25.7 percent of overall revenues. During the fourth quarter, the company formed Holiday RV Assurance Services, Inc., an Arizona finance and insurance (F&I), in-house subsidiary to provide various F&I products on a national basis.

In Holiday RV's 1996 annual report, Newton wrote that the company's board of directors believed that—in light of Holiday RV's financial strength and overall performance—the market value of the company represented by its share price of $1.99 at year-end, did not reflect the intrinsic value of the company. Furthermore, they held that although Holiday RV had not shown consistent earnings from quarter to quarter, a comparison with other "pure play" publicly owned dealer chains—such as Republic Industries and CarMax—clearly indicated the quality of Holiday RV's performance.

Toward a New Century: 1997 and Beyond

During Holiday RV's 1997 fiscal year, industry unit growth declined for both new recreational vehicles and for recreational watercraft. The company's total revenues fell 9.1 percent to $68.0 million from $74.8 million for the previous year. Inventory build-up in eastern stores led to gross profit erosions for some product segments throughout the year. The good news was that the company, having refocused on increasing its profit margins and adjusting product lines, continued to grow business without having to incur long-term debt. The net result was that Holiday RV's earnings per share were the highest in its corporate history.

Among the significant events of the year were the introduction of a vanity credit card, dubbed Superstores MasterCard, which featured a point system that enabled cardholders to receive discounts on future purchases for RVs and boats. The company also hired Prudential Securities, Inc. as an exclusive financial advisor to explore strategic alternatives, such as possible acquisitions, mergers, or even the sale of the company, for enhancing shareholder value. The company continued its on-going process of looking for further acquisitions and possible mergers while analyzing why, during a booming economy, the RV industry was not more profitable, and why growth in the industry had been comparatively slow over the past 20 years. In an interview in the October 1997 issue of the *Wall Street Corporate Reporter,* Newton opined that his industry's slow growth was due in part to the pricing of products. With the average motor home in America selling for $68,000, the cost of RV products had grown at almost twice the rate of inflation. "The real mission for us," Newton emphasized, "is to develop affordable products that appeal to a wider population."

One of the ways Holiday RV planned to grow the company by meeting the needs of a wider population was to launch a line of private-label recreational vehicles in 1999. The proprietary product line, named Virginia Road, would include travel trailers and fifth-wheel trailers equipped with uniquely designed features. According to the *Wall Street Corporate Reporter,* Newton believed that private-brand marketing allowed for consistency at each Superstore location on a nationwide level. He thought that with a private brand, Holiday RV could influence research and development of RVs and respond from a retailer's, rather than solely from a manufacturer's, point of view to what consumers really wanted. For Newton, the Virginia Road line offered an entry "into the realm of mass merchandising . . . through a joint-venture marketing effort with a mass marketer."

In January 1998 Holiday RV also sought to increase shareholder value through the repurchase of up to $1 million of its common stock. By May 1998, the company's stock was riding high. On April 29, 330,000 Holiday RV shares traded hands: a volume the company had not seen in years. That the company had indeed turned a corner was clear when 1998 third-quarter results were released in August 1998. Net revenue had reached $57.78 million, a ten percent increase over the $52.42 million reported for the same period in 1997. Furthermore, at the end of the third quarter net income peaked at $400,025, an increase of 47 percent over the $271,568 in net income posted for the same period in 1997. Holiday RV, the only public company in the highly fragmented, cyclical recreational vehicle and recreational boat industry, made a quick turnaround to increased revenue for the third consecutive quarter and increased profitability for the fourth consecutive quarter—while maintaining a greater than 90 percent Customer Satisfaction Index. This achievement augured well for Holiday RV's continuing success.

Principal Subsidiaries

Holiday RV Assurance Services, Inc.

Further Reading

"Holiday: Every Penny Counts," *Orlando Business Journal,* May 8, 1998.

"Holiday RV," *Savvy Investor,* April 1997.

Krueger, Jill, "Holiday RV Chief Kindlund Positions for Retirement," *Orlando Business Journal,* May 10, 1996, pp. 3–4.

——, "Holiday RV Shifts Gears, Launches Private Label Vehicle Line," *Orlando Business Journal,* June 13, 1997, p. 16.

Magary, Don, "1995 Industry Executive of the Year: Newt C. Kindlund, Leaving Footprints in the Sand," *RV News,* January 1996.

O'Hanlon, John, "Focused on Growth," *Wall Street Corporate Reporter,* October 17, 1997, p. 12.

—Gloria A. Lemieux

HOSPITALITY
WORLDWIDE
SERVICES, INC.

Hospitality Worldwide Services, Inc.

---

450 Park Avenue, Suite 2603
New York, New York 10022
U.S.A.
(212) 223-0699
Fax: (212) 223-0865

Public Company
Incorporated: 1991 as Light Savers U.S.A., Inc.
Employees: 340
Sales: $85.4 million (1997)
Stock Exchanges: American
Ticker Symbol: HWS
SICs: 1522 General Contractors-Residential Buildings
Other Than Single Family; 1799 Construction-
Miscellaneous Special Trade Contractors; 4212 Local
Trucking Without Storage; 4215 Courier Services;
4225 General Warehousing & Storage; 7389 Business
Services

Hospitality Worldwide Services, Inc. is the hotel industry's largest renovation contractor and procurement service provider. Today, Hospitality Worldwide consists of six subsidiaries, all positioned to service the hospitality industry. The company offers hotel owners and operators a highly attractive one-stop shopping package, including complete renovations; procurement of furniture, fixtures, operating supplies, and equipment; and the ability to order online. Hospitality Worldwide Services also offers logistical planning for products ordered directly from the manufacturer and sent to warehouses around the world. Additionally, the company offers ground-up construction, development, and asset management services.

A Start in Fixtures

From its inception in 1991 to August 1995, Hospitality Worldwide Services was a specialized firm whose principal line of business was to design and market decorative, energy efficient lighting fixtures for the hotel and hospitality industry. The company's primary marketing tool was Con Edison's Apple-power Rebate Program, which offered substantial rebates to those who used energy-saving devices. However, in 1994 Con Edison substantially reduced its rebate program, robbing Light Savers of its marketing strategy and thus reducing its income.

As a result, the company's board of directors decided to get out of the lighting business. The first move in this direction came in 1995 with the purchase of AGF Interior Services. AGF was a Florida-based renovation and construction company that, through its wholly owned subsidiary, Hospitality Restoration and Builders, moved Light Savers into the hospitality industry. Later that same year, Light Savers sold its lighting business and changed its name to Hospitality Worldwide Services to reflect its new strategy as a renovation services firm.

New Acquisitions, Start-Ups, Joint Ventures

Until January 1997, the company's only line of business was to provide a complete package of renovation resources, ranging from pre-planning, to construction and remodeling activities, to the budgeting and scheduling needed to deliver furnished rooms on time. In that year, the company also raised net profits of $32.1 million through its sale of stock and purchased Leonard Parker Company. This acquisition moved Hospitality Worldwide Services into the procurement service business and made it the leading outsourcing company for the lodging industry, serving both real estate investment trusts and large hotel chains. Formed in 1969, Leonard Parker Company was the largest independent provider of procurement services to owners, developers, and operators of hotel properties worldwide. The company had projects in the United States, Southeast Asia, Central and South America, Africa, Europe, the Caribbean, and the Mideast, and corporate offices in Miami, Los Angeles, Johannesburg, South Africa, Dubai, United Arab Emirates, Singapore, and Amsterdam.

Leonard Parker Company primarily procured furniture, fixtures and equipment, and operating supplies and equipment for hotels. For most projects, it handled the billing and financial aspects of projects, prepared budgets, negotiated pricing and payment terms with manufacturers, issued purchase orders, and oversaw shipping, delivery, and installation services in connection with new hotels and renovations. It also acted as the intermediary between the property owner and designers, architects, vendors, contractors, and manufacturers. Based on its size and volume of business, Leonard Parker Company enabled Hospitality Worldwide Services, through its core business, Hospitality Restoration and Builders, to provide customers savings on such items as carpeting, bedding, wallcovering, artwork, and decorative lighting. With more then $302 million annually in procurement services, Leonard Parker Company became Hospitality Worldwide Services' second core business.

Leonard Parker Company brought with it a second acquisition, Parker Reorder Company, a procurement service organization similar to Leonard Parker Company in targeting the hospitality industry. However, Parker Reorder Company's scope of services focused upon reordering operating supplies and equipment: the daily purchasing of guest room supplies, china, glassware, linens, flatware, uniforms, engineering supplies, paper products, chemicals, and other regular use items. Parker Reorder Company and Leonard Parker Company customers had access to Parker Reorder, a computer software system, the first of its kind, designed to offer customers the ability to reorder supplies online. Parker FIRST (Fully Integrated Reorder Systems & Tracking) was initiated in 1995 and completed in 1997 with development money provided by Hospitality Worldwide Services. It became available for commercial release in the first quarter of 1998.

In 1998, Bekins Distribution Services, headquartered in St. Louis, Missouri, also joined the Hospitality Worldwide Services team. Bekins had been in business over 20 years as a provider of furniture, fixtures, and equipment for customers, including retail stores, convenience stores, and hotels who were opening, renovating, or relocating facilities. With its network of warehouses at more than 1,000 locations around the United States, Bekins boasted ''just-in-time'' shipping, whereby customers could control the flow of interior products from factory to distribution points to final destination. Under the auspices of Hospitality Worldwide Services, Bekins Distribution Systems began to expand its transportation department to handle the increased traffic expected from Hospitality Worldwide Services and its subsidiaries, and to reorganize its service department to provide more accurate delivery information.

Hospitality Worldwide Services also began a new business, Hospitality Development Services, in 1998. Hospitality Development Services was a real estate development company that provided in-depth knowledge of hotel markets and construction planning to customers. It worked in tandem with Hospitality Worldwide Services Real Estate Advisory Group, a 1998 acquisition, responsible for new business organization as well as feasibility studies, financing, and asset management. Hospitality Development Services and the Real Estate Advisory Group also worked with Hospitality Worldwide Services' other arms.

Renovating the Hospitality Industry

According to a source within the company, Hospitality Worldwide Services has benefited by not being geographically limited. Jefferies & Co. has said in its reports that Hospitality Worldwide Services was in the ''right place at the right time.''

The year 1996 was the most profitable year ever in the U.S. lodging industry. Even though the demand for rooms slipped slightly in 1997 from 65 percent to 64 percent, the industry's profitability increased to $14.5 billion, up from $11 billion in 1996. A near record number of rooms came on board in 1997—approximately 127,000—equaling the previous high of 1987, and the average daily room rate increased at a rate faster than inflation. Hotel starts rose 16 percent from 1996 levels, with more than 1,200 new hotels opening in 1997, the most ever in a single year.

In the late 1990s, some of the Hospitality Worldwide Services' largest renovation customers included real estate investment trusts, such as Felcor Lodging Trust, the Griffin Group and Servico, Inc. In addition, Hospitality Worldwide Services had longstanding relationships with such clients as Prime Hospitality, Hyatt, Marriott, Chartwell Leisure, Meristar, Patriot American, and Hutchison Wampoa, all of whom were looking to expand their presence in selected lodging markets. In 1998, Hospitality Development Services was in the early stages of a joint venture with Prime Hospitality Corporation to develop 20 AmeriSuites over the next two years. Hospitality Restoration and Builders also signed contracts that same year valued at more than $35 million with Felcor Suite Hotels, Inc.; Servico, Inc.; and The Griffin Group. Leonard Parker Company also agreed to act as the buying agent for Marriott International Inc.'s overseas properties, using software that was multilingual and translated multiple currencies.

Hospitality Worldwide Services also began to seek out opportunities for near-term growth in joint ventures to acquire, renovate, and sell hotels at a profit in the late 1990s. The goal was to seek out undervalued hotels in key markets, upgrade the properties, and sell them for a sizable equity return. Its late 1990s investment of $5 million in the Warwick Hotel, part of a joint venture with Apollo Real Estate Advisors L.P., to restore the Philadelphia hotel to four-star status, was expected at the time of investment to yield $50–$60 million in contracts for purchasing and renovation. A second joint venture with Prime Hospitality called for Hospitality Worldwide Services to provide onsite development, construction, and purchasing services for 20 properties through its subsidiary companies. ING Group Partners was Hospitality Worldwide Services' financial associate in the acquisition, renovation, and refurbishment of a third site, the Clarion Quality Hotel in Chicago.

Room for Growth

In 1998, Coopers & Lybrand, a big six accounting firm tracking the hospitality industry, predicted a 2.2 percent growth in the demand for hotel rooms, down from 1997's 2.3 percent demand, but enough to produce another good year for Hospitality Worldwide Services. Room rates were predicted to rise 5.6 percent while revenue per available room was expected to jump 5.5 percent. Industry profits were projected to rise to somewhere between $16 and $17 billion, a 16 percent rise over 1997's record profits of $14.4 billion. In the highly fragmented market for hotel renovation and purchasing services, of which Hospitality Worldwide Services controlled only 1.5 percent of the market share, all of this meant continued growth possibilities for Hospitality Worldwide Services and its subsidiaries.

In the late 1990s, too, a major industry consolidation was taking place, a trend which boded well for Hospitality Worldwide Services. There were about 32,000 hotels in the United States, half of them full-service institutions. A few years earlier, these upscale hotels had been owned by banks and insurance companies but, by the late 1990s, they were owned by real estate investment trusts, and large hotel firms were buying up the bulk of these properties. As a result, Hospitality Worldwide Services was in a position to cement relationships with fewer owners of more hotels. ''It doesn't have to market its services every time it wants to increase its revenues,'' said one Hospitality Worldwide Services insider. ''It can grow along with real estate investment trusts and other hotel consolidators.''

Hotels also were spending money to update their properties. Lenders, seeking to ensure that hotels maintain the value of their assets, required that hotels reserve three to seven percent of their gross revenue to reinvest in properties. Hotels which, in addition, had to return dividends to shareholders, were choosing outsourcing as a means of providing services at lower cost rather than maintaining large staffs of people. Outsourcing was being relied upon increasingly as a way to handle procurement, logistics, freight, management, and installation of supplies.

Hospitality Worldwide Services had just begun to market its comprehensive service package to the hotel industry at the close of 1998. In that year, the emphasis at Hospitality Worldwide Services was on selling itself to the industry. Most of the services it offered were not done any longer in-house by lodging companies, for whom provision of services was simply a cost of doing business since they made money solely from rooms and catering. The hotel industry increasingly contracted services out to small local providers, good news for Hospitality Worldwide Services because of its convenience and economies of its scale over local providers.

Hospitality Worldwide Services was poised to enter the year 2000 looking to expand by adding new clients, some of them assisted living facilities, others, dormitories and timeshares. It also sought to acquire additional purchasing and renovation companies.

Principal Subsidiaries

Bekins Distribution Services; Hospitality Restoration and Builders; Hospitality Development Services; Leonard Parker Company; Parker Reorder Company; Real Estate Advisory Group.

Further Reading

Chang, Martin J., and James F. Wilson, ''Making Hotels More Hospitable,'' *Equity Research: Property Services*, Jefferies & Company, Inc., September 23, 1997, pp. 1–11.

Giovanetti, Toni, ''Hospitality Worldwide Services Builds Multi-Faceted Service Company, Looks to Expand Scope,'' *Hotel Business*, September 7–20, 1998.

Parets, Robyn Taylor, ''Renovating Hotels for Consolidating Industry,'' *Investor's Business Daily*, September 29, 1997.

—Carrie Rothburd

HSBC Holdings plc

10 Lower Thames Street
London EC3R 6AE
United Kingdom
(0171) 260 0500
Fax: (0171) 260 0501
Web site: http://www.hsbcgroup.com

Public Company
Incorporated: 1865 as Hongkong and Shanghai Banking
    Company, Ltd.
Employees: 130,000
Total Assets: £286.39 billion (US$471.69 billion) (1997)
Stock Exchanges: London Hong Kong
Ticker Symbol: HSBHY (ADR)
SICs: 6712 Offices of Bank Holding Companies; 6021
    National Commercial Banks; 6029 Commercial Banks,
    Not Elsewhere Classified; 6162 Mortgage Bankers &
    Loan Correspondents; 6163 Loan Brokers; 6211
    Security Brokers, Dealers & Flotation Companies;
    6282 Investment Advice; 6311 Life Insurance; 6351
    Surety Insurance; 6371 Pension, Health & Welfare
    Funds; 6411 Insurance Agents, Brokers & Services;
    6733 Trusts, Except Educational, Religious & Charitable

A significant force in international banking, HSBC Holdings plc (also referred to as the HSBC Group) operates in some 79 countries and offers a comprehensive financial service encompassing not only commercial and merchant banking but also capital markets, consumer finance, securities, investments, and insurance. The HSBC Group is increasingly international in nature, despite the group still being centered around the bank from which it evolved (and from which it gained its acronymic name)—The Hongkong and Shanghai Banking Corporation Limited, the top bank in Hong Kong, known colloquially as HongkongBank. About 30 percent of HSBC's asset base is in Hong Kong, 35 percent in the United Kingdom, 19 percent in the Americas, 12.5 percent in the Asia-Pacific region (not including Hong Kong), and 3.5 percent in continental Europe.

Founding of HongkongBank

The history of HSBC begins with the founding of the Hongkong and Shanghai Banking Company, Ltd. in 1865. In the early 1860s, Hong Kong's financial needs were served by European trading houses called ''hongs.'' This system proved increasingly inadequate as the colony's bustling trade—primarily in tea, silk, and opium—burgeoned. By 1864 the first proper banks had been established, but as these were based in London or India and controlled from abroad, there was a growing feeling that a local bank was needed in the colony.

Dissatisfaction led to action when it was discovered that a group of Bombay financiers intended to set up a ''Bank of China'' in Hong Kong, and that this bank, chartered in London, was to offer only a small proportion of its shares to China coast businesses. Thomas Sutherland, the Hong Kong Superintendent of the Peninsula and Orient Steam Navigation Company, proposed the foundation of a new bank modeled on ''sound Scottish banking principles.'' The proposal was promptly taken up by others of the Hong Kong business community; within days a provisional committee had established a banking cooperative capitalized at HK$5 million. The move effectively preempted the proposed ''Bank of China,'' whose representative, when he arrived later in Hong Kong, could find no market for his shares.

The Hongkong and Shanghai Banking Company Limited opened on March 3, 1865, with a second branch inaugurated in Shanghai on April 3. A London office was opened later in the year. Members of the cooperative included American, German, Scandinavian, and Parsee Indian merchant houses, as well as representatives from the Bombay-based David Sassoon & Company and Hong Kong-based Dent & Company. The largest companies in Hong Kong, Jardine Matheson and the American firm Russell & Company, were not represented. The highly favorable response to the bank by foreign interests and compradores (native businessmen who acted as intermediaries with the Chinese community), however, led both to reconsider and join.

An international financial crisis in 1865–66 could have destroyed the bank. Instead, with financial support from its members, the bank took over the operations of failed competitors and hired their staff. Dent, meanwhile, the dominant Hong Kong

Company Perspectives:

The HSBC Group's approach is highly distinctive. At its core around the world are domestic commercial banking and financial services which fund themselves locally and do business locally.

Highly efficient technology links these operations to deliver a wide range of international products, as well as services, adapted to local customers' needs. This structure allows the Group to serve a broad international customer base, while limiting its currency risk in any given location. Customers range from individual depositors and small local businesses to the world's largest corporations.

The geographical distribution of assets reflects the HSBC Group's international approach. The largest concentration of the Group's assets remains in the Asia-Pacific region, including the Hong Kong Special Administrative Region (SAR). Asia-Pacific has consistently been the Group's most profitable area.

member of the group, went bankrupt. However, instead of hurting the cooperative, Dent's failure allowed broader representation by more diverse local interests.

Initially, the bank was established under the local Companies Ordinance as the Hongkong and Shanghai Banking Company Limited. Under the colonial law of the time, a bank had to incorporate either under a royal charter in compliance with the Colonial Banking Regulations or else according to British banking legislation. However, the bank's founders objected to these options, as they had particularly designed their enterprise as a local concern. Eventually a deal was struck with the Treasury whereby the bank (renamed The Hongkong and Shanghai Banking Corporation), under a unique ordinance, could retain Hong Kong headquarters while complying with the Colonial Banking Regulations.

Expanded Rapidly in the Late 19th Century

HongkongBank expanded rapidly throughout the 19th century. By 1900, it had branches in Japan, Thailand, the Philippines, Singapore, and the countries now known as Malaysia, Myanmar, Sri Lanka, and Vietnam. In some Asian cities, HongkongBank was the first to usher in principles of modern Western banking and was indeed Thailand's very first bank, printing that country's first bank notes. In the United States and Europe, HongkongBank branches opened in San Francisco in 1875, New York in 1880, Lyons in 1881, and Hamburg in 1889. Except in New York, where a Canadian bank already operated, HongkongBank was the first foreign bank in each of these cities.

In Hong Kong, operations experienced a setback in the 1870s when the bank made some unwise investments in local Hong Kong industry—its reserves fell from HK$1 million to HK$100,000—but the company soon regained its footing under the leadership of a new chief manager, Thomas Jackson, who brought the bank back to a renewed emphasis on its field of expertise, trade finance. By the end of Jackson's reign, in 1902,

HongkongBank's paid-up capital stood at HK$10 million, and its published reserves at HK$14.25 million, with additional estimated inner reserves of HK$10 million.

The bank had, however, developed another lucrative role— that of banker to governments. By the 1880s, HongkongBank was operating in this capacity to the government of Hong Kong and had acquired the Treasury Chest (the British government's military and foreign service) business for China and Japan. In addition, the HongkongBank issued bank notes for Hong Kong and for the Straits Settlements (Singapore and Penang). Since these notes were not, at the time, legal tender, their popularity reflected the public's trust in HongkongBank. Through a powerful compradore in China, the bank established contacts with local officials in Tianjin and Beijing. The bank was later asked to issue a public loan on behalf of the Chinese government, and directed several more in ensuing years. While some of these loans financed China's war against Japan (1894–95) and the enforcement of peace during internal conflicts such as the Boxer Rebellion in 1900, the bulk were used for infrastructural projects such as railroads, coal mines, and shipping lines.

The bank was able to develop a very favorable rapport with the government and business interests in China mainly because it had a widespread presence in China and was incorporated in Hong Kong. By 1910 it was the favored intermediary of the multinational China Consortium, a result of the demonstrated effectiveness of the Bank's London manager, Sir Charles Addis.

World Wars Led to Numerous Difficulties

World War I deeply divided the bank, still well represented by both Germans and Britons. The German members of its board, identified in the press as "hostile interests," eventually resigned, marking a more or less permanent end to German participation in the company. Still, the bank's Hamburg office remained open for the duration of the war.

The high price of silver after the war led the bank to make a rights issue to finance an expansion. Chief Manager A.G. Stephen presided over the construction of new facilities in Hankow, Bangkok, Manila, and especially Shanghai, where a new office was opened in 1923. An office opened in Vladivostok in 1918 but was forced to close in 1924, when Russian revolutionary forces completed their consolidation of control over Siberia.

The optimism of the early 1920s crashed after 1929 and continued to deteriorate through the 1930s, as Japanese interests moved into China, this time supported by Japanese guns. At first, the Japanese domination of China was limited to the rich hinterlands of Manchuria and consisted mainly of the commercial exploitation of resources. While the bank was permitted to establish offices in the Manchurian cities of Dairen, Mukden, and Harbin, its operations were limited only to foreign trade. Meanwhile, in the rest of China, the bank experienced new competition from an increasingly sophisticated Chinese banking community.

At the same time, the bank was losing business from the Philippine government and was discriminated against in Indonesia and Vietnam by Dutch and French colonial authorities. Despite generous lending and other support tactics for customers involved in rubber and other volatile commodities trades, bank profits continued to deteriorate. In many cases, competitors complained that the bank's extraordinary care ''exceeded the limits of prudent lending.'' The bank was, however, founded on cooperative precepts, and continued to operate on that basis. Still, it was the shareholders who suffered; shareholder's funds fell from £9.1 million in 1918 to £8.6 million in 1940.

The number of Hong Kong dollars in circulation, 80 percent of which were printed by the Hongkong and Shanghai Bank, increased from HK$50 million in 1927 to HK$200 million in 1940. In effect, the bank backed HK$160 million of the colony's currency—a dangerous exposure to the local economy, despite transferring the currency from a silver to sterling standard. The bank became involved in an even more unmanageable currency-stabilization effort in Shanghai, from which it eventually had to bow out, turning the scheme over to a government board.

The Japanese occupation of China, meanwhile, had become extremely brutal. Terror bombings, invasion, and a Japanese military riot in Nanking stifled commerce in China and isolated Hong Kong from its Chinese hinterland. Sensing imminent danger, the bank's chief manager, Vandeleur Grayburn, authorized the immediate transfer of silver reserves into sterling assets in London. On December 8, 1940, shortly after completing the transfer, Japanese troops stormed through Hong Kong's New Territories, and on Christmas won a surrender.

Bank staff in Manchuria, Japan, and Indochina were repatriated, and those in Burma and Singapore escaped to India. Employees in China, particularly Foochow, managed to reach Chungking, where the bank opened a formal office in 1943. The staff in Hong Kong were much less fortunate; most of them who were of European descent were imprisoned.

Under prearranged orders from Grayburn, the bank's London manager, Arthur Morse, assumed managerial control of the bank. Morse transferred the dollar-denominated assets located in Hong Kong to London, fearing that if the Japanese gained control of them, the assets would be frozen by the U.S. government. In light of the circumstances—the bank's board was interned in Hong Kong—Morse was named both chief manager and chairman. During the occupation, Japanese authorities forced the bank to issue additional currency in order to support the local economy. Grayburn and his designated successor, D.C. Edmonston, meanwhile, died in prison.

The war ended so suddenly in August 1945 that Hong Kong remained occupied when Japan surrendered. With colonial authorities back in control, the bank began the difficult and costly task of rebuilding. The amortization of banknotes issued under the occupation cost HK$16 million, and new legislation only permitted the bank to collect debts from enemy interests in depreciated occupation currencies.

Postwar Recovery

Despite its weakened condition, the bank played a major role in the reconstruction of Hong Kong, a task Morse began planning well before the war ended. All the company's branches were reopened—with the exception of Hamburg which, again, had remained open during the war—including those in Japan.

By 1947, however, new problems arose in China, where the wartime alliance between Chiang Kai-shek's nationalists and Mao Tse-tung's communists had degenerated into a civil war. The immediate effects were severe inflation and increasing public disorder.

By October 1949 the communists had gained control of the mainland and the nationalists had fled to Taiwan. When an initial plea by the communists for reconstruction in cooperation with capitalists was suddenly reversed in 1950, industrialists fled China—especially Shanghai—for Hong Kong. The bank maintained offices in Shanghai, Beijing, Tianjin, and Shantou until 1955, when all but the Shanghai branch were closed. The Chinese, it seemed, preferred to do all their business through Hong Kong.

After the war, the British government practiced a ''nonextractive'' economic policy in Hong Kong which, coupled with the entrepreneurial talent of industrialists transplanted from Shanghai and a labor force swelled by thousands of mainland refugees, created a powerful economic base. The bank financed hundreds of new ventures that helped the colony achieve unprecedented export-led growth. The growth of the textile industry in Hong Kong, however, led the bank to fear that it had become overexposed to that one industry.

International Expansion, 1950s Through 1970s

Under Michael Turner, the HongkongBank adopted a new strategy of expansion using subsidiaries during the mid-1950s. Initially made necessary by American banking legislation, the subsidiary form of organization was first used in 1955 to establish a branch in California—one step toward reducing its dependence on Hong Kong.

Because Britain relinquished much of its empire after the war, British companies were forced to rationalize, by merger, acquisition, or nationalization. Indeed, many went bankrupt. Two such companies, the Mercantile Bank (formerly the Chartered Mercantile Bank of India, London and China) and the British Bank of the Middle East (known as BBME, formerly the Imperial Bank of Persia), were purchased by the Hongkong and Shanghai Bank in 1959. The addition of the Mercantile Bank, with an extensive branch network in India, and the BBME, strongly represented in the Persian Gulf, made the Hongkong-Bank the largest foreign bank in most of the countries from the Far East to southwest Asia.

Having reduced its exposure to Hong Kong, the bank moved next to diversify operationally. In 1960 it created Wayfoong, a consumer financing group whose name translates loosely as ''focus of wealth.''

A banking crisis in Hong Kong in 1964 led to a serious run on a competitor, the Hang Seng Bank. As the primary financial institution in Hong Kong and de facto central bank, the HongkongBank, while under no statutory duty to do so, acquired a majority interest in Hang Seng in 1965. Hang Seng subsequently recovered, and was the second largest bank incorporated in Hong Kong into the 1990s.

The HongkongBank's expansion through subsidiaries began in earnest with the creation in 1972 of Wardley Ltd., a merchant bank, and an insurance company called Carlingford. The bank also made numerous other investments—in Cathay Pacific Airways, the World-Wide shipping group, and the *South China Morning Post*. All these investments proved highly profitable in light of Hong Kong's rapid economic growth. In addition, the BBME benefited greatly from the newly prosperous oil-based economies in the Persian Gulf. In 1978, however, BBME branches in Saudi Arabia were taken over by the Saudi British Bank, a Saudi-controlled bank in which BBME retained management control, but only 40 percent ownership.

North American Expansion Marked the 1980s

Under the leadership of Michael Sandberg, the Hongkong-Bank reexamined its position in America as part of a wider strategy to gain greater representation in the major Western economies. The Hongkong and Shanghai Bank of California was sold and the bank purchased a 51 percent share of Marine Midland Bank, a Buffalo, New York-based bank holding company, in 1980. The HongkongBank bought the outstanding shares of Marine Midland in 1987. This acquisition inspired substantial debate in the U.S. Congress about whether banking laws should be strengthened to prevent foreign companies from gaining control over American banks.

The bank expanded in several ways during 1980. In China, the Shanghai branch was expanded and a representative office was established in Beijing. In addition, the BBME relocated from London to Hong Kong, and the bank gained control of Concord International, a leasing and finance group, and Anthony Gibbs, a British merchant bank. The following year, a Canadian subsidiary, the Hongkong Bank of Canada, was established in Vancouver. In 1986 the Hongkong Bank of Canada acquired the business of the Bank of British Columbia, bringing the number of branches across Canada to 61.

A bidding war over the Royal Bank of Scotland Group between the HongkongBank and Standard & Chartered (issuer of Hong Kong's other currency) was halted in 1981 by the British Monopolies & Mergers Commission, which ruled against both bids. Meanwhile, the bank succeeded in establishing a presence in Africa in 1981 through the acquisition of a controlling interest in Equator Bank by its merchant bank subsidiary Wardley; in Cyprus in 1982, also primarily through Wardley; and in Australia in 1985, when it established HongkongBank of Australia. Back in North America, Hongkong-Bank entered into a strategic alliance with California-based Wells Fargo Bank in 1989. Also that year, HongkongBank was registered under the Hong Kong Companies Ordinance, at which time it adopted the name The Hongkong and Shanghai Banking Corporation Limited.

HongkongBank's expansionist policies were not always successful. Its acquisition of Marine Midland, said initially to have boosted the bank's assets from HK$125.3 billion to HK$243 billion, soon proved a debacle. Ill-advised forays into real estate and Latin American lending led to significant losses, prompting the parent company in 1991 to completely overhaul its subsidiary—at a purported cost of US$1.8 billion. Other high-profile failures of the 1980s included the bank's financing of an Australian tycoon, Alan Bond, who went bankrupt.

Formation of HSBC Holdings, Acquisition of Midland Bank (U.K.) and the Early 1990s

In 1984 Great Britain and the People's Republic of China signed a historic agreement, slating for July 1, 1997, the return of Hong Kong to Chinese control, and providing added impetus to HongkongBank's overseas expansion. Keen to beef up its presence in Europe, the bank acquired James Capel, a leading U.K. securities firm, in 1986. Of still greater importance was the beginning in December 1987 of an association between Hong-kongBank and Midland Bank, one of four major British clearing banks. In December 1987 HongkongBank made the friendly acquisition of 14.9 percent of Midland's stock, agreeing not to increase its stake in Midland until the expiration of a three-year agreement in December 1990. Staking its future in Europe to that of Midland, HongkongBank transferred control of its branches on the European continent to Midland and in turn acquired Midland's branches in Canada and South Korea. In 1990 Hongkong Bank of Canada expanded still further through the purchase of Lloyds Bank Canada, becoming the seventh largest bank in Canada by the early 1990s.

HongkongBank and Midland entered into merger talks in 1990, but the talks broke off late in the year because of what were termed "financial difficulties." Nevertheless, Hongkong-Bank held onto its stake in Midland following the expiration of the three-year agreement.

Like many Hong Kong-based companies facing the uncertainties of 1997, HongkongBank made some major organizational changes well before the handover. In 1991 it created a new holding company, HSBC Holdings plc, making HongkongBank a subsidiary of the U.K.-incorporated but Hong Kong-based HSBC Holdings. HSBC stock was set up on both the London and Hong Kong markets, showing the importance Hongkong placed on Europe (and London) for its future. For HongkongBank, the establishment of a new holding company relieved it of management responsibility for the group's more than 500 subsidiaries in 50 countries. The bank thus could focus primarily on the Asia-Pacific region it knew so well.

HSBC completed the long-anticipated takeover of Midland in 1992, gaining full control of what became its flagship in Europe. HSBC made an initial friendly offer in March for Midland. The following month Lloyds stepped in with a larger, hostile offer. HSBC soon put an end to the takeover battle with a 480p per share offer in June, prompting Lloyds to bow out. HSBC ended up paying £3.9 billion (US$7.2 billion) to acquire Midland. As a condition of the acquisition, HSBC was required by the regulatory Bank of England to move its main office to London, which it did in January 1993. The headquarters of HongkongBank remained in Hong Kong.

The acquisition of Midland was a coup, providing HSBC with the significant presence in Europe it had previously lacked. Variously described as a merger and a takeover, the amalgamation virtually doubled HSBC's assets (from £86 billion to £170 billion) and workforce. The venerable Midland, the U.K.'s third largest bank, was not performing to standard at that time, being the least profitable of Britain's "big four" banks. Nevertheless, the financial health and the international experience of the parent company began attracting larger corporate customers to

Midland. In addition, many individuals were subsequently won over by the telephone banking service, First Direct, introduced by Midland in 1989 and strongly backed by HSBC. HSBC's lead in technology—used, for example, to automate credit decisions and limit staff expenditure—also played a part in Midland's recovery.

Although under the HSBC umbrella structure individual subsidiaries largely acted autonomously, the company also moved to coordinate some operations. Soon after the takeover of Midland, HSBC integrated its treasury operations in London, New York, and Tokyo and established common technological standards. Also in 1992 HSBC opened a trading room in London for the dealing business of Midland, James Capel, and HSBC Greenwell. This became the largest treasury trading operation in Europe. That year also saw the establishment of the HSBC Investment Banking Group, which coordinated the merchant banking, securities, and asset management business (HSBC Asset Management) of the entire HSBC Group.

HongkongBank, which had long acted as a quasi-central bank, was relieved of some of these unofficial duties in 1992, when the Hong Kong Monetary Authority was established. The following year HongkongBank divested its holding in Cathay Pacific Airways. In 1994 it became the first foreign bank to incorporate locally in Malaysia through the establishment of Hongkong Bank Malaysia Berhad. In the mid-1990s the bank greatly expanded its personal banking business through the opening or upgrading of personal banking units in Australia, Bangladesh, Brunei, Hong Kong, Indonesia, Mauritius, New Zealand, the Philippines, Saipan, Singapore, Sri Lanka, Taiwan, and Thailand. The bank also expanded its presence in China during this period, maintaining good relations with the Chinese government—which was extremely important as 1997 approached.

HSBC Holdings continued to expand in the mid-1990s under the leadership of John Bond, appointed chief executive in January 1993 (and group chairman in June 1998). In 1995 HSBC and Wells Fargo established Wells Fargo HSBC Trade Bank in California, a joint venture (40 percent owned by HSBC) providing trade finance and international banking services in the United States. Marine Midland was bolstered in 1996 with the acquisition of Rochester, New York-based First Federal Savings and Loan Association for US$620 million. Latin America was the subject of several 1997 transactions: the purchase of a 10 percent stake in Banco del Sur del Peru; the founding of a new subsidiary in Brazil, Banco HSBC Bamerindus S.A., which took over assets of Banco Bamerindus do Brasil; the increase in investment in Banco Santiago in Chile to 6.99 percent; the acquisition of Roberts S.A. de Inversiones of Argentina (renamed HSBC Roberts S.A. de Inversiones); and the purchase of a 19.9 percent stake in Grupo Financiero Serfin of Mexico.

Although HSBC seemed to suffer no ill effects from the handover of Hong Kong to Chinese control on July 1, 1997, it did feel the effects of the Asian economic crisis of the late 1990s. The group was particularly hard hit in troubled Indonesia, where it had to set aside about US$2.5 billion in provisions for bad loans. Nevertheless, its earlier moves into Europe and the Americas paid off handsomely, as higher profits in these regions helped offset weaker results in Asia. Meantime, the Hong Kong Monetary Authority, in an attempt to thwart currency speculators, made a significant intervention in the Hong Kong stock market in August 1998, purchasing large stakes in several prominent companies. The government of Hong Kong thereby became HSBC Holdings' single largest shareholder, with an 8.9 percent stake.

In October 1998 HSBC announced that it had signed a 999-year lease for a new 1.1 million square foot headquarters building at Canary Wharf in London, scheduled for completion by early 2002. The following month HSBC said that it would unify the HSBC Group under the HSBC name and logo, thereby establishing a more global corporate identity. Among the units whose marketing names would change to HSBC were Banco HSBC Bamerindus, the British Bank of the Middle East, Hongkong Bank Malaysia, Hongkong Bank of Australia, Hongkong Bank of Canada, HSBC Banco Roberts, Marine Midland, Midland Bank, HSBC Equator Bank, HSBC Investment Banking, and even the flagship HongkongBank itself. Eventually the legal names of many HSBC Group subsidiaries would also be changed. In a press release, Bond said: "We want the HSBC brand to be known in every country and in every sector in which we operate as synonymous with integrity, trust, and excellent customer service. I am confident that a unified brand and the strong recognition it will bring for HSBC's exceptional strengths is an important step forward as we work to maximise shareholder value." The implementation of this significant change was sure to require much of HSBC's attention at the turn of the century.

Principal Subsidiaries

Commercial Banking: Banco HSBC Bamerindus S.A. (Brazil); British Arab Commercial Bank Limited; The British Bank of the Middle East (Channel Islands); Egyptian British Bank S.A.E. (Egypt); Hang Seng Bank Limited (Hong Kong; 62.1%); The Hongkong and Shanghai Banking Corporation Limited (Hong Kong); Hongkong Bank Malaysia Berhad; Hongkong Bank of Australia Limited; Hongkong Bank of Canada; HSBC Banco Roberts S.A. (Argentina; 99.85%); Marine Midland Bank (U.S.A.); Midland Bank plc; The Saudi British Bank (Saudi Arabia); Wells Fargo HSBC Trade Bank, N.A. (U.S.A.). Investment Banking: Guyerzeller Bank AG (Switzerland; 71%); HSBC Asset Management Americas Inc. (U.S.A.); HSBC Asset Management Europe Limited; HSBC Asset Management Hong Kong Limited; HSBC Equator Bank plc; HSBC International Trustee Limited (Channel Islands); HSBC Investment Bank Asia Limited (Hong Kong); HSBC Investment Bank plc; HSBC Private Bank (Jersey) Limited (Channel Islands); HSBC Private Equity Europe Limited; HSBC Securities Asia Limited (Hong Kong); HSBC Securities Japan Limited; HSBC Trustee (Hong Kong) Limited; HSBC Trustee (Jersey) Limited (Channel Islands); HSBC Unit Trust Management Limited; Midland Bank Trust Company Limited; Midland Bank Trustee (Jersey) Limited (Channel Islands); Trinkaus & Burkhardt KGaA (Germany; 73%); Wardley Financial Services Limited (Hong Kong). Capital Markets: HSBC Greenwell; HSBC Securities, Inc. (U.S.A.). Finance: Forward Trust Group Limited; HSBC Forfaiting Asia Pte Limited (Singapore); HSBC International Trade Finance Limited; Mortgage And Finance Berhad (Brunei Darussalam); Wayfoong Credit Limited (Hong Kong);

Wayfoong Finance Limited (Hong Kong); Wayfoong Mortgage And Finance (Singapore) Limited. Insurance, Retirement Benefits, Actuarial and Personal Financial Services: Hang Seng Life Limited (Hong Kong); HSBC Gibbs Limited; HSBC Gibbs Personal Insurances Limited; HSBC Insurance (Asia-Pacific) Holdings Limited (Hong Kong); HSBC Insurance Holdings Limited; La Buenos Aires Compañia Argentina de Seguros S.A. (Argentina); Midland Life Limited. Bullion Dealing and Commodity/Brokerage Services: Wardley Broking Services Private Limited (Singapore). Property: Wayfoong Property Limited. Shipping Services: HSBC Shipbrokers Limited.

Further Reading

Blanden, Michael, "After the Dust of Battle," *Banker,* August 1992, p. 36.

Chambers, Gillian, *Hang Seng: The Evergrowing Bank,* Hong Kong: Hang Seng Bank, 1991.

Collis, Maurice, *Wayfoong: The Hong Kong and Shanghai Banking Corporation,* London: Faber and Faber, 1965.

"An Empire at Risk," *Economist,* September 7, 1996, pp. 71–72.

Engardio, Pete, "Global Banker," *Business Week,* May 24, 1993, pp. 42–46.

Engardio, Pete, and Paula Dwyer, "Hongkong & Shanghai Vs. the World," *Business Week,* August 7, 1995, pp. 59–60.

"Far Eastern Promise and the Global Gamble," *Investors' Chronicle,* January 29, 1993.

Graham, George, "HSBC Reaps Fruits of Growth Strategy," *Financial Times,* February 24, 1998, p. 26.

"Greater Than the Sum of His Parts," *Financial Times,* March 1, 1994.

Green, William, "Bland—And Proud of It," *Forbes,* July 7, 1997, pp. 94–96, 98–99.

Holmes, A.R., and Edwin Green, *Midland: 150 Years of Banking Business,* London: Batsford, 1986.

"HongkongBank's Global Gamble," *Economist,* March 21, 1992, pp. 107–08.

"Hong Kong/China Boom Spawns a Global Banking Colossus," *QL Stockmarket Letter,* July 1, 1993.

"The HSBC Group: A Brief History," London: HSBC Holdings plc, [1995], 31 p.

"HSBC Maps Strategy for US Market," *South China Morning Post,* January 14, 1993.

Irvine, Steve, "The Culture That Powers Hongkong Bank," *Euromoney,* February 1997, pp. 44+.

Jones, Geoffrey, *The History of the British Bank of the Middle East,* 2 vols., Cambridge: Cambridge University Press, 1986–87.

King, Frank H.H., *The Hongkong Bank in the Period of Development and Nationalism, 1941–1984: From Regional Bank to Multinational Group,* New York: Cambridge University Press, 1991, 991 p.

King, Frank H.H., editor, *Eastern Banking: Essays in the History of the Hongkong and Shanghai Banking Corporation,* London: Athlone Press, 1983, 791 p.

King, Frank H.H., Catherine E. King, and David J.S. King, *The Hongkong Bank Between the Wars and the Bank Interned, 1919–1945: Return from Grandeur,* New York: Cambridge University Press, 1988, 705 p.

——, *The Hongkong Bank in Late Imperial China, 1864;ne1902: On an Even Keel,* New York: Cambridge University Press, 1987, 701 p.

King, Frank H.H., David J.S. King, and Catherine E. King, *The Hongkong Bank in the Period of Imperialism and War, 1895–1918: Wayfoong, the Focus of Wealth,* New York: Cambridge University Press, 1988, 720 p.

Leung, James, "HongkongBank Extends Personal Touch," *Asian Business,* February 1997, p. 22+.

"Loan Masters," *Economist,* August 28, 1993, pp. 65–66.

Lucas, Louise, "Hongkong Bank Chief to Quit in HSBC Rejig," *Financial Times,* October 16, 1998, p. 25.

——, "Profits Growth Limited at HongkongBank," *Financial Times,* August 5, 1997, p. 20.

Meyer, Richard, "Lessons from Buffalo," *Financial World,* July 23, 1991, pp. 37–39.

Morris, Kathleen, "Back to the Future," *Financial World,* June 20, 1995, pp. 42–44.

Muirhead, Stuart, *Crisis Banking in the East: The History of the Chartered Mercantile Bank of India, London and China, 1853–93,* Aldershot, England: Scolar Press, 1996, 379 p.

Sender, Henny, and John McBeth, "Living Dangerously: Hongkong Bank Is Mired in an Indonesian Nightmare," *Far Eastern Economic Review,* February 29, 1996, pp. 52–53.

Silverman, Gary, "Look British, Think Chinese: Hongkong Bank Stays No. 1," *Far Eastern Economic Review,* December 28, 1995, pp. 64–65.

Tanzer, Andrew, "The Bank," *Forbes,* December 11, 1989, pp. 43–44.

Vander Weyer, Martin, "Hongkong Officer Corps Builds a Global Empire," *Euromoney,* April, 1993, pp. 52–56.

"Waiting for the Griffin to Pull Its Weight," *Financial Times,* March 16, 1993.

"You Organise Your Bank Around Your Customers," *Daily Telegraph,* March 22, 1993.

"Your Future Is Our Future," Hong Kong: The Hongkong and Shanghai Banking Corporation Limited, 1997, 36 p.

—Robin DuBlanc
—updated by David E. Salamie

Iams Company

**7250 Poe Avenue
Dayton, Ohio 45414
U.S.A.
(937) 898-7387
Fax: (937) 264-7160
Web site: http://www.iams.com**

Private Company
Incorporated: 1946
Employees: 1,200
Sales: $300 million (1996 est.)
SICs: 2047 Dog & Cat Food

Iams Company is a manufacturer of premium dog and cat foods which are distributed only through veterinarians, animal breeders, and specialty pet stores. It is the number two company in the high-end pet food niche, and the seventh largest pet food enterprise overall in the United States. The company sells two brands, Iams dog and cat foods, and Eukanuba. Iams has manufacturing facilities in Lewisburg, Ohio; Aurora, Nebraska; Henderson, North Carolina; and a plant for its international division in Coevorden, the Netherlands. The company distributes its pet foods in more than 70 countries worldwide. Iams also maintains a pet research center in Lewisburg, Ohio, where veterinarians, chemists, and nutritionists study dog and cat diets on laboratory animals raised as pets. Occupying a booming segment of the pet food market, Iams in the late 1990s was one of the fastest growing pet food companies in the world.

Early History

The Iams Company was named for its founder, Paul Iams, the son of a Dayton animal feed store owner. Iams graduated from The Ohio State University in 1938, and with few job prospects because of the Great Depression, he returned from college and went to work for his father. He peddled his father's inexpensive dog food to area kennels and veterinary clinics, but Iams became convinced that dog owners would pay more for a better product. Iams left his father's business to work selling

soap for Procter & Gamble, then served four years in the Navy. After the war, Iams made plans to manufacture a high quality dog food. He founded the Iams Company in 1946, and came out with its first premium dog food, Iams 999, in 1950.

Paul Iams was convinced that dogs needed a higher protein, higher fat food than was commercially available. This insight stemmed from a visit to a mink ranch in 1946. Iams noticed that the dogs who worked on the mink ranch seemed exceptionally healthy, with beautiful, shiny coats. It turned out the dogs were eating the same food the minks got. Iams reproduced something like the minks' diet in his dog food. A self-taught nutritionist, he continued to research pet diet and methods of processing protein. Iams came out with an improved brand, Iams Plus, in 1961. This was called the pet food industry's first complete diet, because it did not require any additives. And because of a process Paul Iams developed, the new food was both high in protein and low in harmful minerals, in stark contrast to other dog foods available at the time.

Iams distributed Iams Plus through dog breeders, kennels, and veterinarians. Sales grew as word got around about the high quality of the product. The company did not advertise, and through the 1960s only sold in five Midwestern states. The business might have continued on this small scale were it not for the vision of a new manager, Clay Mathile, who joined the company in 1970.

Strategic Changes in the 1970s

Mathile was an Ohio native who had worked as an assistant purchasing agent for the Campbell Soup Company. He bought meat for Campbell's, and so knew something of that industry. Paul Iams was looking for a partner to help run his business, and in 1970 a mutual friend introduced him to Mathile. Mathile was not sure he wanted the job, but he quickly became convinced of the quality of the Iams brand. Paul Iams gave him a bag of dog food after their first interview, and Mathile passed it on to his father, who owned what he described as a ''scruffy-looking'' mixed breed dog. Several weeks later, Mathile visited his father and found a beautiful, bouncy animal in place of the disheveled Queenie. It turned out it was the same dog, but looking quite

Company Perspectives:

The Iams Company was built on a simple mission: to enhance the well-being of dogs and cats by providing world-class quality foods.

different as a result of the Iams food. Mathile agreed to become the manager of the Iams Company for a five percent share of the profits. Sales stood at something under $1 million a year, but Mathile was convinced that he could make the company grow.

Unfortunately, it was a bad time for the pet food industry. While costs were increasing, national wage and price controls kept the company from passing on its costs to consumers. Other companies kept up by switching to lower-cost ingredients, but Iams and Mathile realized that that would destroy what made the Iams brand unique. They continued to use the same high-cost ingredients, and by 1973 they were selling the dog food at a loss. The following year was another one in the red, and Paul Iams wanted to sell the company and get out. Mathile convinced him to sell only half—to him—and he and his wife bought a 50 percent share for $100,000.

Mathile worked on a more effective marketing campaign for Iams. Previously, word-of-mouth had been the only advertising. Mathile bought a quarter-page ad in *Dog World* magazine, and began visiting dog shows to promote the product. Soon the company's distribution was nationwide, and by 1975, Iams was back in the black.

Besides working on marketing and distribution, Mathile made some alterations in the product itself. At that time, the dog food looked, according to company literature, like "potting soil mixed with corn flakes." Iams' careful protein rendering process made the food come out in this unique form. But it was apparently a little offensive to some new consumers. In an interview in the July 1988 *Nation's Business*, Mathile described the trouble dogs had with Iams Plus: "They'd sniff it up their noses, and they'd spit it out, and they'd cough." Mathile got advice from a pet-food equipment manufacturer, and by 1976, Iams was putting out more traditional pellet-shaped dog food

With the new, improved product, sales doubled in two years, and doubled again in 1979. Mathile had also shepherded a new brand onto the market, called Eukanuba. The name was taken from a favorite expression of Paul Iams, who heard it from the jazz star Hoagie Carmichael, and it means "the best." Eukanuba was a high-protein, high-fat dog food like Iams Plus, but was supposed to be more palatable. It sold well from the start. The Iams company soon outgrew its Dayton headquarters and built a new plant in Lewisburg, Ohio.

National and International Growth in the 1980s

With a new brand, national distribution, growing facilities, and skyrocketing sales, the company was doing very well. At this time, founder Paul Iams decided to retire. In 1981, he sold his half of the company to Clay Mathile and his wife. With the company's direction entirely in his hands, Mathile worked to make Iams more efficient. He hired new top managers and put together a board of directors. The directors he first chose were friends, but Mathile soon decided he needed a more professional team. So he brought together a new board, this time taking talent from large national businesses such as Tupperware and Dayton Hudson.

The company's sales by 1982 had grown to at least $10 million, and the whole pet food market was experiencing remarkable vigor. There were 48 million dogs in American households in 1982, and 44 million cats. The dog and cat food category was second only to the cereal category in the prepared foods market. As big manufacturers like Ralston-Purina and Gaines competed for supermarket space, Iams continued to sell through veterinarians and breeders. Sales of all brands through these outlets grew quickly in the 1980s, and Iams sales growth sometimes topped 25 percent a year. Perhaps fueled by a rising general interest in health food, more consumers were turning to better quality food for their pets.

The Iams Company increased its advertising in the 1980s and continued to market its brands with educational pamphlets distributed through breeders and veterinarians. The company brought out its first cat food in 1981, and soon followed with foods tailored to life stages, such as kitten and puppy food, and food for less active older animals. Following Clay Mathile's growth strategy, the company expanded its manufacturing capacity, updating its plants and building a new factory in Aurora, Nebraska, in the mid-1980s. The company's annual production capacity doubled between 1985 and 1989. Iams began to sell its brands overseas as well. Exports were five percent of sales in the late 1980s, and growing. In 1988 the company launched its first mass-market advertising, spending an estimated $8 million on its campaign.

By 1990, the company's annual sales were estimated at $210 million. Profits were high as well, with estimated pre-tax margins of 25 percent. Because the Iams and Eukanuba brands were premium quality, consumers paid far more for them than for the supermarket variety of pet food. In 1991, for example, a 40-pound bag of Eukanuba dog food sold for between $36 and $40 retail, more than twice the price of Purina. But the Iams Company's manufacturing cost was still only around $10 for the 40-pound bag, so the mark-up was handsome. Manufacturers of supermarket pet foods saw profit margins far lower, even as their sales grew too in the 1980s.

Competition in the 1990s

Dozens of new premium brands of dog and cat food entered the market in the late 1980s, and Iams had to try harder to maintain its place. The company got a new president in 1990, Tom McLeod, formerly president of the bakery division of Sara Lee. McLeod understood that the 1990s might be a more competitive period for the company, as its success was copied. Yet he refrained from changing the company's marketing strategy by, for example, trying to sell in supermarkets. Nonetheless, to increase its presence, the company began to contact consumers through direct mail, and to reach them with public service ads.

In 1993 Iams advertised in newspapers, advising consumers, "If you're in the market for the best pet food, get out of the supermarket!'' The ads listed area pet stores where Iams brand pet foods were sold, and offered a free bag of Iams or Eukanuba in exchange for an empty bag of a supermarket brand cat or dog food. But competing directly with supermarket brands was a difficult game, and Iams customers by and large were a very discriminating group who could be reached other ways. The next year the company launched a direct-mail campaign as a way to build brand loyalty. Iams contacted new pet owners with an educational letter about cat or dog nutrition. The letters were addressed to the pet itself, and treated the animal as a new family member, its owners as parents. The approach generated enthusiastic response, and garnered the company a valuable database of concerned and loving pet owners.

In 1996 the company changed its target slightly. Iams buyers were typically high income families, often with purebred animals. The new campaign tried to reach the millions of pet owners that adopted animals from shelters. Iams sponsored a Pet Adoptathon, with some 700 participating animal shelters in the United States and Canada, and aired public service ads that concentrated simply on the joy of having a pet. The company hoped to reach new pet owners with flyers and samples. But the ads themselves did not try to sell pet food. The message was more a celebration of pet ownership. The potential market for Iams was huge, as an estimated 15 percent of the almost 64 million pet-owning households adopted their pets from shelters, and a full 25 percent of all pet owners claimed that they would adopt their next pets.

By 1996, Iams's sales were estimated to stand at more than $300 million, so the company's sales growth in the 1990s was still momentous. Iams was second to Colgate-Palmolive's Hill's Science Diet, which marketed vigorously through veterinarian endorsements. Though other major pet food makers vied to cut into the premium market, Hill's and Iams remained the solid leaders in that niche, and there still seemed to be room for growth.

Iams made a big move in 1997, starting construction on its first overseas plant. Since its first European sales in 1984, Iams had increased its international sales to the point where it needed a self-sufficient overseas operation. The plant, located near the German border in Coevorden, the Netherlands, was to manufacture Iams and Eukanuba from raw materials gathered in Europe.

This would cut the company's import costs, and speed up delivery of European orders. And Iams gambled that having a European plant would shield the company from potential future import delays or restrictions. In addition, Iams increased its domestic capacity by building a new plant in Leipsic, Ohio.

The company remained privately held, financing its growth through its profits. Iams sales had been expanding rapidly since the early 1980s, but by the end of the 1990s there still seemed to be no end in sight. Competition from lower-priced brands had not so far hurt the company. With exceptionally loyal customers, an expanding base of U.S. pet owners, and potential markets abroad, Iams seemed to have a formula for continued success.

Further Reading

Bird, Laura, ''Iams and Hill's Wage a High-Fibre, Low-Cal War Against Ralston Purina and Carnation,'' *Adweek's Marketing Week*, October 1, 1990, pp. 20–23.

Cuff, Daniel F., ''Head of Sara Lee Division Joining Maker of Pet Food,'' *New York Times,* April 16 1990, p. D5.

Haran, Leah, ''Iams Unleashing Efforts in Shelters,'' *Advertising Age*, April 1, 1996, p. 42.

Hauck, Katherine, ''Smart Pet Tricks,'' *Prepared Foods*, October 1990, pp. 51–52.

''Iams Ad Lures Supermarket Shoppers,'' *Supermarket News*, May 17, 1993, p. 22.

''Iams of Dayton Builds Loyalty Database of Loving Pet Owners,'' *Direct Marketing*, November 1995, pp. 15–16.

Manges, Michele, ''For Today's Pampered Pets, It's a Dog-Eat-Steak World,'' *Wall Street Journal*, May 18, 1989, p. B1.

Nelton, Sharon, ''Going to the Dogs (and Cats),'' *Nation's Business*, July 1988, pp. 26–27.

Otto, Alison, ''It's Raining Cat and Dog Food,'' *Prepared Foods*, April, 1989, pp. 40–45.

Parker-Pope, Tara, ''For You, My Pet,'' *Wall Street Journal*, November 3, 1997, pp. A1, A10.

Parlin, Sandra, ''Chowing Down: Iams Builds Its First Foreign Pet Food Plant,'' *Food Processing*, May 1998, p. 156.

Schifrin, Matthew, ''Mom's Cooking Was Never Like This,'' *Forbes*, August 19, 1991, pp. 50–51.

—A. Woodward

IKEA International A/S

Ny Strandvej 21
DK-3050 Humlebaeck
Denmark
(45) 49 15 50 00
Fax: (45) 49 15 50 01
Web site: http://www.ikea.com

Private Company
Incorporated: 1943 as IKEA, Ingvar Kamprad
Employees: 36,400
Sales: US$5.86 billion (1997)
SICs: 5712 Furniture Stores; 5719 Miscellaneous Home
    Furnishing Stores

Based in Denmark, IKEA International A/S is one of the world's top retailers of furniture, home furnishings, and housewares. The company designs its own items, and sells them in the more than 140 IKEA stores that are spread throughout approximately 30 different countries worldwide. The company also peddles its merchandise through mail-order, distributing its thick catalogs once a year in the areas surrounding its store locations. IKEA is characterized by its efforts to offer high-quality items at low prices. To save money for itself and its customers, the company buys items in bulk, ships and stores items unassembled using flat packaging, and has customers assemble many items on their own at home. The company is owned by founder Ingvar Kamprad's Netherlands-based charitable foundation, Ingka Holding B.V.

The Early Years

IKEA was founded in 1943 in Sweden by Ingvar Kamprad. Kamprad was born in 1926 as the son of a farmer in Småland, a region in southern Sweden. Småland was historically one of the country's poorest regions, and its inhabitants were known for their hard work, thriftiness, and inventiveness. In 1943, at the age of 17, Kamprad upheld this characterization when he decided to become an entrepreneur and created a commercial company called "IKEA, Ingvar Kamprad." The word IKEA was an acronym of his name and address: Ingvar Kamprad and Elmtaryd, Agunnaryd—the name of his farm and the name of the village it was located within. Kamprad's new company was essentially a one-man effort, and sold fish, vegetable seeds, and magazines to customers in his region. He delivered the items to customers using first a bicycle and later the milk round.

In 1947, IKEA issued its first primitive mail-order catalog, within which the newly invented ballpoint pen was added to the assortment of products Kamprad was offering. Then in 1950, Kamprad set the foundation for the future direction of IKEA by adding furniture and home furnishings to the mail-order line. A year later, an expanded version of the IKEA catalog became available. In 1952, the stability of home furnishings in the IKEA product line was solidified when Kamprad took his items to the St. Eric's Fair in Stockholm and won over customers with the high-quality, low-priced furniture items in his line.

Up to that point, IKEA items had been obtained from other sources and sold by Kamprad, making his enterprise solely a retail operation. In 1953, however, Kamprad made the decision to buy a small furniture factory and open a small furniture and home-furnishing showroom in Älmhult. The IKEA headquarters were moved from the village of Agunnaryd to Älmhult. IKEA began designing its own furniture items in 1955, and soon began taking advantage of the benefits of flat packaging and self-assembly by customers. Success followed quickly, and in 1958 the tiny showroom was replaced by a then giant store of 13,000 square meters. One year later, a restaurant was added to the store, to accommodate the needs of an ever-increasing number of customers who were traveling long distances to IKEA.

The mail-order business continued to flourish as well, helping to further expand IKEA's customer range. This prompted the opening of the first IKEA store outside Sweden, near Oslo in Norway, in 1963. Business continued to increase, boosted in part by a 1964 article in the Swedish magazine *Allt i Hemmet* (All for Your Home), which listed the results of quality tests that had been run on furniture; IKEA received the highest ratings available.

Innovations and Expansion Throughout the 1960s and 1970s

The event that marked the true turning point of the business, however, came in 1965 when Kamprad opened a store just outside the major city of Stockholm, to show what could be done in the way of designing and selling modern low-priced furniture in a large market. The store, located on a greenfield site at Kungens Kurva just ten kilometers southwest of Stockholm, was extraordinary for two reasons. First, it was very large, with some 33,000 square meters of total space and 15,000 square meters of selling space, and it consisted of two connected buildings. One building, circular in shape, had four floors connected ingeniously so that customers could move easily from floor to floor. This building acted as the main display area for furniture. The second building consisted of three floors and a basement and acted as the stockroom and service unit, where there was also a selling area for smaller pieces of furniture and home furnishings. Customer services ranged from a baby carriage hire service, a children's nursery, and a restaurant with seating for 350, to cloakrooms, toilets, a bank, and parking for 1,000 cars.

More important than the physical characteristics of the new IKEA store was the manner in which it revolutionized furniture manufacturing and selling. Kamprad continued the practice of selling most furniture in flat-pack form, as he said, ''to avoid transporting and storing air.'' To make this possible, the furniture was specially designed by IKEA staff in workshops in the Älmhult headquarters and warehouse. For the mass production of the component parts of the flat-pack furniture, Kamprad had to bypass traditional furniture manufacturers and instead use specialist factories. Unfinished pine shelving, for example, came directly from saw mills, cabinet doors were made in door factories, metal frames came from machine shops, and upholstery materials came directly from textile mills. Almost all of the components of each piece of furniture could be put together by the customers themselves, but in some cases IKEA staff could help the customer assemble the furniture at home. IKEA's innovations ranged from table legs which fixed into place with snap locks, to kitchen chairs that were assembled with one screw. A large number of IKEA products carried the label of the Swedish Furniture Research Institute, a byword for good quality and design.

Another innovative marketing tool employed in the new IKEA store in Stockholm was a self-service method of selling, which was largely unknown in the furniture and home furnishing retail trades at the time. Customers were invited to walk around the whole store and select items by themselves. There were information desks and written materials about products, but no sales assistants to persuade customers to buy. In these early days of IKEA, customers had to pay for their purchases in cash to improve the finances of the firm. The customer was given a docket for each item and collected the flat-packed merchandise at the delivery dock. There was no home delivery service; the customer had to provide his or her own transport. Car racks could be bought, and later self-drive vans could be rented.

The IKEA formula was an instant success, particularly for kitchenware and children's furniture, and soon more IKEA stores were launched. Additional stores were opened in Sweden in 1966 and 1967, and in 1969 a store was opened in Denmark. This was followed by the first store openings outside the Scandinavian territory—in Switzerland in 1973, and in Germany in 1974. Soon there were ten IKEA stores in five European countries. The stores employed a total of 1,500 people, and sales in 1974 were SKr 616 million. Sweden remained the company's main market, accounting for 75 percent of total sales.

Kamprad soon realized the potential for IKEA's expansion into new markets worldwide. In 1973, he once again packed up and moved the company's headquarters—this time to Copenhagen, Denmark, which was a more central location for European expansion. The first major expansion was in Germany. After the first store in 1974, ten more were opened by 1980, more than were in operation in Sweden, and by 1990 there were 17 stores in Western Germany. Elsewhere in Europe, stores were opened in Austria in 1977, and in the Netherlands in 1979. The company was expanding outside of Europe, as well. In 1975 the first IKEA in Australia was opened; in 1976 a store opened in Canada; and in 1978 a store was placed in Singapore.

Worldwide Growth in the 1980s and 1990s

With worldwide expansion moving along successfully, IKEA continued to enter new markets around the globe in the 1980s. Stores were placed in the Canary Islands in 1980, in France and in Iceland in 1981, in Saudi Arabia in 1983, in Belgium and in Kuwait in 1984, in the United Kingdom and in Hong Kong in 1987, and in Italy in 1989.

One of the company's most challenging expansion efforts, however, began in 1985 when a store of 15,700 square meters was opened in the United States in Philadelphia, Pennsylvania. The move was a test to see whether a European retail concept, however enterprising in its methods and outlook, could succeed in a vastly different U.S. market. The answer was yes. If anything, the American consumer was more receptive to innovative ideas and merchandise than many of the more conservative European customers. The experience of the previously opened Canadian stores was useful in getting the concept on its feet in the United States.

Another major challenge was taken up in 1990 when IKEA stores were opened in eastern Europe. A store was opened in Budapest in a joint venture with a Hungarian firm, Butorker, and in the same year another small store was opened in Warsaw, Poland. In 1991, stores were placed in the Czech Republic and the United Arab Emirates, and the following year IKEA stores appeared for the first time in Mallorca and Slovakia, along with the opening of a pilot store in the Netherlands. This rapid expansion in a decade and a half helped to greatly change the pattern of sales. In 1975, the Scandinavian markets represented around 85 percent of the company's total sales. By 1990, however, this proportion had dropped to just over 26 percent, and sales in Germany alone had risen to account for more than 27 percent of the company's total. The rest of Europe contributed another large chunk of overall sales—34 percent—and stores in other regions accounted for just over 12 percent of the total.

While IKEA's geographic expansion provided it with more stability—the company no longer had to rely on its saturated Swedish markets for the majority of its income—the expansion also presented minor supply problems. The component parts had to be made to strict specifications, and the originality of the Kamprad approach was to replace the craftsman philosophy with an engineering philosophy. In the early years of growth—while using Sweden, Denmark, and Finland as the main sources of supply—IKEA also saw the advantages of using supplies from eastern European countries. Contracts were signed with state-controlled and other independent factories in East Germany, Poland, and Yugoslavia for the supply of furniture components. Since payment was made in "hard" currency, strict specifications could be enforced and the dates of payment could be flexible, thus improving IKEA's cash flow. In the 1970s, some 20 to 25 percent of total supplies came from eastern Europe in this fashion. By 1990, however, the proportion of supplies obtained from eastern Europe had fallen to around 15 percent, even though that portion was part of a much larger total than had been the case in the past. In 1990, there were around 1,500 suppliers in 45 different countries, presenting a problem of planning and logistics, because production took place in fewer locales.

To counter any problematic situations arising from the fact that IKEA's operations were situated all around the world, management organized the company as a whole into four different main areas with interlocking functions. The first area—*Product Range and Development*—was primarily carried out by IKEA of Sweden. New or improved products had always been an essential part of the success of the company, and the work was undertaken by separate product groups within IKEA of Sweden. Thus, product development tasks were completed in a more centralized fashion, and then filtered down to all other areas of IKEA's operations. Second, *Purchasing* of materials for production and other small retail items was conducted by agents responsible for placing orders to the specifications laid down by IKEA of Sweden and the product development teams. Third, the *Distribution Service* undertook the transport and distribution of the finished products to 12 regional distribution centers and stores throughout the world. Finally, *Retailing* functions were carried out by those operating under the same retail concept, ensuring that selling methods and customer service were of the same standards in all IKEA stores.

In addition to its strong corporate organization of operations, another factor in IKEA's success during the expansion years was its effective—and at times unusual—advertising and sales promotion campaigns around the world. Targeted customers were mainly 20- to 35-year-olds, and the high quality of modern Swedish design was emphasized. The IKEA catalogs played a primary role in advertising success. The catalogs were attractive and easy to use, emphasizing quality of design and the efficiency of IKEA products. During the busy years of geographic expansion, every household in the area surrounding a new store received a copy of the catalog. Although direct mail-order sales always represented a very small portion of total sales and the catalogs did not offer the whole IKEA range, they were always a key factor in attracting new customers to the stores.

IKEA advertisements themselves were unusual in their contradiction of the traditional image of the Swedish as conservative and rather serious. In France, for example, one slogan used was "Ils sont fous ces Suédois"; in Germany, the "unmögliche Möbelhaus aus Schweden"; in the United Kingdom, "the mad Swedes are coming." In the United States, advertising campaigns were even more outrageous, and almost every advertisement included a reindeer, leaving no doubt as to the origin of the campaign. The combination of offbeat advertising and well-designed merchandise had a very effective impact on the group of customers IKEA was targeting.

The Mid-1990s

IKEA continued to open stores in new locations throughout the world. It became interesting to see a company which offered the same basic products at all stores do so well in so many different cultures with different tastes. In 1994, IKEA opened its first store in Taiwan. Two years later, the company placed new stores in Finland, Malaysia, and Spain. By 1998, IKEA had also opened a store in mainland China.

In 1997, IKEA joined thousands of other companies online when it introduced its site on the World Wide Web, aptly named the "World Wide Living Room Web Site." The web site not only offered information about the company, its origin, and its future vision, but also made it possible for customers to see IKEA's merchandise on their computers at home. Part of the company's catalog was available for viewing online, and information about new product lines and pictures of the items were present.

The company also continued its practice of being environmentally friendly, which was actually a practice that the company had embraced since its beginnings. In the 1990s, when media hype about recycling and saving the environment was at its height, IKEA had already taken steps to cut down on waste years before. In order to save money in the production phase, IKEA had long strived to be as economical as possible and use only the amount of materials that was absolutely necessary when producing items. The company had also been saving money (and trees) by using flat-packaging for the storage and transport of items, which dramatically reduced the amount of cardboard packaging materials used by the company. The company's web site challenged customers to "search for new and economical uses of our precious environmental resources to adapt ourselves to the forests, lakes, air and mountains. Not the other way around.''

The End of the Century and Beyond

As the end of the 20th century neared, there were a few possible causes for concern in the future. First, some feared that the saturation point in the number of stores may have been reached already in some countries—for example Sweden, Germany, Belgium, and the Netherlands. This would mean that the potential for continued future growth at the same rate would possibly decrease, unless IKEA continued to aggressively enter new markets around the world. In these other developed countries that were less saturated by the IKEA concept, possible expansion was linked to trends in the birth rate, new housing starts, and the age structure of the population.

Furthermore, there existed the complex question of the company's future finances. Ingvar Kamprad had stated that he would be satisfied if his business was sufficiently successful to provide him with ''bread, schnapps and crayfish.'' Throughout the company's history, most profits were ploughed back into the firm. To avoid problems of outside shareholders and succession, in the 1970s Kamprad had donated the company to a charitable foundation in the Netherlands called Ingka Holding B.V. The move had been made to help prevent the company from being taken over and/or split up when Kamprad died. Some analysts believed that if expansion was to continue and IKEA was to keep ahead of the growing number of direct competitors, other methods of finance would have to be found in the future.

Outsiders felt that IKEA's next course of action would have to be going public on the stock market. But according to a July 1998 article in the *South China Morning Post,* ''Kamprad has no intention of releasing his grip on his empire, to the dismay of many investment banks, salivating over the successful retail chain that attracts 140 million visitors each year.'' As a private entity, IKEA was free to engage in expansion without the pressure of having shareholders demanding quick profits. This meant that the company could take things at its own pace, and potentially fare better in the long run.

Further Reading

''Private Man Behind Private IKEA Keeps Tight Grip on Growing Empire,'' *South China Morning Post,* July 30, 1998.

—James B. Jefferys
—updated by Laura E. Whiteley

indigo

Indigo NV

5 Limburglaan 6229 GA
Maastricht
The Netherlands
(31) 43-356-5656
Fax: (31) 43-356-5600
Web site: http://www.indigonet.com

Public Company
Incorporated: 1977
Employees: 760
Sales: $106.85 million (1997)
Stock Exchanges: NASDAQ
Ticker Symbol: INDGF
SICs: 3555 Printing Trades Machinery; 6794 Patent
    Owners & Lessors

Indigo NV is a pioneering developer and manufacturer of digital printing systems using patented liquid ink technology. Indigo's line of printers enable high-speed, short-run, high-quality color printing on materials ranging from paper to plastic and foil. The company's plateless, liquid ink design provides picture quality rivaling that of traditional offset printing, while matching the flexibility and speed of use of competing dry ink-based xerographic printing systems. With Indigo's printing systems, customers—including the commercial printing and product packaging industries—can produce small orders of specialized print runs without the high cost associated with offset printing. In this way Indigo printers enable users to print labels, packaging, cards, and other products geared toward specific markets.

Indigo's product lines are centered around its E-Print 1000 and Omnius series of digital printers. The company develops and distributes Yours Truly software designed to derive full benefit from the capabilities of digital printing. Indigo also manufactures consumable items, including the color inks developed for its printing systems. In September 1998 Indigo announced the launch of two new printing systems, the e-Print Pro, a low-cost entry into digital printing, and UltraStream, billed as the world's fastest digital printer. Both printers were expected to ship in 1999.

Although Indigo is incorporated in the Netherlands, its manufacturing and research and development facilities are based in Rehovot, Israel, and its stock is quoted on the NASDAQ stock exchange. The company also maintains corporate offices in Woburn, Massachusetts, and facilities in Canada and Belgium. Being a digital printing pioneer has not been extremely profitable for Indigo. After a surge in revenues in the mid-1990s, the company has seen its sales level off in the late 1990s; the company has struggled for profitability, posting losses in 1996 and 1997, after a profitable 1995. But with the financial backing of investment heavyweight George Soros, who increased his holding from 18 percent to 30 percent in 1997, Indigo has the resources to build its still nascent market, while possessing a protective wall of more than 100 international patents for its industry leading technology. Founder Benzion Landa maintains more than 50 percent of Indigo's stock through a family trust. In 1998 Indigo denied reports that it has been negotiating a possible takeover by Israeli printing specialist Scitex.

Digital Printing Pioneer in the 1980s

The printing industry's reliance on liquid ink—and its ability to produce high resolution, high color images—faced a stumbling block with the arrival of the digital era. Digital processes offered vast possibilities for production enhancements, and the printing industry readily adopted computer-driven tools where these could be adapted to the printing process. Yet, if traditional offset printing remained the technology of choice for long print runs, the cost and effort involved in the setup phase limited its practical application for much of what digital printing could offer. Other printing processes, especially xerographic printing, were more adaptable; these electronic printing processes were able to process shorter print runs and even to process a different image for each printed page more easily than offset printing. But xerographic printing remained based on powdered ink, which sacrificed image clarity and color quality for flexibility of use.

In 1977 Canadian-born Benzion Landa established Indigo in the small Israeli community of Rehovot, near Tel Aviv. Later reincorporated in the Netherlands for financial purposes and quoted on the United States' NASDAQ stock exchange, Indigo

Company Perspectives:

Only Indigo combines the quality *of offset printing with the* power *of digital imaging, and the* versatility *of practically limitless substrates.*

was nevertheless firmly rooted in Israel's growing high technology industry. Landa's company initially focused on research efforts for developing technology that the company could sell to other manufacturing industries. At the same time Indigo was working on developing liquid ink products suitable for the quickly growing digital printer/plotter market. By the early 1980s Indigo unveiled its ElectroInk, a liquid ink that when heated was transformed into plastic. Throughout the decade Indigo continued to invest heavily in its research and development activities, building a patent portfolio that the company itself would refer to as a "patent fence." By the early 1990s the company had refined its ElectroInk technology to the point where it was ready to compete not only with xerographic imaging, but as well with traditional short-run printing techniques.

At the start of the 1990s Indigo prepared to move from a primarily research-driven and consumables concern into a full-scale printing equipment manufacturing company. The company's first product would be a digital plotter/duplicator, bringing the tiny company (its 1991 sales totaled less than US$5 million, generating a profit of $440,000) head to head with such industry giants as Xerox and Canon. At the same time Indigo was attracting interest among other manufacturers in the industry, and the company began to generate revenues through licensing its technology. Nevertheless, Indigo remained focused on bringing its own products to market.

Digital Printing Revolution in the 1990s

In 1993 Indigo prepared to launch the E-Print 1000, a medium-speed sheet-fed press capable of four-color (later, up to six-color) printing directly from a computer file. The E-Print marked a revolution in the printing industry, eliminating the expense and labor of the plate-printing setup process, while offering a print resolution up to 800 dots per inch on a variety of paper stock. The E-Print enabled inexpensive short-run color printing. Images not only could be readily changed, they could be changed from page to page, requiring neither additional setup or pauses in the print run. Instead of printing to metal plates, the E-Print printed to a roller, which then transferred the ink directly to paper. Because the ink could be removed completely from the roller, a different image could be printed with each turn of the roller. At the same time, Indigo's ElectroInk-based color inks offered print quality rivaling that of traditional printing processes. Indigo began marketing the E-Print 1000 in 1993.

As preparation for its move into full-scale manufacturing, Landa brought Indigo's headquarters to the Netherlands, placing the company closer to the European market, especially Germany, long the seat of the modern printing industry. Landa next began seeking the financing Indigo needed to move the E-Print into full production.

This financing would come from none other than George Soros, the world-renowned investment giant of the 1990s. In 1993 Soros bought up 12.5 percent of Indigo for some $50 million. Soros's backing also would prove to be an ingredient in Landa's next project, that of taking Indigo public. In 1994 Indigo joined the NASDAQ stock exchange, selling 52 million shares at $20 per share. The offering reduced Landa's personal holding in Indigo to 70 percent. As the stock continued to climb—marking one of the year's initial pubic offering (IPO) successes—Landa's paper worth soon would reach some $2 billion. The IPO netted the company nearly $88 million.

The company's revenues remained more modest, reaching only $73 million in 1994, which nonetheless represented an increase from just more than $13 million the year before. Indigo reached a number of strategic agreements, in particular with Japan's Toyo Ink Manufacturing company, which agreed to manufacture and sell the E-Print for the Asian market. Sales of the $400,000 E-Print were climbing steadily, meanwhile, nearing 300 machines sold by 1995.

Turning fully to the printing press market, Indigo ended production of its series of plotters in 1995. In its place the company prepared to launch another revolutionary product series: the Omnius press. Whereas E-Print focused on medium-volume single-sheet printing, Omnius brought digital printing to a variety of surfaces, including plastic, cardboard, film, and, especially, cans, bottles, and other packaging surfaces. The Omnius's chief market target was the packaging industry. Based on the same technology as the E-Print, the Omnius enabled economical color printing for print runs under 100,000 on such surfaces as soda cans or product boxes—making the machine an ideal marketing tool. Packagers could use Omnius to produce personalized and market-specific labels, cartons, and the like, while avoiding the expense of offset printing. Gearing up for the anticipated boom in sales, Indigo rapidly expanded its work force.

On the basis of the new press Indigo's stock started to soar, reaching $48 per share by the summer of 1995, representing a multiple of some 60 times estimated earnings for the year. Nonetheless, investors soon would become impatient with the company. At the end of 1995, Indigo disappointed. Sales had not reached the expected levels, and the company found itself overstaffed. Despite a strong rise in revenues to $165 million, the company posted its fourth year of losses, of some $40 million. In an effort to move into profitability, Indigo scrambled to restructure its operations, eliminating a large proportion of its work force between the end of 1995 and the first half of 1996. Soros, unshaken, increased his investment to some 18 percent of Indigo's shares.

Equally important to Indigo's revised strategy were its efforts to improve its products, especially their print volumes, and thereby improve its clients' profitability. This had become especially necessary for the company to win new clients, who shied from the high initial investment cost of the E-Print and Omnius systems. Indigo would spend much of the following two years working toward these ends, successfully raising print volumes by some 57 percent on average. The company also would take steps toward lowering the prices of its machines, and it searched for ways to lower the entry barrier to win new customers. Launched in 1997, the company's Easy Entry program introduced variable pricing for the E-Print 1000, ranging from $199,000 to $379,000. The company also began marketing used equipment as a means of lowering the price barrier for customers.

The company's losses continued, however, as revenues slumped to $86 million, while net losses topped $73 million. To finance its activities, the company performed a private placement of shares, raising approximately $103 million in 1996. A new private placement in 1997 would add an additional $28 million. George Soros continued to be the company's ally, building his investment in the company to some 30 percent. Founder Benzion Landa's personal stake remained at more than 50 percent. In 1997 the company saw an improvement in its financial position, as revenues again topped the $100 million mark, and Indigo managed to cut its losses by some 39 percent, ending the year with a net loss of $45 million.

Through 1998 Indigo continued to improve its profit returns, while introducing two new products: the TurboStream add-on module for the E-Print system, providing a significant volume boost; and the Omnius CardPress, designed specifically for the electronic card market. With more and more businesses offering their own credit cards and customer fidelity cards, the growth in telephone cards, as well as the coming smart card explosion, the CardPress seemed to add yet another revolutionary product to Indigo's portfolio. In September 1998 Indigo announced two new products, both based on its existing technology. The e-Print Pro was described as the world's lowest cost digital color press, and the UltraStream promised to be the world's fastest digital press. Both new products were expected to ship in 1999. At the same time, Indigo, which had steadily improved its ink, both in quality and efficiency, announced new pricing plans for its consumable products, offering what it claimed to be the lowest cost-per-page level in the digital press industry. While being a pioneer had not yet been entirely profitable for the company, Indigo continued to be a favorite of financial analysts, who remained convinced that the printing industry would soon catch up to Indigo's digital press revolution.

Principal Subsidiaries

Indigo International Inc. (U.S.A.).

Further Reading

Coy, Peter, ''A Package for Every Season,'' *Business Week,* February 6, 1995.
Jaffe, Thomas, ''Mood Indigo,'' *Forbes,* July 17, 1995, p. 322.
Rossant, John, ''Out of the Desert, into the Future,'' *Business Week,* August 21, 1995, p. 78.

—M. L. Cohen

Inso Corporation

31 St. James Ave.
Boston, Massachusetts 02116
U.S.A.
(617) 753-6500
Fax: (617) 753-6666
Web site: http://www.inso.com

Public Company
Incorporated: 1993 as InfoSoft International, Inc.
Employees: 469
Sales: $81.9 million (1997)
Stock Exchanges: NASDAQ
Ticker Symbol: INSO
SICs: 7372 Prepackaged Software; 7379 Computer Related Services, Not Elsewhere Classified

Inso Corporation is a high technology company based in Boston, Massachusetts, with three major product areas: Electronic Publishing Solutions, Dynamic Document Exchange, and Lexical and Linguistic Products. Historically, the company began as the software division of textbook publisher Houghton Mifflin Company, and it produced proofing tools, information products, and information management tools primarily for original equipment manufacturers (OEMs) to incorporate into their own software products. Soon after the company went public in 1994, it found that changing market conditions would result in severely limited growth prospects for its language-oriented products, and it began to implement a strategic change in direction. In 1998 it completed the divestiture of its Lexical and Linguistic Products.

Instead of selling products to OEMs, as it had been doing, Inso would provide electronic publishing solutions and file-viewing and conversion products to the top 2,000 corporations as well as to OEMs. An ongoing program of acquisitions begun in 1994 expanded Inso's line of document exchange, web publishing, and electronic publishing products. By 1997, the company had decided to commit the bulk of its resources to developing products in two key areas, which it identified as

Electronic Publishing Solutions and Dynamic Document Exchange. As corporate web sites became more complex and distributed computing put networked computers in nearly every corporate workstation, Inso developed solutions to meet the electronic information and publishing needs of its large corporate clients. In 1997 Inso released its Dynabase Dynamic Web Publishing System, a comprehensive, integrated solution for professional web publishing that was especially useful in the management and delivery of information for large, dynamic web sites.

Inso's file-viewing and conversion products, as well as its "on-demand" web publishing products, allowed organizations to share documents across networks, intranet and Internet environments, and electronic mail systems with different applications and operating system platforms. Products in this area, which Inso called Dynamic Document Exchange, included the Quick View Plus enterprise viewing product, the Outside In viewing technology, the ImageStream graphics filters, the Word for Word text filters, and the Outside In HTML Export product. These products generally made it possible to view and manipulate files originating in different applications and operating system environments, including web environments. They eliminated the need for lengthy conversions or the installation of proprietary technology on customers' desktops.

Houghton Mifflin Division Spun Off, 1994

Houghton Mifflin's software division was established in 1982. On November 10, 1993, it was spun off and incorporated in Delaware as InfoSoft International, Inc. The company name was later changed to Inso Corporation in May 1995. On March 8, 1994, it became an independent public company when it completed an initial public offering of its common stock, with three million shares offered at $15 per share. Steven R. Vana-Paxhia was named president and CEO. He had been director of the software division of Houghton Mifflin since 1990, and before that was managing director of Macmillan's Berlitz Translation Service since 1987.

When Inso went public, all of its revenues were derived from proofing tools, information products, and information

215

Company Perspectives:

As electronic information exchange has become the life-blood of today's global businesses, the Web has emerged as the key transmission channel. To succeed in this environment, businesses must quickly consolidate and publish information. Inso Corporation gives companies a way to automate the publishing and management of this critical data. With Inso's End-to-End Publishing Solution, businesses have a system for generating, organizing, distributing, and continually updating their intellectual property.

---

management tools—"legacy products" from the Houghton Mifflin days. The company had a contract with Microsoft Corporation, which incorporated the products into its own software, that represented a substantial part of Inso's revenues. Its marketing efforts were directed at OEMs.

At the same time, the consolidation of the desktop application market was perceived as severely limiting the growth prospects for Inso's OEM-focused linguistic products. The company was also anticipating an explosion in distributed computing, which would result in making every networked desktop a potential user of document exchange and electronic publishing solutions.

As a result, over the next four years the company went through a product transition to become primarily a company that sold and licensed products that enabled large corporations to exchange and publish all types of information. The company's primary market became the world's 2,000 largest corporations, and by 1997 Inso had more than 700 of the world's biggest firms as customers and nearly $30 million in revenues from the corporate market.

Acquired Systems Compatibility Corporation in 1995

Over the next four years Inso would expand its line of document exchange, web publishing, and electronic publishing products through a series of acquisitions and through internal development. Acquisition talks with Systems Compatibility Corporation began in 1994, and in April 1995 Inso acquired the privately held company for $12.5 million. Systems Compatibility Corporation was renamed Inso Chicago Corporation. The acquisition was the first step in Inso's product transition strategy, and in May the company adopted its present name. In its first full year as an independent company, Inso reported net income of $6 million on net revenues of $43.4 million for 1995.

From 1995 to 1997 Inso significantly increased the amount of money it spent on research and development (R&D). It realized that its ability to compete in an industry that was subject to rapid technological change required a commitment to the development of new products and the evolution of new technologies. In 1995 Inso spent $10.2 million on R&D, or 23 percent of revenues. In 1996 R&D spending nearly doubled to $19.1 million, or 27 percent of revenues. By 1997 the company was spending 35 percent of its revenues on R&D, some $29

million. Much of the 1997 investment went toward research and development of new products for use on or in conjunction with the Internet and the World Wide Web. Inso also remained heavily involved in development efforts for XML and other electronic publishing standards.

Made Two Major Acquisitions in 1996

In January 1996 Inso acquired ImageMark Software Labs, Inc., a privately held firm based in Kansas City, Missouri, for $5.5 million. It would continue to operate as Inso Kansas City Corporation. In July Inso acquired privately held Electronic Book Technologies, Inc. for $27.8 million in cash plus an additional $10.6 million to be paid over time. It was renamed Inso Providence Corporation.

Net revenues for 1996 increased to $70.5 million, but the company reported a net loss of $21.3 million, due primarily to a $38.7 million acquisition charge for purchased technology under research and development by ImageMark Software Labs, Inc. and Electronic Book Technologies, Inc. During 1996 Microsoft accounted for 35 percent of the company's revenues.

Several Acquisitions Occurred in 1997

In February 1997 Inso acquired Mastersoft from Adobe Systems Inc. for nearly $3 million in cash. It became part of Inso Chicago. Mastersoft was Adobe's document access and conversion business. Acquired technologies included Word for Word document conversion, the Viewer 95 file access and display technologies, and various end-user products formerly marketed under the name Adobe File Utilities. At the same time, Adobe Systems and Inso entered into related technology cross-licensing agreements.

Level Five Research, Inc., a privately held company, was acquired in April for $5 million in cash. It was renamed Inso Florida Corporation. It was primarily a developer of software and systems that applied intelligent technologies to data access management.

Also in April, a new venture was established to further the development and marketing of the *Information Please Almanac* product line, which the company had acquired from Houghton Mifflin in 1995 for $3.6 million. During 1995 and 1996, Inso licensed the book rights for the *Information Please Almanac* series back to Houghton Mifflin in exchange for initial guaranteed royalties of $1 million in 1995 and $700,000 in 1996. In April 1997 the Information Please LLC partnership was formed, with Inso retaining a 19.8 percent ownership in the venture. Inso transferred its ownership of the Information Please brand and its intellectual properties for the almanac to the partnership, and some of Inso's employees became employees of the partnership.

In November 1997 Inso acquired the privately held Henderson Software, Inc., for $750,000 in cash. Henderson was a provider of Computer Graphics Metafile viewing and filtering solutions.

Web Growth Affects Company's Direction, 1997

During 1997, the company took note of the growth of the World Wide Web and decided to focus its development investment exclusively on the areas of Dynamic Document Exchange and Electronic Publishing Solutions. Sales and marketing efforts were focused on what the company called Global 2000 corporations. Inso served a $500 million market for its publishing products, a market which the company believed would grow at a 40 percent or higher annual growth rate for the next three years.

Net revenues rose to $81.9 million as the company reported a net loss of $440,000. During the year Inso recognized an acquisition charge of $6.1 million for purchased technology under research and development by Level Five Research, Inc., Mastersoft products and technologies, and Henderson Software, Inc. In 1997 the company also marked the end of its major proofing tools contract with Microsoft Corporation, which represented 28 percent of Inso's revenues that year.

Performance during the first half of 1997 was considered disappointing by the company's management. In terms of the company's markets, some new markets failed to materialize as planned, and the impact of the web on CD-ROM publishers and online services had an effect on Inso's performance. Also, several of Inso's search-and-retrieval engine customers had difficult years, which resulted in lower sales for new products and lower royalties from existing products. Internally, management pointed to the company's below-standard execution of planned new product introductions, which resulted in delays. In the marketing area, the company was unable to shift resources from established channels to new channels quickly enough and with enough precision.

Recognizing that it was trying to do too many things simultaneously, Inso's management refocused on the three words that had resulted in past success: focus, simplify, and execute. The company quickly moved to decrease emphasis on its nonstrategic businesses so that it could focus on faster-growing product lines. Every element of the product life cycle process was examined and simplified. Nonessential platforms and features of existing products were trimmed. In sales and marketing, the company moved to rebuild its sales organization to concentrate on corporate customers while simplifying and focusing every aspect of its marketing program.

Reorganization Focuses on Web Content Management and Publishing

In the second quarter of 1997 a reorganization began. More investment was placed in Dynamic Document Exchange and Electronic Publishing Solutions. The sales organization was rebuilt to align it with growth opportunities and customer needs. These efforts resulted in a restructuring charge of $5.8 million in 1997.

Prior to 1997, the company had enjoyed six years of growth averaging 25 percent annually. Its performance in the first half of 1997 caused it to lose credibility with Wall Street and with its shareholders. To regain shareholder confidence and build value for its shareholders, Inso needed to demonstrate that its strategic shift from linguistic tools to Dynamic Document Exchange and Electronic Publishing Solutions was in place.

Although its proofing tools contract expired in 1997, Inso would continue to have a relationship with Microsoft. As Inso president and CEO Steven R. Vana-Paxhia noted in the com-

pany's 1997 annual report, it was Microsoft's "inclusion of our technology in their outstanding products [that] legitimized Inso as a serious software company." However, with Inso's new strategic direction, its new products were no longer candidates to be features of Microsoft products. Instead, Inso sought to complement Microsoft's products, such as by selling its Quick View Plus in conjunction with Microsoft Exchange. There were still several contracts between the two companies, and Microsoft would continue to be one of Inso's largest customers.

Electronic Publishing Solutions Division, 1997

Electronic Publishing Solutions (EPS) enjoyed its first full year of operations in 1997 following the acquisition of Electronic Book Technologies (EBT), which provided the core of Inso's EPS business. EBT was a desirable acquisition for Inso because of its excellent engineering team and strong portfolio of products, and it provided a perfect complement to Inso's Dynamic Document Exchange business.

EPS's sales growth in 1997 was driven by several factors. At the start of the year a completely new sales team was assembled for domestic and international markets. Key markets included automotive and aerospace manufacturers, traditional publishing companies, computer hardware and software, and telecommunications.

Major EPS products included the DynaText publishing system, which appealed to Global 2000 corporations who needed to deliver critical information to key personnel at a specific time and in a specific format. DynaBase was a content management and dynamic publishing system for the web that was launched in 1997. This integrated web publishing tool was designed for teams of people who were building and maintaining large, dynamic web sites. It provided customers with an open, standards-based, and fully integrated web publishing system for developing, managing, automating, and dynamically publishing high-impact, professional web sites. Inso estimated that some 100,000 web sites could benefit from this product.

As the web publishing market continued to grow, DynaBase was expected to be Inso's fastest-growing product ever. Strong opportunities existed for Inso to help its customers convert from authoring formats to industry-standard structured formats using HTML Export, XML Export, and DynaTag, the basis for Inso's Dyna family of information management and distribution products.

Shortly after DynaBase was introduced, Inso successfully sold it to a variety of book publishers, magazine publishers, newspaper publishers, new media and television publishers, and financial services publishers. *Network Computing* magazine gave the product a favorable review, saying "Of the products we put to the test in our labs, Inso Corp.'s DynaBase offers the most complete solution for managing web documents, developing dynamic pages and publishing Web sites." DynaBase would win *Network Computing'*s "Best Web Content Management Software" award in 1997 and again in 1998. Version 3.0 of the DynaBase web content management and dynamic web publishing system was introduced in August 1998.

During 1997 Inso held Customer Council meetings with corporate clients and discovered that the company's potential clients were interested in building strategic relationships with Inso. Inso was perceived by them as a leading provider of electronic publishing solutions. As a result, purchases of the company's EPS products were increasingly being made as part of an overall solution.

Toward the end of 1997, the company introduced the industry's first end-to-end XML (eXtensible Markup Language) publishing solution, which incorporated Inso's Dynamic Document Exchange and Electronic Publishing Solutions products. It was driven by the need for customers to get more out of their web applications. Inso was already shipping products with full support for XML when its competitors were just beginning to demonstrate support for this new development in web language after HTML.

Inso's Data Migration Initiative, based in Boston, was established to facilitate the migration of business information from proprietary formats, such as WordPerfect, Word, and other word processing formats, to standard structured formats. During 1997 the company made progress in developing this enabling technology with contributions from several of Inso's development centers.

Several new versions of the company's Dynamic Document Exchange products were released in 1997, including both Outside In and Quick View Plus. Outside In was the company's family of file-viewing, filtering, and conversion technologies that supported conversion to HTML of more than 200 file formats. In addition to being used in the company's electronic publishing solutions products, it was also incorporated in Microsoft Windows 95 and 98, Lotus Notes, Novell GroupWise, Oracle InterOffice, and other products.

Acquisition Program Continued Through 1998

In March 1998 Inso acquired the privately held ViewPort Development AB of Sweden for $2.5 million in cash. Through its wholly owned subsidiary Synex Information AB, ViewPort was a developer of browser engines and application development toolkits for viewing SGML information. Synex became part of the Inso Electronic Publishing Solutions development organization and continued to operate as a wholly owned subsidiary from its headquarters in Stockholm, Sweden. Inso estimated it would take an acquisition charge of about $2 million for acquired technologies still under research and development.

In April 1998 Inso sold its linguistic software assets to Lernout & Hauspie Speech Products N.V. It marked the divestiture of what Inso termed its ''legacy products,'' products that represented Inso's core business when it was established as an independent company. Inso recognized a gain of $12 million on the sale.

In August 1998 Inso extended the range of electronic publishing solutions it could offer customers with the acquisition of the MediaBank media asset management system and related technologies from Bitstream, Inc. for $12 million in cash. The acquisition would enable Inso to extend its reach into the graphics communications market. The MediaBank system covered a wide range of media elements, including text, documents, images, movies, graphics, sounds, and fonts used in the publishing process. At the same time, Inso announced that BitStream

would license Inso its forthcoming PageFlex client/server software application, which enabled the design and production of customized and personalized documents for one-to-one information publishing. Inso also acquired InterSEP OPI (Open Prepress Interface) server, an image replacement technology used to accelerate the handling of high-resolution images in publishing workgroups.

To further enhance the value of DynaBase, its web content management and publishing system, Inso began entering into technology and marketing partnerships with other vendors of web-based products. In September 1998 it announced agreements with four leading vendors whose products would be compatible with DynaBase's web content management and dynamic publishing platforms. Engage Technologies, a subsidiary of CMG Information Services, Inc., was a vendor of online advertising management and visitor profiling technologies. Through its agreement with Inso, it would extend the personalization and advertising features of DynaBase 3.0. NewsEdge Corporation, a leading provider of global news and current awareness solutions for business, would offer its NewsEdge Review Topics to DynaBase customers for automated intranet and extranet distribution using DynaBase 3.0. Publishing Connections, Inc., a systems integration firm specializing in pagination and web publishing systems, would enable DynaBase customers to automate the web publishing of print-oriented content through conversion into XML. The fourth partner, Resonate Inc., specialized in enterprise traffic management solutions that enabled multiple Internet servers to act as a single Internet server system. Through its partnership with Inso, Resonate would allow Inso's customers to increase the speed and throughput of DynaBase by using server and web site information to intelligently direct traffic using multiple servers.

In September 1998 Inso introduced the Outside In Server 1.0 for integration with Netscape and Microsoft web servers. The editors of the *Seybold Report on Internet Publishing* selected the new server for a ''Seybold Editors' Hot Pick Award.'' The server automatically converted, on demand, more than 200 Windows, UNIX, Mac, and DOS file formats into HTML, GIF, and JPEG, so that documents could be written and maintained in their native formats and also be made instantly accessible as high-quality HTML pages to web browser users.

Company's Outlook

As 1998 drew to a close, Inso did not see the need to move into substantially new technology areas in the near future. The company felt there were significant growth opportunities in its current markets and was planning to devote its resources to providing those markets with more products in its Dynamic Document Exchange and Electronic Publishing Solutions businesses. Inso was poised to take advantage of several trends. These included the increasing size and complexity of corporate web sites, the evolution and growing momentum of the XML standards, and the continuing rapid increase of the use of e-mail. Each of those trends would increase the market opportunities for Inso's Dynamic Document Exchange and Electronic Publishing Solutions products. However, as the company noted in its annual report, it faced competition from both larger and smaller firms in both areas.

Principal Subsidiaries

Inso Chicago Corporation; Inso Dallas Corporation; Inso Florida Corporation; Inso Kansas City Corporation; Inso Providence Corporation; Information Please LLC (19.8%).

Further Reading

"Inso Announces Availability of Version 3.0 of the Award-Winning DynaBase Web Content Management and Dynamic Web Publishing System," company news release, August 24, 1998.

"Inso Announces Outside In Server, the Industry's First Solution for On-Demand Conversion to HTML of Virtually Any Business Document," *PR Newswire,* September 1, 1998.

"Inso Announces Quick View Plus 5.0 Enterprise Edition," *PR Newswire,* September 8, 1998.

"Inso Corporation Announces Second Quarter Results," company news release, July 16, 1998.

"Inso Corporation Announces Technology and Marketing Partnerships with Engage Technologies, NewsEdge Corp., Publishing Connections, Inc., and Resonate Inc.," *PR Newswire,* September 1, 1998.

"Inso Corporation Acquires MediaBank from Bitstream Inc.," *PR Newswire,* August 28, 1998.

"Inso Corporation Acquires Synex Information AB," *PR Newswire,* March 12, 1998.

"Inso's DynaBase Integrated Web Publishing System Wins a Network Computing Magazine 'Well-Connected' Award," Boston: Inso Corporation, May 11, 1998.

"Products of the Year: Inso Dynabase," *Network Computing,* May 15, 1998.

Savage, Betty, "Inso Corporation Acquires MasterSoft Products from Adobe Systems," *PR Newswire,* February 5, 1997.

—David Bianco

Jacobs Engineering Group Inc.

111 S. Arroyo Parkway
Pasadena, California 91105
U.S.A.
(626) 578-3500
Fax: (626) 578-6916

Public Company
Incorporated: 1957 as Jacobs Engineering Co.
Employees: 9,600
Sales: $2.1 billion (1998)
Stock Exchanges: New York
Ticker Symbol: JEC
SICs: 8711 Engineering Services; 8741 Management
    Services; 7349 Building Maintenance Services, Not
    Elsewhere Classified

Jacobs Engineering Group Inc. designs, builds, and operates on a contract basis a wide variety of processing plants primarily for use in the petroleum, minerals, and environmental waste industries. Jacobs Engineering was moving in the 1990s from a medium niche in the world of industrial engineering to compete with such giants as Fluor Corporation and Bechtel Corporation on major domestic and international projects. Jacobs Engineering provided an unmatched rate of return on equity for its shareholders in the late 1990s and, most remarkably, carried no long-term debt.

Company Origins

Of Lebanese descent, Joseph J. Jacobs viewed his own entrepreneurial success in the context of the traditional emphasis among the Lebanese on commerce and self-reliance. Jacobs grew up in Brooklyn, New York, the son of a Lebanese notions peddlar who became wealthy during World War I by selling straight razors. When the safety razor was subsequently invented the Jacobs family fortune went downhill and young Joseph Jacobs was forced to scramble for extra dollars wherever he could. With strong encouragement from his mother, Jacobs

stayed in school and eventually graduated from the Polytechnic Institute of Brooklyn in 1937 with a degree in engineering.

Unable to find steady work in the midst of the Great Depression, Jacobs began teaching at Polytechnic while working on advanced degrees. In 1942, he earned a doctorate in chemical engineering and took a position as senior chemical engineer at Merck & Company in Rahway, New Jersey, where he was involved in the development of vitamin processing and the manufacture of DDT and penicillin. Strongly influenced by the Lebanese tradition of being in business for oneself, Jacobs started his own business in 1947 following a stint at Chemurgic Corporation in Richmond, California. Founding the Jacobs Engineering Company as both a consulting agency and as a manufacturers' representative for makers of large-scale equipment in the processing industry, Jacobs relocated the firm to Pasadena in anticipation of the phenomenal growth that would soon occur in southern California.

Because of a potential conflict of interest between his role as consultant and his work as a broker, Jacobs took pains to advise his clients of his dual professions and to maintain the highest possible standards of integrity with both groups of business associates. Regarding honesty as one of the basic tenets of his business philosophy, Jacobs told the Newcomen Society in 1980, ''Play it straight, deal with honesty and integrity, and you'll get your share. My Lebanese heritage . . . is never really very far from me.''

At first, the sales work expanded more quickly than the consulting end of the business, and by 1954 Jacobs had added four more men to handle sales while he and Stan Krugman concentrated on design consultation. Among their initial consulting clients were such companies as Eston Chemical, Southwest Potash Company (later AMAX Inc.), and Kaiser Aluminum & Chemical, for which Jacobs Engineering provided varied services including feasibility studies, the analysis of proposed new processes, and the development of flowsheets.

Larger Contracts in the 1950s and 1960s

In 1956 Jacobs Engineering landed its largest contract to date. Kaiser Aluminum, wishing to build a new and quite large

220

alumina plant for which its own in-house engineers lacked the requisite technological experience, asked Jacobs Engineering to assume design responsibilities for the project. Although this was new territory and represented a somewhat daunting venture, Jacobs Engineering did the job, hiring an extra 20 designers to help with the complex project, and Kaiser built it as specified and to the satisfaction of everyone involved. Moreover, a decade later when Kaiser wanted to expand the plant threefold they called in Jacobs Engineering to come up with the additional designs. In 1960, Jacobs Engineering won another important contract, this time from Southwest Potash for the design and construction of a potash flotation plant. Until this point in the company's history, Jacobs Engineering had not taken on any construction work, regarding the industry as unprofessional. However, the job for Southwest Potash dispelled that idea for Joseph Jacobs, and his company then offered a full range of both engineering and construction services.

A near disaster in 1962 illustrated the qualities that enabled Jacobs Engineering to grow from a tiny local outfit to one of international importance. The company built another plant for Southwest Potash, this one in Vicksburg, Mississippi, which was equipped with a novel process for making potassium nitrate. When the plant developed serious problems shortly after start-up, Jacobs and a team of his top engineers moved to Vicksburg for six months so that the problems could be corrected as quickly as possible. After months of intensive repair work the plant proved to be of sound design, making Southwest Potash a happy customer and adding to Jacobs Engineering's growing reputation for going the extra distance to achieve its clients' full satisfaction. It was a demonstration of commitment and agility that few of the larger companies in the field could have matched, and on such quality performances Jacobs Engineering based its growth.

Parlaying its reputation for hard work and integrity into a period of sustained growth during the 1960s, Jacobs Engineering snatched smaller contracts away from the industry's larger competitors and convinced larger potential customers of their capabilities. By 1967 Jacobs Engineering had opened offices around the country, encouraging each to emulate the main office's entrepreneurial bent and willingness to take risks and assume responsibility. Joseph Jacobs' hope was that each of the branch offices would duplicate the parent company's own strengths, and by and large they were able to do so. By 1970 Jacobs Engineering had grown to the point where it was advantageous to take the company public. Primarily as a way of rewarding employees with stock options, Jacobs Engineering went public; however, the founder's family maintained control of approximately 40 percent of the stock, and the company tried to retain the atmosphere of a family-run business.

Continued Expansion in the 1970s

Sales in 1972 reached $70 million and Jacobs Engineering began to pursue international as well as domestic contracts. As early as 1964, Jacobs Engineering had been interested in a projected potash recovery plant to be built by Jordan on the Dead Sea. Trading on the experience gained in working for Southwest Potash, Jacobs Engineering was selected to prepare a technical evaluation of the project and, after a decade-long hiatus due to the Arab-Israeli war of 1967, eventually signed a contract to design and build a $450 million plant for the Jordanian government. According to *Business Week,* Joseph Jacobs, speaking fluent Arabic, was instrumental in landing this huge job. The project was handled by Jacobs Engineering's international division based in Dublin, Ireland, which subcontracted much of the heavy construction work to a British company. Because Jacobs Engineering handled the assignment without a hitch, it was asked upon completion in the late 1970s to operate the plant as well.

Merging with the Pace Companies of Houston, Texas, in 1974, Jacobs Engineering recorded skyrocketing sales of $250 million in fiscal 1977, quadruple that of five years earlier. The Pace Companies brought to Jacobs Engineering a strong presence in the Gulf Coast industries of petroleum refining and petrochemicals, which remained staple ingredients of Jacobs Engineering's revenue mix thereafter. With the addition of Pace and its resounding success in the Middle East, Jacobs (which changed its name to Jacobs Engineering Group) set its sights on yet bigger game, hoping one day to rival industry leaders such as Fluor and Bechtel.

Believing that his company had become too large to remain under his personal guidance, Joseph Jacobs made several attempts in the late 1970s to delegate executive authority along the lines favored by his much larger competitors. In 1976 Jacobs hired the first of a series of company presidents and later added a string of executive vice-presidents intended to help the firm pursue further large international contracts like the Jordanian potash project. "Jacobs' concern with management may be coming just in time," wrote *Business Week,* a sentiment shared by those who believed that a single entrepreneur could not handle the administration of a mature corporation.

Subsequent events proved that thinking wrong, at least in the case of Jacobs Engineering. As Joseph Jacobs reduced his involvement in day-to-day management, the company went after ever larger contracts just as the country plunged into the severe recession of 1982–83. Profits shrank and then disappeared in a small but steady wave of red ink, while revenues fell by an astonishing 50 percent to around $200 million in 1984. The cause of this disaster was twofold. The sudden infusion of extra management saddled the company with a high overhead; worse yet, the enlarged executive staff naturally sought to justify its existence by a corresponding increase in revenues. Jacobs Engineering found itself bidding on so-called fixed-price contracts, as opposed to cost-reimbursable jobs favored by Joseph Jacobs. In the weak economic conditions, competition was brutal for the available fixed-price contracts, which typically included the gigantic engineering projects now pursued by Jacobs Engineering. Thus, Jacobs Engineering was awarded a smaller number of larger-than-average contracts yielding little if any profit.

Scaling Back in the 1980s

Distressed by swollen overhead costs and managerial complacency, in 1985 Joseph Jacobs came "roaring back from retirement," as *Forbes* put it, to save his once gleaming creation. The chairman fired almost half of the company's 2,300 employees, including 8 of 14 vice-presidents, and generally returned the company to its old-fashioned methods of the previous three decades—a time when "we made all our decisions standing in the hall," as Jacobs told *ENR* magazine. Starting with a fresh determination not to bid on fixed-price contracts regardless of their appeal, Jacobs Engineering ceded the biggest projects to its bigger rivals, concentrating instead on medium-sized process plants and specialty construction, such as a research and development center for Lockheed Missiles and Space Company in Austin, Texas, a $65 million project, and an addition to the Community Hospital of San Gabriel, California, costing around $20 million. In particular, Jacobs Engineering began lobbying for the many projects suddenly available in the area of environmental safety and clean-up, which typically require a high level of technical competence but not necessarily a contractor of great size. In other words, Joseph Jacobs left to his competitors the battle for mere revenue dollar volume and restored his company's emphasis on what he called the "net return on brainpower"—a ratio based on the amount of profit divided by number of employees to measure the profitable productivity per each of his highly skilled engineers.

The results of this program were astonishing. Between 1987 and 1991 Jacobs Engineering returned an industry best 22.4 percent on shareholders equity while also managing to increase sales by an average of 37 percent annually, which also topped the industry by a wide margin—all this without incurring any long-term debt. Annual reports in the early 1990s revealed that the company had literally zero debt; according to a 1992 *Forbes* index of leading engineering firms which listed the median debt to capital ratio as 25 percent, with several companies reporting figures well over 40 percent, Jacobs Engineering's ratio was given as 0.0 percent.

In the early 1990s, Jacobs Engineering Group enjoyed a balanced sales mix, having long since shed its former dependence on the petroleum industry. Again, with the emphasis on smaller, high-tech, higher margin contracts, Jacobs Engineering provided a broad variety of engineering services. From its earlier work in the minerals, fertilizers, and petrochemical segments, Jacobs Engineering had diversified into the areas of pharmaceuticals, biotechnology, and sterile facilities, along with the already mentioned opportunities in environmental protection projects. The company was the third largest domestic hazardous waste contractor, with 25 percent of its professional staff dedicated to environmentally driven projects. A 1987 buyout of Robert E. McKee Corporation (formerly the construction arm of Santa Fe Southern Pacific Corporation) gave the company added strength in the construction end of its business.

In 1992 Jacobs stepped down as CEO, and Noel Watson, an employee at Jacobs Engineering for 32 years, replaced him at the head of the company. Watson focused the company on two of its most profitable and growing segments: government-financed environmental cleanup jobs and facilities design and construction for the biopharmaceutical industry. In 1993 ten percent of Jacobs' annual revenue came from government contracts, but those contracts generated 20 percent of the company's pretax profits. Jacobs pursued this area in the mid-1990s with several government projects. In a joint venture with industry leader Fluor, Jacobs was awarded a contract in 1993 to clean up former uranium production facilities in Fernold, Ohio. The $2.2 billion contract was expected to generate as much as $40 million in profit for Jacobs. The company was also developing

clean-up plans with the U.S. Navy for several sites in the southwestern United States and with the Department of Energy for a weapons plant in Colorado. With clean-ups at military bases and weapons sites on the rise, Jacobs anticipated its environmental division would grow 20 to 30 percent a year throughout the 1990s.

Expansion in the 1990s

Watson also targeted the biotech industry for further investment. As the young biotech industry matured in the 1990s, Jacobs Engineering wanted to be in the position to build the specialized plants they would need for product development To that end, Jacobs purchased Triad Technologies and Sigel Group in the early 1990s, two companies that expanded Jacobs' expertise in designing and constructing biotechnology facilities.

Once again aiming to compete with the industry leaders, Jacobs needed a stronger presence internationally. With foreign contracts accounting for only 16 percent of Jacobs' annual revenues in 1992, Jacobs lagged far behind the overseas activity of rivals Foster Wheeler, Fluor, and Bechtel. To narrow the gap, Jacobs purchased the U.K. companies H&G Process Contracting and H&G Contractors in 1993. Humphreys & Glasgow, as the companies were collectively known, were among Europe's most widely recognized contractors.

By 1993 the company had fully recovered from the hard years of the mid-1980s. Not only did the company earn $6.5 million on revenues of $26.6 million in fiscal 1992, but it also held a record backlog of $1.8 billion in contracted business.

Some of that profitability went toward funding further acquisitions. In 1994 Jacobs bought CRS Sirrine Engineers and CRSS Constructors for $38 million. The purchase moved Jacobs Engineering into design and construction for the paper and semiconductor industries. Although the company paused to catch its breath in 1995 and make headway on its backlog, in 1996 Jacobs' acquisitions spree continued. That year it further expanded its presence in Europe by purchasing 49 percent of Serete Group, an engineering company that primarily served in the government sector and specialized in communications. In 1997 Jacobs formed a joint venture with Stone & Webster that would also extend its reach internationally. Named Stone & Webster/Humphreys & Glasgow Ltd., the venture would design and construct power plants in India. The same year, Jacobs purchased CPR Engineering and incorporated the specialist in paper plant engineering as a division.

As Jacobs Engineering grew in size, it maintained an impressive performance record. In 1997 it boasted an almost 16 percent five-year return on capital, and it beat out its rivals in terms of sales growth: a five-year average of 12.4 percent. For fiscal year 1998 the company reported record revenues of $2.1 billion and record net income of $54 million. The company expected a continued rise in revenues and income based on its backlog of $3.33 billion.

Late in 1998 Jacobs was discussing a possible merger with Sverdrup Corporation; if the merger were accomplished the resulting company would have 1998 revenues of approximately $3 billion. According to Watson, "Together, we would immediately emerge as a national leader in three very important and expanding markets: public sector buildings, civil engineering and infrastructure, and federal sector operations and maintenance.''

Principal Subsidiaries

Jacobs Constructors, Inc.; J.E. Merit Constructors, Inc.; Robert E. McKee, Inc.; Jacobs Applied Technology, Inc.; The Pace Consultants, Inc.; Triad Technologies, Inc.; Payne & Keller Company, Inc.

Further Reading

Barnett, Chris, ''Managing by Instinct,'' *Nation's Business,* December, 1985.
''Jacobs Buys Santa Fe's McKee,'' *ENR,* July 30, 1987.

''Jacobs Engineering's Goal: Quintupling by 1986,'' *ENR,* August 13, 1981.
''Jacobs Engineering Enters Merger Talks with Sverdrup Corp.,'' *Wall Street Journal,* November 6, 1998, p. A8.
''Jacobs Eyes Smaller Jobs,'' *ENR,* December 2, 1982.
Jacobs, Joseph J., *Jacobs Engineering Group Inc.: A Story of Pride, Reputation and Integrity,* New York: Newcomen Society in North America, 1980.
''A Loner Relaxes His Grip,'' *Business Week,* November 21, 1977.
Lubove, Seth, ''Thank You, Jack Welch,'' *Forbes,* January 13, 1997, pp. 102–03.
Poole, Claire, ''Faster, Better, Cheaper,'' *Forbes,* January 6, 1992.
''Potash Project Taps Dead Sea Salts,'' *ENR,* May 28, 1981.
Taylor, John H., ''After the Pink Slips,'' *Forbes,* August 2, 1993, p. 51.

—Jonathan Martin
—updated by Susan Windisch Brown

J&R Electronics Inc.

23 Park Row
New York, New York 10038
U.S.A.
(212) 938-2000
(800) 221-8180
Fax: (212) 238-9191
Web site: http://www.jandr.com

Private Company
Incorporated: 1971
Employees: 600
Sales: $283 million (1997 est.)
SICs: 5731 Radio, Television & Consumer Electronics
   Stores; 5734 Computer & Computer Software Stores

J&R Electronics Inc. is the largest home entertainment/computer superstore completely based in New York City. This privately owned company includes J&R Computer World and J&R Music World. J&R's retail outlets are all located on one short street in downtown Manhattan.

From Audio to Office Products and Computers: 1971–89

The business was founded as an audio equipment store in 1971 by Joe Friedman, an electrical engineer, and his wife Rachelle, a chemistry student at Brooklyn's Polytechnic Institute of New York, who later described herself and her husband as "two newlyweds who really knew little about business." Founding the company with money they received as wedding gifts, they located it in a 500-square-foot storefront at 33 Park Row, on the northern edge of Manhattan's financial district and just to the south of City Hall Park. "I would set up experiments, come down to the store for two hours, stay there alone, then rush back, and finish my experiments," Rachelle Friedman reminisced in 1995. "My husband used to come down on his lunch hour. If we both weren't there, the store was closed."

The Friedmans soon learned that their audio customers also were seeking phonograph records. They rented a space in the basement of the building and began taking orders, quickly developing a reputation as a source for hard-to-find classical and jazz records. Whether selling audio equipment or records, it was not uncommon in J&R's early days for either husband or wife to hop in their car and drive to a distributor to pick up a single item for a single customer. They spent their first Christmas Eve in the business gift-wrapping items people had placed on hold or purchased with a small deposit.

Rachelle Friedman started J&R's catalog business in 1974, and it soon proved a big success. Meanwhile, Joe Friedman was stocking the store with more equipment, which in turn required more space. In 1979 the couple acquired 23 Park Row, moved their operations to the new location, and opened what would become a consumer electronics superstore. In 1980 they added game-oriented, low-end computers to their stock, and in 1984 they filled a small section of the store with telephones, telephone answering devices, and key business systems. J&R's inventory of office business products quickly expanded with the addition of fax machines, cellular phones, and word processors. In time, this department also added specialty phones, typewriters, calculators, and copiers.

Further Expansion: 1989–95

Eventually the Friedmans came to feel that they would not succeed in the computer field unless they moved computers into a separate environment with separate salespeople. Accordingly, in 1989 J&R moved its computers and videos from the lower level of the main store to 15,000 square feet in 15 Park Row, a stationery supply building two doors distant. This space included a showroom in the back corner featuring 40 ergonomically designed workstations with full computer/printer setups, a mezzanine devoted to software, books, and magazines, and a "tech room" staffed by five computer specialists offering advice on troubleshooting and networking. The decor was an arrangement of gray carpet, shiny steel surfaces, and low-level lighting designed for a comfortable environment. The grand opening of what was named J&R Computer World was held in 1990.

Another section of the main floor of the new building was devoted to J&R's office equipment, including a select line of home-office furniture and office stationery supplies (the latter dropped in 1991). There also was an ample stock of fax machines, telephones, answering machines, copiers, computer printers, word processors and a few electronic typewriters, electronic organizers, and calculators. The relocation included a freestanding security system that eliminated the need to place models in display cases where shoppers were unable to touch and test them. The spacious basement of the new location was earmarked for inventory.

At some point in the early 1980s, inspired by the breakup of AT&T Corp., J&R opened a "phone outlet" next to the main store, so with the addition of Computer World the enterprise now consisted of three buildings with some 85,000 square feet of retail space divided into special stores for audio and video hardware, portable electronics products, car stereos, telephones, home-office equipment, computers, popular music, jazz, and classical music. "The record companies are always telling us to open other stores, but we have a different philosophy than other retailers," Rachelle Friedman told a reporter. "We want to be the best we can be by staying on the block rather than becoming a chain. This way we maintain control, which the chain stores lose. . . . When we used to visit chain stores, we felt that the boss doesn't work there, and it showed."

By the end of the 1980s J&R's mail-order service had grown to require 40 salespeople handling toll-free telephone-number inquiries and orders. To serve these customers, J&R had added a 75,000-square-foot warehouse across the street from its original 50,000-square-foot facility in Maspeth, Queens. The company was distributing one million catalogs every three months, plus variations that were being issued every six weeks.

J&R celebrated its 20th anniversary in 1991 with a two-day cruise that brought all of the company's 400-odd employees together. The Friedmans disclosed that the main store would be gutted and expanded, resulting in a 45,000-square-foot music superstore with such amenities as listening posts and a stage for in-store performances.

From her fourth floor office, Rachelle Friedman could hear every announcement made over the loudspeaker; she also walked around, checking on operations and greeting customers. Her husband was even more peripatetic, maintaining no office and making the rounds of the entire complex. *Billboard* estimated J&R's music revenues in 1990 at $20 million, with 75 percent generated from the store and the other 25 percent from mail-order, which included a wholesale division. Although compact discs were the main recorded-music item, J&R also at this time maintained a large budget section for vinyl LPs and 45s, cassettes, and videos.

J&R Computer World was proving to be a success, with Wall Street brokers and investment bankers crowding into the store at midday to get time on one of the 40 state-of-the-art PC workstations. Chrome-appointed columns, glass brick, and neon were being employed to impart an upscale, high-tech ambience, and promotional films ran on video monitors suspended overhead. "Everything is shown, everything is user-friendly, everything is touchable from the hardware to the software," said the company's marketing manager.

Monitors were connected to a common system, showing the same image for comparison. Nearly 50 salespeople were working on commission. Three technicians were available to configure systems and offer follow-up support. Through a service firm, J&R also offered home repair and maintenance. The store was a factory-authorized dealer for most leading computer brands. The mezzanine carried 5,000 software titles. J&R Computer World also leased equipment and had a corporate sales department, with conference rooms off the main sales floor.

By 1993 J&R had moved into a fourth building on Park Row, with a total of 100,000 square feet of selling area divided into four music software outlets, a main electronics outlet, a video outlet, a portable electronics outlet, the computer store, and a home-office store. The mail-order business now was shipping about 1.5 million catalogs every six weeks. The Friedmans, while not disclosing figures, acknowledged that sales and profits had grown in every year of the business's operation, despite the 1987 Wall Street crash and the 1980–82 and 1990–91 recessions.

To publicize its wares through print advertisements, J&R was employing a targeted rather than scattershot approach. Music offerings, for example, appeared on the back page of the *New York Times* Sunday arts and entertainment section, and computers and related equipment took up most of the back page of the Tuesday science and Friday business sections of the *Times*. On weekends, J&R's reputation for rock-bottom prices drew a different crowd in sneakers and jeans. Speaking of lower Manhattan, Joe Friedman said, "This area is totally dead on Saturday and Sunday, but those are our busiest days because people come from other areas of the city. It shows we are a destination store." By 1995 the National Association of Record Merchandisers twice had given J&R its Retailer of the Year award.

In the Sunday *Times* Styles section, Liz Logan reported in 1993 that she visited J&R Office World—the home-office store—looking for a telephone answering machine. She found the gray-carpeted, gray-walled interior "curiously soothing" and was pleasantly surprised to encounter salespeople who were "neither elusive nor pushy—just there, waiting to help. . . . When, after preliminary browsing, I was ready to be helped, a salesman answered my questions and volunteered useful information without a trace of hucksterism." She concluded, "The thing that I'm still amazed about is this: Nobody at J&R tried to sell me a warranty extension."

In 1992 J&R purchased another building on Park Row to convert into a separate audiovisual store, housing about 25,000 square feet of hardware. With the opening at Christmas 1993, the existing audio store was converted to a single 45,000-square-foot audio and video software store—the largest in New York, according to Rachelle Friedman. The new store enabled J&R to demonstrate high-end audio entertainment and home theater in floor displays and to include more audio and video soundrooms.

A cosponsor of the 1995 world chess championship in New York City, J&R reported strong demand and increased sales in products directly connected to the event, including all chess software, CD-ROM software, and self-standing chess games. The competition was held at the observation deck of the World Trade Center, only a short walk from Park Row. J&R banners were prominent at the match site, even inside the soundproof glass-walled room where champion Garry Kasparov dueled challenger Viswanathan Anand. A booth on the southern side of the floor featured mail-order catalogs, product literature, and a Sony Magic Link desktop communicator/organizer demonstration unit.

Spreading Out Still Further, 1997–98

In 1997 J&R enlarged the main music store from two floors to five and built an addition to the computer/home-office store. This brought the retailer's floor area to 300,000 square feet. Also that year, J&R demolished the nine-story Clark Building at the corner of Park Row and Ann Street, just west of 15 Park Row, to make way for a new building to house a major expansion of its computer and home-office holdings. The destruction of the ornate, 103-year-old building provoked anger among preservationists, who had urged the Friedmans, in vain, to try to preserve the building's facade and renovate the interior for the new store.

J&R's plan called for a six- or seven-story building with 50,000 square feet of space, to be constructed in its place and to open in 1999. The building, which was to house products geared to the small-office/home-office consumer, initially was to be called Office World, but J&R came to believe Computer World better encompassed the wide variety of products found in both areas, including multifunction units, copiers, and video-conferencing equipment, as well as PCs and accessories. J&R also was planning to harmonize its music stores in a new, high-tech design.

J&R's warehouses also were expanded in the 1990s, reaching 210,000 square feet of space for mail-order and shipping operations. Aside from the original one-story building and the five-story loft-building addition, the company in 1997 bought 80,000 square feet in a one-story building adjoining the original one. High ceilings, convenient loading docks, and adequate parking were the main attractions of the new site.

In the fall of 1998 J&R's retail outlets were situated in eight buildings that occupied most of Park Row. On the eastern end, 33 Park Row housed classical music offerings, including compact and laser discs, cassettes, and video. The store at 31 Park Row held video and audio, including television sets and video-cassette recorders, camcorders, and both video and audio furniture and accessories. The space at 27 Park Row stocked small appliances, personal care, and home security items, exercise equipment, watches, and keyboards. Jazz compact discs and cassettes were located at 25 Park Row. The main music store, at 23 Park Row, contained popular music compact discs, cassettes, and videotapes. The home-office store, 17 Park Row, housed telephones, answering machines, beepers, word processors, fax machines, calculators, copiers, databases, and pens. The computer store, 15 Park Row, held hardware, software, and multimedia.

Further Reading

Bessman, Jim, "For J&R Music, It's No Small World," *Billboard,* June 10, 1989, p. 60.
——, "J&R's Chess Match Co-Sponsorship Is a Strategic Retail Move," *Billboard,* October 14, 1995, p. 57.
Lewis, Jeff, "J&R Pushes Back Opening of an Expanded Store," *HFN/Home Furnishings News,* May 18, 1998, p. 49.
Logan, Liz, "A Cure for Answering-Machine Meltdown," *New York Times,* November 7, 1993, Sec. 9, p. 16.
Lueck, Thomas J., "Building Demolition Provokes a Clash with Preservationists," *New York Times,* March 6, 1997, p. B8.
McConville, James A., "Dynamic Duo," *HFD/Home Furnishings Daily,* January 18, 1993, pp. 69–71.
——, "J&R Computer World Aims for Perfect Fit," *HFD/Home Furnishings Daily,* May 28, 1990, p. 98.
——, "J&R to Open Computer/Home Office Store," *HFD/Home Furnishings Daily,* June 12, 1989, p. 98.
Oser, Alan S., "Short Spaces Stand Out in West Queens Market," *New York Times,* May 20, 1998, p. B8.
Sullivan, R. Lee, "Selling a Solution," *DM/Discount Merchandiser,* April 1991, pp. 56–57.
Verna, Paul, "J&R at 20: Mom-and-Pop Stop Goes On," *Billboard,* November 23, 1991, p. 45.
Wall, Craig, "How J&R Turned an Audio Den into a CE Superstore," *Dealerscope Merchandising,* August 1995, pp. 1+.

—Robert Halasz

Johnson Controls, Inc.

5757 North Green Bay Avenue
Post Office Box 591
Milwaukee, Wisconsin 53201-0591
U.S.A.
(414) 228-1200
Fax: (414) 228-2302
Web site: http://www.jci.com

Public Company
Incorporated: 1885 as Johnson Electric Service Company
Employees: 72,300
Sales: $12.59 billion (1998)
Stock Exchanges: New York
Ticker Symbol: JCI
SICs: 3429 Hardware, Not Elsewhere Classified; 3494
   Valves & Pipe Fittings, Not Elsewhere Classified;
   3495 Wire Springs; 3559 Special Industry Machinery,
   Not Elsewhere Classified; 3585 Air Conditioning,
   Warm Air Heating Equipment & Commercial &
   Industrial Refrigeration Equipment; 3613 Switchgear
   & Switchboard Apparatus; 3691 Storage Batteries;
   3822 Automatic Controls for Regulating Residential
   & Commercial Environments & Appliances; 3823
   Industrial Instruments for Measurement, Display &
   Control of Process Variables & Related Products

Johnson Controls, Inc. is a diversified company made up of two main business groups: automotive systems, including seating, overhead and instrument panels, doors, and batteries; and building management and control systems. Johnson is the world's largest independent maker of automotive seating and interior systems, and is a leading supplier of batteries for the original equipment and automotive replacement markets in North America. The company is number one worldwide in building control systems, services, and integrated facility management, serving school districts, hospitals, and other nonresidential building owners. The Automotive Systems Group generates nearly three-fourths of overall revenues, with the Controls Group responsible for the remainder. Over the course of more than a century, Johnson Controls has an impressive track record, including the consecutive payment of dividends since 1885 and 52 straight years of sales increases through fiscal 1998.

Origins in Control Devices

Warren Seymour Johnson was born in Rutland County, Vermont and grew up in Wisconsin. Johnson worked as a printer, surveyor, school teacher, and school superintendent before he was appointed a professor at the State Normal School in Whitewater, Wisconsin, in 1876. He was known as a highly original teacher but Johnson's main interest was his laboratory, where he experimented in electrochemistry. In 1883 he produced the first Johnson System of Temperature Regulation, an electric thermostat system which he installed at the State Normal School.

When Johnson received a patent for the electric telethermoscope, he persuaded Milwaukee, Wisconsin, hotelier and heir to the Plankinton Packing Company, William Plankinton, to become his financial backer in producing the device. Their partnership, the Milwaukee Electric Manufacturing Company, allowed Johnson to resign his professorship so he could devote all his time to his inventions. Although retired from teaching, he would always be called "the Professor." On May 1, 1885, the company was reorganized as the Johnson Electric Service Company, a Wisconsin corporation, in Milwaukee. Plankinton became president and Johnson, vice-president and treasurer.

The Professor continued to invent additional control devices, but he also designed products such as chandeliers, springless door locks, puncture-proof tires, thermometers, and a hose coupling for providing steam heat to passenger railcars. The creations for which the young company received the most recognition were the Professor's impressive tower clocks. He developed a system powered by air pressure that increased the reliability of such clocks. The company built its first big clock in 1895 for the Minneapolis courthouse and a year later built the clock for the Milwaukee City Hall tower. Johnson's largest tower clock was installed in the Philadelphia City Hall. A large-

---

Company Perspectives:

Johnson Controls, Inc.'s corporate objectives are Customer Satisfaction: we will exceed customer expectations through continuous improvement in quality, service, productivity, and time compression; Technology: we will apply world-class technology to our products, processes, and services; Growth: we will seek growth by building upon our existing businesses; Market Leadership: we will only operate in markets where we are, or have the opportunity to become, the recognized leader; Shareholder Value: we will exceed the median return on shareholders' equity of the Standard & Poor's Industrials.

---

scale floral clock for the Saint Louis World's Fair in 1904 received international acclaim and enhanced the growing reputation of the company. The clocks' success helped prove the usefulness of the pneumatic operations the company was utilizing in its control applications.

At the Paris World's Fair of 1900, Johnson's wireless-communication exhibit won second prize. In the same competition Guglielmo Marconi, developer of the wireless telegraph, placed third. The Professor, his sons, and inventor Charles Fortier began to test a variety of alloys in wireless sets. The men built a 115-foot tower several miles south of Milwaukee, but many attempts to transmit messages to the company's downtown factory were unsuccessful. Lee DeForest, whose audio tube would later provide the breakthrough for radio, also worked on the project.

Company directors elected Johnson president of the company in 1901, and a year later the firm's name was changed to Johnson Service Company. Even as president, Johnson was not able to convince the board to provide financial backing for his interest in establishing a national automobile company. Johnson saw the automobile as a way to ensure that the company was not completely dependent on temperature-regulating equipment. In 1907 he introduced a gasoline-powered engine. Johnson was the first to receive a U.S. contract to deliver mail with a horseless carriage. At the outset, according to an often-told story, the wary postmaster agreed to pay Johnson an amount equal to his horses' feed bills for the mail service. The company's failure to expand those automobile interests was a source of frustration to Johnson until his death in 1911. He had assigned more than 50 patents—most of them concerned with harnessing power generated by fluid, air, or steam pressure—to Johnson Service Company.

Harry W. Ellis was elected president in 1912. Ellis, who had been manager of the Chicago branch office, decided to concentrate on opportunities for growth in the controls field. He sold all of the company's other businesses, improved the efficiency of factory operations in Milwaukee, and introduced a modern accounting system.

In 1885, the year the company was incorporated, it had sold the rights to sell, install, and service its temperature-control-regulation systems to two firms. The firms did not perform up to expectations, but the situation was not changed for years. By 1912 Johnson had regained the rights to do business directly throughout the country and had established 18 U.S. branch offices, six Canadian offices, and direct agencies in Copenhagen, Berlin, Saint Petersburg, Manchester, and Warsaw.

Early 20th-Century Growth

The Professor had insisted that only trained Johnson mechanics could install his company's devices and Ellis reinforced this policy. He insisted that the company was to serve not just as a producer of regulation equipment but as a single source for design, installation, and service. Johnson's temperature-control business expanded in tandem with the country's building boom. Skyscrapers became popular as structural steel replaced iron and other building systems were refined. During World War I, the company's temperature-control business was classified by the War Industry Board as nonessential to the war effort, since it was seen as a means of providing comfort. Johnson contracts dropped off as civilian construction was sharply reduced. The firm looked to government buildings for business and began seeking contracts to retrofit old buildings with new temperature-control systems.

In 1919 the company's new contracts exceeded $1 million. Although a business depression meant that few new office buildings were being constructed, movie theaters, department stores, and restaurants were introducing air-cooled interiors. By 1928 the company's new contracts passed the $4 million mark.

The Great Depression dealt a serious blow to the construction industry, and most new building-control installations in the 1930s aimed for economy. Projects in schools and government buildings that were assigned by the Public Works Administration also had fuel savings as a goal. Johnson's new Dual Thermostat, which allowed a building to save fuel by automatically lowering temperatures at times when the building was unoccupied, was in demand.

Joseph A. Cutler was elected president of the company in 1938. A former engineering professor at the University of Wisconsin, his presidency, like Ellis's, would last almost 25 years.

After the United Stated entered World War II, Johnson was classified as part of an essential industry, evidence of the change in the way the public perceived building controls. Johnson's contributions to the war effort included installing temperature-and-humidity control systems in defense facilities and the engineering of special military products. The company also made leak detectors that were used to test barrage balloons used over military installations, ships, and landing barges; developed the radiosonde to help combat pilots encountering unknown flying conditions to gather weather data; and manufactured echo boxes, devices that tested radar sets.

Post-World War II Boom

After World War II ended, civilian construction boomed and with it the company's new contracts. Along with this boom came a renewed interest in air conditioning. By 1949 the company's sales were $10 million.

In 1956 Johnson began to build and install pneumatic control centers that allowed a single building engineer to monitor panels displaying room temperatures, ventilating conditions, water temperatures, and the outdoor temperature. To ensure a steady and reliable source of customized control panels for these centers, Johnson purchased a panel-fabrication company in Oklahoma in 1960. Operations at company headquarters in Milwaukee were also expanding, so the company bought and eventually expanded an additional building there for its brass foundry, metal fabrications, assembly operations, and machining work.

Richard J. Murphy was elected company president in 1960, the year the company celebrated its 75th anniversary. Murphy had started with the company as a timekeeper in 1918 and had moved up through the ranks. Although his presidency lasted only six years, he was responsible for many innovations. Murphy established an international division, with subsidiaries in England, France, Australia, Belgium, Italy, and Switzerland. Each international office was managed as a virtually independent business, as were operations in the United States and Canada. In 1964 construction of the first foreign manufacturing plant began in Italy.

Since World War II, Johnson had enjoyed an excellent reputation for its work in atomic research plants and other installations requiring exceptional levels of reliability. In 1961 the Systems Engineering & Construction Division was established. It provided equipment for all 57 Air Force Titan II launch complexes and most other major missile programs. The National Aeronautics and Space Administration contracted with Johnson throughout the 1960s for mission-control instrumentation for the Apollo-Saturn program.

In 1962 Johnson, along with its main competitors Honeywell and Powers Regulator, were charged in a federal antitrust suit with price-fixing in the sale of pneumatic temperature control systems. The suit's resolution in a consent decree, coupled with new competitors entering the controls market, meant increasingly competitive bidding. Johnson occasionally won contracts on which it ended up making little or no profit.

Acquisitions in the 1960s

By the early 1960s it became apparent to Johnson management that electronics technology could be used to control all aspects of maintaining a building. To improve its in-house electronics capability, the company purchased the electronics division of Fischbach & Moore in 1963. Because of its increasing involvement in projects requiring exacting quality standards and high-quality components, Johnson acquired Associated Piping & Engineering Corporation and Western Piping and Engineering Company in 1966. The companies fabricated expansion joints and piping for nuclear and fossil fuel generating plants and many other industrial applications.

Fred L. Brengel became the sixth Johnson president in 1967. He had joined the company as a sales engineer in 1948 and served as manager of the Boston branch office and sales manager of the New England and Midwest regions before becoming vice-president and general sales manager in 1963.

The same year Brengel was elected president, Johnson introduced the T-6000, a solid-state, digital data logger that used "management by exception"—the system announced when its variables were outside specified limits so an engineer's attention was only called for when needed. The T-6000 not only performed heating, ventilating, and air conditioning functions, but also monitored fire and smoke detection, security, and emergency lighting systems.

Just a year after Brengel assumed the presidency, Johnson acquired Penn Controls, a 50-year-old company that manufactured controls for original equipment manufacturers (OEMs), distributors, and wholesalers. With its Penn acquisition, Johnson improved its competitive edge by having its own supply of electrical products for installation projects. Penn also had manufacturing plants and subsidiaries in Canada, the Netherlands, Argentina, and Japan, which helped Johnson expand its international markets. The year it acquired Penn, the company's sales rose about 20 percent, to $155 million.

Johnson introduced the JC/80, the industry's first minicomputer system that managed building controls, in 1972. One of the many advantages of the JC/80 was that operators of the system needed only a minimal amount of technical training. The JC/80, which could cut fuel requirements by as much as 30 percent, was introduced at the ideal time, just a year before international embargoes on oil would change the way people viewed energy consumption. Virtually overnight, people became interested in reducing energy costs.

The company adopted its present name—Johnson Controls, Inc.—in 1974. By 1977 it had captured approximately 35 percent of the estimated $600 million market for commercial-building control systems. It had 114 branch offices in the United States and Canada and more than 300 service centers, staffed by 10,000 engineers, architects, designers, and service technicians. In spite of a worldwide recession, the company's sales rose to almost $500 million that year.

Expanded into Batteries in 1978

Although Johnson fared well in the boom market for energy conservation products, new companies were beginning to crowd the building-controls field. To diversify, the company merged with Globe-Union, the country's largest manufacturer of automotive batteries, in 1978.

Founded in Milwaukee in 1911, Globe Electric Company had as its original aim the fulfillment of the battery needs of streetcars, rural light plants, and switchboards. In 1925 Globe's treasurer, Chester O. Wanvig, entered an agreement with Sears, Roebuck and Company President General Robert Wood to produce automobile replacement batteries for the company. Globe shareholders declined the opportunity and Wanvig organized the Union Battery Company to serve Sears. In 1929 Globe Electric and Union Battery consolidated, with Wanvig as president. By the late 1930s Globe-Union had ten manufacturing plants across the United States.

In the late 1950s Globe-Union invented the thin-wall polypropylene battery container, a major technological breakthrough that won the company a leadership position in the industry. The thickness of the battery walls was reduced and the container was lighter and stronger than hard-rubber cases. In 1967 Sears used this technology in its DieHard battery, made by Globe-Union. By 1971 Globe-Union had become the largest U.S. manufacturer of automotive replacement batteries, with its sales climbing past $100 million that year. The company turned to nonautomotive battery applications in 1972 when it formed an industrial products unit. One of its best-known creations was the Gel/Cell, a line of sealed, portable lead acid units for the standby power needs of security and telecommunications applications.

Johnson's merger with Globe-Union doubled its sales, broadened its financial base, and gave it leadership in a new field. Three years after the merger, sales surpassed $1 billion. In the early 1980s Johnson took the lead in developing controls for "intelligent buildings," which featured state-of-the-art technology to manage energy, comfort, and protection needs. Despite the entrance of many new companies into this sector, Johnson remained a leader in the field. In the latter part of 1989, Johnson announced a joint venture with Yokogawa Electric Corporation to manufacture control instrumentation and to integrate and service industrial automation systems for the North American market.

Acquired Hoover Industrial in 1985

Johnson greatly expanded its automotive business in 1985 when it acquired Hoover Industrial, a major supplier of seating and plastic parts for automobiles and a new entrant in the plastic-container industry. Although company officials denied it, industry analysts speculated that the acquisition may have at least in part been an attempt to thwart a possible takeover attempt by Miami financier Victor Posner. One of Posner's companies owned almost 20 percent of Johnson in 1985.

At the time of its purchase, Hoover was changing its emphasis from supplying seating components to building completely assembled automotive seating. The company had an excellent reputation for its just-in-time delivery system, which meant the company supplied its automotive customers with needed parts and components precisely when they needed them to avoid customer storage charges.

The same year it purchased Hoover, Johnson also acquired Ferro Manufacturing Corporation, a supplier of automotive seating components and mechanisms. Hoover and Ferro units unrelated to Johnson's major businesses were sold shortly after the acquisitions were completed.

With its new components in place, Johnson became known as a parts supplier that could design, engineer, assemble, and deliver modular systems to their customers' plants "just-in-time." In addition to supplying components to the major domestic carmakers, Johnson also supplied several of the U.S. operations of Japanese auto manufacturers, including Toyota, Honda, and Nissan, and a Toyota-General Motors joint venture.

James H. Keyes was elected chief executive officer in 1988, after serving as president since 1986. A certified public accountant, he joined Johnson as an analyst in 1966 and held several key executive positions, including treasurer and chief operating officer.

Johnson expanded its plastics business in 1988 by acquiring Apple Container Corporation and the soft drink bottle operations of American National Can Company. In mid-1989 the company spent $166 million to purchase Pan Am World Services, a leading provider of high-tech and other facility-management services for military bases, airports, and space centers. This acquisition was intended to bolster Johnson's nascent business of providing engineering and protection services for commercial buildings.

Johnson's controls business had had an international presence, concentrated in Europe and the Far East, since the 1960s. During the mid-1980s Johnson also began to expand its plastic-container and seating businesses into Europe. This aggressive expansion was facilitated primarily through acquisitions. By 1990 Johnson claimed leadership positions in both markets.

In 1989, meanwhile, Johnson's battery group acquired Varta, the largest automotive-battery maker in Canada. That same year the battery division unveiled the EverStart, a new automotive battery that carried its own emergency backup power system. It was called the first real breakthrough in battery technology in decades.

Although there were rumors about possible takeovers of Johnson in the late 1980s, the company's management was committed to rebuffing all such attempts. President Keyes told *Forbes* in March 1989, "It depends on whether you take a short-term view and want to improve returns immediately, or you take a long-term view and seek to maintain market leadership. We've chosen the latter approach."

Automotive Systems Became Predominant in the 1990s

During the 1990s Johnson Controls' automotive businesses would become by far the company's most important business sector. The decade began, however, with the introduction of the Metasys facility management system. In development for three years at a cost close to $20 million, Metasys was a breakthrough system designed for buildings as small as 50,000 square feet and tied together the entire control system through a distributed computer-controlled network.

In 1991 Johnson acquired several European car seat component manufacturers, furthering its overseas expansion. That year also marked the company's involvement in a landmark sex discrimination lawsuit settled by the U.S. Supreme Court. During the 1980s Johnson Controls had switched from a voluntary to a mandatory policy barring women of childbearing age from jobs involving exposure to high levels of lead at its 15 car battery plants. The company was concerned that pregnant women exposed to a potentially harmful substance might sue if the exposure resulted in birth defects. The Supreme Court, however, in a 6–3 ruling, said that decisions about the welfare of future children "must be left to the parents who conceive, bear, support, and raise them rather than to the employers who hire those parents." The Court ruled that Johnson Control's policy was discriminatory against women and therefore could not stand.

Of all of the company's diversified operations, its battery unit was the least profitable, partly because prices for batteries had not increased in a decade, and partly because the unit's unionized plants had to compete with nonunion plants of other companies. In mid-1991 Johnson Controls attempted to sell the battery division but could not find a buyer. The unit was further battered when it lost its contract to supply DieHard batteries to Sears in late 1994. Since that time contracts were signed or renewed with such retailers as AutoZone and Wal-Mart, and the company also supplied the largest battery distributor in the nation, Interstate Battery System of America. In October 1997 a contract was signed to supply Sears with DieHard Gold batteries, the top of that product line. The battery unit also began to target overseas markets more aggressively, opening a plant in Mexico in 1994, forming a joint venture in China in 1996 to make batteries for Volkswagen, and creating another joint venture in 1997 with Varta Battery AG of Germany to make batteries in South America.

In the mid-1990s Johnson Controls made a number of significant acquisitions in the area of automotive systems that helped to greatly increase sales in the company's automotive segment—a 94 percent increase from 1995 to 1998 alone. In 1995 Johnson spent $175–$200 million for a 75 percent interest in Roth Freres SA, a Strasbourg, France-based major supplier of seating and interior systems to the European auto industry. In October 1996 the company paid about $1.3 billion for the Prince Automotive unit of Prince Holding Corporation in the largest acquisition in Johnson Controls history. Based in Holland, Michigan, Prince Automotive brought to Johnson an innovative supplier of automotive interior systems and components, such as interior ceilings, overhead consoles and switches, door panels, armrests, and floor consoles. The addition of Prince meant that Johnson Controls could now make virtually all major interior auto components.

Also in 1996 the company made a number of moves to expand in the Asia-Pacific region. A joint venture was formed in China with Beijing Automotive Industry Corp. to run a car seating and interior system factory in Beijing. Another joint venture was launched in India to supply seats and trim for Ford Escorts built there. In addition, Johnson Controls purchased Aldersons, a unit of Sydney, Australia-based Tutt Bryant Industries PLY Ltd. that supplied interior systems to Australia's four major automakers.

To help to pay down the heavy debt incurred by the purchase of Prince Automotive, Johnson Controls sold its plastic container division to Schmalbach-Lubeca AG/Continental Can Europe, a unit of German conglomerate Viag Group AG, for about $650 million in February 1997. That year also saw a major expansion of the company's automotive business in South America, where its number of plants increased from 2 to 11 during the year.

Joint ventures and acquisitions continued in 1998. In April the company announced the formation of a venture with Recaro North America Inc. (a unit of German seat manufacturer Recaro GmbH & Company) whereby Johnson Controls would supply brand-name specialty seats for the first time—under the Recaro brand. In July Johnson acquired the Becker Group, a supplier of interior systems in both North America and Europe, for $548 million and the assumption of debt. The addition of Becker propelled Johnson Controls to the number one position in Eu-

rope in interior systems. In a move to divest a noncore unit and to help pay down additional debt taken on to purchase Becker, Johnson Controls sold its plastics machinery business to Cincinnati Milacron Inc. for about $190 million in September 1998.

In July 1998, John M. Barth was named president and chief operating officer, with Keyes remaining chairman and CEO. For fiscal 1998 Johnson Controls reported record sales of $12.59 billion, an increase of 13 percent over the previous year, and record net income of $302.7 million, an increase of 16 percent. The company's emphasis on its more profitable Automotive Systems Group (over its Controls Group) and its aggressive expansion through acquisitions and joint ventures had served Johnson Controls well in the 1990s. If there was any cause for concern about the firm's future it was in the increased debt level Johnson Controls had incurred to fund this growth—total debt having more than doubled from fiscal 1994 to fiscal 1997.

Principal Subsidiaries

Apple Container Corp.; Becker Group; Creative Control Designs, Inc.; G-U Export, Inc.; Globe International Delaware, Inc.; Globe-Union, Inc.; Hoover Universal Inc.; Hyperion Corp.; IKIN L.L.C.; Interior Product Services, Inc.; Interstate Battery System International, Inc.; Intertec Systems L.L.C.; J.C. Capital Corporation; Johnson Control Products, Ltd.; Johnson Controls Battery Group, Inc.; Johnson Controls DISC, Inc.; Johnson Controls Engineering, Inc.; Johnson Controls Facilities, Inc.; Johnson Controls Holding Company, Inc.; Johnson Controls International, Inc.; Johnson Controls Investment Company, Inc.; Johnson Controls Management Company; Johnson Controls Management Systems, Inc.; Johnson Controls Network Integration Services, Inc.; Johnson Controls Nevada, Inc.; Johnson Controls Northern New Mexico L.L.C.; Johnson Controls Richland, Inc.; Johnson Controls Services Company; Johnson Controls Technology Company; Johnson Controls World Services Inc.; Johnson Controls-RMS, Inc.; Johnson International Trade Co.; Johnson Service Co.; Joventa USA Inc.; Maintenance Automation Corporation; NAV L.L.C.; NYLLE L.L.C.; P & ET Container, Inc.; Prince Corporation; Readiness Management Support L.C.; SAVID L.L.C.; SECH L.L.C.; Setex, Inc.; TechnoTrim, Inc.; Trim Masters Inc.; Vintec Co.; XYZ Container Corporation Johnson Controls lists additional subsidiaries in Argentina, Austria, Australia, Barbados, Belgium, Brazil, Canada, Cayman Islands, China, Czech Republic, France, Germany, Hong Kong, Hungary, India, Indonesia, Italy, Japan, Luxembourg, Malaysia, Mauritius, Mexico, Netherlands, Norway, Poland, Portugal, Singapore, Slovakia, South Africa, Spain, Sweden, Switzerland, Thailand, Turkey, United Kingdom, Venezuela, and the Virgin Islands.

Principal Operating Units

Automotive Systems Group; Controls Group.

Further Reading

Berss, Marcia, "Watizzit? Johnson Controls Is a Strange Mixture—Car Seats, Thermostats, Plastic Bottles, and Automobile Batteries. But It Works," *Forbes,* August 28, 1995, p. 100.

Byrne, Harlan S., "Johnson Controls: Strong Market Positions Help It Ride Out the Recession," *Barron's,* February 24, 1992, pp. 51–52.

Dubashi, Jagannath, "Slump Control: Johnson Controls Thought One Good Deal Would Eliminate Two Pet Peeves," *Financial World,* May 29, 1990, p. 49.

Gardner, Greg, "JCI Buys Itself a Prince," *Ward's Auto World,* August 1996, p. 35.

Marsh, Peter, "A Sitting Target for Two Rivals," *Financial Times,* April 15, 1996, p. 10.

——, "Standing Up to Seating Challenge," *Financial Times,* February 23, 1998, p. FTS7.

Miller, James P., "Johnson Controls' Container Business Will Be Sold to Unit of Germany's Viag," *Wall Street Journal,* December 10, 1996, p. A3.

Right for the Times: Johnson Controls 100th Anniversary, Milwaukee, Wis.: Johnson Controls, Inc., 1985.

Rose, Robert L., "Johnson Controls Agrees to Purchase of Becker Group," *Wall Street Journal,* April 28, 1998, p. B22.

——, "Johnson Controls Gets a Big Boost from the Bottom," *Wall Street Journal,* February 3, 1997, p. B4.

——, "Johnson Controls Plans to Expand into Asia, Pacific," *Wall Street Journal,* September 26, 1996, p. B2.

——, "Johnson Controls to Buy Prince Unit As Car-Interior Industry Consolidates," *Wall Street Journal,* July 19, 1996, p. A3.

Rose, Robert L., and Robert L. Simison, "Johnson Controls and UAW Reach Pact," *Wall Street Journal,* February 21, 1997, pp. A3, A4.

Tetzell, Rick, "Mining Money in Mature Markets," *Fortune,* March 22, 1993, p. 77.

Wermiel, Stephen, "Justices Bar 'Fetal Protection' Policies," *Wall Street Journal,* March 21, 1991, pp. B1, B5.

—Mary Sue Mohnke
—updated by David E. Salamie

Kansas City Southern Industries, Inc.

114 West 11th Street
Kansas City, Missouri 64105
U.S.A.
(815) 556-0303
Fax: (816) 556-0459
Web site: http://www.kcsi.com

Public Company
Incorporated: 1887 as Kansas City Southern Railway
    Company
Employees: 4,080
Sales: $1.1 billion (1997)
Stock Exchanges: New York
Ticker Symbol: KSU
SICs: 4011 Railroads—Line Haul Operating; 7374 Data
    Processing & Preparation; 6282 Investment Advice;
    6719 Holding Companies, Not Elsewhere Classified

Kansas City Southern Industries, Inc. (KCSI) controls a number of operations in its transportation and financial services divisions. Kansas City Southern Railway (KCSR) is KCSI's primary subsidiary, operating direct transportation service over approximately 4,000 miles of track primarily in the central and southern United States. As of the late 1990s, KCSI derived a substantial portion of its revenues from its fund management subsidiaries Janus Capital Corporation and Berger Associates, Inc., which together had assets of approximately $70 billion. KCSI also held 41 percent of DST Systems Inc., which supplied the financial services industry with record-keeping and computer services.

Entrepreneurial Beginnings

KCSI was founded on January 8, 1887, by Arthur Edward Stilwell, a native New Yorker and grandson of one of the builders of the Erie Canal. Stilwell's original goal was to provide passenger service and transport for local meat-packing houses and granaries. An astute entrepreneur—he was able to secure initial funding for the railway in a matter of hours—he recognized that considerable opportunity existed in the transport of coal, lead, and zinc from southern mines. In just over six months, he raised $2.5 million and in 1891 extended the line southward to Fort Smith, Arkansas. Two years later, despite a severe nationwide depression in the railroad industry, Stilwell secured $3 million in backing from a commodities broker in Amsterdam, the Netherlands, to extend the line directly south to the Gulf of Mexico, where goods could then be shipped to eastern markets by sea.

Stilwell's original intent was to extend the railroad to Shreveport, Louisiana, and use the tracks of other lines to continue the journey to the Gulf. Noting that coastal towns were periodically subject to violent hurricanes, Stilwell changed his mind and decided to route his lines to Lake Sabine, a well-protected body of water seven miles inland from the Gulf. He then built a port on the lake and dug a canal to connect it to the Gulf. Port Arthur, named after Stilwell, became the second largest grain port in the United States after New York City.

Stilwell left Kansas City Southern Railway Company in 1900, a year before oil was discovered in Beaumont, Texas. He was replaced by Leonore F. Loree, who made concerted but unsuccessful efforts in the late 1920s to merge the Missouri-Kansas-Texas Railroad, the St. Louis Southwestern Railroad, or Cotton Belt, and KCSR. Loree established KCSR's reputation as a well-run, professional business. His sound financial and operating philosophy helped the company weather the Great Depression of the 1930s, and in 1939 KCSR company purchased the Louisiana and Arkansas Railway, extending its territory through Baton Rouge to New Orleans, Louisiana, and westward to Dallas, Texas. KCSR's strength during the Depression led General Motors in 1939 to choose the railroad to test the first diesel-electric locomotive for passenger service in the United States.

Post-World War II Prosperity

A bitter battle ensued in 1944, when local businessmen wrested control of KCSR from East Coast investors, demanding the resignation of then Chairman Charles P. Couch. The nomination of William N. Deramus as president ushered in a new era for the company, during which it focused on developing business in existing territories that were experiencing a post-World War II industrial boom. By the early 1950s KCSR was one of the most profitable railroads in the country.

Building on a solid base of well-maintained railways, Deramus was instrumental in incorporating innovative technology to keep ahead of competition. He acquired surplus World War II radio equipment, helping KCSR become a pioneer in the use of microwave signals to control portions of the rail system from a centralized location. During the 1950s KCSI also became an innovator in developing computerized data processing systems to control the flow of paper work through the system, an expertise it later applied to providing computerized accounting systems for the railroad industry.

A profitable partnership between Deramus and his son William N. Deramus III began in 1955, when the young Deramus was president of the Chicago Great Western and Katy Railway. The father-and-son team began a joint study of a proposed propane line along the right-of-way of their respective railways. This led to a key role for both entrepreneurs in building the Mid-America Pipeline (MAPCO), which grew to become a major U.S. energy company. KCSR's small interest in MAPCO ended, however, when shares in MAPCO were distributed as dividends to KCSI stockholders in 1973 and later in 1982.

Diversification in the 1960s

In 1961 William N. Deramus III left his post at Chicago Great Western and joined his father in senior management of Kansas City Southern. Their partnership instituted a series of far-reaching transformations within the company, centering on the incorporation of Kansas City Southern Industries as a holding company, which in turn purchased Kansas City Southern Railway through a two-for-one stock swap with its investors. "The prospects for significant growth in the railroad industry are lacking," the younger Deramus told the International Commerce Commission (ICC) in 1962, "and the interest of shareholders can be better shared by diversification." At the time, this transaction was the largest in a trend among railroads to diversify in an attempt to remain viable in the face of growing competition from the trucking and airline industries.

The new Kansas City Southern Industries began a series of acquisitions starting in 1963 with the purchase of a 40 percent interest in Television Shares Management Corp., a Chicago-based mutual funds manager that attracted KCSI in part for its holdings in the electronics and aerospace industries. John Hawkinson was appointed president, and the name of the acquisition was changed to Supervised Investors Services Inc. (SIS).

As the volume of mutual fund transactions grew at SIS, Raymond P. Bammes and others at KCSI capitalized on KCSR's experience in computerized data processing to develop data management systems for mutual funds. A new company, DST Systems Inc., was incorporated in 1968 to market these systems to the financial services industry. In 1983 DST Systems Inc. went public, filing an initial public offering of 1.38 million shares. All shares were sold, and KCSI retained approximately an 86 percent interest. DST Systems grew to become one of the cornerstones of KCSI's financial services division.

In 1966 KCSI ventured into the broadcast media industry, purchasing six television and radio stations in Illinois and Missouri. The company acquired KRCG-TV and KWOS-radio in Jefferson City, Missouri; KMOS-TV in Sedalia, Missouri, for a purchase price of $3 million; and WEK-TV and WEEQ-TV in Peoria, Illinois, for $3 million.

In 1969 a new member of KCSI's legal department, Irvine O. Hockaday, discovered that Lee National Corporation had purchased 20 percent of KCSI stock and was secretly trying to gain control of the company. KCSI sued Lee National for $40 million to prevent the takeover on grounds that Lee National was an investment firm and was therefore barred from purchasing securities without prior Securities and Exchange Commission (SEC) approval. Lee countersued with two civil suits asking $110 million in damages; the company charged that KCSI management was engaged in a conspiracy to thwart Lee's legal attempts to participate in control of the company.

Ultimately, due to Hockaday's efforts, Lee National agreed in November 1970 to transfer its 21.5 percent interest back to KCSI in exchange for $23 million in cash, real estate, and other securities. Largely as a result of his handling of the Lee National affair, Hockaday was named president and chief operating officer of KCSI in 1971, replacing William N. Deramus III, who continued as chairman and chief executive officer.

The late 1960s were difficult years for KCSR. In 1967 the railway terminated its passenger service after three consecutive years of losses totaling over $7.2 million. KCSI had been expending the bulk of its energies in diversification ventures and ignoring the needs of the railway. Furthermore, during an industrywide probe of the effects of railroad diversification in 1971, the ICC's Bureau of Enforcement proposed an investigation into KCSI's activities.

Among other things, the ICC alleged, "If there has not been a deliberate policy to deprive the railroad of its non-operating assets and to drain off its operating revenues, management, in pursuit of its independent enterprises, has been so indifferent to the financial well-being of the railroad company as to accomplish the same result." The ICC went on to accuse KCSI of wasting $9 million in the spinning off of its north Baton Rouge development project and the transfer of most of the carrier's $44 million nonoperating assets to the holding company. Another issue was the use of $9 million of the railroad's cash in the purchase of Howe Coal Co. in the late 1960s, an investment that led to a $15.4 million write-off when the coal company became unprofitable. Despite these setbacks, KCSI reported a net income of $12.8 million in 1971, up from $5.9 million a year earlier.

Another lawsuit was brought forward in 1971, challenging the merger of Supervised Investors Services and Kemperco Inc. and asking payment of profits made through the stock swap. The consolidation between SIS and Kemperco resulted in Kemper Financial Services. One of the largest mutual fund managers in the United States, it handled more than $30 billion in dividends.

Rejuvenating the Railway in the 1970s and 1980s

By 1973 KCSR was in worse shape than it had been in 1962. Neglect of the railway division by KCSI was addressed when a civil engineer, Thomas S. Carter, was appointed president of KCSR. Carter asked the KCSI board for $75 million to improve rail beds, which he promptly received. The impetus for this massive rehabilitation program was a 20-year contract to transport coal to power plants in Louisiana and Texas. Continuing his renovation program using only money generated by KCSI operations, Carter invested more than $200 million by 1978 to make the 1,500-mile track one of the safest and most efficient in the nation. As a result of the improved rail lines—as well as a new coal delivery contract—coal tonnage grew from just above one percent of KCSR's cargo in 1973 to approximately 20 percent in 1982 and 33.1 percent in 1991.

KCSR's profits grew in the early 1980s, thanks to an increase in coal transport and a favorable mix of other freight traffic yielding high revenues. Likewise, DST and Pioneer Western Corp.—which marketed insurance and investment services through its subsidiary, Western Reserve Life Insurance Co.—grew rapidly from 1975 to 1981, in part because of the expanding mutual funds industry. In 1983 the company bought a majority interest in Janus Capital Corp. and Janus Management Corp., a Denver-based mutual funds company that managed nearly $120 million in assets for private accounts. Also in 1983 KCSI joined Telecom Engineering to form LDX Group Inc., a telecommunications holding company formed as an umbrella company for KCSI's erratically profitable broadcasting subsidiary, LDX Network Inc.

In 1986 William N. Deramus IV became president of KCSR, and by the company's centennial in 1987, the Deramus family boasted a 75-year history with the railroad. That same year KCSI unsuccessfully bid $2.6 billion for Southern Pacific Corp., a railway ten times the size of KCSR that was considering a merger with Santa Fe Railway.

KCSI reported a net loss of $33 million in 1988, after paying $50 million to settle lawsuits filed by Energy Transport Systems Inc., which was involved in a project to build a coal slurry pipeline from Wyoming to Texas. The transport company alleged that KCSR had conspired with other railroads to block construction of the pipeline, which would have competed with KCSR's coal transport business. In a separate but related suit, the court ordered KCSI to pay $844 million in damages to the state of South Dakota. The U.S. Circuit Court of Appeals later overturned the judgment and the matter was settled by mid-1989.

Export coal volume grew tremendously in 1989, and KCSR was poised to handle overflow from eastern ports into ports on the Gulf of Mexico, notably Port Arthur. The railroad acquired total ownership of the facilities in Port Arthur in 1991. In April of that year, a nationwide labor dispute threatened the railroad; a one-day strike ensued that was immediately halted by congressional intervention. A National Mediations Board was installed to settle differences and decreed that railroads could operate two-man crews, regardless of the number of cars and length of trains. As a result of this determination, KCSR was able to pare down the number of its train operators by one-third from 600 employees to 400.

KCSI's strong showing in its financial services division in the late 1980s reflected the booming growth of the mutual funds industry. When KCSI entered the financial services market in 1962, managed assets were about $50 billion nationwide. By the end of 1991 managed assets had grown to nearly $1.4 trillion. Janus Capital Corp. sold about 10 percent of all growth funds in 1991, prompting *U.S. News & World Report* to name it the top fund family in the United States.

KCSR's railroad tracks ran through a generally prosperous area of the Sun Belt and benefited considerably from local traffic. In the early 1990s the company had streamlined its railway operating procedures and, with total control of the facilities, was poised to handle an increased volume of coal transport, its primary moneymaker. KCSI had also tightened its financial services division, paring off unprofitable ventures. The company had learned from its nonproductive endeavors and planned to concentrate its energies in the areas in which it excelled: transportation and financial services.

Prosperity in the 1990s

Janus Capital and Berger Associates enjoyed tremendous growth in the early 1990s, as investment in mutual funds continued to rise throughout the United States. In 1992 revenues at Janus rose 134 percent, contributing a third of KCSI's operating income. The following year the company's fund businesses outstripped the railroad business for the first time in providing income for KCSI. The fund management provided $112 million out of KCSI's total of $175 million in pretax income.

Although DST Systems suffered some setbacks in the early 1990s, it held a strong position in its area of expertise and was expanding its services. DST's operating income dropped 33 percent in 1992 after losing Vanguard as a customer. The mutual fund leader had accounted for 10 percent of DST's business, and the company had to scramble for new accounts to make up the loss. DST was the leader in providing third-party services to the mutual fund industry in 1993, holding 40 percent of the market. The company was moving into new service areas in an attempt to supply all of the back-office needs of the mutual fund industry. To offer portfolio accounting and stock transfer services, DST entered into joint ventures with Kemper Financial and State Street Boston. It also moved into new industries by adding a subsidiary called Vantage Computer Systems to provide record keeping and custom software to the life and property insurance industry. Its 50 percent-owned Argus Health Systems used DST computers to process medical claims.

The success of its financial asset management segment allowed KCSI to invest in improvements to its railroad segment. Between 1987 and 1993 the company spent $500 million to modernize track and facilities and to purchase modern diesel locomotives. In 1992 KCSI purchased MidSouth Corp. for $220 million. The acquisition added approximately 1,200 miles of track in Mississippi and Alabama, almost doubling the size of the railroad. More importantly, it extended KCSR's line from Dallas to Birmingham, Alabama, complementing its traditional north-south line between New Orleans and Kansas City. The extension strengthened KCSR's position in the lucrative chemical hauling and intermodal segments.

Throughout the early and mid-1990s, KCSI debated splitting up the company to concentrate on either the railroad or the financial asset management segments. The trend toward diversification in the 1960s had led KCSI into the unusual combination of industries, and an equally strong trend in the 1990s toward divestiture and single-industry companies encouraged KCSI to sell one off. Plans to sell the railroad accelerated in 1993, and the company reached an agreement to sell with Illinois Central in July 1994. Three months later, however, the deal fell through and debate about the company's structure continued.

In 1995 KCSI sold 51 percent of DST to the public. The money gained in the initial public offering helped reduce the company's debt ratio.

In 1997 KCSI teamed with Transportacion Maritima Mexicana S.A. de C.V. (TMM) to bid on Mexico's northeast railroad concession. At $1.4 billion, the KCSI/TMM bid won the 50-year concession to operate the northeast line of Ferrocarriles Nacionales de Mexico. With the addition of this line, KCSR linked lines stretching from Chicago to Mexico City, forming what was being called "The Nafta Railroad."

In 1998 both the railroad and the financial asset management segments of KCSI were healthy. Plans to divide the two segments continued, although KCSI was then working on spinning off the financial asset management segment rather than the railroad.

Principal Subsidiaries

Kansas City Southern Railway Company; Carland, Inc.; Berger Associates, Inc. (87%); Janus Capital Corporation (83%); DST Systems Inc. (41%).

Further Reading

Boland, John, "On the Right Track," *Barron's*, November 19, 1979.
Dubashi, Jagannath, "Throwback," *Financial World*, July 20, 1993, pp. 24–25.
Fink, Ronald, "If It Ain't Broke...," *Financial World*, August 2, 1994, pp. 26–27.
Gross, Lisa, "Who Needs a Merger?," *Forbes*, September 13, 1982.
Haverty, Mike, "Mexico's Railway Privatization; KCS Maps 'The NAFTA Railroad,' " *Railway Age*, January 1997, pp. 49–51.
Jaffe, Thomas, "Fundamental Analysis 101," *Forbes*, August 14, 1995, p. 175.
"Kansas City Southern to Record Loss for '88," *Wall Street Journal*, January 5, 1989.
LaMonica, Paul R., "Last Train to Fundville," *Financial World*, April 8, 1996, pp. 30–33.
Malone, Frank, "A Lean Little Road with a PIP of a Program," *Railway Age*, June 25, 1979.
O'Hanlon, James, "The Little Railroad That Went Astray," *Forbes*, July 24, 1978.
"On a Fast Track," *Barron's*, April 26, 1982.
Shedd, Tom, "Rail-Oriented Traffic Base Helps As KCS Seeks to Stay Independent," *Modern Railroads*, February 1984.

—Elaine Belsito
—updated by Susan Windisch Brown

Kelly Services, Inc.

999 West Big Beaver Road
Troy, Michigan 48084
U.S.A.
(248) 362-4444
(877) 602-6182
Fax: (248) 244-4154
Web site: http://www.kellyservices.com

Public Company
Incorporated: 1946 as Russell Kelly Office Services, Inc.
Employees: 800,000
Sales: $3.85 billion (1997)
Stock Exchanges: NASDAQ
Ticker Symbol: KELYA
SICs: 7363 Help Supply Services

Kelly Services, Inc. is one of the oldest and largest staffing support companies in the United States. It serves numerous markets, providing temporary employees with general office skills; experience in accounting, engineering, and information technology; and the ability to work in many manufacturing and distribution positions. In addition, Kelly Assisted Living Services provides in-home care for people physically unable to live on their own. Kelly Scientific Resources supplies professionals experienced in biology, chemistry, geology, biochemistry, and physics, and the Wallace Law Registry provides paralegals and lawyers for temporary or long-term assignments.

Early History

Kelly Services was founded in 1946 by William Russell Kelly. After dropping out of the University of Pittsburgh, Kelly worked as a car salesman before being called to serve in the U.S. Army. As a fiscal management analyst for the Army's Quartermaster Market Center during World War II, Kelly became acquainted with office procedures and a wide variety of newly developed business machines. When he left the Army at the end of the war, Kelly set up Russell Kelly Office Services, Inc., a general office services bureau in Detroit, Michigan. At

first he took in typing, copying, and inventory calculating work from other firms and performed the duties in his own office, using his machines and employees.

Eventually, however, Russell Kelly began sending employees and machines to his clients' offices to work onsite. At a certain point, his clients began to acquire their own office machines, and it was no longer necessary for Kelly to provide equipment. As he later told the *New York Times,* though, clients "were impressed by the way my girls had been trained. It just seemed to be a natural development to send out the girls and forget about the machines." With this innovation, an industry was born. In 1947, the first full year of operation for Kelly, his company racked up $92,000 in sales, and Kelly asked his brother Richard to assist him.

In 1952 the rapidly growing Russell Kelly Office Services was reincorporated in Delaware as Personnel Service, Inc., and three years later, Richard Kelly opened the company's first branch office in Louisville, Kentucky. By the end of 1955 Kelly boasted 35 offices in cities across the nation, and the company opened a new, larger national headquarters in Highland Park, Michigan. Two years later, to reflect the all-female composition of Kelly's work force, the company changed its name to Kelly Girl Service, Inc.

By 1961 the company had $19.4 million in sales, and in 1962, revenues topped $25 million. Kelly went public that year with an offering of 100,000 shares, of which Russell Kelly retained two-thirds. The company had expanded to include 148 wholly owned and operated offices across the country, with other Kelly brothers pioneering operations in Florida and New York. Kelly also began to expand away from its earlier, exclusive emphasis on office work, adding a marketing division to provide employees for a wider variety of tasks, such as demonstrating new products door-to-door or acting as hostesses at conventions.

Demand Rises in the 1960s

Business owners began to realize that temporary employees fit their business cycles, since they were available to work during peak periods of business activity. As a result, the demand for temporary employees grew rapidly. Kelly's biggest problem became not placing its employees, but finding them. To recruit new Kelly Girls, the company ran newspaper advertisements appealing to "bored or needy housewives," according to the *New York Times*. Women who responded to the ads were brought together in conference rooms in suburban hotels for a sales pitch, augmented by an inspirational film urging the women to join Kelly Girl Service, "the next time you get fed up with the household routine."

Most of the women who responded favorably to this approach and joined up, the company reported, had worked briefly before quitting to marry and have children. A survey of Midwestern Kelly offices in the early 1960s yielded a profile of the average Kelly girl as a 37-year-old who had been born in a city, graduated from high school, worked in an office for 7.8 years, and then married and had two children. For those who were not yet married, Russell Kelly suggested to the *New York Times* in pre-politically correct 1963, that the company provided an added benefit: "Instead of working in an office where all the men are married, they have the chance to 'case the field' and work in as many offices as they wish in order to expose their charms to potential husbands."

The company's reliance on homemakers led to seasonal shifts in the workforce, particularly during the summer, when children were out of school. This caused temporary shortages of employees in early June, before the "co-eds" arrived home from college, and in the late summer, after they left on vacation and before the mothers returned. To supplement the housewife corps, one Kelly branch office looked even further afield than the suburbs, adding women from England to its roster of employees. In 1963 Kelly's New York office reported that 80 British women were employed there, up from 35 the year before. In addition, the company implemented a work-travel plan for foreigners, which allowed them to see the country by transferring from city to city, earning money as they moved.

By 1964 the company had expanded its operation to include 169 offices in 44 states. Though the bulk of these offices were licensee operations, the company made it a point to retain direct control in larger cities, such as New York, Chicago, Los Angeles, and Philadelphia, and it moved to reacquire direct ownership of some eastern licensee offices. Sales during the year increased by more than 20 percent, and the company predicted year-end revenues of $37.5 million.

Also in 1964 Kelly expanded its scope of services further, adding a light industrial division to provide blue-collar employees to industrial firms and a technical services division to offer temporary drafting and data processing help to architects, engineers, and researchers. Among the services already offered by

Kelly were manual accounting, electronic punch-card accounting, key punching, and mailing.

By providing more highly skilled employees, Kelly Girl Service looked to increase its fees. In keeping with this goal, a survey in early 1965 indicated that more than one-third of Kelly's temporary employees had a college degree. By 1966 the company had added engineers to its pool of available labor, as the demand for these employees grew rapidly in the industrial build-up during the Vietnam War. To reflect the broader scope of the company's offerings, Kelly Girl Service changed its corporate name to Kelly Services, Inc. in 1966, relegating the reference to "girls" to its office services sector, which became known as the Kelly Girl Division.

In 1968 Kelly opened its first office outside the United States, when it began operations in Toronto, Canada. The following year, the company moved to yet another larger headquarters building in Southfield, Michigan. Seeing its sales depressed by a brief recession at the onset of the 1970s, the company implemented cost-control measures to offset the impact of the slow-down in the economy. Because Kelly's customers were caught with unnecessarily large staffs when activity in the economy dropped, the demand for temporary employees decreased sharply in 1970 and 1971.

Expansion Continued in the 1970s

Sales and revenues began to recover in 1972, however, as the economy on the whole picked up and acceptance of temporary workers increased. In October of that year, Kelly opened its first European office, in Paris. This was followed in 1973 by the establishment of a London office.

Kelly's sales passed the landmark $100 million level in 1973, and the company continued to expand with new offices, including a second outlet in Paris, which opened in early 1974. For the rest of that year, Kelly was again beset by a general economic downturn, as the U.S. economy suffered the effects of the Middle East oil embargo. Since employers had pared their staffs significantly after past slowdowns, however, the impact on demand for temporary help was lessened somewhat. Kelly still managed to notch records in sales and earnings for 1974.

The recession deepened in the first half of 1975, though, curtailing company growth more sharply and resulting in a decrease in sales and earnings for the year. The company responded by consolidating several offices, cutting back on promotional expenses, and postponing work on special projects.

By the final quarter of 1975, however, the pace had begun to quicken, and Kelly rebounded to report record revenues of $150 million in 1976. In May of that year, the company followed up on a pilot project it had conducted in several cities when it purchased a small healthcare services firm and launched a new division, Kelly Home Care, whose name would soon be changed to Kelly Health Care. With the aging of the American population and the increasing demand for healthcare services, Kelly looked forward to strong growth in this sector of the market, and indeed, it opened 20 healthcare offices during the division's first year in operation.

In 1977 Kelly again reported record growth, as its sales nearly doubled in just two years. This strong performance came about as the American work force was entering a period of change that would eventually benefit the temporary industry enormously. Companies began to realize that the actual cost of hiring an employee was much higher than the mere cost of his or her salary. When items like recruitment and training, administrative overhead associated with payroll, fringe benefits such as health insurance and vacations, Social Security payments, pension plan contributions, taxes, and other expenses were taken into consideration, an employee's actual cost could reach 150 percent of her wages. To keep personnel expenditures down, companies began to reduce their permanent staffs, relying more heavily on temporary employees to fill in only when there was a genuine need for extra help. This structural shift toward leaner staffs in all sectors of the economy resulted in a bonanza for the temporary employment industry and helped to fuel dramatic growth throughout the decades of the 1970s and 1980s.

In 1978 Kelly revenues topped a quarter of a billion dollars for the first time, and the company moved into a new high-rise world headquarters in Troy, Michigan. Also that year the company implemented "service descriptions," a profile of the skills and background required to fulfill the duties of a given job, to help it better match temporary employees to a customer's needs.

Kelly topped off a decade of remarkable growth during 1979, when its sales grew by $90 million, an amount greater than its total sales in 1970. With the addition of branch offices in Vermont and South Dakota, the company planted its flag in all 50 states.

Kelly also prepared for the gradual technological transformation of the American office that took place in the late 1970s and early 1980s, when the typewriter was being replaced by the word-processing computer. It would no longer be sufficient to simply test a potential secretary's typing speed. Rather, temps would now be required to make use of one or more of a variety of word-processing programs and packages.

As a first step toward the extensive education and skills testing that would become necessary in the computer age, Kelly formed a professional training department and developed video training facilities in 1979. This grew into Guided Discovery Learning, a multimedia word-processing training program that was implemented in 1981. The program was put in place to aid the company in its "major thrust into the expanding field of word processing," as Russell Kelly put it in that year's annual report. The expansion mandated by new technology was matched by Kelly's withdrawal from its outmoded data processing business, as the company closed its Service Bureau Division.

Kelly experienced an unaccustomed decline in its revenues and earnings in 1982, when it suffered the effects of a national recession and a severely decreased demand for temporary help. Sales also shrank for Kelly Health Care, the company's nursing division, as lower demand for temporary medical workers in hospitals and nursing homes offset the growth of the company's home healthcare practice. Most of Kelly's healthcare offices obtained Medicare certification in 1982, qualifying them to provide services paid for by the federal healthcare program for the elderly.

Maintaining Quality in the 1980s

By 1983 Kelly was once again reporting record gains. With the opening of offices in five new cities, the company's number of branches reached 550. Also during 1983, Kelly moved to install in all of its Kelly Girl offices a computer simulation program that could be used to test potential temps on word-processing programs produced by Wang, IBM, and Lanier. The company made this large investment in response to the loss of confidence in temporary workers that ensued when secretaries unfamiliar with particular word-processing programs were sent out on jobs to use them and proved unable to do so. As a follow-up to this effort, Kelly unveiled a new advertising campaign in business publications in January 1984, in an attempt to upgrade the image of temporary help.

Also in 1984 Kelly expanded its operations to its first new country since the addition of the United Kingdom office in 1973, when it opened a branch in Dublin, Ireland. In addition, the company moved its healthcare division out of the Medicare and Medicaid markets and repositioned its nurses and other personnel as a privately paid service. Called Kelly Assisted Living Services, Inc., the program featured nurses who made home visits and aides who handled household chores for elderly or disabled people who were not seriously ill, allowing them to avoid institutionalization.

By 1985 the Kelly network comprised 650 offices worldwide, filling jobs with 160 different service descriptions. In keeping with the trend toward extensive testing of temporary employees to guarantee their abilities, the company introduced the Kelly Dexterity Indexer System in its light industrial division to electronically examine the broad arm and hand movements, as well as the more precise wrist and finger movements, of its manual laborers.

Throughout 1986 the company worked to install Kelly PC-Pro—the next generation of its clerical skills testing program, which covered the 11 leading word-processing packages—in its offices around the world. The program was introduced to customers in early 1987. In addition to training in the Kelly office, the company also equipped its word processors with manuals to the programs employees would be using on the job and a hot-line number to call in case they ran into trouble. These efforts helped Kelly to record sales of more than $1 billion in 1986.

The company's growth during the mid-1980s was constrained not by demand, which grew steadily, but by the shrinking labor pool, which made recruitment of temporary workers ever more difficult. During the summers of 1985 and 1986, for instance, Kelly was unable to hire enough summer workers to fill the positions that were vacant. As a result, in 1987 the company expanded its recruiting efforts to a population of workers previously underutilized by the temporary industry—retired people. In 1987 Kelly introduced the ENCORE Program in an attempt to woo members of this demographic group back to the workforce. Additional recruitment programs eventually reached out to military wives, displaced homemakers, single parents, and college students.

Along with its steady expansion through the opening of new branch offices, whose numbers reached 800, Kelly embarked on a stint of acquisitions in 1988. The company entered the Australian market by purchasing existing temporary agencies in four cities—Sydney, Melbourne, Brisbane, and Adelaide—and also acquired a company in Quebec City, Quebec.

This continued growth prompted Kelly to reorganize for more effective operations in early 1989. Company activities were arranged under two headings, Kelly Temporary Services and Kelly Assisted Living. Throughout the decade of the 1980s, the business of Kelly Services had grown at an explosive rate, as annual sales tripled and earnings quintupled during that time.

New Markets in the 1990s

Foreign acquisitions continued in 1990, when Kelly Services purchased Competence ApS, a temporary agency in Denmark; Free-lance Uitzendburo in the Netherlands; and Adstaff Associates, Ltd. in New Zealand. During the following year, Kelly purchased Xpert Recruitment, Ltd. in Great Britain and added Acton Staff Management to its Australian holdings. In addition, the company opened an office in Juarez, Mexico.

In 1991 Kelly reorganized further, forming four operating divisions in its temporary help area, as performance suffered in the general business slowdown of the early 1990s. Although sales remained essentially the same, earnings fell from $71 million in 1990 to $39 million in 1991. The downturn continued in 1992; sales rose to $1.7 billion, but earnings stayed flat at $39 million.

The improvement in the economy in the early 1990s meant increased sales for Kelly. Uneasy about hiring full-time employees after the trauma of downsizing, companies turned to temporary services to supplement their workforces. By the mid-1990s Kelly's performance had improved, with sales and earnings rising steadily. As a percent of sales, however, income never regained the heady five percent level of the late 1980s. It hovered around the 2.5 percent level, with income in 1995 of $70 million on sales of $2.7 billion.

One reason income did not rise as quickly as sales in the mid-1990s was Kelly's investment in acquisitions. In 1994 the company purchased ComTrain, a company that specialized in the development of software for testing and training. That same year Kelly acquired the employee-leasing company Your Staff. The purchase added a new twist to Kelly's offerings: the company did not merely fill positions for the customer, it provided entire human resource staffs to monitor the temporary help and provide such services as administering payroll and benefits. Outsourcing became an important business segment for Kelly. Its outsourcing division, Kelly Management Services, managed its customer's support departments, providing direction for mailing and shipping, payroll, accounts payable, and records management. In 1995 Kelly expanded into the legal market with its purchase of the Wallace Law Registry, a temporary help service that provided clerks, paralegals, and even lawyers.

The company moved into yet another new market in 1995 when it created Kelly Scientific Resources, a subsidiary that specialized in providing science professionals for temporary assignments. The subsidiary expanded in 1996 when Kelly bought the temporary help service Oak Ridge Research Institute and incorporated it into Kelly Scientific Resources. With customers primarily in the defense and energy industries, Oak Ridge gave the new subsidiary an established customer base and experience in placing scientists. Kelly Scientific Resources opened an office in Canada in 1997 and another in Paris, France, in 1998, making it the only global scientific staffing company. With 2,600 scientists on its payroll and approximately $1 million in sales in 1998, it was also the world's largest.

Kelly also continued to expand internationally in the mid- to late 1990s. By 1996 the company owned subsidiaries in Australia, New Zealand, Canada, Mexico, and several in Europe. In 1997 Kelly acquired a temporary service in Russia. It also expanded into Italy, which had just changed its employment laws to allow the use of temporary services.

Kelly faced heavy competition in Europe, however, where temporary services had flourished in an environment of strict employment laws. European companies commonly used temporary help rather than hire full-time employees that would be difficult to fire in a downturn. In 1996 two established temporary services, Adia in Switzerland and Ecco in France, merged to form Adecco. Not only did the new company threaten Kelly's foothold in Europe, it also challenged Kelly's position as third largest temporary service in the United States. By 1997 Adecco was the fourth largest temporary service in the United States, and its strong growth looked likely to push it past Kelly Services within a year.

Although Kelly was not growing as fast as some of its competitors in the late 1990s, it was still reporting record sales and earnings. In 1997 sales reached $3.85 billion, with earnings of $80.8 million. Sales in 1998 were expected to exceed $4 billion.

Principal Subsidiaries

Kelly Assisted Living Services, Inc.; Kelly Professional Services, Inc.; Kelly Properties, Inc.; Your Staff, Inc.; Kelly Canada Services, Ltd.; Kelly Services Ltd. (Australia); Kelly Services (France); Kelly Uitzendburo (Netherlands); Kelly Services, Ltd. (U.K.); Kelly de México S.A. de C.V.

Principal Divisions

Kelly Marketing; Kelly Technical; Kelly Temporary Services, Ltd.

Further Reading

Brandstrader, J.R., "It's an Ill Wind . . . ," *Barron's,* March 25, 1996, pp. 18–20.
Curry, Gloria, "Temporary Help Market Continues to Grow," *Office,* July 1993, pp. 8–10.
Cooper, Richard, "Personality: The Kelly Girls Are Two Men," *New York Times,* April 14, 1963.
Loehwing, David A., "More Warm Bodies," *Barron's,* December 17, 1962.
Sansoni, Silvia, "Move Over, Manpower," *Forbes,* July 7, 1997, p. 74.
Segre, Claudio, "The British Secretary Is New Status Symbol for Some U.S. Bosses," *Wall Street Journal,* February 5, 1963.
Willatt, Norris, "Manpower Abroad," *Barron's,* January 4, 1965.
Zweig, Jason, "Kelly Girls and Kelly Grandmas," *Forbes,* January 8, 1990.

—Elizabeth Rourke
—updated by Susan Windisch Brown

Koninklijke Nedlloyd N.V.

Boompjes 40
3011 XB Rotterdam
Netherlands
(31) 10 400 71 11
Fax: (31) 10 404 61 90
Web site: http://www.nedlloyd.com

Public Company
Incorporated: 1970
Employees: 13,000 (excluding 11,000 employees of P&O Nedlloyd)
Sales: NLG 3.46 billion (US$1.79 billion) (1997)
Stock Exchanges: Amsterdam Frankfurt (Nedlloyd shares also trade in the United States in the form of ADRs and in London on SEAQ)
SICs: 4731 Freight Transportation Arrangement; 4783 Packing & Crating; 4789 Transportation Services, Not Elsewhere Classified; 4499 Water Transportation Services, Not Elsewhere Classified; 4449 Water Transportation of Freight, Not Elsewhere Classified; 4491 Marine Cargo Handling; 3731 Ship Building & Repairing; 4225 General Warehousing & Storage; 4226 Special Warehousing & Storage, Not Elsewhere Classified

Koninklijke Nedlloyd N.V. (Royal Nedlloyd) is one of the leading international logistics services companies in Europe. Based in Rotterdam, The Netherlands, Nedlloyd has refocused its organization onto its logistics offerings—including warehousing, transportation, and specialty and other logistics services—through such subsidiary companies as Mammoet, Van Gend & Loos, and others. Nedlloyd and its subsidiaries offer extensive logistics design and implementation services, from warehousing to delivery and the formation of distribution networks, while adding special focus to chemical logistics, fashion services (clothing transportation), and customs activities.

During the 1990s Nedlloyd has undergone a thorough restructuring to recoup profitability while preparing the company for the upcoming single European market competition. Ned-

lloyd has jettisoned its noncore activities, including its interests in airline company Martinair; oil drilling and exploration under Neddrill; and other interests, including a share in Smit International, and the company's holdings of North Sea Ferries. The most significant split was the company's decision to merge its worldwide container (shipping) activities with those of the United Kingdom's Peninsular and Oriental Steam Navigation Company (P&O), to form the new independent company P&O Nedlloyd. Royal Nedlloyd holds a 50 percent share and a continued active interest in the operations of P&O Nedlloyd.

Shipping Foundations in the 19th Century

The formation of Nedlloyd occurred in 1970 as the result of the amalgamation of four major Dutch ship-owning companies, but its origins could be traced back to the founding of the Koninklijke Nederlandsche Stoomboot Maatschappij (KNSM) in 1856; the company joined Nedlloyd in 1981. In the mid-19th century, when the British, Russian, and French merchant fleets were occupied with the Crimean War, there was an acute shortage of vessels available to carry out everyday trade. Christian Ramann, a young German businessman, persuaded two Dutch merchants, C.A. von Hemert and M.S. Insinger, of Amsterdam's potential as a major European port. The trio successfully applied for a royal charter to establish liner services between Amsterdam and several Baltic ports—including St. Petersburg, Gothenburg, Copenhagen, and Königsberg—and between Amsterdam and Bordeaux via Le Havre. The resulting company, KNSM, started its Baltic service on October 1, 1856, with two chartered sailing ships. Expansion was rapid, and by 1863 the company was operating 11 ships totaling 4,200 tons.

In 1870 the Stoomvaart Maatschappij Nederland (Nederland Line) was founded for the purpose of trading with and in the Far East. The company got off to a bad start when its first ship, S.S. *Willem II,* caught fire in 1871, but the vessel was not seriously damaged. In 1883 Rotterdam Lloyd, a company that was to become both a competitor and a collaborator, was founded.

Meanwhile, KNSM entered a difficult phase. In 1869 it decided to enter the lucrative migrant trade to North America, but by the time its new ships, S.S. *Stad Haarlem* and S.S. *Amsterdam,* were delivered in 1875, the combination of a severe

---

Company Perspectives:

Nedlloyd aspires to obtain a leading position as an international logistics services company, with the emphasis on providing tailor-made logistics solutions both in the area of European Transport and Distribution and in worldwide Container Logistics. Nedlloyd aims to offer its shareholders a competitive return on their investment in the Company. Nedlloyd's client friendly and well-motivated staff may rely on the Company optimally protecting their employment in the widest sense, which includes offering competitive employment conditions. Nedlloyd considers it its social duty to limit the burden its activities may place on the environment wherever possible.

---

economic depression in the United States and a European boom severely reduced the number of immigrants to North America. KNSM put the new ships into service but losses increased and the ships were sold in 1879, leaving KNSM seriously in debt. The managing directorship of Ernst Heldring restored the fortunes of KNSM. He consolidated existing services and added new ones, helping KNSM to develop successful trade with North America. European governments commonly used mail contracts during the 19th century to subsidize their national shipping lines. This was part of a strategy to consolidate their overseas possessions and expand their spheres of interest. In 1888 the Dutch government, intent on strengthening its links with the Indonesian archipelago, awarded the Indonesian mail contract to a new company, the Koninklijke Paketvaart Maatschappij (KPM). KPM was founded jointly by Nederland Line and Rotterdam Lloyd expressly for the purpose of developing interisland trade in Indonesia. The service began on January 1, 1891, with 30 ships on 13 regular routes.

KPM's early years were difficult: it sought to establish trade with the smallest and most inaccessible islands of the archipelago and suffered fierce competition from British ship owners. After overcoming these initial difficulties, KPM started to expand and during the early years of the 20th century began services between Indonesia and Australia and Indonesia and Thailand (then known as Siam). In 1911, with a fleet approaching 100 ships, KPM introduced fast weekly services between several Far Eastern ports. Following a temporary halt in its progress during World War I, KPM became the largest shipowner in the Far East by the late 1920s.

Postal service also played an important part in the development of KNSM. Koninklijke West-Indische Maildienst (KWIM) had been established to deliver mail to and from the Dutch West Indies. It expanded too rapidly, however, and left itself vulnerable to competitors. By 1913 KNSM had gained effective control of KWIM, seeing the opportunity to become a leading player in the West Indies. KNSM also hoped to expand its services through the Panama Canal and across the Pacific, but World War I intervened before this became possible.

KPM, Rotterdam Lloyd, and Nederland Line also had shares in the Java-China-Japan Line (JCJL), a company founded in 1902 to take advantage of the growing traffic between India and the Far East. JCJL's major shareholder was the Nederlandsche Handel Maatschappij, a government-backed bank that provided capital for Dutch overseas investors. JCJL's progress was steady rather than spectacular; by 1939 its services were limited to 11 vessels. JCJL came into its own, however, after World War II and the Dutch withdrawal from Indonesia.

In 1908, KPM, Rotterdam Lloyd, and Nederland Line came together, this time through a holding company, to found Koninklijke Hollandsche Lloyd (KHL)—a consolidation of the South America Line that had been established in 1899. By 1914 those companies that eventually came together to form the Nedlloyd Group were, for the most part, in sound financial condition and had extended their sphere of activity to the Far East, Australasia, and the Americas. During World War I, the allied forces exercised the "Right of Angary"—that is, the right of a belligerent state to utilize the property of a neutral state. Consequently, the portion of the Dutch fleet that had escaped the German navy (138 ships altogether, including 22 KNSM vessels) was used to support the Allied cause.

The immediate postwar years were prosperous for Dutch ship owners. They benefited from restraints imposed on German competitors and from Europe's determination to rebuild its stocks of basic commodities. By 1920, however, freight rates had started to fall and shipping companies were feeling the pinch. The Nederland Line, Rotterdam Lloyd, KPM, JCJL, KNSM, and three other small companies came together to form Vereenigde Nederlandsche Scheep-vaartmaatschappij (United Netherlands Navigation Company, or VNS), a joint venture that was intended to help restore prewar services and to strengthen the competitive position of Dutch shipowners in anticipation of a German shipping revival.

The fortunes of VNS companies varied during the interwar years. KPM recovered quickly; most of its fleet was fully intact after the war and the company rapidly resumed business on its old routes. Before long it was the largest shipping company in the Far East and during the boom years between 1925 and 1930 it added 60 new vessels to its fleet. KPM also entered the tourist market during this period, opening hotels in Bali and other Far Eastern countries.

The early 1930s were for shipping, as for most industries, a time of contraction. Most Dutch shipowners, including Nederland Line, KPM, and Rotterdam Lloyd, went through a period of severe cost-cutting. KPM was the only company to begin its recovery before the start of World War II; in 1937 it brought two state-of-the-art cargo ships into service and started up the Zuid Atlantische Lijn, which linked Durban, Montevideo, Buenos Aires, Santos, Rio de Janeiro, and Capetown.

At the outbreak of World War II, all Dutch ships in European waters were instructed to make their way to British ports if they were able to do so. Vessels outside European waters continued with their existing activities until it was decided how they could aid the Allied cause at sea. The future Nedlloyd Group companies served the Allied war effort, incurring severe losses of personnel and ships. In 1939 the KNSM fleet, for example, comprised seven passenger vessels and 76 cargo ships; six years later it had fallen to three passenger vessels and 39 cargo ships. KPM lost 98 vessels in the conflict, having begun the war with 146 ships.

Insurrection in Indonesia and the subsequent declaration of the Republic of Indonesia on December 27, 1949, precipitated the most immediate postwar change in Dutch shipping. KPM's success had been based on their services in the Indonesian archipelago and, in view of the political upheavals there, the company did not find postwar business in the area profitable. Accordingly, KPM's Far Eastern fleet was merged with JCJL in 1947. The latter company had lost 6 out of 11 vessels during the war but, with the help of "Victory" ships, had quickly resumed its old services between Indonesia, Hong Kong, China, and Japan, and had added the Philippines to its route. The new JCJL-KPM company was called Koninklijke Java-China Paketvaart Lijnen (KJPCL), but it eventually became known by the English title Royal Interocean Lines.

The remaining portion of KPM's fleet tried to continue its Indonesian interisland services but was under constant harassment from the Indonesian government, which seized some of its ships and expelled the company in 1957. The remaining 40 ships initially were put in dry dock, but some were later sold and others used as tramp ships. In 1966 the remnants of KPM joined Royal Interocean.

The rise of civil aviation accelerated the withdrawal of future Nedlloyd companies from passenger services. In 1964 both Nederland Line and Rotterdam Lloyd sold their passenger ships. The company's final passenger ship was not sold, however, until 1974 when Royal Interocean's *New Holland* left the fleet.

Merging in the 1970s

The modern era in Nedlloyd's history began in 1970 with the full integration of the activities of Royal Interocean Lines, Rotterdam Lloyd, Nederland Line, VNS, and their subsidiaries into the Nedlloyd Group. In 1977 the name was changed to the Koninklijke (or Royal) Nedlloyd Group.

In 1981 the Royal Nedlloyd Group took over KNSM, which, with a history of 125 years of service, was the world's oldest shipping line still operating independently. During the postwar era, KNSM had rapidly rebuilt business halted by the hostilities and reestablished its routes, particularly in Central and South America. It was not able, however, to withstand the severe shipping slump of the late 1970s and early 1980s.

During the 1980s, Nedlloyd was affected by the recession in liner shipping, and divestment rather than expansion became the company's watchword. The company's strategy of concentrating on shipping and inland transport and disposing of peripheral activities eventually became profitable: after losses in 1990, Nedlloyd returned to the black in 1991. Nedlloyd remained in fragile financial condition (no dividend was paid in 1991), but liner shipping, out of all of its core activities, exhibited the most improved performance.

In 1983, the company, in an attempt to bolster its inland transport business, decided to move further down the transport chain and provide transport service not only from port to port but also from the factory gate to the final consumer. Feeling it necessary to purchase regional transport companies to improve its services, Nedlloyd bought Van Gend and Loos a Dutch company active in storage, distribution, and specialized trans-

port in 1986. Nedlloyd also purchased the Spanish shipping company Fernando Roqué in 1987, the German companies Andreas Christ and Union-Transport in 1989, and Great Britain's Transflash, also in 1989. These acquisitions were criticized later for being inconsistent with the company's policy of concentrating on its core activities, that is, container logistics through a global network of shipping links, and transport, forwarding, inventory management, and distribution, including those for specific industries and products, principally in Europe.

While attempting to take advantage of the greater integration of the European market, Nedlloyd also targeted road transport companies in northern Europe, especially in Germany. The financial demands of acquisitions and new building (seven large ultramodern container ships were ordered in 1989 and 1990, with five ships delivered in 1991 and 1992, and two to be delivered in 1994 and 1995, respectively) were high and Nedlloyd sold noncore activities to help finance them.

Success Amidst Difficulties: The 1990s

Despite the active divestment policy in 1991, the Nedlloyd supervisory board was criticized by Torstein Hagen, a Norwegian citizen who held almost 30 percent of Nedlloyd shares in early 1992. Hagen believes that Nedlloyd, rather than focusing on core business, overexpanded into areas it did not fully understand. Campaigning periodically since 1988 for a seat on the Nedlloyd supervisory board, Hagen was thwarted initially by Dutch takeover barriers, but the board eventually agreed to grant Hagen's wish in the spring of 1992. The move was blocked by the employees' council but the board sought to overturn the decision in the Dutch courts.

In 1992 economic conditions affecting the freight industry remained difficult: freight rates in most markets had fallen dramatically, the weakness of the dollar—the currency of the shipping industry—also was expected to affect earnings adversely, and economic slowdown in major European markets was impeding business. This combination of factors made the short-term future of Nedlloyd uncertain.

The continued economic crisis soon forced Nedlloyd to undertake an extensive restructuring of its activities. A first wave of reorganization brought the company back into the black by 1994—for net profits of NLG 92 million on sales of NLG 6.6 billion, after 1993's loss of NLG 112 million. By the late 1990s the company had eliminated its interests in oil exploration and drilling, selling its Neddril subsidiary to the United States' Nobel Drilling Corporation, and in commercial airlines (after selling its share of Dutch airliner Martinair), passenger and other ferry lines, represented by North Sea Ferries. The most significant phase of the company's restructuring occurred as much as a step toward meeting increasing globalized competition. In 1996 Nedlloyd reached agreement with the Peninsular and Oriental Steamship Company (P&O) to merge the two companies' container shipping operations. The resulting 50–50 partnership company, P&O Nedlloyd, began operations in 1997 and featured one of the largest container shipping fleets in the world, with revenues of nearly US$4 billion per year. Initial returns were less than dramatic, however: by year-end 1997, Nedlloyd posted profits of US$37 million (NLG

72 million) on deconsolidated turnover of US$1.79 billion (NLG 3.46 billion).

Nonetheless, Nedlloyd had successfully transformed itself into a tightly focused, Eurocentric logistics powerhouse in time for the arrival of the single European currency slated for January 1999. As the premier logistics operator in the Benelux countries, as well as Germany, Nedlloyd began actively seeking to extend its operations throughout France and Spain and beyond the European Community into Switzerland and much of Eastern Europe. If the economic crisis, which, starting in late 1997, looked to cripple much of the Asian economies for the rest of the decade, also was hurting Nedlloyd's P&O Nedlloyd revenues in 1998, the company's core European logistics activities were showing strong advances.

Principal Subsidiaries

European Transport and Distribution: Nedlloyd Unitrans GmbH (Germany); Nedlloyd NTO GmbH (Germany); Van Gend & Loos B.V.; Nedlloyd Districenters International B.V.; Nedlloyd Flowmasters B.V.; Nedlloyd Road Cardgo B.V. (a.k.a. Nedlloyd Chemical Logistics); Nedlloyd Fashion Services B.V.; Gerlach & Co. B.V. Ocean Shipping: P&O Nedlloyd (U.K.; 50%). Other activities: Mammoet Transport B.V. (66%); Gerlach Art Packers & Shippers B.V.; Europe Consolidated Terminals B.V. (30.56%).

Further Reading

Cockrill, Philip, "K.N.S.M.—The Royal Netherlands Steamship Company (1856–1981)," Newbury, Berks: published by the author, 1981.

Cockrill, Philip, and Halebos, J., "Koninklijke Paketvaart Maatschappij (1891–1941) with the Java-China-Japan Line to 1970," Newbury, Berks: published by Philip Cockrill, 1982.

Lloyds Shipping Economist (various issues), London, England.

Mulder, P., "De schepen van de KNSM 1856–1981," *Boer Maritiem,* Weesp., 1983.

—Debra Johnson
—updated by M.L. Cohen

Koppers Industries, Inc.

436 Seventh Avenue
Pittsburgh, Pennsylvania 15219
U.S.A.
(412) 227-2001
Fax: (412) 227-2333
Web site: http://www.koppers.com

Private Company
Incorporated: 1944 as Koppers Inc.
Employees: 1990
Sales: $593.1 million (1997)
SICs: 2999 Petroleum & Coal Products, Not Elsewhere
Classified; 2861 Gum & Wood Chemicals; 1241 Coal
Mining Services; 3624 Carbon & Graphite Products;
3743 Railroad Equipment

Although Koppers Industries, Inc. began as a manufacturer of byproduct recovery coke ovens in 1912, its circuitous route through a number of acquisitions and diversified products classifies it as an early predecessor to a modern-day conglomerate. From its long association with the Mellon family interests in Pittsburgh's heavy industry, to its forays into chemicals, plastics, wood products, road building, and even buttons, the company struggled to secure an identity in the face of cyclical markets and dependence on capital goods spending. While the impressive returns earned during the 1970s expansion into chemicals were interrupted by a depressed market in the 1980s, Koppers underwent several incarnations before becoming the pared down company of the late 1990s. From a successful stint in road building, paving, and repairs to its present status as a leading supplier of carbon-based materials and treated wood products, as well as coke products—its initial foray into manufacturing—Koppers has come full circle with a strong identity and a firm bottom line.

Starting Off with a Bang, 1920s to 1955

In the 1920s an entrepreneur from Virginia purchased a small coke oven company in an attempt to build a consortium of companies to integrate all aspects of coal production. Henry B. Rust then solicited support from Andrew Mellon, one of the nation's leading financiers and industrialists, and was soon operating a vast network of holding companies engaged in mining, railroad transportation, shipping, utilities, and steel mills. Rust's conglomerate, named Kopper United, successfully exploited all the potential uses of coal and subsequently became the favorite of Mellon's industry operations. Their empire, however, was short-lived. The Depression came and with it Roosevelt's Public Utility Holding Company Act, which forced the company to sell Eastern Gas & Fuel Associates. By losing this division—which directed the coal, utility, and railroad operations—the company relinquished control of its integrated coal orientation. Of the remaining former empire, the manufacturing and engineering divisions evolved into Koppers Inc.

The traditional business of manufacturing byproduct coke ovens and products related to coal such as tar became, once again, Koppers' major source of income. Yet sensing the company had lost its direction, the Koppers board of directors (with the Mellon family representing a major presence) appointed Brehon Burke Somervell, a World War II four-star general, to assume control of the operations. As chief executive officer, Somervell proposed that the company follow a delineated course of action by imposing a strict military hierarchy. Minutiae of detail demarcating job responsibilities, limits of authority, and centralized powers were codified in books. While many found this method of leadership incompatible with the industry, Somervell's plan was to create an environment conducive to generating new technologies. The General's tenure at Koppers was shortened by illness; upon his death in 1955 he had only directed the company for five years.

Postwar Change, Late 1950s to 1969

Although the rigid organizational structure was abandoned after Somervell's death, the World War II veteran had successfully launched a campaign into the new areas of chemicals and plastics. Fred Foy, a company executive who had served under the General during the war, assumed Somervell's position and continued his predecessor's program of diversification. Before joining Koppers, Foy worked as vice-president at J. Walter

---

Company Perspectives:

Koppers Industries is a diversified company—heavily based in metallurgical coke manufacturing, coal tar processing, and wood preserving technology—organized to supply the key chemicals and materials required for successful manufacturing, processing, and construction.

Thompson and also worked at Ford. By 1956 sales gained from the company's plastic operations heralded a long awaited revitalization of the almost 50-year-old company. Unfortunately, intense competition from large companies in petroleum caused a volatile price war. After this price war ended, Koppers reported low profit figures.

The results from the plastic campaign did not represent Koppers' only disappointment; the old product line also suffered from poor performance figures. Shares earning $5.01 in 1956 now earned a little more than half that. To prevent any further profit decrease Foy, along with his energetic young president Fletcher L. Byron, held a policy planning meeting. Together the two executives decided on strict measures to reduce costs and consolidate businesses. Nineteen plants producing low profits were closed and the Engineering and Construction division, which built plants for the steel and iron industries, acquired a general contracting firm. This subsidiary, purchased for $20 million, released the division from sole dependence on the cyclical steel industry by encouraging business in other fields. By 1960 the first nine-month earnings figures posted a healthy 50 percent increase. While much of these encouraging numbers resulted from sales in the Engineering and Construction division, closer inspection revealed that a backlog of orders carried over from the previous year had artificially increased the new year's figures.

The entry into the chemicals field, initiated under General Somervell, remained a disappointment. While some 60 percent of the $300 million in sales could be traced to chemicals, Koppers' profits remained far behind competing chemical companies. This discrepancy resulted from the company's dependence on old-line products at the expense of new technologies. While competitors manufactured innovative plastics such as styrene, polystyrene, and polyethylene, Koppers produced age-old products such as roofing pitch and road-paving items. A major integration of plastics operations had not occurred until the mid-1950s, well behind the industrywide movement. To remedy this situation, Foy announced plans to market an innovative plastic building panel and double capacity projections for polystyrene production. By bolstering the chemical operations through the sale of new plastics, as well as attempting to provide an entry for old products into new markets, Foy hoped to mitigate the effects of chronic fluctuations in the market for engineering and construction products.

Working alongside Foy in this major revision of company operations was the indefatigable Byron. The company president had joined Koppers as an assistant to a division manager soon after World War II and in the following 13 years he assumed eight

different positions of increasing responsibility. The son of a coal buyer at the American Steel & Wire Company, Byron decided at an early age that his career was in the steel industry. After college he joined the same company that employed his father and began working as a sales trainee. During World War II Bryon took a leave from the company to work as a coordinator for a research project at the Naval Ordnance Laboratory in Washington. After participating in the conceptualization of surface-to-air missiles, Byron decided at the end of the war to return to the steel company. When American Steel responded with only lukewarm enthusiasm, Byron applied for a job at Koppers.

In three years he was promoted to plant superintendent after helping negotiate a compromise to a strike at a West Virginia plant. In a daring act of independence, Byron spent $500,000 to replace aging equipment without the authority of his supervisor. When the replacement equipment upgraded plant productivity so that in just over a year profits jumped from negative figures to $2 million, Byron's grateful superiors forgave him his impetuosity. The company then sent the young executive to a management training program at the Harvard Business School, where he was exposed for the first time to an intellectual environment full of different ideas and philosophies. This exposure eventually led to the implementation of a highly decentralized, yet intellectually demanding, approach to business that would characterize Byron's tenure at Koppers.

In 1960 Foy, retaining titles of both chairman and CEO, promoted Byron to president. This promotion came after initially rejecting the candidate as too young. Four years later the Byron-Foy team had successfully molded a company whose revenues surpassed the $1 billion mark. By identifying expandable markets, Koppers began producing piston rings for high-speed diesel engines which accounted for over 50 percent of net income in one year. Similarly, Koppers ranked fifth among domestic producers of polyester resins and ranked high among those producing phthalic anhydride. One particularly successful branch of Koppers polyester resin business was the manufacture of buttons.

Growth and Decline, 1970–81

Koppers' foray into plastic building panels proved less successful because marketing of the unusual product demanded time-consuming and expensive planning. Similarly, an attempted partnership to produce polyethylene from Koppers plastic division using ethylene manufactured by the Sinclair Oil Company also failed to generate hoped for profits. Despite an impressive beginning the joint venture fell victim to intensive competition from other oil companies. This failed venture ended Koppers' participation in the thermoplastic and petrochemical markets.

Notwithstanding these disappointments, Koppers' overall performance in the 1970s caused common stock shares to triple in value as management announced a two-for-one split. By 1979 earnings reached a high of $3.21 a share. To encourage growth, Byron guided Koppers into several high technology projects. Purchasing 30 percent of Genex Corporation, a recombinant-DNA research company, Byron's strategy suggested many benefits for Koppers' organic chemical production. It was hoped that the research would discover the process to genetically engineer resorcinol, a product previously manufactured by a traditional method. Additional plans were underway to explore synfuel processes such as coal gasification.

By 1980, however, company equity dropped from 20.3 percent to 17.1 percent. A depressed market started by a recession once again had adverse effects on company performance. Apart from the cyclical nature of the market, industry observers began blaming internal structural problems for Koppers' ailing profit margins. While Byron's decentralized policy of encouraging middle managers to assume greater responsibility in decision-making actually allowed for a certain number of mistakes, the costs of these mistakes started to reflect on productivity. Miscalculations and faulty equipment forced writeoffs and reduced profit margins.

While Byron promised better returns once an assured turn in the economy revived capital spending, he continued to pursue his unorthodox policy of management. This policy promoted the delegation of authority to such a degree that much of Byron's time was actually spent outside the area of daily decision-making. By giving priority to the intellectual and civic responsibilities believed to be incumbent upon himself as a business leader, Byron functioned more as a spiritual guide than an actual company director. Not only did he traverse the country on a lecture circuit to prominent universities and businesses, he also conducted trimonthly seminars for his own young executives to examine the philosophies of such thinkers as John Kenneth Galbraith, John Maddox, and Michael Harrington.

By 1981 profits dropped $2.4 million to a total of $51.8 million. Instead of patiently waiting for the recession to end, management announced an effort to reduce capital outlays and sell unprofitable businesses. Selling up to 18 percent of poorly performing operations in all four of the major divisions, as well as allotting just $110 million for capital spending, Koppers' management hoped to find immediate relief for the company's disappointed shareholders. High technology research remained a protected project as maturing operations in the wood and forest division were terminated. The ascension of Charles R. Pullin to the positions of chairman and CEO gave further impetus to this consolidation effort.

New Leadership, New Goals, 1982–89

A former president of Koppers' Road Material group Pullin, unlike his predecessor, thoroughly immersed himself in day-to-day operations. The new company leader had grown up in West Virginia as the son of a steel worker. A high school summer job with the state highway department directed his ambitions toward the road building industry. From the time he joined Koppers in 1946 as a technical service engineer to his final promotion to top management, Pullin was employed in the road building industry. Although some of that time was spent at another construction company, he returned to Koppers when the new road materials division needed an experienced leader.

While Pullin continued to invest money in high technology research, Koppers' most impressive results emerged from the division closest to Pullin's experience, namely, Road Building. Two new ventures in innovative production increased research spending to $88 million in 1984. These projects included the

exploration of engine technology and the development of plant disease diagnostic equipment. Koppers' recovery, however, did not result from revenues generated from these new technologies; rather it was traditional blacktop roadway production that symbolized the beginning of the company's revitalization. During the first six months of 1984 the Road Building division generated $274.5 million of the $811 million in total revenues. By developing an integrated operation, independent of subcontractors, Koppers emerged as the first nationwide paving company. Furthermore, the five-cent-a-gallon fuel tax included in the Surface Transportation Act allocated funds for the rehabilitation of the nation's highways. Koppers moved to capitalize on this growing market.

When road building emerged as the mainstay of company profits, Pullin reduced Koppers' investment in technological research. The 30 percent stake in Genex failed to produce the sought after financial rewards. As a result, it was sold along with several other mature businesses. Some $360 million in assets were generated from the sale of the coke ovens, button, and several wood product operations. This housecleaning included the sale of Koppers' original steel industry construction business; a hard decision for many of Koppers' executives. In addition, Pullin slashed capital spending by reducing Koppers' workforce.

Thus as nationwide spending for bridge and road construction increased 17 percent between 1983 and 1986, Koppers successfully exploited the market trend. The price of common stock, decreasing in 1985, increased to a high of $27 per share in 1986. Yet Koppers' focus and fortune was still evolving, and change—both large and small—was on its way. Market volatility, economic conditions, and several leadership and ownership changes began in the summer of 1988 when Koppers was acquired by BNS Acquisitions (a subsidiary of Beazer Limited) for $226.8 million and renamed Beazer East, Inc. A few months later, the management of Beazer, Inc. and KAP Investments, Inc. (a wholly owned subsidiary of Koppers Australia) led a leveraged buyout of the company's assets, financed through warrants, issuance of stock, and various loans. When the dust settled, Koppers Industries had been born again.

A Refocused Direction, the 1990s

With the new, improved version of Koppers Industries in the early 1990s, road paving, once the boon of the company's bottom line, was out; and concentration was placed on three major divisions: carbon materials and chemicals, railroad and utility products, and coke products. While the lion's share of the company's revenues (50 percent) came from the rail and utility products division, by the mid-1990s this figure fell by 10 percent while carbon materials and chemicals rallied—bringing both divisions to a dead heat of 40 percent of sales. Coke products also claimed a bit of the rail and utility's slice, by increasing to 15 percent of sales. Koppers was full-steam ahead, however, for all divisions—acquiring the nation's most modern coke facility in Monessen, Pennsylvania, in March 1995; the U.S.'s largest railroad crosstie treating plant in Somerville, Texas, in April; Aristech Chemical Corporation's coke chemical division a year later; the U.K.'s Bitmac, Ltd., a tar distillation company, in August 1996, and still more.

Sales for 1995 and 1996 were robust, as Koppers' strategic acquisitions eliminated middle-men and supplied its divisions with the majority of their raw materials. As a result, annual sales climbed 10 percent from 1994's $476.4 million to $525.7 million in sales in 1995, and grew another 12 percent for 1996's $588.5 million. Internationally, Koppers was strong in both Australia and Denmark as its joint ventures, Koppers Australia and Tarconord, respectively, were major suppliers of carbon pitch and related products. In 1997 Koppers bought out its longtime Australian partner, Broken Hill Proprietary Company Limited, for full control of Koppers Australia, as well as having KAP Investments and a group of company investors spend $52.5 million to purchase all of Koppers' voting and non-voting shares from Cornerstone-Spectrum Inc., an affiliate of Beazer East, Inc. Sales before the extraordinary charge for the stock purchase were $593.1 million, up just slightly from 1996's $588.5 million, while earnings were slashed due in part to the closure of a coke plant in Woodward, Alabama, and a wood-treating facility in Feather River, California.

Despite its tumultuous history, Koppers Industries carved niches for itself in a myriad of manufacturing areas. From coal and coke to carbon pitch, phtalic anhydride, and creosote, from buttons to road paving, from railroad crossties to utility poles—Koppers produced them all, with the same dedication to quality and long-range goals. Though Koppers streamlined its businesses in the 1990s to just three divisions (Carbon Materials and Chemicals, Railroad and Utility Products, and Coke Products), each was a leader in its industrial segment with 21 facilities in the United States, and another 14 in the South Pacific (mostly in Australia and New Zealand).

Principal Subsidiaries

Koppers Australia; Tarconord (50%); KSA Limited Partnership (50%).

Principal Divisions

Carbon Materials and Chemicals; Railroad and Utility Products; Coke Products.

Further Reading

Boselovic, Len, "Koppers Gets Approval to Reopen Pennsylvania Coke Plant," *Knight-Ridder/Tribune Business News,* April 19, 1995.

Holmgren, R. Bruce, "Upgrade Bag Line to Hike Output, Get Close Weights," *Packaging,* May 1989, p. 44.

"Koppers to Delay IPO Until 1998," *Pittsburgh Business Times,* June 9, 1997.

"Koppers Industries Releases First Quarter Earnings," *PR Newswire* (online), April 24, 1998.

"Loaders Standardized at Wood Treating Plant," *Wood Technology,* August 1996, p. 30.

Minahan, Tim, "Supply Chain Key to Growth at Koppers," *Purchasing,* April 17, 1997, p. 81.

Robertson, Scott, "Koppers Set to Close Woodward Coke Plant," *American Metal Market,* December 17, 1997, p. 3.

—updated by Taryn Benbow-Pfalzgraf

Kraft Jacobs Suchard AG

Klausstrasse 4
CH-8008 Zurich
Switzerland
(01) 385-11 11
Fax: (01) 382-16 45

*Wholly Owned Subsidiary of Kraft Foods International,
Inc.*
Incorporated: 1982 as Jacobs Suchard AG
Employees: 16,799
Sales: US$8.7 billion (1997)
SICs: 2022 Natural, Processed & Imitation Cheese; 2035
Pickled Fruits & Vegetables, Salad Dressings,
Vegetable Sauces & Seasonings; 2064 Candy &
Confectionery Products; 2066 Chocolate & Cocoa
Products; 2095 Roasted Coffee; 2098 Macaroni,
Spaghetti, Vermicelli & Noodles; 2099 Food
Preparations, Not Elsewhere Classified

Kraft Jacobs Suchard AG—part of Philip Morris Companies
Inc. by way of Kraft Foods, Inc.—is a leading European food
company. Formed in 1993 through the combination of Jacobs
Suchard AG and Kraft General Foods Europe, Kraft Jacobs
Suchard (KJS) specializes in three food categories: coffee (42
percent of operating revenues), confectionery (30 percent), and
cheese/grocery (28 percent). Key coffee brands include Carte
Noire, Gevalia, Grand' Mère, Hag, Jacobs, Jacques Vabre,
Kenco, Saimaza, and Splendid. In confectionery, noteworthy
brands include Callard & Bowser, Côte d'Or, Daim, Freia,
Lacta, Marabou, Milka, Suchard, Terry's, and Toblerone. Fi-
nally, well-known brands in cheese/grocery include Dairylea,
El Caserío, Kraft, Miracle Whip, O'boy, Philadelphia, Sot-
tilette, and Tang.

Of KJS's immediate predecessor companies, Kraft General
Foods Europe was formed in 1989 from the merger of Kraft
Europe (founded in 1927 and purchased by Philip Morris in
1988) and General Foods Europe (founded in 1954 and bought

by Philip Morris in 1985). Jacobs Suchard's history dates back
to 1825, having its origins in three spirited entrepreneurs:
Philippe Suchard and Johann Jakob Tobler, confectioners; and
Johann Jacobs, a coffee merchant. The Suchard and Tobler
companies joined forces in 1970 to form Interfood, which Jacobs' coffee company joined 12 years later to form Jacobs
Suchard. Philip Morris acquired Jacobs Suchard in 1990.

Suchard Formation in 1825

Philippe Suchard opened his small confectionery shop in
Neuchâtel, Switzerland, in 1825, and the following year expanded his business by opening a chocolate factory in Serrières.
Suchard was an innovator. Before trying the candy business, he
had taken part in founding a shipping company on the Rhine
River, had attempted to raise silkworms to make silk scarves,
and had tried to establish a Swiss colony in the United States,
near Carthage, New York. Later he provided housing for people
working in his Serrières factory at a time when they did not have
a union to voice their needs and demands. Suchard soon had
built his business into the leading Swiss chocolate maker. Four
years before its founder's death, the Suchard Company opened
its first plant outside Switzerland, in Lörrach, Germany, in
1880, the first in a series of international expansion efforts. In
1901 Suchard established the Milka chocolate brand, one of
Europe's oldest and most popular brands of milk chocolate.

Suchard's son-in-law, Carl Russ, led the business into other
countries, opening another factory in 1888, in Bludenz, Austria,
two factories in France in 1903, one in Spain in 1909, one in
Italy in 1923, and one in Belgium in 1929. Although the chocolate industry fell on hard times during World War I, by 1931
Suchard had begun to move into sugar confectionery, under the
Sugus brand. This venture helped the company weather the
Great Depression. After World War II, Suchard's chocolate
business again flourished and the company enjoyed relatively
stable success.

Tobler Established in 1867

The Tobler company, which merged with Suchard in 1970,
began in 1867 when Jean Tobler, formally Johann Jakob

Tobler, opened a small shop called Confiserie Spécial in Switzerland. A year later, he opened a confection factory in the capitol city of Bern. An avid traveler, Tobler was involved in various ventures while continuing to build his chocolate business, which prospered quickly. In 1908 Jean Tobler's son, Theodor, put the Toblerone chocolate bar on the market. One of the most valuable additions to the Tobler line of chocolates, it became Tobler's hallmark product.

In 1922 Tobler first expanded outside Switzerland, to Paris. It was not until 1951, however, 29 years after moving into France, that Tobler made its second international move, this time into Stuttgart, West Germany. In 1967 Tobler extended into Great Britain. Tobler and Suchard continued to develop their respective chocolates and businesses until 1970, when the companies merged to become Interfood.

The joint effort focused on internationalizing business operations and broadening product lines. In 1980 Interfood would acquire Andes Candies, based in the United States, and in 1982 it would purchase Callebaut, a well-known Belgian producer of candy coatings and other products.

Jacobs Launched in 1895

The Jacobs coffee company, based in Bremen, Germany, can be traced to Johann Jacobs, born in 1869. This third industrious entrepreneur in Jacobs Suchard's story opened a shop offering chocolates, tea, biscuits, and coffee in 1895. Jacobs opened a roasting plant of his own in 1906, and seven years later registered the Jacobs brand of coffee. In 1929 Johann Jacobs handed over the leadership of the company to his son Walther.

Much of Jacobs' subsequent growth is attributed to a vital marketing decision made by Walther Jacobs: the company began delivering freshly roasted coffee directly to retail shops. After World War II, this system of direct delivery was stepped up, along with production and sales, until in the mid-1960s more than 1,000 vehicles delivered Jacobs' fresh-roasted coffee to over 60,000 shops. In 1966 Jacobs began marketing different brand names of its coffee products, beginning with Krönung and growing to include Tradition, Privat, and Edel Mocca.

Klaus Jacobs, Walther's son and the third Jacobs generation to lead the company, took over in 1970. Jacobs had expanded into Austria in 1961 and would expand into Switzerland in 1971. The company, under Klaus's leadership, had plans to expand further into non-German-speaking countries and needed a home office to operate from. In 1973 a management and consulting subsidiary was established in Zürich. Subsequently, Jacobs moved into Denmark, France, and Canada during the 1970s by acquiring roasting and production companies in those countries. Jacobs acquired Jacques Vabre in 1973, and then again set its sights on France and bought Café Grand' Mère, in 1982.

Jacobs Suchard Formed in 1982

By this time it seemed to Interfood and Jacobs leaders alike that a merger was in order. Both companies had ambitious goals for international expansion. Chocolate and coffee, though hardly the same business, offered some scope for cooperation, and a merger would bring both companies economies of scale. The merger, which created the public company Jacobs Suchard AG, was accomplished in 1982. Its head office was established in Zürich, since Interfood was determined to stay Swiss, and Klaus Jacobs (whose family controlled 55 percent of the company) was made chairman of the board, since Jacobs was by far the larger of the two companies. The new company's logo featured the letters J and S placed closely together to also form a T, for Tobler.

Jacobs Suchard immediately began to cut costs; Jacobs eliminated most of the company's middle management positions and used capital it raised by selling shares to acquire many established and successful businesses. One of the most prominent of them was the international Monheim Group, which Jacobs Suchard took over in July 1986. Included among Monheim's subsidiaries was Van Houten, a West German company manufacturing consumer chocolate, cocoa, industrial cocoa butter, and cocoa powder. Another Monheim member was General Chocolate, in Belgium, which marketed specialty sweets under the Meurisse brand. Jacobs Suchard Belgium began handling Van Houten's and General Chocolate's consumer business; its industrial affairs were absorbed into Jacobs Suchard in Zurich.

By the end of 1986 Jacobs Suchard was operating quite successfully with its European additions. On the North American continent, however, save for Andes Candies, the company was doing very little business. So Jacobs Suchard set out to participate more aggressively in the lucrative American candy market.

Late 1980s Acquisitions

In December 1986 Jacobs Suchard completed a takeover of E.J. Brach for almost US$750 million. The American candy company, in existence more than 80 years, was the third largest candy company in the United States. Jacobs Suchard saw this acquisition as a profitable enterprise in itself and, perhaps more importantly, as a door through which to introduce its goods to the North American market.

In March 1987 the company took over the Belgian chocolate company Côte d'Or, a controversial deal since the Belgian company was the last of its kind still owned by Belgians. From the late 1960s into the 1980s Belgian candy companies had one by one been bought by foreign interests, including Callebaut's 1982 purchase by Interfood. Nestlé had also bid for control of

Côte d'Or, but the families who owned the Belgian "national icon" chose Jacobs Suchard. Jacobs Suchard, vowing to sustain the high quality of Côte d'Or's chocolate, absorbed Côte d'Or into Jacobs Suchard's Belgian operations. Jacobs Suchard also expanded its product market into Italy and Greece, in preparation for the integration of the European Economic Community in 1992.

In 1988 Jacobs Suchard bid for control of Rowntree, one of the United Kingdom's largest candy companies. In April of that year Jacobs Suchard began buying the largest percentage of shares, 29.9 percent, allowed by British law without placing a bid for the whole company. Nestlé was on the scene again, eager to bid, but Rowntree was not eager to be bought by either company. Nestlé finally bought the company for about US$4.5 billion, topping Jacobs Suchard's offer by US$400 million; Jacobs Suchard decided to stop bidding after a two-month battle and sold its Rowntree holdings to Nestlé for US$285 million.

Jacobs Suchard bought a Panamanian bank, Banco Aleman-Panameno, in 1985, and acquired the majority interest in West Germany's Ibero-Amerika Bank in July 1986. Both had close ties to Latin America's green-coffee business, upon which the company heavily depended. Direct participation in the banks was intended to provide Jacobs Suchard with greater knowledge about the green-coffee business.

During the first few years following the 1982 merger that created Jacobs Suchard, the company saw three phases in its development. In the beginning only key areas, such as personnel and finance management, were integrated, in an effort to bring Interfood and Jacobs together while disturbing their individual operations as little as possible. In 1983 the company reevaluated techniques for marketing its chocolate and coffee products in light of one another, and of the various countries in which they were sold, and made plans to capitalize on its popular brands and the changing desires of consumers. With consolidation taking a firm hold in management and marketing, in 1986 Jacobs Suchard redefined its business structure to include three business units: core business, finance and trading, and diversification, focused mainly on North America.

After spending approximately US$1 billion in acquisitions in 1987 and 1988 alone, Klaus Jacobs made four more purchases in 1989, including Italian maker of canned meat Simmenthal and Spanish coffee producer Saimaza. By the end of 1990 Jacobs had concentrated the company's European production in just six manufacturing centers (down from 22 in 1989); streamlined its European product line; and improved European sales by strengthening its less expensive brands, such as Milka. Jacobs Suchard also moved to capture a healthy portion of the growing Asian chocolate market. In 1989 the company hired 100 salesmen to push Milka chocolate in the Tokyo area alone.

Philip Morris Acquires Jacobs Suchard in 1990

Philip Morris Companies began a major push into the food industry in 1985 when it purchased General Foods Corp. Three years later Kraft, Inc. was acquired in a second huge acquisition. In 1989 Philip Morris combined the two companies into Kraft General Foods. Both of the acquired companies had longstanding European food units. Kraft Europe had been founded in 1927, while General Foods Europe debuted in 1954. With the creation of Kraft General Foods also came the creation of Kraft General Foods Europe.

Only one year after Kraft General Foods Europe was formed, Philip Morris acquired Jacobs Suchard. In August 1990 Philip Morris completed the SFr 5.4 billion (US$3.8 billion) purchase, the largest foreign acquisition of a Swiss firm to that date. The addition of Jacobs Suchard made Philip Morris the second largest food company in the world, trailing only Nestlé, and the third largest in Europe, trailing Nestlé and Unilever.

Philip Morris placed Raymond Viault in charge of Jacobs Suchard as CEO. Viault had previously engineered a turnaround of Maxwell House Coffee Co., a subsidiary of Kraft General Foods. Initially, Jacobs Suchard became a unit of Kraft General Foods International and operated separately from Kraft General Foods Europe. There was, however, a shuffling of assets. Several Jacobs Suchard businesses not of interest to Philip Morris—including E.J. Brach, Nabob Foods of Canada, the Dutch group Van Houten, and various real estate properties—were sold back to Klaus Jacobs. Non-European Jacobs Suchard operations in Hong Kong, Japan, Australia, Argentina, and Brazil were transferred to other subsidiaries of Kraft General Foods International. At the same time, several Kraft General Foods businesses in Europe were handed over to Jacobs Suchard, including German decaffeinated-coffee company Café Hag, the Onko brand of coffee, Swedish coffee roaster Gevalia, and French chewing gum manufacturer Hollywood. The future of Jacobs Suchard was clearly European.

Soon after joining the Philip Morris family, Jacobs Suchard went on a spending spree, scooping up more than a dozen companies in 1992 and 1993 alone. The most significant of these was the US$1.5 billion 1993 purchase of leading Scandinavian confectionery maker Freia Marabou, which had been created only two years earlier through the merger of Freia of Norway and Marabou of Sweden. Most of the other acquisitions were in the areas of coffee and confectionery: coffee makers Splendid of Italy and Fiesta of Greece, as well as confectionery makers in Czechoslovakia, Spain, Hungary, the United Kingdom, Poland, Lithuania, and Bulgaria. Moreover, Jacobs Suchard's acquisition activity ranged beyond its two core food groups, picking up Maarud Cheese of Norway, Scandinavian snack maker Estella, and a Spanish maker of cheese. The company also established two joint ventures in 1993: in Turkey, Marsa, which produced margarine and edible oils; and in Poland, Mazowsze Chorzele, a maker of cheese.

In late 1993 Philip Morris decided to merge its two main European food units, in a move designed to improve productivity, cut costs, streamline management, and unify marketing. Viault was named president and chief executive of the new group, dubbed Kraft Jacobs Suchard AG, which was headquartered in Zürich, Switzerland. KJS, which inherited the mantle of third largest food maker in Europe, had three core areas of concentration: coffee, confectionery, and cheese, with several other minor "grocery" areas. At first, KJS was a subsidiary of Kraft General Foods Europe, but in 1995 Kraft General Foods was reorganized into a new entity known as Kraft Foods, Inc., with KJS becoming a unit of Kraft Foods International, Inc., itself a unit of Kraft Foods, Inc.

The creation of Kraft Jacobs Suchard did nothing to slow down the company's acquisitiveness, which was particularly acute in eastern Europe. In 1994 KJS took control of the largest chocolate producer in Romania, Poiana-Produse Zaharoase. The following year brought confectioners in the Ukraine (Ukraina) and Russia (Petroconf) into the KJS fold. In 1994 the company also purchased the Lyon's instant coffee brand from Allied-Lyons of the United Kingdom, and KF Co-Op Cirkel of Sweden, maker of coffee and spices. In 1996 and 1997 KJS also made several divestitures of noncore businesses, including Malaco candy in Scandinavia, Hayat mineral water in Turkey, Fiesta croissants in Greece, and the Spanish confectionery company acquired in 1992.

Future KJS growth was also expected to come from its Middle East and Africa unit, headquartered in London. By 1998 this unit was marketing KJS products in more than 70 countries. Saudi Arabia and Kuwait were two of KJS's strongest markets. In each, the company held the number one market position in cream cheese and the number two position in coffee. The rapidly growing Kraft Jacobs Suchard appeared well positioned to compete with the Nestlés and Unilevers of its world.

Principal Subsidiaries

Kraft Jacobs Suchard Management & Consulting AG; Kraft Jacobs Suchard (Schweiz) AG; Kraft Jacobs Suchard Service AG (Switzerland); Taloca AG; Kraft Jacobs Suchard Oesterreich Gesellschaft MBH (Austria); Suchard Schokolade Ges. mbH Bludenz (Austria); KJS Namur S.A. (Belgium); Kraft Jacobs Suchard S.A. (Belgium); Kraft Jacobs Suchard Bulgaria AD; Kraft Jacobs Suchard spol. s r.o. (Czech Republic); Kraft Freia Marabou ApS (Denmark); Kraft Freia Marabou Danmark A/S (Denmark); Oy Estrella AB (Finland); Oy Kraft Freia Marabou Finland AB; Café Grand' Mère S.A. (France); Café Hag S.A. (France); Kraft Jacobs Suchard France; Grundstucksgemeinschaft Kraft Jacobs Suchard GbR (Germany); Kraft Jacobs Suchard Erzeugnisse GmbH & Co. KG (Germany); Kraft Jacobs Suchard Manufacturing GmbH & Co. KG (Germany); Kraft Jacobs Suchard Produktion GmbH (Germany); Mirabell Salzburger Confiserie-und Bisquit GmbH (Germany); Jacobs Suchard Pavlides S.A. (Greece); Kraft Jacobs Suchard Hungária Kft. (Hungary); Kraft Jacobs Suchard Ireland Ltd.; Krema Limited (Ireland); Côte d'Or Italia S.p.A. (Italy); Kraft Jacobs Suchard S.p.A. (Italy); AB Kraft Jacobs Suchard Lietuva (Lithuania); Kraft Jacobs Suchard BV (Netherlands); Kraft Jacobs Suchard Central & Eastern Europe Service BV (Netherlands); A/S Freia (Norway); A/S Maarud (Norway); Kraft Freia Marabou Norden A/S (Norway); Kraft Jacobs Suchard Polska Sp. z o.o. (Poland); Kraft Jacobs Suchard Portugal Productos Alimentares Lda. (Portugal); Kraft Jacobs Suchard Romania S.A.; Jacobs Suchard Figaro, a.s. (Slovak Republic); Kraft Jacobs Suchard Iberia, S.A. (Spain); AB Estrella (Sweden); Kraft Freia Marabou AB (Sweden); Marsa Kraft Jacobs Suchard Sabanci Gida Sanayi ve Ticaret A.S. (Turkey); Kraft Jacobs Suchard Ukraina Open Joint Stock Company (Ukraine); The Kenco Coffee Company Limited (U.K.); Kraft Jacobs Suchard (Holdings) Limited (United Kingdom); Kraft Jacobs Suchard Limited (U.K.); Suchard Limited (U.K.).

Principal Operating Units

Western Europe Region; Northern Europe Region; Central and Eastern Europe/Middle East and Africa Region.

Further Reading

Deveny, Kathleen, "Philip Morris Picks Viault to Be Chief of Jacobs Suchard," *Wall Street Journal,* August 17, 1990, p. C8.

Deveny, Kathleen, and Craig Forman, "Philip Morris Seeks to Gain in Europe with $3.8 Billion Bid for Suchard Stake," *Wall Street Journal,* June 25, 1990, p. A3.

Edlin, Christa, *Philippe Suchard (1797–1884): Schokoladefabrikant und Sozialpionier,* Meilen: Verein fur Wirtschaftshistorische Studien, 1992, 84 p.

Feldman, Amy, "Arrogance Goeth Before a Fall," *Forbes,* September 30, 1991, pp. 82 + .

Jonquières, Guy de, "Bittersweet Taste of Expansion," *Financial Times,* October 2, 1995, p. 20.

——, "Kraft, Jacobs Suchard to Link," *Financial Times,* September 9, 1993, p. 32.

Sesit, Michael R., "Many Suchard Minority Holders Steamed over Philip Morris Offer," *Wall Street Journal,* July 16, 1990, p. C1.

Wicks, John, "Jacobs Suchard Keeps on Growing," *swissBusiness,* September/October 1993, pp. 18 + .

——, "Under New Management," *swissBusiness,* September/October 1991, pp. 41 + .

—updated by David E. Salamie

Kubota

Kubota Corporation

1-2-47 Shikitsu-higashi
Naniwa-ku
Osaka 556-8601
Japan
(06) 648-2111
Fax: (06) 648-3862
Web site: http://www.kubota.co.jp

Public Company
Incorporated: 1930 as Kubota Limited
Employees: 15,399
Sales: ¥1.03 trillion (US$7.80 billion) (1998)
Stock Exchanges: Tokyo Osaka New York Paris
    Frankfurt Luxembourg
Ticker Symbol: KUB
SICs: 1541 General Contractors-Industrial Buildings &
    Warehouses; 3299 Nonmetallic Mineral Products, Not
    Elsewhere Classified; 3321 Gray & Ductile Iron
    Foundries; 3324 Steel Investment Foundries; 3498
    Fabricated Pipe & Fabricated Pipe Fittings; 3511
    Steam, Gas & Hydraulic Turbines; 3531 Construction
    Machinery & Equipment; 3523 Farm Machinery &
    Equipment; 3569 General Industrial Machinery &
    Equipment, Not Elsewhere Classified; 3585 Air
    Conditioning, Warm Air Heating Equipment &
    Commercial & Industrial Refrigeration Equipment;
    6719 Offices of Holding Companies, Not Elsewhere
    Classified

Kubota Corporation prides itself on being flexible and adjusting as necessary to compete under changing economic conditions. Kubota, originally a small manufacturer of iron castings, took advantage of the emphasis on industrialization that Japan's aggressive foreign policies required. The company came up with novel techniques to produce cast-iron pipes at the turn of the century to serve developing municipal water systems. When the market for piping peaked, around 1912, Kubota began to manufacture machine tools in time to take advantage of the demand for heavy industry that World War I prompted. Depression between the wars led to more innovative production techniques and more diversification. Overcoming the devastation of World War II, the company took advantage of major trends, rapid reindustrialization, and the partnership between government and business in the same way: by innovating and diversifying.

Today Kubota Corporation has operations that fall within three product groups: internal combustion engines and machinery, which includes farm equipment and engines as well as construction machinery; industrial products and engineering, which includes pipe and fluid systems engineering, environmental control plants, industrial machinery, and industrial castings; and building materials and housing, which includes cement roofing materials and other housing equipment as well as prefabricated houses. The company's operations include 14 factories in Japan and overseas subsidiaries and affiliates in Brazil, Canada, the United States, France, Germany, Spain, the United Kingdom, Australia, Indonesia, Malaysia, the Philippines, Taiwan, and Thailand. Kubota is determined to stay on top of its markets through its established methods and has committed more resources to research and development so it can continue its role as an innovator in heavy industry.

Castings Origins

Gonshiro Oode was the fourth and last child of a very poor Inno Island farmer who supplemented his family's income by working as a coppersmith. In 1885, when he was only 14 years old, Oode left home to try to get a job in Osaka. This was a difficult task because the boy had no relatives or friends in the city to help him during an era when one's contacts determined where one worked and lived. Eventually, however, Oode was accepted as an apprentice at the Kuro Casting Shop. His apprenticeship was indeed the bottom of the ladder; it initially consisted of babysitting and running errands. But Oode was diligent, and he was soon promoted to a position in which he could learn metal-casting processes.

Three years later, Oode joined Shiomi Casting, which produced metal domestic items. The job change enabled him to learn more about metal-casting techniques. By saving every penny possible, Oode was able to accumulate ¥100 in a year and a half.

Company Perspectives:

Ever since the founding of the company back in 1890, Kubota has been contributing to the progress of society through its manufacturing activities and technological developments. Its business operations have expanded into a wide range of fields covering machinery, pipe systems, basic structural materials, environmental facilities, and housing materials. As the twenty-first century approaches, Kubota is squarely facing the world's environmental problems, the biggest threat to the future of mankind. To ensure the peaceful coexistence of man with nature and protect the earth's environment while also achieving economic growth, the company is working to help create a truly affluent society. Kubota zealously pursues these goals throughout the whole range of its business activities. Here at Kubota, where we strive to make a positive contribution to the lives of individual people, society and the world's environment by being a company full of vitality, we look forward to receiving your continued guidance and support.

With the capital he had saved, Oode founded his own company, Oode Casting, in 1890. His timing was propitious. In 1868 the restored Meiji Emperor had abandoned Japanese isolation and opened contact with the outside world. That was the beginning of the industrialization of Japan's economy which spurred the development of the iron and steel industries. By 1890 metal for manufacturing was in great demand, and Oode Casting was successful from the beginning. Oode moved his business to larger quarters three times in the company's first five years.

Although the company has never been a ''war plant,'' except during World War II, part of Oode Casting's success was due to Japan's aggressive foreign policies. Japan invaded Korea on the Asian mainland in 1894, setting off the Sino-Japanese War. The Japanese army needed modern equipment, and Oode Casting could provide it. Oode expanded by hiring more than ten employees, and he changed the company's name to Oode Casting Iron Works.

After Japan's modern forces won the Sino-Japanese War, Oode continued to expand his company. He increased his product line, adding castings for domestic items and for cutting machines.

In 1897 a customer, Toshiro Kubota, took a typically Japanese step to promote Oode's success. Kubota asked if he could adopt Oode as his son. The move meant that he would officially sponsor the younger man and that Oode would be able to inherit from him. Both his natural parents were dead by then, and Oode agreed to the plan. He took the Kubota family name and changed his company's name to Kubota Iron Works to reflect his new relationship.

Developed New Pipe Production Methods in Early 20th Century

With Toshiro Kubota's patronage, Gonshiro Kubota was able to devote more time to developing new techniques. His invention of a new method of producing cast-iron pipe in 1900 established his company's reputation. Gonshiro Kubota had long grappled with how to produce pipe domestically for a modern national water system, which had become a national priority about 20 years before. Importing the necessary iron pipes was delaying the project. He invented a jointless-type cylindrical outer mold to produce jointless cast pipes by the vertical round-melt casting method and set up mass production in 1901. In 1904 Gonshiro Kubota invented another method, vertical rotary-type casting. His new processes made domestic cast-iron pipe production possible.

In 1904 war once again meant a boost for Japanese heavy industry and Kubota. Czar Nicholas II began the Russo-Japanese War when he backed the claims of Russian lumber exploiters along the Yalu River, which was in Japan's sphere of influence on the Chinese mainland. Japan easily defeated Russian forces. While the war was brief and one-sided, it promoted what has been called ''a second industrial revolution'' because Japanese leaders committed the country to modernization. Building the country's infrastructure called for more pipes and more cast iron. Kubota thrived.

Kubota had already committed himself to manufacturing machine tools when World War I broke out. In order to meet the needs of developing heavy industry, Kubota turned to manufacturing steam engines and iron-making machines. The company's main Osaka factory concentrated almost exclusively on producing machinery, and new factories were opened in Amagasaki and Okajima to produce the traditional lines of iron pipes and castings.

Some of that production was sold abroad for the first time: in 1917 Kubota exported 2,000 tons of iron pipe to Java, beginning the company's entry into Southeast Asian markets. Shortly afterward, in 1918 and 1919, Kubota opened regional offices in Tokyo, Kyushu, and Kure to improve his sales network. By 1919 the company had 1,500 employees.

Kubota emphasized innovation and use of state-of-the-art technology to remain competitive during the recession that followed World War I. The company invented heat-resistant castings and automatic carbon feeders. Kubota himself made trips abroad in 1919 and 1927 to learn new methods of producing high-grade cast pipes. His trips led to practical applications of a revolutionary centrifugal casting method. In 1937 the company opened the Sakai Engine Plant, the largest plant to that point in Asia. Sakai was noteworthy for using the conveyor belt to automate production. Kubota also entered new product lines in the years between the wars, including agricultural and industrial motors.

Demand for cast-iron pipes once again increased after World War I as domestic infrastructure projects were readdressed. Kubota took over the Sumida Iron Works in Tokyo as a subsidiary in 1927 and thereby gained a major share of the pipe market.

The acquisition made it easier to meet new foreign demands for Kubota's high-quality cast-iron pipes. The company expanded its presence in Southeast Asia in 1929, when it began to export pipes to Dutch territorial Indochina. In 1932 it began to establish a name in Europe as well when it filled an order from Groningen, Holland, for 2,400 tons of 30-inch cast-iron pipes for a city waterworks project. Kubota became an effective competitor abroad because of its reputation for quality, a highly motivated sales force, and an emphasis on after-sales service.

Incorporated As Kubota Limited in 1930

In 1930 the company underwent a reorganization to insure that it would continue to be successful when its self-made founder was no longer managing. Kubota Limited was incorporated that year. It was not long after the company's incorporation that the threat of war loomed once again. The 1930s were a decade of Japanese expansion. The country was dominated by military and industrial groups who looked abroad to compensate for overpopulation and a shortage of raw materials. In November 1936 the increasingly authoritarian Japanese government signed the Anti-Comintern pact with Germany, becoming part of a coalition of European and Asian powers. In September 1940 Japan joined Germany and Italy in the Tripartite Pact, which divided Asia and Africa into spheres of influence. Under the pact, Japan was to get Southeast Asia. With Germany's initial defeat of the European imperial powers, it appeared to Japanese expansionists that Southeast Asia was available for the taking, and they moved in to stake their claim. Japan's attack on Pearl Harbor, Hawaii, on December 7, 1941, signaled its intentions.

War was once again good for heavy-industrial producers such as Kubota. Now producing engines as well as pipes and machine tools, the company benefited handsomely from the war effort.

The war ultimately devastated the country, however, and led to the postwar rule of the Allied victors. One advantage of General Douglas MacArthur's tenure was his determination to put the country back on its feet. Kubota's agricultural-equipment division and cast-iron pipes for restoring the country's basic services brought the company back to prosperity.

Agricultural Equipment Manufacturing Developed After World War II

Shortly after the war ended, Kubota's power tiller, the K-2, won a prestigious prize in the Okayama Agricultural Power Equipment Competition. The prize confirmed Kubota's preeminent position in the agricultural-machine industry. Kubota went on to develop machinery especially suited for Japanese agriculture, culminating in the production of the first domestically produced tractor and a special tractor for rice cultivation in 1960. Kubota also developed a wide range of rice transplanters. By the end of the 1960s, the company could offer a fully integrated mechanized system for rice production: earthmoving, rice-planting, harvesting, and threshing machines.

Kubota also continued to innovate in its traditional product areas. In 1954 the company expanded its pipe manufacturing operations by adding asbestos cement pipe and vinyl pipe to its product list. In 1959 Kubota became the first Japanese company to develop a spiral-welded steel pipe.

In 1952 the company entered the plant-construction business when it designed and constructed a cement-mixing plant for the Yoyokawa Agricultural Water Utilization Office of the Ministry of Agriculture and Forestry. This successful venture established Kubota's reputation for building new, technologically modern facilities, and the company built up-to-date plants for a variety of clients.

Entered Building Materials Sector in the 1960s

In 1960 Kubota advanced into a new related area when it developed Colorbest, a roofing and external wall material that is lightweight and nonflammable. Within 30 years the new material had captured 75 percent of its market. Other building materials, including home siding, aluminum-cast fences and gates, and interior home products such as enameled cast-iron bathtubs, were later added to Kubota's housing materials and equipment division, making the company a major producer of building products. Kubota management recognized the postwar development of the company by adopting a new slogan, "Everything from Nation Building to Rice Growing."

By the 1960s, Japan had made a remarkable recovery. Its industry was advancing at an unparalleled rate, and Japanese exports increased almost fourfold over the decade. The massive postwar investment in heavy machinery and a rebuilding effort that involved developing state-of-the-art factories were partly behind the industrial resurgence.

Also important in Japan's recovery was the relationship that Japanese businesses had with government and with banks. Norihiku Shimizu, a Japanese economist, called the collaboration "Japan, Inc., the biggest company in the world." What Japan, Inc. meant for Kubota was the opportunity to establish policies with government and business leaders, favorable national policies, and a higher rate of debt than in other industrialized countries. The average Japanese company has a debt to equity ratio of 80 to 20, just the opposite of those of U.S. companies.

Postwar Expansion Overseas

Like other major Japanese industrial producers, Kubota took advantage of this economic climate by expanding overseas. The company established subsidiaries in Brazil in 1957, Taiwan in 1961, the United States in 1972 and 1973, Iran in 1973, France in 1974, and Thailand in 1977. The company opened overseas offices in Taipei, Los Angeles, Bangkok, New York, Athens, Jakarta, London, and Singapore. A casting plant using the latest techniques and computer technology was constructed in East Germany in 1985.

Just as the company had made Japanese rice cultivation more efficient in the 1950s, the agricultural machinery division looked at conditions in foreign countries to provide custom-made solutions to indigenous agricultural conditions wherever it competed. It also adapted its pipe technology and water control systems to flood control in Third World countries.

Japan's success in competing in world markets, however, provoked a backlash. By the end of the 1960s, other nations where Kubota was doing business were condemning Japan for taking advantage of the relatively free foreign markets while restricting foreign access to its own expanding economy. The international outcry—and the 10 percent U.S. import surcharge—along with a severe recession due to the shock of 1973 when the cost of the oil imports that Japanese industry relied on rose dramatically, meant that changes had to take place in the Japanese way of doing business.

At Kubota, more resources were devoted to research and development. The office of business planning and development was established in 1982 to promote innovation, and a research and development headquarters was established in 1984. By the end of the 1980s 1,500 employees were working on new product and technical development. The advances developed by the research team were especially pronounced in the electronics area, where Kubota became a major producer of industrial sensors, scales using microcomputer technology, optical-fiber technology used in steel mills, computer equipment, and other electronic equipment.

In the computer sector, Kubota was especially active in the area of disk drives, purchasing hard drive maker Akashic Memories Corporation in 1987 and forming a joint venture, Maxoptix Corp., with Maxtor in 1989 to make erasable optical-storage disks. Kubota also purchased minority stakes in MIPS Computer Systems Inc., a Sunnyvale, California-based maker of high-speed microprocessors for minicomputers; and Boulder, Colorado-based Exabyte Corp., maker of computer tape drives. Kubota expanded its computer interests in 1989 when its Ardent Computer Corporation merged with Stellar Computer to form Stardent Computer Inc., producer of graphics supercomputers. Meanwhile, the company began manufacturing in the United States for the first time with a plant in Gainesville, Georgia, making attachments for front-end loaders.

1990s and Beyond

Kubota promoted a different image for its centennial in 1990 by replacing the name Kubota Limited with Kubota Corporation. That year the company invested $50 million for a 5.4 percent stake in Columbus, Indiana-based Cummins Engine Co., a maker of heavy-duty diesel engines. Kubota hoped the alliance with Cummins would enable it to build engines for its European operations. Also in 1990 Kubota was sued by the cofounders of Ardent who alleged that Kubota fraudulently obtained computer technology by forcing the merger that created Stardent and then transferring technology to a subsidiary, Kubota Graphics. Kubota vigorously denied the allegations.

As the 1990s continued Kubota pulled back from its ventures in U.S. high tech. First, in 1991, the $130 million the company had invested in Stardent and its predecessor companies failed to turn the venture around and Stardent's chairman decided to call it quits. Kubota Graphics was likewise dissolved in 1994. Citing increased competition and industry overproduction, Kubota withdrew from the hard drive business in 1997 when it sold Akashic Memories to StorMedia Inc. of Santa Clara, California, and it divested its stake in Maxoptix through a management buyout. Meanwhile, the company received a boost from increased orders for earthquake-resistant ductile iron pipe and water storage tanks for emergency use, following the Great Hanshin Earthquake of 1995.

The slumping Japanese economy hurt Kubota's results in the later 1990s. During fiscal 1998 the Asian economic crisis had an impact as well, and net sales fell from ¥1.14 trillion in 1997 to ¥1.03 trillion in 1998. Similarly, net income fell from ¥28.95 billion to ¥21.78 billion. Nevertheless, Kubota's long tradition of successful adaptation seemed likely to see it through the troubled times. Such innovations as roofing materials that integrate solar cells and others that incorporate television antennas were keeping the company's product mix from growing stale. In addition, Kubota was quickly reacting to the recessionary Japanese market by continuing to explore overseas markets, such as the 1998 formation of a joint venture to manufacture farm equipment in China.

Principal Subsidiaries

Kubota Tractor Australia Pty Ltd.; Kubota Brasil Ltda. (Brazil); Kubota Canada Ltd.; Kubota Metal Corporation (Canada); Jiangsu Biaoxin Kubota Industrial Co., Ltd. (China); Kubota Europe S.A. (France); Kubota (Deutschland) GmbH (Germany); Kubota Baumaschinen GmbH (Germany); P.T. Kubota Indonesia; P.T. Metec Semarang (Indonesia); Sime Kubota Sdn. Bhd. (Malaysia); Kubota Agro-Industrial Machinery Philippines, Inc.; Kubota Servicios España S.A. (Spain); Shin Taiwan Agricultural Machinery Co., Ltd.; The Siam Kubota Industry Co., Ltd. (Thailand); Kubota (U.K.) Limited; Kubota Tractor Corporation (U.S.A.); Kubota Credit Corporation, U.S.A.; Kubota Manufacturing of America Corporation (U.S.A.); Auburn Consolidated Industries, Inc. (U.S.A.); Kubota America Corporation (U.S.A.); Kubota Electronics America Corporation (U.S.A.); Kubota Finance (U.S.A.), Inc.

Principal Divisions

Farm & Industrial Machinery Consolidated Division; Pipe & Fluid Systems Engineering Consolidated Division; Environmental Control Plant Consolidated Division; Materials Consolidated Division; Housing Materials & Utilities Consolidated Division; Air Condition Equipment Division.

Further Reading

Bulkeley, William M., and Udayan Gupta, "Japanese Find U.S. High Tech a Risky Venture," *Wall Street Journal,* November 8, 1991, pp. B1, B2.

Chipello, Christopher J., and Jacob M. Schlesinger, "Kubota Forges Ahead on High-Tech Push," *Wall Street Journal,* July 19, 1990, p. A6.

"Gonshiro Kubota: The Founder of Kubota, Ltd. Profile and Achievements," *Kubota Times,* First Quarter 1990.

Gross, Neil, "Why Kubota Hitched Its Tractor to Cummins," *Business Week,* July 30, 1990, pp. 20–21.

Introducing Kubota, Ltd., Osaka: Kubota, Ltd., 1989.

Kelly, Kevin, and Mark Ivey, "Turning Cummins into the Engine Maker That Could," *Business Week,* July 30, 1990, pp. 20–21.

Levine, Jonathan B., "Ardent's Daddy Warbucks," *Business Week,* June 12, 1989, pp. 26–27.

Nakamoto, Michiyo, "Kubota Refocuses Computer Side," *Financial Times,* October 26, 1994, p. 33.

—Ginger G. Rodriguez
—updated by David E. Salamie

L.A. T Sportswear, Inc.

1200 Airport Dr.
Ball Ground, Georgia 30107-5010
U.S.A.
(770) 479-1877
Fax: (770) 720-2240
Web site: http://www.latsportswear.com

Public Company
Incorporated: 1978
Employees: 356
Sales: $72.6 million (1997)
Stock Exchanges: NASDAQ
Ticker Symbol: LATS
SICS: 2329 Men's & Boy's Clothing, Not Elsewhere
   Classified; 2339 Women's Misses & Jr. Outerwear,
   Not Elsewhere Classified; 5136 Men's Clothing &
   Furnishings; 5137 Women's & Children's Clothing

L.A. T Sportswear, Inc. is a major manufacturer and distributor of imprintable and decorable knitted sportswear. The distribution arm of the business is one of the fastest-growing distributors in the industry. Its manufacturing division makes T-shirts, sweatshirts, one-piece rompers, dresses, and coordinating separates, offering both imprinted as well as blank sportswear, principally in the form of T-shirts and sweatshirts. The company distributes its own products under its Full Line Distributors division, which also distributes the products of 13 other garment and accessory manufacturers including Fruit of the Loom, Hanes, Russell, and Fieldcrest/Cannon. The company's primary customers include small independent imprinters, embroiderers, advertising specialty companies, and sporting goods stores.

L.A. T Sportswear was founded by Isador E. Mitzner in 1978, operating as a broker of overstocked and discontinued T-shirts and other screenprintable garments. The company was controlled in common by The Connection Group, Inc. and SPZ, Inc., both based in Georgia. L.A. T expanded into the distribution of baseball and golf caps, in addition to developing a business as an independent manufacturers' sales representative. In 1982, L.A. T contract-manufactured its first proprietary line of activewear for infants and toddlers, marketed under the Rabbit Skins label. Following the success of its Rabbit Skins products, the company purchased the cut and sew operations of its contract manufacturer and began manufacturing operations. Six years later, the company introduced a line of fashion-oriented imprintable sportswear for women, which expanded into a unisex product line offered under the L.A. T Sportswear label. The company began screenprinting its infant and toddler sportswear which was marketed to mass merchandisers, theme parks, resort specialty shops, and college book stores, among others.

In 1987 the company formed the Full Line division out of the merger of two small independent distribution locations in Texas and southern California. A relatively small line of imprintable golf shirts and sport shirts had been marketed by the independents prior to the merger. The Full Line division increased the product line to include T-shirts, sweatshirts, caps, jackets, bags and aprons, athletic jerseys, and shorts. Full Line added distribution centers in the Atlanta, Pittsburgh, and the San Francisco Bay metropolitan areas.

Expansion in the Early 1990s

By 1990, L.A. T's net sales had reached $34.4 million. In that year T-Shirt Brokerage Services, Inc., a cap and apparel broker, was spun off from the company, as was The Ball Ground Reps, Inc., a commission sales representative for various manufacturers. A new distribution center was opened in Chicago just as the company prepared for tight margins due to the major T-shirt mills' heavy inventories for 1994. The company offered a new product—an adult French Terry clothing line—and was encouraged by its successful performance. L.A. T sought market niches in an industry dominated by larger mills that produced enormous inventories of imprinted sportswear—where L.A. T's ability to produce on a shorter product run basis allowed for more innovative product design or fabric introductions, which differentiated the company from its competitors.

In January 1994, the company offered 1.2 million shares of common stock at $10 per share in its initial public offering.

Company Perspectives:

L.A. T Sportswear, Inc. targets market and product niches where the major mills don't compete. The company's strategy aims to create a more complete line of new and innovative products, including the expansion of sales of private label products—a market too small for the major producers. The company is committed to carrying complete inventories in significant depth to minimize out-of-stock occurrences, and will concentrate on the addition of distribution locations to further expand one-day UPS delivery to 90 percent of the U.S. The company continues to focus on improving customer service and internal operations.

Following the IPO, The Connection Group, Inc. was merged into SPZ, Inc., at which time the companies reorganized from S Corporation status to C Corporation status.

By 1995 the Rabbit Skins label had become one of the leading producers in the infant/toddler market, accounting for half of the manufacturing division's sales. The Rabbit Skins line consisted of 36 styles and 724 individual items, manufactured using a variety of fabrics including 100 percent cotton and cotton/polyester blends. The company was committed to offering products of high quality fabrics and stylish designs. A screenprinted product program with Wal-Mart stores was a primary reason for increased sales in its manufactured sales sector. Michael's Stores was another major account which the company supplied with a new line of popular fleece products. Printed products included garments bearing the licensed names, logos, and mascots of major colleges and universities. Following the development of screenprinting capability which decorated the Rabbit Skins line, sales of the company's decorated products grew to 15 percent of the division's sales; blank Rabbit Skins products accounted for the remaining 85 percent of sales. The adult L.A. T Sportswear label accounted for about 20 percent of that division's sales, consisting of relatively upscale garments such as dresses, leggings, fashion T-shirts, pantsuits, and tops. L.A. T for Kids ages five to ten accounted for approximately 10 percent of that label's sales. L.A. T became one of the few manufacturers to supply specialty sportswear to all three age brackets. Almost one-third of the company's blank products were sold through its manufacturing division to screenprinters. Sales to distributors, including the company's own distribution division, craft stores, and mass merchants, made up the remaining outlet for blank products.

The Full Line distribution division grew in product line and in the number of manufacturers it represented, utilizing catalogue distribution (275,000 catalogues were sent in 1994) as a primary marketing device. The catalogues were made available at trade shows, supplemented by mailings to potential screenprint and other customers. Trends in activeware consumption were recognized in overall growth of 15 percent annually as consumers identified with various groups and events, and began dressing more casually. The company distributed products made from nationally recognized manufacturers such as Fruit of the Loom, Hanes, Russell, Jonathan Corey, Print-ons, Augusta Sportswear, Anvil, and Yupoong, as well as its own products. Geographically,

the division grew from its original distribution centers in Anaheim, California, and Houston, to include centers in Pittsburgh, Atlanta, San Francisco, Chicago, Miami, and St. Louis.

Targeting the 1996 U.S. Summer Olympic Games

L.A. T signed a letter of intent with the Hanes division of Sara Lee Corporation to use trademarks, licensed to Sara Lee by the U.S. Olympic Committee and the Atlanta Committee for the Olympic Games, in connection with the 1996 Summer Olympic Games. The company used the Hanes label and trademarks for the promotion of its fashion knitware for youth and adults with the intention of distributing the products through its mass-market accounts and mid-tier retailers. The company was optimistic that other licensee agreements for special events would be generated from the Olympic venue exposure.

The company began experiencing major setbacks in 1995 due to several factors, including disappointing revenues related to the Olympics products. That market became saturated when the number of sub-licensees grew, and the company had overestimated the amount of inventory required to fill that market niche. In addition, stiff competition caused prices to fall—and adding to the losses an offshore manufacturing program failed when problems relating to the quality of their manufactured products affected sales and production, and delivery cycles were delayed. The program was discontinued by late 1995 during a period when the U.S. market was hit by increased import competition and a soft market. Further complicating matters, the company struggled with the implementation of a new computer system which supported catalogue sales and distribution. The conversion took much longer than expected to install, resulting in system failures, disputes with customers, the loss of critical data, and impaired collection efforts. Losses reached approximately $3.6 million in 1995, compared with net income of $2.9 million reported in the previous year. Operating expenses extended to $21 million. L.A. T fell out of compliance with its bank agreement, which was financed with Bank South. The company had been allowed a $30 million credit line, and once that limit had been reached they began renegotiating with Bank South while also seeking out the possibility of replacement financing through other lenders. The company eventually established a three-year, $35 million credit line with Mellon Bank, secured by "virtually all the assets of the company," according to David Shelton, chief financial officer for L.A. T.

In an effort to restructure operations, L.A. T realigned its management team and discontinued certain product lines. Vice-president and board director Jeffrey S. Lebedin resigned and Robert C. Aldworth became executive vice-president and COO. Operations were closed at the San Francisco; Byffe, Alabama; and Chicago distribution facilities and it was decided that the printing facility should discontinue operations by the summer of 1996. Profits continued to decline in 1996, when sales dropped 20.3 percent, as the company struggled to regain ground lost during the restructuring period.

1997: Returning to Profitability

By the third quarter of 1997 L.A. T was reporting a net profit of $184,000. Addressing the company's rebound, CEO and Chairman Isador Mitzner told the *Daily News Record* that

"Although the industry remains sluggish and we continue to face stiff price competition, we are encouraged by a second straight profitable quarter compared to prior-year losses."

In response to the intense competition in the screenprint garment distribution business, L.A. T reaffirmed the need to provide good quality, competitive pricing, prompt delivery, a wide selection of products, and a high level of customer support. Internal operations were streamlined through improved flexibility in inventories which negated the prior tendency to maximize quantities of goods in order to best serve customers. New methods of tracking allowed the cutting and sewing departments to produce at levels more consistent with demand, reducing inventories in many cases. As of December 1997, L.A. T was positioned to fill a backlog of orders valued at approximately $1.9 million. Reflecting the diversity of its sales base, the company reported that in 1997 its largest customer accounted for less than two percent of sales, and the company's ten largest customers accounted for less than eight percent of sales. L.A. T's active customer list had grown to over 26,000 customers.

Nationally, the company's primary competitors in the screenprint garment distribution business included Broder Brothers, Staton Wholesale, California Shirt Sales, and South Carolina Tees. Regionally, distributors such as San Mar, Alpha Shirts, and Stardust competed for the company's business. L.A. T recognized that in order to compete with these companies and others it needed to focus on product design, quality, pricing, and responsiveness to customer service demands. Chairman and CEO Isador Mitzner stated in company reports that "through better inventory control, we have added 125 new styles for 1998, without significantly increasing our overall inventory investment. This merchandising strategy is appealing to our customer base. With our day to day operations significantly improved, the Company will focus on a sales strategy, beginning in the second quarter of 1998, in an effort to improve our revenues. The success of this mission should create the opportunity to return the Company to profitability in 1998."

Principal Divisions

Full Line Distributors.

Further Reading

Combining Manufacturing with Distribution of Specialty Activewear, Atlanta: L.A. T Sportswear, Inc., 1995.
"L.A. T Posts $426K Loss in First Quarter," *WWD*, May 20, 1996, p. 13.
L.A. T Sportswear, A Corporate Profile, Atlanta: L.A. T Sportswear, Inc., 1995.
"L.A. T Sportswear Earnings Dip," *Daily News Record*, August 22, 1996, p. 10.
"L.A. T Sportswear, Inc. Back in Black," *Daily News Record*, November 10, 1997, p. 17.
"L.A. T Sportswear, Inc. Signs Letter with Sara Lee on Olympic Apparel," *Daily News Record,* July 1, 1994, p. 8.
"Noncompliance—L.A. T Sportswear, Inc. Did Not Respect Its Bank Credit Line Agreement Due to Loss in FY 1995," *WWD*, April 3, 1996, p. 14.

—Terri Mozzone

Lefrak Organization Inc.

97-77 Queens Boulevard
Rego Park, New York 11374
U.S.A.
(718) 459-9021
Fax: (718) 897-0688
Web site: http://www.lefrak.com

Private Company
Incorporated: 1905
Employees: 16,000
Sales: $2.75 billion (1997 est.)
SICs: 1382 Oil & Gas Field Exploration Services; 6513
    Operators of Apartment Buildings; 6552 Land
    Subdividers & Developers, Except Cemeteries; 7812
    Motion Picture & Video Tape Production; 7922
    Theatrical Producers (Except Motion Picture) &
    Miscellaneous Theatrical Services

Lefrak Organization Inc. was, by the late 1990s, one of the largest private real estate development companies in the world. It was the nation's eighth largest owner of multifamily apartment buildings in the United States, with 61,000 units—all or most in New York and New Jersey—including Lefrak City and the residential portions of Battery Park City and Newport. The organization, a family holding company consisting of hundreds of subsidiaries, also controlled millions of square feet of office and retail space in projects that it developed. In addition, the Lefrak Organization was the holding company for Lefrak Oil & Gas Organization (LOGO), engaged in exploration, and Lefrak Entertainment, which operated the record label LMR, owned stage and movie theaters, and produced movies and Broadway and television shows.

From Glazier to Mass Market Builder: 1905–60

Russian-born Harry Lefrak came to the United States from Palestine as a youth about 1900, arriving in New York City with $4 in his pocket. He had learned glazing and carpentry from his grandfather and father and with the latter founded what was to become known as the Lefrak Organization in 1905, concentrating its efforts on manufacturing customized lamps for Louis Comfort Tiffany. After some personal reverses, Harry Lefrak sold the glass factory in 1919 and began erecting row houses in Brooklyn, eventually constructing entire blocks of homes in the Bedford-Stuyvesant area. As Brooklyn filled up, the Lefrak Organization switched to building apartment houses for middle-income families, constructing more than 400 such buildings in the metropolitan area.

The Lefrak Organization became a partnership in 1940 when Samuel Lefrak, Harry's only son, joined the firm, buying a piece of the business. He became president in 1948, on the threshold of the great homebuilding boom that followed World War II. But he was still only a small-time Brooklyn builder in January 1951, when he scraped together the $50,000 binder needed to support his $5 million winning bid at public auction for 29 pieces of real estate and 20 mortgages being liquidated. To raise the $500,000 down payment required by law, he pledged the ten most valuable properties as collateral. To finance the rest of the sum he had to sell the other properties for less than their assessed valuation, but the ten properties he retained yielded enough cash to win further loans for the large-scale building projects he envisioned.

By the late 1950s Lefrak's gamble had proved to be a resounding success. In 1957 the Lefrak Organization erected buildings with a total of 2,000 apartments, mostly in Queens and Brooklyn; in 1958 the number grew to 2,500, and in 1959 it reached 4,600. By 1960, 250 corporations established under the partnership owned and collected rents from more than 200 buildings, most of them constructed by Lefrak. The organization bought land and materials at bulk prices, did its own architecture, engineering, painting, plastering, and carpentry, and bought forests and clay and gypsum quarries to operate its own lumber mills, brick factories, and cement plants. Mechanical services were the only major part of a project contracted out. Although Sam Lefrak generally eschewed government-assisted programs, his organization built the first project under New York's Mitchell-Lama law in 1957, a 520-unit Brooklyn development that used low-interest, state-guaranteed loans and tax abatements.

Some of the Lefrak Organization's apartment buildings were owned outright or jointly in Baltimore, Washington, Philadelphia, Boston, Dallas, Minneapolis, and Los Angeles, but most were in the New York metropolitan area, where labor, materials, taxes, debt, and land costs were more expensive than anywhere else in the nation and where most builders felt the middle-income apartment monthly market-rent range—$30 to $40 a room—was not worth building for. By vertical integration and obsessive attention to cost control, the Lefrak Organization was able to turn a profit building mostly six-story brick walk-ups in Brooklyn and Queens for this market. By 1963 it was the landlord for about 250,000 people and was receiving more than $5 million a month in rentals.

Sam Lefrak's management style was to employ so many executives that he said he could not remember how many vice-presidents there were. They made few major decisions but carried out Lefrak's own decisions to build, buy, or borrow. Speaking of his executive vice-president, he said, "I make the deal and he cleans it up." Another executive was leasing and renting administrator of the organization's buildings and also headed a self-insuring subsidiary. The legal department kept Lefrak informed on building codes and also sought code revisions from state legislators. Other departments were devoted to architecture, construction, and field engineering.

To hold down costs the Lefrak Organization bought land years in advance of a project, warehoused steel and bricks at distress prices, thoroughly tested sites to save on building expenses, and fostered steady cash flow to hold down interest rates on its loans. The organization's size and wealth enabled it to take a hard line with subcontractors, suppliers, and manufacturers. Sam Lefrak even looked into the feasibility of building a nuclear power plant to reduce electricity costs. A former associate called him a "ferocious negotiator"; a rival developer preferred the term "vicious negotiator."

Big New York Projects, 1960–96

In 1960 the company announced its largest endeavor yet: Lefrak City, a high-rise residential development on a swampy but strategically located 40-acre Queens site purchased for $7 million. Built with no government aid of any sort, not even Federal Housing Authority mortgage insurance, it was the largest privately financed apartment development in the world. Completed in 1967 at a cost of $150 million, Lefrak City included 20 18-story towers with 5,000 apartments. There also were two office buildings. Although drab and uninviting in appearance, Lefrak City offered two-bedroom apartments for about $220 a month and efficiencies for as little as $102 a

month. Amenities available (for additional fees) included terraces, parking, a swimming pool, and air conditioning.

During the 1960s Lefrak Organization projects included two high-rise urban development housing projects on Manhattan's West Side and Westchester Plaza, a large-scale development in suburban Mount Vernon. In 1972 the Lefrak Organization put up its first major midtown Manhattan office building, and by 1976 it was the company's single most valuable property. With the run-up in fuel prices that followed the 1973 oil embargo, Sam Lefrak decided to secure his own supplies of fuel by founding Oklahoma-based Lefrak Oil & Gas Organization (LOGO), which in 1981 was drilling nearly 100 wells in the United States.

The Lefrak Organization in 1976 had an asset value estimated at between $500 million and $700 million and net worth of perhaps $100 million. Debt service was running about $30 million and annual net cash flow at about $10 million to $12 million. The holding company consisted of some 350 separate companies and was owned by Sam Lefrak, his wife, and their four children, including Richard, president of the parent firm. Arsam Investment Co. was engaged in several venture capital deals. Lefrak Communications operated LMR, the record label that launched Barbra Streisand, and also invested in music publishing and television and movie production. By this time Sam Lefrak had changed the spelling of his name to LeFrak (pronounced le*frak*) instead of Lefrak (pronounced *lef* rak). He later said the change had been necessary because other Lefraks at his club had been cited for nonpayment of dues.

The last Lefrak Organization development in New York City was Battery Park City. In 1969 the company, over heavy competition, won the right to co-develop this ambitious state project on a mile-long, 92-acre site along the Hudson River in lower Manhattan, formed by landfill from the construction of the World Trade Center. Plans called for a collection of office buildings, stores, and apartment towers, financed by issuing state agency "moral obligation" bonds backed by rents from office leases. With the advent of the 1973–74 recession and the subsequent default of the bonds, the project stalled.

Lefrak and his partners were able to obtain FHA insurance, sell bonds to the public, and complete the 1,712-apartment Gateway Plaza complex, consisting of three 34-story towers and three low-rise buildings, in 1981. After that red tape and lawsuits took a further toll, and Battery Park City, in reduced form and without further Lefrak Organization participation, was not completed until the 1980s. "The bureaucrats tortured him," a real estate executive and former city official later told a reporter. The bureaucrats had another story: they disliked the drab towers he had built, and when they told him he would have to bid against other developers for further work, he replied that "he didn't want to stand in a delicatessen line."

Heavily Jewish Lefrak City underwent white flight in the mid-1970s, after the Lefrak Organization was sued for alleged discrimination against blacks. By 1980 two-thirds of its residents were blacks. By 1990 only nine percent of the residents were white (compared with 82 percent in 1970). The complex suffered from rising crime and vandalism, and its biggest commercial tenant, the Social Security Administration, departed in

1989. Yet by 1996 increasing immigration from the former Soviet Union had resulted in a resurgence of the Jewish community. The black population included not only longtime residents but a large number of West African Muslims who had settled in Lefrak City over the past decade and were considered a stabilizing factor. New York City's Department of Environmental Protection had, in 1991, moved into the office space formerly occupied by the Social Security Administration.

Newport: 1986–98

In the 1980s the Lefrak Organization's attention turned from the city to the blighted Hudson River waterfront in New Jersey, opposite from lower Manhattan. In partnership with the Glimcher Co. and Melvin Simon and Associates, Lefrak in 1986 began converting 600 acres of abandoned railroad tracks along the Jersey City shoreline into a $10 billion mixed-use complex named Newport. The privately financed project received tax abatements and a $40 million federal urban development grant, the largest ever.

By 1990 the Lefrak Organization had erected four high-rise buildings with 1,624 apartments and condominium units, a huge shopping mall with a multiplex cinema, and a 1,000-boat marina. A 475,000-square-foot office building also was completed. An economic downturn put an end to further building, however, with only one-third of the project completed, and LeFrak refused to pay property taxes due to Jersey City, arguing he had not received promised services. The dispute was later resolved.

Lefrak resumed work in 1995 with the start of construction for Towers of America, a group of four residential buildings on a peninsula jutting into the Hudson. By autumn 1998 two had been completed and work had begun on a third. Ground was broken in May 1998 for a 575,000-square-foot Lefrak-financed office building, even though no leases had been signed—making it the first speculative building to rise in the metropolitan area in 20 years. The company also began construction in 1998 of a 200-room Marriott hotel in Newport. A riverside esplanade, marina, and heliport already were in place. When completed, Newport was to include 9,000 apartments, 4.5 million square feet of office space, two million square feet of retail space, and 1,200 hotel rooms.

A 1992 *Business Week* article listed the Lefrak Organization's real estate empire as consisting of 92,000 apartment units, primarily in the New York metropolitan area; five million square feet of office space, mostly small buildings, but including a high-rise at 40 West 57th Street in Manhattan; and five million square feet of retail space, including Ashley Plaza in Charleston, South Carolina, and Tri-State Mall in Wilmington, Delaware. Lefrak Oil & Gas held 300 oil- and gas-producing properties in Louisiana, Texas, and Oklahoma; two years later, it bought 200 more oilfields. Lefrak Entertainment Co.'s Broadway productions had included *Nine* and *Crimes of the Heart* (both of which won awards and were co-produced by Sam Lefrak's daughter Francine). Its recording artists had included Dolly Parton and Stevie B. as well as Barbra Streisand.

According to an annual survey by *National Real Estate Investor,* however, the Lefrak Organization had an apartment ownership interest in only 61,127 units in 1992. The number given by this publication for 1998 was 61,000. Sam LeFrak's son, Richard, had been president of the Lefrak Organization since at least 1987 and was in charge of day-to-day administration. *Forbes* estimated the worth of the LeFrak family holdings in 1998 at $1.7 billion.

Further Reading

Carlson, David B., "Sam Lefrak: He Builds Them Cheaper by the Dozen," *Architectural Forum,* April 1963, pp. 102–05.

"Formula for Profit—Middle-Income Rents," *Business Week,* May 28, 1960, pp. 199–200, 202.

"Harry Lefrak, Builder, Is Dead; Known for Middle-Income Units," *New York Times,* July 2, 1963, p. 29.

Hevesi, Dennis, "On the Hudson, A City Within Jersey City," *New York Times,* September 13, 1998, Sec. 11, pp. 1, 6.

Karp, Richard, "The World According to Sam Lefrak," *FW/Financial World,* April 2, 1991, pp. 62–65.

Lavelle, Louis, "Lefrak Beginning $60M Tower in N.J.," *Bergen Evening Record,* May 14, 1998, p. B1.

Lowenstein, Roger, "LeFrak's City," *Wall Street Journal,* December 15, 1987, pp. 1, 26.

Onishi, Norimitsu, "Stabilizing Lefrak City," *New York Times,* June 6, 1996, pp. B1, B4.

Rudnitsky, Howard, and Rudolph, Barbara, "New Boys in the Oil Patch," *Forbes,* March 16, 1981, pp. 108, 110.

"Sam Lefrak: Real Estate Bargain Hunter," *Business Week,* May 31, 1976, pp. 50–54.

Steinem, Gloria, "The Lefrak Way of Life," *New York Times Magazine,* July 31, 1966, pp. 18, 20, 22, 25.

Stodghill, Ron II, "Sam Lefrak: Enjoying the Last Laugh," *Business Week,* September 7, 1992, pp. 68, 70.

—Robert Halasz

Levy Restaurants L.P.

980 N. Michigan Avenue, Fourth Floor
Chicago, Illinois 60611
U.S.A.
(312) 664-8200
Fax: (312) 280-2739
Web site: http://www.startrekexp.com/bkgd/levy.html

Private Company
Incorporated: 1978
Employees: 1,168
Sales: $165 million (1997 est.)
SICs: 5812 Eating Places; 7389 Business Services, Not Elsewhere Classified

A fast-growing foodservice operator based in Chicago, Levy Restaurants L.P. operates nearly two dozen restaurants in the United States and provides specialty concessions to an equal number of sports complexes, amusement parks, and convention centers. Levy Restaurants began as a traditional restaurant operator, developing popular dining concepts that tapped into just-emerging dining trends. During the 1980s, the company also began providing specialty catering services, a business that eventually developed into its mainstay operating segment. This concession business, operated through Levy Restaurants' Sports and Entertainment Group, supplies gourmet food to corporate skyboxes, luxury suites, and private clubs at baseball, football, and basketball venues throughout the United States. In addition, the concession division supplies food to amusement centers, convention halls, zoos, and parks. Levy Restaurants' smallest business segment—its Consulting and Advisory Services Group—provides consulting services to other restaurant operators seeking to develop new dining concepts. Lawrence F. Levy owned the company.

Origins

The Levy brothers began their involvement in the restaurant business in Chicago, where they built the core of their food service business around a faltering delicatessen during the late 1970s. In the months prior to going into business together, Larry and Mark Levy had established careers independent of one another. Although both had relocated from St. Louis to Chicago, they had made the journey separately and upon arrival had begun working for different companies. Mark joined the insurance business and Larry delved into real estate, each accumulating enough financial wherewithal to jointly open a delicatessen named D.B. Kaplan's with a third partner in 1976. Initially, the business was intended to be a sideline venture for each brother. Said Larry: "I had always loved deli food and thought there was no good deli food in Chicago. I found a backer to do it, and I thought I would continue at my other company." In a matter of months, however, closer, hands-on involvement was required. The operation of the delicatessen and its 285-item menu quickly proved too much an undertaking for the Levys' third partner, prompting Larry and Mark to fire him. Mark quit his insurance job and, along with his wife, took on the responsibility of D.B. Kaplan's daily operation. Immediately afterwards, according to the brothers, the delicatessen showed strong signs of improvement, transforming from a money-loser to a profitable enterprise under the direct stewardship of Mark Levy. Two years later, in 1978, Larry quit his job as well and joined his brother in the restaurant business, embarking on a career that allowed his natural talents to flower.

At an early age, Larry Levy showed himself to be an entrepreneur at heart. Before he was ten years old, Levy sold magazine subscriptions and handmade pot holders door to door. During his high school years, he developed a discount card that his fellow students could use when buying merchandise from selected merchants. While attending the Kellogg School of Management at Northwestern University during the late 1960s, Levy shuttled through the dormitories selling sandwiches and charter airline tickets to Europe, making extra money while he earned his M.B.A. degree. "I've always been an entrepreneur," Levy explained years after D.B. Kaplan's success spawned a small empire of restaurant properties. "When I found the restaurant business," he said, "my entrepreneurial skills met passion. It's something I truly love doing."

After Levy left his real estate job in 1978, he and his brother formed Levy Restaurants and the Levy Organization, a commercial real estate company. With the establishment of these two companies, the corporate vehicles for expansion were in place, but the success of the delicatessen did not give birth to a chain of D.B. Kaplan clones. Instead, the two brothers developed new restaurant concepts, pursuing a strategy that would lead to a heterogeneous patchwork of restaurants all owned by Levy Restaurants. During the first years of Levy Restaurants, the Levys developed several major restaurants in Water Tower Place, one of Chicago's premier high-rise shopping malls. One of the restaurants located in Water Tower Place was Chestnut Street Grill, a grilled seafood restaurant that quickly became highly popular. It was one of the first Chicago restaurants to feature grilled seafood, offering the public a welcomed alternative to deep-fried or sautéed fish. A number of other restaurants were opened, each one buttressed by a distinctive concept that, in several cases, represented a harbinger of national restaurant trends. Grilled seafood became the rage during the 1980s, and the Levys were one of the first restaurateurs to capitalize, if not engender, the trend, as they were with the craze for upscale, Italian restaurants with wood-burning ovens. In the early 1980s, the Levy Organization built an office and residential tower in Chicago and inside established Spiaggia, an upscale Italian eatery featuring a wood-burning oven, built by the restaurant division in 1984. By paying close attention to detail, emphasizing service, and carefully crafting attractive concepts, the Levys recorded eye-catching success, emerging as well-known, well-respected restaurateurs on a national scale by the mid-1980s.

Concession Business in the 1980s

Within a decade, the Levys had established a thriving, diverse family of restaurants, but neither brother was satisfied with his solid success in a notoriously capricious area of business. Together, they began moving into a different niche of the foodservice industry as they added to their collection of restaurants. The Levys became involved in specialty catering, providing foodservice at Chicago's Ravinia Festival, an outdoor music amphitheater, and in the corporate suites at Comiskey Park, the home of Major League Baseball's Chicago White Sox. Begun as a sidelight venture, the foray into concession foodservice expanded as the original restaurant division grew. Walt Disney Company selected the Levys to create, own, and operate two restaurants at its Pleasure Island complex in Orlando, leading to the opening of the Fireworks Factory and the Portobello Yacht Club in 1985. The diversification proved to be intrinsic to Levy Restaurants' later success, evolving into an indispensable component of the Levy empire.

The importance of the company's concession business emerged during the late 1980s. At the time, Mark and Larry Levy found themselves waging against fierce competition as the number of heavily conceptualized restaurants throughout the country proliferated. Several of the Levys' restaurants were closed, abandoned in some cases because the concept created had failed to draw diners and in other instances the restaurants folded because of encroaching competitors. The late 1980s stumble did not represent a crisis, but it did serve as a turning point for the company's future direction. The Levys rethought their strategy in the foodservice business and opted to pursue a different course. Explained Larry Levy: "We said we could compete with everybody else in the world as concept creators,

or we could look at how successful we had been with White Sox and Ravinia and saw that it could be a much bigger business." Although the Levys would continue to establish new restaurants, in the years ahead the emphasis would be on developing the concession side of their foodservice activities. Gradually, the concession division grew to equal, and then exceed, the size of the restaurant division in terms of annual sales.

1990s Growth

As the brothers moved forward with their plan, they focused on private dining and catering in sports arenas, amusement parks, zoos, and convention centers, marketing themselves as restaurateurs able to provide restaurant-quality food in locales previously dominated by traditional concessionaires. The strategy worked, generating ample new business. In 1991, Levy Restaurants began operating foodservice facilities in Chicago's McCormick Place convention center, the largest convention center in the United States, and added a wealth of other clients, such as Lincoln Park Zoo, Wrigley Field, Arlington International Racecourse, and the Centel Western Open, one of the Midwest's premier golf tournaments. By 1992, much had been achieved in a short time to bring about the type of company envisioned by the Levys in the late 1980s. Annual revenues for Levy Restaurants hovered around $100 million, with 45 percent of the total collected by the company's family of concept restaurants and 55 percent coming from its fast-growing concession business.

The mid-1990s were marked by progress for both facets of the company's business, but particularly its specialty concession business. When Cleveland's Jacobs Field opened in the spring of 1994, Levy Restaurants served as the specialty foodservice provider, operating all the food and beverage service for the stadium's 375-seat Terrace Club private dining room and 450-seat bar, its 124 private suites, and the ball park's Club Lounge, with 2,100 adjacent outdoor Club Seats for season ticket holders. Later in the year, Levy Restaurants began catering at Arrowhead Stadium, home of the National Football League's Kansas City Chiefs, and the following year the company began catering for suites and preferred seating at the new Oregon Arena, home of the National Basketball Association's Portland Trailblazers. The restaurant division was active as well, with its most notable achievement being the establishment in Los Angeles in 1994 of DIVE!, a restaurant concept created in partnership with director Steven Spielberg and Jeffrey Katzenberg, a former Disney executive. Managed by Levy Restaurants, DIVE!, on the outside, looked like a neon-lighted submarine crashing through 30-foot walls of water, with 35-foot lighthouses flanking each side. Inside, where diners selected from a menu of gourmet submarine sandwiches, the concept was carried to the fullest extent, complete with portholes, cinematic aquatic scenes outside the portholes, and a computer system that simulated a submarine dive every 45 minutes. The Los Angeles DIVE! generated $10 million in sales during its first year of operation and led to the opening of a second DIVE! in Las Vegas in June 1995.

By 1995, Levy Restaurants was a sprawling operation, with 23 conventional restaurants and 17 specialty concessions. Annual sales swelled to $150 million. Amid the flurry of activity that took place during the mid-1990s, Levy Restaurants was reorganized, as management came to grips with the growth of new business segments. The company was restructured, whittled down from five divisions to three divisions. For a number of years the company had been providing consulting services on an informal basis to other restaurant operators, assisting them in developing concepts, but by the mid-1980s these services had developed into a genuine business for Levy Restaurants and were organized into the company's new Consulting and Advisory Services Group. The other two divisions were the company's Restaurant Group, which operated the traditional concept restaurants that had been Levy Restaurants' hallmark since the late 1970s, and the Sports and Entertainment Group, which managed the company's specialty concessions.

Three years after the restructuring, a significant leadership change occurred that marked the end of a long-lived partnership and set the stage for Levy Restaurants entry into the 21st century. In August 1998, Mark Levy sold most of his interests in Levy Restaurants to start a new, self-funded investment firm, ending his 22-year business partnership with his brother. Larry Levy, who continued to serve as chairman and chief executive officer, remarked, "we wanted to do two separate things. Now we are both happy." On that amicable note, Larry Levy, without his brother as vice-chairman, looked toward the future, envisioning great things to come for his diversified foodservice company. With sales expected to reach $200 million at the end of 1998, Levy Restaurants stood poised to collect considerably more revenue in the years ahead, particularly from its Sports and Entertainment Group, which had signed contacts with a half-dozen major sports venues in Denver, Los Angeles, Atlanta, Indianapolis, Miami, and Cleveland. "More than half our business hasn't opened yet," Levy noted in the wake of his brother's departure. With the arrival of this new business fueling confidence for the future, the company charted its plans for the coming century, gradually creating an entirely different company than the small, delicatessen operator that had started business in 1976.

Principal Divisions

Restaurant Group; Sports and Entertainment Group; Consulting and Advisory Services Group.

Further Reading

Heimlich, Cheryl Kane, "This Joint's No Dive: Movie Moguls Target Miami for Restaurant," *South Florida Business Journal,* June 16, 1995, p. 3A.
"Levy Enters the Big Leagues with Specialty Concessions," *Nation's Restaurant News,* August 10, 1992, p. 30.
Scarpa, James, "Grandstand Play," *Restaurant Business,* June 10, 1993, p. 101.
Walkup, Carolyn, "Lansing Vows to 'Raise the Bar' at Reorganized Levy," *Nation's Restaurant News,* November 20, 1995, p. 3.
——, "Larry Levy: Always an Entrepreneur," *Nation's Restaurant News,* September 20, 1993, p. 127.
——, "Larry Levy: Chairman, Chief Executive, Levy Restaurants, Chicago," *Nation's Restaurant News,* January 1995, p. 12.
——, "Levy Brothers Split; Business Growth to Proceed," *Nation's Restaurant News,* August 10, 1998, p. 3.
——, "Now Batting in Cleveland: Chicago's Levy Restaurants," *Nation's Restaurant News,* April 25, 1994, p. 7.

—Jeffrey L. Covell

Littelfuse, Inc.

800 East Northwest Highway
Des Plaines, Illinois 60016
U.S.A.
(847) 824-1188
Fax: (847) 391-0894
Web site: http://www.littelfuse.com

Public Company
Incorporated: 1938
Employees: 2,845
Sales: $275.2 million (1997)
Stock Exchanges: NASDAQ
Ticker Symbol: LFUS
SICs: 3613 Switchgear & Switchboard Apparatus; 3625
   Relays & Industrial Controls; 3679 Electronic
   Components, Not Elsewhere Classified

Littelfuse, Inc., aptly named, is a company that designs, manufacturers, and sells a wide range of electronic, automotive, and industrial products throughout the world. Headquartered in Des Plaines, Illinois, a suburb near Chicago, Littelfuse has manufacturing facilities throughout the United States, and in China, England, Korea, Mexico, the Philippines, and Switzerland, as well as sales and distribution centers in the United States, Brazil, Hong Kong, Japan, the Netherlands, and Singapore. While so many of its fuses and circuit protection devices are "smaller than a speck of pepper," as the company has stated, Littelfuse's ubiquitous products—found in telecommunications, computers, appliances, medical equipment, automobiles, and a myriad of other industrial and electronic products—have kept lives running smoothly for years, though few are aware of Littelfuse's products and even less recognize the company by name.

Starting Off Small, 1920s to 1959

Edward V. Sundt, the founder of Littelfuse, was a man of many trades. The youngest child of a Baptist minister, Sundt

was raised in western Manitoba where he later worked as a lumberman, farmer, and a member of the famed Royal Canadian Mounted Police. Sundt attended Brandon College in Manitoba, where he studied engineering. After graduation he moved to Chicago in 1923 and found work at General Electric and later Stewart-Warner. In his work with lamps and vacuum tubes, Sundt found meters repeatedly burned out during tests. Tinkering after hours with a variety of test meters, Sundt developed and eventually patented a small "fast-acting" protective fuse for use in test meters in 1926. At the time, the world was awash in new discoveries and daring adventures. While Sundt had toiled on his fuses, Kodak had produced the first 16mm movie film and Robert Goddard had fired the first liquid-fueled rocket. The next year, as Ford rolled out its 15-millionth Model "T," Sundt founded his own company. With $150 from selling his Chevrolet, Littelfuse Laboratories set up shop in a second floor room on Wilson Avenue, in Chicago.

Though Sundt's discovery did not seem spectacular or send shockwaves around the world, its importance was monumental in the newly evolving electronic marketplace. Though no fuses had been sold, by April 1928 Sundt and an equally dedicated coworker, Ben Kollath, had developed 10 different fuses of varied amperes as well as a couple mountings for protecting the most common meters used in electronics. After placing an ad in *Radio News*, the fledgling company finally received its first order worth $1.10. Littelfuse's innovative fuses were the first of their kind and soon very much in demand.

By the beginning of the next decade, America's obsession with the automobile led to the introduction of similar fuses for horseless carriages, just as the new phenomenon of "technocracy" became less myth and more reality in a country that boasted nearly 35 percent of the world's industrial production. Sundt and Kollath had continued to experiment and modify fuses for wider applications throughout the 1930s. In 1938 the company was incorporated, and the "Laboratories" dropped from the name. Littelfuse, Inc. had a new name and a new partner, as Thomas Blake, who had been keeping the company's books, joined Sundt and Kollath.

When global peace began to crumble and nations went to war, Littelfuse turned from manufacturing strictly small instrument-

Company Perspectives:

Littelfuse's mission is to be the world's leading circuit protection company: to anticipate and respond to the customers' needs with continuous innovation and improvement in productivity, quality, and service; to provide for the development of associates and teams to achieve superior performance; to always act responsibly, with fairness and integrity, and expect the same in all our business activities; and to create superior value for our customers and shareholders.

related fuses, with a traditionally limited use and marketplace, to producing circuit protection fuses for the communications and aviation industries. This technology, desperately needed and immediately put to use for wartime production, put Littelfuse on the map—though only temporarily. With the dawn of the 1950s, World War II faded from memory and orders suddenly stopped. Luckily Americans had turned to another newfangled invention, the television. Seemingly on the cusp of another new direction, Littelfuse began producing television fuses for the country's 1.5 million TV sets. The company had also expanded further into the automotive market with a series of new switches, relays, and electromechanical devices. Year-end sales for 1950 hit $1.96 million and Littelfuse's move into television fuses was an excellent choice. By 1951 there were more than 15 million TV sets in American homes and just three years later, over 29 million. The company's further diversification into the automotive industry proved just as propitious, since Americans owned 60 percent of all cars in the world by the mid-1950s, despite only having one-sixth of the world's population.

New Horizons, 1960–80

Littelfuse's continued growth and need for expansion funds propelled it to the next business level—becoming a publicly traded company—in the early 1960s. Its IPO came in 1962 with 10 million shares at $7 per share, and the next year the company moved to a new state-of-the-art facility in Des Plaines, Illinois. The year also brought the first of what would be a string of awards for the company: *Factory Magazine*'s "Top Ten Plants" award. In addition, Littelfuse made big news with the introduction of its new MICRO and PICO fuses, advanced subminiature fuse lines recognized by the Martin company as suitable for the world's newest obsession after automobiles and television: space exploration. Again at the forefront of a new industry, Littelfuse jumped headlong into micro-circuitry, and its latest innovations more than passed muster with NASA as both MICRO and PICO fuses were incorporated into the ambitious Gemini Space Program.

A year later, in 1964, came further recognition for the company's subminiature fuse lines, when Littelfuse was awarded a Gemini II launch vehicle flag as one of only 31 companies in the United States who supplied parts crucial to the launch of the Gemini Space Program. Littelfuse was considered not only a "critical parts supplier" for its MICRO fuse, but the fuse was deemed as a life-saving component of Gemini's Man-in-Space exploration initiative.

In 1965 most North Americans became aware of relay switches and related products with the failure of one such relay switch in Ontario which threw 30 million people into an electrical blackout (New York City's blackout occurred 12 years later). Thoroughly unaffected by the melee, Littelfuse was in the midst of further much-needed expansion, opening its second Illinois manufacturing plant, this one in Centralia, in southern Illinois. The end of the year not only brought stunning sales, at $7.43 million, but the retirement of founder Edward Sundt. Thomas Blake, who had been president since 1954, took over as chairman of the board. By 1965 sales had leapt to $11 million and in 1968, due to its ever-increasing market exposure and success, the company was acquired by the Texas-based Tracor, Inc., an international technological defense and instrument manufacturer. The acquisition also marked the beginning of the company's European expansion through a new plant in Wear, England, and an additional facility in Tyne, Washington.

With the early 1970s came the second of Littelfuse's major awards, General Electric's coveted "Outstanding Supplier" award, due mostly to the company's manufacturing of shock-proof and waterproof refrigerator door switches. The same year the company opened its third Illinois manufacturing facility, in Watseka, west of Kankakee and near the Indiana border, then moved southwest in 1973, opening a new manufacturing facility in Piedras Negras, Mexico. In 1974 came a major new product introduction with a line of indicator lights called Littelites, for use in industrial machinery, office and business machines, appliances, instrumentation equipment, and a somewhat obscure piece of equipment, the computer. Though the first "electronic brain" or automatic computer was developed in the United States back in 1942, few envisioned the role computers would later play in the lives of virtually everyone on the planet. For its part, Littelfuse was once more at the precipice of a revolution, developing fuses that helped bring computers further into the mainstream for business.

In 1976 Littelfuse debuted an unusual blade-type fast-acting fuse, another first for the market, called the Autofuse, used in automotive manufacturing. Developed for miniature fuse blocks found in all automotive vehicles, the Autofuses were a huge hit with General Motors, and soon became standard for auto manufacturers throughout the United States, Europe, and Japan.

Acquisition and Its Aftermath, 1980–89

The early 1980s brought both global and domestic expansion for Littelfuse, with the 1981 acquisition of a fuse and related products manufacturer in the Netherlands, Olvis Smeltzeringenfabriek B.V. (later renamed Littelfuse Tracor, B.V.) and the 1982 purchase of seven acres of land adjacent its Des Plaines headquarters. An existing 48,000-square-foot building on the property was renovated for additional warehouse and packaging space. The next year, 1983, found Littelfuse in court fighting a wave of counterfeit products bearing the company's name. Filing suit against several outfits manufacturing, importing, and selling bogus Autofuses, Littelfuse sought and was granted an Exclusion Order to prohibit importation of the patented fuses—one of only 28 such grants issued since 1974—and a boon for the company and its products. This year also marked the building of another new manufacturing plant with all the latest technological breakthroughs and most recent state-of-the-art advances in automation, robotics, microprocessor-based testing and controls, CAD/CAM systems, and more. Additionally, Littelfuse spent millions on a new testing laboratory to maintain the highest possible standards.

At the end of the decade, Howard B. Witt joined Littelfuse; in the long term he was to have a profound impact on the company. The 1980s brought a host of technological advances, with IBM's debut of the first personal computer, or PC, in 1981 and the Apple MacIntosh and its silly ''mouse'' launched in 1984. After returning to the drawing board for several new applications and design breakthroughs of its own, Littelfuse debuted the FLNR and FLSR Slo-Blo power fuse product lines in 1985. The highly automated fuse lines offered what the company deemed ''excellent time delay,'' as well as ''dual element and current-limiting characteristics'' for a wide range of electrical products. The company was also honored by another award, the ''Q1,'' bestowed by Ford Motor Company to Littelfuse's Watseka plant in Illinois for high quality. The following year, 1986, Ford again presented the company with a Q1 for the Des Plaines headquarters plant, while General Motors awarded the company's Mexico plant with its coveted ''Certified Supplier Award'' for the enduringly popular appliance switch. Also in 1986, came the opening of another Illinois plant, in Arcola, as well as several new product introductions including the Minifuse, which replaced the popular Autofuses and took up far less space; the Maxifuses which replaced traditional fusible wire and links; and the superminiature Flat-Pak fuse lines for computers, televisions and VCRs.

In the midst of the leveraged buyout craze of the late 1980s, Littelfuse's parent company Tracor was bought by Dallas-based defense contractor Westmark Systems, Inc., in 1987. Yet a short time later it became clear that Westmark's highly leveraged purchase of Tracor and Littelfuse, combined with a downturn in the defense industry, put all of the companies in jeopardy. Top officers of both Westmark and Tracor, along with their senior creditors, began discussions of voluntary bankruptcy. Littelfuse, meanwhile, continued to gain recognition and turn out increasingly sophisticated fuses, including the world's smallest glass tube fuse in 1988, a full one-third of the size of previous glass tubes. Littelfuse England also became the first division of the company to receive an ISO 9002 rating, followed quickly by Littelfuse Switzerland, and the opening of a new sales office in Singapore.

A Brighter Future, the 1990s and Beyond

Despite the financial wrangling in the early 1990s, Littelfuse maintained operations and ushered in not only a new president and CEO, Howard B. Witt, but another first in the power fuse industry with the debut of the LDC series class ''L'' fuse, the only such fuse to meet UL criteria for certain AC and DC applications. The next year, 1991, Tracor and Westmark Systems Inc. were awash in financial difficulties and filed for reorganization under Chapter 11. After the companies were awarded bankruptcy protection, Littelfuse evolved from reorganization and became an independent company. Though the move was a costly one, and its stock price went as low as $7 per share, Littelfuse soon picked up speed in sales and shareholder value. By 1992 net sales were $149.8 million with net income of

$700,000, while shareholder value leapt to $19.25 per share. In 1993 Witt was appointed chairman of the board, in addition to his duties as president and CEO. Net sales for the year had climbed to $160.7 million, up nearly $11 million from 1992, while net income soared to $10 million. Both sales and income were pushed by a 15 percent sales increase in North America, a 30 percent sales hike in Europe, and a phenomenal 49 percent jump in Asian sales.

Littelfuse's sales in the mid-1990s continued to climb: 1994 brought in $194.5 million with net income $15.2 million, while 1995's net sales rose just under 13 percent to $219.5 million with a 25 percent income increase to $19.3 million. Littelfuse had also moved forward with a stock buy-back plan, repurchasing 3.5 million shares by the end of 1995. For both 1994 and 1995 shareholder value continued to fare well.

In 1996 Littelfuse celebrated its fifth year of independence and 70th year in business with a jump in net income of 13 percent to $21.7 million on net sales of $241.4 million, up from the previous year's $219.5 million. The 10 percent rise in net sales was predominantly generated by a robust automotive market and an ongoing improvement in the global electronics marketplace. Littelfuse's net income per share also climbed, to a very healthy 17 percent increase, while the company had repurchased 671,000 warrants and 285,000 shares of common stock for $26.8 million to reduce outstanding shares to 12 million.

Internationally, Littelfuse's performance was stellar—with a 29 percent sales growth spurt in the Asia-Pacific region, nine percent in Europe, and six percent in North America, while having tripled international sales since 1991. For the first time, the company found overseas electronic sales represented more than half its total sales in 1996. In response to the trend, the company had opened a new sales office in Hong Kong, as well as a technical center in Japan, and planned a manufacturing facility and warehouse in Suzhou, China, near Shanghai. The new plant not only allowed Littelfuse access to local markets in China, but it was hoped that the company's continued success in Japan and China would stimulate weaker sales in neighboring Korea. Other international expansion included enlarging its Great Britain facility, and opening a distribution and engineering center in São Paulo, Brazil, as a foundation for South American operations.

New products, such as the newly designed PTCs, or positive temperature coefficient devices, were in part why Littelfuse continued to be at the forefront of the electronics industry. The PTCs, made from a conductive polymer, were originally conceived by the Raychem Corporation, and subsequently developed by Littelfuse to reset themselves after current overflows and eliminate costly downtime. Though surface-mounted and primarily for use in computers and telecommunications equipment, PTCs had applications beyond these categories, including automotive use. With an estimated worldwide marketplace of over $200 million, an alliance between Raychem and Littelfuse provided each with an advantage in the youthful market.

A myriad of products, from barrier fuses (to protect petrochemical electronic networks) in Europe to the automotive industry's innovative fusible links, or from the development of the Powr-Gard product line to the emergence of PTCs, had kept

Littelfuse on the cutting edge of electronics. With the production of more advanced cars and trucks in the late 1990s, especially electric cars, came a greater demand for electrical fuses—a cornerstone of Littelfuse's past and future. With nine out of 10 automobiles using Littelfuse's protective circuits, Littelfuse succeeded as an OEM (original equipment manufacturer) as well as a supplier for the MRO (maintenance and repair) market.

With very strong results for 1997, including a stock split in the second quarter and shares reaching an all-time high of $35.50 in the fourth quarter, Littelfuse headed into 1998 and beyond with elevated hopes for its continued growth and success. Though some market and currency fluctuation could be expected, Littelfuse had enjoyed a compounded annual sales rate of 13 percent for the previous five years, and management expected to remain in this range for 1998 and 1999. Investments and acquisitions, like Samjoo, Korea's largest manufacturer of electronic fuses, and an expansion of the company's research and manufacturing facility in Grenchen, Switzerland, promised to keep Littelfuse on the cutting edge—a comfortable niche the company had occupied for over seven decades.

Further Reading

"Littelfuse Announces South Korean Acquisition," June 3, 1997, http://www.littelfuse.com.
"The Littelfuse Story," *Group Insurance Review,* February 1956.
"The Littelfuse Story: 1927 to 1970," *Fusette,* June 1970, pp. 4–5.

—Taryn Benbow-Pfalzgraf

Maclean Hunter Publishing Limited

777 Bay Street
Toronto, Ontario M5W 1A7
Canada
(416) 596-5000
(800) 268-9199
Fax: (416) 596-5526

Wholly Owned Subsidiary of Rogers Communications Inc.
Incorporated: 1891 as J.B. McLean Publishing Company,
  Ltd.
Employees: 800
Sales: C$235.7 million (1997)
SICs: 2721 Periodicals: Publishing, or Publishing &
  Printing; 4899 Communication Services, Not
  Elsewhere Classified

Maclean Hunter Publishing Limited is a leading publisher of Canadian consumer magazines and business publications. It is perhaps best known as the producer of *Maclean's,* Canada's English-language weekly news magazine, with a readership of 2.3 million. Other consumer magazines include *L'actualité,* Canada's French-language current affairs magazine; women-oriented *Chatelaine* (English language), *Châtelaine* (French), *Flare,* and *Modern Woman; Ontario Out of Doors;* and, through Today's Parent Group, several parenting magazines, including *Today's Parent* and *Great Expectations.* Maclean Hunter publishes more than 40 specialized business periodicals, newsletters, and directories, including *Canadian Grocer, The Medical Post, Canadian Printer,* and *Marketing.* The company also holds a 60 percent stake in Canadian Business Media Ltd., whose publications include *Canadian Business,* the country's number one business magazine. Maclean Hunter also owns MH Media Monitoring Limited, the leading media tracking source in Canada; and Canadian Ad-Check Services Inc., which specializes in co-op advertising administration, audit, reporting, and retailer payment services.

Maclean Hunter was founded in the late 19th century as a publisher of trade publications, and over the succeeding decades grew into a Canadian communications giant with operations in North America and Europe and with interests in broadcasting, cable television, and various other communication services, generating revenue of C$1.74 billion in 1993. In April 1994 Rogers Communications Inc. purchased the company, then known as Maclean Hunter Limited, for more than C$3 billion—the largest acquisition in Canadian telecommunications history. Rogers sold some of the Maclean operations, merged others into various Rogers units, and created Maclean Hunter Publishing Limited as its periodical publishing subsidiary.

Canadian Grocer *Launched in 1887*

Maclean Hunter began in 1887, when John Bayne Maclean left his post on the *Toronto Mail* to found Grocer Publishing Co. and publish the *Canadian Grocer,* a specialized publication filled with commercial news about the food industry. The first 16-page issue was sent free to grocers all over Canada, who were invited to purchase subscriptions for $2 a year. Within three months, the fledgling publication became profitable and Maclean began to publish weekly. At that time, he also brought his brother, Hugh, into the business as a partner. Expansion followed in 1888 with the establishment of *Dry Goods Review.*

Success in the grocery area led Maclean to move into other trades, and in 1888, *Hardware & Metal* was established at the invitation of a group of hardware store owners. By 1890 Maclean was publishing four business journals, and had set up his own typesetting and composition operations. In 1891, the J.B. McLean Publishing Company, Ltd. was incorporated. (Maclean was not always consistent in spelling his own last name.)

By 1893 Hugh Maclean was running the business in Toronto, while his brother J.B. worked in New York City on a short-lived art publication called *Art Weekly.* In the early 1890s, the company began to open advertising sales offices in cities outside Toronto, branching out to Montreal in 1890, and across the Atlantic Ocean to London in 1895. In 1899 John Maclean bought out his brother's one-third share in their company for $50,000.

Expanded into General Interest Publications in Early 20th Century

By 1903 J.B. McLean Publishing Company had grown to employ about 50 people. Two years later, the company was successfully publishing six business papers, including *Bookseller and Stationer, Printer and Publisher,* and *Canadian Machinery & Manufacturing News,* and its founder was anxious to make his mark in a wider field. Using the profits from his commercial journals, he purchased a magazine published by an advertising agency, called *Business: The Business Man's Magazine.* Shortening its name to the *Business Magazine,* Maclean published his first issue in October 1905. The 144-page general interest publication was made up entirely of condensed articles from other publications. Three months later, the magazine's name was again changed, this time to *Busy Man's Magazine,* with a subtitle that explained its purpose: "The Cream of the World's Magazines Reproduced for Busy People." Maclean edited it personally while also overseeing the company's other publications.

At the start of 1907, the J.B. Maclean Publishing Company introduced another general-interest publication, the *Financial Post.* The weekly was a joint venture between Maclean and Stewart Houston, a well-connected lawyer who wrote and edited the newspaper, which started out with 25,000 copies.

In the first decade of the 20th century, Maclean's publishing enterprise grew quickly. Under the autocratic and frugal leadership of its founder, who became known as "the Colonel" after he was given command of a regiment during the Boer War in 1899, the company had a high turnover of employees, frustrated by low salaries and the Colonel's constant meddling. In 1911, however, Maclean promoted the man whose name would one day join his in the corporate logo, Horace T. Hunter, to general manager. Hunter raised salaries and brought a decentralized approach to management, improving the company atmosphere and employee productivity. Also in 1911, Maclean changed the title of *Busy Man's Magazine* to *Maclean's.* He continued to act as chief editor for the flagship publication.

Not long after the end of World War I, in August 1919, Maclean's only son died unexpectedly, eliminating the possibility that his company would become a dynasty. Also that year, Maclean renamed the enterprise the Maclean Publishing Company Limited. Soon afterward, in 1920, Maclean sold 30 percent of the company to Hunter, now a vice-president, for $50,000, and another ten percent of the stock to his general manager, H. Victor Tyrrell. Other editors and executives were also given the opportunity to buy company stock. At the same time, Maclean undertook a long-overdue company restructuring and bought the one-third of the *Financial Post* that the company did not already control.

In the years following World War I, the Canadian consumer-magazine industry was overwhelmed by an influx of magazines produced in the United States that paid no import duties to enter the country. Nevertheless, throughout the 1920s, Maclean's enterprise continued to grow. In 1922, the company officially branched out from publishing into the related field of commercial printing, an activity that actually had been going on for some time. In 1909 the company had purchased an entire square block of property in Toronto to provide enough space for a printing plant for all its magazines, and over the years, the plant had begun to take on outside work. In 1927 the company first ventured outside Canada with its acquisition of *Inland Printer* and *Rock Products* in the United States, and in the following year it introduced *The Chatelaine*—later simply *Chatelaine*—a women's magazine that soon gained a loyal following.

Survived Great Depression and World War II Shortages

In 1930 the company moved into French-language publishing for Canadians when Maclean purchased *Le Prix Courant.* During this period, Maclean's company felt the impact of the Great Depression. Helped by a government duty on imported magazines, which allowed Canadian publishers to regain some of the market share they had lost to U.S. publishers, Maclean was able to avoid laying off employees by putting workers paid by the hour on shortened schedules, and cutting wages and vacation pay. Maclean Publishing Company's salaried employees suffered two ten-percent cuts in pay. In 1935 the import duties were lifted with a change in Canada's government, and U.S. publications gained predominance once more on newsstands. By 1936, however, Maclean's employees numbered nearly 900, and wages and hours had both increased. By the end of the decade, the company boasted 30 publications.

With the coming of World War II, Maclean coped with wartime rationing and shortages of goods and workers, and a drastic decline in advertising revenue. With the conversion of the economy to a wartime footing, production of consumer goods was drastically curtailed, resulting in a scarcity or disappearance of many goods, and the need for consumer product advertising thus dried up. The company attempted to compensate by encouraging "sustaining" advertising, to maintain the image and familiarity of a brand name, and through the increased use of advertising by the government. The company's business publications became tools in the war effort, monitoring the nationwide war production effort, and publicizing government policies and regulations. Even such publications as *Mayfair,* a society magazine, were transformed, advising women on war charities and economical use of food. In addition, the company produced a free edition of *Maclean's* for distribution to Canadians on active duty overseas, which eventually gained a circulation of 30,000.

In 1945 the company's name was changed to Maclean-Hunter Publishing Company to reflect the contribution of Horace T. Hunter, its president since 1933. Three years later, the company made its most dramatic physical expansion up to that point, when it opened a $3 million printing plant in a Toronto suburb, Willowdale. Throughout the postwar years, the company once again found its consumer publications facing stiff competition for advertising dollars from such U.S. imports as the Canadian editions of *Time* and *Reader's Digest.* By 1948 two-thirds of all magazines purchased in Canada came from other countries.

In 1950 John Maclean died, and Hunter acquired 60 percent control of the company, in which he continued to serve as president for two more years. In 1952 Floyd S. Chalmers, who had been with the company since 1919, became president. Throughout the 1950s, Canadian magazines found themselves challenged by new modes of communication, such as television, as well as by U.S. publications. In 1956 Canadian publishers got some help from their government when it imposed a 20 percent tax on advertising in non-Canadian magazines, but this was repealed the following year under U.S. pressure. By the end of the decade, nonetheless, Maclean-Hunter was publishing 51 different titles.

Diversified in the 1960s

The 1960s marked a turning point for Maclean-Hunter. What had until then been a staid enterprise, engaged almost exclusively in publishing, became a diversified company, operating in a wide variety of communications fields. In 1960 the company made an unsuccessful attempt to obtain a license for a television station in Toronto, but in the following year it was able to enter the broadcasting industry through its purchase of 50 percent of the radio station CFCO in Chatham, Ontario. The station had been one of the pioneers in Canadian radio, having been founded by a butcher with an interest in radio in 1926. It had used a homemade transmitter until 1948.

Maclean-Hunter also diversified into the event planning industry. In 1961, the company organized a convention for members of the plastics industry, despite the fact that Canada's main trade association for plastics was headed by a rival trade publisher, who refused to lend the association's support to the show. The show, which became an annual event, was not a great success, nor would it be for many years. Nevertheless, Maclean-Hunter forged ahead in the show-management field, forming Industrial & Trade Shows of Canada, later known as Industrial Trade & Consumer Shows Inc., in 1962.

At this time, the company also expanded its holdings in the media information services field. Maclean-Hunter had long owned *Canadian Advertising Rates & Data,* a service publication for advertising agencies, and in 1958 it had acquired *British Rate & Data.* Both were doing well, and the company was looking for new areas of growth. The U.S. market was out of the question, dominated as it was by one well-established firm, Standard Rate & Data Service, so Maclean-Hunter moved into continental Europe with the French publication *Tarif Media.* In 1961 it sold 50 percent of this publication to the U.S. company Standard Rate & Data Service, and with this partner formed a European joint venture to launch a West German service, *Media Daten.* Eventually, European operations came to include Austria, Switzerland, and Italy.

The company's Canadian operations, however, were not faring as well. Although the company had continued to expand its French-language offerings, adding its first general interest publication for the Quebec market in 1960, *Châtelaine-La Revue Moderne,* and following with *Le Magazine Maclean* in 1961, its English-language consumer magazines lost $1.8 million in that same year. This was, as ever, due partly to the domination of the Canadian market by U.S. publications. Despite this, Maclean-Hunter introduced another English-language consumer publication in 1963, targeted at younger women. It was called *Miss Chatelaine.*

A year later, in 1965, the Canadian periodical industry received some government support when the tax deduction for the business expense of advertisements in non-Canadian publications—with the exception of *Time* and *Reader's Digest*—was abolished. This opened up the field somewhat by discouraging the proliferation of U.S.-owned Canadian editions, and driving some of these publications out of business.

Also in 1965, stock in Maclean-Hunter was publicly traded for the first time. Up until this time, the company's shares had been closely held by Maclean's designated successors and a small number of members of senior management, but it became clear that internal mechanisms for distributing stock in the company were no longer adequate, and a sale of 15 percent of the shares was arranged. Of the 15 percent, 40 percent was allotted to meet high employee demand.

The company expanded further into nonpublishing fields in the mid-1960s, acquiring Design Craft Ltd., which produced exhibits for trade shows, as a natural complement to its existing interests in that area. It continued to purchase radio stations, adding CHYM, a rural station, in 1964, and CKEY of Toronto, the company's first urban radio property, in 1965. Also in 1965, the broadcasting company's interests were augmented by the acquisition of CFCN radio and television, of Calgary.

Entered Cable TV in 1967

Further ventures into the broadcasting field came in 1967 with Maclean-Hunter's entry into the cable television business. The company entered a partnership with Frederick T. Metcalf, who had already built a cable system in Guelph, Ontario, and the result was Maclean Hunter Cable TV. The first market targeted for expansion was Toronto. The company's steady progress in diversification was ratified in 1968 when its name was updated from Maclean-Hunter Publishing Company Limited to Maclean-Hunter Limited.

In the first years of the 1970s, the company ventured into book distribution, purchasing a book wholesaler; into the printing of business forms, with the acquisition of Data Business Forms; and into the paging business, by buying Airtel, provider of personal pagers to relay messages. In 1973 Maclean-Hunter purchased a 50 percent interest in KEG Productions Ltd., which put together television programs on wildlife. The company created "Audubon Wildlife Theater" and "Profiles of Nature," both successful and long-running series.

In the mid-1970s, with further expansion in the Canadian market blocked by the Canadian Radio-Television & Telecommunications Commission, Maclean-Hunter set its sights on cable television in the United States, buying Suburban Cablevision of New Jersey. Unlike Canadian cable systems, which existed to provide clear reception of ordinary network television in remote locations, the New Jersey operations set out to attract customers by offering them access to programs not available on regular television, such as special sporting events. This new concept proved popular, and Suburban Cablevision grew from ten franchises to 43.

In 1975 Hunco Ltd., the Hunter family holding firm, owned a 51 percent controlling interest in Maclean-Hunter. This block of stock was sold to the board of Maclean-Hunter in January 1976, when chairman Donald F. Hunter, facing death from a brain tumor, sold nearly 3.5 million of his family's four million shares to a holding company set up to ensure that the company would be safe from unwanted takeover attempts in his absence. The era of family control was over.

Bill C-58 (1976) Revitalized Maclean's

Perhaps the most important event of the mid-1970s for Maclean-Hunter took place outside the company: the passage of Bill C-58 in 1976. This amendment to the Income Tax Act removed the exemptions on tax-deductible advertising from *Time* and *Reader's Digest,* and stipulated that three-quarters of a publication's owners must be Canadian and four-fifths of its contents must be original and nonforeign, in order for advertising within it to qualify for a tax exemption. This gave new life to the Canadian magazine industry, in particular *Maclean's.* The flagship publication had long suffered in its head-to-head battle with *Time,* and in addition had fallen into an identity crisis under a series of editors. The magazine, which had lost credibility and had been losing money heavily since the early 1960s, had become a source of embarrassment to all concerned. With the support of Bill C-58, however, *Maclean's* was able to rally in the latter part of the 1970s, and in 1978 stepped up from a biweekly to weekly publication.

By that time, Maclean-Hunter had diversified to such a large extent that income from publishing accounted for only half of all company revenues. Notwithstanding these changes, the company continued to expand its magazine operations in the late 1970s, acquiring four special interest publications in 1978, including *Ski Canada* and *Racquets Canada,* and founding *New Mother* and its French-language counterpart *Mère Nouvelle* in 1979.

Steady expansion of Maclean-Hunter operations continued into the 1980s, with the purchase of a four-fifths interest in a U.S. form printer, Transkrit Corporation, in 1980; the acquisition of *Progressive Grocer* journal in 1982; the launch of *City & Country Home* in 1982; and the purchase of *Hospital Practice* in 1983. In 1981 Maclean-Hunter Limited dropped the hyphen in its name, becoming Maclean Hunter Limited.

Moved into Newspaper Publishing in 1982

In 1982 the company fulfilled a longstanding ambition to include the newspaper business in its ever-widening scope of operations when it purchased a 51 percent share of the *Toronto Sun,* a daily tabloid newspaper. A year later its involvement with the *Sun* led to purchase of the *Houston Post,* in Texas.

Throughout the late 1980s, Maclean Hunter continued to grow in its chosen fields, primarily through acquisitions, as in its purchase of the Yorkville Group in 1985 and Davis & Henderson Ltd. in 1986, both printers. In 1986, it started work on 49 percent-owned Barden Cablevision, which covered all of Detroit, Michigan, and subsequently began construction of a system in the United Kingdom. By 1989, newspaper holdings included *Sun* papers in three Canadian cities outside Toronto, and in 1990 the company purchased Armstrong Communications, a cable system, in Ontario.

In December 1988 Maclean Hunter made the largest acquisition in its history, taking over Selkirk Communications Ltd., a Toronto-based broadcasting and cable company, for an estimated $600 million. It subsequently negotiated deals worth a total of $310 million to sell off large segments of the target company to three other companies, including its rival, Rogers Communications. Although the Canadian Radio-Television and Telecommunications Commission approved the deal the following year, it ordered Maclean Hunter to invest $21.2 million—the size of the financial gain the company stood to make on the purchase and breakup—in a capital fund to be used to strengthen and improve Canadian broadcasting.

As Maclean Hunter entered the new decade, a recessionary economy and a concomitant decline in ad revenues resulted in lower profits. Likewise, the company's stock earnings plummeted to 14 cents per share, a 75 percent drop. According to some analysts, the company's move towards product diversity also contributed to the decline. The cost of the Selkirk acquisition, for instance, while strengthening the company's presence in the broadcasting and cable television markets, offset revenue growths from other segments of the company.

Acquired by Rogers in 1994

Maclean Hunter itself became the object of an acquisition in early 1994. Hoping to create a C$3 billion communications conglomerate that would serve a third of Canada's 7.2 million cable subscribers and provide a Canadian analog to U.S. communications giants Time Warner and McGraw-Hill, Rogers looked to purchase all of Maclean Hunter's shares, which were valued at C$3.2 million. The magnitude of the possible merger and the repercussions in the communications world provoked a variety of responses. Rogers' aggressive chief and founder Ted Rogers expressed the belief held by many that the new conglomerate would help Canada as a whole by securing its place on the information highway and, in the short term, consolidating the country's cable-TV industry and enhancing customer service. Others, however, feared the ramifications such a merger would present for the Canadian populace. Ian Morrison, president of Friends of Canadian Broadcasting, for instance, suggested that the competitive advantage gained by Rogers would hinder the free flow of information and raise prices in the Canadian entertainment industry. "When does a monopoly ever reduce the cost to the consumer?" he told the *Globe and Mail*'s Harvey Enchin and John Partridge.

In an attempt to prevent the hostile takeover, Maclean Hunter chose not to adopt a common strategy known as a "poison pill", in which a targeted company sells its assets and loads itself with debt. Rather, after Rogers made an offer of

$17 per share, Maclean Hunter chief executive officer Ronald Osborne attempted to obtain more money for shareholders by breaking up the company and selling the individual pieces at a higher rate. But no one could top Rogers' offer. After a month of heated rhetoric between the two companies, Rogers amended his offer, agreeing to pay a special dividend of 50 cents a share, raising the value of the deal by C$90 million. On March 9, negotiations were finally completed, with the C$3.07 billion acquisition consummated in April; eight months later the takeover was approved by the federal broadcast regulator.

Reborn As Maclean Hunter Publishing

After taking full control of the communications giant, Rogers elected to sell—in 1994 and 1995—Maclean Hunter's U.S. cable-television assets, several radio stations, magazines in the United States and Europe, and some printing operations. To gain regulatory approval, Rogers also had to divest CFCN-TV; it sold the station to Shaw Communications Inc. in September 1995. Maclean Hunter's Canadian cable-television systems were integrated into Rogers Cablesystems Limited. Maclean's paging operations were subsumed by Rogers Cantel Mobile Communications Inc., an 81 percent-owned unit of Rogers Communications. In 1996 Rogers sold off several additional operations acquired with Maclean Hunter, including printers Davis & Henderson and Transkrit and the 62 percent interest in Toronto Sun Publishing Corporation (which therein included a 60.2 percent stake in the *Financial Post*).

Rogers set up a new subsidiary, Rogers Multi-Media Inc. (soon renamed Rogers Media Inc.), which included the remaining Maclean Hunter assets and which consisted of two units. Rogers Broadcasting Limited included four Maclean radio stations (in addition to Rogers' several other radio stations, television stations, and other broadcasting interests). Maclean Hunter, in a roots-returning maneuver, was reborn as Maclean Hunter Publishing Limited, producer of several consumer magazines and more than 35 business publications. Revenue for the new Maclean Hunter was C$203.7 million in 1995, the company's first full year as a Rogers subsidiary.

By 1997 revenue had increased to C$235.7 million. Part of the increase was attributable to acquisitions. In February 1997 Maclean Hunter paid C$8.3 million for seven professional periodicals in healthcare, including *Family Practice* and *Patient Care*. During 1998 Maclean Hunter gained full control of Today's Parent Group, producer of the national parenting magazine *Today's Parent*, as well as *New Mother* and its French-language counterpart, *Mère Nouvelle*. Soon added to this group of parenting magazines was *Today's Grandparent*, which was launched in January 1999 and was aimed at Canadians between 50 and 70 with grandchildren under the age of 13. Maclean Hunter also launched two other new periodicals in 1998: *Advisor's Edge*, which debuted in June and targeted financial planners, and *Corporate Travel Management*, which premiered in November and was aimed at managers responsible for company travel policy.

Principal Subsidiaries

Canadian Ad-Check Services Inc.; MH Media Monitoring Limited; Toronto Life Publishing Co. Ltd.; Canadian Business Media Ltd. (60%); Today's Parent Group.

Further Reading

Enchin, Harvey, "It's Official: CRTC Okays HM Takeover," *Globe and Mail,* December 20, 1994, p. B1.

Enchin, Harvey, and John Partridge, "Rogers, Maclean Hunter Sign Deal," *Globe and Mail,* March 9, 1994, p. A1.

——, "Rogers Tempers His Takeover Bid," *Globe and Mail,* February 25, 1994, p. B1.

Gold, Douglas, "Money Managers Like MH Deal," *Globe and Mail,* March 9, 1994, p. B8.

McKenna, Barrie, "Rogers Not Splitting MH Print Empire," *Globe and Mail,* September 16, 1994, p. B4.

Partridge, John, "Media Stocks Hit Hard," *Globe and Mail,* February 23, 1991, p. B1.

——, "Profits Plunge for Newspaper, Media Giants," *Globe and Mail,* July 26, 1990, p. B7.

Perry, Robert L., *Maclean Hunter at One Hundred,* Toronto: Maclean Hunter Limited, 1987.

—Elizabeth Rourke and Jason Gallman
—updated by David E. Salamie

Madge Networks N.V.

Wexham Springs
Framewood Road
Wexham, Slough
SL3 6PJ
England
(44) 1753 661000
Fax: (44) 1753 661011
Web site: http://www.madge.com

Public Company
Incorporated: 1986
Employees: 600
Sales: US$482.1 million (1996)
Stock Exchanges: NASDAQ
Ticker Symbol: MADGF
SICs: 3577 Computer Peripheral Equipment, Not
    Elsewhere Classified; 2661 Telephone & Telegraph
    Apparatus; 7372 Prepackaged Software

Madge Networks N.V. is one of the world's leading suppliers of networking hardware. Headquartered in England (the company's tax home is in The Netherlands), Madge Networks has developed an array of Token Ring, Ethernet, ATM, ISDN, and other products providing extensive solutions for the corporate LAN (local area network), WAN (wide-area network), intranet, internet, and video conferencing markets. The company's products range from ISA- and PCI-bus adapter cards for personal computers to work group switching hubs, routers, and ISDN backbone carriers, with an emphasis on providing convergence solutions among Ethernet, Token Ring, ISDN, and the emerging ATM networking technologies. In addition to its Wexham, England headquarters, Madge operates main offices in Eatontown, New Jersey, and San Jose, California, as well as offices in more than 25 countries throughout the world.

Founded in 1986, Madge Networks has helped pioneer the networking market, the emergence of which has come to define internal and external communications among corporations in every industry. Madge Networks is one of the world's leading proponents of Token Ring technology, producing the ISA, PCI, and PC Card adapters, switches, stacks, and other devices required for its implementation. In the late 1990s Madge Networks also has taken a leading role in developing the standards and first implementations of emerging High Speed Token Ring (HSTR) technology. This new protocol provides for a dramatic increase in data transmission bandwidth, while remaining backward compatible with first-generation Token Ring technology.

Sale of the company's Lannet subsidiary to Lucent Technologies in July 1998 has reduced Madge Networks' presence in the Ethernet market, a rival networking technology to the Token Ring standard. Instead, Madge has tightened its focus to emerging video conferencing technology and ISDN carrier applications, producing switching, routing, WAN-LAN interfacing equipment to facilitate both intracorporate and intercorporate video conferencing. In the ISDN market—using digital telephone lines to increase data, voice, and video transmission bandwidth—Madge Networks has developed a line of Edge Switching Nodes (ESNs) and other carrier equipment.

Madge Networks continues to be led by founder Robert Madge. The company has been traded on the NASDAQ stock exchange since 1993. In 1997 the company posted more than US$482 million in revenues.

A Token Ring Pioneer in the 1980s

One-time horseback riding instructor Robert Madge entered the computer industry with Britain's Intelligent Software Ltd., designing computer-driven chess games. In 1986 Madge sought to set up his own business, opening shop on his family's Buckinghamshire, England farm. Unlike many computer industry start-ups, Madge brought no new technology to the market; instead, the company concentrated on exploiting a technology then being developed by IBM and dubbed the Token Ring networking protocol. Token Ring presented an alternative to the more widely implemented Ethernet technology. Whereas Ethernet broadcasted data to every endpoint on a network, Token Ring's data could be deposited at specific user terminals; the technology often would be compared with the action of a train

Company Perspectives:

Sophisticated networking is now at the very heart of a successful business. And no company is better placed to help you reap the benefits of the latest networking technologies than Madge Networks.

as it picks up and drops off passengers. Token Ring would become established as a more efficient, and more stable, networking protocol, despite the dominance of Ethernet in the early period of the networking industry.

The Ethernet field was already crowded with competitors by the mid-1980s. Madge's choice of Token Ring proved a shrewd one. Loath to take on the IBM powerhouse, other companies avoided the Token Ring market. Meanwhile, Madge could develop a profitable business operating in IBM's shadow. Madge Networks introduced its first Token Ring products by 1987. The company quickly opened up a second headquarters in San Jose, California, placing the company closer to the heart of the worldwide computer industry, a move that provided additional benefits: the company's U.S. customers believed Madge to be a large British company; Madge's U.K. customers, on the other hand, saw Madge as a successful U.S. company. Indeed, Madge's early decision to establish a U.S. presence later would be credited as essential to the company's survival and success.

Not content with simply selling Token Ring products, Madge led his company to extending the technology, introducing new products, such as the Smart Ringnode in 1989 and the company's Fastmac technology in 1990, that would bring it to the forefront of Token Ring research and development. By the early 1990s the company had outpaced even IBM's development efforts—and the larger company would begin recommending Madge's products to its own customers. An early boost came from the licensing of Madge's Fastmac technology to Cisco Systems in 1990.

Madge made a name for itself in the early 1990s as well by taking on Olof Soderblom, inventor of Token Ring technology and holder of the so-called Soderblom patent. Until 1990, Token Ring developers had been paying license fees to Soderblom's company. Madge, however, had refused from the start to make license payments, reasoning that the Token Ring products developed by his company, which, adhering to the IEEE 802.5 standard, featured a peer-to-peer local network technology, bore no resemblance to the Soderblom patents, which described remotely connected networks over telephone wires. In July 1990 Madge Networks won its legal battle with Soderblom and established the Madge name in the Token Ring industry.

The company's revenues for 1990 reached $18 million. One year later, Madge's revenues nearly doubled, to $34 million. The rise of computer networking, however, had only just begun to be seen. By the following year Madge's revenues would near $100 million. At the end of 1992 the company had managed to increase its share of the Token Ring market to seven percent—

still minor compared with IBM's 76 percent share. Yet Madge continued to build momentum, as IBM struggled to keep up with advancing technology. Until the early 1990s, Madge had been focusing on producing adapter cards, which were fitted to individual computers to connect them to the network; the company's expanding product line soon included the hubs and switching components needed to route data and allow the adapter cards to communicate.

Market Momentum in the 1990s

Madge Networks would rise rapidly through the 1990s, boosted by the boom in computer networking and by its own leading Token Ring technology. Madge successfully chipped away at IBM's Token Ring market lead, building Madge's share to more than 16 percent by mid-decade. Overall, IBM's market share quickly dropped below 50 percent—a movement aided in part by licensing agreements between Madge and networking specialist Cisco Systems.

In the 1990s Madge continued to expand its international presence, opening new offices in Germany, Hong Kong, Japan, and France and building its San Jose office into a second headquarters. To fuel the company's growth, Madge Networks went public in 1993, offering more than six million shares on the NASDAQ stock exchange. By 1994 Madge Networks' revenues had topped $213 million—an impressive growth, but still minor in comparison with its main market competitors, Cisco Systems, 3Com Corp., Bay Networks, and Cabletron Systems. In addition, many *Fortune* 1000 companies sought a broader range of networking products than Madge could offer. Although Madge had performed well in the Token Ring arena, its Ethernet capacity was lacking—even as Ethernet became the networking technology of choice in the mid-1990s.

In 1995 Madge Networks and Lannet Data Communications, an Israel-based networking specialist with a focus on LAN switches for Ethernet-based networks, agreed to merge operations in a stock swap valued at some $300 million. Lannet's operations were merged into Madge Networks, creating Madge's Ethernet division. With combined revenues of $283 million, Madge and Lannet were the smallest of the top five networking market leaders, but the combined company's product line offered a complete array of Token Ring and Ethernet products.

The merger gave Madge the ability to combine the rival networking technologies into hybrid systems—and the capacity to bridge the company's products into the latest networking technology, ATM, or asynchronous transfer mode. By the mid-1990s companies were straining the limits of the existing networking technologies. As corporations joined more and more of their work force to the company network, their networks quickly ran short of bandwidth for transmitting data. The arrival of new networking applications—in particular, video conferencing and video data transfers—not only pushed bandwidth needs to the extreme, but threatened to cripple networks entirely. ATM's more efficient use of packet technology offered the prospective of dramatic bandwidth gains. Adoption of the technology would require corporations to rebuild their networking infrastructure, and Madge Networks readied not only its own ATM products, but also the hubs and switches needed to bridge existing Token Ring and Ethernet equipment to the new technology. The Lannet merger enhanced Madge's portfolio of LAN switches, needed to connect Ethernet and Token Ring stations to corporate ATM installations.

Aiding Madge's growth was the 1995 agreement with Cisco Systems, by then global networking leader, to incorporate Madge's Token Ring switches into Cisco's products and to license other parts of Madge's Token Ring technology for future Cisco designs. At the same time, Madge gained access to Cisco-developed LAN and WAN switching software. Following on the Cisco agreement, Madge also prepared to step up its manufacturing capacity, with a new facility in Ireland.

The Madge-Lannet combination seemed to be the right match: by the end of 1995 the company, now with some 1,400 employees, achieved revenues of more than $400 million, all but 15 percent coming from outside its U.K. base. The company entry into 1996 continued its expansion efforts, including adding to its Israeli manufacturing capacity with a new $10 million plant in Jerusalem. In February 1996 Madge moved to plug another hole in its product line with the acquisition of Teleos Communications Inc., bringing that company's ISDN and WAN access products. Based in Eatontown, New Jersey, Teleos, which posted revenues of $24 million in 1995, cost Madge $165 million in a pooling of interests transactions. At the same time, Madge again deepened its relationship with Cisco Systems, broadening the company's licensing agreements to include Cisco's IOS software.

At the end of 1996 Madge rolled out a new line of products to enhance its portfolio and bring the company into a new and increasingly important market: video conferencing. Madge's products placed the company in position to offer bridge solutions between the formerly independent data and video transmission technologies. Although the video conferencing market had yet to mature, Madge's move appeared to place it firmly near the lead to compete for what analysts considered a future boom market.

Yet, for the short term, Madge's growth was slowing. After years of strong expansion, the company's revenues for 1996 reached only $482 million. In 1997 the company began posting losses; analysts suggested that the company, in attempting to broaden its product line, had lost its product focus. By August 1997 the company was forced to restructure, laying off some 650 employees. During the mid-1990s, Madge had attempted to transfer the bulk of its headquarters operations to the United States, building up employee capacity around its San Jose offices. The conflict of time zones, however, proved difficult for the company to overcome; the choice was made to concentrate the company's activities in the similar England-Israel times zones, and the company's U.S. offices were scaled back.

Madge's restructuring continued to occupy the company into 1998. In late 1997 the company spun off its Ethernet division into a separate subsidiary, once again named Lannet. After denying early reports that it was looking to divest its Ethernet business, Madge agreed to sell Lannet to Lucent Technologies for $117 million in July 1998. During this period, Madge also moved to exit the manufacturing business, selling its Ireland plant to Celestica, an electronics contract manufacturer. The total cost of Madge's restructuring passed $50 million, but the company's renewed commitment to Token Ring technology appeared to have stabilized the company's balance sheet. By mid-1998 Madge had once again returned to profitability.

In the late 1990s Madge's attention focused on developing the next-generation Token Ring technology, High Speed Token Ring, offering scalable bandwidth from 16 Mbps (megabit per second) to 100 Mbps, with future speeds reaching into the gigabit ranges. Abandoning the Ethernet market appeared to be somewhat risky, given that technology's popularity, but Madge could continue to build on its strengths—and renewed focus— in Token Ring technology.

Further Reading

Bosma, Martin, ''Hollandse Madge Jaagt op Omzet IBM in Silicon Valley,'' *Trouw,* June 23, 1995, p. 6.

Burke, Steven, ''Lone Wolf Wins Early Round in Token-Ring Patent Fight,'' *PC Week,* July 2, 1990, p. 1.

Loudermilk, Stephen, ''Token-Ring Vendor Madge Aims to Grab Market Share from IBM,'' *PC Week,* November 23, 1992, p. 133.

''Madge Networks N.V. Completes Lannet Transition with Sale to Lucent Technologies,'' Wexham, England: Madge Networks N.V., July 9, 1998.

''Madgical Mystery Tour,'' *Economist (U.S. Edition),* December 16, 1995, p. 67.

Musich, Paula, ''Switching Match: Madge, Lannet to Unite,'' *PC Week,* June 26, 1995, p. 12.

——, ''Trying to Beat the Heat, Madge Restructures,'' *PC Week,* August 18, 1997, p. 123.

Wirbel, Loring, ''Madge Buys Teleos, Swaps Software with Cisco,'' *Electronic Engineering Times,* February 12, 1996, p. 28.

—M. L. Cohen

Mammoet Transport B.V.

De Ruyterkade 7
1013 AA Amsterdam
The Netherlands
(31) 20 6387171
Fax: (31) 20 6386949
Web site: http://www.mammoet.com

*Jointly Owned Subsidiary of Koninglijke Nedlloyd N.V.
and Decafin SpA.*
Incorporated: 1971
Employees: 810
Sales: NLG 320 million (US$160 million) (1996 est.)
SICs: 4789 Transportation Services, Not Elsewhere
Classified; 4499 Water Transportation Services, Not
Elsewhere Classified

Mammoet Transport B.V. is one of the world's leading "heavy-lift" and special transport companies, with a fleet of specialized transport and lifting vehicles, vessels, and equipment with lifting capacities ranging up to 13,000 tons or more. Based in The Netherlands, Mammoet operates through its primary subsidiaries Mammoet Decalift International B.V., handling land-based projects, and Mammoet Shipping B.V., handling oceangoing transport, and through a network of subsidiaries located worldwide. The combination of land-based and oceangoing transport capacity enables the company to offer the logistics planning and implementation of large-scale and long-distance transportation projects. Mammoet specializes in large-scale operations such as the transportation of nuclear reactor cores, power plants, pre-constructed mining operations, and other "mammoth" projects, often to remote locations lacking the roads and other infrastructure needed to transport the extreme weights associated with these structures.

The company's land-based equipment ranges from its fleet of computer-driven SPMTs (self-propelled modular transporters), with total capacity of more than 11,000 tons, to conventional heavy-duty platform trailers with total capacity of more than 12,000 tons. The company's vehicle fleet includes

more than 85 road trailer systems; more than 70 heavy-duty road trailers with capacities ranging from 25 to 100 tons; more than 100 heavy-duty road trucks; and a fleet of forklifts with capacities ranging up to 20 tons. Mammoet also operates its self-designed Hydra-Jack lifting system, composed of nearly 20 units with total lifting capacities exceeding 7,000 tons. The company's fleet of some 200 cranes offers lifting capacities ranging from ten to 2,000 tons.

The company's land operations form the complement to its extensive oceangoing fleet of heavy cargo vessels, under the direction of the Mammoet Shipping subsidiary. Mammoet Shipping operates as the managing agent for Mammoet Heavy Lift Partners, a pool of vessel owners, including several Mammoet subsidiaries and affiliates, and Mitsui-OSK Lines of Tokyo. The combined fleet includes Mammoet's "Happy" transporters: the Happy Buccaneer and the more recently (1997) commissioned Happy River, Happy Rover, and Happy Ranger, with lengths of 138 meters (145 for the Buccaneer) and with steer-based wheelhouses complemented by traditional bow-based wheelhouses for Suez and Panama canal passages. The company also owns or manages a number of other vessels, including the Project Orient, the Project Arabia, the 161-meter Enlivener and Encourager, and the 153-meter Envoyager. In 1998 the company added the Sailer Jupiter, owned by partner Mitsui-OSK Lines (which also owns the Envoyager, Enlivener, and Encourager), to its fleet of vessels.

Mammoet operates as the heavy transport subsidiary of The Netherlands' logistics and transportation company Koninglijke Nedlloyd, which controls approximately two-thirds of Mammoet, and Italy's Decafin SpA. Mammoet remains a profitable arm of Nedlloyd, despite heavy investments needed for the subsidiary's 1997 launch of its new Mammoet Engineering operation. In the late 1990s Mammoet added approximately NLG 320 million to Nedlloyd's annual sales.

Mammoth Mergers in the 1970s

Mammoet was the product of the merger of three family-owned Netherlands transport companies—HTM Goedkoop, Van Wezel, and Stoof—between the years 1971 and 1973. All three companies had long histories in goods transportation. The oldest, Goedkoop, traced its foundation back to 1805 and was one of the chief instigators of the Mammoet merger. Goedkoop's specialty historically had been water-based transport, plying its fleet of barges and tugboats through The Netherlands' highly developed canal system. Under the leadership of Jan Goedkoop, the decision had been made to expand into land-based transport. In this way, the company would be able to offer a complete range of transport services, with a focus on the heavyweight sector. Joining Goedkoop in 1971 was Van Wezel, which dated its origins to 1845; the merged company took on a new name, Mammoet Transport B.V., using the Dutch word for "mammoth" to emphasize the company's intended market. The new company represented as much a pooling of equipment as a gathering of know-how in the growing and increasingly complex heavy-lift transport market.

The third founding member of the company joined later that year, when Stoof, located in the southern city of Breda, was taken over by Mammoet Transport. The family-owned Stoof had been founded in 1927, delivering packages with horse-drawn carts. The company began moving into heavier transports in the years following World War II and over the following two decades had become a specialist in heavyweight and complicated logistical transports. Stoof's land-based operations complemented Mammoet's water-based transport capacity, enabling Mammoet to position itself as a transport provider covering the full range of steps—whether on land or over sea—from factory floor to final destination. At the time of the new takeover, Stoof had begun operations on its first international contract, the transport of nuclear power reactor vessels to Sweden. That experience would prove necessary for enabling Mammoet to become a worldwide heavy-lift specialist.

The transport of oversized and heavyweight objects became a more and more common occurrence in the 1970s, as construction and production techniques enabled the fabrication of larger and larger structures. Other factors came into play: the oil crisis of the early 1970s prompted most of northern Europe to begin massive offshore oil exploration and exploitation operations in the North Sea. The increased offshore and sea-based activity would further encourage Mammoet's international ambitions. In 1973 the company established a specialized seagoing arm, Mammoet Shipping B.V., as a partnership with Dutch shipbuilding giant KNSM (Royal Netherlands Steamship Company). Within this partnership, Mammoet acquired its first specialized heavy lift vessel, the Happy Pioneer. A former sludge carrier, the Happy Pioneer opened new international opportunities for Mammoet. Although the company originally had expected to serve primarily the European market, it was able to press the Happy Pioneer into service on longer runs. By 1974 the

company had begun delivering to the Far East, transporting components of a nuclear power station to South Korea. The Happy Pioneer was indeed a pioneer, being the first transport ship to include lifting equipment permanently affixed to the starboard (right) side of the vessel—a feature that soon would become commonplace in the international shipping industry.

Over the next several years Mammoet gradually became a subsidiary of KNSM, as the larger company acquired Mammoet's shares. By 1976 Mammoet was a full subsidiary of KNSM. The merger into the larger company gave Mammoet the capital to expand its equipment. Two important additions to the company's fleet were the Happy Rider and Happy Runner, both of which were custom-built and delivered in 1976, and both of which were designed with starboard-side integrated lifting systems. While Mammoet was expanding its oceangoing fleet, it also was innovating on land. In the mid-1970s the company was able to take the lead in the international heavy-lift industry with the development of its Hydra-Jack system, which used an arch framework to provide a combination of hydraulic and electric powered lifting units capable of lifting far heavier weights than standard crane systems.

While Mammoet was expanding its business among its European neighbors, during the second half of the 1970s it also was establishing an important presence in the Middle East, in particular among the oil-producing Gulf States, including Saudi Arabia, Kuwait, the United Arab Emirates, Qatar, and Oman. In 1979 Mammoet's position was enhanced further by the takeover of Dutch rival Big Lift, a subsidiary of Holland American Line, which was moving then to concentrate its focus on its cruise ship business. Big Lift not only brought Mammoet a stronger position in Europe, it also brought Mammoet the joint venture Alatas Big Lift. Later named Alatas Mammoet, this subsidiary, based in Saudi Arabia, would prove crucial for the growth of Mammoet's Middle East operations.

Back home in Europe, Mammoet added a new partnership, Mammoet/BBI, providing trailer transport operations between the United Kingdom and continental Europe. Founded as a 50/50 partnership in 1977, Mammoet/BBI would become wholly owned by Mammoet Transport in 1983. At that time the company was renamed as Mammoet Ferry Transport B.V., specializing in English Channel and North Sea cargo transport.

New Owners for the 1980s

The 1981 merger of parent KNSM with Koninglijke Nedlloyd (a.k.a. Royal Nedlloyd) gave Mammoet Transport a new parent and a new role as the rapidly expanding Nedlloyd's Heavy Transport division. After acquiring full control of the Mammoet/BBI partnership in 1983, Mammoet, under its Mammoet Shipping arm, next formed Mammoet Heavy Lift Partners in 1984. Created as a pool of heavyweight-capable oceangoing vessels, owned not only by Mammoet Transport, but also by Germany's Project Carriers (later Hansa Linie) and Sloman Neptun Schiffahrts, Mammoet Heavy Lift Partners would come under operational control of Mammoet Shipping, which acted as managing agent. While operating Mammoet and other partners' vessels (including those of later partner Mitsui-OSK Lines of Tokyo, which joined in 1989), the Heavy Lift Partners also operated a number of charter vessels. This arrangement gave Mammoet one of the world's foremost fleets of heavy-lift ocean vessels. At the end of the decade, this position was consolidated further with the merger of Mammoet Transport and Hansa Linie's shipping interests into Mammoet-Hansa-Linie A.G. Bremen.

Expansion During the 1980s and 1990s

In 1986 Mammoet expanded its Dutch presence with the acquisition of 50 percent control of Walter Wright, the transport subsidiary of Verenigde Bedrijven Bredero. Formed as Walter Wright Mammoet, the remaining 50 percent of Walter Wright would be acquired the following year. In 1987, also, Mammoet made moves to enter the North American markets, acquiring what would become Mammoet Western Inc., based in California. The company's U.S. holdings would be strengthened before the end of the decade with the purchase of 50 percent of Davenport & Sons Inc., based in Rosharon, Texas. This acquisition was regrouped under the name Davenport Mammoet Heavy Transport Inc. A separate subsidiary was set up in Canada. Although some 55 percent of Mammoet Canada Limited would be held by third parties at the start of the 1990s, in 1993 the company acquired full ownership of its Canadian subsidiary. Meanwhile, the company also acquired majority interests in its Davenport subsidiary, building to 90 percent in 1990 and to nearly 92 percent in 1993, before taking full control in 1995.

The booming economies in the Asian Pacific region presented new opportunities for Mammoet. In addition to the vessels added to the Heavy Lift Partners group by youngest member Mitsui, Mammoet had been expanding the company's presence, with a minority share in Skanza Mammoet Transport Sdn Bhd, based in Malaysia. In 1994 Mammoet increased its share of this company to 88 percent. In that same year, Mammoet Shipping opened its Korean office. Mammoet's growth was reflected in the order for three new vessels placed in 1995. Parent Nedlloyd, however, after an extensive expansion drive, had been struggling for profits. In 1995 Mammoet Transport was merged with the heavy-lift operations of Italy's Decafin, forming Mammoet Decalift International B.V. Mammoet Transport continued to hold the majority (67 percent) of these operations. Such was not the case with its Mammoet Shipping subsidiary, which in 1995 was placed under the majority control of Spliethoff's Bevrachtingskantoor. From 51 percent control at the start of 1995, Spliethoff would build to a 70 percent holding by the end of that year.

After establishing new subsidiaries in South Africa in 1996 and in the Philippines in 1997, Mammoet took delivery of its three new vessels, the Happy Rover, the Happy Ranger, and the Happy River. These new vessels were joined by partner Mitsui's new Sailor Jupiter, which set sail in the first half of 1998. By then Mammoet long had been established as the world's premier heavy-lift transporter, with annual sales of approximately NLG 320 million per year. Whereas the Asian region had formed an increasingly important role in Mammoet's activities, the effect of that region's economic problems in the late 1990s on Mammoet—and parent Nedlloyd—remained to be seen.

Principal Subsidiaries

Mammoet Decalift International B.V.; Mammoet Shipping B.V.; Mammoet Stoof VOF; StoTra B.V.; Mammoet Transport N.V. (Belgium); Mammoet Transport (UK) Ltd.; Mammoet Transport Norge A/S; Mammouth Transport France S.a.r.l.; Mammoet Ferry Transport B.V.; Mammoet Ferry Transport GmbH (Germany); Alatas Mammoet Co. Ltd. (Saudi Arabia); Mammouth Gulf (United Arab Emirates); Navigation Mammouth Gulf (Qatar); Mammoet Transport USA LLC; Mammoet Western Inc.; Davenport Mammoet LLC; Mammoet Canada Inc.; Mammoet Kew (South Africa); Mamut de Colombia S.A.; Mammoet Transport B.V. (Japan); Mammoet Shipping (Korea); Walter Wright Mammoet Ltd. (Hong Kong); Vermerk Limited (Bangladesh); Syarikat Walter Wright (B) Sdn Bhd (Brunei); Walter Wright Mammoet (PH) Inc. (Philippines).

Further Reading

"Mammoet Company Profile," Amsterdam: Mammoet Transport B.V., 1997.

—M. L. Cohen

McDonald's Corporation

McDonald's Plaza
Oak Brook, Illinois 60523
U.S.A.
(630) 623-3000
Fax: (630) 623-5004
Web site: http://www.mcdonalds.com

Public Company
Incorporated: 1955
Employees: 267,000
Sales: $11.41 billion (1997)
Stock Exchanges: New York Midwest Frankfurt Munich
    Paris Tokyo Zürich Geneva Basel
Ticker Symbol: MCD
SICs: 5812 Eating Places

Since its incorporation in 1955, McDonald's Corporation has not only become the world's largest quick-service restaurant organization, but has literally changed Americans' eating habits. On any given day, about eight percent of the U.S. population will eat a meal at a McDonald's restaurant; in a year, 96 percent of Americans will visit a McDonald's. The company stands head and shoulders above its competition, commanding by far the leading share—42 percent—of the U.S. fast-food market (Burger King is number two with 19 percent). Internationally, McDonald's runs more than 23,500 restaurants in 114 countries. Eleven major markets—Australia, Brazil, Canada, England, France, Germany, Hong Kong, Japan, the Netherlands, Taiwan, and the United States—account for 87 percent of overall sales and 92 percent of operating income. McDonald's growth is best described as phenomenal; McDonald's has recorded increases in revenues, income, and earnings per share every quarter since it went public in 1965.

Early History

In 1954 Ray Kroc, a seller of Multimixer milkshake machines, learned that brothers Richard and Maurice (Dick and

Mac) McDonald were using eight of his high-tech Multimixers in their San Bernardino, California, restaurant. His curiosity was piqued, and he went to San Bernardino to take a look at the McDonalds' restaurant.

The McDonalds had been in the restaurant business since the 1930s. In 1948 they closed down a successful carhop drive-in to establish the streamlined operation Ray Kroc saw in 1954. The menu was simple: hamburgers, cheeseburgers, french fries, shakes, soft drinks, and apple pie. The carhops were eliminated to make McDonald's a self-serve operation, and there were no tables to sit at, no jukebox, and no telephone. As a result, McDonald's attracted families rather than teenagers. Perhaps the most impressive aspect of the restaurant was the efficiency with which the McDonalds' workers did their jobs. Mac and Dick McDonald had taken great care in setting up their kitchen. Each worker's steps had been carefully choreographed, like an assembly line, to ensure maximum efficiency. The savings in preparation time, and the resulting increase in volume, allowed the McDonalds to lower the price of a hamburger from 30 cents to 15 cents.

Believing that the McDonald formula was a ticket to success, Kroc suggested that they franchise their restaurants throughout the country. When they hesitated to take on this additional burden, Kroc volunteered to do it for them. He returned to his home outside of Chicago with rights to set up McDonald's restaurants throughout the country, except in a handful of territories in California and Arizona already licensed by the McDonald brothers.

Kroc's first McDonald's restaurant opened in Des Plaines, Illinois, near Chicago, on April 15, 1955. As with any new venture, Kroc encountered a number of hurdles. The first was adapting the McDonald's building design to a northern climate. A basement had to be installed to house a furnace, and adequate ventilation was difficult, as exhaust fans sucked out warm air in the winter, and cool air in the summer.

Most frustrating of all, however, was Kroc's initial failure to reproduce the McDonalds' delicious french fries. When Kroc and his crew duplicated the brothers' method—leaving just a little peel for flavor, cutting the potatoes into shoestrings, and rinsing the strips in cold water—the fries turned into mush.

After repeated telephone conversations with the McDonald brothers and several consultations with the Potato and Onion Association, Kroc pinpointed the cause of the soggy spuds. The McDonald brothers stored their potatoes outside in wire bins, and the warm California breeze dried them out and cured them, slowly turning the sugars into starch. In order to reproduce the superior taste of these potatoes, Kroc devised a system using an electric fan to dry the potatoes in a similar way. He also experimented with a blanching process. Within three months he had a french fry that was, in his opinion, slightly superior in taste to the McDonald brothers' fries.

Once the Des Plaines restaurant was operational, Kroc sought franchisees for his McDonald's chain. The first snag came quickly. In 1956 he discovered that the McDonald brothers had licensed the franchise rights for Cook County, Illinois (home of Chicago and many of its suburbs) to the Frejlack Ice Cream Company. Kroc was incensed that the McDonalds had not informed him of this arrangement. He purchased the rights back for $25,000—five times what the Frejlacks had originally paid—and pressed on.

Kroc decided early on that it was best to first establish the restaurants and then to franchise them out, so that he could control the uniformity of the stores. Early McDonald's restaurants were situated in the suburbs. Corner lots were usually in greater demand because gas stations and shops competed for them, but Kroc preferred lots in the middle of blocks to accommodate his U-shaped parking lots. Since these lots were cheaper, Kroc could give franchisees a price break.

McDonald's grew slowly for its first three years; by 1958 there were 34 restaurants. In 1959, however, Kroc opened 67 new restaurants, bringing the total to more than 100.

Kroc had decided at the outset that McDonald's would not be a supplier to its franchisees—his background in sales warned him that such an arrangement could lead to lower quality for the sake of higher profits. He had also determined that the company should at no time own more than 30 percent of all McDonald's restaurants. He knew, however, that his success depended upon his franchisees' success, and he was determined to help them in any way that he could.

In 1960 McDonald's advertising campaign, "Look for the golden arches," gave sales a big boost. Kroc believed that adver-

tising was an investment that would in the end come back many times over, and advertising has always played a key role in the development of the McDonald's Corporation—indeed, McDonald's ads have been some of the most identifiable over the years. In 1962 McDonald's replaced its "Speedee" the hamburger man symbol with its now world-famous golden arches logo. A year later, the company sold its billionth hamburger.

Phenomenal Growth in the 1960s and 1970s

In the early 1960s, McDonald's really began to take off. The growth in U.S. automobile use that came with suburbanization contributed heavily to McDonald's success. In 1961 Kroc bought out the McDonald brothers for $2.7 million, aiming at making McDonald's the number one fast-food chain in the country.

In 1965 McDonald's Corporation went public. Common shares were offered at $22.50 per share; by the end of the first day's trading the price had shot up to $30. A block of 100 shares purchased for $2,250 in 1965 was worth, after 11 stock splits, about $1.8 million in 1997. McDonald's Corporation is now one of the 30 companies that make up the Dow Jones Industrial Average.

McDonald's success in the 1960s was largely due to the company's successful marketing and flexible response to customer demand. In 1965 the Filet-o-Fish sandwich, billed as "the fish that catches people," was introduced in McDonald's restaurants. The new item had originally met with disapproval from Kroc, but after its successful test marketing, he eventually agreed to add it. Another item that Kroc had backed a year previously, a burger with a slice of pineapple and a slice of cheese known as a "hulaburger," had flopped. The market was not quite ready for Kroc's taste; the hulaburger's tenure on the McDonald's menu board was short. In 1968 the now legendary Big Mac made its debut, and in 1969 McDonald's sold its five-billionth hamburger. A year later, as it launched the "You Deserve a Break Today" advertising campaign, McDonald's restaurants had reached all 50 states.

In 1968 McDonald's opened its 1,000th restaurant, and Fred Turner became the company's president and chief administrative officer. Kroc became chairman and remained CEO until 1973. Turner had originally intended to open a McDonald's franchise, but when he had problems with his backers over a location, he went to work as a grillman for Kroc in 1956. As operations vice-president, Turner helped new franchisees get their stores set up and running. He was constantly looking for new ways to perfect the McDonald's system, experimenting, for example, to determine the maximum number of hamburger patties one could stack in a box without squashing them and pointing out that seconds could be saved if McDonald's used buns that were presliced all the way through and weren't stuck together in the package. Such attention to detail was one reason for the company's extraordinary success.

McDonald's spectacular growth continued in the 1970s. Americans were more on-the-go than ever, and fast service was a priority. In 1972 the company passed $1 billion in annual sales; by 1976, McDonald's had served 20 billion hamburgers, and systemwide sales exceeded $3 billion.

McDonald's pioneered breakfast fast food with the introduction of the Egg McMuffin in 1973 when market research indicated that a quick breakfast would be welcomed by consumers. Five years later the company added a full breakfast line to the menu, and by 1987 one-fourth of all breakfasts eaten out in the United States came from McDonald's restaurants.

Kroc was a firm believer in giving ''something back into the community where you do business.'' In 1974 McDonald's acted upon that philosophy in an original way by opening the first Ronald McDonald House, in Philadelphia, to provide a ''home away from home'' for the families of children in nearby hospitals. Twelve years after this first house opened, 100 similar Ronald McDonald Houses were in operation across the United States.

In 1975 McDonald's opened its first drive-thru window in Oklahoma City. This service gave Americans a fast, convenient way to get a quick meal. The company's goal was to provide service in 50 seconds or less. Drive-thru sales eventually accounted for more than half of McDonald's systemwide sales.

Survived 1980s ''Burger Wars''

In the late 1970s competition from other hamburger chains such as Burger King and Wendy's began to intensify. Experts believed that the fast-food industry had gotten as big as it ever would, so the companies began to battle fiercely for market share. A period of aggressive advertising campaigns and price slashing in the early 1980s became known as the ''burger wars.'' Burger King suggested that customers ''have it their way''; Wendy's offered itself as the ''fresh alternative'' and asked of other restaurants, ''where's the beef?'' But McDonald's sales and market share continued to grow. Consumers seemed to like the taste and consistency of McDonald's best.

During the 1980s McDonald's further diversified its menu to suit changing consumer tastes. Chicken McNuggets were introduced in 1983, and by the end of the year McDonald's was the second largest retailer of chicken in the world. In 1987 ready-to-eat salads were introduced to lure more health-conscious consumers. The 1980s were the fastest-paced decade yet. Efficiency, combined with an expanded menu, continued to draw customers. McDonald's, already entrenched in the suburbs, began to focus on urban centers and introduced new architectural styles. Though McDonald's restaurants no longer looked identical, the company made sure food quality and service remained constant.

Despite experts' claims that the fast-food industry was saturated, McDonald's continued to expand. The first generation raised on restaurant food had grown up. Eating out had become a habit rather than a break in the routine, and McDonald's relentless marketing continued to improve sales. Innovative promotions, such as the ''when the U.S. wins, you win'' giveaways during the Olympic games in 1988, were a huge success.

In 1982 Michael R. Quinlan became president of McDonald's Corporation and Fred Turner became chairman. Quinlan, who took over as CEO in 1987, had started at McDonald's in the mailroom in 1963, and gradually worked his way up. The first McDonald's CEO to hold an M.B.A. degree, Quinlan was regarded by his colleagues as a shrewd competitor. In his first year as CEO the company opened 600 new restaurants.

McDonald's growth in the United States was mirrored by its stunning growth abroad. By 1991, 37 percent of systemwide sales came from restaurants outside of the United States. McDonald's opened its first foreign restaurant in British Columbia, Canada, in 1967. By the early 1990s the company had established itself in 58 foreign countries and operated more than 3,600 restaurants outside of the United States, through wholly owned subsidiaries, joint ventures, and franchise agreements. Its strongest foreign markets were Japan, Canada, Germany, Great Britain, Australia, and France.

In the mid-1980s, McDonald's, like other traditional employers of teenagers, was faced with a shortage of labor in the United States. The company met this challenge by being the first to entice retirees back into the workforce. McDonald's has always placed great emphasis on effective training. It opened its Hamburger University in 1961 to train franchisees and corporate decision-makers. By 1990, more than 40,000 people had received ''Bachelor of Hamburgerology'' degrees from the 80-acre Oak Brook, Illinois, facility. The corporation opened a Hamburger University in Tokyo in 1971, in Munich in 1975, and in London in 1982.

Braille menus were first introduced in 1979, and picture menus in 1988. In March 1992 Braille and picture menus were reintroduced to acknowledge the 37 million Americans with vision, speech, or hearing impairments.

Quinlan continued to experiment with new technology and to research new markets to keep McDonald's in front of its competition. Clamshell fryers, which cooked both sides of a hamburger simultaneously, were tested. New locations such as hospitals and military bases were tapped as sites for new restaurants. In response to the increase in microwave oven usage, McDonald's, whose name is the single most advertised brand name in the world, stepped up advertising and promotional expenditures stressing that its taste was superior to quick-packaged foods.

McRecycle USA began in 1990 and included a commitment to purchase at least $100 million worth of recycled products annually for use in construction, remodeling, and equipping restaurants. Chairs, table bases, table tops, eating counters, table columns, waste receptacles, corrugated cartons, packaging, and washroom tissue were all made from recycled products. McDonald's worked with the U.S. Environmental Defense Fund to develop a comprehensive solid waste reduction program. Wrapping burgers in paper rather than plastic led to a 90 percent reduction in the wrapping material waste stream.

1990s Growing Pains

It took McDonald's 33 years to open its first 10,000 restaurants—the 10,000th unit opened in April 1988. Incredibly, the company reached the 20,000-restaurant mark in only eight more years, in mid-1996. By the end of 1997 the total had surpassed 23,000—by that time McDonald's was opening 2,000 new restaurants each year—an average of one every five hours.

Much of the growth of the 1990s came outside the United States, with international units increasing from about 3,600 in 1991 to more than 11,000 by 1998. The number of countries with McDonald's outlets nearly doubled from 59 in 1991 to 114 in late 1998. In 1993 a new region was added to the empire when the first McDonald's in the Middle East opened in Tel Aviv, Israel. As the company entered new markets, it showed increasing flexibility with respect to local food preferences and customs. In Israel, for example, the first kosher McDonald's opened in a Jerusalem suburb in 1995. In Arab countries the restaurant chain used "Halal" menus, which complied with Islamic laws for food preparation. In 1996 McDonald's entered India for the first time, where it offered a Big Mac made with lamb called the Maharaja Mac. That same year the first Mc-Ski-Thru opened in Lindvallen, Sweden.

Overall, the company derived increasing percentages of its revenue and income from outside the United States. In 1992 about two-thirds of systemwide sales came out of U.S. McDonald's, but by 1997 that figure was down to about 51 percent. Similarly, the operating income numbers showed a reduction from about 60 percent derived from the United States in 1992 to 42.5 percent in 1997.

In the United States, where the number of units grew from 9,000 in 1991 to 12,500 in 1997—an increase of about 40 percent—the growth was perhaps excessive. Although the additional units increased market share in some markets, a number of franchisees complained that new units were cannibalizing sales from existing ones. Same-store sales for outlets open for more than one year were flat in the mid-1990s, a reflection of both the greater number of units and the mature nature of the U.S. market.

It did not help that the company made several notable blunders in the United States in the 1990s. The McLean Deluxe sandwich, which featured a 91 percent fat-free beef patty, was introduced in 1991, never really caught on, and was dropped from the menu in 1996. Several other 1990s-debuted menu items—including fried chicken, pasta, fajitas, and pizza—failed as well. The "grown-up" (and pricey) Arch Deluxe sandwich and the Deluxe Line were launched in 1996 in a $200 million campaign to gain the business of more adults, but were bombs. The following spring brought a 55-cent Big Mac promotion, which many customers either rejected outright or were confused by because the burgers had to be purchased with full-priced fries and a drink. The promotion embittered still more franchisees, whose complaints led to its withdrawal. In July 1997 McDonald's fired its main ad agency—Leo Burnett, a 15-year McDonald's partner—after the nostalgic "My McDonald's" campaign proved a failure. A seemingly weakened McDonald's was the object of a Burger King offensive when the rival fast-food maker launched the Big King sandwich, a Big Mac clone. Meanwhile, internal taste tests revealed that customers preferred the fare at Wendy's and Burger King.

Late 1990s Comeback?

In response to these difficulties, McDonald's drastically cut back on its U.S. expansion—in contrast to the 1,130 units opened in 1995, only about 400 new McDonald's were built in 1997. Plans to open hundreds of smaller restaurants in Wal-Marts and gasoline stations were abandoned since test sites did not meet targeted goals. Reacting to complaints from franchisees about poor communication with the corporation and excess bureaucracy, the head of McDonald's U.S.A. (Jack Greenberg, who had assumed the position in October 1996) reorganized the unit into five autonomous geographic divisions. The aim was to bring management and decision-making closer to franchisees and customers.

On the marketing side, McDonald's scored big in 1997 with a Teenie Beanie Baby promotion in which about 80 million of the toys/collectibles were gobbled up virtually overnight. The chain received some bad publicity, however, when it was discovered that a number of customers purchased Happy Meals just to get the toys and threw the food away. For a similar spring 1998 Teenie Beanie giveaway, the company altered the promotion to allow patrons to buy menu items other than kids' meals. McDonald's also began to benefit from a 10-year global marketing alliance signed with Disney in 1996. Initial Disney movies promoted by McDonald's included *101 Dalmatians, Flubber, Mulan, Armageddon,* and *A Bug's Life.* Perhaps the most important marketing move came in the later months of 1997 when McDonald's named BDD Needham as its new lead ad agency. Needham had been the company's agency in the 1970s and was responsible for the hugely successful "You Deserve a Break Today" campaign. Late in 1997 McDonald's launched the Needham-designed "Did Somebody Say McDonald's?" campaign, which appeared to be an improvement over its predecessors.

Following the difficulties of the early and mid-1990s, the late 1990s were perhaps shaping up as transition years for a corporate turnaround. Several moves in 1998 seemed to indicate a reinvigorated McDonald's. In February the company for the first time took a stake in another fast-food chain when it purchased a minority interest in the 16-unit, Colorado-based Chipotle Mexican Grill chain. The following month came the announcement that McDonald's would improve the taste of several sandwiches and introduce several new menu items; McFlurry desserts—developed by a Canadian franchisee—proved popular when launched in the United States in the summer of 1998. McDonald's that same month said that it would overhaul its food preparation system in every U.S. restaurant. The new just-in-time system, dubbed "Made for You," was in development for a number of years and aimed to deliver to customers "fresher, hotter food"; enable patrons to receive special-order sandwiches (a perk long offered by rivals Burger King and Wendy's); and allow new menu items to be more easily introduced thanks to the system's enhanced flexibility. The expensive changeover was expected to cost about $25,000 per restaurant, with McDonald's offering to pay for about half of the cost; the company planned to provide about $190 million in financial assistance to its franchisees before implementation was completed by year-end 1999.

In May 1998 Greenberg was named president and CEO of McDonald's Corporation, with Quinlan remaining chairman; at the same time Alan D. Feldman, who had joined the company only four years earlier from Pizza Hut, replaced Greenberg as president of McDonald's U.S.A.—an unusual move for a company whose executives typically were long-timers. The following month brought another first—McDonald's first job cuts—as the company said it would eliminate 525 employees from its headquarters staff, a cut of about 23 percent. In the second quarter of 1998 McDonald's took a $160 million charge in relation to the cuts. McDonald's announced in September 1998 that it planned to purchase $3.5 billion of its common stock by year-end 2001. This flurry of 1998 activity boded well for the future of an American—and increasingly a global—institution.

Principal Subsidiaries

McDonald's Australian Property Corporation; McDonald's Deutschland, Inc.; McDonald's Development Italy, Inc.; McDonald's Property Company Limited; McDonald's Restaurant Operations, Inc.; McDonald's System of France, Inc.; McDonald's Sistemas de España, Inc.; Restaurant Realty of Mexico, Inc.; McDonald's Australia Limited; McDonald's Properties (Australia) Pty., Ltd.; Restco Comercio de Alimentos Ltda. (Brazil); McDonald's Restaurants of Canada Limited; McDonald's Danmark A/S (Denmark); McDonald's France, S.A.; McDonald's GmbH (Germany); McDonald's Immobilien GmbH (Germany); McDonald's Restaurants Limited (Hong Kong); Italian Restaurant Financing S.R.L. (Italy); MDC Inmobiliaria de Mexico S.A. de C.V.; McDonald's Nederland B.V. (Netherlands); McDonald's LLC (Russia); McDonald's Restaurants (Swisse) S.A. (Switzerland); McDonald's Restaurants (Taiwan) Co., Ltd.; McDonald's Restaurants Limited (U.K.).

Further Reading

Bigness, Jon, "Getting the Sizzle Back at McDonald's," *Chicago Tribune,* August 30, 1998.

Branch, Shelly, "McDonald's Strikes Out with Grownups," *Fortune,* November 11, 1996, pp. 157+.

——, "What's Eating McDonald's?," *Fortune,* October 13, 1997, pp. 122+.

Burns, Greg, "Fast-Food Fight," *Business Week,* June 2, 1997, pp. 34–36.

Byrne, Harlan S., "Welcome to McWorld," *Barron's,* August 29, 1994, pp. 25–28.

Canedy, Dana, "McDonald's Burger War Salvo," *New York Times,* June 20, 1998, pp. D1, D15.

Cohon, George, with David Macfarlane, *To Russia with Fries,* Toronto: M & S, 1997, 335 p.

Donlon, J.P., "Quinlan Fries Harder," *Chief Executive,* January/February 1998, pp. 45–49.

Gibson, Richard, "McDonald's Makes Changes in Top Management," *Wall Street Journal,* May 1, 1998, pp. A3, A4.

——, "Some Franchisees Say Moves by McDonald's Hurt Their Operations," *Wall Street Journal,* April 17, 1996, pp. A1, A10.

——, "Worried McDonald's Plans Dramatic Shifts and Big Price Cuts," *Wall Street Journal,* February 26, 1997, pp. A1, A6.

Gibson, Richard, and Bruce Orwell, "New Mission for Mickey Mouse, Mickey D," *Wall Street Journal,* March 5, 1998, pp. B1, B5.

Kroc, Ray, *Grinding It Out: The Making of McDonald's,* Chicago: H. Reguery, 1977, 201 p.

Leonhardt, David, "McDonald's: Can It Regain Its Golden Touch?," *Business Week,* March 9, 1998, pp. 70–74, 76–77.

Love, John F., *McDonald's: Behind the Arches,* New York: Bantam Books, 1986, 470 p.

Machan, Dyan, "Polishing the Golden Arches," *Forbes,* June 15, 1998, pp. 42–43.

Papiernik, Richard L., "Mac Attack?," *Financial World,* April 12, 1994, pp. 28–30.

Serwer, Andrew E., "McDonald's Conquers the World, *Fortune,* October 17, 1994, pp. 103+.

Watson, James L., ed., *Golden Arches East: McDonald's in East Asia,* Stanford: Stanford University Press, 1997, 256 p.

—Anne C. Hughes
—updated by David E. Salamie

Mentor Corporation

5425 Hollister Avenue
Santa Barbara, California 93111
U.S.A.
(805) 681-6000
Fax: (805) 964-2712
Web site: http://www.mentorcorp.com

Public Company
Incorporated: 1969
Employees: 1,612
Sales: $215.2 million (1998)
Stock Exchanges: NASDAQ
Ticker Symbol: MNTR
SICs: 3842 Surgical Appliances & Supplies; 3841
    Surgical & Medical Instruments

A fast-growing company, Mentor Corporation produces breast implants, tissue implants, facial implants, and penile implants for the treatment of impotence, as well as incontinence products and ophthalmology products. Mentor initially produced products for incontinence, recording its first success with a disposable catheter introduced in 1974. By virtue of a series of acquisitions in the 1980s and through its own product development activities, the company diversified into plastic surgery products and ophthalmology products. Mentor developed its first penile prosthesis in 1980 and gained entry into the market for breast implants through the acquisition of Heyer-Schulte in 1984, a transaction that more than doubled the company's sales. Entry into the manufacture of ophthalmology products, which were used in cataract and glaucoma surgery, was achieved through the acquisition of Mentor O&O in 1990. Between 1990 and 1998, Mentor's sales increased energetically, rising from $50 million to more than $200 million. The company markets its products to physicians, hospitals, health care providers, and general consumers in the United States and abroad.

Founded in 1969

The dominant personality behind Mentor's creation and its ensuing success was Chris Conway, who earned as many de-

tractors as he did supporters. Conway began his career as a research fellow in neurology at the University of Minnesota's medical school in 1965. His jump into the corporate world began four years later, when he and his friend and laboratory coworker Eugene Glover developed a pacemaker-like device for bladder control. With an innovative medical device at the ready, the two academics mulled over the idea of starting their own company. The intent, so they claimed, was not to get rich, but to gain independence. Conway left no doubt concerning the value he placed on independence. "The idea of working for a company," he once remarked, "was abhorrent to me."

Conway and Glover resolved to go ahead with their entrepreneurial plan in 1969, but before they did so the pair enlisted the help of others. Conway invited his next-door neighbor Tom Hauser, a marketing specialist at Honeywell, to join the partnership, and next asked Gerald Timm, an assistant professor of neurology, to join as well. With the product and the personnel lined up, Conway's next challenge was to find the money to back the venture. He turned to the stock market, hoping to cultivate enough interest in the proposed business to raise sufficient cash to get started, but after being turned down by Piper Jaffray, Conway decided look elsewhere. He eventually found what he needed through the assistance of an aggressive local broker named Jerry Shapiro, and his new company, Mentor Corporation, was up and running.

Not long after getting started, Conway began to attract the attention that would prompt Barbara Rudolph of *Forbes* magazine to write: "Despite the image he likes to project, Conway has succeeded by stepping on toes, alienating his friends, and suing his competitors." The first incident occurred in mid-1971 when Conway sued Gerald Timm for breach of contract. Years later Timm said, according to Rudolph, "I hear that Conway has changed over the years, but when I knew him he could be amoral." Of the 1971 lawsuit, Conway only offered, "I sued him for disloyalty," but whatever the personal feelings behind the 1971 dispute, one thing was certain: Mentor was struggling profoundly. From the start, sales were anemic, largely because the medical establishment shunned Mentor's bladder pacemaker. As a result, the company appeared to be headed for a quick and ignoble end to its brief corporate life, but before financial collapse foundered Mentor, Conway changed his strategy and greatly improved Mentor's prospects.

Conway decided to eschew the type of pioneering work that spawned Mentor's bladder control product and instead graft the new onto the old by developing product innovations for established markets. In other words, instead of inventing something to replace the wheel, Conway resolved to develop a better wheel. The new strategy meant the creation of new products, which, in turn, meant Conway needed more money. Again, Conway was successful, raising $300,000 through private placements that funded the development of a new and improved disposable catheter. The Mentor Urosan featured a lining that made it less likely to tighten around the skin, which won the business of the previously indifferent medical establishment. Sales quickly escalated, enabling Mentor to graduate from its status as a fledgling upstart to an established, financially stable company.

Expansion and Diversification in the 1980s

By 1980, sales of the Mentor Urosan and other urological products had pushed Mentor's annual revenue volume up to $3 million and had necessitated an increase in the number of its employees to 25. These figures represented modest totals for a decade's work, but from 1980 forward financial and physical growth would be achieved at a much faster pace. The cause of such growth was the company's foray into plastic surgery products, begun in 1980 when Mentor started the development of an implantable penile prosthesis. In 1983, Mentor received approval from the Food and Drug Administration to begin marketing its penile implant, marking the formal beginning of the company's involvement in implantable prostheses. Although Mentor's entry into plastic surgery products represented a pivotal step in a new direction, pointing the company toward a business area that eventually accounted for roughly 50 percent of its total business, a far more immediate boost to its stature arrived one year after the company began marketing its penile implants. In 1984, Mentor purchased the Heyer-Schulte division of American Supply Hospital, an acquisition that more than doubled the company's sales and greatly diversified its product lines overnight. The Heyer-Schulte division produced several implantable products, most notably breast implants, which bolstered Mentor's line of plastic surgery products. The acquisition also gave Mentor a new headquarters location in Santa Barbara, the home of Heyer-Schulte, although Mentor kept its Minneap-

olis manufacturing facility in operation and continued with its expansion in later years.

A decidedly stronger company by 1985, Mentor prepared to expand its horizons further as the latter half of the 1980s approached. Some moves were successful, while others were not, but the net result was robust growth. In 1985, the company developed the Mentor condom, which used the same adhesive-seal technology that had made its male external catheters successful. The Mentor condom earned national recognition, prompting the company to entertain the idea of developing a consumer health products division. Distribution channels were explored for the sale of the Mentor condom on a national scale, with the hope being that once the distribution network was established, the company could then funnel other consumer health products through the same distribution channels. The plan never worked, however, primarily because Mentor never found any other consumer health products it was willing to acquire. Consequently, the Mentor condom line was sold to Carter-Wallace in 1989.

A more lasting addition to the Mentor enterprise arrived the same year the company developed its ill-fated condom line. In 1985, the company acquired its supplier of latex catheter products, a Minnesota-based company named Arcon Corporation. It was a move toward vertical integration that gave Mentor greater control over its manufacturing processes, and was followed in 1988 by the acquisition of another manufacturer, Polymer Technologies Corporation. Based in California, Polymer Technologies produced silicone materials for the manufacture of surgical products, an acquisition that gave Mentor further control over the manufacture of materials used in its product lines.

The 1990s and Beyond

Propelled by the diversification into plastic surgery products and the steps taken toward vertical integration, the company that entered the 1980s with $3 million in annual sales, exited the decade with sales eclipsing $50 million. Not willing to abandon the pursuit of further growth, the company pushed forward as the decade began and resumed its acquisitive activities. In 1990, Mentor purchased Mentor O&O, which coincidentally shared the same name with its new parent company and, to exacerbate the confusion, shared the same founding year as its acquirer, yet was a separate company unaffiliated with Mentor Corporation until 1990. The acquisition represented yet another move toward diversification, providing Mentor entry into the ophthalmology field. Mentor O&O's prominent product was Polytef, an injectable material used for vocal cord treatments that presented market potential for the treatment of urinary incontinence, one of Mentor's early strengths. Before the year was through, Mentor completed another acquisition, purchasing Teknar, Inc., a manufacturer of urological and ophthalmic ultrasound equipment.

After acquiring Mentor O&O, Conway and his management team felt it was time to reorganize Mentor and create an operational structure that reflected the diversity of its product lines. The company chose to create subsidiary structures that divided its different business areas into separate operating units. Toward this end, Mentor H/S, Inc. was incorporated as a wholly owned subsidiary in 1991 to operate as a stand-alone business for the company's plastic surgery activities. A similar arrangement followed in 1993 when the company incorporated Mentor Urology. Lastly, the company grouped its international activities into Mentor International, which, in turn, comprised a number of subsidiary branch offices. Although Mentor had been involved in overseas business during the 1980s, achieving steady sales growth throughout the decade, its international activity gained new momentum early in the 1990s. In 1991, the substance of what would become Mentor International took shape when the company opened direct sales offices in Germany, Australia, the United Kingdom, and in Canada. Two years later, Mentor's international business was given further support with the selection of its first European manufacturing site, located in The Netherlands. The facility, situated in Leiden, opened in 1994.

As the company restructured its operations domestically and abroad, it also looked at its U.S. manufacturing facilities and found an opportunity to increase production capacity, reduce costs, and lower overhead. These objectives were achieved by consolidating its manufacturing facilities in 1993, which entailed the closure of production operations in Santa Barbara, St. Louis, and in Stewartville, Minnesota. Manufacturing was subsequently moved to the company's production facilities in Minneapolis and Dallas.

After more than three years of reorganization and consolidation, Mentor expanded again in 1994, acquiring the intraocular lens product line from Optical Radiation Corporation. The acquisition gave the company a manufacturing facility in Puerto Rico and broadened its capabilities in the ophthalmology field, enabling Mentor to offer surgeons an extensive line of products for treating cataracts. Although ophthalmology represented one of the smallest segments of Mentor's business during the 1990s, accounting for roughly 15 percent of the company sales at the end of the decade, the expansion of the business segment was seen to be a lucrative opportunity for growth. Cataract surgery ranked as the most frequently performed surgical operation in the world and accounted for roughly 70 percent of the average ophthalmologist's annual income. Consequently, the strengthening of Mentors' ophthalmology business offered great potential for growth as the company entered the late 1990s and prepared for the 21st century, but the same could be said of the company's largest business segment, its plastic surgery products business. Accounting for 50 percent of the company's sales in the late 1990s, plastic surgery products were also demonstrating vigorous sales growth, increasing at a better than 23 percent pace. Mentor controlled approximately 55 percent of the growing U.S. breast implant and reconstruction market, while its ultrasonic liposuction equipment, which was also included in the company's plastic surgery products segment, promised to generate considerable sales.

Against this backdrop, Mentor occupied an enviable position as it planned for the future. The company was building its presence in burgeoning markets and it held an entrenched position in growing markets. From this perspective, Mentor appeared poised for pronounced gains in sales and profits, with its diversity offering several avenues of expansion for the future.

Principal Subsidiaries

Mentor H/S, Inc.; Mentor Urology; Mentor International.

Further Reading

Ferguson, Tim W., "Ponce de Leon, Come Back," *Forbes,* December 18, p. 270.
"Mentor Corp.," *Insiders' Chronicle,* January 20, 1992, p. 3.
"Mentor Corp.," *Insiders' Chronicle,* March 30, 1992, p. 3.
Pouschine, Tatiana, "The Survivors," *Forbes,* December 7, 1992, p. 148.
Rudolph, Barbara, "Nice Guys Finish Last," *Forbes,* October 22, 1984, p. 114.

—Jeffrey L. Covell

Meritage Corporation

6613 North Scottsdale Road, Suite 200
Scottsdale, Arizona 85250
U.S.A.
(602) 998-8700
(800) 210-6004
Fax: (602) 998-9162
Web sites: http://www.montereyhomes.com
          http://www.legacy-homes.com

Public Company
Incorporated: 1985 as Monterey Homes Corporation
Employees: 180
Sales: $149.38 million (1997)
Stock Exchanges: New York
Ticker Symbol: MTH
SICs: 6552 Subdividers & Developers, Not Elsewhere
    Classified; 1521 General Contractors, Single-Family
    Houses; 1531 Operative Builders

Meritage Corporation, formerly Monterey Homes Corporation, is a leading homebuilder in the United States, designing, constructing, and selling distinctive single family, entry-level, luxury, and move-up homes. Under the Monterey Homes name, the company's primary marketplaces include the Phoenix and Tucson, Arizona metropolitan areas. The Monterey division builds single-family, move-up, and semi-custom, luxury homes. Under the Legacy Homes name, the company's primary marketplaces include the Dallas/Fort Worth, Austin, and Houston, Texas metropolitan areas. Legacy builds lower-end, entry-level, and move-up homes. Under the Meritage Homes of Northern California name, the company's primary marketplaces include the San Francisco and Sacramento, California metropolitan areas.

Home-Grown Company Starting Out, 1985–87

Monterey Homes was founded in 1985 by two graduates of Chaparral High School and Arizona State University, William

W. Cleverly and Steven J. Hilton, to build semi-custom luxury homes in the affluent Phoenix-area suburb of Scottsdale. The company became only the second Arizona-based company that had originated in the area, joining Dix Corporation, owned by Valley resident Von Dix. The following year, the company began building operations in the City of Phoenix, as well as the surrounding metropolitan area, as a custom builder, competing against some 75 other builders in the market.

In the Right Place at the Right Time, 1988–91

In 1988, Cleverly and Hilton won the Best of Show Award in the Street of Dreams home show and began looking for their first major project. The following year, a slow-down in the housing market weakened many established homebuilders, giving young, lean companies such as Monterey a chance to establish themselves, and Dix closed his company down that year, joining local rival AM Homes as its president. Things looked good for the fledgling company. And then their big break came when a rival, Malouf Bros., passed on buying 72 lots at Scottsdale Country Club, with a golf course designed by golf legend Arnold Palmer. Cleverly and Hilton stepped in with their innovative designs, and the country club owner, Alan Mishkin, was so impressed with their designs, he not only sold them the lots, he became a major investor in the company.

Following the company's opening move of being in the right place at the right time, in 1991, the company picked up a piece of property ideally located near the Scottsdale Fashion Square shopping center, the Galleria, and the Neiman-Marcus store in the posh neighborhood. The parcel was obtained from The Resolution Trust Corp., a federal savings and loan bail-out agency, which inherited the property when Sun State Savings and Loan became insolvent. The Village at Pavoreal was built there, and Cleverly and Hilton, standing by their products, both purchased homes there. In a similar move, the company purchased a subdivision from Dividend Development Corp. after the latter ran into financial problems. Monterey launched Mira-Bella there, with 123 lots. Other projects during 1991 included Monterey at Mountain View in Scottsdale.

The Roaring 1990s

Skye Top was the company's premier project in 1992, located at The Troon Country Club in Scottsdale. The 96 homes there ranged from 1,658 to 2,524 square feet and varied in price from $179,500 to $220,000. Paloma Montana at Pinnacle Peak was also built that year, and featured 3,200- to 3,600-square-foot homes ranging in price from $329,500 to $399,500.

Later that year, the company built La Reserve on the location where the landmark Brophy House once stood. The 70-year-old landmark, built in 1920 by Frank Cullen Brophy, president of the Bank of Douglas (progenitor of Arizona Bank and, later, Security Pacific of Arizona), once hosted balls, parties, and intimate tea gatherings featuring such Hollywood legends as Ethel Barrymore and Helen Hayes. The home of the former Bisbee store clerk had fallen into disrepair over the years, years during which Cleverly grew up, a mere one mile away, occasionally traipsing across the Brophy property and being run off by the owner or the caretaker. Cleverly and his company built homes on the property, attempting to capture the spirit of the house and saving as much of the citrus grove as possible.

In 1993, the company built ''7600 Lincoln'' at that address, a gated, guarded community of 113 homes. By 1994, the company had gradually expanded to include the building of quality move-up homes. The Scottsdale Mountain community was built, featuring 21 homes in the McDowell Mountains, laid out in the washes and lush vegetation of the Sonoran Desert. The homes, each with an unobstructed view of Phoenix a thousand feet below, ranged from 3,361 to 4,178 square feet and varied in price from $362,900 to $399,900. The beautiful and isolated area brought competition from Ryland Homes, A.F. Sterling Homes, and SunCor Development Co., among others. Total revenue for Monterey Homes for the year climbed to $61 million. In both 1993 and 1994, the company was listed in *Inc.* magazine as one of the country's 500 fastest-growing privately held companies; was recognized by Arthur Anderson as one of the top 100 privately held firms in Arizona; and was among the top 15 Valley homebuilders.

In 1995, the company's first condominium project, The Vintage, was built in Scottsdale, with living space ranging in size from 1,232 to 1,678 square feet and in price from $114,900 to $145,900. That year, total revenue reached $133 million. In

April 1996, the company entered the Tucson, Arizona metropolitan area market, building move-up and semi-custom homes ranging in price from $120,000 to $380,000 and from 1,600 to 4,500 square feet.

On the last day of that year, the two related privately owned Arizona homebuilding companies, Monterey Homes Arizona II Inc. and Monterey Homes Construction II Inc., owned by Cleverly and Hilton, became a publicly traded company on the New York Stock Exchange through a reverse merger with Homeplex Mortgage Investments Corporation, a real estate investment trust. The company sold itself to Homeplex, which changed its name to Monterey Homes Corp., for approximately $11 million. Cleverly and Hilton became co-CEOs, with the former becoming chairman, and the latter becoming president. Alan D. Hamberlin, previously financial vice-president of Coventry Homes, president of Courtland Homes, and Homeplex's chairman and CEO of six years, became a member of the company's board of directors. The reverse acquisition came after nearly two years as Homeplex searched through some 30 homebuilders in an effort to acquire operating companies it could use to move its highly liquid capital base. Previously Homeplex, incorporated in May 1988 in Maryland as Emerald Mortgage Investments Corporation, had provided short-term and intermediate-term mortgages on improved and unimproved properties and owned residual mortgage assets. The merger lost Homeplex its real estate investment trust status, but Monterey went public for a very inexpensive $1 million and without the fuss.

During 1996, the company was ranked Number 27 in the *Business Journal*'s ''Top 50 Homebuilders in the Valley [of the Sun, Arizona].'' At the end of the year, the company had closed on 307 homes and sold 283 homes with an aggregate sales value of $90.2 million. Total revenue for the year reached $85 million for just Monterey, with a net income of $6.1 million. Total revenue for both companies reached $173 million.

By 1997, the company was in the number one spot in its price range ($180,000–$500,000+) and one of the top five builders of quality move-up homes in the Phoenix area, building homes ranging in size from 1,600 to 4,500 square feet.

In a strategic effort to diversify its homebuilding operations, the company in July made its first acquisition, acquiring Legacy Homes Ltd., a privately held, Dallas-based builder of entry-level and move-up homes, with operations in the Austin, Houston, and Dallas/Fort Worth areas. Along with the acquisition came Legacy Enterprises Inc. Monterey paid approximately $1.5 million in cash and 667,000 shares of common stock for the Texas company.

Legacy was founded in 1988 by John R. Landon, a former employee of Nash/Phillips Copus, one of the largest builders in the country at the time, to build mostly move-up houses in Dallas. Landon, who started his company with a mere $50,000 in capital, became the chief operating officer and the third co-CEO in Monterey Homes, as well as president of the company's Texas division. Legacy entered the Austin metropolitan market in 1994, constructing 124 and 103 homes in 1996 and 1997, respectively, ranging from 1,600 to 3,100 square feet and averaging $124,000 in price. In early 1997, the Legacy Homes subsidiary entered the Houston metropolitan marketplace, with 1,900- to 3,300-square-foot homes averaging $135,000 in price. Legacy's sales in 1995 and 1996 were $62 million and $84 million, respectively. The acquisition doubled the company's revenues. By the end of fiscal 1997, Monterey Homes had closed on a total of 644 homes and sold 693 homes with an aggregate sales value of $157.5 million. Net income reached $14.2 million on revenues of $149.4 million.

In late 1997 and early 1998, the industry saw some consolidation in the Arizona and Texas markets, with Monterey's Arizona-based competitor Continental Homes being acquired by Dallas-based D.R. Horton Inc. in a $422 million stock swap. In March 1998, Del Webb Corp. stunned the industry as it announced it was looking for a buyer for the veteran company, known for its Sun City developments throughout the West and Southwest. The price tag was announced at $1.2 billion.

In May 1998, the company established its headquarters in Plano, Texas, moving planning, acquisition, and strategic functions there, but leaving the financial and administrative functions in its executive offices in Scottsdale, Arizona. The following month, the company acquired California-based builder Sterling Communities. Sterling, engaged in the construction and sale of high-quality, single-family homes in the San Francisco Bay and Sacramento areas, closed on 105 homes and generated earnings of $2.7 million before taxes on total revenues of $31 million in 1997. Sterling President Steve Hafener remained in charge of the California operations. The acquisition, which cost the company approximately $15 million in cash and assumption of debt, brought the company an immediate entry into the booming northern California market.

In mid-September, the combined company, consisting of Monterey Homes, Legacy Homes, and Sterling Homes, changed its name to Meritage Corporation, remaining on the New York Stock Exchange and under the ticker MTH. The Sterling Homes division was renamed Meritage Homes of Northern California.

As 1998 drew to a close, the company had a record year-end backlog, demand in the company's existing markets in both Arizona and Texas continued to be robust, and the company was looking to extend its operations into new markets, through start-ups and continued acquisitions. Some 121,000 people moved to the Dallas/Fort Worth area alone in 1997, and the company looked strong as it headed into the 21st century.

Principal Subsidiaries

Legacy Homes; Meritage Homes of Northern California; Monterey Homes.

Further Reading

Allen, Marilyn, "City's Lights Twinkle Below Monterey Homes," *Tribune Newspaper*, August 27, 1994, p. D1.
——, "Eagle Mountain Blends with Setting," *Tribune Newspaper*, October 12, 1996, p. D1.
——, "The Heart of Town," *Tribune Newspaper*, October 14, 1995, p. D1.

——, "Homes Fit Desert Lifestyle," *Tribune Newspaper*, August 2, 1997, p. G1.
——, "Miss a Basement?: Visit Canada Vistas," *Tribune Newspaper*, April 27, 1996, p. D1.
——, "Monterey Homes Have That Custom Touch," *Scottsdale Progress Tribune*, June 20, 1992, p. 29.
——, "Monterey Park Has Plenty of Choices," *Tribune Newspaper*, June 8, 1996, p. D1.
——, "Paloma Montana Lives up to Its Name," *Scottsdale Progress Tribune*, May 2, 1992, p. 33.
——, "Portales Offers Quiet Living," *Tribune Newspaper*, January 20, 1996, p. E1.
——, "Semi-Custom Home Features Flexibility," *Scottsdale Progress Tribune*, February 1, 1992, p. 33.
——, "7600 Lincoln Residents Near All the Amenities," *Scottsdale Progress Tribune*, April 10, 1993, p. C1.
——, "Skye Top View Inspires Awe," *Scottsdale Progress Tribune*, April 18, 1992, p. 29.
——, "The Vintage Offers Convenience, Comfort," *Tribune Newspaper*, September 23, 1995, p. D1.
"*The Arizona Republic* AZ Inc. Column," *Knight-Ridder/Tribune Business News*, May 6, 1998, p. OKRB981260A.
Breyer, R. Michelle, "Area New Home Sales Soar," *Austin American-Statesman*, p. D1.
Brown, Steve, "Dallas-Area Housing Boom Expected to Last Through '98," *The Dallas Morning News*, p. 2D.
"Change of Name to Meritage Is Approved by Stockholders," *Wall Street Journal*, September 18, 1998, p. C19(W)/A4(E).
"Changes in Stock Listings," *Wall Street Journal*, September 18, 1998, p. C14.
Coulson, Linda, "Builders Move in with Customers," *Scottsdale Progress Tribune*, April 20, 1991, p. 25.
——, "MiraBella Joins the Family of Monterey Homes," *Scottsdale Progress Tribune*, June 29, 1991, p. 29.
Doerfler, Sue, "Eagle-Eye Views: Fountain Hills Development Offers an Aerie Retreat," *AZ Home*, November 9, 1996, p. AH1.
——, "From the Home Office: Trend Is Here to Stay," *AZ Home*, November 16, 1996, p. AH1.
——, "In Love with the View," *AZ Home*, September 10, 1994, p. AH1.
——, "Palos Verdes Offers Scottsdale for Less," *AZ Home*, July 13, 1996, p. AH1.
——, "Still Space for Luxury Living Deep in the Heart of Scottsdale," *AZ Home*, February 1, 1997, p. AH1.
Hartzel, Tony, "Area Cities Experience Booming Growth," *Dallas Morning News*, p. 31A.
Higgins, Stephen, "Scottsdale Builders Put New Ideas to Work: Their Patio Homes Made to Order for Smaller Lots," *Scottsdale Progress Tribune*, February 18, 1989, p. 25.
"Homeplex Mortgage Investments Corp.," *Business Journal—Serving Phoenix & the Valley of the Sun*, June 28, 1996, p. 60B.
"Homeplex Reports Sharp Earnings Decline," *American Banker*, November 8, 1995, p. 14.
Hovey, Juan, "Under-Promise, Over-Deliver," *Big Builder*, July 1998, p. 32.
Jenkins, Susan, "Design," *Builder*, October 1997, p. 194.
Lyon, Jon, "Monterey Homes: New Directions Lead to Positive Results," *Arizona Daily Star*, May 18, 1997, p. H5.
McDonald, Michele, "Monterey Moving On Up: Home Builder Preserves Success," *Scottsdale Progress Tribune*, November 12, 1993, p. B1.
"Monterey Homes Awards Three Local Realtors with Prize Money from Commission Plus Program Drawing," *Arizona Journal of Real Estate*, January 1996, p. 1.
"Monterey Homes Corp.," *Wall Street Journal*, May 7, 1998, p. A9(W)/A14(E).

"Monterey Homes Corp.," *Wall Street Journal*, January 16, 1998, p. B7(W)/B5(E).

Netherton, Martha, "Builders Continue Record Pace: Construction of Single-Family Homes Keeps up with Growth," *Business Journal—Serving Phoenix and the Valley of the Sun*, January 23, 1998, p. 1.

Reagor, Catherine, "*The Arizona Republic/Phoenix Gazette* Real Estate Column," *Knight-Ridder/Tribune Business News*, June 7, 1996, p. 6070225.

——, "Side Job Evolves into a Custom Fit," *Arizona Republic*, February 8, 1998, p. D1.

Ruber, Ilana, "Homeplex Headed for Proxy Fight," *Business Journal—Serving Phoenix & the Valley of the Sun*, June 9, 1995, p. 1.

"Sterling Communities Agrees to Sell Assets to Monterey Homes," *Wall Street Journal*, June 29, 1998, p. B7H.

Talley, Karen, "OTS Spurs Writedown of Mortgage-Backeds," *American Banker*, August 26, 1997, p. 8.

"Valley's Housing Market Heats with Thermometer," *Arizona Republic*, July 27, 1995, p. D1.

Vandeveire, Mary, "ADFlex Leads Positive AZ Stock Price Gain," *Business Journal—Serving Phoenix & the Valley of the Sun*, August 8, 1997, p. 41.

——, "Monterey Homes, Homeplex Agree to $11M Merger," *Business Journal—Serving Phoenix & the Valley of the Sun*, December 27, 1996, p. 1.

—Daryl F. Mallett

Miller Industries, Inc.

3220 Pointe Parkway
Suite 100
Norcross, Georgia 30092
U.S.A.
(770) 446-6778
Fax: (770) 446-5255
Web site: http://www.millerind.com

Public Company
Incorporated: 1991 as Miller Group
Employees: 2,200
Sales: $292.4 million (1997)
Stock Exchanges: New York
Ticker Symbol: MLR
SICs: 4789 Transportation Services, Not Elsewhere
    Classified; 3713 Truck & Bus Bodies; 3799
    Transportation Equipment, Not Elsewhere Classified

Miller Industries, Inc. is the world's leading integrated provider of towing equipment and services. The company manufactures bodies for tow truck and car carriers; operates a towing service called RoadOne; acts as a distributor of towing equipment; and offers financial services to customers, as well as to other towing and distribution companies. Formed by William Miller in the early 1990s, Miller Industries rapidly gained a 40 percent share of what had been a fragmented industry. Despite a strong showing in the mid-1990s, in 1997 it faced a series of challenges that included a class-action lawsuit (later dismissed) and a Justice Department antitrust investigation. Nonetheless, the company persevered, and made a forthright public relations response to the situation, issuing press releases regarding both legal challenges.

The Early Years: Resurrecting Dead Giants

Miller Industries Chairman William Miller—called ''Bill'' by clients and associates—grew up in Detroit, Michigan, in the 1950s and 1960s. Because his father, like many others in Detroit, worked at an auto-manufacturing plant, Miller planned to

become a line supervisor for Ford Motor Company. His high school guidance counselor, however, saw further potential in him, and suggested that he obtain a college education. Yet it was Miller's father who indirectly cemented his decision to go to college, when he made the comment: ''At my plant, the guys with college degrees walk around all day doing nothing and making lots of money.'' Miller enrolled at the University of Michigan in Ann Arbor, where he earned a degree in engineering, and later an M.B.A.

After college, Miller went to work for a variety of large companies, including Bendix Corporation, Neptune International, Wheelabrator-Frye, and Allied Signal—then called Signal Companies, Inc. In each case, he found work fixing troubled units for the companies, and in the course of this experience caught the entrepreneurial bug himself. Miller later told *Forbes,* in November 1996: ''The big companies weren't geared toward the shareholders. They were geared toward a bureaucracy.'' His first position at the helm of a company came in February 1987, when he assumed the presidency of Flow Measurement, a maker of industrial flow meters. Miller assumed that role until April 1994, when he stepped down to focus his energies solely on Miller Industries, which he had been forming for a few years prior. Upon leaving Flow Measurement, however, Miller maintained ownership of 80 percent of the capital stock of the company.

The creation of Miller Industries came as the result of careful and thoughtful planning. After considering many different options, Miller decided that the best business strategy would be to find a once-great brand name in a fragmented industry, resurrect the brand name, and grow market share by consolidating smaller companies. Soon he hit upon the answer: tow trucks. In the manufacturing segment of that industry, there were three big names—Century, Challenger, and Holmes International—but each had seen better days. Suffering from debt incurred by leveraged buyouts, the three giants were dying, and around them had sprung up numerous smaller competitors. Surveying the situation, Miller decided that he would resurrect the three giants and once again gain control of the market.

Thus, in 1990 Miller began bringing these mordant giants back to life. First he bought Holmes, a bankrupt company that had once held a 75 percent share of the tow-truck industry in the

Company Perspectives:

Miller Industries is the world's largest integrated provider of vehicle towing and recovery equipment, systems and services with executive offices in Atlanta, Georgia and manufacturing operations in Tennessee, Pennsylvania, Mississippi, France and England. Miller Industries markets its towing and recovery equipment under the well-recognized Century, Challenger, Holmes, Champion, Eagle, Vulcan, Jige, and Boniface brand names and markets its towing services under the national brand name RoadOne.

United States. Soon thereafter he purchased Challenger and Century. Together the three became part of the newly formed Miller Group—for a total price of $25 million, of which Miller borrowed $20 million. He soon set about consolidating his acquisitions, shutting down three of the five existing production factories and getting rid of some 300 distributors. He also rationalized the production process so that in many cases the same part would fit in any Miller vehicle.

In 1991, the Miller Group lost $4.7 million, but this was perhaps to be expected, considering its several large acquisitions and the fact that the enterprise was just being launched. Just three years later, however, in the fiscal year that ended in April 1994, Miller showed a profit of $4.3 million. At that time, Miller Industries was formed using the foundation that the Miller Group had created.

In August 1994, Miller took his company public, with an initial offering of some 10.7 million shares—40 percent of the company—which yielded $30 million before fees. Five million dollars of this went to repay Miller's personal investment in 1990; $16.5 million paid off debt incurred in the purchases of Holmes, Challenger, and Century; and the remainder went back into the business. According to a November 1996 *Forbes* article, "In just four years he had increased the market value of the company close to threefold."

To encourage stock purchases, Miller had given each Miller employee a single share of the company at the time of the IPO. One employee who had received stock options from Miller told *Forbes* that his options—which at the time of the article in November 1996 were worth $11,500—would pay the college tuition of his son, who was then only six years old.

Moving Forward in the Mid-1990s

Given the scope of Miller's achievements, it was perhaps no wonder that he and his company were accorded almost reverential status within the industry. In November 1996, a North Carolina tow truck distributor told *Forbes* that Miller "came along, and he healed the sick." Miller himself, however, approached his success with humility: responding to reports that his company would show a profit of $13.5 million on sales of $225 million in the fiscal year that ended April 30, 1997, he told the *Atlanta Journal and Constitution,* "You can't look backwards; you have to constantly look forward."

In the mid-1990s, Miller Industries grew dramatically through a series of acquisitions that gave it an increasingly large share of the towing industry. In 1996, it acquired two European subsidiaries, tow truck makers Jige in France and Boniface Engineering in the United Kingdom. Also acquired was Vulcan International, Inc., a leading U.S. manufacturer of towing equipment. In the period between July 1996 and July 1997, Miller acquired ten towing equipment distributors. The company announced its intent to use the new distributors in concert with its existing distributors to form a North American network for towing and recovery equipment, specialty truck equipment, and related components.

Miller Industries created RoadOne, a towing service company, in February 1997, and in less than six months it had acquired 34 towing service companies with combined historic revenues of $80 million annually. RoadOne was, from the beginning, the largest towing company in the United States, with service in 15 states. According to the company's annual report that year, Miller planned to establish a national towing service network. In 1997, the company also set up its Financial Services Group, which offered equipment financing and other financial services to Miller Industries distributors and their customers. The company planned to continue its expansion into these realms of business in the following year.

On November 10, 1997, Miller announced the acquisition of its 50th towing service company under the RoadOne name. "In just eight months," Bill Miller stated in a press release, "we have reached an important milestone in our RoadOne strategy. Acquiring our 50th towing service company in this short period of time is a tribute to the team of people that has come together to execute the strategy."

By virtually any measure, it was impressive growth, and Wall Street responded. For some companies, a big step such as the introduction of a new product or service line might have caused at least a momentary drop in stock value, but on the day Miller Industries announced the establishment of RoadOne, its stock rose ¾, to 20¾. The *Atlanta Journal and Constitution* reported in February 1997 that Miller had been the biggest gainer among Georgia public companies in 1996. In May 1997, Robert Luke of the *Atlanta Journal and Constitution* wrote that "Wall Street thinks Miller can maintain the momentum, much like Bill Gates has at software giant Microsoft." Whereas Microsoft's shares were trading at 45 times estimated 1997 profits, Miller Industries's stock was trading as high as 65 times earnings.

Miller told the *Atlanta Journal and Constitution* that he thought the company would top out at 70 percent market share. Diversification would be a key: "The company needs to be able to go in more than one direction in order to become a $1 billion company," according to Miller. He also stated that he hoped to be able to show $100 million in profit by the end of the century. Miller Industries estimated that consumers were spending $2 billion annually on towing services, while businesses were spending an estimated $7 billion annually. With regard to RoadOne, Miller said, "We could see 10,000 affiliates."

Although the diversification strategy was necessary if the company wanted to increase the value of its stock, the broad reach of Miller Industries' services would soon expose the company to legal liabilities. As it turned out, Luke's favorable comparison to Microsoft—which itself underwent a widely publicized antitrust investigation in the late 1990s—would prove to be ironic.

Challenges at the Century's End

In August 1997, *Forbes* once again praised Miller's recent accomplishments, but added a cautionary footnote, stating: "No question that Miller has been a hot growth company. But the picture's changing." By purchasing distributors, Miller had begun competing with the companies which purchased its equipment. This meant, in effect, that it was competing with its own success. Furthermore, *Forbes* noted that by embarking "on a consolidation binge in towing services," it was again competing with its customers. Finally, a number of motor clubs—which were typically a large source of towing-service income—were "wary" of Miller Industries.

Two months later, in October 1997, the news was even worse. A group of stockholders brought a class action suit against the company, charging that Miller himself, along with several of his officers, had "disseminated false financial statements" about the company's growth in order to sell stock. While Miller Industries was still in the throes of this legal challenge, it received word in January 1998 that it faced an even more formidable adversary: the U.S. Department of Justice, which had initiated an antitrust investigation. At the crux of the government's probe was a charge which turned Miller's strategy of diversification into a liability. Apparently, by purchasing so many companies in various segments of the tow truck industry, the Justice Department held that Miller was in danger of creating a monopoly.

Miller Industries responded to the legal challenges, as well as to concerns about its stock, with a forthright public relations campaign. In a press release, for instance, it noted that its earnings in the third quarter of 1997 were lower than expected. It also issued communiqués reporting the progress of the Justice Department investigation. President and CEO Jeffrey I. Badgley said, "We believe that this industry is highly competitive, and are prepared to support our belief. We will cooperate fully with any investigation if asked to do so. In the meantime, we intend to continue to focus on operating our business for the benefit of our customers and shareholders."

In taking a positive approach to a negative situation, Miller Industries was—perhaps without recognizing the fact—borrowing a page from Georgia's own Ivy Ledbetter Lee (1877–1934), often referred to as the "Father of Public Relations." While he was working as a public relations consultant for the Pennsylvania Railroad in 1906, a train owned by the company had an accident. The railroad followed standard procedure, which was to pretend that nothing had happened; Lee, however, went against tradition by inviting reporters to visit the scene of the accident—at the railroad's expense, no less—and promised to provide them with all the information they needed. Soon the newspapers were printing positive stories about the company, and the railroad executives realized the wisdom of Lee's innovative approach.

In mid-1998, it remained to be seen whether Miller's forthright strategy would yield similar results. Certainly there had not been a spate of negative news stories in the *Atlanta Journal and Constitution* or elsewhere, and though the antitrust investigation continued, the company had good news to report on another front. According to a May 20, 1998, press release, a Tennessee judge had granted Miller Industries' motion to dismiss the class action suit. Half the legal battle was over, and Miller would continue its public relations campaign and carry on business as usual until the results of the antitrust case—and the company's future—were decided.

Principal Subsidiaries

Century Holdings, Inc.; Champion Carrier Corporation; Miller Industries International, Inc.; Boniface Engineering Limited (U.K.); Jige International (France); Miller Financial Services Group, Inc.; Vulcan International, Inc.

Further Reading

Abram, Malcolm X., "Antitrust Inquiry for Towing Firm," *Atlanta Constitution,* January 10, 1998, p. E5.

Foster, Christine, "The Tow Truck Savior," *Forbes,* November 4, 1996, pp. 184–86.

Keaten, James, "Miller Industries to Buy 32 Towing Companies," *Marietta Daily Journal,* February 5, 1997, p. B4.

Kerfoot, Kevin, "Miller Industries Acquires Greeneville Facility," *Tennessee Manufacturer,* April 1997, p. 1.

Luke, Robert, "Georgia-Based Wrecker Manufacturer Prepares for More Bang-Up Growth," *Atlanta Journal and Constitution,* May 19, 1997.

Quinn, Matthew C., "Miller Industries to Buy 30 Towing Services in 15 States," *Atlanta Journal and Constitution,* February 5, 1997.

Waxler, Caroline, "Lifts Needed," *Forbes,* August 25, 1997, pp. 268–69.

—Judson Knight

Minnesota Mining & Manufacturing Company (3M)

3M Center
St. Paul, Minnesota 55144-1000
U.S.A.
(651) 733-1110
(800) 364-9436
Fax: (651) 736-2133
Web site: http://www.3M.com

Public Company
Incorporated: 1929
Employees: 75,639
Sales: $15.07 billion (1997)
Stock Exchanges: New York Pacific Chicago Tokyo
    Amsterdam Swiss
Ticker Symbol: MMM
SICs: 2672 Paper Coated & Laminated, Not Elsewhere
    Classified; 2834 Pharmaceutical Preparations; 2891
    Adhesives & Sealants; 2899 Chemical Preparations,
    Not Elsewhere Classified; 3089 Plastics Products, Not
    Elsewhere Classified; 3291 Abrasive Products; 3643
    Current-Carrying Wiring Devises; 3679 Electronic
    Components, Not Elsewhere Classified; 3842 Surgical
    Appliances & Supplies

The largest manufacturer in Minnesota, the 89th largest U.S. company overall, and a member of the Dow Jones ''30,'' Minnesota Mining & Manufacturing Company (officially abbreviated as 3M) is Wall Street's epitome of high-tech/low-tech business and solid blue chip performance. Its daunting inventory of some 50,000 products runs the gamut from Post-it Notes and Scotch tape to transdermal patches of nitroglycerin. Its equally daunting global presence extends to subsidiary companies in more than 60 countries and markets in nearly 200, as well as net sales from international operations of $7.8 billion, or 52 percent of the company's total 1997 revenue. 3M owes its formidable strength to its unusual corporate culture, which comfortably fosters innovation and interdepartmental cooperation, backed by a massive research & development budget, which in 1997 exceeded $1 billion. Because of this, 3M ranks as a leader in—and in many cases a founder of—a number of important technologies, includ-ing pressure sensitive tapes, sandpaper, protective chemicals, microflex circuits, reflective materials, and premium graphics. In 1998, the company realigned into three organizations: Industrial and Consumer Markets; Health Care Markets; and Transportation, Safety and Chemical Markets.

Rough Start As Sandpaper Maker: 1900s–10s

3M was formed in 1902 in Two Harbors, Minnesota, a thriving village on the shores of Lake Superior, by five entrepreneurs in order to mine the rare mineral corundum and market it as an abrasive. The ill-planned venture—sparked by a flurry of other forms of mining operations in northeastern Minnesota—nearly bankrupted the company, for its mineral holdings turned out to be not corundum but low-grade anorthosite, a virtually useless igneous rock. This unsettling discovery (by whom or when is unclear) was never disclosed in the company records and, for whatever reason, did not deter the owners from establishing a sandpaper factory in Duluth, another more or less ill-fated scheme that placed the company further in jeopardy (3M faced a host of abrasives competitors in the East and was soon forced to import a garnet inferior to that owned by domestic manufacturers, which resulted in a lower quality product).

In May 1905 a principal investor named Edgar B. Ober, determined to save the company, convinced friend and fellow St. Paul businessman Lucius Pond Ordway to join with him in rescuing 3M from almost certain demise by paying off $13,000 in debt and pumping in an additional $12,000 in capital. Together Ordway and Ober purchased 60 percent of the company; over the next several years, Ordway, a self-made millionaire, spent an additional $250,000 on a company that had yet to produce a profit, and Ober, who proceeded to oversee 3M, went without a salary. Ordway's continued backing, despite a strong desire to cut his losses early on and his decision to move the firm to St. Paul in 1910, ensured 3M's eventual health during the boom years following World War I.

Early Dual Leadership Instills Legacy of Innovation: 1920–40s

Of greatest significance to both the company's foundation and future were the hirings in 1907 and 1909 of William L. McKnight and A.G. Bush, respectively. Former farmhands trained as bookkeepers, the two worked as a team for well over 50 years and developed the system that helped make 3M a success. McKnight ran 3M between 1916 and 1966, serving as president from 1929 to 1949 and chairman of the board from 1949 to 1966. He created the general guidelines of diversification, avoiding price cuts, increasing sales by ten percent a year, high employee morale, and quality control that fueled the company's growth and created its unique corporate culture. In some ways, the sales system overshadowed the guidelines. McKnight and Bush designed an aggressive, customer-oriented brand of salesmanship. Sales representatives, instead of dealing with a company's purchasing agent, were encouraged to proceed directly to the shop where they could talk with the people who used the products. In so doing, 3M salesmen could discover both how products could be improved and what new products might be needed. This resulted in some of 3M's early innovations. For instance, when Henry Ford's newly motorized assembly lines created too much friction for existing sandpapers, which were designed to sand wood and static objects, a 3M salesman went back to St. Paul with the news. 3M devised a tougher sandpaper, and thus captured much of this niche market within the growing auto industry. Another salesman noticed that dust from sandpaper use made the shop environment extremely unhealthy. Around the same time, a Philadelphia ink manufacturer named Francis G. Okie wrote McKnight with a request for mineral grit samples. According to Virginia Huck, "McKnight's handling of Okie's request changed the course of 3M's history. He could have explained to Okie that 3M didn't sell bulk mineral. . . . Instead, prompted by his curiosity, McKnight instructed 3M's Eastern Division sales manager, R.H. Skillman, to get in touch with Okie to find out *why* he wanted the grit samples." The reason soon became clear: Okie had invented a waterproof, and consequently dust-free, sandpaper. After purchasing the patent and then solving various defects, 3M came out with WetorDry sandpaper and significantly expanded its business, eventually licensing two other manufacturers, Carborundum and Behr-Manning, to keep up with demand. It also hired the inventor as its first full-time researcher. This marked the creation of one of the nation's first corporate research and development divisions.

Sending salesmen into the shops paid off a few years later in an even more significant way, by giving 3M its first non-abrasives product line. In 1923 a salesman in an auto body painting shop noticed that the process used to paint cars in two tones worked poorly. He promised the painter that 3M could develop an effective way to prevent the paints from running together. It took two years, but the research and development division invented a successful masking tape—the first in a line of pressure-sensitive tapes that now extends to over 900 varieties. The invention of Scotch tape, as it came to be called and then trademarked, established 3M as a force for innovation in American industry. Taking a page from its sandpaper business, 3M immediately began to develop different applications of its new technology. Its most famous adaptation came in 1930, when some industrious 3M workers found a way to graft cellophane, a Du Pont invention, to adhesive, thus creating a transparent tape.

Transparent Scotch tape, now a generic commodity, provided a major windfall during the Depression, helping 3M to grow at a time when most businesses struggled to break even. Another salesman invented a portable tape dispenser, and 3M had its first large-scale consumer product. Consumers used Scotch tape in a variety of ways: to repair torn paper products, strengthen book bindings, mend clothes until they could be sewn, and even remove lint. By 1932 the new product was doing so well that 3M's main client base shifted from furniture and automobile factories to office supply stores. During the 1930s, 3M funneled some 45 percent of its profits into new product research; consequently, the company tripled in size during the worst decade American business had ever endured.

3M continued to grow during World War II by concentrating on understanding its markets and finding a niche to fill, rather than shifting to making military goods, as many U.S. corporations did. However, the war left 3M with a need to restructure and modernize, and not enough cash on hand to do so. To meet its building needs, in 1947 3M issued its first bond offerings. Its first public stock offering, coupled with its tremendous growth rate, attracted additional attention to 3M. In 1949, when President McKnight became chairman of the board (with A.G. Bush also moving from daily operations to the boardroom), it marked the end of a tremendous era for 3M. Under McKnight, 3M had grown almost 20fold. By its 50th year, it had surpassed the $100 million mark and was employing some 10,000 people.

Growing Reputation: 1950s

Such growth could not be ignored. Now that 3M was publicly traded, investment bankers took to recommending it as a buy, business magazines sent reporters to write about it, and other companies tried to figure out how 3M continued to excel. McKnight's immediate successor as president, Richard Carlton, encapsulated the company's special path to prosperity with the phrase: "we'll make any damn thing we can make money on." Yet the 3M method involved a great deal more than simply making and selling. Its metier had been, and continues to be, finding uninhabited markets and then filling them relentlessly with high-quality products. Therefore, research and development received money that most companies spent elsewhere—most companies still did not have such departments by the early 1950s—and the pursuit for ideas was intense.

Carlton kept the company focused on product research (today, 3M rewards its scientists with Carlton Awards), which led to another innovation in the 1950s, the first dry-printing photocopy process, ThermoFax. 3M breezed through the 1950s in impressive fashion, with 1959 marking the company's 20th consecutive year of increased sales. Yet, for all its growth and diversity, 3M continued to produce strong profits from its established products. In a way, this was almost to be expected, given 3M's penchant for being in "uninhabited" markets. As noted by John Pitblado, 3M's president of U.S. Operations, "almost everything depends on a coated abrasive during some phase of its manufacture. Your eyeglasses, wrist watches, the printed circuit that's in a TV set, knitting needles . . . all require sandpaper.''

Skyrocketing 1960s to Earthly Ups and Downs in the 1970s and 1980s

In the 1960s 3M embarked on another growth binge, doubling in size between 1963 and 1967 and becoming a billion-dollar company in the process. Existing product lines did well, and 3M's ventures into magnetic media provided excellent returns. One venture, the backdrops used for some of the spectacular scenes from the 1968 movie *2001: A Space Odyssey,* earned an Academy Award. During the 1970s a number of obstacles interfered with 3M's seeming odyssey of growth. Among these were the resignations of several of the company's top executives when it was revealed that they had operated an illegal slush fund from company money between 1963 and 1975, which included a contribution of some $30,000 to Richard Nixon's 1972 campaign. Sales growth also slowed during the decade, particularly in the oil crunch of 1974, ending 3M's phenomenal string of averaging a 15 percent growth rate. 3M responded to its cost crunch in characteristic fashion: it turned to its employees, who devised ways for the company to cut costs at each plant.

The company also had difficulties with consumer products. Particularly galling was the loss of the cassette tape market, which two Japanese companies, TDK and Maxell, dominated by engaging in price-cutting. 3M stuck to its tradition of abandoning markets where it could not set its own prices, and backed off. Eventually, the company stopped making much of its magnetic media, instead buying from an overseas supplier and putting the 3M label on it (3M instead focused attention on data storage media for the computer market, in which it continues as a world leader). The loss of the cassette market was not overwhelming: revenues doubled between 1975 and 1980, and in 1976 3M was named one of the Dow Jones Industrial 30.

Unfortunately, price-cutting was not the only problem confronting 3M as it entered the 1980s. Major competitors seemed to face the company on all fronts: the niches of decades past seemed extinct. When Lewis Lehr became company president in 1981, he noted that ''there isn't a business where we don't have to come up with a new technology.'' He promptly restructured 3M from six divisions into four sectors: Industrial and Consumer, Electronic and Information Technologies, Graphic Technologies (later renamed Imaging and combined with Information and Electronic), and Life Sciences, containing a total of some 40 divisions. He also established a goal of having 25 percent of each division's earnings come from products that did not exist five years before. Lehr's concern was not to keep the company going, for 3M was still well-respected, with a less than 25 percent debt-to-equity ratio and reasonable levels of growth. Shareholders, too, had little to complain about, for 1986 marked the 18th consecutive year of increased dividends. Rather, Lehr wanted to ensure that 3M would continue to develop new ideas. The major product to come out of the 1980s was the ubiquitous Post-it, a low-tech marvel created by Art Fry.

Challenges of the 1990s

L. D. DeSimone, who joined 3M in 1958 as a manufacturing engineer and moved into management while working in international operations, was named CEO in 1991. He took the helm of a ship being buffeted by economic recession and stiff price competition: sales rose an annual average of just two percent from 1991 to 1993. Kevin Kelly wrote in a 1994 *Business Week* article, ''It turned out that the creative juices that had transformed 3M into a paragon of innovation and the inventor of everything from ubiquitous yellow Post-it notes to surgical staples weren't producing new products fast enough.''

DeSimone pushed research staff to work more closely with marketers and transform existing technology into commercial products. Connecting with customers' needs took on more urgency. Product turnaround time was slashed; product development rivaled basic research. Customer-driven products gleaned from the new system included the Never Rust Wool Soap Pad made from recycled plastic bottles and a laptop computer screen film which enhanced brightness without heavy battery drain.

On the international front, foreign sales produced more than 50 percent of total 3M sales for the first time in company history in 1992. The Asia Pacific region yielded nearly 27 percent of the $7 billion foreign sales volume. A major restructuring of European operations was completed in 1993: manufacturing plants were closed and consolidated and the workforce was trimmed in response to declining operating income.

The company achieved record sales, operating income, net income, and earnings per share in 1994. More than $1 billion of the $15 billion in total sales came from first-year products. DeSimone raised the bar: at least 30 percent of future sales were to come from products introduced within the past four years.

On a more somber note, in 1994 3M took a $35 million pretax charge against probable liabilities and associated expenses related to litigation over 3M's silicone breast implant business operated through former subsidiary McGhan Medical Corporation. 3M was named in more than 5,800 lawsuits claiming injuries caused by leakage or rupture of the implants.

In 1996, 3M dismantled the Information, Imaging and Electronics sector which accounted for a fifth of its business. It was the largest restructuring effort in company history. The divisions making floppy disks and other data-storage media, x-ray film and specialty imaging equipment were spun off as an independent, public company, and the audio and videotape operations shut down entirely. 3M retained the businesses making electrical tapes, connectors, insulating materials, overhead projects, and transparency films. The company cut about 5,000 jobs.

Since DeSimone took command, 3M had pumped $1.2 billion into the Information, Imaging and Electronics division, yet operating profit margins remained only a third of the Industrial and Consumer Products and Life Sciences divisions. Persistent pricing pressures from competitors such as Kodak plus rising raw material costs prompted DeSimone to pull the plug on the audio and videotape business. A smaller, leaner operation—the new $2 billion Imation Corporation—was deemed to have better prospects in the equally fierce data-storage marketplace.

Future Forecast

Following restructuring, 3M concentrated product development efforts on about two dozen core technologies. In 1997 the company achieved one of DeSimone's goals: 30 percent of total sales were generated from products introduced within the past four years. But 3M's numbers began slipping again in 1998. Michelle Conlin wrote in an October 1998 *Forbes* article, "Are these unavoidable downward blips on a rising curve? Or are they signs of deeper trouble? 3M has been glacially slow to respond to the economic meltdown in Asia, where it gets 23% of its business. In the U.S. a flood of cheaper products made by competitors like Korean polyester film outfits SKC and Kolon have cut into 3M's sales."

Conlin conceded that 3M had promising products, such as bendable fiber-optic cable and a fluid to replace ozone-depleting chlorofluorocarbons, already in the pipeline. In the long run, 3M has little to worry about. Despite its gargantuan size, the company maintains a distinctively entrepreneurial environment and, through one of its several legendary "rules," allows its employees to spend up to 15 percent of company time on independent projects, a process called "bootlegging" or "scrounging." As *In Search of Excellence* authors Thomas J. Peters and Robert H. Waterman, Jr., have written, because heroes abound at 3M, because scrounging is encouraged, because failure is okay, because informal communications are the norm, because overplanning and paperwork are conspicuously absent, because of these and a half-dozen more factors "functioning in concert—over a period of decades," innovation works at 3M. A near fixture on *Fortune*'s annual list of the most admired companies in America, 3M is that most prized of conglomerates: a perennial money-maker with the innovative culture and managerial drive to ensure that it remains so.

Principal Subsidiaries

Dyneon L.L.C. (54%); Eastern Heights State Bank (99%); 3M Unitek Corporation; 3M Argentina S.A.C.I.F.I.A.; 3M Australia Pty. Ltd.; 3M Oesterreich GmbH (Austria); 3M Belgium S.A./N.V.; Seaside Insurance Limited (Bermuda); 3M do Brazil Limitada; 3M Canada Inc.; 3M A/S (Denmark); Suomen 3M Oy (Finland); 3M France, S.A.; 3M Deutschland GmbH (Germany); 3M Hong Kong Limited; 3M Italia Finanziaria S.p.A. (Italy); Sumitomo 3M Limited (Japan; 50%); 3M Health Care Limited (Japan; 75%); 3M Korea Limited; 3M Mexico S.A. de C.V.; Corporate Services B.V. (Netherlands); 3M Nederland B.V. (Netherlands); 3M (New Zealand) Limited; 3M Norge A/S (Norway); 3M Puerto Rico, Inc.; 3M Singapore Private Limited; 3M South Africa (Proprietary) Limited; 3M Espana, S.A.; 3M Svenska AB (Sweden); 3M (East) A.G. (Switzerland); 3M (Schweiz) A.G. (Switzerland); 3M Taiwan Limited; 3M Thailand Limited; 3M United Kingdom Holdings P.L.C.; 3M Venezuela, S.A.

Principal Operating Units

Industrial and Consumer Markets; Health Care Markets; Transportation, Safety and Chemical Markets.

Further Reading

"And Then There Were Two," *Economist,* November 18, 1995, pp. 74–75.

Conlin, Michelle, "Too Much Doodle?" *Forbes,* October 19, 1998, pp. 54–55.

DeSilver, Drew, "Aftershock Layoffs Seen for 3M's Spin-Off," *Minneapolis/St. Paul CityBusiness,* November 17, 1995, pp. 1, 45.

Dubashi, Jagannath, "Technology Transfer: Minnesota Mining & Manufacturing," *Financial World,* September 17, 1991, pp. 40–41.

Fredrickson, Tom, "3M Unifies Its Empire in Europe," *Minneapolis/St. Paul CityBusiness,* August 13–19, 1993, pp. 1, 29.

Gilyard, Burl, "Tale of the Tape," *Corporate Report Minnesota,* January 1998, pp. 35–38.

Goldman, Kevin, "Scouring-Pad Rivals Face 3M Challenge," *Wall Street Journal,* January 11, 1993, p. B5.

Houston, Patrick, "How Jake Jacobson Is Lighting a Fire Under 3M," *Business Week,* July 21, 1986, pp. 106–07.

Huck, Virginia, *Brand of the Tartan: The 3M Story,* New York: Appleton-Century-Crofts, 1955.

Kelly, Kevin, "The Drought Is Over at 3M," *Business Week,* November 7, 1994, pp. 140–41.

——, "It Really Can Pay to Clean Up Your Act," *Business Week,* November 7, 1994, p. 141.

——, "3M Run Scared? Forget About It," *Business Week,* September 16, 1991, pp. 59, 62.

Larson, Don, *Land of the Giants: A History of Minnesota Business,* Minneapolis: Dorn Books, 1979.

"The Mass Production of Ideas, and Other Impossibilities," *Economist,* March 18, 1995, p. 72.

Mattera, Philip, "Minnesota Mining and Manufacturing Company," *World Class Business: A Guide to the 100 Most Powerful Global Corporations,* New York: Henry Holt and Company, 1992, pp. 465–67.

McSpadden, Wyatt, "3M Fights Back," *Fortune,* February 5, 1996, pp. 94–99.

Meyers, Mike, "3M Reports 9% Increase in Net Income on Worldwide Sales Gain of 2.3 Percent," *Star Tribune,* May 4, 1993, p. 1D.

Mitchell, Russell, "Masters of Innovation: How 3M Keeps Its New Products Coming," *Business Week,* April 10, 1989, pp. 58–63.

Moskowitz, Milton, et al, "3M," *Everybody's Business: A Field Guide to the 400 Leading Companies in America,* New York: Doubleday, 1990.

Our Story So Far: Notes from the First 75 Years of 3M Company, St. Paul, Minn.: 3M Public Relations Department, 1977.

Peters, Thomas J., and Robert H. Waterman, Jr., *In Search of Excellence,* New York: Harper and Row, 1982.

"3M Co.," *Minneapolis/St. Paul CityBusiness,* February 17, 1995, p. 26.

"3M Co.," *Minneapolis/St. Paul CityBusiness,* December 13, 1996, p. 24.

"3M Co.," *Minneapolis/St. Paul CityBusiness,* November 7, 1997, p. 36.

"3M: New Talent and Products Outweigh High Costs," *Financial World,* February 18, 1992, p. 19.

"3M: 60,000 and Counting," *Economist,* November 30, 1991, pp. 70–71.

Weinberger, Betsy, "3M Breaking New Ground with Plan for China Plant," *Minneapolis/St. Paul CityBusiness,* April 9, 1993, pp. 1, 24.

Weiner, Steve, "A Hard Way to Make a Buck," *Forbes,* April 29, 1991, pp. 134–35, 137.

—Jay P. Pederson
—updated by Kathleen Peippo

MITRE Corporation

202 Burlington Road
Bedford, Massachusetts 01730
U.S.A.
(781) 271-2000
Fax: (781) 271-3402
Web site: http://www.mitre.org

Nonprofit Company
Incorporated: 1958
Employees: 3,500
Sales: $488.1 million (1997)
SICs: 8733 Noncommercial Research Organizations;
8734 Testing Laboratories; 8744 Facilities Support
Management Services; 9711 National Security

MITRE Corporation is a federally funded nonprofit organization that performs systems engineering and integration work for the command, control, communications, and intelligence systems of the Department of Defense. MITRE also performs systems research and development work for the Federal Aviation Administration and other civil aviation authorities. It maintains facilities in Bedford, Massachusetts, and McLean, Virginia.

Electronic-Systems Pioneer: 1958–70

MITRE was formed in 1958 as a federally funded "think tank," with its staff detached from the Massachusetts Institute of Technology's Lincoln Laboratories, which had been established by the Pentagon in 1951. Some 480 laboratory personnel were transferred to the new organization, whose first task was to develop the nation's first automated, real-time air defense system for the U.S. Air Force, which had been unable to find a for-profit company to do the job. Later, in 1989, Charles S. Zrabet—president and chief executive officer at the time—recalled MITRE's beginnings: "They wanted a dedicated laboratory that had the multi-disciplines of radar, computers, and communications. It was a new technology, and there was no expertise for this anywhere."

In its early years MITRE played a vital role in helping design electronic systems that detected and tracked Soviet-bloc missiles and aircraft and intercepted communications. It played a major part in designing the hardened, underground North American Air Defense (NORAD) facilities intended to protect against a possible nuclear attack by enemy aircraft and/or ballistic missiles. In order to process and interpret information quickly for military purposes, MITRE, together with the Electronic Systems Division (ESD) of the U.S. Air Force Systems Command, came to possess, by 1962, one of the most powerful computers in the world. The computer was an IBM 7030 that, including peripheral equipment, covered a space the equivalent of a basketball court. Also in 1962, MITRE and ESD sponsored the first congress of information system sciences ever held.

During the Vietnam War, MITRE endured criticism by opponents of the war for its role in developing a so-called electronic fence, composed mainly of acoustics and sensors, that was supposed to help pinpoint the movement of Viet Cong and North Vietnamese forces into South Vietnam. Despite the unpopularity of the war and the doomsday scenarios of the Cold War era, Zrabet told a reporter in 1985 that in his many years at MITRE he could not remember a time when an employee left due to objections to the moral or political nature of the organization's work.

Not all of MITRE's work was related to the military, however. During the 1960s it began to work on systems used for civilian air-traffic control. As electronic command and control systems proliferated, in 1963 the organization established a Washington-area office in addition to its Bedford, Massachusetts facility. This new office was later moved to McLean, Virginia. Because the technology it developed for the military was also useful for civilian applications, MITRE helped civil agencies develop information systems for transportation, medicine, law enforcement, space exploration, and environmental remediation. In 1971, for example, it began developing a two-way, interactive cable-television system.

Expansion in the 1970s and 1980s

Throughout the 1970s and 1980s, MITRE continued to work on air defense and other command, control, communications,

Company Perspectives:

In partnership with government clients, MITRE addresses public interest issues of critical importance, combining system engineering and information technology to develop innovative, actionable solutions that make a difference.

and intelligence (C3I) systems used by Department of Defense clients. C3I networks were frequently referred to as the brains or nervous systems of weaponry. They consisted of command centers on both the ground and in airplanes, the radar and satellites scanning the battlefield, and the communications equipment linking the other components. MITRE also became heavily involved in satellite communications technology, and in the late 1980s was working on Millstar, a system designed to provide worldwide communications for the military which was not only invulnerable to enemy efforts to jam it, but also capable of surviving nuclear attack.

On the one hand, to preserve the credibility of the United States' deterrent to nuclear attack, it was essential that the C3I systems function so that the military could counter any enemy first strike with a retaliatory attack. These systems had to be able to distinguish a real strike from, for example, blips on the radar screen that turned out to be geese. In addition, nuclear weapons sites had to be protected from entry by unauthorized personnel, which might include thieves or terrorists. Thus, during the 1970s a four-year research effort by MITRE and ESD scientists established automatic speech, handwriting, and fingerprint verification systems to screen all personnel and deny access to would-be intruders.

During the late 1980s MITRE was also taking part in projects to replace the federal telecommunications system, design a new computer system for the Securities and Exchange Commission, upgrade medical information systems for the National Institutes of Health, and store radiological images on computer tape—rather than film—for Georgetown Hospital. MITRE also designed the Federal Bureau of Investigation's National Crime Information System.

Military projects remained MITRE's bread and butter, however. Its heyday was during the Reagan Administration's buildup of the 1980s, when one of the military's highest priorities became improving command and control systems so that the United States retained the capacity to retaliate against a massive nuclear strike. By the end of the decade MITRE was exploring sensor technology to cope with radar-evading stealth aircraft.

MITRE's revenues doubled between 1980 and 1984, reaching $287 million by the end of that period, when the workforce rose to 5,000. The company actually outgrew its own facilities in Bedford, Massachusetts, and had to move its operations into several leased buildings. MITRE's revenues then rose to $463 million in 1988, when it had 5,800 employees and $62 million in a reserve fund. As the Cold War came to a close at the end of the decade, military spending began to decline and competition

for contracts became fiercer. Commercial engineering firms argued that they could do MITRE's work at a lower cost. They complained about the organization's lack of public accountability, particularly its freedom from the federal government's competitive bidding process and its exemption from taxes. They also resented MITRE's power over for-profit companies in its capacity to help review proposals from such contractors and to monitor how well the work was carried out.

MITRE in the 1990s

Amid the uncertainties of a new decade, MITRE continued to collaborate closely with the Air Force's (renamed) Electronic Systems Center (ESC) at Hanscom Air Force Base. In 1994 MITRE and ESC personnel were engaged in laboratory simulations intended to improve the capabilities of AWACS and Joint-STARS aircraft to use both onboard and offboard sensors in providing a synthesized picture of the battlefield. Two years later, a journalist visiting the Air Force base received a demonstration of three-dimensional, virtual-reality imaging techniques that might be used to meet a variety of military needs. These ranged from allowing planners to configure an air command center in the field to using robotics to assist surgeons in performing simple operations from a remote site. The visualization lab also created a computer model of a section of Seoul, South Korea, in a 24-hour period as a demonstration of what could be done quickly to aid forces conducting a hostage rescue mission.

MITRE continued to count on steady work from the Federal Aviation Administration. In 1993 this agency awarded the organization a new three-year, $222 million contract to continue operating its Center for Advanced Aviation System Development in McLean and to provide support for further development of the National Airspace System. MITRE also held contracts to help upgrade the federal government's telephone network and apply a Defense Department navigation system to commercial aviation. Meanwhile, MITRE offered its services to help the military clean up bases and was working with the FBI to improve the National Crime Information Center by, among other things, developing a system to send mug shots directly to police patrol cars.

About 70 percent of MITRE's work, however, remained in C3I applications for the military. As one of ten federally funded research and development centers scheduled to lose $100 million of $1.35 billion in government funds, the organization reacted by laying off 300 of its 5,500 employees in October 1994. In response to objections raised by members of Congress and the Defense Department, MITRE also cut back on some of its federally funded expenses and canceled holiday parties for executives. It continued to give employees generous relocation allowances, however, and provided automobiles to company officers for personal use. In 1996 a government audit described $4.7 million of $5.3 million in management expenses incurred during fiscal 1994 as ''unnecessary and in some cases extravagant.''

MITRE disarmed its critics in January 1996 by divesting itself of $70 million worth of federal nonmilitary contracts. This work was spun off to Mitretek Systems Inc., a new nonprofit organization dedicated to research for nonmilitary federal agencies and state and local governments in such areas as environmental remediation and telecommunications. MITRE would continue working for the military and the FAA but, according to its new president and chief executive officer, Victor A. De-Marines, would no longer work for other nonmilitary agencies or private-sector companies.

Further Reading

Black, Chris, "Audit Hits Firm's Use of US Funds," *Boston Globe,* January 26, 1996, p. 37.

Day, Kathleen, "The Think Tank That Went Out for a Spin," *Washington Post,* February 23, 1996, p. B1.

Debons, Anthony, and Horne, Esther E., "NATO Advanced Study Institutes of Information Science and Foundations of Information Science," *Journal of the American Society for Information Science,* September 1997, pp. 794–803.

Gwynne, Peter, "Fail Safe," *Newsweek,* January 17, 1977, p. 42.

Hughes, David, "Mitre, Air Force Explore Data Fusion for Joint-STARS," *Aviation Week & Space Technology,* March 7, 1994, pp. 47–51.

——, "USAF Finds C3I Uses for Virtual Reality," *Aviation Week & Space Technology,* March 18, 1996, pp. 50–52.

Lewis, Diane, "Mitre Plans to Lay Off 300 Workers with Nearly Half of Cuts in Bedford," *Boston Globe,* October 12, 1994, p. 43.

Marcus, Jon, "Defense-Oriented MITRE Adjusts, Finds Work with the FBI," *Boston Globe,* April 13, 1993, p. 47.

Stein, Charles, "Mitre Booms As Military Takes Brains over Brawn," *Boston Globe,* April 23, 1985, p. 27.

Sugawara, Sandra, "The Mighty Voice of Mitre," *Washington Post,* August 20, 1989, p. H1.

Wilgoren, Debbi, "Mitre Corp. Picks Insider As New CEO," *Washington Post,* March 2, 1990, p. 10.

—Robert Halasz

MOLSON

The Molson Companies Limited

40 King Street West, Suite 3600
Toronto, Ontario M5H 3Z5
Canada
(416) 360-1786
Fax: (416) 360-4345
Web site: http://www.molson.com

Public Company
Incorporated: 1844 as Thos. & Wm. Molson &
   Company
Employees: 14,700
Sales: C$1.55 billion (US$1.09 billion) (1997)
Stock Exchanges: Montreal Toronto Vancouver
Ticker Symbol: MOL
SICs: 2082 Malt Beverages; 5211 Lumber & Other
   Building Materials Dealers; 6512 Operators of
   Nonresidential Buildings; 7941 Professional Sports
   Clubs & Promoters; 7999 Amusement & Recreation
   Services, Not Elsewhere Classified

Established in 1786, The Molson Companies Limited is perhaps best known for its brewery, which is the oldest in North America. Molson Breweries supplanted longtime leader Labatt Brewing Company Limited as Canada's leading brewery in 1989 and claimed slightly less than half of the country's beer market in the late 1990s. Molson has nurtured a distinctly Canadian character: its flagship beer brand is "Molson Canadian," its beers are brewed only in Canada, and its advertising aggressively pitches the "I am Canadian" line. Molson Breweries is also the leading exporter of beer into the United States and is involved in partnerships with two major U.S. brewers, Coors Brewing Company and Miller Brewing Company, as well as with Foster's Brewing Group Ltd. of Australia.

In addition to its brewing interests, Molson Companies owns the Montreal Canadiens National Hockey League team and the Molson Centre, the Canadiens' home arena. It also owns Beaver Lumber Company Limited—a 145-unit retail chain offering lumber, building materials, and supplies—but plans to sell this noncore asset, the last of its retailing operations.

Origins in Montreal Brewery

The history of Molson brewing began soon after 18-year-old John Molson emigrated from Lincolnshire, England, during the late 18th century. He arrived in Canada in 1782 and became a partner in a small brewing company outside Montreal's city walls on the St. Lawrence River a year later. In 1785 he became the sole proprietor of the brewery, closed it temporarily, and sailed to England to settle his estate and buy brewing equipment. Upon his return in 1786, with a book entitled *Theoretical Hints on an Improved Practice of Brewing* in hand, the novice started brewing according to his own formula. By the close of the year, Molson had produced 80 hogsheads (4,300 gallons) of beer. In 1787 Molson remarked, "My beer has been almost universally well liked beyond my most sanguine expectations." His statement in part reflects the quality of the brew, but it also indicates that Molson had excellent timing; he faced little competition in the pioneer community.

Before electrical refrigeration became available, Molson was confined to a 20-week operating season because the company had to rely on ice from the St. Lawrence River. Nevertheless, production grew throughout the 1800s as the Montreal brewery steadily added more land and equipment. Population growth and increasingly sophisticated bottling and packaging techniques also contributed to Molson's profitability in the early days.

It was not long before Molson became an established entrepreneur in Montreal, providing services in the fledgling community that contributed to its growth into a major Canadian city. Molson first diversified in 1797 with a lumberyard on the brewery property. A decade later he launched the *Accommodation,* Canada's first steamboat, and soon thereafter he formed the St. Lawrence Steamboat Company, also known as the Molson Line. The steam line led to Molson's operation of small-scale financial services between Montreal and Quebec City; eventually the services became Molson's Bank, chartered in 1855.

In 1816 John Molson signed a partnership agreement with his three sons—John Jr., William, and Thomas—ensuring that the brewery would remain under family control. He was elected the same year to represent Montreal East in the legislature of Lower Canada and opened the Mansion House, a large hotel in Montreal that housed the public library, post office, and Montreal's first theater.

The Molsons established the first industrial-scale distillery in Montreal in 1820. Three years later, the youngest brother, Thomas, left the organization after a severe disagreement with his family. In 1824 he moved to Kingston, Ontario, where he established an independent brewing and distilling operation.

The elder John Molson left the company in 1828, leaving John Jr. and William as active partners. He served as president of the Bank of Montreal from 1826 to 1830, and in 1832 he was nominated to the Legislative Council of Lower Canada. Possibly his most fortuitous venture was his contribution of one quarter of the cost of building Canada's first railway, the Champlain and St. Lawrence. He died in January 1836 at age 72.

Thomas Molson returned to Montreal in 1834 and was readmitted to the family enterprise. Over the next 80 years new partnerships formed among various members of the Molson family, prompting several more reorganizations. The first in the third generation to enter the family business was John H.R. Molson, who joined the partnership in 1848. He became an increasingly important figure in the company as William and John Jr. devoted more of their time to the operation of Molson's Bank.

In 1844 the Molson brewery, now called Thos. & Wm. Molson & Company, introduced beer in bottles that were corked and labeled by hand. Beer production grew faster than bottle production, though, necessitating the company's purchase of a separate barrel factory at Port Hope, Ontario, in 1851. In 1859 Molson started to advertise in Montreal newspapers, while also setting up a retail sales network and introducing pint bottles.

The company became John H.R. Molson & Bros. in 1861 following the establishment of a new partnership with William Markland Molson and John Thomas Molson. In 1866 the Molsons closed their distillery, citing poor sales, and in 1868 they sold their property in Port Hope.

By 1866, the brewery's hundredth year in Molson hands, its production volume had multiplied 175 times but profit cleared on each gallon remained the same—26¢. In the early years of the 20th century, the company incorporated pasteurization and electric refrigeration into its methods. In addition, electricity replaced steam power, and mechanized packaging devices sped

the bottling process. In 1911 the company became Molson's Brewery Ltd. following its reorganization as a joint-share company. The Molson family would continue to hold a major stake in the company through the late 1990s. The family's direct interest in banking ended in 1925 when Molson's Bank merged with the Bank of Montreal.

The first half of the 20th century was a period of rapid growth for Molson. Production at the Montreal brewery rose from three million gallons in 1920, to 15 million in 1930, to 25 million in 1949. Molson adopted modern marketing and advertising methods to enhance market penetration and in 1930 began producing its first promotional items—despite founder John Molson's contention that "An honest brew makes its own friends."

Additional Breweries Built and Acquired Starting in 1955

In the mid-1950s Molson management recognized a need to expand operations significantly. By concentrating their resources, other Canadian breweries had finally begun to compete successfully against perennial leader Molson. Molson decided that the appropriate strategy was to have a brewery operating in each province, as distribution from its base in Quebec to other provinces was subject to strict government regulations. With operations in the other provinces, Molson could further build its market throughout Canada. This large-scale expansion began when Molson announced a second brewery would be built on a ten-acre site in Toronto. Modernizations at the Montreal facility had, it was felt, fully maximized output there. The new Toronto installation opened in 1955 and became the home of Molson's first lager, Crown and Anchor. In the next few years Molson acquired three breweries: Sick's Brewery, bought in 1958; Fort Garry Brewery in Winnipeg, 1959; and Newfoundland Brewery, 1962.

The expansion effort resulted in good returns for Molson investors; between 1950 and 1965 earnings more than doubled. Even so, Molson leaders recognized that expansion potential within the mature brewing industry was limited, and further, that growth rates in the industry would always be slow. It was clear that even the most successful brewing operation soon would reach the limits of its profitability. Thus Molson began an accelerated diversification program in the mid-1960s that heralded in Canada the era of the corporate takeover.

Diversification Began in 1968

In 1968 Molson made its first major nonbrewing acquisition in more than a century. Ontario-based Anthes Imperial Ltd. was a public company specializing in steel materials, office furniture and supplies, construction equipment rentals, and public warehousing. The Anthes executive staff was known to be highly talented in acquisitions and strategic management, two areas in which Molson needed expert help to pursue its goal of diversification. However, because the various Anthes companies required different management and marketing strategies, the acquisition did not benefit Molson as much as its directors had hoped. Soon Molson sold off most of the Anthes component companies. The company had learned that future acquisitions should be of firms that were more compatible with Molson's longstanding strengths in marketing consumer products and services.

Molson did retain one important component of Anthes: its president. As Molson's chairman, Donald "Bud" Willmot directed a series of successful acquisitions in the early 1970s. Management felt that the ideal candidate must be a Canadian-based firm and must be involved in above-average growth. The do-it-yourself material supplies market appeared to be the ideal candidate: there seemed to be a new trend—consumers doing their own home improvements—and Molson recognized the potential for rapid growth of this market in urban areas, which at that time had few or no lumberyards or similar outlets. Molson began acquiring small hardware, lumber, and home furnishings companies. In 1972 it spent $50 million buying more than 90 percent of the shares of Beaver Lumber, a large Canadian company. During the remainder of the decade Beaver acquired several smaller hardware and lumber operations. Molson's service center division grew to encompass 162 retail stores, most of them franchises, selling everything from paint to home-building supplies. In the mid-1980s Beaver began importing competitively priced merchandise from Asian countries.

In July 1973 the company's name was changed to The Molson Companies Limited, a reflection of its diversification. The beer-making operations were renamed Molson Breweries of Canada Ltd.

Although Beaver's sales climbed steadily throughout the 1970s, rapidly making it a leader in its industry, profits lagged behind what Molson had anticipated, and initially the company considered the Beaver purchase only a modest success. Struggling at first to integrate the brewing and home improvement divisions, Molson eventually learned that the two industries, and marketing therein, are very different. The beer industry operates in a controlled market; governments regulate sale and manufacture of alcoholic products. The hardware industry, on the other hand, operates in a relatively free market. Furthermore, in brewing, manufacturing efficiency is the key to a profitable enterprise, but the success of a home improvement retail operation hinges on the ability to provide a broad variety of products at competitive prices.

The challenge of integrating two companies operating in such different markets led Molson to a careful reassessment of its diversification criteria; in the future, the company would concentrate on marketing specific product brands. W.J. Gluck, vice-president of corporate development wrote: "We only wanted to go into a business related to our experience—a business in which marketing, not manufacturing, is the important thing." The search for another acquisition began.

Expansion into Chemicals, Sports, and Entertainment in 1978

In 1978 Molson offered $28 per share of stock in Diversey Corporation, a manufacturer and marketer of institutional chemical cleansers and sanitizers based in Northbrook, Illinois. Contending that their company—which boasted $730 million in annual sales—was worth more, Diversey stockholders contested the sale, but eventually accepted Molson's original $55 million offer. Diversey was Molson's first large acquisition in the United States, though most of its clients and manufacturing plants were in fact located outside the United States in Europe, Latin America, and the Pacific basin. Molson also bought into sports and entertainment in 1978, buying a share in the Club de Hockey Canadien Inc. (the Montreal Canadiens) and the Montreal Forum, as well as hosting Molson Hockey Night in Canada and other television shows through its production company, Ohlmeyer Communications.

Molson opened the 1980s with the $25 million purchase of BASF Wyandotte Corporation, a U.S. manufacturer of chemical specialties products related to food services and commercial laundries. The subsequent merger of BASF and Diversey made Molson's chemical products division its second largest earnings contributor. Prior to the merger, Diversey was a weak competitor in the U.S. sanitation supplies market. BASF Wyandotte, however, was a leader in the U.S. kitchen services market. Thus the marriage was a sound move for Diversey, which had found a relatively inexpensive way to increase its share of its market in the United States.

Having concentrated on diversification, Molson found that it had missed the globalization of the brewing industry that had begun in the 1970s. While other major competitors had expanded internationally through acquisition, Molson had not completed a single foreign acquisition. Although the conglomerate remained profitable throughout the 1980s, it became clear to the board of directors—led by eighth-generation heir Eric Molson—that the company would need to make some international connections to remain a major, independent participant in the beer market.

1988 Merger of Molson Breweries and Carling O'Keefe

In 1988 the board hired Marshall "Mickey" Cohen as president and CEO. A career civil servant who had entered the private sector in 1985, Cohen was brought into Molson with one objective: to raise the 202-year-old company's sagging returns. His first move was to revive ailing merger talks between Molson and Elders IXL Ltd., Australia's largest publicly traded conglomerate. Elders (subsequently renamed for its beer-making subsidiary, Foster's Brewing Group Ltd.) had recently capped off a five-year amalgamation of global brewing companies with the purchase of Canada's number three brewery, Carling O'Keefe. The proposed merger of number two Molson with Carling was called "the biggest and most audacious deal in Canadian brewing history" in a 1989 *Globe and Mail* story, but it required Molson to share control of the resulting company (50–50 between Molson and Foster's). Whereas it had been difficult for Cohen's predecessors to agree to relinquish more than two centuries of control, Cohen had no such compunctions.

The resulting union gave Molson access to Foster's 80-country reach, while Foster's bought entree into the lucrative U.S. market, where Molson was the second largest importer after Heineken NV. The merger also helped lower both participants' production costs: the combined operations were pared from 16 Canadian breweries down to nine, and employment was correspondingly cut by 1,400 workers. As a concession to its larger pre-merger size—Molson's brewery assets were valued at $1 billion, whereas Carling's only amounted to about

$600 million—Cohen also managed to wring $600 million cash for Molson Companies out of the deal.

Some analysts surmised that the CEO would use the funds to further supplement the multinational beer business, but he surprised many with the $284 million acquisition of DuBois Chemicals Inc., the United States' second largest distributor of cleaning chemicals, in 1991. The addition boosted Diversey's annual sales by 25 percent to $1.2 billion and augmented operations in the United States, Japan, and Europe. Unfortunately, the merger proved more troublesome than expected, and a subsequent decline in service alienated customers. While Diversey's sales increased to $1.4 billion in fiscal 1994 (ended March 1994), its profits declined to $72.6 million and the subsidiary's president jumped ship. Cohen took the helm and began to formulate a turnaround plan.

Hoping to boost the Molson brand's less-than-one-percent share of the U.S. beer market, Molson and Foster's each agreed to sell an equal part of its stake in Molson Breweries to Miller Brewing Company, a leader in the American market. Miller's $349 million bought it a 20 percent share of Molson Breweries and effectively shifted control of Canada's leading brewer to foreigners in 1993 (Molson's stake in Molson Breweries having been reduced to 40 percent). Cohen expected the brand to retain its distinctly Canadian character (the beer would continue to be manufactured exclusively in Canada), but hoped that it would benefit from Miller's marketing clout.

Molson's financial results were mediocre at best in the early 1990s. Sales rose from $2.55 billion in fiscal 1990 to $3.09 billion in fiscal 1993, but earnings vacillated from $117.9 million in fiscal 1990 to a net loss of $38.67 million the following year, rebounding to $164.69 million in fiscal 1993. The company blamed its difficulties on Diversey's money-losing U.S. operations, which faced strong competition from industry leader Ecolab Inc. The following year's sales and earnings slipped to $2.97 billion and $125.67 million, respectively, as Diversey continued to lose money in the United States.

Nevertheless, Cohen remained determined to turn Diversey's operations around. Late in 1994 he announced a decision to divest Molson's retail home improvement businesses to focus on the brewing and chemicals operations. By this time Molson's retail sector included Beaver Lumber, a 45.1 percent interest in the Quebec-based Réno-Dépôt Inc. chain, and a 25 percent stake in Home Depot Canada. The last of these was rooted in Molson's 1971 purchase of the Ontario-based Aikenhead's Home Improvement Warehouse chain. In 1994 Home Depot Inc. purchased a 75 percent stake in Aikenhead's, whose stores were then converted to Home Depots.

Refocused on Brewing in the Mid-1990s

The exit from retailing proved to be a slow one, however, and Molson dramatically shifted course in 1996 when it sold Diversey, jettisoning its troubled chemicals operations. Most of Diversey was sold to Unilever PLC, with the entire chemical unit bringing about US$1.1 billion to Molson. Nonetheless, charges related to the sale and for restructuring both Molson Breweries and Beaver Lumber resulted in a net loss of C$305.5 million (US$225 million) for fiscal 1996. Management

shakeups led to Cohen's exit from Molson in September 1996 and to Cohen's replacement, former company executive Norman Seagram, lasting only until May 1997, when James Arnett took over as president and CEO. Arnett, a corporate lawyer based in Toronto, had been a director of Molson. Meanwhile, the historic Montreal Forum was replaced in 1996 as the home of the Montreal Canadiens by the newly built Molson Centre, a 21,400-seat state-of-the-art arena, which was wholly owned by the Molson Companies.

Under Arnett's leadership, it quickly became apparent that brewing was once again number one at Molson. The company finally began to unload its retail interests, starting with the March 1997 sale of its interest in Réno-Dépôt. In April 1998 Molson's stake in Home Depot Canada was sold to Home Depot Inc. for C$370 million (US$260 million). Two months later Molson announced that it would sell Beaver Lumber as well, and it placed Beaver within its area of discontinued operations.

The long-neglected Molson Breweries had suffered from steadily declining market share, falling from 52.2 percent of the Canadian market in 1989 to 45.8 percent in mid-1997. John Barnett had been named president of Molson Breweries in November 1995, and he used his 25-plus years of brewing experience to aggressively attempt to reverse the decline. He decentralized the unit's operations (which included seven Canadian breweries) and began niche marketing, targeting particular brands at specific Canadian regions.

While Barnett moved to shore up Molson Breweries, Arnett acted quickly to regain full control of the unit. In December 1997, Molson Companies, Foster's, and Miller Brewing reached an agreement that restructured their relationships. Molson and Foster's repurchased Miller's 20 percent stake in Molson Breweries, returning each to 50 percent shares in the unit. The deal also had Molson and Foster's purchasing a 24.95 percent stake in Molson USA, with Miller retaining a 50.1 percent interest. Molson USA was charged with distributing Molson and Foster's brands in the United States. The new relationship also called for Molson Breweries to continue to manage the Miller brands in Canada.

Then in June 1998 Molson regained full ownership of Molson Breweries by paying C$1 billion (US$679.4 million) in cash to Foster's. Through the deal, Molson also gained Foster's stake in Coors Canada Inc., manager of Coors brands in Canada. Molson's interest in Coors Canada was thus increased to 49.9 percent.

With the Canadian beer market in an extended flat period and with Labatt's share of the market nearly equal to that of Molson's, Arnett was counting on Canadians preferring 100 percent Canadian-owned Molson brands to those of Labatt, which had been purchased by Belgium's Interbrew S.A. in 1995. Although this strategy seemed somewhat questionable, retaking full control of Molson Breweries certainly proved that The Molson Companies was fully focused on brewing. The company was likely to seek to build its brewery operations through acquisition, particularly once the sale of Beaver Lumber was finally completed.

Principal Subsidiaries

Molson Breweries; Beaver Lumber Company Limited; Club de Hockey Canadien, Inc.; Molson Centre Inc.; Coors Canada Inc. (49.9%).

Further Reading

Banks, Brian, "Continental Draft: Molson Brews Up a Strategy to Export Its Canadian Success to the Mighty US," *CA Magazine,* December 1991, pp. 28–31.

Cheers for 200 Years!: Molson Breweries, 1786–1986, Vancouver: Creative House, 1986.

Daly, John, "Miller Time for Molson: The Largest Brewer Gives Up Canadian Control," *Maclean's,* January 25, 1993, p. 30.

DeMont, John, "A Global Brew," *Maclean's,* July 24, 1989, pp. 28 + .

Denison, Merrill, *The Barley and the Stream: The Molson Story,* Toronto: McClelland and Stewart, 1955.

Forsyth, Neil, *The Molsons in Canada: The First 200 Years,* Public Archives Canada, 1986.

Galarza, Pablo, "Molson: Talk About Frothy," *Financial World,* November 7, 1995, p. 18.

Greenberg, Larry M., "Canada's Top Brewers Draft Ways to Fight New Rivals," *Wall Street Journal,* March 16, 1993, p. B4.

——, "Molson Buys Rest of Brewing Unit for $679.4 Million," *Wall Street Journal,* June 24, 1998, p. B6.

Joslin, Barry, "Anatomy of a Merger," *Business Quarterly,* Autumn 1990, pp. 25–29.

Molson's, 1961 [175th Anniversary, 1786–1961], Montreal: Molson's, 1961.

Mullin, Rick, "Unilever Pays $568 Million for a Big Piece of Diversey," *Chemical Week,* January 31, 1996, p. 9.

Perreault, Michel G., *The Molson Companies Limited: A Corporate Background Report,* Ottawa: Royal Commission on Corporate Concentration, 1976.

Slater, Michael, "Number One at Last," *Globe and Mail,* November 17, 1989, p. 50.

Stevenson, Mark, "My Dear, Best Friend," *Canadian Business,* March 1994, pp. 52 + .

Waal, Peter, "Molson Muscle?," *Canadian Business,* July 31, 1998, p. 18.

Wells, Jennifer, "Thirst for Growth: Molson Tries to Halt a Decline in Beer Sales," *Maclean's,* September 1, 1997, pp. 44 + .

Wells, Jennifer, and Ann Brocklehurst, "The End of a Dream: Molson Jettisons a Money-Losing U.S. Subsidiary," *Maclean's,* February 5, 1996, pp. 38–39.

Woods, Shirley F., *The Molson Saga, 1763–1983,* Toronto: Doubleday Canada, 1983.

—April Dougal Gasbarre
—updated by David E. Salamie

Morris Travel Services L.L.C.

240 East Morris Avenue
Salt Lake City, Utah 84115
U.S.A.
(801) 487-9731
Fax: (801) 483-6677
Web site: http://www.morristravel.com

Private Company
Incorporated: 1971
Employees: 450
Sales: $200 million (1997 est.)
SICs: 4724 Travel Agencies

Morris Travel Services L.L.C. is the largest travel agency in the western United States and one of the largest in the nation. It provides a full range of travel services and products for individual, family, government, and corporate customers through its more than 50 retail offices in Utah, Idaho, Montana, Nevada, Oregon, and Washington. Morris Travel also is well-known for creating Morris Air, a low-cost charter service to Hawaii and western states. Later Morris Air became a separate company and a regular airline that then was acquired by Southwest Air. The nation's business community has honored founder June M. Morris because of her contributions to the travel and airline industries.

Origins

June M. Morris was born in Manti, Utah. After graduating from West High in Salt Lake City and attending the University of Utah and Stevens-Henager College of Business, she gained experience managing a travel agency for the Utah Auto Association.

In 1970 she started Morris Travel as a one-person operation working out of spare office space in her husband Mitchell Morris's film processing firm. Mitchell Morris helped the new firm with cash for operating expenses when some Morris Travel customers failed to pay their bills.

In 1975 June Morris hired her son Richard W. Frendt. In the May 22, 1988 *Deseret News*, Frendt recalled that, "At the time,

Morris was just four or five people, so it didn't seem like a business with a future." However, he accepted the job: "$16,800 a year and all the travel benefits. It seemed like a fortune back then."

Frendt also recalled the turning point when Morris Travel gained Sperry Univac as a corporate customer. "That doubled our business and gave us the idea that we could really do it. We doubled in size every year after that."

Expansion in the 1980s

In 1983 Morris Travel recruited two new individuals who helped build the small Utah company. Randy Hunt, formerly with United Airlines, helped land some major accounts as the new Morris executive vice-president.

The other person, Mark Slack, joined Morris Travel in 1983 as its corporate controller. A 1980 graduate of Southern Utah University with a B.S. in accounting and business administration, Slack had worked as a CPA for Ernst and Young before starting with Morris Travel. He wrote all of Morris Travel's accounting policies, established its internal controls, and installed a new computer system for the company. After being promoted to financial vice-president, Slack renegotiated Morris's bank contracts, which saved the company $10,000 a year from lowered credit rates. In addition, all accounts were moved to one bank and made part of a cash management system.

In 1987 Morris Travel acquired Bountiful's Faldmo Tours, Ogden's Fishburn Travel, TourWest in Utah County, Logan's Travel Chalet, and Salt Lake City's Travel Express, five agencies that had been incorporated in 1984 under the name Travel Express. That acquisition increased corporate sales some $30 million to reach approximately $90 million. At the same time, June Morris sold Morris Travel to two company officers and Travel Express shareholders. Since Travel Express had become a franchise of the national travel chain called Ask Mr. Foster, the newly merged firm became known as Morris/Ask Mr. Foster.

Before the merger with Travel Express, Morris Travel was Utah's largest travel agency, but the merger resulted in the company's first major sales outside of Salt Lake.

Morris made Richard Frendt its new president in the 1987 reorganization. However, in 1989 Morris Travel elected Mark Slack as its new president and the following year made him the CEO and chairman of the board.

Morris Air

Meanwhile, in 1983 June Morris had started Morris Air Services as a division of Morris Travel to offer charter services to Hawaii by leasing seats, mainly on Hawaiian Airlines. Customers jumped at the opportunity to fly roundtrip to Hawaii and receive five nights hotel accommodations on Waikiki Beach for just $399. Once in 1985 an incomplete Morris charter from Salt Lake City to Honolulu filled the remaining seats by offering the same $399 deal for only $99.

Later the charter service expanded to various West Coast cities. "From the day we started, our flights were based on low fares, and our strategy was to make air travel affordable to people who were not traveling," said June Morris in the August 1993 *Nation's Business*.

In 1987 Morris Air Services was spun off as a separate firm, but it continued a close association with Morris Travel. In 1989, for example, both companies moved into their new 60,000-square-foot office building at 260 East Morris Avenue in south Salt Lake.

In 1993 Morris Air Services became a regular airline known simply as Morris Air, which owned some of its own planes and leased others. At age 62, June Morris was "the only female CEO in the jet airline business in the USA," according to an August 30, 1993 *USA Today* cover story. In December 1993 Southwest Airlines, headed by Herb Kelleher, acquired Morris Air.

Since some people may have thought that Morris Air and Morris Travel were affiliated businesses, Mark Slack in the December 14, 1993 *Deseret News* emphasized that they had separated in 1987 and therefore Morris Travel was not influenced by Southwest Airlines purchasing Morris Air. "Our management and 400 service representatives at our 35 offices throughout Utah and Idaho will continue to be available at the same locations and phone numbers," said Slack.

Expansion and Challenges in the 1990s

In 1990 the Salt Lake Chamber of Commerce honored Morris Travel as the "Outstanding Business of the Year." In the same year Morris changed its name from Morris/Ask Mr. Foster to Morris Travel, Associate of Carlson Travel Network.

Morris Travel expanded into Pocatello, Idaho, in 1991. After signing a contract with the J.R. Simplot Company and merging with a 24-year-old firm called Travel Inc., Morris in 1991 also moved into Boise, Idaho. Sales in 1991 reached $130 million, and the growth continued.

In 1992 Morris Travel left the Carlson Travel network and joined the American Express Network with its 1,700 owned and representative worldwide travel agencies. As the largest representative travel agency of the American Express Travel Related Services Company, Morris was able to offer more services to its customers. Executives of the American Express Travelers Cheque Division in Salt Lake City welcomed the new affiliation. "Morris will provide us with increased opportunities for high quality customer service in our Travelers Cheque business," said Senior Vice-President James F. Welch in the March 20, 1992 *Deseret News*.

The Utah state government in 1992 contracted with Morris Travel to provide its travel needs. Operating from an office in the State Office Building, Morris booked flights and made other arrangements for the state's employees, county agencies, and state-supported colleges and universities. Morris Travel and the state renewed the four-year contract in 1996.

In 1993 the company opened its new office in St. George, Utah. The following year, Morris entered the Oregon market for the first time by acquiring Portland's TravelLink, an agency with two offices and $7 million in annual sales.

Also in 1994, Morris Travel created a new company called Morris Vacations to sell low-fare charter tours mainly to Mexico and other destinations, following Southwest Airlines' decision to cancel low-cost flights to Mexico in the fall of 1984.

During the early 1990s, many travelers changed their preferences for vacation spots. Fewer chose Hawaii, due in part to higher prices for roundtrip airline tickets. Australia and the Caribbean islands became more popular, as did Britain because of a more favorable exchange rate. In addition, more people traveled to Russia after the 1991 collapse of the Soviet Union and the so-called end of the Cold War.

Another relatively new destination for Morris Travel customers was Branson, Missouri, which in the 1990s replaced Nashville as the hot spot for country western music fans. In addition, Mormon customers booked more trips to church history sites, such as Palmyra, New York, where Joseph Smith, Jr., founded The Church of Jesus Christ of Latter-Day Saints in 1830, and Nauvoo, Illinois, where most church members lived before crossing the plains to Utah in 1847.

Major changes in operations, personnel, and ownership occurred at Morris Travel in 1995. First, the company in March 1995 reduced its number of workers after all major U.S. airlines announced they were capping commissions to travel agents for booking domestic flights. Agents began receiving $25 for a one-way ticket and $50 for a roundtrip, instead of the earlier ten percent commission. This commission change resulted from the airlines losing $10 billion in the previous four years. And since Delta Airlines, the major hub operator out of the Salt Lake Airport, was particularly hurt financially, that impacted the Salt Lake City travel agencies. For example, Morris Travel suffered a 20 percent income decrease because of the airlines' decision. Morris Travel sold about 60 percent of its airline tickets for Delta flights.

In May 1995 Morris Travel chose Dave Kooyman as its new board chairman, replacing Mark Slack, who remained the firm's president and CEO. A 22-year veteran of the travel industry,

Kooyman had served on the Morris Travel board for eight years.

A new owner of Morris Travel emerged a few months later. For an undisclosed price, Yamagata Enterprises, a Nevada corporation owned by Gene Yamagata, purchased Morris Travel. Yamagata, a Las Vegas resident who had grown up on a Jerome, Idaho farm, owned two other companies: Vegas Eagle Canyon Airlines to provide flights over the Grand Canyon and Forever Living Products of Japan. Mark Slack, who remained president of Morris Travel, stated in the August 17, 1995 *Deseret News* that Yamagata Enterprises "will provide us with the necessary capitalization to further develop state-of-the-art automation systems and enhance our highly trained sales and support team. In addition, the new ownership brings great stability for the future of Morris Travel, including the opportunity to expand into new markets."

On October 5, 1995, Mark Slack signed a statement that Morris Travel Services L.L.C., a Nevada limited liability company, had the right to use all Morris names, including Morris Travel Express, Morris Travel, Morris Vacations, Morris Incentives, Faldmo Tours, Diamond Travel, and the June Morris School of Travel.

Morris Travel in 1995 started a new program called "Worry-Free Low Fare Guarantee" to ensure its customers they would receive the lowest possible airline fares. Even after a ticket was purchased, the firm would notify a customer if a lower fare was found. The $10 fee for this program also provided flight insurance, one day parking near the Salt Lake Airport, and a five-minute prepaid phone card.

In 1995 Morris Travel acquired Seattle's Diamond Travel with its six offices which emphasized vacation travel. That was followed by the 1996 purchase of Seattle's Corporate Travel Service, a firm with $7 million in annual sales.

Also in January 1996, Morris Travel merged with Beehive Travel, another Salt Lake City travel agency, to create the newly named Morris-Beehive Travel, the nation's 15th largest travel agency with offices in six states. Morris Travel in 1995 had $145 million in sales with 400 employees, while Beehive recorded $43 million in sales with 150 employees. According to Clifford Snyder, Jr., Beehive's former CEO, in the January 5, 1996 *Deseret News*, "It's been an obvious marriage that we've been pursuing on both sides for some time. The timing is excellent for the marriage to happen. . . . With the way the travel industry is heading, and the way many industries are heading, synergy and strength of operations are critical for future strategies. These two highly successful companies combining will create a terrific and powerful force in the Western United States."

To provide services for its expanding corporate customers, Morris Travel in 1996 created a new Morris Meetings and Incentives Division. The division offered special programs for sales meetings, executive retreats, and company conferences sponsored by firms like the Utah Jazz, Huntsman Chemical, KSL-TV, and Southland Life. For example, Morris staff traveled to destination hotels to arrange all the details, from securing audiovisual equipment to creating special conference menus. Morris offered these services through Convention Ser-

vices & Technologies, a meeting management firm in operation since 1988.

Morris continued its acquisitions in the late 1990s. In 1997 it purchased single-office New Horizon Travel in Cedar City, Utah. Morris in 1997 also acquired Anderson-Elerding Travel with six offices in Montana: Billings, Cut Bank, Havre, Helena, and two in Great Falls.

In August 1997 Morris Travel announced that it had become the largest travel agency in the West based on volume. Previously, Associated Travel of Los Angeles and Seattle's Mutual Travel outranked Morris, but their purchase by the U.S. Office Products Company of Texas resulted in Morris becoming number one. It employed some 500 individuals who worked at over 50 offices in Utah, Idaho, Washington, Oregon, Montana, and Nevada. The company also announced it had created a new logo and opened a new office in Spanish Fork, Utah, to serve customers there and in Provo and Orem.

In September 1997 Morris announced it had been chosen by Autoliv Inc. to provide its corporate travel needs. Autoliv manufactured car safety products, such as seat belts and air bags, for the world's largest auto makers.

To better serve its customers, Morris offered a software program called Perk Passport available on compact disc for $19.95. Anyone could browse the photos, movies, and audio of different vacation sites and get the latest information on travel specials. After selecting a deal from this virtual travel marketplace, customers then phoned or e-mailed a Morris office to make their reservations or get more detailed information.

The company also set up a web site for better access in the Information Age. It included addresses and phone numbers for all Morris offices, details on various travel support systems, and links to other web sites featuring information on different destinations and travel bureaus around the world.

Morris also teamed up with Woodside Travel Trust (WTT) to provide support for business travelers traveling overseas. According to Morris Travel's web site, WTT since its origin in 1973 had become "the largest travel management company in the world." WTT partners like Morris Travel gave their clients the advantage of accessing services at over 4,000 locations in more than 60 nations. Whether customers were concerned about passport and visa issues, car rentals, hotel reservations, or getting the best price on airfares, the Morris Travel/Woodside Travel Trust joint venture furnished the necessary information.

To help businesses keep track of their travel expenses, Morris Travel supplied the Navigator system of investigative tools and travel management consulting. That included proprietary reporting systems to provide companies with customized statistical reports on their travel activities. Morris consultants also were available to help firms improve their travel policies and procedures. State-of-the-art software programs helped companies automatically monitor travel expenses.

Morris Travel in 1998 continued to grow because of such innovative technology and good leadership under the direction of President Mark Slack. As Utah's largest travel agency and one of the nation's largest, Morris remained dedicated to meeting the travel needs of its individual, family, corporate, and government customers.

Further Reading

Brown, Matthew, ''Frendt Has Taken Travel Firm a Long Way,'' *Deseret News,* May 22, 1988.

Denalli, Jacquelyn, ''An Airline of Her Own,'' *Nation's Business*, August 1993, pp. 14, 16.

Knudson, Max B., ''Lots of Name Jockeying Hasn't Hurt Business a Bit at Morris Travel Agency,'' *Deseret News*, January 3, 1993, p. D9.

''Morris Travel Now Largest in West,'' *Deseret News,* August 12, 1997.

Thomson, Linda, ''Las Vegas Entrepreneur Purchases Morris Travel,'' *Deseret News,* August 17, 1995.

——, ''Morris Travel Merges with Beehive Travel,'' *Deseret News,* January 5, 1996.

——, ''$1.5 Million Morris Restructuring to Result in Layoffs and Fee Changes,'' *Deseret News,* March 3, 1995.

—David M. Walden

Motown Records Company L.P.

Worldwide Plaza
825 Eighth Avenue, 29th Floor
New York, New York 10019
U.S.A.
(212) 445-3353
Fax: (212) 333-8203
Web site: http://www.motown.com

Wholly Owned Subsidiary of PolyGram N.V.
Incorporated: 1959 as Motown Record Corporation
Employees: 130
Sales: $90 million (1996 est.)
SICs: 3652 Phonograph Records & Prerecorded Audio
Tapes & Disks

The *New Republic* has called it "the most successful Black-owned business in American history." Many first think of the company's trademark sound—the bluesy, impassioned recordings that dominated popular music in the 1960s. A part of the PolyGram group since 1993, Motown Records Company L.P. has struggled to replicate its early success while celebrating its heritage in re-issued recordings, television specials, and the nostalgic Motown Cafe and Motown Museum.

Roots of the Motown Sound

Berry Gordy, Jr.,was born in Detroit on November 28, 1929, the first Thanksgiving Day of the Great Depression. He learned the rudiments of music from an uncle while an early taste for gambling may have foretold his calling to the riskiest of businesses, the music industry.

Gordy entered a variety of occupations from contracting for his father to shining shoes and hawking newspapers. After ditching a promising career in boxing in favor of the freer musician's lifestyle, he began writing songs full-time. He persuaded his family to let him record a jingle he had written for their printing business.

Before his musical career could begin in earnest, however, he was drafted and spent the next couple of years in Korea. When he returned to Detroit he opened the 3D-Record Mart/House of Jazz with the help of family members. The shop languished until jazz enthusiast Gordy warmed to the simpler blues records that were popular at the time. Still, his conversion came too late to save the store.

After a stint as a cookware salesman, Gordy settled down to write songs again, taking advantage of one of his father's apartments, available rent-free. After marrying and starting a family, however, he took a job on the Ford assembly line. Nevertheless, while fastening trim he was composing songs in his head.

Gordy and his writing partners Roquel Billy Davis and sister Gwen Gordy eventually made connections at a variety of small music labels. "All I Could Do Was Cry," recorded by Etta James on Chess Records, became a hit and made Gordy and Davis a sought-after commodity. Jackie Wilson's hit "Reet Petite," by Davis and Berry Gordy, became one of the most popular songs in the country. Still, after several consecutive hits, the writing team had little financial gain to show for their work.

Gordy therefore set out to build his publishing company, Jobete, and own record label, Tamla Records, in 1959. Gordy had discovered Smokey Robinson's group, the Miracles, and after the local success of their first single, he began acting as their manager as well as producer. (Robinson, invaluable to Gordy, stayed with the company for years, becoming a Motown executive.) Gordy next achieved an instant success with newcomer Marv Johnson singing "Come to Me." United Artists bought the recording and soon Gordy had signed another act to that label.

Gordy launched another label, Motown Records, with "Bad Girl," a collaboration with his friend Smokey Robinson. Motown, affectionately named after the "Motor City," Detroit, would be the label used for group acts, rather than solo artists which were still being recorded on Tamla. Gordy found himself short of cash to release his new record and hustled desperately to raise funds until Chess Records bought the recording. "Bad Girl" proved a hit for the Miracles only to be followed by the even more successful "Way Over There," which achieved hit status on a national level.

Company Perspectives:

"Like most of you, I have joyously lived my life watching Motown Records transcend from a small record company housed in a two-story building in Detroit, Michigan, to an institution that has set musical standards for Pop and R&B music as they exist today.

I have always been inspired by the entrepreneurial brilliance of Berry Gordy Jr., the legacy of Motown and the classic foundation it was built upon. It is with this set of high standards in mind that I am prepared to guide Motown Records into the 21st century and establish it once again as a leader in today's competitive creative entertainment environment." —George Jackson, president and CEO (1997)

Gordy and his companion (he was divorcing his first wife) moved into a house at 2678 West Grand Boulevard, dubbed "Hitsville," that served as the company's headquarters. Gordy cowrote one of the first hits recorded in the house's improvised studio, "Money (That's What I Want)." Motown was likened to a Detroit assembly line, where artists came in as unknown, raw talent and were built into stars. International Talent Management, Inc. was created to oversee their development. Gordy borrowed concepts, such as quality control, from the Detroit car plants and applied them to his business. He even used the division of labor principles he had seen at work on the assembly lines: performers performed, songwriters wrote songs, and producers recorded them, with little switching between roles. In spite of its mechanistic efficiency, the "Motown Family," which included many of Gordy's own relatives, embraced its employees in a sort of familial paternalism.

Greatest Hits of the 1960s

The 1960s would be Motown's golden years. When the decade started, "Shop Around" by the Miracles was the second bestselling single in America (it sold a million copies). The next year, Motown signed the Supremes, then known as the Primettes. The Temptations, Marvin Gaye, and Stevie Wonder soon followed. In 1962, the Marvelettes gave Motown their first number one pop hit, "Please Mr. Postman."

The innovative Motortown Revue toured the country promoting the label's acts. In 1963, the writing and producing team of Brian and Eddie Holland and Lamont Dozier began working together, soon creating a unique string of hits, such as "Heat Wave" by Martha Reeves and "Baby I Need Your Loving" by the Four Tops. Motown also released Martin Luther King, Jr.'s speeches on the Gordy imprint in 1963. After King's slaying, Motown artists played a benefit concert for the Poor People's March to Freedom.

Mary Wells left the label after gaining a level of fame. However, the Supremes finally hit it big in 1964 when "Where Did Our Love Go" reached number one. The follow-up, "Baby Love," became Motown's first number one song in Britain. "Come See About Me" gave the "girl group" three top hits in a row.

In 1964 several Motown stars toured Europe. By introducing standards into the repertoire of the Supremes, Motown was also able to book its acts on the lucrative nightclub circuit, including New York's famed Copacabana, previously dominated by established stars such as Frank Sinatra.

Motown's fortunes rolled ahead, and its stable of productive writers grew. In his autobiography, Gordy credited much of the label's marketing success to employees like Barney Ales, a master salesman of Italian descent. The expanding company moved its administrative offices to downtown Detroit.

In 1968, the Holland-Dozier-Holland writing/production team defected in a flurry of multimillion-dollar litigation. After Motown's initial $4 million complaint, HDH filed a countersuit accusing Motown of failing to pay all royalties due. The parties finally settled in 1972.

In spite of the change in writing staff, the hits kept coming for acts such as Marvin Gaye and Gladys Knight and the Pips, who, oddly, both reached the number one slot with different versions of "I Heard It Through the Grapevine" within a year of each other. During the last week of 1968, Motown had half of Billboard's Top Ten singles. In 1969, it signed what would become one of the most popular acts of the 1970s, the Jackson 5. After maintaining a West Coast office for several years, the company relocated its corporate headquarters to Los Angeles in order to help foster movie deals.

The Soulful 1970s

The Jackson 5's first single, "I Want You Back," reached number one on the charts in January 1970. By April, their second single, "ABC," had displaced the Beatles' "Let It Be" from the first position. A third top hit, "The Love You Save," followed in June and their fourth single, "I'll Be There," also made number one—an unprecedented feat for a new act. At the same time as the Jackson's upbeat success, singer Marvin Gaye insisted upon producing a protest album, *What's Going On,* which sold surprisingly well.

Meanwhile, Diana Ross had left the Supremes to launch a solo career. Her development was a high priority at Motown. In 1971 she starred in a film Motown coproduced, *Lady Sings the Blues,* based on the life of the legendary jazz singer Billie Holliday. It garnered four Academy Award nominations. In 1974, another Motown Productions feature, *Mahogany,* also starred Ross. The video unit would also turn out a respectable body of made-for-TV specials and a miniseries.

Motown Record Corporation was restructured in 1973. At the time it was taking in about $46 million per year. Motown Industries oversaw Motown Records, Jobete Music, MPI (Motown Productions), and ITMI (International Talent Management, Inc.). Gordy appointed sales executive Ewart Abner president of Motown Records. Abner had earlier been president of another legendary, independent black-owned label, Vee Jay Records in Chicago.

In the mid-1970s, Stevie Wonder won three consecutive Album of the Year awards; his *Songs in the Key of Life* entered the Pop charts at number one. Still, Wonder was not beyond producing an expensive flop. His follow-up documentary soundtrack album, *Journey Through the Secret Life of Plants,* sold only 100,000 copies and was three years in the making. In 1975, a tumultuous year, Barney Ales returned to replace Abner as Motown Records president. An untimely upheaval came when the Jackson 5, concerned that Motown had not been promoting their records sufficiently, signed with CBS.

By the late 1970s, many of Motown's original roster of stars, writers, and producers had been courted away by other labels. The business had changed, and the process of making and selling records had become much more complicated. "Three Times a Lady," by the Commodores, was Motown's only Top Ten single for 1978.

On the brink of insolvency, Motown was forced to take a bank loan to continue operating. Fortunately for the struggling firm, Diana Ross, Stevie Wonder, and Smokey Robinson all delivered hit singles, enabling the company to pay off its loan within a year. Lionel Richie had left the Commodores to become a star in his own right, but the Motown artist and repertoire staff had uncovered a new generation of popular acts from Rick James to DeBarge. Jay Lasker replaced Barney Ales in 1979, ending Ales's long association with the company.

Eking out the Hits in the 1980s

Another parting came in 1981, when Diana Ross left Motown to record for RCA. She consented to appear, however, in a television retrospective staged for Motown's 25th anniversary, *Motown 25: Yesterday, Today, Forever* in 1984. The show gathered many of the label's legendary acts for a soul-affirming celebration and won an Emmy award in the process.

After interminable collection problems with independent distributors, Motown finally allied with a major record company, MCA, in May 1983. Within a couple of years, MCA had made overtures to buy Motown. MCA's offer seemed to undervalue Motown's hidden assets, such as its master recordings, and Gordy canceled the deal in December 1985.

The record business of the 1980s was difficult for Motown to master. Hundreds of thousands of dollars were then being spent to promote singles, and the music video became the chief tool in the music industry's publicity arsenal. Jay Asker, who had been reluctant to spend money on music videos, stepped down as president in 1987. While 25 Motown records made number one in the 1970s, Motown only reached that position eight times in the 1980s.

Sales negotiations with MCA resumed in 1988. This time, only the record company was offered, not publishing rights or film and television operations. MCA and the investment group Boston Ventures bought Motown Records for $61 million on June 29. Motown Productions was renamed Gordy-de Passe Productions. It and the Jobete publishing company became subsidiaries of the newly formed Gordy Company.

The Nostalgic 1990s

As difficult as the 1980s were, during the next decade the challenges increased. The average cost for music videos rose to $750,000 each. The company's only number one hits came from a new group, Boyz II Men. The company's president and CEO since 1988, Jheryl Busby, focused on Motown's back catalog, compiling box sets and other value-added anthologies in contrast to the budget-oriented re-releases of the 1980s. A new venture, the Motown Cafe, also focused on nostalgia. The first cafe opened in New York City in mid-1995.

PolyGram NV paid $301 to acquire Motown Records in late 1993. However, the label failed to turn a profit, much less regain its former hit-producing capacity. With declining sales of its catalog, which still brought in $45 million per year, and no major stars besides Boyz II Men, PolyGram CEO Alain Levy named Andre Harrell president and CEO of Motown in November 1995, offering $35 million in a five-year contract. A media account executive by day, Harrell had also developed a career as a hip-hop artist and started his own label, Uptown Records (which, like Gordy, he sold to MCA for a reported $50 million). Harrell's hugely expensive self-promotional campaign incensed many in the company, including some performers.

Motown lost nearly $70 million in 1996, with annual sales of about $90 million. Harrell, who had moved the company headquarters across the country to New York City, resigned his position in August 1997. Film producer George Jackson, who was responsible for Krush Groove, became president and CEO of Motown Records in late 1997. He was authorized to cut Motown's bloated staff. In addition, a new Boyz II Men album promised a positive beginning for his tenure.

PolyGram merged the rhythm and blues interests of its Mercury subsidiary with Motown in early 1998. The move eliminated some personnel (mostly from Mercury) due to redundancies and infused Motown's roster with a few new acts such as Brian McKnight.

In mid-1997, Berry Gordy finally parted with some of his publishing rights when EMI bought a 50 percent stake in his 15,000-song catalog for $132 million.

Further Reading

Early, Gerald, "One Nation Under a Groove," *New Republic,* July 15, 1991.

Gordy, Berry, *To Be Loved: The Music, The Magic, the Memories of Motown,* New York: Warner, 1994.

Holmes, Marian Smith, "Who Could Resist the Kind of Music They Made at Hitsville?" *Smithsonian,* October 1994.

Johnson, Roy S., "Motown: What's Going On?" *Fortune,* November 24, 1997.

Mason, Kiki, "Pop Goes the Ghetto," *New York,* October 23, 1995.

"Refreshing Motown's Reputation, and Remembering the Hit Factory," *Music Business International,* February 1996.

Roberts, Johnnie L., "Pitsville, USA," *Newsweek,* December 2, 1996.

Stark, Susan, "Stop! In the Name of Lunch!" *Detroit News,* October 10, 1995.

Waller, Don, *The Motown Story,* New York: Charles Scribner's Sons, 1985.

White, Adam, "Gordy Speaks," *Billboard,* November 5, 1994.

—Frederick C. Ingram

Trust The Leaf®

Murdock Madaus Schwabe

10 Mountain Springs Parkway
Springville, Utah 84663
U.S.A.
(801) 489-1500
(800) 962-8873
Fax: (801) 489-1700
Web site: http://www.naturesway.com

Private Company
Incorporated: 1969 as Nature's Way Products Inc.
Employees: 200
Sales: $75 million (1997 est.)
SICs: 2833 Medicinals & Botanicals

Murdock Madaus Schwabe is an international leader in the herbal or natural products industry. Used for foods or folk medicines for thousands of years, herbal products became more commercialized after World War II and increasing numbers of companies were created to produce and distribute herbal formulas. Originally a small family business, Murdock Madaus Schwabe has partnered with other companies to create a huge international business with hundreds of products. It has prospered by making its products available through retail stores, including health food stores, discount stores such as Wal-Mart, and grocery store chains.

Company Origins

In 1968, while President Lyndon Johnson struggled to lead the nation in the Vietnam War, Lalovi Murdock of Arizona faced her own crisis—a serious case of breast cancer. Weakened by chemotherapy and surgery, she told her husband, Tom Murdock, she could not handle another operation. Seeking an alternative to the medical establishment's cancer therapies, Tom Murdock met a Navajo medicine man who reportedly had used steeped chaparral leaves to fight cancer. Tom then picked and prepared some leaves and convinced Lalovi to try the homemade chaparral drink.

Next Tom Murdock found a better way to prepare chaparral for human consumption. He took barrels of dried leaves of the common desert plant to California, where he used a friend's milling and tableting devices to make chaparral tablets. His wife took the tablets and also began a strict diet of healthy fresh foods and a daily exercise routine. Soon she improved. However, she was reluctant to tell her doctors how it happened.

Tom Murdock began selling chaparral tablets to chiropractors, naturopaths, osteopaths, and health food stores. Company literature proclaimed that "Tom Murdock was the first to sell commercially encapsulated herbs to retail stores." Thus Nature's Way Products Inc. was born in 1969 as a family business in Phoenix, Arizona. Working out of their home, the Murdocks sold about $50,000 worth of chaparral tablets during their first year in business.

Early Expansion and Diversification

With the help of Lalovi Murdock, whose cancer went into remission, and sons George and Ken Murdock, who joined the firm in 1970, Nature's Way doubled its sales to about $100,000 the second year in business. The firm bought an old Latter Day Saints (Mormon) church cannery and moved out of the Murdock home.

Nature's Way's second major product was Alfa-Con, a brand of alfalfa concentrate tablets. The company removed the indigestible parts of the alfalfa plant to produce tablets usable by humans. Advertising of that product led to huge orders, which were very difficult for the young company to meet.

Starting in 1971, the company benefited from the work of John R. Christopher, a leading naturopath and pioneer in the nation's herbal renaissance. The author of several herbalism books and a well-known lecturer, Christopher granted Nature's Way the exclusive right to use over 20 of his herbal formulas in 1975. His original B/P Formula, which combined cayenne, parsley, ginger root, golden seal root, garlic clove, and Siberian ginseng root, was among the products sold by Nature's Way. Although Christopher died in 1983, his principles and contributions would continue to guide Nature's Way in the 1990s.

Company Perspectives:

Mission Statement: To benefit the quality of human health and promote positive health care choices by developing, manufacturing, and marketing preventative, curative and nutritive health care products of primarily natural origin.

In the early 1970s the Murdock family decided to diversify its business interests. In a profile on him and his success Geroge Murdock recalled, "We were beginning to see some of the problems of the health food industry, the persecution of the FDA, and the fact that we couldn't make any claims for our herbal products."

Thus the family started a food storage business called Rainy Day Foods in California. Mormon leaders for years had encouraged church members to maintain at least a year of food storage, and that demand helped fuel the expansion of Rainy Day Foods. In November 1973 Rainy Day Foods moved to Provo, Utah. By early 1974 Rainy Day Foods was booming, with over 100 employees, while Nature's Way had only three or four workers. In March 1974 Nature's Way moved from Phoenix to Provo to share facilities with the family's food storage business.

Interestingly, several other herbal firms originated in Utah, including Nature's Herbs, Nature's Sunshine, Nu Skin, Sunrider, and USANA. This unusual concentration of herbal firms in Utah was due in part to the Mormons' historic and contemporary use of herbs.

By 1976 Rainy Day Foods was still profitable, but the Murdock family began to feel that it was a risky business. So they developed another product called Weekenders, a compact can-in-a meal for campers. When that business failed, however, the family decided to focus on Nature's Way again. The percentage of Americans using natural products had increased from just two or three percent in the late 1960s to at least ten percent by 1976. "We noticed that some of the little backyard companies that had started out like we had, were now multimillion-dollar corporations," noted George Murdock, adding "We had missed out on this growth potential by not paying attention to what was happening in the health food industry."

With the help of businessman Doug Snarr, the Small Business Administration, and Walker Bank, the Murdocks invested $1 million cash in Nature's Way. Brothers Ken and George Murdock bought out their father's share of the business, and the company began to expand its product line to several hundred products.

Nature's Way also changed its distribution methods. Instead of selling herbal products directly to thousands of retail stores, the firm began selling through major jobbers or brokers. While the new middle marketers received their share of the profits, the firm's increased sales made up for that loss.

After debuting the company's new display rack featuring its main products at a trade show in Las Vegas in 1977, Nature's Way sold over 100 of the $500 racks. George Murdock in his 1981 profile commented, "In just one year we became the largest supplier of herb products to health food stores in the world. In the process we established our own advertising company, a multilevel direct sales company, and a separate line of herbal products for doctors." Nutrition Professionals was the new division formed to meet the needs of health professionals. Murdock International was created as a holding company over the various family businesses, including Nature's Way, Rainy Day Foods, and Health Products International.

The multilevel marketing arm of the company was NaturaLife International, incorporated as a subsidiary on May 27, 1976. In 1979 K. Dean Black became president of NaturaLife. Black had been helped by the herbal formulas of Tei Fu Chen, a native of Taiwan who was working for NaturaLife. The two wanted to market Chinese herbal formulas, but Murdock officials disagreed, preferring to stay with American herbal products in the John Christopher tradition. So in 1982 NaturaLife began the process of breaking away from Murdock. The company's name was changed to The Sunrider Corporation, with Chen as the founding chairman. Sunrider grew into a multinational firm that in 1987 moved its headquarters to Torrance, California.

Meanwhile, in 1984 Murdock moved into a new 107,000-square-foot plant in the Springville Industrial Park a few miles south of Provo. Designed for the production of pharmaceutical grade products, the facility was enlarged in 1988 and 1990.

Murdock International announced in 1987 that it was creating Murdock Pharmaceuticals, Inc. to make and distribute over-the-counter (OTC) products, including the Efamol PMS Program, Efamol Evening Primrose Oil, and other items. Murdock aggressively marketed the Efamol PMS Program through national magazines and a referral system. "The response to our national advertising for the Efamol PMS has been overwhelming," reported Candace Jacobson, Murdock International's customer service manager, in the September 23, 1987 *Provo Community Journal.* "There are so many women who now realize they are suffering from PMS [premenstrual syndrome], who are looking for relief.... This product is unique in that it treats the source of the problem rather than temporarily masking the symptoms."

New Products and Distribution Methods in the 1990s

In July 1992 Murdock began shipping its new homeopathic "Medicine from Nature" product line. In the October 26, 1992 *Brandweek,* Murdock's Vice-President of Marketing Jeff Hilton commented on promoting herbal and homeopathic products: "We did focus groups in Boston and Los Angeles and found a strong interest in self-care. People are frustrated with a medical system based on crises rather than on wellness and prevention.... The homeopathic medicines traditionally sold here have come in small vials and might have been sort of scary-looking to the novice. Ours look very commercial by design.... We wanted the package to invite rather than intimidate.... In our research we found little overlap—people use either homeopathy or herbs. We're hoping we can encourage some cross-pollination, that customers who have used our herbal products will try homeopathy."

Seven new homeopathic formulas, for motion sickness, nervous stress, sore throat, bronchial congestion, child fever and restlessness, and water retention, were designed by Dana Ullman, M.P.H., as over-the-counter products. The author of *Discovering Homeopathy* and three other books on the subject, Ullman directed the Homeopathic Educational Services in Berkeley, California, and served as Murdock's homeopathic spokesman. He also authored a well-received booklet called *A Guide to Homeopathic Medicine for Pharmacists* that was published in 1993 by Murdock as part of its marketing program.

The company promoted its homeopathic and other products through such national magazines as *New Age Journal* and *Vegetarian Times,* radio programs, and TV shows such as *Jeopardy, Geraldo,* and the *Rush Limbaugh Show.*

Homeopathy had been founded in the late 1700s in Europe and remained popular until the early 1900s, when orthodox medicine increased its dominance of the healthcare system. However, it rebounded by the 1980s as more people sought alternatives to drugs promoted by MDs and the pharmaceutical industry. In spite of critics, homeopathic formulas found increasing popularity through chain stores such as Wal-Mart, natural food stores, and independent pharmacies.

By the early 1990s some health food stores, which sold products made by Murdock and other firms, were expanding and using modern advertising methods. According to Jeff Hilton, the health food industry experienced a "true transformation." Hilton explained: "Instead of the traditional mom-and-pop kind of store, we're seeing natural-food grocery stores that sell organic produce, natural cereals and supplements, including vitamins, minerals and herbs. . . . While these health-food superstores are still a small percentage of health-food outlets, they're accounting for a larger percentage of sales." Moreover, Hilton observed, "Health-food stores used to be intimidating places: dark, often cramped, with shelf after shelf of mysterious bottles. Today the industry has gotten smarter, shedding its counterculture image and sharpening its merchandising, packaging and advertising. Our company has grown along with the industry. We're currently in about 1,750 health-food stores across the country, including 1,200 General Nutrition Centers. . . . Baby boomers are our core customers. Today's 30–50-year-olds are educated customers who make health a priority in their lives."

In 1994 Murdock created a new division called NaturaLife to market its supplements to the growing mass market of drug, food, and discount stores, while Nature's Way products continued to be reserved for health food stores.

By 1998 the Nature's Way brand encompassed seven product lines. First, its over 70 Herbal Singles products included Aloe Vera, St. John's Wort, Kava Root, Kelp, and Ginger Root. Second, Herbal Formulas featured combinations of herbs aimed at treating Digestion, Blood Sugar, and Heart ailments. Third, the firm sold Standardized Extracts such as Black Cohosh, Korean Ginseng, Green Tea, and Valerian. The company's fourth line, World Select Brands, included Slim & Trim (a weight loss drink mix), Thisilyn (milk thistle extract), and Ginkgold (Ginkgo biloba extract). Its Vitamin supplements line contained single vitamins or minerals, multivitamins, and other

items such as Antioxidant Formula, Cod Liver Oil, and Lactase Enzyme. Thirty products were found in the Medicine From Nature Homeopathics line, and the company's seventh type of product was its Fastactives Liquids, which included over 30 herbs in either alcohol- or glycerine-based formulas.

Other Developments in the 1990s

In 1990 Loren D. Israelsen was chosen as the president of Murdock HealthCare Corporation to replace Ken Murdock, who remained board chairman. A San Francisco native and graduate of the Brigham Young University Law School, Israelsen had joined the firm eight years earlier.

In the summer of 1992 the Food and Drug Administration, in cooperation with the Utah Department of Agriculture, stopped Nature's Way from shipping nearly five million capsules of evening primrose oil. According to the July 2, 1992 *Deseret News,* John Scharmann, the director of the FDA's Denver District, said that "no scientific data exists that establishes the safety of the substance" and that the FDA's decision was based on two cases in the U.S. Ninth Circuit Court of Appeals.

Nature's Way's Loren Israelsen argued that the court cases only banned the sale of evening primrose oil when it was "so misbranded or adulterated that it presents a health risk." He maintained that "We sell it only as a single dietary supplement, and it's not added to any other product. . . . It's been approved for use in 40 other countries. . . . And we think we've got scientific evidence that proves it's safe." Nature's Way would later begin selling evening primrose oil again as one of its Standardized Extracts.

Like many companies, Murdock formed joint ventures or partnerships with other firms in the 1990s. In 1992 its articles of incorporation were amended to include not only Ken Murdock and Loren Israelsen as executives, but also men from two German companies, Madaus AG in Cologne and Dr. Willmar Schwabe GMBH & Co. in Karlsruhe. With over 70 years of experience with medicinal plants, Madaus had established a reputation as a leading firm in the botanical pharmaceutical industry, especially from two standardized extracts, EchinaGuard and Thisilyn. The Dr. Willmar Schwabe company was well-known for studying the benefits of herbal products; it conducted over 280 studies showing the usefulness of Ginkgold, a standardized extract from the leaves of the Ginkgo biloba tree. Marketed in the United States only by Nature's Way, Ginkgold outsold all other Ginkgo products combined.

On December 10, 1993, Murdock International shareholders voted to change the company name to MMS America Corporation. At the same time the Murdock Holding Group changed its name to the MMS Holding Company. According to Utah Corporation Division records, Derek Hall was the president of both MMS America Corp. and MMS Holding Company in 1993. The following year MMS America Corp. was listed as the parent name, with a business name of Murdock Madaus Schwabe.

Murdock in the 1990s continued partnerships started in 1985 with two other foreign companies. The first was London-based Efamol Ltd., a world leader in researching essential fatty acids. Efamol conducted much of its work at a research center in Nova

Scotia. The Montreal, Canada, firm of Institut Rosell, Inc. also partnered with Murdock by making the Utah firm its sole distributor of its acidophilus products in the United States and overseas. Institut Rosell created its trademarked Primadophilus supplement in four potencies to help users repopulate their intestines with normal bacteria needed for digestion.

In 1994 the Nature's Way brand celebrated its 25th anniversary. Derek Hall, Nature's Way president and CEO, in his anniversary address in the company newsletter, commented on the challenges facing the natural products industry: "One important freedom we hope to celebrate this year is a continuation of our freedom of choice—especially as it relates to our freedom to choose what kind of health care products we want to use, manufacture and sell.... These rights are a very emotional issue for nearly 100 million Americans who take dietary supplements.... Our industry is experiencing rapid growth.... Unfortunately, it has attracted those who would risk our industry's integrity for a fast buck.... We must never underestimate our value as an industry in the ongoing debate on an affordable, quality health care system."

In 1995 Murdock expanded its Springville base of operations. It spent $6 million to double the size of its production, distribution, and office facilities to a total of over 230,000 square feet. The project included a two-level production system with the ability to have the same equipment on both floors. It also featured state-of-the-art clean rooms to prevent any dust or contamination of its products. Hall said in the August 9, 1995 *Deseret News* that because there was room to add another 120,000 square feet: "This plant should last us through the turn of the century.... We're the leading and the largest herbal manufacturer in the U.S."

In 1996 Murdock Madaus Schwabe chose Gary Hume as its new president and CEO with the responsibility to manage 326 international employees. Before joining Murdock Madaus Schwabe, Hume was president of Tree of Life South West, a large distributor of natural products.

Environmental and Educational Programs in the 1990s

"Murdock Healthcare views its support of rain forests and environmental causes as an urgent part of our corporate mission and social responsibility," wrote Loren Israelsen, Murdock Madaus Schwabe's president, in a January 18, 1990 *Deseret News* article on the firm's creation of a special account to accomplish those goals. Specifically, every time a Nature's Way product was purchased, part of the price was placed in the account, which then could be used to purchase threatened rain forest lands, back university researchers, or underwrite other related projects. For example, Murdock financially sponsored an international environmental symposium held in New York City in January 1992, as well as the March 1998 International Symposium on St. John's Wort in Anaheim, California.

Murdock Madaus Schwabe also backed the nonprofit Seacology Foundation based in Springville. Founded and chaired by Dr. Paul Cox, a Brigham Young University botany professor, Seacology's resources were used to preserve Samoa's rain forest and build schools, hospitals, and other facilities to help the Samoan people, who were feeling pressure to sell their forests to outside logging companies. This was a prime example of the Seacology Foundation goal of "saving the world one village at a time," according to the April 14, 1997 *Deseret News*. Ken Murdock served as Seacology's president.

Murdock Madaus Schwabe also supported educational institutions, including Phoenix's Southwest College of Naturopathic Medicine, Portland's National College of Naturopathic Medicine, the Texas Chiropractic College, Seattle's John Bastyr University of Naturopathic Medicine, and such professional groups as the American Botanical Council and the Herb Research Foundation.

The company participated in the nonprofit Utah Natural Products Alliance, headed by Loren Israelsen, Murdock Madaus Schwabe's former president. The alliance represented Utah firms selling herbal and natural medicines, dietary supplements, and exercise equipment. After the FDA seizure of Murdock's evening primrose oil, the company spent at least $250,000 to lobby Congress and to support the Utah Natural Products Alliance in promoting the 1994 Dietary Supplement Health and Education Act sponsored by Utah Senator Orrin Hatch. Nicknamed the "health freedom act," it was passed to protect vitamin/health foods producers from overregulation by the FDA.

This was just one example of how Murdock Madaus Schwabe and other firms have supported the alliance in various state and federal public policy issues concerning the natural products industry. The alliance in 1998 claimed that Utah's natural products industry, with $2.3 billion in annual sales, was larger than the state's mining, skiing, agriculture, banking, and insurance industries.

Increased Demand for the Natural Products Industry

Murdock Madaus Schwabe enjoyed increasing consumer demand for its products and growing recognition by experts on the importance of herbalism and alternative healing. In 1990, according to one report, Americans visited alternative healers, such as herbalists or chiropractors, more often than family doctors and internists. According to the January 28, 1993 *New England Journal of Medicine,* a nationwide survey of 1,539 adults found that 34 percent reported using alternative health methods.

In addition, Harvey Hartman, the president of Hartman & New Hope, a firm that researched the natural foods industry, said in the June 28, 1998 *Deseret News* that the industry was "going mainstream." His firm's survey of 43,000 American households found that 68 percent had used at least one natural product and 38 percent had used at least seven.

The *Natural Foods Merchandiser* magazine reported that in 1997 retail sales alone of natural products exceeded $14 billion in the United States. Those figures omitted items sold through multilevel marketing, used by many Murdock Madaus Schwabe competitors, including Nature's Sunshine, Nu Skin, USANA, Morinda, Neways, Enrich International, and E'ola.

Tom Murdock in 1969 had little idea what his pioneering herbalism work would lead to. In 1998 Ken Murdock, in cooperation with foreign partners, followed in his father's footsteps as Murdock Madaus Schwabe remained a leader in an industry that was expected to expand even more in the years ahead.

Further Reading

Bird, Sharon, ''Dr. John R. Christopher,'' *Central Utah Journal,* March 9, 1983, pp. 1–4.

Campbell, Joel, ''Nature's Own,'' *Deseret News* (Web Edition), June 28, 1998.

Carricaburu, Lisa, ''Utah's Natural-Products Firms Blossom from Need,'' *Salt Lake Tribune,* August 16, 1998, pp. E1–E2.

Debrovner, Diane, ''Micromedicine [Homeopathy],'' *American Druggist,* June 1993, pp. 36–41.

Haddock, Sharon M., ''Saving Rain Forests Is Professor's Forte,'' *Deseret News* (Web Edition), April 14, 1997.

Jarvik, Elaine, ''War Over Vitamins, Health Foods Escalates,'' *Deseret News* (Web Edition), August 12, 1993.

Johnson, G. Wesley, and Marian Ashby Johnson, ''Nature's Way,'' *Centennial Utah,* Encino, Calif.: Cherbo Publishing Group, 1995, pp. 156–58.

''Murdock Pharmaceuticals New Company of the Murdock International Group,'' *Provo Community Journal,* September 23, 1987, p. 13.

''Nature's Way Growing and Healthy,'' *Deseret News* (Web Edition), August 9, 1995.

Nelson, Lee, ''George Murdock,'' *Mormon Fortune Builders,* Provo, Utah: Council Press, 1981, pp. 195–213.

Schwartz, Judith D., ''Selling Middle America on Nature's Way of Curing Illness,'' *Brandweek,* October 26, 1992, p. 30.

''Springville Health Company Sets Up Rain-Forest Fund,'' *Deseret News* (Web Edition), January 18, 1990.

Vice, Jeff, ''Utah, U.S. Order Springville Firm to Stop Shipping Food 'Additive','' *Deseret News* (Web Edition), July 2, 1992.

—David M. Walden

National
Audubon
Society

National Audubon Society

700 Broadway
New York, New York 10003-9562
U.S.A.
(212) 979-3000
Fax: (212) 979-3188
Web site: http://www.audubon.org

Nonprofit Company
Incorporated: 1905 as National Association of Audubon
　Societies for the Protection of Wild Birds and
　Animals
Employees: 300
Operating Revenues: $62 million (1997 est.)
SICs: 8699 Membership Organizations, Not Elsewhere
　Classified; 2721 Periodicals; 8641 Civic & Social
　Associations; 8733 Noncommercial Research
　Organizations

The National Audubon Society (NAS or the Society), one of the largest private conservation organizations in this country, seeks to advance public understanding of the value and need of conserving soil, water, plants, and wildlife, as well as to encourage progress through intelligent use of natural resources. Incorporated in 1905 as a nonprofit organization, this leading grassroots Society organizes citizen action in support of specific conservation goals and conducts environmental research as well as programs on conservation issues. In North America, NAS has over 550,000 members and 518 chapters across North America; on a nationwide basis the Society manages 104 Audubon Wildlife Sanctuaries and Nature Centers. NAS produces elementary classroom curricula for its "Audubon Adventures" program, which reaches half-a-million children in 16,000 classrooms across the nation. "Audubon's Animal Adventures" is rated as one of the highest original series of the Disney Channel and won the Genesis Award for the "Outstanding Cable Television Children's Series." "Wild Wings: Heading South," airs on PBS and on BBC; the series features "electronic field trips" on the World Wide Web and enables children in 1,000 schools

in the United States and Great Britain to learn about and track migrating birds in the Old World and the New World. A curriculum for another program, "Wild Wings: Heading North," enables 12,000 students in U.S. schools to track and study migrating geese in real time, via the Web, during the four months of the birds' migration. The Society has over 105 books available for purchase and publishes the bimonthly *Audubon* magazine. NAS also sponsors staff-led "Nature Odysseys" to destinations around the world. The Society takes scientifically informed positions on all environmental issues in which it engages, works in conjunction with its chapters for wise environmental policies and laws, and initiates or joins in legal actions against activities destructive to the environment.

Awakening Awareness to Exploitation: 1886–1905

The roots of the National Audubon Society go as far back as 1886 when, according to Frank Graham, Jr.'s book titled *The Audubon Ark: A History of the National Audubon Society*, "the first Audubon Society was the ephemeral creation" of George Bird Grinnell, the proprietor of *Forest and Stream*, the 19th century's leading hunting and fishing journal in the United States. The young editor published hard-hitting editorials about the slaughter of wild birds and animals; he became a leader in the campaign that outlawed market hunting and the mindless killing of birds to meet fashion demands for bird plumes—or even entire birds—to decorate hats, clothing, and coiffures. In the February 11, 1886 issue of *Forest and Stream* Grinnell encouraged his readers to join him in forming the Audubon Society for the protection of wild birds and their eggs. He named the Society in honor of John James Audubon (1785–1851)—the ornithologist, explorer, and wildlife artist whose widow had been young Grinnell's teacher in New York City. Membership was open to everyone refusing to wear bird feathers as ornaments and/or willing to prevent the killing of wild birds not used for food and the destruction of their eggs.

The Audubon Society collected no dues, owned no property, lobbied no legislatures, and sued no malefactors. After a year, the organization emerged as a separate publication called the *Audubon Magazine*, which sold for six cents a copy or 50 cents for an annual subscription. The first issue reported that "Within the past few years, the destruction of our birds has increased at a rate which is alarming. This destruction now takes place on such a large scale as to seriously threaten the existence of a number of our most useful species.'' By 1887, the Society was a New York organization of 39,000 members. Overwhelmed by the response, Grinnell had neither the time nor the staff at *Forest and Stream* to keep up with additional correspondence and administrative details; he disbanded the group in 1888.

But Grinnell's concern for bird preservation was not a dead issue. In 1896, several of Boston's fashionable ladies recruited some prominent naturalists and ornithologists to form a society for the protection of birds: the Massachusetts Audubon Society was to discourage ''the buying and wearing, for ornamental purposes, of the feathers of any wild birds and to otherwise further the protection of native birds.'' Members of the Society distributed leaflets to educate the public, wrote letters to newspaper editors, and spoke to politicians. To recruit junior members, as Grinnell had done, the Society supported a Bird Day in the schools by sending teachers the forms needed to enroll youngsters at no cost, provided they signed a pledge card that read: ''I promise not to harm birds or their eggs, and to protect them both whenever I am able.'' After a few months, an Audubon Society was established in Pennsylvania and, by 1899, 15 other states had formed Audubon Societies.

While various states implemented legislation to protect birds, Senator Hoar of Massachusetts and Representative John F. Lacy focused on the passage of national legislation prohibiting interstate shipment of birds and other animals killed in violation of state laws; Congress passed the Lacy Act in 1900. Although at that time only five states had passed laws to protect birds, between 1895 and 1905, 32 additional states adopted model bird protection laws. In 1899 ornithologist Frank Chapman's publication of *Bird-Lore* magazine, gave the Audubon movement a unifying national forum. Furthermore, in 1900 Chapman sponsored the first national Christmas Bird Count. By the end of the century, more than 42,000 birders participated in this annual census and provided valuable data to ornithologists.

William Dutcher, an early leader of the Audubon movement, urged the state-based Audubon Societies to unite in order to have greater national clout. In 1901 some of these societies formed a loose alliance called the ''National Committee of the Audubon Societies of America'' and chose Dutcher as chairman. Then, in 1905, the National Committee incorporated as the National Association of Audubon Societies for the Protection of Wild Birds and Animals (Audubon), with William Dutcher as the president who ''almost singlehandedly pulled the movement together,'' Graham commented in *The Audubon Ark*. Dutcher found a staunch ally in Abbott H. Thayer, an artist whose book

about the protective coloration of animals inspired the new art of camouflage during World War I. Thayer provided Dutcher with the financial means to take forceful action against bird killers. The public contributed $1,400 to the Thayer Fund, which Dutcher enthusiastically used to set up a warden system to enforce conservation laws.

Evolving Advocacy, Action, and Research: 1906–35

The Audubon Society was instrumental in obtaining the passage in New York of the Audubon Act (1911), which prohibited the sale of feathers of native wild birds in the state, and of the federal Migratory Bird Treaty Act (1918), which prohibited the killing or capturing of most non-game bird species. During the first decades of the 20th century, NAS succeeded in saving from possible extinction many species; for example, the American and snowy egrets, terns, gulls, waterfowl, and some species of insectivorous birds. The Society also campaigned for the U.S. government to protect vital wildlife areas by establishing a National Wildlife Refuge system.

In 1910 President Dutcher was succeeded by T. Gilbert Pearson, whose 30 years in office were characterized by creative support of a warden and sanctuary system, nature education for children, political action, and a close working relationship with biologists in the federal government. During his tenure, NAS received the 26,000 acres of Louisiana marshlands that became the Paul J. Rainey Sanctuary, the oldest Audubon sanctuary. When Pearson left the Audubon presidency, the Audubon board chose Kermit Roosevelt, son of conservationist President Theodore Roosevelt, as president. The board also created the position of executive director and offered it to John Hopkinson Baker, a practical businessman and field birder who gave up his investment business to accept the new position. Baker built an elite staff composed mainly of naturalists in their 20s and 30s, strengthened the association's avian research, emphasized nature education, encouraged campaigns for the protection of nesting colonies, and gave a high priority to the education of children.

Among the schoolchildren who joined the Junior Audubon program was Roger Tory Peterson, a bird lover and talented artist. Whenever Peterson saw a new bird, he noted its distinguishing characteristics—such as thickness of the bill, a bar in the wing, color in the tail, a crest, a bright patch on throat or rump—in sketches that he used as guides during his field trips. Peterson tried to publish his collection of sketches but did not succeed until he received an offer from Houghton Mifflin to publish the guide without advance payment and—because of the high cost of making plates of the sketches—no royalties for the first thousand copies sold. The first 2,000 copies of *A Field Guide to the Birds,* published in April 1934, included only species found in the eastern United States, but the book sold within a week; 5,000 additional copies were printed and sold almost immediately. Each plate represented a group of related species; slim black pointers indicated distinguishing characteristics and the text gave information on each bird's voice, range, and habitat. ''The Peterson System of Identification,'' endured as the basic method of identifying birds. Baker hired Peterson as Audubon educational director and art director of *Bird-Lore* magazine. The artist-naturalist visited classrooms and museums and created leaflets that would appeal to children of different age groups. When he left Audubon to enlist in World War II, nine million American children were members of the Junior Audubon program NAS President Pearson had designed in the fall of 1910.

Widening the Scope of Concern: 1936–59

During the 1930s NAS sponsored many scientific research projects on endangered birds, such as the ivory-billed woodpecker and the roseate spoonbill. In the summer of 1936 the Audubon Association opened a camp on Hog Island in Maine's Muscongus Bay to educate adults about conservation of natural resources. Audubon Camp's summer sessions were an immediate success. Meanwhile, Baker persuaded Chapman to sell the *Bird-Lore* magazine to the Audubon association. In 1941 the name of the magazine was changed to *Audubon Magazine* and later shortened to *Audubon*. A year earlier the board of directors changed the name of ''National Association of Audubon Societies for the Protection of Wild Birds and Animals'' to ''National Audubon Society'' (NAS or the Society). In 1953 NAS adopted the flying great egret as its emblem.

Although most of NAS's state organizations remained aloof from Baker's operations, vigorous little urban ''bird clubs'' sprang up across the country. These clubs considered themselves nominal NAS affiliates but were devoted mostly to outings led by local naturalists. For instance, St. Louis Bird Club President Wayne Short organized bird walks and asked some of the leading naturalists (including Roger Peterson) who had brought their color motion-picture cameras into their favorite wildlife haunts, to be part of a series of lectures during the winter months. Within a few years, an average of a thousand people attended each lecture.

World War II brought wartime problems that cut into the Society's membership and programs. Baker accepted Short's offer to set up a program, called ''Audubon Screen Tours,'' that would visit various cities during the winter months. Within a few years, more than 50 cities, from New England to California, were in the program. Baker, promoted to president in 1944, was always on the alert for land acquisition and dealt successfully on the personal level with potential financial contributors. He was also among the first to foresee the danger inherent in technological innovation; it was he who warned against the growing enthusiasm for unrestricted use of DDT, the insecticide the U.S. Army used to protect its troops against lice, malarial mosquitoes, and a typhoid epidemic. According to the May 26, 1945 issue of the *New Yorker*, Baker said that ''If DDT should ever be used widely and without care, we would have a country without freshwater fish, serpents, frogs, and most of the birds we have now.''

National Presence: 1960–89

When Carl Buchheister succeeded Baker in 1959, NAS entered one of the most intense series of legislative struggles in the modern conservation era. Buchheister built up NAS's branch and chapter system; then he encouraged lobbies in state legislatures and in Congress for the passage of laws to protect wildlife, natural habitats, and the environment; the Society issued leaflets, booklets, and other informational materials on natural history and the environment. During his tenure NAS staff and members played a leading role in the enactment of the Clean Air and Clean Water Acts, the Wild and Scenic Rivers Act and the Endangered Species Acts. In 1961 NAS formed a Nature Centers Division by merging with Nature Centers for Young America, Inc. These Centers worked with school boards and other community organizations to give children living experiences of outdoor life.

In 1962 NAS took the lead in the defense of marine biologist Rachel Carson, whose book, *Silent Spring*, touched off a furious controversy by documenting how DDT and its new sister poisons were contaminating the earth. The eventual result was a virtual ban of DDT in this country. NAS's *Audubon* magazine published a series of articles on pesticide legislation and regulation and became a force in the struggle for pesticide reform. When Buchheister retired in 1967, he had consolidated the Society nationally, made friends with state leaders, directed the upgrading of the Society's magazine, and led the staff into increased participation in national issues, such as elimination of air and water pollution, support of land-use planning, need for energy conservation, and opposition to the giving away of public lands. Growth in membership broadened NAS involvement in environmental issues. For example, for 11 years NAS worked with the people of Washington state for the creation in 1968 of North Cascades National Park in order to save that area of high jagged mountains, deep forests of giant trees, and rushing rivers. NAS leadership passed on to Elvis T. Stahr in 1968, to Russell W. Peterson in 1979, and to Peter A.A. Berle in 1985.

President Stahr brought his considerable talents and Washington connections to serve as environmental leader and advocate for reform. He prevented the building of a dam that would have destroyed Kentucky's Red River Gorge. He also led NAS's support of a coalition formed by other national organizations to save Florida's Everglades National Park from almost certain destruction. A mammoth jetport projected to be built north of the park would have restricted and polluted the flow of fresh water vital to the Everglades. Stahr's influence in Washington and NAS's painstaking collection of environmental facts brought about the federal government's cancellation of the project. In addition, when the Internal Revenue Service threatened the tax-deductible status of the Society and of other nonprofit organizations, Stahr organized and chaired the ''Coalition of Concerned Charities,'' composed of some 60 national nonprofit organizations that were not founded primarily to influence legislation. His leadership led to the 1976 Tax Reform Act, which allowed nonprofit organizations to spend up to one million dollars annually for lobbying expenditures. During Stahr's tenure, NAS membership grew 340 percent, from 88,000 members to 388,000. The Society's assets, excluding properties, rose from $8.1 million to $18.5 million.

In 1979, Russell W. Peterson, after a long career in industry and government, began his NAS presidency with the slogan ''Think Globally, Act Locally.'' In *The Audubon Ark*, Graham quoted him as commenting that ''Environmental degradation knows no borders. . . . One nation's radioactive waste dumped in the ocean may end up in another country's tuna sandwiches.'' Peterson's enthusiasm for facing global issues (such as the threat posed to the global environment by nuclear arms and the population explosion), was not shared by the majority of NAS staff and members who remained more interested in wildlife protection than in global politics, but his vision for NAS involvement in global issues would surface as an NAS guideline before the end of the century. Peterson's more obvious contribution, during his tenure, was introducing NAS to the world of television through a cooperative arrangement with Ted Turner, creator of the Turner Broadcasting System. The young Turner's sense of showmanship and Peterson's eagerness to spread the Audubon message resulted in a television-film series, titled *The World of Audubon*, about people working to protect wildlife and the environment.

In 1985 Peter A.A. Berle left his work in a law firm to work as the next NAS president because, according to Graham's quote, he saw "the job as a chance to make a difference in an area of great importance." Berle knew that NAS operated at a loss but it was only in 1987 that he and the board of directors realized the extent of the NAS deficit. As they struggled to balance income and expenses, contemporary events—such as the world's oil glut eliminating the license fees NAS received from companies extracting natural gas from the Rainey Sanctuary, the rapid rise of liability-insurance premiums for the Society's physical properties (sanctuaries, summer camps, nature centers, etc.), and increases in the cost of paper and postage—severely crippled NAS operations. To avoid a total collapse, the board proposed a restructuring of the Society's regional operations but was met with an uproar among chapter leaders because they had not been consulted. Berle asked Chairman Donal C. O'Brien, Jr., to "democratize" the board by adding representation from the chapters. Tightened expenditures and aggressive fundraising made for a dramatic fiscal turnaround. On June 30, 1988, NAS had an annual budget of over $32 million in place. The deficit had disappeared and a new sense of mission revived among the Society's chapters and staff.

The 1990s and Beyond

To meet the need for new headquarters, in 1990 NAS bought, remodeled the interior, and restored the exterior of a century-old Romanesque Revival loft building in Manhattan. The renovated Audubon House that opened in 1992 symbolized NAS goals for conservation of both natural resources and the urban environment: it was a model of the energy-efficient, environmentally responsible workplace. For instance, Audubon House's energy-efficient features—from the thermal shell to the lighting reductions—were designed to reduce the Society's annual energy costs by 64 percent.

During the early 1990s, Berle continued to foster grassroots active participation in the Society's goals. NAS membership rose to over 550,000 men and women who gave the Society high visibility and nationwide political leverage for the protection of ancient forests in the Pacific Northwest, the prevention of oil drilling in the Arctic National Wildlife Refuge, the preservation of wetlands and reauthorization of the Endangered Species Act. The grassroots element also played a decisive role in defining the future of the Society. In 1994 Chairman O'Brien and other members of the board, NAS members, chapter lead-

ers, and staff joined forces to forge the *Strategic Plan for Audubon 2000* (The Plan), a plan that was to make the Society one of the strongest and most effective grassroots organizations for environmental advocacy at the community, state, and national levels.

Berle was succeeded by John Flicker, who assumed the office of NAS President/CEO in 1995. Flicker had served 21 years with The Nature Conservancy (an organization that bought and managed wildlife habitats). Among other accomplishments, he had designed and promoted the $3 billion Preservation 2000 land-acquisition program. Under his leadership NAS scored dramatic victories and substantial progress in its National Campaigns; for example, legislation to revise the priorities of the National Wildlife Refuges; return of the Everglades to a healthy, thriving ecosystem; passage of a new, stronger Endangered Species Act; policies to halt destruction of wetlands; and prevention of water-diversion projects that would destroy natural habitats on Nebraska's Platte River. Flicker supported decentralization of senior staff and stressed the need for heavy investment in the Society's distinctive grassroots network as the primary instrument of environmental advocacy. "A decentralized state program structure is better able to address uniquely local needs and opportunities," wrote Flicker in his *1997 Annual Report*. He also stressed expansion of educational programs to nurture appreciation of nature and understanding of the essential link between ecological health and the well-being of human civilization.

For more than a century, NAS and the conservation movement had grown and evolved together. The 21st century would bring new challenges to a worldwide culture of conservation but the National Audubon Society, as a grassroots powerhouse, was geared to lead the conservation movement into a bright and sustainable future.

Further Reading

Atteberry, Ann, "Birders Flock to Wildlife Refuges in Southeast Texas," *Dallas Morning News*, July 19, 1998, p. G6.

——, "Off the Beaten Bayou in Cajun Country," *Dallas Morning News*, October 1, 1995, p. G8.

Bandrapalli, Suman, "So, Who's Coming to Dinner? It Depends on What You're Serving," *Christian Science Monitor*, February 5, 1998, p. 11.

Begley, Sharon, "Audubon's Empty Nest: Bye-Bye Little Birdie; Hello Corporate Savvy," *Newsweek*, June 24, 1991, p. 57.

"Building Audubon Centers," *Audubon*, September 1997, p. 112.

Evans, Brock, "A Time of Crisis: The Giveaway of Our Public Lands," *Vital Speeches*, September 1, 1995, pp. 689–95.

Flicker, John, "Building Diversity at Audubon," *Audubon*, March 1998.

——, "Tracking Birds on the Net," *Audubon*, May 1998.

Graham, Frank, Jr., *The Audubon Ark: A History of the National Audubon Society*, New York: Alfred A. Knopf, 1990, 336 p.

Isbell, Connie M., "Growing Up in the Fisheries Crises," *Audubon*, May 1998.

Lemonik, Michael D., "Winged Victory," *Time*, July 11, 1994, p. 53.

—Gloria A. Lemieux

National Beverage Corp.

One North University Drive
Fort Lauderdale, Florida 33324
U.S.A.
(954) 581-0922
Fax: (954) 473-4710
Web site: http://www.nbcfiz.com

Public Company
Incorporated: 1985
Employees: 1,200
Sales: $400.7 million (1998)
Stock Exchanges: American
Ticker Symbol: FIZ
SICs: 2086 Bottled & Canned Soft Drinks

A leading second-tier beverage company, National Beverage Corp. develops, produces, and sells branded soft drinks, juice products, and bottled water, distributing its products nationwide from 14 manufacturing facilities scattered throughout the United States. National Beverage acquired its first branded soft drink, Shasta, in 1985 and added Faygo, a regional brand, in 1987. With these two brands, the company began developing a diversity of flavored beverages, supplying its products to retail grocery chains, warehouse clubs, food service outlets, convenience stores, and vending machines. Other branded beverage products were added in later years, including Big Shot, a regional soft drink, Everfresh juice products, LaCROIX carbonated and still water, à Santé sparkling mineral water, Body Works, an isotonic sports drink, and Spree, an all-natural, carbonated soft drink. Unlike many of its competitors, National Beverage manufactures its own beverage products instead of contracting production to other bottlers. The operation of its own bottling plants allows the company to perform bottling services for private label brands, giving it an important secondary source of income. During the late 1990s, National Beverage was 77 percent-owned by its founder and chief executive officer, Nick A. Caporella.

Origins

Few companies in the history of business were created for the reasons that gave birth to National Beverage. At its founding, the company served as a mechanism to resolve an acrimonious struggle between two corporate barons, beginning as a hollow corporate shell whose sole purpose was to rid another company of an unwanted suitor. The dispute that eventually spawned National Beverage had its roots in the late 1970s, when a Fort Lauderdale company named Burnup & Sims Inc. was thriving as an installer of cable television and telecommunications systems. Headed by a Pennsylvania coal miner's son named Nick Caporella, the company was performing phenomenally well, demonstrating a level of profitability that delighted Wall Street and one investor, Miami financier Victor Posner, in particular. Posner watched Burnup & Sims's earnings nearly triple between 1978 and 1981 and decided to secure a piece of the rising profits. Posner began buying shares in Burnup & Sims, accumulating a sufficiently sized stake in the company to suggest to Caporella that a hostile takeover was imminent. Caporella was adamantly opposed to any interference or involvement on Posner's part and, as events unfolded, he displayed remarkable perseverance and ingenuity in parrying what he perceived as an assault by Posner.

At first, as Posner's holding in Burnup & Sims gradually increased, it appeared Caporella was unwilling to fight. In 1982, when Posner's stake eclipsed 29 percent, Caporella quit in disgust, vacating his chief executive position at Burnup & Sims and taking 17 executives with him. The cable television and telecommunications company kept its doors open with no one inside to run the company, but, at the urging of Burnup & Sims's board of directors, Caporella returned after a month and obtained a temporary federal restraining order to bar Posner from interfering with the company's business. The restraining order, however, was only a temporary measure. Caporella wanted to achieve more than keeping Posner at arm's distance; he wanted to eliminate all of Posner's influence. From Caporella's perspective, Burnup & Sims's survival depended on Posner's removal from any association with the company. When Burnup & Sims's earnings collapsed in 1982, Caporella

Company Perspectives:
Flavors are the primary focus of the company, with superior quality as the masthead of the corporate philosophy. National Beverage's full line of branded, multi-flavored soft drinks, including colas, teas, bottled waters and juice products, satisfy a wide range of consumers.

complained, "Our operating subsidiary presidents stopped working. They felt humiliated." At fault, according to Caporella, was Posner, a "dark cloud" that threateningly loomed over Burnup & Sims's headquarters.

For the solution to his problem, Caporella searched for a white knight—a company willing to buy Burnup & Sims and thereby thwart Posner's threatening advances. He found no company willing to take on the role of Burnup & Sims's savior, but his search did lead to an effective, if somewhat confusing, solution. As Posner's percentage crept up to 43 percent, Caporella decided to create his own white knight and use his newly formed company to dilute Posner's ownership percentage in Burnup & Sims. National Beverage Corp. would be Caporella's white knight.

Through a partnership controlled by Caporella, National Beverage Corp. was formed in 1985. The partnership retained 55 percent ownership of the new company and sold 40 percent to Burnup & Sims for $38.2 million plus 1.8 million in new Burnup & Sims shares. The shuffle of stock put the new Burnup & Sims stock under Caporella's personal control and consequently watered down Posner's Burnup & Sims holding from 43 percent to roughly 35 percent. The strategy worked, but its execution also created the need to put National Beverage into business. To fulfill the second part of his plan, Caporella had his new corporate shell acquire Shasta Beverages from Sara Lee Corporation. National Beverage paid $40 million for the soda subsidiary plus the 1.8 million Burnup & Sims shares.

After this second flurry of transactions, National Beverage was a going enterprise, its existence tied to Burnup & Sims in what outside observers described as a sister-to-sister relationship. Caporella, now with two companies under his control, was pleased by the results, but Posner still controlled 35 percent of Burnup & Sims—too much in Caporella's view. He performed another securities trick, selling another 5.2 million new Burnup & Sims shares to National Beverage in June 1986, which further diluted Posner's stake to 23 percent. Caporella was overjoyed by the accomplishment, declaring, "It's like being reborn." Posner, however, did not make his full retreat until 1988 when Cincinnati financier Carl Lindner purchased Posner's shares and transferred them to Burnup & Sims. Caporella by this point had already turned his attention to National Beverage, deciding to rethink his operating strategy for Burnup & Sims while he worked to expand his new company. Intending to use Shasta as a foundation, Caporella aimed for a lofty objective, vowing to develop National Beverage into a $1 billion beverage company.

1987 Acquisition of Faygo

Caporella's bid to develop a billion-dollar beverage company began with Shasta, a national brand that was first sold in 1889. To broaden National Beverage's distribution coverage, Caporella next added Faygo, a popular carbonated beverage in the Midwest, acquiring the regional brand in 1987 from Tree Sweet Products Corp. The acquisition of Faygo, which first appeared in 1907, and Shasta also gave National Beverage 12 bottling plants scattered throughout the United States, each located near major markets. As the company moved forward, it used its bottling facilities to bottle its own drinks and to bottle private-label brands. The use of its own bottling plants—a luxury not all beverage companies enjoyed—provided National Beverage with an important secondary source of income, as grocery chains turned to National Beverage for the production of their private-label brands and smaller, regional beverage companies contracted National Beverage to bottle their brands.

With Shasta and Faygo, Caporella controlled a beverage company with annual revenues in excess of $300 million, a total far below the billions collected by National Beverage's giant rivals, The Coca-Cola Company and Pepsi-Cola Company. The presence of these two conglomerates, whose corporate reach extended around the globe, dictated to a large degree the strategy employed by Caporella. Coca-Cola and Pepsi controlled an overwhelming share of the U.S. market, each holding such a dominant and entrenched position that they were, in effect, only in competition with one another. Second tier beverage companies like National Beverage could not realistically hope to usurp either of the two giants, which Caporella realized. He was determined to avoid a direct battle for national market share against either of the beverage industry's behemoths, and instead sought to carve a niche for National Beverage as a producer of flavored sodas

By the end of the 1980s, National Beverage was filling and labeling 1.5 million cans of soft drinks in its packaging plants and marketing these beverages in a rainbow of flavors. Financially the company was doing well, particularly in light of the weakened state both Shasta and Faygo were in prior to their purchase. Financial health, however, was not the only concern National Beverage faced during the late 1980s. A nagging issue, and one that drained National Beverage's financial strength, was the company's relationship with Burnup & Sims. In the aftermath of the struggle between Posner and Caporella, Burnup & Sims and National Beverage emerged as two companies woven tightly together. The transfer of stock from both Caporella-managed companies left Burnup & Sims owning 42.1 percent of National Beverage and made National Beverage a 55.6 percent owner of Burnup & Sims. Shareholders and outside observers had expected the two companies to be disentangled shortly after Posner sold the last of his shares in 1988, but it was not until April 1990 that a plan was announced for the separation of the companies. Although the unusually close relationship between the two companies had certain advantages for National Beverage, such as the use of Burnup & Sims's capital for expansion, the union created its own particular problems. Cross-management of the two companies had proven costly and intercompany debt also hobbled National Beverage's progress, making some resolution to the situation a necessity.

National Beverage a Separate Company for the 1990s

According to the plan first revealed in April 1990, National Beverage was to be spun off as a separate company and its stock offered for sale to the public. The long-awaited deal occurred in September 1991, but its completion only added fuel to yet another nagging issue. In the September 1991 attempt to separate the companies, National Beverage's ownership in Burnup & Sims was only reduced from 55 percent to 36 percent and only 23 percent of National Beverage was sold to the public, which prompted most institutional investors to shun the beverage company's stock. When the dust had settled, Caporella ended up owning 77 percent of National Beverage, making his original $1.6 million investment in National Beverage worth $38 million. Additionally, Caporella's $900,000-a-year salary was paid by Burnup & Sims, by the company some believed had been weakened in order to strengthen National Beverage. To make the situation more distasteful to some, Caporella received one percent of National Beverage's revenues to run the company, a salary that amounted to $3 million following the 1991 public offering. One Burnup & Sims shareholder had had enough, and filed a lawsuit against Caporella, charging that Burnup & Sims shareholders had suffered financially from Caporella's dealings. "He's Victor Posner's twin," railed the disgruntled shareholder, a Miami insurance agent named Albert Hahn who held 50,000 shares of Burnup & Sims stock. Caporella fought back, explaining, "If it wasn't for me, my cash, and my idea, we [Burnup & Sims shareholders] would have been left to the ruin and rape of Victor Posner. I took the gamble and bought a losing company [Shasta] with a dying brand. I would like to have the recognition of a doctor who performed an operation and saved a patient."

As had been the case since National Beverage's formation, publicly waged disputes attracted the bulk of attention, diverting it away from the day-to-day operations of the beverage company. Although the company's stock was not performing well because of the contentious squabbles punctuating its history, the company itself was making some headway. Amid the rancor surrounding him, Caporella was still intent on fashioning National Beverage into an industry heavyweight, declaring in 1992, "I am going to have a humongous big beverage company some day." At the time, National Beverage ranked as the sixth largest beverage company in the United States, but because of the enormous power wielded by Pepsi and Coca-Cola, sixth largest in the United States translated to a mere 1.7 percent national market share. Nevertheless, the company had flowered into a flavored-soda maker and added several brands to its portfolio since the 1987 acquisition of Faygo. Spree, an all-natural, carbonated soft drink, joined the company's fold by the beginning of the 1990s, and was followed by the acquisition of Big Shot, a regional, multiflavored soft drink line established in 1935. By 1992, the company was producing 108 flavors and 34 product lines, marketing more beverage flavors than any other beverage company in the world. Meanwhile, National Beverage's private-label bottling business had received a tremendous boost in 1991 when the U.S. Navy contracted the company to produce the Navy's own private-label brand of soft drinks called "Sea."

By the mid-1990s, National Beverage had increased its stature within the U.S. beverage industry, becoming the nation's fifth largest producer in 1996. By this point, the company had diversified into the production and sale of teas, bottled water, and juice products, adding to the scores of soft drink flavors it produced. The company's diversification into non-carbonated beverages gained its greatest momentum from two acquisitions completed in the mid-1990s, the purchase of WinterBrook Corp. and Everfresh Beverages Inc. WinterBrook, a Bellevue, Washington-based company, operated as the holding company for three brands, Cascadia, WinterBrook Clear, and LaCROIX, a brand of carbonated and still water. LaCROIX was the most important addition to National Beverage, giving the company a branded water beverage that ranked as a top seller in several Midwestern markets and enjoyed a noticeable presence on airline beverage carts. The acquisition of Everfresh moved the company solidly into the juice production business, helping Caporella to shape National Beverage into what he described as "a total beverage company."

By 1998, sales had surpassed $400 million, far below the $1 billion goal Caporella had been aiming for during the previous decade. Although the late 1990s did not see Caporella sitting atop the "humongous big beverage company" he was hoping to create some day, National Beverage was enjoying annual sales growth of roughly 10 percent as it prepared for the 21st century. With this encouraging growth propelling it forward, and a consistent record of profitability supporting it, National Beverage and its growing roster of brands appeared solidly positioned for the years ahead.

Principal Subsidiaries

BevCo Sales, Inc.; Big Shot Beverage Co.; Everfresh Beverages, Inc.; Faygo Beverages, Inc.; LaCROIX Beverages, Inc.; National BevPak; National Retail Brands, Inc.; PACO, Inc.; PETCO, Inc.; Shasta West, Inc.; Shasta Beverages, Inc.; Shasta Beverages International, Inc.; Shasta Food Services; Shasta Military Sales; Shasta Midwest, Inc.; Shasta Northwest, Inc.; Shasta Sales, Inc.; Shasta Sweetener Corp.; Shasta USA; Shasta Vending; Winnsboro Beverage Packers, Inc.

Further Reading

Davis, Tim, "Creative Groundskeeping," *Beverage World,* March 1993, p. 50.

Lappen, Alyssa A., "One Down, One to Go? Burnup and Sims' Nick Caporella Managed to Neutralize Victor Posner. Now Who Will Neutralize Caporella?," *Forbes,* August 11, 1986, p. 67.

Lubove, Seth, "No Respect," *Forbes,* August 3. 1992, p. 78.

"National Beverage Buys Winterbrook, Everfresh," *Beverage World,* April 1996, p. 26.

"National Beverage Spin-Off Set," *South Florida Business Journal,* December 24, 1990, p. 4.

Sedore, David, "Caporella Big Winner in Burnup Split," *South Florida Business Journal,* March 18, 1991, p. 1.

——, "Wanted: Investor to Retire Burnup & Sims Debt," *South Florida Business Journal,* July 30, 1990, p. 6.

—Jeffrey L. Covell

National Semiconductor Corporation

2900 Semiconductor Drive
P.O. Box 58090
Santa Clara, California 95052-8090
U.S.A.
(408) 721-5000
(800) 432-9672
Fax: (408) 739-9803
Web site: http://www.national.com

Public Company
Incorporated: 1959
Employees: 13,000
Sales: $2.53 billion (1998)
Stock Exchanges: New York
Ticker Symbol: NSM
SICs: 3674 Semiconductors & Related Devices; 3679
    Electronic Components, Not Elsewhere Classified

National Semiconductor Corporation is one of the leading American manufacturers of semiconductors used in a broad range of electronics applications. During its rapid rise to prominence in the late 1970s, National Semiconductor gained a reputation as perhaps the most efficient producer of semiconductors in the world, turning out a wide array of standardized, reliable parts at very low cost. National's prosperity relied less on high-tech genius than on low-tech frugality and hard work, qualities instilled in the company by its longtime president and chief executive, Charles E. Sporck. In the increasingly crowded world of semiconductors, however, National suffered during the 1980s from Asian price competition, leading to a series of money-losing years. National staged a turnaround in the mid-1990s under Sporck's successor, Gilbert F. Amelio, and is now—under another new leader, Brian Halla—staking its future on sophisticated, higher-margin products, most notably the system-on-a-chip.

Founded in 1959

''Semiconductor'' is the name given to a group of elements which under normal conditions do not conduct electricity, but which when slightly modified can be used as conductors with great precision and reliability. The development of the modern electronics industry, beginning with the 1949 invention of the transistor, has depended on the progressively more subtle use of semiconductors to control and direct electricity in very small packages known as integrated circuits or ''chips.'' In 1959 Dr. Bernard Rothlein, formerly of Sperry Rand Corporation, joined the burgeoning semiconductor industry by creating National Semiconductor in Danbury, Connecticut (the company moved to Santa Clara, California, in 1968). The company was tiny by industry standards, with only $5.3 million in sales by 1965, but it offered a variety of fairly sophisticated semiconductors and was operating at a profit.

Dr. Rothlein's former employer filed a suit against National for patent infringement, however, and the case depressed the company's stock price when it reached the courts in the mid-1960s. The low stock price encouraged a substantial investment by East Coast financier Peter J. Sprague (son of the chairman of Sprague Electric Company), who became chairman of National in 1966 and set out to make the company a major player in the semiconductor industry. Sprague recognized that National needed an injection of strong management if it was to make the transition from small research lab to commercial manufacturer, and in the spring of 1967 he surprised the industry by hiring away five top executives from Fairchild Camera & Instrument Corporation, then the nation's second largest maker of semiconductors.

Sporck Hired in 1967

Chief among the new recruits was Charles E. Sporck, 39-year-old head of Fairchild's semiconductor division, who accepted a 50 percent cut in pay to become National's president (and owner of a chunk of its stock). From then until 1991 National Semiconductor would remain largely the creation of these two men, and especially of the hard-driving Charlie Sporck.

Sporck and National Semiconductor were ideally suited to each other. National had some excellent products but lacked management control, while Sporck was not a technical genius but knew how to run a tight ship, market his wares, and make money. With the full financial and moral backing of Peter

Sprague and the board of directors, Sporck turned National upside down in the 12 months following his arrival. He marked down the value of National's inventory of transistors by $1.5 million (helping the company to a $2 million loss in fiscal 1967) and focused its energies on selling large quantities of standard semiconductors in three different market areas: linear, Transistor-to-Transistor Logic (TTL), and metal-oxide semiconductors (MOS). He also kept a tight lid on corporate overhead, using outside sales representatives whenever possible, farming out basic engineering and accounting work to independent contractors, and generally promoting a corporate ethic of spartan austerity. In an industry rapidly flooding with new competitors, Sporck's penny-pinching would prove the key to National's survival in the coming price wars. As he told *Business Week* in 1970, "We make money because we have to."

Though it might not have been apparent to the casual observer in 1967, National Semiconductor had assembled a trio of powerful business advantages. Most fundamentally, National was in an industry about to undergo tremendous growth, as the spread of computers made the semiconductor critical to every aspect of modern life; it could draw on the financial strength of its investors in order to raise the large amounts of money required for expansion; and the company was run by a man naturally inclined to efficiency and thrift. The combination of these elements allowed National to grow with amazing swiftness, 1965's sales of $5.3 million becoming $42 million in 1970 and $365 million in 1976. For other, less well-prepared companies, the same period was fatal, as bitter price wars erupting in 1969 and 1970 drove even giants such as General Electric and Westinghouse out of the semiconductor business and kept profit levels minuscule everywhere. Silicon Valley was suddenly very crowded, and from among its scores of visionary entrepreneurs only a few would survive to dominate the national scene.

Sporck early on brought a global awareness to National. National was one of the first semiconductor companies to move its assembly operations to the Far East, where labor was available at a fraction of its cost in the United States. The company also sold about 20 percent of its finished products overseas, much of it going to Europe at prices that stirred charges of unfair trade practices. On the other hand, Sporck appeared to have grossly underestimated the long-term potential for competition from the Far East, where the growth of an indigenous semiconductor industry drove prices ever lower on the kind of standardized semiconductors made by National. Sporck's preference for selling a high volume of standard items made possible National's prodigious growth, so long as its competition was limited to American firms operating on similar cost bases; when the Japanese made semiconductors a global business in the 1980s, the same formula brought consistent losses and a desperate appeal from Sporck for federal trade protection. National was at the forefront of political pressure leading to the 1986 Semiconductor Trade Agreement.

Failed 1970s Diversification Efforts

Sporck was aware of National's vulnerability, of course, and beginning in the early 1970s he made a number of attempts to diversify the company's sales base by "integrating forward," making consumer products as well as the semiconductors that went inside them. National leaped into the manufacture of calculators, digital watches, and video games, enjoying initial success as the public responded to the novelty of these high-tech gadgets. Within a few years, however, National's emphasis on low-price mass merchandising again left it vulnerable to the crush of competitors entering these markets. National had no experience in retail manufacturing, and before long its products were saddled with a reputation as low-end junk, without the style or cachet needed to survive in a maturing market. By the time everyone in America was wearing a digital watch National had been driven from the marketplace, suffering minor losses which were fortunately overshadowed by its roaring success in semiconductors.

Two other efforts by Sporck to widen National's product line had more complex histories, though both also ended in failure. In the mid-1970s, National became interested in the possibility of electronic point-of-sale terminals for use in supermarkets. In association with a group of California supermarketers, National developed the "Datachecker" system for the scanning and recording of sales, with which it built a substantial and modestly profitable business over the following decade. Of greater potential was National's decision around 1976 to enter the computer business, originally as a producer of mainframe computers for sale by Itel Corporation, a San Francisco-based marketing and finance company. As many others had tried before, Itel and National were hoping to cut into IBM's domination of the mainframe market by selling similar machines at a much reduced price. At first, National was satisfied simply to make computers for the Itel name; in the late 1970s, however, National tried to push into the market with its own line of mainframes and minicomputers, encouraged by the huge profits it was making on the Itel IBM-compatibles.

National's System 200 and 400 lines of large computers never got off the ground, due in part to renewed competition from the ever vigilant IBM. Itel had similar but more severe problems, forced by IBM price pressure in early 1979 to ask National for cheaper computers with which to compete. Sporck recognized a golden opportunity: he agreed to supply Itel with cheaper computers only if they would agree to buy more machines. Itel foolishly did so, and when the market softened later that year Itel was stuck with computers it could not sell and an obligation to buy a lot more of them. Faced with a complete disaster, Itel essentially gave its inventory and sales force to National in exchange for a release from its contracts; as one former Itel executive told *Fortune,* "National blackmailed us and then stole the business." Be that as it may, Sporck had "stolen" little more than a distraction and headache. National enjoyed sporadic success selling a line of mainframes made by Hitachi in Japan, but again its timing and approach were all wrong. Aside from the inherent difficulties of competing with IBM, the 1980s also witnessed a general decline in the mainframe segment of the computer industry that even IBM was not able to withstand successfully. The monolithic mainframe was being replaced by combinations of mini and microcomputers, and in a shrinking market National's chances of success against IBM fell from slim to none. The company sold its National Advanced Systems division in 1989.

Buffeted by Asian Competition in the 1980s

In the meantime National's semiconductor business continued to boom. Sales for 1981 reached $1.1 billion—tripling in four years—and the company employed 40,000 workers, two-thirds of them in Southeast Asian assembly plants. Its strength continued to be the manufacture of linear and bipolar logic integrated circuits in large quantities and at low cost; as a competing executive told *Fortune,* National was the "sweatshop of our industry—a pipe-rack, low-cost, survival-oriented company." But National was soon faced with a number of grave problems. In 1981, a handful of key National executives left the company to accept more lucrative offers elsewhere, among them Pierre Lamond, for years National's chief designer and engineer. Job-hopping is endemic to the electronics industry, but the defection of Lamond was still a significant blow for National: never strong on technical ingenuity, the company had now lost its brightest designer. Worse yet, competition from the Far East was now at flood tide, and the first to feel its impact would be companies like National who lived by volume and price appeal. National's line of staple items could be reproduced anywhere, and even better than having two-thirds of one's employees in the Far East was to have all of them there. Although the cheapest maker of semiconductors in the United States, National was not the cheapest worldwide.

The recession of 1981–82 plunged National into the red. Its losses totaled only $25 million, but they set the tone for the coming decade. The company was solid in the following few years, suffered a sharp downturn in 1985 and 1986, and then recovered again in late 1987. At this point, Sporck made a purchase that must have given him great personal satisfaction, whatever its permanent value to National Semiconductor. For $122 million National bought the semiconductor division of Fairchild Camera, the same Fairchild from which Sporck and his management team had emigrated back in 1967. Fairchild had been one of the pioneers in semiconductors, but since the departure of Sporck it had staggered through many losing years and was now available at what some observers thought was a bargain price. Sporck felt that Fairchild's strengths in chips for mainframes and supercomputers and its excellent military ties would complement National's relative weakness in those segments of the market. Once again, his timing was poor; the mainframe market continued to shrink and military spending declined from its peak during the Reagan administration. Moreover, Fairchild Semiconductor had lost $265 million in the two years prior to its purchase by National, and the latter already had plenty of its own problems.

From fiscal 1987 through fiscal 1992, National posted an aggregate loss exceeding $500 million. President Sporck and Chairman Sprague took vigorous measures to right their floundering ship, getting out of computers and point-of-sale equipment, dropping the two least profitable semiconductor lines, and in early 1991 replacing Sporck himself with Gilbert F. Amelio.

Under the leadership of Amelio, a former Rockwell International executive who had a Ph.D. in physics from Georgia Institute of Technology, National turned more of its energies toward the market for analog semiconductors, used increasingly by the telecommunications industry. National was already the number one producer of analog chips, which for years had been all but lost in the excitement over digital chips for computer applications, and Amelio hoped that the changing demands of the market would make National's analog expertise far more valuable in the 1990s. The immediate signs were not encouraging. Even after writing off $144 million in the massive reorganization of the company in 1991, National came up with a $120 million loss in the following year.

Shift to Value-Added Chips in the Mid-1990s

Nonetheless, for the next three years, as the restructuring reached its culmination, National Semiconductor was on the rebound, posting healthy profits and seeing revenues increase each year. In addition to selling off nonstrategic assets, Amelio also divided the company's chip lines into two areas: lower-margin, more cyclical logic and memory chips—the so-called commodity chips upon which National gained prominence; and higher-margin, value-added analog and mixed-signal chips. The division seemed to point toward the eventual divestment of the commodity chips, but before he could make this dramatic move, Amelio left National Semiconductor in early 1996 to become CEO of Apple Computer Inc. and attempt another turnaround.

Brought on board in May 1996 as new CEO and president (and soon chairman as well) was Brian Halla, a former executive vice-president at LSI Logic Corp. who had also spent 14 years in marketing at Intel Corporation. The month after his arrival, National announced that it had consolidated its commodity chip lines within a new unit, Fairchild Semiconductor, resurrecting the name of the pioneering Silicon Valley chip company that National had bought in 1987. In March 1997 National completed the divestment of Fairchild whereby it sold the unit to an investment company for $550 million, with National retaining a 15 percent stake in Fairchild.

Halla also staked the company's future on the so-called system-on-a-chip, a new type of technology in development that would include all functions required for one device on a single chip. For instance, a PC would require only one chip rather than the several typically required (though in both cases, memory chips are also needed). This would result in cheaper, more reliable, and smaller systems, and the system-on-a-chip was therefore ideally suited to such proposed consumer products as cellular phones with Internet access built in and PCs small enough to fit into a wallet.

National Semiconductor was not the only company pursuing this technology but it seemed to be the most aggressive. The company made a number of acquisitions designed to gain the combination of technologies needed to make the system-on-a-chip a reality. In March 1997 National paid $74.5 million for Mediamatics, Inc., a Fremont, California-based maker of MPEG audiovisual chips for the PC market. Cyrix Corporation was acquired in November 1997 for about $540 million. Cyrix specialized in lower-price Intel-compatible microprocessors used in sub-$1,000 personal computers. Halla planned to use

Cyrix chips as a base for the system-on-a-chip, which could be the heart of PCs costing less than $400. In May 1998 National paid $104.8 million to acquire ComCore Semiconductor, Inc., a maker of integrated circuits for computer networking and communications.

The acquisition of Cyrix was perhaps the final piece needed to complete the system-on-a-chip puzzle. National announced in April 1998 that the first product using the new technology would be ready in mid-1999. The company also announced that month that it would close some plants and lay off 10 percent of its workforce, or about 1,300 people, because of slackening demand worldwide. Charges related to these moves and to the acquisition of ComCore led to a full-year fiscal 1998 loss of $98.6 million. Revenues declined to $2.54 billion from $2.68 billion in 1997.

Principal Subsidiaries

ComCore Semiconductor, Inc.; Future Integrated Systems, Inc.; Cyrix Corporation; Cyrix Manufacturing, Inc.; Cyrix International, Inc.; Mediamatics, Inc.; Dyna-Craft, Inc.; National Semiconductor International, Inc.; DTS Caribe, Inc.; National Semiconductor Netsales, Inc.; National Semiconductor (Maine), Inc.; Comlinear Corporation; ASIC II Limited; National Semiconductor B.V. Corporation; National Semiconductor France S.A.R.L.; National Semiconductor GmbH (Germany); National Semiconductor (I.C.) Ltd. (Israel); National Semiconductor S.r.l. (Italy); National Semiconductor A.B. (Sweden); National Semiconductor (U.K.) Ltd.; National Semiconductor (U.K.) Pension Trust Company; Cyrix International Limited (U.K.); National Semiconductor Benelux B.V. (Netherlands); National Semiconductor B.V. (Netherlands); National Semiconductor International Finance S.A. (Switzerland); Natsem India Designs Pvt. Ltd. (India); National Semiconductor (Australia) Pty. Ltd.; National Semiconductor (Hong Kong) Limited; National Semiconductor (Far East) Limited (Hong Kong); NSM International Limited (Hong Kong; 51%); National Semiconductor Sunrise Hong Kong Limited; National Semiconductor Japan Ltd.; Cyrix K.K. (Japan); National Semiconductor SDN. BHD. (Malaysia); National Semiconductor Technology SDN. BHD. (Malaysia); DynaCraft SDN. BHD. (Malaysia); DynaCraft Asia Pacific SDN. BHD. (Malaysia); National Semiconductor Pte. Ltd. (Singapore); National Semiconductor Asia Pacific Pte. Ltd. (Singapore); National Semiconductor Manufacturer Singapore Pte. Ltd.; Shanghai National Semiconductor Technology Limited (China; 95%); National Semiconductor Korea Limited; National Semiconductor Canada Inc.; National Semicondutores do Brazil Ltda.; National Semicondutores da America do Sul (Brazil); Electronica NSC de Mexico, S.A. de C.V.; ASIC Limited (Bermuda); National Semiconductor (Barbados) Limited; Cyrix Export Sales Corporation (Barbados).

Further Reading

Amelio, Gil, and William L. Simon, *Profit from Experience: The National Semiconductor Story of Transformation Management,* New York: Van Nostrand Reinhold, 1996, 312 p.

Brandt, Richard, "The Man National Is Putting Its Chips On," *Business Week,* February 18, 1981.

Carroll, Paul B., "For National Semiconductor, Revenue Is the Challenge," *Wall Street Journal,* February 8, 1996, p. B4.

——, "National Semi Resets Agenda with New CEO," *Wall Street Journal,* May 6, 1996, pp. A3, A9.

"Confounding an Industry on Prices," *Business Week,* November 21, 1970.

Epstein, Joseph, "Semi Circle: National Semiconductor's Turnaround Isn't Quite Complete," *Financial World,* October 21, 1996, pp. 82+.

"Fast Footwork in an Industry Talent Hunt," *Business Week,* March 11, 1967.

Gomes, Lee, "Chip Maker to Revamp Cheaper Lines," *Wall Street Journal,* June 21, 1996, p. B7.

"The Hot New Computer Company," *Business Week,* October 22, 1979.

Miles, Robert H., *Corporate Comeback: The Story of Renewal and Transformation at National Semiconductor,* San Francisco: Jossey-Bass, 1997, 388 p.

Murray, Thomas J., "Live Wire at National Semi," *Dun's,* August, 1972.

Reinhardt, Andy, "National Semiconductor's Silicon Dreams," *Business Week,* October 14, 1996, pp. 94, 97.

Richards, Bill, "Computer-Chip Plants Aren't As Safe and Clean As Billed, Some Say," *Wall Street Journal,* October 5, 1998, pp. A1, A13.

Takahashi, Dean, "National Semiconductor to Acquire Cyrix," *Wall Street Journal,* July 29, 1997, pp. A3, A4.

——, "New CEO Strives to Revitalize National Semiconductor," *Wall Street Journal,* January 3, 1997, p. B5.

——, "New Chip by National Semiconductor May Drive PC Prices to Less Than $400," *Wall Street Journal,* April 6, 1998, pp. A3, A6.

Uttal, Bro, "The Animals of Silicon Valley," *Fortune,* January 12, 1981.

—Jonathan Martin
—updated by David E. Salamie

NetCom Systems AB

Skeppsbron 18
P.O. Box 2094
103 13 Stockholm
Sweden
(46) 8 562 000 60
Fax: (46) 8 562 000 40
Web site: http://www.netcom-systems.se

Public Company
Incorporated: 1993
Employees: 871
Sales: SEK 4.03 billion (US$510.6 million) (1997)
Stock Exchanges: Stockholm NASDAQ
Ticker Symbol: NECSY
SICs: 4813 Telephone Communications, Except Radio;
    6719 Holding Companies, Not Elsewhere Classified

NetCom Systems AB is poised to become Scandinavia's leading private provider of telecommunications services, challenging the former government-run telephone monopolies in its native Sweden and throughout Scandinavia. NetCom Systems combines a portfolio of services, including mobile telecommunications, fixed telephony services, Internet access, network systems, and cable television, under principal operating subsidiary Tele2 and its three primary divisions: Comviq, Tele2, and Kabelvision. A young company, NetCom Systems, which represents the former telecommunications holdings of Industriforvaltnings AB Kinnevik, has nevertheless quickly imposed itself on the newly deregulated Scandinavian telecommunications scene. In mid-1998 the company's Comviq GSM mobile telephone service recorded its one millionth customer. Through Tele2, the company's fixed telephony business had grown to more than 300,000 customers by the end of 1997, while the company's Internet services remain the oldest and largest in Scandinavia. NetCom Systems also has been among the first in the region to offer Internet access via satellite. Through its ownership of Kabelvision, Sweden's second largest cable television network, with 320,000 subscribers in 50 cities, NetCom

Systems is preparing to offer both Internet and extended telephony services.

The 1997 deregulation of the Danish and Norwegian telecommunications markets has opened new expansion possibilities for NetCom Systems and its brands, and the company has achieved early success in these countries, principally with the introduction of Tele2's fixed telephony services. By year-end 1997 the company recorded more than 115,000 customers in Denmark. In just the four weeks following the December 1997 deregulation of the Norwegian market, NetCom Systems added more than 25,000 customers. The company also holds a 25 percent stake in NetCom ASA, its publicly listed cellular phone affiliate in Norway. After strong revenue growth since the mid-1990s NetCom has made advances toward stable profitability. Both Comviq and Tele2, the company's primary revenue generators at 52 percent and 42 percent, respectively, have posted operating profits since 1996. NetCom Systems also has shown strong revenue growth: its sales of SEK 4.03 billion in 1997 represent an increase of 41 percent over its 1996 figures. Publicly traded on the Swedish and NASDAQ stock exchanges, NetCom Systems is led by 38-year-old president and CEO Anders Björkman.

Breaking Monopolies in the 1990s

Although formed in 1993, NetCom Systems' involvement in telecommunications began under former parent Kinnevik in the late 1970s. The pending deregulation of the Swedish and Scandinavian telecommunications markets encouraged Kinnevik to begin investing in the new technologies. With the government fixed telephony monopoly still very much in force, Kinnevik's first step was to enter the nascent mobile telecommunications market. In the late 1970s the company built its own analog mobile telephone network. Comviq AB began operations in 1981 and proved that there was a market for mobile telephones. Kinnevik's frequency allocations, however, remained limited to just 20,000 subscribers. Nonetheless, Comviq's analog system, if unable to expand, remained in operation until the mid-1990s.

While operating its analog network, Kinnevik also was investing in the emerging digital and satellite transmission tech-

---

Company Perspectives:

" 'The new nomad must be prepared to accept change in different forms, to change location and living conditions, and to see the rules of the game changing while the game is under way.'

The Swedish poet and philosopher Lars Gustafsson formulated this idea in an essay on nomadic life and the forgotten virtues of that lifestyle. His arguments that all of us—and not just a few of us—will become nomads was an important insight for me. It underscored the importance of being able to feel secure in an environment of change rather than in static structures. The quality of being able to adapt to change will continue to be a decisive strength of NetCom Systems." —Anders Björkman, President and CEO

nologies that would transform the telephone industry in the 1990s. Data transmission became technologically and commercially viable during the early 1980s, not only through traditional telephone lines, but also using satellite broadcasting technology. In 1986 Kinnevik inaugurated its own satellite link for data transmission, setting up subsidiary Comvik Skyport AB for its operations. By the late 1980s, with Swedish telephone deregulation scheduled for 1993, Kinnevik began preparing to enter the voice transmission market as well. The company's first step was a 1989 joint investment agreement with the Swedish National Rails Administration to construct a fiber optic network separate from the telephone monopoly's primarily copper wire-based network. Fiber optic cables provided the additional advantage of far greater bandwidth than traditional cables, essential for the future boom in voice, data, and video transmission. The National Rails Administration's fiber optic network later would reach more than 6,000 kilometers, connecting all of Sweden's urban population. Kinnevik's telecommunications objectives received an additional boost in 1989 when it was awarded a nationwide license to operate a GSM network. GSM, for Global System for Mobile Communications, was a European-wide collaboration to develop a digital network for voice and data transmission covering the entire continent, and beyond. During the 1980s Kinnevik added another important piece of what later would become the NetCom Systems puzzle, with the Kabelvision AB subsidiary and its cable television network. Despite competition, Kabelvision's subscriber base would grow to more than 300,000 by the 1990s.

Following upon the agreement with the National Rails Administration, Kinnevik changed the name of its Comvik Skyport subsidiary to Tele2, not only to group its increasing fixed telephony interests, but also to emphasize its goal of challenging the nation's telephony services monopoly. Tele2 began operations of its data networking services in 1991, while continuing to build its network in preparation for the coming deregulation. Also in 1991 Tele2 received its license to offer telephony services. At the same time, Tele2 discovered a new market— the Internet. Although the explosion of the Internet market would not occur until the mid-1990s—with the appearance of the graphically friendly World Wide Web—in 1991 Tele2 became the first to offer Internet access in Sweden, giving the

company a long lead ahead of competitors, including the telephone monopoly.

Kinnevik's mobile telephone subsidiary changed its name to Comviq GSM and began offering services in September 1992. One of the first GSM operators in Europe, Comviq aimed at building an extensive network of transceivers (antennas), controllers, switches, and other equipment needed to provide full coverage in Sweden. The Swedish regulatory body, the National Post and Telecom Agency, was charged with enforcing a European-wide requirement that all highways and all urban centers with populations of 10,000 or more receive mobile telephone coverage. Comviq initially focused on the most dense urban areas, before rolling out the service to the rest of the country. Initial operations remained fairly modest, however. By the end of 1992 the company had enrolled 2,000 subscribers, a number that would grow to only 21,000 by the end of the following year. With Europe slipping deeper into an extended economic crisis during the first half of the 1990s, real growth in the mobile telephone market seemed to be on hold temporarily. Nevertheless, Comviq continued investing in building its network, utilizing both its own network of radio transmission equipment and the National Rails Administration's fiber optic network.

Deregulation and the Formation of NetCom, 1993

The formal deregulation of the Swedish telecommunications market in 1993 led Kinnevik to regroup its telecommunications activities into a separate subsidiary. Called NetCom Systems AB, the new subsidiary began operations chiefly as a holding company for the former Kinnevik subsidiary Comviq. Tele2 and Kabelvision also were added to the NetCom Systems holding. With the deregulation of the Swedish market, Tele2 could at last begin offering its own telephone services. Tele2 began these operations in March 1993, with international calling services. Customers wishing to use Tele2 needed to dial 007; this requirement, viewed as giving the former government monopoly, now renamed Telia, an unfair advantage, was slated to be dropped in 1999. Also expected to be added in 1999 was telephone number portability, meaning that customers would be able to keep their telephone number regardless of the provider chosen. In 1994 Tele2 began offering domestic telephone services as well. By the end of that year the company had established itself firmly as Sweden's number two telephone company.

The year 1994 proved to be a breakthrough year for Comviq as well, as its subscriber base expanded to 136,000. By the end of 1995 Comviq's subscribers would surpass 450,000. In that year NetCom Systems began acting as an operating company, rather than a holding company. Tele2 and Kabelvision were grouped more directly under NetCom Systems. An early investor in Tele2, Britain's Cable & Wireless, which had controlled 39.9 percent of Tele2's shares, agreed to the restructuring, exchanging its Tele2 shares for a 9.2 percent stake in NetCom Systems. Both Tele2 and Comviq would register dramatic revenue growth from 1994 to 1995, boosting NetCom Systems' total sales to SEK 2 billion in 1995 compared with less than SEK 1 billion for 1994. Apart from the more than tripling of the number of Comviq subscribers, NetCom Systems was equally boosted by 1995's surge in Internet interest. While Tele2 would continue to seek the majority of its sales in telephone services, Internet access quickly became Tele2's second largest revenue source.

As NetCom Systems expanded its activities in Sweden, it also was preparing to enter the markets of its Scandinavian neighbors. Already present in Norway through a 25 percent holding in NetCom ASA, formed with the deregulation of part of Norway's telecommunications market in 1993, NetCom ASA's chief activity became mobile GSM services, adding retail activities in the mid-1990s. NetCom Systems' direct participation in the Norwegian market remained limited to Internet and data transmission services, as the company awaited full deregulation of the Norwegian system, including its telephone system, slated for January 1998. In the meantime, NetCom Systems entered Denmark, with that country's deregulation in 1996, forming Tele2 A/S. The first company to break the 100-year-old government telephone monopoly, Tele2 A/S began building its infrastructure and client base, offering domestic and international telephone services, as well as Internet access and services.

NetCom Spun Off, 1996

In 1996 Kinnevik spun off NetCom Systems as an independent, publicly traded company. NetCom Systems shares were distributed among Kinnevik's shareholders, and NetCom Systems was listed on the stock exchange in Sweden. Listing on the NASDAQ exchange would take place the following year. With the spinoff came new leadership: Anders Björkman, who had served as the company's vice-president since 1995, was named president and CEO in 1996. Under Björkman, NetCom Systems completed the transition from holding company to active operating company. Grouped directly under the newly public company were Comviq GSM AB and Tele2 AB, while the company's Kabelvision operations continued to be listed as an associated company.

Both Comviq and Tele2 continued to post impressive gains into the second half of the decade. Comviq, after seeing its subscriber base stall somewhat in 1996—hovering at 466,000—once again recorded a dramatic increase in 1997, building to more than 810,000 by the end of that year. By mid-1998 the company had recorded its one millionth customer. Aiding Comviq's growth were not only expanded GSM services, including data transmission and e-mail services, but also the successful launch of a prepaid, nonsubscription telephone credit card. The increasing popularity of GSM-based telephones in the rest of Europe also contributed to Comviq's fortunes at home, as customers moved to take advantage of a network that covered nearly the entire European continent.

Tele2 also achieved important growth in 1997, raising the number of customers to more than 310,000. In addition, Tele2 began marketing mobile telephone subscriptions based on the Comviq GSM network. At the same time, Tele2's Internet services were booming, more than doubling the number of subscribers to some 260,000, as the company maintained its position as Sweden's leading Internet services provider. Meanwhile, Tele2 began eyeing the synergy possibilities available through Kabelvision, including not only Internet access, but telephone applications as well. To strengthen these opportunities, NetCom Systems reorganized the company's operations in December 1997. All of the company's subsidiaries, including Kabelvision, now were grouped into a single subsidiary, Tele2 AB. The company's Danish and Norwegian subsidiaries, as well as its recently launched networking services subsidiary, NatTeknik, were placed under Tele2 AB. Each division would continue to operate under their well-established brand names.

NetCom and the Future

The deregulation of the Norwegian telephone system occurred on January 1, 1998. NetCom Systems, through subsidiary Tele2 Norge AS, appeared to make strong gains into the new market, adding some 25,000 customers in just the first four weeks of operation. The company also boosted its network services position throughout Scandinavia by purchasing the Swedish, Danish, Norwegian, and Finnish Datametrix operations from Innova International Corporation. After announcing its one millionth Comviq GSM customer in mid-1998, NetCom Systems continued adding products, including an enhanced version of its prepaid GSM card, and testing of satellite telecommunications services. As in most Western European countries, the deregulation of long-held government telecommunications monopolies introduced enormous new opportunities. NetCom Systems' more than two decades of experience suggested that the company was prepared to meet the competition to conquer at least its Scandinavian region.

Principal Subsidiaries

Tele2 AB (Tele2; Comviq; Kabelvision); Tele2 A/S Denmark; Tele2 Norge AS; NatTeknik; NetCom ASA (Norway; 25%).

Further Reading

"NetCom Systems Not Affected by Economic Fluctuations," *Dagens Industri,* January 15, 1997, p. 7.
"New NetCom Systems Head to Pursue Existing Strategy," *Dagens Industri,* October 2, 1996, p. 12.

—M. L. Cohen

Norelco Consumer Products Co.

101 Washington Blvd., P.O. Box 120015
Stamford, Connecticut 06912
U.S.A.
(203) 351-5000
(888) 466-7352
Fax: (203) 967-9433
Web site: http://www.norelco.com

Division of Philips Electronics North America
Corporation
Founded: 1947
Employees: n/a
Sales: $150 million (1995 est.)
SICs: 5122 Razors & Blades, 3652 Household Audio &
Video Equipment, 3635 Household Vacuum Cleaners,
3634 Electric Housewares & Fans, 3631 Household
Cooking Equipment, 3630 Household Appliances

Norelco Consumer Products Co. is a division of Philips Electronics North America Corporation, a subsidiary of Philips Electronics N.V. of the Netherlands. Norelco is a leading manufacturer of men's personal grooming products, including electric razors, beard and moustache trimmers, and hair clippers. Over the past 50 years, Norelco has achieved many key milestones and continues to lead all electric razor manufacturers. Norelco is dedicated to developing grooming solutions for men through research, leading-edge technology, and innovation.

A Late Start in the Shaver Industry

Norelco sold the first single-headed rotary electric razor in the United States in the late 1940s when Gillette, the originator of disposable blade razors, dominated the shaving industry. Its chief rivals within the electric segment at that time were Remington, Schick, and Sunbeam. Norelco's parent company, Philips Electronics North America, had first established American operations in 1933 and introduced its first razor, the Philips Philishave, in 1939.

The shaver market, whether electric or blade, had always been consumer-driven, with purchasers making selections based largely on brand recognition and loyalty. Thus, as a relatively late entry in the shaver market, Norelco focused its competitive energies on advertising. Since most electric razor sales occurred in the year's fourth quarter, at holiday gift-giving time, Norelco put large amounts into its fourth quarter ad campaign in an attempt to decisively influence gift purchases.

The 1950s were good years for electric razor manufacturers as a whole. Electric razor sales peaked in 1956 at about $140 million, and sales for Norelco increased in keeping with the upward trend. A leader in electric razor innovation, Norelco introduced its Speedshaver, a double-headed rotary razor that featured a pop-up trimmer for sideburns and moustaches and "microgroove" shaving heads in the 1950s. Yet by 1961, the industry had shrunk to less than $100 million, a decline blamed primarily on Gillette, which aggressively marketed its disposable razors and stole potential business away from the electrics.

Advertising Success in the 1960s

Norelco entered the 1960s with 18 percent of the diminished electric market, ranking fourth in its category, behind Remington and Schick, each with 30 percent, and Sunbeam with 20. During this decade, Norelco began to increase its advertising budget and to build its campaign around sports programming. Dedicating more than 50 percent of its $3 million in advertising to broadcast television, Norelco focused on the NFL games, with promotions accompanying the ads: free footballs, a book about professional football, sweepstakes for trips to the playoffs, and the Super Bowl games. From football, Norelco branched out to other sports events, becoming a year-round advertiser, while still continuing its emphasis on fourth quarter advertising. In 1961, it launched its well-known, long-running holiday campaign, which featured Santa riding a razor across a snowy landscape and calling the brand "Noelco."

Shortly after the Santa campaign took off, Richard Kress, the man who would lead Norelco to dominate the electric razor market and who would head the company for nearly three decades, came aboard as head of advertising for the company in

1963. The enigmatic and energetic Kress, who became president in 1971, held an MBA in business administration from Wharton and had a background in advertising, yet claimed to be a bad speaker. To overcome his "handicap," he staged stunts to motivate his sales force, such as rappelling down buildings, flying across streets as "Norelco Man," and once went a few rounds with a professional boxer at a yearly sales convention. The quixotic executive doubled the ad budget to $6.2 million, adding sponsorship of horse racing's Triple Crown and such popular television shows as "Smothers Brothers," "Mission: Impossible," "My Three Sons," "The Carol Burnett Show," "Lost in Space," "Gunsmoke," "Gilligan's Island," "Candid Camera," and "The Ed Sullivan Show." Kress's new marketing methods, accompanied by improved shaver technology and greater acceptance of electric razors by women, spurred a mid-1960s upswing in sales of electric shavers. Seven million razors were sold in 1965, of which Norelco seized the lion's share.

The Leader in a Declining Market in the 1970s

After the FTC ruled that advertisers could name the competition in the 1970s, the long-term rivalry among the shaver industry's top competitors became public. Schick ran an ad in 1973 claiming that lab tests proved that its Flexamatic shaved closer than Norelco's VIP Tripleheader. The ad was part of a campaign geared at increasing Schick's 8.3 percent share of the then $175 million electric market to 20 percent by year-end. Norelco, number one with a little less than 50 percent of the market, responded by challenging the test's methodology and filed a lawsuit, along with Remington, then number three with about 33 percent. Identifying the competition did nothing, however, to help Schick; the National Advertising Review Board ruled in 1974 that the Schick ads were "false in some details" and "misleading in overall implications." Schick's market share dropped by 1975, while Norelco's fate improved. Despite a general decline in electric razor sales from early 1970s highs of 5.5 million to 4.5 million by 1975, Norelco increased its share of the smaller pool. This overall decline was attributed to a number of factors, including the economy; the popularity of competitive gadgets, such as the pocket calculator; the huge ad budgets backing wet shave systems; and public confusion following the shaving closeness wars.

Secure with its growing lead in the electric market, Norelco turned to take on Gillette in the wet shave market with its "We beat the blades" campaign. It backed its challenge by advertising: "We dare any blade to match shaves with a Norelco," and an ad budget that, by the end of the 1970s, had risen to $10 million. A visually direct attack on wet shaving systems, the 1974 "Gotcha!" campaign, showed a man getting nicked by a blade razor, and may have contributed as much as a ten percent increase to Norelco's growing command of the market—from 48 percent in 1974 to 58 percent in 1975. Tests conducted by an independent research organization, billed as the "most intensive consumer and laboratory testing ever developed for the product category," also helped to support Norelco's claim that its electric razors gave a shave as close as blades. The competitive tactic succeeded where Gillette's had failed and helped make Norelco the first choice among electric shaver buyers.

By the close of the 1970s, an estimated 30 to 35 percent of the American shaving population used electric razors and Kress

announced in *Advertising Age* that the electric razor market had shaken off its bitter internecine ad rivalry and was "beginning to grow again." By 1978, Norelco was selling more than three million men's shavers and 450,000 women's razors annually, capturing an estimated 60 percent of the market segment. In that year, Norelco chose to invest more than $20 million to campaign for a host of new products headed by its premium-priced line of Silver Rotary Razors, which it pitted against Gillette's new wet-shave razor. It purchased longtime rival Schick, began to market men's and women's bladed razors under the Schick brand name, and extended its "Gotcha!" campaign to its new Solid State Charge Rotary Razor, the first to convert automatically to any electrical current in the world.

Product Innovation, Diversification and Reorganization in the Early 1980s

Norelco pursued product innovation and diversification in the early to mid-1980s. Seeking to capitalize upon the aging of the American population and its increased health consciousness, it introduced many new items in the area of healthcare, such as blood pressure testing machines, electronic digital scales, and a vibrating board to provide back relief. As early as the 1970s, Norelco had introduced its coffeemaker, a direct competitor for the Mr. Coffee machines, to whom it ran second in market share. Now it added other kitchen appliances, such as toaster ovens and food processors, and irons, its biggest success.

In the area of personal care, Norelco introduced its Rotatract Lift and Cut Rotary Razor in 1980, advertised as "Twin blade closeness with no 'Gotcha.'" This put Norelco in direct competition with the wet shave industry. It later brought out its Chic and Satin lines for women: a curling brush, compact hair dryer, and a brush/massage head for the shower, and further segmented its market with the introduction of the "Black Pro" shaver designed to lift curly whiskers and meet the needs of black men via a custom-engineered "razor bump." It also added its Man Care collection of hair dryers and shoe polishing kits, leveraging off its share of the electric market.

Much of this innovation was spurred by the increasingly competitive nature of the market in the mid-1980s once Remington, Ronson, and Braun began to sell both shavers and kitchen appliances in the United States. Norelco's market share in razors dropped to 56 percent by 1985 in the United States, and in Canada, where competition came from Braun as well as Remington, its market share dropped from 60 percent in 1980 to 45 percent in 1986. Braun's pressure came at the high end of the market, while the others came especially in the low- and mid-priced segments. Norelco responded by upgrading its product line, as well as by adding low-priced shavers in 1985, backing up its razors with a 25 percent increase in consumer advertising, 60 percent of which was allocated to TV and 40 percent to print ads. However it found the introduction of less expensive products hurt sales and profits since its bestselling razor was not its traditional $55 shaver but its new $19 model. It thus quickly dropped its lower-end razors in favor of higher-priced, higher-styled units, shifting its emphasis from price to product.

When Richard Kress suddenly resigned as president of consumer products in 1986, profits were down in both the electric razor and coffee machine markets for Norelco, where Braun had also pushed the upper end. That year saw major restructuring at Norelco, which had gone from $100 million in sales in 1968 to $250 million during Kress's tenure. U.S. Appliances, which marketed Schick razors and had been under the aegis of the Norelco Consumer Products Division, was transferred to the Philips Home Products division, which had been created in 1986 to launch a full-line of Dutch-made appliances. Kress continued as corporate advisor to North American Philips, while John Beggs became president in 1987, followed in 1991 by Patrick Dinley.

The original rationale for creating the Philips Home Products Division had been to provide a distinctive identity for the company's higher-end products. However, in 1988, in order to take advantage of economies of scale and savings in distribution, U.S. Appliances was transferred back to Norelco, which resumed marketing and administrative responsibilities for Schick electric shavers and Philips small appliances. This change was accompanied by a series of others at Norelco. From 1987 to 1989, it increased its ad budget threefold from 10 to 30 million and, at the same time, cut in half the number of products it offered, exiting all of its markets except men's and ladies's shavers, coffeemakers, steam irons, and clean-air machines.

Continued Diversification and Innovation

By the early 1990s, advertising levels had risen across the shaver industry to meet the growing high-end market. Norelco reintroduced its old Santa spots in 1992, updated with the latest computer animation, and, in 1997, it added sponsorship of the NHL Stanley Cup Playoffs, with accompanying advertising in print. By the mid-1990s, Norelco, with an ad budget of $30 million, was spending more than the rest of its competitors combined. The men's market had reached $357 million wholesale ($160 million retail) by the late 1990s, while the women's market was a $63 million wholesale category.

Norelco's new generation of razors continued to reflect the trend toward upgraded products. Its three distinct Tripleheaded shaving systems: the company's Reflex Action, Micro Action, and Double Action, all had Norelco's Lift & Cut technology and many had pop-out trimmers for beards, moustaches, and sideburns; some were battery powered, others rechargeable. In 1996, it expanded its Silhouette series of women's shavers, upgrading the line with additional features such as ergonomic design, a bikini trimmer, and rechargeable and/or battery options. In 1995, Norelco added its Maverick line of beard trimmers.

Norelco continued to diversify into other product lines as well in the 1990s. In 1993 it debuted its Satinelle Hair Removal System for women, promoted via infomercial. In 1995 it introduced a line of dental care products and its Voyager line of travel items, including irons, garment steamers, a styling brush, a travel razor, alarm clocks, and a hot beverage maker. It also

expanded its line of kitchen electrics, made by Philips N.V., marketing an assortment of high-end and volume-oriented products. In 1995, Philips purchased bankrupt Regina vacuums for $17 million to provide its products entry into the U.S. floor care market and assigned responsibility for distribution, sales, and marketing of Regina products to Norelco. In 1997, Norelco launched sound conditioning machines, Norelco Natural Sounds, and electric aromatherapy diffusers, called Norelco Natural Aromas, along with Naptime Sounds for its Baby Sound Selector.

Norelco's ventures in the realm of beauty and wellness products reflected its desire to appeal more to a female audience. These personal care products were marketed under the Philips brand name. Yet at the same time, Norelco was rolling out new packaging for its mainstay—men's grooming products—which continued to be sold under a newly designed Norelco label. Norelco was once again reinventing its marketing strategy, positioning itself to gain access to a larger portion of its markets, while relying, as always, upon brand recognition and heavy advertising to sway consumers its way.

Further Reading

Eckhouse, Kim, "Philips and Norelco Unwrap New Packaging," *HFN—The Weekly Newspaper for the Home Furnishing Network*, June 29, 1998, p. 43.

Fanelli, Louis A., "Norelco Aiming to Slice into Wet Shave Market," *Advertising Age*, June 9, 1980, p. 4.

Frinton, Sandra, "New Rule at Regina," *HFN—The Weekly Newspaper for the Home Furnishing Network*, June 26, 1995, p. 29.

Gittlitz, Ian, "Norelco Pumps Dollars into Home Health Care," *Housewares*, June 7, 1983, p. 3.

——, "Norelco: Using Brand Name to Get New Markets," *Housewares*, March 27, 1984, p. 1.

"Kress Successor to Face Challenge of Maintaining Norelco," *HFD— The Weekly Home Furnishings Newspaper*, October 20, 1986, p. 59.

Millstein, Marc, "Norelco Looks to the 90s: Banks on Strategy of Consolidation, Innovation," *HFD-The Weekly Home Furnishings Newspaper*, December 4, 1989, p. 64.

"NAP Restructures Genie for Small Appliances Move," *HFD-The Weekly Home Furnishings Newspaper*, April 21, 1986, p. 85.

Perry, Brian, "N.A.P. Shifting Two Philips Lines," *HFD-The Weekly Home Furnishings Newspaper*, November 9, 1987, p. 1.

——, "Norelco: Ready to Recharge," *HFD-The Weekly Home Furnishings Newspaper*, November 30, 1987, p. 1.

Phillips, Lisa E., "DMB&B Charged for Norelco Task," *Advertising Age*, March 16, 1987, p. 39.

Purpura, Linda M., "Norelco Kitchen Appliances Set for Expansion in 1991," *HFD-The Weekly Home Furnishings Newspaper*, March 5, 1990, p. 1.

——, "Norelco's Santa Rides Again," *HFD-The Weekly Home Furnishings Newspaper*, October 19, 1992, p. 92.

Ratliff, Duke, "Shaver Ads for Yule," *HFD-The Weekly Home Furnishings Newspaper*, November 7, 1994, p. 42.

—Carrie Rothburd

Northwest Airlines Corporation

5101 Northwest Drive
St. Paul, Minnesota 55111-3034
U.S.A.
(612) 726-2111
Fax: (612) 727-7617
Web site: http://www.nwa.com

Public Company
Incorporated: 1926 as Northwest Airways
Employees: 49,000
Sales: $10.23 billion (1997)
Stock Exchanges: NASDAQ
Ticker Symbol: NWAC
SICs: 4512 Air Transportation, Scheduled

Northwest Airlines Corporation is the holding company for Northwest Airlines, Inc., described as "America's oldest carrier with continuous name identification" and the world's fourth oldest airline. It has flown across the Pacific for 50 years, more than anyone else. Northwest serves as the United States' northern regional air carrier, and flies 1,700 flights each day to 400 cities in 80 countries. More than 97 percent of the revenue of Northwest Airlines Corporation comes from Northwest Airlines, Inc.

Roaring to Life in the 1920s

After passage of the Kelly Airmail bill in 1926 the Ford Transport Company, a subsidiary of the auto manufacturer, was awarded the Chicago to St. Paul airmail route. They commenced business on June 7 of that year, but a series of airplane crashes over the summer forced Ford to sell the company to Northwest Airways by October. Northwest ran Ford's open-cockpit, single-engine biplanes until the winter weather compelled them to cease operations. In the spring of 1927 Northwest resumed business. By July the company was hauling passengers on their short trunk routes. Once again, however, the harsh northern winter obliged them to close for the season.

During the flying seasons of 1928 to 1933 Northwest secured an expansion of routes through the Dakotas and Montana, and eventually to Seattle, Washington. The man largely responsible for the company's westward growth was Croil Hunter. While Hunter only occupied a position in middle management, it was his initiative to enter new markets and win new airmail routes that gave Northwest its early preeminence. By 1933 Hunter was vice-president and general manager of the airline.

In the years before World War II Northwest directed its expansion eastward to New York. The company survived the government's temporary suspension of airmail contracts in 1934 with virtually no loss in business, and began operating mail services and passenger routes along the northern corridor. Moreover, new and modified airplanes enabled Northwest to continue operations through the winter. The planes were modified further when it became obvious that finding light-colored, downed planes in the snow was a difficult task. The tail fins of all the company's planes have since been painted a bright, contrasting red. In 1937 Croil Hunter, who had been credited with the airline's success, was named president of the company.

In the attempt to establish northern routes to Asia, Northwest pilots made expeditions to Alaska and across the Aleutian Islands. The northern route had been passed up by Pan Am, which was unable to win landing rights in the Soviet maritime provinces and Japan. Instead, Pan Am decided to open a route to the Philippines and China, via Hawaii and Guam. Pan Am crossed the ocean first, but Northwest held the promise of a faster route.

When the Americans became involved in World War II in 1941, Northwest was chosen to operate the military support routes to the strategically important Aleutian Islands. The airline's experience with cold weather aviation and its predominance in the region made it a logical choice. The Army Air Corps flew its C-46s, C-47s, B-25 and B-26 bombers directly from the production line to Northwest facilities in Minneapolis, Minnesota, and Vandalia, Ohio, in order for them to be modified for cold weather and long distance routes. Northwest's expertise in this area contributed significantly to the effectiveness of the Allied war effort.

During the war passenger flights were strictly limited to people with priority status. Regardless of the suspension of commercial business, however, Northwest benefited from the war. With a healthy military allowance from the War Department, Northwest improved its facilities and upgraded its technology.

Postwar Competition

When the war ended Northwest lobbied the Civil Aeronautics Board to award the airline rights to fly to the Orient from Alaska. This so-called "great circle" route was actually about two thousand miles shorter than Pan Am's transpacific route. When Congress rejected airline magnate Juan Trippe's proposal to make Pan Am America's international flag carrier, the Civil Aeronautics Board was free to certify Northwest for "great circle" routes to the Orient.

With the government's reaffirmation of competition within the industry, all the companies hurried to modernize their airline fleets. It was both a matter of cost-efficiency and prestige. Northwest looked to the Martin Company, with its new 202 airliner, to replace the aging DC-3 model, and complement the company's fleet of Boeing 377 Stratocruisers. The Stratocruiser, with its lower level bar and intimate "honeymoon suites," was extremely popular with newlyweds and business travelers. The Martin 202, however, did not remain in service for very long; its reputation for malfunctioning became widespread. Fortunately, the 202 was quickly replaced with the new DC-4.

When the Korean War started in 1950, Northwest employed many of its DC-4s to assist the United Nations forces. They ferried men and transported equipment, including bomber engines and surgical supplies, to various points in Japan and Korea. The military utilization of the airline, which lasted for several years, was carried out without any interruption of its regular commercial services.

In 1952 Hunter relinquished the presidency to Harold R. Harris, but retained his position as chairman of the board. After two uneventful years Harris was replaced by Donald Nyrop. After he received his law degree, Nyrop served in the military transport group during World War II. Later, he headed the Civil Aeronautics Board. For many years after joining Northwest he set an austere tone for the organization. For example, the Minneapolis headquarters was located in a large windowless building that he planned would become a maintenance hangar at some point in the future. Nyrop also had a chart showing the inverse relationship between the number of vice-presidents and profits. Needless to say, Northwest had a minimal number of vice-presidents.

On the other hand, Nyrop brought Northwest into the jet age quickly, purchasing the Lockheed L-188 prop-jet Electra, the DC-8, and the Boeing 707 and 727. Through the early 1960s Northwest consolidated its service across the northern United States and along the "great circle" to its Asian destinations. Profits were consistent and growth remained slow and cautious.

Perhaps the one outstanding event of the period occurred on Thanksgiving Eve of 1971. A man who identified himself as Dan Cooper boarded a Northwest 727 in Portland, Oregon, bound for Seattle, Washington. He claimed to have a bomb and demanded $200,000 and two parachutes. His demands were met and the airplane departed. Somewhere over southwestern Washington, at about 25,000 feet, Cooper ordered the airplane's rear bottom door opened. He walked down the stairs and jumped into the densely clouded, cold and black night. Cooper and most of the money were never found. He was, however, rumored to have died in a New York hospital in 1982.

In 1978, after 24 years in charge, Donald Nyrop retired. He was replaced by Joseph M. Lapensky, an accountant who was promoted from within the company. Many industry analysts expected Lapensky to continue Nyrop's management policy. In fact, Lapensky must be regarded as an interim figure, one who represented a definite but subtle change in direction for the company.

Soaring Under Deregulation

Lapensky inherited the leadership on the eve of deregulation. For many of the large airlines the new era of competition resulted in the loss of large amounts of revenue. Northwest, however, was quite firmly established in its various markets, and remained largely unchallenged. Lapensky's most important problem, however, was the ruptured state of labor relations which resulted from his predecessor's attempts to weaken the unions. In one instance, when Northwest employees threatened to strike, Nyrop decided to confront the unions. He enlisted the help of a 15-airline mutual aid fund established to enable the companies to withstand the effects of a long-term strike. When Nyrop realized the effort was stalemated, he gave in to union demands. Nyrop's union problem became Lapensky's union problem, and before long Lapensky retired.

In October 1983 Steven G. Rothmeier became Northwest's new president. Rothmeier gained Lapensky's favor after writing a paper on a deregulated airline market as a student at the University of Chicago. Rothmeier's case study of Northwest had so impressed people at the airline that they offered him a job in 1983. Like Lapensky, he rose through the company, albeit quickly, to the top executive position. Under new management the airline formed a holding company, Northwest Airlines, Inc., which assumed responsibility for the airline and its subsidiaries. On January 1, 1985, Rothmeier was named chief executive officer, confirming his position as the leader of Northwest.

In 1985 United Airlines proposed to buy the Asian and Pacific routes of Northwest's competitor Pan Am. Rothmeier led the opposition to the sale, arguing that it would leave only two airlines competing in Asia. Northwest invested many years of negotiation and costly waiting to achieve and maintain its Pacific markets. According to Rothmeier, it was hardly fair that

United could simply purchase a competitive share. Regardless of the opposition, the sale of Pan Am's Asian routes to United was approved in 1986.

Northwest, which had suffered from not having a computerized reservations system, purchased a large share of TWA's PARS system, which the two companies jointly operate. The company has also made arrangements with four smaller independent airlines to generate more "feeder" traffic to Northwest.

In 1986 Northwest purchased its regional competitor Republic Airlines. The $884 million sale barely won federal approval since the two airlines operated many of the same routes. At first the Civil Aeronautics Board was concerned that Northwest would operate monopolies in too many markets. Republic had established hubs in Detroit and Memphis, in addition to Minneapolis. However, Republic's north-south route structure provided the ideal "feeder" for Northwest's longer-haul east-west structure, despite a certain amount of overlap. As a result of this merger, John F. Horn was named president of Northwest and NWA, Inc. Rothmeier, still chief executive officer, assumed the position of chairman, vacant since Lapensky's retirement in May 1985.

Prior to the merger, Republic flew to over 100 cities in 34 states, Canada, and the Caribbean. Northwest's network covered 74 cities in 27 states and 16 countries in Western Europe, the Far East, and the Caribbean. Until the purchase of Republic Airlines, Northwest had always been "underleveraged," or virtually free of debt. Northwest's management used to be proud of this fact, but came to recognize that, for tax and other purposes, it was good to carry "some debt."

In 1989 financiers Alfred Checchi and Gary Wilson bought control of Northwest in a $3.65 billion leveraged buyout deal, after which the airline became a private company. One year later, former Beatrice CEO Frederick Rentschler was named Northwest's new CEO. One of the first tasks facing the new management was rectifying the service record of the airline, whose poor service and on-time performance record in recent years led dissatisfied business travelers to give it the unfortunate nickname "Northworst." Flush with optimism over the company's future, Checchi and Wilson embarked on a program of acquiring the assets of other airlines and committed $450 million through the year 1995 to improving service. They purchased Eastern Airlines' Washington, D.C. hub, bought Asian routes from Hawaiian Airlines, and made their desire to deal further well-known—at various times, they began negotiations to buy all or major portions of Continental, Midway, and Qantas.

However, Northwest was soon struck by business and image setbacks. Two 1990 incidents—the conviction of several Northwest pilots for flying under the influence of alcohol and a runway collision of two Northwest jets, killing eight, which was later blamed on crew error—tarnished the airline's public reputation further. The airline's hopes to expand through acquisitions proved hampered by its $4.2 billion debt, the product of the leveraged buyout coupled with debt extant from the purchase of Republic, which left the airline with a negative net worth. Moreover, Northwest was hit by the general financial troubles that affected the industry in the late 1980s, including

rising fuel costs, declining traffic caused by a weakening economy, and pricing wars. In 1990 and 1991, when these problems were exacerbated by recession and war in the Middle East, Northwest lost $618 million. As leading airline United began aggressive expansion into the Pacific market, Northwest's inability to match United's purchases left it vulnerable in its traditionally strongest area.

Management attempted a number of plans to raise operating funds, including pursuing incentive funds from the state of Minnesota, in which the airline is based; in 1991, the company received $835 million in aid from the state for opening two maintenance bases there. In order to stave off bankruptcy, the company also embarked on an aggressive cost-cutting campaign, cutting service by a third at its Washington, D.C. hub and seeking concessions from its six unions, although many of its workers already received wages below the industry average.

Northwest appeared to have escaped the catastrophic effects of recession and deregulation that felled such competitors as Eastern and Pan Am, but its massive debt left it at a disadvantage at a time when other airlines were employing a strategy of buying routes and expanding globally. However, Checchi and Wilson's creative debt-cutting measures and their expenditures to improve the airline's service record bore some fruit: in 1991 the airline finished first in on-time performance, a category in which it had been dubbed the worst.

In 1992 Northwest and KLM Royal Dutch Airlines applied to the United States Transportation Department to merge the operations of the two companies and function as one. Since the United States had recently signed a treaty with the Netherlands allowing companies a good deal of leeway, the Transportation Department approved the combination, allowing Northwest and KLM to coordinate prices, available seats, sales forces, and data, while sharing revenues. An added bonus was the injection of KLM's equity stake in the company. The alliance nearly doubled the pair's share of transatlantic traffic, to 12 percent.

Fortunately for Northwest, the industry pulled out of its slump by 1994. A public stock offering early in the year reflected investors' optimism. Northwest posted revenues of $8.33 billion for the year and income of $830 million. These figures rose to $9.09 billion and $902 million in 1995.

New Horizons for the New Century

Although the Northwest/KLM alliance proved fruitful for investors on both sides of the Atlantic—Wilson and Checchi's 20 percent stake grew from $40 million to nearly $1 billion and KLM's $400 million investment reached a value of $1.6 billion—a bitter power struggle unfolded behind the scenes. KLM's overtures for more control of Northwest prompted Wilson and Checchi to insert "poison pill" provisions into Northwest's charter preventing KLM from acquiring more than its 19 percent share of the company. This in turn prompted a lawsuit from KLM, which also lobbied to loosen the regulations preventing foreign companies from owning controlling interests in U.S. airlines. In addition, KLM President Pieter Bouw's separate discussions with the pilots' union—the two parties together controlled half of Northwest—infuriated Wilson, according to *Fortune*.

Even this relationship could be mended, however. Bouw resigned as KLM president in May 1997. By August, KLM had dropped its poison pill lawsuit and agreed to sell back its Northwest shares gradually through the year 2000. The working bonds seemed as strong as ever: the pair announced their considerable cargo operations would cooperate more closely, and the expanded KLM alliance gave Northwest a passage to India (via Amsterdam) beginning in June 1997.

At the same time, Northwest's Pacific operations were threatened by political forces abroad. Northwest had already suffered from an excess of capacity in Japan, and the Japanese government sought to curtail the carrier's rights to fly passengers beyond Japan to other Asian destinations. Nevertheless, Northwest's $10.23 billion in revenues brought in a net income of $596.5 million. At approximately $2 billion, its debt had been reduced to half the 1993 level.

A strike by Northwest pilots, eager to claim their share of the company's bounty and opposed to various management strategies, finally grounded the airline in late August 1998. Northwest laid off 31,000 employees during the crisis and did not resume full operations until September 21. The shutdown resulted in a $224 million loss for the third quarter of 1998 on revenues of $1.93 billion (the carrier had earned $290 million in the third quarter of the previous year).

Although its confrontations with KLM and its labor problems seemed to have been resolved, Northwest would have to successfully navigate the U.S. government's interests as well as those of the Japanese. Northwest's announced intentions to purchase control of Continental Airlines, the fifth largest U.S. carrier, prompted scrutiny from the Justice Department, as did its "predatory" price competition against budget carriers such as Pro Air and Reno Air.

Principal Subsidiaries

Northwest Airlines, Inc.; Northwest Aerospace Training Corporation (NATCO); NWA Leasing, Inc.; NWA Aircraft Finance, Inc.; Northwest Capital Funding Corporation; Montana Express; Northwest Aircraft, Inc.; MLT Inc.; Northwest PARS Holdings, Inc.

Further Reading

Davies, R.E.G., *Airlines of the U.S. Since 1914*, New York: Putnam, 1972.

De Young, Dirk, and Tim Huber, "Northwest Deal Will Boost Cargo," *Minneapolis-St. Paul CityBusiness*, August 1, 1997.

Gwynne, S.C., "Flying into Trouble," *Time*, February 24, 1997.

Jackson, Robert, *The Sky Their Frontier: The Story of the World's Pioneer Airplanes and Routes, 1920–1940*, Airlife, Ltd., 1983.

Johnson, Tim J., "Northwest Strike Sparks PR Battle," *Minneapolis-St. Paul CityBusiness*, September 7, 1998.

Kelly, Kevin, "A Midcourse Correction for Northwest," *Business Week*, July 13, 1992.

Laibich, Kenneth, "Winners in the Air Wars," *Fortune*, May 11, 1987.

"Negotiations Leave Northwest Airlines Circling," *Corporate Report-Minnesota*, August 1997.

Tully, Shawn, "The Big Daddy of CFO's," *Fortune*, November 13, 1995.

Tully, Shawn, and Therese Eiben, "Northwest and KLM: The Alliance from Hell," *Fortune*, June 24, 1996.

Zagorin, Adam, "Hunting the Predators," *Time*, April 20, 1998.

Zellner, Wendy, "How Northwest Gives Competition a Bad Name," *Business Week*, March 16, 1998, p. 34.

—John Simley and James Poniewozik
—updated by Frederick C. Ingram

Norwood

Norwood Promotional Products, Inc.

106 E. Sixth Street, Suite 300
Austin, Texas 78701
U.S.A.
(512) 476-7100
Fax: (512) 477-8606
Web site: http://norwood-promotional.com

Private Company
Incorporated: 1973 as Radio Cap Company
Employees: 1,900
Sales: $175.84 million (1997)
SICs: 3161 Luggage; 2353 Hats, Caps & Millinery; 2759
Commercial Printing, Not Elsewhere Classified; 3086
Plastics Foam Products; 3085 Plastics Bottles; 3949
Sports & Athletics Goods, Not Elsewhere Classified;
2329 Men's & Boys' Clothing, Not Elsewhere Classified;
2339 Women's, Misses', & Juniors' Outerwear, Not
Elsewhere Classified; 5085 Industrial Supplies

Norwood Promotional Products, Inc. is the leading player in the highly fragmented promotional products marketplace. Norwood, through the companies in its two divisions, manufactures or customizes a variety of products which are imprinted with the names of businesses and generally given away as a form of advertising. Sales of promotional products total nearly $10 billion annually in the United States, and there are several thousand companies in the field, many of them small "mom and pop" operations. Norwood's strategy has been to acquire other companies whose products are complementary in an attempt to become a "one stop" source of goods. The company went public in 1993, but following several years of disappointing results, it was taken back off the market in a merger with a newly formed corporation backed by founder Frank Krasovec.

Beginnings

Norwood's origins date to 1973, when the Radio Cap Company was founded in San Antonio, Texas. Radio Cap produced caps which were customized with names of different businesses, which then typically gave them away as part of a promotional campaign. Promotional products such as these were widely used by businesses and salespeople as a way of keeping a company's name before its customers. In giving them a useful item such as a pen, calendar, cap, etc. which would be used over time, the hope was that the customer would better remember the advertiser's name and come back for more business. There was no single large promotional products supplier nationwide, and products were mainly produced by small regional companies. Typical orders would only be worth several hundred dollars, and the range of products requested varied widely. Products were sold through regional distributors, who obtained stock from a number of different suppliers. Many items were manufactured overseas and then imprinted with advertisers' names by companies in the United States. Key factors in the promotional products business were price, quality, and timely shipment of products, with many orders requiring quick turnaround.

In 1976 Frank Krasovec, along with several other investors, purchased Radio Cap. Krasovec, whose background included experience in a variety of businesses including cable television and real estate, bought out his partners in 1983, giving the name Norwood to the new holding company into which Radio Cap was placed. Shortly after this, the manufacturer of Koozie beverage insulators was added to the Norwood stable. This logo-imprinted plastic foam giveaway product, into which a cold beverage container could be placed, was a popular promotional item, and would be a mainstay of the company's product line for years to come. Manufacture of other promotional products, including mugs and glassware, was added over time at the Radio Cap plant in San Antonio.

In October 1989, Krasovec restructured and recapitalized Norwood, at which point the company's name was officially changed to Norwood Promotional Products, Inc. Norwood continued to gradually expand its product line, adding a range of imprinted writing instruments by 1991. In May 1992, the company acquired Barlow Specialty Advertising, Inc., a manufacturer of recognition awards and other promotional products, some marketed under the Salm name. The latter were fancier,

Company Perspectives:

The Company's business strategy is to continue to improve its market position in each of its existing product lines and to expand into new product lines and distribution channels. Key elements of this strategy include: (i) expanding product offerings by developing new products and innovative imprinting and decorating techniques and applications; (ii) increasing penetration of existing markets through enhanced customer service and coordinated marketing efforts among its operating companies; (iii) making selective acquisitions to add new product lines and expand distribution; (iv) introducing new management and operating systems to reduce order processing times, increase production efficiency and increase processing capacities of existing and acquired businesses; and (v) exploring new markets, primarily through international marketing and alternative distribution arrangements.

more expensive items, and gave Norwood a wider price range of goods to offer. Other Barlow wares included keychains and money clips. Norwood also purchased a ceramic mug imprinting facility located in Pittsburgh in early 1993.

Summer 1993: Norwood Goes Public

An initial public offering of stock on the NASDAQ exchange took place in June 1993, as Norwood sought money to refinance and repay debts, and to further expand. Krasovec would retain his positions of chairman and CEO, and keep about 18 percent of the company's stock, with Robert Whitesell continuing as COO and president, with a three percent stock interest. Following the offering, Norwood began negotiations for several acquisitions. The company purchased Key Industries, Inc. and ArtMold Products Corporation in May and July 1994. Key was an established supplier of inexpensive promotional paper, pen, magnet, button, and plastic items, while ArtMold focused on golf-related products, higher-priced writing instruments, and other desk accessories.

Norwood's acquisitions continued in 1995, with purchases of The Bob Allen Companies (subsequently renamed Air-Tex Corp.) in March, Designer Plastics, Inc. in June, BTS Group, Inc. in July, and Ocean Specialty Manufacturing Corp. in November. Bob Allen/Air-Tex was an Iowa company that specialized in promotional sportswear, luggage, gun cases, and accessories. Designer, also known as Designer Line, produced promotional bags, while BTS was a maker of special awards, recognition gifts, and other items. Ocean (renamed The California Line by Norwood) made a range of products including memo and cork boards, buttons, magnets, and other desk accessories.

Norwood's annual sales had been rising steadily, with its fiscal 1989 sales total of $26.6 million increasing to $103.9 million in 1995. The company's net profits generally kept pace, growing from $1.2 million to $4 million. Along with the increased revenues generated by its new acquisitions, Norwood was enjoying the benefits of strong growth within the promo-

tional products marketplace. Estimated annual U.S. sales of promotional products grew from $5.3 billion in 1992 to $7 billion in 1995, and continued to rise. Norwood also was expanding its product line and increasing the number of distributors it supplied, reaching a majority of the over 10,000 distributors of promotional products by the mid-1990s. In 1995 the company published its first catalog of corporation-wide "best sellers." Norwood was also recognized that year by the promotional products industry association as the number one company in the United States in sales. December 1995 saw a secondary offering of stock, with 2.75 million shares made available to secure more funds for debt repayment.

Acquisitions continued apace in 1996, with Tee-Off Enterprises, Inc. purchased in January and Alpha Products, Inc. in April. Tee-Off was a custom imprinter of golf balls, and also produced other golf-related products. Alpha, formerly a subsidiary of Aladdin, Inc., made imprinted insulated drinkware, and its acquisition served to strengthen Norwood's Koozie line of beverage insulators, which remained the leading seller in its family of products. Alpha also had a retail sales division, a first for Norwood. However, it soon became apparent that the company's capabilities in this area had been exaggerated, and a year later Norwood sold off that part of Alpha's operation.

In August 1996, following apparent difficulties integrating its Ocean Specialty and Designer Line businesses, and predicting lower quarterly earnings, Norwood announced it was restructuring. Sales and marketing functions were realigned, and two pairs of the company's subsidiaries were merged. Air-Tex Corp. (which had previously been combined with Designer Line) was folded into the Radio Cap Co., while ArtMold (which also controlled Tee-Off) was subsumed by Key Industries, Inc. Other acquisitions had previously been aligned in this way, so that Norwood was left with a total of three direct subsidiaries, which it called divisions, the other being Barlow Promotional Products, Inc. CEO Krasovec, in a conference call with stock analysts, remained upbeat, claiming that Norwood was in the "best shape we've been in," and anticipated annual sales of $500 million in as little as five years' time.

1997–98: Acquisitions Continue; Norwood Goes Private

Following an aborted attempt to acquire a German promotional products company, Norwood completed two further purchases in February 1997, buying Wesburn Golf and Country Club, Inc., and DM Apparel, Inc. Wesburn's line of imprinted golf balls gave Norwood the lead in the promotional golf ball game, when added to the company's Tee-Off business. DM Apparel, a jacket company, further extended Norwood's clothing offerings. With revenues continuing to fall below expectations in 1997, the company decided to make further changes, and realigned its management structure in August. Robert Whitesell resigned his posts of president and COO, with Krasovec adding the president position to his CEO and chairman roles. He had sold his remaining real estate interests in July 1996 to devote his complete attention to Norwood. The company's limited retail operations also were sold or closed, leaving sales of Norwood's 2,400 plus products completely up to the more than 11,000 distributors it now serviced. A further consolidation of the company's operating divisions realigned these into two, Radio Cap Co. and Barlow. The company's corporate office, which had remained in San Antonio, Texas, was moved to Krasovec's home base of Austin.

Though the company was still making a profit, Norwood's stock had been stagnant for some time. Citing his frustration with the apparent indifference of investors, Krasovec decided to take Norwood private again. Forming a new limited liability company called FPK LLC, Krasovec announced in March 1998 a plan to purchase Norwood's outstanding shares of stock for $20.70 a share. FPK formed a unit which would merge with Norwood, the latter continuing as the name of the surviving company. Krasovec stated that, "The completion of this transaction is a significant event in Norwood's history. By being a private company, the managers of the Norwood family of supplier companies will be better able to collectively and individually direct resources to provide creative solutions and service to our customers in these fast changing times." Following the approval in August of the company's shareholders, the transaction was completed by the end of October.

Norwood Promotional Products, having grown into a stronger, more diverse company, and the largest single supplier of promotional products in the United States, appeared poised for greater success with its restructuring of operations and return to private ownership. The promotional products marketplace was still highly fragmented, but continued to expand as advertisers recognized the value of such products in their overall promotional mix. Frank Krasovec, Norwood's founder and longtime chief, was now devoting his full attention to the company, and had an experienced management team on board. With all of these elements in place, it seemed likely that Norwood would regain its momentum and continue on an upward trajectory as the 1990s drew to a close.

Principal Subsidiaries

Air-Tex Corp.; ArtMold Products Corp.; Barlow Promotional Products, Inc.; BTS Group; Concept Enterprises, Inc.; Key Industries, Inc.; Radio Cap Company.

Further Reading

Breyer, R. Michelle, "Dominance Isn't a Gimme; Savvy Propels Promotional Materials Maker Norwood," *Austin American-Statesman*, January 26, 1996, p. D1.
——, "Norwood Sees Third-Quarter Earnings Dip," *Austin American-Statesman*, August 16, 1997, p. D2.
——, "Weak Wall Street Showing Prompts Norwood to Return to Private Life," *Austin American-Statesman*, March 17, 1998, p. D1.
Fohn, Joe, "Norwood Promotional Products, Inc.," *San Antonio Express-News*, January 19, 1997, p. 29G.
Haines, Renee, "Hip on Hype—Norwood Promotional Products Catching Investors' Attention," *San Antonio Express-News*, March 26, 1995.
Levaux, Janet Purdy, "The New America: Norwood Promotional Products, Inc., San Antonio, Texas—Leading with Products That Raise Profiles," *Investor's Business Daily*, February 22, 1996, p. A6.
Menshesa, Mark, "Norwood Secures Large Loan Package," *San Antonio Business Journal*, November 4, 1994, p. 6.
"Norwood Promotional to Sell Alpha Products in Restructuring Effort," *Dow Jones Online News*, August 12, 1997.
Nowlin, Sanford, "Norwood Plans $20 Million Public Offering," *San Antonio Business Journal*, May 21, 1993, p. 1.
Windle, Rickie, "Wall Street Darling in a Gimme Cap," *Austin Business Journal*, February 2, 1996, p. 10.

—Frank Uhle

1-800-FLOWERS, Inc.

1600 Stewart Avenue
Westbury, New York 11590
U.S.A.
(516) 237-6000
(800) FLOWERS; (800) 356-9377
Fax: (516) 237-6060
Web site: http://www.1800flowers.com

Private Company
Incorporated: 1987
Employees: 2,500
Sales: $300 million (1997 est.)
SICs: 5992 Florists

1-800-FLOWERS, Inc., headquartered in Westbury, New York, is one of the world's largest florists. Recognized for the quality of its flowers and customer service, the company guarantees the freshness of its floral arrangements for one week. As a leading integrated marketer, the company maintains 150 franchised and company-owned retail stores, 2,500 domestic affiliates, 1,300 overseas affiliates, a web site (www. 1800flowers.com), and other interactive services through 15 electronic retail partners, including America Online. A phone order system also is available 24 hours a day, seven days a week. The company's retail outlets, designed to resemble European flower shops, are located in such major markets as New York, Los Angeles, Chicago, Dallas, Atlanta, San Francisco, San Diego, Orlando, San Antonio, St. Louis, and Phoenix.

James McCann: Social Worker Turned Florist

1-800-FLOWERS was transformed from a small struggling business into a successful international operation by James McCann. As a young man living with his family in Queens, New York, McCann had initially hoped to become a police officer and studied at John Jay College of Criminal Justice in New York in the 1970s. He eventually became a social worker, however, accepting a job as the administrator of a youth home in Rockaway, New York. Finding that he needed to supplement his income from social work, he also went into business for himself in 1976, purchasing Flora Plenty, a small flower shop, using $10,000 that friends and relatives had lent him. "In the early days," McCann explained in *Forbes,* "you have no choice; you have all of your net worth in the business. I was running a cash business with a cigar-box mentality. I would never be able to give a bank a financial statement, because I had no clue. But I knew that if I wanted to build an enterprise with some legacy value, I had to make the leap into the legitimate world, doing everything the way you're supposed to."

McCann's little shop grew into a 14-store chain earning about $50,000 a year by the 1980s. McCann then made Flora Plenty a C Corporation and put himself on the payroll. Using his real estate and stock market assets—as well as mortgaging his home (several times)—McCann acquired 1-800-FLOWERS in 1987. Headquartered in Dallas, Texas, 1-800-FLOWERS was then struggling financially, losing about $400,000 monthly.

McCann paid $7 million for the poorly managed 1-800-FLOWERS, then spent another $9 million covering the company's debts and liquidating assets. Nevertheless, McCann was able to turn the company around, largely by marketing flower delivery through telephone orders. At first, 1-800-FLOWERS utilized FTD, a florist delivery cooperative with thousands of members, including McCann's company. Thus, 1-800-FLOWERS retained a 20 percent fee from each order placed through FTD. In 1993, however, FTD launched a floral phone service of its own, and McCann positioned 1-800-FLOWERS to compete directly with FTD. Using previously untapped toll-free telephone technology, McCann capitalized on consumers' needs for convenience and competitive pricing. McCann offered his customers a seven-day freshness guarantee, as well as a 100 percent satisfaction guarantee. He also established a Frequent Flowers Club for repeat customers. While FTD's service lost approximately $13 million during this time, 1-800-FLOWERS had achieved $100 million in annual sales by 1993.

The Business Takes Root by 1992

Over time, McCann contracted new affiliates and established telecenters throughout the United States. As technological advancements permitted, he also became active in electronic retailing. In 1992, 1-800-FLOWERS launched its first online store site on CompuServe's Electronic Mall. Eventually the company joined with a strategic Internet development partner, Fry Multimedia of Ann Arbor, Michigan, to create a site driven by Microsoft Site Server Commerce. By the end of 1997, ten percent of the company's annual sales came from interactive marketing—about $30 million—and *PC Magazine* recognized the company's web site as one of the top 100 web sites in 1997.

In October 1994, 1-800-FLOWERS purchased the Conroy's Flowers franchise system, established in 1961 and headquartered in Long Beach, California. One of the larger retail floral chains in the western United States and with the most stores in the 1-800-FLOWERS retail system, Conroy's Flowers played an important role in the company's success. For example, *Entrepreneur Magazine* named Conroy's/1-800-FLOWERS the best floral franchiser in its 1996 listing of top 500 franchisers. (Considered one of the foremost small business magazines, *Entrepreneur* began ranking franchises in 1980. By 1996, its Franchise 500 list was viewed as an authoritative source about the franchise industry in America, if not the world.)

In August 1995, 1-800-FLOWERS established a toll-free telephone number for its customers around the world. In cooperation with AT&T's USADirect 800 service, the florist provided customers in more than 130 countries with the technology to purchase flowers and gifts for friends and relatives in the United States without paying international and in some cases local telephone charges. By utilizing AT&T Language Line operators, 1-800-FLOWERS communicated with customers in more than 20 languages, a great convenience for U.S. citizens traveling abroad, business professionals, and U.S. military personnel stationed overseas.

The 1995 Documercial

During the 1995–96 holiday season, 1-800-FLOWERS initiated its first documercial. A combined infomercial and documentary, *The Fresh Flower Half Hour* appeared in three large markets in early morning and late night time slots. On December 4, 1995—as part of the company's $30 million marketing plan—1-800-FLOWERS launched the half-hour television program covering the operations of the company, floral care, and home decorating. Appearing for the Christmas holiday buying season, *The Fresh Flower Half Hour* aired on network affiliates in New York, Phoenix, and San Antonio markets before national broadcasting.

Entertaining and informative, the half-hour program profiled the business activities of 1-800-FLOWERS, including coverage of its Floraversity training program and procedures for handling and caring for flowers. *The Fresh Flower Half Hour* also featured home decorating advice and four two-minute direct response opportunities to purchase a holiday flower tree arrangement.

Sales for the 1995–96 Christmas season broke records for the company. Though retail sales nationally had been uneven or disappointing for many retailers, 1-800-FLOWERS saw its sales grow 39 percent over the previous year's. The company also enjoyed strong sales during the Valentine's Day holiday in 1996, accumulating an increase of 32 percent above sales for 1995.

Among the reasons for the increased sales were population and consumer attitude shifts. Industry observers noted that aging baby boomers were becoming more accepting of sending flowers as gifts, and more women, in particular, were buying flowers as gifts for others. While in the past most flower purchasers were men, busier lifestyles demanded more convenient forms of gift-giving just when sending flowers became easier. Fortuitously, 1-800-FLOWERS offered its customers service by telephone, via interactive media, or in person at one of the 150 company-owned/franchised retail stores throughout the United States.

The company's sales from Mother's Day—the highest volume sales day in the floral industry—increased 31 percent from 1995 to 1996. Sales and order volumes for this holiday—traditionally about 16 percent of the company's annual revenue—swelled in all of the florist's marketing platforms. Telephone calls broke the million mark, setting a record for the company, and interactive sales increased by 314 percent over the same time for the preceding year. December 1996 online sales exceeded those of the previous year by three times, and web site sales increased tenfold.

Interactive Marketing in 1997

By 1997, 1-800-FLOWERS conducted about ten percent of its business through interactive marketing online. The company expected its share of the online market to grow as additional convenience-conscious customers became more familiar with new technologies. Thus, the florist developed a system of online gift reminders to save customers the embarrassment of forgetting a birthday or anniversary. Based on this program's success, 1-800-FLOWERS also started mailing reminder postcards—about 100,000 monthly in 1997.

To compete more effectively in the interactive market, 1-800-FLOWERS contracted with Network Computer, Inc., a subsidiary of Oracle Corporation, to install 2,000 of the company's computers—connected to an NC Enterprise Server—at 1-800-FLOWERS establishments in April 1997. The first corporate client to adopt Ellison's Oracle-backed Java computing system in place of a mainframe terminal environment, 1-800-FLOWERS then operated seven telecenters throughout the nation.

Within a few months, 1-800-FLOWERS announced a new four-year agreement with America Online. As that service's exclusive online florist, the company anticipated more than $250 million in sales from this arrangement. The florist also redesigned its award-winning web site, the fifth revision of the site in three years, to facilitate holiday shopping in November 1997. Changes to the site included a one-click-to-product process that simplified shopping online. Specifically, this streamlined process allowed customers to order merchandise from the web site's home page; in the past, online shoppers needed to browse through several pages before placing an order. The new system offered web site visitors faster service and greater convenience in an effort to turn more browsers into buyers.

In addition, the web site now included an updated look and expanded content; for example, the site featured a new registration area, an expanded floral reference and how-to area, a retail store locator, and information on the company's franchising efforts. The company also planned to add more features to the web site in January 1998, notably real-time credit card authorization.

In December 1997, 1-800-FLOWERS introduced an enhanced version of its BloomLink system to network online with its franchisees. BloomLink initially served as a vehicle for order processing, but partnering with AT&T, 1-800-FLOWERS transformed it into a web-based communications system that offered basic ordering capabilities, a home page on the web for individual florists, online training programs, e-mail and chat groups, and wholesale purchase opportunities with farms worldwide. As a comprehensive, open architecture system, BloomLink allowed florists to interact with other communication networks or point-of-sales systems with software provided by 1-800-FLOWERS at no charge.

December 1997 sales through the Internet reached a record-setting $4 million, about ten percent of the company's total holiday sales. Customers placed approximately 80,000 orders through the company's web site and through online services such as America Online, the Microsoft Network, and CompuServe. In all, Internet sales rose 150 percent from the preceding year, with men representing two-thirds of the online buyers.

With nine million customers nationwide in 1997, 1-800-FLOWERS neared sales of $300 million. The increased growth in sales—about 25 percent since 1996—prompted 1-800-FLOWERS to open new stores in New Hyde Park, Selden, West Babylon, Bay Ridge, and Brooklyn, New York, and on Manhattan's East Side—with more outlets planned.

Entering the Catalog Market: 1998

1-800-FLOWERS entered the catalog market in 1998 with the purchase of an 80 percent interest in Plow & Hearth, a home-and-garden products marketer. Plow & Hearth founder Peter Rice continued to administer the 18-year-old company as a subsidiary of the florist.

In 1998 1-800-FLOWERS also added a new management level. Owing to its consistent growth and expansion over the years, the company appointed four employees to serve as vice-presidents: Donna Iucolano, director of interactive services; Bill Shea, company treasurer; Tom Hartnett, director of store operations; and Vinnie McVeigh, director of worldwide call center operations. (Previously, Chris McCann, brother of Jim McCann, held the only vice-president position, and he became a senior vice-president at the time of the new appointments.)

The Future

Jim McCann—who won much recognition for his work at the florist, being named Direct Marketer of the Year, Retailer of the Year, and Entrepreneur of the Year—talked of making 1-800-FLOWERS a public company in the future. He hoped to triple the company's size as well. He told *LI Business News:* "We just want to get bigger and better at what we do at a pace we could handle."

Principal Subsidiaries

Teleway; Plow & Hearth (80%).

Further Reading

Campbell, Tricia, "The Drama of Selling," *Sales & Marketing Management,* December 1997, p. 92.

"In Online Odyssey, 1-800-FLOWERS Lands on Microsofts's Plaza Mall," *Interactive Marketing News,* November 15, 1996.

Johnson, Stephen S. "Flower Power," *Forbes,* July 4, 1994, p. 144.

Martorana, Jamie, "New Management Team Blooming at 1-800-FLOWERS," *LI Business News,* July 27, 1998, p. 9A.

McCann, Jim, "Building Relationships On-Line Is True Promise of Interactive Marketing," *Marketing News,* October 27, 1997, p. 10.

——, *Stop and Sell the Roses,* New York: Ballantine Books, 1998.

McCune, Jenny C., "On the Train Gang," *Management Review,* October 1994, p. 57.

McKenna, Patrick. "Ellison's Network Computers Heading to 1-800-Flowers," *Newsbytes,* April 7, 1997.

Miller, Paul, "Flowering Hearth: 1-800-FLOWERS Buys 80 Percent of Plow & Hearth," *Catalog Age,* May 1998, p. 5.

Oberndorf, Shannon, "Flower Power Half Hour," *Catalog Age,* March 1996, p. 28.

"Online: 1-800-FLOWERS," *Report on Electronic Commerce,* January 14, 1997.

Pellet, Jennifer, and George Schira, "This Bud's for You," *Chief Executive* (U.S.), March 1997, p. 24.

"Ringing up Sales with Cable," *MEDIAWEEK,* March 27, 1995, p. S30.

Warshaw, Michael, "Invest in Yourself; Get Professional Help and Diversify Your Fortune, Says the Owner of Industry Giant 1-800-FLOWERS," *Success,* April 1997, pp. 27–28.

—Charity Anne Dorgan

O'Reilly Automotive, Inc.

233 South Patterson
Springfield, Missouri 65802
U.S.A.
(417) 862-6708
Fax: (417) 874-7145
Web site: http://www.oreillyauto.com

Public Company
Incorporated: 1957
Employees: 7,000
Sales: $316.39 million (1997)
Stock Exchanges: NASDAQ
Ticker Symbol: ORLY
SICs: 5013 Motor Vehicle Supplies & New Parts; 5531
   Automobile & Home Supply Stores

O'Reilly Automotive, Inc. sells a variety of new and re-manufactured auto parts, accessories, equipment, and supplies to both "do-it-yourself" (DIY) customers and professional car mechanics and service technicians (professional installers). A small portion of its business consists of selling parts wholesale to independent auto parts stores. O'Reilly also provides machining services but does not do any other repair services or sell tires. A family firm, O'Reilly serves customers in mainly smaller communities in the Midwest and the South. Operating about 500 stores in ten states, O'Reilly in 1998 was one of the nation's top ten auto parts chains.

Origins

O'Reilly Automotive was founded by the descendants of Michael Byrne O'Reilly, an Irishman who fled the terrible potato famine in 1849. He came to St. Louis, earned a law degree, and worked as a title examiner.

His son was the first in the family to work in the auto parts industry. Charles Francis O'Reilly began in 1914 as a traveling salesman for Fred Campbell Auto Supply in St. Louis. In 1927 Charles's request for a transfer to the Springfield, Missouri area was granted. By 1932, in the depth of the Great Depression,

Charles was a manager of Link Motor Supply and his son Charles H. "Chub" O'Reilly already had worked two years for Link. The father and son provided the crucial leadership to make Link the main auto parts store in the Springfield region.

In 1957 Link planned to retire Charles F. O'Reilly, age 72, and reassign his son Chub O'Reilly to Kansas City as part of a corporate reorganization in which Link was bought by Meyers Motor Supply in Joplin, Missouri. In a phone interview, Chub O'Reilly said he did not want to live in Kansas City because it was "too big" with all its "hustle and bustle" and heavy traffic. In addition, he did not want to uproot his family and be separated from those he loved.

Hence, the father and son broke away from Link and formed their own company. They founded O'Reilly Automotive in November 1957 with 12 employees, some of whom owned stock in the new firm. Charles F. O'Reilly was the first president, and Charles H. O'Reilly was the vice-president. In Springfield they rented their first building at 403 Sherman, an old structure they extensively remodeled. With the help of some excellent salesmen who also left Link, sales at O'Reilly reached $700,000 in 1958, the company's first full year in business.

When it began operations, O'Reilly Automotive faced the challenge of persuading major brand auto parts companies to sell them parts. Link Motor Supply Company tried to stop the manufacturers from selling to O'Reilly, but the O'Reilly founders gained the cooperation they needed because of their many years of working closely with the manufacturers' sales representatives. Early in its history, then, O'Reilly was able to sell A.C. Delco batteries and other brand name products.

In 1957 O'Reilly Automotive sold almost all its items wholesale to various garages and industrial customers who employed professional mechanics or installers. Gradually, however, they sold more parts retail to individuals who wanted to fix up their own cars.

Growth from 1960 to 1989

In October 1960 O'Reilly started Ozark Automotive Distributors to buy parts directly from manufacturers and then distribute those parts to O'Reilly and to independent automotive jobbers in

---

Company Perspectives:

O'Reilly Automotive intends to be the dominant supplier of auto parts in our market areas by offering our retail customers, professional installers, and jobbers the best combination of price/quality provided with the highest possible service level. In order to accomplish this mission, O'Reilly will provide a benefit and compensation plan that will attract and keep the kind of people who will enable the company to reach its goals of growth and success.

---

the Springfield area. The following year O'Reilly Automotive's and Ozark's combined sales reached $1.3 million.

At first O'Reilly Automotive grew slowly. For example, its initial branch store in Springfield was not opened until July 1965. Ten years later, in 1975, O'Reilly's annual sales reached $7 million, and the company built a new 52,000-square-foot warehouse at 223 South Patterson in Springfield to serve its nine stores, all located in southwest Missouri. Chub O'Reilly said building the company's first warehouse was a "tremendous change." Later the firm increased the capacity of the Springfield distribution center to 297,000 square feet and built other distribution centers in Kansas City, Missouri (93,183 square feet) and Oklahoma City (122,800 square feet). By 1980 all four of Chub O'Reilly's children (Charles, Lawrence, and David O'Reilly and Rosalie O'Reilly Wooten) had become leaders in the growing family business.

In the early 1980s modest expansion occurred. In February 1983 O'Reilly opened its first store outside of Missouri in Berryville, Arkansas, a small town close to the southern Missouri border and thus close to the other O'Reilly stores. The Berryville store, the firm's 38th store, was gained as part of a seven-store acquisition of a parts company based in Harrison, Arkansas.

In 1986 the company decided for the first time to start stores in cities with more than 100,000 people. In August 1986 O'Reilly opened its first store in the Kansas City, Missouri metropolitan area. Eventually O'Reilly operated stores in other cities, such as Omaha, Oklahoma City, Tulsa, Des Moines, Wichita, and Kansas City, Kansas, but the firm continued its basic strategy of locating most of its stores in smaller communities.

Growth in the 1990s

O'Reilly became a public corporation in April 1993 with the initial public offering of its stock. The following year the company began to remodel stores to conform to a standardized design featuring better lighting, increased parking, higher ceilings, and separate counters for professional installers.

In 1997 O'Reilly added ten new stores in both Nebraska and Oklahoma, eight in Kansas, seven in Iowa (the first in that state), four in Missouri, and one in Arkansas, for a company record high of 259 stores. As of December 31, 1997, O'Reilly owned 131 of those stores, leased 69 from others, and leased 59 stores from O'Reilly family real estate investment partnerships. With 1997 product sales of $316.4 million, up 22.1 percent

from 1996, and 1997 net income of $23.1 million, an increase from 1996 net income of $19 million, O'Reilly proclaimed in its annual report that 1997 was "Our best year ever." Other statistics supported that conclusion, for the firm's total assets ($247.6 million) and stockholders' equity ($182 million) reached record levels. Also in 1997, O'Reilly conducted a two-for-one split of its common stock. At the end of 1997 O'Reilly employed 3,945 nonunionized individuals at its parts stores, distribution centers, and headquarters, but a major expansion was imminent.

In January 1998 the firm spent $47.8 million, or $4.35 per common share, to complete the acquisition of the Houston-based public company called Hi-Lo Automotive, Inc. (NYSE: HLO), which had sales of about $238 million for the year ending on December 31, 1997. The merger came after Hi-Lo ended its announced merger with Discount Auto Parts, Inc. Donaldson, Lufkin & Jenrette Securities Corporation advised O'Reilly on this merger, and NationsBank provided the financing. The St. Louis law firm of Gallop Johnson & Neuman, L.C. gave O'Reilly legal counsel on this and other concerns.

The purchase of Hi-Lo furnished O'Reilly with 189 new stores in California, Texas, and Louisiana. Hi-Lo's properties also included a 375,000-square-foot distribution center in Houston. As soon as the deal was complete, O'Reilly began converting Hi-Lo stores to the new owner's systems and strategies. Chub O'Reilly said that this was a major challenge, in part because the company had to replace Hi-Lo's older computers with new IBM computers. With good advance planning, however, this conversion took place rapidly as about 200 Team O'Reilly members left headquarters to supervise the changes at the Hi-Lo stores.

In April 1998 O'Reilly sold its seven Hi-Lo California stores to a competitor, Auto Parts Wholesale, doing business as Carquest of California. "The sale of these stores will allow us to concentrate our efforts on Hi/Lo's core business in Texas and Louisiana," stated President and Chief Operating Officer Larry O'Reilly in an April 30 press release.

The Hi-Lo acquisition, by far the largest in O'Reilly's history, propelled the company into the ranks of the nation's top ten auto parts chains. At the end of the first quarter ending March 31, 1998, O'Reilly operated 460 stores in nine states: Arkansas (17), Illinois (one), Iowa (ten), Kansas (46), Missouri (111), Nebraska (11), Oklahoma (78), Louisiana (17), and Texas (169). The company planned in 1998 to add another 38 stores, as well as its fifth distribution center in Des Moines, Iowa, a warehouse with 160,000 square feet. O'Reilly estimated its 1998 sales would exceed $615 million. O'Reilly also planned to open 80 new stores in 1999.

O'Reilly's competitors in the do-it-yourself market included chains such as Pep Boys, AutoZone, Parts America (formerly called Western Auto), independent stores, car dealerships, and large discount stores (like K-Mart) that carried auto parts. Competing in the professional installer market were car dealers, AutoZone, independent stores, and national warehouse distributors and associations, such as Carquest, Parts Plus, and the National Automotive Parts Association (NAPA).

O'Reilly felt in 1998 that it was prepared to expand and thus help consolidate what it called in its 1997 10-K SEC Report a "still highly fragmented" industry. The ability of chains like

O'Reilly and its major competitors to engage in efficient purchasing, inventory, and advertising because of economies of scale gave them a major advantage over small independent parts dealers. The chains also could spend more money on training their store personnel, a necessity as cars became more and more complex with the use of microcomputers and other high-tech electronics. The days of the simple "grease-monkey" were long gone.

O'Reilly's inventory management and distribution system was a good example of a modern high-tech operation. Each O'Reilly store was linked by computer to a distribution center. Bar codes enabled the company to record automatically when a part was sold and then order a replacement part from a distribution center. O'Reilly had an inventory of more than 105,000 SKUs (stock keeping units), so the necessity of such a computerized system was obvious.

Like other firms, O'Reilly worked to make sure its computer systems were prepared to deal with the "millennium bug" and thus be able to recognize the year 2000. The firm's management expected the Y2K project to be "substantially complete by early 1999," according to its 1997 annual report.

To keep its customers happy, O'Reilly started its "Right Part, Right Price, Right Now" policy, which gave customers a five percent discount on the retail price if one of the company's 15,000 most commonly requested items was not available immediately. Items usually were available from another store or a warehouse within 24 hours. According to O'Reilly annual reports, "The Company believes that its principal strengths are its ability to provide both the DIY and Professional Installers same day or overnight availability to more than 105,000 SKUs."

O'Reilly served its professional installer customers by using vans or small trucks to deliver parts and supplies, granting trade credit to qualified individuals, employing sales representatives specializing in the professional installer market, and conducting seminars on technical, safety, and business issues. The firm also published *Tech Talk* three times a year, *Tools & Equipment* twice a year, and the *Finisher's Choice* (paint and body catalog) quarterly for its professional installer market.

The company relied on purchasing parts and supplies from about 350 vendors, including name brand companies such as A.C. Delco, Gates Rubber, Prestone, Quaker State, STP, Armor All, and Turtle Wax. Most products were covered by manufacturers' warranties, but O'Reilly also provided warranties on some products. O'Reilly sold some of its own private label parts as well.

For several years O'Reilly has sponsored race cars as part of its advertising program. At state fairs, smaller local races, and major shows, O'Reilly has promoted its name and image on stock cars and high-powered race cars. For example, in June 1998 the 27th annual O'Reilly Spring Nationals were held at the Tulsa International Raceway. On its web site, O'Reilly listed the dates of more than 100 events between June and November 1998 at which the company was sponsoring contestants, including some truck and tractor pulls and bike racing competitions.

In 1998 O'Reilly remained a family firm. Its officers included Chub O'Reilly, chairman emeritus; Charlie O'Reilly, board chairman; David O'Reilly, president and chief executive officer; Larry O'Reilly, president and chief operating officer; Rosalie O'Reilly Wooten, executive vice-president; and Ted Wise, executive vice-president.

The auto parts industry has recognized the leadership of O'Reilly officers. The Automotive Warehouse Distribution Association honored David O'Reilly and the *Automotive Aftermarket* magazine presented both David and Larry O'Reilly with Retailers of the Year awards. Such recognition was based in part on the fact that O'Reilly Automotive consistently had increased its annual sales and net income from 1989 through 1997. Based on that financial performance and the major acquisition of Hi-Lo in 1998, O'Reilly Automotive seemed well prepared to continue its role as a major auto parts supplier in its chosen markets.

Principal Subsidiaries

Ozark Automotive Distributors, Inc.; Hi-Lo Automotive, Inc.

Further Reading

"O'Reilly Auto Parts History," July 21, 1996, http://www.oreillyauto.com/history.html.

—David M. Walden

Owens-Illinois, Inc.

One Sea Gate
Toledo, Ohio 43666
U.S.A.
(419) 247-5000
Fax: (419) 247-1132
Web site: http://www.owens-illinois.com

Public Company
Incorporated: 1907 as The Owens Bottle Machine
    Corporation
Employees: 32,400
Sales: $4.66 billion (1997)
Stock Exchanges: New York
Ticker Symbol: OI
SICs: 3089 Plastic Products, Not Elsewhere Classified;
    3221 Glass Containers

Owens-Illinois, Inc. is one of the largest manufacturers of glass containers and plastic packaging in the world. About half of the glass containers made worldwide are made by Owens-Illinois. It holds the top position in glass containers in the United States, North America, South America, Australia, New Zealand, and India, and the number two position in Europe (behind Compagnie de Saint-Gobain). In 1997, 71 of overall sales stemmed from glass. The remaining revenue was generated from the company's plastics group, which is a leading worldwide maker of plastics packaging, including containers, closures, prescription containers, labels, and multipack carriers for beverage bottles. With 144 manufacturing plants in 24 countries, an increasingly global Owens-Illinois generates about 37 percent of sales outside the United States.

Early History

The Toledo-based company was incorporated in Ohio in 1907 as The Owens Bottle Machine Corporation, the successor to a New Jersey firm of the same name founded in 1903. It took the name Owens-Illinois Glass Company following the 1929 merger of Owens Bottle and the Illinois Glass Company of Alton, Illinois, a small manufacturer of glass products for the drug and medical fields. Like most can and bottle making companies, Owens-Illinois weathered the years of the Great Depression without a production slowdown. Throughout the 20th century the container industry as a whole proved itself to be almost unaffected by dramatic swings in the economy.

In 1935 Owens-Illinois acquired the Libbey-Glass Company and entered the consumer tableware field. The Libbey division was responsible for making tumblers, glass pitchers, dishes, and bowls. Soon afterward Owens began conducting experiments with glass fibers, learning that one of its chief competitors, Corning Glass, was doing similar research. The two firms agreed to cooperate and formed Owens-Corning Fiberglass in 1938. Development of marketable fiberglass products quickly followed. Corning and Owens, with their virtual monopoly on fiberglass technology, profited greatly. Following a 1949 antitrust ruling that barred Corning and Owens from controlling Owens-Corning, the joint venture was taken public in 1952, with shares distributed, one-third each, to Owens, Corning, and the public. Subsequently, both Owens-Illinois and Corning Glass sold their shares in Owens-Corning.

During the period immediately following World War II, Owens-Illinois remained primarily a glassmaker, its few deviations from the bottle business being limited to those areas on the immediate periphery of glass containers. This was all soon to change, however. A number of antitrust rulings in the late 1940s restricted companies such as Owens-Illinois from increasing market share through wholesale acquisitions of subsidiaries in their respective industries. Growth, it seemed, would have to come from fields outside glass.

Meanwhile, from 1948 through 1958, Owens-Illinois made asbestos pipe and boiler insulation under the brand Kaylo. Though it sold this fairly small business to Owens-Corning in 1958, the company's production of an asbestos-laden product would result in extended litigation in the 1980s and 1990s.

Company Perspectives:

Owens-Illinois is one of the world's leading manufacturers of packaging products. It is the largest manufacturer of glass containers in North America, South America, and India, and the second largest in Europe. Approximately one of every two glass containers made worldwide is made by Owens-Illinois, its affiliates, or its licensees. The company's plastics group manufactures a wide variety of plastic packaging items including containers, closures, trigger sprayers, finger pumps, prescription containers, labels, and multipack carriers for beverage containers.

Owens-Illinois is the leader in technology, the high-productivity/low cost producer, and the leading supplier in almost all of the markets it serves.

Diversification in the 1950s and 1960s

The first significant diversification move came in 1956 when Owens purchased the National Container Corporation, America's third largest box maker at the time. The move into forest products, though gradual, was as predictable as it was necessary. It made good economic sense to make a forest products company part of the Owens-Illinois holdings. Not only was the parent firm supplied cardboard boxes at reduced rates, but the paper and pulp sector turned profits of its own.

In the 1950s Owens-Illinois took another step outside the glass container field, into a promising new area—plastics. The company had for some time made plastic caps and closures, but up until the mid-1950s the technology for making plastic containers was not available. This changed very quickly.

Most popular at that time was the plastic squeeze-bottle which could be used as a container for prepared mustard and other sauces. Owens-Illinois, however, directed its energy toward semirigid plastic containers, and this strategy was successful. In 1958 Owens-Illinois persuaded a number of large bleach and laundry detergent companies to switch to the new bottles. The plastic bottles were immediately popular with consumers and continued to gain favor during succeeding decades. Each year plastic containers claimed a more substantial share of counter space in American supermarkets.

Despite the important advances in paper and plastics, the company was still very much committed to glass manufacturing. The 1960s were years of tremendous growth in both can and bottle manufacturing. Although the two industries were rivals for the growing consumer beverage market, there was enough soft beverage and beer business for all the container companies. The intense competition was for the lion's share, and the initial demand for the new pop-top can seemed to relegate glass containers to a distant second place.

Then the ever bothersome returnable bottle, with its thick glass and mandatory deposit, gave way to the lighter "one-way" bottle. The new construction ushered in a renaissance for the glass industry, allowing it to challenge the can

industry more effectively. Since the one-way bottle was not returned for refilling it could be made of thinner glass. This meant production cost and production time were reduced, thereby increasing profit margins. Although many industry analysts thought the glass beverage container was destined to failure in the early 1960s it did not surrender its market share to the pull-tab can; bottle sales tripled that decade.

Still, Owens-Illinois was aware that diversification efforts would have to be accelerated if growth was to continue. The burgeoning of the beverage market during the 1960s was not to be repeated, and expansion in glass manufacturing slowed considerably. The company involved itself in such far-removed fields as sugar cane farming in the Bahamas and phosphate rock mining in Florida. During the late 1960s Lily Tulip Cups, maker of everything from wax-lined milk cartons to disposable cups, was acquired. Moves such as these prompted Owens-Illinois to drop the word "glass" from its corporate name, becoming Owens-Illinois, Inc.

Modernizing Facilities in the 1970s

As beverage sales leveled off in the 1970s, the container industry found itself in the midst of a worldwide recession. Many large can and bottle customers, which included large breweries and soft drink companies, began manufacturing their own containers. Many can and bottle manufacturers had unwisely increased the size of their container-producing facilities and were now confronted with overcapacity, an unwieldy workforce, and tumbling prices. The problem was particularly acute in bottle manufacturing where production was more labor-intensive.

Owens-Illinois attempted to solve this problem through technology, investing in new industrial equipment that could make 20 bottles in the time it used to take to make six, and therefore cutting labor costs. Also, the company dedicated more factory space, often entire plants, to single product lines for one customer. However, these were stop-gap measures and did not solve the overall problem. Wholesale modernization was necessary.

As Owens-Illinois entered the 1980s its production costs advantage, once the envy of the industry, had been eroded. While the company developed revolutionary new container machinery, it allowed the majority of its conventional glass plants to deteriorate. Edwin D. Dodd, the company's chief executive officer, divested marginal interests, which were draining resources and performing poorly, and supervised a $911 million four-year plant modernization program.

More importantly, the company's attitude toward its own industry changed, particularly regarding bottle manufacturing. Historically a large volume dealer concerned with maintaining its huge market share, Owens-Illinois began to emphasize profit margins rather than its share of the bottle manufacturing market. Unprofitable plants, even relatively new ones, were closed or sold; production of the two-way returnable bottle was discontinued in favor of the exclusive manufacture of the "one-way" bottle; and the minimum order level was raised while the customer base was reduced to a number of large-volume, blue-chip customers. The results of this policy were impressive.

Capacity was reduced by 24 percent and the workforce was cut by 30 percent. Owens-Illinois was again able to reclaim its productive edge over competitors.

Owens-Illinois's regard for the natural environment drew the attention and praise of consumer advocate Ralph Nader. In his 1971 study on water pollution, Nader cited Owens-Illinois as the industrial company with the best record on environmental issues. The compliment was well-deserved. The company's glass factories were among the safest and cleanest in the business; it led the industry in recycling; and it advocated a national system of resource recovery to deal with the mounting solid waste problem.

Owens-Illinois environmental policies came about largely through the work of a former chief executive officer, Raymond Mulford, who died in 1973. He had encouraged community participation on behalf of his staff and factory workers and devoted nearly half of his time in later years to social and environmental programs. Most company plants were located in small towns, and Mulford insisted they be an asset, not a liability, to the community. This meant confronting the issue of pollution control long before it was a national concern.

By the early 1980s the modernized Owens-Illinois company was the most formidable member of the glass container industry. It outproduced its competitors by 33 percent. Yet, to increase profit margins and efficiency, company operations were streamlined. The company invested heavily in research and developed production methods that reduced the labor content of a finished glass product from 40 percent to 20 percent. A total of 48 plants were closed and 17,000 workers laid off. The jobs of 46,000 other employees, however, were saved.

Many of Owens-Illinois's rivals did not spend the money necessary to compete. Thatcher Glass, once number two in the industry, went bankrupt in 1981, its failure the product of a poorly executed leveraged buyout and an unwillingness to rebuild old furnaces and install new technology. Other manufacturers, such as Anchor-Hocking and Glass Containers Corporation, found themselves in similar predicaments.

Robert Lanigan, the CEO of Owens-Illinois during the 1980s, emphasized the manufacture of plastic bottles and the increasingly popular plastic-shield glass bottle. He also continued the diversification program and acquired two nursing home chains and the Alliance Mortgage Company, a mortgage banking concern. Owens-Illinois's policies were aimed at reducing the company's vulnerability to a takeover. Since the container industry was a mature, slow-growth one, return on stockholder's equity was, in the mid-1980s, less than ten percent. Thus Owens-Illinois's stock price was well below book value; at the same time, it had an attractive annual cash flow of $300 million.

KKR Leveraged Buyout in 1987

In the end, Lanigan's efforts could not stave off a takeover. On December 11, 1986, Kohlberg Kravis Roberts & Company (KKR), a holding company specializing in taking firms private, offered to purchase Owens-Illinois for $55 per share. Owens-Illinois refused the offer and threatened to initiate a reorganization, including the sale of over $1 billion in assets, in order to protect the company from subsequent takeover attempts. KKR responded by raising its bid to $60 per share. When investment houses acting on behalf of Owens-Illinois failed to find buyers willing to outbid KKR, Owens-Illinois officials were forced to negotiate.

In mid-February 1987, Owens-Illinois announced that it had agreed to be acquired by a KKR subsidiary, the Oil Acquisition Corporation, for $60.50 per share, or about $3.6 billion. In order to finance the leveraged buyout a number of banks agreed to extend a short-term, or "bridge," loan of $600 million to KKR, to be paid back over 18 months through an issue of high-yield bonds.

KKR had first established a relationship with Owens-Illinois in 1981, when it purchased cupmaker Lily Tulip from Owens-Illinois. While some members of the Owens-Illinois board opposed the takeover (and opposed becoming a private company), it was generally agreed that the short-term interests of the stockholders were served.

Over the next few years KKR-led Owens-Illinois divested several noncore operations, in part to pay down the hefty $4.4 billion debt on the company books following the LBO and in part because a prime reason to diversify—fending off raiders—was now moot. In addition to jettisoning the forest products and mortgage banking unit, Owens-Illinois sold its healthcare businesses in 1991 for $369 million.

Meanwhile, the company moved to significantly bolster its share of the U.S. glass container market through a $750 million 1987 acquisition of Jacksonville, Florida-based Brockway Inc. The merger of two of the three largest U.S. glass container makers was initially blocked by the U.S. Federal Trade Commission (FTC), which contended that the combination would create a company with too much control of the market, with a 38 percent share. Owens-Illinois took its case to federal court, winning an appeal in 1988. The following year, however, an FTC administrative law judge ruled that the company should be forced to sell Brockway, leading to another Owens-Illinois appeal. Finally, in March 1992 the chairman of the FTC overturned the earlier ruling, allowing the acquisition to stand.

Somewhat ironically, in December 1991 a federal jury had found that Owens-Illinois and Brockway (along with Dart Industries Inc.) had conspired to fix prices on glass containers in the 1970s and 1980s. A settlement on the damages was soon reached out of court, with the terms not disclosed.

Public Again in 1991

In December 1991 KKR took Owens-Illinois public once again, through an initial public offering (IPO) that raised about $1.3 billion. The proceeds were used to further pay down debt, which by 1993 stood at $2.5 billion. KKR maintained a stake of about 26 percent through the late 1990s.

Over the next several years after the IPO, Owens-Illinois concentrated on building up its core glass container and plastic packaging operations. Much of the growth would come in the form of acquisitions—particularly overseas—but the company also spent more than $1.5 billion in capital expenditures from 1993 through 1997 to improve productivity and increase capacity of existing facilities. The company's involvement in the plastics industry also expanded, evolving into a plastics group producing containers, closures, prescription containers, labels, and multipack carriers for beverage bottles. The 1992 acquisition of Specialty Packaging Products, Inc. brought Owens-Illinois a leading U.S. manufacturer of trigger sprayers and finger pumps, with annual sales of $100 million.

During the mid-1990s the company continued to affirm its concentration on glass containers and plastic packaging through several strategic divestments. In 1994 and 1995 it sold off its specialty glass segment. Also in 1994 Libbey Glass was spun off, becoming the publicly traded Libbey Inc. Owens-Illinois in December 1993 sold 51 percent of specialty packaging and laboratory equipment maker Kimble Glass Inc. to Gerresheimer Glas AG. It sold the remaining 49 percent stake to Gerresheimer in March 1997.

Mid-1990s Global Expansion

A serious international presence began in 1993 with an expansion of South American operations, leading to the company's capture of the number one position in glass containers on that continent. Another top position, in India, was gained in 1994 through the acquisition of glass container maker Ballarpur Industries. Three years later Owens-Illinois spent about $586 million for AVIR S.p.A., the largest manufacturer of glass containers in Italy. By this time the company also held leading positions in this segment in the United Kingdom, Poland, Hungary, Finland, Estonia, and had gained the number two position overall in Europe.

Back home, Owens-Illinois paid about $125 million in February 1997 to acquire the glass container assets of Anchor Glass Container Corporation, in the process increasing its share of the U.S. market to more than 40 percent. Also during 1997 the company completed a major refinancing, which included the retirement of about $1.9 billion in high-cost debt. In April 1998 Owens-Illinois paid $3.6 billion in cash for the worldwide glass and plastics packaging businesses of BTR plc of the United Kingdom, in the largest acquisition in company history. Added thereby to the Owens-Illinois empire was ACI Glass Packaging, the only maker of glass containers in Australia and New Zealand, with additional operations in China and Indonesia; and U.S.-based Continental PET Technologies, a leading supplier of plastic food and drink containers in the United States, Australia, New Zealand, the United Kingdom, the Netherlands, and such emerging markets as Brazil, China, Hungary, Mexico, and Saudi Arabia. The Commission of the European Communities approved the purchase but with the stipulation that Owens-Illinois sell BTR's glass container operations in the United Kingdom, known as Rockware Glass.

Throughout the 1990s the company had to contend with ongoing asbestos litigation stemming from its Kaylo insulation business of 1948–58. By the end of 1997 Owens-Illinois had settled claims involving about 210,000 claimants, with an average payment per claim of $4,200. The company had itself sued more than two dozen insurance companies who had refused to cover these claims. By 1997 Owens-Illinois had reached settlements with a number of these insurers, resulting in about $308.4 million in coverage for the company. It expected to receive substantial additional payments as the remaining suits reached settlements. Owens-Illinois was still a named defendant in asbestos claims involving about 14,000 claimants by the end of 1997, and new claims were filed each year, although the number was steadily decreasing.

Even prior to the acquisition of BTR's packaging units, Owens-Illinois had more than doubled its sales outside the United States. In 1997 non-U.S. revenue accounted for 37 percent of overall company revenue, which had reached a record $4.66 billion. With its concentration on the core areas of glass containers and plastic packaging and with its aggressive program of international expansion, Owens-Illinois appeared to have in place a solid plan for 21st-century growth.

Principal Subsidiaries

Owens-Illinois Group, Inc.; OI Health Care Holding Corp.; OI General Finance Inc.; OI Closure FTS Inc.; OI Plastic Products FTS Inc.; Owens-Illinois Prescription Products Inc.; Owens-Brockway Plastic Products Inc.; Owens-Illinois Labels Inc.; Owens-Brockway Packaging, Inc.; OI Ione STS Inc.; Owens-Brockway Glass Container Inc. The company also lists subsidiaries in the following countries: Bolivia, Brazil, Bermuda, China, Colombia, Czech Republic, Ecuador, Estonia, Finland, Hungary, India, Italy, Mexico, the Netherlands, Peru, Poland, Spain, Thailand, the United Kingdom, and Venezuela.

Further Reading

Henderson, Angelo B., ''Owens-Illinois Agrees to Acquire Glass, Plastic Line of BTR for $3.6 Billion,'' *Wall Street Journal,* March 2, 1998, pp. A13.

Norman, James R., ''Smart Timing,'' *Forbes,* November 25, 1991, pp. 170+.

Willoughby, Jack, ''Owens-Illinois: Wishful Recap,'' *Financial World,* May 14, 1991, pp. 21+.

—updated by David E. Salamie

PACCAR Inc.

PACCAR Building
777 106th Avenue NE
Bellevue, Washington 98004
U.S.A.
(425) 468-7400
(888) 337-6811
Fax: (425) 468-8216
Web site: http://www.paccar.com

Public Company
Incorporated: 1924 as Pacific Car & Foundry Company
Employees: 17,000
Sales: $6.75 billion (1997)
Stock Exchanges: NASDAQ
Ticker Symbol: PCAR
SICs: 3711 Motor Vehicles & Car Bodies; 5531 Auto &
Home Supply Stores; 7513 Truck Rental & Leasing,
Without Drivers; 6719 Holding Companies, Not
Elsewhere Classified

As the second largest medium and heavy truck manufacturer in the world, PACCAR Inc. sells Class 6, 7, and 8 trucks under the Kenworth, Peterbilt, Foden, Leyland, and DAF nameplates. As of the late 1990s, PACCAR also manufactured and sold industrial winches, operated finance and leasing subsidiaries, and sold automotive parts and accessories through its A1's Auto and Grand Auto retail outlets.

Company Origins

The history of PACCAR began with a steel foundry established in Bellevue, Washington (near Seattle) in 1904. At that time, the major industries in Seattle were forestry and shipping, neither of which had any use for primary steel products. Unable to find a market for the steel, the company's founder, William Pigott, decided to establish a second facility to manufacture finished steel products. In 1905 the company began production of "bunks," the steel clasps used to secure logs to railroad flat cars. Shortly afterwards, the company began to produce railroad cars, and took the name Pacific Car & Foundry Company.

Over the ensuing 20 years Pacific Car & Foundry developed a variety of special transportation equipment but remained primarily involved in railroad car production. Pacific Car was incorporated in April 1924, and was acquired four years later by the American Car & Foundry Company. In May 1931 Pacific Car acquired the Arrow Pump Company and plants belonging to the Bacon & Matheson Drop Forge Company.

Severe economic conditions during the Great Depression forced American Car & Foundry to close its Pacific Car plant at Renton, south of Seattle. William Pigott's son, Paul, repurchased the facility in 1934, and initiated production of refrigerated box cars. The box cars, or "reefers," were bought by railroads and agricultural combines to transport perishable goods to distant markets. Production of the company's refrigerator cars was highly profitable despite continuing poor economic conditions, generating enough surplus capital to permit the acquisition in 1936 of Heisers Incorporated, a manufacturer of motor buses.

During World War II Pacific Car produced railcars for the transportation of war materiel from production plants to major ports. The company also manufactured special vehicles and mechanical components. Following a reorganization in 1943, the company retired its common stock, and compensated stockholders with new preferred shares. The reorganization brought Pacific Car under close family control.

Expands into Truck Manufacturing in the 1940s and 1950s

In January 1945, as the war neared its end, Pacific Car & Foundry purchased the Kenworth Motor Truck Corporation, located in Seattle. Kenworth specialized in the production of powerful diesel trucks and achieved a reputation for quality.

Transportation needs in the western United States grew during the late 1940s and 1950s. Despite the growth of smaller communities in the West, it was uneconomical for railroad companies to construct new lines. This created a demand for

Company Perspectives:

PACCAR maintains exceptionally high standards of quality for all its products: they are well-engineered, are highly customized for specific applications and sell in the premium segment of their markets, where they have a reputation for superior performance and pride of ownership.

large trucks capable of climbing steep mountain grades and crossing long stretches of flatland. Kenworth trucks were perfectly suited for this kind of work and, while expensive, they were also highly dependable and popular.

In 1953 Pacific Car & Foundry bought the Seattle facilities of the Commercial Ship Repair Company. Five years later the company purchased the assets of the Dart Truck Company, a Kansas City-based manufacturer of large ''off-highway'' construction equipment, such as earth movers and giant dump trucks; then in the following year, 1954, Pacific Car acquired the Peterbilt Motors Company, a truck manufacturer like Kenworth, located in Newark, near San Francisco.

When Paul Pigott died in 1961, Robert O'Brien was named to succeed him as president of the company. O'Brien placed greater emphasis on truck sales and structural steel production. As a result of these efforts, Pacific Car experienced an average 23 percent annual increase in earnings between 1961 and 1966. In 1965 Robert O'Brien was promoted to chairman of the board and was replaced as president by Charles Pigott, grandson of the founder.

Pacific Car purchased a Canadian producer of automotive transmissions and industrial winches called Gearmatic and in early 1967 completed its acquisition of Sicard Incorporated, a manufacturer of snow removal equipment and airport vehicles.

Workers at all three Pacific Car plants in Seattle staged a crippling labor strike from April 5 to July 22, 1968. This precipitated a 12-week strike at the Gearmatic Division in British Columbia and a three-week strike at the Dart facility in Kansas City. The strikes cost Pacific Car over $1 million in lost production but caused no lasting damage to the vehicle divisions.

Pacific Car & Foundry continued to produce railroad cars at its Renton Division. Although railroad car production contributed only a fraction to company earnings, it remained stable and profitable. Structural Steel, the weakest Pacific Car division, was one of the first U.S. steel manufacturers to suffer from the effects of outdated technology and a market restricted by imported steel. Although efforts were made to cut costs and increase productivity, Structural Steel continued to perform marginally.

In November 1971 Pacific Car & Foundry created a holding company, incorporated in Delaware, called PACCAR Incorporated. On February 1, 1972, PACCAR absorbed Pacific Car & Foundry. Company divisions such as Kenworth and Peterbilt retained their names, but other subsidiaries (particularly in finance) adopted the PACCAR name.

Unlike competing truck manufacturers, PACCAR was insulated from severe shifts in market demand by maintaining virtually no manufacturing facilities. Kenworth and Peterbilt trucks were merely assembled from parts produced by Eaton, Rockwell International, Cummins Engine, and Caterpillar Tractor, among others. This permitted PACCAR to avoid costly investments in manufacturing facilities and easily reduce production when demand fell. In addition, PACCAR had the freedom to purchase components from a variety of competing manufacturers, allowing it to custom build trucks to a customer's specifications and take full advantage of the newest products.

Challenges in the 1970s and 1980s

Inflation and high oil prices in 1974 led trucking companies to use their equipment more efficiently, which, in turn, caused a decline in new truck orders. Demand for higher quality Kenworth and Peterbilt trucks, however, was not seriously affected and production losses during 1974 were due more to the reoccurrence of strikes than to poor market conditions. Many labor disputes between 1974 and 1978 were caused by wage negotiations as labor contracts expired.

In November 1979 PACCAR failed in an attempt to gain control of the Harnischfeger Corporation, which produced cranes and earth-moving equipment. But 11 months later PACCAR successfully completed a takeover of Fodens Ltd., a British manufacturer of heavy-duty trucks. Fodens, which had been bankrupt since July, sold trucks in Britain, Europe, and Africa. The company's operations were taken over by a newly created PACCAR subsidiary, Sandbach Engineering.

A second oil crisis in 1979 and the subsequent implementation of deregulation in the trucking industry once again compelled operators to utilize their equipment more efficiently. This caused sales of Class 8 trucks (those over 33,000 pounds in gross vehicle weight, and the only type produced by Kenworth and Peterbilt) to fall 58 percent between 1979 and 1982. However, despite an overall 35 percent drop in sales, PACCAR remained profitable.

The Freightliner subsidiary of Daimler-Benz and the merged operations of Volvo White and General Motors became particularly aggressive in the mid-1980s, forcing PACCAR's share of the Class 8 truck market to drop from 23 percent in 1983 to 18 percent in 1986. Plagued by overcapacity, PACCAR was forced to close a Kenworth plant in Kansas City in April 1986 and a Peterbilt plant in Newark, California, the following October.

In an effort to reduce its dependence on the depressed Class 8 truck market, PACCAR announced its intention to purchase Trico Industries, a manufacturer of oil exploration equipment based in Gardena, California. After initial resistance, Trico agreed to be acquired in 1986 for $65 million.

During this time PACCAR also announced that it was negotiating with the Rover Group, the state-owned British automotive company, for the purchase of its British Leyland truck division. However, Rover management, with substantial support in the British parliament, elected to sell the truck division to DAF, a Dutch automotive concern.

PACCAR continued to experiment in new markets and in early 1987 concluded an agreement with Volkswagen do Brasil to import Class 7 trucks (26,001- to 33,000-pound gross vehicle weight) for sale in the United States. The Class 7 market, however, was overwhelmingly dominated by Navistar, General Motors, and Ford. PACCAR was also interested in acquiring the Bell Helicopter division of Textron, a unit it first attempted to purchase in 1985.

A recovery in demand for Class 8 trucks in early 1987 reinforced PACCAR's position that Kenworth and Peterbilt should not be merged. Truck production continued to provide PACCAR with about 90 percent of its operating income. Despite efforts at diversification, the company had yet to find a viable alternative to the cyclical demand and production of Class 8 trucks.

Later that year PACCAR moved into the automotive parts and accessories retail market with the purchase of A1's Auto Supply, a Washington-based wholesale distributor and aftermarket retailer. The company created a new subsidiary, PACCAR Automotive, Inc., to run the stores. In 1988 PACCAR bought Grand Auto, Inc., another auto parts and accessories retailer, and folded the new stores into the PACCAR Automotive subsidiary. Based in California, the new acquisition rounded out PACCAR's presence in the auto parts market in the western United States.

The 1990s: Maintaining Profits

The cyclical nature of truck sales again plagued the company in the early 1990s. As demand for trucks fell, so did PACCAR's sales. From a high of $3.5 billion in 1989, revenues fell to $2.8 billion in 1990 and then to $2.3 billion in 1991. The company managed to remain profitable, however, with net income falling from $242 million in 1989 to $40 million in 1991. The company avoided red ink in part by laying off 11 percent of its employees in 1990. PACCAR Automotive also cut back its operations in 1991 when it abandoned its wholesale auto parts sales to focus on its retail outlets.

PACCAR's finances improved slightly in 1992, when profits rose to $65 million. That year the company added to its oil field equipment manufacturing with the purchase of a 21 percent stake in Wood Group ESP.

The cycle rolled back upward in the mid-1990s, when aging fleets needed replacement and interest rates were relatively low. PACCAR enjoyed a series of record years, with revenues rising to $3.5 billion in 1993, $4.5 billion in 1994, and $4.8 billion in 1995. Profits rose commensurately, reaching $253 million in 1995. Robert Stovall, in a 1994 *Financial World* article, named PACCAR "the premier long-term investment in the heavy hauling business."

The prosperity encouraged expansion, and in 1993 PACCAR acquired a line of winches from heavy equipment manufacturer Caterpillar. The same year it brought a new plant in Washington on line to help meet the increased demand for trucks. In 1994 the company began selling in New Zealand for the first time and entered new countries in Asia and Central and South America. The company made its Mexican joint venture VILPAC, S.A., a wholly owned subsidiary in 1995.

In 1996 industrywide truck sales were down 25 percent from the year before. PACCAR responded by cutting back on production: It shut down truck manufacturing at a Seattle plant and closed a plant in Quebec that had been hurt by a strike the year before. The company's control over the heavy truck manufacturer VILPAC came in handy when PACCAR was able to move some of the Canadian production to the Mexican facilities.

PACCAR greatly expanded its presence in Europe in the late 1990s. In 1996 the company spent $543 million to acquire DAF Trucks N.V. Based in the Netherlands, DAF sold over 24,000 trucks in Europe in 1996 and employed around 5,000 people. In 1998 PACCAR bought Leyland Trucks Ltd., an acquisition it first pursued back in the mid-1980s. Founded in 1896, Leyland Trucks brought over 100 years of experience and 1997 sales of $272 million to PACCAR. The acquisitions were funded in part by the sale of Trico Industries, PACCAR's oil field equipment manufacturer, to EVI in 1997.

The acquisitions helped push PACCAR's revenues to $6.5 billion in 1997. Net income also increased, leaping 71 percent from the year before to approximately $345 million. Although truck sales were up, PACCAR's other businesses contributed to the company's prosperity. Earnings from retail automotive parts rose, and the company boasted 143 A1's Auto and Grand Auto stores by 1998. Financial and leasing subsidiaries also performed well in the late 1990s.

Principal Subsidiaries

DAF Trucks N.V.; Leyland Trucks Ltd.; PACCAR Automotive, Inc.; PACCAR of Canada, Ltd.; PACCAR Financial Corp.; PACCAR Financial Limited (U.K.); PACCAR Leasing Corporation; PACCAR Australia Pty. Ltd.; PACCAR Sales North America, Inc.; PACCAR Financial Pty. Ltd.; PACCAR Financial Services Ltd. (Canada); VILPAC, S.A. (Mexico).

Principal Divisions

Dynacraft; Kenworth Truck Company; PACCAR Parts; PACCAR Technical Center; PACCAR Winch Division; Peterbilt Motors Co.; PACCAR International.

Further Reading

Flint, Jerry, "In Good Times, Prepare for Bad," *Forbes,* July 1, 1996, p. 46.

Grones, Alex, *PACCAR: The Pursuit of Quality,* Bellevue, Wash.: Documentary Book Publishers, 1981.

PACCAR Reports Record 1997 Sales and Earnings," *Business Wire,* February 3, 1998.

Stovall, Robert H., "Carrying the Goods of Recovery," *Financial World,* July 5, 1994, p. 78.

—updated by Susan Windisch Brown

PacifiCorp

700 Northeast Multnomah
Portland, Oregon 97232-4116
U.S.A.
(503) 731-2000
(800) 547-2540
Fax: (503) 731-2136
Web site: http://www.pacificorp.com

Public Company
Incorporated: 1910 as Pacific Power & Light Company
Employees: 12,305
Sales: $6.27 billion (1997)
Stock Exchanges: New York Pacific Boston Midwest
  Philadelphia
Ticker Symbol: PPW
SICs: 4911 Electric Services; 6719 Holding Companies,
  Not Elsewhere Classified

Owner of Pacific Power & Light, Utah Power & Light, and the Australian utility Powercor, PacifiCorp is one of the largest electric utility holding companies in the United States. In the late 1990s, PacifiCorp provided electric power to 1.3 million customers in parts of Washington, Oregon, Utah, Wyoming, California, Montana, and Idaho, and more than half a million customers in Australia. PacifiCorp planned to use its expertise in the trading of bulk power to take advantage of the increasing deregulation in the U.S. power industry.

Company Origins

PacifiCorp began in 1910 as Pacific Power & Light Company, which was formed through the merger of several financially troubled electric utilities in the Pacific Northwest. Pacific included utilities in Astoria, Pendleton, and The Dalles, Oregon; Yakima, Walla Walla, and Pasco, Washington; and Lewiston, Idaho. It had a total of 14,344 electric, gas, and water customers and first-year revenues of $832,200.

The electric industry was in its infancy in 1910. Most large towns had their own electric companies, which often provided gas, steam, or water service as well. Because it was difficult for these small firms to raise enough capital to expand or improve service, holding companies sprang up across the United States, buying smaller companies and integrating them into regional electric utilities. Holding companies like Electric Bond & Share, which owned Pacific, provided capital and expertise.

Customers in Pacific's mostly rural area wanted the electricity-powered conveniences: lights, electric ranges, toasters, vacuum cleaners, washing machines, and water pumps. Pacific successfully marketed and sold electric appliances to help increase electricity sales, although the Great Depression slowed Pacific's sales until 1941. During the Depression employees were forced to take pay cuts, and stockholders' dividends were cut.

Except for the worst years of the Great Depression, rural electrification was an important source of company growth. By 1938 Pacific's system included 10,000 farms. In addition to lighting, farmers used electric power to run irrigation pumps, which created more farm land and more demand for electricity. Pacific often wired the houses and sheds of its new customers and supplied the power.

By 1941 Pacific was in a solid financial position, with income of $740,000 on sales of $6.7 million. It had 73,000 customers, including 4,400 electrified farms. In 1942 it joined the newly formed Northwest Power Pool, formed with several other regional power companies to coordinate resources when capacity was stretched.

One of the biggest of U.S. President Franklin D. Roosevelt's New Deal projects was the development of regional hydroelectric systems, such as the Pacific Northwest system, which included the Bonneville dam and the Grand Coulee dam. Paul B. McKee, president of Pacific starting in 1933, realized that the massive government projects presented Pacific with tremendous opportunities for growth—partly because the projects would stimulate the regional economy, but also because the company could buy a share of the low-cost hydroelectric power that the dams would produce. McKee also dealt with a strong government-ownership movement in Washington and northern

Oregon from the Depression through the mid-1950s. More than 100 votes were held on establishing public utility districts or municipal ownership, and Pacific won most of them. It had fairly strong support from the public because of its good service record and its efforts to stimulate economic growth in the regions it served.

Mergers in the 1950s and 1960s

In 1950 Electric Bond & Share spun off Pacific as an independent, publicly traded company. Pacific pushed aggressively to build itself into a self-sufficient organization, moving to secure its power supply. The Pacific Northwest area was booming, and Pacific was unsure it would be able to renew its contract to buy cheap government power, so it began building its own hydroelectric generating stations. It completed Yale dam in southwest Washington in 1953, but the company still generated only 50 percent of its power. That generating dearth lead to Pacific's first major merger, with Mountain States Power Company.

Mountain States, founded in 1917, served western Oregon, northern Idaho, western Montana, and Wyoming. In 1940 the company reorganized because the lingering effects of the Depression left it unable to meet its bond debts. It became an independent company that year, when its holding company spun it off as a result of the Public Utility Holding Company Act of 1935. Throughout the 1940s Mountain States acquired nearby systems and built lines into rural areas that had no service. It pushed electric appliances hard, increasing demand. From 1941 to 1953 the company's customer load nearly doubled, leaving it unable to meet demand for electricity. Mountain States had no hydroelectric sites it could develop economically, did not have the capital to build new generating plants, and worried it might fold.

In 1954 Mountain States merged into Pacific, creating a company twice as large as it had been, with service territory spread over five states. The merger also brought Pacific two small telephone companies, one in Oregon and one in Montana. Pacific immediately began building generating plants in Wyoming, where Mountain States had been unable to meet demand. Large coal veins nearby fueled the new plants near Glenrock, Wyoming. Pacific also built a third hydroelectric plant on the Lewis River in Washington and a large coal-fired steam plant near Centralia, Washington.

In the late 1950s and early 1960s Pacific bought coal leases that gave it more than one billion tons of reserves. In 1961 the company merged with California Oregon Power Company (COPCO). COPCO, which served southern Oregon and northern California, was formed in 1911 and acquired by Standard Gas & Electric in 1925. In 1947 COPCO became independent again, partly as the result of the 1935 holding company act. With the COPCO acquisition, Pacific jumped to 411,000 customers from 318,000, and reached annual revenues of $90 million.

During the 1960s Pacific struggled to integrate the COPCO system and meet demand, which was growing at seven percent a year. The region's hydroelectric potential was already tapped, so the company added thermal generating plants.

Increased Diversification in the 1970s

In the early 1970s Pacific decided to build up its small but profitable phone operations. In 1973 the company bought a majority interest in Telephone Utilities, a company in rural Washington that had assembled a network by buying small local telephone companies that had been ignored by the Bell System. In 1979 Pacific bought Alascom from RCA Corporation for $210 million. Alascom, which provided long-distance and local telephone service in Alaska, proved to be a good investment, as Alaskan toll calls grew 23 percent to 25 percent annually for the next several years. In 1981 Pacific bought about 48 percent of the second largest independent phone equipment manufacturer in the United States when it bought General Dynamics' phone manufacturing operations for nearly $50 million. In 1982 Pacific changed the name of Telephone Utilities to Pacific Telecom and its own name to PacifiCorp, of which Pacific Power became a subsidiary. By 1983 Pacific Telecom had revenues of $341 million.

Pacific also continued expanding its coal mining and energy exploring operations. In 1976 it formed Northern Energy Resources Company (NERCO) to manage its coal properties and mining operations. Because Pacific already had bought so many coal and mineral properties, NERCO was one of the biggest producers of coal, silver, and gold in North America at the time it was formed. It continued to grow through acquisitions, spending $15.2 million in 1981 for a Fairbanks, Alaska, exploration company that owned mineral rights to 5.5 million acres of Alaska. NERCO had become the sixth largest U.S. coal miner. In 1982 NERCO acquired Clements Energy Incorporated, an oil and gas exploration company.

Pacific ran into trouble in the late 1970s and early 1980s because of inflation, runaway construction costs, shifts in energy supplies and costs, and then a recession. However, a collapse in energy demand left Pacific Power with excess capacity and investments in several nuclear power plants under construction that were no longer needed. The collapse of the Washington Public Power Supply System (WPPSS), financed by Pacific Power and three other utilities, attracted nationwide attention. PacifiCorp's diversification helped it weather a $292 million write-off in 1983 for investments in WPPSS and another $260 million write-off on three other nuclear plants.

By 1982, 46 percent of PacifiCorp's revenue came from nonutility operations, which offered a rate of return two to three times greater than the company's electric unit. At the same time, the company decided to push electricity sales to make use of its huge excess generating capacity. It took out ads touting electric home heating, tried to increase economic development in its territory by helping communities form industrial development groups, and sold surplus power to industry and neighboring utilities at wholesale rates. To reduce expenses PacifiCorp cut 600 positions from electricity operations between 1982 and 1984. NERCO launched a drive in 1983 to sign industrial customers to long-term coal contracts to make up for declining sales to utilities. Its earnings also were helped by the 1982 purchase of two gold and silver mines in Nevada. In 1984 PacifiCorp formed Inner PacifiCorp, Inc., to hold NERCO, Pacific Telecom, and other nonelectric businesses.

By 1985 conditions had improved for PacifiCorp's electric business. Electrical income was up nearly 85 percent since 1981, compared with 34 percent for Pacific Telecom and 29 percent for NERCO, which was hurt by declining coal prices. That year PacifiCorp formed a financial services arm, buying Northwest Acceptance Corporation for $53 million and changing its name to PacifiCorp Financial Services. It then bought Hyster Credit for $120 million. It lost, however, $44 million in an oil and gas exploration venture and $78 million in various venture capital and telecommunications manufacturing investments. In 1987 NERCO bought 42 oil and gas wells in southern Louisiana, and PacifiCorp bought Thomas Nationwide Computer Corporation for $25 million. Net income for 1987 was $266 million.

Power Swapping Initiated in the Late 1980s

In 1987 PacifiCorp agreed to merge with Utah Power & Light Company, which ran along Pacific's southern flank, in a $1.85 billion stock swap, but the merger did not actually occur until 1989 because of regulatory hurdles. To get regulatory approval for the merger, PacifiCorp accepted conditions imposed by the Federal Energy Regulatory Commission, agreeing to open its transmission system to outside producers under certain circumstances. The company received criticism within the utility industry for the move, which other companies feared would set a harmful precedent. For PacifiCorp the agreement was worth a small amount of competition from independent producers. Utah Power's transmission system was connected to the southwestern and California markets, and the merger allowed PacifiCorp to move surplus power out of Wyoming and into those markets. The companies also fit together well because PacifiCorp's demand peaked in winter, while Utah Power's peaked in summer.

PacifiCorp operated Utah Power as a separate subsidiary, with about 535,000 customers in a 90,000-square-mile area in Utah and parts of Idaho and Wyoming. Pacific Power served about 682,000 customers in a 63,000-square-mile area in parts of Oregon, Wyoming, Washington, Idaho, Montana, and California. Utah and Oregon provided most of the company's electric revenue, with 37.2 percent and 29.6 percent, respectively, in 1989.

In 1989 PacifiCorp offered to buy the troubled Arizona Public Service Company for nearly $2 billion in cash and stock. When the plan faltered, PacifiCorp offered to buy Arizona Public's parent company, Pinnacle West Capital Corporation, which rejected PacifiCorp's $1.87 billion bid as inadequate. The purchase would have given PacifiCorp an electric grid stretching from the Canadian to the Mexican border. Arizona Public eventually agreed to seasonal power swaps with PacifiCorp, so both companies could take advantage of differences in their peak demand times. Also in 1989 Pacific Telecom agreed to buy Wisconsin's North West Telecommunications Incorporated for $250 million in cash and securities, completing the purchase in mid-1990. Net income for 1989 was $466 million on sales of $3.6 billion.

By 1990 PacifiCorp provided electricity to 1.2 million customers. Its generating capacity was 86 percent coal-powered and 13 percent hydroelectric. NERCO was one of the top ten

U.S. coal producers, with most of its coal sold to electric utilities under long-term contracts. Pacific Telecom provided local telephone service for 352,000 access lines in parts of ten states. In 1991 NERCO bought Union Texas Petroleum's oil and gas operations in the Gulf of Mexico, dramatically increasing its petroleum reserves.

The 1990s: Refocusing on Power

The 1992 National Energy Act, which allowed independent energy developers to generate, buy, and sell electricity, transformed PacifiCorp's plans for the future. With their low-cost coal-fired and hydroelectric plants and their experience in bulk trading of energy, PacifiCorp was in an enviable position to take advantage of the new law. Although competition was only introduced in the industrial market in the early 1990s, eventually deregulation would reach the individual consumer market. PacifiCorp readied itself in several ways for the coming of full deregulation.

In the early 1990s PacifiCorp sold several nonutility subsidiaries that had been underperforming. The first to go was PacifiCorp's gold and silver mining operation, which was sold in 1992. The following year, the company sold NERCO, its coalmining management subsidiary. In 1995 PacifiCorp sold its long-distance telephone provider Alascom to AT&T. Not only did these sales bring in cash that could be used in strategic acquisitions, it also helped the company focus on its electric utilities and its wholesale marketing of electricity.

As a first step in entering a competitive market, PacifiCorp established a marketing office for wholesale power in Las Vegas in 1994. The following year it reorganized its utility operations to reflect the new emphasis on competitive sales: Discrete units were created for electricity generation, wholesale transactions and transmission, and retail sales. In addition, PacifiCorp bought the remaining shares of Pacific Telecom, making it a wholly owned subsidiary.

The company's preparations for complete deregulation took an unusual turn in 1995. That year PacifiCorp bought the Australian electric utility Powercor for $1.6 billion. The recently privatized company made it the perfect test ground for how to transform a regulated electric utility into a competitive electric retailer. Like PacifiCorp's electric operations in the United States, Powercor served a large and diverse customer base with primarily coal-generated electricity. In addition to its usefulness as a learning tool, the Powercor acquisition gave PacifiCorp an entrée into the global marketplace.

Acquisitions continued at a rapid pace in the following years. In 1997 PacifiCorp bought TPC, a natural gas exploration and marketing company, for $435 million. The same year it began a joint venture with the natural gas company KN Energy that would offer power and communications services. The new company, Enable LLC, would send each customer a single bill for these services. In 1998 PacifiCorp moved to acquire The Energy Group, a diversified energy company with operations in the United Kingdom, Australia, and the United States. With an offer of $10.7 billion, PacifiCorp was the clear leader in the bidding process. Because the purchase would be primarily financed through increased debt, Standard & Poor's took a dim view of the acquisition, placing the ratings of PacifiCorp and its subsidiaries on CreditWatch with negative implications. To offset some of the purchase price, PacifiCorp agreed to sell Pacific Telecom to Century Telephone.

Principal Subsidiaries

PacifiCorp Holdings, Inc.; PacifiCorp Financial Services, Inc; Powercor Australia Limited, Pacific Power & Light Company; Utah Power & Light Company.

Further Reading

Burkhart, Lori A., ''PacifiCorp to Acquire The Energy Group for $9.6 Billion,'' *Public Utilities Fortnightly,* August 1997, p. 12.

Frisbee, Don C., ''The PacifiCorp Story,'' New York: Newcomen Society of the United States, 1985.

Marks, Anita E., ''Dennis Steinberg: The Utility Man,'' *Worldbusiness,* July/August 1996, pp. 42–43.

''Nomura Exit Clears Way for PacifiCorp's TEG Takeover,'' *Euroweek,* February 13, 1998, p. 30.

—Scott M. Lewis
—updated by Susan Windisch Brown

Pentair, Inc.

Waters Edge Plaza
1500 Country Road B2 West, Suite 400
St. Paul, Minnesota 55113-3105
U.S.A.
(612) 636-7920
Fax: (612) 639-5203
Web site: http://www.pentair.com

Public Company
Incorporated: 1966 as Pentair Industries Incorporated
Employees: 10,433
Sales: $1.84 billion (1997)
Stock Exchanges: New York
Ticker Symbol: PNR
SICs: 3981 Diversified Conglomerate; 3451 Screw
   Machine Products; 3482 3546 Power Driven Hand
   Tools; 3553 Woodworking Machinery; 3561 Pumps
   & Pumping Equipment; 3569 General Industrial
   Machinery & Equipment, Not Elsewhere Classified;
   3644 Noncurrent-Carrying Wiring Devices; 3679
   Electronic Components, Not Elsewhere Classified;
   3825 Instruments for Measuring & Testing of
   Electricity & Electrical Signals

Pentair, Inc. is a diversified manufacturer of woodworking equipment, vehicle service equipment, power tools, water pumps and systems, water conditioning control valves, automated lubrication systems and equipment, and electrical and electronic enclosures. Its enviable record of growth (since 1969, return on common equity has averaged nearly 17 percent) is due to its highly distinctive, corporate strategy of buying underperforming—even foundering—concerns and then implementing capital and management improvements to effect quick turnarounds. In the early years of the company's history, the plan was adopted for purposes of sheer survival, but as the company prospered despite periods of debt load, it became apparent that regular acquisitions through leveraged financing would be the company's mainstay. Firmly committed to both shareholders and employees, Pentair has rebuffed three takeover attempts during its history and has pledged to remain independent and devoted to long-term growth. Pentair divides its subsidiaries into three groups: Professional Tools and Equipment; Water and Fluid Technologies, and Electrical and Electronic Enclosures. Autonomously operated, subsidiaries in these groups (which include market leaders Delta International Machinery Corp., Porter-Cable Corporation, Fleck Controls, Hoffman Enclosures Inc., and Schroff) maintain 50 locations in North America, Europe, and Asia.

Balloons, Then Canoes, Then Paper

Pentair was founded in July 1966 in Arden Hills, Minnesota, as a five-person partnership with the purpose of manufacturing high-altitude research balloons. The company founders—three engineers, a foreman, and a salesman—were all former employees of a local branch of Litton Industries. The partners incorporated as Pentair Industries, Inc. in August and completed an initial public offering in January 1967 to sustain their seriously undercapitalized business. Further complicating matters at the time was the lagging market for inflatables. Following the guidance of cofounder and acting manager Murray Harpole, the company decided to purchase a neighboring, virtually bankrupt business for the small sum of $14,500. With some modest engineering applications this new venture, the American Thermo-Vac Company, promised at least one saleable product: vacuum-formed, high-quality canoes. By the fall of that year red-and-white Penta Craft canoes were being successfully manufactured and sold. However, both the canoe and inflatables businesses were fraught with problems; by the end of 1967, the company had few assets, zero profits, and little direction.

As Del Marth later reported, "By June, 1968, before Pentair was two years old, the corporate dream had become a nightmare. The company had no product to speak of, it was nearly out of money, one cofounder had died and three others had abandoned the venture." What sustained the company was Harpole's pledge to commit himself entirely to the business for at least five years—this and the entry of high-risk investor Ben Westby. Although Westby did not formally join the company until May 1968, he had been in close contact with Harpole for

---

Company Perspectives:

Pentair's willingness to change has been an integral part of its success and ability to build shareholder value. Over the last three years, Pentair has reinvented itself with the goal of being a sharply focused, industrial growth company. This process has led the Company to form three new operating groups—Professional Tools and Equipment; Water and Fluid Technologies; and Electric and Electronic Enclosures—replacing the Specialty Products and General Industrial Equipment groups established in 1991. This reorganization allows Pentair to communicate its financial performance in a way that parallels its operating structure, and it reflects the sharper strategic focus that will guide the Company's growth and development in the years ahead.

---

some time and had accompanied the founder on a business trip to Wisconsin, to consider the purchase of then debt-ridden, privately owned Peavey Paper Mills, Inc.

A manufacturer of absorbent tissue paper, Peavey was acquired in June and became Pentair's first wholly owned subsidiary. The deal that Westby and Harpole had arranged was important for two reasons. First was the low cost: $10,000 down, $20,000 due in one year, and an additional five percent of after-tax profits for the first five years. Second, and most importantly, was the paper mill's potential: annual sales of $4 million even in its current state of disrepair and mismanagement. Of course, with this ostensibly one-of-a-kind deal came a particularly painful and hidden price: Peavey's $1.5 million in debt. Despite this preventable surprise, a lesson in cautious and thorough research, the acquisition was made profitable within three months due primarily to Harpole's management and labor-negotiation skills. The purchase also left Pentair free to divest itself of its first two, nonproducing businesses. Now a viable paper company with substantial assets, Pentair began attracting considerable notice from the investment community and, with both a three-year Procter & Gamble contract and a preliminary agreement to acquire a Trinidad paper mill, Pentair closed the year on a high note.

1970s Paper Acquisitions

In 1969, due to Pentair's new status as an acquisition-oriented, international corporation, company stock soared from $2 per share to $25 and a 3-for-1 split was declared. Before the end of the year, however, operations at the Trinidad paper mill were halted due to social and political unrest in that country. The contract with Procter & Gamble to produce absorbent wadding for use in its disposable Pampers fueled the company's growth for the next few years. Still Harpole and Westby considered Pentair's position tenuous. Ensuing diversifications into leather goods, meat-rendering, and computer software by and large failed to give the company the stability required for uninterrupted long-term growth. Then came the acquisitions of Niagara of Wisconsin Paper, Miami Paper, and Flambeau Paper Corporations, in 1972, 1974, and 1978, respectively. Initial annual sales for the three totaled some $90 million. Although Pentair

had sold Peavey in 1976 due to plant and market limitations, it had now established itself as a major supplier of coated groundwood, book grade, and commercial printing papers, producing some 350,000 tons annually.

Pentair signaled its arrival as a major corporation by declaring its first quarterly cash dividend in 1976. Four years earlier the company had sustained a debt-to-equity ratio of greater than 7-to-1, but by 1979, after paying down debt with paper profits, it had more than reversed these numbers and gained some valuable banking partners in the process.

The 1970s were also notable for several management developments, including the departure of Westby in 1974 and the hiring of D. Eugene Nugent, an ITT executive, as vice-president of operations in 1975. Harpole, singularly aware that tenacious and disciplined management had become the key to Pentair's success, handpicked Nugent as his likely successor. Both agreed that maintaining a lean corporate staff, which then numbered only ten despite more than 1,000 employees and widespread operations, would be a continuing goal for the company. (Management actually became proportionally leaner as employee levels continued to rise.) As Jeffrey Trachtenberg stated, reporting on Nugent's management style for *Forbes* in 1984, "Big corporation management stifles risk-taking at the operational level. Pentair's setup is that of a slim holding company running herd over a pack of operating subsidiaries. . . . It pushes decision-making out where it belongs, among the operating managers."

Diversification Highlighted in the 1980s

The "pack" Trachtenberg referred to was the early fruition of a carefully thought out strategy by Harpole and Nugent to diversify into industrial products manufactured primarily for industrial users. As early as 1978 the two had commenced their search for such businesses to offset the capital-intensive and cyclical paper group, which, led by Niagara, nonetheless represented a fairly consistent source of cash flow. According to Harpole, whose *Living the American Dream* recounts the corporation's history, he and Nugent "had to be successful on their first venture because the investment community was skeptical of our ability to expand beyond paper." The initial goal was for a company with annual sales of $25 to $100 million, preferably floundering and consequently available at a bargain price. Unfortunately, the realization of the goal was postponed, largely due to a time-consuming battle against a takeover threat by Steak and Ale founder Peter Wray, an attempt that ended only after Pentair agreed to a $4.5 million settlement in early 1981. By the middle of that year Pentair had researched and considered more than 125 manufacturers before deciding in October to acquire Porter-Cable Corporation (the portable power tools division of Rockwell International) of Jackson, Tennessee, for $16 million. Another debt-laden but revenue-heavy paper mill acquisition in 1983, as well as the 1984 purchase of Rockwell's woodworking machinery division renamed Delta International, boosted earnings to $21 million on annual sales of $545 million, vaulting the paper-and-tools company into the *Fortune* 500 rankings. The company had flourished beyond anyone's expectations.

With Nugent established as CEO and Harpole imparting a legacy stretching well beyond his retirement as chairperson in

1986, Pentair fortified itself for years to come with additional forays into industrial products, beginning with the acquisition of McNeil Corporation and its two major divisions: Lincoln, a St. Louis-based maker of lubricating products and automotive service equipment, and F.E. Myers, an Ohio-based producer of water pumps. Lincoln was eventually split into Lincoln Automotive and Lincoln Industrial. The transaction expanded the industrial group considerably, so that it accounted for 32 percent of sales and 43 percent of operating profits. In 1988 Pentair completed one of its largest purchases, that of Federal-Hoffman Corporation (FC Holdings, Inc.), a Minnesota-based manufacturer of sports ammunition as well as metal and composite electrical enclosures. Divided into Federal Cartridge and Hoffman Engineering, FC Holdings commanded $300 million in annual sales, or nearly 40 percent of Pentair's total sales for the previous year. A decade after its stated objective to strengthen through diversification, the company had reduced its dependency on paper sales to just 30 percent while multiplying its total equity tenfold.

Late in 1985, the company announced an ambitious $400 million joint venture between Pentair and Minnesota Power of Duluth to form Lake Superior Paper Industries (LSPI). The venture was to be the company's first sustained ''ground-floor-up'' business, with the culmination of years of technical expertise, industry-specific knowledge, and financial clout put to the test. LSPI, the newest and most efficient paper mill in North America, began start-up operations in late 1987 and, by March 1988, was producing supercalendered, publication-grade paper (SCA) for a highly competitive U.S. market. The difficulty of the market and the huge capital outlay worried investors from the start. Nevertheless, ''while others either wrung their hands or snickered,'' wrote Alyssa Lappen for *Forbes*, ''Nugent pressed ahead with a capital investment project that now claims customers ranging from Sears and J.C. Penney to *Rolling Stone*. Foreign competitors like West Germany's Haindl Papier and Feldmühle have been squeezed, while more customers line up for Pentair's paper every day.'' In its second year of operations, LSPI was operating at 87 percent of its 245,000-ton-per-year capacity and had positioned itself as the domestic leader of SCA. By the end of 1991, production had risen 93 percent and earnings had increased 58 percent over 1990 levels.

Mid-1990s: Exit from Paper, Several Acquisitions

In August 1992 Winslow Buxton, former president of Niagara of Wisconsin, succeeded Nugent as CEO; Buxton was then named chairman as well in January 1993. One of his initial goals, inherited from Nugent, was to acquire another manufacturing company with sales from $200 to $500 million while elevating overall corporate sales to $2 billion by 1996. Sales growth in 1990 of only one percent and a fractional sales loss in 1991 made such an acquisition a near imperative, given Pentair's history. But it would take until January 1994 for Buxton to find a suitable match. That month Pentair acquired Schroff GmbH from Fried. Krupp AG Hoesch-Krupp, the company's first acquisition in almost seven years. Schroff, a maker of electronics enclosures, fit well alongside the Hoffman electrical enclosures unit.

In September 1994 Pentair announced that it was examining the future of its paper businesses. The cyclical nature of the paper industry proved to be a drag on the company's stock. Pentair could no longer afford to ride the ups and downs of a noncore business (only 10 percent of 1994 operating income came from paper), and management decided to jettison all the paper operations. In April 1995 Pentair sold Cross Pointe Paper Corporation to Noranda Forest, Inc. for $203.3 million. Two months later came the sale of Niagara of Wisconsin, the 50 percent interest in LSPI, and a 12 percent stake in Superior Recycled Fiber Industries to Consolidated Papers, Inc. for $115.6 million and the assumption of debt.

Freed to concentrate on its industrial manufacturing units, Pentair went on a targeted spending spree, in the process building upon its already strong businesses. The acquisitions also led to a January 1998 restructuring of Pentair units into three operating groups: Professional Tools and Equipment; Water and Fluid Technologies; and Electrical and Electronic Enclosures. The first of these operating groups developed around Lincoln Automotive, Delta International, and Porter-Cable. In November 1995 Biesemeyer Manufacturing Corporation, maker of precision woodworking accessories, was acquired and became a subsidiary of Delta. In June 1996 Pentair added a German manufacturer of portable power tools, Flex Elektrowerkzeuge GmbH, which became part of Porter-Cable. Pentair acquired another manufacturer of vehicle service equipment, Century Manufacturing Company, in November 1996. Subsequently added to Century were P&F Technologies Ltd., a manufacturer of automotive refrigerant recycling systems, in July 1997; and T-Tech Industries, specializing in automotive transmission fluid exchanger systems, in April 1998.

The Water and Fluid Technologies group developed around Lincoln Industrial and F.E. Myers. Pentair paid $130 million for Fleck Controls, Inc. in October 1995, gaining a leading maker of control valves for water systems. Pentair bought reciprocating pump maker Aplex Industries, Inc. in January 1996 and made it a subsidiary of F.E. Myers. In December of that year, Italian water conditioning control equipment manufacturer SIATA S.p.A. was acquired and became part of Fleck Controls. In August 1997 Pentair spent $200 million to acquire General Signal Pump Group, a maker of fluid handling products and systems. This business was subsequently combined with F.E. Myers to form the Pentair Pump Group. Also, in January 1998 Pentair purchased ORSCO, Inc., producer of precision oil dispensing systems. ORSCO became a wholly owned subsidiary of Lincoln Industrial.

Pentair's Electrical and Electronic Enclosures group centered around Hoffman and Schroff. Growth for this unit mainly came in Europe, where Schroff was the leader in electronic enclosures. Pentair bought Transrack S.A. of France in January 1997 and Walker Dickson Group Limited of Scotland in October 1998. Earlier in 1998 the company had attempted to acquire electronics enclosure maker VERO Group plc of Southampton, England, but was outbid by Applied Power, Inc. of Butler, Wisconsin.

While building up these three core areas, Pentair also made one other significant divestment of a peripheral business, selling Federal Cartridge to Blount International, Inc. for $112 million in October 1997. Looking to increase profitability, Pentair announced in June 1998 that it had launched an effort to cut costs by $60 million over a two-year period. With an increased emphasis on cost control and a disciplined approach to acquisitions that resulted in synergistic growth within core areas, Pentair was well-positioned for increasing growth and profits into the 21st century.

Principal Subsidiaries

Aplex Industries, Inc.; Biesemeyer Manufacturing Corporation; Century Manufacturing Co.; Delta International Machinery Corp.; Fleck Controls, Inc.; Hoffman Enclosures Inc.; HS Systems, Inc.; McNeil Corporation; ORSCO Acquisition Corp.; Pentair Pump Group; Penwald Insurance Company; Porter-Cable Corporation; Schroff Inc.; Telestack Company; Pentair Canada, Inc.; Pentair Halifax, Inc. (Canada); Pentair Nova Scotia Co. (Canada); Lincoln Czech Republic; Fleck Europe, SAS (France); Schroff SAS (France); Transrack S.A. (France); EuroPentair, GmbH (Germany); Flex Elektrowerkzeuge GmbH (Germany); Lincoln GmbH (Germany); Schroff, GmbH (Germany); Pentair Financial Services Ireland; Schroff S.r.L. (Italy); SIATA S.p.A. (Italy); Schroff K.K. (Japan); APNO, S.A. de C.V. (Mexico); Hoffman Engineering, S.A. de C.V. de SrL (Mexico); Hoffman-Schroff PTE Ltd. (Singapore); Pentair Asia, PTE Ltd. (Singapore); Schroff Scandinavia AB (Sweden); Schroff Co. Ltd. (Taiwan); Hoffman Engineering Co Limited (U.K.); Lincoln U.K. Ltd.; Pentair U.K. Ltd.; Schroff U.K. Ltd.; Pentair FSC Corporation (U.S. Virgin Islands).

Principal Operating Units

Professional Tools and Equipment Group; Water and Fluid Technologies Group; Electrical and Electronic Enclosures Group.

Further Reading

Beal, Dave, "Paperless Pentair Extends Its Reach," *St. Paul Pioneer Press,* February 11, 1996.

Calian, Sara, "Pentair, After Switching Businesses, Is Often Ignored, but Finds Some Fans," *Wall Street Journal,* May 17, 1993, p. C6.

Carideo, Anthony, "Many Are Expecting a Turnaround in '92," *Star Tribune,* August 26, 1991.

Fraser, Jill Andresky, "The Five Rules of Debt," *Corporate Finance,* December 10, 1991.

Harpole, Murray J., *Living the American Dream: Pentair, Inc.—The First Twenty-Five Years,* St. Paul, Minn.: St. Thomas Technology Press, 1992.

Hoonsbeen, Mark, "Paperless Tiger," *Twin Cities Business Monthly,* April 1996.

Jaffe, Thomas, "Paper Profits," *Forbes,* August 25, 1986.

Lappen, Alyssa A., "Gene's Dream," *Forbes,* May 30, 1988.

Marth, Del, "Friendly Takeovers," *Nation's Business,* May 1986.

Mullins, Robert, "Pentair Aims to Grow Fleck Controls After Acquisition," *Business Journal—Milwaukee,* November 11, 1995, p. 26.

"Paper Losses Mean a Real Income Drop for Pentair," *Star Tribune,* February 5, 1991.

"Pentair Agrees to Buy Anoka Holding Firm," *Star Tribune,* November 15, 1988.

Peterson, Susan E., "Pentair on the Prowl: The Conglomerate Has Been Seeking a Major Acquisition for More Than a Year," *Star Tribune,* June 20, 1992.

——, "Pentair's '91 Revenues Dip, but St. Paul Company Reports a 28.2 Percent Increase in Net Income," *Star Tribune,* January 31, 1992.

Sikora, Marty, "Pentair's Persistent Demand for Value," *Mergers & Acquisitions,* July/August 1995, p. 48.

Trachtenberg, Jeffrey A., "It's Not Glamorous, but It Works," *Forbes,* May 21, 1984.

Youngblood, Dick, "Pentair Transforms Itself Once More," *Star Tribune,* September 18, 1995.

—Jay P. Pederson
—updated by David E. Salamie

PetroFina S.A.

52 rue de l'Industrie
B-1040 Brussels
Belgium
(32-2) 288 91 11
Fax: (32-2) 288 34 45
Web site: http://www.fina.com

Public Company
Incorporated: 1920 as Compagnie Financière Belge des
    Pétroles
Employees: 14,675
Sales: BFr 727.03 billion (US$20.25 billion) (1997)
Stock Exchanges: Brussels Paris Amsterdam Frankfurt
    London Zürich Basel Geneva New York
Ticker Symbol: FIN
SICs: 1311 Crude Petroleum & Natural Gas; 2819
    Industrial Inorganic Chemicals, Not Elsewhere
    Classified; 2851 Paints, Varnishes, Lacquers, Enamels
    & Allied Products; 2911 Petroleum Refining; 5541
    Gasoline Service Stations

PetroFina S.A., Belgium's largest corporation, is the 15th largest publicly traded integrated oil and gas company in the world. PetroFina is a leading exploiter of North Sea oil and gas, with other exploration and production interests in Italy, Azerbaijan, the Gulf of Mexico, Texas, Louisiana, Alaska, Canada, Libya, Angola, the Democratic Republic of Congo, and Vietnam. Downstream, the company boasts some of the most efficient refineries in the world, in particular at Antwerp in Belgium, Port Arthur in the United States, and Immingham in the United Kingdom (the Lindsey Oil Refinery, which is jointly owned by PetroFina and Total S.A.); other refineries are located in Rome, Italy; Luanda, Angola; and Big Spring, Texas. Under the Fina brand, the company operates about 6,300 service stations in Europe and the southeastern and southwestern United States. PetroFina is also active in the field of petrochemicals, where it ranks among the top four producers of polypropylene in the world. In the area of paints, the company owns about 80 percent of the Sigma Coatings Group, known worldwide for its marine and protective coatings. PetroFina lost most of its assets during World War II, and has achieved its current position virtually from nothing in a matter of half a century.

Romanian Roots

PetroFina was founded in 1920—as Compagnie Financière Belge des Pétroles—by a group of Belgian financiers headed by the Bank of Antwerp. Its existence became possible when four Romanian oil companies, confiscated from their German owners after World War I, came up for sale at an advantageous price. PetroFina's founders were aware of the importance of petrol in the age of motorized transport. Romania, an oil-rich but cash-poor country, presented a convenient entry into an already overcrowded industry. The assets on offer included oil wells, refineries, and distribution networks. On taking control, PetroFina merged three of the four companies to form Concordia, whose 1921 output, at 128,500 tons, represented 11 percent of Romania's total crude oil production. Five years later Concordia's production had tripled.

PetroFina marketed its products in Western Europe through Purfina, an Antwerp-based company jointly established with the American Pure Oil Company, but wholly owned by PetroFina starting in 1923. To serve central Europe and the Balkans, PetroFina set up Socombel, which supplied small independent outlets until PetroFina acquired its own outlets over the next few years. The company also owned a small fleet of tanker ships.

In 1923 the Banque de l'Union Parisienne became an important shareholder in PetroFina, resolving a dispute over the prewar claims of a French company on Concordia's Vega refinery. The arrangement was attractive both to France, anxious to acquire an oil supply independent of the U.S. and British companies, and to PetroFina, which wanted access to the capital markets of Paris.

French PetroFina, a subsidiary started in 1924, won a monopoly on the import into France of Soviet oil products, in which Purfina's Ertvelde refinery also dealt. French PetroFina soon entered the refinery business, constructing a large plant at Dunkirk; this received most of its crude oil from the United

---

Company Perspectives:

Our mission: To maximize added value throughout the entire industrial and commercial process by pursuing a clear strategic line, using company resources efficiently and safely and yielding the necessary profit to remunerate shareholders and ensure the Company's growth; to play a constructive role within the communities in which we operate, by positioning our activities within their development objectives and by ensuring high added value quality employment, through continuous learning.

States, since until 1936 PetroFina's own oil fields were subject to Romanian government prohibitions on crude oil exports. At the approach of war, however, French PetroFina reached an agreement with Romania whereby the company financed arms supplies in return for crude oil.

The Depression of the 1930s affected PetroFina less by its direct impact than by changes it prompted in Belgian commercial law. Legislation passed in 1935 and designed to insulate the banking system from industrial ups and downs obliged the Bank of Antwerp to transfer its shares in PetroFina to the specially formed Antwerp Company. PetroFina, created by financiers and for its first 15 years managed by them, now became an oil company run by oilmen.

Substantial World War II Losses

Having survived the Depression with its assets comparatively intact, PetroFina suffered catastrophic losses during World War II. The Germans bombed and later dismantled the Dunkirk refinery. Of PetroFina's five tankers, only one survived the war. The most serious losses, however, were in Romania. Invading German forces seized the oil fields and refineries, and after the war the Soviet Union appropriated all of PetroFina's Romanian assets, together with its outlets in Hungary and Bulgaria.

PetroFina had not lost quite everything. Distribution subsidiaries, including those in western Europe and Africa, had survived, as had the Ertvelde refinery. The most important element of continuity from prewar days was that PetroFina had managed to retain its workforce, whose expertise would be the company's major strength in the postwar reconstruction period.

Postwar Reconstruction and Expansion

In the years immediately following the war, PetroFina—led by president Laurent Wolters—concentrated on rebuilding its distribution network, acquiring three new ships, modernizing its Belgian depots, and restructuring outlets in France, the United Kingdom, the Netherlands, and the Belgian Congo (later known as Zaire, still later as the Democratic Republic of Congo). With virtually no products of its own, it formed an alliance with British Petroleum PLC (BP), which by contrast had oil but lacked adequate distribution facilities. Under an agreement which lasted from 1946 to 1980, BP supplied the oil, crude or refined, that PetroFina required. Lacking funds to rebuild the

Dunkirk refinery, PetroFina turned it over to BP in exchange for products.

Faced with an unprecedented demand for petrol, the Belgian government decided in the late 1940s that the country's refinery capacity needed drastic upgrading. PetroFina and BP spawned the Société Industrielle Belge des Pétroles (SIBP) to build a huge refinery at Antwerp, which opened in October 1951 with a capacity of two million tons per annum, equivalent to Belgium's entire consumption. In the next 20 years the refinery's capacity was to increase by a factor of eight, making it by far the largest in Belgium, and among the largest in Europe.

PetroFina undertook its first postwar explorations in Mexico, starting in 1949. The Mexican venture proved short-lived. Canadian Fina Oil (Canada Fina) and Canadian PetroFina started exploring on opposite sides of Canada in the early 1950s; in 1961 Canada Fina would become a subsidiary of Canadian PetroFina. Exploration also took place in Africa, including Angola, Zaire, and Egypt, during the 1950s.

In 1956 PetroFina gained a foothold in the United States. American PetroFina was set up in cooperation with the Panhandle Oil Corporation of Texas to operate Panhandle's oil wells, refineries, and distribution network. By the end of 1957 the company was extracting 11,000 barrels per day (b/d), had refining capacity for 50,000 b/d, and controlled over 1,000 retail outlets.

The 1950s saw PetroFina's refinery base and distribution networks expanding into Germany, Italy, Sweden, Norway, Switzerland, and Tunisia, as well as North America. It typically entered new markets through acquisitions, financed through rights issues. A dozen large tankers were added to the fleet, the availability of several of which gave PetroFina an edge when the 1956 closure of the Suez Canal added 25 days to the sea journey taken by most of Europe's oil.

Alongside PetroFina's main activities, complementary interests were being developed. Palmafina, a margarine and soap-making subsidiary dating from before the war, joined a U.S. collaborator in a new venture, Oleochim, founded in 1957 to produce fatty acids and glycerine at Ertvelde.

Moved into Chemicals and Paints in the 1950s and 1960s

In 1954 PetroFina had taken a share in Petrochim, a petrochemical venture by a consortium of Belgian chemical companies. Four years later, ready to exploit its research findings, Petrochim began constructing a factory near the SIBP refinery at Antwerp. When the factory failed to achieve the economies of scale needed for profitability, PetroFina took control together with a partner with extensive petrochemical experience, the American Phillips Petroleum Company. In 1964 PetroFina and Phillips launched Petrochim on a BFr 5 billion investment program involving the construction of one of the largest ethylene production facilities in the world; an extraction unit for benzene, toluene, and xylenes; and a synthetic rubber manufacturing plant.

PetroFina's petrochemical interests grew during the 1960s, with an emphasis on vertical integration. Pipelines were built to take Petrochim's ethylene to the factories that used it, and PetroFina and Phillips invested in one such factory, Polyolefins. Set up in 1966 to make high density polyethylene, Polyolefins would increase its output by a factor of five in its first 15 years.

PetroFina became a major force in U.S. petrochemicals with its 1963 acquisition of Cosden Petroleum Corporation, a leading polystyrene manufacturer with valuable patents and a wealth of expertise. Between 1963 and 1979, Cosden's petrochemical sales were to grow from US$18 million to US$500 million, necessitating ambitious construction projects, notably Cosmar, a styrene plant in Louisiana feeding Cosden's original polystyrene plant at Big Spring and an additional plant at Calumet City.

The year 1963 also saw PetroFina's entry into the paint market with Oleochim's purchase of Astrolac. This move fitted neatly into the portfolio: paints and varnishes were needed for PetroFina's ships and plant, and PetroFina's refineries could supply many of their ingredients.

North Sea Oil and Gas Began Flowing in the Late 1960s

Around the same time, PetroFina was joining forces with Phillips Petroleum for explorations in the North Sea, the extent of whose resources were then only suspected. Together with Agip of Italy, the partners acquired the rights to a 5,000-square-kilometer area in the British sector. The giant Hewett gas field, discovered in 1967, was shared with the owners of an adjacent block. Gas started to flow in 1969, by which time two other gas fields had been found. In 1965 the Phillips-PetroFina-Agip group acquired exploration licenses for the Norwegian sector. Phillips was the operator and PetroFina had a 30 percent participation. Success came with the discovery of Ekofisk. Other fields were found nearby, but Ekofisk was the richest oil field ever discovered in Western Europe.

During the 1960s and 1970s, the average capacity of a PetroFina refinery tripled. Of the refineries belonging to the companies it had bought, PetroFina closed some and upgraded others. Large, modern plants, such as the Lindsey oil refinery in England, co-owned with Total, were constructed. This rationalization, resulting in a reduction in the number of sites, threatened to increase transport costs. Therefore PetroFina began in the late 1960s to make reciprocal arrangements with other companies. Soon PetroFina, with only four European refineries of its own, was refining in 26 different European locations.

In 1970 Laurent Wolters, who had presided over PetroFina's rise from its postwar ashes, became chairman. He was succeeded as president and chief executive by Jacques Meeus, the nephew of Laurent Meeus, one of the founders of PetroFina.

Bringing the Ekofisk field into production was the major project of the 1970s. Requiring innovative engineering, it cost 15 times as much as any of PetroFina's previous exploration and production enterprises. It signaled a move towards processing and marketing the products of the group's own wells rather than purchased crude.

In 1975, the year that Adolphe Demeure de Lespaul succeeded Meeus, Ekofisk's oil began to flow along an undersea pipeline to a terminal on Britain's Teesside. Two years later gas began to be piped to a purification plant at Emden in Germany for distribution to France, Holland, and Belgium. By 1979 11.3 million cubic meters of gas and 17 million tons of oil were coming from Ekofisk.

The shortages following the OPEC oil crisis of 1973 gave PetroFina's North Sea explorations an additional impetus. The Maureen field was discovered in 1973, and in 1976 a series of exciting discoveries began in T-Block, including the Thelma, Toni, Tiffany, and Treena fields.

At home in Belgium, the 1970s were years of continuing expansion for PetroFina's petrochemical interests. Drawing on American PetroFina's plastics expertise, the company achieved total vertical integration right through to consumer goods manufacturing. From 1972, for example, styrene was brought by canal from the Petrochim factory at Antwerp, itself fed by the SIBP refinery, to the Belgochim plant at Feluy, where it was made into polystyrene granules. These in turn were sent to PetroFina's Synfina site at Manage, to be made into household items such as toys.

In 1977 PetroFina and an Italian partner, Montedison S.p.A., established a new company, Montefina, into which Belgochim was integrated. Montefina built a plant at Feluy to make polypropylene, a versatile plastic with applications in the automotive industry. A research laboratory was set up on the same site at Feluy, one of the largest plastics plants in Europe.

In the United States too, PetroFina was expanding its petrochemical interests. By the end of the 1970s it had 14 percent of total U.S. capacity for both styrene and polystyrene, and co-owned Hercofina, one of the largest producers of terephthalates, a primary ingredient of polyester fibers. Raw materials for Hercofina came from the Port Arthur refinery which American PetroFina had acquired in 1973.

Consolidated Paint Interest in Sigma Coatings in 1972

In 1972 the group consolidated its paint production facilities into Sigma Coatings, which by the end of the 1970s would have 20 paint factories in Europe, North and South America, and the East. In the same year, PetroFina fused its fatty acids concerns, Oleochim and Palmafina, into Oleofina. At first co-owned, this leading manufacturer of glycerines and glycerides later became a fully owned PetroFina subsidiary.

In the 1970s, during the OPEC crisis, PetroFina, in common with other companies, could at times operate neither its fleet nor its refineries at full capacity. In 1977, faced with losses and also with debts incurred to finance exploration and production, PetroFina began preparing itself to weather the inclement market conditions. Refineries were upgraded with the latest equipment. Distribution subsidiaries improved buying and inventory policies to the extent that they showed a profit in the difficult year of 1979. The 1980 investment program was financed entirely from retained earnings.

Oil extraction in Ekofisk peaked in 1980. To recover less accessible reserves, the operators began to inject water into the ground, also mitigating the subsidence of the seabed (subsidence is the sinking of the seabed from the pumping of oil and gas beneath it); as a result, the platforms later needed jacking up by six meters. Meanwhile, the Maureen field off the coast of Scotland came onstream in 1983. The purchase of Charterhouse Petroleum in 1986 gave the group extensive new reserves and exploration licenses in the U.K. sector of the North Sea. In 1990 PetroFina bought important North Sea exploration and production interests from Elf Aquitaine and Lasmo.

Across the Atlantic, PetroFina Canada was sold to the Canadian national oil company, Petro-Canada, at the beginning of the 1980s, but PetroFina held a quarter-share in the explorations of Texas Oil & Gas for four years from 1982. In 1988 Tenneco's onshore production capabilities in Texas, Louisiana, and New Mexico were purchased, doubling PetroFina's U.S. reserves overnight.

Upgraded Refineries in the 1980s

PetroFina sought to compensate for the gradual decline in Ekofisk production not only by exploring elsewhere, but also by improving processing techniques, both in its refineries and in its petrochemical plants. At the Antwerp refinery, where PetroFina bought out BP's share in 1988, investment enabled more and more products to be squeezed out of each ton of crude, and improved the proportion of petrol and other high-value products to those of heavy fuel oil. Similar investment went on at other refineries, some of which were also equipped to switch production between petrol and propylene according to demand. U.K. and Belgian refineries were modified to produce lead-free or lead-reduced petrol. The *Economist,* March 14, 1987, credited PetroFina with "some of the oil industry's most efficient refineries."

In petrochemicals, too, the emphasis everywhere was on larger, more efficient plants. In 1983 PetroFina bought out its partner in the synthetic rubber factory, and in 1985 it did the same at the ethylene and polyethylene plants at Antwerp, becoming one of Europe's largest producers of high density polyethylene. Buying a polypropylene plant near Houston, Texas, in 1984, the group acquired nine percent of the total U.S. capacity for manufacturing this chemical.

The mid-1980s were record years for chemical sales, but towards the end of the decade PetroFina was hit by falling prices. At the same time there was surplus production in the oil market and a squeeze on refining margins. In the first half of 1990 profits fell 12 percent, but these problems were eventually offset by an upsurge in the productivity of PetroFina's newer North Sea oil and gas interests.

1990s and Beyond

Adolphe Demeure, who had died in 1985, had been succeeded by Jean-Pierre Amory as chairman and chief executive. Amory was in turn succeeded as chairman by Albert Frère in 1990. For the first time since the 1930s, a financier was in charge; Frère was the chairman of the holding company Groupe Bruxelles Lambert (GBL), PetroFina's largest shareholder (with about a 31 percent stake). Alongside Frère, François Cornélis became CEO. In 1991 Cornélis became vice-chairman as well, a title he shared with Etienne Davignon; the latter was

the chairman of Société Générale de Belgique S.A. (SGB), the second largest holder of PetroFina stock (with approximately 11 percent). In 1989 GBL and SGB (along with lesser PetroFina shareholders Groupe Fortis AG and Sofina S.A.) entered into an agreement—binding until 2004—whereby the companies would "act in concert" on such matters as the strategic plans of PetroFina, acquisitions and divestments, and any third-party takeover attempts. GBL and SGB also had the right of first refusal whenever the other party intended to sell PetroFina shares. The two companies controlled half the seats on the PetroFina board of directors—PetroFina's future was clearly in Frère and Davignon's hands.

In the early 1990s greater-than-normal subsidence at the Ekofisk field alarmed the Norwegian government, which threatened to shut down a major offshore facility jointly owned by PetroFina. Under a redevelopment plan, a new platform for treating and transporting oil and gas was installed in 1997. PetroFina continued to seek additional production sites in the 1990s, beginning production in both Italy and Vietnam during the decade. The company's facilities in Angola were devastated in 1993 and 1994 as a result of the civil war there. In mid-1998 PetroFina announced it would downsize its presence in southern Africa to just Angola and the Democratic Republic of Congo; it divested its downstream operations in Gabon, Burundi, and Rwanda. In 1997 PetroFina took a 28 percent stake in an exploration project in British Columbia, Canada, as well as a five percent interest in an offshore Caspian Sea field in Azerbaijan. In Alaska, the Badami field (on the North Slope, east of Prudhoe Bay) began production in August 1998, through a venture 70 percent-owned by British Petroleum and 30 percent-owned by PetroFina. The company's oil and gas production reached 88.7 million barrels of oil equivalent in 1997, with oil production comprising 53.9 million barrels, a 7.6 percent increase over the previous year. Overall reserves remained steady, thanks to declining reserves of natural gas; oil reserves increased to 607 million barrels by 1997.

In the chemical sector, PetroFina in 1995 gained full control of the Montefina polypropylene venture, which it renamed Fina Chemicals Feluy S.A. In September 1997 the company announced a partnership with BASF Aktiengesellschaft to construct the world's largest liquids steam cracker near the Port Arthur refinery in Texas to produce ethylene and propylene. The two companies formed a limited partnership, 60 percent-owned by BASF and 40 percent-owned by PetroFina, to build the US$900 million facility. In October 1998 PetroFina announced that it had entered into two cooperative agreements with the Solvay Group of Belgium in the area of high-density polyethylene (HDPE). PetroFina aimed to double its overall petrochemical production by the year 2008, planning to spend US$800 million to do so. Meanwhile, in paints, PetroFina merged Sigma Coatings with the paint operations of the Lafarge group. As a result the new Sigma Coatings—of which PetroFina owned about 80 percent, and Lafarge around 20 percent—was one of the three largest makers of decorative paints in Europe.

Fina, Inc.—the new name of American Fina as of 1991—acquired a 34 percent interest in Southwest Convenience Stores, LLC (SCS) in 1996. SCS ran more than 160 Fina service stations, all of which operated alongside 7-Eleven convenience stores, in the southwestern United States. In early 1997 Petro-

Fina announced plans to acquire the 15 percent of Fina that it did not already own. In a related maneuver PetroFina stock began trading on the New York Stock Exchange (NYSE) in September 1997; the company thereby became the first Belgian company on the NYSE. In August 1998 PetroFina completed its purchase of the Fina stake, spending about US$265 million in the process. Fina, Inc. became a wholly owned subsidiary of PetroFina and its stock ceased trading on the American Stock Exchange. By gaining full control of Fina and adding a listing on the NYSE, PetroFina simplified its organizational structure, raised its profile in the United States, and gained greater access to the markets of the world's leading economy. The NYSE listing also necessitated that the company, traditionally low in profile and somewhat secretive, conform to the more stringent financial reporting requirements of U.S. securities laws.

PetroFina's future direction was unclear as it headed into the late 1990s, a period marked by falling petroleum prices leading to intense global consolidation in the oil industry. In August 1998, a few days after British Petroleum PLC and Amoco Corporation agreed to a blockbuster merger, Frère told French and Belgian newspapers that PetroFina needed a partner to survive. Then in early December 1998—nearly simultaneous with the announcement of another huge merger, that of Mobil Corporation and Exxon Corporation—PetroFina announced that Total S.A. had agreed to acquire the company through a US$12.9 billion stock deal, creating in the process Total Fina, an oil company ranking number three in Europe and number six worldwide. The deal came after reports that either Elf Aquitaine or Italy's ENI S.p.A. would take over PetroFina. Instead, Frère struck a deal with Elf's rival which gave him a 12 percent stake in Total.

Principal Subsidiaries

EtmoFina S.A.; Fina Europe S.A.; Fina Insurance; Fina Exploration Norway S.A.; Fina Exploration Norway SCA; Fina Marine S.A.; Fina Raffinaderij Antwerpen N.V.; Fina Research S.A.; Fina Oleochemicals N.V.; Fina Chemicals Antwerpen N.V.; Fina Chemicals Feluy S.A.; PetroFina International Group S.A.; Sigma Coatings S.A.; Fina Antwerp Olefins N.V. (65%); Fina Petroleos de Angola S.A.R.L. (62.9%); Fina GmbH (Austria); Brittany Holdings Ltd. (Bermuda); Fina do Brasil Petroleo Ltda. (Brazil); Fina Rep S.P.R.L. (Republic of Congo); Fina Congo S.A.R.L. (Republic of Congo; 60%); SEP Congo S.A.R.L. (Republic of Congo; 36.6%); Fina France S.A.; Sigma Coatings S.A. (France); Fina Deutschland GmbH (Germany); Fina Holding Deutschland GmbH (Germany); Fina Italiana S.p.A. (Italy); Raffineria di Roma S.p.A. (Italy; 57.5%); Petro-Fina Japan Office; Fina Exploration Libya B.V.; Fina Road Services (Luxembourg); Fina International N.V. (Netherlands); Fina Nederland B.V. (Netherlands); Mafina B.V. (Netherlands); Sigma Coatings B.V. (Netherlands); Norpipe Oil AS (Norway; 28.44%); Norsea Gas A/S (Norway; 12.9%); Fina Portuguesa - Oleos e Carburantes, S.A. (Portugal); Fina Far East Pte Ltd (Singapore); Fina Iberica S.A. (Spain); Fina Aviation-Chemicals S.A. (Switzerland); Fina plc (U.K.); Fina Exploration Ltd. (U.K.); Lindsey Oil Refinery Ltd. (U.K.; 50%); Norsea Pipeline Ltd. (U.K.; 23.75%); American PetroFina Holding Co. (U.S.A.); Fina, Inc. (U.S.A.); PetroFina Delaware, Inc. (U.S.A.); Cos-Mar, Inc. (U.S.A.; 50%); Fina Exploration Minh Hai B.V. (Vietnam).

Further Reading

Bahree, Bhushan, and Martin du Bois, "Total to Acquire Petrofina in $12.9 Billion Stock Deal," *Wall Street Journal,* December 2, 1998, p. A17.

Dafter, Ray, "The Enigmatic Independent," *Financial Times,* November 3, 1983.

du Bois, Martin, "Petrofina Investors Weigh Uncertainties over Oil Field Investment and Dividend," *Wall Street Journal,* November 13, 1992, p. A7B.

——, "Petrofina Takes Measures to Avoid Takeover Attempts," *Wall Street Journal,* April 8, 1993, p. A10.

du Bois, Martin, and Bhushan Bahree, "Elf Aquitaine in Talks to Buy Petrofina in Stock Deal," *Wall Street Journal,* November 19, 1998, p. A16.

Dumoulin, Michel, *Petrofina: Un groupe petrolier international et la gestion de l'incertitude, vol 1: 1920–1979,* Louvain La Neuve, Belgium: Peeters, 1997, 235 p.

Fritsch, Peter, "Petrofina Offers to Buy Rest of Fina for $256 Million," *Wall Street Journal,* February 26, 1997, p. C18.

Hagerty, Bob, "Frère's Long Climb Results in a Jewel," *Wall Street Journal Europe,* May 4, 1990.

——, "Petrofina Hopes to Lure U.S. Investors," *Wall Street Journal Europe,* October 22, 1990.

——, "Petrofina's Big Holders Expected to Press for More Openness," *Wall Street Journal Europe,* May 7, 1990.

Hill, Andrew, "Flaws in the Elf Takeover Theory," *Financial Times,* April 27, 1993, p. 26.

Kovski, Alan, "Fina to Get More Muscle, Not Job Cuts, in Petrofina Takeover," *Oil Daily,* February 19, 1998, p. 5.

Locquet, Gérard, ed., *Contribution à l'histoire de Petrofina,* Brussels: PetroFina S.A., 1980.

Morris, Gregory D.L., Debbie Jackson, and David Hunter, "Steady Aim Makes for Fast Growth at Petrofina," *Chemical Week,* October 6, 1993, pp. 48–50.

PetroFina: 1920–1995, Brussels: PetroFina S.A., n.d.

Smith, Leigh, "Petrofina's Secrets of the Deep," *Lloyd's List,* December 18, 1989.

Wrong, Michela, "Fina Treads Carefully in Angola's Oilfields," *Financial Times,* April 16, 1996, p. 31.

—Alison Classe
—updated by David E. Salamie

PG&E Corporation

PG&E Corporation

77 Beale Street
San Francisco, California 94105-1814
U.S.A.
(415) 973-7000
(800) 743-5000
Fax: (415) 973-0585
Web site: http://www.pge.com

Public Company
Incorporated: 1905 as Pacific Gas and Electric Company
Employees: 26,200
Sales: $15.4 billion (1997)
Stock Exchanges: New York Pacific London Basel
    Zürich Amsterdam
Ticker Symbol: PCG
SICs: 4931 Electric & Other Services Combined; 6719
    Holding Companies, Not Elsewhere Classified

PG&E Corporation is one of the largest power and gas distributors in the United States, with several energy-related subsidiaries. The company's most important subsidiary, Pacific Gas and Electric Company, was the second largest investor-owned gas and electric utility in the United States in terms of sales in 1998. It had a service area covering about 94,000 square miles—most of northern and central California—and a population of more than 13 million people. The company was positioning itself to be a nationwide power distributor rather than a power supplier in the approaching deregulated utility environment.

Early History

Pacific Gas and Electric Company (PG&E) was formed in 1905 by John Martin and Eugene de Sabla, Jr., to acquire and merge power companies in central California. Martin and de Sabla, who had earlier been involved with gold mines in the Yuba River region north of Sacramento, California, began in the 1890s to use hydroelectric power to operate their mines. De Sabla located customers and raised the capital for their first

hydroelectric plant in Nevada City, California, in 1895; Martin handled the engineering with help from William Stanley, developer of the Westinghouse alternating-current electrical system. The plant proved successful and convinced them there was a market for electrical power in Sacramento and San Francisco. They built another plant in 1898 and in 1899 formed Yuba Power Company to build a third, more powerful facility.

In 1900 the three plants were consolidated into Bay Counties Power Company, with de Sabla as president and general manager. In 1901 the company built a 140-mile transmission line, the world's longest at that time, to power an electric railway in Oakland, California. The line, suspended across the San Francisco Bay, carried 60,000 volts—a very high voltage for the time—and attracted great publicity. The company then joined its three plants into a single power grid, although it remained primarily a power-generating company, not a distribution-based utility.

In 1903 de Sabla and Martin formed California Gas & Electric Company (CG&E) to buy power companies and merge them into a large electric grid that could use economies of scale to its advantage. In the next few years CG&E bought many power companies, backed by capital from New York financiers. CG&E's acquisitions included long-established utilities like Oakland Gas Light & Heat Company, serving Oakland and Berkeley, and United Gas & Electric Company, serving communities south of San Francisco. In 1905 de Sabla and Martin bought San Francisco Gas & Electric Company (SFG&E), the dominant utility in San Francisco, giving the company a power grid in the most important city in central California. They merged SFG&E with CG&E to form Pacific Gas and Electric Company, capitalized at about $45 million. The San Francisco company had steam power plants, which complemented PG&E's hydroelectric plants by carrying peak loads when demand was high or when freezes or droughts cut hydroelectric output.

Steady Expansion: 1900–60

PG&E continued buying power companies and merging electric grids. By 1914 it owned the largest integrated regional system on the Pacific Coast and was one of the five largest utilities in the United States. It supplied 1.3 million people in a

37,000-square-mile area and had 36 percent of California's electric and gas business. During most of this period the company's steam-power capacity was growing faster than its hydroelectric capacity, partly because of the falling price of California crude oil. In 1912 PG&E began to increase its hydroelectric capacity. Using water from the South Yuba and Bear Rivers, it built a series of six plants with a projected capacity of 190,750 horsepower. A 110-mile transmission line strung across steel towers carried 100,000 volts to PG&E's switching station at Cordelia, California.

PG&E also continued to grow through mergers. In 1927 it bought the Sierra and San Francisco Power Company, and in 1930 it bought its only major competitor, the Great Western Power Company. In 1935 PG&E consolidated the operations of the companies it had bought.

PG&E and most other electric utilities were not greatly affected by the Great Depression because of their status as monopolies. Most sales that were lost to declining industry were made up by increasing residential sales.

In 1948 Pacific signed an interchange agreement with Southern California Edison Company that stated that either company would sell the other excess electricity when needed until 1962. PG&E continued to expand, buying Vallejo Electric Light & Power Company in 1949 and Pacific Public Service Company in 1954. By 1955 PG&E's network extended into 46 counties in northern and central California. It supplied electricity to 168 cities and towns and gas to 146 cities and towns. Pacific operated 57 hydroelectric plants and 12 steam plants generating about 84 percent of its total electric output, but bought 68 percent of its gas from El Paso Natural Gas Company. The company had 18,000 employees. Total revenue for 1954 was $386 million.

In 1957 PG&E and the General Electric Company constructed the small Vallecitos atomic power plant. Plans for a large nuclear power plant at Bodega Bay, north of San Francisco, were scrapped in the early 1960s because of public opposition. The company constructed a 63,000-kilowatt nuclear power plant at Humboldt Bay near Eureka, California, in 1963. From 1968 to 1970, Pacific participated in a design study of a 350,000-kilowatt sodium-cooled nuclear power plant. The company contributed $10 million over the following ten years to a joint U.S. government-industry project to build the first large sodium-cooled reactor. It also began construction of two pressurized-water nuclear power plants at Diablo Canyon, expected to total one million kilowatts. The plants were scheduled to be finished in 1975 and 1976.

Controversy in the 1970s

By 1973 PG&E was the second largest utility in the United States, with 65 hydroelectric plants and 12 steam electric plants and total revenue of $494 million. The Diablo Canyon nuclear power plants, however, were running years behind schedule. PG&E entered the 1970s expecting demand to increase by six to seven percent annually, as it had for years; but California was growing rapidly, and demand grew faster than PG&E had projected. In addition, natural gas, which fueled the steam electric plants, was in short supply in California. The energy crisis of the early 1970s sent the price of gas skyrocketing, and the company's natural gas business shriveled. Between 1975 and 1984 PG&E lost 60 percent of its industrial gas sales.

PG&E announced the urgent need to convert its plants to oil, which was also in short supply. At a cost of $100 million, the conversion involved building moorings for oil supertankers at seven of PG&E's 12 steam electric plants. To pay for the conversion, the company asked for a $233 million rate increase by 1975, the largest in California history.

The California Public Utilities Commission (CPUC), the state body that regulates PG&E, traditionally had been one of the toughest in the United States. From 1966 to 1974, however, when Ronald Reagan was governor of California, the CPUC became more sympathetic to utilities. One decision by the Reagan-appointed commission allowed utilities to increase rates without public hearings as the price of oil increased. By early 1974, with the price of oil soaring, rate increases were enacted almost monthly. As a result, PG&E's $233 million rate increase received wide news coverage and was opposed vigorously by consumer groups, which used public outrage to push for utility reform. Jerry Brown, Reagan's successor, appointed reform-oriented commissioners to the CPUC. In 1975 the CPUC ordered PG&E to offer a minimal amount of electricity at subsidized rates to all residential customers. The move was opposed by PG&E and its largest customers, whose electric rates would pay for the subsidy.

PG&E also faced opposition from environmentalists. The Environmental Defense Fund (EDF) confronted the utility, claiming PG&E would not need to build more power plants if it used its existing capacity more wisely. Both sides ran television commercials to push their viewpoints. The EDF eventually helped pressure PG&E into using alternative energy suppliers, such as windmill farms, and use-strategies such as redirecting customer demand to stretch generating capacity further. By the late 1970s PG&E was offering incentives to customers who fulfilled their energy requirements at nonpeak hours.

In 1979 the CPUC granted PG&E a $269 million annual rate increase, but it also pushed the company to buy more power from alternative energy sources. In 1980 the CPUC granted a $530 million gas- and electric-rate increase, but over the next few years it ordered the company to give several refunds. Net income for 1980 was $525 million. In 1981 the CPUC authorized the company to begin a six-year, interest-free home loan program for customers who installed insulation or energy-saving devices.

Rising Rates in the 1980s

One of the two Diablo Canyon nuclear plants was finished in 1981, but PG&E did not receive permission to begin testing because of concerns that the plant, located just two miles from an earthquake fault, was not safe. Questions were also raised about quality control during the plant's construction. Protesters blockaded the plant for two days while the U.S. Nuclear Regulatory Commission considered approving its start-up. Permission was granted in late 1981, and in 1982 the company hired Bechtel Power Corporation to manage the project while it was completed and licensed. In late 1983 uranium fuel was finally loaded into the Diablo Canyon reactor, and testing began in 1984. The company then requested rate increases to pay for the plant, which cost $5.8 billion, 18 times initial projections.

At the same time the company continued buying electricity from alternative sources. Under the 1978 Public Utility Regulatory Policies Act, U.S. electric utilities were required to buy power offered by independent producers at prices set by state utility commissions. In 1982 PG&E signed a contract to buy most of the wind-generated power from a wind farm in Solano County, California. In 1983 it agreed to buy all the electricity from a solar-energy power plant being built by a subsidiary of Atlantic Richfield Company. By mid-1986 PG&E had signed 695 contracts to buy 20 percent of alternative capacity planned for the United States, more than half of PG&E's own capacity. The company had so many alternative generating contracts that it had excess capacity.

In 1982 PG&E appointed Richard Clarke as head of utility operations. Clarke won CPUC approval to overhaul the structure of natural gas rates for PG&E's industrial customers. That move helped reverse a long decline in gas sales and doubled the utility's net income to $1 billion during the next four years. Also in 1982 the CPUC ordered PG&E to suspend its large fuel-oil contract with Chevron USA Inc. PG&E had signed a long-term contract with Chevron during the early 1970s, when natural gas prices and power-demand projections were high. In 1981, however, capacity increased due to alternative electric sources, and natural gas prices dropped. In part because PG&E had contracted to buy more expensive fuel oil, residential electric rates rose six percent in 1981. The CPUC used contingency provisions in PG&E's oil contract that allowed for suspension of deliveries if a government agency ordered it.

In 1984 the CPUC granted the company $697 million in rate increases, a 1.7 percent hike. Net income for 1984 was $975 million. In 1985 the CPUC ordered PG&E to lower its natural gas rates by $316.9 million per year. The following year the company acquired the 48.9 percent of Pacific Gas Transmission Company that it did not already own in a stock swap valued at $164 million, and in 1986 Pacific Gas Transmission became a wholly owned subsidiary of PG&E.

In 1986 Richard Clarke became chairman and chief executive officer of PG&E, and George Maneatis became president. While PG&E's managers had traditionally begun as engineers, Clarke was an attorney-turned-manager, and his experience as an attorney served his company's interest in the ensuing years.

California had become the most competitive power market in the United States, partly because of high rates the CPUC had mandated for independent power generators. Because PG&E had to buy relatively high-priced power from independents, the company's electricity rates were forced up. To protect residential customers from the rising costs, the CPUC raised industrial

power rates and used them to subsidize residential rates. In the mid-1980s a long-term plan for industry deregulation began by allowing large industrial customers to buy power from independent suppliers. As a result, many large industrial customers devised plans to build their own power stations, or to import power from other states where electricity was 15 percent to 30 percent cheaper. With the loss of many of its large industrial customers, PG&E was forced to lay off approximately 2,500 employees in 1987. To be more competitive, Clarke pressed the CPUC to make changes that would allow his company to offer better rates to large customers and to set up a major accounts program that would give individual attention to PG&E's biggest customers.

In 1988 PG&E reorganized into five new business divisions. Four of the divisions focused on primary markets: electric supply, gas supply, distribution, and nonutility business. The electric supply division generated, transported, bought, and sold electricity for the distribution division and for other wholesale customers throughout the western United States. The gas supply division acquired natural gas for the distribution and electric supply divisions and for large customers outside PG&E's service area; it operated about 5,000 miles of pipeline from southern California to Alberta, Canada, as well as underground storage tanks. The distribution division provided gas, electric, and steam service to customers and was responsible for maintaining the customer base. The nonutility operations included natural gas exploration and production, enhanced oil recovery, real estate development, and power plant operations. The company formed a subsidiary, PG&E Enterprises, to manage the nonutility businesses. The fifth division, engineering and construction, provided services to the other divisions and was responsible for designing and building most of the company's dams, power plants, and other transmission and distribution systems. The new structure was designed to help managers identify costs, know their customers, understand their competition, and respond quickly to technological and regulatory changes.

In 1988 the company took a $576 million charge to pay for cost overruns during the construction of the Diablo Canyon nuclear plant. The charge reduced net income for 1988 to $62.1 million.

Also in 1988 PG&E-Bechtel Generating Company, a joint venture of PG&E and Bechtel Power, began construction of its first power plant, in Montana. The joint venture was formed to build and operate plants outside of PG&E's territory. By 1990 the venture had completed the Montana plant, had one under way in Pennsylvania, and was planning another in New Jersey.

PG&E was well prepared for the major earthquake that hit the San Francisco area in 1989. Although power was cut off from 1.4 million customers, it was restored to one million of them within 12 hours. The company sustained $100 million in damage, mostly to transmission and generating equipment, with distribution and communications barely disrupted.

The 1990s: Preparing for Full Deregulation

In 1990 the company added a sixth division, nuclear power generation, which was responsible for the Diablo Canyon nuclear power plants and the support services they required. Earnings were strong in 1990, with an increase of 10.5 percent from 1989. PG&E had held the operating costs of its utility business at 1986 levels, while utility revenues had increased 20 percent during the years 1986 to 1990. In anticipation of an increasingly competitive market, the company began a program in 1990 to reduce its management staff by 300 over the next three years. The utility business accounted for about 70 percent of PG&E's earnings in 1990, but the company, through PG&E Enterprises, continued to pursue nonutility ventures that offered a potentially higher return than the strictly regulated utility operations.

The flight of large industrial customers to independent suppliers continued to hurt PG&E in the early 1990s. Since the mid-1980s, the company's annual revenues from such customers had dropped by $400 million. As a result, PG&E's need for gas dropped, leaving the company short on its longstanding contracts with gas producers. In 1992 three Canadian gas producers sued PG&E for not fulfilling its contracts for gas purchases. The following year, PG&E paid $210 million to settle the suit.

In 1994 Stanley T. Skinner, who had been a PG&E employee for years, became chief executive officer. Skinner pushed ahead company plans to adapt to increasing deregulation. Although PG&E was the nation's largest investor-owned utility, it faced out-of-state competition with prices 25 percent lower than its own. Cost-cutting was a major goal for the company; it had laid off 1,500 employees in 1993 and planned to lay off another 1,500 in 1994. The company cut its spending on energy conservation programs by $100 million in 1994. Skinner also planned not to renew contracts with alternative energy suppliers, which the company had been forced to make in the regulated environment. In 1994 PG&E paid $1.6 billion for power from solar, wind, and other alternative sources. According to Skinner, once freed from regulation the company could buy that power from traditional sources for half the price.

To offset potential losses of its California customers, PG&E moved to beef up its nonregulated business in the mid-1990s. PG&E Enterprises formed U.S. Generating Co., a joint venture with Bechtel Group, to build power plants in the United States and eventually in China, India, and South America. Other strategies included selling plant management and advising overseas customers on energy conservation. In 1995 PG&E moved into energy commodity purchasing and portfolio management with the creation of a new subsidiary, PG&E Energy Services.

In 1996 subsidiary Pacific Gas Transmission acquired a 389-mile natural gas pipeline in Australia for $136 million. The following year PG&E increased its natural gas supply business by purchasing Valero Energy for $1.5 billion.

In 1996 California law reduced the rate of return it allowed PG&E to earn from its Diablo Canyon nuclear plant from 17 percent to 6.77 percent. In addition, the company agreed to accelerate the depreciation on the Diablo plant from 20 years to five in 1998. Because Diablo contributed almost 40 percent of the company's earnings, these two changes would result in a significant loss of earnings for PG&E in 1998.

In 1997 PG&E terminated the implementation of a new customer information system, which it had bought from IBM for $100 million. The company said the plan had failed because the system could not adapt quickly enough to changes wrought by deregulation. In another blow in 1997, PG&E was found guilty by a California court of 739 counts of negligence and fined $2 million. According to court documents, PG&E had been cutting its budget for tree trimming; inadequate trimming near power lines was found to have caused at least one wildfire.

PG&E Energy Services expanded rapidly in the late 1990s, opening 17 offices across the United States in 1997 alone. Targeting its services to commercial, agricultural, and industrial customers, the subsidiary hired McCann-Erickson Worldwide that year to create a national advertising campaign. By 1998 PG&E Energy Services had signed contracts for a total of more than $1 billion with such customers as McDonald's, Atlantic Richfield Co., Safeway, and Blockbuster Video. Another of the company's unregulated businesses, U.S. Generating Company, became a wholly owned subsidiary in 1997 when PG&E bought out Bechtel's interest in the joint venture.

PG&E's efforts to make its utility business competitive were showing signs of progress in 1998. That year it signed a contract with Ultramar Diamond Shamrock worth $2 billion to provide power to the customer's refineries, pipelines, and gas stations. Also in 1998 PG&E bought 18 non-nuclear power plants from New England Electric for $1.6 billion.

Principal Subsidiaries

Pacific Gas & Electric Co.; Calaska Energy Co.; Eureka Energy Co.; Natural Gas Corporation of California; PG&E Generating Co.; PG&E Resources Co.; Pacific Gas Transmission Company; Alberta and Southern Gas Company Limited (Canada); Pacific Gas Properties Company; PG&E Enterprises; Mission Trail Insurance (Cayman) Ltd.; Pacific Energy Fuels Co.

Further Reading

Cuneo, Alice Z., "Two Utility Acc'ts Plan $60M in Ads," *Advertising Age,* May 19, 1997, pp. 4, 81.

Hughes, Thomas P., *Networks of Power,* Baltimore": Johns Hopkins University Press, 1983.

Mitchell, Ruddell, "PG&E: One Step Ahead of Future Shock," *Business Week,* November 14, 1994, pp. 68–69.

Moad, Jeff, "PG&E Dumps CIS Project," *PC Week,* April 28, 1997, pp. 1–2.

"Pacific Gas and Electric, San Francisco, CA" *Forbes,* August 24, 1998, p. 76.

"PG&E's Biggest Power Play Yet," *Business Week,* March 23, 1998, p. 42.

"PG&E Energy Nabs Arco," *Electricity Journal,* May 1998, p. 6.

"Short Circuit," *Forbes,* July 28, 1997, p. 248.

—Scott M. Lewis
—updated by Susan Windisch Brown

Play by Play Toys & Novelties, Inc.

4400 Tejasco
San Antonio, Texas 78218
U.S.A.
(210) 829-4666
Fax: (210) 824-6565
Web site: http://www.pbyp.com

Public Company
Incorporated: 1986
Employees: 620
Sales: $74.20 million (1997)
Stock Exchanges: NASDAQ
Ticker Symbol: PBYB
SICs: 3942 Dolls & Stuffed Toys; 3069 Fabricated
   Rubber Products, Not Elsewhere Classified

A noted toy manufacturer, Play by Play Toys & Novelties, Inc. designs, develops, markets, and distributes stuffed toys and novelties for the amusement and retail industries throughout the world. The company licenses widely recognized characters from children's entertainment, professional sports team logos, and corporate trademarks to create its product lines. Play by Play Toys holds licensing agreements with most of the major players in children's entertainment. The company licenses many prominent characters, including Mickey Mouse, Winnie the Pooh, Bugs Bunny, Tweety, Sylvester, Tasmanian Devil, Animaniacs, Spiderman, Batman, Wolverine, and other properties from Disney Enterprises Inc., Warner Brothers, and Marvel Entertainment Group Inc. The company's Play-Faces line of sculpted toy pillows also features licensed characters. Play by Play Toys also designs, develops, and distributes electronic and nonlicensed stuffed toys, as well as sells and distributes a variety of nonlicensed novelty items.

Arturo Torres, Entrepreneur: The First Ten Years

Arturo Torres left his native Cuba for America in 1961 with aspirations of becoming a cowboy. Instead he found a job washing dishes at a Pizza Hut in Texas. Before long, though, his drive and determination took him from the kitchen to the board room. By the 1980s, this Cuban refugee operated 240 Pizza Huts and Taco Bells. Ever the entrepreneur, Torres founded Play by Play Toys in 1986 as a vending-machine prize supplier. Within six years, he sold his restaurant franchises for $125 million, and by 1995 he made Play by Play Toys a public company, with subsidiaries and expansion plans.

In 1996, Play by Play Toys sold its restaurant subsidiary, Restaurants Universal Espana S.A., for $1.6 million to Croitex S.A., a firm based in Spain. Though the toy manufacturer's two owned-and-operated restaurant units generated about five percent of consolidated sales, Play by Play Toys lost $259,000 in fiscal 1995 because of the restaurants' performances, which continued losing money—$111,000—in the first half of fiscal 1996. Without the restaurants, Play by Play Toys expected greater focus and concentration on its core business of toys.

Acquiring the Ace Novelty Company: 1996

In May 1996, Play by Play Toys purchased Bellevue, Washington-based Ace Novelty Company for $44 million in cash, debt, and some liability assumption. Play by Play Toys financed its purchase of Ace Novelty and obtained working capital using a $65 million credit facility. Chemical Bank acted as the agent of the credit facility, and Heller Financial and Texas Commerce Bank also participated in the loan. Ace Novelty effectively became a subsidiary of Play by Play Toys, retaining its own management team and identity in the marketplace. "We're forming an Ace Novelty subsidiary, which will keep a separate identity within our company," Play by Play Toys chief financial officer Joe Guerra revealed in *Amusement Business*. "We believe there is quite a bit of value in the Ace name and reputation, and we want to maintain that identity in the market."

Nevertheless, the acquisition made Play by Play the largest supplier of stuffed toys and novelties in the United States and expanded the properties licensed by Play by Play Toys. (Ace Novelty licensed entertainment characters for the amusement and retail markets, including the Warner Brothers' Looney Tunes and *Space Jam* characters.) In the deal Play by Play Toys also obtained Ace's operating assets, business operations, facilities, warehouses, and distribution centers in Bellevue, Washington; Los Angeles, California; Chicago, Illinois; and Burnaby, British Columbia, Canada.

Completed in June 1996, the acquisition of Ace Novelty—and its many character licenses—added greatly to Play by Play Toys' international sales strength, as well as to the company's activity in the retail market. Play by Play Toys' net sales rose significantly in fiscal 1997's fourth quarter—94.2 percent—owing to the acquisition, among other factors.

The acquisition of Ace Novelty reorganized Play by Play Toys' activities in the amusement and retail markets. Formerly, the company directed about 60 percent of its business to the amusement industry and the remaining 40 percent to the retail market. Since the purchase of Ace Novelty, Play by Play Toys increased its activity in the amusement market by 15 percent, reducing its retail business to approximately 25 percent. As a result, during the winter months when the seasonal amusement industry was quietest, Play by Play Toys' sales volume fell as fixed overhead costs and a percentage of sales rose. Nevertheless, the company saw growth in the third quarter of 1997, especially in international markets. Demand for Play by Play products abroad further developed the company's international facilities and infrastructure.

Play by Play negotiated a multiyear licensing agreement with Warner Brothers Consumer Products (UK) Limited, a unit of Warner Brothers Entertainment Company, in August 1996. The agreement permitted Play by Play Toys to distribute a broad line of stuffed toys based on popular Looney Tunes, Tiny Toons, and Animaniacs characters to western European markets. This arrangement complemented Play by Play Toys' domestic marketing plans. The popularity of Warner Brothers characters in western Europe also promised to enhance the company's international expansion. Previously, Play by Play Toys licensed Looney Tunes and Animaniacs characters from Warner Brothers for the distribution of plush toys in Spain's retail market and for the distribution of its Play-Faces sculpted pillows in Europe.

The agreement further strengthened the relationship between Play by Play Toys and Warner Brothers. In 1996 the toy maker won the Looney Tunes President's Award for Excellence in Achievement.

Acquiring the TLC Gift Company: 1996

Another key acquisition, the purchase of TLC Gift Company in the United Kingdom, also added to the company's performance overseas. Acquiring this company solidified Play by Play Toys' position in the amusement market, as well as expanded its penetration of European markets.

In November 1996, Play by Play Toys finalized the acquisition of the TLC Gift Company, based in Doncaster, England. A leading distributor of specialty plush and novelty products, TLC Gift Company supplied both the retail and amusement markets throughout Europe. TLC Gift Company acted as the exclusive distributor of Play by Play Toys Europe in the United Kingdom since 1995. The new arrangement allowed the British company to increase its revenues by $5 million in a one-year period. After the acquisition, TLC Gift Company became a wholly owned subsidiary of Play by Play Toys Europe. Thus, the company's headquarters moved from Great Britain to Play by Play Toys Europe's location in Valencia, Spain.

New Products in 1997

The company developed new products in 1997, notably Talkin' Tots, its first product for the large doll market. Talkin' Tots, two dolls that communicate (they talk and sing) through infrared sensors, also marked the company's first venture into television advertising. Play by Play Toys also promoted its Tornado Taz through television ads. A plush version of the popular Looney Tunes character, Tornado Taz shook, spun, and spoke with the voice of the late Mel Blanc. New products such as Talkin' Tots, Tornado Taz, and a plush version of the popular Looney Tunes beanbags sold well and strengthened both the company's retail and amusement product lines.

In 1997 Play by Play Toys added some classic characters to its product line through new licensing agreements. In September 1997, Play by Play Toys signed an agreement with Warner Brothers Consumer Products giving it exclusive worldwide rights in the design, manufacture, and distribution of Baby Looney Tunes products. The company created play and pull toys around these characters for infants, toddlers, and pre-schoolers. Play by Play Toys anticipated expanding this product line throughout 1998. With $50 million in revenue potential, the product line, manufactured in conjunction with WB Toys, included a developmental line of play toys and toddler pull toys for early childhood. These toys allowed Play by Play Toys to enter the pre-school market, an expanding industry segment, as well as established the company as a greater presence in the retail market. Manufactured and distributed to retailers, the products debuted in 1998.

Play by Play Toys launched a public offering of two million shares of common stock, priced at $16 per share, in November 1997, the proceeds of which were used to reduce debt and enhance corporate growth. The toy manufacturer's sales hit $137 million in 1997, and the company's stock doubled in value. At this time, Play by Play Toys changed advertising agencies, awarding a $5 million contract to New York-based Anda and Scotti. The firm assumed responsibility for the toy maker's television and print creative campaigns for the consumer and trade markets.

International Growth in 1998

The company's overseas subsidiary Play by Play Toys & Novelties UK signed an agreement with Walt Disney UK for the distribution of its plush product line in the United Kingdom and Ireland in 1998. Valued at $5 million the first year, this contract positioned Play by Play Toys as a dominant player in the European market. At the time of the agreement, Francisco Saez Moya, president of Play by Play Toys & Novelties Europe, noted, "We are very excited that we have been awarded the rights to distribute the Disney product line in the U.K. and Ireland. . . . We are quickly becoming the dominant player in the burgeoning European market with our wide range of product lines that include Baby Looney Tunes, Garfield, Tom and Jerry, The Muppets, Coca-Cola, Sesame Street, and now Disney. In line with our growth strategy, this distribution agreement brings us one step closer to becoming the leading European distributor of high quality plush toys based on classic character licenses." By 1998 Play by Play Toys dominated the carnival prize market, with a commanding 50 percent market share.

Future Plans

At the end of 1998, Play by Play Toys planned to continue its extension into the toy market worldwide. The company expected to acquire additional character licenses in the future, as well as to expand its product lines in both the retail and amusement sectors. In addition, other new product introductions could be expected from the toy manufacturer in upcoming years.

Principal Subsidiaries

Ace Novelty; Play by Play Toys & Novelties UK; Play by Play Toys & Novelties Europe; TLC Gift Company (Europe).

Further Reading

"Agency News," *ADWEEK* (Eastern edition), November 3, 1997, p. 62.

Kahn, Jeremy, "Getting Flush on Plush," *Fortune,* March 30, 1998, p. 34.

"Play by Play Completes Acquisition of TLC Gift Company," *Business Wire,* November 8, 1996, p. 11081073.

"Play by Play Toys & Novelties Announces Completion of Acquisition of Ace Novelty Co. Inc.," *Business Wire,* June 24, 1996, p. 6241190.

"Play by Play Toys & Novelties, Inc., Files Registration Statement with the Securities and Exchange Commission to Offer 3.2 Million Shares of Common Stock," *Business Wire,* November 1997, p. 11031184.

"Play by Play Toys & Novelties, Inc., Prices Secondary Offering of 2,000,000 Million Shares of Common Stock," *Business Wire,* November 26, 1997, p. 11261072.

"Play by Play Toys & Novelties, Inc., Reports Fiscal 1997 Third Quarter and Nine Months Results," *Business Wire,* June 16, 1997, p. 6161156.

"Play by Play Toys & Novelties, Inc., Reports Record Fiscal 1997 Fourth Quarter and Year End Results," *Business Wire,* October 23, 1997, p. 10231202.

"Play by Play Toys & Novelties, Inc., Signs Major Amusement Licensing Agreements with Warner Brothers of Europe," *Business Wire,* August 12, 1996, p. 8120212.

"Play by Play Toys & Novelties Obtains Rights to Distribute the Walt Disney Company's Plush Products in the United Kingdom and Ireland," *Business Wire,* February 5, 1998, p. 2051130.

"Play by Play Toys & Novelties Signs Exclusive Worldwide Licensing Agreement with Warner Brothers Consumer Products," *Business Wire,* September 8, 1997, p. 9080213.

"Play by Play Toys & Novelties Signs Letter of Intent with Warner Brothers Consumer Products," *Business Wire,* November 17, 1997, p. 11171254.

"Play by Play Toys Sells Its Restaurant Subsidiary," *Nation's Restaurant News,* April 29, 1996, p. 12.

Waddell, Ray, "Ace Name to Remain in Play by Play Deal," *Amusement Business,* May 13, 1996, p. 1.

—Charity Anne Dorgan

Post Properties, Inc.

One Riverside
4401 Northside Parkway
Suite 800
Atlanta, Georgia 30327-3057
U.S.A.
(404) 846-5000
Fax: (404) 504-9388
Web site: http://www.postproperties.com

Public Company
Incorporated: 1971
Employees: 1,600
Sales: $203.4 million (1997)
Stock Exchanges: New York
Ticker Symbol: PPS
SICs: 6798 Real Estate Investment Trusts

Post Properties, Inc. is known throughout the "Sun Belt" states for its landscaped apartment homes, but in business terms it is a real estate investment trust, or REIT. Typically, an apartment developer merely builds dwellings, but does not manage them. Similarly, most apartment management companies are not in the development business. A defining feature of Post is that it participates in all phases of the creation and operation of its apartment communities, from initial site selection to construction to leasing to ongoing maintenance and management. As of 1998, Post had more than 29,000 apartment units in Georgia, Florida, Virginia, Tennessee, and—thanks to its 1997 acquisition of Dallas-based Columbus Realty Trust—Texas. Using a formula involving "garden-style" apartment dwellings—usually three-story structures which cover a relatively large area of land—the company has experienced steady growth. In the mid- to late 1990s, however, Chairman John Williams began taking Post in a new direction. Keeping with the "New Urbanism" movement in the United States, Post Properties began constructing and/or renovating multi-story high-rises in urban centers.

A Business Started at the Breakfast Table

Post founder John A. Williams began his multimillion-dollar enterprise at an International House of Pancakes (IHOP) restau-

rant. "Armed with slides of development sites and lots of chutzpah," wrote Jeanie Franco Hallem in 1987, Williams "would commandeer a table for the morning and meet prospective investors." Williams began his work day with a 6:30 a.m. breakfast meeting, he told Hallem. "We would say good-bye at 7:30 a.m., then my second appointment would arrive. Normally I had two or three breakfasts."

Williams's background included attending the Georgia Institute of Technology, where he earned his B.S. in industrial management in 1964. At the age of 20, he went to work as a financial systems analyst for Georgia Power, the state's leading electrical utility. A year later, he moved to the Southern Company, where he worked as a sales engineer—a job that put him into contact with developers throughout metropolitan Atlanta. In the late 1960s, Atlanta was on the verge of phenomenal growth, which would continue through the end of the century. Williams would become a significant part of that growth. In 1969, at the age of 26, Williams decided that he wanted to start his own business. In 1971, with just $25,000, he founded Post Properties.

Growing with the Post Formula in the 1970s and 1980s

Much of Williams's formula for success with Post Properties revolved around careful attention to detail. The company purports to have started the landscaping concept for apartment complexes. "I can promise you," Williams told *Business Atlanta* in 1987, "in '71 or '72, you didn't see flowers" in apartment complexes. Ben W. Johnson, in a *National Real Estate Investor* editorial nearly a decade after the 1987 *Business Atlanta* piece, expressed similar ideas: "We've lived in Post communities for five years now," he wrote, "and we've been pretty darned impressed (and spoiled) by the company's attention to the big things, like attitude (the customer comes first), and the little (beautiful landscaping and grounds maintenance)."

Post's overall formula, however, was about much more than flowers. Its upscale apartment communities featured amenities with its "yuppie" clientele in mind. For instance, Post Lenox Park in Atlanta's Buckhead district includes a 24-hour business center with a fax machine, copier, and computer. The company also puts on a number of social events for its renters, many of whom are single and transient; and, of course, service is paramount. For example, a 1987 *Business Atlanta* article detailed a time when an apartment air conditioner broke down in the heat of the summer. The company's maintenance team had to order a part that would take a few days to arrive. But, because Post's stated policy is "one-day service," the company remedied the situation by sending a limousine to pick up the residents and take them to a hotel.

On the management end, the company grew steadily, but carefully. In the early 1970s, prior to the mid-decade recession, there was a lot of capital available in real estate. Many developers entered too many deals, and many people entered into the business of developing who probably should not have done so. The result was exposure to debt, and lenders who possessed little staying power. Post, on the other hand, selected its financing carefully, grew slowly, and thus was able to account for fully 100 percent of Atlanta's new apartment construction in 1975 and 1976—during the recession. Such a feat could hardly have been replicated in the period of fast growth the city of Atlanta experienced in the 1980s, 1990s, and beyond, but by then Post had become a more significant player in both the Atlanta market and in other cities.

The "New Urbanism" in the 1990s

Post went public in the summer of 1993, with its stock priced at $25.50 per share. The company had to make another 1.38 million shares available because the initial offering of 9.2 million shares was so far oversubscribed.

Post had certainly succeeded with its well-manicured "garden" apartment complex formula; but by the 1990s it appeared that the company had possibly succeeded just a bit too much. Numerous other apartment developers in Atlanta and elsewhere were catching on to the idea pioneered by Post and others, spawning thousands of rapidly built units in cookie-cutter complexes that one observer—noting the sameness and apparent regimentation in the design—called "yuppie prisons."

The company itself had become aware of the phenomenon, and had begun to look in new directions. It issued a statement, under the heading "The Future," at its site on the World Wide Web: "In recent years, we have become concerned about the future of garden apartments, particularly those located in suburban areas. Such apartments have become a ubiquitous element of modern suburban sprawl, and have increasingly taken on the undifferentiated characteristics of a commodity product." Due to its misgivings about the potential for garden apartments to

appreciate in value, in the late 1980s the company began to explore urban "in-fill locations"—that is, areas in once-vacant urban centers that were beginning to become residential again.

The rebirth of the United States' cities and towns, termed "New Urbanism," spelled an end to years of decay in the nation's downtown centers. Interstate highways, the growth of suburbs, and the destruction of historic landmarks during the 1960s and 1970s in favor of box-like glass and concrete buildings had all contributed to the flight of residents from the urban centers. This was particularly true of downtown Atlanta, whose nighttime population consisted mainly of conventioneers and the homeless. In the late 1980s, Post became part of efforts to turn this situation around, and in 1991 it entered into a joint venture with developer Ackerman & Co. to build Renaissance City Center in a blighted area near the Atlanta Civic Center.

With the advent of the 1996 Summer Olympics nearing, Atlanta became the first major city in decades to create a new downtown park—Centennial Park, which was built in an area of abandoned factories and housing projects near the CNN Center, the Georgia World Congress Center, and other important Olympic venues. In March 1996, the *Atlanta Journal and Constitution* reported that Post had expressed an interest in building apartments adjacent to the park, which was expected to become a magnet to downtown development in coming years. Following the Olympics in 1997, Post proposed a number of additional projects, including a six- or seven-story apartment building near Peachtree Battle Shopping Center and a mixed-use development in a decayed area near the Lindbergh Center MARTA (Metropolitan Atlanta Rapid Transit Authority) rail station. Neither development was likely to be a traditional Post product in the eyes of most Atlantans, but both projects were in line with the company's new focus.

Moving Beyond Atlanta in the Late 1990s

In August 1997, Post announced a merger with Columbus Realty Trust. The $600 million company, based in Dallas, Texas, would expand Post's holdings by more than a third, from over 21,000 units to more than 29,000. In a company press release about the merger, Williams stated that Post considered Dallas to be "one of the few major metropolitan markets in the country with the long-term appeal of our home base, Atlanta." Industry analysts agreed that Post's expansion into markets outside its typical geographic area was a smart move, and noted that the decision was made in order to expand, rather than because the company was not faring well in the Atlanta area.

Post's expansion beyond Atlanta, however, may have been partly due to other environmental factors as well. A May 1997 *Atlanta Journal and Constitution* article indicated that increasing levels of government regulation regarding development had made Atlanta "a more and more difficult place to build." The company stated its desire to reduce the percentage of its overall holdings that were based in Atlanta from the 70 percent level. Rather than doing this by divesting some of its Atlanta holdings, the company wished to expand into other markets and obtain holdings elsewhere that would increase the company's percentage of non-Atlanta properties.

In October 1997, the *Constitution* reported that development of the Peachtree property was being held up due to inadequate sewers. An Atlanta official was quoted as saying that the city "would prefer to see a sewer developed along Peachtree Street," and it appeared that Post might have to bear the sewer expansion's financial burden in order to speed up the process. The problem provided evidence of the sort of bureaucratic boondoggle that was driving Post away from its Atlanta base. Fellow developer Blaine Kelley told the *Constitution* that the developers were "not willing to pay for a major overhaul of the city system down a city street."

Around the nation, evidence of Post's presence began to appear in formerly depressed downtown areas. In November 1997, Max Jarman of the *Arizona Republic* reported that "The missing link to successful redevelopment of downtown Phoenix is about to be added to the chain," noting that Post Properties had taken over a $75 million, 800-unit project in that area. The facility would be built on an 11-acre site, and would incorporate several historic buildings such as the old Gold Spot Market and the bishop's house for the Episcopal diocese. It was thought that when completed, the project would help bring a new wave of downtown residents into the area, who would then support the city's restaurants, drugstores, and other service businesses.

In Denver, Colorado, another project was under way, and Erika Gonzalez wrote in the *Rocky Mountain News* that Post Properties would "breathe new life" into the site of a hospital closed since 1993. The project, which would cost $80 million, would include 1,100 residential units, 70 loft apartments, 50,000 square feet of retail space, and two 500-space parking garages.

Throughout the country at the end of the 1990s, Post left its mark on many once-dead urban centers. In 1998, in its Atlanta base, Post was putting the finishing touches on a development which exemplified the "New Urbanism." Riverside, located off Northside Parkway near the Chattahoochee River, would feature living spaces modeled on New York brownstones, with retail shops on the first floor and apartments above. Residents would be able to live, work, and socialize in the same place, without once having to get in their cars—an idea almost previously unheard of in Atlanta. "There is quite frankly nothing like it in existence in the Southeast," Williams told Martin Sinderman of the *Atlanta Business Chronicle.*

The development, meanwhile, had sparked controversy—not over its design, but its "history." The latter was an entirely fictionalized account which Post presented in advertisements that were pen-and-ink drawings of the buildings and browning photos of the imaginary residents. The advertisements' fine print, however, revealed that the history was simply a tale spun to add interest to the project. Hence, for instance, it was not true that one building in the complex "was a grist mill and a boarding house a century ago. During the Civil War, that building became a hospital—one that camouflaged a small arsenal that played a crucial role in the Battle of Peachtree Creek." In reality, the building—like the rest of Riverside—had been built in the late 1990s. Although the "hoax" inspired quite a few letters to the editor, few residents seemed truly concerned. As for Williams, he said that the whole affair "was a lot of fun for us."

Post, in fact, decided to move its corporate headquarters to Riverside in June 1998. There, the company continued to focus its energies on fulfilling its stated mission: "To provide a superior apartment living experience for our residents." As the 20th century drew to a close, Post Properties seemed to possess the past experience and future focus to succeed well into the years to come.

Further Reading

Boyd, Jennifer, "More 4th Ward Apartments," *Business Journal—Charlotte,* April 6, 1998, p. 1.

Friedman, Alan, "Post Initial Offering in Big Demand," *Marietta Daily Journal,* July 20, 1993.

Gonzalez, Erika, "Builder Breaks Ground at St. Luke's Site," *Rocky Mountain News,* December 16, 1997, p. 8B.

Hallem, Jeanie Franco, "Post U.S.A.," *Business Atlanta,* September 1987, p. 34.

Harte, Susan, and Maria Saporta, "Post Properties Goes West," *Atlanta Constitution,* August 5, 1997, p. E1.

Jarman, Max, "Vital Urban Housing to Fill Bleak Area," *Arizona Republic,* November 14, 1997, p. A1.

Johnson, Ben W., "Giving Post-Haste a Whole New Meaning," *National Real Estate Investor,* June 1996, p. 4.

Lawson, Richard, "Post Ready to Move Ahead on Bennie-Dillon Revitalization," *Nashville Business Journal,* May 8, 1998, p. 1.

Lunsford, Darcie, "CityPlace Sparks Downtown Homes," *South Florida Business Journal,* May 1, 1998.

McCarthy, Mike, "Downtown Apartments: Major Developer Plans to Build 800 Units," *Business Journal—Sacramento,* April 17, 1998, p. 1.

Salter, Sallye, "Post Properties to Use Funds from Stock Offering to Cut Debt," *Atlanta Constitution,* May 14, 1993, p. F5.

——, "Two Peachtree Road Projects Held Up by Sewer Inadequacy," *Atlanta Constitution,* October 16, 1997, p. D2.

Saporta, Maria, "Post Hoping to Hang Its Hat at More Places Outside Town," *Atlanta Journal and Constitution,* May 23, 1997, p. E3.

Schneider, Craig, "A Charming, Fictional Story: Plan Invents Past in Present," *Atlanta Journal and Constitution,* March 23, 1998, p. E1.

Sinderman, Martin, "Post Now Embracing 'New Urbanism' Movement," *Atlanta Business Chronicle,* May 1, 1998, p. 17B.

Sotto, Cindy M., "Post Downtown Is a Go," *Atlanta Business Chronicle,* May 27, 1991, p. 1.

Westfall, Jill Elizabeth, "Apartment of the Week," *Atlanta Journal and Constitution,* September 7, 1997, p. H53.

Wilbert, Tony, "Bidders Lining Up for MARTA," *Atlanta Business Chronicle,* January 16, 1998, p. 1A.

——, "Post to Develop Apartments Near Peachtree Battle," *Atlanta Business Chronicle,* September 19, 1997, p. 1A.

—Judson Knight

The Procter & Gamble Company

One Procter & Gamble Plaza
Cincinnati, Ohio 45202
U.S.A.
(513) 983-1100
Fax: (513) 983-9369
Web site: http://www.pg.com

Public Company
Incorporated: 1890
Employees: 79,000
Sales: $37.15 billion (1998)
Stock Exchanges: New York Cincinnati Amsterdam Paris
    Basel Geneva Lausanne Zürich Frankfurt Brussels
    Tokyo
Ticker Symbol: PG
SICs: 2045 Prepared Flour Mixes & Doughs; 2079
    Edible Fats & Oils, Not Elsewhere Classified; 2095
    Roasted Coffee; 2096 Potato Chips; Corn Chips &
    Similar Snacks; 2099 Food Preparations, Not
    Elsewhere Classified; 2676 Sanitary Paper Products;
    2834 Pharmaceutical Preparations; 2841 Soap &
    Other Detergents, Except Specialty Cleaners; 2842
    Specialty Cleaning, Polishing & Sanitation
    Preparations; 2844 Perfumes, Cosmetics & Other
    Toilet Preparations; 7812 Motion Picture & Video
    Tape Production

The Procter & Gamble Company (P&G) is a giant in the area
of consumer goods. The leading maker of household products in
the United States, P&G is also active in 140 countries world-
wide; about half of the company's revenues are derived outside
North America. P&G markets about 300 brands in all, in several
areas: baby care (Luvs, Pampers); beauty care (Cover Girl,
Head & Shoulders, Ivory, Oil of Olay); fabric and home care
(Cascade, Mr. Clean, Spic and Span, Tide); feminine protection
(Always, Tampax); food and beverages (Crisco, Folgers, Jif,
Hawaiian Punch, Pringles); healthcare (Crest, Nyquil, Pepto-
Bismol, Scope, Vicks); and tissue and towels (Bounty,
Charmin, Puffs). Committed to remaining the leader in its

markets, P&G is one of the most aggressive marketers in the
consumer goods industry and is the largest advertiser in the
world. Many innovations that are now common practices in
corporate America—including extensive market research, the
brand-management system, and employee profit-sharing programs—were first developed at Procter & Gamble.

Launched with Candles and Soap in 1837

In 1837 brothers-in-law William Procter and James Gamble
formed a partnership, Procter & Gamble, in Cincinnati, Ohio, to
manufacture and sell candles and soap. Both men had emigrated
from the United Kingdom. William Procter had moved to Ohio
from England in 1832 after his woolens shop in London was
destroyed by fire and burglary; Gamble came from Ireland as a
boy in 1819 when famine struck his native land. Both men
settled in Cincinnati, then nicknamed "Porkopolis" for its
booming hog-butchering trade. The suggestion for the partnership apparently came from their father-in-law, Alexander
Norris, who pointed out that Gamble's trade, soapmaking, and
Procter's trade, candlemaking, both required the use of lye,
which was made from animal fat and wood ashes.

Procter & Gamble first operated out of a storeroom at Main
and Sixth streets. Procter ran the store while Gamble ran the
manufacturing operation, which at that time consisted of a
wooden kettle with a cast-iron bottom set up behind the shop.
Early each morning Gamble visited houses, hotels, and steam-
boats collecting ash and meat scraps and bartering soap cakes
for the raw materials. Candles were Procter & Gamble's most
important product at that time.

Procter & Gamble was in competition with at least 14 other
manufacturers in its early years, but the enterprising partners
soon expanded their operations throughout neighboring Hamilton and Butler counties. Cincinnati's location on the Ohio River
proved advantageous as the company began sending its goods
downriver. In 1848 Cincinnati was also linked to the major
cities of the East via rail, and Procter & Gamble grew.

Around 1851, when P&G shipments were moving up and
down the river and across the country by rail, the company's
famous moon-and-stars symbol was created. Because many
people were illiterate at this time, trademarks were used to

distinguish one company's products from another's. Company lore asserts that the symbol was first drawn as a simple cross on boxes of Procter & Gamble's Star brand candles by dock hands so that the boxes would be easily identifiable when they arrived at their destinations. Another shipper later replaced the cross with an encircled star, and eventually William Procter added the familiar 13 stars, representing the original 13 U.S. colonies, and the man in the moon.

The moon-and-stars trademark became a symbol of quality to Procter & Gamble's base of loyal customers. In the days before advertising, trademarks were a product's principal means of identification, and in 1875 when a Chicago soapmaker began using an almost identical symbol, P&G sued and won. The emblem, which was registered with the U.S. Patent Office in 1882, changed slightly over the years until 1930, when Cincinnati sculptor Ernest Bruce Haswell developed its current form.

During the 1850s Procter & Gamble's business grew rapidly. In the early part of the decade the company moved its operations to a bigger factory. The new location gave the company better access to shipping routes and stockyards where hogs were slaughtered. In 1854 the company leased an office building in downtown Cincinnati. Procter managed sales and bookkeeping and Gamble continued to run the company's manufacturing. By the end of the decade, the company's annual sales were more than $1 million, and Procter & Gamble employed about 80 people.

Prosperity During Civil War

Procter & Gamble's operations were heavily dependent upon rosin—derived from pine sap—which was obtained from the South. In 1860, on the brink of the Civil War, two young cousins, James Norris Gamble and William Alexander Procter (sons of the founders), traveled to New Orleans to buy as much rosin as they could, procuring a large supply at the bargain price of $1 a barrel. When wartime shortages forced competitors to cut production, Procter & Gamble prospered. The company supplied the Union Army with soap and candles, and the moon and stars became a familiar symbol with Union soldiers.

Although Procter & Gamble had foreseen the wartime scarcities, as time wore on, its stockpile of raw materials shrank. In order to keep up full production the company had to find new ways of manufacturing. Until 1863 lard stearin was used to produce the stearic acid for candlemaking. With lard expensive and in short supply, a new method was discovered to produce the stearic acid using tallow. The lard and lard stearin that was available was instead developed into a cooking compound. The same process was later adapted to create Crisco, the first all-vegetable shortening. When P&G's supply of rosin ran out

toward the end of the war, the company experimented with silicate of soda as a substitute, which later became a key ingredient in modern soaps and detergents.

Launched Ivory Soap in 1878

After the war Procter & Gamble expanded and updated its facilities. In 1869 the transcontinental railroad linked the two coasts and opened still more markets to Procter & Gamble. In 1875 the company hired its first full-time chemist to work with James Gamble on new products, including a soap that was equal in quality to expensive castile soaps, but which could be produced less expensively. In 1878 Procter & Gamble's White Soap hit the market and catapulted P&G to the forefront of its industry.

The most distinctive characteristic of the product, soon renamed Ivory soap, was developed by accident. A worker accidently left a soap mixer on during his lunch break, causing more air than usual to be mixed in. Before long Procter & Gamble was receiving orders for "the floating soap." Although the office was at first perplexed, the confusion was soon cleared up, and P&G's formula for White Soap changed permanently.

Harley Procter, William Procter's son, developed the new soap's potential. Harley Procter was inspired to rename the soap by Psalm 45: "all thy garments smell of myrrh, and aloes, and cassia, out of the ivory palaces whereby they have made thee glad." Procter devoted himself to the success of the new product and convinced the board of directors to advertise Ivory. Advertising was risky at the time; most advertisements were placed by disreputable manufacturers. Nevertheless, in 1882 the company approved an $11,000 annual advertising budget. The slogan "99$\frac{44}{100}$% pure" was a welcome dose of sobriety amidst the generally outlandish advertising claims of the day. Procter, committed to the excellence of the company's products, had them analyzed and improved even before they went to market. This practice was the origin of P&G's superior product development. Procter believed that "advertising alone couldn't make a product successful—it was merely evidence of a manufacturer's faith in the merit of the article."

The success of Ivory and the ability of Procter & Gamble to spread its message further through the use of national advertising caused the company to grow rapidly in the 1880s. In 1886 P&G opened its new Ivorydale plant on the edge of Cincinnati to keep up with demand. In 1890 James N. Gamble hired a chemist, Harley James Morrison, to set up a laboratory at Ivorydale and improve the quality and consistency of Procter & Gamble's products. P&G soon introduced another successful brand: Lenox soap. Marketed as a heavier-duty product, the yellow soap helped P&G reach sales of more than $3 million by 1889.

The 1880s saw labor unrest at many U.S. companies, including Procter & Gamble, which experienced a number of strikes and demonstrations. Thereafter, the company sought to avert labor problems before they became significant. Behind P&G's labor policies was a founder's grandson, William Cooper Procter. William Cooper Procter had joined the company in 1883 after his father, William Alexander Procter, requested that he return from the College of New Jersey (now Princeton University) just one month before graduation to help with the company's affairs. Procter learned the business from the ground up, starting in the soap factory.

Innovative Employee Benefits Introduced

In 1885 the young Procter recommended that the workers be given Saturday afternoons off, and the company's management agreed. Nevertheless, there were 14 strikes over the next two years. In 1887 the company implemented a profit-sharing plan in order to intertwine the employees' interests with those of the company. Although the semiannual dividends were received enthusiastically by employees, that enthusiasm rarely found its way back into the work place. The next year William Cooper Procter recommended tying the bonuses to employee performance, which produced better results.

In 1890 The Procter & Gamble Company was incorporated, with William Alexander Procter as its first president. Two years later the company implemented an employee stock-purchase program, which in 1903 was tied to the profit-sharing plan. By 1915 about 61 percent of the company's employees were participating. The company introduced a revolutionary sickness-disability program for its workers in 1915 and implemented an eight-hour workday in 1918. Procter & Gamble has been recognized as a leader in employee-benefit programs ever since.

Meanwhile, new soaps, including P&G White Naphtha, which was introduced in 1902, kept P&G at the forefront of the cleaning products industry. In 1904 the company opened its second plant, in Kansas City, Missouri, followed by Port Ivory on Staten Island, New York. In 1907 William Cooper Procter became president of the company after his father's death.

Procter & Gamble soon began experimenting with a hydrogenation process which combined liquid cottonseed oil with solid cottonseed oil. After several years of research, Procter & Gamble patented the procedure, and in 1911 Crisco was introduced to the public. Backed by a strong advertising budget, Crisco sales took off.

World War I brought shortages, but Procter & Gamble management had again foreseen the crisis and had stockpiled raw materials. William Cooper Procter was also active in the wartime fundraising effort.

During the 1920s the flurry of new products continued. Ivory Flakes came out in 1919. Chipso soap flakes for industrial laundry machines were introduced in 1921. In 1926 Camay was introduced and three years later Oxydol joined the P&G line of cleaning products. The company's market research became more sophisticated when F.W. Blair, a P&G chemist, began a six-month tour of U.S. kitchens and laundry rooms to assess the effectiveness of Procter & Gamble's products in practical use and to recommend improvements. After Blair returned, the economic research department under D. Paul Smelser began a careful study of consumer behavior. Market research complemented Procter & Gamble's laboratories and home economics department in bringing new technology to market.

Soon after Richard R. Deupree became president of the company in 1930, synthetic soap products hit the market. In 1933 Dreft, the first synthetic detergent for home use, was introduced, followed by the first synthetic hair shampoo, Drene, in 1934. Further improvements in synthetics resulted in a host of new products years later.

Brand Management Debuted in 1931

In 1931 Neil McElroy, a former promotions manager who had spent time in England and had an up-close view of Procter & Gamble's rival Unilever, suggested a system of "one man—one brand." In effect, each brand would operate as a separate business, competing with the products of other firms as well as those of Procter & Gamble. The system would include a brand assistant who would execute the policies of the brand manager and would be primed for the top job. Brand management became a fixture at Procter & Gamble, and was widely copied by other companies.

The Great Depression caused hardship for many U.S. corporations as well as for individuals, but Procter & Gamble emerged virtually unscathed. Radio took Procter & Gamble's message into more homes than ever. In 1933 Procter & Gamble became a key sponsor of radio's daytime serials, soon known as "soap operas." In 1935 Procter & Gamble spent $2 million on national radio sponsorship, and by 1937 the amount was $4.5 million. In 1939 Procter & Gamble had 21 programs on the air and spent $9 million. That year P&G advertised on television for the first time, when Red Barber plugged Ivory soap during the first television broadcast of a major league baseball game.

In 1940 Procter & Gamble's packaging expertise was given military applications when the government asked the company to oversee the construction and operation of ordinance plants. Procter & Gamble Defense Corporation operated as a subsidiary and filled government contracts for 60-millimeter mortar shells. Glycerin also became key to the war effort for its uses in explosives and medicine, and Procter & Gamble was one of the largest manufacturers of that product.

Postwar Growth Fueled by Tide

After World War II the availability of raw materials and new consumer attitudes set the stage for unprecedented growth. Procter & Gamble's postwar miracle was Tide, a synthetic detergent that, together with home automatic washing machines, revolutionized the way people washed their clothes. The company was not ready for the consumer demand for heavy-duty detergent when it introduced the product in 1947; within two years Tide, backed by a $21 million advertising budget, was the number one laundry detergent, outselling even the company's own Oxydol and Duz. Despite its premium price, Tide remained the number one laundry detergent into the 1990s. In 1950 Cheer was introduced as bluing detergent, and over the years other laundry products were also marketed: Dash in 1954, Bold in 1965, Era in 1972, and Solo in 1979.

The 1950s were highly profitable for the company. In 1955, after five years of research, Procter & Gamble firmly established itself in the toiletries business with Crest toothpaste. Researchers at the company and at Indiana University developed the toothpaste using stannous fluoride—a compound of fluorine and tin—which could substantially reduce cavities. In 1960 the American Dental Association endorsed Crest, and the product was on its way to becoming the country's number one toothpaste, nudging past Colgate in 1962.

Procter & Gamble began acquiring smaller companies aggressively in the mid-1950s. In 1955 it bought the Lexington, Kentucky-based nut company W.T. Young Foods, and acquired Nebraska Consolidated Mills Company, owner of the Duncan Hines product line, a year later. In 1957 the Charmin Paper Company and the Clorox Chemical Company were also acquired.

In 1957 Neil McElroy, who had become Procter & Gamble president in 1948, left the company to serve as secretary of defense in President Dwight D. Eisenhower's cabinet. He was replaced by Howard Morgens who, like his predecessor, had climbed the corporate ladder from the advertising side. In 1959 McElroy returned to Procter & Gamble as chairman and remained in that position until 1971, when Morgens succeeded him. Morgens remained CEO until 1974.

Paper Products Push Included Pampers

Morgens oversaw Procter & Gamble's full-scale entry into the paper-goods markets. A new process developed in the late 1950s for drying wood pulp led to the introduction of White Cloud toilet paper in 1958, and Puffs tissues in 1960. Procter & Gamble's Charmin brand of toilet paper was also made softer.

Procter & Gamble's paper-products offensive culminated in the 1961 test marketing of Pampers disposable diapers. The idea for Pampers came from a Procter & Gamble researcher, Vic Mills, who was inspired while changing an infant grandchild's diapers in 1956. The product consisted of three parts: a leak-proof outer plastic shell, several absorbent layers, and a porous film that let moisture pass through into the absorbent layers, but kept it from coming back. Test-market results showed that parents liked the diapers, but disliked the 10 cents-per-Pamper price. Procter & Gamble reduced the price to six cents and implemented a sales strategy emphasizing the product's price. Pamper's three-layer design was a phenomenal success, and within 20 years disposable diapers had gone from less than one percent to more than 75 percent of all diapers changed in the United States. Procter & Gamble improved the technology over the years, and added a premium brand, Luvs, in 1976.

In the 1960s Procter & Gamble faced charges from the Federal Trade Commission alleging that its Clorox and Folgers acquisitions violated antitrust statutes. In a case that found its way to the Supreme Court, Procter & Gamble was finally forced to divest Clorox in 1967. The Folgers action was dismissed after Procter & Gamble agreed not to make any more grocery acquisitions for seven years, and coffee acquisitions for ten years.

In the late 1960s public attention to water pollution focused on phosphates, a key group of ingredients in soap products. After initial resistance, Procter & Gamble, along with other soapmakers, drastically reduced the use of phosphates in its products.

In 1974 Edward G. Harness became chairman and CEO of Procter & Gamble and the company continued its strong growth. Many familiar products were improved during the 1970s, and new ones were added as well, including Bounce fabric softener for the dryer in 1972 and Sure antiperspirant and Coast soap in 1974.

In 1977, after three years of test marketing, Procter & Gamble introduced Rely tampons, which were rapidly accepted in the market as a result of their superabsorbent qualities. In 1980,

however, the Centers for Disease Control (CDC) published a report showing a statistical link between the use of Rely and a rare but often fatal disease known as toxic shock syndrome (TSS). In September 1980 the company suspended further sales of Rely tampons, taking a $75 million write-off on the product.

Ironically, P&G was able to capitalize on the resurgence of feminine napkins after the TSS scare. The company's Always brand pads quickly garnered market share, and by 1990 Always was the top sanitary napkin, with over one-fourth of the market.

Early 1980s Brought Food and OTC Drug Acquisitions

In 1981 John G. Smale became CEO of Procter & Gamble. He had been president since 1974. Smale led the company further into the grocery business through a number of acquisitions, including Ben Hill Griffin citrus products. The company also entered the over-the-counter (OTC) drug market with the 1982 purchase of Norwich-Eaton Pharmaceuticals, makers of Pepto Bismol and Chloraseptic. The company completed its biggest purchase in 1985, with the acquisition of the Richardson-Vicks Company for $1.2 billion, and bought Dramamine and Metamucil from G.D. Searle & Company. These purchases made Procter & Gamble a leader in over-the-counter drug sales.

In 1985, unable to squelch persistent rumors linking Procter & Gamble's famous moon-and-stars logo to Satanism, the company reluctantly removed the logo from product packages. The logo began to reappear on some packages in the early 1990s, and the company continued to use the trademark on corporate stationary and on its building.

During fiscal 1985, Procter & Gamble experienced its first decline in earnings since 1953. Analysts maintained that Procter & Gamble's corporate structure had failed to respond to important changes in consumer shopping patterns and that the company's standard practice of extensive market research slowed its reaction to the rapidly changing market. The mass-marketing practices that had served Procter & Gamble so well in the past lost their punch as broadcast television viewership fell from 92 percent to 67 percent in the mid-1980s. Many large companies responded to the challenge of cable TV and increasingly market-specific media with appropriately targeted "micro-marketing" techniques, and Procter & Gamble was forced to rethink its marketing strategy. In the late 1980s Procter & Gamble diversified its advertising, reducing its reliance on network television. Computerized market research including point-of-sale scanning also provided the most up-to-date information on consumer buying trends.

In 1987 the company restructured its brand-management system into a "matrix system." Category managers became responsible for several brands, making them sensitive to the profits of other Procter & Gamble products in their areas. Procter & Gamble brands continued to compete against one another, but far less actively. The restructuring also eliminated certain layers of management, quickening the decision-making process. The company became more aware of profitability than in the past. A company spokesperson summed it up for *Business Week:* "Before it had been share, share, share. We get the share and the profits will follow.'' In the later 1980s, Procter & Gamble was no longer willing to settle just for market share.

In the late 1980s healthcare products were one of the fastest-growing markets as the U.S. population grew both older and more health-conscious. To serve this market, Procter & Gamble's OTC drug group, which had been built up earlier in the decade, entered a number of joint ventures in pharmaceuticals. Procter & Gamble teamed up with the Syntex Corporation to formulate an OTC version of its best-selling antiarthritic, Naprosyn. Cooperative deals were also struck with the Dutch Gist-Brocades Company for its De-Nol ulcer medicine; Up-John for its antibaldness drug, Minoxidil; and Triton Bioscience and Cetus for a synthetic interferon.

Acquired Noxell and Blendax in 1988

In September 1988 Procter & Gamble made its first move into the cosmetics business with the purchase of Noxell Corporation, maker of Noxema products and Cover Girl cosmetics, in a $1.3 billion stock swap. Procter & Gamble also planned to further develop its international operations. In 1988 the company acquired Blendax, a European health and beauty-care goods manufacturer. The Bain de Soleil sun-care product line was also purchased that year. By 1989 foreign markets accounted for nearly 40 percent of group sales, up from 14 percent in 1985.

P&G's brand equity was threatened by the weak economy and resultant consumer interest in value in the late 1980s and early 1990s. This value orientation resulted in stronger performance by private labels, especially in health and beauty aids. Private labels' market share of that segment grew 50 percent between 1982 and 1992, to 4.5 percent.

To combat the trend, P&G inaugurated ''Every Day Low Pricing'' (EDLP) for 50 to 60 percent of its products, including Pampers and Luvs diapers, Cascade dish soap, and Jif peanut butter. The pricing strategy was good for consumers but was compensated for with lower promotion deals for wholesalers. Some retailers objected to P&G's cut in promotional kickbacks to the point of actually dropping products, but others welcomed the value-conscious positioning. P&G redirected the money it saved from trade promotions for direct marketing efforts that helped bring coupon and sample programs to targeted groups for brands with narrow customer bases like Pampers, Clearasil, and Oil of Olay.

In the 1990s Procter & Gamble also hopped on the so-called green bandwagon of environmental marketing. It reduced packaging by offering concentrated formulations of products in smaller packages and refill packs on 38 brands in 17 countries.

While P&G expanded its presence in cosmetics and fragrances through the July 1991 acquisition of the worldwide Max Factor and Betrix lines from Revlon, Inc. for $1.03 billion, it also divested holdings in some areas it had outgrown. In 1992 the corporation sold about one-half of its Cellulose & Specialties pulp business to Weyerhaeuser Co. for $600 million. While vertical integration had benefited P&G's paper products in the past, the forestry business had become unprofitable and distracting by the 1990s. The corporation also sold an Italian coffee business in 1992 to focus on a core of European brands.

P&G hoped to introduce products with pan-European packaging, branding, and advertising to capture more of the region's well-established markets. Meanwhile, Pantene Pro-V was introduced in 1992 and quickly became the fastest-growing shampoo brand in the world.

Major Restructuring Began in 1993

Company sales surpassed the $30 billion mark in 1993. Under the leadership of chairman and CEO Edwin L. Artzt and president John E. Pepper, Procter & Gamble that year launched a major restructuring effort aimed at making the company's brand-name products more price competitive with private label and generic brands, bringing products to market faster, and improving overall profitability. The program involved severe cost-cutting, including the closure of 30 plants around the world and the elimination of 13,000 jobs, or 12 percent of P&G's total workforce. The $2.4 billion program, which culminated in 1997, resulted in annual after-tax savings of more than $600 million. It also helped to increase Procter & Gamble's net earnings margin from 7.3 percent in 1994 to 10.2 percent in 1998.

During the restructuring period, the company continued its brisk pace of acquisitions. In 1994 P&G entered the European tissue and towel market through the purchase of Vereinigte Papierwerke Schickedanz AG's European tissue unit, and added the prestige fragrance business of Giorgio Beverly Hills, Inc. That year also saw Procter & Gamble reenter the South African market following the lifting of U.S. sanctions. The company altered its geographic management structure the following year. P&G had divided its business into United States and international operations but would now organize around four regions—North America, Latin America, Asia, and Europe/Middle East/Africa. In July 1995 Artzt retired, and was replaced as chairman and CEO by Pepper. Durk I. Jager was named president and chief operating officer.

In 1996 Procter & Gamble purchased the Eagle Snacks brand line from Anheuser-Busch, the U.S. baby wipes brand Baby Fresh, and Latin American brands Lavan San household cleaner and Magia Blanca bleach. In celebration of the 50th anniversary of Tide's introduction, the company held a ''Dirtiest Kid in America'' contest. Also in 1996 P&G received U.S. Food & Drug Administration (FDA) approval to use olestra, a controversial fat substitute, in snacks and crackers. The company had developed olestra after 25 years of research and at a cost of $250 million. The FDA go-ahead came after an eight-year investigation and included a stipulation that foods containing the substitute include a warning label about possible gastrointestinal side effects. P&G soon began test-marketing Fat Free Pringles, Fat Free Ritz, and other products made using olestra.

In July 1997 Procter & Gamble spent about $1.84 billion in cash to acquire Tambrands, Inc. and the Tampax line of tampons, thereby solidifying its number one position worldwide in feminine products. The company sold its Duncan Hines baking mix line to Aurora Foods of Ohio for $445 million in 1998.

In September 1998 P&G announced a new restructuring initiative, dubbed Organization 2005. In 1996 the company had set a goal of doubling sales from $35 billion in 1996 to $70 billion by 2005. But sales stood at just $37.15 billion by 1998, only a four percent increase over the previous year, although seven percent-per-year increases were needed to maintain the desired pace of growth. A key element of this restructuring was a shift from an organization centered around the four geographic regions established in 1995 to one centered on seven Global Business Units based on product lines: Baby Care, Beauty Care, Fabric & Home Care, Feminine Protection, Food & Beverage, Health Care & Corporate New Ventures, and Tissues & Towels. According to a company press release announcing the new structure, "This change will drive greater innovation and speed by centering strategy and profit responsibility globally on brands, rather than on geographies." Jager would lead this reorganization, as it was announced at the same time that he would become president and CEO on January 1, 1999, with Pepper remaining chairman until September 1, 1999, when Jager would also assume that position.

Principal Subsidiaries

Fisher Nut Company; The Folger Coffee Company; Noxell Corporation; The Procter & Gamble Cellulose Corporation; The Procter & Gamble Distributing Company; Procter & Gamble Eastern Europe, Inc.; Procter & Gamble Far East, Inc.; Procter & Gamble FED, Inc.; The Procter & Gamble Global Finance Company; Procter & Gamble Health Products, Inc.; Procter & Gamble Interamericas Inc.; The Procter & Gamble Manufacturing Company; The Procter & Gamble Paper Products Company; Procter & Gamble Pharmaceuticals, Inc.; Procter & Gamble Productions, Inc.; Procter & Gamble Scandinavia, Inc.; Richardson-Vicks Inc.; Rosemount Corporation; Shulton, Inc.; Tambrands Inc.; Productos Sanitarios S.A. (Argentina); Procter & Gamble Inc. (Canada); Procter & Gamble S.A. (France); Procter & Gamble Hong Kong Limited; Procter & Gamble-Hutchison Ltd. (Hong Kong); Procter & Gamble India Limited; Procter & Gamble Italia, S.p.A. (Italy); Procter & Gamble de Mexico, S.A. de C.V.; Procter & Gamble Philippines, Inc.; Procter & Gamble A.G. (Switzerland); Procter & Gamble Manufacturing (Thailand) Limited; Procter & Gamble Health & Beauty Care-Europe Limited (U.K.); Procter & Gamble Limited (U.K.); The Procter & Gamble U.K. Tissue Company; Thomas Hedley & Co. Limited (U.K.).

Principal Operating Units

Baby Care; Beauty Care; Fabric & Home Care; Feminine Protection; Food & Beverage; Health Care & Corporate New Ventures; Tissues & Towels.

Further Reading

Canedy, Dana, "A Prescription to Keep P&G Growing Strong: Big Household Name Tries to Be a Drugstore, Too," *New York Times,* November 4, 1997, p. D1.

Galuszka, Peter, and Ellen Neuborne, "P&G's Hottest New Product: P&G," *Business Week,* October 5, 1998, p. 92.

Henkoff, Ronald, "P&G: New and Improved!," *Fortune,* October 14, 1996, p. 151.

"The House That Ivory Built: 150 Years of Procter & Gamble," *Advertising Age,* August 20, 1987.

Johnson, Bradley, "Retailers Accepting P&G Low Pricing," *Advertising Age,* June 22, 1992, p. 36.

Kirk, Jim, "The New Status Symbols; New Values Drive Private-Label Sales," *Adweek* (Eastern Ed.), October 5, 1992, pp. 38–44.

Laing, Johnathan R., "New and Improved: Procter & Gamble Fights to Keep Its Place on the Top Shelf," *Barron's,* November 29, 1993, pp. 8–9, 22, 24, 26.

Lawrence, Jennifer, "Jager: New P&G Pricing Builds Brands," *Advertising Age,* June 29, 1992, pp. 13, 49.

——, "Laundry Soap Marketers See the Value of 'Value!,' " *Advertising Age,* September 21, 1992, pp. 3, 56.

Lenzner, Robert, and Carrie Shook, "The Battle of the Bottoms," *Forbes,* March 24, 1997, p. 98.

Levin, Gary, "P&G Tells Shops: Direct Marketing Is Important to Us," *Advertising Age,* June 22, 1992, pp. 3, 35.

Lief, Alfred, *It Floats: The Story of Procter & Gamble,* New York: Rienhart & Company, 1958.

Miller, Cyndee, "Moves by P&G, Heinz Rekindle Fears That Brands Are in Danger," *Marketing News,* June 8, 1992, pp. 1, 15.

Mitchell, Alan, "The Dawn of a Cultural Revolution," *Management Today,* March 1998, pp. 42–44, 46, 48.

Parker-Pope, Tara, "P&G, in Effort to Give Sales a Boost, Plans to Revamp Corporate Structure," *Wall Street Journal,* September 2, 1998, p. B6.

——, "P&G Targets Textiles Tide Can't Clean," *Wall Street Journal,* April 29, 1998, pp. B1, B4.

Parker-Pope, Tara, and Joann S. Lublin, "P&G Will Make Jager CEO Ahead of Schedule," *Wall Street Journal,* September 10, 1998, pp. B1, B8.

Parker-Pope, Tara, and Jonathan Friedland, "P&G Calls the Cops As It Strives to Expand Sales in Latin America," *Wall Street Journal,* March 20, 1998, pp. A1, A9.

Procter & Gamble History, Cincinnati, Ohio: The Procter & Gamble Company, 1996.

"Procter's Gamble," *Economist,* July 25, 1992, pp. 61–62.

Saporito, Bill, "Behind the Tumult at P&G," *Fortune,* March 7, 1994, p. 74.

Schiller, Zachary, "And Now, a Show from Your Sponsor," *Business Week,* May 22, 1995, p. 100.

——, "Ed Artzt's Elbow Grease Has P&G Shining," *Business Week,* October 10, 1994, p. 84.

——, "Make It Simple," *Business Week,* September 9, 1996, p. 96.

——, "No More Mr. Nice Guy at P&G—Not by a Long Shot," *Business Week,* February 3, 1992, p. 54.

——, "Procter & Gamble Hits Back: Its Dramatic Overhaul Takes Aim at High Costs—and Low-Price Rivals," *Business Week,* July 19, 1993, p. 20.

Schisgall, Oscar, *Eyes on Tomorrow: Evolution of Procter & Gamble,* Chicago: J. G. Ferguson Publishing Co., 1981.

Swasy, Alecia, *Soap Opera: The Inside Story of Procter & Gamble,* New York: Times Books, 1993.

Weinstein, Steve, "Will Procter's Gamble Work?," *Progressive Grocer,* July 1992, pp. 36–40.

"Weyerhaeuser Is Set to Acquire Pulp Assets from Procter & Gamble," *Corporate Growth Report,* August 31, 1992, p. 6212.

Wilsher, Peter, "Diverse and Perverse," *Management Today,* July 1992, pp. 32–35.

—Thomas M. Tucker and April Dougal Gasbarre
—updated by David E. Salamie

QUESTAR

Questar Corporation

180 East First South
P.O. Box 45433
Salt Lake City, Utah 84147-0433
U.S.A.
(801) 324-5000
(888) 880-1690
Fax: (801) 324-5483
Web site: http://www.questarcorp.com

Public Company
Incorporated: 1984
Employees: 2,437
Sales: $933.27 million (1997)
Stock Exchanges: New York
Ticker Symbol: STR
SICs: 4923 Gas Transmission & Distribution; 1311
Crude Petroleum & Natural Gas; 6719 Holding
Companies, Not Elsewhere Classified

Questar Corporation is an integrated natural gas company whose major subsidiaries search for, produce, and market oil and natural gas; conduct interstate gas transmission; and distribute gas to the retail market in Utah, southwestern Wyoming, and southeastern Idaho. Other affiliates provide data processing and telecommunications services. The subsidiaries Questar Pipeline Company and Questar Gas provided the bulk of Questar's revenues in the late 1990s, yet non-gas-related subsidiaries, such as Questar InfoComm, Inc., were receiving increasing attention from the company.

Company Origins

Questar Corporation was organized in Utah in April 1984. On October 2, 1984, it became the holding company for Mountain Fuel Supply Company, a public utility that is the backbone of Questar and other gas transmission and exploration and production subsidiaries. Mountain Fuel Supply had grown out of another company, one formed by the Ohio Oil Company in 1928.

In 1922, the Ohio Oil Company discovered natural gas reservoirs in the Baxter Basin area near Rock Springs, Wyoming. Because of these substantial reservoirs, Ohio Oil decided to develop its company in the West. They merged with two other companies to form the Western Public Service Corporation in October 1928. One of their primary subsidiaries was Mountain Fuel Supply, which handled gas production, owned and leased natural gas territory, and controlled gas purchase agreements in other territories. These territories, which included both proven and suspected natural gas reservoirs, covered 125,000 acres in Colorado, Utah, and Wyoming.

In December of that same year, Western Public Service acquired the Utah Gas and Coke Company, which owned and operated the manufactured gas distribution system in Salt Lake City. These acquisitions provided the company with established distribution systems that could be used for natural gas as well. Western Public Service acquired the distribution rights in Ogden, Utah, and several other towns in Utah and Wyoming. Extensive pipeline systems were needed to transport the gas 200 miles from the Baxter Basin reservoirs to Salt Lake City and Ogden. Some came from their subsidiary Wasatch Gas, and the rest were built by Western Public Service.

With natural gas reserves ready, pipelines and distribution networks in place, and growth in the West raising demand for energy, Western Public Service expected 1929 and the following years to be stellar ones. The stock market crash in October, however, dashed the company's hopes. Western Public's stock price fell from $46 a share in September 1929 to $3 a share in 1932. By 1932, the company's net income had only reached $313,000. Most of that income was generated by commercial customers; natural gas was too expensive for the average Depression-era family.

In 1935 Western Public Service merged with its subsidiaries Aspen Mountain Gas, Utah Gas and Coke Company, Wasatch Gas, Ogden Gas, Uinta Pipe Line, and Mountain Fuel Supply, ending the holding company structure. The new organization, incorporated under the name Mountain Fuel Supply Company, avoided many of the bureaucratic entanglements required by the federal Public Utility Holding Company Act. The consolidated company moved its general office from Pittsburgh to Salt Lake City.

World War II vastly increased the demand for natural gas, not only from residential customers who found the rising price of coal too expensive but also from the new munitions plants and defense installations. In 1941, Mountain Fuel refused new applications for heating services from industrial customers to conserve its resources for the war effort. The following year, the federal War Production Board indicated the company should refuse new residential heating customers also. Pent-up demand at the end of the war led to boom years at Mountain Fuel, although the continued scarcity of steel made it difficult for the company to extend its pipelines for several years.

As the company expanded its distribution service over the next several decades, it kept up with increasing demand with several substantial natural gas discoveries in Wyoming, Colorado, and Utah. The first, in the Clay Basin region northeast of Utah, was made in the mid-1930s. In 1946 the Church Buttes field was discovered in southwestern Wyoming. Another prolific source was discovered in the Brady field, about 30 miles southeast of Wyoming, in 1972.

Expansion in the 1970s

Throughout the 1970s, Mountain Fuel Supply altered the organization of its subsidiaries to create distinct profit centers. According to the *Questar 1991 Fact Book,* this reorganization was done to "provide greater financial and operating flexibility." To begin, in 1971, Mountain Fuel Supply created Entrada Industries, Inc., to operate the corporation's nonutility endeavors. Within months, Entrada acquired Interstate Brick Company, which manufactured and marketed brick and tile products.

In 1975 Mountain Fuel Resources, later renamed Questar Pipeline Company, was organized and incorporated as a wholly owned subsidiary of Entrada Industries. With Federal Power Commission approval, this new company acquired a gas transmission system in Colorado and Utah from Cascade Natural Gas Corp. The $8.5 million investment gave Mountain Fuel Resources over 200 miles of transmission, gathering, and underground storage lines and enabled them to connect gas fields in western Colorado with their existing transmission system in eastern Utah. From 1976 to 1978, Mountain Fuel Resources invested $33 million in the construction of a new underground storage reservoir. The reservoir, located in the Clay Basin gas field of northeastern Utah, was approved by the FPC and served an interstate market.

In addition to these projects, Mountain Fuel Resources joined with six other companies to create the Trailblazer pipeline system, a 793-mile, 36-inch diameter pipeline that runs from Beatrice, Nebraska, to western Wyoming. Mountain Fuel Resources designed, constructed, and operated the 88-mile Overthrust Segment, which extended from Whitney Canyon, north of Evanston, Wyoming, to Rock Springs, Wyoming.

Mountain Fuel Supply continued its restructuring in 1976 with the organization of Wexpro Company, a subsidiary held by Entrada Industries. Having designed the subsidiary to conduct development drilling and production operations, Mountain Fuel Supply transferred to Wexpro all of its nonutility oil-producing properties in January 1977. Wexpro worked under a joint operating agreement with Mountain Fuel. In 1983 a settlement agreement with the states of Utah and Wyoming stipulated that Wexpro was authorized to engage in development drilling on oil and gas properties that were productive as of August 1, 1981.

Reorganization in the 1980s

Celsius Energy Company, another Entrada Industries subsidiary, was organized in 1982 to conduct oil and gas exploration and production operations in the Rocky Mountain region. By 1984 Celsius owned oil and gas leases or rights on over two million acres of potential oil and gas lands. Together with Wexpro and their parent company, Mountain Fuel Supply, Celsius had full or partial working interests in 340,000 acres of producing fields by 1984. These fields, located in New Mexico, Nevada, Wyoming, Montana, North Dakota, and Nebraska, contained about 150 oil wells and 425 gas wells held by the company in full or jointly with others.

Mountain Fuel Supply's transmission system had grown by 1984 to include almost 1,500 miles of gas transmission pipeline, and its distribution system to over 12,000 miles of street mains and service and connecting pipelines. Its maximum delivery capacity had reached over 900 million cubic feet per day.

In 1984 the company transferred from Mountain Fuel Supply to Mountain Fuel Resources various interstate transmission operations and assets. Approved by the Federal Energy Regulatory Commission (FERC), this transfer was designed to reduce regulatory duplication and improve operating efficiency.

The company's corporate structure continued to evolve when the shareholders of Mountain Fuel Supply accepted an agreement of reorganization and plan of merger in 1984, which created a new holding company, Questar Corporation. Mountain Fuel Supply became one of the corporation's subsidiaries and began to concentrate solely on natural gas distribution. In 1985 the corporation's data processing and communication needs were taken over by a new subsidiary, Questar Service Corporation.

In the 1980s the gas industry changed significantly as a result of deregulation. Once the controls on gas prices were loosened, exploration for gas dramatically increased, resulting in the abundant gas supply of the late 1980s and early 1990s. This abundant supply lowered prices and changed gas companies' marketing strategies. Many began purchasing gas at low wellhead prices and storing it in anticipation of seasonal price fluctuations. Questar Pipeline took advantage of this development by creating new storage service at its depleted Clay Basin gas field. The FERC accepted an open-access blanket certificate, and by 1992 customers had subscribed to 90 percent of the available firm storage. Further deregulation ordered by the FERC in 1992 allowed companies to buy gas directly from producers and transport and store the gas with someone else. These changes gave an additional boost to the Clay Basin storage field.

In addition, regulations changed not only for gas prices but also for the industry's business practices. In 1985 the FERC issued the first of a series of orders devised to encourage competition in the pipeline industry and increase the scope of their business. In effect, pipeline companies had to alter their operations from buying and reselling gas to transporting gas for third parties. Questar was challenged to make drastic changes in internal structure to accommodate the new orders. As of 1991 the FERC was refining the new shape of the industry, primarily through regulations concerning "comparability of service" rulemaking. According to Questar's 1991 annual report, the company had "been able to minimize . . . negative side effects" of these new rulings. The company also felt that "pipelines will be able to manage and perhaps prosper in the new industry environment."

The low gas prices of the mid-1980s combined with a slow economy in Utah to create some difficult challenges for Questar. Not only did the company have to contend with lowered demand and lower prices, various incidents, including labor disputes and flooding of the Great Salt Lake, led to the company losing some of its largest customers.

The company's stability going into this tumultuous period, however, helped it survive the problems and even take advantage of certain opportunities. The lowered gas prices had led to lower assessed values on oil- and gas-producing company assets. Questar found it had the resources to buy companies it could not have afforded before. In 1987 Questar acquired 53 percent of Universal Resources Corp. for $16.24 million. Soon thereafter, Questar bought the company's remaining shares for $14.19 million, although by assuming Universal Resources' debt, the total value of the acquisition was about $100 million. The purchase of the exploration and production company brought with it holdings primarily in Oklahoma, Kansas, and Texas, but also smaller properties in few Midwestern and Rocky Mountain states. With producing fields in the midcontinental United States and established natural gas marketing in the West, Universal Resources seemed a natural addition to Questar.

Questar managed to find another advantage in Utah's depressed economy in the 1980s. With lower construction costs, Mountain Fuel was able to build new transmission lines. Between 1986 and 1988, Mountain Fuel extended service to southern Utah with a 209-mile pipeline, making natural gas available for the first time to over 20,000 customers in the area. An extension to the line in 1988 brought the distribution system 74 miles further southwest.

Diversification in the Late 1980s and Early 1990s

The gas industry, which relies heavily on the demand for heating, varies with cyclical weather patterns, as do its revenues. To stabilize its revenues, Questar diversified in the late 1980s into non-gas-related businesses. Taking advantage of the

expertise gained with radio communications while operating its interstate gas transmission, the corporation established a new subsidiary, Questar Telecom Inc., in 1989. This company provided customers a combination of two-way radio and mobile telephone service called specialized mobile radio, or SMR. Following a strategy of buying smaller SMR providers and combining them to improve customer service and achieve economies of scale, Questar Telecom had already become one of the largest providers of SMR in the western United States by 1992. Although the enterprise was not yet working at a profit, Questar planned to double its investment in the operation in the next few years, counting on increased efficiency and the steadily growing demand for personal communications to make the operation into a consistent revenue source.

Questar supported the development of another new technology, natural gas vehicles (NGV). Vehicles powered by natural gas generate far fewer emissions that contribute to urban air pollution than petroleum-powered vehicles, making them appealing to environmentalists. Mountain Fuel Supply sponsored tests at the National Center for Vehicle Emissions Control in Ft. Collins, Colorado, that showed when vehicles burned natural gas instead of petroleum, carbon monoxide emissions were reduced by 94 percent, oxides of nitrogen by 16 percent, carbon dioxide by 22 percent, and reactive hydrocarbons by 67 percent.

Mountain Fuel Supply planned in 1991 to allocate approximately $4 million to further development of NGV-related facilities. Mountain Fuel began by initiating marketing efforts on fleet vehicles because the cost of converting a vehicle to natural gas was more economical for vehicles with high annual mileages. According to Questar's 1991 annual report, Mountain Fuel representatives discussed NGV conversions with operators of more than 40 fleets consisting of nearly 6,000 vehicles. Mountain Fuel also converted 500 of its own fleet to natural gas.

As of 1991, Questar owned one-third of a related venture, FuelMaker Corporation, a company that marketed a refueling device for NGVs. The device connected directly to the user's gas supply at home or business and automatically refueled the vehicle in about five hours. Utilities and other businesses bought the original 2,000 units, and FuelMaker began expanding production capabilities to 6,000 units per year.

To improve returns, Questar sold Interstate Brick Company in 1990 for approximately book value. The company had not been consistently running at a profit for the previous few years.

In 1991 Mountain Fuel Supply connected service to its 500,000th customer, having doubled its customer base since 1970. It also continued to expand its service area, receiving franchises to 18 communities in western Utah. The services tapped into the Kern River Pipeline and were expected to begin providing gas by the winter of 1992–93.

Renewed Growth in the 1990s

In the early 1990s demand for natural gas was growing because of its cleanliness and domestic availability. Nationwide gas usage grew every year from 1986 to 1991 despite an economic recession and a series of warm winters. In addition, Utah's economy improved in the 1990s, and Questar enjoyed a dramatic increase in retail business. Between 1990 and 1997,

Questar's customer base rose by 150,000, reaching 642,000 customers in 1997. This rate of growth doubled the industry average.

Exploration and production also improved in the 1990s. Although the lowered gas prices had hurt Questar's exploration and production companies in the 1980s, cost-cutting and employee incentives combined with rising gas prices in the 1990s to raise the E&P companies' income. Net income for Questar's E&P companies rose from approximately $11 million in 1989 to $41 million in 1997. The renewed prosperity allowed Questar to acquire several new holdings, expanding its reserves in the Rocky Mountains and the Midwestern United States and moving for the first time into Canada, namely Alberta and British Columbia. The company saw the early 1990s as a window of opportunity for exploration, in part because wells drilled prior to 1993 qualified for federal tax credits. Using funds from internal sources and short-term loans, the company increased exploration and production. Exploratory and development drilling received approximately $65 million in 1992, spent primarily on drilling in tight sands gas areas.

In 1994 Nextel Communications Inc. bought Questar Telecom for 3.8 million shares of Nextel stock. Using the price of Nextel stock at the time, Questar received approximately $100 million for the subsidiary. The sale, however, did not represent Questar's intention to abandon its diversification into the information technology and communications field. Questar Service expanded its operations in the mid-1990s and changed its name to Questar InfoComm in 1995. In addition to providing information and communications services to internal and external clients, Questar InfoComm moved into the local telecommunications market in 1996. Questar InfoComm initiated a joint venture with NEXTLINK, an operator of local telephone and data networks, to provide local telecommunications services to businesses in Utah.

Questar's expansion continued into the late 1990s. The company initiated a five-year spending program amounting to $2 billion, focusing on pipeline construction and reserve acquisition. Approximately $260 million was devoted to the TransColorado Pipeline, which neared completion in 1998. Questar Pipeline bought a 700-mile oil pipeline between New Mexico and California in 1998, renaming it the Questar Southern Trails Pipeline and beginning its conversion to gas transmission. The same year, Questar acquired HSRTW, Inc., an oil- and gas-exploration and production company with 150 billion cubic feet of proven natural gas reserves.

Because of the continued deregulation of the energy market, Questar wished to create a single brand image that customers would identify with its varied products and services. To that end, Mountain Fuel changed its name in 1998 to Questar Gas. The company also planned to combine Celsius Energy and Universal Resources under the name Questar Exploration and Production in 1999.

Principal Subsidiaries

Questar Regulated Services Company (holding company for Mountain Fuel Supply Company and Questar Pipeline Company); Entrada Industries Incorporated (holding company for Wexpro Company; Universal Resources Corporation; Questar Gas Management Company; Questar Energy Services, Inc.; Questar Energy Trading Company; and Celsius Energy Company); Questar InfoComm, Inc.

Principal Divisions

Regulated Services; Market Resources.

Further Reading

Baum, David, "Questar Corp: Rapid Development Fuels New Business," *InfoWorld,* September 18, 1995, p. 76.
Edgerton, Jerry, "Build Your Wealth Drip by Drip," *Money,* August 1997, pp. 88–97.
Questar 1991 Fact Book, Salt Lake City: Questar Corporation, 1992.
"Questar to Pay $157.5 for Its Rival's Business," *New York Times,* July 29, 1998, p. C4.

—Susan Windisch Brown

Quest Diagnostics Inc.

One Malcolm Avenue
Teterboro, New Jersey 07608
U.S.A.
(201) 393-5000
Fax: (201) 393-5717
Web site: http://www.questdiagnostics.com

Public Company
Incorporated: 1967 as MetPath Inc.
Employees: 16,300
Sales: $1.53 billion (1997)
Stock Exchanges: New York
Ticker Symbol: DGX
SICs: 8071 Medical Laboratories

Quest Diagnostics Inc. is one of the largest clinical laboratory testing companies in the United States. It offers a broad range of routine and esoteric services used by the medical profession in the diagnosis, monitoring, and treatment of disease and other medical conditions. The company's customers include independent physicians and physician groups, health maintenance organizations and other managed-care groups, hospitals, and government agencies. It was spun off from Corning Inc. in 1996.

Corning Medical Products and MetPath to 1982

The origins of Quest Diagnostics were in the laboratory glassware of Corning Glass Works. Its Pyrex glassware—which spawned a lucrative cookware line—put the company in the laboratory business as far back as World War I. When instrumentation began to replace test tube, flask, and beaker chemistry in the 1960s, Corning added to the primitive meters it was already making a high-powered pH-measuring instrument designed to find how well a critically ill patient's lungs were exchanging oxygen and carbon dioxide. The new blood-gas apparatus could not, in 1977, be produced fast enough to keep up with demand.

By 1975 Corning also had begun marketing white blood cell analyzers to automate one of the last blood tests still being performed manually in clinical laboratories. In 1976 the company had a medical products division making electrodes, pHmeters, electrometers, biomedical instruments and systems, photometers, electrophoresis equipment, and densitometers in Medford, Massachusetts, and in Palo Alto, California. In 1977 Corning's health and sciences activities were consolidated into a single operating division with sales amounting to $221 million and net income at 12 percent of the parent company's total. In 1981 these figures were $374 million and 32 percent, respectively.

Corning's clinical laboratory testing did not begin, however, until it acquired MetPath Inc. in 1982. Paul A. Brown, a pathologist who later said he was "amazed at the sky-high test prices charged by hospitals and clinics," founded what was originally Metropolitan Pathological Laboratory in 1967 with $500 and initially ran it out of his Manhattan apartment. Two years later he invested in a $55,000 device that automatically performed 12 common blood tests, charging $5.50, compared with more than $40 charged by hospitals and medical laboratories. In 1972 Brown spent more than $1 million on two AutoChemist units, which raised the number of blood tests MetPath could perform automatically to 25 and saved significantly on costly chemical reagents needed for analysis. The company began turning a profit in 1971 and, beginning in 1974, made money each year. Corning Glass Works bought ten percent of its stock in 1973.

By 1975 MetPath had one of the best equipped and largest medical laboratories in the world and was the largest U.S. company devoted entirely to clinical laboratory services. It was offering, in 11 cities, more than 600 laboratory tests to physicians, hospitals, and institutions and performing more than two million lab tests a month from specimens of more than 150,000 patients. The tests were being processed at a highly automated central laboratory in Hackensack, New Jersey, with 80 percent of the results delivered to the client within 24 hours after collection of the specimen. Overall, MetPath's average billing per patient transaction was only $9.

MetPath was, by 1979, challenging Damon Corp. for first place in the clinical laboratory testing field, which had grown

---

into a $12-billion-a-year business. The company had net income of $3.8 million in fiscal 1978 (the year ended September 30, 1978) on revenues of $53.4 million. A new, $25 million laboratory, easily the industry's largest and capable of analyzing up to 30,000 samples a day, was completed in Teterboro, New Jersey, in 1978. Fifty local offices made daily collections at doctors' offices and clinics, shipping them via same-day air freight to the laboratory. The results were transmitted to telecommunications terminals at each of the company's local offices. For a package of 29 common tests, MetPath was charging only $20.

MetPath was tops in the clinical laboratory testing field by 1982. The Teterboro laboratory's four IBM mainframe computers were sending results to terminals in 70 branches and 550 doctor's and hospital offices. MetPath had acquired small testing laboratories throughout the country to become collection points for samples and had built a second clinical laboratory near Chicago's O'Hare Airport. The expansion raised the company's debt so precipitously, however, that in 1982 it was sold to Corning Glass Works for stock worth about $145 million.

MetPath and Other Units: 1982–95

Although MetPath remained autonomous and its revenue kept growing—fueled by Medicare funding, a new emphasis on preventive medicine, and a wave of medical malpractice suits, which encouraged doctors to order more tests—the company found itself overwhelmed by freight costs. It also had lost business to smaller labs as testing equipment became smaller and more affordable. MetPath's operating profit margin fell from ten percent in 1981 to four percent in 1985, when it wrote off the Chicago-area lab and closed some local offices. Instead, it transformed its testing facilities into a network of regional laboratories close to the physicians being served and capable of quicker response to customer needs. By 1988 MetPath was again solidly in the black, although SmithKline Beckman Laboratories was doing twice as much annual business in the clinical testing field as MetPath's $350 million.

Corning regrouped its products and services in 1989 into four industry segments. The science and optical products units were moved from the former Health and Science segment to Specialty Materials, with the remaining businesses forming the Laboratory Services segment. Laboratory Services had net sales of $580.8 million in 1989 and income before tax of $99.2 million. At the end of 1990 the Laboratory Services segment was placed into a subsidiary named Corning Lab Services Inc.

MetPath, now able to handle more than 1,400 different clinical tests, remained the major unit. It strengthened its regional network in 1991 by the addition of smaller labs, including Clinical Pathology Facility, Inc. in Pittsburgh and Continental Bio-Clinical Laboratories in Grand Rapids, Michigan. Corning Lab Services acquired Southgate Medical Laboratory System, a Cleveland-based operator of clinical testing laboratories in Ohio, Indiana, and Pennsylvania, in 1992, and clinical laboratories in Denver, Dallas, and Phoenix from Unilab Corp. in 1993. (Corning had taken a major stake in Unilab—a major western U.S. clinical testing network—in 1992.) Another Corning Lab Services operation was St. Louis-based Metropolitan Reference Laboratories Inc. Founded in 1987, it was testing medical samples from ten midwestern and southern states by 1993.

Also in 1993, Corning acquired, for its Laboratory Services subsidiary, Damon Corp., the nation's fifth largest owner of clinical testing laboratories, with 14 in the United States and one in Mexico and about 220 satellite labs in remote U.S. locations. This made Corning Lab Services the nation's second largest laboratory testing company.

Founded in Needham, Massachusetts, in 1961 by Dr. David Kosowsky, Damon bought many small labs and had $22.8 million in revenue and $1.3 million in net income in 1968, just before going public. It was first in its field in 1978, doing $76 million a year in clinical laboratory analysis, but was then overtaken by MetPath and by 1982 was struggling financially. After being taken private in a 1989 leveraged buyout, it lost money for three successive years because of large interest payments tied to the buyout debt. In 1992, however, the company earned $18 million on sales of $317 million. Corning, which paid $575 million for Damon, sold the company's California laboratories in 1994.

Corning Lab Services was renamed Corning Life Sciences, Inc. in 1994, and MetPath was renamed Corning Clinical Laboratories. That year the parent company acquired Maryland Medical Laboratory Inc., one of the Baltimore area's largest diagnostic and testing operations, with annual sales of nearly $100 million, for about $140 million worth of stock. Maryland Medical was conducting regional testing for AIDS, immunogenetics, virology, veterinary diagnostics, molecular biology, and computer sciences. Also in 1994, Corning acquired Nichols Institute, another clinical laboratory testing operation, for about $325 million. Both acquisitions became part of Corning Clinical Laboratories, which in 1994 accounted for $1.7 billion of the parent company's $4.8 billion in sales and was the nation's largest clinical laboratory company.

The business climate for Corning Clinical Laboratories was far from ideal, however, as public demand intensified for cost containment in healthcare. MetPath and Metwest—a California-based spinoff from MetPath—agreed in 1993 to pay the federal government $39.8 million to settle charges that they had submitted Medicare claims for unnecessary blood tests. In 1995 Corning Clinical Laboratories agreed to pay the federal government $8.6 million for tests that doctors never ordered, and in 1998 Quest Diagnostics—Corning Clinical Laboratories' successor—agreed to pay $6.8 million to settle a similar case. In 1996 Damon—which had been renamed Damon Clinical Laboratories

Inc.—agreed to pay $119 million in criminal and civil fines after pleading guilty to charges that it had defrauded Medicare by seeking reimbursements for unnecessary blood tests.

Fines, the tougher regulatory climate, the growth of managed-care networks limiting the ability of Corning Clinical Laboratories to increase prices, and the difficulty by the diverse companies acquired in processing bills put the unit in the red in 1995. Despite net revenues of $1.63 billion in 1995, Corning Clinical Laboratories lost $52.1 million, after the parent company took a charge of $62 million to increase accounts receivable because of the billings problems. Moreover, Corning Clinical Laboratories' long-term debt reached almost $1.2 billion.

Quest Diagnostics: 1996–97

In 1996 Corning decided to spin off its laboratory testing and pharmaceutical services businesses to shareholders, creating two independent public companies. The laboratory testing business became Quest Diagnostics Inc. Corning, on the last day of 1996, distributed all outstanding shares of common stock of the new company to Corning stockholders, with one share distributed for each eight shares of Corning. Revenues for 1996 came to $1.62 billion, with a loss of $626 million after taking into account special charges of $668.5 million, including a $445 million write-down of intangible assets. Long-term debt declined, however, to $515 million because Corning assumed more than $700 million of Quest's debt when it spun off the company. In 1997 Quest had a net loss of $22.3 million on revenues of $1.53 billion. The loss reflected special charges totaling $55.5 million in connection with eliminating and consolidating company facilities to reduce excess capacity.

In 1997 Quest Diagnostics had a network of 15 regional laboratories located in major metropolitan areas across the United States and an esoteric testing laboratory and research and development facilities (Nichols Institute) in San Juan Capistrano, California. In addition, Quest had several smaller branch laboratories, including one in Mexico, approximately 150 local laboratories, and about 800 patient service centers. The company was processing about 54 million requisitions for testing each year.

Routine testing services and operations, performed at the regional laboratories, included procedures in the areas of blood chemistry, hematology, urine chemistry, virology, tissue pathology, and cytology. This accounted for about 89 percent of Quest Diagnostics' net laboratory revenues in 1997. Esoteric testing by Nichols Institute was being performed in cases where the information provided by routine tests was not specific enough or was inconclusive as to the existence or absence of disease. This generated about nine percent of the company's net laboratory revenues in 1997.

The balance of Quest's net revenues in 1997 was derived from the manufacture and sale of clinical laboratory test kits by Nichols Institute and from clinical trials and informatics businesses. Quest Informatics was collecting and analyzing laboratory, pharmaceutical, and other data to help large healthcare customers identify and monitor patients at risk for certain diseases.

Principal Subsidiaries

CLMP Inc.; Damon Investment Holdings, Inc.; DPD Holdings, Inc.; Laboratory Holdings Inc.; Nichols Institute Diagnostics; Nichols Institute Diagnostics Ltd. (U.K.); Nichols Institute Diagnostics Trading S.A. (Switzerland); Nichols Institute Diagnostika GMBH (Germany); Nichols Institute International Holding B.V. (Netherlands); Nomad-Massachusetts, Inc.; Quest Diagnostics Inc.; Quest Diagnostics of Pennsylvania Inc.; Quest Holdings Inc. (Maryland); Quest Holdings Inc. (Michigan); Quest MRL Inc.

Further Reading

Blanton, Kimberly, "Needham Lab Fined $119 Million for Fraud," *Boston Globe,* October 10, 1996, pp. A1, A24.

Chilthelen, Ignatius, "Clinical Case," *Forbes,* March 20, 1989, pp. 178, 180.

"Damon Corp." *Boston Globe,* June 8, 1993, p. 38.

Gross, Daniel, "Corning's Experiment," *Crain's New York Business,* January 22, 1996, p. 26.

Gross, Shera, "Rapid Growth Spurs Metropolitan Lab Move," *St. Louis Business Journal,* November 16, 1992, p. 13.

Holusha, John, "Corning to Spin Off Labs and Drug Units," *New York Times,* May 15, 1996, p. D4.

Kindel, Stephen, " 'It Takes a Lot of Patience,' " *Forbes,* September 13, 1982, pp. 82–84.

——, "Management, Know Thyself," *Forbes,* August 16, 1982, pp. 69–71.

"Machines to Analyze White Blood Cells Are Put on Market," *Wall Street Journal,* January 27, 1975, p. 8.

Magnet, Myron, "Corning Glass Shapes Up," *Fortune,* December 13, 1982, pp. 96, 100.

McConnell, Bill, "Corning Inc. Buys Maryland Medical Laboratories for $149 Million," *Warfield's Business Record,* May 6, 1994, p. 12.

"MetPath: Price-Cutting with a Super-Lab Creates New Growth," *Business Week,* February 26, 1979, pp. 126, 132.

Mullaney, Christine, "MetPath Approach in Budding Industry Pays Off," *Investment Dealers' Digest,* October 7, 1975, pp. 29–30.

Sims, Calvin, "Blood Labs Agree to Pay $39.8 Million," *New York Times,* September 14, 1993, pp. D1, D5.

—Robert Halasz

The Really Useful Group

19/22 Tower Street
London WC2 H9S
United Kingdom
171-240-0880
Fax: 171-240-1204
Web site: http://www.reallyuseful.com

Private Company
Incorporated: 1977 as The Really Useful Company
Employees: 4,000
Sales: n/a
SICs: 7922 Theatrical Producers (Except Motion Picture)
& Miscellaneous Theatrical Services; 3652
Phonograph Records & Prerecorded Audio Tapes &
Disks; 7929 Bands, Orchestras, Actors, & Other
Entertainers & Entertainment Groups

The Really Useful Group is the umbrella corporation over a welter of entertainment and leisure companies that operate worldwide. The core of the company's business is marketing of the work of Andrew Lloyd Webber, Britain's most successful composer, known for blockbuster musicals such as *Jesus Christ Superstar, Joseph and the Amazing Technicolor Dreamcoat, Cats, Evita, Phantom of the Opera,* and others. The company receives a percentage of the profits from every new Lloyd Webber production, and is responsible for promoting and producing the shows. In addition, the company owns the rights to much of Lloyd Webber's work, and exploits these through film, video, and recording ventures. The Group owns a record company, Really Useful Records, which principally releases recordings of Lloyd Webber's music. The Really Useful Picture Company, the Group's film production arm, develops and produces works for both television and the big screen. Many of the Picture Company's ventures revolve around Lloyd Webber musicals, such as a documentary commissioned by the BBC about the making of *Sunset Boulevard.* Other film ventures are about other people's music, including a made-for-television film about the Beatles and a series on music made in collaboration with the Walt Disney Company. The Group also owns several theaters around the world, including three in London, and theaters in Germany, Switzerland, and Australia. The company also has a games division. The Really Useful Group's offices are found in London, New York, Los Angeles, Sydney, Hong Kong, Singapore, and Frankfurt. The bulk of the company's profits come from North America, with a substantial portion also made in continental Europe, and smaller contributions coming from Japan, Australia, Singapore, and other Asian venues, and from the United Kingdom.

Lloyd Webber's Beginnings

The history of The Really Useful Group cannot be separated from the history of Andrew Lloyd Webber himself. Lloyd Webber was born in 1948, son of William Lloyd Webber, director of the London College of Music. William Lloyd Webber was a talented organist, and his broad musical tastes and special fondness for church music may have influenced his son's early work, especially the biblically themed *Jesus Christ Superstar* and *Joseph and the Amazing Technicolor Dreamcoat.* Young Andrew was given music lessons from the age of four, and he soon began composing his own tunes. He published his first piece of music at age nine, called *The Toy Theatre Suite.* Andrew Lloyd Webber made it to prestigious Oxford University, but he quit after one term. His only real interest was in writing musicals. After he dropped out of college, Lloyd Webber subsisted off money from his grandmother, took a few composing courses, and wrote pop songs and several musicals with a friend, Tim Rice. Rice was a talented lyricist, and the two made a dynamic combo. They had limited success with their first efforts, eventually staging a 30-minute "pop cantata"— *Joseph and the Amazing Technicolor Dreamcoat*—in St. Paul's Cathedral. This piece was covered favorably in the newspapers, and because of it Rice and Lloyd Webber were picked up by the agents David Land and Sefton Myers of New Talent Ventures. Land and Myers provided Rice and Lloyd Webber with a living wage in exchange for 25 percent of their earnings over the next three years. Rice and Lloyd Webber then recorded a few songs, and searched for a big idea that would put them on the map. When they recorded a song called "Superstar" about Jesus Christ, it became a cult hit, and in 1969 MCA Records commissioned the pair to write a full-length musical based on the life of Christ. The two-album recording of *Jesus Christ Superstar* debuted in 1970. It flopped in England, but sold astonishingly well in the United States.

Rice and Lloyd Webber were becoming a hot item, and so they were snapped up by a new backer, Robert Stigwood. Stigwood bought a 51 percent stake in New Talent Ventures, Rice and Lloyd Webber's original agency, and negotiated the rights to 25 percent of the pair's earnings over the next five years, plus the rights to film and stage productions of their works in the English-speaking world. The stage version of *Jesus Christ Superstar* debuted on Broadway the next year, an immediate smash hit. It was Stigwood who boosted the show, toured it all over the United States, and launched a dozen lawsuits against pirate productions. By 1975, Rice and Lloyd Webber had each made an estimated $2.4 million off *Jesus Christ Superstar*. Their next show, a full-length version of their earlier *Joseph,* was also a huge hit, staged in dozens of countries. Then in 1978, Rice and Lloyd Webber produced *Evita,* a musical based on the life of Eva Perón. Another smash, this show eventually made an estimated $240 million. The album sold 3.5 million copies, and the film rights were sold for $1.6 million.

Lloyd Webber was an immense artistic success, living his dream of composing musicals. His work had made him wealthy by the time he was 23. After *Evita,* his second five-year contract with Stigwood was up, and Lloyd Webber decided to take control of his own finances. He set up a variety of different companies, each dedicated to a separate aspect of his business. He set up a company called Escaway (an elision of "escape" and "getaway") to manage his personal finances; his Steampower Music Company owned the rights to his music publishing. The company he formed to take over what Stigwood had done he named The Really Useful Company, after James the Really Useful Engine on the popular British children's television show "Thomas the Tank."

Start of Really Useful in the 1970s and 1980s

The Really Useful Company operated out of the profits from Lloyd Webber's new shows. He parted with lyricist Rice at the same time he severed his connection with Robert Stigwood, and moved on to create another sensation, *Cats. Cats* debuted in 1981, and was still playing in New York ten years later. It was estimated to have made $640 million worldwide in these ten years, and it sold millions of recordings. Lloyd Webber also produced *Song and Dance* in 1982, which ran for two years in London and 14 months on Broadway. This was followed by *Starlight Express* in 1984. In 1985, The Really Useful Company was flush with profits from these shows, and Lloyd Webber announced he would offer public shares in the company.

The new publicly owned company, called The Really Useful Group, promised investors a share in Lloyd Webber's upcoming works for the next seven years. The company was also still raking in profits from *Cats.* Lloyd Webber retained 40 percent of the stock in Really Useful, and sold the rest on the London Stock Exchange beginning in January 1986. The stock started out at $4.79 a share, and had risen almost 60 percent by the autumn of 1987. Revenues for its first year as a public company were $29 million, and the profit came to $8.5 million. The Group's managing director was Brian Brolly, who had formerly been Paul McCartney's business manager.

The company flourished when Lloyd Webber's *Phantom of the Opera* debuted in 1989. The new show packed in audiences in New York, London, Los Angeles, and Vienna. Meanwhile, *Cats* continued to do well. Yet there was some evidence that things were not running altogether smoothly at the company. Director Brolly quit the company, apparently over differences with Lloyd Webber. Brolly then sold his shares in the company, and they were bought up by publishing magnate Robert Maxwell. Maxwell spent some $16.5 million for the 14.5 percent stake in Really Useful. Despite his large investment, Maxwell claimed he did not want a say in the company, but merely saw it as a good investment.

Maxwell bought his stake in the company in August 1989, and by February 1990, Lloyd Webber had apparently decided that he was in danger of losing artistic control of his work to outside investors. Lloyd Webber asked to buy back the shares he had sold to the public, and take Really Useful private again. Though there had been no real conflict with Maxwell or any other investor, Lloyd Webber explained that he wanted to do new things, such as make movies, and he did not want to feel bound by investor expectations. Company literature also explained that Really Useful felt its "core activities were not understood by, or suited to, the financial markets." After negotiating with major stockholders, who included Maxwell and the Australian tycoon Robert Holmes à Court, Lloyd Webber bought back all Really Useful's stock in March 1990.

Private Again in the 1990s

After the stock buyback, Really Useful began to transform itself into a bigger and more ambitious operation. In 1991, the record and entertainment conglomerate Polygram bought a 30 percent stake in The Really Useful Group. Polygram paid $110 million for its shares, and this money relieved Really Useful of debt. The partnership did not seem to threaten Lloyd Webber's artistic control the way the earlier investor relationships had, and the company forged into new territory. Really Useful opened a television production division shortly after the Polygram deal went through. The division, which became the Really Useful Picture Company, developed and produced TV documentaries and dramas, mainly music- and arts-oriented. Because it had the rights to Lloyd Webber's work, some of its programming revolved around his musicals. But the division also coproduced and cofinanced other television projects, and eventually produced feature films in partnership with the BBC, Disney, The Children's Film Foundation, and the American entertainment channel A&E.

The Really Useful Group began to expand geographically as well. Lloyd Webber's theatrical productions proved easily exportable, and the shows traveled across Europe and into Asia. In 1993, the company ventured for the first time into Southeast Asia, where audiences were for the most part unprepared for Western musicals. Really Useful used its Australian arm to mount an Australian production of *Cats,* and then brought the show to Singapore. Marketing and production cost $11 million, and the eight-week run at Singapore's Kallang Theater was considered a big risk, since local shows played there for no more than ten days. However, southeast Asia seemed like the last big market left unexplored.

By 1996, the company had successfully penetrated this new market, and it had permanent offices in Singapore, Hong Kong, and Sydney, as well as in Frankfurt, New York, and Los Angeles. At one time that year, 31 Lloyd Webber musicals were being staged in 12 countries across the globe. Over 90 percent of the company's earnings came from outside the United Kingdom that year.

Close to half of Really Useful's profits came from its North American operations. The New York and Los Angeles divisions began to take on more responsibilities. In Los Angeles, Really Useful Films worked on Hollywood feature films, including an animated *Cats* and a coproduction with Warner Brothers of *Phantom of the Opera.* The division of The Really Useful Group headquartered in New York, called The Really Useful Company, mainly oversaw North American theater and concert production. This included managing the many hectic details of traveling shows, such as getting waivers for English artists to work in the United States and producing advertising and booking theaters for new productions. The New York company also produced some works by artists other than Lloyd Webber, such as a musical adaptation of the film *A Star Is Born.*

In 1997, The Really Useful Group restarted its London-based record branch. The record division had released chart-topping albums in the 1980s and 90s, including a number one single in 1991, of a song from *Joseph.* Since that time, the division had not progressed, and it had no plans outside producing Lloyd Webber works. The company recruited a top executive from EMI, and announced that it was ready to sign on new talent. Meanwhile, Really Useful Group trimmed back other areas. Some staff was cut from the main London office in January 1997, and the New York office also reduced staff and moved out of prestigious Rockefeller Center into a smaller mid-town office. In August, the president of Really Useful Company resigned. This was at a time when there were no upcoming New York productions of Lloyd Webber works, and action in the parent company seemed centered on upcoming film deals and on a sequel to *Phantom of the Opera.*

Midway through 1998, Lloyd Webber seemed to be repeating his actions of 1990, when his fear of losing artistic control led him to take his company private. In June Lloyd Webber began negotiating with Polygram to buy back the 30 percent share that company held in Really Useful Group. Polygram had apparently worked well with Really Useful. They were both entertainment companies, and their goals were similar, but Polygram was bought out by Seagram's in May 1997, leaving some speculation that the stake in Really Useful might fall into other hands. Nonetheless, Lloyd Webber affirmed in an interview with *Variety* that even if he should somehow lose control of his company, the company would be nothing without him. Lloyd Webber's creative talent was the essential product of The Really Useful Group, and its future success seemed to hinge on his continued unfettered artistic output.

Principal Subsidiaries

Aurum Press Limited; Palace Theater London Limited; The Really Useful Picture Company; The Really Useful Record Company Limited; The Really Useful Theater Company Limited; Interactive Instructional Systems, Inc. (U.S.A.); The Really Useful Company, Inc. (U.S.A.).

Further Reading

Bronson, Fred, "60 Lbs. of Mouth Organs," *Billboard*, October 19, 1996, p. ALW6.
Dawtrey, Adam, "Really Useful Group Tuning in TV Division," *Variety*, September 30, 1991, p. 40.
Evans, Greg, "Occasionally Useful," *Variety*, August 4, 1997, p. 41.
Hudson, Richard L., "Robert Maxwell Buys 14.5% Stake in Really Useful," *Wall Street Journal*, August 7, 1989, p. B4.
Hunter, Nigel, "And Now for Something Really Useful . . ." *Billboard*, October 19, 1996, p. ALW6.
Mantel, Jonathan, *Fanfare: The Unauthorized Biography of Andrew Lloyd Webber*, London: Michael Joseph, 1989.
Murdoch, Blake, "Mack, Lloyd Webber Target Southeast Asia," *Variety*, May 17, 1993, p. 101.
Pitman, Jack, "Lloyd Webber to Get $13-Mil Via Stock Float," *Variety*, January 15, 1986, pp. 1, 230.
"Stock Offering in A Major," *Time*, December 16, 1985, p. 50.
"The Really Useful Group PLC," *Fortune*, September 28, 1987, p. 80.
Watson, Peter, "Lloyd Webber: Composer As Industry," *New York Times*, April 1, 1990, pp. H1, H10.
White, Adam, "Andrew Lloyd Webber's RUG Restarts Its Record Branch," *Billboard*, November 1, 1997, p. 57.
Wolf, Matt, "Lloyd Webber Aims to Nab RUG Stake," *Variety*, June 1, 1998, p. 48.

—A. Woodward

Reebok International Ltd.

100 Technology Center Drive
Stoughton, Massachusetts 02072
U.S.A.
(781) 401-5000
Fax: (781) 297-7402
Web site: http://www.reebok.com

Public Company
Incorporated: 1979 as Reebok U.S.A.
Employees: 6,948
Sales: $3.64 billion (1997)
Stock Exchanges: New York
Ticker Symbol: RBK
SICs: 2329 Men's & Boys' Clothing, Not Elsewhere
Classified; 2339 Women's, Misses' & Juniors'
Outerwear, Not Elsewhere Classified; 2393 Textile
Bags; 3149 Footwear, Except Rubber, Not Elsewhere
Classified

Reebok International Ltd. is one of the world's leading athletic footwear and apparel makers. The company first gained prominence by opening up a new market for athletic shoes—aerobic exercise shoes for women interested in fashion as well as function—and subsequently built upon that success by expanding into other sports and products and by seeking business around the world. Reebok currently sells footwear and apparel in the sports, fitness, and casual sectors, under such brands as Reebok, Weebok, Greg Norman, Rockport, Ralph Lauren, and Polo Sport. The company also operates about 150 factory direct stores, including Reebok, Rockport, and Greg Norman stores.

British Roots

Reebok began its growth into a worldwide enterprise in 1979 when Paul B. Fireman, a marketer of camping and fishing supplies, noticed the products of a small British athletic shoemaker, Reebok International, at a Chicago sporting goods show. Looking for a business opportunity, Fireman acquired the North American license for the company's products, founding Reebok U.S.A.

The British parent company, the oldest manufacturer of athletic shoes in the world, got its start in the 1890s in Bolton, England, when Joseph William Foster began handcrafting shoes with spiked soles for runners. By 1895 he was the head of J.W. Foster and Sons, Inc., providing shoes to world-class athletes, including the 1924 British Olympic running team. In 1958 two of Foster's grandsons founded Reebok, named after an African gazelle, to manufacture running shoes in Bolton, and this company eventually took over the older firm.

After Fireman acquired the right to sell Reebok products made in Britain in the United States, he introduced three top-of-the-line models of running shoes, with price tags of $60, the highest on the market. Sales topped $1.5 million in 1981, but after two years in the extremely competitive U.S. market, Fireman's enterprise was out of money, and he sold 56 percent of his fledgling company to Pentland Industries PLC, another British shoe company. Reebok used the infusion of cash to open a factory in Korea, thereby significantly lowering production costs.

1982 Debut of Aerobic Exercise Shoes

The company's fortunes began to change dramatically, however, in 1982 with the introduction of a shoe designed especially for aerobic exercise. Unlike traditional athletic shoes, which were made of unglamorous materials in drab colors, Reebok aerobics shoes were constructed of soft, pliable leather and came in a variety of bold, fashionable colors. Reebok's Freestyle aerobics shoe was the first athletic shoe designed and marketed specifically for women, and it quickly became hugely popular. By selling its shoes to women, Reebok had opened up a new market for athletic shoe sales. This market would continue to expand as women began to wear their comfortable athletic shoes on the street, for daily life. In addition, the company both contributed to and profited from the boom in popularity of aerobics in the early 1980s, sponsoring clinics to promote the sport and its shoes.

In 1983, the year following the introduction of the shoe for aerobics, Reebok sales shot to $13 million. The company had become the beneficiary of a full-fledged fad. By the following year, sales of Reebok shoes had reached $66 million, and Reebok U.S.A. and its corporate sponsor, Pentland Industries, made arrangements to buy out Reebok International, the company's

British parent, for $700,000. In addition, the company expanded its offerings to include tennis shoes, although shoes for aerobics continued to make up more than half of Reebok's sales in 1984.

By 1985 Reeboks had gained a large following of trendy young consumers, and the shoe's standing as a fashion item was solidified by the appearance of actress Cybill Shepherd wearing a bright orange pair of Reeboks under her formal black gown at the presentation of the Emmy awards. Such celebrity endorsements, as well as an advertising budget of $5 million, helped to push the company's 1985 sales to more than $300 million, with profits of nearly $90 million. Fireman, Reebok's founder, set up an office in California to help the company stay on top of trends and maintain its shoe's popularity.

In July 1985 Reebok International stock was offered publicly for the first time, selling over the counter at $17 a share. By this time international sales of Reebok shoes were contributing 10 percent of revenues. By September the company was unable to meet the continuing high demand for its products and was forced to restrict the number of shoes available to individual stores until it could expand production at its South Korean factories.

Consumers who were able to purchase Reebok shoes were finding that their high price tag did not guarantee high quality, as the shoes' soft leather uppers sometimes fell apart within months. Reebok launched an attempt to improve quality control in 1986, increasing its number of onsite factory inspectors from 7 to 27. Although the company's production reached four million pairs a month by mid-1986, a backlog of $400 million in orders existed, and plans were made for further expansion of production capacity. In keeping with this gain, Reebok's advertising budget grew to $11 million, and the company began advertising on television for the first time.

Diversification in the Mid-1980s

Anticipating an inevitable decline in the popularity of its aerobics shoes—which contributed 42 percent of the company's sales in 1985—as the aerobics trend peaked and slacked off, Reebok moved to further protect its sales position in 1986 by diversifying its product offering. The company began by introducing sports clothing and accessories, limiting sales to $20 million so that growth could be controlled. In addition, the company inaugurated a line of children's athletic shoes, called Weeboks, at the end of 1986. Perhaps the most significant innovation was the introduction of a basketball shoe. In entering this market, Reebok was stepping up its competition with rival athletic shoemakers Nike and Converse, which controlled a large part of the lucrative basketball shoe market. By the end of 1986, revenues from basketball shoes totaled $72 million and made up 8.6 percent of Reebok's total sales.

In June 1986, Reebok was rebuffed in its first attempt to expand through the acquisition of other companies, when Stride Rite Corp., another shoe manufacturer, rejected Reebok's offer. Reebok was successful, however, in its negotiations for the purchase of Rockport Company, a leading maker of walking shoes with sales of around $100 million that had gotten its start in the early 1970s. Rather than integrate the new company's operations closely with its own, Reebok maintained a separation between the two, even to the extent of allowing the companies' products to compete with each other.

Later that year, in an effort to better manage its growth, the company was restructured into three areas: footwear, apparel, and international products. Sales tripled in 1986 to reach $919 million, and the company's stock began trading on the New York Stock Exchange at the end of the year.

By the start of 1987, Reebok's backlog of orders for all its lines of shoes had grown to $445 million, indicating that demand for its products continued to be strong. With Fireman, as chairman, receiving record compensation tied to the company's profits, Reebok's growth continued unabated, and the company embarked on a string of purchases of other shoe companies. In March 1987 Reebok made arrangements to buy Avia Group International, Inc., another maker of aerobic shoes, for $180 million. Following this move, the company sold $6 million worth of stock to raise money to help offset the cost of its acquisition, reducing Pentland Industries' interest in the company from 41 to 37 percent. The company's pace in buying other footwear manufacturers did not slow, as Reebok-owned Rockport acquired a bootmaker, the John A. Frye Company, in May 1987. This 125-year-old company, which also marketed hand-sewn shoes, had yearly sales of about $20 million. One month later, after forming a Canadian subsidiary, Reebok Canada Inc., Reebok used it to purchase the ESE Sports Company, Ltd. Reebok closed out 1987 by finalizing plans to acquire the U.S. division and the U.S. and Canadian rights to the trademark of an Italian apparel company, Ellesse International S.p.A., for $25 million, a more modest version of an earlier plan to acquire the entire company.

In addition to purchases of other shoemakers and apparel companies, Reebok continued to expand its own offerings in 1987, as part of an effort to maintain and protect its market share by providing a wide variety of products. The company introduced shoes designed specifically for walking, in hopes of establishing a presence in a field that Reebok chairman Fireman believed would be the next fad in fitness, and also began offering volleyball shoes and dressier styles for women. This trend continued in the next year with the introduction of shoes for golf.

In an attempt to shed its reputation as a company noted for fashion products, as opposed to serious high-performance athletic shoes, Reebok entered the fray of high-tech design innovations, an area previously dominated by its competitor Nike, with the introduction of energy return system shoes. At the end of 1987, Reebok held a quarter of the market for basketball shoes and dominated the field in aerobics, tennis, and walking shoes.

Late 1980s Doldrums

In 1988 Reebok's long and meteoric rise began to show signs of flagging as the company's historically high profit margins went into a slump. Reebok's strength in the youth market, focused primarily on basketball shoes, was shaken by a massive advertising campaign by competitor Nike, which spent $7 million in advertising in the first quarter of 1988 when Reebok spent only $1.7 million.

In an effort to regain lost ground, Reebok went on the offensive, publicizing its products in several ways. The company gave away shoes to young people known as style makers and renovated urban playgrounds. In addition, Reebok sponsored a series of rock concerts to raise money for human rights groups and inaugurated a Reebok Human Rights Award. Starting in August 1988, Reebok also devoted a portion of its $80 million advertising budget to an innovative and esoteric television and print campaign, built around the theme "Reeboks let U.B.U.," which featured people expressing their personalities in unique ways while wearing Reeboks. The campaign was unsuccessful, however, and by the end of 1988 earnings had fallen by one-fifth on sales of $1.79 billion.

In March 1989 the company unveiled a new $30 million advertising campaign entitled "The Physics Behind the Physique." This push was focused on women, traditionally Reebok's strongest customer base, and connected sweaty physical exertion with sex and narcissism. These relatively rapid shifts in emphasis from performance to fashion and back again began to muddle the consumer's idea of what the company stood for, and Reebok continued to see its portion of the market slip as its sales growth waned. Commentators observed that the company appeared to have lost its focus.

Reebok also underwent a period of turmoil in its administrative and executive structure during this time. In August 1989 the company's head of marketing, Mark Goldston, left after less than a year with the company, and two months later, its president, C. Joseph LaBonte, brought in by Fireman only two years earlier, resigned as well. In addition to these changes at home, Reebok moved to strengthen its international management team at this time.

Reebok sold its Frye boot subsidiary in 1989. The company then made its only purchase outside the footwear and sportswear industries, buying a manufacturer of recreational boats, Boston Whaler, Inc., for $42 million in 1989.

The Pump Introduced in 1989

Although Reebok's market share had fallen behind Nike's, to 22 percent by the end of 1989, the seeds of Reebok's resurgence were sown in mid-November with the introduction of "The Pump," a basketball shoe with an inflatable collar around the ankle to provide extra support. Although the expensive shoes made up only a small portion of Reebok's overall sales, the popularity of the new technology lent a sorely missed air of excitement to the company's brand name.

Reacting to its previous difficulties and continuing challenges in both the fashion and performance shoe markets, Reebok rearranged its corporate structure at the beginning of 1990, splitting its domestic division into two areas, one focusing on performance products and the other on fashion products. A month later, the company further restructured by merging its international and U.S. units into one global business.

Reebok split with its ad agency, Chiat/Day/Mojo, in an effort to regain lost market share. To do so, the company built on its recent success with The Pump technology by expanding The Pump to other lines of footwear, including aerobics, cross-training, running, tennis, walking, and children's shoes. In addition, facing a relatively mature and highly competitive U.S. market for athletic shoes, Reebok looked to foreign markets, which made up a quarter of the company's sales, for further growth.

Results were immediate—overall European sales grew 86 percent in 1991 alone. By 1992 Reebok products were available in approximately 140 countries outside the United States, holding a number one ranking in sales for nine of those countries, including the United Kingdom, Canada, and Australia. U.S. growth stood at less than 10 percent. The company needed to project its image as a leader in innovative athletic apparel through products in other sports categories that would display the latest in Reebok technology.

Reebok premiered football and baseball shoes in 1992, and more than 100 players in the major leagues donned the company's footwear. Marketing momentum increased as Notre Dame's Fighting Irish captured the Cotton Bowl championship on New Year's Day, 1993, sporting the Reebok football shoes supplied them throughout the season. The development of a shoe for basketball players on playground courts—branded the Blacktop—became very successful in 1991. Reebok acquired two other sports apparel manufacturers, consolidating their products with Reebok's own line of clothing and accessories; sold subsidiaries Boston Whaler and Ellesse; and positioned Reebok, Rockport, and Avia to be the principal operating units of the future. In early 1993 Reebok struck an agreement with golf legend Jack Nicklaus to create a unique line of golf shoes. Reebok also generated tremendous sales with its debut of a casual, non-athletic footwear line called Boks during the fall of 1992.

Reebok took steps to enhance its reputation through sponsorship of targeted sporting events and support of human-rights programs. The company became the sponsor of the Russian Olympic Committee through 1996 and the International Hockey Federation Olympic Winter Games for 1994. Reebok's commitment to human rights led to the establishment of the Witness and Volunteer Programs in 1992. In 1993 Reebok increased its budget for a global publicity campaign, estimated at $115 million. During the 1993 SuperBowl, the company aired a 60-second commercial premiering "Planet Reebok," a campaign associating Reebok products with intense competition and high performance. Reebok renewed relations with Chiat/Day/Mojo to promote individual products and began a weekly Top 30 countdown radio program based on the ''Planet Reebok'' theme.

1990s Struggles

The repositioning of Reebok away from fitness/fashion toward an emphasis on high-end performance sneakers, which began in 1992, proved troublesome. The company signed up several high-profile athletes to endorsement contracts. Most notable among these was emerging basketball superstar Shaquille O'Neal, but the subsequently launched ''Shaq Attaq'' sneaker—a white sneaker when black shoes were the hot commodity at a hefty $130 price tag—failed miserably. Instead of catching up to Nike, Reebok was now falling further behind, its market share declining to 20 percent by 1995. That year institutional shareholders, irked by several years of flat profits, pressured Reebok to bring in an outsider to run the company but Fireman retained his position as chairman, CEO, and president.

The company found some success with the 1996-debuted Shaqnosis basketball shoe, but generally flat sales of athletic shoes in the mid-1990s exacerbated Reebok's problems. The push into performance sneakers also translated into large increases in expenses, resulting in decreasing net income, from $254.5 million in 1994 to $164.8 million in 1995 to $139 million in 1996. In June 1996 Reebok sold Avia to American Sporting Goods. The company in October 1996 pulled the plug on the Boks brand, after earlier in the year gaining the rights to design, develop, manufacture, and distribute men's, women's, and children's footwear under the Ralph Lauren label.

In February 1997 Reebok suffered much embarrassment when it was forced to apologize for naming a women's running shoe the ''Incubus.'' Unbeknownst to the shoe's designers, an incubus is an evil spirit that in medieval times was believed to have sex with sleeping women. The outlook for the company brightened some with the development of successful products utilizing new shoe technology. In April 1997 the DMX series made their debut following three years in development. The DMX shoe—available in running, walking, and basketball models—featured air that moved underfoot to provide better cushioning, and was an attempt by Reebok to take on Nike's blockbuster ''Air'' line. Also introduced in 1997 were running, walking, basketball, and women's fitness shoes featuring 3D Ultralite technology, Reebok's entry into the lightweight performance footwear sector.

Despite the apparently resurgent new-product development activity at Reebok, a company turnaround was far from complete. During the early months of 1998 the company had to contend with a marketplace flooded with athletic footwear, leading to inventory surpluses and price cuts. In response, Reebok took a restructuring charge of $23.7 million in the first quarter of 1998 for costs related to eliminating management layers, combining business units, and cutting its workforce by 500, or 10 percent. At the same time the company was in the process of severely trimming its roster of costly celebrity-athlete endorsements, aiming to reduce the number to about 20. In June 1998 Reebok terminated its contract with O'Neal, who had already been shopping around for another sponsor, one that would pay him more than the $3 million he had been receiving each year from Reebok. By this time, Allen Iverson had replaced O'Neal as Reebok's top

basketball endorser, through a deal estimated at $5 million per year. August 1998 brought another management change as Carl Yankowski was brought in as president and chief executive of the Reebok brand. The fourth person to hold that position in the last decade, Yankowski had previously spent time as an executive at PepsiCo Inc., Polaroid Corp., and Sony Electronics Inc. It remained to be seen whether Yankowski would be able to reverse the fortunes of the struggling shoe manufacturer.

Principal Subsidiaries

Ralph Lauren Footwear Co., Inc.; RBK Thailand, Inc.; Reebok Aviation, Inc.; Reebok CHC, Inc.; Reebok Eastern Territories, Inc.; Reebok Foundation, Inc.; Reebok International Securities Corp.; Reebok Securities Holdings Corp.; The Reebok Worldwide Trading Company, Ltd.; The Rockport Company, Inc.; Avintco, Inc.; RFC, Inc.; Reebok Austria GmbH; Rockport Gmbh (Austria); Reebok Belgium SA; Reebok Do Brasil Servicos a Participacoes Ltda (Brazil); Rockport do Brasil - Comercio, Servicos e Participacoes Ltda. (Brazil); R.C. Investments Ltd. (Canada); Reebok Canada Inc.; Reebok France S.A.; Rockport France S.a.r.L.; American Sports and Leisure Vertriebs GMBH (Germany); Reebok Deutschland GmbH (Germany); Reebok (China) Services Limited (Hong Kong); Reebok Far East Ltd. (Hong Kong); Reebok Trading (FAR EAST) Limited (Hong Kong); Reebok India Company; Reebok Technical Services Private Limited (India); Reebok Ireland Limited; Reebok Italia S.r.l. (Italy); Rockport International Trading Co. Italy S.r.l.; Reebok Japan Inc.; Rockport Japan Inc.; Reebok Korea Limited; Reebok Korea Technical Services Company, Ltd.; Reebok (Mauritius) Company Limited; Rockport Mexico S.A. DE C.V.; Reebok Distribution B.V. (Netherlands); Reebok (Europe) B.V. (Netherlands); Reebok International Finance B.V. (Netherlands); Reebok Nederland B.V. (Netherlands); Rockport (Europe) B.V. (Netherlands); Rockport (Nederland) B.V. (Netherlands); Reebok (Philippines) Services Co., Inc.; Reebok Poland SA; Reebok Portugal Artigos Desportives Lda; Reebok Russia (Retail), Inc.; Reebok Leisure SA (Spain); Reebok (South Africa) (Proprietary) Limited; Reebok (Switzerland) Ltd.; Reebok (Taiwan) Services Company; Subsidiary enterprise Reebok Ukraine; J.W. Foster & Sons (Athletic Shoes) Limited (U.K.); RBK Holdings plc (U.K.); Reebok Eastern Trading Limited (U.K.); Reebok International Limited (U.K.); Reebok Sports Limited (U.K.); Reebok UK Limited; The Rockport Company Limited (U.K.); Rockport International Limited (U.K.).

Principal Operating Units

The Reebok Division; The Rockport Company; Greg Norman Division.

Further Reading

Grimm, Matthew, ''Deft Reebok Strides into Women's Walking,'' *Brandweek*, August 24, 1992.

——, ''Reebok's Big Idea,'' *Brandweek*, January 25, 1993.

Jensen, Jeff, ''Better Days Ahead on Planet Reebok,'' *Advertising Age*, June 26, 1995, p. 4.

Labich, Kenneth, ''Nike Vs. Reebok: A Battle for Hearts, Minds and Feet,'' *Fortune*, September 18, 1995, p. 90.

La Monica, Paul R., ''Reebok International: Flat of Foot,'' *Financial World*, August 3, 1993, p. 18.

Pereira, Joseph, "Can Air Pockets Help Reebok Catch Nike in High-Performance Sneaker Marathon?," *Wall Street Journal,* March 27, 1997, pp. B1, B19.

——, "Reebok Trails Nike in Fight For Teens' Hearts and Feet," *Wall Street Journal,* September 23, 1988.

Pulliam, Susan, and Joseph Pereira, "Reebok CEO Fireman Faces Criticism by Institutional Holders," *Wall Street Journal,* September 14, 1995, pp. C1, C2.

Reidy, Chris, "Reebok Delivers a Boot," *Boston Globe,* July 1, 1998, p. A1.

Sellers, Patricia, "Reebok Gets a Lift," *Fortune,* August 18, 1997, p. 180.

Sloan, Pat, "Reebok Takes Off Around the Planet," *Advertising Age,* January 25, 1993.

Smith, Geoffrey, "Reebok Is Tripping Over Its Own Laces," *Business Week,* February 26, 1996, pp. 62, 64, 66.

Smith, Geoffrey, and Mark Maremont, "Can Reebok Regain Its Balance?," *Business Week,* December 20, 1993, pp. 108–9.

"The Sneaker Wars," *Forbes,* March 25, 1993.

Tedeschi, Mark, "Paul Fireman" (interview), *Sporting Goods Business,* January 6, 1997, pp. 62–63.

Therrien, Lois, "Reeboks: How Far Can a Fad Run?," *Business Week,* February 24, 1986.

Vickers, Marcia, "After Tripping on Its Laces, Reebok Is Focused Again," *New York Times,* March 2, 1997, p. F3.

Watkins, Linda M., "Reebok: Keeping a Name Hot Requires More Than Aerobics," *Wall Street Journal,* August 21, 1986.

"Where Nike and Reebok Have Plenty of Running Room," *Business Week,* March 11, 1991.

Wulf, Steve, "A Costly Blunder," *Sports Illustrated,* July 6, 1992.

—Elizabeth Rourke and Edna M. Hedblad
—updated by David E. Salamie

Renault S.A.

34, quai du Point du Jour
92109 Boulogne-Billancourt
Cedex
France
(33) 1 41 04 50 50
Fax: (33) 1 41 04 67 90
Web site: http://www.renault.com

Public Company
Incorporated: 1945 as Régie Nationale des Usines
    Renault
Employees: 147,185
Sales: FFr 207.91 billion (US$38 billion) (1997)
Stock Exchanges: Paris
SICs: 3711 Motor Vehicles & Car Bodies; 3714 Motor
    Vehicle Parts & Accessories; 3713 Truck & Bus
    Bodies; 3799 Transportation Equipment, Not
    Elsewhere Classified; 6141 Personal Credit
    Institutions

One of the world's pioneering auto makers, Renault S.A. is also one of Europe's largest. Renault's annual sales of more than FFr 207 billion (approximately US$38 billion) and its payroll of more than 147,000 employees in 1997 also make it one of France's flagship corporations. Renault manufactures automobiles, vans, and trucks, farm, industrial, and forestry machinery, machine tools, engines, and other large-scale production components for the automobile and other industries, as well as heavy trucks through the company's Mack Truck (the number three heavy truck maker in the United States) and Renault V.I. subsidiaries. In addition to the company's Automobile and Industrial Vehicle divisions, Renault's Finance division is one of France's largest credit providers, principally toward the purchase of the company's automobiles.

After a rocky period in the mid-1990s, marked by the former government-run company's privatization and capped by stagnating sales and the failed attempt to fuse the company with Sweden's Volvo, Renault has recaptured both its market position and its spirit. Upon setting a new company production record of 2.2 million vehicles in 1998, Renault announced intentions to double that number by the year 2010, while increasing the share of its foreign sales to 50 percent of total sales—compared with just 20 percent in 1997. Under CEO and Chairman Louis Schweitzer, Renault has taken strong steps to meet its goal, including the opening of a FFr 4 billion production facility in Brazil in December 1998.

Automobile Pioneer

The closest parallel in the French automobile industry to Henry Ford was Louis Renault. His youthful interest in mechanical contrivances, especially steam engines and electrical devices, was accepted by his well-to-do family and he was allowed to have his own workshop on the family's property.

Soon after he finished his military service and his father had passed away, Louis convinced his older brothers Fernand and Marcel each to invest FFr 30,000 to build an automobile firm, which would be called Renault Freres. In 1899 Renault Freres received its first down payments for motor cars at FFr 1,000 per vehicle. Primarily an assembly operation in the early years, Renault Freres expanded operations as fast as it could acquire components and erect buildings. Engines, tires, radiators, gears, steel, and electrical equipment all came from other companies. Already by 1899, the industry had generated a considerable range of specialist component firms. Marcel Renault soon joined the active management of the company to lessen some of Louis's workload, since he preferred to work in the shop rather than attend to commercial details. By 1901 the company had become the eighth largest firm in the automobile industry, based on the manufacture of a small, inexpensive, and reliable car. Its success should not be measured only by its sales and profits, however, but by its imitators; Louis Renault's transmission system was eagerly copied by other small car manufacturers.

Perhaps the most important ingredient in the firm's early success was the publicity Renault's cars received as a consequence of their racing prowess. Both Marcel and Louis Renault were expert racing drivers and they were victorious in numerous

---

Company Perspectives:

Renault's strategy is asserted and propagated throughout the company on the basis of the following seven strategic goals: To be the best on the market in terms of quality of products and services; To develop a coherent and open group; To present a young, strong and innovative product range; To expand internationally; To reduce overall costs for an uncertain future; To work better as a team; To be profitable so as to guarantee independence and financial development; These goals, which are regularly reviewed and enlarged, have enabled the Group to achieve its turn-around, and constitute the foundation of Renault's strategy.

---

international events. Unfortunately in 1903, while competing in the Paris-Madrid race, Marcel Renault was killed. Louis immediately withdrew his cars from the racing circuit and his company did not compete again for several years.

After 1905 Renault's taxicab became his largest selling product. Work began on this line late in that year when the company won an order for 250 chassis. The large orders for cabs soon made Renault the most important French automobile producer.

The firm did considerable export business during this period. In 1912, for example, nearly 100 Renault cabs were in service in Mexico City, and Renaults outnumbered all of the other types of taxicabs in Melbourne. By 1914 the company had 31 dealers in foreign countries, from Yalta to Shanghai. Louis Renault himself did not take as much interest in these marketing matters as he did in the technical aspects of his business. He considered himself more of an inventor than anything else and took out in his own name about 700 patents for devices that he had made personally or that had been developed in his factory.

Like several other automobile firms, Renault participated in the development of aviation in France. In 1907 the company began to experiment with aircraft engines, attempting to extract the most power possible from lightweight, air-cooled motors. While somewhat successful technically, this activity brought no profits at the time. Nevertheless, the discoveries and the experience that resulted found their justification in the war that soon followed. During World War I the company became an important manufacturer of all sorts of military equipment, including aviation engines and the light tanks that proved so effective in 1918.

Postwar Technocracy

After the war the Renault factory expanded. Nonetheless, though the firm remained among the top producers in France during the interwar period, Louis Renault was slow to adopt new technical and organizational ideas. This reluctance significantly hindered the company's growth. Then, when Paris was liberated near the end of World War II, Louis Renault was jailed on a charge of Nazi collaboration. He died in prison before his case could be examined and the de Gaulle provisional govern-

ment nationalized his company. The government installed some inspired technocrats to operate the company along commercial lines, and they made it into a showpiece of French industry. The firm built up its own production of machine tools and its factory was the first in Europe to use automation. In 1948 the company began to manufacture a miniature car called the Quatre Chevaux (4 CV or hp), which had been planned secretly during the war by Renault technicians.

The Quatre Chevaux proved to be a symbol of the social philosophy that has guided Renault ever since, first under Pierre Lefaucheux and then under his successor Pierre Dreyfus. An idealistic kind of technocrat, Dreyfus regarded the car as a social instrument that every family had a right to possess. Therefore, the firm concentrated on a large production of relatively small and inexpensive cars, the models gradually growing in size as French incomes and living standards rose. The other feature of this social philosophy was the idea that a firm owes its workers not only a wage, but also as full and happy a life as possible. With state support Renault led the field in welfare and labor relations.

It is possible to view the introduction of the Quatre Chevaux either as an example of effective business management or as the use of a state firm to provide a lower-cost product. During the 1950s and 1960s the company maintained its record for effective product innovation. The Dauphine was manufactured to fit into the market opening between the inexpensive economy models and the higher-priced models. The new model soon became quite popular and outsold all others for the next five years. A second distinctive aspect of Renault's success has been its emphasis on exports. It was one of the first companies in the automobile industry to make a serious effort to develop a sales organization in the United States.

Because of the interest in Renault cars within the United States, the company was aiming initially to penetrate the market by supplying 1,000 cars per month. But the United States ordered no fewer than 3,000 cars in only one month. Consequently, Renault increased their daily production rate from 300 to approximately 500 units; company production facilities were near capacity for months in advance. Continued expansion into the world automobile markets remained one of the company's main concerns for years, and plans were made, therefore, for the construction of plants abroad. Sales agreements using existing local networks were made in Brazil, Argentina, Algeria, and India.

By the end of 1959 Renault was estimated to be the sixth largest automobile manufacturer in the world. At the beginning of 1960, when the U.S. automobile market began to shrink, sales of the Dauphine dropped by 33 percent in comparison with the previous year. It was a period of stagnation on the U.S. domestic market and, as a result, Renault was faced with the problem of adjusting to the specific requirements of the American motorist.

In France, meanwhile, preparations were underway for new car models, which would be known as the R-4 and the R-8. These were vehicles that had a third side window on a four-door body. Subsequently, an error was made on a project that was to have been a large six-cylinder vehicle. Once the accounts had been completed it was discovered that the price of the car ought to have been 25 percent higher than originally planned. The swift and decisive intervention of Renault's chairman, Pierre Dreyfus, established the parameters of the new car, which was to have four cylinders, a functional styling, and a competitive price. The result was the R-16, which remained in production until the mid-1970s and had features that are still retained on more recent models. As a parallel development to car production, Renault also had begun to manufacture the Estafette, a commercial vehicle for door-to-door deliveries, which was replaced by another model in the beginning of the 1980s.

During the 1970s Renault went through a period of significant expansion. The success of the R-5, a particularly well-designed and highly reliable vehicle, allowed Renault to stay at the top of the European league of manufacturers. At the same time, a widely based program initiated in 1977 enabled the firm to purchase 46.4 percent of the shares in American Motors in 1980. The U.S. company then began production of the Alliance and the Encore, corresponding to European versions of the Renault.

The relationship began in 1979 when the two corporations signed an agreement. American Motors became the exclusive North American importer and distributor of Renault cars, and the French corporation would market American Motors products in France and several other countries. This was followed by the direct purchase of approximately $500 million in American Motors securities. American Motors chairman Gerald Meyers resigned in 1982 and was replaced by Paul Tippett, Jr., who then named Renault's Jose Dedeurwaerder as president and chief operating officer. Other Renault personnel took their places in the corporation and on the board of directors as the first modern trans-Atlantic company was established.

Regrouping in the 1980s and 1990s

By the mid-1980s, however, Renault's small deficit had turned into a US$1.5 billion loss. Georges Besse arrived in 1985 with a mandate to prevent any further losses. Besse, a pragmatic engineer who had rescued the state-owned Pechiney Metals Group, was unable to go much beyond symbolic measures in helping the company. The Socialist government in France had backed away from tough industrial decisions that it feared would hurt the party in national elections. In addition, Besse's timing was unfortunate since powerful French communists had been arguing that Renault should worry more about upgrading French operations and protecting French jobs than spending money abroad on American Motors. The communists claimed that there was an imbalance between investments needed at home and expansion abroad. AMC's losses in 1986 made those arguments more compelling in the view of many Frenchmen. Nonetheless, Besse was able to cut some 20,000 jobs from the payroll, while instilling a new profit-driven culture in the government-owned company.

In November 1986 Besse was assassinated by the French terrorist organization "Direct Action." This unfortunate event, however, was not the only one that had an adverse effect on Renault. The company also was suffering from a series of poor marketing judgments that had reduced its share of the domestic auto market. Once the largest car manufacturer in Europe, Renault had slipped to sixth place. Besse's successor, Raymond Levy, pushed through Besse's restructuring of the company,

eliminating an additional 30,000 jobs and leading the company toward its privatization in the 1990s.

In March 1987 Renault announced that it would withdraw from the U.S. market by selling its share in American Motors to the Chrysler Corporation. Under this agreement, which American Motors voted to accept, Renault received upwards of US$200 million for its AMC shares and bonds over a period of five years. The company also received royalties from Chrysler's marketing of AMC's newly launched Premier. In exchange, Renault agreed to export between US$2 billion and US$3 billion worth of automatic components to Chrysler.

In 1990, the former Régie Nationale des Usines Renault converted its status to that of Renault S.A., a first step toward privatization. At the same time, the company entered into agreement with Volvo to merge the two companies' operations—including an exchange of shares that would give the Swedish automotive maker as much as 20 percent of Renault. This ambitious cross-ownership plan fell through spectacularly in 1993 when Volvo's shareholders rejected the plan.

The Volvo failure would prove only the tip of what would become a somber period. Hit by an extended European recession, facing dwindling market share and increasing global competition, Renault would slip into losses by 1996. Yet, under a new CEO and chairman, Renault already had begun to strike back against misfortune. In the early 1990s, despite the poor economic climate, Renault began expanding its international presence, building new operations and cooperation agreements in such countries as Turkey, China, and the Czech Republic, as well as strengthening the company's Latin American operations and entering the Russian market. Whereas Renault had done little to enter the growing Asian countries, the company now began to move toward building a presence in these developing markets.

More importantly, Renault—driven more and more by the need to provide profits, as the French government's position was reduced from 80 percent to just 45 percent by 1995—went back to the drawing board for its new car designs. Indeed, during the 1990s the company would appear to recapture the spirit of innovation that had produced the indomitable R-4 and R-5 with the introduction of the Clio in 1992, which would take the lead as France's bestselling car. In 1993 the company debuted the Twingo, another success. In the larger-sized realm, Renault continued to dazzle auto buyers with the popular Megane (the number two selling car in France), the minivan Espace, and 1997's hit Kangoo.

The company's net loss of FFr 5 billion, chiefly due to rising production costs, in 1996 proved only temporary. A streamlining of the organization and the reduction of production costs by nearly FFr 4,000 per automobile would return the company to profitability in 1997. In 1998 the company could forecast an all-time production record of 2.2 million vehicles. According to CEO Schweitzer, however, by the year 2010 this record would seem ancient history. Continued cost-cutting measures were expected to produce some FFr 20 billion in savings, while the company's strategy called for production to reach more than four million vehicles per year, with foreign sales to account for some 50 percent of the company's total, compared with just 20 percent in the late 1990s. As a primary step toward this goal,

Renault prepared to open a new FFr 4 billion production facility in Brazil in December 1998.

Principal Subsidiaries

Renault Vehicles Industriels; Renault Industries Equipements Et Techniques (99.9%); Renault Agriculture; Europcar; Société Nouvelle De Roulements (86%); Chausson (35%); Diffusion Industrielle Et Automobile Par Le Crédit-Diac; Société De Financement Pour L'Extension de L'Industrie-Sofexi; Compagnie Financière Renault; Renault Crédit International; Mack Truck Inc.

Further Reading

Debontride, Xavier, ''Brésil, Turquie, Russe: Renault rêve son avenir à long terme,'' *Les Echoes,* September 30, 1998, p. 54.

Laux, James M., *In First Gear: The French Automobile Industry to 1914,* Liverpool: Liverpool University Press, 1976.

McLintock, J. Dewar, *Renault: The Cars and the Charisma,* Cambridge: Stevens, 1983.

Routier, Airy, ''Le diététicien de Renault,'' *Challenges,* April 1998, p. 78.

—updated by M. L. Cohen

Republic Engineered Steels, Inc.

410 Oberlin Road S.W.
P.O. Box 579
Massillon, Ohio 44648-0579
U.S.A.
(330) 837-6000
Fax: (330) 837-6083
Web site: http://www.repsteel.com

Private Company
Incorporated: 1989
Employees: 3,800
Sales: $802 million (1998 est.)
SICs: 3325 Steel Foundries, Not Elsewhere Classified;
    3312 Blast Furnaces & Steel

Republic Engineered Steels, Inc. is the country's largest integrated producer of carbon and alloy bar, stainless, tool, and remelted specialty steels. As of 1998, the company operated 10 plants in Ohio, Pennsylvania, Maryland, Indiana, Illinois, and Connecticut. Republic primarily served the automotive, forging, industrial, and off-highway machinery, hydraulic equipment, aerospace, bearing, hand tool, and machine shop markets.

Company Origins

Republic traces its history to the establishment of the Berger Manufacturing Company in Canton, Ohio, in 1886. Berger was subsumed by United Alloy Steel Company, which was formed in 1916. Over the next 40 years, several companies were founded that would later merge to form Republic Steel. Union Drawn Steel was established in Beaver Falls, Pennsylvania, in 1889 and built a new plant in Gary, Indiana, in 1917. Another precursor to Republic, the Central Steel Corporation, was founded in Massillon, Ohio, in the early 1900s and built the world's first electrified steel plant. Central Steel grew rapidly, particularly during World War I when demand for steel skyrocketed. In 1926 Central Steel merged with Union Drawn and United Alloy to form the Central Alloy Steel Corporation.

In 1930 Cyrus Eaton, a Cleveland industrialist, formed Republic Steel Corporation from a merger between Central Alloy Steel Corporation and the Interstate Iron and Steel Company, a Chicago-based company that had been founded in 1905. With the merger, Republic Steel became the third largest steel producer in the country, competing with United States Steel Corporation and the Bethlehem Steel Corporation. Republic Steel's research staff and skilled workforce, as well as its concentration of electric furnaces suitable for making a new product—stainless steel—provided certain commercial advantages over its larger rivals.

Republic Steel's fortunes were affected by the conditions that influenced the development of all domestic steel producers in the years that followed: the economic constraints of the Great Depression and the growing movement to organize steelworker labor. The steel industry suffered intensely in the Great Depression, with production dropping to pre-1900 levels. Rail production, for example, fell by 1933 to its lowest level since 1865. Full-time employment industrywide fell from 158,000 to 18,000 in 1932 and wages bottomed out at 33 cents an hour for steelworkers. Conditions were ripe for labor organization.

Several steelworker strikes were stymied between 1932 and 1935 for various reasons, but the passage of the National Labor Relations Act in 1935 gave labor organizers renewed confidence. In June 1936 the Steel Workers Organizing Committee (SWOC) was formed and, with $500,000 from the supporting miners union, began recruiting members among the workers at the largest steel mills in the United States, including Republic Steel. Industrialists opposed union formation, and threats and violence against union sympathizers were not uncommon. By 1937, however, the SWOC had organized the nation's largest steel company, United States Steel Corporation, and was representing workers at the bargaining table with U.S. Steel management. Republic Steel and the management at several other steel companies did not recognize the SWOC, who had not achieved as great a membership among their workers as at U.S. Steel. In May and June 1937, the SWOC called for a strike at these "Little Steel" companies. On Memorial Day, 1937, steelworkers demonstrating at Republic Steel's mill in south Chicago were confronted by police. In what was later called the Memo-

---

Company Perspectives:

It is the mission of Republic Engineered Steels, Inc. to be customer focused and the supplier of choice. To this end we are committed to continuously improving our processes and working together to provide long-term growth, security, and profitability for our employees and shareholders.

---

rial Day Massacre, ten workers died and approximately 100 were injured, mostly from bullet wounds in the back. The SWOC continued to gain momentum, however. By the time the SWOC had ratified its constitution and changed its name to the United Steel Workers Union in 1942, it had established a collective bargaining agreement with Republic Steel.

World War II brought sudden prosperity to Republic Steel. To meet demands for steel in Europe and in anticipation of the United States entering the war, production had risen dramatically in 1940 and 1941. With steel needed for everything from bullets to tanks to aircraft carriers, Republic's steel works were soon running nonstop, and the company employed a record number of people.

Republic Steel saw a slight drop in production immediately after the war ended, but pent-up demand for consumer goods made with steel, such as cars and appliances, soon had the steel works booming. Steelworks in Japan, Germany, and England had mostly been destroyed during the war, which left the United States as the world's only significant producer of steel. Republic Steel faced no competition from imports and was able to increase exports to countries struggling with postwar reconstruction. The 1950s and 1960s were years of unparalleled prosperity for Republic Steel.

In 1972 and 1973 Republic Steel, along with the nation's other two steel giants, Bethlehem Steel and U.S. Steel, forged an agreement with the United Steel Workers Union that would have far-reaching effects for the steel industry. The "experimental negotiating agreement" prohibited strikes and lockouts and guaranteed steelworkers a minimum three percent raise plus cost-of-living increases every year. Although management was pleased with having eliminated the threat of strikes, it did not anticipate the rampant inflation of the 1970s and the subsequent skyrocketing of employee wages.

Republic Steel, like the rest of the industry, began to show the first signs of trouble in the 1970s. The unprecedented prosperity of the previous decades had encouraged complacency in the steel industry. Payrolls were bloated, graft was rampant, little investment had been made in technological advances. When finally faced with competition from imported steel and steel products in the 1970s, the steel industry was in no condition to respond decisively. Republic was forced to begin laying off employees and closing steelmaking facilities.

In an effort to compete more effectively with the threats that imported steel products were presenting, Republic Steel was acquired by the LTV Corporation in 1984 and merged with

Jones & Laughlin to form LTV Steel Co. However, the merger did not resolve the companies' problems, and LTV declared bankruptcy in July 1986. Still in bankruptcy in October 1988, LTV management decided to concentrate on the flat rolled steel business. The other major area of business, the bar division, was offered for sale.

Employee Buyout in 1989

Management and employees of the bar division, concerned that a highly leveraged buyer would be more likely to liquidate the division's assets than invest the capital needed to operate it as a going concern, tendered a formal bid to buy the bar division through an Employee Stock Ownership Plan (ESOP). LTV accepted the bid in May 1989, and the purchase was formally signed effective November 28, 1989. Russell W. Maier, who had been president of the bar division, became president and chief executive officer of the new Republic Engineered Steels, Inc.

Maier had been with Republic Steel since before the merger that formed LTV Steel. Starting in 1960 as an industrial engineer, Maier was promoted to a series of positions with increasing responsibility. In 1983, he was named chief operating officer; after the merger, he served as executive vice-president of LTV until becoming president and general manager of the bar division in 1985. According to the *New York Times,* Maier initially fought the idea of employee ownership, but came to believe that a combination of employee ownership and full employee participation in decision-making resulted in employee suggestions that led to significant cost savings.

The original initiative for the buyout was said to have come from the steelworkers union, the United Steelworkers of America (USWA). The complex ESOP was designed by New York investment firm Lazard Freres, and the purchase price was set at $280 million. The bar division's 5,000 employees, union and management, contributed an average of $4,000 each or a total of $20 million. Another $190 million was borrowed from the Bank of Boston and Security Pacific Bank, and the remaining $70 million was borrowed from LTV. The transaction left the new Republic in a highly leveraged position, but committed to its own operating future. Federal tax policies advantageous to the ESOP-owned Republic permitted greater use of cash generated from operations. Significant cash obligations for the young company included its debt service, contributions to its ESOP, and a postretirement health benefit fund. In the years that followed, Republic made a major reduction in its debt.

In conjunction with the purchase, a new labor agreement was reached between the USWA and Republic management. Appendix H-1 to the agreement acknowledged the need for the involvement of all employees in the success of the business. A committee, consisting of union representatives, salaried employees, and management, and known as the H-1 committee, determined to develop a new corporate culture, conducive to respect and trust between the groups, and oriented toward the profitability of Republic.

The H-1 committee established a companywide education program to enable the new employee-owners to understand the

ESOP structure, to make sense of the financial statements, and to grasp the basic elements and goals of Republic's business plan. Republic provided most of the multimillion-dollar cost of the program, which involved an hour of business instruction each month for each employee-owner for 30 months.

Reorganization and Cost-Cutting in the Early 1990s

Republic's sales for its first stub year, through June 1990, were approximately $379 million. The next six months, from July 1990 through December 1990, saw a sharp drop to $310 million. Republic blamed the general economic environment and responded by reorganizing into four separate business centers, each with profit accountability: Steel Division, Rolling Division, Cold Finished Division, and Specialty Steel Group.

In addition, in June 1991, Republic announced a target of $80 million in cost reductions. Employee suggestions on operations were actively sought as alternatives to job cuts. By February 1992, more than 1,000 suggestions had been submitted, valued by Republic at $60 million in savings. One suggestion alone that made dramatic savings, approximately $3.6 million, was a new plan for the separation of different types of scrap steel for more efficient and reliable use in recycling.

By including "Engineered" in its new corporate name, Republic signified its intent to meet demanding specifications from its customers, more than 50 percent of whom were in the automotive industry. The products of Republic's Rolling Division and Cold Finished Division could be produced in a wide variety of sizes, grades, shapes, and finishes. The Specialty Steel group produced precision bar steel that met critical requirements for aerospace as well as energy and defense applications.

Republic's principal competitors in these markets included U.S. Steel/Kobe joint venture, the Timken Co., MacSteel Co., Bethlehem Steel's bar division, Inland Steel's bar division, and North Star. Low cost minimills like Koppel Steel and Nucor were an increasing threat to Republic as well.

As a privately held company, Republic was not required to release its results of operations to the public. It did, however, disclose financial information on a quarterly basis—including operating income, which was positive for all but one quarter in the first year after its formation. In any event, within its first 13 months, Republic was able to build a cash reserve of approximately $90 million, out of which it paid down $37 million of its debt.

Republic made only one stock dividend payment, shortly after the ESOP was formed. Since the stock was not publicly traded, employee-owners could only sell their stock back to the company, and then only upon retirement. A minimal gain of a few hundred dollars might be recognized by the individual. But to most of the employee-owners in the early days, job security was more critical than capital gains. Although Republic was not the first steel company in the United States to respond to financial troubles with employee ownership, its experiment was conducted on a much broader scale than that of Weirton Steel, for instance, which preceded it. As CEO Maier looked to the future in the early 1990s, he was "cautiously optimistic."

Maier recognized that the future of Republic was tightly bound with that of the automotive industry that it served and the U.S. economy as a whole.

Renewed Expansion in the Mid- to Late 1990s

Although the steel industry remained slow in the early 1990s in the United States, Republic managed to generate a healthy cash flow. Because of the complex federal tax structure for companies with ESOPs, Republic reported losses of $42 million over its first three years. To allocate common stock placed in ESOP trust at the company's formation, Republic was required to take quarterly noncash charges of $8 million. Although this requirement led to a red bottom line, it left Republic with cash to make capital improvements and to reduce its debt. Within a few years, the company had paid off all of the $260 million of short-term debt used to finance the leveraged buyout, partly through a long-term bond issue in 1993. In addition, the company invested in much-needed modernization of its plants.

The ample cash flow also helped Republic expand through acquisitions. In 1993, the company purchased Western Steel Group, a maker of cold finished bar. The following year, Republic expanded its stainless tool steel and forged products business by acquiring the principal assets of Baltimore Specialty Steels Corporation. The deal with parent company Armco, Inc. was made for an undisclosed sum. Republic transformed operations at the plants acquired from both of the troubled acquisitions. By creating flexible, self-directed teams, Republic was able to eliminate 40 percent of the workforce while maintaining the same level of production.

In 1995 Republic floated an initial public offering of eight million shares of common stock. With the $64 million it gained from the IPO, Republic repurchased the employees' preferred stock, thus freeing itself from the guaranteed dividends of 16.5 percent instituted with the creation of the ESOP. Although the initial public offering introduced outside influence, the employees still owned 58 percent of the common stock, thus retaining control of the company.

Also in 1995 Republic began construction of a CAST-ROLL facility in Canton, Ohio. The only plant of its kind in North America, the facility cost approximately $165 million. The state-of-the-art plant reduced the time needed to create billets of different sizes and metallurgical grades. By closely linking such processes as ladle refining and rolling operations, the new facility could ready molten steel for shipping in one sixth the time needed using traditional methods.

In 1997 the ESOP stock was fully allocated and Republic no longer had to take quarterly charges toward it, leaving the company with a much-improved bottom line. Republic split its businesses into three independent divisions: Hot Rolled Bar Division, Cold Finished Bar Division, and Stainless and Specialty Steels Division. The same year, Republic signed a four-year technology exchange agreement with the Japanese company Sanyo Special Steel. Sanyo agreed to provide technical assistance to Republic in its steel melting practices and in fine-tuning the operation of its CAST-ROLL facility.

In 1998 Republic agreed to be acquired by an investor group led by the Blackstone Group and Veritas Capital Partners. Blackstone and Veritas planned to merge Republic with Bar Technologies, Inc., which the investors also owned. BarTech produced hot rolled engineered and cold finished steel bar products, primarily for the automotive machinery and tool industries. The new company, which was due to be finalized by the end of 1998, would be named Republic Technologies International.

Principal Subsidiaries

Nimishillan and Tuscarawas Railway Company; Oberlin Insurance Company.

Principal Divisions

Hot Rolled Bar Division; Cold Finished Bar Division; Stainless and Specialty Steels Division.

Further Reading

Drown, Stuart, "Republic Attempts Recasting," *Beacon Journal,* August 26, 1991.

Kilborn, Peter T., "New Paths in Business When Workers Own," *New York Times,* November 22, 1991.

"Republic Engineered Steel Company Earnings," *New York Times,* August 25, 1998, p. C8.

Rosen, Robert, *Leading People: Transforming Business from the Inside Out,* New York: Viking Penguin, 1996.

Serrin, William, *Homestead: The Glory and Tragedy of an American Steel Town,* New York: Random House, 1992.

Sheridan, John H., "Counting on Cash," *Industry Week,* September 2, 1996, pp. 10–15.

—Marcia McDermott
—updated by Susan Windisch Brown

Republic Industries, Inc.

110 S.E. Sixth Street
Fort Lauderdale, Florida 33301
U.S.A.
(954) 769-7200
Fax: (954) 769-6408
Web site: http://www.republicindustries.com

Public Company
Incorporated: 1981
Employees: 56,000
Sales: $10.3 billion (1997)
Stock Exchanges: New York
Ticker Symbol: RII
SICs: 7514 Passenger Car Rentals; 5511 Auto New &
    Used; 5531 Auto Parts Dealer—Retail

Until H. Wayne Huizenga became chairman of the board of Republic Industries, Inc. in the summer of 1995, the Fort Lauderdale-based car rental and dealership company was little known. Republic originated in the waste disposal business, then moved quickly into used cars and trucks. Huizenga, the driving force behind Waste Management (now WMX Technologies Inc.) and Blockbuster Entertainment Corporation, was determined to make Republic Industries another success story, and he did, propelling the company from $48 million in sales in the early 1990s to over $10.3 billion in 1997. Republic became the nation's largest auto retailer in a $1 trillion industry, owning just shy of 320 new car dealerships, a fleet of over 310,000 rental cars in the United States, Canada, the Caribbean, Latin America, Australia, Europe, Africa, and the Middle East (including Alamo Rent A Car, National Car Rental, and CarTemps USA companies), 26 AutoNation USA superstores, and had plans to add the 12-outlet Driver's Mart chain to the fold in 1998.

A Brief History of Huizenga, 1960s to 1994

When Huizenga began buying used car dealerships, his intention was to revolutionize the industry—to replace dishon-

esty with truthfulness, and the tacky and disreputable with good, solid sales, and to keep customers coming back for a lifetime. It was a tall order—and one generally sneered at by most analysts; few doubted Huizenga's business acumen, just his choice of business. Like many times before, Huizenga took delight in his critics' disbelief or outright dismissal, since he had proven them wrong before and figured he would have the last laugh once again.

H. Wayne Huizenga grew up in Chicago, the son of Dutch immigrants. The family business was garbage hauling and Huizenga bought his first garbage truck in 1962 in his early 20s. He built a business buying up dumpsters he rented to others, and his insistence on cleanliness and courtesy set him apart from others in area garbage hauling. In 1966, just four years after purchasing his first garbage truck for $5,000, Huizenga and his family formed Waste Management and used company stock to buy up small waste haulers throughout the Chicago area, then the Midwest, then the rest of the country. By 1984, when Huizenga sold Waste Management to move onto newer, greener pastures, the company was a $3 billion conglomerate.

In the mid-1980s Huizenga experimented in various businesses, including bottled water, lawn fertilizer, and even another form of waste management—portable toilets—then bought controlling interest in an up-and-coming yet troubled venture called Blockbuster Video in 1987. Along with a colleague named Steven R. Berrard, Huizenga built the little-known Blockbuster, with 19 outlets, into an empire of 3,700 stores and sold it for $8.4 billion to entertainment giant Viacom in 1994. Before settling on Republic Industries, Huizenga bought several sport franchises in the early 1990s, including the Florida Marlins, the Miami Dolphins, and the Florida Panthers.

Wayne's World, 1995

Well before Huizenga took over Republic, he was considered a controversial figure. He was undeniably successful, and those who had worked with him walked away with millions, yet both WMX Technologies and Blockbuster suffered a host of problems after Huizenga sold them. Waste Management, given its trade, was rumored to have ties with organized crime—

+---+
| **Company Perspectives:** |
| |
| *Republic's mission is to build shareholder value by creating* |
| *customers for life in each of its business segments. The* |
| *company is growing through internal expansion, strategic* |
| *acquisitions, and by leveraging the strengths that exist in its* |
| *complementary lines of business.* |
+---+

which Huizenga vehemently denied—and was repeatedly investigated by the SEC and environmental agencies, though all charges were later dropped. Blockbuster, though the leader in the video rental industry, ran into major financial problems from too-rapid expansion in terms of both new stores and diversifying into music. Critics repeatedly charged Huizenga was a master of building up and bailing, jumping in to cash out when the going was good. Others, of course, begged to differ—including Huizenga who stated in a *U.S. News & World Report* article that when he left both WMX Technologies and Blockbuster each was ''. . . in great shape, and to be blamed for their problems years after I left is ridiculous.''

Yet the residue of financial difficulties explained why few took serious note of Huizenga's latest ventures in 1995, Republic, and a new hotel chain called Extended Stay America. Though Republic's primary business was something he knew—waste disposal—the ''extended stay'' hotel was a concept yet to take hold in America. As Huizenga built his hotels across the country, he also moved into the highly fragmented and lowly field of used cars with Republic. Some thought he had lost his mind and others figured he bit off far more than he could chew. But Huizenga's vision was to take the unwieldy and unpopular used car industry and to make it a standardized, respectable business by introducing a ''no-haggle'' pricing policy and quality cars. If the lemons and the slimy tactics were eliminated, what was left was a business like any other with the same potential for profit. Huizenga's goal was to knock $1,000 off the price of every used car sold, through efficiency and the no-haggle pricing.

Another piece in the puzzle came with Huizenga's interest in AutoNation Incorporated, a growing chain of used auto superstores in direct competition with the similar CarMax, owned by Circuit City. The first AutoNation superstore opened its doors in 1995, and soon CarMax's management cried foul, suing Republic for copyright infringement and a series of issues Huizenga dismissed as without merit. By the end of the year, Republic's year-end sales were hard to ignore at $5.2 billion, giving Huizenga plenty of paper to move forward with his next move—from used cars to new cars. Huizenga began buying up car dealerships at a dizzying pace throughout the country. Yet many of his acquisitions came with a welcome twist: the owners of the dealerships joined Republic's management team with long-term contracts. Some dealers, sensing Huizenga's network was the wave of the future, actually sought him out. Republic's purpose was made clear—to eliminate waste from car buying processes like factory rebates, cash-back bonuses, and all the usual tricks of the trade by offering customers the same no-haggle pricing Huizenga had instituted in his used car outfits.

Onward and Upward, 1996 and Beyond

In 1996 Republic still moved at breakneck pace, buying hundreds of car dealerships, building over a dozen AutoNation superstores, and diversifying further into the automotive industry by acquiring several car rental agencies. First came Alamo Rent A Car, followed by National Car Rental, Spirit Rent-A-Car, Value Rent-A-Car, Snappy Car Rental, and EuroDollar Rent A Car the next year. The move was part of Huizenga's total picture for the entire automotive industry—from new to used to rental vehicles—to be, literally, America's one-stop-shop for cars and trucks. New cars would be leased to dealers, then after the leases expired, moved to the rental arena, then moved to the used car lots. With its own reconditioning centers, Republic knew the history of each vehicle and could then offer customers seven-day money back guarantees as well as 99-day bumper-to-bumper warranties.

To Huizenga, it was a simple enough plan—waste not, want not—but to others it was idealistic if not impossible. Never one to cave to public opinion, Huizenga continued his quest. While other car dealerships were cannibalizing their own markets, many began to see the logic in Republic's buying spree though feared Huizenga having such a stranglehold on the automotive industry. Also in 1996 came a two-for-one stock split in June. Though there were some bumps in the road, such as calling off a planned acquisition of ADT Ltd., an electronic security company, year-end sales spoke loud and clear at nearly $6.6 billion. Soon after the ADT deal fell through Huizenga's thinking changed from enlarging Republic's electronic security division to unloading it to concentrate on his automotive empire.

The sale came in October 1997, and the next logical step was to do the same with Republic's waste disposal division. Instead of selling the division, however, Huizenga and Berrard readied it for a spinoff. By the close of 1997 Republic was in the midst of streamlining operations and year-end sales had leapt to $10.3 billion, with a staggering jump in income to $439.7 million. Huizenga's naysayers, however, squawked about the company's $244.1 million pre-tax charge, which consisted of $150 million for combining new and used car operations into one automotive retail division, while an additional $94.1 million was spent to integrate Republic's rental operations. Huizenga's other ventures, such as the Extended Stay America hotel chain, were experiencing difficulties, while two other companies run by former colleagues, Boston Market and Discovery Zone, had plummeting stock and bankruptcy woes, respectively. Though Huizenga had invested in the companies, he had nothing to do with running them and their failure was ancillary addendum to his résumé.

Huizenga's impact, however, on the United States' nearly 23,000 auto dealers in the late 1990s was profound, and more shocking was his direct aim at the automakers themselves. No one ever had the audacity to take on the Big Three nor the Japanese automakers, but Huizenga's approach was basically a non-approach: he bought what he wanted, when he wanted it, and where he wanted it. If his acquisitions stepped on toes, the general attitude was ''so what.'' Ford, GM, Chrysler, and Nissan made no waves and allowed Republic to gobble up dealerships, but Toyota and Honda protested. Each was met with a battery of former state's attorneys general hired by Republic.

Toyota settled quickly, and though litigation with Honda continued, Huizenga was not concerned. One automaker, however, did win a concession: after buying six Saturn dealerships in Arizona and Florida, Huizenga agreed to sell the dealerships back to Saturn in 1997 because the cars, though "a great brand" were not big enough sellers. Saturn claimed it wanted to keep the brand exclusive. Both parties claimed victory.

Yet the future seemed bright as Republic wrapped up the July 1998 IPO of Republic Services, the waste disposal division. The original business of the once-fledgling Republic Industries, the waste disposal division's spinoff of 36.1 percent of its outstanding shares netted proceeds of around $1.4 billion. The remaining shares were later distributed to Republic stockholders the next year. Another big boon in 1998 was the overturning of a $50 million jury award to CarMax. Not only was the award voided, but the judge ruled that Republic had not infringed on any CarMax trademarks, and that the case was closed for good—another victory for the fast-moving Huizenga and his phenomenal Republic Industries.

Near the end of the century Huizenga and Republic were still dogged by critics. Some claimed Huizenga could not do for the auto industry what he did for Waste Management or Blockbuster, because the auto market was not growing in leaps or bounds but was a mature industry slated to gain only a percentage point or two over the next several years. Further, pundits were convinced Huizenga and his henchmen would bail on Republic and leave a house of cards. In response to such claims Huizenga told *U.S. News & World Report*'s Dan McGraw, "I worked for Waste Management for 24 years and Blockbuster for eight. The whole notion that we're going to bail is crazy. We've told the manufacturers that if we leave, we give the franchises back." To the car dealers and franchisees who joined Republic over the last several years, Huizenga's statement seemed like an ironclad parachute. With Huizenga predicting revenue of $50 to $60 billion by 2003, few took him seriously, though most were wary. Is Wayne on the Wane, as Susan Pulliam of the *Wall Street Journal* predicted? Only time will tell.

Principal Subsidiaries

AutoNation USA; Alamo Rent A Car; National Car Rental; CarTemps USA; Snappy Car Rental, Spirit Rent-A-Car; Eurodollar Rent A Car; Republic Services; and nearly 300 car dealerships throughout the United States.

Further Reading

Deogun, Nikhil, "Republic Industries Appoints Berrard President, Co-CEO," *Wall Street Journal,* October 24, 1996, p. B3.
"Ford or Honda, New or Used, He Wants to Sell It," *New York Times,* October 16, 1997.
Frank, Robert, "Huizenga Faces Challenge in Meshing Eclectic Empire. . . ," *Wall Street Journal*, July 3, 1996, p. B6.
"Judge Says Republic Industries Won't Have to Pay CarMax $50 Million," *PR Newswire,* November 5, 1998.
Lowenstein, Roger, "Intrinsic Value—Republic Tender: In Huizenga We Trust," *Wall Street Journal,* July 11, 1996, p. C1.
McGraw, Dan, "Car Guy: Will He Own the Road?," *U.S. News & World Report,* October 20, 1997.
Pulliam, Susan, "Is Huizenga Losing His Magic Touch?," *Wall Street Journal,* July 10, 1997, p. C1.

—Taryn Benbow-Pfalzgraf

RockShox, Inc.

401 Charcot Avenue
San Jose, California 95131
U.S.A.
(408) 435-7469
Fax: (408) 435-7468
Web site: http://www.rockshox.com

Public Company
Incorporated: 1989
Employees: 300
Sales: $102.2 million (1998)
Stock Exchanges: NASDAQ
Ticker Symbol: RSHX
SICs: 3751 Motorcycles, Bicycles & Parts

RockShox, Inc. is the worldwide leader in the design, manufacture, and marketing of high performance suspension products for the bicycle industry, with ten front suspension forks and three rear shocks offered in 1998 under its own brand names, such as "Boxxer," "Deluxe," "Indy," "Jett," "Judy," "Mag," "Quadra," "Ruby," and "SID."

Founding, 1989

RockShox, Inc. was founded by Paul Turner and Steve Simons in 1989 and incorporated in North Carolina. It was later reincorporated in California. Turner, who raced motorcycles in his teen years during the 1970s, went on to found an aftermarket engine parts company in 1977 at the age of 18. He then went to work for Honda Motor Company as their factory motocross team mechanic, an opportunity which provided Turner with experience working with the top racers in the field, as well as suspension designers and other motocross industry leaders.

Turner quickly advanced to working as a consultant for Honda, moving to northern California and there developing race engines and chassis. He also began racing in triathlons on racing bicycles and mountain bicycles. As someone who spent years riding plush suspended motocross bikes, the switch to rigid mountain bikes was difficult and Turner felt they were archaic in comparison, so he did his own modifications on a simple, lightweight motorcycle fork design which became the first generation of RockShox products. Turner went on to become vice-president of advanced research and development for the company he started in 1989.

Entrepreneur and veteran motorcycle racer Steve Simons in 1974 designed a new shock absorber for Moto-X Fox which went on to become a bestselling product in the industry. Utilizing this success, Simons went on to found his own company, Simons Inc., which developed suspension modifications and complete front forks, and obtain two patents on suspension forks, one of which he licensed to the major motorcycle and shock companies. In 1988, his spinoff company called Simons Precision became so successful in the machining industry that the original company was sold so that Steve could focus on the machine shop. In 1989, Paul Turner approached him to lend his manufacturing expertise to a bicycle suspension idea that became the genesis of RockShox. Simons agreed, becoming president of the company that year.

Also that year, Turner brought Greg Herbold aboard as test rider and company spokesperson. Herbold, known affectionately as "HB," was the first downhill world champion on one of the first suspension forks ever made. That August, the company released its first 100 suspension forks, called the "RS1," for shipment to the consumer marketplace.

In September 1990, the company celebrated its first World Championship Cross Country when bicycler Ned Overend won with a suspension fork. That fiscal year, the company brought in total revenues of $1.6 million on the strength of the one product they were manufacturing, the RS1.

With each evolutionary step the company's product line took, RockShox, Inc. enjoyed a corresponding increase in sales and was profitable every year from inception through at least 1996. From approximately 1984–95, the mountain bike market was the fastest-growing segment of the worldwide bicycle industry, with manufacturers such as Cannondale Corporation, GT Bicycles, Schwinn, Huffy Corporation, Montague, and others producing the distinctive new style of bicycle. The com-

Company Perspectives:

A masterpiece is not created overnight, and it isn't just a lucky guess or the product of blood, sweat and tears. It goes deeper. True innovation is a combination of passion, education, experimentation, foresight, resources, vision, resolve, determination, experience, belief, timing, talent, insight, courage, conviction, and a little good luck. RockShox innovation is borne from a team of masters whose joint creative force is exponentially greater than the sum of its parts.

pany focused its first seven years to the high-end mountain bicycle market (those retailing for $600 or more).

In September 1992, the company introduced a new adjustable hydraulic suspension component for mountain bikes called the "Mag 21," which featured high-pressure seals that lasted five times longer than previous seals, with a fork twice as rigid, able to handle all types of terrain. Total revenues for the year ending in March 1993 climbed to $30.5 million, with a net income of $2.7 million.

In the early to mid-1990s, most mountain bikes were sold with no suspension. Many bikers went back to dealers to pick up suspension forks when they became available, giving the company a huge surge in aftermarket business. But, in the later 1990s, suspension bicycles began to have better penetration in the market, decreasing the aftermarket share. In 1993, the company released the Quadra fork which retailed for $90. In the fiscal year ending March 1994, the company's total revenue reached $37.9 million, with a net income of $4.7 million.

In September 1994, the company released the Judy XC and Judy SL forks, with their revolutionary oil cartridge suspension technology. In the fiscal year ending in March 1995, the company's total revenues dropped to $14.3 million, and a net loss of $2.3 million was posted.

In March 1995, the company received an influx of capital investment from MCIT PLC and The Jordan Company. June of that year saw the company introduce its new "Deluxe" product line of rear suspensions, featuring a coil over a hydraulic damper. The following month, the Super Deluxe product was released, featuring a coil over a hydraulic damper with an oil reservoir.

By the end of that year, the mountain bike fad had subsided somewhat, and the segment dropped for the first time in a decade, down from $1.6 million to $1.5 million that year, but it still continued to grow. That year, a total of 8.2 million mountain bicycles were sold worldwide through independent bicycle dealers. Of that total, the company estimated it held a 35 percent market share. Of the 2.2 million sold in the United States, RockShox Inc. held 50 percent of the market. By the end of the fiscal year ending March 1996, the company's total revenue bounced back from the previous year's dismal showing, reaching $83.5 million, and the company posted a net income of $5.7 million.

In April 1996, the company introduced the Indy C product, featuring a Type 2 Spring system, targeted at the mid-priced mountain bike market. May saw the Indy XC product, and June featured the Indy SL.

In July of that year, bicyclist Paola Pezzo won an Olympic Games gold medal in the first-ever Olympic mountain bike event while using the company's Judy products on his bike. That month, the company also released the Coupe Deluxe product, featuring a coil over a hydraulic damper, similar to the Deluxe product.

In October the company completed its initial public offering, selling 4.8 million shares of common stock and netting approximately $64.5 million. The company began trading under the symbol RSHX on the NASDAQ stock exchange. By the following month, analysts estimated the company held 45 percent of the mountain bicycle suspension market, outselling its nearest competitor by 50 percent, and 460 of the 660 mountain bikes models available with front suspension utilized RockShox.

Roy Turner (no relation to Paul) joined RockShox in February 1997 as the Race Program Manager, working to use his broad experience in suspension technology and race team support to help the company provide teams and athletes with the best possible technical service. He started his career in professional Supercross racing as a lead technician for Team Honda in 1973, going on to become regarded as the top technician in the areas of chassis, suspension, and engine tuning. Team Kawasaki recruited him away and he quickly went from lead technician to team manager, a position he held for 12 years, where he was responsible for the development and overall success of the multimillion-dollar Kawasaki professional supercross racing program.

In the fiscal year that ended in March 1997, the company had shipped over one million suspension forks, posted net sales of $106.2 million, a 27 percent increase from 1996, with a net income of $6.9 million.

Branching Out, 1997 and Beyond

Although high-end mountain bikes continued to be the fastest-growing sector of the bicycle market, the company began branching out with a myriad of new product innovations which expanded the company's reach to include mid-priced mountain bikes, road bikes, and full-suspension bikes. In April 1997, the company released the Judy S product, featuring the Elastomer Spring system of suspension. The following month, the Judy T2 was released. Also in May, the company joined five others, including telecommunications equipment manufacturer Yurie Systems Inc., as *Business Week*'s Hot Growth Companies of the year. In September of that year, Olympic gold medalist Paola Pezzo won his first World Championship using the company's SID cartridge/air spring suspension on his bike.

In November, the company named George Napier, former president and CEO of Meridian Sports Inc., COO of Wilson Sporting Goods Co., and a RockShox board member since January 1997, to the position of president and CEO. Napier succeeded cofounder Steve Simons, who remained as chairman and chief technical officer.

In the fiscal year that ended in March 1998, the company had again shipped over one million suspension forks, posted net sales of $102.2 million, a four percent decline from 1997, and net income posted at $5.1 million.

The mountain bike segment of the market continued to be sluggish as late as mid-1998. But, by the year 2000, analysts estimated that some 9.5 million mountain bikes would be sold throughout the world, with RockShox capturing 40 percent of the worldwide market. Nearly 2.5 million of those would be in the United States, and the company hoped to hold 55 percent of the market at that time.

As the company headed into the end of the 20th century, its sales and name recognition remained strong, and it continued to struggle to contain costs and remain a powerhouse in the bicycle industry.

Further Reading

Barrett, Amy, et al, ''Hot Growth Companies,'' *Business Week*, May 26, 1997, p. 90.

Leventon, William, ''Mountain Bike Suspension Allows Easy Adjustment,'' *Design News*, July 19, 1993, p. 75.

''Rockshox Inc.,'' *Wall Street Journal*, November 25, 1997, p. B11(W).

''Rockshox Inc.,'' *Wall Street Journal*, January 13, 1998, p. B5(W).

Thompson, T. ''Rockshox Inc.,'' Merrill Lynch Capital Markets, July 31, 1998.

—Daryl F. Mallett

Rocky Shoes & Boots, Inc.

39 E. Canal Street
Nelsonville, Ohio 45764
U.S.A.
(740) 753-1951
Fax: (740) 753-4024
Web site: http://www.investquest.com/InvestQuest/r/
   rcky

Public Company
Incorporated: 1932 as The William Brooks Shoe
   Company
Employees: 1,700
Sales: $95 million (1997)
Stock Exchanges: NASDAQ
Ticker Symbol: RCKY
SICs: 3143 Men's Footwear, Except Athletic; 3144
   Women's Footwear Except Athletic

Rocky Shoes & Boots, Inc. is one of the few remaining shoemakers in the United States with a domestic manufacturing facility. The company designs, develops, manufactures, and markets premium quality men's and women's footwear. The company's product line includes such rugged outdoor footwear as waterproof hunting and hiking boots, nonmilitary occupational footwear, and hand-sewn casual footwear. The company also markets, through several distribution channels, accessories, such as socks and inner sole supports under a number of brand names, including Rocky, Stalkers, Cornstalkers, Safari, Bear Claw, Snow/Stalkers, and Outback.

The company's product line is organized into three primary categories: rugged outdoor footwear, including hunting and hiking boots, with suggested retail prices generally ranging from $60 to $190 per pair; nonmilitary occupational footwear, with suggested retail prices generally ranging from $40 to $160; and hand-sewn casual footwear, with suggested retail prices generally ranging from $90 to $150 per pair. The company's products also include Thinsulate thermal insulation; Cambrelle cush-

ioned linings, which are manufactured from a material that breathes, absorbs perspiration, and resists mildew and odors; Vibram rubber outsoles, which are long-wearing, flexible, and slip-resistant and incorporate Air-O-Magic air-cushioned footbeds. The company maintains a factory outlet store in Nelsonville, Ohio, but its products are also sold in department stores, sporting goods stores, and through mail-order catalogs in the United States and Canada. Manufacturing facilities are located in Ohio, Puerto Rico, and the Dominican Republic.

The William Brooks Shoe Company, 1932–59

In 1932, William Brooks founded The William Brooks Shoe Company in Nelsonville, Ohio, about 60 miles southeast of Columbus, joined by his brother F. M. "Mike" Brooks. Both men had lost their jobs during the Great Depression when Godman Shoe Co. of Columbus went bankrupt. In 1937, Mike's 17-year-old son, John W. Brooks, joined the company, taking a break only to serve four years in the U.S. Army during World War II. The two brothers ran the business until the mid-1950s when they had a falling out. Bill, the original founder, bought out Mike, and the two never spoke again.

The Irving Drew Shoe Co., 1959–74

In 1959, convinced that the U.S. shoe industry was going under, Bill began looking for a buyer for the business. Mike's son, John, offered to buy it, but his uncle refused, saying he was doing him a favor, and pointing to the hundreds of other domestic shoe companies, and the first imports, which were a lot cheaper, starting to come from Japan. Bill sold the business to The Irving Drew Shoe Co., a women's-shoe company, headquartered in Lancaster, Ohio, and John remained in the company as an employee.

For 25 years, ownership was out of the Brooks family. John remained on through the entire Irving Drew ownership period, eventually rising to plant manager. Eventually, Irving Drew began to struggle as offshore shoe manufacturing boomed and competitors lowered their margins and, concurrently, their prices. After losing money for three years running, The Irving Drew Shoe Co. announced its closing in 1974. John, realizing

Company Perspectives:

Innovativeness, quality, and durability are hallmarks of the Rocky brand name. The company continually monitors the development of innovative raw materials and has distinguished its branded products by incorporating new fabric technologies into the design of its footwear. Rocky places an emphasis on the manufacture of waterproof footwear and is currently the largest customer of Gore-Tex waterproof fabric for footwear. The company was also the first footwear manufacturer to market an all-Cordura nylon fabric hunting boot.

that his dream of owning his own company might finally come to fruition, with five children to raise and a modest salary, put a meager $500 of his own money into the venture, and borrowed $640,000 from various banks to purchase the company, worth about $1.3 million, from Irving Drew.

John W. Brooks Inc. and the Return of The William Brooks Shoe Co., 1975–93

After the purchase in 1975, John formed John W. Brooks, Inc. as an Ohio corporation, reacquired the operating assets of the original company, and moved the principal executive offices back to Nelsonville, renaming the company The William Brooks Shoe Co. in honor of his uncle. Then he called his son Mike.

Against John's worry that the business might not work out, Mike, who had left college early and went to Milan, Italy, where he spent a year studying shoe design at the well-known Ars Satoria trade school, and had already worked at U.S. Shoe Corp. and at two tanning companies, quit his job at a tannery in Milwaukee, Wisconsin, the very next day, taking a huge pay cut, and moving his family back to Nelsonville. There, Mike found disaster . . . no bank financing yet, aging machinery, three years of losses, the plant in disarray, morale at an all-time low because of layoffs, meager raises, and workers' medical insurance in a bad state.

Mike turned things around quickly, designing a new pair of hiking boots, and going out on the road to sell them. He worked to speed up production and ease the company's cash needs and spent time roaming the factory floor, attempting to buoy the spirits of a demoralized workforce. Then the cavalry arrived. Dave Fraedrich, hired by John right out of college, came aboard as a financial guru and Bob Hollenbaugh, a childhood friend of Mike, became manager of shipping, personnel, and purchasing. The three became a triad and worked together, plotting company strategies over beer in the evenings.

The father-and-son team quarreled for years about the way to run their business. Mike began to think about taking the company public right away, because the company was always highly leveraged and never had enough capital to do anything properly. But John, a bitter survivor of the Great Depression and the stock market crash of the 1930s, refused to expand, wanting to keep control of the company in the family. The two were at an

impasse for nearly a year and a half. Their options were: sell a piece of the business to raise funds, continue running the company undercapitalized, or sell it outright. Business continued as well as possible.

In 1975, the United States was emerging from the worst downturn since the 1930s. Meanwhile, imports from steel to semiconductors flooded into the U.S. market. The Midwest was hit hard, with so many manufacturing facilities closed down that it was named the Rustbelt. Furthermore, the shoe industry went from its plateau of the 1950s into a steep dive. In 1970, imported shoes accounted for 30 percent of the market. By 1980, imports had climbed to 50 percent and were still going up. During those ten years, over 300 domestic shoe plants shut their doors for good.

The company's regular customers, Sears and J.C. Penney, bought nearly 80 percent of the company's output. The company was bringing in nearly $8 million a year, but could not continue to run things the way they were. Plummeting import prices were killing the U.S. shoemaker, salaries were dropping, the plant was decrepit, the machinery was failing, and something had to be done. In 1979, during a meeting in Chicago with a buyer for Sears, Mike finally realized the battle was being lost. He had asked for a 50 cent per pair increase in the purchase price. The buyer balked and asked to speak with John. John drove out with Mike the following week, 400 miles, since he hated to fly, and the meeting degenerated from the start. John, worried about losing the account, waffled on the price; Mike stuck to his story. Sears agreed to the price increase, but only until it could find a cheaper alternative, probably a Korean shoemaker.

As the company struggled in the early 1980s, the shoe market bounced back. Numerous upstart companies entered the fray; others began to prosper. Distinctive products with brand names and premium prices became the rage. Shoes were sold through new retail channels, not just the old shoe stores and department stores. Advertising costs soared. "Athletic" shoes became a new rage. Nike led in athletic shoes; Timberland led in boots. However, old-time manufacturers in the Midwest and elsewhere in the United States kept going under, and another 300 manufacturers closed up shop.

Back when Mike created his new red-laced hiking boots to sell to Sears, he called them "Rocky," thinking it sounded strong and bold and All-American. He had a new box designed, with a picture of a bighorn sheep on it, put the boots in it, and put Bob Hollenbaugh out on the streets to sell them. Approaching independent dealers in the Ohio and surrounding areas, Hollenbaugh made sales at margins far higher than Sears would give.

In 1983 the company began marketing "occupational" shoes, such as those worn by police officers and mail carriers, under the Rocky brand. It opened up new markets and new distribution methods. Mike was also watching Timberland. He knew he had to reinvent the wheel, by making a new and distinctive product and then selling it through the path of least resistance. The company also had to broaden and deepen its line past just the four Rocky boots it was then offering.

Slowly, the company continued to build, shoe by shoe. In 1984, the company introduced the Rocky Stalkers boots. In

1987, Five Star Enterprises Ltd., a Cayman Islands corporation, was formed by John and Mike, two other executive officers of the company, and Eric M. Beraza, a retired executive officer of the company, to produce shoe and boot uppers at a manufacturing facility located in La Vega, The Dominican Republic. The following year, Lifestyle Footwear, Inc., a Delaware corporation, was established as a subsidiary of Rocky Co. and commenced operations at a manufacturing facility in Aquadilla, Puerto Rico. Also that year, the company released its Rocky Cornstalkers boots.

A strategic victory was created by Hollenbaugh as he beat the bushes out on the road, lining up hundreds of reps, meeting hundreds of buyers, creating a distribution network unparalleled by any other U.S. shoemaker. Hunting and sporting goods stores, mostly in the Midwest, carried the "Made in the USA"-labeled, waterproof boots, and were willing to pay a bit more for them. Hollenbaugh developed catalogs, learned the advertising industry, and spearheaded campaigns in outdoor magazines. Sales rose as the company, in 1988, reached $20 million in annual revenue.

The following year, Mike created a new line of products that could hold its own against Korean and Taiwanese imports when he found Gore-Tex, a patented membrane which allowed moisture escape, but kept water droplets out, created by W.L. Gore & Associates. Mike quickly created Gore-Tex boots, which everyone loved and no one could duplicate without serious money being put into the project, because Gore & Associates asked for all footwear customers to fork over a $25,000 licensing fee. Other manufacturers became furious; Mike Brooks loved it and showed up the next day with a $25,000 check and a bottle of champagne he shared with CEO Bob Gore, knowing his investment in the latter company had paid off.

In August 1991, John walked into Mike's office and said he was retiring, and walked out, leaving $11.25 million in debt to Mike and his four siblings and their spouses. He gave up his controlling interest in the family business and divided it equally among Mike and his two brothers and two sisters, all of whom worked for the company, retaining a small interest in the Dominican plant. It cleared the way for Mike to take the company public. That year, as he struggled to do so, total sales reached $29.8 million, with a net income of $577,000. Total sales for 1992 climbed to $32.5 million, with net sales nearly tripling over the previous year, to $1.6 million.

Rocky Shoes & Boots, 1993 On

In February 1993, Mike Brooks did take the company public, spending nearly three-quarters of a million dollars in the process, changing the name to Rocky Shoes & Boots and initiating the company's initial public offering. Selling approximately 1.9 million shares at $10 apiece on the NASDAQ under the symbol RCKY, and bringing in nearly $14 million, the company was able to help pay off its debt and add a bit of working capital. The five family members, along with three longtime employees, retained a 47 percent interest in the company, and John cashed in his interest shortly thereafter, remaining with the company as a semi-retired employee. Net income for 1993 nearly reached $1.8 million on net sales of $41.2 million.

In 1994, the company released the "4 Way Stop" line of occupational shoes designed for food service workers, who often encounter wet, slippery conditions, featuring an exclusive "downspout" design sole that causes liquid to flow through the sole and out the sides, increasing traction and exceeding the U.S. government's standards for slip-resistance by a factor of two. In August of that year, the company opened a 25,000-square-foot building in Nelsonville, Ohio, adjacent to the company's manufacturing facilities, which included 12,500 square feet of office space and a 12,500-square-foot factory outlet store, to replace a 3,000 square foot one. Opened in September, the expanded store primarily sells first-quality, irregular, and closeout Rocky footwear and accessories, as well as footwear and apparel from other manufacturers. Other achievements that year included the company investing $2.7 million in new equipment and changeover to modular manufacturing, and adding six lines of boots to the Rocky Safari series of lightweight hiking boots. The company achieved records that year, with net sales increasing 28 percent to $52.9 million, and sales of Rocky rugged outdoor footwear increasing 42 percent to $28.7 million. Net income for 1994 repeated at just above $1.8 million.

In January 1995, both Rocky Shoes and competitor Wolverine World Wide entered the apparel business, launching workwear lines of clothing. The company also signed a licensing agent, The Kravetz Group, to help it market and license its products. The company also introduced the Rocky Professionals line of occupational shoes, with dress-shoe-styling designed for safety forces and general occupational markets. This line featured waterproof leather uppers, lightweight soles and materials, slip-resistant polyurethene-injected soles, breathable linings, and superior lateral stability. The retail market for shoes struggled in 1995, as footwear stocks dipped. Rocky attributed a fourth-quarter 1995 sales drop to a decrease in hand-sewn casual shoe sales for a private-label customer, among other things. Retail sales from the factory outlet store were approximately $2.7 million, making up some 7.6 percent of net sales for the year. In fiscal 1995, the company ended the year with $60.2 million in total revenue, with net income dropping slightly to $1.4 million.

John W. Brooks, the consummate shoemaker, passed away in February 1996, ending a nearly 60-year career in the shoe industry. His company continued as three new styles were introduced by mid-1996, including Snow Stalkers, Sidewinders, and Tuff Terrainers. The company also changed its fiscal year from June 30th to December 31st. Total revenue for 1996 reached $73.2 million, with a net income of $2.8 million. During the first quarter of 1997, sales were especially strong in the Outdoor and Handsewn categories.

In January 1998, the company installed a System 21 Style enterprise resource planning (ERP) system from JBA International, as part of an effort to improve the company's reporting and tracking capabilities. Also early that year, the company discontinued the sale of footwear uppers to a private label customer. By June, the company, with its Nelsonville, Ohio-based facility, employing some 250 people, was one of the last remaining U.S. footwear companies with a domestic production plant. In August, the company announced it would repurchase up to 300,000 shares of stock in the following year. In September, Hurricane Georges affected the company's manufacturing facilities in Puerto Rico and the Dominican Republic when production was interrupted for approximately one week, and Hurricane Mitch hammered Puerto Rico, the Caribbean, and Central America again. But the company continued into the end of 1998, expecting to post new record income and sales, and continuing on into the 21st century as a venerable leader in the U.S. shoe industry.

Principal Subsidiaries

Five Star Enterprises Ltd.; Lifestyle Footwear, Inc.

Further Reading

Berg, Susan M., ''Made in the USA,'' *Business First—Columbus*, June 12, 1998, p. 39.

''Earnings and Stock News,'' *Business First—Columbus*, May 16, 1997, p. 48.

''Earnings and Stock News,'' *Business First—Columbus*, May 23, 1997, p. 36.

''Earnings and Stock News,'' *Business First—Columbus*, September 4, 1998, p. 66.

''Insider Trading,'' *Business First—Columbus*, January 29, 1996, p. 27.

''Insider Trading,'' *Business First—Columbus*, December 5, 1997, p. 64.

''Rocky Shoes & Boots Inc.,'' *Business First—Columbus*, August 1, 1995, p. 58A.

''Rocky Shoes & Boots Inc.,'' *Business First—Columbus*, January 23, 1995, p. 15.

''Rocky Shoes & Boots Inc.,'' *Business First—Columbus*, July 26, 1996, p. 62A.

''Rocky Shoes & Boots Inc.,'' *Business First—Columbus*, July 25, 1997, pp. 60A, S60.

''Rocky Shoes & Boots Inc.,'' *New York Times*, October 6, 1997, p. C12(N)/D12(L).

''Rocky Shoes & Boots Inc.,'' *Wall Street Journal*, May 13, 1998, p. C16(W)/B22(E).

''Rocky Shoes & Boots, Inc. Announces Preliminary Third Quarter Sales,'' *PR Newswire*, October 9, 1998, p. 8374.

''Rocky Shoes & Boots, Inc. Announces Stock Repurchase Program,'' *PR Newswire*, August 31, 1998, p. 831CLM008.

''Rocky Shoes Has Rights Plan,'' *Wall Street Journal*, November 12, 1997, p. B11B(E).

Rudolph, Ron, Bob Woodward, and Eric Perlman, ''Foot Retrofit,'' *Snow Country*, Spring 1995, p. 20.

''Rugged Footwear Brands Step into Apparel Business,'' *Sporting Goods Business*, January 1, 1995, p. 26.

Shook, Carrie, ''LCI Reaches for the Sky,'' *Business First—Columbus*, September 5, 1994, p. 10.

——, ''Max & Erma's Climbs Up,'' *Business First—Columbus*, September 26, 1994, p. 12.

——, ''Neoprobe Hits 52-Week High,'' *Business First—Columbus*, July 31, 1995, p. 26.

——, ''P. J. Phillips on Way Up,'' *Business First—Columbus*, June 13, 1994, p. 34.

——, ''R. G. Barry Loses Steam,'' *Business First—Columbus*, December 12, 1994, p. 24.

——, ''Rocky Shoes & Boots Climbs,'' *Business First—Columbus*, September 25, 1995, p. 20.

——, ''Rocky Shoes & Boots Makes Gain,'' *Business First—Columbus*, October 16, 1995, p. 22.

——, ''Symix Stock Makes Gain,'' *Business First—Columbus*, July 24, 1995, p. 16.

''Taking Stock,'' *Business First—Columbus*, December 6, 1996, p. 34.

''Taking the ERP Trail,'' *Computerworld*, January 12, 1998, p. 39.

Walter, Rebecca, ''Rocky Shoes IPO Strained Family Ties,'' *Business First—Columbus*, December 12, 1994, p. 1.

——, ''When the Baby Is the Family Business,'' *Business First—Columbus*, December 5, 1994, p. 1.

—Daryl F. Mallett

Rodamco N.V.

Coolsingel 120
3011 AG Rotterdam
The Netherlands
(31) 10 224 12 24
Fax: (31) 10 224 21 15
Web site: http://www.rodamco.nl

Public Company
Incorporated: 1979
Employees: n/a
Sales: NLG 15.19 billion (US$7.45 billion) (1998)
Stock Exchanges: Amsterdam Paris Frankfurt
Ticker Symbol: D.ROM
SICs: 6512 Nonresidential Building Operators; 6719
 Holding Companies, Not Elsewhere Classified

Rodamco N.V. of The Netherlands steers one of the largest property investment funds in the world, with investments in 14 countries and total assets of more than NLG 15 billion. Rodamco conducts its activities through four primary subsidiaries reflecting its worldwide areas of interest, including Rodamco Europe, Rodamco North America, and Rodamco Pacific; the fourth subsidiary, RoProperty Services BV, provides the management activities for Rodamco's holdings. In the late 1990s Rodamco began preparations for splitting up the funds into these four segments as independently listed real estate investment funds.

Rodamco's investment focus favors large-scale investments, with an emphasis on commercial shopping centers and other retail locations. In 1998 fully 69 percent of the company's holdings was in retail shopping complexes. Office buildings comprise the company's second largest group of investments, at 14 percent. In addition, Rodamco owns participations in industrial and renovation projects, which form five percent and nine percent, respectively, of Rodamco's total assets. Despite its European roots, Rodamco's North American investments form a major proportion of its portfolio, accounting for some 40 percent of total assets for 1998. Rodamco's European holdings represented 46 percent of total assets in 1998. The Pacific region remained the third largest investment area, at 14 percent of total assets, helping to limit Rodamco's exposure somewhat to the late 1990s economic crisis affecting much of that region.

Among Rodamco's holdings are featured sites such as the Suria KLCC Retail Centre shopping complex at the foot of the Petronas Towers, in Kuala Lumpur, Malaysia; the Centre Commercial Vélizy 2, in Vélizy Villacoublay, France; the Walt Disney World Swan, in Orlando, Florida; and the Sheraton Hotel and Towers in Chicago, Illinois. In addition to its investment, Rodamco provides management services for many of its properties, generating management fees as well as rents as income. Despite a shaky period at the beginning of the 1990s, Rodamco's investments have long been profitable for the company and its shareholders, representing a solid if conservative return on investment. In 1998 the company posted net profits of NLG 590 (US$289) million.

Rodamco remains under the direction of founding parent company Robeco, the largest Dutch investment fund, which itself was acquired by Rabobank in 1997. The principal institutional shareholder is the Algemeen Burgerlijk Pensionfonds (ABP), the Dutch civil service pension fund, which holds more than 20 percent of Rodamco.

''Ro'': Formed in 1979

Rodamco's parent Robeco, which stands for Rotterdam Beleggings (Investment) Consortium, was formed in 1929. A group of wealthy Rotterdammers were attracted by the dip in the Wall Street stock exchanges, and they decided to pool their resources to take advantage of the soft U.S. stock prices. When the dip turned into the Great Depression, the group incorporated their holdings as Robeco. This incorporation enabled the group's fund to survive the Depression. By the early 1970s Robeco had more than simply survived: it had grown to become the largest Dutch investment vehicle, including having captured some 70 percent of the country's ''household'' investors. Beyond The Netherlands, Robeco had grown to become one of the largest investment funds in Europe.

419

Company Perspectives:

These are exciting and challenging times for Rodamco. We have established our place at the forefront of international real estate companies and are now faced with the tasks of systematically evaluating priorities among new investment opportunities and carrying out timely divestitures.

With its current management structure, geographical diversification and the position of RoProperty, its strong international asset manager, Rodamco is strategically positioned to profit from healthy real estate markets, to weather the declines in weak ones and to seize opportunities wherever they arise. The prime objective is to increase our annual net profit per share.

The oil crisis of the early 1970s and the resulting worldwide recession convinced Robeco, which had built its portfolio in large part on the household goods market, to expand its investment holdings into the traditionally more stable real estate market. Through the 1970s Robeco made a number of significant purchases, notably of a US$120 million property and management portfolio purchased from Pakhoed, the Netherlands-based storage and transport business, and the property investment trust WAP, adding a portfolio of European and North American real estate holdings.

In the late 1970s Robeco found its dominance of the Dutch household investment market challenged as a number of Dutch banks launched their own investment funds. Robeco determined to meet this challenge by diversifying its product offerings, setting up several market-specific investment vehicles. One of these new funds would be formed with a US$230 million real estate portfolio spun off by Robeco in 1979 as Rodamco. In addition to diversifying its funds, Robeco also made it easy for investors to transfer their investments among the company's various products.

Growth in the 1980s

From its start, Rodamco's investments focused on the international scene. While some 45 percent of the company's initial portfolio was concentrated in The Netherlands, at least 38 percent of its assets were situated in the United States. Rodamco also had footholds in much of Western Europe, but in particular in neighboring Belgium and Germany, and in France. The company aimed to expand its European holdings, despite restrictions still in place among European Community countries in the late 1970s; Rodamco also eyed an expansion into the Swiss market.

Like other Robeco vehicles—the names of each of which were required to feature the prefix "Ro" and the suffix "co," for the sake of euphony—Rodamco was listed as an independent corporation, with an initial sale of 3.7 million shares, for a purchase price of NLG 100 per share, on the Amsterdam exchange. Over the following decade Rodamco would add its listing to most of the Western European exchanges in which it held investments and to the over-the-counter market in the

United States. Like Robeco, Rodamco's investors group was as international as its portfolio. While some 60 percent of the fund's shareholders were Dutch, Rodamco—given liberal Netherlands' investment policies, especially the lack of withholding and stock exchange taxes—was immediately popular with the worldwide investment community. This international focus would serve the company well as the European market countries moved toward 1992's open market.

By the late 1980s Rodamco had increased its initial portfolio of NLG 500 million to assets of more than NLG 3 billion. This growth was the result not simply of shrewd investments, but of a Robeco-led policy of takeovers, including the NLG 1 billion purchase of the British real estate firm Haslemere Estates in 1986. In 1987 Rodamco's acquisition of Hexalon brought it that investment firm's U.S.-based assets.

The stock market crash of October 1987 sent investors reeling toward real estate—and Rodamco. By 1988 Rodamco's war chest had grown sufficient for a new target: the nearly US$2.4 billion acquisition of Hammerson Property & Development Corp. of the United Kingdom, which complemented prime shopping center assets in England with a strong portfolio of international property investments. Rodamco also began to prepare to expand its assets toward a broader international scope, including enhancing its Western European portfolio, while beginning to build on its portfolio in the booming Asian economies.

The vigor with which the investment community turned to real estate was reflected in Rodamco's staggering growth in the last years of the 1980s. By the beginning of the new decade Rodamco had jumped from a total assets package of just NLG 3 billion to a portfolio worth more than NLG 10 billion—earning Rodamco a place among the top four real estate investment funds in the world.

Crash and Repair in the 1990s

The real estate euphoria was short-lived. At the start of the 1990s the investment community woke with a hangover of massive overbuilding that would cripple the real estate market through much of the first half of the 1990s. An example of the glut in new buildings was represented by Houston, Texas, and other cities—flattened by the bust in the oil market in the 1980s, these cities found themselves confronted with large numbers of nearly empty office buildings.

By September 1990 the real estate crash had caught up to Rodamco. As part of Robeco, Rodamco had offered shareholders the ability to transfer investments among Rodamco and the other Robeco vehicles, as well as offering a degree of liquidity through redemption of shareholder investments. With the flight from real estate investments, however, Rodamco was forced to suspend its stock redemption policies. The stock market reacted strongly, and in September 1990 Rodamco was forced to suspend trading of its stock for four days. When trading reopened, Rodamco's share price had fallen by some 25 percent. Rodamco's share price would continue to face pressure, losing nearly 50 percent of its value over two years. Rodamco's actions, which led to unsuccessful shareholder lawsuits, would haunt the fund through the first half of the decade.

The continued depressed real estate market also would affect the company's bottom line, as its growth turned negative.

In 1992 Rodamco found some redemption of its own, when the Algemeen Burgerlijk Pensioenfonds (ABP), representing the country's civil service pension fund, bought up a 12.5 percent stake in Rodamco, and an additional 20 percent in individual Rodamco divisions, for some NLG 2.5 billion. This new injection of capital enabled Rodamco to continue building its portfolio, including eyeing properties for the first time in the recently independent Eastern European market, but especially in expanding the company's Far Eastern portfolio. Whereas the company's investments had tended to remain in Australia, the fund now began liquidating these holdings in favor of the booming real estate markets in such "tiger" economies as Singapore, Malaysia, and Thailand, as well as in China, Taiwan, Hong Kong, and Japan.

Continued growth of the Asian Pacific region played a significant role in Rodamco's future plans. The company expected to increase its Asian Pacific investments to represent some 25 percent of its total portfolio; its United States investments, which ranged up to 40 percent of total assets, would be brought back to some 35 percent, with Europe representing the remainder of the company's asset portfolio. By 1994 Rodamco appeared to have recovered from the real estate crash—and regained the confidence of its investors. That year brought the company into Eastern Europe for the first time, with the NLG 70 million purchase of a shopping center in the Brandenburg region of former East Germany. Nevertheless, the fund remained guarded as to further Eastern European expansion.

Spain, on the other hand, presented a more attractive opportunity. In 1994 Rodamco purchased its first two shopping centers, for NLG 175 million. Rodamco would raise the number of its Spanish shopping center investments to 12 by the late 1990s, giving it one of the most important positions in the Spanish shopping center market. Indeed, shopping centers and retail stores would retain the largest part of Rodamco's portfolio, as the company shied away from an office building market still suffering from an under-occupancy rate of more than ten percent.

Into the mid-1990s Rodamco returned to health and once again to significant acquisitions, including the NLG 800 million takeover of France's Cegep real estate fund in 1996 and the NLG 1.3 billion acquisition of the assets of Britain's Imry project development and investment group in 1997. These acquisitions made it difficult, however, for the company to reach its goal of placing 25 percent of its assets portfolio in the Far East. This difficulty would, in fact, serve the company well: in

October 1997 many of the previously booming Asian economies collapsed, leading to a collapse in the region's real estate market as well.

While the booming economies of the U.S. and European markets helped protect Rodamco, its Asian portfolio would nevertheless suffer through the crisis, which would extend through 1998 and threaten to take down much of the world's economy as well. Rodamco was forced to write off nearly NLG 200 million of its Asian investment portfolio. As a result, Rodamco once again turned its interest to the European and U.S. market, as well as its Dutch home market.

In 1998 Rodamco began making preparations to split up its assets into four separately listed funds, three of which reflected the company's regional interests, that is, Europe, the Americas, and Asia, with the fourth representing the company's property management interests. In this way, Rodamco would be able to offer its investors the flexibility to place their shares in the region of their choice.

Principal Subsidiaries

Rodamco Europe BV (Rodamco Retail Nederland BV; Rodamco UK BV; Rodamco France BV; Rodamco Deutschland BV; Rodamco België BV; Rodamco Espana BV; Rodamco Hungary BV); Rodamco North America BV; Rodamco Pacific BV (Rodamco Australia BV; Rodamco Indonesia BV; Rodamco Philippines BV; Rodamco China BV; Rodamco Malaysia BV; Rodamco Singapore BV; Rodamco Thailand BV); RoProperty Services BV.

Further Reading

Billingham, Erica, "Rodamco UK to Go It Alone," *Estates Gazette,* June 13, 1998, p. 55.
"Rodamco Lijdt Pijn in Azie," *Dagblad de Limburger,* June 10, 1998, p. 2.
"Rodamco, Son of Robeco," *Economist,* March 10, 1979, p. 114.
Schutten, Henk, "Rodamco heeft klap doorstaan," *Het Parool,* August 6, 1994, p. 9.
Shapiro, Harvey D., "Professor Kortweg's Theory of 1992," *Institutional Investor,* December 1988, p. 177.
——, "Will Rodamco Find Redemption with Investors?," *Institutional Investor,* December 1990, p. 33.
Tamminga, Menno, "Vastgoedfonds Rodamco gaat winkelen op Engelse markt," *NRC Handelsblad,* February 8, 1997, p. 21.
van Rijsingen, Jos, "Rodamco erg optimistisch voor beleggers," June 12, 1997, p. 20.

—M. L. Cohen

Rohm and Haas Company

100 Independence Mall West
Philadelphia, Pennsylvania 19106-2399
U.S.A.
(215) 592-3000
Fax: (215) 592-3377
Web site: http://www.rohmhaas.com

Public Company
Incorporated: 1917
Employees: 11,592
Sales: $4.00 billion (1997)
Stock Exchanges: New York
Ticker Symbol: ROH
SICs: 2821 Plastics Materials, Nonvulcanizable
Elastomers & Synthetic Resins; 2869 Industrial
Organic Chemicals, Not Elsewhere Classified

Rohm and Haas Company is a specialty chemical company that is best known for the invention of Plexiglas, a product it no longer makes. Polymers and acrylics are its staple products, accounting for 70 percent of sales. Generating 20 percent of revenues are what the company calls "chemical specialties," which include agricultural chemicals, biocides, and ion exchange resins. The remaining 10 percent of sales derive from chemicals used in the manufacture of electronic materials, such as integrated circuits and printed wiring boards. Long active overseas, Rohm and Haas maintains 26 manufacturing plants in 20 countries, with half of company revenues being generated outside the United States.

Origins in Leather Softening

The story of Rohm and Haas begins in 1904 when a German man named Otto Röhm noticed that the stench from the local tannery was similar to the smell of the gas water produced by the Stuttgart Gas Works, where he was dissatisfied with his job as an analytical chemist. The bad odor of the gas water came from the combination of carbon dioxide and ammonia, and

Röhm wondered if these chemicals could be used to soften (bate) leather. At the time, tanners bated leather, as they had for centuries, with fermented canine feces which varied in composition and hence yielded inconsistent results. The unpredictability of the bating process, coupled with the inherently disgusting nature of the bating agent, made tanners eager to break with tradition. Nevertheless, not even the German chemical industry, the most advanced in the world at the time, understood the chemical nature of bating, and no satisfactory replacement for the bating agent had been discovered.

Hoping to make a name for himself in chemistry, Otto Röhm attempted to solve the problem. By 1906 he had developed a solution of gas water and salts that appeared to sufficiently soften leather. He then wrote to his friend Otto Haas, a young German who had immigrated to the United States a few years before. Haas agreed to join Röhm in his venture, with the understanding that Haas would bring the process back to the United States. The new bating agent was christened Oroh, derived from the two owners' initials.

By the time Haas returned to Germany, there was bad news waiting for him. Oroh was not performing as well as expected. The two men went back to the laboratory and studied the chemical process of bating, a process that had been debated a good deal in the leather industry. Röhm eventually concluded that the two prevailing schools of thought, the first, that the bating action was caused by bacteria and the second, that the action was caused by lime reacting with bate, were both partially correct. Reaction with a bate removed the lime used to dehair the hide, and then something in the organic bate softened the hide. But what?

In 1907 Eduoard Buchner discovered enzymes, the chemical compounds from living cells that caused fermentation. Röhm saw the applicability of Buchner's Nobel prize-winning work to his own research on leather chemistry. He realized that enzymes in organic bate softened leather by decomposing it, while his product merely delimed it.

Röhm set out to isolate enzymes cheaply, and by 1907 had applied for a patent for a bate made with enzymes derived from animal pancreas. Combining his own initials with the Greek word for juice, Röhm called the solution Oropon. He then developed a technique to measure the strength of Oropon so that the solution could be sold in standard strengths.

That year Röhm and Haas legally formed a German company bearing their names and established their first plant in Essenlingen, a city outside of Stuttgart. The first order of business was to manufacture large quantities of Oropon, which they made by squeezing animal pancreas in a manual press and collecting the juice.

As more tanneries began to use Oropon, Haas and Röhm were able to hire men to squeeze the pancreas for them, and turned their attention to marketing the product in Germany, England, and France. This early marketing effort established a style of salesmanship that still characterizes Rohm and Haas: technically proficient salesmen working closely with manufacturers. The company did so well that in 1909 Haas was able to return to open a branch in the United States. Due to the large number of tanneries in the area Haas decided to settle in Philadelphia.

By 1914 Haas was able to expand by opening a plant in Chicago in order to serve Midwestern tanners. His product line had increased to leather finishes, fat-liquors, and a mordant for dyeing. The timing of this expansion was fortunate since, with the advent of World War I, there was a dramatic need for leather chemicals to replace the ones that had come from Germany, still the world's leading chemical producer.

Formation of the U.S. Rohm and Haas in 1917

Röhm and Haas's chemicals were needed for army boots, yet the firm's German origins meant that it was under surveillance by the U.S. government. This was due to the fact that a few companies run by German-Americans were discovered to be in collaboration with the Kaiser's Germany. Although there was no evidence that Haas was a collaborator, the government nevertheless ordered that 50 percent of the company's stock (held jointly by the two owners) be sold to outsiders. A tanners' group, which was afraid of a disruption in the production of necessary leather chemicals, arranged to buy the shares—Röhm's share—and become a friendly partner with the firm. At the same time, Haas incorporated the U.S. branch as Rohm and

Haas Company, a separate company independent of the German firm (which itself evolved into Röhm GmbH, currently owned by Huls Group, which is owned by Veba A.G.).

While this legal maneuvering was taking place Rohm and Haas diversified into textile chemicals and then, in 1920, acquired one of its suppliers which was going out of business. That same year Haas purchased the North American rights to a German synthetic tanning agent and also supervised his company's expansion into synthetic insecticides. When the Great Depression began Rohm and Haas management's growth policies helped the company through this difficult period. The company expanded its product line but still concentrated on serving the leather and textile industries, which continued to produce goods albeit at a reduced rate throughout the depression. This, coupled with Haas's policy of high liquidity and low dividend payments, meant that the company not only survived the depression without layoffs but also managed to grow.

In 1927 Haas established a company called Resinous Products with a German scientist, Kurt Albert, who had developed a synthetic resin that was useful in making varnishes. Like Oropon this new product replaced a variable and unpredictable organic product. The new company was run separately from Rohm and Haas, and from its research into resins came a whole range of chemicals used in the coating and plywood industries.

Haas was satisfied with the success of his two business ventures but unhappy with the ownership agreement, so he arranged to purchase the shares held by the tanners' association and set up a trust for Röhm who had been deprived of his interest in Rohm and Haas Company.

1935 Discovery of Plexiglas

Haas reaped many benefits from his continued association with Röhm. One of them was the introduction of Plexiglas, which was discovered by accident in Röhm's laboratory located in Darmstadt, Germany. Röhm had started his work with acrylics in 1927. He had originally intended them for use as drying oils in varnishes, but soon realized that they could also be used as a coating for safety glass. In 1935 one of his research associates was experimenting with an acrylic polymer to see if it would bind two sheets of glass. Instead of acting as an adhesive, however, the polymer dried into a lightweight, clear plastic sheet that was immediately considered a promising glass substitute.

It was another three years until Plexiglas could be manufactured inexpensively and applications for it found. Röhm himself experimented with various uses: he replaced the glass in his car and even the glass in his spectacles with Plexiglas. Among the many uses Röhm's researchers explored were musical instruments. One such instrument, the acrylic violin, while striking in appearance produced a terrible sound. The Plexiglas flute was more successful. The most important applications of Plexiglas, however, were not for see-through flutes but for airplanes.

It was through such frivolities as the acrylic violin that company researchers learned how to stretch and shape Plexiglas sheets into cockpit enclosures. By 1934, when these techniques were almost perfected, the Nazi government had placed restrictions on the transmission of technical reports abroad. Haas got around these restrictions by sending one of his own chemists from the United States over to the company's German laboratory and having this man memorize the technology.

The U.S. Army Air Force was immediately interested in Plexiglas because it was lightweight and durable, and the design of war planes was altered to take advantage of this new, shatterproof material. Rohm and Haas, anticipating the entrance of the United States into the war, enlarged its capacity to manufacture Plexiglas so that the discovery made in Nazi Germany could benefit the Allies.

During the war Plexiglas accounted for two-thirds of Rohm and Haas's sales. In the last year before the war, sales had reached $5.5 million and by the end of the war this figure had swelled to $43 million. However, Plexiglas was not the company's only contribution to the war effort. In 1934 Herman Bruson, an employee hired by Haas, discovered a synthetic oil additive. It was not until the war that the significance of his discovery was revealed. Designers of military aircraft had difficulty finding a hydraulic fluid that would function at a sufficiently wide temperature range, until a review of potentially useful patents turned up Bruson's formula. Bruson often took credit for the Russian victory at Stalingrad since his hydraulic fluid kept Russian equipment from freezing, unlike the German hydraulic fluid which was rendered useless by the cold.

When the war ended Rohm and Haas experienced a dramatic decrease in the demand for Plexiglas and, as a result, the company struggled to expand the civilian uses of acrylic polymers. Plexiglas began to be used for illuminated signs and car lights, along with additives for coatings and fuel. The company's major undertaking in the decade following the war was building a huge plant in Houston, Texas, that was used to make the ingredients for acrylics. Along with acrylics the company also attempted to increase its holdings in markets for insecticides and fungicides. Exports, especially fungicides, were used to expand the company's European markets which Haas had previously left underdeveloped in order not to compete with his friend Röhm.

In 1959, the 50th year of Rohm and Haas's U.S. operation, Otto Haas retired, leaving the company in excellent shape. He was described as a hard-driving administrator who was, by turns, kind and unfair to his employees. One incident that typified Haas's attitude towards his employees took place during World War II when a new guard refused to allow Haas into a company munitions plant without a pass. Haas immediately fired the man and then rehired him the next day with a raise in pay. John Haas, Otto's son, was a less colorful president. John's style of administration stressed teamwork among the top executives, while his father's administration had stressed obedience.

Ill-Fated 1960s and 1970s Diversification

One of the first projects John Haas undertook was the ill-fated diversification into fibers and health products. At the time Rohm and Haas was the main producer of Plexiglas in the country, and had a successful product mix of paper, leather, textile, and agricultural chemicals. The expansion into fibers was motivated by the fear that one of the large chemical companies would challenge the company in the Plexiglas and acrylic

emulsion markets that Rohm and Haas dominated. Yet the challenge from the major chemical companies never materialized, and it was the measures taken to prevent the company from being hurt that caused the damage. The new divisions, health and fibers, were profitable in only one of their 14 years of existence.

The fibers division was especially costly. The company intended to enter the crowded field through technological breakthroughs and specialized markets; this was how it had succeeded with leather chemicals and acrylics. The company had high hopes for a new synthetic fiber named Anim/8, which was supposed to give fabrics added stretch without altering their appearance. Anim/8 failed in part because Rohm and Haas misunderstood the nature of the fibers market. While an aerospace manufacturer might pay the higher dollar amount for a superior hydraulic fluid, consumers did not care that Anim/8 had slight advantages over its competitors, Spandex and Lycra, when it was 20–30 percent more costly. Secondly, Rohm and Haas entered the field just as women were abandoning girdles and other undergarments that were a major market for stretch fabrics. The coup de grace was the crash of the entire synthetic fabric industry in 1975 when, as company president Vincent Gregory said, "You couldn't give the stuff away."

Bridesburg Tragedy

Earnings were depressed in the late 1960s and early 1970s as the losses incurred by the two new divisions canceled out the gains made by specialty chemicals. The company's troubles were not only of a financial nature, however. In 1975, just as the synthetic fabric industry was reaching its nadir, Rohm and Haas was deluged with bad publicity surrounding the deaths of workers who were exposed to a carcinogenic chemical called BCME. In 1962 a suspicious pattern of lung cancer deaths emerged at the company's Bridesburg, Pennsylvania, plant where resins for water purification purposes were produced. The company took measures to minimize employee exposure to chemicals at the plant, but its efforts were not sufficient. In 1974 the Health Research Group, founded by Ralph Nader, accused Rohm and Haas of concealing the dangers at the plant, 54 employees of which had died of cancer, probably induced by BCME.

Vincent Gregory, who had become president in 1970, was confronted with a difficult situation. Not only did he have a public relations fiasco on his hands, but he also had to accept some of the blame for the company's financial situation since he should have divested Rohm and Haas of the fiber and health divisions immediately upon his appointment. By 1975 the company began to lose money and there was speculation that Gregory would be relieved of his duties. However, the chairman of the board, John Haas, assumed his share of the blame for having started the ill-fated diversification into areas that were unfamiliar to the company. The board decided that Gregory had had "an expensive education," and retained him to help revitalize the company.

1980s Turnaround

The solution to the company's difficulties turned out to be a combination of cost-cutting (including extensive layoffs), the sale of unprofitable plants, and a few judicious acquisitions.

One acquisition was the Borg-Warner PVC modifier plant (the modifiers make PVC more malleable), a business that was inexpensive to purchase but that had not been profitable for a period of time. Rohm and Haas, with its experience in plastics, returned the plant to profitability by 1982, a year after it was purchased for $35 million.

The company decided to keep their slow-growing but profitable staples such as Plexiglas and paint and floor finishes. For faster growth it turned to herbicides, which the company started working with in the 1930s. A herbicide called Blazer, used on soybeans, had the largest sales in its specialized market. By building on its experience with resins Rohm and Haas made coatings for electronic components a part of its product line through the purchase of a 30 percent stake in Shipley Co. Inc. in 1982. These acquisitions marked the company's return to its early strategy: relying on businesses and product lines it was well acquainted with, concentrating on value-added chemicals, and increasing its market share rather than its size. This old-fashioned approach resulted in record profits. In 1985 sales were down slightly, but given the difficult economic conditions that existed that year for chemical companies the performance of Rohm and Haas was regarded by many industry analysts as satisfactory.

The late 1980s saw revenues increase to $2.66 billion by 1989, while earnings reached a record $230 million in 1988 before falling to $176 million in 1989. In mid-1988 Gregory retired as chairman and CEO, with J. Lawrence Wilson selected to succeed him. The popular Wilson—a cost-cutter quoted by the *Wall Street Journal* as saying, ''I'm probably a bit of a cheapskate''—had once been in charge of Rohm and Haas's European operations and had been serving as vice-chairman and director of corporate business.

1990s and Beyond

The recession of the early 1990s created more difficult conditions for Rohm and Haas, but the company managed to keep its earnings from falling as far as some of its rivals. The tight ship that Wilson ran helped make Rohm and Haas one of the most efficient specialty chemical companies in the industry. A net loss of $5 million in 1992 resulted from a reduction in earnings of $179 million caused by the adoption of a new accounting standard for retirement benefits. That year, sales surpassed the $3 billion mark for the first time, totaling $3.06 billion.

Meanwhile, Rohm and Haas made a number of moves in the 1990s to bolster and extend its existing product areas. In 1992 the company paid $175 million to Unocal Corp. for that firm's emulsion polymers business, which included acrylic polymer lines for paints, coatings, and varnishes. That same year, Rohm and Haas joined with Elf Atochem of France to form AtoHaas Americas, a joint venture that included the Plexiglas business of Rohm and Haas and Elf Atochem's Altuglas operation. In mid-1998, however, Rohm and Haas sold its half-interest in this venture to its partner, thus divesting itself of its most famous product. Though Plexiglas was long a company staple, Rohm and Haas had determined that its future lay in more specialty chemistry. In yet another 1992 move, Rohm and Haas issued $170 million in stock to purchase the 70 percent of Shipley it

did not already own, thereby lifting the company's profile in the field of chemicals for the electronics industry.

During 1993, when Rohm and Haas's net earnings fell to $107 million—in part because of the skyrocketing prices of raw materials used to make specialty chemicals—Wilson announced a reengineering effort aimed at further curtailing costs. By 1996 1,300 jobs were eliminated, mainly through attrition. Sales that year reached $3.98 billion, while record net earnings of $363 million reflected both the strength of the economy and the effectiveness of the restructuring. In July 1996 Rohm and Haas formed a 50–50 joint venture with Röhm, its one-time German sister company, called RohMax. The venture, which involved the manufacture and sale of petroleum additives, was short-lived, however, as Rohm and Haas sold its interest to Röhm less than two years later.

In June 1997 Rohm and Haas purchased a 25 percent stake (later increased to 31 percent) in Newark, Delaware-based Rodel, Inc.—an expansion of its electronic materials sector. Rodel specialized in precision polishing technology for the semiconductor and other industries. Additional electronic chemicals expansion came in the form of the 1997 acquisition of Pratta Electronic Materials, Inc., of Manchester, New Hampshire, which was involved in wiring board materials; and the January 1998 formation of a joint venture between Shipley and LG Chemical Ltd. of Korea for the manufacture and sale of microelectronic chemicals in Korea. Shipley owned 51 percent of the new entity.

Later in 1998 Rohm and Haas announced that for financial reporting purposes it had reorganized its businesses into three sectors: performance polymers, chemical specialties, and electronic materials. In July 1998 the company purchased a minority stake in Isagro Italia, a subsidiary of Isagro S.p.A. specializing in crop protection products. That same month Rohm and Haas announced a plan of succession to create the management team that would lead the company in the early 21st century. John P. Mulroney, president and chief operating officer since 1986, would retire at year-end 1998 and be replaced by J. Michael Fitzpatrick, who previously held the position of vice-president and chief technology officer. Wilson would retire by the end of 1999, with Rajiv L. Gupta, vice-president for electronic materials and Asia-Pacific, taking over as chairman and CEO. Rohm and Haas was long overdue for a major acquisition to build upon its solid core businesses, and it was quite possible that the new leadership would be more aggressive in pursuit of such a move.

Principal Subsidiaries

Rohm and Haas Capital Corporation; Rohm and Haas Credit Corporation; Rohm and Haas Equity Corporation; Rohm and Haas Finance Company; Rohm and Haas Latin America, Inc.; Rohm and Haas Performance Plastics Inc.; Rohm and Haas Puerto Rico Inc.; Rohm and Haas Texas Incorporated; Shipley Company L.L.C.; Rohm and Haas Australia Pty. Ltd.; Rohm and Haas (Bermuda), Ltd.; Rohm and Haas Holdings Ltd. (Bermuda); Rohm and Haas Quimica Ltda. (Brazil); Rohm and Haas Canada Inc.; Beijing Eastern Rohm and Haas Company, Limited (China; 60%); Rohm and Haas Colombia S.A.; Rohm and Haas France S.A.; Rohm and Haas Deutschland GmbH

(Germany); Rohm and Haas China, Inc. (Hong Kong); P.T. Rohm and Haas Indonesia; Rohm and Haas Italia S.r.l. (Italy); AgLead (Japan; 60%); Japan Acrylic Chemical Company, Ltd. (Japan); Rohm and Haas Japan K.K.; Shipley Far East Limited (Japan); Rohm and Haas Mexico S.A. de C.V.; Rohm and Haas New Zealand Limited; Rohm and Haas Philippines, Inc.; Rohm and Haas (Scotland) Limited (75%); Polytribo, Inc. (60%); Rohm and Haas Singapore (Pte.) Ltd.; Rohm and Haas Espana S.A. (Spain); Rohm and Haas Nordiska AB (Sweden); Rohm and Haas Taiwan Inc.; Rohm and Haas Chemical (Thailand) Ltd.; Duolite Int. Limited (U.K.); Rohm and Haas (UK) Limited; Shipley Europe Limited; Quimica Conosur Sociedad Anonima (Uruguay); Rohm and Haas Foreign Sales Corporation (U.S. Virgin Islands).

Principal Operating Units

Polymers and Resins; Monomers; Formulation Chemicals; Electronic Chemicals; Ion Exchange Resins; Biocides; Plastics Additives; Agricultural Chemicals.

Further Reading

Basralian, Joseph, ''Rohm & Haas: Little Cause for Pricing Panic,'' *Financial World,* November 8, 1994, p. 18.

Cochran, Thomas N., ''Rohm & Haas Co.: Its Key Parts Shine Brighter than Its Overall Record,'' *Barron's,* August 15, 1988, pp. 37–38.

Freedman, Alix M., ''Rohm & Haas Names Wilson As Next Chief,'' *Wall Street Journal,* December 3, 1986, p. 16.

Hochheiser, Sheldon, *Rohm and Haas: History of a Chemical Company,* Philadelphia: University of Pennsylvania Press, 1986.

Lane, Randall, ''Tough in the Clutch,'' *Forbes,* January 4, 1993, p. 107.

Peterkofsky, David, ''Rohm & Haas Deal Likely to Bolster Emulsions Hand,'' *Chemical Marketing Reporter,* December 16, 1991, pp. 5, 24–25.

Randall, William S., and Stephen D. Solomon, *The Tragedy of Bridesburg,* Boston: Little Brown, 1977.

Webber, Maura, ''The Price May Not Be Right for Rohm and Haas' Taste,'' *Philadelphia Business Journal,* May 9, 1997, p. 6.

Wood, Andrew, ''Rohm and Haas Sees Earnings Bloom, but Returns Disappoint,'' *Chemical Week,* September 21, 1994, pp. 42, 44.

—updated by David E. Salamie

SABRE Group Holdings, Inc.

4255 Amon Carter Boulevard
Fort Worth, Texas 76155
U.S.A.
(817) 931-1000
Fax: (817) 931-5582
Web site: http://www.sabre.com

Public Subsidiary of AMR Corporation
Incorporated: 1996
Employees: 8,500
Sales: $1.78 billion (1997)
Stock Exchanges: New York
Ticker Symbol: TSG
SICs: 4724 Travel Agencies; 6719 Holding Companies,
   Not Elsewhere Classified; 7372 Prepackaged
   Software; 7373 CAD Systems and Services; 7374
   Data Processing and Preparation; 7375 Information
   Retrieval Services; 7389 Business Services, Not
   Elsewhere Classified

SABRE Group Holdings, Inc. is a leading distributor of electronic travel-related products and services in the world. The company provides information technology (IT) solutions to the travel and transportation industry, which allow travel agents worldwide to electronically access booking information for airlines, railways, cruises, tours, hotels, and rental cars. In doing so, SABRE operates one of the largest privately owned real-time computer systems. The company also offers individual customers the option to set up travel reservations on the Internet, through its easySABRE and Travelocity services. A very large majority share of SABRE is retained by AMR Corporation, which is also the parent company of American Airlines.

The Early Years

Although SABRE Group Holdings, Inc. has only been a freestanding entity for a few years, its beginnings date back to 1946, when American Airlines brought computer technology to the travel industry with the Magnetronic Reservisor. One of the first computerized reservations systems, Magnetronic Reservisor was advanced to include basic computer file technology, so that a reservation agent could automatically check availability and sell or cancel seats. Later in the decade, American Airlines and IBM joined together to announce the Semi-Automated Business Research Environment—SABRE. The system cost an exorbitant $40 million, including expenses for initial research and development as well as the actual installation of the system.

After being introduced, SABRE evolved into an electronic gateway to provide access to reservation information about all types of travel-related items, including airlines, cars, and hotel reservations. The technology used to make reservations was also adapted to act as a means for customers to secure items such as flowers, theater tickets, and bon voyage gifts. Additionally, other services were provided to varied markets such as insurance providers, retailers, broadcasters, financial institutions, and manufacturers.

Growth in the 1980s and 1990s

In 1985, consumers with their own personal computers were introduced to the easySABRE system, which offered individuals the access and ability to make travel-related arrangements in the comfort of their own homes. For the most part, however, the company provided its services to corporate clientele. In fact, until 1988, SABRE only provided services to AMR Corporation (AMR)—its parent company—and one of AMR's other subsidiaries, American Airlines. SABRE's software and systems management services helped distinguish American as one of the most technologically advanced airlines.

At the end of the 1980s, however, SABRE's services began to be offered to other companies, including more than 130,000 travel agency terminals worldwide. The business gained by the addition of these travel agent customers came to represent over 50 percent of SABRE's IT revenue. By the mid-1990s, in fact, the company estimated that more than 40 percent of all travel agency airline bookings were made through SABRE, representing 65.8 percent of the company's revenues.

In the 1990s, SABRE outsourced its IT services to over 450 clients in 73 countries. Through this non-reservation-based area, SABRE worked with its parent, AMR, and with other transportation and financial services companies which had data problems. The company maintained three regional offices across the globe: one in Dallas/Ft. Worth, Texas; one in Sydney, Australia; and one in London, England. Each of these units was responsible for all aspects of SABRE's business and also provided support to local offices in their respective regions.

Independence in the Mid 1990s

April 1996 brought the beginnings of SABRE's repositioning as a separate legal entity from AMR. The decision to do so was made based on SABRE's position as one of the nation's largest computerized reservation services, as well as on its strong growth in the IT field. A prospectus was filed with the U.S. Securities and Exchange Commission which covered an initial public offering of as much as $550 million of Class A common stock. Approximately 20 percent of this stock was offered by late summer in 1996, causing parent company AMR's stock to jump 5.5 percent.

For 1996, SABRE's executives noted that the company's performance during its first year as a public company was the best in its history. Booking volumes outside the United States grew at a compound annual rate of 28 percent, and during 1996, the company introduced new products for both of their primary areas of business—Information Technology Solutions and Electronic Travel Distribution.

In the midst of continued positive change and growth for SABRE, one of its travel agent reservation software products was identified in an investigation of its fellow AMR subsidiary, American Airlines. Allegations were made that the company had programmed bias into the computer reservation system used by travel agencies, meaning that add-on software used when booking with SABRE's product was biased toward American's flights. The allegations were made against American by Northwest Airlines and The Department of Transportation in October 1996. Developed by SABRE, ''Preference MAAnager'' was said to have violated rules against building bias into computer reservation system displays. This particular software could reorder flights on the agents' screens to either highlight, or show only American flights—even though the Department of Transportation had made it illegal to bias a reservation system in 1984. In 1992, however, the department had decided that travel agents could install add-on software, such as ''Preference MAAnager'', from third-party vendors. A Department of Transportation administrative law judge later ruled that American was not technically violating federal rules by offering ''Preference MAAnager'' free to travel agents.

Innovations in Technology: 1996–98

In March 1996, the company joined together with Worldview Systems Corporation to create and introduce ''Travelocity'' (http://www.travelocity.com) for use by those individuals looking to make their own travel arrangements online. This Internet device communicated directly with the SABRE reservation system, and was soon the largest travel site on the World Wide Web that was not an airline-run site. The web site's system was developed for those individuals who wished to peruse and purchase travel industry offerings via their personal computers. Attempting to lure customers on to the web by offering extras that were not available from a traditional agent, Travelocity had a traveler-paging option to provide the customer with information about up to five flights. Other features available online through Travelocity included an instant travel reservation system, a lowest-fare finding device, electronic ticketing, consolidator fares for pre-purchased bulk sales to travel agencies, international booking capability, and a travel agency directory.

After its introduction, Travelocity soon registered in excess of 1.6 million members, and began logging about 15 million web-page hits monthly. This helped the site earn a ranking among the Top 25 web sites used at work, according to two separate research firms—RelevantKnowledge and Media Metrix. For every online booking transaction, SABRE received approximately five percent from the airline, car rental company, or hotel (arrangements made through a travel agent earned $3 per purchase). Travelocity made more than $100 million in travel-related bookings on the web in 1997—its first full year of operation. Industry analysts noted the sudden increase in travel industry revenues that originated online from sites like Travelocity, and predicted that the percentage of industry revenues garnered online would only continue to increase in coming years. According to the Travel Industry Association of America, the $827 million worth of bookings which were made in 1997 represented a mere one percent of earnings in the travel industry. The Travel Industry Association predicted this figure could reach five percent by the year 2000, however.

Also launched in 1996 was SABRE Business Travel Solutions (SABRE BTS), the company's online corporate travel management service. This gave business travelers and/or their travel counselors an easy and convenient way to make or change their own travel plans according to corporate policies through their computers, with 24-hour access and travel agency support. In addition to automating travel planning and reporting, SABRE BTS was also designed to cut up to 30 percent of the costs associated with business travel management. The products offered consisted of integrated modules for travel booking, policy compliance, and expense reporting. Enabled to track all travel-related spending ranging from pre-planning to reimbursement, businesses could save as much as 30 percent in total travel management costs by using SABRE BTS. An additional feature of SABRE BTS was an overhead map of the airplane with all available seats mapped out, noting such details as exit rows, first class, and location of the galley. Any specific seat could be reserved, changed, or canceled by the user at any time before travel. By March 1998, SABRE BTS was used by 120 customers—more than any other system for corporate travel management.

SABRE was awarded six patents in July 1997 by the U.S. Patent and Trademark Office, for new information management systems technology. Covered by the patents were the Availability Processor for reservation inventory control applications, CRSSim technology for business-generating computer reservations systems, the Shell Communication Interface Program, the SQL Mapper, and Interactive Analysis System—or Datawise—technologies.

In 1998, SABRE BTS was redesigned to offer new features such as the ability to access departure/arrival gates and times, restrictions, cancellation terms, and ticketing guidelines. The user could receive an automated pre-travel authorization of booked reservation via e-mail. Also included was an updated car rental and hotel booking process, which allowed travelers at separate company sites the ability to add personal preferences, like frequent flyer numbers.

Announcement of an alliance with MobileStar Network Corp. was made in August 1998, which would supply travelers greater mobile access to their travel plans through wireless high-speed access to the SABRE BTS online booking tool. Connecting through their laptop via a PC card device with a small radio and ethernet local area network adapter, the new SABRE system allowed users to connect with its network without the bother of having to find an analog phone line. That same month, SABRE BTS was upgraded once again to include information such as online hotel maps, weather information, and group travel-related information. SABRE also announced plans to team up with IBM to develop a "next generation" corporate travel management solution. This combination of SABRE BTS's policy compliance tools and online booking, and IBM's web-based Electronic Expense Reporting Solution, would provide the consumer with easy installation, ongoing customer support, and the convenience of web-access to all of their booking and expense reporting tools.

Planet SABRE, the industry's first Internet-enabled application for travel agencies, was introduced in early February 1997. Using the same technology that had been developed for Travelocity, Planet SABRE integrated every tool a travel agent could need into one customizable desktop display. This easy-to-use Microsoft Windows 95-based software suite greatly simplified the booking of travel arrangements. Through Planet SABRE or Turbo SABRE, the company offered a private web site for travel agents called SABRE AgentExplorer. The site featured a customized city pair chart showing the lowest published airfare available for those pairs of cities most frequented by their customers. The bulletin board also showed details regarding the fares, which included the previous lowest fare and the airline offering the fare, among others.

The End of the Century and Beyond

A $4.3 billion, 25-year contract between US Airways Group Inc. and SABRE Group Holdings, Inc. was signed December 12, 1997, selling off US Airways' information technology assets. The deal was arranged so that SABRE could run US Airways' data center operations, communications and help desks, and software applications, while also providing hardware and personnel. Additionally, the contract called for significant support by SABRE for the airline's ground and flight operations, maintenance and engineering activities, internal reservations system, sales, and cargo. All US Airways' software was scheduled to be converted to a SABRE application by 1999.

February 1998 brought another multimillion-dollar agreement for the company. ABACUS International Holdings Ltd. and SABRE signed a joint venture agreement called ABACUS International, a new Singapore-based travel services company. In this agreement, SABRE was to invest $139 million in cash, plus about $100 million in assets, while becoming the provider of computer reservations for the company. In a second agreement, over 7000 ABACUS travel agencies across the world adopted a customized version of the SABRE reservations service, which was called "ABACUS powered by SABRE." This venture added almost 150,000 terminals in more than 40,000 travel agencies in 108 countries, and positioned SABRE to become a key player in Asian travel technology.

In a 1998 effort to bolster customer confidence in the safety of SABRE's online reservation and purchase systems, the company introduced its Shop Safe Guarantee. By using the site's secure server, this service would be provided in the event of credit fraud and reimburse the individual's liability fee, up to $50. Travelocity joined the Better Business Bureau (BBB) online initiative, dedicated to ethical online marketing practices. The site's BBB online profile could be viewed through the Travelocity web site.

Throughout many different industries, SABRE has been recognized as a leader in information technology solutions and operations. Among the awards the company has earned are the ORSA Award—"The Best Operations Research Group in the Country (U.S.A.)" (first recipient), by the Operations Research Society of America; the Franz Edelman Award—"Best Operations Research Project in the World," by the Institute of Management Sciences; the *Network World* User Excellence Award; the UNIX-Expo Award—International Excellence in Open Systems; the Datamation Client Server Award; the Partners in Leadership Award; the Strategic Mission Award; the ESPRIT Award; the Object Management Group Object Application Award; the Business Traveler International Magazine Award; and the People's Voice Award.

Just a few short years after SABRE incorporated as a publicly held company, the company's personnel and expertise had led it to become one of the largest travel service providers in the world. Through its combination of strengths, SABRE was able to provide its customers with cutting-edge technology, and over 150 products and services that could be used by many groups ranging from airlines to foodservice providers. Its unequaled customer service offered support 365 days per year to those clients with SABRE intelligent workstations, communications networks, and printers. As the 20th century came to a close, SABRE seemed to be poised for further growth and innovation in the future.

Further Reading

Berry, Kate, "Travel Stock Jumps on Sales, Internet News," *Wall Street Journal,* April 20, 1998, p. B11L.

Browning, E. S., and Scott McCartney, "Heard on the Street: AMR's Offering of SABRE Shares Seeks to Tap Hidden Value in Reservations, Consulting Unit," *Wall Street Journal,* October 7, 1996, p. C2.

Caldwell, Bruce, "Separation Anxiety for IT?," *Information Week,* April 22, 1998, p. 18.

Flint, Perry, "SABRE Unleashed," *Air Transport World,* November 1996, pp. 95–96.

Foley, John, "SABRE's Challenge," *Information Week,* August 18, 1997, p. 83.

Mauer, Jennifer Fron, "AMR Strike Could Be a Boon for Online Travel Industry," *Dow Jones News Service,* February 14, 1997.

McCartney, Scott, "AMR Moves Closer to Spinoff of SABRE Group," *Wall Street Journal,* August 9, 1996, p. C2.

——, "U.S. Charges American Airlines Puts Bias Toward Carrier in Reservation Service," *Wall Street Journal,* October 29, 1996, p. A8.

—Melissa West

Schuff Steel Company

420 S. 19th Avenue
P.O. Box 39670
Phoenix, Arizona 85069
U.S.A.
(602) 252-7787
Fax: (602) 251-0315
Web site: http://www.schuff.com

Public Company
Incorporated: 1976
Employees: 645
Sales: $138.2 million (1997)
Stock Exchanges: NASDAQ
Ticker Symbol: SHUF
SICs: 1791 Structural Steel Erection; 3441 Fabricated
Structural Metal

Schuff Steel Company is one of the largest construction companies in the southwestern United States. The company is a rapidly growing, fully integrated fabricator and erector of structural steel for commercial and industrial construction projects such as high- and low-rise buildings and office complexes, hotels and casinos, convention centers, sports arenas, shopping malls, hospitals, dams, bridges, mines, and power plants. The company also specializes in the fabrication and erection of heavy steel plate, including large-diameter water pipe, water storage tanks, pollution control scrubbers, tunnel liners, pressure vessels, and a variety of customized projects. Other services offered include complete, turnkey steel construction, featuring engineering, detailing, shop fabrication, and field erection, which enables the company to pursue a fast track, design-as-they-go operating strategy. The company operates primarily in the southwestern United States, with a concentration in Arizona, Nevada, and southern California, as well as in South America and Mexico.

Through the First Decade: 1976–86

David Schuff had worked in the steel industry for a number of years. His son, Scott, worked during the summers with his father, beginning at the age of 13. After Scott's graduation from high school in 1976, the father and son team founded Schuff Steel Company. The company was originally created to operate as a steel erector, and it outsourced the fabrication portion of its projects. The company was incorporated that year in Arizona.

In 1983 the company helped build the Kaiser Clinic in Los Angeles. The following year, major projects for the company included The Quality Royale Hotel (San Diego, California); and, in Arizona, Thunderbird Samaritan Hospital (Glendale); Valley Lutheran Hospital and Desert Samaritan Hospital (Mesa); Arizona State University's Engineering Building (Tempe); and a test facility for Motorola (Chandler).

As the company grew, it began to integrate its services. To do so, in 1985, the company acquired its first fabrication facility, located in Phoenix. Major projects for 1985 included The Scottsdale Center (Scottsdale, Arizona); the Radisson Hotel Centennial (Mesa); a huge tower office complex at Central & Thomas Avenues (Phoenix); and a manufacturing facility for Fab 9 (Albuquerque).

Major projects in 1986 included a Southern California Edison facility (Irvine); the McKellar Research Center, the Intercontinental Hotel, and an International Rectifier building (San Diego) in California; a desalization plant (Yuma), Tucson's City Center, AT&T's Mesa Two Data Center and Hughes Helicopter's ADC Building (Mesa), and the Biltmore Financial Center I and the Civic Plaza Expansion (Phoenix) in Arizona.

Almost Bust: 1987

In 1987 the company hit hard times. In a 1997 interview in the *Business Journal,* Scott Schuff said, ''We were probably three hours away from going out of business. In a year-and-a-half, we lost $3.5 million.'' The losses were attributed to a slump in the real estate market and a communications breakdown between project managers and top management, among other things. Schuff responded by beginning weekly project status meetings and diversifying the company's markets and projects. Major projects for the year included, in California, McDonnell Douglas Building 58 and Building 5 (Long Beach); Plaza Alicante (Garden Grove); Hughes Research Laboratory (Malibu); Palomar Hospital (Escondido); Ralph's Grocery Distribution Center (Los Angeles); a Nordstrom department store

---

Company Perspectives:

Schuff Steel Company is a rapidly growing steel fabrication and erection company providing a fully integrated range of steel construction services, including design engineering, detailing, joist manufacturing, fabrication and erection, and the level of project management expertise necessary to accommodate fast track, "design-as-you-go" projects.

(Santa Ana); and Chesapeake Park Plaza and the Omni International Hotel (San Diego). Projects in Arizona included Broadway Proper Hilton Hotel (Tucson); Flagstaff Medical Center (Flagstaff); an SRP Service Center (Tolleson); Western Savings Financial Plaza (Mesa); and Western Savings Corp. Headquarters, Phoenix General Hospital, Camelwest Plaza, Talley Plaza, and Camel Point Urban Complex (Phoenix).

Concrete Growth: 1988–98

The company jumped forward again after its 1987 slump, with major projects in 1988 including a Veterans Administration Hospital and General Dynamics (San Diego); Jamboree Center II (Irvine); Scottsdale Princess Hotel (Scottsdale); and Mountain Bell Tower and the Interstate 17/Papago Interchange (Phoenix). The following year, the company built the Golden Nugget Hotel & Casino (Las Vegas); Waddell Dam Siphon Pipe; Riverside (in California) In-Patient Hospital; the San Diego Corporate Center; and SRP Information Systems Building and The Mercado (Phoenix).

In 1990 the company began doing earnest business in Las Vegas, working on the Holiday Casino expansion, the Flamingo Hilton, and the Holiday Riverboat. Work in Phoenix continued, with the Biltmore Fashion Center's Phase III and Phoenix Plaza Tower's Phase II construction commencing. In southern California, the company built Alvarado Hospital in San Diego and Western Digital LSI II in Irvine. The Pima County Office Building in Tucson and Scottsdale Fashion Square were among the company's other large projects in Arizona that year.

David Schuff turned over the company's operations to Scott in 1991, naming the younger Schuff president and chief executive officer, while David remained as chairman. In the Las Vegas market, the company moved away from casino work for the year, constructing Hughes Center Buildings A and B and Valley Bankwest, but picked up a contract for the Flamingo Laughlin Hotel and Casino in that Colorado River city. Major engineering and construction projects included Roosevelt Dam's lake tap, shaft, and tunnels; Sky Harbor International Airport Terminal 4 Parking Garage in Phoenix; and the Palo Verde Nuclear Plant Administration Buildings. Other major projects that year included the NEC Mega Line and Energy Center Buildings (Sacramento) and the Puritan Bennett Office Building (Carlsbad) in California; Smith's Grocery Warehouse (Tolleson), The Shops at Arizona Center (Phoenix), and The Scottsdale Galleria in Arizona; and a cereal manufacturing plant in Albuquerque.

Major projects for 1992 included the Sharp Hospital's Women's Center (San Diego), Community Hospital of Chula Vista, and Kaiser Regional Data Center (Corona) in California; and McCarran Airport, the Sands Hotel & Casino Convention Center, and the Minami Tower, all in Las Vegas. Total revenue for the year reached $47 million, with a net income of $325,000. The following year, with projects like the Children's Hospital (San Diego) and the Jet Propulsion Laboratory's Observation Lab (Pasadena) in California, three major construction sites in Henderson, Nevada, Sierra Health Services in Las Vegas, and a solid waste station in Phoenix, the company's total revenue for 1993 grew to $58.6 million.

In 1994 the company experienced more growth, building Barney's of New York (Beverly Hills), an Anheuser Busch Plant (Ontario), and a Smith's Grocery Distribution Center & Dairy facility (Riverside) in California; a Ramada Express (Laughlin), Gary's Wild Wild West Casino (state line), and the rehabilitation of the Tropicana Hotel, the MGM Grand Hotel & Casino, and Boulder Station Hotel & Casino (Las Vegas) in Nevada; a blast simulator at White Sands (New Mexico), and the Incredible Universe superstore in Phoenix. Total revenue climbed another ten million, to $68.2 million, with a net income of $3.8 million.

The year 1995 brought the company more work in Las Vegas, as it built the Texas Gambling Hall, Arizona Charlie's Casino, and the long-awaited Hard Rock Cafe Hotel. Skywest Airlines contracted the company to build a facility in Salt Lake City, Utah. California added a state compensation insurance fund building in Santa Ana and a NUMMI Bumper facility in Fremont. Arizona construction included the Salt River 21-inch-diameter siphon pipe (Mesa), Motorola's Building 99 and Schreiber Foods' warehouse (Tempe), SRP's Navajo Maintenance Facility (Page), and the St. Joseph Medical Center (Phoenix). In October of that year the company received a $25 million contract from Intel Corp. for the steel erection work on the latter's $1.4 billion chip fabrication facility in Phoenix, Arizona, moving Schuff to the top of the steel erector company rankings in the 1995 Top 600 Specialty Contractors List. The project required the fabrication of 10,000 tons of structural steel. Total revenue for 1995 moved forward to $62.1 million, with a net income of $2.5 million.

Big projects in 1996 included the Woodland Hills Theatre Complex, a Toyota distribution center (Ontario), and the Gates Computer Science Building (Palo Alto) in California; the Maingate Center (Tucson); The Galleria at Sunset Mall (Henderson) and Sunrise Mountain View, the Howard Hughes Office Building, The Orleans Hotel & Casino, and the State of Nevada's Department of Water & Power Poles facility (Las Vegas) in that state; and the Vandenburg Air Force Base Launch Complex. Total revenue for 1996 skyrocketed to $103.9 million, with a corresponding jump in net income to $10.1 million.

What About Barry and BOB?: 1997–98

In January 1997 the company acquired 100 percent of the outstanding capital stock of B & K Steel Fabrications, Inc., a steel fabricator headquartered in Gilbert, Arizona, for $1.2 million in cash and promissory notes. By July the company was one of the largest privately held companies in Arizona. On July 7, the company reincorporated in Delaware, shifting its status from an S Corporation. Schuff Steel completed an initial public offering, raising $16 million, which it used to purchase new equipment for its new Gilbert fabrication facility and to fund acquisitions. The stock began trading on the NASDAQ under the ticker symbol SHUF.

In August 1997 the company received a $6 million contract for the design and fabrication of 4,000 tons of structural steel for the expansion of an aluminum smelter facility owned by Aluar (Aluminios Argentinos) in Puerto Madryn, Argentina, a port city on the Atlantic Ocean, 400 miles south of Buenos Aires. The following month the company was awarded $15.7 million in new contracts for five steel fabrication and erection projects. Two of the projects were started in October 1997. The first was a subcontract to fabricate and erect the structural steel for an addition to a laboratory facility in Thousand Oaks, California, for Baxter International Inc., a large medical technology supplier. The second was to fabricate and erect the steel for the expansion of an existing manufacturing facility for Sony Corp. in San Diego. The third project, started in December 1997, called for the fabrication and erection of the 380,000-square-foot City Mills Mall in Orange, California, which required 1,200 tons of structural steel. In January 1998 erection began on eight 240-foot-long, 26-foot-deep trusses as part of the company's contract for the fabrication and erection of steel for Bakersfield Arena, an ice hockey rink for the expansion of the Bakersfield Convention Center in California. The final and largest of the five projects, begun in mid-1998, had Schuff Steel providing the fabrication and erection of all the structural steel for a new U.S. Federal Building and Courthouse in downtown Phoenix, Arizona. The project required 3,100 tons of structural steel, which framed an atrium attached to an eight-story concrete frame building.

Exciting projects in 1997 included the Paris Hotel & Casino and the New York, New York Casino Coaster Platform in Las Vegas, as well as Sky Harbor International Airport's Terminal 4 (Barry Goldwater Terminal) expansion. The major project of the year, however, was constructing the steel framework of the massive Bank One Ballpark, located in downtown Phoenix (lovingly referred to as BOB). A state-of-the-art baseball stadium, BOB featured a Schuff-built fully retractable roof and massive scoreboards and would become the home playing field for Major League Baseball's 1998 expansion team, the Arizona Diamondbacks franchise. Total revenue for 1997 was $138.2 million, with a net income of $8.7 million.

In March 1998 the company began building a 50-story replica of the Eiffel Tower in a $14 million project at the Paris Hotel & Casino in Las Vegas. The project required more than 2,000 tons of structural and plate steel, 300,000 bolts, 264 flights of stairs, and approximately 180,000 man-hours for fabrication and erection. The tower was erected over the casino, with three of the four tower legs penetrating into the casino area. Each 28-foot square tower leg was fabricated in modules that were shipped to the project site for ground assembly prior to erection. The base is 193 feet square, with the tower rising 540 feet above ground and featuring restaurants and retail areas at the 104-foot elevation and an observation deck at the 460-foot level.

In June 1998 the company completed a private placement of $100 million. Net proceeds were used to repay debts and finance part of the acquisition of Addison Structural Services, Inc. The Albany, Georgia-based privately held company was purchased

for approximately $59.4 million. The acquisition provided Schuff Steel with structural steel fabrication and erection services and capability for manufacturing short- and long-span joists, trusses, and girders for industrial and commercial projects; as well as fabrication facilities in Albany, Georgia, and Lockhart, Florida, and a joist manufacturing plant in Quincy, Florida.

In July 1998 the company and its subsidiaries were awarded five contracts worth more than $7.2 million, including a train station and parking structure in Millbrae, California; orange juice storage tanks in Florida; casino expansions in North Las Vegas and Reno, Nevada; a one million-square-foot liquor distribution center in Hialeah, Florida; a student center and library for Soka University in Aliso Viejo, California; and multiple-screen theaters in Cherry Hill, New Jersey and Fairfield, California.

Early in September of that year, the company completed the acquisition of Six Industries, Inc., a privately held company headquartered in Houston, Texas. The company and its subsidiaries were purchased for an aggregate price of $17.9 million in cash and promissory notes. The acquisition included: the Aitken, Inc. subsidiary, which manufactured strainers, filters, separators, and other types of measuring equipment used in the oil, gas, petrochemical, and pipeline industries, as well as provided a wide array of steel fabrication services and other related products to the oil, gas, and petrochemical industries; and The Rowell Welding Works, a division that manufactured pressure vessels and related fabrication for chemical and petrochemical plants, refineries and power plants, oilfields, water treatment, and aggregate handling facilities. The acquisition also included The Marauder Company, a division that fabricated structural steel for large industrial contractors in Houston and other locations situated near the Gulf of Mexico, and was also a key supplier of structural steel products to Fluor Daniel for petrochemical facilities. In addition, Marauder provided structural steel for other major international design firms. Wayne Harris, president and CEO of Six Industries, agreed to stay on to continue to manage Six's day-to-day operations. The acquisition further expanded Schuff Steel's geographic and market diversity, giving the company Marauder's long-term relationships in the petrochemical market, access to profitable new industrial equipment markets, and additional fabrication capacity.

By the end of 1998, with 95 percent of the steel fabrication and erection industry being highly localized ''Mom and Pop'' shops, Schuff's unique position in the steel industry, its aggressive growth strategy, and its strong competitive advantages were expected to be key factors behind its continued financial and operational growth as it headed into the 21st century.

Principal Subsidiaries

Addison Structural Services, Inc.; Quincy Joist; Six Industries, Inc.

Further Reading

''*The Arizona Republic* AZ Inc. Column,'' *Knight-Ridder/Tribune Business News,* July 9, 1998, p. OKRB981900C.
Balzer, Stephanie, ''Fabricator Steels Against Failure,'' *Business Journal—Serving Phoenix & the Valley of the Sun,* October 10, 1997, p. 41.

——, "Public Companies Prep for October Forum," *Business Journal—Serving Phoenix & the Valley of the Sun,* October 3, 1997, p. 22.

"Correction," *American Metal Market,* January 22, 1997, p. 2.

Gilbertson, Dawn, "Arizona Steel Company Issues Public Stock Offering," *Knight-Ridder/Tribune Business News,* May 13, 1997, p. 513B0994.

Hassler, Darrell, "Schuff Steel Acquires Southeastern Facilities," *American Metal Market,* June 12, 1998, p. 3.

——, "Schuff Steel in $50.6M Deal with Addison," *American Metal Market,* May 27, 1998, p. 4.

Kravetz, Stacy, "Schuff Steel Stock Skids 26% on News of 2nd-Period Loss," *Wall Street Journal,* August 14, 1998, p. B4(W)/A4(E).

"Phoenix-Based Schuff Steel to Build Eiffel Tower Replica," *Knight-Ridder/Tribune Business News,* March 3, 1998, p. 303B0941.

Rose, Frederick, "Schuff Steel to Buy Addison Structural in Prelude to Planned Acquisition Spree," *Wall Street Journal,* March 20, 1998, p. B7C(E).

Sacco, John E, "Schuff Steel to Build Eiffel Tower Replica," *American Metal Market,* March 13, 1998, p. 3.

"Schuff Steel Amends Offer, Adds Shares," *American Metal Market,* June 18, 1997, p. 6.

"Schuff Steel Co.," *New York Times,* May 22, 1998, p. C4(N)/D4(L).

"Schuff Steel Co.," *Wall Street Journal,* May 11, 1998, p. B14.

"Schuff Steel Company Completes Acquisition of Six Industries, Inc.," *PR Newswire,* September 3, 1998, p. 903CGTH019.

"Schuff Steel Extends Expiration Date of Exchange Offer," *PR Newswire,* September 4, 1998, p. 904CGF027.

"Schuff Steel Gets 5 Pacts," *American Metal Market,* July 10, 1998, p. 3.

"Schuff to Acquire Addison," *Wall Street Journal,* May 22, 1998, p. B2(E).

"Schuff Wins Five Pacts Valued at $15.7 Million," *American Metal Market,* September 24, 1997, p. 3.

Tulacz, Gary J., "Schuff Steel Co: In the Chips," *ENR,* October 16, 1995, p. 81.

—Daryl F. Mallett

Schwan's Sales Enterprises, Inc.

115 West College Drive
Marshall, Minnesota 56258-1747
U.S.A.
(507) 532-3274
Fax: (507) 537-8450
Web site: http://www.schwans.com

Private Company
Incorporated: 1948 as Schwan's Dairy
Employees: 6,000
Sales: $2.9 billion (1997 est.)
SICs: 2024 Ice Cream & Frozen Desserts; 2037 Frozen
   Fruits, Fruit Juices & Vegetables; 2038 Frozen
   Specialties, Not Elsewhere Classified

A highly successful dairy and frozen food company, Schwan's Sales Enterprises, Inc. holds 90 percent of the national school market for frozen pizzas and boasts one of the most extensive home delivery operations in the country, with a truck fleet exceeding 2,000. The trucks deliver to customers in 49 states a variety of frozen foods, including ice cream, pizza, meats, vegetables, and juices. From the 1960s through the early 1990s, revenues for the holding company have doubled virtually every three to four years, due to a wise acquisition policy and a continually expanding truck fleet and sales force. Sales growth has since been more moderate, but steady. Schwan's is comprised of some dozen operating divisions, the most successful of which is Tony's Pizza, the number two frozen pizza in the United States, behind Tombstone. The driving force behind most of the company's long and healthy history was consummate entrepreneur Marvin M. Schwan, who left behind a $1.3 billion estate when he died in 1993. The Schwan family still owns the company.

Family Enterprise from the Start

Marvin's father, German immigrant Paul Schwan, entered the ice cream business following World War I when he accepted a delivery job with a creamery in the southwest Minnesota town of Marshall. In 1944 the elder Schwan was financially able to launch his own venture. That year he bought half interest in a milk bottling plant, which happened to be adjacent to the Marshall Ice Cream Company, his most recent employer. The new firm, Neisen and Schwan's Dairy, was a family enterprise from the start, founded on personalized delivery service to area homes. At the age of 14, Marvin accepted a milk delivery route and supplemented his income on weekends by packaging ice cream bars, fudgesicles, and popsicles. Realizing that he could boost his productivity by 25 percent, Marvin purchased a bag-opening machine with his own funds; his father recognized both the advancement in productivity and Marvin's initiative and reimbursed his son for the capital expenditure. By 1948 the business, which both supported local dairy farmers and provided a valuable service to households, was well known and respected. With the help of Marvin's own investment, Paul bought out his partner, renamed the business Schwan's Dairy, and opened a new plant in town. Paul's wife, Alma, assisted in the daily operations by running the Schwan's Dairy Store, a small restaurant that offered homecooked meals and Schwan's dairy products. Marvin left Marshall at this time to attend a two-year college, but returned on weekends to assist with the business. His father, meanwhile, had begun experimenting with surplus cream and perfected his own recipes for chocolate and vanilla ice cream, which he soon began manufacturing in 2½-gallon containers.

Marvin's decision to return full-time to the business in 1950 was perhaps the single greatest reason for the modest dairy's development into a national concern. After barely weathering a retail price freeze on milk during 1951–52, Schwan's swiftly rebounded when Marvin discovered that he could undercut the comparatively higher ice cream prices of neighboring towns. Experienced in home delivery and alert to the current rise in freezer purchases by rural families, he had only to purchase a truck and establish a route. Within a year, he added a second truck to his delivery operation and quickly began to promote the Schwan's name as synonymous with the best ice cream—now available in a dozen flavors—in southern Minnesota. Distinctive yellow trucks, the simple cursive logo, the round returnable ice cream containers, and the courteous assistance of the drivers helped attract a remarkably loyal and longstanding customer base.

By the mid-1950s Schwan, faced with the realities of high overhead for his growing fleet and sales force, positioned the company for greater profits and a greatly expanded market by adding first a depot in the southeast portion of the state and then a freezer-warehouse in the central portion. Schwan's faced its second major crisis in 1957 when the Redwood River reached flood stage in Marshall, severely damaging equipment in the central plant and halting operations for four days. A federal disaster loan allowed the business to recover, which it did rapidly under Marvin, who had effectively become the company's general manager. By the early 1960s sales had easily surpassed $4 million and the full-time workforce had swelled from the original five to well over 100. The company met the challenge of another crisis in 1962, that of a nearby fire which threatened to destroy the plant's north wall and with it a 10-ton condenser, and redoubled its efforts to grow into a stable, thriving company. The site of the auto dealership that was destroyed by the fire was soon purchased by Schwan's to allow for an expanded headquarters and by 1963, round-the-clock operations were initiated, elevating ice cream production to some 11,000 gallons daily.

Acquisitions Began in 1963

In *Self-Made: The Stories of 12 Minnesota Entrepreneurs,* authors Carol Pine and Susan Mundale accord special significance to the year 1963 for the company. Aside from marking the 15th anniversary of the business as a solely owned family enterprise, 1963 was the year in which Marvin adopted a long-term acquisition policy to ensure that the company could experience aggressive growth while remaining profitable. Among the first acquisitions were a prepared sandwich company and a condensed fruit juice company, both of which were incorporated under the new holding name of Schwan's Sales Enterprises, Inc. Two years later, Schwan discovered that one of his Wisconsin salesmen had begun carrying Roma brand frozen pizzas on his route. With the rising popularity of prepared pizza, the small label promised additional diversity and sales for the delivery company and so Schwan signed a contract to market the pizzas in a four-state region. By 1969—the year of Paul Schwan's death—pizza sales were approaching those of ice cream and, consequently, Schwan was eager to expand his territory. Prevented from doing so by Roma, Schwan placed an ad in the *Wall Street Journal* disclosing his interest in purchasing a complete pizza manufacturing plant. He received a response from Kansas-based Tony's Pizza. After determining that the Tony's pizza recipe required improvement, Schwan acquired the company in 1970, made the necessary alterations, and then launched the division with a somewhat new marketing scheme: selling the pizzas via a special fleet of trucks directly to retail stores rather than chain warehouses. As in his home delivery routes, the emphasis was on providing the customer with quality, freshness, and service. Each driver was given the latitude to enhance sales for his route and profits for each route were tallied daily, weekly, and monthly.

The pizza acquisition proved a resounding success and fueled much of the company's growth during the 1970s, despite heavy competition from Jeno's and Totino's. Another turning point for the company came in 1974, in the wake of a devastating fire at the ice cream plant. Schwan saw the tragedy as an opportunity to rebuild in a more suitable location and almost moved his business. Fortunately for the citizens of Marshall (25 percent of whom now work for him), Schwan decided to recommit himself to the community that had helped him to prosper. By 1979 he had built his delivery system into a 1,000-truck fleet. Ever conscious of the bottom line, he converted the entire fleet to LP gas at this time to combat the rising costs for conventional fuel. Finally, he ended the decade by diversifying beyond the food business with the acquisition of Syncom Magnetic Media, a computer tape and diskette manufacturer based in Mitchell, South Dakota.

As Schwan's entered the 1980s, roughly half of its sales came from pizza. The remaining half came from its line of home-delivered products, which had now expanded to include meats, frozen fish, bread, frozen fruit, and french fries in addition to a full line of dairy products. While the ongoing success of the latter half of operations was virtually ensured, the former—represented primarily by Tony's—was pitted against serious Minnesota rivals Totino's (acquired by Pillsbury in 1975) and Jeno's. Totino's, benefiting from the Pillsbury name and a large sales apparatus, led the national market share with 22 percent, followed by Tony's and Jeno's, each with approximately 13 percent of the market. The competition between the big three had been fierce for several years, and in 1981 Schwan's launched a serious attack on the number one position with a highly controversial ad campaign, which playfully hinted that the other leading pizza manufacturers employed a glue-like substance in their cheese while only Tony's contained 100 percent real cheese. Despite outcries from its competitors, Schwan's benefited from the exposure, and the campaign went on to win the top Minnesota advertising award of the year. However, 1981 was also the year in which the company sustained its greatest personal loss, the death of an employee and the injury of eight others following an anhydrous ammonia leak at the main plant.

Expanded into Institutional Pizza in the Mid-1980s

By the mid-1980s, with sales approaching $500 million, Schwan entered the institutional pizza market and quickly carved out his own sizeable niche, thereby circumventing the need for competing head-to-head, at high cost, in the retail grocery market. Schwan had discovered that cheese surpluses were being delivered to the nation's public schools by the Department of Agriculture. He reasoned, correctly, that the schools would be willing to trade their allotments for discounted school lunch pizzas, to be manufactured by Schwan's with the government cheese. Schwan greatly strengthened his foothold in this new market with the acquisition in 1986 of his major school lunch competitor, Sabatasso Foods. In 1988 he established a virtual monopoly with the additional acquisition of Better Baked Pizza. During this same period of rapid growth, Schwan had instituted a portable pricing and inventory system that squeezed even greater profit margins from his home delivery business. As always, Schwan's intent was to maintain his business as a self-financing operation, ensuring the private company's longevity and eminent profitability.

In 1982, Pine and Mundale wrote that although "almost every other kind of home delivery system has gone the way of the dinosaur, Schwan's Sales Enterprises has grown and prospered." The statement remained just as true more than a decade later, due to Schwan's business acumen, the quality of his products, and, probably above all, the effectiveness of his drivers. Although the job of driving for Schwan's was notoriously rigorous, involving long hours and considerable physical labor, Schwan was known as an extremely fair boss and, with one-third of all executives drawn from the Marshall workforce, employee loyalty was strikingly high.

In 1992 Schwan's acquired two more companies, bringing its total to 12. One, Monthly Market, was a for-profit food cooperative catering to fund-raising groups; the other, Panzerotti, was a stuffed pastry business. Although no annual revenues were disclosed with either of the sales, both businesses would likely benefit by their integration with the Schwan's delivery system. Other Schwan's businesses at the time included a pastamaker and an egg roll company. Also by this time, according to a 1998 article in *Minneapolis St. Paul City-business,* the company owned three leasing companies: Business Credit Leasing, established in 1979, and Manifest Group, founded in 1988, both leased office equipment; while Secured Funding Source was established in 1991 as a lessor of medical equipment. In March 1993 Schwan's expanded its pizza business through the purchase of San Diego-based Chicago Brothers Frozen Pizza, makers of deep-dish pizza.

Newsworthy in the Mid-1990s

The normally secretive company found itself much in the news in the mid-1990s. First, Marvin Schwan died suddenly of a heart attack in May 1993 at the age of 64. Marvin's brother Alfred took over as chairman, CEO, and president. Alfred Schwan had been the company's director of manufacturing in Salina, Kansas, where Schwan's had a pizza plant. He soon had to contend with a public relations and litigation nightmare following a nationwide outbreak of salmonella poisoning in September and October 1994, an outbreak eventually traced to contaminated Schwan's ice cream, which the company quickly recalled. An investigation by state and federal health authorities concluded that a tanker truck containing pasteurized ice cream pre-mix had not been washed out after previously carrying raw, unpasteurized eggs. Officials later estimated that more than 240,000 people became ill as a result of eating the tainted product, a figure that company officials disputed as being eight times too high. The company was cleared of direct wrongdoing in the case as it had purchased the pre-mix from a supplier and an independent trucking firm had made the delivery. Nonetheless, before officials allowed the ice cream plant to reopen in early November 1994, Schwan's had to agree to change some of its procedures. The company began using only company-leased "dedicated" tankers to truck in the ice cream pre-mix, began

pasteurizing the pre-mix on its arrival at the plant, and began testing the pre-mix and the finished product for salmonella. It was also reported that month that Schwan's had paid out almost $1 million to thousands of customers who signed a legal release stating that they would not sue the company. In February 1995 a tentative settlement was reached in a class-action lawsuit whereby Schwan's agreed to pay from $80 to $75,000 to customers who became ill after eating the contaminated ice cream. The amount would depend upon the severity of the illness. Schwan's estimated in 1996 that the total number of people filing claims would be about 30,000. By that time sales of the company's ice cream products had returned to previous levels, indicating that it had survived the crisis.

In March 1995 Ken Noyes was named president and chief operating officer of Schwan's. Noyes, a 12-year company veteran who had previously headed up the company's leasing operations and its food service division, became the first nonfamily member in the post of president. Also in 1995 Schwan's leasing operations expanded through the acquisition of Universe Leasing, a lessor of tractor trailers. The company made further inroads into the financial world in 1995 when it established Spectrum Commercial Services Inc., a Bloomington, Minnesota-based private lender offering alternative financing for companies unable to have all of their needs met by a bank or other traditional lender.

Right on the heels of the salmonella crisis came a family feud resulting in more unwelcome publicity. Marvin Schwan's will left two-thirds of his 100 percent holding in Schwan's Sales Enterprises to the Marvin M. Schwan Foundation, a funder of conservative Lutheran religious and educational causes. It also called for the company to purchase the foundation's shares after his death. Alfred Schwan and the company board approved a plan to repurchase the stock through payments totaling $1.8 billion spread out over 15 years, with a final balloon payment of $600 million in 2009. Four children of Marvin Schwan filed a federal lawsuit in May 1995 against Schwan's, Alfred Schwan, and Larry Burgdorf, the latter two being trustees of Marvin Schwan's estate. The suit contended that the amount being paid to the foundation was inflated by more than $250 million and jeopardized the financial health of the company. The deal also restricted the heirs' ability to cash in their company shares until after the 15 years were concluded; by that time, the children feared that Schwan's would be reduced to a shell of its former vibrant self. They also contended that the trustees had unfairly changed their father's estate plan. Alfred Schwan and Burgdorf countered that they were merely carrying out Marvin Schwan's wishes and had created a deal that was best for the company and its family owners. In November 1997 a settlement was reached in the lawsuit. While terms were not disclosed, it was reported that the descendants of Marvin Schwan remained the owners of Schwan's and that the plaintiffs were allowed to sell some of their shares in the company.

In February 1998 Noyes became the third CEO in company history when he replaced Alfred Schwan in that position. Schwan remained chairman. Schwan's, back in its more familiar reclusive mode, was looking for growth overseas in the late 1990s. It had already established itself as a market leader in the frozen pizza sector in Europe, having entered the U.K. market in 1992. Schwan's then in 1997 acquired La Roue du Pays d'Auge, a

French maker of wood-fired pizzas as well as pasta. That year the company began selling its Freschetta brand of bake and rise frozen pizza in Europe, after the product was a runaway hit in the United States following its 1995 debut. Schwan's also entered the Malaysian market in 1997 when it began selling Tony's pizza there. It appeared that the Schwan's of the 21st century would have an increasingly international flair.

Further Reading

Blemesderfer, S. C., and Eric J. Wieffering, "Pizza Hut Delivers Blow to Schwan's," *Corporate Report Minnesota,* February 1992.

Clark, Don, "Stuck: Pizza Firm Scolded for Glue Comparison," *St. Paul Pioneer Press,* January 30, 1981.

Emerson, Dan, "Soft-Serve Financing," *Minneapolis St. Paul City-business,* February 6, 1998.

Fritz, Michael, "Schwan's Song," *Forbes,* April 3, 1989.

Gibson, Richard, "Dirty Trucks May Have Hurt Ice Cream Mix," *Wall Street Journal,* October 21, 1994, p. B1.

Jones, Jim, "Tainted Pizza Ad Wins Top Award," *Minneapolis Star,* June 25, 1981.

——, "3 State Frozen Pizza Firms Fight to Become Big Cheese," *Minneapolis Star,* November 13, 1978.

Kennedy, Tony, "Legacy of Litigation," *Minneapolis Star Tribune,* December 10, 1995, p. 1D.

——, "Marvin Schwan's Heirs Settle Lawsuit," *Minneapolis Star Tribune,* November 29, 1997.

——, "Schwan Children Expand Allegations in Lawsuit," *Minneapolis Star Tribune,* April 10, 1996, p. 1D.

——, "Schwan's Buys Two State Food Firms, Including Tino Lettieri Pastry Business," *Minneapolis Star Tribune,* June 24, 1992.

——, "Schwan's Names Insider Ken Noyes President, Chief Operating Officer," *Minneapolis Star Tribune,* March 30, 1995, p. 1D.

——, "Schwan's Paying Customers Who Agree Not to Sue: Total Approaches $1 Million," *Minneapolis Star Tribune,* November 19, 1994, p. 1A.

Kramer, Julie, "1 Killed, 8 Hurt in Marshall Ammonia Leak," *Minneapolis Tribune,* August 22, 1981.

Lambert, Bruce, obituary of Marvin M. Schwan, *New York Times,* May 12, 1993, p. B7.

McClintock, Lindsay, "Schwan's Song," *Grocer,* May 10, 1997, p. 17.

McGrath, Dennis J., "Schwan's Turns Ice Cream into Lots of Cold Cash," *Minneapolis Tribune,* October 29, 1978.

Pine, Carol, and Susan Mundale, "Frozen Assets: How Marvin Schwan Led His Ice Cream Company Along the Rocky Road to Success," *Corporate Report,* September 1982.

——, "Marvin Schwan: The Emperor of Ice Cream," in *Self-Made: The Stories of 12 Minnesota Entrepreneurs,* Minneapolis: Dorn Books, 1982.

"Schwan's Buys 2 Minnesota Food Firms," *St. Paul Pioneer Press,* June 25, 1992.

Slovut, Gordon, "Report Says '94 Schwan's Outbreak Affected 240,000," *Minneapolis Star Tribune,* May 16, 1996, p. 1A.

——, "Schwan's Plant Gets Go-Ahead to Reopen, *Minneapolis Star Tribune,* November 8, 1994, p. 1B.

"Towering Pizza," *Frozen and Chilled Foods,* June 1998, p. 8.

—Jay P. Pederson
—updated by David E. Salamie

SkyMall

SkyMall, Inc.

1520 E. Pima Street
Phoenix, Arizona 85034
U.S.A.
(602) 254-9777
Fax: (602) 254-6075
Web site: http://www.skymall.com

Public Company
Incorporated: 1989
Employees: 200
Sales: $60.8 million (1997)
Stock Exchanges: NASDAQ
Ticker Symbol: SKYM
SICs: 5961 Mail Order Houses; 2741 Miscellaneous
    Publishing

SkyMall, Inc. is the largest in-flight catalog company in the United States, offering its "SkyMall" catalog on most U.S. domestic passenger air carriers. On United Airlines flights, the catalog is called "High Street Emporium"; on US Airways (USAir), it is known as "Selections." Headquartered on seven acres of property in Phoenix, Arizona, the company makes products and services available to more than 400 million airline passengers per year, marketing and selling a broad selection of premium merchandise provided by participating merchants. The merchandise of each participating merchant is presented in a separate section of the *SkyMall* catalog to allow browsing from "store to store," providing the convenience and variety of an upscale shopping mall environment. The company produces four catalogs per year, with the fourth quarter holiday issue being the largest. The company operates a toll free telephone order center, with 24-hour-per-day coverage, taking between 2,000 and 6,000 calls per day, including those made from airplanes on air-to-ground phones.

Some of the major air carriers partnering with SkyMall Inc. have included Alaska Airlines, Aloha Airlines, America West Airlines, Continental Airlines, Delta Air Lines, Frontier Airlines, Hawaiian Airlines, Horizon Air, Midway Airlines, Reno Air, Skywest/Delta Connection, Southwest Airlines, Sun Country, Trans World Airlines Inc. (TWA), United, and USAir.

Dream Investors: 1989–90

The idea for SkyMall Inc. was formulated in 1989 by Robert M. Worsley, a former accountant with Big Six firm Price Waterhouse LLP. According to a 1996 article in *Forbes,* Worsley, who went on to become the president and chief executive officer, "got the idea for SkyMall on a flight from Seattle to Phoenix back in 1989. Paging through the Giftmaster Inc. (a tiny subsidiary of Minneapolis-based Carlson Companies Inc.) catalog from the airline seat pocket, he was startled by its poor merchandise."

Figuring he could offer better products, Worsley approached companies like The Sharper Image and Land's End and offered to carry their products. They agreed. Worsley incorporated SkyMall Inc. in Arizona and began mailing out his 100-page business plan to 50 venture capitalists and individual investors. In February 1990, *WordPerfect* co-creator Alan Ashton agreed to help finance the company, pitching in $250,000. Worsley and two other investors each invested $25,000 in the fledgling company.

Worsley spent nearly $3 million in his start-up phase, buying a 21,000-square-foot warehouse in Phoenix, Arizona and installing state-of-the-art technology such as NeXT personal computers and Sun Microsystems servers, at the adjacent customer service center. The first catalog, distributed on Eastern Airlines in 1990, carried products from Bits & Pieces, Hammacher Schlemmer, The Nature Company, Spiegel, and The Wine Enthusiast, which were purchased by SkyMall at a 35 percent discount, so that the company might match the prices featured in the individual merchant's catalogs and the products were stocked in the warehouse in Phoenix. Revenues for 1990 were a mere $200,000.

Going Down in Flames: 1991–94

By February 1991 the company's catalogs were being carried on TWA, and Continental Airlines added the catalogs in April. July was a boom month for SkyMall, with Alaska, Atlantic Southeast, Delta, Horizon, SkyWest, and USAir all starting to carry the company's catalogs. The air carriers were paid a percentage of sales. The early catalogs averaged between 60 to 80 pages, but the extra weight of all that paper forced SkyMall to cover the airlines' extra fuel costs for carrying the catalogs when the commissions fell short.

That year, Worsley got a call from Carlson's senior vice-president, Walter Erickson, inquiring if SkyMall would be interested in purchasing Giftmaster, which was bringing in some $6 million in annual sales and was barely breaking even. Ashton and Worsley bought the competition for a few million dollars, moving its operations to SkyMall's Phoenix headquarters and slowly replacing the Giftmaster catalogs with SkyMall catalogs.

Worsley's original intent was to deliver goods, such as dress shirts and ties, to customers who shopped midflight when they arrived at their destination airport, similar to pizza delivery. Unfortunately, most of his customers preferred to have their purchases delivered to their homes, leaving SkyMall holding expensive inventory and no delivery system. Losses mounted. In December 1991, Worsley begam experiencing chest pain and passed out in his kitchen and was carried out of the SkyMall Christmas party on a stretcher. Diagnosed with stress, doctors ordered him to cut back on work, but he took off weekends only, opening airport delivery services in Atlanta, Chicago, Dallas, Denver, Los Angeles, and San Francisco to try to unload excess inventory. Total revenue for 1991 reached $5.4 million, but the company was losing a half-million dollars per month.

By early 1992 SkyMall dominated the U.S. domestic in-flight industry. United joined the bandwagon in June and, that November, the company signed an agreement with Toronto-based TMS Marketing that brought its catalogs to Air Canada's flights. But that year the company posted a net loss of $9.6 million on total revenue of $16.1 million; in 1993 another $5.8 million loss on $27.1 million in revenue was posted.

Ashton and another investor poured $25 million into the company to keep it afloat. Worsley desperately tried to make a profit for the company, selling his own inventory backlog in the company's catalogs. However, fate seemed to be conspiring against the hardworking entrepreneur. By the end of 1993 the company's computer system was misplacing orders and miscounting inventory; 20 trailers sat in the Phoenix parking lot, crammed to the ceiling with products; more than 400 creditors were owed approximately $9 million; First Boston canceled its planned initial public offering (IPO) of SkyMall stock; a Baby Bell company backed out

of buying the sinking ship; and Ashton finally refused Worsley the $6 million more the beleaguered CEO requested. Desperate, the SkyMall CEO locked himself in his office for three straight days and came up with the plan to save his dying company: SkyMall would stop carrying inventory and begin having it shipped directly from the merchants to the customers, significantly decreasing the company's operating expenses. In addition, the company would begin charging merchants $20,500 per page to appear in the SkyMall catalog.

Ashton liked the idea, but was not going to invest another dime in the company. So SkyMall employees, including Worsley and his family, began calling the company's creditors one at a time to discuss reduced payment schedules. The airport stores were closed; Hammacher Schlemmer, SkyMall's biggest catalog customer, helped by buying $1 million of SkyMall inventory, and the rest was liquidated; and Worsley called in OrderTrust to capture customer orders from SkyMall's ordering system and route them directly to merchants' fulfillment systems.

Turnaround: 1994

Although the company would post in fiscal 1994 a $12.2 million loss on total revenues of $30.3 million, slowly things started to turn around as the company implemented Worsley's new plan. During 1994, Amtrak began carrying the company's catalog on selected train routes. February brought America West into the SkyMall repertoire; Midway came on board in June; and that July, Hawaiian Airlines added SkyMall's 136-page catalogs to its flights from the mainland to Hawaii and on inter-island flights. By September, SkyMall had dropped all of its airport delivery segment.

Clear Skies: 1995–Date

Growth continued in 1995, with Sun Country adding the catalogs to its flights in January and Frontier adding the catalogs in September. Revenues for the year reached $43.1 million and, for the first time in many years, the company posted a net income of a modest $758,000.

In 1996 the company was reincorporated in Nevada. Southwest Airlines added the company's catalogs to its flights beginning in July. SkyMall acquired the Internet service company GiftOne in November of that year, gaining the capability to help customers manage gift-giving by sending e-mail reminders of family events and gift suggestions based on profiles of gift recipients provided by the shopper. The catalog grew to an average 148 pages. Following a test run of catalogs on Japan Air Lines (JAL) during the year, the company entered the international market, releasing a Japanese-language edition on United flights. Finally, in December 1996, the company completed its IPO, selling two million shares and bringing in approximately $14 million. Total revenue for the year reached $43.7 million, with a net income of an impressive $2.2 million. Worsley breathed a sigh of relief for the first time in a long while.

Following a busy 1996 holiday season, the company used some of the IPO influx of cash to expand its call center, building a 15,000-square-foot service center, formerly a warehouse area. The company also rebuilt existing offices on the company's campus in the Sky Harbor park and redesigned exterior space for parking and employee recreation. The upgraded facility held 211 sales and customer service agents. Additional room to grow still existed, as the company also owned an adjacent 12,000-square-foot shopping center that it rented out to a Payless ShoeSource store and other retailers, as well as 4.5 acres of vacant land.

In mid-1997 the company entered the "e.commerce" arena, launching in partnership with MCI Communications Corp., OrderTrust LLP, and LitleNet, an interactive shopping system on its own World Wide Web site (www.skymall.com). When "virtual malls" were first launched on the Internet, they did not fare so well. Notable early failures included MecklerWeb from Mecklermedia Corp. and another site by The Internet Shopping Network, a subsidiary of Home Shopping Network, Inc. in 1994, and MCI's MarketplaceMCI and IBM's World Avenue in 1995. Some virtual malls, such as IMall Inc.'s IMall and Time Warner Inc.'s DreamShop, managed to struggle along, but the prospects for virtual malls looked bleak at the start. Major competition for SkyMall's business partner LitleNet included CyberSource Corp., as well as package shipping giants Federal Express Corp. and DHL Systems Inc., who helped companies manage the logistics of processing and fulfilling electronic orders. Federal Express made its debut in e-commerce in 1996 when it announced Business Link, a web commerce offering eventually known as Virtual Order, which featured a company's web catalog site and tracked orders for the company's order processing center using its well-known tracking software, attracting e-commerce customers such as Sun Data Inc. (a Norcross, Georgia-based systems integrator and hardware distributor and reseller) and Garden Escape (a web-based merchant selling everything from plant bulbs to wheelbarrows).

Unfazed, SkyMall slogged ahead, going to work with LodgeNet Entertainment Corp. to provide interactive shopping services in more than 250,000 hotel rooms across the United States via LodgeNet's broadband network. Other partners, such as Microsoft Corp., IIS, emaginet, and EDI, were quickly attracted to the project. Slow to start (accounting for approximately one percent and three percent of the company's net merchandise sales in the fourth quarter of 1997 and the first quarter of 1998, respectively), it continued to grow and was another source of income for SkyMall.

During 1997 the company captured 70 percent of and first position in the American air carrier market, placing approximately 17 million catalogs on the flights of a majority of U.S. domestic airlines carrying some 400 million passengers. Reno Air was added in April. The catalog grew in size again, to average about 168 pages, and total revenue reached $60.8 million, with a net income of $2.6 million.

The e.commerce market growth created a few glitches for SkyMall. In December 1997 the company's call center staff was frustrated because the computer system was taking minutes, rather than seconds, to input and save a single order, and calls were backing up. Worsley rolled up his sleeves, called in the IT (information technology) department, and spent most of the next three weeks working with programmers to troubleshoot the system, eventually fixing it.

By April 1998 the company had exclusive relationships with every major domestic airline in the United States to place its catalogs in aircraft seat pockets, save two: American Airlines, the second largest airline in the United States, with about 20 percent of the market, which did not provide its passengers with a catalog; and Northwest Airlines, which carried a catalog by Genesis Direct. In August, American announced, after 18 months of negotiations with various catalog companies, including SkyMall, that it, too, would be carrying Genesis Direct catalogs on its flights.

The Federal Aviation Administration expected U.S. passenger enplanements to increase from 595 million in 1997 to 924 million in 2009, a 3.7 percent compound annual growth rate, and the Direct Marketing Association estimated the catalog market as a $45 billion industry. SkyMall Inc. appeared to be in good position to monopolize the marketplace in the 21st century.

Further Reading

"*The Arizona Republic* Earnings Arizona Column," *Knight-Ridder/Tribune Business News,* August 14, 1998, p. OKRB982260B.

Balzer, Stephanie, "Public Companies Prep for October Forum," *Business Journal—Serving Phoenix & the Valley of the Sun,* October 3, 1997, p. 22.

Callaway, Erin, "Putting a New Spin on Web Shopping: SkyMall Outsources Its E-commerce Operation for Better Customer Service," *PC Week,* June 30, 1997, p. 143.

——, "Taking Web-Based Retailing Skyward," *PC Week,* April 27, 1998, p. 92.

Davies, John, "Catalog Service Extended to Air Canada Flights," *Journal of Commerce and Commercial,* November 5, 1992, p. 2B.

Eng, Paul M., "Bits & Bytes," *Business Week,* March 18, 1991, p. 124A.

——, "Coffee, Tea, or Shopping Spree," *Business Week,* March 18, 1991, p. 124A.

Moser, Karen D., "Client/Server Net Keeps Catalog Firm Flying High," *PC Week,* March 8, 1993, p. 73.

Oliver, Suzanne, "Spoiled Rotten," *Forbes,* July 15, 1996, p. 70.

Orr, Alicia, "Catalogers Find Customers in the Sky," *Target Marketing,* June 1992, p. 12.

Ruber, Ilana, "In-Flight Shopping Orders Up Profits, Puts Catalog Firm on Solid Ground," *Business Journal—Serving Phoenix & the Valley of the Sun,* July 4, 1997, p. 27.

——, "Southwest Passengers to Get SkyMall Catalog," *Baltimore Business Journal,* May 31, 1996, p. 13.

"Shop on the Fly," *Travel Weekly,* July 28, 1994, p. 36.

"Skymall Inc.," *Wall Street Journal,* October 17, 1997, p. B11(W)/B9(E).

"Skymall Inc.," *Wall Street Journal,* April 28, 1998, p. B22(W)/B27(E).

"Skymall Reports," *Aviation Week & Space Technology,* January 10, 1994, p. 17.

Vandeveire, Mary, "ADFlex Leads Positive AZ Stock Price Gain," *Business Journal—Serving Phoenix & the Valley of the Sun,* August 8, 1997, p. 41.

——, "The Sky's the Limit for Expanding SkyMall Inc.," *Business Journal—Serving Phoenix & the Valley of the Sun,* October 31, 1997, p. 6.

Wagner, Mitch, "SkyMall Guns for Virtual Shoppers at 30,000 Feet," *Computerworld,* June 30, 1997, p. 43.

Western, Ken, "Phoenix-Based SkyMall Scrambles to Meet Holiday Retail Demand," *Knight-Ridder/Tribune Business News,* December 24, 1997, p. 1224B1093.

Yoegel, Rob, "Fulfilling Orders Off the Web," *Target Marketing,* February 1998, p. 56.

—Daryl F. Mallett

Smurfit-Stone Container Corporation

150 North Michigan Avenue
Chicago, Illinois 60601-7568
U.S.A.
(312) 346-6600
Fax: (312) 580-4919
Web site: http://www.smurfit-stone.net

Public Company
Incorporated: 1983 as Jefferson Smurfit Corporation
Employees: 32,400
Sales: $8 billion (1998 est.)
Stock Exchanges: NASDAQ
Ticker Symbol: SSCC
SICs: 2421 Sawmills & Planing Mills, General; 2493
Reconstituted Wood Products; 2499 Wood Products,
Not Elsewhere Classified; 2611 Pulp Mills; 2621 Paper
Mills; 2631 Paperboard Mills; 2653 Corrugated & Solid
Fiber Boxes; 2655 Fiber Cans, Tubes, Drums & Similar
Products; 2656 Sanitary Food Containers, Except
Folding; 2673 Plastics, Foil & Coated Paper Bags; 2752
Commercial Printing, Lithographic; 2754 Commercial
Printing, Gravure; 2759 Commercial Printing, Not
Elsewhere Classified; 3497 Metal Foil & Leaf; 3569
General Industrial Machinery & Equipment, Not
Elsewhere Classified; 5093 Scrap & Waste Materials

Smurfit-Stone Container Corporation is the world's largest manufacturer of paperboard and paper-based packaging products, including containerboard, corrugated containers, folding cartons, paper bags and sacks, and kraft paper. The company's facilities number some 350 in 18 countries. Smurfit-Stone was formed in 1998 through the merger of Stone Container Corporation and Jefferson Smurfit Corporation. Ireland's Jefferson Smurfit Group plc had held a 47 percent stake in the latter. Following the merger, Jefferson Smurfit owned about 33 percent of Smurfit-Stone.

Stone Container Started As Shipping Supplies Jobber

Stone Container's beginnings go back to 1926 when Joseph Stone, a Russian immigrant, left his position as a salesman for a paper jobber and, with his life savings of $1,500 and his sons Norman and Marvin, created J.H. Stone & Sons. Together the three men set up shop in a former wholesale grocery operation at 120 North Green Street, just west of Chicago's downtown, in an office they shared with a customer and family friend. Building on the selling experiences of Joseph and Norman Stone, the Stones became jobbers of shipping supplies—wrapping paper, bags, tissue paper—and related industrial supplies. The company was a success. During the first fiscal year, which ran 15 months, sales totaled $68,000 and profits equaled $13,500. In 1928, Jerome Stone, the youngest of the three Stone brothers, came into the business. The same year, J.H. Stone & Sons began jobbing corrugated boxes.

As Joseph Stone began to slow down, his three sons began to run the company together. If there was a disagreement, the single loser always then agreed to support the decision of the majority. With a simple management system in place, the Stones built their early success on service. They kept little in stock and only occasionally bought for inventory. As the company grew, it moved to larger quarters several times in the early days all within Chicago, ending up on 74th Street, with 55,000 square feet, in 1937.

Entered Manufacturing During the Great Depression

The Great Depression pushed J.H. Stone & Sons into manufacturing. The National Recovery Act, which President Franklin D. Roosevelt signed into law in 1933, outlawed price cutting. Jobbers such as J.H. Stone & Sons would not get their merchandise at a discount, and Stone's customers would have to pay a premium for Stone's services.

The company needed a cheaper source of supplies, so the Stones explored manufacturing. The opportunity came late in 1933, when the company's principal supplier closed a nearby plant and offered to sell the Stones five pieces of obsolete equipment that converted corrugated sheets into boxes. Accepting the offer, J.H. Stone & Sons paid $7,200 for "Big Betsy," as the machines came to be known, and the services of a technician to help with installation. In 1936 the company moved one step closer to self-sufficiency with the purchase of a second-hand corrugator, for $20,000. The same year, founder

Joseph Stone died. Volume grew and in 1938 the Stones decided to erect their own plant. The 150,000-square-foot building in Chicago was the first plant anywhere devoted exclusively to the manufacture of corrugated boxes. Completed in the summer of 1939 at a cost of $382,000 it was built to order for Stone & Sons by the Central Manufacturing District, an authority of the City of Chicago. Also that year, the company reached $1 million in sales for the first time.

In all of these early ventures, the Stones paid with cash on hand or paid off their loans early. To pay for the new plant, they took a 20-year loan at six percent interest, but they paid off the debt in less than three years.

During World War II, when the government was sending aid and arms overseas, almost everything was packed in corrugated boxes. Since J.H. Stone & Sons' war priority rating was high, it had no problem with material shortages. The Stones continued to expand in the face of a good market. In 1943 Norman Stone learned of a corrugated box company in Philadelphia, Pennsylvania, that was for sale. Light Corrugated Box Company was two-thirds the size of J.H. Stone; it was also Stone's first venture outside of the Chicago area. After acquiring the company for $1.2 million, the brothers found they needed a resident manager, and for the first time, they brought in a nonfamily general manager, David Lepper.

After World War II the growing company incorporated as Stone Container Corporation. Demand skyrocketed, and raw materials grew short. Chief executive officer Norman Stone saw both opportunities for expansion and a need to control raw materials. With these in mind, Stone Container acquired two mills in 1946, the first being a $1.2 million box-board mill in Franklin, Ohio. Since Stone container did not need box-board, the raw material used in rigid boxes and folding cartons, the box-board machines were converted to the production of jute linerboard, then used as the outer layers in corrugated containers. The second was a $575,000 Coshocton, Ohio, mill that produced corrugating medium—the fluted material sandwiched between linerboard layers in corrugated containers—from straw. To pay for the two Ohio mills, Stone Container borrowed $2 million, and paid off the loan in one year.

Went Public in 1947

In 1947 Stone Container issued 250,000 shares of common stock and became a publicly owned company. No longer completely family owned, the brothers began working to attract outsiders to management positions.

The company found that its two big Ohio paper mills had enough capacity to supply the Chicago and Philadelphia plants and to sustain an additional corrugated-container plant. Stone Container, therefore, built a new corrugated-container plant, in the industrial area of Mansfield, Ohio. The plant was completed just before the Korean War began in 1950.

During the Korean War demand was high, and Stone Container sought to expand capacity. In 1950 Norman Stone heard of a mill at Mobile, Alabama, that had been taken over by the Reconstruction Finance Corporation, a federal agency. Within a year, Stone Container had bought the mill and converted it to the manufacture of jute linerboard.

During the 1950s the expansion of supermarkets and self-service outlets began to change the face of retailing. Containers became more than a means of conveying merchandise from producer to consumer. Producers began to see boxes as a means of advertising. On the crest of that wave, Stone became a pioneer in advertising on the exteriors of boxes.

Expanded Geographically and Diversified, 1950s–70s

The 1950s were also a period of aggressive geographic expansion for Stone Container. Since it was not economical to transport corrugated boxes more than about 125 miles, Stone Container located plants near its customers. First the company would identify a market, then it would build or buy a box plant in that area, and finally it would find the paper supply to feed the plant with raw materials. Among the box companies Stone Container acquired during the 1950s were: W.C. Ritchie & Company of Chicago in 1955, Western Paper Box Company of Detroit in 1956, and three companies in 1959: Campbell Box & Tag Company of South Bend, Indiana; Acme Carton Company of Chicago; and Delmar Paper Box Company.

Along with geographic expansion came diversification. Until 1954, Stone Container had confined its operations to the manufacture and sale of corrugated containers and paperboard. By 1960 it was selling folding cartons, fiber cans and tubes, tags, and special paper packages, due in great measure to the acquisition of W.C. Ritchie & Company, a manufacturer of high-grade paperboard-product packages.

While Stone was expanding rapidly and becoming a force in the industry its primary raw material, jute linerboard, was losing ground to the lighter, stronger kraft linerboard. To stay competitive, Stone had to buy kraft linerboard from other paper companies. Although the kraft linerboard shortage became apparent in the late 1950s, CEO Norman Stone was not able to address the problem until 1961, when Stone Container organized and took a 65 percent equity share in South Carolina Industries (SCI). Through SCI, Stone Container built a completely new kraft linerboard mill at Florence, South Carolina, a mill capable of producing 400 tons of board a day. Begun in 1962, during an economic recession, and financed through Northwestern Mutual Life Insurance, the SCI mill was completed in 1964 at a cost of $24 million, more than Stone Container's entire net worth at the time.

By the early 1960s Stone Container was consolidating its gains. The advertising revolution was complete, and in 1961 nearly all of its containers were designed specifically for a customer's product and market. The same year, Stone moved its corporate offices to North Michigan Avenue in Chicago, an office tower that was renamed the Stone Container Building. In 1962 the company was listed on the New York Stock Exchange. With the opening of the South Carolina mill in 1964, Stone for the first time became a fully integrated company, supplying virtually all of its own raw materials.

During the economic slowdown of the late 1960s and early 1970s, the company continued expanding. It spent $35 million in capital expansion, diversified with a plastics packaging division, and in 1974 bought Lypho-Med, a dry-freeze pharmaceutical manufacturer. Although operations kept expanding, Stone Container resolutely stayed out of the forestry business. According to Chairman Jerome H. Stone, who spoke with *Paper Trade Journal* in January 1977, the investment would have been too much. "For us to become self-sufficient we would need 300,000 acres of land. At $300 to $400 per acre we would have to justify an investment of $100 million. At the present time I don't see any way of obtaining a reasonable return on that investment." According to Stone, the Florence mill had 110 good suppliers of wood during the 1960s and 1970s.

In the early 1970s Roger Stone, then vice-president of the containerboard division and later CEO, saw industry leaving the Northeast. He realized that his primary customer base was shrinking and that he needed to reorient production in some geographic sectors toward a more consumer-based market. To that end Stone set out to boost sales of boxes to customers making nondurable consumer products—such as foods, beverages, and toys—to 75 percent of total sales.

By 1975 the Stone family's ownership was some 62 percent of the company's stock. Yet the Stones continued to work hard to assure that Stone Container was a truly public company. They promoted heavily from within. Three family members were in the company's upper echelons: Jerome as chairman and chief executive officer, Roger as president and chief operating officer, and Alan as vice-president, marketing.

Expansion continued, and in 1975 the company entered the Minneapolis-St. Paul, Minnesota, corrugated-container market by buying National Packaging for $6.05 million. In the face of expansion, however, earnings slumped, falling from a 1974 high of $1.87 per share to $.90 in 1978.

In 1979 Roger Stone became CEO of Stone Container. Son of Marvin Stone, one of the original founders, he was the second youngest of five cousins. Roger Stone had joined Stone Container as a sales representative in 1957, and become president in 1975.

In 1979 Boise Cascade proposed a merger, offering some $125 million in cash and stock to buy Stone Container's outstanding shares, more than twice the company's market value. The Stone family, which at that time owned about 60 percent of 7.7 million shares, mulled over the offer, and initially CEO Roger Stone was in favor of accepting it. With signs of an upturn in the paper market, however, Stone Container pulled out of the deal and decided to remain public. With that commitment to the future of the Stone Container Corporation, Roger Stone began an aggressive expansion campaign that would eventually make the company one of the largest paper manufacturers in the world.

Roger Stone Led 1980s Acquisition Campaign

Roger Stone's idea was to buy capacity from disenchanted or financially distressed producers. In that way he would neither increase industrywide capacity, possibly leading to a bust in container prices, nor incur the tremendous costs of building new plants and buying new machines. In a May 1, 1981, interview with *Financial World* Stone said, "We were willing to make that commitment when demand was down. That is when you should commit, when nobody else really wants to." In 1979, a low point in the business cycle, Stone ordered a $55 million expansion of the then wholly owned, ultra-efficient Florence linerboard plant. Then in 1981 he had Stone Container buy an equity position in Dean-Dempsy Corporation, a wood-chip fiber source. The Dean-Dempsy acquisition made Stone Container the 13th largest producer of boxes in the United States.

The rest of the 1980s saw Roger Stone making larger acquisitions. His was a leveraged buyout strategy. With banks and junk bond innovator Michael Milken and the then powerful Drexel Burnham Lambert supplying ready cash, and chief financial officer Arnold Brookstone devising ingenious financial strategies, Stone Container quintupled its annual capacity to 4.8 million tons by 1987, at a cost that was one-fifth that of new plants. Like his predecessors, Roger Stone bought during down times, and paid his debts when prices rose. His feeling for the business cycle was keen.

In October 1983 Stone Container paid $510 million for Continental Group's containerboard and brown-paper operations; 1983 was a bad year in the industry and Continental needed cash. Stone was able to buy three highly efficient paper mills, 15 corrugated box plants, five bag plants, and the cutting rights to 1.45 million acres of timberland for about one-third of the replacement value of the mills alone. Paid for with a $600 million loan, boosting debt to 79 percent of capital, and the first equity offering since 1947, which cut the family's share from 57 to 49 percent, the Continental purchase doubled Stone Container's annual capacity to 2.3 million tons and made Stone the nation's second largest producer of brown paper behind International Paper. After the Continental purchase, containerboard prices increased, and Stone was able to pay down its debt significantly.

In October 1985 Stone paid $457 million to buy three containerboard mills and 52 box-and-bag plants from Champion International Corporation. With this purchase, Stone's debt again soared, to about 70 percent of capitalization. The deal also gave Champion the option to buy 12 to 14 percent of Stone's stock at a higher price in the early 1990s. The Stone family, however, still owned 37 percent of the company.

In 1987 Stone paid $760 million to buy Southwest Forest Industries, a containerboard company that also made newsprint. The acquisition of Southwest's two large pulp and paper mills, 19 corrugated container plants, and assorted plywood and veneer plants, lumber mills, railroads, and private fee-timber made Stone the nation's largest producer of brown paper, including corrugated boxes, paper bags, linerboard, and kraft paper.

According to some analysts, the acquisitions were taking a toll. Stone had more than $1.44 of debt for each $1 of equity. To shake some of the debt, Brookstone spun off Stone Container's wood products businesses as Stone Forest Industries (SFI). By selling shares in the new company, which was still controlled by Stone Container, the company obtained cash and spun off a portion of its own debt. While Brookstone was dealing with the debt, the economy was running hot. Stone Container plants were operating nearly at full capacity, and the company was able to meet its obligations. The family's share fell to 30 percent.

In 1988, after the SFI acquisition, CEO Roger Stone set a goal of making the Stone Container Corporation a major force in packaging, newsprint, and market pulp—the material used to make fine paper—throughout North America and Europe. Stone predicted that after European economic integration in 1922 there would be an explosion in packaging as firms shipped goods around the continent. He wanted Stone Container to be there when it happened. In pursuit of this strategy, Stone Container made the biggest acquisition in its history. In March 1989 Stone paid $2.2 billion in cash and securities for Consolidated-Bathurst Inc. (CB), Canada's fifth largest pulp-and-paper company. The purchase made Stone Container the world's second largest producer of pulp, paper, and paperboard; a major player in newsprint; and gave Stone Container a foothold in the European market through CB's Europa Carton subsidiary and U.K. plants.

While some analysts worried about debt, which increased to 70 percent of capital, and fluctuations in the newsprint market, which tumbled alarmingly just as the deal was going through, others lauded the strategic benefits of becoming a truly international company, especially with the coming economic integration of the European Community. Unlike earlier acquisitions, in the Consolidated-Bathurst deal Stone had paid full price for a well run company—a 47 percent premium over the market price at the time. Investors worried about the $3 billion debt load, and prices for newsprint slipped 14 percent in the year following the acquisition. With investors jittery about debt and an economic slowdown in the works, stock prices fell from a 1988 high of $39.50 to $8.50 in October 1990. In 1989 the company disposed of some debt by selling $330.4 million in noncore assets.

1990s Struggles

In 1990 cash flow remained more than adequate to meet obligations, although a substantial reduction in net income—from $285.8 million in 1989 to $95.4 million in 1990—did not bode well for the future. In fact, the company was in the red for the next four years, with a peak net loss of $358.7 million in 1993. Stone Container was certainly hurt by low prices in the early 1990s, but it was the debt burden that nearly caused the company to collapse. Roger Stone had financed the purchase of Consolidated-Bathurst with bank loans, planning to refinance with junk bonds once interest rates dropped. While interest rates did fall, the market for junk bonds temporarily dried up, leaving Stone Container holding the inflexible bank debt.

In 1993, with rumors flying about bankruptcy, the company attempted to improve its balance sheet through a $500 million stock offering. After the plan was disclosed in April, however, the company's stock plummeted in value, forcing the postpone-

ment of the offering. By this time, total consolidated debt stood at $5 billion. The level was reduced later in 1993 when the company negotiated the conversion of $400 million in debt into 23 million shares of common stock. Later in 1993 Stone Container raised about $125 million from the sale of its interest in Empaques de Carton Titan, a Mexican maker of corrugated containers, and the divestment of two short-line railroads. Around this same time the company sold 25 percent of Consolidated-Bathurst, renamed Stone-Consolidated, to the public, raising about $575 million. In 1995 Stone-Consolidated merged with Rainy River Forest Products, Inc., a Toronto-based pulp and paper company; in the process, Stone Container's interest in Stone-Consolidated was reduced further, to 46.6 percent. Meantime, the Stone family saw its ownership in Stone Container fall to 15 percent.

Stone Container briefly returned to profitability in 1995 when it posted net income of $255.5 million on record sales of $7.35 billion. But falling prices once again battered the company, leading to losses of $126.2 million in 1996 and $417.7 million in 1997. Also troubling was the fact that debt remained very high: the $3.94 billion in 1997 translated into a debt to capitalization ratio of 89 percent. In May 1997 Stone-Consolidated merged with Abitibi-Price Inc. to form Abitibi-Consolidated Inc., the world's largest newsprint maker, 25.2 percent owned by Stone. Later that year Stone Container announced its intention to refocus on paperboard and paper packaging, its historical core interests. In doing so the company planned to divest its stake in Abitibi-Consolidated, its 50 percent interest in Canadian corrugated container maker MacMillan-Bathurst, newsprint operations in Snowflake, Arizona, and five plants that made bleached market pulp. Stone Container also hoped to reduce debt by more than $1.5 billion through these sales, cutting its debt to capitalization ratio to 40 percent.

In February 1998 the company and the Federal Trade Commission entered into a consent order, settling FTC charges that Stone had tried to fix linerboard prices in 1993. Stone did not admit guilt in entering into the order. In May 1998 came the announcement of the merger between Stone Container and Jefferson Smurfit Corporation, which was consummated in November of that year. In September Stone Container bought out the 50 percent interest in MacMillan-Bathurst held by MacMillan Bloedel Ltd. for C$185 million, and then immediately sold the interest to a Canadian subsidiary of the Jefferson Smurfit Group (parent company of Jefferson Smurfit Corporation) for the same amount. Also in September Stone Container sold its Snowflake newsprint unit to Abitibi-Consolidated for about $250 million. This ended Stone's direct involvement in the newsprint business, although it had not yet sold its 25.2 percent stake in Abitibi-Consolidated.

History of Jefferson Smurfit Corporation

Ireland-based packaging conglomerate Jefferson Smurfit Group plc built a U.S. base through a series of shrewd acquisitions of financially troubled paper companies, which Smurfit swiftly turned around. It made its first move into the United States in 1974 when it acquired a 40 percent interest in Time Industries Inc., a small ($32 million in sales) Chicago-based maker of paperboard and packaging products. By 1977 Smurfit had gained full ownership of Time Industries, which was renamed Smurfit Industries Inc. From 1979 to 1981 Smurfit spent $52 million to gradually take full control of Alton Box Board Co., another paperboard and packaging specialist, based in Alton, Illinois. In September 1982 Smurfit formed a 50–50 joint venture to take over the packaging operations of Diamond International Group, then bought out the partner's shares to gain full control in 1983. The total cost to Smurfit to acquire the $200-million-in-sales company was $86 million.

Also in 1983 Smurfit created Jefferson Smurfit Corporation (JSC) as its holding company for its U.S. interests, which were consolidated therein. In addition, it sold 22 percent of the common shares of JSC to the public in November 1983, raising more than $50 million for the payoff of debt.

In 1986 Smurfit made several more acquisitions which were added to JSC's holdings. The two most important were the purchase of an 80 percent interest in Publishers Paper Company (renamed Smurfit Newsprint Corporation), a major newsprint maker, purchased from The Times Mirror Company for $132 million; and the $1.2 billion leveraged buyout of Container Corporation of America (CCA) through a joint venture with New York investment house Morgan Stanley. Through this aggressive acquisition strategy, JSC's revenues increased from $630.4 million in 1985 to $1.1 billion in 1987.

In 1989 JSC restructured as a privately held corporation, owned equally by Jefferson Smurfit Group and the Morgan Stanley Leveraged Equity Fund II L.P. (MSLEF). In 1994, however, Smurfit needed funds to pay for its $1.04 billion acquisition of the paper and packaging unit—Cellulose du Pin—of France's Compagnie de Saint-Gobain. To do so, it took JSC public once again, after which Smurfit held a 47 percent interest in JSC, MSLEF held 36 percent, and the public 17 percent. The following year JSC purchased the 20 percent of Smurfit Newsprint it did not already own. By 1997 Jefferson Smurfit Corporation had sales of more than $4 billion, with 43 percent of revenues coming from its containers/containerboard sector, 28 percent from folding carton and boxboard, 11 from reclamation and wood, nine percent from newsprint, and another nine percent from industrial and consumer packaging.

Smurfit-Stone Container Created in 1998

The November 1998 merger was set up as a complicated takeover of Stone Container by JSC, with the latter changing its name to Smurfit-Stone Container Corporation. Following the stock transaction, Jefferson Smurfit Group owned about 33 percent of Smurfit-Stone, MSLEF owned nine percent, with the remaining ownership interest in the hands of the public. Michael W.J. Smurfit was named non-executive chairman of Smurfit-Stone, with Roger Stone serving as president and CEO of the new firm, which would boast revenues exceeding $8 billion while contending with debt of more than $6.7 billion. The management planned to shed, within 18 months, about $2.5 billion in noncore assets, most notably Stone's interest in Abitibi-Consolidated and JSC's newsprint operations. The aim was to concentrate on paper-based packaging. In late November 1998 Smurfit-Stone announced a restructuring in which it would cut as many as 3,600 jobs (10 percent of its workforce) and take a fourth-quarter charge of as much as $350 million.

Further Reading

Byrne, Harlan S., ''Stone Container: Battered Paper Maker Strives to Slash Debt, Halt Losses,'' *Barron's,* July 12, 1993, pp. 41–42.

Byrne, John A., ''Guess Who Gets the Last Laugh,'' *Forbes,* June 20, 1983, pp. 140+.

DeKing, Noel, ''Smurfit Moves to the Top Through Acquisitions, Skilled Management,'' *Pulp and Paper,* December 1988, pp. 110–13.

Deutsch, Claudia H., ''Bags and Boxes Full of Profits,'' *New York Times,* August 14, 1988, p. F1.

Dubashi, Jagannath, ''Fearless in the Forest,'' *Financial World,* April 19, 1988, pp. 19+.

——, ''A Mill Too Far?,'' *Financial World,* May 28, 1991, pp. 24–26.

Gubernick, Lisa, ''Paper Shuffler,'' *Forbes,* February 11, 1985, p. 79.

Labich, Kenneth, ''An Irishman Feasts on American Trees,'' *Fortune,* July 20, 1987, pp. 62–64, 68.

Lashinsky, Adam, ''Stone's Rocky Road to Recovery,'' *Crain's Chicago Business,* October 19, 1992, pp. 3+.

Lund, Herbert F., ''Stone Container's First 50 Years Just a Springboard to Much Greater Growth,'' *Paper Trade Journal,* January 1, 1977.

Mies, Willard E., ''Stone Container Doubles Capacity Through Bold Acquisition Move,'' *Pulp and Paper,* December 1983, pp. 65+.

Miller, Drew, ''Jefferson Smurfit Corp.: Well-Integrated and Poised for Growth,'' *Pulp and Paper,* April 1997, pp. 44+.

Miller, James P., ''Stone Container Agrees to a Merger with Jefferson Smurfit in Stock Deal,'' *Wall Street Journal,* May 11, 1998, p. B4.

Moskal, Brian S., ''A Paper Tiger?: Roger Stone Gambles Again,'' *Industry Week,* November 25, 1988, pp. 20+.

Schifrin, Matthew, ''Back from the Brink and Ready to Roll,'' *Forbes,* February 13, 1995, pp. 110+.

Siler, Julia Flynn, ''Suddenly, Stone Container Feels Boxed In,'' *Business Week,* October 15, 1990, pp. 79, 81–82.

Simon, Ruth, ''They Thought We Were a Little Crazy,'' *Forbes,* September 21, 1987, pp. 50+.

Stone, Marvin N., and Jerome H. Stone, *Stone Container Corporation,* New York: The Newcomen Society in North America, 1975, p. 24.

Taub, Stephen, ''Stone Container: Survival Not Set in Stone,'' *Financial World,* February 15, 1994, pp. 14–15.

—Jordan Wankoff
—updated by David E. Salamie

Suiza Foods Corporation

3811 Turtle Creek Boulevard
Suite 1300
Dallas, Texas 75219
U.S.A.
(214) 528-9922
Fax: (214) 528-9929
Web site: http://www.suizafoods.com

Public Company
Incorporated: 1988 as Kaminski/Engles Capital Corp.
Employees: 7,050
Sales: $1.80 billion (1997)
Stock Exchanges: New York
Ticker Symbol: SZA
SICs: 6719 Offices of Holding Companies, Not
   Elsewhere Classified; 2023 Dry, Condensed &
   Evaporated Milk Products; 2024 Ice Cream & Frozen
   Desserts; 2026 Fluid Milk; 2086 Bottled & Canned
   Soft Drinks & Carbonated Waters; 2095 Roasted
   Coffee; 2099 Food Preparations, Not Elsewhere
   Classified; 3085 Plastic Bottles; 3089 Plastic Products,
   Not Elsewhere Classified

Suiza Foods Corporation has seemingly come out of nowhere to become one of the leading fresh milk and dairy food companies in the United States. The trade magazine *Dairy Foods* ranked Suiza as the number four dairy company as of year-end 1997 (behind Kraft Foods, Land O'Lakes Inc., and Dean Foods Corp.), moving up from the number 19 position in only one year. The company's spectacular growth—revenues increased from $341 million in 1993 to a forecasted $3.4 billion in 1998—has been fueled by an aggressive program of acquisition through which it is serving (along with Dean Foods) as a major consolidator of the dairy industry. Just since its initial public offering in April 1996, Suiza Foods has completed more than 40 acquisitions. Most of the companies purchased have been milk processing concerns, but Suiza has also added operations involved in fruit drinks, coffee, juices, yogurt, packaged ice cream, ice cream novelties, and bottled water. The company's brands are primarily of the regional variety, with nationally known brands including International Delight (gourmet coffee creamers), Second Nature (egg substitute), Naturally Yours (sour cream), Mocha Mix (non-dairy creamer), and Coffee Rich, Farm Rich, and Poly Rich (creamers). In addition to its involvement in various food sectors, the company has quickly gained a leading position in the consumer goods plastic packaging industry, with an emphasis on containers used for milk, water, and other beverage products. About 70 percent of company revenues are derived from dairy operations, with the remainder from packaging. Suiza Foods Corporation is essentially a holding company for its various subsidiary operations. The company also holds a 12 percent stake in Boulder, Colorado-based Horizon Organic Dairy Inc., the largest producer of organic dairy products in the United States.

Packaged Ice Beginnings

Suiza Foods had its start in 1988 when an investment firm, Kaminski/Engles Capital Corp., formed by Gregg L. Engles and Robert Kaminski purchased the Reddy Ice packaged ice business from The Southland Corporation, owner of the 7-Eleven convenience store chain, for $26 million. It was ironic that Reddy Ice would be the company that Suiza Foods was founded upon, since Southland also traced its beginnings to Reddy Ice, which was launched in 1927 by 7-Eleven founder Joe C. Thompson. By the late 1980s, Southland had fallen on hard times, and the selling of its ice business was part of a divestiture program. Later in 1988 Kaminski/Engles bought Sparkle Ice from The Circle K Company, another convenience store chain, and combined it into Reddy Ice. Over the next several years, more than a dozen additional ice making and distribution operations were purchased and melded into Reddy Ice, creating abundant opportunities for consolidating facilities and achieving economies of scale. This pattern would be followed to an even larger extent by Engles in the dairy sector.

Engles's background was in investment banking, but he specialized in mergers and acquisitions, which was quickly apparent. In late 1993 Engles and a group of partners in Suiza Holdings L.P. acquired Suiza-Puerto Rico for $99.4 million, including $85 million in cash. Suiza-Puerto Rico's operations included Suiza Dairy Corp., the largest dairy company in Puerto Rico. Suiza Dairy ("Suiza" is Spanish for "Swiss") had been founded in 1942 by Héctor Nevares, Sr., and was owned by the Nevares family until the purchase by the Engles-led partnership. The company held 58 percent of the milk market on the island, had 850 employees, and generated annual revenues of $185 million. Suiza-Puerto Rico was also involved in the manufacture of fruit drinks and the distribution of third party brand name ice cream and other dairy products.

The dairy sector quickly became Engles's industry of choice. He had been searching for an area ripe for consolidation. In 1998, in explaining to *Dairy Foods* why he chose dairy, he said: "In large measure, because that's the opportunity that presented itself. I don't know of a bigger industry consolidation going on today. But I like dairy. It's dynamics are good. This industry is one in which there are real economic benefits in size and scale, but no one really has it, no one has capitalized on that." The U.S. dairy industry of the 1990s was highly fragmented, with numerous family-owned operations that were ideal acquisitions candidates.

Engles's formula for growth was evident right from his first foray into dairy (and actually was earlier applied to ice packaging). His plan was to purchase the leading dairy in a region, then fill in with additional acquisitions in that region. By consolidating operations, closing plants, and cutting jobs, the first dairy acquired would gain market share, increase its efficiency, and become more profitable. In Puerto Rico, Engles followed his purchase of Suiza Dairy with the June 1994 $7 million acquisition of Mayaguez Dairy, Inc., the island's number three dairy. Mayaguez was subsequently consolidated into Suiza Dairy, whose market share increased to 66 percent, and the plan was put into practice.

In April 1994 Engles, through his Dallas-based investment banking firm Engles Management Corp., spent $48 million to acquire Lakeland, Florida-based Velda Farms, Inc., providing a regional base for the state of Florida. Velda Farms, which was founded in 1955, manufactured and distributed fresh milk, ice

cream, and related products under its own brand names to about 9,500 food service accounts, convenience stores, club stores, and schools.

Suiza Foods Formed in October 1994

Engles incorporated Suiza Foods Corporation in October 1994 as a holding company for Suiza-Puerto Rico, Velda Farms, and Reddy Ice. Engles was named chairman and CEO, while Cletes O. "Tex" Beshears—Engles's right-hand man— was named president and chief operating officer as well as a director. Beshears had been a vice-president at Southland and COO of its dairy group from 1980 to 1988. From 1965 to 1980 Beshears was division manager for a number of Southland's regional dairy operations, including Velda Farms. The headquarters for Suiza Foods were established in Dallas.

Suiza Foods was set up as a holding company, with a thoroughly decentralized management style. As with its previous acquisitions, the Suiza plan was to seek out companies with strong management teams that could be left in place for a smooth transition and the retention of local market experience, relationships, and knowledge. By and large, the company had no plans for creating national brands, concluding that the continuation of longstanding local and regional brands was critical for success in the dairy industry.

The newly formed corporation immediately set out on the acquisition trail. In November 1994 Velda Farms added to its dairy operations the Florida division of Flav-O-Rich Inc., which was purchased from Mid-American Dairymen, Inc. for $3.6 million. Similarly, Velda bought Skinner's Dairy Inc. of Jacksonville, Florida, in January 1996.

To help fund additional acquisitions and pay down debt, Suiza Foods went public in April 1996 through an initial public offering—priced at $14 per share—that raised about $48.6 million. Company stock was traded on the NASDAQ stock exchange under the symbol SWZA. An additional $10 million was secured in August 1996 through a private placement of common stock to the T. Rowe Price Small Cap Value Fund. Then in January of the following year Suiza raised another $89 million through a secondary public offering, priced at $22 per share. Proceeds were again used to reduce debt. In March 1997 Suiza Foods began trading on the New York Stock Exchange under the symbol SZA. Company stock ended 1997 trading at $59.56 per share, after reaching a high of $62.50.

Meanwhile, in July 1996 Suiza acquired Garrido y Compania, Inc., the second largest coffee processor in Puerto Rico and operator of the island's largest office and hotel coffee service. The company paid $35.8 million for Garrido, which became part of Suiza-Puerto Rico. In September 1996 Suiza gained a regional milk producer in southern California through the $55.1 million acquisition of Swiss Dairy Corp., based in Riverside. The family owned and operated dairy was founded in the 1940s and had sales of about $126 million in 1995. Suiza Foods added another western dairy to its growing stable in December 1996 when it paid $27 million for Model Dairy, also family owned and operated since opening in 1906. Reno, Nevada-based Model Dairy was the largest milk distributor in northern Nevada. These acquisitions helped increase Suiza Foods' revenues from $431 million in 1995 to $521 million in 1996.

Acquisition Pace Quickened Starting in 1997

In July 1997 Beshears was named vice-chairman of Suiza and William P. "Bill" Brick added the post of president to his title as COO (which he had assumed from Beshears in October 1996). Brick, like Beshears, had experience in the dairy industry prior to joining Suiza in July 1996 as an executive vice president.

During the later months of 1997 and all of 1998 Suiza Foods grabbed headlines with its ever-more acquisitive methods. In the second half of 1997 alone, the company acquired Dairy Fresh L.P. (renamed Dairy Fresh, Inc.) for $106.3 million (in July); Garelick Farms, Inc. for $299.6 million (also in July); the Nashville, Tennessee, dairy division of Fleming Companies, Inc. (in August); Country Fresh, Inc. for $135 million in stock and debt (in October); and The Morningstar Group, Inc. for $960 million in stock and debt (in November). Winston-Salem, North Carolina-based Dairy Fresh generated about $125 million in annual revenues through the processing of milk and ice cream products. The Fleming dairy division, which Suiza renamed Country Delite Farms, Inc., had revenues of $76 million. In February 1998 Suiza paid $248 million for Land-O-Sun Dairies, L.L.C., a Johnson City, Tennessee, processor of fluid milk and ice cream with revenues of $464 million. Dairy Fresh, Country Delite, and Land-O-Sun together formed the largest dairy manufacturing and distribution network in the Southeast.

Garelick Farms included three dairy companies in the Northeast—Franklin, Massachusetts-based Garelick, Fairdale Farms, Inc. in Bennington, Vermont, and Grant's Dairy, Inc. of Bangor, Maine—in addition to Mendon, Massachusetts-based bottled water firm Miscoe Springs, Inc. Garelick's operations also included 17 plastic bottle manufacturing operations located from Maine to Texas, which Suiza consolidated within a new subsidiary, Franklin Plastics, Inc. Collectively, the Garelick operations generated more than $370 million in revenues and provided Suiza a solid base for growth in the Northeast.

The acquisition of Country Fresh provided Suiza its first penetration of the Midwestern market. Based in Grand Rapids, Michigan, Country Fresh was a processor of milk, juice, and ice cream products, which it distributed in Michigan, Ohio, and Indiana. The company had annual revenues of $353 million. In early 1998 Suiza expanded its presence in the Midwest through the February acquisition of Oberlin Farms Dairy, Inc. of Cleveland, Ohio, and the March purchase of Louis Trauth Dairy, Inc., of Newport, Kentucky. Oberlin had revenues of $76 million, while Louis Trauth had sales of $67 million.

The merger—through a stock swap—with Morningstar was different in that it diversified Suiza's operations. Morningstar's history paralleled that of Suiza Foods. It, too, was born in 1988 through a Southland divestment. Since being sold that year to private investors, Morningstar had grown through acquisitions and become a publicly traded company (just as Suiza had). It had revenues of about $528 million through its manufacturing and distribution of branded and long shelf life dairy and nondairy specialty foods. Morningstar's array of brands included International Delight gourmet coffee creamers, Second Nature

no-cholesterol egg substitute, Naturally Yours sour cream, Mocha Mix nondairy creamer, and Jon Donaire cheesecakes and desserts. The company also licensed the Lactaid brand for a line of lactose-free and lactose-reduced dairy products, as well as supplied its customers with private label creamers, cottage cheese, prewhipped toppings, sour cream, and yogurt.

As a result of its aggressive acquisition strategy, Suiza Foods more than tripled its revenues for 1997, posting net sales of $1.8 billion. The company reported net income of $28.8 million. It now laid claim to the top position in U.S. dairy products, although Dean Foods also boasted that it was number one.

Following the merger with Morningstar, Suiza shuffled its top management. Brick shifted over to become executive vice-president and president of the dairy group, making room for L. Hollis Jones to become president and COO, the position he had held at Morningstar. Jones, however, left Suiza in February 1998, becoming an exclusive consultant for Suiza, with a focus on acquisitions and strategic developments. Taking over as president and COO was G. Irwin Gordon, who had been a Suiza executive vice-president.

Acquired Continental Can in 1998

Suiza Foods' acquisition of Garelick Farms—more specifically Franklin Plastics—had presented the company with another opportunity. Up until that purchase, Suiza was involved in the plastic packaging industry only through those dairies it had acquired that made their own containers (such as Neva Plastics, which was acquired along with Suiza-Puerto Rico). Franklin Plastics, however, served outside customers as well. Suiza decided to build upon the expertise of Franklin by applying its consolidation strategy to plastic packaging. In an acquisition announced in January 1998 and consummated in June of that year, Suiza acquired Continental Can Company, Inc. for about $345 million. Norwalk, Connecticut-based Continental Can had revenues of $546 million and 15 plastic packaging plants in the United States, which when added to those of Franklin provided Suiza with a nationwide packaging network. Continental Can also had nine European plants that manufactured food cans and plastic packaging, and it was possible that these operations would eventually be divested. Suiza was also considering an eventual public offering of a minority interest in its packaging operations to improve its already strong financial state.

In March 1998 the company's board of directors adopted a shareholders' rights plan aimed at making a hostile takeover of Suiza more difficult. Two months later Suiza completed the sale of Reddy Ice—the business upon which the company was founded—to privately held Packaged Ice, Inc. of Houston, Texas, for $172 million. The move was intended to allow the company to focus on its core dairy and plastic packaging operations, with the proceeds slated for additional acquisitions in those sectors. In a somewhat similar move, Suiza in July 1998 exchanged its Jon Donaire desserts business for the retail refrigerated and frozen creamer business of Rich Products Corporation of Buffalo, New York. While desserts were outside Suiza's core food areas, the Coffee Rich, Farm Rich, Poly Rich, and Rich Whip brands acquired fit in perfectly with the other brands Suiza had acquired through Morningstar.

Suiza Foods added two more dairies to its northeastern region in 1998 by way of the June purchase of West Lynn Creamery, Inc., which had revenues of $215 million; and the August acquisition of the fluid dairy division of Cumberland Farms, Inc. of Canton, Massachusetts, which generated sales of about $200 million. In July 1998 Suiza spent about $12 million for a 12 percent stake in Boulder, Colorado-based Horizon Organic Dairy Inc., holder of 65 percent of the U.S. organic dairy product market. The transaction was made in concurrence with Horizon's initial public offering. Horizon also entered into dairy processing and distribution agreements with Suiza subsidiaries Model Dairy and Garelick Farms. Suiza Foods topped off 1998 with the December purchase of Broughton Foods Corporation for $123 million. Based in Marietta, Ohio, Broughton was a leading manufacturer and distributor of milk, ice cream, and other dairy products in Michigan, Ohio, West Virginia, Kentucky, Tennessee, and sections of the eastern United States. The company had revenues of about $200 million in 1997. Suiza planned to integrate Broughton facilities into its regional operations in the Midwest and Southeast. With its various 1998 acquisitions, Suiza was expected to post 1998 revenues of more than $3.4 billion, nearly double that of the preceding year.

As a new century approached, Suiza Foods was likely to continue building upon its dairy manufacturing and distribution network through major acquisitions in new regions and fill-in purchases in existing regions; as well as seek out additional opportunities to expand its product offerings—consumer branded, value-added, and private label—in all areas of the dairy case. Further acquisitions were also expected to beef up Suiza's plastics packaging operations. The company held more than 10 percent of the $25 billion fluid milk market in the United States, and Engles aimed to increase that figure to 30 percent by 2003. During that period, Engles believed a dominant, $5–$7 billion U.S. dairy company would emerge—and he was working to make sure it was Suiza Foods.

Principal Subsidiaries

Broughton Foods Company; Continental Can Company, Inc.; Country Delite Farms, Inc.; Country Fresh, Inc.; Dairy Fresh, Inc.; Fairdale Farms, Inc.; Franklin Plastics, Inc.; Garelick Farms, Inc.; Garrido y Compania, Inc.; Grant's Dairy, Inc.; Land-O-Sun Dairies, L.L.C.; Louis Trauth Dairy, Inc.; Miscoe Springs, Inc.; Model Dairy, Inc.; The Morningstar Group, Inc.; Neva Plastics Manufacturing Corp.; Oberlin Farms Dairy, Inc.; Suiza Capital Trust; Suiza Dairy Corporation; Suiza Fruit Corporation; Suiza Management Corporation; Swiss Dairy Corporation; Velda Farms, Inc.; West Lynn Creamery, Inc.

Further Reading

Byrne, Harlan S., "Dairy King," *Barron's,* February 23, 1998, p. 20.

Donovan, William J., "Texas' Suiza Foods to Acquire Rhode Island's Garelick Farms," *Providence Journal-Bulletin,* June 24, 1997.

Fink, James, "Coffee Rich Blends with Dallas Company," *Business First of Buffalo,* July 20, 1998, pp. 1+.

Fusaro, Dave, "Enigmatic Acquisition Machine," *Dairy Foods,* March 1998, pp. 18+.

——, "Suiza Foods," *Dairy Foods,* April 1998, pp. 69+.

"Horizon Organic Inc. Completes Its IPO and a Sale to Suiza," *Wall Street Journal,* July 6, 1998, p. C22.

Kuhn, Mary Ellen, "Dairy's Slam Dunk!: Dean and Suiza Capitalize on Consolidation with Aggressive Expansion Agendas," *Food Processing,* June 1998, pp. 22+.

Lipin, Steven, "Suiza Foods to Buy Morningstar Group for $777 Million in Stock, Plus Debt," *Wall Street Journal,* September 29, 1997, p. A4.

Montano, Agnes J., "Suiza Foods' Subsidiary Buys Flav-O-Rich Division," *San Juan Star,* November 29, 1994.

Nethery, Ross, "Food Company Raising $200M," *Dallas Business Journal,* October 21, 1994.

"New Faces in New Places," *Dairy Foods,* July 1998, pp. 10+.

Pico, Maria Bird, "Suiza Plans $80 Million Stock Offering," *San Juan Star,* November 4, 1994.

"Riverside, Calif., Dairy Has Gone Through 48 Years of Changes," *Press-Enterprise* (Riverside, California), October 14, 1996.

"Sell-Off by Bevy of Suiza Insiders Raises Concerns over Stock's Fate," *Wall Street Journal,* August 5, 1998.

Smith, Rod, "Dean, Suiza Continue Strategy to Acquire Dairy Market Share," *Feedstuffs,* June 15, 1998, p. 7.

——, "Suiza Building Platforms to Shape Dairy Industry," *Feedstuffs,* May 11, 1998, pp. 6+.

"Suiza Foods Restructures Top Mgmt., Names Gordon President," *Nation's Restaurant News,* March 16, 1998, p. 116.

"Suiza Foods to Buy Plastics Manufacturers and Dairy Companies," *Wall Street Journal,* June 24, 1997, p. A12.

Templin, Neal, "Suiza Foods Says Butterfat Prices Hurt Its Earnings," *Wall Street Journal,* September 16, 1998, p. A8.

Wren, Worth, Jr., "Two Southland Spinoffs Expected to Merge: Suiza Will Acquire Morningstar in a $960 Million Deal," *Fort Worth Star-Telegram,* September 30, 1997.

Zehr, Douglas, "Delaware Group to Buy Suiza Dairy," *San Juan Star,* September 30, 1993.

—David E. Salamie

Sullivan & Cromwell

125 Broad Street
New York, New York 10004-2498
U.S.A.
(212) 558-4000
Fax: (212) 558-3588
Web site: http://www.sullcrom.com

Private Company
Founded: 1879
Employees: 1,265
Gross Billings: $395 million (1997 est.)
SICs: 8111 Legal Services

Sullivan & Cromwell is one of the nation's elite law firms. For more than a century it has been closely involved in the affairs of some of the largest industrial and commercial enterprises in the United States. Sullivan & Cromwell also has been closely involved in the formulation and execution of U.S. foreign policy and the development and growth of global capital markets. It was tied, in terms of gross revenue, for fifth position among U.S. law firms in 1996.

Under Cromwell's Guiding Hand: 1879–1920

Sullivan & Cromwell was founded in 1879 by Algernon Sydney Sullivan and William Nelson Cromwell. The middle-aged Sullivan was senior partner; he had enabled the youthful Cromwell, formerly a bookkeeper, to attend law school. The firm established offices at the corner of Broad and Wall Streets, opposite the New York Stock Exchange. It earned about $22,500 in its first year. Law clerks were unpaid, and the payroll came to only $950.

Sullivan was a trial lawyer who thought corporations should be outlawed, but the firm increasingly turned from litigation (charging $950 for a criminal case and, if it lost the case, $250 for the appeal) to counseling clients on purely business problems. The major work involved rescuing companies stricken by reverses, forming new companies and merging existing ones

into larger units, and obtaining financing, primarily from the foreign sources whose capital was then essential to the American economy. Among the earliest companies Sullivan & Cromwell helped organize was the Edison General Electric Co. in 1882. The firm also helped rescue Henry Villard's Northern Pacific Railroad from bankruptcy in this decade.

After Sullivan died in 1887, Cromwell chose William J. Curtis as junior partner. Curtis was instrumental in persuading New Jersey's legislature to pass an act making the state a haven for corporation filings. In addition to lowering fees, the act made it legally possible for one corporation to own stock in another one, which led to the formation of holding companies. Holding companies replaced the trusts that had been broken up by legislation and court decisions. The first companies to incorporate under New Jersey's new corporation law were Sullivan & Cromwell clients.

By 1900 Sullivan & Cromwell had 14 lawyers, working four to a room in bullpens surrounding the library. The firm was involved in the creation of the U.S. Steel Corp. in 1901, for which Cromwell received $2 million worth of stock in return for $250,000 in cash. By this time utilities were replacing railroads as the most powerful force in the U.S. economy. Sullivan & Cromwell helped them form holding companies with a trail of subsidiaries; in the case of Union Electric Co., the firm created more than 1,000 subsidiaries. The firm also added to its reputation for saving troubled corporations by means of the "Cromwell Plan," which involved an orderly liquidation and reorganization of companies such as American Water Works, Decker, Howell & Co., and Price, McCormick & Co. Essentially, the plan aimed at holding off creditors as long as possible in times of market panic while awaiting economic recovery.

Sullivan & Cromwell also represented foreign clients, including the French interests that had tried and failed to build a canal in Panama linking the Atlantic and Pacific Oceans. Cromwell's task was to bail out the French company by arranging the sale of its property—which included a railroad—to the U.S. government. Cromwell launched a successful lobbying campaign to convince senators and other powerful insiders that Panama rather than Nicaragua was the right place for a canal. After the Colombian Senate rejected the treaty needed to proceed, Cromwell became a behind-the-scenes agent for the revolution that resulted in Panama's independence from Colombia. The firm's French client then was able to collect $40 million from the United States for its property. Sullivan & Cromwell billed the company $800,000 for its services but had to settle for an arbitration award of $167,500 and expenses.

Cromwell increasingly absented himself from the firm's quarters, and Alfred Jaretzki became managing partner of Sullivan & Cromwell about 1900. By 1915, when Royall Victor succeeded Jaretzki, Cromwell was living in Paris, where the firm had established an office in 1911. He spent most of World War I and considerable time after the war, until 1937, in France. Even when in New York, he rarely came to Sullivan & Cromwell's offices, becoming a semirecluse residing in a midtown mansion crowded with tapestries, paintings, and statuettes. He survived until 1948, after which Rockefeller Center pulled down his residence to erect a high-rise office building.

Prosperity, Depression, Hot and Cold Wars: 1920–53

During the 1920s Sullivan & Cromwell's basic business was "green goods": drafting the indenture agreements under which financial institutions advanced money to corporations and foreign governments. It was active in restoring the international commercial links broken by World War I; between 1924 and 1931 the firm handled 94 securities issues involving more than $1 billion in loans to European parties, especially in Germany. Many of these loans fell into default during the world economic depression of the 1930s. By the end of 1928 Sullivan & Cromwell had offices in Paris, Berlin, and Buenos Aires. John Foster Dulles succeeded Victor as managing partner in 1926.

When the firm moved to larger quarters at 48 Wall Street in 1929, there were 63 lawyers, of whom 14 were partners and 37 were associates. Four women lawyers—the firm's first—were hired in 1930. During the 1920s and 1930s Sullivan & Cromwell revived its trial practice under the leadership of Harlan Fiske Stone, who later became U.S. attorney general and chief justice of the United States.

During the 1930s and most of the 1940s Sullivan & Cromwell was the largest law firm in the world. Through the Depression years Dulles established a litigation group to fight a New Deal measure designed to break up public utility holding companies. After the firm's legal challenge failed in the courts, the firm stayed busy dissolving the holding companies it had once helped put together. It also was very active in the legal work made necessary by stringent new federal regulations in the securities field. Overseas, Sullivan & Cromwell closed its Berlin office in 1935, but Dulles was criticized—both at the time and after World War II—for trying to maintain good relations with the Nazi regime to serve its clients. Among these clients was General Aniline & Film Corp., the biggest subsidiary in the Western Hemisphere of the notorious German cartel I.G. Farben, which employed slave labor during the war.

Dulles resigned as Sullivan & Cromwell's chairman in 1949 and was succeeded by Arthur H. Dean. The firm's influence on foreign policy reached its zenith in 1953, when Dulles became secretary of state and his brother Allen (also a Sullivan & Cromwell partner) became director of the Central Intelligence Agency. Dean took leave to serve the government in a number of posts, including as negotiator in the talks that ended the Korean War in 1953.

Specialized Units: 1950–90

During the 1950s Sullivan & Cromwell's most lucrative work was in the area of antitrust defenses. It successfully defended five of the largest investment banking firms in the nation against antitrust charges filed by the federal government. The general practice division dealt with the complexities of increasingly large public stock offerings. In 1956 it handled Ford Motor Co.'s $643 million initial public offering, the largest ever to that time. Sullivan & Cromwell reopened its Paris office—closed during World War II—in 1962 and opened a London office in 1972. The firm also opened a Park Avenue office in midtown Manhattan in 1971 to handle estates and personal affairs and one in Washington, D.C., in 1977. It moved headquarters to 125 Broad Street, overlooking New York Harbor, in 1979.

William Ward Foshay succeeded Dean as chairman in 1972. Sullivan & Cromwell now consisted of litigation, general practice, and tax groups, plus a group for the administration of estates and trusts. A mergers and acquisition group was formed in 1980. The firm opened offices in Melbourne in 1983, Los Angeles in 1984, and Tokyo in 1987.

To settle a class action suit Sullivan & Cromwell agreed in 1977 to recruit, hire, and pay women lawyers on the same basis as men. The firm at that time had 59 partners, all men, and 116 associates, of whom 26 were women. The first woman partner was appointed in 1982, and by the summer of 1987 there were four, but no blacks. The firm was continuing its quaint practice—unique among major law firms—of simply charging its clients a fee it considered "appropriate" rather than submitting hourly billing. A management committee of ten partners was in charge of setting Sullivan & Cromwell's policies, and a smaller committee of seven decided on how the firm would distribute more than half of its annual profits. The firm had a mandatory three-year phaseout retirement plan that went into effect when the partners reached age 67.

John R. Stevenson, who like his predecessors had considerable diplomatic experience, became chairman and senior partner of Sullivan & Cromwell in 1979. He retired in 1987 and was succeeded by John E. Merow. Merow took the helm during one of the most tempestuous periods in the firm's history. George C. Kern, Jr., head of the mergers and acquisitions unit, was accused by the Securities and Exchange Commission of violating disclosure rules while defending a company against a hostile bid. In addition, a court-supervised disciplinary panel was investigating charges that a partner had bribed and bullied witnesses in the court battle over the estate of the pharmaceuticals heir J. Seward Johnson, and an investor group accused the firm of improperly withholding vital information while fighting the group's lawsuit against a corporate client of Sullivan & Cromwell.

Some of the lawyers working for Sullivan & Cromwell's competitors suggested that the blue-chip firm's troubles stemmed from an air of arrogance. One likened opposing Sullivan & Cromwell to "having a thousand-pound tuna on the line." "They know the rules," another told a reporter, "but sometimes they act as if the rules just don't apply to them.'' All the above matters, however, apparently were disposed of without penalty to the firm. Kern continued to be Sullivan & Cromwell's star because his mergers and acquisitions unit was the firm's most profitable group, bringing in as much as one-third of all billings. In 1986 alone the unit was involved in more than $50 billion worth of acquisitions.

Before 1968 Sullivan & Cromwell's banking practice consisted of a couple of partners in estates and trusts performing routine work such as rolling over term loans. A separate banking practice was established in 1968. Within Sullivan & Cromwell's lucrative mergers and acquisitions group, bank mergers emerged in the 1980s as a major source of activity and profit for Sullivan & Cromwell. The firm helped structure more than 60 major banking mergers in the United States, valued at more than $40.2 billion, during this decade.

Sullivan & Cromwell in the 1990s

In 1991 Sullivan & Cromwell played a part in nearly every major banking deal, including the merger of Manufacturers Hanover Corp. and Chemical Banking Corp. and the acquisition of C&S/Sovran Corp. by NCNB Corp. to form NationsBank Corp. There were seven Sullivan & Cromwell partners and 25 staffers in all engaged in this field at the time.

By the mid-1990s Sullivan & Cromwell partner H. Rodgin Cohen was presiding over the firm's banking practice area, supervising nine partners and ten to 12 associates. The caseload was heavier than ever because of the increasing globalization of banking and the worldwide convergence of financial services. Cohen was recognized as ''king of the bank lawyers''— ''Mount Everest surrounded by the Appalachians,'' according to one mergers and acquisitions banker. Either he or one other lawyer represented one of the principals in 18 of the top 25 bank deals in the United States in 1997. Cohen was one of the partners serving on the executive committee charged with overseeing the firm.

In mergers and acquisitions, Sullivan & Cromwell was ranked fourth among law firms in 1997, acting as legal adviser in $91.5 billion worth of announced deals through October. The firm ranked third among underwriting legal advisers during this period, involved in domestic new issues totaling $14.6 billion in proceeds. New offices were established in Hong Kong in 1992 and in Frankfurt, Germany, in 1995.

In 1996 Sullivan & Cromwell had four divisions. General practice (corporate and financial work) was the largest and included mergers and acquisitions as one of its many units. The other divisions were litigation, tax, and estates and personal. (A fifth, practice development, had been added by 1998.) Securities work accounted for 25 percent of the firm's activity, mergers and acquisitions, 22 percent, and litigation, 21 percent. Half of the firm's clients were outside of the United States. Sullivan & Cromwell had 484 lawyers, including 114 partners, in November 1997. It has maintained a longstanding policy of not recruiting its partners from other firms.

Principal Operating Units

Departments: Estates and Personal Practice Group; General Practice Group; Litigation Practice Group; Practice Development Group; Tax Practice Group. Practice Areas: Asset-Based Finance; Broker/Dealer Regulation; Commercial Banking; Commercial Real Estate; Commodities, Futures and Derivatives; Corporate Reorganization/Bankruptcy; Environmental Law; Insurance and Tort Liability; Intellectual Property; International Trade and Investment; Investment Management; Labor and Employment; Mergers and Acquisitions; Project Finance.

Further Reading

Brill, Steven, *The American Lawyer Guide to Law Firms, 1981–1982,* New York: n.p., 1982, pp. 738–43.

Geyelin, Milo, ''Big Law Firm's Gaffe Over Sealed Records Raises Troubling Issues,'' *Wall Street Journal,* October 4, 1995, pp. A1, A6.

Gray, Patricia Bellow, ''Legal Nightmare: Multiple Allegation of Impropriety Beset Sullivan & Cromwell,'' *Wall Street Journal,* August 3, 1987, pp. 1, 14.

Lisagor, Nancy, and Lipsius, Frank, *A Law Unto Itself,* New York: William Morrow, 1988.

Lubasch, Arnold H., ''Top Law Firm Bans Sex Discrimination,'' *New York Times,* May 8, 1977, p. A13.

Matthews, Gordon, ''Sullivan & Cromwell Rides Merger Wave,'' *American Banker,* January 10, 1992, pp. 1, 10.

McCullough, David, *The Path Between the Seas,* New York: Simon and Schuster, 1977.

Rosenberg, Geanne, ''Bring in the Lawyers,'' *Investment Dealers' Digest,* November 3, 1997, pp. 19–20, 23.

Siegel, Matt, ''The Bank Merger Masters,'' *Fortune,* May 25, 1998, p. 44.

Sullivan & Cromwell, 1879–1979: A Century at Law, New York: privately printed, 1979.

Teitelman, Robert, ''King of the Bank Lawyers,'' *Institutional Investor,* November 1994, pp. 64–70, 72.

—Robert Halasz

◆ SUMITOMO BANK

The Sumitomo Bank, Limited

4-6-5 Kitahama
Chuo-ku
Osaka 541-0041
Japan
(06) 227-2111
Fax: (06) 229-1083
Web site: http://www.sumitomobank.co.jp

Public Company
Incorporated: 1912
Employees: 15,111
Assets: ¥64.67 trillion (US$487 billion) (1998)
Stock Exchanges: Tokyo Osaka Paris London
Ticker Symbol: SUBJY (ADR)
SICs: 6081 Branches & Agencies of Foreign Banks;
    6712 Offices of Bank Holding Companies

Once the banking division of one of Japan's largest and oldest *zaibatsu* conglomerates, The Sumitomo Bank, Limited is one of the largest financial institutions in the world and ranks number two among Japanese banks, trailing only Bank of Tokyo-Mitsubishi Ltd. Offering wholesale, retail, and investment banking services, Sumitomo Bank has more than 350 offices in Japan and 92 overseas branches, offices, and subsidiaries in about 30 countries. Sumitomo is the central coordinating body for the now-independent but former *zaibatsu* members of the Sumitomo group and has assumed the new identity of *keiretsu* (banking conglomerate).

Early History

The Sumitomo group of enterprises is one of the oldest surviving business entities in the world, dating to the early 1600s. Sumitomo was originally founded near Kyoto as a medicine and book shop. The discovery by a family member of a new method for copper smelting led the company into the expanding and highly profitable copper trade. The acquisition and development of large copper mines had made Sumitomo one of Japan's largest companies by 1868, when battling clans restored the Meiji emperor to power.

Although Sumitomo supported the losing side in that struggle, the company managed to develop good relations with the new government and later purchased some state enterprises as part of a national modernization campaign. As the company grew, Sumitomo's director general, Teigo Iba, advocated diversification into new fields of business. Flush with money from Sumitomo's copper operation, Iba set up a banking division in 1895 called the Sumitomo Bank.

Acting as the private banker for the ever-expanding Sumitomo enterprises, the Sumitomo Bank experienced smooth and rapid growth. In 1912, in need of further capital, the bank was incorporated and made a share offering. In doing so it became the first Sumitomo division to go public. Between 1916 and 1918 the bank established branch offices in San Francisco, Shanghai, Bombay, New York, and London, and an affiliate, the Sumitomo Bank of Hawaii.

Japan emerged as a major world power following its victory in the Russo-Japanese War in 1905 and, later, after World War I. This new prestige afforded companies like Sumitomo new business opportunities throughout Asia as Japan became a colonial power on par with Great Britain, the United States, the Netherlands, and France. The Sumitomo Bank established an interest everywhere the Sumitomo group went—Korea, Formosa (Taiwan), and China.

The Sumitomo Bank spun off a division of its own in 1923, when its warehousing arm was incorporated as the Sumitomo Warehouse Company. Two years later the Sumitomo group broadened its financial activities by taking over the management of Hinode Life Insurance, which was renamed Sumitomo Life Insurance the following year. Despite the creation of separate Sumitomo corporations—Sumitomo Machinery Works, Sumitomo Fertilizer Works, Sumitomo Mining, and so on—the Sumitomo group remained a closely knit conglomerate called a *zaibatsu* (literally, a "money clique") whose constituent companies owned collective majorities of shares in each other.

Company Perspectives:

The Sumitomo Bank will be the leading provider of the highest quality financial products and services to our customers on a worldwide basis to gain and maintain their respect and confidence. We will also be a consistent contributor to the development of our local, national and global community through maintaining long-term steady growth.

In order to achieve this, we are committed to the following principles: to give the top priority to our customers and to respond to their needs; to respect our staff as individuals and to create an open and challenging work environment; to consistently stimulate positive thinking, innovation, creativity and efficiency in our business practices; to provide opportunities for the personal development of our staff in which keen insight, pride in our work, professionalism and integrity are fostered; to ensure the highest standards of sound management and ethical conduct throughout our bank and fulfilling our social responsibility and increasing public trust in us.

The power of the various *zaibatsu* was greatly resented by a quasi-fascist element in the military that rose to power during the 1930s. Advocating Japanese supremacy in Asia as well as a more equitable distribution of wealth, these militarists were bent on the eventual nationalization of the *zaibatsu*. But because the *zaibatsu* made up Japan's military-industrial complex, they were essential to the militarists' plans for conquest.

The *zaibatsu* were uncomfortable in their cooperation with the militarists: they stood to profit from Japan's expansion, but they also faced disintegration if the plan worked. Nonetheless, the Sumitomo Bank helped to finance the military's preparation for combat. Many Japanese considered the war a patriotic cause, seeking to remove western imperialists from Asia. But most Japanese companies, regardless of their reservations, were treated according to their cooperation with the militarists after World War II, and the Sumitomo companies were no exception.

Postwar Reorganization

Despite the militarists' desires, the Sumitomo group, having taken over a number of formerly independent or associated companies, became larger and more concentrated as a result of the war. After the war the Allied occupation authority imposed a series of antimonopoly laws that broke the *zaibatsu* into hundreds and even thousands of smaller companies. Each was forbidden to use its prewar name or to engage in cross-ownership of stock. The Sumitomo Bank was reorganized under this plan in 1948 as the Bank of Osaka.

A relaxation in industrial laws in 1949, and again in 1952, permitted the former Sumitomo companies not only to conduct business with each other, but also to resume use of the Sumitomo name and cross-ownership of stock. The *zaibatsu* re-formed, and the Sumitomo Bank became its coordinating entity.

The man placed in charge of the company after the war was Shozo Hotta, who believed that the bank should differentiate itself from other banks by emphasizing business efficiency. He also personally evaluated business ventures that he felt the Sumitomo Bank should back. As the bank grew during the 1950s, it became better able to support larger industrial ventures such as Matsushita Electric, Toyo Kogyo, and Daishowa Paper. Many of these investments were highly successful, particularly the Matsushita venture. During Japan's first period of export-led growth, from 1955 to 1965, Matsushita grew several times over to become the nation's largest electronics manufacturer.

Adopting the new goal of "quality and quantity," the Sumitomo Bank expanded its corporate business, recognizing the diminishing opportunities for growth from its historical affiliates such as NEC, Matsushita, and other Sumitomo companies. In addition, much of the bank's business was concentrated in the Kansai area around Osaka, leaving Tokyo and Yokohama, both rapidly growing markets, largely unexploited by Sumitomo.

In a separate effort to expand, the Sumitomo Bank merged with the Kawachi Bank in April 1965. Retaining the Sumitomo name, the banks' combined deposits surpassed those of their competitor, Fuji Bank.

Hotta was named chairman of the bank in 1971, when he was replaced as president by Koji Asai. Asai and his successor, Kyonosuke Ibe, each had a comparatively short tenure, Ibe being replaced by Ichiro Isoda. Although Hotta was removed from the day-to-day administration of the bank, the organization strongly reflected his personality: bureaucratic and authoritarian. Often described as the father of the restoration of the Sumitomo Bank, Hotta had nevertheless created for it a poor public image, which Isoda was determined to change.

Toyo Kogyo and Atake Crises, 1970s

Higher earnings permitted the bank to increase lending to Matsushita, Toyo Kogyo, and Daishowa, as well as to companies outside the Sumitomo group such as Idemitsu Kosan, Uraga Dock Company, Taisho Pharmaceutical, and Ataka & Company. Again, many of these investments were highly profitable. Those to Ataka, Daishowa, Uraga, and Toyo Kogyo, however, were not. Toyo Kogyo, in particular, was in very serious condition. The manufacturer of Mazda trucks, Toyo Kogyo had bet its future on the success of the Wankel rotary engine, a prewar German design that was supposed to be highly fuel efficient. It proved otherwise, and became a costly problem for Toyo Kogyo, especially in combination with the 1973–74 oil crisis. Sumitomo nevertheless supported Toyo Kogyo during its reorganization.

More serious, however, was the impending failure of Ataka & Company, a major Japanese trading firm. Because it stood to lose substantial amounts of money if Ataka went bankrupt, the Sumitomo Bank pledged to support Ataka until it could again be made solvent. Hotta entrusted Isoda with responsibility for rehabilitating Ataka. Isoda in turn appointed Yasushi Komatsu, managing director of the bank, to head Ataka. A more outgoing, congenial man than Hotta, Isoda enlisted help from the Ministry of Finance, the Bank of Japan, Ataka's customers, and even competitors of the Sumitomo Bank. Under a coordinated effort, Ataka was completely restructured; its unprofitable and under-performing divisions were sold off and cost-cutting procedures were initiated for those that remained. A year after assuming control over Ataka, the bank arranged a merger with C. Itoh, Japan's largest general trading company.

The Sumitomo Bank's handling of the Toyo Kogyo and Ataka affairs greatly enhanced its image among business and govern-ment leaders, as well as with the public. The bank's character changed at a crucial time, as the Japanese economy was entering a period of stable growth. A buyer's market emerged in banking, and with little remaining room for growth, each bank was forced to compete vigorously for market share. Had Isoda tried to cut losses by permitting both companies to go bankrupt, the bank would almost certainly have lost major clients to competitors. Instead, Sumitomo demonstrated an unusual degree of dedication to its customers and won more confidence than any advertising campaign could have hoped to generate.

The company's ability to support its clients through hard economic times was tested in the late 1970s when the industrial base in Kansai began to deteriorate. The textile industry, long in a state of decline in Japan, finally felt the effects of cheaper foreign competition. Within the Sumitomo group, business was down for Sumitomo Light Metals, Sumitomo Cement, Sumi-tomo Metal, and Sumitomo Chemical.

Still, by this time, the Sumitomo Bank had become Japan's largest bank in terms of deposits. That position was later lost, however, not due to a failure in business, but due to the merger of the Dai-Ichi Bank and the Kangyo Bank, forming Dai-Ichi Kangyo Bank. A similar merger between Sumitomo and the Kansai Sogo Bank was cancelled in 1978 because the resulting bank would have been too deeply influenced by the Kansai economy.

Reorganized in 1979

In 1979 the Sumitomo Bank carried out a general reorgani-zation on the recommendations of the American consulting firm MacKenzie & Company. The bank was divided into four divi-sions: business, sales, international, and planning and adminis-tration. In addition, greater freedom was given to division heads in order to achieve greater decentralization.

Isoda ordered the expansion of international financial ser-vices and the establishment of an in-house securities business. Toward that end, Sumitomo purchased the Swiss Banca de Gottardo in February 1984, and later became the leading Japa-nese bank in foreign markets. Meanwhile, the bank rescued another troubled company in the early 1980s when it helped turn around Asahi Breweries, Ltd.

Isoda became chairman in 1983, when he was replaced as president by Koh Komatsu, an imaginative manager who had distinguished himself during the 1960s by rehabilitating Sumi-tomo's operations in California.

In 1986, observing Citicorp's experience with bank compe-tition in the United States, Komatsu decided that Sumitomo needed to diversify its customer base geographically. Having made little progress moving into Tokyo, the bank proposed a merger with an established institution in the region. The partner bank eventually settled upon was the Heiwa Sogo Bank, an institution with about 100 branches that operated until 7:00 P.M.—four hours later than other banks.

1986 Goldman, Sachs & Co. Investment

Sumitomo, already an established leader in international banking and finance, announced in December 1986 that it had made a $430 million, or 12.5 percent, investment in the New York-based investment bank Goldman, Sachs & Co. The in-vestment, which amounted to a controlling interest, greatly alarmed American banks, which charged that a foreign competi-tor had been permitted to enter a field the Glass-Steagall Act had barred American banks themselves from. The Federal Re-serve later ruled that Sumitomo's investment was legal, but that Sumitomo could not increase its interest, exercise management rights, or expand to other countries.

Trouble came for Komatsu the following year, when reports of friction among bank divisions and depressed earnings led the board of directors to replace him as president with Sotoo Tatsumi. The new president pledged to remove excessive layers of bureaucracy that had recently compromised the bank's re-puted speed and efficiency. Emphasizing a new competitive spirit, Tatsumi was charged with consolidating the gains made under Komatsu, to rationalize the company's busy expansion of the previous year.

1990s Banking Crisis

From 1985 through 1989, Japan's economy went through a period of extreme speculation as land prices and share prices soared beyond reason. When the "bubble" burst in the early 1990s, the banking industry in Japan was hit hard. Sumitomo Bank was no exception, and was one of the first to feel the effects. In October 1990 Isoda resigned as chairman, taking personal responsibility for the bank's involvement in a stock manipulation scandal centering around Itoman & Co., an Osaka-based trading company with longstanding ties to the Sumitomo group. The bank operated without a chairman until early 1993 when Tatsumi took on that post with the appoint-ment of Toshio Morikawa as president. Morikawa had served as vice president for international operations.

In January 1993, meantime, Sumitomo made the unprece-dented move of writing off ¥100 billion (US$895 million) in bad loans, a number of them related to the Itoman affair. Another consequence of the 1990s Japanese lending crisis was an increase in violence against the country's bank employees, incidents that were believed to be related to the banks' attempts to collect bad debts from customers. Among the several inci-dents involving Sumitomo Bank was the September 1994 mur-der of the director of the bank's Nagoya branch.

As the 1990s proceeded and the Japanese economy contin-ued to stagnate, the banking crisis only deepened. For the fiscal year ending in March 1995, Sumitomo posted a net loss of ¥335 billion (US$3.8 billion), the first major Japanese bank since World War II to record a loss. The loss resulted from Sumitomo writing off ¥826 billion (US$9.4 billion) in bad loans, a precedent-setting move. Up until this point Japanese regulators had discouraged such writeoffs for fear of weakening confidence in the financial system. Sumitomo, however, wanted to move as quickly as possible to relieve itself of its bad-loan albatross.

In February 1996 Sumitomo Bank took over the U.S. commercial loan portfolio and offices of Daiwa Bank Ltd. in a US$3.37 billion asset transfer. The previous December U.S. regulators had ordered Daiwa to discontinue its U.S. operations following the disclosure of the bank's involvement in a US$1.1 billion trading scandal. Subsequent discussions between Sumitomo and Daiwa about a full-scale merger were put on hold. Also in 1996 the bank opened a representative office in Shenyang, China, becoming the first Japanese bank to open an office in China. In addition, Sumitomo Bank began preparing for Japan's ''Big Bang,'' which was announced in November 1996 and promised to comprehensively reform the Japanese financial system and open it up to international competition by 2001. Meanwhile, Sumitomo faced a new competitor following the April 1996 merger of The Mitsubishi Bank, Ltd. and Bank of Tokyo, Ltd. to form Bank of Tokyo-Mitsubishi Ltd., which became the new number one Japanese bank. Sumitomo Bank was number two.

In June 1997 Morikawa replaced Tatsumi as chairman, and Yoshifumi Nishikawa was appointed president. Continuing to resolve its bad loans burden, Sumitomo in September 1997 sold ¥40 billion (US$330 million) in problem loans to Goldman, Sachs. Unfortunately, that year also brought the beginnings of the Asian financial crisis, which saddled Sumitomo and other Japanese banks with additional bad debt from loans made in such troubled nations as Indonesia and South Korea. Furthermore, new disclosure rules forced Japanese banks to write off more bad loans. For the 1998 fiscal year, therefore, Sumitomo wrote off another ¥1.04 trillion (US$7.66 billion), leading to a full-year pretax loss of ¥502.7 billion (US$3.7 billion). More bad news came in February 1998 when the bank was one of several named in a scandal involving the bribing of Japanese finance ministry officials.

In anticipation of the ''Big Bang,'' Sumitomo Bank and Daiwa Securities announced in July 1998 a series of alliances in the areas of investment banking, derivatives, and asset management. In October 1998 Sumitomo exited from U.S. retail banking when it sold Sumitomo Bank of California to Zions Bancorp. In late 1998 the Japanese government attempted to mitigate the ongoing banking crisis by passing legislation allowing regulators to inject public money into banks that have depleted their capital through problem loan writeoffs. The bailout program eased fears about bank failures and appeared likely to counter the cautious business lending stance adopted by many Japanese banks. In November Sumitomo announced that it would apply for such an injection. In concurrence with its request for public money, Sumitomo was considering launching a tough restructuring program through which it would cut staff, close additional overseas branches, and initiate other cost-cutting efforts. Through such a restructuring and an infusion of money, it seemed possible that Sumitomo Bank might finally be able to relieve itself of its 1980s hangover.

Principal Subsidiaries

Americas: Sumitomo Bank of New York Trust Company (U.S.A.); Sumitomo Bank Capital Markets, Inc. (U.S.A.); Sumitomo Bank Financial Services, Inc. (U.S.A.); Sumitomo Bank Leasing and Finance, Inc. (U.S.A.); Sumitomo Bank Investment Management (New York), Inc. (U.S.A.); Sumitomo Bank Securities, Inc. (U.S.A.); The Sumitomo Bank of Canada; Banco Sumitomo Brasileiro S.A. (Brazil); Central Pacific Bank (U.S.A.). Europe, Middle East and Africa: Sumitomo Finance International PLC (U.K.); Sumitomo Bank (Schweiz) AG (Switzerland); Sumitomo Finance (Middle East) E.C. (Bahrain); Banca del Gottardo (Switzerland); Sumitomo Bank (Deutschland) GmbH (Germany); Finanziaria Sumitomo (Italia) S.p.A. (Italy); Sumitomo Finance (Dublin) Limited (Ireland); SBCM Limited (U.K.). Asia and Oceania: Sumitomo Finance (Asia) Limited (Hong Kong); SBCM Limited Hong Kong Branch; Sumitomo International Finance Australia Limited; Sumitomo International Finance Australia Limited Melbourne Branch; Sumitomo Financial Futures (Singapore) Pte. Ltd.; SB Merchant Bank (Singapore) Limited; P.T. Bank Sumitomo Niaga (Indonesia); P.T. Exim SB Leasing (Indonesia); P.T. Bank Merincorp (Indonesia); P.T. Merincorp Securities Indonesia; China International Finance Company Limited; Sumigin Metro Investment Corp. (Philippines); Bangkok Sumigin Consulting Company (Thailand).

Principal Operating Units

Branch Banking Group; Corporate and Institutional Banking Group; International Banking Group; The Americas Division; Capital Markets Group; Treasury Group.

Further Reading

Baker, Gerard, ''Sumitomo Bank Posts £1.8bn Loss in Wake of Bad Debts,'' *Financial Times,* January 28, 1995, pp. 1, 18.
Brauchli, Marcus W., and Masayoshi Kanabayashi, ''Exit of Sumitomo Chief Marks End of Era,'' *Wall Street Journal,* October 15, 1990, p. A12.
Chandler, Clay, ''The Bank That Broke with Convention,'' *Financial Times,* May 26, 1995, p. 24.
——, ''Sumitomo Bank Selects President in Bid to Surmount Troubled Past,'' *Wall Street Journal,* April 29, 1993, p. A10.
Karmin, Craig, ''Goldman Gets Jump with Japanese Banks,'' *Wall Street Journal,* March 26, 1998, p. B13.
Neff, Robert, and William Glasgall, ''An $8 Billion Write-off—And a Celebration,'' *Business Week,* February 13, 1995, p. 56.
Sapsford, Jathon, ''Japan's Banks to Begin Signing Up for an Injection of Public Money,'' *Wall Street Journal,* November 17, 1998, p. A17.
——, ''Japan's Latest Bank Plan Buoys Credit Hopes,'' *Wall Street Journal,* October 8, 1998, pp. A11, A13.
——, ''Sumitomo, Daiwa Venture Looks Abroad,'' *Wall Street Journal,* July 29, 1998, p. A11.
Shale, Tony, ''Sumitomo's Dangerous Liaisons,'' *Euromoney,* December 1990, pp. 16+.
Shirouzu, Norihiko, ''More Banks in Japan Implicated in Scandal,'' *Wall Street Journal,* February 17, 1998, p. A14.
Tanzer, Andrew, '' 'The Other Banks Feel Threatened,' '' *Forbes,* October 2, 1989, pp. 80+.

—updated by David E. Salamie

Sunburst Hospitality Corporation

10770 Columbia Pike
Silver Spring, Maryland 20901
U.S.A.
(301) 979-3800
Fax: (301) 979-3991
Web site: http://sunbursthospitality.com

Public Company
Incorporated: 1941 as Quality Courts United, Inc.
Employees: 4,851
Sales: $114.6 million (1997)
Stock Exchanges: New York
Ticker Symbol: SNB
SICs: 7011 Hotels & Motels

Sunburst Hospitality Corporation is one of the top ten publicly owned real estate companies involved in building and managing hotels in the United States. As of October 1998, Sunburst owned and operated 86 hotels with 11,850 rooms in 27 states and had 11 more hotels and 1,114 rooms under construction or development. The company's hotels served primarily the mid-priced segment of the market and included the Clarion, Quality, Comfort Inn, MainStay, Econo Lodge, and Roadway brands. Sunburst was spun off from Choice Hotels in October 1997, becoming Choice's largest franchisee in the process.

Early History

Sunburst Hospitality Corp. was a direct descendant of one of the oldest lodging chains in the country, Quality Courts. In the early 1940s, motels were known as roadside tourist camps and had an unsavory reputation. That opinion was reinforced by FBI Director J. Edgar Hoover, who wrote in *American* magazine that "a majority of the 35,000 tourist camps in the U.S. threaten the peace and welfare of the communities upon which these camps have fastened themselves and all of us who form the motoring public. Many of them are not only hideouts and meeting places, but actual bases of operations from which gangs of desperadoes prey upon the surrounding territory."

To counter that image, a group of independent motel owners and operators formed Quality Courts United, Inc., a nonprofit membership corporation, in 1941. The organization established standards for and policed the industry while also promoting and marketing its members' motels. In January 1963, it reincorporated as a for-profit corporation called Quality Courts Motels and changed from a membership to a franchise structure. In April, the company made its first stock offering, selling shares to member motel owners and operators and their employees.

One of those shareholders was Stewart Bainum, whose Park Consolidated Motels, Inc. operated five motels franchised under the Quality Courts Motels name. Bainum was a college dropout and former plumbing contractor. After World War II, he moved from Chicago to the Washington, D.C., suburbs to take advantage of the building boom in the area and entered the construction business. In 1960, he built a nursing home in Wheaton, Maryland, a D.C. suburb, and three years later he went into the motel business. Within five years he was president of Park Consolidated Motels, Inc., based in Silver Spring, Maryland.

In April 1968, Bainum merged Quality Courts with his motel company and also incorporated his nursing home business as Manor Care, Inc. He moved Quality Courts' headquarters from Florida to Maryland and became president and chief executive officer. Within a few months the company announced that it was running 422 motels—12 of which were company-owned with the rest franchised—and was planning to expand into the western part of the country and Canada where there were fewer motels.

The 1970s: From Boom to Almost Bust

As the motel industry enjoyed a boom, Quality Courts established an international division which soon had four motels under development, in Belgium, Germany, and Canada. With properties in 33 states, the company looked beyond motels to related fields, acquiring Revere Furniture and Equipment Company, which sold motel furniture and supplies, and Contempo Associates, a motel interior design firm. In addition, the company's construction subsidiary won a contract to build military housing. Profits were strong, and Quality Courts built a new headquarters and a showroom for Revere in Silver Spring.

Late in 1972, Quality changed its name to Quality Inns International, Inc. to reflect its broader scope of business. However, the "international" portion of the business, and the plans to open 20 hotels in Europe, were stalled by the oil embargo in 1973–74 and the economic downturn that followed. Quality Inns canceled its European expansion plans, stopped construction on projects underway, sold properties most affected by the gas shortage, and worked to strengthen relations with its franchise operators.

During 1976, as deficits grew, the company discontinued The Revere Group and sold other real estate holdings, cutting Quality Inns' losses in half by the end of 1976. At the same time, the company launched a national TV and magazine advertising campaign and initiated a major franchising program, which brought Chicago's illustrious Blackstone Hotel into the chain.

By 1977, revenues were up and Quality Inns was the tenth largest American hotel chain based on number of rooms. In 1978, the company purchased the Royale Inns of America chain and formed a joint venture with a Mexican bank to open 40 motels in Mexico. The following year, Quality Inns became the world's seventh largest lodging chain, with 324 owned and franchised properties.

1980–86: A Merger and Expansion

In 1980, Bainum hired Robert Hazard, Jr., as president and CEO and Gerald Petitt as executive vice-president and chief operating officer. The two men had worked together at IBM, American Express, and more recently at Best Western, which, within a six-year period Hazard had expanded from 800 hotels to 2,600. The company they were to head was considered an also-ran among the top chains, with 350 properties and some 40,000 rooms.

In December, Bainum completed the merger of his nursing home and motel businesses in a $37 million deal in which Manor Care acquired Quality Inns, forming a $125 million lodging conglomerate. The *Washington Post* called the new company "an instant success," noting that within six months the original $7 stock price was worth more than $40. During 1981, Manor Care reorganized as a holding company for three subsidiaries: Quality Inns, Inc., which owned and operated hotels; Quality Inns International, Inc., which franchised hotels under the Quality Inn name; and Manor Healthcare Corporation.

The new hotel management team set out to double the size of Quality Inns in three years. Hazard and Petitt pioneered the concept of segmenting the market, dividing their hotels and motels into three separate chains serving different types of travelers. The Quality Inn brand was assigned to medium-priced properties. For expense account customers and luxury tours, the company created the full-service, deluxe Quality Royale brand. Those who watched their travel budget were serviced by the new, low-priced Comfort Inn brand.

To ensure that all three sectors would live up to the Quality name, the company instituted a strict quality-control system and dropped 30 franchises for failing to measure up. In their first year at Quality Inns International, Hazard and Petitt added 10,168 rooms to the chain. In the meantime, Manor Care's other hotel subsidiary, Quality Inns, Inc., was operating 28 company-owned hotels as a franchisee and looking for a president.

Early in 1982, a $2 million computerized reservation system went into operation to generate more business for the chain. In November, the company had 615 hotels and motels, making it the third largest chain in the industry. That number was achieved even as the company dropped 150 hotels. Most of the additions were existing hotels, and many of these were lured from other chains.

In 1984, Manor Care increased its holdings in the hotel industry when it became the largest shareholder in a British chain of hotels, with nearly a one-third stake in Prince of Wales Hotels, P.L.C. This purchase provided the company with a toehold in Europe, from which to launch further expansion. That summer, the company's SUNBURST reservation system set a new company record, booking $10.85 million in a single month, and Quality announced all-suite prototypes for each of its hotel brands. "We are breaking new ground in the all-suite war by being the first major lodging chain to introduce a mid-priced all-suite product and luxury-budget all suite product simultaneously," a company press release announced.

Quality Inns International continued to innovate, introducing smoke-free rooms and Prime Time, a senior discount program good at all its hotels. The company also increased its international business.

1987–88: Management Change and Shifting Emphases

In 1987, founder Stewart Bainum turned over control of Manor Care to his son, Stewart Bainum, Jr. The new chairman continued the company's emphasis on the healthcare side of the business, selling four hotels and Manor Care's stake in the Prince of Wales hotel chain in England.

During the end of the decade, Quality added new offerings at both ends of the lodging business. For the upscale market, Quality formed Clarion Hotels and Resorts, a joint venture with the Associated Inns and Restaurants Company of America (AIRCOA). The new arrangement merged the franchise operations of Quality's four Royale hotels with the 33 Clarion Hotels owned by AIRCOA and provided the properties with worldwide marketing and reservation systems. "We're not entering a market by building a building, but by providing services to luxury hotels that are already built," Petitt told the *Washington Post* in a 1987 article.

For the budget end of the market, Quality introduced McSleep Inn, with rooms renting for $20 to $29 a night. In 1987, after a year-long legal battle with McDonald's, Quality Inns renamed the chain Sleep Inn. The case made legal history as the first time a court granted McDonald's trademark rights outside the food industry. The budget segment of the lodging industry, with rooms averaging $32 a night, was big news in the business. According to a 1989 article in the *New York Times,* while hotel rooms overall had increased by only two percent a year since 1981, the number of budget rooms grew by 20 percent in 1988, with a projected growth in 1989 of 17 percent. The demand led to consolidation, with the big chains buying smaller budget operations. Quality Inns International joined in the hunt.

1990–94

Following an unsuccessful bid to buy the Ramada and Howard Johnson hotel franchises in the summer of 1990, Manor Care did acquire the Rodeway Inns International franchise system, with 148 budget motels, for nearly $15 million. Quality Inns International, was now the largest hotel franchise system in the world, and in July the company changed the subsidiary's name to Choice Hotels International, Inc. to reflect the wider lodging options it offered.

Manor Care's hotel buying binge continued that fall, when it completed the acquisition of Econo Lodges of America, with 615 motels, along with 85 related Friendship Inns, for $60 million. With seven brand names, including Quality, Comfort, Clarion, Sleep, Econo Lodge, Friendship, and Rodeway Inns, Choice now held one quarter of the low-cost hotel room market. The company began heavy television advertising efforts, with ads featuring celebrities popping out of suitcases. As Choice Chairman Robert C. Hazard, Jr., told *Forbes,* "Our goal is 1 million hotel rooms and 10,000 hotels worldwide by the year 2000."

The rapid pace of acquisitions left Choice with the daunting task of integrating the new chains into its old system. The main link between the disparate parts became a new $5 million computerized reservation program. Rather than have franchises competing with each other for business, as so often occurred in hotel companies with segmented brands, Choice reservation clerks had information about all the company's brands in a city or area, and kept customers within the Choice system.

Choice's fastest-growing brand was Comfort Inn, which had become a giant chain in its own right. In 1993 the company opened its 1,000th Comfort Inn. Fiscal 1994 was Choice's best to date, as it added 325 hotels. Its chains represented one in every ten hotels in the United States. Overseas, Choice hotels now numbered 600; guests could even ride an elephant to the Quality property in the Himalayas. Three things were credited with the success: the reservation system, national advertising, and the quality control program.

Meanwhile, the hotel division was buying more hotels and had spent over $125 million in cash since 1992, to acquire 26 properties, bringing the total under management to 51. The new properties were renovated and turned into hotels in each of Choice's market segments or converted into assisted living facilities for Manor Care. Donald J. Landry, Quality Inns president, predicted the subsidiary would double its acquisitions in the next year. "We are an all-cash, quick-close buyer, with a record of closing the deals we place under contract," he told

National Mortgage News in a December 1994 article. He added, "Our 'deep pockets' enable us to close in a timely manner without financing or leaseback contingencies and to renovate, refurbish and reposition properties as needed."

The division was also testing different, less expensive ways to serve food to hotel guests. In Dallas, for example, a mini-food court, named Choice Picks, offered guests well known brands of pizzas, coffees, and sandwiches. In Mobile, Alabama, the division eliminated its full banquet kitchen, opting to buy food for banquets already prepared: food had only to be heated in a special oven. Both concepts reduced inventory and personnel costs.

In December 1994, Manor Care reorganized its structure once again. It consolidated Quality Inns, Inc. and its 51 properties with the Choice Hotels International Inc. and created a single business dealing with lodging. In fiscal 1994, franchise revenues were $161 million, with the company-owned hotels bringing in another $78 million. Dan Landry became president of Choice Hotels International, and Robert Hazard, Jr., and Gerald Petitt were named co-chairmen.

1995–96: Spinoff from Manor Care

Landry began repositioning Choice as a hospitality company, not just a huge franchiser. "We want to be the market leader serving those who serve travelers," he said in a May 1995 *Lodging Hospitality* article, meaning everything from car rental companies to cruise lines. He worked to increase brand awareness, introduced some of the food service innovations tested in the company-owned hotels, phased out the Friendship brand, and announced a new brand, MainStay Suites. This was an extended stay hotel with daily rates of $40 to $60. That concept was targeted at people wanting lodging for longer periods of time.

On November 1, 1996, deciding its future lay in the healthcare business, Manor Care spun off the $342 million Choice Hotels International subsidiary. That new publicly owned company, with some 3,145 hotels worldwide, was the second largest hotel company in the world. William Floyd, an executive from Taco Bell, was named CEO of Choice Hotels International, with Landry remaining as president and COO.

Spinoff from Choice Hotels International

Within a few months, Choice management decided to separate the real estate management operations from the franchising operations, following a new trend in the lodging industry. On October 16, 1997, Sunburst Hospitality Corporation began trading shares on the New York Stock Exchange. At the time, it owned and operated 76 hotels in the United States and had 20 more under development. The overseas hotels it previously owned were spun off with Choice's franchising business.

The new company developed, owned, and managed hotels. Within a year it had increased its number of hotels to 86, with 11 more being built or under development in 27 states, and was the number one owner/developer of MainStay Suites, the extended stay concept Landry introduced three years earlier. However, the stock market drop in 1998 halted the development plans for MainStay. The company announced it had sold one property and identified others it might sell. Although all its properties were Choice brands, Sunburst was not limited in the hotels it owned. Despite the economy and the overbuilding in the industry, Sunburst's hotels were individually successful, and the MainStay concept appeared to be a popular option, meeting a specific need.

Principal Subsidiaries

Boulevard Motel Corp.; Cactus Hotel Corp.; Choice Management & Realty Services, Inc.; Comfort California, Inc.; Gulf Hotel Corp.; QCM Beverages; Sunburst Hotel Corp.

Further Reading

Abrahamson, Dan, "Non-Smokers Are Targeted in a $3-Million Multimedia DR Campaign by Quality Inns," *DM News,* November 1, 1986, p. 18.
Behr, Peter, "Manor Care: Merger Magic with an Expanding Giant," *Washington Post,* June 22, 1981, Bus. Sec. p. 1.
Berg, Eric N., "At Budget Hotels, Growing Pains," *New York Times,* November 17, 1989, p. D1.
"Choice Names Landry President," *Travel Weekly,* December 26, 1994, p. 102.
Cuff, Daniel F., "A Wake-up Call at Quality Inns," *New York Times,* September 13, 1981, p. C4.
Deady, Tim, "Stock Slump Cramps Hotel Companies," *Washington Business Journal,* September 25, 1998, p. 3.
Evans, Judith, "Choice Hotels President Will Head Spinoff," *Washington Post,* June 27, 1997, p. G2.
Faiola, Anthony, "Choice Hotels Make a Wide Turn," *Washington Post,* July 3, 1995, p. F1.
Hughes, Bill, "The Mature Traveler: 10% Off, Period—And No Fine Print," *Los Angeles Times,* November 9, 1986, Travel Sec., p. 13.
Janjigian, Robert, "Clear Choice: Hotel Company of the Year," *Hospitality Design,* December 1993, p. 54.
Kopecki, Dawn, "Splits, Mergers Stir Hotel Firms," *Washington Times,* November 3, 1997, p. D12.
Koss-Feder, Laura, "Choice Changes Strategy After Spinoff," *Hotel & Motel Management,* April 22, 1996, p. 1.
Knight, Jerry, "Quality Inns Plans 'Mod' Motel Suites," *Washington Post,* June 15, 1983, p. D8.
Marcial, Gene G., "Will Manor Care Spin Off Choice Hotels?," *Business Week,* September 26, 1994, p. 112.
McDonald, Michele, "Quality Inns Signs Pact to Operate 8 U.K. Hotels," *Travel Weekly,* May 3, 1984, p. 1.
"Merger Complete," *Washington Post,* December 2, 1980, p. D9.
Nance, Sheryl, "McDonald's Wins Bout," *National Law Journal,* October 17, 1988, p. 39.
Pearson, Trevor, "Manor Care Renovates Hotels," *National Mortgage News,* December 5, 1994, p. 30.
"Quality Inns Enters All-Suite Market with Three-Tier Approach," *Business Wire,* August 8, 1984.
"Quality Inns International Inc.," *Washington Post,* April 14, 1980, Bus. Sec., p. 40.
"Quality Inns Reports Record-Breaking Summer," *Business Wire,* October 1, 1984.
Rosato, Donna, "No. 2 U.S. Hotel Franchiser Choice Hotels Taps Taco Bell Executive for Its Top Post," *USA Today,* October 10, 1996, p. 6B.
Rowe, Megan, "Choice Chooses Change," *Lodging Hospitality,* May 1995, p. 26.
Saponar, R.C., "Hotel Chain to Announce Plan to Enter New Market Segment," *Nashville Business Journal,* October 23, 1989, p. 2.
"A Sleeping Giant," *Success,* November 1994, p. 99.
Smith, Todd, "Rodeway Acquisition Puts Manor Care Ahead," *Washington Times,* July 6, 1990, p. C1.
Sullivan, Colleen, "A New Direction for Quality Inns," *Washington Post,* April 18, 1977, p. D12.
"Thinking Big at Quality Inns," *New York Times,* December 24, 1983, p. 29.
Walsh, Sharon Warren, "Quality Inns, Clarion Set Hotel Venture," *Washington Post,* January 22, 1987, p. C1.
Walsh, Sharon Warren, "Quality Inns' 'McSleep' Motels Arouse McDonald's Anger," *Washington Post,* September 21, 1987, p. F6.

—Ellen D. Wernick

Sun International Hotels Limited

Coral Towers
Paradise Island
Bahamas
(242) 363-6000
(800) ATLANTIS [from U.S.A.]; (800) 321-3000 [from Canada]
Fax: (242) 363-5401
Web site: http://www.sunint.com

Public Company
Incorporated: 1993
Employees: 13,000
Sales: $558.91 million (1997)
Stock Exchanges: New York
Ticker Symbol: SIH
SICs: 7011 Hotels & Casinos

Sun International Hotels Limited (Sun International) is headquartered on Paradise Island, The Bahamas. The company owns almost 70 percent of 800-acre Paradise Island and, through its subsidiaries, is an international leader in family entertainment and gaming destinations on Paradise Island, the location of the world's largest island resort; the Indian Ocean countries known as the Comoro Islands and Mauritius; and the United States. The company operates nine hotels containing approximately 4,500 rooms and three casinos with gaming space containing more than 6,000 slot machines and 350 gaming tables.

The Early Years: 1993–94

Solomon (Sol) Kerzner, born in South Africa of Russian emigrants, built that country's first five-star hotel in 1964. Then, in partnership with South African Breweries, in 1969 he established the chain of Southern Sun Hotels, which revolutionized tourism in South Africa with the nation's first leisure resort, Sun City. By 1983 Southern Sun operated 30 luxury hotels with more than 5,000 rooms and posted a net income of about $35 million, an annual compound growth in earnings per share of over 30 percent. Then, in 1983, Sol decided to concentrate on casino resorts within the company's portfolio and sold his shares in Southern Sun in order to focus on Sun International (South Africa), which grew to 33 resorts in Africa and Mauritius, among other locations. In 1993, Sol formed Sun International Hotels Limited in order to acquire Paradise Island Resort and Casino, the Ocean Club Golf & Tennis Resort, and the Paradise Paradise Beach Resort from American-based Resorts International Inc.

Butch Kerzner, Sol's son, took the lead in managing the complex transactions necessary to acquire properties and finance the company's wide range of activities, thereby freeing his father to focus on the design and development of Sun International's global destination resort and casino business. The $125 million Paradise Island acquisition was completed in May 1994.

Decline and Rise of Paradise Island: 1994–96

The Paradise Island Resort opened in 1921 but, prior to Sun International's acquisition, experienced a steady decline in its business. The 1969 occupancy rate of 77 percent had fallen to 62 percent by 1993 and room rates had spiraled down from $122 in 1989 to $95 in 1993. Sun International seized the opportunity to develop almost an entire island and invested $140 million in an Initial Development Program geared to the reconstruction of its Paradise Island facilities in an ocean-themed environment based on the myth of Atlantis. According to Plato, Atlantis was an island fortress ruled by the five sets of twins of Poseidon, the god of the sea. There, within concentric rings of water and land, Atlanteans lived a life of harmony and abundance. This evolved civilization flourished for years until it was suddenly lost to the sea, submerged by an unforeseen volcanic eruption.

In December 1994, only seven months after completion of the Paradise Island acquisition, Sun International launched the renovated 1,147-room Atlantis Resort and Casino with its unique 14-acre saltwater marine life habitat, home to over 14,000 fish representing more than 100 species. By December 1995, Atlantis achieved an average occupancy of 85 percent at a room rate of $122.

Company Perspectives:

"We have a pretty basic strategy that is in no danger of making its way into business-school textbooks. Quite simply, we develop unusual destinations where people have fun and where we make money. We like to operate in markets that enjoy barriers to entry or where we can truly distinguish ourselves from the competition."
—Solomon Kerzner, Chairman/CEO

The east end of Paradise Island was dominated by the "boutique" resort known as the Ocean Club. Sun International's initial redevelopment of Paradise Island included returning the Ocean Club to its former grandeur. The Ocean Club had been built in the 1930s as an estate called Shangri-la on what was then known as Hog Island in The Bahamas. In 1962 Huntington Hartford, heir to the Great Atlantic & Pacific Tea Company fortune, bought the estate and built a small, elegant 52-room resort and restaurant. He managed to have the island renamed Paradise Island. Sun International completely redid the colonial-style clubhouse and refurbished the guest rooms and villas. The resort's famous Versailles Gardens and their Italian-marble statues of world figures, as well as the 12th-century French cloister, were carefully preserved.

In the "new" Ocean Club—which included four suites and five two-bedroom villas—guests enjoyed the ultimate in luxury and all the amenities offered in Europe's finest hotels. Ocean Club guests could access complimentary shuttle transportation on Paradise Island, use the casino at Atlantis, play tennis at the Paradise Island Tennis Club, and enjoy championship 18-hole golf at the Paradise Island Golf Club. For value-conscious tourists, Sun International operated the Paradise Paradise Beach Resort, a 100-room beachfront resort hotel.

North American Operations: 1995–97

In early 1994 Sol Kerzner met Chief Ralph Sturges of the Mohegan Nation. The Mohegan Indians had struggled for many years to obtain federal recognition as a nation. Sol joined them in their quest for federal recognition and the development of a casino resort. Sun International formed a 50 percent partnership with Trading Cove Associates (TCA) and entered into a management agreement with the Mohegan Nation to develop and manage a casino resort and entertainment complex to be known as Mohegan Sun Casino, in Uncasville (near Montville), Connecticut. Construction began in October 1995 and was completed within a year. Although Mohegan Sun began to operate during the slow season, from October 12, 1996 through December 31, 1996, the property recorded net revenues of $97 million.

The casino's architectural features and designs incorporating natural elements—such as timber, stone, and water—symbolized various elements of Mohegan Indian culture and history. For instance, guests entered Mohegan Sun through one of four major entrances, each one distinguished by a separate seasonal theme—winter, spring, summer, or fall—and connoting the importance of seasonal changes in tribal life. The

600,000-square-foot Mohegan Sun complex included 150,000 square feet of gaming space for 3,000 slot machines and 180 gaming tables.

In December 1996, Sun International completed the acquisition of Griffin Gaming & Entertainment, Inc. (renamed Sun International North America, Inc.), and became the new owner of the oldest casino on the Boardwalk: the Resorts Casino Hotel in Atlantic City. Sun International planned a major expansion to transform the property into a themed destination resort, the first of its kind in Atlantic City.

Thus, in the short span of two years Sun International positioned itself as one of the leading gaming and resort operators on the East Coast of North America. The redevelopment of Paradise Island in 1994 established the company's presence in the North American market. In October 1996 the $300-million Mohegan Sun Casino further enhanced this presence when it opened to a crowd of 60,000 people. The company's December 1996 purchase of Resorts International Hotel & Casino established the company in the Atlantic City market.

Indian Ocean Operations: 1995–97

Sun International also carried on business in Mauritius, the largest island of the Republic of Mauritius, a small, multiethnic, independent country consisting of several islands located in the Indian Ocean, and in the Comoro Islands, also located in the Indian Ocean off the east coast of mainland Africa. Sun International owned a 22.8 percent equity interest in Sun Resorts Limited, a Mauritian company publicly traded on the Mauritius Stock Exchange. Sun Resorts Limited owned five beach resort hotels in Mauritius: the luxurious 175-room Le Saint Géran Hotel, Golf Club & Casino; the exclusive 200-room Le Touessrok Hotel & Ile Aux Cerfs; the 248-room La Pirogue Hotel & Casino; the 333-room Le CoCo Beach; and the 238-room Sugar Beach Resort. Furthermore, Sun Resorts Limited owned the 182-room Le Galawa Beach Resort & Casino in the Comoros. Sun International managed all six of these resorts.

At Le Saint Gérant, which had more staff than guests, service was impeccable, dining was superb, and every activity and recreation imaginable was offered. The resort was situated on a private peninsula with soft white sand beaches. The hotel was a member of Leading Hotels of the World. Conference facilities accommodated up to 150 people; the Sun Kids Club was available for children and for babysitting. Le Touessrok Hotel & Ile Aux Cerfs, nestled on a cluster of tiny islands, was considered one of the most romantic and elegant resorts in the world. There were 200 rooms and suites, many of them connected to the main building by wooden bridges, and eight restaurants. Le Saint Gérant and Le Touessrok offered deluxe accommodations; the European travel trade considered them to be among the finest beach resorts in the world. They were a haven for celebrities and dignitaries, such as Prince Andrew, Prince Phillip, and Princess Caroline of Monaco.

On the other hand, the La Pirogue, Le CoCo Beach, Sugar Beach, and Le Galawa resorts catered to mid-market and budget travelers. La Pirogue, situated on a beachfront tropical-garden paradise, offered a variety of accommodations with a full complement of amenities and comforts, three restaurants, a casino, a children's club, all water sports, and one of the longest beaches in Mauritius. Le CoCo Beach, brilliantly patterned and boldly designed, was a resort with a Calypso beat and stood out as one of the great bargains on the island. The resort offered the widest possible range of recreational activities on land and at sea, themed entertainment, meeting facilities for 400 people, and a large number of services. In the Sugar Beach Resort were 66 beach villa rooms, 80 Manor House rooms, two suites, and 90 villa rooms with a view of the sea. Each room was furnished in the colonial style: cane furniture, rattan towel rails, and other authentic touches. The "Paul & Virginie" restaurant offered fresh and grilled seafood; a new restaurant opened in December 1998 delighted guests with its colonial architecture and delicious Italian and Mediterranean dishes. A full range of recreational activities, including a certified scuba school, and all traditional services were available. A new conference center opened in December 1998.

Situated on one of the best beaches on Grande Comoro Island, the 181-room Le Galawa Beach Hotel & Casino offered not only excellent service but also the largest selection of recreational activities—including a full range of water sports as well as tennis and other games—in the Indian Ocean. Themed dinners, great entertainment, delicious cuisine, and a casino made the resort a perfect, first-class choice for every member of the family. The Indian Ocean properties maintained an occupancy of 74 percent during 1997. Sun Resorts Limited, the Mauritian company that owned these six properties managed by Sun International, increased its net income by 28 percent over that of the previous year.

Reporting on fiscal year 1996, Chairman/CEO Sol Kerzner wrote that there now existed "a solid foundation on which to build our company. . . . Having turned the Paradise Island operations around in 1995, we expect earnings growth to continue as Atlantis' reputation continues to spread." In 1996, Atlantis's average occupancy rose to 87 percent at a room rate of $158. So it was that in November 1996, seeking to capitalize on the success of Atlantis, Sun International began construction of an approximately $480 million expansion project, dubbed Atlantis Phase II, which was to double the company's room base on Paradise Island, significantly increase its casino capacity and convention space, and expand the attractions of experiencing the ocean-themed adventures available at Atlantis.

Continual Profits and Expansion: 1997 and Beyond

In 1997 Sun International's earnings per share of $2.14 was 35 percent above 1996 earnings and almost 150 percent higher than those achieved in 1995. Paradise Island, the company's flagship and the primary driver of its earnings, had the most profitable year in its 30-year history. The Atlantis resort and casino recorded an 88 percent average occupancy rate at a $173 average room rate that was a ten percent increase over the 1996 average rate. The Ocean Club established its position in the high end of the market. While maintaining an average occupancy of 76 percent, the Ocean Club had an average room rate of $420, an increase of 18 percent over 1996. Paradise Paradise Beach Resort had average occupancy and average daily room rates of 85 percent and $83, respectively.

Furthermore, in order to profit from the boom in the timeshare industry and to diversify the product mix available at

Atlantis, the company formed a joint venture with Vistana, Inc. to build a 375-unit, luxury timeshare resort—known as Villas at Atlantis. Sun International contributed seven acres of land on the harbor side of the island adjacent to Atlantis; Vistana agreed to a $7 million cash equity. Sales of the first group of 175 units began during the second half of 1998; the project was to be completed in late 1999.

Resorts Casino Hotel in Atlantic City increased operating income by 32 percent over the previous year but, because of the former low operating base, this growth amounted to earnings before interest and tax deductions of only $35 million for the year. In his 1997 annual report, Sol Kerzner pointed out that "this result was not unexpected" and that Resorts Casino "had been acquired for its development potential." According to Amy S. Rosenberg's story, dated May 6, 1998, in the *Philadelphia Inquirer*, in 1996 Sun International had proposed a $500 million plan to transform the casino hotel into "a mega-resort unlike anything else on the Boardwalk," but scaled back those plans to a $150 million renovation, including construction of a 600-room tower consisting of a re-themed Victorian-style resort known as the Beach Club. In 1998, however, Sun International scaled back renovation to a cost of $15 million to $20 million. Rosenberg quoted President Butch Kerzner as explaining that "In addition to renovating the existing hotel rooms, we are seriously evaluating the possibility of developing a larger project on our undeveloped real estate [in Atlantic City] through which we could more fully realize the enormous potential of the concept of the Beach Club. Because of the condition of old areas of the buildings, we finally determined the project could not get done for $150 million. We are still committed to the Atlantic City project. The market has been very good," Butch added.

The Mohegan Sun Casino had an outstanding first full calendar year of operations. The complex hosted over 6.6 million arrivals, served more than 3.5 million meals, and enrolled more than 600,000 people in the slots club. The property posted gross earnings of $150.8 million, representing a 47 percent cash-flow return on investment, the highest return ever achieved in the industry for an investment of this size. Sun International found that the average length of stay was 110 minutes and concluded that it had penetrated only the geographic markets in close proximity to the casino. The Tribe's ownership of 240 acres of land offered almost unlimited potential for development of a hotel-casino complex. Furthermore, Mohegan Sun enjoyed the relative protection of the tribal-state compact between the Mohegan Tribe and the state of Connecticut: if that state were to legalize any gaming operation other than one sponsored by an Indian tribe on Indian land, the Mohegan Tribe would no longer be required to make payments from its slot-machine revenues to the state. As of fiscal 1998, the Mohegan Tribe and the Pequot Tribe (operators of Connecticut-based Foxwoods, one of the leading gaming facilities in the United States in terms of the number of slot machines) annually gave 25 percent of their revenues from slot machines to the state.

In February 1998, the Mohegan Tribe appointed TCA to develop a $450 million expansion of Mohegan Sun by building a 1,500- to 2,000-room luxury hotel and a convention center. According to Lyn Bixby's story in the February 11, 1998 issue of the *Hartford Courant*, The Tribe also announced that it was buying out the contract of their professional management team.

"Self-sufficiency has always been a goal. We're ahead of where we wanted to be," said Jayne Fawcett, tribal council vice-chairwoman. "Our goal is to have the premier gaming resort in the world by the summer of 2000," Fawcett commented. TCA and the Tribe agreed that, as of January 1, 2000, TCA would turn over management of the Mohegan Sun Resort Complex to the Tribe. These developments were published in the Tribe's newspaper, *Ni Ya Yo*, a title meaning "It is so."

In December 1998, Atlantis Phase II was completed on schedule and Sun International unveiled its creation of mythical Atlantis. Among the arcadia of lagoons populated by almost 50,000 fish and containing numerous waterfalls, rose a new casino straddling the lagoon between the 1,138-room Atlantis and the new Royal Towers, a 1,202-room deluxe hotel. The result was the creation of the world's largest island resort. And at *The Dig*, centerpiece of the Royal Towers, visitors could visit an imaginative, full-sized re-creation of the ruins of Atlantis and explore the incredible inventions of the ancient Atlanteans during an interactive, total-immersion entertainment experience. Walking through a series of interconnected passageways, boulevards, and chambers with gigantic picture-windows, visitors could view deep-water environments inhabited by a wide variety of live underwater life ranging from piranhas and sharks to jellyfish and eels. Furthermore, a $15 million, 10-acre marina with 40 berths catered to luxury yachts up to 200 feet long—thereby positioning Paradise Island as the Monte Carlo of the Caribbean.

As the 21st century drew near, Sun International Hotels Limited stood out as a symbol of what a father and his son could create in in the realm of world-class resort entertainment. Given the company's illustrious past, what would happen to the busi-ness in the next century doubtless would be profitable, dramatic, and even surprising.

Principal Subsidiaries

Sun International Bahamas Limited; Sun International Representation, Inc.; Sun Cove Limited; Sun Resorts Limited (Mauritius; 22.8%); Sun International North America, Inc.

Further Reading

"Atlantis Expansion Nearly Complete," *Miami Herald*, November 5, 1998.

Barker, Tim, "Vistana Is Staying Busy with Expansions and New Projects," *Orlando Sentinel*, March 23, 1998, p. 11.

Bixby, Lyn, "Mohegan Sun Casino to Add 1,500 to 2,200 Hotel Rooms," *Hartford Courant*, February 11, 1998, p. 11.

Blackerby, Cheryl, "Atlantis Resort Developer Sol Kerzner," *Palm Beach Post*, April 20, 1998, p. 18.

Burke, Patricia, "Resorts Casino Hotel Atlantic City New Jersey," *Hotel Casino Index*, September 9, 1998.

"Indian Gambling," *International Gaming and Wagering Business*, August 1, 1997.

"The New Slot Market," *International Gaming and Wagering Business*, April 1, 1998.

Powers, Mary Buckner, "CM Overcomes Massive Site Changes to Keep Bahamas Resort on Schedule," *Engineering News-Record*, October 19, 1998, p. 40.

"Resort's TV Ad Is Veritable Epic," *Wall Street Journal*, November 6, 1998.

Rosenberg, Amy S., "Sun International Hotels Scales Back Atlantic City Project—Again," *Philadelphia Inquirer*, May 6, 1998.

"Sun Hotels May Be Set to Rise," *Business Week*, December 15, 1997, p. 18.

—Gloria A. Lemieux

Sunkist Growers, Inc.

14130 Riverside Drive
Sherman Oaks, California 91423
U.S.A.
(818) 986-4800
Fax: (818) 379-7405
Web site: http://www.sunkist.com

Member-Owned Cooperative
Incorporated: 1893 as the Southern California Fruit
    Growers Exchange
Employees: 950
Sales: $1.01 billion (1997)
SICs: 0174 Citrus Fruits; 5148 Fresh Fruits &
    Vegetables; 5142 Packaged Frozen Foods; 2037
    Frozen Fruits & Vegetables; 2033 Canned Fruits &
    Vegetables

One of the ten largest marketing cooperatives in the United States, Sunkist Growers, Inc. is a not-for-profit organization operated for the California and Arizona citrus growers who compose its membership. During the late 1990s when Sunkist's membership comprised 6,500 citrus farmers, making it the largest marketing cooperative in the fruit and vegetable industry in the United States, it controlled nearly 60 percent of the domestic market for navel oranges. The cooperative markets oranges, lemons, grapefruit, and tangerines in the United States and abroad, using its "less-than-perfect" fruit to produce processed citrus products such as juices, peels, and oils for use in food products. Sunkist, through its members, boasts the two largest citrus processing plants in the western United States. Owned and controlled by its member-growers, the only individuals eligible to sit on its board of directors, Sunkist markets the world-recognized Sunkist brand name and coordinates the timing of the harvest and release of its members' fruit to achieve superior prices. The majority of the member-growers farm 40 acres or less.

19th-Century Origins

Sunkist's formation in the late 19th century was a function of the burgeoning growth recorded by California's citrus industry during the period. The larger the young industry became, the greater the need for a cooperative of Sunkist's ilk. Commercial citrus production began in the region roughly a half-century before the birth of Sunkist, when the first commercial orchard took root in 1840. From this starting point, a series of events fanned the fires of growth, transforming that single orchard situated in what would later become downtown Los Angeles into a thriving industry and an integral component of the state's economy. The forces that promoted the growth of the citrus industry provided the reason for Sunkist's creation. The first significant event occurred in 1848, when the beginning of California's Gold Rush lured prodigious waves of fortune seekers into the region. As the state's population increased exponentially, its ability to meet the food demands of its new residents was stretched beyond capacity. Vitamin-rich fruits and vegetables were in short supply, causing many of the new Californians to develop scurvy. Citrus production was increased as a response, but an even greater boon to the fledgling citrus industry occurred 20 years later when the transcontinental railroad was completed in 1870. Within ten years of the first rail shipment, the volume of California citrus moving east had grown to more than 2,000 rail cars annually. In another five years the volume had doubled. California citrus had become big business.

At roughly the same time the eastward and westward rail lines reached their meeting point in Promontory, Utah, the first seedless, navel oranges arrived in California. Two parent trees were shipped from Brazil to southern California by American missionaries and planted in Riverside in 1873, marking the introduction of what would prove to be a highly prized variety of orange into an already rapidly expanding market. Finally, the opening of the Atchison, Topeka, and Santa Fe rail lines in 1885, which connected Los Angeles to the rest of the country, provided the last significant factor propelling the growth of the citrus industry before Sunkist's debut as a cooperative. As the 1880s gave way to the 1890s, "a veritable boom in orange planting" was underway, according to an early Sunkist historian. The industry was growing by leaps and bounds, measured in part by the dramatic increase in citrus planting activity. Between 1880 and 1893 California's citrus acreage increased from 3,000 to more than 40,000, underscoring the heightened demand for oranges and lemons. As the revenue generated from citrus production escalated, however, there was one sector of the industry excluded from sharing in the riches. Alarmingly, the growers were watching others get rich from the citrus they grew, and as the 1890s began, they found what little power they had quickly slipping away. Collective action was the response, and Sunkist emerged as the lasting answer.

The orange growers began to watch their share of the citrus revenue dwindle when production exceeded the local market demand. With local markets glutted, the orange growers realized their survival depended on shipping their fruit to distant markets, but this realization was far easier to apprehend than it was to put into action. Amid the packinghouse owners, distributors, agents, and speculators—the "middlemen" of the citrus trade—the growers ranked a distant last in terms of exercising any control over the industry. They were independent, small-scale farmers presiding over modest five-, ten-, or 15-acre groves without the organization and training to distribute their produce effectively. The growers' weak bargaining position worsened in 1891 when agents decided they would no longer buy fruit F.O.B., or freight-on-board, a purchase term meaning the buyer pays the transportation charges and assumes all risk of damage and delay in transit not caused by the shipper. Instead, the agents declared they would handle the citrus only on consignment, a decision that shifted the risk from distributor to the scattered ranks of independent citrus growers. Forced either to accept the offers of local speculators or consign their fruit to commission agents in the East, the California citrus growers were cornered into an untenable position. Successive years of widespread financial losses—the "Red Ink" years—followed during the early 1890s, forcing the growers to marshal their forces and organize against a system they believed was unjust.

A number of attempts to band growers together occurred before the commission houses refused to purchase fruit F.O.B., with the first attempt taking place in 1885 when The Orange Growers Protective Union of Southern California was formed. Other attempts at collective action followed during the ensuing years, but all failed for one reason or another. Their brief existences, however, did lay the foundation for the one cooperative organization that would endure, the Southern California Fruit Growers Exchange, Sunkist's predecessor. Formed in 1893, the Exchange was organized as a federated structure, member-owned and –operated, comprising regional marketing cooperatives, known as district exchanges. During its first season, the Exchange represented 80 percent of the orange growers of southern California and shipped 6,000 carloads of the 7,000 shipped by all of the state's growers. By regulating shipments and directing the fruit where demand was the highest, the Exchange made an immediate impact on the financial well-

being of its member-growers, quickly erasing the painful memory of the Red Ink years. By the end of the first season growers realized an average net price of roughly $1 per box of oranges, a return that far eclipsed what many would have earned without the Exchange's existence. It was the common belief that without the Exchange, growers would have fallen short of earning $.25 per box, the realization of which prompted many nonmembers to seriously consider joining the Exchange's ranks. By the end of the century the cooperative was firmly established as the indispensable ally of the formerly powerless orange growers in southern California. There were 1,700 members from 75 local packing associations and 12 district exchanges working together, bringing in $3.7 million in sales.

As the Exchange prospered and expanded in southern California, others noted the superior return member-growers were earning from their groves, namely, those growers working the land to the north. In California's San Joaquin Valley citrus growers were suffering from many of the same problems that had plagued their counterparts in the south. By 1905, after more than a decade of watching the southern growers prosper under the beneficent control of the Exchange, the northern growers clamored to join the Exchange. In response, the Exchange extended its purview to encompass the entire state. With the addition of member-growers in the north, the Exchange changed its name to reflect its broader geographic base, adopting the California Fruit Growers Exchange as its new corporate title, and stood solidly positioned as one of the most promising cooperative organizations in North America. Although the Exchange on paper owned very little (the furniture in its Los Angeles office representing its only asset), there was a powerful force operating behind what appeared to be a barren corporate shell. The cooperative owned no citrus groves or property, it held no financial interest in packinghouses, district exchanges, or other local property, yet it represented 45 percent of California's citrus industry through its 5,000 grower-members. In all, the cooperative governed more than 14,000 carloads of citrus when it adopted its new name, with sales returns eclipsing $7 million.

Birth of the Sunkist Name and the Great Depression

Geographic expansion was followed by diversification, something the cooperative would do with vigor following World War II. Its first meaningful step in this direction occurred in 1907, when the Exchange formed its own timber supply company. Unable to secure a steady supply of reasonably priced wood for packing crates, the cooperative created the Fruit Growers Supply Company, which set the precedent for the Exchange's synergistic approach to the business of agriculture in later years. The inaugural year of the Fruit Growers Supply Company also marked the Exchange's first foray into advertising. In 1907 the cooperative launched a major advertising campaign—reportedly the first time a perishable food product was advertised—that, for the first time, included the use of the Sunkist brand name. The Sunkist trademark, registered in 1909, became one of the most effective marketing tools for the cooperative from this point forward, on its way toward becoming one of the most recognizable trademarks in the world.

Over the course of the next two decades the Exchange grew into a formidable force, its highlight achievements punctuating the progress of a cooperative with far-reaching capabilities. In 1914 the cooperative's product division was founded with a small marmalade factory, followed by entries into the production of citrus byproducts and the production of orange juice. Advertising became more sophisticated as the years passed, emphasizing the health and nutrition advantages inherent in citrus consumption, and the cooperative bolstered its membership rolls, becoming the unrivaled representative of growers throughout California. By the end of the 1920s the Exchange comprised more than 13,000 citrus fruit growers who produced more than 75 percent of the California citrus crop. Geographic expansion had carried the Exchange's membership ranks into neighboring Arizona, where the cooperative could look forward to providing its marketing and distributing services to untapped citrus-growing regions. In California, the cooperative had won over a considerable majority of the state's citrus producers. In 1932, amid the torturous economic environment of the Great Depression, three out of every four citrus growers in California were members of the Exchange.

The economic collapse of the 1930s sent shockwaves throughout the United States, creating a maelstrom of economic turmoil. Citrus growers were not excluded from the pervasive financial panic sweeping the nation. By 1933 citrus prices had dropped to or below the cost of production, making profit an impossibility, but instead of retreating and slowing its shipments the Exchange continued to offer normal volumes throughout the Great Depression. The cooperative extended additional credit, reasoning that there was nothing to be gained by curtailing its activities. "It seemed better to take the risk," explained a Sunkist official at the time, "than permit the fruit to remain, and probably waste, in California, for sales lost with a perishable commodity are never regained." Careful management carried the cooperative through the difficult 1930s, and by its 50th anniversary in 1943, the frenetic activity of world war had vanquished any remnants of economic ruin. Midway through World War II, Sunkist was as robust an organization as it ever had been. Within the cooperative there were 200 local packinghouses feeding into 25 local district exchanges, packing more than 37 million boxes of oranges, lemons, and grapefruit. During the economic boom period of the 1950s and 1960s, growth, diversification, integration, and the modernizing and streamlining of operations became the key words describing a corporate world fast on the move. Sunkist, from 1945 forward, began to take on new shape, broadening and expanding to compete effectively in the new world surrounding it.

Post-World War II Progress

One of the most important developments during the postwar period was increasing the awareness and regard for the Sunkist brand name in the minds of consumers. Toward this end, the cooperative registered a marketing triumph, effectively removing the cooperative from the business of commodity selling, in which the winners and losers were determined by whoever priced their products the lowest. As recognition and respect for the Sunkist brand increased through sophisticated advertising efforts, consumers demonstrated their willingness to pay more for a Sunkist orange than for the non-Sunkist variety. The cooperative had stamped successfully the Sunkist trademark on fresh oranges first in 1926 and in 1951 began branding its trademark on frozen concentrates and other canned citrus juices. In 1952 the cooperative made the ultimate acknowledgement of

the importance of the Sunkist name by changing its own name from the California Fruit Growers Exchange to Sunkist Growers, forever allying the cooperative and its member-growers with the ubiquitous brand.

Another decisive postwar move was the cooperative's penetration of foreign markets, particularly its foray into Japan. At first, however, the cooperative's biggest foreign market was in Europe, where nearly eight million cartons were shipped annually during the early 1960s. By the late 1960s Sunkist was shipping more than 12 million cartons abroad annually, while at home the company controlled roughly 80 percent of the citrus crop in the Far West. The energy crisis of the early and mid-1970s severely hobbled Sunkist's burgeoning export business, as the costs of shipping fruit overseas tripled, but overall the 1970s were years of robust growth. In 1974 the cooperative licensed its name to the Ben Myerson Candy Co., Inc., which began producing fruit jellied pectin made from Sunkist's citrus byproducts. Three years later an agreement was reached with General Cinema Corporation to market citrus-flavored carbonated drinks bearing the Sunkist trademark, as the cooperative sought to realize the full financial benefits of its esteemed brand. Because of these and other efforts, sales swelled 50 percent between 1973 and 1979, eclipsing the $500,000 mark in 1977. By this point there were 6,500 ranches signed on as Sunkist members in California and Arizona, with the groves ranging in size from five acres to as much as 10,000 acres. Expansion overseas had led to the establishment of three foreign subsidiaries, and the company's domestic efforts were supported by 37 fresh fruit sales offices scattered throughout the country.

Sales reached their next milestone of $1 billion in 1990, following a decade that saw the number of member-growers decrease while the average size of member farms increased. The decline in membership had begun during the 1960s, when there were nearly 15,000 member-growers, but the decline had become more precipitous as the cooperative entered the 1980s. By 1983 membership was down to 5,000 and its share of the Far West citrus crop had fallen from nearly 80 percent to 56 percent, as the encroachment of commercial firms into the Western citrus industry altered the face of citrus farming. Sunkist officials realized that the cooperative's survival depended on maintaining a large volume base and that any further erosion of the cooperative's membership rolls would cause decided injury to the 90-year-old organization. To gain new members, membership requirements were eased during the decade, overhead costs were reduced, and in 1988 the cooperative formed a new subsidiary, Sunkist Real Estate, Inc. Through Sunkist Real Estate, members received real estate, financial, and investment services, as well as short-term financing. Gradually, the cooperative's membership rose.

Although the 1990s began with the longest, coldest freeze in California's history, the decade was a positive one for the cooperative. After three decades of investment, export business accounted for roughly a third of the cooperative's sales volume during the decade, which represented a considerable amount of overseas business considering that annual revenue eclipsed $1 billion during the 1990s. By the end of the decade, as the cooperative settled into its second century of operation, there were 6,500 citrus farmers in California and Arizona who counted themselves as Sunkist growers. As the company prepared for the 21st century, its decades of leadership in the U.S. citrus industry pointed to a similarly influential role in the decades ahead. Perhaps the cooperative's greatest strength was its name, however, a brand imprinted on the minds of consumers that promises to endure.

Principal Subsidiaries

Fruit Growers Supply Company; Sunkist Real Estate, Inc.

Further Reading

Merlo, Catherine, *Heritage of Gold: The First 100 Years of Sunkist Growers, Inc.,* Sherman Oaks, Calif.: Sunkist Growers, Inc., n.d.
Paris, Ellen, "Sunset in the Groves?," *Forbes,* March 23, 1987, p. 35.
"Sunkist Bursting Out All Over," *Supermarket News,* February 9, 1998, p. 12.
"Sunkist Reports Record Year for California Citrus Sales," *Knight-Ridder/Tribune Business News,* February 11, 1998, p. 2.

—Jeffrey L. Covell

The Sunrider Corporation

1625 Abalone Avenue
Torrance, California 90501
U.S.A.
(310) 781-3808
Fax: (310) 222-9271
Web site: http://www.sunrider.com

Private Company
Incorporated: 1983
Employees: 500
Sales: $700 million (1997 est.)
SICs: 2833 Medicinals & Botanicals

Operating in over 27 nations in 1998, The Sunrider Corporation is one of the world's largest herbal products firms. Based on Chinese formulas, Sunrider's nutritional and body-care products are created from over 100 kinds of herbs grown and processed by the company. Sunrider products are manufactured in plants in California, Taiwan, Mainland China, and Singapore and then sold around the world by distributors using multilevel marketing and traditional sales methods. Although the firm has experienced serious legal and public relations problems, it has grown and prospered because of the twin appeals of better health and financial independence. Combining ancient Chinese herbalism with modern manufacturing technology, Sunrider continues to play a key role in the herbal renaissance of the late 20th century.

Origins of Sunrider

Three people with very different backgrounds founded Sunrider: Tei Fu Chen, Oi-Lin Chen, and K. Dean Black. Tei Fu Chen was raised in poverty in Taiwan following World War II. He reported having an early interest in health because of his own childhood illnesses, noting that his health was restored using ancient Chinese herbal formulas and martial arts training. Tei Fu Chen met his wife Oi-Lin Chen, a Hong Kong native, when they attended Kaoshiung Medical College in Taiwan. Oi-Lin earned a medical degree there, while Tei Fu studied traditional Chinese healing and herbalism and earned a bachelor's degree in pharmacy at Kaoshiung. Although Tei Fu Chen would use the title "Dr." following the Chinese customary use of this term for one with his training in traditional Chinese medicine, he never claimed to be a medical doctor. Later Tei Fu Chen served in the Taiwanese military and lived in California.

Chen and his wife moved to Utah County, Utah, in 1976, having converted to the Latter-Day Saints (Mormon) church. Tei Fu Chen attended Brigham Young University (BYU) from 1975 to 1977 as an undergraduate chemistry student and also taught martial arts there. He left BYU to work at an herbal products company called Nature's Sunshine, then in 1979 began working for Murdock International, another Utah County herbal company later renamed Murdock Madaus Schwabe.

Meanwhile, Oi-Lin Chen completed a medical internship in Pennsylvania and then passed her board exams to become a licensed M.D. in Utah. In Orem she set up her medical practice in her family's home. By this time her husband's parents and sisters had moved to Utah County.

Around this time Tei Fu Chen met the other key Sunrider person, K. Dean Black, who had grown up in Salt Lake City and Denver in a Mormon family. In 1971 he received a Ph.D. in human development at Pennsylvania State University, with specialization in gerontology. After teaching at BYU, in 1979 he became the president of NaturaLife International, a Murdock subsidiary that had been incorporated in 1976 in Utah.

In an interview, Black reported that Chen's herbal products helped him recover from hayfever and food allergies. "I was just amazed at what was going on," said Black. Chen explained to Black how the herbs helped restore balanced metabolism and optimal health.

Murdock allowed Chen's Chinese herbal formulas to be sold in stores but did not actively promote them, preferring instead the American herbal products based on the work of Utah naturopath John Christopher. Murdock's reliance on Christopher's concepts frustrated Chen and Black, who continued in vain to make believers out of the Murdock officials. Eventually Murdock prohibited Chen and Black from meeting together on

470

company time. Murdock insisted that "America was not ready for Chinese herbs," said Black.

Both Chen and Black decided to break away from Murdock. On October 8, 1982, shareholders in NaturaLife International voted to name Tei Fu Chen, Oi Lin Chen, and Yung Yeuan Chen, all of Orem, Utah, as directors. However, it was not until October 15, 1983, that the articles of incorporation were amended to change the company's name to The Sunrider Corporation. In February 1984 the firm under the name NaturaLife International filed its annual report with the Utah state government; it listed Tei Fu Chen as chairman of the board and K. Dean Black as president. With Black's departure as president in 1984, Tei Fu Chen became both chairman and president. The transition was completed.

NaturaLife products had been distributed by the multilevel marketing (MLM) system, also known as network marketing, used by Amway, Mary Kay Cosmetics, and Avon. In a 1998 telephone interview, Sharon Farnsworth of Sandy, Utah, maintained that she had one of the largest NaturaLife organizations with about 13,000 self-employed distributors, and she thus became a key player in the early Sunrider MLM effort; Farnsworth continued into the 1990s as one of the firm's main distributors with a downline in several nations.

Sunrider's position in Utah was influenced by two general trends. First, the Mormon heritage of herbal use under founder Joseph Smith and his successor Brigham Young continued into the 20th century and clearly influenced some individuals to use and sell Sunrider products. Several commentators have pointed out that Utah was a leading state in the natural products industry, with over 40 companies selling herbal products and vitamin supplements.

Second, "Utah is an important state in multi-level marketing," according to David Owen, the author of an article in the October 1987 issue of the *Atlantic*. Owen pointed out that a former BYU communications professor was the president of a consulting firm that worked with mostly MLM firms. Moreover, he observed, there was a "heavy evangelical element in MLM," and "Mormons are a big presence in MLM." Dennis Lythgoe in a 1997 newspaper article reiterated Owen's point: "Utah has often been called 'the network marketing capitol of the world.'"

Chinese Herbal Products and Philosophy

In the 1980s Sunrider marketed a wide range of natural products said to be based on Chinese formulas thousands of years old. According to the company's literature, its whole food products marketed by its Sunergy Division included Nutrien, "a whole food concentrate for general nourishment," and an Ori-

ental tea called Calli, billed as "the perfect whole food beverage to follow meals and encourage digestion." Other Sunergy products were whole food formulas designed to regenerate and strengthen specific body systems, such as Alpha20C for the immune/lymphatic system, Lifestream for the circulatory/cardiovascular system, Prime Again to help the reproductive system, and Assimilaid for the digestive system. Yet other Sunergy items were herbal concentrates, such as white willow bark (Salix alba), dong quai (Angelica sinensis), Korean white ginseng (Panax ginseng), goldenseal root (Hydrastis canadensis), and Siberian ginseng root bark (Eleutherococcus senticosus).

A second Sunrider division, Vitalite Weight Management, produced whole food concentrates for weight control. The three basic Vitalite products were Vitalite Breakfast Drink, Vitalite Lunch, and Vitalite Dinner (a soup). Sunrider's third division, Kandesn Skin and Personal Care, sold shampoo, hair conditioner, aftershave, cleansing bars and creams, and hand and body lotions.

Sunrider founder Tei Fu Chen based his products on the concept of regeneration, that is, restoring the body to optimal health by using concentrated herbal extracts. Chen favored food herbs and preventing disease over the American herbal tradition of using medicinal herbs to treat disease.

After Dr. Dean Black left Sunrider in 1984, he formed his own Springville, Utah, company called The BioResearch Foundation, which produced newsletters, books, videotapes, and audiotapes promoting the validity of herbalism and alterative healing. Although no longer officially part of Sunrider, Black gave presentations to groups of natural products users and distributors, including Sunrider distributors.

Growth and Legal Problems in the 1980s

In 1987 Sunrider recorded $24 million in annual sales and had 125 employees and 40,000 distributors worldwide. "Our goal is to become the largest and best health products company in the United States," said Kerry Nielson, Sunrider's director of operations, in a 1987 book on the history of Provo and Orem.

In 1987 the Chens decided to expand in the Los Angeles area. The headquarters shifted to Torrance, while a new plant was being built in the City of Industry. Utah economic development leaders tried to convince Sunrider to expand in Utah, but the Chens found no building already in place to handle their needs. Sunrider's leaders also wanted a new location near a Pacific port, since some Sunrider ingredients were imported from Asia.

Meanwhile, several government agencies, including the U.S. Food and Drug Administration, the Utah Department of Agriculture, the Utah Division of Consumer Protection, and the Utah Health Department's Bureau of Epidemiology, were investigating Sunrider. In Utah and California, salmonella bacteria were found in the firm's Nutrien product, which may have caused illness in several consumers. None of those cases were life threatening. Sunrider responded by recalling all Nutrien products on February 5, 1988, and offering to reimburse customers for the recalled products. A couple of weeks later the company issued a second recall—of Vitalite products containing Nutrien.

Sunrider also shut down its Orem plant where the salmonella-contaminated products were made. A new plant with new equipment was opened in Orem in late February 1988, after state regulators gave their approval. The new plant produced Nutrien. Although no lawsuits occurred over this problem, the recalls and new plant cost the company about $5 million.

On March 14, 1988, the Utah Department of Agriculture closed Sunrider's Orem plant and continued working with Sunrider to resolve several problems. The department had cited the firm for nine violations of state regulations, including false product labels, sanitation violations, and using unapproved additives.

The main problem of course was the salmonella contamination from raw soybean products imported from Taiwan. Unlike other firms that heated soy to kill bacteria, Sunrider used unheated soy products in order to preserve its nutrients.

Unable to find a U.S. supplier of its soy ingredient, Sunrider later in 1988 decided to eliminate its Nutrien and Vitalite products as part of an agreement with the Utah Department of Agriculture. Sunrider also agreed to pay $20,500 to the state of Utah for these violations, a reduced fine given the company's cooperation.

Meanwhile, a six-part television series of short reports broadcast by Salt Lake City's KSL Channel 5 added to the Sunrider controversy. Reporter Con Psarras began the series called "Herbal Medicine: Miracle or Mirage" as part of the Sunday evening news on February 7, 1988. The series looked into Tei Fu Chen's background and qualifications and of course the usefulness or dangers of using herbal products. Some Sunrider distributors claimed the company's products could cure a wide range of serious illnesses. Those claims were consistently discouraged by the corporation, according to its attorney, Cecil McNab.

The KSL-TV programs, along with the numerous newspaper articles on the government investigations of Sunrider, generated a lot of controversy in Utah in 1988. Sunrider advocates appeared on TV and talk radio shows to rebut the criticisms, while critics took up the offensive. Not surprisingly, Dr. William Jarvis entered the fray. Jarvis was a Loma Linda University health education professor and president of the National Council Against Health Fraud, a major organization opposed to the misuses of herbs and various forms of alternative medicine. Dr. K. Dean Black defended Sunrider, concluding that "KSL and its reporter began their investigation with a negative and biased story in mind, and sought only to support it."

In the midst of these legal difficulties, the Chen family experienced considerable conflict over herbal products and corporate issues. In 1989, Dr. Jau-Fei Chen, Tei Fu Chen's sister, started a rival herbal firm called E-Excel International, Inc. in Provo, Utah. Jau-Fei was supported by her parents, who no longer supported Tei Fu Chen and his Sunrider business. Dr. Jau-Fei Chen in 1988 earned her Ph.D. in microbiology at Brigham Young University. The internal conflicts within the Chen family continued to play a role in Sunrider's legal problems in the 1990s.

However, these legal and family problems did not stop Sunrider from expanding in the 1980s. In 1984 the company began operating in Canada, followed by Hong Kong and Taiwan in 1987, Thailand in 1988, and Australia, New Zealand, and Korea in 1989.

Expansion and Challenges in the 1990s

In 1990 Tei Fu Chen received an honorary doctorate of agriculture from the Chinese Culture University in Taipei, the largest university in Taiwan, the Republic of China. By 1990 Sunrider's sales had reached more than $200 million based on operations in the United States, Canada, Taiwan, Malaysia, Hong Kong, Japan, Korea, Australia, Thailand, and New Zealand.

Sunrider finally shut down all its Orem, Utah, facilities in 1991. It laid off 150 workers, who were not transferred to the company's more advanced plant in the City of Industry, California. However, many Sunrider distributors remained in Utah, and The Sunrider Corporation, doing business as Sunrider International, remained registered as a Utah corporation.

Meanwhile, Sunrider's legal battles continued. In 1989, the firm agreed to pay the state of California $175,000 and to cease claims that its products had any effect on medical conditions or disease.

A Phoenix, Arizona, jury in 1992 decided that Sunrider had broken the state's racketeering laws and at the same time awarded $650,000 to a woman who said she had been deceived by Sunrider representatives and had become sick after using company products.

In 1995 the Sunrider Corporation, Tei Fu Chen, and Oi-Lin Chen were charged with tax evasion, conspiracy, filing false company tax returns, and smuggling. The company was charged with overstating the costs of importing materials in order to understate company profits. Moreover, in 1997 the Sunrider owners were found guilty of tax evasion for not paying taxes on more than $126 million of taxable income earned between 1987 and 1990. Tei Fu Chen received a prison sentence of two years, plus six months home detention. His wife was sentenced to two years probation, including six months home detention. The Chens also paid $93 million to the federal government for back taxes, interest, and penalties.

Not surprisingly, Sunrider since its founding in 1982 has had its share of critics, often from the medical profession. One example was Stephen Barrett, M.D., a well-known critic of alternative medicine. Barrett in 1998 reported that Sunrider was among the 100-plus companies using multilevel marketing to sell health products. Other such companies included Melaleuca of Idaho Falls, Idaho; Matol Botanical International in Canada; Provo, Utah's Nu Skin International; and Nature's Sunshine also in Provo. Barrett concluded in his Quackwatch web site that, "Consumers would be wise to avoid multilevel products altogether. Those that have nutritional value . . . are invariably overpriced and may be unnecessary as well. Those promoted as remedies are either unproven, bogus, or intended for conditions that are unsuitable for self-medication."

In spite of such critics, Sunrider and other herbal corporations in the 1990s were aided by more studies showing the potentially beneficial uses of herbs and even more acceptance of alternative medicine in the medical establishment. For example, in 1993 the federally funded National Institutes of Health organized its Office of Alternative Medicine. In 1997 a federal advisory panel strongly approved the use of acupuncture for certain conditions, such as headaches, lower back pain, and stroke rehabilitation. The Bellevue, Washington-based consulting firm of Hartman & New Hope estimated that the natural products and supplement industry accounted for over $14.8 billion in 1997.

According to an article in the *Journal of the American Medical Association,* a survey of approximately 1,000 Americans found that 40 percent said they had used some form of alternative medicine not available from their medical doctor. Alternative medicine was found to be equally popular among both men and women and among various age and racial groups.

A strong consumer or self-help movement also helped Sunrider grow. Twenty or 30 years prior most Americans put all of their trust in medical doctors, but as more people started asking questions about different companies and professions, they began to take more responsibility for their own life and health. Such emphasis on wellness, fitness, and personal responsibility influenced some to seek out companies such as Sunrider that catered to those values.

International Growth

Sunrider moved into several new international markets in the 1990s. The company's strong Asian business expanded with the 1997 creation of Sunrider Philippines, headquartered in Pasig City near Manila. In 1998 Sunrider celebrated its fifth year in Indonesia, where over 47,000 distributors were registered in 27 provinces. The company also opened a $13.2 million manufacturing plant in Singapore to support its growing worldwide business.

The People's Republic of China (PRC) in Beijing on April 21, 1998 announced a ban on multilevel and direct marketing in China. Nevertheless, Sunrider continued to sell its products through hundreds of Chinese dealers with wholesale and retail stores. Sunrider's Chinese operations had begun three years earlier, and by 1998 the firm operated manufacturing plants in the cities of Tianjin and Huang Pu.

Sunrider entered the Latin American market in 1992 when it began operations in Mexico City. In 1996 the company opened an office in Bogota, Columbia, and in 1998 established its Sao Paolo, Brazil, office.

In 1992 Sunrider started operating in Western Europe. Based in London, Sunrider Europe supported distributors in the United Kingdom, Ireland, France, Germany, Belgium, Austria, Italy, the Netherlands, and Finland. The company in 1994 expanded into the Eastern European market by commencing business operations in Budapest, Hungary. In 1997 the company opened Sunrider Hungary's new office to accommodate the growing number of individuals interested in starting their own business after the end of the Cold War and the collapse of communist state-controlled economies. Also that year the Sunrider Latvia subsidiary was started in the capital of Riga and operations began in Russia. The following year the company opened an office in Warsaw, Poland. In 1998 Sunrider planned to commence operations in Belarus, India, South Africa, and the Ukraine.

Expanded Product Lines

By 1998 Sunrider was offering some of its original products, plus new lines developed in the 1990s. "Eat Healthy" products included Dr. Chen's Secret Sauce in regular and vegetarian flavors without preservatives or artificial flavors, NuPuffs, SunBar, and NuPlus. "Drink Healthy" items featured the original Calli tea, plus newer VitaFruit, Fortune Delight, Sunectar, and SunnyDew products. Sunrider also sold Vitalite Weight-Management products, herbal nutritionals items, and vitamin and mineral supplements.

In addition, the company produced Kandesn 2000 eyeshadow and other cosmetics as well as the Oi-Lin Signature Line of lipsticks and perfumes. Its SunSmile items included herbal toothpaste, teeth whitening gel, lip moisturizer, mouth refresher drops, and a fruit and vegetable rinse.

Sunrider literature proclaimed that, "Because Sunrider controls its entire production process, our products are incomparable in their exclusivity, quality and the conditions under which they are manufactured." The company's largest plant was its 188,000-square-foot facility on Sixth Avenue in City of Industry, California. Sunrider plants featured automated devices to clean, grind, formulate, extract, and concentrate herbal raw materials to make finished powdered or encapsulated products.

In 1998 Sunrider continued to develop new products, and held annual conventions in California, where distributors from around the world could see the company's manufacturing facilities and also its 300,000-square-foot headquarters on nine acres of land in Torrance. The firm planned to expand its headquarters another 50,000 square feet in 1999. Visitors to the Sunrider Museum of Harmony learned about the ancient traditions of Chinese history and art and especially the story of Chinese herbalism and medicine.

In spite of its serious legal problems, in 1998 Sunrider continued to expand, especially in international markets. Due to increasing consumer demand for better health based on natural products, as well as the fact that more individuals were seeking financial opportunity with a home-based multilevel marketing business, Sunrider was riding a strong wave into the next century.

Principal Subsidiaries

Sunrider Australia; Sunrider New Zealand; Sunrider Brazil; Sunrider Canada; Sunrider China; Sunrider Colombia; Sunrider Europe; Sunrider Hong Kong; Sunrider Hungary; Sunrider Indonesia; Sunrider Israel; Sunrider Japan; Sunrider Korea; Sunrider Latvia; Sunrider Malaysia; Sunrider Mexico; Sunrider Philippines; Sunrider Poland; Sunrider Taiwan; Sunrider Thailand; Sunrider Russia.

Principal Divisions

Sunergy Division; Vitalite Weight Management; Kandesn Skin and Personal Care.

The Sunrider Corporation

Further Reading

Cannon, Kenneth L., II, "Sunrider International," *Provo & Orem: A Very Eligible Place: An Illustrated History,* Northridge, Calif.: Windsor Publications, 1987, pp. 108–09.

Carricaburu, Lisa, "Utah's Natural-Products Firms Blossom from Need," *Salt Lake Tribune,* August 16, 1998, pp. E1–E2.

Emshwiller, John R., "Sunrider May Have Concocted Tax Fraud," *Salt Lake Tribune,* January 8, 1997, p. B4.

Lythgoe, Dennis, "Multilevel Marketing-Simple Economics," *Deseret News* (Web Edition), October 17, 1997.

McMullin, Eric, "Sunrider Builds Plant, Drops Soy-Based Line," *Salt Lake Tribune,* September 19, 1988, p. B4.

Owen, David, "Dreams and Downlines," *Atlantic,* October 1987, p. 84.

Rogerson, Kenneth S., "Sunrider Calls It Quits in Utah. . . ," *Deseret News,* February 12, 1991, p. B1.

Rolando, Joe, "Sunrider Recalls Nutrien; Salmonella Is Suspected," *Salt Lake Tribune,* February 20, 1988, p. A12.

Sunrider International Company Profile, Torrance, Calif.: Sunrider, 1998.

"Sunrider Owners Guilty of Tax Evasion," *Daily News of Los Angeles,* September 6, 1997.

—David M. Walden

Supercuts Inc.

550 California Street
San Francisco, California 94104
U.S.A.
(612) 947-7777
Fax: (612) 947-8800
Web site: http://www.supercuts.com

Wholly Owned Subsidiary of Regis Corporation
Incorporated: 1975
Employees: 1,500
Sales: $96 million (1997 est.)
SICs: 7231 Beauty Shops

One of the largest barbershop chains in the United States, Supercuts Inc. operates approximately 1,200 stores in the United States and Puerto Rico. Supercuts was founded in 1975 and grew in large part through franchising for the ensuing 15 years, attracting a steady clientele who preferred the company's discount prices and unisex approach to hair styling. In the early 1990s, as the company underwent a series of management changes, company-owned stores took the center stage after years of relying on franchisee-led expansion. The shift into establishing company-owned stores led to crippling financial losses for the chain, as the number of company-owned stores increased from 45 to 500 during a two-year span. In 1996, when Supercuts was coming off a more than $7 million loss and found itself $25 million in debt, Regis Corporation acquired the chain. Regis, based in Minneapolis, owned 2,000 hair salons operating under the names MasterCuts and Trade Secret. In 1998, 754 of the Supercuts in operation were owned by franchisees, with the balance owned by the company itself.

Mid-1970s Origins

Supercuts was founded in 1975 by Frank Emmett and Geoffrey Rappaport, two entrepreneurs who reworked the business of cutting hair and created a concept capable of nationwide expansion. Compared with high-fashion hair salons and neighborhood barbershops, the prototype Supercuts store developed by Emmett and Rappaport was fundamentally distinct, differing from each end of the hair-styling industry spectrum. The idea behind Supercuts was to provide an inexpensive and quick haircut, without appointment and available to everyone—men, women, and children. Further, the basic services offered at a Supercuts store—shampoo, haircut, blow-dry, and styling—would be offered individually, enabling customers to choose those services they specifically wanted and be charged for only the services they chose, something akin to dining from an à la carte menu. In essence, the concept represented the standardization of cutting hair: streamlining the process for maximum efficiency and then marketing the services to a broad customer base. Supercuts customers could get their haircut with the same ease as going to the supermarket and expect the same type of service no matter which Supercuts they frequented. To make this concept work, Emmett and Rappaport created a framework that served as a pattern for all Supercuts stores to follow. The particulars of this blueprint distinguished Supercuts from nearly all other competitors.

Emmett's and Rappaport's novel "product" was the development of an efficient hair-cutting technique that reduced the time required to complete a haircut to 20 minutes. It was a technique that other hair stylists could learn readily, providing the company with a standard that could be disseminated to all Supercuts hairstylists. To become a Supercuts hairstylist, an individual first was required to be a licensed cosmetologist, then had to undergo training in the Emmett-Rappaport hair-cutting technique. Recertification every seven months was another stipulation, but the rewards for adhering to the standards of Supercuts had their advantages for willing hair stylists. At the time of Supercuts formation, the prevailing compensation method in the hair-cutting industry was on a commission basis. Hair stylists earned their money according to how many heads they cut, which meant that financial success was dependent on the individual hair stylist's success in building his or her own clientele. Not so at Supercuts, where hair stylists were genuine employees paid a regular salary, along with benefits.

The first Supercuts opened in the fall of 1975 in Albany, California, and quickly attracted a steady stream of business.

Three years later Emmett and Rappaport were ready to expand and in a burst of energy established five more stores in 1978. At this point, the burgeoning company did not possess all of the characteristics of its systemic approach to the business of cutting hair, but those qualities did begin to appear after the end of 1978. By the end of their company's third year of business, Emmett and Rappaport, encouraged by the resounding success of their concept, decided to begin franchising Supercuts. Over the course of the ensuing decade—their last as Supercuts owners—Emmett and Rappaport governed the proliferation of their concept into a sprawling chain, one that grew for the most part through franchising. In an eight-year span, slightly more than 20 new Supercuts stores were opened by Supercuts the corporation, but this same period also saw nearly 500 Supercuts open up through franchise agreements. By the mid-1980s the chain was the second largest of its kind in the country, trailing only Memphis-based Fantastic Sam's.

Combined, company-owned stores and franchised units were generating more than $120 million in sales per year, their presence blanketing much of the United States. In less than a decade Emmett and Rappaport and their franchisees had begun to exert a stranglehold on the nation's major markets, with Supercuts stores entrenched in 39 states, but the company's statistical strengths alone did not tell the whole story. By the end of 1986 there were profound and, as it would turn out, incurable problems between the founders and the franchisees. A divisive feud had festered during the chain's prolific growth, and by the beginning of 1987 the task of resolving the acrimony had been passed to new owners.

1987 Knightsbridge Acquisition

A group of Chicago-based venture capitalists operating under the name Knightsbridge Partners purchased Supercuts from Emmett and Rappaport in 1987. Led by David Lipson, former executive vice-president and chief financial officer of Beatrice Companies Inc., Knightsbridge invested in companies involved in food, consumer products, and consumer services and had first approached Emmett and Rappaport in November 1986 about acquiring Supercuts. The founders rejected the proposal, as well as others, but three months later their position had changed and it was Emmett and Rappaport who approached Knightsbridge, inviting the investment firm to offer another bid. An agreement was reached, and as the details of the deal were negotiated Knightsbridge began looking for an executive to manage their soon-to-be-acquired investment. Lipson and his colleagues turned to an executive referral service and the name they were given to contact was Betsy Burton, most recently the marketing executive for Pontiac, Michigan-based Perry Drug Stores Inc.

Burton signed on as chairman, chief executive officer, and president, assuming the responsibility of assuaging the difficulties between Supercuts franchisees and corporate executives in San Rafael.

Burton, in her mid-30s when she was tapped as the leader of Supercuts, held a B.A. in psychology from the College of William and Mary and an M.B.A. from the University of Chicago. She began her professional career as a merchandising manager for health and beauty aids for a Midwestern retail chain named Jewel Companies, Inc., distinguishing herself enough to be recruited in 1981 by Bee Discount, a retail chain of beauty and barber supply stores. Eventually rising through the corporate ranks to become president and chief operating officer, she left Bee Discount to become president of Victory Beauty Supplies, the largest beauty supply distributor in the Midwest. Her record of success continued at Victory, where she was credited for doubling sales. As part of her compensation for invigorating business, grateful Victory management awarded Burton part-ownership in the company, which she subsequently cashed in when Victory was sold to Alberto-Culver Co. in 1985. Her bank account fattened by the sale of her ownership stake, Burton joined Perry Drug Stores Inc. as senior vice-president of marketing. In February 1987, while working for Perry Drug, Burton's telephone rang, signaling her next career move to Supercuts.

With the money she gained from her heralded efforts at Victory, Burton not only assumed the three most powerful executive positions at Supercuts, she also took on a financial interest in the company, acquiring ten percent of the beleaguered hair salon chain. The challenge in front of her was unifying the franchisees and corporate management, something that was intrinsic to the vitality of the company. "My challenges are set out in front of me," Burton explained when she took the helm in late 1987. "The first task is to develop a partnership with the franchisees. The company doesn't make money unless the franchisees make money," she remarked. Burton also looked past the internal strife and set the tone for future growth once the difficulties were resolved. "The growth of chains is rapid," she noted, "but there's still room for more growth. Expansion will help the existing stores. We're not even near saturation. We will try to increase density in underpenetrated markets." On this confident note, Burton began moving forward, hoping to make her tenure at Supercuts as successful as her previous managerial stints.

When Burton first slipped behind her desk at San Rafael, the adversarial relationship between corporate headquarters and the franchisees had erupted into a contentious legal squabble that hobbled the company. As the chain grew robustly during the first half of the 1980s, the independent shop owners became increasingly angered about their treatment from Supercuts executives. The franchisees were convinced that their thoughts and ideas concerning the operation of Supercuts were being ignored, and in response they took collective action and formed an association of independent Supercuts owners. Meanwhile, productivity waned as emotions flared and chainwide profitability began to suffer. Against this backdrop the change in ownership occurred, and by the time Burton took the helm the association of franchisees had filed a lawsuit against Supercuts the corporation, threatening further difficulties for the company. Burton realized that the situation was grave, requiring immediate resolution. Before the Knightsbridge deal was officially concluded, Burton began to preach harmony, hoping to demonstrate to the independent shop owners that she was on their side. She hosted a reception for franchisees, met several of their demands, and convinced the franchisees to settle their class action lawsuit, which centered on the use of advertising dollars. "It was heart-warming," she remarked shortly after the reception. "It's a tremendous feeling. People are asking to expand. They want to know what our plans are."

With the rift between management and franchisees resolved, Burton next turned her attention toward regaining the momentum lost during Supercuts' mid-1980s downward spiral. She reduced corporate staff by 50 percent and assembled her own management team. After realizing that Supercuts had been operating without any formal budgeting procedures, she put in place measures to curtail overspending. In addition, she began selling beauty supplies in Supercuts stores, something Emmett and Rappaport had shied away from because, in their minds, it detracted from the company's no-frills concept. "It seemed to me," Burton explained, "that selling hair-care products in the shops was an ideal way to build another profit center without increasing overhead by more than the few thousand dollars it would take to stock the goods." Given the opportunity to increase profits, Supercuts' franchisees welcomed the new facet to their business operations, as they did the $500,000 Burton spent on the company's training program. The changes and the renewed team spirit worked wonders, injecting life into a previously anemic enterprise. During the first two years of Burton's stewardship, franchisees recorded double-digit sales increases. All told, franchisee revenues swelled from $126 million to $170 million, spurred in part by the 100 new franchised stores that were added during the two-year span. By the beginning of the 1990s optimism and confidence soared, reflected in Burton's five-year master plan of reaching $500 million in sales and a store count of 1,200 by 1995. The harmonious spirit that had lifted Supercuts' fortunes had even spread upward to the company's highest ranks: in 1990 Burton and Lipson married. It seemed the perfect beginning for a rejuvenated company, but the camaraderie did not last. Less than a year after her wedding and the launching of her five-year master plan, Burton quit.

Troubled Early 1990s

Burton's enchantment with her tenure at Supercuts soured in 1991. At the time, the company's financial growth and physical expansion was brisk. Lipson, perhaps spurred by the company's energetic progress, wanted to take Supercuts public, a proposal Burton was wholly against. As the leader of the company, Burton did not relish the idea of shareholders possessing a voice in the governance of Supercuts, but Lipson was firmly attached to the idea and would not be swayed from converting the company to public ownership. In response, Burton resigned five months before Supercuts' initial public offering of stock in October 1991. Shortly after Burton departed, she and Lipson divorced, leaving Lipson in the same position he had occupied four years earlier: in need of someone to manage Supercuts.

To replace Burton, Lipson selected Edward Faber, the flamboyant president of ComputerLand during the early 1980s who was credited with rapidly increasing franchise sales for the computer retailer. Expected to invigorate franchise sales as he had at ComputerLand, Faber did not remain with Supercuts long enough to achieve any substantial goals. He resigned from the company 11 months after he took control, explaining that he lacked the energy for the job. Supercuts, too, was beginning to slouch in the shoulders, bereft of steady support to franchisees that had reached its acme during the years of Burton's leadership. With nowhere else to turn, Lipson named himself as Supercuts' new chief executive officer, taking over with a bold new plan that promised to change the face of Supercuts as it had existed since 1975. Lipson proclaimed a new focus on establishing company-owned stores, moving the company away from its nearly 20-year-long dependence on franchised units to fuel growth. Lipson's dramatic turnaround was predicated on his belief that the rampant franchisee-led growth that occurred during the 1980s was made possible by the liberal lending habits of banks during the decade, a characteristic that no longer described bank lending practices during the 1990s. Consequently, Lipson looked to company-owned stores as the driving force for Supercuts' future, and in early 1993 he hoped to open 120 new company-owned stores before the end of the year.

As a foundation on which to build, Lipson had 45 company-owned stores, far fewer than the more than 720 franchised Supercuts that were in operation when he took over as chief executive officer. For potential location sites for the company-owned stores he would open, Lipson looked to the Midwest and the Northeast, where the company's presence was weakest, and away from California, Texas, and Florida, where Supercuts stores were concentrated. Lipson, as he set his plan in motion, displayed a prodigious appetite for expansion, establishing one new store after another in rapid fashion. By the beginning of 1996 the total number of Supercuts stores had risen to nearly 1,200, close to the target goal set by Burton five years earlier; the goal had been achieved, however, in a manner contrary to the mode of growth projected by Burton. All of the new stores were company-owned stores, lifting the total count of such stores to 500, a remarkable increase from the 45 company-owned stores in operation roughly two years earlier. The prolific expansion did not come without its costs, the most alarming of which was the more than $7 million loss recorded in 1995. The chain was reeling under the strain of too-rapid expansion, and the person to blame was the architect of the frenetic expansion: Lipson. At the beginning of 1996 Lipson was ousted from the company, his vision of financial success achieved through an armada of company-owned stores having proved illusory.

In the wake of Lipson's departure, Supercuts was a rudderless company coming off of fours years of misguided management. The task of steering the company in the right direction fell to the chain's new owners, who arrived in mid-1996. In July, Minneapolis-based Regis Corporation, operator of nearly 2,000 hair salons, purchased Supercuts. Regis acquired Supercuts in a stock swap valued at approximately $120 million, a deal that also forced Regis to assume $25 million in debt racked up by the weakened Supercuts chain. Under Regis's ownership, Supercuts was operated as a separate business unit, retaining its name and many of its senior executives, led by Steve Price, who took over as president and chief executive officer after Lipson's departure. A number of company-owned stores closed in the months after the acquisition was finalized in October 1996, particularly in the New York area. During the ensuing two years, the chain avoided major expansion and steadied itself after years of tumult, striving to distance itself from its troubled past and chart a course for a less disruptive future.

Further Reading

Berss, Marcia, "Haircut, Anyone?," *Forbes,* April 26, 1993, p. 128.

Brown, Katie, "Venture Firm Takes Control of Supercuts," *San Francisco Business Times,* September 28, 1987, p. 1.

Liedtke, Michael, "Minneapolis' Regis Corp. Buys Supercuts Inc. of San Francisco," *Knight-Ridder/Tribune Business News,* July 16, 1996, p. 7.

Stevens, Mark, "Turnaround Tricks: Getting a Company Back on Its Feet," *Working Woman,* December 1990, p. 45.

—Jeffrey L. Covell

The Swatch Group SA

Seevorstadt 6
CH-2502 Bienne
Switzerland
(41) 32 343 68 33
Fax: (41) 32 343 69 22
Web site: http://www.swatchgroup.com

Public Company
Incorporated: 1984 as Société Suisse de
    Microelectronique & d'Horlogerie
Employees: 17,729
Sales: SFr 3.05 billion (US$2.03 billion) (1997)
Stock Exchanges: Zurich
SICs: 3873 Watches, Clocks, Watchcases & Parts; 5094
    Jewelry & Precious Stones; 5944 Jewelry Stores

The Swatch Group SA—known as Société Suisse de Microelectronique & d'Horlogerie or SMH until 1998—is the world's leading supplier of watch movements and finished watches, accounting for as much as 25 percent of total world production, while capturing more than ten percent of all watch sales. The Swatch Group is more than its flagship Swatch brand—which alone accounts for half of the company's profits, and, in the late 1990s has given its name to a 15-store chain of retail Swatch Megastores. The Swatch Group also includes many of the world's most prestigious names in watch design, including Omega and Blancpain (luxury); Rado and Longines (high end); Tissot, Certina, Mido, Balmain, Hamilton, and Calvin Klein (mid-market); and FlikFlak, Lanco, and Swatch in the 'basic' or low-end market. In addition, the company's exclusive Endura label crafts custom-designed watches.

In an era of increasing market segmentation, Swatch remains a tightly vertically integrated company, manufacturing not only watches, but their movements and motors and other basic components. The company produces components—through a range of subsidiaries, including ETA, itself Switzerland's largest movements manufacturer—for much of the Swiss watchmaking industry, as well as for the member brands of the Swatch group. In total, Swatch has nearly 450 reporting business units, principally in Switzerland, but implanted throughout the world. Its 50 production centers are located in Switzerland, the United States, France, Italy, Germany, Thailand, Malaysia, China, and the Virgin Islands.

Beyond watches and their components, Swatch has long flirted with high technology, fabricating microprocessors, smart-card technology, portable telephones, and other future-oriented designs, such as wristwatches that double as telephones, credit cards, even concert tickets. In October 1998, Swatch debuted its latest venture, or adventure, as some would have it: the Smart car, a project in partnership with the Daimler Benz corporation. The chief architect behind these projects and the Swatch group's success has been Nicolas Hayek, who, at more than 70 years of age remains company chairman. Hayek is credited with leading Swatch from the bankruptcy of its founding companies to more than SFr 3.05 billion in annual sales in 1997.

Out of Time in the 1970s

Switzerland's traditional dominance of the international watchmaking market foundered in the 1970s. The arrival of digital technology and the use of quartz-based timing in so-called quartz analog watches gave rise to a new breed of cheap Asian watches and to a new generation of giant Japan and Hong Kong-based industrial manufacturers. The Swiss market, with its tradition of small, often family-owned firms, and its continued focus on more expensive, labor-intensive mechanical movements, was caught by surprise by the gains made by such brands as Seiko and Citizen.

While Swiss watchmakers had been among the first to debut digital watches—priced at the high end of the market at their debut in the late 1960s—most of the Swiss industry considered these and quartz-based timing a fad that would swiftly pass. Instead, demand for these easily produced watches (in contrast to the meticulous craftsmanship needed for most mechanical watches) encouraged a whole new crop of worldwide competitors to enter the field. By the mid-1970s, the market had become glutted, prices plunged, and the entire industry underwent a crisis, even as demand for digital watches and their LED or

LCD faces vanished. The appearance of the first quartz analog watches, which supplanted mechanical movements with quartz-based ''modules'' while retaining traditional analog watch-faces, however, would prove more enduring. Here again, however, the Swiss industry clung to mechanical movements, convinced that the quartz fad would soon end as well.

By the end of the 1970s, the Swiss watchmaking industry was in serious trouble. Many spoke of exiting the watchmaking market altogether, or limiting craft-based production to the high-end and luxury markets. Two of the largest Swiss watchmakers were among those facing collapse. Both Allgemeine Schweizerische Uhrenindustrie (ASUAG) and Société Suisse pour l'Industrie Horlogère (SSIH) had been formed in the 1930s depression era, grouping, in SSIH's case, such long-revered names in watchmaking as Omega and Tissot. Omega, founded in the mid-19th century, had achieved prominence as one of the world's top luxury brands, with its mechanical watches and timepieces not only an Olympic Games standard, but also the choice of U.S. astronauts.

As French-speaking SSIH concentrated on watches, its German-speaking rival ASUAG focused on movements and other component parts, while also adding watchmaking subsidiaries and brands. By the 1960s, both ASUAG and SSIH were among the world's largest watchmaking firms. ASUAG itself had built a position as one of the Swiss industry's chief suppliers of movements and watch components. Yet, by the beginning of the 1980s, faced with an onslaught of cheaply produced quartz-based and digital watches, both ASUAG and SSIH were facing bankruptcy proceedings. In addition to the glut of cheap watches, ASUAG and SSIH had suffered from important economic factors: the devaluation of the U.S. dollar in the mid-1970s vastly increased the cost of importing Swiss watches into what had been one of the industry's chief marketplaces; at the same time, Switzerland could not hope to compete with the low wage and production costs available in the Far East.

In the late 1970s, both companies, joined by the Swiss industry as a whole, attempted to reverse their fortunes, investing massively in quartz module production facilities. By the end of the decade, the industry had succeeded in bringing all quartz component manufacture needs within the country's borders. ASUAG had been among the earliest to adopt this new manufacturing trend, and had succeeded in becoming an important supplier of quartz movements. Yet the move proved too late. As the decade closed, more than half of the 1,600 Swiss watchmakers present at the start of the decade had gone out of business. SSIH, which had become the country's largest watchmaker, was bleeding: after suffering large losses in 1980, it received a US$150 million bailout from its banks. Nevertheless, its losses continued.

By 1982, it was the turn of ASUAG and SSIH to face liquidation procedures. Foreign competitors hovered around the two companies, eager to buy up such famous watch brands as Longines, Hamilton, Tissot, Rado, and Omega. Observers of the Swiss industry seemed resigned to see watchmaking fade into the fabric of Swiss history.

The Hayek Era of the 1980s

Many credit the survival of ASUAG and SSIH's operations to the actions of one Nicolas Hayek. (Hayek himself would claim to have rescued the entire Swiss watchmaking industry, to the indignation of many of his competitors.) Hayek was the head of Hayek Engineering, which had built a reputation in the 1970s as a leading manufacturing consultant. In 1982, Hayek was hired by ASUAG and SSIH's creditors to investigate the Swiss watchmaking industry and, as Hayek claimed, ''produce a report saying it's impossible to produce in Switzerland because the Japanese are much cheaper, labor is cheaper'' (*European*, June 19, 1997).

Despite the banks' desire to shut down the Swiss watchmaking industry, and sell off its jewels to recoup some of their losses, the so-called Hayek Study would lead the Swiss industry into a new era. Chief among Hayek's recommendations was to merge the two longtime rivals into a single company. Hayek's second recommendation proved perhaps still more radical: the production of a new type of watch directed at the low-cost (under US$50) watch market. The banks agreed to the merger, creating the ASUAG/SSIH entity in 1983. But the banks refused Hayek's idea for the new type of watch. Instead, they offered to sell 51 percent of the merged company to Hayek for SFr 151 million. Hayek accepted the gamble, renaming the company as Société Suisse de Microelectronique & d'Horlogerie, or SMH.

Hayek counted on an innovation made by the company's ETA watch movement subsidiary, led by Ernst Thomke. At the height of the watch market explosion in the 1970s, a great deal of competition had focused on making the thinnest watch in the world. ETA would win, developing the technology to produce a watch that was less than 1 mm in thickness. The watch, marketed as the Delirium, proved a success, with sales of more than 5,000, despite a price tag of nearly US$5,000. At the start of the 1980s, Thomke's attention too turned toward rescuing not only parent company ASUAG but also SSIH, as a means of rescuing ETA itself—the failure of these two watchmaking powerhouses would mean the failure of ETA as well. Thomke devised a radically new watch concept, based on the technology developed for the Delirium, and to be manufactured entirely by automated production methods. It was this concept that Hayek brought to SMH's creditors as the means to rescue the newly merged company.

This watch was, of course, the Swatch. More than a watch, the Swatch represented a entirely new marketing concept, featuring colorful designs and flashy advertising that not only broke from the conservative mold of the Swiss industry, but also caught its Asian competitors entirely off guard. Greeted by industry skepticism, the Swatch proved a huge success. The automated production process had succeeded in keeping costs down, propelling SMH into profitability by mid-decade. By 1986, SMH's revenues had climbed to SFr 1.25 billion. The Swatch's colorful designs encouraged customers to purchase multiple watches—and inspired an entire collecting craze consciously fueled by the company itself. In the late 1990s, rare Swatch designs would sell for nearly US$20,000—for a watch that cost less than US$50 when it was first produced.

The Swatch success would inspire the Swiss watchmaking industry as a whole; meanwhile, SMH scored a new hit in the second half of the decade with the introduction of the Rock-Watch, again conceived by Thomke, and released by SMH brand Tissot. Similarly, SMH introduced the children's watch Flik Flak, inspired by the Swatch with its multiple designs. SMH's success proved infectious for its other units, as brands such as Omega and Hamilton revitalized and refocused. Not all of SMH's initiatives were so fortunate: the company's attempt to move into merchandising, introducing a line of Swatch-inspired clothing and accessories, and a chain of in-store Swatch Boutiques, met with little interest. The company abandoned this project and returned its focus to watches and watch movements.

Industry Leadership in the 1990s

By the beginning of the 1990s, SMH was well on its way to becoming the world's largest producer of watches and watch movements. Under Hayek and Thomke, the company had made substantial gains, and the once scoffed at Swatch had sold more than 250 million watches worldwide. Thomke left the company in 1991, after helping reestablish such brands as Tissot, Rado, and Omega. These brands were joined by the 1991 acquisition of the renowned Blancpain brand of luxury watches. The Swatch success story seemed to have a strange side effect: renewed interest in mechanical watches, and especially in the high end and luxury category of watches.

Hayek, meanwhile, was already looking in new directions for SMH. In the 1990s, the company would begin investigations on entering the portable telephone market—with announcements of a Swatch watch with built-in telephone. Hayek had also begun searching for a partner for a project that seemed as radical as the Swatch had been: a new type of car. The so-called Swatchmobile was to be an ecologically friendly vehicle based on a new type of car engine—inspired in part by watch technology. SMH originally entered an agreement with Volkswagen to begin designing the proposed automobile. This agreement fell through, however.

In the mid-1990s, SMH found a new partner for its Swatchmobile in Daimler Benz. In 1994 the two companies announced the creation of the joint partnership Micro Compact Car for the production of the Smart car. Initially scheduled for shipping in October 1997, the Smart car would finally enter production in June 1998, with initial sales in October 1998. The car's minuscule design and Swatch-like design features, as well as an innovative sales approach, caused a sensation at its launch.

The late 1990s would bring to fruition other of SMH's projects. In May 1998, the company planned to launch its Swatch Talk, a new Swatch design featuring a built-in portable telephone. The Swatch Talk was joined by two other products—the Swatch Telecom and Swatch Access—designed to launch the company into the telecommunications market at a time of the European market's deregulation. SMH also began building a new distribution channel for its expanding Swatch brand, opening the first of a proposed 15-store chain of Swatch Megastores in New York and Geneva.

In 1998, SMH adopted the new name of the Swatch Group in recognition of its world-renowned product. The company had grown into an industry powerhouse representing more than 25 percent of total watch and watch component sales, while capturing ten percent of global watch revenues. The Swatch Group, with its forays into automobile production and telecommunications, had also developed a strong vertically integrated organization, producing the full range of watches and watch components, including batteries and microprocessors. In 1997, Swatch posted revenues of SFr 3.05 billion, and net profits of SFr 332 million.

Principal Subsidiaries

Finished Watches: Blancpain; Omega; Longines; Rado; Tissot; Calvin Klein; Certina; Mido; Hamilton; Pierre Balmain; Swatch; Flik Flak; Lanco; Endura. Watch, Movement, and Component Production: ETA, Habillage; Frédéric Piquet; Renata; Comadur; Nivarox-FAR; SMH Assembly. Microelectronics, Components, and Systems: EM Microelectronic-Marin; Oscilloquartz; Micro Crystal; Omega Electronics; SMH Autombile. Other Subsidiaries: Asulab; CDNP; ICP; LASAG; Columna; Swiss Timing; SMH Real Estate; Swatch Telecom; Micro Compact Car (50%).

Further Reading

Domberg, John, "Up from Swatch," *Business Month*, March 1988, p. 54.
Fuhrman, Peter, "Jewelry for the Wrist," *Forbes*, November 23, 1992, p. 173.
"The Many Faces of Swatch," *Harvard Business Review*, March–April 1993, p. 108.
Short, David, "At the Court of the King of Swatch," *European*, June 19, 1997, p. 28.
"Swatch: Ambitious," *Economist*, April 18, 1992, p. 74.

—M. L. Cohen

Thomas Publishing Company

5 Penn Plaza
New York, New York 10001
U.S.A.
(212) 290-7200
Fax: (212) 290-7362
Web site: http://www.thomaspublishing.com

Private Company
Incorporated: 1898
Employees: 500
Sales: $450 million (1997 est.)
SICs: 2721 Periodicals, Publishing; 2731 Books,
      Publishing; 8732 Market Research, Commercial

Celebrating its centennial in 1998, Thomas Publishing Company is a niche reference book publisher dedicated to marketing product information and other materials relevant to both domestic and international industry. It is best known for its *Thomas Register of American Manufacturers.* The company also publishes 27 product news magazines, 23 major buying guides, and is the acknowledged originator of both the industrial product classification system and the reader service card.

Founded in 1898

Thomas Publishing was started in 1890 by Harvey Mark Thomas. It has been family-owned and -managed ever since. The company was incorporated on January 28, 1898, at 106 Wall Street, New York City. Later in the year Thomas's *American Grocery Trades Reference Book* was launched. It was the predecessor of the *Thomas Grocery Register (TGR),* and in 1993 it became the *Thomas Food Industry Register (TFIR).*

When it was first published, the *American Grocery Trades Reference Book* was the first directory of the food industry. Over the years the *American Grocery Trades Reference Book* evolved from a one-volume directory of grocery merchants to a three-volume, industrywide buying guide. The 1998 edition listed more than 30,000 companies and 120,000 suppliers and featured more than 6,000 product classifications. Long before

then, of course, it was recognized as the single most comprehensive, nationwide buying guide for the food industry. As the company's original publication, it led to the development of Thomas Publishing's extensive line of industrial buying guides, including the well-known *Thomas Register of American Manufacturers,* which is the company's flagship publication.

Thomas Register of American Manufacturers *Introduced in 1905*

What became the company's best-known publication, the *Thomas Register of American Manufacturers,* was launched as the *Thomas' Register of American Manufacturers and First Hands in All Lines* in 1905. The original publication featured product classifications grouped by state. In 1969 Thomas added a catalog section to the *Thomas Register,* which included advertisers' catalogs in separate volumes. This publication would become known as ThomCat.

In 1984 the content of the *Thomas Register* became available online through Dialog Information Services, and the 75th anniversary edition was published in 1985. It contained more than 61,000 individual advertisements by 17,000 companies. To mark the occasion, Thomas Publishing donated 1,000 sets of the 19-volume work to the U.S. Department of Commerce. That same year, *Inbound Logistics* magazine was first published as an outgrowth of the Inbound Traffic Guide section of the *Thomas Register.* In 1993 the content of the *Thomas Register* was first published in CD-ROM format and in 1995 was made available on the Internet.

Published annually, the 1998 edition of the *Thomas Register* included 34 volumes containing sourcing information on nearly 56,000 industrial products and services. Together with detailed specifications and availability information from manufacturers, the work included more than 1.7 million individual product or service sources. The publication also included a complete three-volume Company Profiles section and a comprehensive eight-volume Catalog File section. More than 152,000 U.S. and Canadian firms were listed.

In 1915 the *Thomas Register* acquired an eight-person sales force, marking the start of the independent sales contractor system for Thomas Publishing. The newly acquired sales force included Sam Hendricks, a former competitor who had founded the *Hendricks Register.* Over the year Thomas Publishing's sales force grew to over 1,000 independent sales contractors, of which about 600 were devoted to selling the *Thomas Register.* In 1923 Thomas Publishing moved to the Printing Crafts Building on 461 Eighth Avenue in New York City, now known as Five Penn Plaza.

First New Product News Tabloid, 1933

In 1933 Thomas began publishing *Industry Equipment News (IEN),* the earliest new product tabloid to be published. It would spawn many imitators. The next year IEN became the first publication to include a "bingo card," a reader reply card which readers could send in to obtain more information from the periodical's advertisers.

The concept for IEN was brought to Harvey Mark Thomas, publisher of the then 26-year-old *Thomas Register of American Manufacturers,* by F. Morse ("Mo") Smith. Smith noticed that the new product sections of most business publications tended to be the most well-read, indicating a basic need for new product news. It was a need that Harvey Mark Thomas also recognized, and together with Smith and editor Bill Irish they developed the first product news magazine.

The first edition of *Industry Equipment News* was mailed in May 1933. By the end of the year it was clear that the publication had achieved sufficient reader acceptance to begin taking advertising. The publication was noted for several innovations in product news reporting. It featured a tightly written style that allowed for the maximum number of new products in each issue. It employed an oversized tabloid page format with ads surrounding a center column of editorial content. The pages reported on a wide range of new products from all industries, so that readers could find solutions to their manufacturing needs.

IEN aimed to make it easy for prospective buyers to contact manufacturers, and it assigned a number to each ad and editorial item. In 1934 IEN introduced the "bingo card," the now familiar reader service card that could be sent back to the magazine to obtain additional product information from the manufacturers. IEN later improved upon the bingo card by providing a write-in card on which readers could spell out in greater detail their specific needs.

IEN's circulation policy was also innovative. It was offered free to all qualified subscribers, thus speeding up the process of getting new product information to decision-makers in industry. IEN was among the first publications to use free "controlled circulation" exclusively, a method which became the dominant way specialized business periodicals were distributed.

Almost from its very beginning, IEN began to expand internationally. In 1938 Mo Smith licensed IEN in Canada and the United Kingdom. Some 40 years later IEN began an international network with editions being published in different countries by local partners. Still expanding in the 1990s, this international network covered pan-Europe, France, Germany, Holland, the Mideast, Brazil, Latin America, Japan, and Korea.

Continuing its tradition of innovation, Thomas created an Internet database of product news called the Product News Network (PNN). It was launched in March 1998 with 50,000 products and was expected to expand dramatically. Another source of product news, IENOnline, was scheduled to launch in the spring of 1999. IENOnline would be a web site that would uniquely interact with the print publication.

Thomas Marketing Information Center (TMIC) Established, 1969

In 1969 Thomas established the Thomas Marketing Information Center (TMIC) to market industrial information and databases the company had collected. In 1977 TMIC began offering industrial marketing research services to outside companies. In the early 1990s TMIC published the company's first manufacturing software guides.

Thomas International Publishing Co. (TIPCo) was established to develop international ventures for the company. In its first year TIPCo teamed up with INCOM K.K. of Japan to produce the first foreign-language version of IEN. It was the company's first joint venture. The next year it established a joint venture in Brazil with T/L Publicacoes Industrials Ltda. to produce Portuguese editions of IEN and the *Thomas Register.* In 1975 TIPCo established joint ventures in Belgium and Germany. In 1978 a joint venture was established in France, called Editions Elsevier-Thomas S.A. By 1998 Thomas was publishing 21 titles in seven languages worldwide. TIPCo also published the *Thomas Register of European Manufacturers,* and the first CD-ROM edition of that title was published in 1996.

Thomas Regional Directory Company Established, 1976–77

Thomas Regional Directory Company began as a division of Thomas Publishing in 1976. The idea for publishing regional information had been circulating around Thomas for some time, because it spoke to the core of Thomas's publishing mission: to provide industrial purchasing information to buyers and specifiers. During 1976 Philip O'Keefe, who eventually became president of Thomas Regional Directory Company, and a group of Thomas staffers developed a regional publication for northern New Jersey, a heavily industrialized area. In March 1977, Thomas Regional Directory Company published its first regional industrial buying guide covering the North Jersey region. Eventually it would publish 19 regional editions covering much of the United States.

With the success of the North Jersey volume, Thomas Regional Directory Company was officially incorporated as a subsidiary of Thomas Publishing Company in 1977. By the early 1980s, Thomas Regional had published other regional industrial buying guides. In 1986 Philip O'Keefe resigned as president of

Thomas Regional and was replaced by Eileen Markowitz, previously a vice-president with Ziff-Davis Publishing Co.

Ever since the early 1990s, more and more directories were being published on CD-ROM as librarians and small business owners were discovering the benefits of this electronic format. After forming a task group to study CD-ROMs, Thomas Regional published its first Thomas Regional Electronic Network Directory (TREND) in November 1996. That year Thomas Regional released a total of 19 CD-ROMs, one for each region.

At the same time, the TREND team oversaw the development of the Thomas Regional Internet site. This site would become the web's largest and most comprehensive database of regional industrial suppliers, providing information on more than 480,000 industrial companies. The company's new CD-ROMs would provide seamless web connectivity to Thomas Regional on the Internet, so that the company's CD-ROM customers would have access to the entire web database. Thomas Regional's busy publishing schedule—one print guide and one CD-ROM every three weeks—was handled by an in-house staff of 75 people, which also took care of updating the Thomas Regional web site.

Began Publishing American Export Register, *1980*

Known as the *American Export Register* since it was acquired by Thomas Publishing, the *American Register of Exporters and Importers* was first published in 1948 by another publisher. It was designed to help European industry recover from World War II by providing contact information for American suppliers of goods and services. Thomas acquired the publication in 1979 from its current publisher, S. John Cousins, and renamed the 1980 edition the *American Export Register.*

The 1998 edition of the *American Export Register* contained more than 1,100 paid advertisers, 5,500 product and service categories, and more than 44,000 listings for U.S. companies. The work was published annually and circulated to nearly 200 countries, reaching more than 20,000 users worldwide.

In March 1998 the *American Export Register* became the first and only directory for exporters to make its information available on both a multilingual CD-ROM and on the Internet. The electronic formats, published in English, French, German, Italian, Spanish, and Portuguese, facilitated contact between international buyers and American exporters through fax forms and hotlinks. In addition, the electronic products contained the linecards, catalogs, brochures, and videos of the American export companies.

Toward the end of 1998 the American Export Group announced that a new Chinese-language edition of the *American Export Register* would be published in China in 1999 by a new venture called International Business Directories, Inc. The new edition was endorsed by the Chinese Ministry of Foreign Trade and Economic Cooperation and would be distributed to 20,000 qualified purchasers of imported industrial products and services.

Thomas Launched Managing Automation, *1986*

In 1986 a new magazine devoted to advanced manufacturing, *Managing Automation,* was first published by Thomas Publishing. It grew out of a recognition on the part of IEN management that automating a manufacturing facility was a complex process. While automation was becoming essential to the survival of manufacturing in America, there was a marked lack of information about the necessary automation solutions. As a result, *Managing Automation* focused on the increased use and influence of computers on integrated manufacturing. It covered the factory and manufacturing from the point of view of systems integration.

To define its audience, *Managing Automation* developed a new circulation definition system. Instead of using traditional definitions such as job title, function, or SIC code, the new system categorized readers on the basis of their involvement in various stages of the automation process.

Over the next decade and more, integration of the manufacturing process advanced rapidly, from factory floor integration to plantwide integration to efforts to integrate the entire supply chain globally. *Managing Automation* changed, too, from a focus on individual hardware components toward systems and software-controlled supply chain integration.

Thomas Began Publishing Software Guides, *1992*

Thomas began publishing software guides and a directory of software manufacturers in 1992. The first guide, *Computerized Maintenance Management Systems (CMMS) Software Directory and Comparison Guide,* was published in 1992 by the Thomas Marketing Information Center. The publication grew into a family of guides that would help users compare and select manufacturing software. These software guides were later published in electronic format by the Managing Automation Software Guides division of the Thomas Magazine Group.

A second software guide and directory was published in 1995. It covered factory software and was published under the title *Manufacturing Execution Systems (MES) Directory and Comparison Guide.* It was published by Managing Automation Software Guides, first in print form, then in 1996 on CD-ROM. The CMMS guide was also made available in CD-ROM format.

In 1997 Thomas debuted the *Manufacturing Enterprise Applications (MEA) Comparison* CD-ROM. It contained detailed information on 150 software systems and suppliers of enterprise-wide software. Also included on the CD-ROMs were electronic advertisements. With widespread acceptance of the CD-ROM versions of its software guides, Thomas stopped publishing them in print form.

In addition to publishing new manufacturing software guides in 1997, Thomas acquired three computer-assisted design (CAD) titles originally launched by Autodesk: *PartSpec, PlantSpec,* and *CADBlocks.* These titles provided design engineers, plant engineers, and architects with an online library of product drawings for use in their own designs.

In December 1997 Thomas entered into a partnership with Advanced Manufacturing Research, Inc., a respected industry and market analysis firm specializing in enterprise applications and related trends and technologies. The partnership created Total Applications Selection Kits (T.A.S.K.) for mid-size manufacturers to provide complete solutions to the software selection process. T.A.S.K. provided all of the necessary research, tools, advice, and information for identifying, comparing, selecting, and purchasing the appropriate software.

To facilitate adding new information to its database of manufacturing software, Managing Automation Software Guides published in January 1998 an editorial questionnaire on the Internet in a secure web site for software suppliers to provide Thomas with updated information on their systems and companies.

Web Sites and Online Services

After moving back to 5 Penn Plaza, originally 461 Eighth Avenue, in 1993, Thomas Publishing made the content of the *Thomas Register* available on the Internet at www. thomasregister.com in 1995. In early 1998 the web site was relaunched. The redesign helped increase site traffic by 20 percent a month to 13 million page views per month.

In 1997 a joint venture was established between Thomas Publishing and General Electric Information Services (GEIS) of Rockville, Maryland, to provide web-based procurement solutions to buyers and sellers worldwide. Called the Trading Partner Services Register, or TPN Register, the system allowed users to conduct business electronically using Thomas's classification system and Internet programs. It was reported that the service could reduce procurement cycles by up to 50 percent and reduce costs by 30 percent.

TPN Register grew out of a 1996 partnership between a Thomas subsidiary, Electronic Purchasing Information Corporation (EPIC), and GEIS. The two companies teamed to create ConnectUs, a public database that allowed firms to choose suppliers internationally. With ConnectUs, companies could make online purchases using a purchasing card and electronic data interchange (EDI) messages. Thomas had created the Electronic Purchasing Information Corporation (EPIC) to develop ways to enhance and administer electronic commerce using information contained in Thomas Publishing's databases.

In 1998 SoluSource was introduced as a "next generation" online service to help design engineers. It was based on Thomas's vast library of original equipment manufacturer (OEM) catalogs. It incorporated specially designed search tools and functionality-based indexing that facilitated side-by-side product comparisons.

By 1998 all of Thomas's major directories were available as databases on the World Wide Web, including the *Thomas Register of American Manufacturers,* the *Thomas Register of European Manufacturers, Thomas Regional Directories,* and the *Thomas Food Industry Register.* The Thomas databases could be accessed for free by users, with advertisers footing the bill.

Celebrated 100th Anniversary, 1998

Thomas Publishing celebrated the company's 100th anniversary in 1998. A number of commemorative activities were scheduled, including a nationwide industrial marketplace study

of leading companies; donations of Thomas's electronic products to colleges and universities; and sponsorship of a nationwide essay contest among students of purchasing.

Throughout its 100-year history, Thomas Publishing has created products to bring buyers and sellers together. Its pioneering supplier directory and other new products helped establish it as the industrial information authority throughout the 20th century. As a result, Thomas Publishing was positioned as the recognized leader in providing U.S. industry with product information through both print and electronic publishing.

Principal Subsidiaries

Thomas International Publishing Company, Inc.; Thomas Regional Directory Company; Thomcomp Incorporated.

Further Reading

"America's Leading Export Directory Becomes First to Publish Multi-Lingual CD and Internet Site," March 16, 1998, http://www.thomaspublishing.com/praer.html.

Brennan, Patricia L., "Thomas Register Marks 75th Year As the Leader of Buying Guides for Businesses," *Indianapolis Business Journal,* June 17, 1985, p. 2B.

"Efficient Procurement," *Industry Week,* April 7, 1997, p. 120.

Fitch, Thomas P., "Two Vendor Info Networks Boost Electronic Business," *Corporate Cashflow Magazine,* April 1996, p. 5.

Hargraves, Allison, "Thomas Register Marks 75th Year," *Pittsburgh Business Times and Journal,* February 25, 1985, p. 4S.

"Industrial Equipment News," http://www.thomaspublishing.com/annivienist.html.

Kaydo, Chad, "Does Nepotism Work?," *Sales and Marketing Management,* July 1998, p. 16.

O'Leary, Mick, "Thomas Brings Register—and More—to the Web," *Database,* June–July 1998, p. 80.

"Pop Goes Purchasing," *Industry Week,* February 5, 1996, p. 43.

Raffaele, Elizabeth, "Thomas Publishing Sues Industry.Net over Copyright," *Pittsburgh Business Times and Journal,* February 10, 1997, p. 9.

"Thomas Food Industry Register," http://www.thomaspublishing.com/annivtfir.html.

"Thomas Publishing Announces China Directory," October 1, 1998, http://www.thomaspublishing.com/praerchina.html.

"Thomas Publishing Company Timeline," http://www.thomaspublishing.com/annivtpcotime.html.

"Thomas Publishing Company Celebrates 100 Years of Bringing Buyers and Sellers Together," March 11, 1998, http://www.thomaspublishing.com/100release.html.

"Thomas Regional Directory Company," http://www.thomaspublishing.com/annivregion.html.

"Thomas Regional Settles Internet Copyright Infringement Lawsuits Brought Against IndustryNet," February 26, 1998, http://www.thomaspublishing.com/indnet.html.

"Thomas Register of American Manufacturers," http://www.thomaspublishing.com/annivtr.html.

"ThomasNet Launches SoluSource," June 9, 1998, http://www.solusource.com/release.html.

Walsh, Mark, "Thomas Gains Purchase on Web, but Success Comes at a Cost," *Crain's New York Business,* May 4, 1998, p. 32.

—David Bianco

TIG Holdings, Inc.

65 East 55th Street
New York, New York 10022
U.S.A.
(212) 446-2700
Fax: (212) 371-8360
Web site: http://www.tig1.com

Public Company
Incorporated: 1993
Employees: 1,100
Total Assets: $6.86 billion (1997)
Stock Exchanges: New York
Ticker Symbol: TIG
SICs: 6331 Fire, Marine & Casualty Insurance; 6339
   Insurance Carriers, Not Elsewhere Classified; 6719
   Offices of Holding Companies, Not Elsewhere
   Classified

TIG Holdings, Inc. is engaged primarily in the business of property/casualty insurance and reinsurance, mainly through its TIG Insurance Co. and TIG Reinsurance Co. subsidiaries. The major lines of coverage, in the late 1990s, were workers' compensation, automobile liability and physical damage, general and other liability, and commercial multiple peril. Policies were being sold through independent agents and brokers. TIG Holdings' initials derived from Transamerica Insurance Group, a unit of Transamerica Corporation before 1993.

Transamerica's Property/Casualty Holdings: 1928–84

Transamerica Corporation was the holding company founded by A. P. Giannini in 1928 to control the Bank of America and other properties, including Pacific National Fire Insurance Co., which was founded in 1911 and commenced business in 1915. Based in San Francisco, Pacific National Fire Insurance was, in 1940, conducting business in all 48 states, offering fire, motor vehicle, inland marine, aircraft, and numerous other kinds of property/casualty insurance, including damage from earthquakes, tornadoes, explosions, and riot and civil commotion. In 1932 it acquired all business of the Associated Fire Marine Insurance Co. except for automotive. Pacific National Fire Insurance earned $5.1 million in premiums in 1940 but lost $301,000. In 1950 it earned $11 million in premiums and had net income of $1.1 million.

Transamerica acquired Philadelphia-based Manufacturers Casualty Insurance Co. in 1950. This company was incorporated in 1915. In 1950 it earned premiums of $12 million and recorded a net loss of $1.1 million. It controlled Manufacturers Fire Insurance Co., also of Philadelphia, which in 1949 earned premiums worth $1.3 million and had net income of $134,511. Also in 1950, Transamerica acquired more than 92 percent of Paramount Fire Insurance Co. Based in New York City, this company was incorporated in 1938 and wrote a variety of property/casualty policies. In 1949 it had total earnings of $950,252.

Transamerica was considerably slimmed down in 1958, after a congressional law forced the holding company to divest itself of its banking interests. Among what remained were seven insurance companies: Occidental Life Insurance Co. and six fire and casualty companies writing nearly all forms of insurance other than life. Manufacturers Casualty and Manufacturers Fire were merged into Pacific National Fire in 1958, and Paramount Fire Insurance was merged into it in 1959. The company changed its name to Pacific National Insurance Co. in 1962 and Transamerica Insurance Co. in 1963.

Among Transamerica Insurance's holdings was American Surety Co., 93 percent acquired by Transamerica Corporation in 1960. Incorporated in New York in 1881, this large company and its affiliates wrote almost every kind of insurance. In 1960 American Surety earned $53.2 million in premiums and had net income of $2.6 million. This company, which included Canada Surety Co., was merged into Transamerica Insurance at the end of 1963.

In addition, when parent Transamerica Corporation purchased Pacific Finance Corporation in 1961, it also acquired four property/casualty subsidiaries: Olympic Insurance Co., Mt. Beacon Insurance Co., Marathon Insurance Co., and Spartan Insurance Co. These companies were still part of Pacific Finance when it became Transamerica Financial Corporation in 1968, but the following year they passed to Transamerica Insurance, which also controlled Premier Insurance Co., Wolverine Insurance Co., and Wolverine's subsidiary, Riverside Insurance Co. of America. In 1970 Transamerica Insurance collected $220.7 million in insurance premiums and had net income of $2.2 million. By this time the company had moved from San Francisco to Occidental Life's quarters in downtown Los Angeles.

During the 1960s the parent Transamerica became a conglomerate by purchasing several businesses unrelated to financial services, including the United Artists movie studio and Trans International, a charter airline. Occidental Life remained Transamerica's most lucrative unit, but the property insurance companies accounted for only about five percent of earnings. During the early 1970s this line of business became even less important to the parent. Transamerica Insurance's revenues grew from $246.7 million in 1971 to $328.6 million in 1974, but net income, after rising to $11.3 million in 1972 and 1973, fell to $7 million in 1974. In 1975 the company's $354.5 million in direct premiums written accounted for 15 percent of the company's total revenues, but its net income was only $5 million.

Specialized Forms of Coverage: 1984–92

During the late 1970s Transamerica Insurance's earnings improved markedly, reaching a peak of $53.6 million in 1979 on $701.6 million in net premiums written. By the mid-1980s, however, the entire property/casualty industry was suffering from nearly six years of rate-cutting and underwriting losses. Transamerica Insurance reported an after-tax loss of $58.8 million on net premiums written of $856.6 million in 1984, forcing parent Transamerica Corporation to contribute $100 million of new capital to the subsidiary.

Some of the money was being allocated to specialized, potentially more profitable lines of insurance. The company, for example, wrote the property and liability coverage for the 1984 Summer Olympic Games, held in Los Angeles. To reduce its liability, the company required the Olympic Committee's drivers to attend a special safety training program stressing defensive driving techniques. By the end of the summer, Transamerica Insurance had received a little more than 1,900 claims, which was considered tolerable in terms of its exposure to loss. But the company took on this role as its civic and patriotic duty and did not expect to make money.

In 1986 property and casualty insurance accounted for just one percent of the parent company's record $194.2 million in income from continuing operations. Property and casualty volume came to about $1 billion that year, split almost evenly between commercial, personal, and specialty lines. That year Transamerica Insurance began writing coverage for sports and leisure events jointly with K&K Insurance Group. The agreement began with auto racing but grew to cover professional and amateur athletics, including the professional golfers' tour, the National Football League, the National Basketball Association, further Olympic Games, and college basketball's final four. It also covered fairs, theme parks, country festivals, and theater.

In addition, Transamerica Insurance covered the National Trust for Historic Preservation, which owned and cared for 17 historic house museums open to the public, including George Washington's estate in Mount Vernon, Virginia. It also provided coverage for about 60 historic properties operated by National Trust member organizations. In 1987 Transamerica Insurance Group was established and incorporated as the parent of Transamerica Insurance Co. That year it acquired Fairmont Insurance Co. and its subsidiaries, Fairmont Reinsurance Co. and 51-percent-owned River Thames Insurance Co., Ltd. Transamerica Insurance Group moved its headquarters in 1988 from Los Angeles to a suburb, Woodland Hills.

In 1990 Transamerica Insurance Group was the nation's 27th largest property and casualty insurer and included the ninth largest reinsurance company. It had 48 offices in the United States and in the United Kingdom and 4,600 employees, not counting 4,100 independent insurance agents and brokers with whom it did business. Revenues that year came to $2.13 billion, and earnings were $61.1 million, or 23 percent of Transamerica Corporation's total. (The parent company had shed many of its acquisitions and was once again primarily a financial services firm.)

Transamerica Insurance Group entered the movie business in 1989 or 1990 by acquiring Completion Bond Co., a firm that insured financial backers that a movie would be delivered on schedule and within budget, or the firm would pay to finish the movie itself. By 1990 Completion Bond had guaranteed more than 500 films with aggregate budgets exceeding $1.6 billion. Through a U.S. insurance broker and a British entertainment carrier, Transamerica Insurance also was offering coverage for live theater, television production, and concerts, including cast insurance. These lines of coverages were extensions of its established lines of specialty insurance, including sports, leisure, and venues. Other specialty markets in which the group was engaged included excess workers' compensation and reinsurance.

In 1991 Transamerica Insurance Group accounted for nearly a third of the parent corporation's revenue and had 65 offices nationwide, but its earnings of $63 million were considered insufficient. Premiums had fallen about 25 percent because of price-cutting in the property/casualty field, and the group had suffered losses because of fraud in the southern California workers' compensation market and movie cost overruns. Transamerica Corporation announced the following year that it would sell or spin off the unit to focus on its finance and life insurance businesses.

TIG Holdings: 1993–98

Transamerica Insurance Group became TIG Holdings Inc. in 1993, when 44.2 million shares of common stock were sold at $22.63 a share in an initial public offering that raised $1 billion. The holding company's headquarters were installed in New York City, while the Woodland Hills operation—renamed TIG Insurance Co.—was moved to Las Colinas, Texas, a suburb of

Dallas. Transamerica Corporation initially kept a 27 percent stake in the new company but sold it before the end of 1993.

Aided by $70 million in deferred tax liabilities, TIG decided to build on one of its major strengths: reinsurance, which in 1992 accounted for 23 percent of Transamerica Insurance Group's net premiums. That division had a profitability ratio considerably better than that of the overall industry. On the other hand, workers' compensation had accounted for 25 percent of net premiums, and 56 percent of that business was in California, where an observer said the "regulatory climate has been an absolute disaster for insurers." In 1993 TIG Holdings lost $128 million on total revenues of $1.88 billion. The following year the company slashed expenses and had net income of $51.5 million on revenues of $1.78 billion. In 1995 TIG had net income of $118.3 million on revenues of $1.88 billion.

Despite the 1994–95 turnaround, TIG Holdings' return on equity remained below the 15 percent generally regarded as acceptable. In February 1996 the company announced it would lay off 550 of its remaining 1,920 employees. TIG's chairman cited "sustained rate pressure in every segment" of its business, worsened by falling interest rates, which reduced the amount of income generated on invested premiums. The company took a $100 million pretax charge to cover outlays for severance, office lease terminations, and the write-off of some capitalized expenses and said it would discontinue certain coverages failing to meet profitability standards, including some lines of workers' compensation. Gross written premiums in the California workers' compensation market already had fallen from $180 million in 1993 to $64 million in 1995. In all, about 12 percent of overall net premiums written in 1995 were unprofitable.

The company's efforts to raise its profit margin did not bear fruit. Expenses actually rose in 1996 because of the restructuring charge, and TIG Holdings had net income of only $79 million that year on revenues of $1.83 million. Expenses fell $55 million in 1997, but revenues dropped by $68 million, and net income came to only $52 million. In early 1998 the company took a $145 million pretax charge to increase its reserves for claims. This was made necessary, TIG officials said, by the poor performance of the reinsurance unit, which had high-risk professional liability coverages on its books. Following this announcement a class action suit against TIG was filed by two firms, alleging violations of federal securities laws on the ground that the company's reserves had been understated.

TIG Holdings was, in 1997, primarily engaged in the business of property/casualty insurance and reinsurance through 14 domestic insurance subsidiaries and 45 offices writing basically all lines of such insurance in all 50 states. Commercial specialty insurance accounted for 41 percent of net premiums, reinsurance for 36 percent, and retail for 23 percent. Twenty-six percent of direct written premiums were written in California.

Based in Stamford, Connecticut, TIG Reinsurance Co. tended to underwrite lines of business in which it had specific expertise, such as general liability, auto liability and physical damage, and workers' compensation. TIG Insurance Co. had two divisions, Commercial Specialty and Retail, both based in Irving, Texas. Workers' compensation accounted for more than half of all commercial specialty net premiums written in 1997. Other specific units in this division included sports and leisure, primary casualty, excess casualty, special-risk operations, and Lloyds' syndicates. Retail provided property and liability coverage for individuals and small businesses, with the main market automobile liability and physical damage. Homeowners' insurance was offered mainly by the division's independent agents unit, which was sold to Nationwide Mutual Insurance Co. on the last day of 1997.

Principal Subsidiaries

TIG Holdings 1, Inc. (including its subsidiary, TIG Excess & Surplus Lines, Inc., and this subsidiary's subsidiary, TIG Specialty Insurance Co.); TIG Insurance Group (including among its subsidiaries TIG Insurance Co., which included among its subsidiaries Countrywide Corporation, TIG American Specialty Insurance Co., TIG Lloyds Insurance Co., TIG Premier Insurance Co., and TIG Reinsurance Co.).

Further Reading

Apodaca, Patrice, "Insurer Guarantees That Movies Have an Ending—Happy or Otherwise," *Los Angeles Times,* April 10, 1967, p. D7.

——, "Transamerica Seeks Buyer for Casualty Group," *Los Angeles Times,* July 21, 1992, pp. D1, D5.

Brenner, Lynn, "Transamerica Unit Gets Infusion of New Capital," *American Banker,* June 10, 1985, p. 18.

Carpenter, C. A., "Transamerica Focuses on Reorganization," *Journal of Commerce,* May 13, 1987, p. 11A.

Dauer, Christopher, "Insurers Mark 5-Year Partnership," *National Underwriter* (Property & Casualty/Risk & Benefits Management Edition), January 28, 1991, pp. 25–26.

"A Department Store That Sells Money," *Business Week,* May 23, 1964, p. 45.

Dolan, Carrie, "Transamerica Unit Fetches About $1 Billion," *Wall Street Journal,* April 20, 1993, p. A3.

Haggerty, Alfred G., "Historic Sites Covered by Transamerica," *National Underwriter* (Property & Casualty/Risk & Benefits Management Edition), March 27, 1989, pp. 6, 63.

——, "Problems Seen in Transamerica Sale," *National Underwriter* (Property & Casualty/Risk & Benefits Management Edition), July 22, 1992, pp. 1, 37.

Mullen, Liz, "Transamerica to Sell Its Final 27% Stake in Spinoff Insurance Concern,' *Los Angeles Business Journal,* November 29, 1993, p. 5.

Scism, Leslie, "TIG Holdings to Combine 2 Divisions, Cut 550 Jobs, Take 1st-Period Charge," *Wall Street Journal,* February 23, 1996, p. A7B.

Sclafane, Susanne, "TIG Holdings Hit with Class-Action Suit," *National Underwriter* (Property & Casualty/Risk & Benefits Management Edition), March 16, 1998, pp. 2, 55.

——, "TIG Holdings Takes $145 M Hit on Re Reserves," *National Underwriter* (Property & Casualty/Risk & Benefits Management Edition), February 9, 1998, pp. 1, 54.

Tobenkin, David, "His Vision Wasn't Quite 20/20," *Los Angeles Business Journal,* February 11, 1991, p. 22 and continuation.

"Transamerica Corp.," *Forbes,* May 15, 1966, pp. 18–19.

"Transamerica's Olympics Coverage a Success," *National Underwriter* (Property & Casualty/Risk & Benefits Management Edition), November 12, 1984, p. 67.

—Robert Halasz

TOOLEX

Toolex International N.V.

Derun 4315
5500 AD Veldhoven
The Netherlands
(31) 40 2581581
Fax: (31) 40 2541985
Web site: http://www.toolex.com

Public Company
Incorporated: 1997
Employees: 453
Sales: NLG 400.9 million (US$200 million) (1997)
Stock Exchanges: Amsterdam NASDAQ
Ticker Symbol: TLXAF
SICs: 3559 Special Industry Machinery, Not Elsewhere
    Classified; 6719 Holding Companies, Not Elsewhere
    Classified

The merger/takeover of The Netherlands' ODME by Sweden's Toolex Alpha in October 1997 created Toolex International N.V., the premier manufacturer and distributor of optical disc production systems in the world. The optical disc market includes compact discs, CD-ROMs, CD-Rs (recordables) and CD-RWs (rewritables); in the late 1990s the optical disc market expanded to include the new digital versatile disc (DVD) format and its recordable and rewritable forms (DVD-R, DVD-RAM). Both ODME and Toolex Alpha had been leaders in complementary optical disc segments; their merger into Toolex International forms an industry leader offering a full range of optical disc manufacturing and peripheral equipment, including its own full-scale, turnkey disc processing machinery and component process equipment for integration into third-party production systems.

Prior to the takeover of privately held ODME, the smaller Sweden-based Toolex Alpha had been listed publicly on the Amsterdam and NASDAQ stock exchanges. Toolex International retains these public listings, but has as its headquarters the former ODME site in Veldhoven, The Netherlands. Former ODME chief Lambert Dielesen is Toolex International's president and CEO.

In 1997 Toolex International posted pro-forma revenues of NLG 400.9 million and net profits of NLG 40.3 million.

Recording Revolutions in the 1980s

For lovers of vinyl records, 1984 was a bad year. It was that year that a new recording format was introduced—the optical disc, most popularly known for the compact disc recording format. More than a new recording material, the compact disc presented the first digital recording medium for the consumer market. The compact disc technology involved converting analog sound to digital information—1s and 0s—which could then be stored on the disc using specially formulated dyes and other coating materials. A laser was then used to read this information, feeding it to a compact disc player's DAC (digital-to-analog converter) to produce sound waves.

The digital medium added a number of advantages, not least of which was the possibility to reproduce an infinite number of copies of a recording with no loss to the quality of the recording. With analog technology, a copy remained inferior to the original "master" recording, while the copying process also was likely to introduce additional noise and potential distortion to the sound quality. Although many audio purists would complain about a resulting lack of warmth offered by compact disc recording, the new digital recording technology represented a breakthrough in many areas and would ultimately lead the way to transforming music itself.

Developed primarily by Philips and Sony, compact disc technology was slow to be embraced by a consumer public that proved reluctant to convert their existing home stereo systems—and their library of recordings—to the new and more expensive compact disc. The success of the compact disc also depended on the willingness of other members of the recording industry to support the format. An early adopter of the technology was Toolex Alpha, based in Sweden.

Toolex Alpha already had accumulated more than 20 years of experience providing equipment for the recording industry. The company's specialty was the machines needed to produce the final recorded product. Under director of research and development, Curt Lindell, Toolex Alpha made an early mark on the recording industry when it developed an automatic press for manufacturing LPs (long-playing records) in the 1970s. In the early 1980s Lindell was instrumental in leading Toolex Alpha into the digital era. Among the first to adopt the optical disc format and to begin producing support equipment for the new technology, Toolex Alpha would provide an important industry breakthrough with the introduction of the first injection-molding machine adapted to the production of compact discs and later optical disc formats. Lindell and Toolex Alpha also were responsible for shifting the industry from primarily separate production systems to the smaller, inline production systems that would become an industry standard in the 1990s.

The rise of the compact disc recording format began in earnest in the late 1980s, spurred in part by the steady decreases in the prices of consumer CD players. Many new companies appeared during the 1980s to join the optical disc manufacturing industry. Among them was The Netherlands' OD&ME (for Optical Disc and Manufacturing Equipment; later ODME), established in Veldhoven in 1987. ODME started out as a single product company, manufacturing the monoliner, an integrated compact disc production system. The small private company would grow substantially in 1991, however, when ODME bought up ODM, the optical disc mastering equipment manufacturing subsidiary held by Philips and Du Pont. ODM's specialty had been in mastering, that is, in the preparing of the master recording—typically called a glass master—from which copies are produced. ODM added its master production equipment to ODME's product range. The addition also added more than twice the number of employees to ODME's payroll, a process that proved less than smooth, as the merging firms realized a clash of cultures.

Gaining the Lead in the 1990s

Nevertheless, the merger enabled ODME to continue to expand its range of products. In 1992 it introduced a new production system, the miniliner, that offered small capacity production runs, not only to smaller producers, but also to major manufacturers seeking to supplement production capacity during seasonal and other demand peaks. The addition of ODM was instrumental in ODME's growth: by the mid-1990s ODME had captured world leadership of the mastering equipment market, with 40 percent, and a strong position in the disc reproduction market, equaling Toolex Alpha's 25 percent. Toolex Alpha, meanwhile, had carved out a leadership position in optical disc fabrication, extending its injection molding system and introducing new replication systems.

Both ODME and Toolex Alpha would benefit from the introduction, in 1991, of a new optical disc-based product, the

CD-ROM (read-only memory). Capable of containing a variety of data, including audio, video, and other data formats, the CD-ROM was adapted perfectly to the growing computer industry. Indeed, by the mid-1990s, as prices of CD-ROM readers dropped rapidly, the CD-ROM would become an important driver for the entire computer industry, creating a new surge in demand among the consumer public eager to join the "multimedia" revolution.

Meanwhile, new optical disc formats were under development. Whereas the compact disc and the CD-ROM were both read-only, that is, they could not be used for consumer recording purposes, the optical disc industry was preparing three new recording optical disc formats. The first to arrive was the CD-R format, which permitted a disc to be recording a single time. The original CD recorders were priced in the thousands of dollars, but a subsequent plunge in prices would prove remarkable—less than three years after their introduction, the cost of a consumer CD-R system would drop below $200. By then, the CD-R was joined by the next optical disc revolution, the CD-RW, or rewritable compact disc. This new format permitted multiple recordings to a single disc—up to 1,000 times or more. Introduced in 1996, the price drop of the new CD-RW consumer systems would be still more dizzying: by 1998 entry-level CD-RW systems were priced at less than $300.

ODME continued to build its market leadership in private, enjoying not only the steady growth in compact disc demand, but also the rapid rise in CD-ROM, CD-R, and CD-RW formats, each of which could be produced with adaptations to existing optical disc manufacturing systems. The smaller Toolex Alpha, also performing strongly, chose to ride the growth of the optical disc industry into a different direction: a listing as a public company. In 1996 Toolex Alpha placed its stock on the United States' NASDAQ stock exchange and, at the same time, on the Amsterdam stock exchange. The company chose the Dutch exchange over the Swedish exchange for the former's greater exposure on the worldwide market.

Mid-Decade Woes

Toolex Alpha would quickly experience the downside of its public exposure. After a successful introduction and share prices at a respectable NLG 40 (approximately $20), Toolex Alpha's market fortunes would dwindle rapidly. Toolex Alpha had failed to meet a deadline for delivery to a number of customers in the Far East; these customers suspended their orders, forcing the company to take a loss of some SK 27.6 million (approximately US$3 million). At the same time, the company, faced by rising marketing and sales costs, was finding its profits further pressured. By October 1996 the company announced lower revenue and earnings projections. The company's stock tumbled, dropping by more than half its value. The company also came under suspicion for insider trading activities on the Dutch stock exchange, further hurting the reputation of the company and its stock.

The timing of Toolex Alpha's troubles was especially poor as the industry began gearing up for the introduction of what promised to be the next revolution in optical disc technology: the DVD, or digital versatile disc. A DVD was capable of storing from four gigabytes to as much as 11 gigabytes of data, compared with the roughly 600 megabytes of an ordinary compact disc. The increase in storage capacity opened a new realm of possibilities, not only in audio data—offering the potential of adding information such as Dolby surround sound coding—but also, and especially, in video. A single DVD was capable of storing an entire full-length feature film, providing far higher image and sound quality than a videocassette, while also presenting the possibility of including such data as multiple language soundtracks, multiple versions of a film, subtitling language choices, etc.

DVD presented other advantages: the discs themselves were the same size as compact discs, meaning that production systems could be adapted or extended to produce all of the various optical disc formats, without the need to replace an entire production line. For the consumer, DVD readers promised backwards compatibility with existing audio CDs and with CD-ROMs. Introduced in 1996, DVD would build momentum, as the industry worked out standards, and as consumers awaited the building of an extensive DVD-based film library and less expensive DVD readers.

For Toolex Alpha and ODME, as with the rest of the optical disc industry, the need to expand into the DVD arena—particularly with the arrival of recordable and rewritable DVDs expected for 1999—was clear. The cost of research and development of new systems designs, however, presented a possible stumbling block. At the same time, the economic crisis striking the Asian economies was slowing demand for existing systems, reducing revenue flow. Both Toolex Alpha and ODME sought a means for expanding their product lines toward a full service solution, without driving up the research and development costs to supplement their existing systems.

In July 1997 Toolex Alpha and ODME announced the takeover of the larger ODME by the smaller Toolex Alpha. The fact that ODME, at roughly $150 million in revenues, was twice as large as Toolex Alpha raised a few eyebrows. As the merger progressed, however, it became clear that the two companies had performed somewhat of a "reverse takeover." While the new company adopted the name of Toolex International, its headquarters were moved to the former ODME's Veldhoven offices. The former ODME president was named head of Toolex International—indeed, ODME executives would quickly fill the principal executive and director positions at Toolex International. Meanwhile, the newly merged company continued trading under the Toolex name.

As details of the merger became clear, the industry responded positively to the formation of what became the industry's largest independent supplier of optical disc production systems. The products of both companies were seen as strongly complementary, while the company's pooled research and development resources gave the company a strengthened position to meet the coming DVD revolution.

Following the merger, Toolex International's operations were organized into five production divisions: Mastering; Prerecorded Replication Systems; Recordable and Rewritable Replication Systems; and Peripherals, including pre-mastering, electroplating, physical testing, and injection molding systems, and both Toolex and third-party consumable products. A sixth business unit formed the company's Sales division, operating a network of sales and service offices in more than 15 countries.

By mid-1998 the merger appeared to be a success. Toolex International's revenues were running well ahead of the formerly separate companies' revenues, as 1997 sales for the merged operations reached NLG 401 million, some 14 percent more than the companies' separate 1996 sales. This growth came despite the collapse of many of the Asian economies in late 1997 and 1998.

Looking Forward

In February 1998 Toolex International moved to expand its product line still further, with the acquisition of the Laser Optics Division (LOD) of Del Mar Avionics, of Irvine, California. This acquisition brought LOD's patented, low-cost production systems into the Toolex International product family. A second acquisition made at the same time, of the company's former Hong Kong distributor, Special Zone Limited, represented the company's push to increase its Far East sales presence in the face of the economic crisis there. Toward the end of 1998 the company also was preparing to expand its direct sales presence in the Japanese and Chinese markets. In June 1998, in addition, the company's new TREX division, grouping the company's Recordable and Rewritable Replication Systems, introduced a next-generation CD-R design, dubbed SAN CD-R. This new production method was expected to provide significant cost reduction for recordable CD production—and was likely to be a new boost for this growing market.

Principal Subsidiaries

Toolex Alpha AB (Sweden); ODME International BV (Netherlands); Apex Systems Inc. (U.S.A.); Toolex, Inc. (U.S.A.); Media Morphics BV (Netherlands); ContTec GmbH (Germany); ODME Consumables (BV).

Further Reading

Frost, Tim, "Putting a New Spin on the Recordable Compact Disc," *One to One,* June 1998, p. 67.
"It Takes Two'lex," *One to One,* November 1997, p. 5.
Paulussen, Chris, "Toolex marktleider in CD-productiesystemen," *Eindhovens Dagblad,* February 11, 1998, p. 9.
Scholtes, Peter, "ODME grijpt bij Toolex de macht," *Eindhovens Dagblad,* September 30, 1997, p. 9.
"Toolex Alpha," *Tape-Disc Business,* September 1997, p. 150.

—M. L. Cohen

The Toro Company

8111 Lyndale Avenue South
Bloomington, Minnesota 55420-1196
U.S.A.
(612) 888-8801
Fax: (612) 887-8258
Web site: http://www.toro.com

Public Company
Incorporated: 1914 as the Toro Motor Company
Employees: 3,911
Sales: $1.05 billion (1997)
Stock Exchanges: New York
Ticker Symbol: TTC
SICs: 3524 Lawn & Garden Equipment; 3494 Valves &
    Pipe Fittings, Not Elsewhere Classified; 3052 Rubber
    & Plastic Hose & Belting; 3648 Lighting Equipment,
    Not Elsewhere Classified

Long respected as a manufacturer of premium-priced lawn-mowers, snowblowers, and irrigation systems, The Toro Company touts itself as "one of the world's leading producers of integrated solutions for outdoor landscapes." Toro is an industry leader in both turf maintenance and underground irrigation capacities for golf courses, sports fields, and other "professional" establishments and holds a strong position in the home-owner and consumer markets with such brand name lines as Toro, Lawn Boy, Toro Wheel Horse, and Lawn Genie. An increasingly diversified Toro now generates more than 55 percent of its revenue from professional turf maintenance products, with residential products accounting for the balance. The company also generates an increasing share of its total revenues outside the United States—about 22 percent in fiscal 1997.

Early History

Founded in Minneapolis in 1914, the Toro Motor Company was established by executives of the Bull Tractor Company—among them J.S. Clapper, Toro's first president—primarily to manufacture engines and other machined parts for use in the parent company's line of Bull tractors. When Bull Tractor folded in 1918—approximately the same time that Deere & Company and other competitors were fortifying their positions in the agricultural market—Toro was forced to fend for itself. The United States' entry into World War I in 1917, however, created a demand for steam engines for merchant supply ships, a need that Toro helped to fill through the conclusion of the war. In 1920 Toro Motor became Toro Manufacturing Company. The first product to carry the company's name was the Toro (two-row) cultivator that converted to a tractor. A widespread economic depression among American farmers during the early 1920s, however, left the company overstocked and in need of new products to sell. In 1921 the opportunity came for Toro to reinvent itself and become profitable for the long term. The greens committee chairman for an exclusive Minneapolis country club had approached the company with an unusual request: Could a specialized tractor replace the horse-powered system then used for cutting the greens and fairways? The solution was a tractor equipped with five 30-inch lawnmowers, which enabled the groundskeeper to cut a 12-foot wide swath in a third of the time required by the earlier method. This relatively simple invention led directly to the machine-driven, gang-reel mower, the forefather of the modern power mower industry.

By 1925 the Toro name had become synonymous with turf maintenance among nearly all of the major golf courses in the nation. Business was booming. The rapid growth of the company was due in large part to the establishment of a distributorship system in which regional business owners/sales representatives promoted quality Toro products while offering knowledgeable advice and service. In 1929, 13 distributorships were in place and Toro decided to go public, realizing that its research and development edge had to be maintained to thwart rising competition. The October 1929 stock market crash impeded the company's progress, but only temporarily.

In 1935 the company became Toro Manufacturing Corporation of Minnesota; two years later its engineers unveiled its most important product to date, the 76-inch Professional, an ingenious compromise between the maneuverability of walk-behind mowers and the speed and capacity of the large gang-reel units. The popular product was replaced ultimately by the Super-Pro and the 58-inch Pro.

In the years prior to World War II, the company succeeded in forming several overseas distributorships and in introducing its first power mower for the domestic consumer market. By 1942 sales had grown to $2 million and the company's commercial line—its mainstay—now served not only golf courses, but parks, schools, cemeteries, and estates. Like most American manufacturers during that period, Toro concentrated its resources on the war effort, contributing parts for tanks and other machinery. When 1945 came, Toro retooled under new owners.

Aggressively Targeted Consumer Market Following World War II

Robert Gibson, Whitney Miller, and David Lilly, all veterans and all friends since their days at Dartmouth College, purchased the company in 1945 and fueled it for the next several years with youthful ambition and systematic expansion. To maintain the loyalty of their workers, who then numbered around 50, they named longtime employee Kenneth Goit as president. Following much-needed plant reorganization and modernization, the three owners led the company aggressively into the homeowner mower business, which market studies had shown to be a particularly promising area. From 1946 to 1950 sales climbed from $1.4 million to $7 million. Several factors contributed to this remarkable increase. The solid expansion of Toro's distribution network, which had grown to 88 members, who in turn sold to approximately 7,000 retailers, made the company a large-scale presence. In addition, the company developed and marketed Sportlawn, a popular walk-power reel mower. Finally, and most importantly, Toro acquired Milwaukee-based Whirlwind, Inc. in 1948. Whirlwind was a prominent manufacturer of a consumer rotary mower, a new design that Toro proceeded to enhance with safety features.

In 1950 Lilly succeeded Goit as president. A number of firsts highlighted the decade, including Toro's pioneering lawn and garden television advertisements, the erection of a test facility in Bloomington, Minnesota, and the creation of the Wind Tunnel housing for its Whirlwind mower, which made rear-bagging feasible for the first time. Sales increases uniformly reached double-digit percentages, despite a lukewarm entry into snow-

removal equipment and a poor performance by the Tomlee Tool Company, acquired in 1954.

Toro indisputably came of age in the 1960s, aided by the power of its ad campaigns and the strength of its research and development department. Its power mower line was widely regarded by the public as the standard in engineering excellence. After achieving this goal, the half-century-old company was ready for a new dynamism. The retirement of "Mr. Toro," a charismatic salesman named "Scotty" McLaren, also augured a change in direction. The invention of the single-stage Snow Pup snow-thrower in 1962 signaled the company's recommitment to establishing a winter product line, but the results were less than satisfactory (Toro would succeed eventually, years later, with the Snow Master). Further diversification within the golf market was another possibility. One campaign centered on the production of a deluxe golf car, the Golfmaster, that would utilize all of the company's significant design expertise. As Trace James reported in *Toro: A Diamond History,* "Toro had purchased the materials and manufactured the parts to build 1,000 Golfmasters. However, by the time the first 250 of these beauties came off the assembly line, they were so loaded with features that golf courses could not afford to buy them. Toro was left with work in progress for 750 cars." Through persistent sales efforts, however, the company was able to rid itself of all but four cars and turn a profit.

Expanded into Irrigation Products in 1962

Finally, in 1962, Toro purchased a company that would virtually ensure Toro's lasting preeminence in the golf course industry. California-based Moist O'Matic, a manufacturer of irrigation products, brought sales above the $20 million mark that year and ultimately gave Toro the number one position in golf course irrigation equipment. This same year the company relocated to its present headquarters in Bloomington. By the end of the decade, with a greatly strengthened commercial division and the introduction of the electric start feature for its consumer mowers, Toro's sales surpassed $50 million.

The 1970s began with David McLaughlin assuming the presidency from Lilly. Growth during the decade for The Toro Company (so named in 1971) was phenomenal. The consumer snow removal business, after persistent re-engineering and re-marketing, began to thrive. Commercial turf maintenance, with the introduction of the all-hydraulic Greensmaster and Groundsmaster, experienced a renaissance. As a flurry of new products went on line, the Toro workforce swelled to substantially more than 1,000 employees. Net earnings from 1977 to 1979 almost tripled and sales reached an all-time high of $357.8 million. McLaughlin forged ahead with greatly expanded production of snowblowers. Suitable weather in which buyers could utilize the new product line proved elusive, however. Snow was a relative scarcity during the winters of 1980 and 1981 and, consequently, so were snowblower sales. Because Toro had positioned a full 40 percent of its business in this market, it suffered devastating losses, a total of $21.8 million between fiscal 1981 and fiscal 1982. To make matters worse, McLaughlin had moved Toro into the mass merchandising arena and away from its reliance on the dealer network—where lower sales but greater profits were the norm.

Further Diversified in the 1980s

Melrose replaced McLaughlin in 1981 and went to work quickly, cutting salaried staff by nearly half, closing plants, and instituting a ''just-in-time'' inventory system to prevent future overproduction. During the mid-1980s he systematically diversified, acquiring two lighting manufacturers and establishing an outdoor electrical appliance division. The 1986 purchase of Wheel Horse (a manufacturer of lawn tractors) and Toro's entry into the lawn aeration business helped push sales to more than $500 million the following year. Rounding out the decade was the company's 1989 purchase of one of its chief lawnmower competitors, Outboard Marine Corporation's Lawn Boy, for $98.5 million. Melrose, along with recently elected President Morris, had succeeded in reducing the company's dependency on snowthrower sales, which fell to just nine percent of revenues, while maintaining the Toro name as the industry market leader.

The investment community, however, remained oblivious, in large part, to the dramatic turnaround, and this was reflected in Toro's depressed stock price. Robert Magy, in his article ''Toro's Second Season,'' recounted Melrose's befuddlement at the sluggish reaction of the investment community to Toro's recovery. This puzzlement led to the hiring in 1989 of a Chicago-based investor relations firm. ''In October, the agency surveyed analysts and institutional investors in several major markets and discovered that few of them had any knowledge of Toro, and that among those who believed they did know something about the company, several thought it had collapsed early in the last decade.'' Thus work of a different sort, higher-profile public and investor relations, awaited Melrose. Although he quickly proved to be an effective and energetic company spokesperson, Melrose did err with overly optimistic earnings predictions.

Early 1990s Struggles

Toro's 1990 introduction of the Toro Recycler (a high-performance mulching mower) and its high expectations for Lawn Boy as a lower-priced complement to the existing product line were among the many reasons why Melrose anticipated the company would achieve billion-dollar status by 1992. Instead, the company saw sales drop from $750 million in 1990 to $711 million in 1991 to $635 million in 1992. A series of profit projections, all of which had to be revised downward, seriously dampened the company's credibility during the early part of this period. Particularly harsh criticism came from *Star Tribune* writer Tony Carideo. ''With each piece of negative news, Toro has trotted out explanations: A bad economy. Not enough rain. Too much rain. Not enough snow. A really bad economy. Well, maybe. But how about this? Toro makes a product that costs too much because there's a lot of R&D and advertising cost in it and because it's sold through an antiquated distributor-dealer network that raises the price even higher.'' Carideo's article appeared January 28, 1992, just after Toro had announced a major consolidation and restructuring of its Lawn Boy and Toro businesses, including a plant closing and some 450 layoffs.

Restructuring charges for fiscal 1992 led to a net loss of $21.7 million for the year. Recognizing that its current mix of products left it vulnerable to the cyclicality of the consumer market (not to mention the weather), Toro executives determined to place a greater emphasis on a wide range of professional turf-related product areas. Expanding upon its irrigation lines, Toro entered the fertilizer market in 1992 with the Toro BioPro brand environmentally friendly liquid fertilizer. A further step into this arena came in 1996 when the company acquired Liquid Ag Systems Inc., a pioneer in ''fertigation'' systems that simultaneously watered and fertilized tuft areas, including farmland. In 1994 Toro began manufacturing recycling equipment for landscape contractors and housing developers when it acquired Olathe Manufacturing and formed a new Recycling Equipment Division. Among the initial products offered by the division was a grinding machine that turned tree stumps into sawdust, which could simply be plowed right into the ground.

Toro significantly bolstered its irrigation lines during this period through acquisitions. In December 1996 the company acquired the James Hardie Irrigation Group from James Hardie Industries Limited of Australia for $118 million, one of Toro's largest acquisitions ever. Hardie's irrigation business was strongest in agricultural markets and commercial markets other than golf courses, which was Toro's major market. Hardie also made drip irrigation systems, a rapidly growing area and one that expanded upon Toro's irrigation lines. Another positive aspect of the acquisition was Hardie's strong international presence. The purchase made Toro the world's largest supplier of irrigation products and systems. The February 1998 acquisition of Drip In Irrigation further expanded Toro's drip irrigation lines.

Two additional 1997 acquisitions expanded Toro's professional product offerings still further. In September Toro bought the manufacturing, sales, and distribution rights to Dingo Digging Systems; the Dingo utility loader, designed for landscape contractors, was a versatile and compact product featuring more than 35 attachments. In November the company purchased Beatrice, Nebraska-based Exmark Manufacturing Company, Inc., a maker of mid-sized walk-behind power mowers and zero-turning-radius (ZTR) riding mowers for professional landscape contractors.

1998 ''Profit Improvement Plan''

Thanks to its increasing emphasis on professional products and a more aggressive pursuit of overseas markets, Toro had rebounded nicely from the dark days of the early 1990s. By fiscal 1997 net sales surpassed $1 billion for the first time and net earnings were a healthy $36.5 million. The 1998 fiscal year, however, did not start out so rosy, primarily because of its consumer product lines, the sales of which fell 8.5 percent in 1997. In May 1998 Toro initiated a ''profit improvement plan'' aimed mainly at overhauling its struggling consumer business. In addition to scaling back significantly on the number of models it offered in the areas of mowers, tractors, and other garden equipment, Toro closed a manufacturing plant in Sardis, Mississippi, and sold its recycling equipment business to Leeds, Alabama-based Precision Husky Corporation, having determined that this particular product line was incompatible with the company's core products. Perhaps the most dramatic change came in the form of the expansion of Toro's distribution network for Toro-branded lawnmowers to include selected home retail centers for the first time. This shift was likely long overdue given consumers' increasing preference for shopping at mass merchant outlets.

At the turn of the millennium, Toro was a company significantly different from that of just a decade earlier. The increasing emphasis on professional turf maintenance products provided the company with a steady income and profit generating force not nearly as susceptible to the vicissitudes of the consumer market—in particular, the consumer market for such seasonal items as lawnmowers and snowthrowers. A turnaround of its consumer business through the profit improvement plan should enable Toro to weather any early 21st-century storms.

Principal Subsidiaries

Toro Credit Company; Lawn-Boy Inc.; Toro Probiotic Products, Inc.; Toro Sales Company; Toro Southwest, Inc.; Toro International Company; Hahn Equipment Co.; Professional Turf Products of Texas, Inc.; Integration Control Systems & Services, Inc.; Turf Management Systems, Inc.; Exmark Manufacturing Company Incorporated; Toro Australia Pty. Limited; Toro Europe (Belgium); Toro Foreign Sales Corporation (Barbados); James Hardie Irrigation Pty. Limited (Australia); Irritrol Systems of Europe S.p.A. (Italy).

Further Reading

Carideo, Anthony, "It's Not All Sunshine for 3 Minnesota Firms," *Star Tribune,* May 6, 1991, p. 1D.
——, "Toro Tackles Question of Luring Buyers Seeking a Cheaper Lawn Mower," *Star Tribune,* January 28, 1992, p. 2D.
Gibson, Richard, "Toro Charges into Greener Fields with New Products," *Wall Street Journal,* July 22, 1997, p. B4.
Howatt, Glenn, "Toro Has First Quarterly Profit in Year; Retail Sales Still Weak," *Star Tribune,* May 22, 1992, p. 7D.
James, Trace, *Toro: A Diamond History,* Bloomington, Minn.: Toro, 1989.
Kirsch, Sandra L., "Toro Co.," *Fortune,* November 20, 1989, p. 106.
Kurschner, Dale, "Toro Battles Snapper for Similar Turf," *Minneapolis-St. Paul City Business,* September 9, 1991, pp. 1, 24.
Magy, Robert, "Toro's Second Season," *Corporate Report Minnesota,* May 1990, pp. 57–63.
Meeks, Fleming, "Throwing Away the Crystal Ball: Most Chief Executives Shy from Making Profit Projections. Toro Co.'s Ken Melrose Now Knows Why," *Forbes,* July 22, 1991, p. 60.
Melrose, Ken, *Making the Grass Greener on Your Side: A CEO's Journey to Leading by Serving,* San Francisco: Berrett-Koehler, 1995.
"Mulching Mowers Cutting an Ever-Widening Swath," *Star Tribune,* May 17, 1991, p. 1D.
Osborne, Richard, "Company with a Soul," *Industry Week,* May 1, 1995, pp. 20–22+.
Peterson, Susan E., "Toro Plans to Close Distribution Center and 2 Plants," *Star Tribune,* July 31, 1992, p. 1D.
——, "Toro Restructuring Will Shut Down Mississippi Plant, Cut 450 Workers," *Star Tribune,* January 22, 1992, p. 1D.

—Jay P. Pederson
—updated by David E. Salamie

Triple P N.V.

Ir. D.s. Tuynmanweg 10
4131 PN Vianen
The Netherlands
(31) (0) 347 353 353
Fax: (31) (0) 347 353 354
Web site: http://www.triple-p.com

Public Company
Incorporated: 1988
Employees: 886
Sales: NLG 292.9 million (US$150 million) (1997)
Stock Exchanges: NASDAQ
Ticker Symbol: TPPPF-BB
SICs: 7373 Computer Integrated Systems Design; 7372
    Prepackaged Software

Triple P N.V. supplies customized computing and networking products and services, primarily to the healthcare, print and publishing, and telecommunications industries. Triple P (the Ps stand for People, Performance, and Partnership) describes its business as operating in three principal areas: Systems, for the provision of networking and relating computing solutions; Services, including hardware and software systems management, maintenance, training, and consulting; and Software Solutions, including the adaptation of third-party software to meet customers' requirements. Systems accounts for some 51 percent of Triple P's revenues, while Services adds 40 percent; the company's Software Solutions division represents the remaining nine percent of sales. The company has targeted primarily small and medium-sized companies often overlooked by Triple P's rivals.

Triple P has experienced its share of growing pains in the late 1990s. After attempts at global growth in the 1990s, Triple P has seen its sphere of operations retract to focus especially on The Netherlands and Belgium. Successive moves to restructure the company, culminating in the divestiture of nearly all of the company's German operations, seem to have returned the company to a concentration on its core activities. Nonetheless, while other companies, including The Netherlands' Baan Co. and Germany's SAP, have undergone strong growth in the surging mid-1990s automation and networking markets, Triple P may have missed the boat. With the September 1997 replacement of company founder Fezi Kaleghi Yazdi with CEO Jan Willem Baud, however, Triple P appears to have turned the tide. In 1997 the company's listing was dropped from the NASDAQ national market; since August 1998, however, Triple P has been readmitted, now to a quotation on the NASDAQ small cap market.

Paper Beginnings in the 1980s

When 36-year-old Fezi Kaleghi Yazdi set his thoughts on paper for the formation of a new company in 1988, he was already well known in The Netherlands' business community. In 1974 Yazdi left his native Iran to supplement his business economics education with technical studies in the United States. En route, however, Yazdi stopped in Holland for a vacation; he never left. While there, he was offered a role acting as a mediator for Dutch business interests in Iran. Yazdi decided to complete his studies in Holland, attending the technical university in Rijswijk, where he studied mechanical engineering.

His studies completed, Yazdi worked a stint with Shell and then joined engineering firm Lummus Crest. In 1982 Yazdi changed hats, taking a position with RSV in that company's automation department. Yazdi's position was to make the department more commercial, but he never got the chance. Within days after starting work at RSV, the company declared bankruptcy. Yazdi, undeterred, saw possibilities for his department, which provided computer automation services to the relatively young business computing market. Seeking a means to buy up the department and recreate it as an independent business, Yazdi met Jan Kuijten, a well-known Dutch financier. Kuijten liked Yazdi's idea, so much so that the pair became partners. The assets of RSV's computer automation department were combined with those of another automation company, Holec Control Systems, and HCS Technology was born. Kuijten took charge of management, and Yazdi was in charge of technical development.

Yazdi and Kuijten went on the acquisition trail, buying up numerous small automation companies and grouping them under the HCS name. Although analysts would later criticize the company for failing to integrate its acquisitions into a more tightly operating whole, the company nevertheless showed impressive revenue growth. In 1987 Yazdi and Kuijten brought HCS to the Amsterdam stock exchange. With the public offering, Yazdi's personal fortune was made. Only a year later, however, the partners would split up. In 1988 Kuijten sought to add a new company—held by his personal holding company—to HCS. Yazdi judged the purchase price to be too high and attempted to block the sale. A power struggle ensued; Yazdi, the loser, left HCS that same year.

At the time, Yazdi and Kuijten were criticized by analysts, as reported in the *NRC Handelsblad,* as "having the goal of making as much money as possible in the short term. Nothing more profound, such as providing optimal service to the customer or continuity. Earning money fast, through acquisitions." Yazdi himself would admit to the same reporter: "Financial goals were the priority at HCS. . . . HCS gathered companies that hung together like loose sand."

Undeterred by his setback with HCS, Yazdi would use the financial lessons he had learned from Kuijten to his advantage in his next high technology venture. In 1988 Yazdi vowed to build a new company, setting his thoughts down on paper for that company's organization and goals. Yazdi would stick with computer automation, focusing on an area he saw as having strong growth potential in the years to come: the telecommunications industry, particularly its convergence with software systems. By the end of the year Yazdi had succeeded in raising investments for the new company, called Triple P, the Ps standing for People, Performance, and Partnership. Yazdi himself invested in the new company, taking on some NLG 6 million in personal debt and holding as much as 60 percent of Triple P.

Yazdi's plans called for a repeat of sorts of the ingredients that had built HCS. For the first two years Triple P would concentrate on acquiring the companies that would provide the "basic ingredients" for Triple P's products and services. The following two years would be spent concentrating the organization and grouping its strengths, while upgrading its product line. The next two years would then be spent taking Triple P on an international growth drive. From the start, Yazdi's goal was to build Triple P into one of the top five Dutch automation firms. Yazdi, however, claimed to have learned other lessons from his stint with HCS. For one, Yazdi (telling *NRC Handelsblad*) would avoid HCS's mistakes: "With us, forming a tight organization with a clear structure comes first. . . . A takeover in itself does not mean that you have the business under control, or that you are in position to keep up with developments in the mar-

ket." Yazdi also vowed to avoid the stock market and, thereby, stockholder pressures for short-term performance.

Yet Triple P would keep one essential ingredient of HCS's rapid growth: the acquisition of struggling or failing companies to build his own as rapidly as possibly. The late 1980s and early 1990s, in fact, provided no lack of struggling and failing companies, giving Yazdi a multitude of takeover possibilities. Indeed, the company showed strong progress in its early years. With its collection of companies, grouped in a decentralized organization, Triple P had grown from Yazdi's 1988 business plan (reportedly drawn up on two sheets of paper) to a company boasting revenues of NLG 125 million in 1991. The company also was showing strong profits—at least according to Dutch accounting requirements. After an NLG 2.9 million profit in 1991, the company's net profits would rise to NLG 4.2 million in 1992. Triple P's acquisitions had taken the company into three primary areas of business: data and telecommunications, computer maintenance, and computer networking services.

Meanwhile, HCS Technology was struggling. After the acquisition of a U.S. company, Savin, HCS was forced to declare bankruptcy. The resulting stockholders' scandal would hurt the reputation of Jan Kuijten and other financiers who had joined in HCS. Because he had left the company more than four years earlier, Yazdi's own reputation was spared.

Stumbling in the 1990s

Triple P's acquisition drive had cut deeply into the company's capital, which had sunk to as low as 14 percent of revenues. The company's projections for growth had proven optimistic: calls for the company to reach sales of NLG 180 million proved overreaching, given that it took into account the acquisition of a company that, Yazdi would explain, fell through at the last moment. Nonetheless, Yazdi's optimism continued, calling for profit growth in 1993 to as much as NLG 6 million—despite forecasting a lack of revenue growth. Indeed, Triple P would miss its target of NLG 160 million for 1993, reporting instead a turnover of NLG 142 million. Nevertheless, Triple P also was able to report a net profit of NLG 5.8 million.

At the beginning of 1994, Triple P moved to consolidate its holdings. Judging that its efforts to integrate its various acquisitions had fallen behind Yazdi's initial two-year plan because of the company's decentralization, Triple P moved its headquarters and the bulk of its operations to Vianen, where the company took over the office building formerly occupied by failing computer manufacturer Nixdorf. For Triple P, the move remained geographic more than organizational. While business units continued to function independently, the company hoped that the new proximity among business units would encourage greater cooperation.

By the end of 1994, Triple P's revenues had more than doubled, reaching NLG 300 million. The company's payroll also had grown dramatically, numbering some 1,400 employees. Chiefly responsible for this impressive growth was the company's acquisition of the struggling European division of American automation house MAI Systems. For a purchase price of NLG 10 million, Triple P added some NLG 150 million in revenues, as well as MAI's business units in Germany, Belgium, France, and The Netherlands, and a second headquarters in Germany. The MAI Europe acquisition was seen as a strategically sound move on Triple P's part, providing synergy with the company's existing developments and adding new strengths in healthcare and transportation automation systems to Triple P's telecommunications focus. At the time of the acquisition Yazdi continued to insist that his company had no plans to go public, preferring to finance its operations privately.

Yet, one year later, Triple P announced plans to pursue a listing on the NASDAQ stock exchange. The choice for the American exchange, rather than for the Amsterdam exchange, was explained by the stronger—some would claim less critical—U.S. interest in high technology stocks. In December 1995, Triple P went public, selling nearly seven million shares—including more than 700,000 of Yazdi's own shares, reducing his holding in the company to just 44.5 percent—for US$10 per share.

The approximately NLG 110 million netted from the initial public offering (IPO) was sorely needed. The acquisition and integration of MAI Europe had cost Triple P dearly, sending company-owned capital levels into the negative to the tune of more than NLG 64 million. The IPO, conducted according to U.S. accounting requirements, also revealed that Triple P had for years been unprofitable, due to its continued acquisition activity (U.S. accounting methods required the company to write down the cost of acquisitions against its income). In 1994, for example, the company's balance sheet showed a loss of some NLG 66 million with the U.S. method, compared with what still could be reported as a profit using the Dutch method. Only in the first nine months of 1995—leading up to the company's decision to go public—did Triple P post a profit according to U.S. standards. With his NLG 10 million share of the IPO, Yazdi was able to pay off his personal debt carried over from the founding of the company.

Triple P seemed to be in good health, finishing 1995 with revenues of more than NLG 347 million and a net profit of NLG 10.5 million. Indeed, as 1996 began, Yazdi was more optimistic than ever, forecasting that the company's revenues would reach NLG 1 billion within three years, with operational profits of some 13 percent. Fueling this expansion would be a combination of internal growth and acquisition. The company also was determined to shift its focus more and more away from hardware and toward software, a market offering higher profit margins. To fund the company's expansion, Yazdi proposed a second public offering, now on a European exchange, for later in the 1996 year.

Triple P appeared to have the wind in its sails. By April 1996 the company was able to announce an agreement with Daimler-Benz, in which Triple P would take over part of the activities, clients, and employees of the German automobile manufacturer's automation arm Debis, chiefly in the area of transportation. The company's stock price reflected its seemingly bright future, with shares of Triple P climbing to some $15.75 per share.

Four months later, Triple P began to take on water. While the automation market itself was booming and competitors such as The Netherlands' Baan Co. and Germany's SAP were booking record growth, Triple P's turnover had stagnated, and its first-half profits had fallen off sharply—by some 87 percent. One culprit behind the company's difficulties was a problem with Triple P's newly developed software package for the healthcare industry: reportedly, the package did not work. The efforts needed to correct the problems with the package would drain millions of guilders in extra costs and lost orders. By August 1996, Triple P was forced to reorganize its operations, jettisoning a number of subsidiary holdings that strayed too far from its core businesses, including a software package for the Belgian automobile sales market and another package for a German beverage distributor, while reducing staff by as much as ten percent. Meanwhile, Triple P's stock price plunged, dropping to just US$5 per share in August and finishing the year at US$3 per share.

Triple P's misfortunes had only just begun. In September 1996 a fire destroyed the company's distribution center. In October the company was forced to cut some 225 employees. The total cost of the reorganization reached some NLG 16.5 million. For the year-end, the company's revenues remained flat at NLG 347 million, and its net profits had slid to a loss of NLG 2.5 million. By mid-1997 the company's shares would drop to around $1.50 per share. According to a report by *Quote* magazine, however, a more critical reading of Triple P's IPO prospectus might have spared some of its shareholders—for the main part, institutional investors and company personnel—their losses. If only because Triple P had continued to invest heavily in so-called "vertical" software, that is, software designed for a specific enterprise, while the market clearly had shifted to the "horizontal" software favored by Baan Co. and SAP, which could be purchased by and adapted to any client, the company had entered the second half of the 1990s in a weakened competitive position. The *Quote* article, however, goes further, suggesting that Triple P misrepresented the scope of its activities in its prospectus.

With the release of the company's 1996 figures in March 1997—including the acknowledgement that the company's capital had fallen to a negative NLG 1.3 million—Yazdi accepted full responsibility for the company's failings, admitting that he "had never been a hero in operational management." Nonetheless, he remained optimistic for the company's future, claiming a return to profitability by the end of the year. At the same time, Yazdi moved to strengthen Triple P's management, bringing in Jan Willem Baud, who formerly had headed the Dutch firm Besi, making his own fortune when that company was brought to the stock market. By the end of June, with Triple P's revenues in free fall, its second quarter losses mounting to NLG 24.8 million, its capital deeply in the red, and the company's stock price bottoming out at US$1.50 per share, Triple P's stock was removed from its listing on the NASDAQ stock exchange. At this time, Yazdi announced that he would step down from the company's leadership in September 1997, after arranging for the company's refinancing.

Yazdi held true to his promise. In September 1997, Baud formally took over control of Triple P's operations. Baud's immediate concern was to steer Triple P through a second and more thorough reorganization, culminating with the sale of most of the company's German holdings, including all of its former MAI activities in that country. The total cost of this new reorganization would reach NLG 28 million.

Under Baud, Triple P appeared to refocus on its core activities. By the end of 1997 the company again was posting a slight quarterly profit, a trend that continued into the second half of 1998. In August 1998, Triple P was restored to a NASDAQ listing, now on the Small Cap market.

Principal Subsidiaries

Triple P Belgium NV/SA; Triple P Deutschland, Druck & Verlag; Triple P/MAI France NV/SA; Triple P USA, Inc.

Principal Operating Units

Telematics; Computer Industries; Mediasystemen; Services.

Further Reading

Den Tex, Niek, "Pech, Pech, Pech'en nog 'ns de vrije val van Triple P," *Quote,* August 31, 1997, p. 34.

Stijl, Herman, "Triple P overweegt nieuwe beursgang," *Het Parool,* February 17, 1996, p. 13.

"Triple P verkoopt Duitse verlieslaters," *Algemeen Dagblad,* December 30, 1997, p. 11.

Van Dinther, M., "Rentree Triple P op koersbord van NASDAQ," *Algemeen Nederlands Persbureau ANP,* August 10, 1998.

Verbraeken, "Triple P van Amerikaanse schermenbeurs verwijdered," *Algemeen Nederlands Persbureau,* June 24, 1997.

Wammes, Hans, "Fezi Khaleghi Yazdi terug in Nederlandse softwarezaken," *NRC Handelsblad,* October 28, 1994, p. 14.

—M. L. Cohen

UnitedAuto

United Auto Group, Inc.

<table>
<tr><td>

375 Park Avenue
New York, New York 10022
U.S.A.
(212) 223-3300
Fax: (212) 223-5148
Web site: http://www.unitedauto.com

Public Company
Incorporated: 1990
Employees: 4,000
Sales: $2.1 billion (1997)
Stock Exchanges: New York
Ticker Symbol: UAG
SICs: 5511 Motor Vehicle Dealers (New & Used)

</td></tr>
</table>

United Auto Group, Inc. is a leading acquirer, consolidator, and operator of franchised automobile and light-truck dealerships and related companies. In 1997 it was the second largest publicly traded retailer of new motor vehicles in the United States and the fourth largest overall. At the end of 1997 it was operating franchises in 12 states and Puerto Rico. All of United Auto Group's franchised dealerships included integrated service and parts operations. One subsidiary was engaged in the purchase, sale, and servicing of automobile loans, and another was marketing a complete line of aftermarket automotive products and services.

Selling the Concept: 1990–93

United Auto Group was founded in 1990 by Marshall S. Cogan, a New York City financier and investor who had amassed a fortune as a Wall Street dealmaker. Cogan, who owned the well-known midtown Manhattan restaurant "21" and controlled Foamex International Inc., a major automotive interiors supplier, traced his interest in consolidating the auto sales industry to a stint with his uncle's Chevrolet dealership in Cambridge, Massachusetts, when he was a teenager.

Cogan founded United Auto Group with two other investors: Apollo Advisors L.P. and Harvard Private Capital Group Inc.,

Harvard University's investment unit. Cogan invested $33 million and his partners, who came to include J.P. Morgan Capital Corp., invested about $70 million in the enterprise. For $5.2 million, they bought a 70 percent interest in New Jersey-based DiFeo Automotive Group, the second largest dealer network in the New York City metropolitan area, with 1991 sales of $375 million, and later added other dealerships, including ones in Nyack, New York, and Danbury, Connecticut. By the end of 1993—United Auto's first full year in business—it was the eighth largest retail automotive dealer in the United States, with total revenues that year of $606.1 million. The company was employing 1,200 people and operating 41 franchises at seven sites in late 1994.

The purpose of the investors was to capitalize on consolidation opportunities within the highly fragmented automotive retailing industry by purchasing and operating family-owned auto dealerships and managing them professionally, controlling costs, and improving customer service. Other companies had begun doing the same in the 1980s, buying up smaller dealers, offering a wide variety of makes and models, and merging service and parts operations, but these efforts capsized in the junk-bond fiasco at the end of the decade. "This was an industry not well-regarded by Wall Street," Cogan recalled. "People avoid auto dealers like they avoid the dentist."

In spite of Wall Street's reluctance, Cogan felt that consolidation made sense, arguing that a big dealership franchiser could make money even during an economic downturn because most of the revenue would come from fixing and financing new cars, not selling them. He also argued that economy of scale would allow such a company to save money on advertising, credit lines, and computer processing. Carl Spielvogel, formerly head of the Bates Worldwide advertising agency, was brought in as United Auto Group's first chairman and chief executive. He said his mission was to turn the company's dealerships into supermarkets where customers could buy any car make, new or used, and get any kind of part or service. His strategy was to acquire dealerships in geographic clusters. "We try to surround a market," he told a reporter, "because it gives you the ability, in particular, to move used cars from one dealership to another."

United Auto Group's courtship of the nation's 23,400 auto dealers, many of them approaching or already at retirement age, was being matched by other ventures, such as Asbury Group, Cross-Continent Auto Retailers, and AutoNation USA, a subsidiary of H. Wayne Huizenga's Republic Industries Inc. United Auto Group paid cash for acquired dealerships: an average of $12 million for each of the three suburban Atlanta dealerships it acquired in 1996. In return, the company wanted the dealer to stay on (at least until professional management was installed) and for the business to keep its prior name.

Automakers traditionally had eschewed dealing with groups of dozens or hundreds of dealerships, opting instead to do business with small, often family-owned corporations tightly monitored under the franchise system. They were not sure they wanted to negotiate with megadealers who ordered cars by the tens of thousands, and they were especially resistant to the idea of selling to retailers who also offered rival car makes. This unwillingness began to change in the mid-1990s, when automakers such as Ford and Chrysler began to feel that large companies could help them cut the cost of delivering cars to dealerships from the factory, which some experts estimated was accounting for up to 30 percent of the retail price of a new car. In 1997 Ford and Chrysler were creating or proposing their own auto superstores, grouping their brands under one roof.

United Auto Group made it clear that selling used cars, which yielded profit margins of up to 15 percent—far more than the five percent profit on a new car—was an essential part of its strategy. One of its innovations was the Security Blanket, a 15-day money-back guarantee—unique for the industry—on all of its used cars, which were being sold on a few of the company's lots. United Auto's used car lots also offered a 132-point car inspection and, unlike their main competitors, made prices negotiable. The vehicles were mostly two- or three-year-old off-lease vehicles, purchased at auction. The company's wholly owned subsidiary, Atlantic Auto Finance Corp., made car loans at attractive interest rates. United Auto opened its first strictly used car outlets in 1996 and, as of early March 1997, had eight freestanding used car superstores in four states as well as 51 new car dealerships, with used car areas, in 11 states.

Broadening Its Base: 1994–98

After earning net income of $1.2 million in 1993, United Auto Group lost $245,000 in 1994 on revenues of $731.6 million and $3.7 million in 1995 on revenues of $805.6 million. The company's fortunes began to turn around in that year, when

DiFeo Group eliminated 17 unprofitable franchises—almost half the total—and about 250 jobs and tied pay plans to net profits and customer satisfaction. In 1996 United Auto had net income of $3 million on revenues of $1.3 billion, with Cogan attributing the turnaround to used cars. The company went public in October 1996, raising $180 million in a sale of common stock at $30 a share.

In March 1997 United Auto Group bought nine auto dealerships with 1996 sales of $430 million from John Stalupp and John Stalupp, Jr. Five of them were in West Palm Beach, Florida, and the other four were located on Long Island, New York. The acquisition price was $53 million in a combination of cash, stock, and promissory notes. By the end of 1997 United Auto had acquired a number of other dealerships, all of them in the South or Puerto Rico, and was the nation's second largest publicly traded auto dealership. It was first in the New York metropolitan area, with 23 dealerships.

Despite the rapid growth of the company, all was not well with United Auto Group. The common stock, which peaked at $35.25 a share in November 1996, plunged to $16 in April 1997, soon after company executives told financial analysts that overhead costs would keep first-quarter earnings from reaching previous projections. Spielvogel resigned his post and was replaced by Cogan, who adopted a strategy of concentrating on the "aftercare" market of parts and services, where profit margins could run much higher than on sales of automobiles. AutoCare was the company's subsidiary for aftermarket products and services.

Typically, fewer than one-third of new car customers were going to their original dealership for service, but Cogan was trying to change that with sales training and a database sending customers reminders about tune-ups and oil changes. At some United Auto Group dealerships, the rate of customers coming back for service rose as high as 60 percent. Another goal that Cogan announced for 1998 was to have 90 percent of United Auto's finance originations, including the loans bought by other lenders, pass through Atlantic Auto Finance's hands and generate fees. In nearly every case customers would make their checks out to the subsidiary, even if another lender actually held the paper.

United Auto Group continued to broaden its base in 1998. In January of that year, for about $28 million, it acquired five franchises with estimated 1997 revenues of $320 million. The company also purchased, for $14.5 million, The Triangle Group, Puerto Rico's second largest auto retailer with estimated 1997 revenues of $160 million. In July United Auto announced it had purchased two San Diego dealerships and had agreed to buy two more. The four franchises had estimated annual revenues of $160 million. Their acquisition brought United Auto's total to 98 franchises nationwide.

Expansion was not coming cheaper, however, and United Auto Group's long-term debt rose from $11.1 million at the end of 1996 to $238.6 million at the end of 1997. Interest expenses of $14.1 million were one reason the company lost $10.1 million on $2.09 billion of revenues in 1997. The firm also suffered when the big U.S. automakers cut prices of new cars, which depressed used car sales and pushed used car prices lower. United Auto Group took a pretax charge of $31.7 million in late 1997, related to the realignment of operations, including the divestiture of nine unprofitable franchises. Its stock fell as low as $9.50 a share in January 1998.

United Auto Group in 1998

As of April 1998, United Auto Group was operating franchised dealerships in Arizona, Arkansas, Connecticut, Florida, Georgia, Illinois, Indiana, Louisiana, Nevada, New Jersey, New York, North Carolina, Puerto Rico, South Carolina, Tennessee, and Texas. The company was selling U.S., European, and Asian brands, ranging from economy cars to luxury automobiles and sports utility vehicles. Eight of its outlets were stand-alone used car retail centers. Vehicle sales accounted for 88 percent of total revenues in 1997. The company sold 50,985 new and 31,253 used vehicles.

United Auto Group had ready access to used vehicles through trade-ins for new cars, vehicles originally leased through its new vehicle dealerships, and used vehicle auctions only open to new vehicle dealers. In addition, only new vehicle franchises were able to sell used vehicles certified by manufacturers under a recently introduced program by which manufacturers supported specific high-quality used cars with extended warranties and attractive financing options.

Aftermarket products and service and parts operations accounted for nine percent of total revenues. Aftermarket products included accessories such as radios, cellular phones, and alarms, as well as extended service contracts and credit insurance policies. Each of United Auto Group's new vehicle dealerships was offering a fully integrated service and parts department. Unlike independent service shops or used car dealerships with service operations, United Auto was qualified to perform work covered by manufacturer warranties. The company believed that its market share would grow at the expense of independent mechanics' shops, which might be unable to address the increased sophistication of motor vehicles and the increased expense of compliance with more stringent environmental regulations. It was actively marketing warranty-covered services to potential customers such as municipalities and corporations with large fleets of automobiles.

Atlantic Auto Finance was renamed UnitedAuto Finance in 1997. Based in Rochester, New York, UnitedAuto Finance accounted for three percent of the parent company's total revenues

that year. It was the subsidiary for purchasing, selling, and servicing primarily prime-credit-quality automobile loans originated by both the parent company and third-party dealerships. UnitedAuto Finance also was receiving fees from financial institutions that purchased installment contracts from customers referred to them by UnitedAuto Finance. At the end of 1997 this subsidiary was serving about 250 dealerships in eight states.

In April 1998 Cogan was United Auto Group's largest stockholder, holding 20.5 percent of the common stock through Trace International Holdings, Inc. Aeneas Venture Corp., an affiliate of Harvard Private Capital Group, held 14.5 percent, and a unit of Apollo Advisers L.P. held 9.4 percent.

Principal Subsidiaries

Atlantic Auto Funding Corp.; UAG Capital Management, Inc.; UAG Finance Company, Inc.; United Auto Enterprises, Inc.; United AutoCare, Inc.; United AutoCare Products, Inc.; United-Auto Finance Inc.; United Lenders, Inc.

Further Reading

Brown, Peter, "Dealer Groups Enter on Exit Strategy," *Automotive News,* February 27, 1995, p. 14.

Halliday, Jean, "For United Auto, Expansion Not As Important As Profits," *Advertising Age,* April 7, 1997, p. S10.

Henry, Jim, "UAG's Cogan Leads Profit-Center Push," *Automotive News,* August 25, 1997, pp. 3, 9.

Incantalupo, Tom, "Major Car Chain Buys 5 LI Dealers," *Newsday,* February 26, 1997, pp. A43–A44.

Messina, Judith, "Spielvogel to Speed Auto Dealers' Growth," *Crain's New York Business,* November 28, 1994, pp. 3, 51.

Naughton, Keith, "Demolition Derby on Wall Street?," *Business Week,* September 9, 1996, p. 48.

Temes, Judy, "Dealer's Auto Motive," *Crain's New York Business,* March 31, 1997, pp. 1, 52.

"United Auto Expanding into California Market," *New York Times,* July 14, 1998, p. D3.

Wernle, Bradford, "United Buys 9 More Stores; Stock Falls," *Automotive News,* March 3, 1997, pp. 1, 47.

"Who Will Deal in Dealerships?" *Economist,* February 14, 1998, pp. 61–63.

Yung, Katherine, "Public Dealerships Shake Up Old-Line Auto Sales Industry," *Detroit News,* February 2, 1997, p. 1C+.

—Robert Halasz

U.S. Foodservice

9755 Patuxent Woods Drive
Columbia, Maryland 21046
U.S.A.
(410) 312-7110
Fax: (410) 312-7591
Web site: http://www.usfoodservice.com

Public Company
Incorporated: 1989 as JPF Holdings, Inc.
Employees: 12,500
Sales: $5.5 billion (fiscal year ended June 28, 1998)
Stock Exchanges: New York
Ticker Symbol: UFS
SICs: 5140 Groceries & Related Products

U.S. Foodservice is the second largest distributor of food and related products in the United States, serving an area containing 85 percent of the nation's population. The company markets more than 40,000 items to over 130,000 restaurants, hotels, hospitals, school cafeterias, and other facilities, including Fenway Park and the U.S. Senate. Formerly JP Foodservice, Inc., the company changed its name in 1998 following its acquisition of Rykoff-Sexton, Inc.

Early History

The history of U.S. Foodservice encompasses the story of how (and where) Americans purchase the food they eat. It reflects the development of an entire industry, shifting from small entrepreneurial wholesalers supplying retail grocery stores to large regional and national distributors offering a broad line of products to institutional clients.

Several of the entities that comprised what is now U.S. Foodservice started in the 19th century. Monarch Foods, for example, traced its roots to Reid-Murdock Co., a Dubuque, Iowa, company founded in 1853 to provision wagon trains heading west. John Sexton & Co. began as a tea and coffee merchant in Chicago in 1883. Sexton soon discovered hotels

and restaurants were his biggest customers and he dropped his retail business altogether. Before the turn of the century, Sexton began manufacturing pickles, salad dressings, preserves, and jellies to guarantee a uniform high level of quality for his institutional customers.

Los Angeles-based S.E. Rykoff & Co. was established in 1911, and the Mazo and Lerch families started their business in northern Virginia in 1927. Most of these wholesalers tended to specialize, selling items to local grocery stores. In the early 1930s, distributors, including Mazo-Lerch Company, began offering frozen foods, primarily frozen French fries and orange juice.

Sowing the Seeds of an Industry: 1940–70

Foodservice distributors served institutional clients that provided food away from home, unlike retail distributors, who sold to grocery stores. The first distinction between the two groups came about in 1951, with the formation of the Association of Institutional Distributors. With fighting going on in Korea, the federal government reinstituted price controls, including a 16 percent ceiling on food distributors' gross profits. About a dozen companies met in Chicago to respond to that action. Because it cost more to distribute to their institutional customers than to grocery stores, the distributors wanted to be considered separately from grocery wholesalers and to have their ceiling raised to at least 21 percent. They were successful in their lobbying efforts.

The federal government also helped open up foodservice markets. Five years earlier, in 1946, the U.S. Congress passed the National School Lunch Act. Suddenly, large numbers of schoolchildren were eating cooked meals away from home, and school cafeterias became the first institutional mass market. One of the few distributors to focus on schools was the Pearce-Young-Angel Company (PYA) in the Carolinas. That same year, Consolidated Foods Corp., the precursor of Sara Lee Corporation, acquired Monarch Foods.

By the late 1950s, most distributors had added frozen foods to their product lines. In 1958, Mazo-Lerch held the first food show, and was one of the first distributors to offer both custom-

Company Perspectives:

The key to our continuing success in the future, as in the past, is our people. It's their skills, dedication and professionalism on behalf of our customers and shareholders that have enabled us to accomplish so much as a company up until now and that will allow us to accomplish even more in the years ahead.

cut meats and beverage dispenser programs. The diversification trend continued over the years, as foodservice distributors provided disposable items such as napkins and tablecloths, followed by china and glassware, then light and heavy equipment.

In 1965, Americans spent just 20 cents of every food dollar for food away from home. Total distributor sales that year were an estimated $9 billion, and the average institutional distributor had an annual volume of $1.5–$2 billion. *Institutional Distributor*, in its first survey of the foodservice distribution industry, found that the average order size of respondents was $80.40, and the average number of customers was 572. The survey also found that nearly half of the respondents sold to both grocery and institutional customers.

National Distributors: 1971–89

The decade of the 1970s saw the move to broadline, multi-branch organizations. Consolidated Foods bought the old Pearce-Young-Angel distribution network in 1971 and merged it with its Monarch Foods subsidiary to form PYA/Monarch, which would eventually become the foundation of US Foodservice. Within a few years, PYA/Monarch had linked data processing operations in its branches with the computer in its headquarters. S.E. Rykoff went public in 1972, one of the few foodservice distributors to do so.

The distribution industry went through a difficult period during the early 1980s, with companies under pressure as a result of inflation and economic slowdown. However, people still needed to eat, and much of the pressure was from competition. Speakers at national conferences focused on customer service, productivity, and professional development. Computers were playing a greater role in the business, enabling a distributor to provide customers with information to help control inventory, determine menu costs, and analyze profitability. As distributors became more professional, restaurant chains such as Marriott and Howard Johnson folded or reduced their self-distribution activities and focused on their restaurant operations.

By 1982, the foodservice distribution was a $69 billion industry. Five companies were considered "national distributors," with a total of 168 distribution centers covering major portions of the country. PYA/Monarch and John Sexton & Co. were two of the five, joined by SYSCO Corporation of Houston, CFS Continental, Inc., and Kraft Foodservice. Despite their dominance geographically, these multi-branch distributors reported combined sales in 1982 of $4.8 billion—seven percent of the industry.

Over the next several years, the big distributors made major acquisitions. S.E. Rykoff bought Sexton & Co. in 1983, in what was then the largest acquisition in the industry. The renamed Rykoff-Sexton took fourth place among foodservice distributors with $800 million in sales. CFS Continental's purchase of Publix Fruit and Produce moved it into third place, with sales in the $1.1 billion range. Number one SYSCO acquired B.A. Railton along with Pegler, increasing its volume to over $2 billion. Meanwhile, in Greenville, South Carolina, number two PYA/Monarch bought Fleming Foodservice of Austin, Texas, raising its 1984 sales volume to an estimated $1.3 billion. By the end of its fiscal year in June 1984, PYA/Monarch was serving some 70,000 foodservice operators, and its 22 distribution centers blanketed 60 percent of the United States.

PYA/Monarch was one of the first distributors to compete as a provider of services as well as products. "The day of the distributor who merely warehouses, delivers, and takes orders for products a customer wants is over," company management told *Institutional Distribution* in a 1984 article. PYA/Monarch's mission statement revealed its goal: "... to be a premier company in every area of operations, providing products and services that can enable a customer to run a more efficient and profitable business."

Using the largest computer in the industry, PYA/Monarch phased in a new state-of-the-art data processing system. Totally centralized, the system made it possible for headquarters to carry out data processing for each of the 22 branches, whose computers now gathered data.

The 1980s saw a tremendous change in the eating habits in the United States. By 1986, Americans were spending one-third of every food dollar outside the supermarket, and the foodservice distribution had grown to a $78 billion industry.

Creation of JP Foodservice, 1989

By April 1989, Sara Lee Corporation had decided to sell off the northern division of PYA/Monarch, citing dissatisfaction with its performance. Although the southeast division was the top food distributor in its region, overall PYA/Monarch ranked third behind SYSCO and Kraft, and Sara Lee was committed to being first or second in each of its businesses.

In June 1989, members of PYA/Monarch management incorporated a new entity, JPF Holdings, Inc. Two weeks later, on July 3, JPF Holdings acquired all the capital stock of the Sara Lee subsidiary, JP Foodservice Distributors, Inc., including the mid-Atlantic and northeastern operations of PYA/Monarch Inc. Under the terms of the leveraged buyout, Sara Lee retained ownership of PYA/Monarch, now operating in the southeast, as well as 47 percent of the shares in JP Foodservice.

Headed by James L. Miller, who had been executive vice-president of PYA/Monarch's northern division, the new company immediately sold three of its branches—Los Angeles, Little Rock, and Paducah—to Kraft Foodservice. The result was a major regional operation with nine distribution centers serving a territory from Virginia north to Maine and west to Nebraska.

Growing a New Company: 1990–96

JP Foodservice Distributors passed the $1 billion mark in its first year, with sales for fiscal 1990 of $1.02 billion. That was a jump of more than 12 percent from the division's sales in fiscal 1989, and made the new company number five among the top 50 distributors selected by *Institutional Distributor*. But Miller and the other managers had borrowed over 95 percent of the $317 million they paid for the company. With that amount of debt, and with a soft economy, JP concentrated on building the lowest cost structure in the industry. The company invested primarily in improving facilities, adding a new $15 million replacement center between Washington, D.C., and Baltimore and building an addition at its Allentown, Pennsylvania warehouse that doubled freezer and cooler capacity. It also used technology to cut costs and provide greater service to its customers. For example, a hand-held electronic device allowed JP customers to monitor their inventory and send information to the company.

In November 1994, five years after it was created, the company adopted the name JP Foodservice, Inc. and went public in November, listed on the NASDAQ under the symbol JPFS. Sara Lee Corporation now held 37 percent of JP common stock. The public offering raised $86 million, and JP restructured and paid off much of its debt.

JP Foodservice had more than 21,000 customers in 25 states in the Mid-Atlantic, Midwest, and Northeast regions of the country and was the sixth largest food distributor. It provided customers with a broad line of products, including canned, dry, frozen, and fresh foods, paper products, detergents, and light restaurant equipment. With its debt problems resolved, the company set a new growth strategy which, in addition to increasing internal growth, included acquiring smaller distributors. Its first purchases were Tri River Foods, Inc. and Rotelle Inc., two Pennsylvania distributors. JP's strategy also called for increasing its line of private label products, which included Hilltop Hearth breads, Cattlemen's Choice meats, and Roseli Italian foods.

Mergers and acquisitions were also continuing in the industry as a whole: early in 1995, Rykoff-Sexton merged with US Foodservice and acquired Continental Foods of Baltimore. Foodservice distribution had grown to become a $124 billion industry, and the ten largest distributors accounted for 18 percent of the business. JP's business, which for fiscal 1995 reached $1.12 billion, was about 55 percent independent (hospital cafeterias, family-owned restaurants) and 45 percent chains. The increasing product demands and bigger menus of the chains and large restaurants were important factors fueling consolidation among distributors.

Toward the end of 1995, the company and its former parent, Sara Lee Corporation, began talks about exchanging PYA/Monarch, Sara Lee's southeastern foodservice subsidiary, for JP stock worth about $946 million. Yet the two companies failed to reach agreement on several factors, including valuation (JP's stock price had gone up in expectation of the merger), structure, and dilution of earnings to existing shareholders, and the deal fell through in February 1996. The experience left both sides bitter, and JP was expected to find a way to reduce Sara Lee's presence or end its investment in the company all together.

That separation occurred before the end of 1996, when JP held a public offering involving the sale of all the common stock held by Sara Lee. On December 31, 1996, JP Foodservice moved to the New York Stock Exchange, trading under the symbol JPF.

1997 On

JP continued buying smaller companies, paying for them with $66 million raised by another stock offering. Acquisitions included Valley Industries of Las Vegas, Arrow Paper and Supply Company, based in Connecticut, Squeri Food Service of Cincinnati, and Mazo-Lerch Company, Inc., the 70-year-old food distributor based in northern Virginia that had held the first food fair in 1953. By the end of the fiscal year in June, net sales were up 17 percent to $1.7 billion, with acquisitions accounting for about six percent of the increase and the remaining 11 percent from internal growth. JP's growth was significantly higher than the three percent for the foodservice distribution industry.

The company credited its internal growth to sales training and promotions and to the expansion of its private and signature brands. During 1997, JP introduced Harbor Banks, a seafood line.

Then, in December 1997, the company jumped into second place among foodservice distributors with the purchase of rival Rykoff-Sexton Inc. for $1.4 billion. Unlike its previous acquisitions, Rykoff-Sexton was much bigger than JP. Sales were expected to triple, to $5.2 billion, and the number of JP customers ballooned from 35,000 to 130,000. As a result, Standard & Poor's added JP to the S&P MidCap 400 Index. The merger also changed JP from a major distributor in the East and Midwest to one operating coast to coast. New territories included the Southeast, the Sun Belt, and the West Coast.

Acquisitions continued even as JP worked to assimilate the Rykoff-Sexton operations, adding Sorrento Food Service, Inc., of Buffalo, and Westlund, a Minnesota custom cut meat specialist. In February, the company changed its corporate name to U.S. Foodservice and its trading symbol to UFS, having already introduced a new logo.

Sales for the 1998 fiscal year that ended in June, were better than expected, totalling $5.5 billion, an increase of seven percent from 1997. Chairman and CEO Jim Miller was justifiably proud of the accomplishments, telling the *Baltimore Sun*, "We not only successfully completed the largest merger ever in our industry, tripling the size of our company, we did so achieving record earnings and meeting or exceeding virtually every goal set out in our merger plan." A few days later, the company announced it was selling the assets of its Rykoff-Sexton manufacturing division as part of its plan to shed its non-core operations.

The making of U.S. Foodservice reflects the trends of its industry: from retail to institutional customers; from specific products to a broadline of offerings; from single distribution centers to multi-unit branches; increased professionalism and customer service; and, most pronounced, the continuing and aggressive expansion through acquisition. In the $141 billion industry, according to a July 1998 article in *Baltimore Business Journal*, the top 50 companies accounted for only 28 percent of sales, and most of those sales, 23.7 percent, were by the ten biggest companies. The successful integration of the larger Rykoff-Sexton company made U.S. Foodservice a favorite among analysts, and the company itself indicated it was still on the lookout for purchases in the highly fragmented foodservice industry.

Principal Subsidiaries

U.S. Foodservice, Inc.; JP Foodservice Distributors, Inc.; RS Funding, Inc.; Targeted Specialty Services, Inc.; BRB Holdings, Inc.; John Sexton & Co.

Further Reading

Bernstein, Charles, "Big 4 Distributors Capture Increasing Share of Market," *Nation's Restaurant News*, November 21, 1983, p. 1.

Civin, Robert, "Foodservice Distribution: The Evolution of an Industry," *Institutional Distribution*, October 1985, p. 67.

Civin, Robert, and Stephanie Weisman Salkin, " 'National' Foodservice Distributors; Do They Really Have an Edge?" *Institutional Distributor*, September 1, 1983, p. 63.

Davis, Jo Ellen, "Food Distribution: The Leaders Are Getting Hungry for More," *Newsweek*, March 24, 1986, p. 106.

DeMarco, Donna, "Price Nabs Foodservice Stock," *Baltimore Business Journal*, July 24, 1998, p. 1.

Faiola, Anthony, "JP Foodservice Has an Appetite for Growth," *Washington Post*, April 3, 1995, Washington Business p. 5.

Gondo, Nancy, "Food Fight," *Investor's Business Daily*, March 23, 1995, p. A5.

Grugal, Robin M., "Tasty Deal: JP Foodservice Goes National After Snapping Up Key Rival," *Investor's Business Daily*, January 23, 1998.

Hyman, Julie, "Big Merger Goes Well for U.S. Foodservice," *Washington Times*, September 14, 1998, p. D28.

"JP Foodservice, Inc.," *Investor's Business Daily*, August 15, 1994, p. A6.

"JP Foodservice, Inc., The Top 50," *Institutional Distribution*, December 1989, p. 102.

"JP/PYA Deal Called Off," *Foodservice Distributor*, March 1996, p. 15.

Martin, Ellen James, "JP Buys Sizable Part of Rotelle," *Baltimore Sun*, November 28, 1995, p. 1C.

McConnell, Bill, "It's a Food Fight! Gourmet Tastes, Booming Restaurant Growth Feed Takeover in Food Service Industry," *Warfield's Business Record*, September 4, 1995, p. 1.

——, "JP Foodservice Unshackled," *Daily Record* (Baltimore), August 17, 1995, p. 1.

Mirabella, Lorraine, "Restaurant Supplier's Profit Soars," *Baltimore Sun*, August 14, 1998, p. 3C.

Mullaney, Timothy J., "JP Foodservice Has Appetite for Rivals," *Baltimore Sun*, January 30, 1995, p. 13C.

"A New Concept for Leadership in Distribution: PYA/Monarch, Inc.," *Institutional Distributor*, July 1984, p. 67.

"No Sara Lee Merger," *Eurofood*, February 28, 1996, p. 20.

"Sara Lee in Talks to Merge Its PYA/Monarch Unit with JP Foodservice," *Associated Press*, November 30, 1995.

"Sara Lee to Spin Off PYA-Monarch Northern Division in Executive Buyout," *Institutional Distribution*, May 1, 1989, p. 40.

Segal, David, "JP Foodservice Buys Pittsburgh Distributor," *Washington Post*, May 31, 1995, p. F3.

Speeks, Mark, "Nuptials Are Off . . . Or Are They? Mergers in Foodservice," *Voice of Foodservice Distribution*, April 1996, p. 29.

Tanyeri, Dana, "The Lerch Tradition: Mazo-Lerch Is Independent, Family-Run, Built to Stay That Way," *Institutional Distribution*, July 1989, p. 8.

"The Top 50," *Institutional Distribution*, December 1990, p. 86.

"U.S. Foodservice Closes on Transfer," *Reuters Limited*, August 31, 1998.

"U.S. Foodservice Company Overview," http://www.usfoodservice.com/overview/index.html.

"What the Analysts Say," *Washington Post*, September 25, 1995, p. F33.

—Ellen D. Wernick

USG Corporation

125 South Franklin Street
Chicago, Illinois 60606-4678
U.S.A.
(312) 606-4000
Fax: (312) 606-4093
Web site: http://www.usg.com

Public Company
Incorporated: 1901 as U.S.G. Company
Employees: 13,000
Sales: $2.87 billion (1997)
Stock Exchanges: New York Midwest
Ticker Symbol: USG
SICs: 3275 Gypsum Products; 3296 Mineral Wool; 3299 Nonmetallic Mineral Products, Not Elsewhere Classified; 6719 Offices of Holding Companies, Not Elsewhere Classified

Gypsum products are the principal goods manufactured by USG Corporation, the largest maker of such products in the world. The manufacture of gypsum is a highly competitive and price-sensitive undertaking, with easy entry and exit from the field. As a result of these conditions USG Corporation—or the U.S.G. Company, as it was originally incorporated—has exerted substantial influence in the building-supplies field because of its market size. Among USG's operating companies are the world's largest maker of gypsum wallboard, the leading distributor of gypsum wallboard in the United States, the world's largest manufacturer of ceiling suspension grid, and the second largest producer of ceiling tile in the world (trailing only Armstrong World Industries, Inc.).

Gypsum Production in the United States

Understanding gypsum production methods is essential to an understanding of USG's corporate character. Gypsum, or hydrous calcium sulphate, is, in pure form, a white mineral commonly called alabaster. Large quantities of gypsum exist throughout North America. One of the first uses for gypsum was as a fertilizer. Gypsum is made suitable for commercial use by a process called calcination, which involves heating the mineral to remove approximately three-quarters of its water. Calcined gypsum, or plaster of Paris, can recrystallize into any shape with the simple addition of water. In the 1890s gypsum manufacturers perfected a method of strengthening plaster by adding a retarder, which controlled the setting time, thus creating a viable competitor to traditional lime plaster. Because gypsum was plentiful, and available at a relatively low price, and because the manufacturing process was so simple, new firms flooded the market and placed constant downward pressure on prices.

In the early years of the 20th century, several key businesses emerged as gypsum-product leaders. The English family of Nebraska; C.G. Root, Emil Durr, S.Q. Fulton, and Charles Pullen of Wisconsin; Waldo Avery and B.W. McCausland of Michigan; and, lastly, the largest manufacturer in the United States, J.B. King of New York, were all important gypsum processors. By 1901 several attempts to organize some of the industry's producers into a corporate combination had failed.

Consolidation in 1901

That year 35 gypsum companies consolidated into the U.S.G. Company. The participating firms traded their assets for securities and acquired a $200,000 loan. Directors of the new company, which controlled about 50 percent of U.S. gypsum output, chose B.W. McCausland as its first president. The company was based in Chicago.

Between 1901 and 1905 each director remained largely concerned with the success of his own plants. This polarization ended in 1905, when McCausland was replaced as president by Sewell Avery, his partner's son. Avery's tenure as president would extend 35 years, until November 12, 1936. Avery then served as chairman, between 1937 and 1951. He and his brother, Waldo Avery, were the company's largest stockholders, controlling about 3.6 percent of the company's stock. During Sewell Avery's presidency, his character permeated the company's culture. Avery was a conservative businessman who had the last word in virtually all matters. In 1931, when Montgomery Ward and Company was on the verge of financial collapse, Avery became chairman of the board of that company, a position he held until 1955.

Avery had managed his father's firm, the Alabaster Company, since 1894. When U.S.G. absorbed Alabaster, he became a U.S.G. director and its Buffalo, New York, sales manager. Avery built a strong research division after his promotion to president from his post as Cleveland sales manager. Staffed by engineers and chemists, the new division sought to find new uses for gypsum. The U.S.G. Company, reincorporated in 1920 as the United States Gypsum Company (US Gypsum), has maintained a market share ranging between 50 percent in 1901 and 33 percent in the late 1990s. In 1909 Avery set out to diversify the company with one of his first acquisitions, the Sackett Plasterboard Company of New York. Augustine Sackett had invented gypsum wallboard and the specialized machinery to make it. This basic wallboard quickly became one of US Gypsum's major products. Wallboard, a layer of gypsum plaster sandwiched between two pieces of paper, is a convenient building material with strong fireproofing and insulating qualities.

US Gypsum improved on Sackett's concept and patented a wallboard that had paper folded over its edges to seal in plaster residue, which often escaped during the wallboard's installation. In 1927 CertainTeed Products Corporation introduced its own wallboard, which did not have enclosed edges, and challenged US Gypsum for market share. CertainTeed's managers believed that their less expensive version had a good chance of success. The result was a price contest between the two companies, beginning in 1927 and ending in 1929. US Gypsum had a much larger market than CertainTeed. It, therefore, was able to sell wallboard at a loss only in those markets that CertainTeed also served. In all other markets US Gypsum kept prices up. CertainTeed, however, was forced to sell its product at a loss in all its markets. By 1929 CertainTeed was beaten. The smaller company was licensed to produce US Gypsum's patented wallboard and was forced to sell the product at the price set by US Gypsum. This incident marked the start of US Gypsum's unrivaled leadership in gypsum materials.

Weathering the Great Depression

In 1928 Avery successfully predicted a recession that eventually became the Great Depression. Avery's instinct for predicting business cycles helped US Gypsum get through the Depression without a single year of losses; this situation was quite unusual for a business involved in the cyclical building industry. Avery moved to protect the company, in part by ordering the construction of new plants closer to East Coast metropolitan centers. Since gypsum is a high-bulk, relatively low-value commodity, transportation costs continue to have a large effect on pricing.

US Gypsum's greatest advantage was size. The company was able to use its size to keep manufacturing and transportation costs down and to compete more effectively. Three specific policies, set by Avery, helped US Gypsum to counter the Depression and maintain its number one position in the industry. According to the February 1936 issue of *Fortune*, diffusion of production facilities allowed US Gypsum to keep transportation costs, and thus total costs down. US Gypsum was also vertically integrated, from mine floor to retailer, and employed highly mechanized techniques when possible. The third element in US Gypsum's success, according to *Fortune*, was a devotion to product diversification. US Gypsum marketed a broad cross section of building materials. Broken down into individual units these products would have been prohibitively expensive to transport. Combined, however, transportation costs were much more reasonable.

Avery took advantage of the company's strong cash position at the beginning of the Depression to purchase nearly a dozen building material firms weakened by the economic downturn. In 1930 US Gypsum bought into the insulation board business with the purchase of the Greenville Insulating Board Corporation of Greenville, Mississippi. Also in 1930, it bought into the metal-lath business with the purchase of the Youngstown Pressed Steel Company of Warren, Ohio, and the metal-lath division of Northwestern Expanded Metal Company. Avery also made US Gypsum, which had already been in the lime business for 15 years, a leading lime producer in 1930 with the acquisition of lime-producing firms such as the Farnam Cheshire Lime Company. Producers of mineral wool and asphalt roofing acquired in 1933, and asbestos-cement siding acquired in 1937, rounded out the Depression-era acquisitions. The company countered the downturn in new construction by exploiting the remodeling and industrial markets. During the Depression, 15 percent of sales were to industrial users. Glassmakers used gypsum as a packing material. Cement producers used it to retard setting, and moviemakers used flaked gypsum as snow.

The 1940 Price-Fixing Suit

In 1940, a new problem confronted the company's management when the U.S. Justice Department filed suit against US Gypsum and six other wallboard manufacturers, charging them with price fixing. The claim stemmed from US Gypsum's 1929 cross-licensing of its patented wallboard. The agreement set prices at which the wallboard must be sold. In 1950 the Supreme Court forced US Gypsum and its six licensees—who produced all of the wallboard sold east of the Rocky Mountains—to cease setting prices, and US Gypsum was enjoined from exercising its patent-licensing privilege.

Between 1946 and 1949 US Gypsum invested over $51 million in expansion under the direction of William L. Keady, who had become president in 1942. In 1949, however, Chairman Avery predicted another depression—incorrectly—and began to rein in expansion. Keady resigned as a result of Avery's intervention. Although there was a slight recession in 1949, the company did not step up capital spending again until 1954. In May 1951, when Sewell Avery resigned as US Gypsum's chairman and CEO, his replacement, Clarence H. Shaver, inherited a company that had a capitalized value of $61 million and produced more than 75 commodities in 47 mines or factories. Avery's imprint was an extreme conservatism marked by strong centralized control, rigid cost-cutting practices, and few benefits for employees.

Expansion in Mid-Century

Toward the end of the 1950s US Gypsum extended its expansion internationally. One of its principal discoveries during the decade was the gypsum deposit in Mexico's San Luis Potosi State. This find, one of the world's largest, was conservatively estimated to contain at least 300 million tons of commercial deposits.

In the 1960s US Gypsum became the first major U.S. corporation to undertake privately funded housing renovation on a large scale. The highly publicized project began in 1964, when US Gypsum purchased six adjoining tenements in the East Harlem Section of New York City. US Gypsum paid $9,125 to renovate each unit; the cost of constructing new units averaged $22,500. US Gypsum's president, Graham J. Morgan, saw these projects as an opportunity to get in on the ground floor of a potential $20 billion market. Morgan felt the renovation would open up because of the Federal Housing Administration's willingness to provide financing for such projects. By 1969 the company had completely remodeled 32 buildings in New York, Cleveland, Chicago, and Detroit.

In 1973 US Gypsum settled a class-action civil antitrust suit brought against it by wallboard users and buyers. Settlement of those cases, which alleged price fixing, cost US Gypsum $28 million. This case led to a criminal indictment of US Gypsum and three competitors in 1973. The criminal trial eventually found its way to the Supreme Court, which ordered a new trial, and in 1980 US Gypsum settled the case, agreeing to pay $2.6 million in taxes on deductions from earlier civil antitrust judgments.

On January 1, 1985, a holding company, USG Corporation (USG), was created, and US Gypsum became the largest of the holding company's nine operating subsidiaries. Chairman and CEO Edward W. Duffy reportedly formed the holding company to protect the bulk of company operations from asbestos litigation against US Gypsum. Asbestos had been a standard additive in wallboard manufacture for decades. US Gypsum had already begun to face property damage suits in 1984 with a $675,000 award to a South Carolina school district.

1980s Takeover Battles

In November 1986 the Belzberg brothers of Canada attempted a hostile takeover of USG. USG immediately instituted a plan to buy back 20 percent of its common stock in an effort to fend off the takeover. By December 1986, however, USG had purchased Samuel, William, and Hyman Belzberg's 4.9 percent stake, for $139.6 million. The Belzberg family's profits on the transaction were in excess of $25 million.

In 1987 USG acquired DAP Inc., maker of caulking and sealants, for $127 million. In October of that year a partnership led by Texans Cyril Wagner, Jr., and Jack E. Brown's Desert Partners attempted to gain control of the company. Wagner and Brown's main business venture was a Midland, Texas, oil and gas partnership with secondary real estate operations. They purchased their 9.83 percent stake in USG as USG tried to recover financially from the Belzberg takeover attempt. In April 1988 a federal court refused to block USG's poison-pill antitakeover plan. In May 1988 USG announced a restructuring and recapitalization plan designed to further block the takeover attempt, and by June the plan had succeeded.

The plan was expensive, however, and $2.5 billion in new debt (on top of previous debt of $851 million) left USG in a precarious financial state. Several noncore assets were sold over the next few years to help pay down debt. In October 1988 USG sold its Masonite Corporation subsidiary, purchased in 1984. International Paper Corporation paid $400 million for Masonite. Sold the following year were the Kinkead division (to Kohler Co.) and Marlite (to Commercial and Architectural Products Inc.). In September 1991 USG sold DAP to U.K.-based Wassall plc for $90 million.

"Prepackaged" Bankruptcy in 1993

These moves proved inadequate, however, as USG's management had not anticipated the depressed state of the housing market in the late 1980s and early 1990s. With revenues declining and the company posting a net loss for 1990, USG defaulted on $40 million in loans in 1991. USG—led by CEO Eugene B. Connolly starting in January 1990—attempted to reorganize outside of bankruptcy court through negotiations with its lenders. Finally, in March 1993 USG was forced to declare Chapter 11 bankruptcy, although it quickly emerged only two months later, following the implementation of a "prepackaged" plan of reorganization. Banks and bondholders ended up owning 97 percent of the common stock of USG, in exchange for the elimination of $1.4 billion in debt. The company was also able to reduce its annual interest payments by $200 million.

USG emerged from bankruptcy with a still high debt load of $1.56 billion, and set a goal of reducing that to $650 million within five years. In 1994 the housing market—and USG's future outlook—had improved enough to enable the company to raise $224 million through a stock offering, the proceeds of which were used to pay down debt. Connolly retired in early 1996, replaced as chairman and CEO by William C. Foote. Later that year USG sold its insulation manufacturing operation. The company returned to profitability in 1996, posting net income of $15 million on net sales of $2.59 billion.

The following year was even better, as sales hit $2.87 billion, while net income increased almost tenfold, to $148 million. Improving economic conditions played a big role in USG's turnaround as did heavy capital expenditures that aimed at achieving organic, profitable growth. From the company's emergence out of bankruptcy through year-end 1997, USG had spent $532 million in capital expenditures, including the beginning of construction in mid-1997 of a new $110 million wallboard plant in Bridgeport, Alabama—USG's largest nonacquisition capital investment ever. In April 1997 USG announced that it would build a plant in Gypsum, Ohio, to manufacture gypsum wood fiber panels—which combined gypsum with cellulosic fibers to create strong, impact-resistant panels—under the Fibrerock brand. In November of that year USG purchased a 60 percent stake in Zhongbei Building Material Products Company, China's largest ceiling grid company. By the end of 1997 total debt had been reduced to $620 million, marking the achievement of the firm's debt reduction target.

Throughout the 1990s the company continued to be involved in litigation relating to personal injury suits and other claims based on asbestos-containing products, which were sold by USG from the 1930s through 1977. The claims were being paid by insurance income under the 1985 Wellington Agreement on asbestos-related claims. In 1988 USG and 19 other former producers of asbestos-containing products replaced the Wellington Asbestos Claims Facility with the Center for Claims Resolution (CCR), which continued in operation through the late 1990s. A class-action lawsuit resulted in a $1.3 billion agreement with the CCR in 1993, but in June 1997 the U.S. Supreme Court invalidated the settlement, finding that the class was defined improperly. USG estimated in 1997 that it was the defendant in about 73,000 personal injury cases and that the average settlement would be about $1,600.

USG had itself sued nearly two dozen insurance companies who had refused to cover these claims. By 1997 the company had reached settlements with a number of these insurers, resulting in about $325 million in coverage for the company. USG expected to receive substantial additional payments—between $200 million and $265 million—as the remaining suits reached settlements.

During 1998 USG continued to spend heavily on capital improvement projects and the construction of new plants. In April the company announced it would build a new $112 million wallboard factory in Aliquippa, Pennsylvania. In September USG announced plans to construct two new, state-of-the-art wallboard plants in Plaster City, California, and Rainier, Oregon, for a total cost of $225 million. Replacing older facilities with modern, low-cost plants aided USG's overall productivity. With the economic boom of the mid- to late 1990s making for an exceptionally strong building industry, and with the company's debt load finally eased, USG was in its best financial shape in years. Perhaps most indicative of its recovery was USG's September 1998 announcement that it would pay a quarterly dividend for the first time in a decade, as well as repurchase as many as five million of its common shares.

Principal Subsidiaries

United States Gypsum Company; USG Interiors, Inc.; L&W Supply Corporation; USG International, Ltd.; USG Foreign Investments, Ltd.; USG Interiors International, Inc.; USG Funding Corporation; La Mirada Products Co., Inc.; USG Foreign Sales Corporation; Gypsum Engineering Company; Alabaster Assurance Company, Ltd.; USG Interiors Australia Pty. Ltd. (Australia); USG Interiors (Donn) S.A. (Belgium); USG Interiors (Europe) S.A. (Belgium); USG Interiors Coordination Centre S.A. (Belgium); USG Belgium Holdings S.A.; Gypsum Transportation Limited (Bermuda); CGC Inc. (Canada); USG Canadian Mining Ltd. (Canada); USG Manufacturing Worldwide, Ltd. (Caymans); Shenzhen USG Zhongbei Building Materials Co. (China; 60%); USG France S.A.; Donn Products GmbH (Germany); USG Interiors Eastern Manufacturing GmbH (Germany); USG Interiors East Sales GmbH (Germany); USG Interiors (Far East) SDN BHD (Malaysia); Yeso Panamericano, S.A. de C.V. (Mexico); USG (Netherlands) B.V.; Alabaster Engineering (Nederland) B.V. (Netherlands); Red Top Technology (Nederland) B.V. (Netherlands); USG Interiors Pacific Ltd. (New Zealand); Panama Gypsum Company; USG Asia Pacific Holdings Pty. Ltd. (Singapore); USG (U.K.) Ltd.

Principal Operating Units

North American Gypsum; Worldwide Ceilings.

Further Reading

Duff, Christina, "Costly Recapitalization Drives USG Corp. to the Wall," *Wall Street Journal,* June 3, 1992, p. B4.

Gilbert, Nick, "USG: Now a Value Play," *Financial World,* May 9, 1995, p. 26.

Greising, David, "USG's Remodeling May Mean Gutting the House," *Business Week,* January 21, 1991, pp. 54–55.

"Gyp," *Fortune,* February 1936.

Miller, James P., "USG Modifies 'Prepackaged' Chapter 11 Plan," *Wall Street Journal,* January 25, 1993, p. A11.

Saporito, Bill, "The Benefits of Bankruptcy," *Fortune,* July 13, 1993, p. 98.

Taub, Stephen, "The 1980s Legacy Still Stalks USG," *Financial World,* August 21, 1990, p. 11.

"U.S. Gypsum: No Nonsense," *Fortune,* September 1955.

—John C. Bishop
—updated by David E. Salamie

VICTOR COMPANY OF JAPAN, LIMITED

Victor Company of Japan, Limited

12, 3-chome, Moriya-cho
Kanagawa-ku
Yokohama 221-8528
Japan
(045) 450-2837
Fax: (045) 450-1574
Web site: http://www.jvc-victor.co.jp

Public Company
Incorporated: 1927
Employees: 31,040
Sales: ¥916.31 billion (US$6.94 billion) (1998)
Stock Exchanges: Tokyo Osaka
Ticker Symbol: VJAPY (ADR)
SICs: 3577 Computer Peripheral Equipment, Not
    Elsewhere Classified; 3651 Household Audio & Video
    Equipment; 3652 Phonograph Records & Pre-
    Recorded Audio Tapes & Discs; 3663 Radio & TV
    Broadcasting & Communications Equipment; 7812
    Motion Picture & Video Tape Production

Victor Company of Japan, Limited (JVC) is one of several Japanese companies that has evolved to dominate the international consumer electronics market. The company has achieved its current position not only through effective marketing but also by consistently developing new products that establish standards within the industry. Like Matsushita Electric Industrial Company, Limited and Sony Corporation, JVC was strongly influenced by a single dominant personality; as the man most responsible for the success of JVC, Kenjiro Takayanagi is also considered one of Japan's most important inventors. Today, JVC makes VCRs, audio equipment, televisions and monitors, video cameras, computer peripherals, and other electronics items—both for the consumer and professional markets. The company is also active in the field of entertainment, where it produces music CDs, video game and karaoke software, and movies. The focus of the company is increasingly on digital technologies. JVC is an independently

operated affiliate of Matsushita Electric, which holds a 52.4 percent stake.

Japanese-American Roots

JVC was founded in 1927, as the wholly owned subsidiary of the Victor Talking Machine Company of the United States, to manufacture and market phonographs in Japan. Victor, however, was purchased in 1929 by the Radio Corporation of America and renamed RCA Victor. As part of an effort to enlist the marketing and sales expertise of well-established Japanese conglomerates, minority shares of the Japanese Victor Company (JVC) were sold to the Mitsubishi and Sumitomo financial groups. JVC was thereafter operated as a U.S.-Japanese joint venture.

In 1930 JVC built a large phonograph-and-record plant in Yokohama, at the time the largest in Asia. Japan, however, soon came under the domination of ultra-rightwing militarists who in 1937 launched Japan into a war with China. The war soon led to hostility with other nations and caused many U.S. interests to reassess their investments in Japan. RCA Victor sold a majority of its shares in JVC to Nihon Sangyo (later the Nissan Motor Company), which assumed managerial control of the company. In an unrelated move, JVC shares held by Mitsubishi and Sumitomo were transferred to the Dai-Ichi Mutual Life Insurance Company.

RCA Victor sold its minority interest in JVC to Tokyo Shibaura Electric (now Toshiba) and Nihon Denko in 1938, making the company an entirely Japanese enterprise. The following year JVC successfully produced the first television set manufactured entirely from Japanese-made components. The television never entered mass production, but it did establish JVC's reputation as a leading electronics company.

The television was developed by an electrical engineer named Kenjiro Takayanagi. Takayanagi began work on the first Japanese-made television at the Hamamatsu Technical College in 1924, and succeeded in projecting images two years later. Takayanagi developed improved designs and was later awarded a full professorship. He was appointed to a number of positions with the Japan Broadcasting Corporation, where he led the

511

Company Perspectives:

JVC is a world leader in audiovisual and related software products. The Company is being transformed from an audiovisual innovator to a digital systems integrator. Its position as one of the few companies in the world with large-scale operations in both hardware and software, along with the innovative technology that led to the development of VHS, provides JVC with a competitive advantage in the development of digital systems. Based on these strengths, JVC looks forward to a new stage of growth in the multimedia age.

---

development of television technologies, often in cooperation with companies such as JVC.

World War II had a dramatic impact on JVC, as it did on nearly every Japanese company. In 1943, as part of a government-imposed industrial reorganization, JVC's name was changed to Nippon Onkyo (Japan Acoustics), and in April 1945 its Yokohama plant was destroyed by aerial bombings. The facility was rebuilt shortly after the war ended, when the company also returned to its former name.

Kenjiro Takayanagi joined JVC as head of the television research department in July 1946. The company resumed full production of radios, phonographs, and speakers in 1950, and introduced televisions in 1953, the year that Takayanagi was promoted to managing director of JVC.

Became Affiliate of Matsushita Electric in 1953

As a result of the anti-monopoly laws imposed by the U.S. military occupation authority, Tokyo Shibaura (the primary owner of JVC) was forced to sell its interest in the company. For the next several years JVC endured labor problems and persistent financial instability. Japan's anti-monopoly legislation was relaxed in stages, so that by 1953 the Matsushita Electric Industrial Company was permitted to purchase a 50 percent interest in the nearly bankrupt JVC.

Konosuke Matsushita, who had founded Matsushita Electric in 1918, decided to maintain JVC's operational autonomy, offering only managerial direction and capital infusions. Initially JVC was considered a good investment for Matsushita because the two companies competed in relatively few areas. As it evolved, however, the relationship between JVC and Matsushita became one of competitive cooperation. Matsushita permitted JVC's managers great latitude in making decisions about investments in research and development, joint production, and licensing agreements. One of the ideas JVC developed was a videotape recorder.

In the field of audio technology, JVC developed the 45–45 system, one of the first systems to enable phonographs to reproduce sound in stereo. In conventional monaural systems, a small needle ran through a V-shaped groove that varied in depth, and the vibration of the needle was amplified to produce sounds. The 45–45 system required that depths vary on both sides of the groove. Two separate mechanisms measured the vibration of

the needle in perpendicular directions. These vibrations were then amplified independently to produce two sounds simultaneously, or in stereo.

JVC introduced 45–45-system stereo phonographs in 1957, and the following year developed a color videotape recorder. The company began commercial production of color television sets in 1960, at a new plant in Iwai. Color television broadcasting began that same year and greatly increased demand for JVC televisions. In order to take better advantage of the company's growth, JVC shares were listed on the Tokyo and Osaka stock exchanges, and capital raised through subsequent share issues enabled the company to increase production capacity. Favorable economic conditions and low production costs allowed JVC to gain substantial market shares in foreign countries, particularly in the United States. In 1968, in an ironic reversal of 1927, JVC established a wholly owned U.S. subsidiary called JVC America, and three years later the company created a West German subsidiary called Nippon Victor (Europe) GmbH.

Kenjiro Takayanagi assumed a more influential role in the management of JVC during the 1960s, further diminishing the company's system of consensus management. Trained as an engineer, however, Takayanagi was not able to avoid the prolonged drop in profits that lasted from 1970 to 1976. The management of Matsushita continued to provide the guidance and support necessary to keep JVC from encountering more serious financial difficulty.

During those six years, JVC devoted considerable resources to the development of a commercial videocassette system. As part of a reorganization program in 1973, the company's management separated the music division from JVC and established it as a subsidiary called Victor Musical Industries. During the mid-1970s JVC established additional subsidiaries in Great Britain, Canada, and the United States.

Introduced VHS System in 1976

A few months before his 76th birthday, in 1974, Kenjiro Takayanagi retired from JVC, but continued to serve the company as an advisor. The video division, which was largely his creation, introduced the video home system (VHS) format videocassette recorder in 1976. The system was introduced after Sony's Betamax VCR, but was superior in several ways. Matsushita Electric, which had been independently developing a third format, was so impressed with the VHS that it abandoned its project and arranged for cross-licensing of the JVC technology.

Matsushita and its allied brands, Quasar and Panasonic, adopted the VHS format and, with JVC, worked diligently to establish VHS as the industry standard. Their efforts succeeded and, despite a full year of monopoly, the Sony Betamax was superseded by the VHS; Sony's market share rapidly diminished.

With the tremendous success of VHS, JVC's profits had risen by a factor of ten by 1982. The video division which had accounted for six percent of total sales in 1976, accounted for 69 percent in 1982. JVC established several additional subsidiaries, particularly in Europe, to handle sales of VHS video recorders and other products.

JVC engineers developed a laser-operated videodisc system in 1978. Although the technology gained favor among consumers, the product's inability to record television broadcasts was such a drawback that it curtailed its further development. A subsequent compact disc (CD) format developed by Sony and Philips, however, proved highly successful for audio reproduction. JVC applied certain videodisc technologies to the CD and developed a VHD videodisc system that was interchangeable with conventional CD players. JVC introduced the VHD to Japan in April 1983, and licensed VHD technology to 13 other Japanese manufacturers in addition to Thorn EMI, AEG-Telefunken, and General Electric. JVC was also expanding its VHS market through the 1982 development of VHS-C, a compact format that became a popular base for camcorders, and the 1987 launch of the Super VHS format, which offered sharper resolution than standard VHS. The 1987 introduction of digital audio tape (DAT) recorders, however, proved to be a failure.

JVC first entered the computer market in 1978 when it began making CRT displays and floppy disks and drives. Six years later, JVC introduced a line of personal computers while production of 3.5-inch disk drives began in 1985. At this time Ichiro Shinji was serving as president of the company, becoming the first person in 25 years to gain promotion to the company presidency from within JVC ranks.

Diversified in the 1990s

In April 1990 Takuro Bojo was appointed president of JVC; at 51 he was the youngest president in company history. Bojo began a diversification drive that aimed at expanding the company beyond the mature consumer electronics sector. The aim would be to expand sales in the areas of professional electronics (such as video cameras), telecommunications devices (such as cordless telephones), and entertainment. The last of these included production of video games and karaoke software as well as music and feature films. JVC's involvement in motion pictures had begun in 1989 with the production of Jim Jarmusch's *Mystery Train*. The company that year also took a stake in Largo Entertainment Pictures, a production company headed by entertainment veteran Larry Gordon which in the early 1990s developed such films as *Point Break* (1991), *Malcolm X* (1993), and *Time Cop* (1994). JVC was also involved in the production of such award-winning films as *The Piano* (1994) and *Carrington* (1996). In 1992, meanwhile, JVC entered into a joint venture with Hughes Aircraft Co. to develop projectors for large-screen televisions.

The early 1990s were difficult ones for most electronics firms in Japan as the country's economy entered an extended slump following the bursting of the bubble economy of the 1980s. Still largely a maker of consumer electronics, JVC was hurt not only by slumping sales of electronics goods in Japan and overseas markets but also by its failure to develop any breakthrough audiovisual products. The company consequently posted pretax losses for 1992, 1993, and 1994. It announced in August 1992 that it would cut 700 workers in its video plants. Less than a year later JVC said it would reduce its staff by 3,000 and cut capital spending by 36.3 percent. Soon after the conclusion of the 1994 fiscal year, Bojo resigned as president, taking

responsibility for the poor financial performance. He was replaced by Takeo Shuzui, a director at Matsushita.

Shuzui led JVC on the comeback trail with a new emphasis on high-value-added digital technology, including digital camcorders, the D-VHS digital videocassette format, digital video disc (DVD) software and hardware, and high-definition television sets. The company thereupon posted healthy profits in 1996 and 1997, resuming dividend payouts in 1996, before returning to the red in 1998 as the Japanese economy entered a recession. In April 1998 JVC Europe Ltd. was established as the headquarters for European operations. This subsidiary joined three others—JVC Americas Corp., JVC Asia Pte. Ltd., and JVC (China) Investment Co., Ltd.—and the parent company as the centers of the five business spheres in which JVC operated: Japan, the Americas, Europe, Asia, and China. Each of the regional headquarters were locally managed. Although the short-term outlook for JVC did not appear favorable given the weakness of the Japanese economy, the company's long-term prospects seemed brighter based on a resurgence in successful product development.

Principal Subsidiaries

Victor Entertainment, Inc.; Victor Media Products, Inc.; Victor Interactive Software, Inc.; Victor Leisure System Co., Ltd.; JVC Advanced Media Co., Ltd.; Victor Arcs Co., Ltd.; Sanin Victor Sales Co., Ltd.; Okinawa Victor Sales Co., Ltd.; Victor Service & Engineering Co., Ltd.; Victor Data Systems Co., Ltd.; Victor Real Estate Co., Ltd.; Victor Finance Co., Ltd.; Victor Logistics, Inc.; JVC Belgium S.A./N.V.; JVC Canada Inc.; JVC (China) Investment Co., Ltd.; JVC France S.A.; JVC Deutschland GmbH (Germany); JVC Video Manufacturing Europe GmbH (Germany); JVC Italia S.p.A. (Italy); JVC Electronics Malaysia Sdn. Bhd.; JVC Nederland B.V. (Netherlands); JVC Finance B.V. (Netherlands); JVC Asia Pte. Ltd. (Singapore); JVC Electronics Singapore Pte. Ltd.; JVC España S.A. (Spain); JVC Manufacturing (Thailand) Co., Ltd.; JVC Components (Thailand) Co., Ltd.; JVC Europe Ltd. (U.K.); JVC (U.K.) Ltd.; JVC Manufacturing U.K. Ltd.; JVC America, Inc. (U.S.A.); JVC Americas Corp. (U.S.A.); US JVC Corp.; JVC Entertainment, Inc. (U.S.A.).

Further Reading

"JVC Undergoing Major Restructuring," *Television Digest,* July 16, 1990, pp. 12+.

Much, Marilyn, "JVC, Who?," *Industry Week,* September 3, 1984, pp. 57+.

Nakamoto, Michiyo, "JVC Records Pre-Tax Loss for Third Consecutive Year," *Financial Times,* May 25, 1994, p. 32.

"Sony and JVC Shoot from the Shoulder," *Economist,* January 18, 1986, pp. 55–56.

Terazono, Emiko, "Victor Resumes Dividend After Four Years," *Financial Times,* May 23, 1996, p. 36.

Trachtenberg, Jeffrey A., "JVC, in Bid to Mute Sony, to Introduce Digital VCR That Plays VHS Tapes," *Wall Street Journal,* April 3, 1995, p. B3.

Turner, Richard, "How Larry Gordon Got His $100 Million Movie Deal," *Wall Street Journal,* August 23, 1989, pp. B1, B5.

—updated by David E. Salamie

Visa International

3155 Clearview Way
San Mateo, California 94402-3798
U.S.A.
(650) 432-3200
Fax: (650) 432-7431
Web site: http://www.visa.com

Private Company
Incorporated: 1970 as National BankAmericard Inc.
Employees: 4,000
Sales: $1.6 billion (1997 est.)
SICs: 6153 Payment Cards, Travelers Cheques, & Travel Vouchers

Visa International has grown from a credit card company into the largest full-service consumer payment system in the world. With around 600 million cards in circulation as of 1998, Visa boasted the most widely recognized general purpose payment card in the world. Worldwide consumer purchases made with Visa reached around $1 trillion in 1997. In the United States, Visa commanded the majority of the market in transactions made with credit cards. The company also offered numerous products and services in the late 1990s, including debit cards, travelers cheques, and a worldwide ATM network.

Company Origins

The driving force behind Visa's explosive growth was Dee Ward Hock. Born in 1930, the son of a lineman for Utah Power & Light Company, Hock was raised in North Ogden, Utah. He attended a local junior college, married his childhood sweetheart soon after school, and worked in a slaughterhouse and for a brick mason. In the early 1950s, Hock joined the consumer finance department of Pacific Finance Company and soon became a local branch manager.

In 1965 Hock began working for National Bank of Commerce in Seattle, eventually becoming assistant vice-president. At the same time, Bank of America was in the process of licensing BankAmericard, its credit card operation, to other banks. National Bank became one of BankAmericard's first licensees, and Hock was promoted to manager of the bank's credit card program. However, many of the new licensee banks complained of delayed payment transfers and lack of adequate measures to prevent user fraud. At a meeting of over 100 bank licensees in 1968, Hock prodded the members to restructure the entire credit card operation. Hock was elected head of the committee to resolve recurring problems.

Hock influenced an industry with a history dating back to 1914 when the first customer charge card was issued by Western Union. This card provided many different services, including deferred payment for preferred customers. Over the years, a variety of hotels, gasoline companies, and department stores issued their customers charge cards, but the first card accepted by a number of different merchants, the Diners Club Card, was introduced in 1950. Merchants were reimbursed for transactions made with the Diners Club Card by deducting a small fee. Customers were billed monthly for the charges they incurred on the card and were required to pay the full amount of the invoice upon receipt.

In 1951 Franklin National Bank on Long Island issued the first bank-based charge card. The card was accepted only by local merchants, but soon more than 100 other banks were issuing cards. Merchants were charged a fee by the issuing bank for any transaction made with the card, and no fee or interest was charged to cardholders who paid the entire bill upon receipt. However, since these early bankcard systems only served a bank's local area, profits remained low.

Bank of America issued its BankAmericard in 1958. The card was successfully marketed throughout the entire state of California. One new factor essential to its success was the credit service. BankAmericard provided its customers with the option of paying the balance of the account in installments, with a monthly finance charge on the remaining balance, rather than requiring a full payment upon receipt of the bill. Of course, the customer could still pay the full balance of the account for the month without any finance charge.

Soon Bank of America was forming licensing agreements with banks outside of California that allowed them to issue the

Company Perspectives:

Today, Visa offers the widest range of financial services in the bankcard industry. Visa's diverse product line includes credit and debit cards, travelers cheques, Visa stored value cards, corporate and business cards, as well as new, state of the art products such as our online products and services, and the Visa Global ATM Network with over 457,000 ATMs in 120 countries.

Tomorrow, Visa will continue to lead the payments industry as our products and services evolve to meet the ever-changing dynamics of the marketplace. In the future, Visa will continue to advance the use of chip cards in electronic commerce, on the Internet, and in other emerging media to ensure that we remain ''The World's Best Way to Pay'' for our Members and their cardholders.

BankAmericard. At approximately the same time, a consortium of banks from Illinois, California, and a number of East Coast states established another bankcard association and began to issue Master Charge (later MasterCard). In light of the success of these two bankcard licensing associations, most local and regional banks terminated their independent bankcard programs and joined either BankAmericard or Master Charge. By 1970, over 1,400 banks offered one of the two cards, and total consumer charges on the cards amounted to $3.8 billion.

Consortium Revamps BankAmericard in 1970s

The success of Bank of America's credit card operation was accompanied by problems, which Hock, in his capacity as head of the banks' committee, was responsible for solving. He urged the member banks to take control of the BankAmericard program, and in 1970 they created National BankAmericard Inc. (NBI), a consortium of banks that issued the BankAmericard. This independent, nonstock membership corporation purchased the entire bankcard operation from Bank of America over the next few years and then began to administer and develop the BankAmericard system. Hock was chosen to lead the new organization.

Hock headed an entirely domestic bankcard system. Outside the United States, BankAmericard was issued by Bank of America's licensee banks in over 15 countries. In 1974 Hock negotiated the sale of all foreign credit card operations held by Bank of America to IBANCO, a group of bank licensees that formed a multinational, nonstock corporation to administer and develop the international operations of the BankAmericard program. He then made the entire domestic BankAmericard system a subsidiary of IBANCO, and served as this group's chief executive officer.

When it came to Hock's attention that in many foreign countries there was resistance to issuing a card associated with Bank of America, despite the fact that the association was nominal only, he decided to change the name of the card and the company. In 1977 BankAmericard was renamed the Visa card. Hock chose the name ''Visa'' because it implied no national

identification, it was relatively easy to pronounce in any language, and it made no reference to a bank, which Hock thought might limit how customers perceived they could use the card. Concurrently, NBI was rechristened Visa U.S.A., and IBANCO became Visa International.

Under Hock's leadership, customer billings for the Visa card rose dramatically, and worldwide name recognition grew at an astronomical rate. The first Visa Classic card was issued in 1977, and in 1979 Visa Traveler's Checks were introduced. Also in 1979, Visa management began to encourage merchants to use an electronic transaction-authorizing system whenever a purchase was made with the card. Visa terminals read a magnetic strip on the card and automatically requested authorization, thereby reducing retail store fraud by almost 85 percent. The Visa Premiere card was introduced in 1981, and in 1983 the Visa Classic card was redesigned to include a hologram for added security against user fraud. In 1977 Visa's market share of the bank card business was 40 percent and MasterCard International's was 60 percent. By 1983, the market share proportions of each company had reversed, with Visa's billings amounting to $59 billion and MasterCard's billings to $42 billion.

Continued Expansion in the 1980s

In 1983 Hock implemented one of the most important and far-reaching services known in the credit card industry: a global network of automated teller machines (ATMs) that allowed Visa cardholders to obtain cash at locations far away from the banks or credit unions that originally issued them the card. The network provided a cash-dispensing service for travelers carrying the Visa card; after inserting the card into an ATM, the customer received cash from a bank account or from a previously established line of credit. Most of the ATMs were situated initially in places convenient for travelers, such as airports and tourist attractions, but soon ATMs were placed in banks themselves, gas stations, grocery stores, and innumerable other locations.

Visa's ATM network was not well received by the banking industry, since many banks operated their own network of automated teller machines. The Plus System Inc., located in Denver, was owned by 34 banks, all of which were Visa members, and had approximately 950 various financial institutions that operated ATMs that only accepted the Plus card. The banks each invested up to $150,000 to exclude customers who banked with competitors. Thus, while the Plus System and other similar ATM networks worked hard to ensure exclusivity for their members, Hock was implementing a network that would be accessible to customers of all 15,000 member banks of Visa.

Dee W. Hock retired as president of Visa in 1984 and was succeeded by Charles T. Russell, vice-president and longtime employee of the company. Russell immediately defused the animosity between Visa and its member banks over the ATMs. During that year, the Visa ATM network was the first to complete a transnational transaction.

Visa continued its phenomenal growth under the leadership of Russell. In 1986 Visa and MasterCard took a 73 percent share of the $275 billion worldwide charge card market, and their combined transactions totaled $3.9 billion, far more than any other financial services company.

In January 1987 Visa won a contract to operate Interlink, the largest retailer, or point-of-sale (POS), network that accepted debit cards in restaurants and stores in the United States. Already managing the California-based Interlink network of transactions since 1984, Visa was ahead of the competition in the burgeoning point-of-sale business. In February of the same year, it reached an agreement to pay $5 million for a 33 percent share in the Plus System of ATMs. By adding the 13,000 machines from Plus, the second largest ATM network in the nation, Visa provided its cardholders with access to almost one-third of the 68,000 ATMs in the United States. The Plus System was acquired completely by Visa in 1993.

One of Russell's most important strategies to maintain Visa's market share involved a commitment to improve the company's communications network. Having started VisaNet in 1972, a comprehensive communications and data processing network, Russell directly supervised a $16 million transformation of the system from that of credit card transaction to general purpose electronic payment, a system capable of dealing with most types of consumer banking transactions. Aware that the continued success of Visa was dependent upon the connection between its electronic mail systems and data processing networks, Russell initiated a comprehensive redesign of the company's data centers. In 1992 Visa converted its Basingstoke, England, and McLean, Virginia, data centers into global "supercenters" capable of processing worldwide volume from either location. This setup was made possible because Visa incorporated transoceanic fiber-optic cables to upgrade its international communications network. As a result of these improvements, a significant increase in volume occurred while the cost per transaction decreased. In 1992 the number of transactions on VisaNet reached a record 807 per second. The network is now capable of processing 1,100 transactions per second at less than a penny per transaction.

Early 1990s: Market Leader

By 1992, Visa's Gold Card, previously the Premiere Card, had become the most widely used and best recognized credit card in the world. Indeed, by all measures of success, 1993 was a banner year for Visa. Total worldwide billings under the Visa name amounted to over $500 billion; more than 300 million cards were issued to customers around the world; more than six billion card and cheque transactions were made, with travelers cheques alone growing to a worldwide sales volume of more than $16 billion; and Visa operated more than 160,000 ATMs in 60 nations.

An aggressive marketing campaign conducted against Visa by MasterCard in 1991 and 1992 appeared to pay off by March 1993. For the first time in 14 years, MasterCard reported a gain in its U.S. market share for charge-card spending, up to 26.8 percent, while Visa's market share decreased from 45.3 percent to 45.1 percent. The competition between Visa and MasterCard, however, was friendly because almost all the banks that owned the MasterCard association also belonged to the Visa association, and no one bank benefited from a gain in market share by one at the expense of the other.

Visa's primary competitor for both the U.S. and international markets was American Express. Whereas the Diners Club card held a 2.2 percent market share of U.S. charge-card spending in 1992 and the Sears Discover card a 6.5 percent share, American Express maintained a 19.4 percent share and was working hard to increase it. Both Visa and American Express intensified the competition for a larger U.S. market share by using the concept of "ambush advertising" in their commercials. Visa, as one of the major sponsors of the 1992 Olympics, used its television ads to remind viewers that the Visa card was more widely accepted than American Express. American Express, for their part, featured an Olympic theme while using a clever play on the word "visa" to promote its own card at Visa's expense.

American Express's advertising did not gain any market share for the company. In fact, American Express lost ground in the early and mid-1990s, with its global market share falling to 13.4 percent in 1992 and down to 10.4 percent in 1995. In addition, merchants who accepted the card fell over the same period. In an effort to increase market share, American Express introduced a bank credit card of its own. Visa, however, thwarted this attempt in the United States by establishing an internal bylaw that banned its members from issuing the American Express card.

When the battle for market share refocused in Western Europe, Visa attempted to introduce a similar bylaw for its European member banks in 1996. American Express had already arranged with several banks in Portugal, Greece, and Israel to offer its card and fought the proposed bylaw through the European Commission. When Europe's competition commissioner announced that Brussels would not accept the bylaw, Visa backed down. In June 1996 it decided not to restrict member banks in Europe from issuing cards that competed with Visa. With credit card usage on the rise in Asia, however, a similar battle was on the horizon.

New Products and Services in the Mid- to Late 1990s

In the mid-1990s Visa developed new products and services that met with varying degrees of consumer enthusiasm. In 1994 the company acquired Interlink, which provided Visa with an online banking service it could offer around the world. A joint venture with Microsoft to offer home banking services and create related software did poorly against Intuit and other competitors in its first few years.

Much more popular was Visa's debit card, a payment option that gained a great deal of momentum in the 1990s. Payments made with the debit cards were withdrawn from the holder's checking account and no interest payments were levied. Visa invested heavily in another new payment option, the chip-based "smart card," with much less satisfying results. Although Visa had endorsed the chip technology in 1992, it did not offer the card until 1996. Named Visa Cash, the card electronically stored money to be used as cash. Consumers could load money onto the card by transferring money from a checking account to the card at an ATM. To encourage member banks to transfer from magnetic stripe cards to the new technology, Visa instituted the Partner Program in 1997. Tests with the card, however, were not encouraging. In a 1998 trial by Citibank and Chase Manhattan on the Upper West Side of Manhattan, consumers rarely loaded their cards a second time. "Smart cards are a technology chasing a business case,'' Richard Speer, CEO of the financial consulting firm Speer & Associates, told the *New York Times* in 1998.

Visa encountered a couple of setbacks in 1997 related to new shopping services on the Internet. Visa and Yahoo, the largest Internet search engine, had reached an agreement to jointly develop an Internet shopping site. Yahoo canceled the agreement in September 1997, costing them $20.5 million. The same year Visa postponed the full introduction of a secure Internet purchasing system. The system, dubbed the Secure Electronic Transaction (SET) protocol, would make electronic money transactions safe through the use of encryption, digital certificates, and digital signatures. In August 1997 Visa began the world's largest pilot program for secure electronic commerce using the SET protocol.

In 1998 federal regulators filed an antitrust suit against Visa and MasterCard, charging that their bylaws preventing member banks from issuing competing cards were creating an uncompetitive marketplace. Visa fought the suit, claiming intense market competition existed. ''We believe the suit filed today by federal regulators will fail in a court of law,'' Paul Allen, executive vice-president and general counsel for Visa U.S.A., said in a press release. ''Because, when it comes right down to it, consumers have unlimited choices when it comes to credit cards.''

In the late 1990s, Visa's focus was on developing its foreign operations, increasing its debit activity, and improving its technological infrastructure. Despite problems with its electronic cash card, the introduction of its SET protocol, and the federal antitrust suit, Visa operated the largest and strongest consumer payment system in the world.

Further Reading

Desmond, Edward, ''Yahoo: Still Defying Gravity on the Web,'' *Fortune,* September 8, 1997, p. 154.

Garfield, Bob, ''AMEX vs. Visa—Round 2: The Agony of Ambushing,'' *Advertising Age,* July 20, 1992, p. 44.

Hansell, Saul, ''Got a Dime? Citibank and Chase End Test of Electronic Cash,'' *New York Times,* November 4, 1998, p. C1.

Louis, Arthur M., ''Visa Stirs Up the Big Banks—Again,'' *Fortune,* October 3, 1983, pp. 196–203.

''A Punch-Up in Plastic,'' *Economist,* June 8, 1996, pp. 77–78.

—Thomas Derdak
—updated by Susan Windisch Brown

Volt Information Sciences Inc.

1221 Avenue of the Americas
New York, New York 10020-1579
U.S.A.
(212) 704-2400
(800) 468-8658
Fax: (212) 704-2424
Web site: http://www.volt.com

Public Company
Incorporated: 1957 as Volt Technical Corp.
Employees: 36,800
Sales: $1.42 billion (1997)
Stock Exchanges: New York
Ticker Symbol: VOL
SICs: 2741 Miscellaneous Publishing; 2759 Commercial
Printing, Not Elsewhere Classified; 2791 Typesetting;
2796 Platemaking & Related Services; 3555 Printing
Trade Machinery & Equipment; 5045 Computers &
Computer Peripheral Equipment & Software; 7363
Help Supply Services; 7371 Computer Programming
Services; 7372 Prepackaged Software; 7373 Computer
Integrated Systems Design; 7374 Computer
Processing & Data Preparation & Processing Services;
8741 Management Services

Volt Information Sciences Inc. is a diversified company in three major businesses: staffing services; telecommunications and information solutions, including the publication of telephone directories; and prepress publishing systems. Its chief business, supplying professional and technical employees to clients on a temporary basis, was being directed in 1997 from 272 branch and onsite offices throughout the United States.

Diversified Technical Company: 1951–80

The company originated as a technical documentation business established in Brooklyn, New York, in 1951. The founders—William Shaw and his brother Jerome—began putting together technical manuals for the military during the Korean War. This involved writing material to instruct untrained draftees in the operation and maintenance of military equipment, making illustrations, and cataloging parts. The company, which was incorporated in 1957 as Volt Technical Corp., also did well after the war, a period during which expensive missile programs were initiated and cost-plus-fixed-fee writing contracts were easy to obtain. Gross revenue grew from $988,401 in fiscal 1957 (the year ended October 31, 1957) to $7.3 million in fiscal 1961. Net income increased from $19,893 to $366,016 during this period.

During the early 1960s less work was available because of a slowdown in the funding of big new defense projects. Volt, which went public in 1962, acquiring five affiliated corporations in an exchange of stock, moved heavily into the services end of the business. By 1963 it was supplying clients with technically trained personnel, and in the mid-1960s, at the request of several aerospace clients who needed nontechnical temporary help, it created Volt Instant Personnel, providing bookkeepers, stenographers, secretaries, and clerks. To keep its newly leased IBM 360 system occupied, Volt was already offering such computer services as systems analysis, programming, and payroll processing. The Vietnam War further stimulated business; during fiscal 1968 revenues reached $39.8 million and net income, $2.1 million. A share of Volt stock soared as high as $110 in 1968—just before a 5-for-1 split—compared with $7.50 in 1966.

The company name was changed to Volt Information Sciences in 1968 to reflect its broader scope. In 1970 Volt was offering, through some 50 offices nationwide, services including engineering, training, data processing, graphics, marketing, and temporary personnel. It also was publishing as well as preparing technical manuals, having purchased the company doing the page makeup when it was close to failure. This company eventually became Autologic, Inc., which began making computerized typesetters. During 1971–72 Volt acquired Autologic's parent, Alphanumeric Publication Systems, Inc., which included another subsidiary engaged in the manufacture and sale of these typesetters and in other computer services.

Volt also started a school at its New York City headquarters in 1966 to teach computer programming and operation. By the 1970s it was developing and administering education and training programs for government and community agencies and industrial concerns. Nevertheless, as the military buildup in Vietnam waned, the company's revenues dropped from $45 million in fiscal 1969 to $33 million in fiscal 1970, during which it lost $1.4 million. Volt lost $3.4 million on only $27 million in revenues in fiscal 1971. It returned to the black in fiscal 1972 but lost money again in fiscal 1973, a year in which the stock fell to below $1 a share. The company's fortunes then turned around, and in the latter years of the decade it had net income as high as $9 million a year. In 1980, when Volt earned $9.3 million on revenues of $171.4 million, a share of its stock traded as high as $40.

Autologic became Volt's Electronic Pre-Press Equipment Division. By 1979 its APS-5 state-of-the-art cold-type photo-typesetter was the world's leading digital cathode-ray-tube typesetter, with output speed of up to 3,000 lines a minute. More than 400 of these machines and those of the earlier APS-4 model had been sold. Volt itself was using this equipment to photocompose telephone directories, technical documents, and other publications produced by its various service divisions.

The company's Technical Publications Division installed Autologic's new text-management system in 1978 and immediately put it to use in the preparation of quick-reaction proposals for customers bidding on government contracts. Next the system was applied to the processing of large complex databases, such as those involved in the preparation and updating of operations-and-maintenance manuals for defense and aerospace products.

Volt's Technical Services Division, enhanced by systems analysts, programmers, and terminal operators, was using computer storage devices and microfilm and microfiche in addition to the printed page to record technical information. Systems developed by Volt now were capable of merging graphics and artwork with tax material in computer-indexed files for storage, display, and transmission in a variety of modes.

Volt believed its telephone directory systems to be the most advanced in use, offering telephone companies substantial savings in product costs and higher directory advertising revenue. The key feature in systems being developed by Volt for these companies was distributed processing. The telephone company processed changes to its tariff structure and transmitted them to the master database maintained by Volt. These changes were further processed by Volt to produce updates to the many telephone network documents affected by tariff modifications. The first long-term contract for these services was signed in 1978.

Volt's Contract Services Group was providing its clients with technical and professional personnel for assignments around the world. These personnel included systems analysts, programmers, computer operators, and technical writers, editors, and illustrators. Volt took care of all administration, salaries, payroll taxes, and fringe benefits, with the client paying a fixed dollar rate for each hour actually worked. The Temporary Personnel Group was a source for all kinds of temporary office and industrial help, including clerks, secretaries and word processors, keypunch operators, bookkeepers and accountants, communications and marketing specialists, truck drivers, forklift operators, welders, and assemblers.

Mixed Fortunes: 1980–95

In 1980 Autologic introduced APS-Micro 5, a high-speed digital typesetter aimed at the mid-range market with a selling price of less than $50,000. Also that year, Volt acquired Delta Resources Inc., a subsidiary of Itel Corp. It formed a subsidiary, Volt Delta Resources Inc., to continue the acquired company's operations, which consisted of designing and leasing customized computer systems for telephone directory assistance. By fiscal 1983 Volt Delta Resources was accounting for 36 percent of the parent company's profits on only 12 percent of its sales.

Volt had record net income of $16.8 million in fiscal 1983 and $13 million in fiscal 1984. In the latter year, however, Autologic lost money. Autologic was producing the typesetting systems used by many of the nation's biggest newspapers, including the *New York Times, Los Angeles Times,* and *USA Today,* but it was falling behind the curve as publishers began to switch to desktop publishing. Moreover, the parent company was incurring heavy interest costs as its long-term debt swelled to a record $124.3 million in 1984. Even as its revenues continued to climb, Volt lost money in fiscal 1985 and 1986. The following year it was back in the black, but Autologic lost $27.5 million.

After three profitable years, Volt lost $1.9 million in fiscal 1990 because of a variety of problems, including military cutbacks following the end of the cold war and cost overruns on contracts associated with entering new markets. The Technical Publication Services Division, aimed particularly at companies in defense and aerospace, fell into debt, discarded its full-service reproduction and printing operations, and was discontinued in 1991.

On the favorable side, Autologic returned to profitability, recording a fat $10.5 million profit in fiscal 1991 on only 12 percent of the parent company's sales. In addition, Volt's group for producing telephone directories and installing equipment for telephone companies had entered new areas. During the mid-1980s it created a joint venture with a subsidiary of Southwestern Bell Publications to sell telephone directory advertising for most of Australia. In addition, in 1987 it formed a company with a subsidiary of Pacific Bell Directory to centralize and automate directory operations for telephone books published in California and Nevada. Both ventures proved profitable, especially the Australian operation. By 1993 Volt also was putting out the entire telephone book in Uruguay, handling advertising sales and prepress preparation as well as the printing.

Volt also was installing the computers necessary for telephone company information systems. By 1993 it had such systems installed for American Telephone & Telegraph Co., GTE Corp., NYNEX Corp., Pacific Telesis Group, and other customers.

By 1994 Volt had a licensing partnership with Bolt, Beranek & Newman Inc., a supplier of speech recognition technology, that allowed a computer to respond to spoken words—such as locations and company names—without human assistance on Volt's automated systems. The biggest share of the company's revenues (60 percent in fiscal 1992) continued to come, however, from the division in charge of technical services and temporary personnel. Volt had developed a database for placing technical personnel that was one of the largest in the country.

Dragging down the parent company's earnings—and helping account for a $2.7 million loss in fiscal 1993—was Volt's construction and engineering division, which lost money three years in a row before turning profitable in 1994. The computer systems unit, supplying hardware and networking equipment, mainly to telephone companies, also lost money in 1993 and 1994 before making a profit in 1995. The telephone directory business, with major investments in Brazil (acquired in 1994) as well as Uruguay, still was losing money in 1995, however. In January 1997 Volt sold its interest in Telelistas Editors Ltda., the Brazilian company that had printed Rio de Janeiro's telephone listings. Later that year it sold its part of the Australian joint venture. In 1995 Volt merged Autologic with a competitor, Information International, Inc., and spun off the new unit, retaining 59 percent of the business.

Renewed Prosperity in the Mid-to-Late 1990s

Volt's rebound in the mid-1990s was outstanding. Revenues increased from $734.5 million in fiscal 1994 to $1.42 billion in fiscal 1997, and net income also rose sharply each year, from $11.8 million to $39.9 million. Technical services and temporary personnel, especially the high-tech staffing unit, continued to be Volt's biggest revenue generator and was also its chief source of profits. This division accounted for 72 percent of sales and 51 percent of operating profits in fiscal 1997. Corporate downsizing and a shortage of high-tech personnel in virtually every industry had made the company one of the nation's ten largest temporary staffing companies, with clients that included Microsoft Corp., Hewlett Packard, and Pacific Telesis.

Volt's Telecommunications Services segment was its second largest source of business, accounting for ten percent of sales and 31 percent of operating profit in fiscal 1997. This segment included Voltecon, a nationwide full-service provider of telecommunications services, including engineering, design, construction, installation, maintenance, removals, and distribution of telecommunications products. It also consisted of Advanced Technology Services, a division established in 1994 to meet the challenges of the "information superhighway" and the merging of voice, data, and video services to telephony, broadband, and other providers of information system services.

The Telephone Directory segment was Volt's third biggest in fiscal 1997, accounting for six percent of its sales and 15 percent of its operating profit. This segment consisted of the division responsible for the production, licensing, commercial printing, database management, sales and marketing services, and contract management software systems to telephone directory and other advertising media publishers, as well as for Volt's own (through the DataNational division) publishing of 67 telephone directories in seven states. The Uruguay unit was printing telephone directories in Argentina and Brazil as well as performing commercial printing in all three countries.

The Electronic Publication and Typesetting Systems segment consisted of Autologic Information International, Inc. Volt's share in this subsidiary accounted for six percent of its sales and 2.5 percent of its operating profit in fiscal 1997. Autologic's products were computerized imagesetting and publication systems equipment and software to automate the various prepress production steps in the publishing process.

The Computer Systems segment accounted for five percent of Volt's sales but less than one percent of its operating profit in fiscal 1997. Through Volt Delta Resources and Volt VIEWtech, it was designing, developing, selling, leasing, and maintaining computer-based directory assistance and other database management and telecommunications systems and related services for the telecommunications industry. It also was providing services, principally computer-based projects, to public utilities.

Volt's stock traded as high as $70 per share during 1997. William Shaw continued to be chairman, president, and chief executive officer of the company, and Jerome Shaw was executive vice-president and secretary. In early 1998 William Shaw owned 24.6 percent of the common stock, Jerome Shaw owned 21.3 percent, and institutions owned about 34 percent. The long-term debt was $55.4 million at the end of fiscal 1997.

Principal Subsidiaries

Autologic Information International, Inc. (59%); DataNational, Inc.; Shaw & Shaw, Inc.; Tainol, S.A. (Uruguay); Volt Delta Resources, Inc.; Volt Holding Corp.; Volt Real Estate Corporation; Volt Technical Corp.; Volt Temporary Services, Inc.; Volt Viewtech, Inc.

Principal Operating Units

Advanced Technologies, Research & Development; Advanced Technology Services; Autologic Information International,

Inc.; DataNational; Directory Systems/Services; Shaw & Shaw; Uruguay; Volt Delta Resources; Volt Services Group; Volt VIEWtech; Voltelcon.

Further Reading

Agovino, Theresa, "Volt's Red Ink Makes Analysts Skittish," *Crain's New York Business,* March 18, 1991, p. 16.

"Alphanumeric Transfers 30% Stakes in 2 Firms to Volt Information," *Wall Street Journal,* April 26, 1972, p. 6.

Loehwing, David A., "No Pi in the Sky," *Barron's,* May 15, 1972, p. 3.

McNatt, Robert, "Economy on Mend Giving Firm Voltage," *Crain's New York Business,* February 8, 1993, pp. 3, 30.

Messina, Judith, "Deregulation Puts a Jolt into Lethargic Volt," *Crain's New York Business,* August 5, 1996, pp. 3, 31.

Morgan, Mary, "Volt Claims Gains Despite Objections," *Rochester Business Journal,* August 26, 1994, p. 2.

"New Lease on Life," *Barron's,* April 25, 1966, pp. 5, 14.

Rosenberg, Jim, "Autologic to Merge with Triple-I," *Editor & Publisher,* July 8, 1995, p. 28.

Storch, Harvey B., "Volt Information Sciences," *Wall Street Transcript,* April 2, 1979, p. 53,848.

—Robert Halasz

Wal-Mart Stores, Inc.

702 Southwest 8th Street
Bentonville, Arkansas 72716-8611
U.S.A.
(501) 273-4000
Fax: (501) 273-6850
Web site: http://www.wal-mart.com

Public Company
Incorporated: 1969
Employees: 825,000
Sales: $117.96 billion (1998)
Stock Exchanges: New York Pacific
Ticker Symbol: WMT
SICs: 5331 Variety Stores; 5311 Department Stores;
    5411 Grocery Stores

Wal-Mart Stores, Inc. is the largest retailer in the world, the fourth largest company overall in the United States, and the nation's largest nongovernmental employer. The retail giant's domestic operations include 1,921 Wal-Mart discount stores (located in all 50 states); 441 Wal-Mart Supercenters, which are combined discount outlets and grocery stores (and which make Wal-Mart one of the country's top food retailers); and 443 Sam's Clubs, the number two U.S. warehouse membership club chain (trailing Costco). International operations, which were commenced only in 1991, include Wal-Mart format stores in Canada and Puerto Rico; Wal-Mart Supercenters in Argentina, Brazil, Mexico, and China; and Sam's Clubs in Argentina, Brazil, Mexico, Puerto Rico, and China. In Mexico, Wal-Mart also operates Aurreras combination stores, Bodegas discount stores, Suburbias specialty department stores, Superamas supermarkets, and Vips restaurants. The company has also established operations in Germany and Korea. In all, one-fifth of Wal-Mart's stores are located outside the United States.

Development of a "Good Concept" in the 1960s

Founder Samuel Walton—who at his death in 1992 was among the richest people in the United States—graduated from the University of Missouri in 1940 with a degree in economics and became a management trainee with J.C. Penney Company. After two years he went into the army. Upon returning to civilian life three years later, he used his savings and a loan to open a Ben Franklin variety store in Newport, Arkansas. In 1950 he lost his lease, moved to Bentonville, Arkansas, and opened another store. By the late 1950s, Sam and his brother J.L. (Bud) Walton owned nine Ben Franklin franchises.

In the early 1960s Sam Walton took what he had learned from studying mass-merchandising techniques around the country and began to make his mark in the retail market. He decided that small-town populations would welcome, and make profitable, large discount shopping stores. He approached the Ben Franklin franchise owners with his proposal to slash prices significantly and operate at a high volume, but they were not willing to let him reduce merchandise as low as he insisted it had to go. The Walton brothers then decided to go into that market themselves and opened their first Wal-Mart Discount City in Rogers, Arkansas, in 1962. The brothers typically opened their department-sized stores in towns with populations of 5,000 to 25,000, and the stores tended to draw from a large radius. "We discovered people would drive to a good concept," Walton later recalled in a 1989 article in *Financial World.*

Wal-Mart's "good concept" involved huge stores offering customers a wide variety of name-brand goods at deep discounts that were part of an "everyday low prices" strategy. Walton was able to keep prices low and still turn a profit through sales volume as well as an uncommon marketing strategy. Wal-Mart's advertising costs generally amounted to one-third that of other discount chains; most competitors were putting on sales and running from 50 to 100 advertising circulars per year, but Wal-Mart kept its prices low and only ran 12 promotions a year.

By the end of the 1960s the brothers had opened 18 Wal-Mart stores, while still owning 15 Ben Franklin franchises throughout Arkansas, Missouri, Kansas, and Oklahoma. These ventures became incorporated as Wal-Mart Stores, Inc., in October 1969.

The 1970s held many milestones for the company. Early in the decade, Walton implemented his warehouse distribution strategy. The company built its own warehouses so it could buy in volume and store the merchandise, then proceeded to build stores throughout 200-square-mile areas around the distribution points. This practice cut Wal-Mart's costs and gave it more control over operations; merchandise could be restocked as quickly as it sold, and advertising was specific to smaller regions and cost less to distribute.

Wal-Mart went public in 1970, initially trading over the counter; in 1972 the company was listed on the New York Stock Exchange. By 1976 the Waltons had phased out their Ben Franklin stores so that the company could put all of its expansion efforts into the Wal-Mart stores. In 1977 the company made its first significant acquisition when it bought 16 Mohr-Value stores in Missouri and Illinois. Also in 1977, based on data from the previous five years, *Forbes* ranked the nation's discount and variety stores, and Wal-Mart ranked first in return on equity, return on capital, sales growth, and earnings growth.

In 1978 Wal-Mart began operating its own pharmacy, auto service center, and jewelry divisions, and acquired Hutchenson Shoe Company, a shoe-department lease operation. By 1979 there were 276 Wal-Mart stores in 11 states. Sales had gone from $44 million in 1970 to $1.25 billion in 1979.

Sam's Clubs Are Established in 1983

Wal-Mart sales growth continued into the 1980s. In 1983 the company opened its first three Sam's Wholesale Clubs and began its expansion into bigger-city markets. Business at the 100,000-square-foot cash-and-carry discount membership warehouses proved to be good; the company had 148 such clubs by 1991, by which time the name had been shortened to Sam's Clubs.

The company continued to grow rapidly. In 1987 Wal-Mart acquired 18 Supersaver Wholesale Clubs, which became Sam's Clubs. The most significant event of that year, however, was the opening of a new Wal-Mart's merchandising concept—taken from one originated by a French entrepreneur—that Walton called Hypermart USA. Hypermart USA stores combined a grocery store, a general merchandise market, and such service outlets as restaurants, banks, shoe shine kiosks, and videotape

rental units in a space that covered more area than six football fields. Prices were reduced as much as 40 percent below full retail level, and sales volume averaged $1 million per week, compared to $200,000 for a conventional-sized discount store.

Making customers feel at home in such a large-scale shopping facility required inventiveness. The Dallas store had phone hot lines installed in the aisles for customers needing directions. Hypermart floors were made of a rubbery surface for ease in walking, and the stores offered electric shopping carts for the disabled. To entertain children, there was a ''ball pit'' or playroom filled with plastic balls—an idea taken from Swedish furniture retailer Ikea.

Hypermart Evolves into the Wal-Mart Supercenter

There were also wrinkles to work out. Costs for air conditioning and heating the gigantic spaces were higher than expected. Traffic congestion and limited parking proved a drawback. Customers also complained that the grocery section was not as well-stocked or maintained as it needed to be to compete against nearby grocery stores. Wal-Mart began addressing these problems by, for example, redesigning the grocery section of the Arlington, Texas, store. Wal-Mart also opened five smaller ''supercenters''—averaging around 150,000 square feet—featuring a large selection of merchandise and offering better-stocked grocery sections, without the outside services such as restaurants or video stores. These stores, dubbed Wal-Mart Supercenters, proved much more successful than the Hypermart format, which was eventually abandoned. Hundreds of Supercenters were subsequently opened during the 1990s.

Wal-Mart received some criticism during this period for its buying practices. One analyst, according to an article in the January 30, 1989 edition of *Fortune,* described the treatment sales representatives received at Wal-Mart: ''Once you are ushered into one of the spartan little buyer's rooms, expect a steely eye across the table and be prepared to cut your price.'' Wal-Mart was known not only for dictating the tone with its vendors, but often for only dealing directly with the vendor, bypassing sales representatives. In 1987, 100,000 independent manufacturers representatives initiated a public information campaign to fight Wal-Mart's effort to remove them from the selling process, claiming that their elimination jeopardized a manufacturer's right to choose how it sells its products.

During this time, however, Wal-Mart's revenues kept going up, and the company moved into new territory. Wal-Mart enjoyed a 12-year streak of 35 percent annual profit growth through 1987. In 1988 the company operated in 24 states—concentrated in the Midwest and South—1,182 stores, 90 wholesale clubs, and two hypermarts. President and Chief Executive Officer David D. Glass, who had been with the company since 1976, was a key player in Wal-Mart's expansion.

In a move motivated by good business sense and public relations efforts, Wal-Mart sent an open letter to U.S. manufacturers in March 1985 inviting them to take part in a ''Buy-American'' program. The company offered to work with them in producing products that could compete against imports. ''Our American suppliers must commit to improving their facilities and machinery, remain financially conservative and work to fill our requirements, and most importantly, strive to improve employee productivity,'' Walton told *Nation's Business* in April 1988. Product conversions—arranging to buy competitively priced U.S.-made goods in place of imports—were regularly highlighted at weekly managers' meetings. William R. Fields, executive vice-president of merchandise and sales, estimated that Wal-Mart cut imports by approximately five percent between 1985 and 1989. Nonetheless, analysts estimated that Wal-Mart still purchased between 25 and 30 percent of its goods from overseas, about twice the percentage of competitor Kmart Corporation.

Criticism for Small Town Impact in the 1990s

Wal-Mart also came under criticism for its impact on small retail businesses. Independent store owners often went out of business when Wal-Mart came to town, unable to compete with the superstore's economies of scale. In fact, Iowa State University economist Kenneth Stone conducted a study on this phenomenon and told the *New York Times Magazine* (April 2, 1989): ''If you go into towns in Illinois where Wal-Mart has been for 8 or 10 years, the downtowns are just ghost towns.'' He found that businesses suffering most were drug, hardware, five-and-dime, sporting goods, clothing, and fabric stores, while major appliance and furniture businesses picked up, as did restaurants and gasoline stations, due to increased traffic.

Nevertheless, Wal-Mart developed a record of community service. The company began awarding $1,000 scholarships to high school students in each community Wal-Mart served. At the same time, the company's refusal to stock dozens of widely circulated adult and teen magazines, including *Rolling Stone,* had some critics claiming that Wal-Mart was willfully narrowing the choices of the buying public by bowing to pressure from conservative special interest groups.

In 1990 Wal-Mart added its first stores in California, Nevada, North Dakota, Pennsylvania, South Dakota, and Utah. The company also opened 25 Sam's Clubs, of which four were 130,000-square-foot prototypes incorporating space for produce, meats, and baked goods. In mid-1990, the company acquired Western Merchandise, Inc., of Amarillo, Texas, a supplier of music, books, and video products to many of the Wal-Mart stores. Late in 1990 Wal-Mart acquired the McLane Company, Inc., a distributor of grocery and retail products based in Temple, Texas. Early in 1991 The Wholesale Club, Inc. of Indianapolis merged with Sam's Clubs, adding 28 stores that were to be integrated with Sam's by year-end. Also, Wal-Mart agreed to sell its nine convenience store-gas station outlets to Conoco Inc.

Wal-Mart's expansion continued, and by 1992 the company opened about 150 new Wal-Mart stores and 60 Sam's Clubs, bringing the total to 1,720 Wal-Mart stores and 208 Sam's Clubs. Some of these stores represented a change in policy for the company, opening near big cities with large populations. Another policy change was instituted by the company when it announced that it would no longer deal with independent sales representatives.

In 1991 Wal-Mart introduced its new store brand, Sam's American Choice, the first products for which were such beverages as colas and fruit juices. The beverages were made by

Canada's largest private-label bottler, Cott Corp., but the colas were supplied from U.S. plants. Future plans called for the introduction of many different types of products that would match the quality of national brands, but at lower prices.

Expanding Outside the United States in 1991

Also in 1991 Wal-Mart ventured outside the United States for the first time when it entered into a joint venture with Cifra, S.A. de C.V., Mexico's largest retailer. The venture developed a price-club store called Club Aurrera which required an annual membership of about $25. Shoppers could choose from about 3,500 products ranging from fur coats to frozen vegetables. Within the year, the joint venture operated three Club Aurreras, four Bodegas discount stores, and one Aurrera combination store.

Expansion in the United States also continued, and from 1992 to 1993, 161 Wal-Mart stores were opened, while only one was closed. Another 48 Sam's Clubs and 51 Bud's Warehouse Outlets were also opened. Expansions or relocations took place at 170 Wal-Mart stores and 40 Sam's Clubs. All told, there was a net addition of 34.5 thousand square feet of retail space. By 1993 the 2,138 stores included 34 Wal-Mart Supercenters and 256 Sam's Clubs.

Founder Sam Walton died on April 5, 1992, of bone cancer. A fairly smooth management transition at Wal-Mart ensued, since Walton had already hand-picked his successor, David Glass, who had served as CEO since 1988.

In January 1993 Wal-Mart's reputation was shaken when a report on NBC-TV's *Dateline* news program reported on child laborers in Bangladesh producing merchandise for Wal-Mart stores. The program showed children working for five cents an hour in a country that lacked child labor laws. The program further alleged that items made outside the United States were being sold under ''Made in USA'' signs as part of the company's Buy American campaign instituted in 1985. Glass appeared on the program saying that he did not know of any ''child exploitation'' by the company, but did apologize about some of the signs incorrectly promoting foreign-made products as domestic items.

In April 1993 Wal-Mart introduced another private label, called Great Value. The brand was initially used for a line of 350 packaged food items for sale in its supercenter stores. The proceeds from the company's other private label, Sam's American Choice, were to be channeled into the Competitive Edge Scholarship Fund, which the company launched in 1993 in partnership with some vendors and colleges. In the same year, Wal-Mart purchased 91 Pace Membership Warehouse clubs from Kmart, which had decided to shut down the Pace chain. Wal-Mart subsequently converted the new units into Sam's Clubs. The Sam's Club chain was thereby solidified—particularly in California, where it gained 21 stores—soon after the emergence of a rival, PriceCostco Inc. The product of the October 1993 merger of Price Co. and Costco Wholesale Corp., Price Costco—later renamed Costco Cos.—would within a few years overtake the Sam's Club chain as the nation's top warehouse membership club.

Mid-1990s Growth Slowdown

In the mid-1990s Wal-Mart continued to grow in the United States, but at a slower pace than previous years. Whereas the company had always posted double-digit, comparable stores, sales increases, starting in fiscal 1994 these sales increases had fallen to levels closer to the retail industry average—four to seven percent. Furthermore, overall net sales had typically risen 25 percent or more per year in the 1980s and early 1990s. For fiscal years 1996, 1997, and 1998, however, net sales increased 13 percent, 12 percent, and 12 percent, respectively. The company was beginning to reach the limits of expansion in its domestic market. This was reflected in the scaling back of the Wal-Mart discount store chain, which reached a peak of 1,995 units in 1996 before being reduced to 1,921 units by 1998. The company staked its domestic future on the Wal-Mart Supercenter chain, which was expanded from 34 units in 1993 to 441 units in 1998. Most of the new Supercenters—377 in total—were converted Wal-Mart discount stores, as the company sought the additional per-store revenue that could be gleaned from selling groceries. Meanwhile, the Sam's Club chain was struggling and was not as profitable as the company overall. As it attempted to turn this unit around, Wal-Mart curtailed its expansion in the United States; there were only 17 more Sam's Clubs in 1998 than there were in 1995.

Another vehicle for company growth was aggressive international expansion. Following its earlier move into Mexico, Wal-Mart entered into the other NAFTA market in 1994 when it purchased 122 Woolco stores in Canada from Woolworth Corporation. Over the next few years Wal-Mart entered Argentina, Brazil, and China through joint ventures. By 1997 Wal-Mart had set up several joint ventures with its Mexican partner, Cifra. That year, these joint ventures were merged together and then merged into Cifra. Wal-Mart then took a controlling, 51 percent stake in Cifra for $1.2 billion. The company thereby held a majority stake in the largest retailer in Mexico, whose 402 stores included 27 Wal-Mart Supercenters, 28 Sam's Clubs, and 347 units consisting of several chains, including Bodegas discount stores, Superamas grocery stores, and Vips restaurants.

In December 1997 Wal-Mart entered Europe for the first time when it acquired the 21-unit Wertkauf hypermarket chain in Germany. The Wertkauf format was similar to that of the Wal-Mart Supercenter. The profitable Wertkauf chain had annual sales of about $1.4 billion and was the eighth largest hypermarket operator in Germany. Also in December 1997 Wal-Mart bought out its minority partner in its Brazilian joint venture, which by that time ran five Wal-Mart Supercenters and three Sam's Clubs. By early 1998 the company also operated nine Wal-Mart Supercenters and five Sam's Clubs in Puerto Rico. Later that year Wal-Mart announced plans to triple its retail base in China by the end of 1999, aiming for a total of nine stores at that time. Moreover, in July 1998 the company announced that it had purchased a majority stake in four stores and six additional development sites in Korea, extending its expansion in Asia. Around this same time, however, a Wal-Mart expansion into the troubled nation of Indonesia under a franchise agreement appeared to have failed.

During fiscal 1997 Wal-Mart's international operations were profitable for the first time. By 1998 international sales had reached $7.5 billion, an impressive figure given that the company had only begun its foreign expansion in 1991; still this figure represented only 6.4 percent of overall sales. Although growth in sales at home were slowing down, Wal-Mart managed to exceed the $100 billion mark in overall revenues for the first time during fiscal 1997 and that year also gained further prestige through its selection as one of the 30 companies on the Dow Jones Industrial Average, a replacement for the troubled Woolworth.

As another possible outlet for shoring up its top position in retailing in the United States and for increasing sales amid its reaching the saturation point for its Supercenters, Wal-Mart in late 1998 began testing a new format, the Wal-Mart Neighborhood Market. In an attempt to compete directly with traditional supermarkets and with convenience stores, this new concept consisted of a 40,000-square-foot store offering produce, deli foods, fresh meats, other grocery items, and a limited selection of general merchandise. The new store also featured a drive-through pharmacy. The company hoped that the Neighborhood Market would allow it to penetrate markets unable to support the huge 100,000-square-foot Supercenters, such as very small towns and certain sections within metropolitan areas. Even if this attempt to penetrate the grocery sector ended in failure, Wal-Mart was sure to remain a giant retailer representing stiff competition for others in the industry.

Principal Subsidiaries

Wal-Mart Stores East, Inc.; Sam's West, Inc.; Sam's East, Inc.; Wal-Mart Property Company; Sam's Property Company; McLane Company, Inc.; Cifra, S.A. de C.V. (Mexico; 51%).

Further Reading

Bowermaster, Jon, "When Wal-Mart Comes to Town," *New York Times Magazine,* April 2, 1989.

Donlon, J.P., "A Glass Act," *Chief Executive,* July/August 1995, pp. 40+.

Fitzgerald, Kate, "Suppliers Rallying Against Negative 'Dateline' Report," *Advertising Age,* January 4, 1993, pp. 3, 38.

Friedland, Jonathan, and Louise Lee, "The Wal-Mart Way Sometimes Gets Lost in Translation Overseas," *Wall Street Journal,* October 8, 1997, pp. A1, A12.

Kelly, Kevin, "Wal-Mart Gets Lost in the Vegetable Aisle," *Business Week,* May 28, 1990.

Koepp, Stephen, "Make That Sale, Mr. Sam," *Time,* May 18, 1987.

Laing, Jonathan R., "Super-Saviors," *Barron's,* May 6, 1996, pp. 17–19.

Lee, Louise, "Discounter Wal-Mart Is Catering to Affluent to Maintain Growth," *Wall Street Journal,* February 7, 1996, pp. A1, A8.

——, "Facing Superstore Saturation, Wal-Mart Thinks Small," *Wall Street Journal,* March 25, 1998, pp. B1, B8.

Malkin, Elisabeth, "Warehouse Stores Move into Mexico," *Advertising Age,* January 18, 1993, p. 13.

Nelson, Emily, "Why Wal-Mart Sings, 'Yes, We Have Bananas!'," *Wall Street Journal,* October 6, 1998, pp. B1, B4.

Ortega, Bob, *In Sam We Trust: The Untold Story of Sam Walton and How Wal-Mart Is Devouring America,* New York: Times Business, 1998.

Ortega, Bob, and Christina Duff, "Kmart Will Sell 91 Warehouse Clubs to Wal-Mart, Shut Rest of Pace Chain," *Wall Street Journal,* November 3, 1993, p. A4.

Saporito, Bill, "And the Winner Is Still . . . Wal-Mart," *Fortune,* May 2, 1994, pp. 62 +.

——, "David Glass Won't Crack Under Fire," *Fortune,* February 8, 1993, pp. 75 +.

——, "Is Wal-Mart Unstoppable?," *Fortune,* May 6, 1991, pp. 50–59.

Schwartz, Nelson D., "Why Wall Street's Buying Wal-Mart Again," *Fortune,* February 16, 1998, pp. 92 +.

Sellers, Patricia, "Can Wal-Mart Get Back the Magic?," *Fortune,* April 29, 1996, pp. 130 +.

Sparks, Debra, "Life After Sam," *Financial World,* December 6, 1994, pp. 52, 54.

Trimble, Vance H., *Sam Walton: The Inside Story of America's Richest Man,* New York: Penguin, 1990, 319 p.

Vance, Sandra S., and Roy V. Scott, *Wal-Mart: A History of Sam Walton's Retail Phenomenon,* New York: Twayne, 1994, 220 p.

"Wal-Mart: Will It Take Over the World?," *Fortune,* January 30, 1989.

Walton, Sam, with John Huey, *Sam Walton, Made in America: My Story,* New York: Doubleday, 1992, 269 p.

"Walton's Mountain," *Nation's Business,* April 1988.

Zellner, Wendy, "A Grand Reopening for Wal-Mart," *Business Week,* February 9, 1998, pp. 86, 88.

——, "The Sam's Generation," *Business Week,* November 25, 1991, pp. 36–38.

Zellner, Wendy, et al, "Wal-Mart Spoken Here," *Business Week,* June 23, 1997, pp. 138–41, 143–44.

—Carole Healy and Dorothy Kroll
—updated by David E. Salamie

Weirton Steel Corporation

400 Three Springs Drive
Weirton, West Virginia 26062-4989
U.S.A.
(304) 797-2000
Fax: (304) 797-2171
Web site: http://www.weirton.com

Public Company
Incorporated: 1982
Employees: 4,873
Sales: $1.40 billion (1997)
Stock Exchanges: New York
Ticker Symbol: WS
SICs: 3312 Steel Works & Blast Furnaces; 3316 Cold
    Rolled Steel Sheet, Strip & Bars

The fortunes of Weirton, West Virginia, a quintessential company town, have fallen and risen with those of Weirton Steel Corporation. A huge steel plant founded there in 1909 became part of National Steel Corporation in 1929, but decades later, in the 1970s, when National Steel faced a declining economy and a declining steel industry, Weirton Steel's future looked grim. In 1983 Weirton Steel's employees saved their town and their company with an innovative employee-takeover plan. In 1984 Weirton Steel became the largest employee-owned company in the nation, enjoying initial success in the later 1980s before running into difficulties in the 1990s. In 1989 Weirton Steel sold about 23 percent of its stock to the public; employees retained the remaining stock. A second offering in 1994 reduced the employee stake to about 49 percent. Weirton is the nation's eighth largest integrated steel company and the largest producer of tin-coated steel. The company is a partner in several joint ventures: with U.K.-based Balli Group plc, it markets and sells Weirton steel products worldwide; with Dutch company Koninklijke Hoogovens NV, it operates a galvanizing plant in Indiana; and with ATAS International, it produces residential steel roofing.

The Creation of a Company Town

In 1905 Ernest Tener Weir, a Pittsburgh, Pennsylvania-area steel employee, enlisted a partner to buy the Phillips Sheet and Tin Plate Company, an ailing steel company in Clarksburg, West Virginia. The plant flourished under Weir's stewardship, and within four years he was looking for a new site to accommodate expansion. The site would have to have access to coal mines, water sources, river and rail transportation, and centers of industry.

Weir found his ideal industrial site in the northern finger of West Virginia that separates Ohio and Pennsylvania, about 39 miles from Pittsburgh. In 1909 Weir began building on 105 acres he purchased near the hamlet of Hollidays Cove. By the end of the year, Weir had ten steel mills operating, and mill workers had started to come in from as far away as Greece and Italy.

The boom continued throughout the decade. By 1920, more than 15,000 people lived in the area. As growth continued, Hollidays Cove expanded rapidly and new communities like Weirton, Weirton Heights, and Marland Heights sprang up nearby. In 1947 all these villages would be incorporated into the city of Weirton.

The vast majority of the town's residents worked in Weir's mills. In return, Ernest Weir met many of their needs. He built homes, supplied utilities, and provided police and fire protection during the town's early decades. Later, he would build churches, a library, and leisure facilities for the use of his employees.

The expansion of the city coincided with the expansion of Weir's mills. In 1910, ten more mills were added. In 1911, Weir acquired the 12-mill Pope Tin Plate Company in Steubenville, Ohio, and in 1915 and 1916, two more hot mills were constructed at Weir's strip steel plant. Weirton's facility thus became the flagship of Weir's enterprise, and in 1918 Weir named his concern Weirton Steel.

Formation of National Steel, 1929

The firm grew throughout the 1910s and 1920s, as expansion allowed the plant to verge toward vertical integration. In 1923, the Weirton coke plant went into operation. In the following years, new furnaces, hearths, and river docks were constructed. In 1925 Weir incorporated Weirton Steel Company. In 1929 Weirton Steel Company merged with Great Lakes Steel Corpo-

Company Perspectives:

Weirton Steel is rich in tradition with a long history of solid performance in an always-competitive industry. Weirton Steel has matured through the decades and today is a modern, high-tech producer of quality steel. And while we are proud of past accomplishments, today we are focused on the future.

ration and Hanna Iron Ore Company to form National Steel Corporation, which immediately became one of the nation's largest steelmakers. Henceforth, Weirton Steel became a subsidiary of National Steel, although it retained its own administration and management, with Weir continuing as chairman and J.C. Williams as president.

Although Weirton Steel workers certainly benefited from Weir's largesse, relations between management and the workforce were often less than harmonious. During the 1920s, Weir successfully fended off the growing unions from his plants. In the 1930s, however, Weir was confronted with twin challenges: the bitter strikes that plagued mines and mills all through Appalachia, and New Deal legislation and institutions that were intended to protect laborers.

The Great Depression wrought havoc in the steel industry; demand for steel declined steadily, causing industry retrenchment. As New Deal measures helped bring about a recovery, labor problems, and not production records, put Weirton Steel in the news in 1933. In the midst of a strike, nearly 1,000 workers were repulsed by tear-gas bombs when they tried to stop cars carrying workers from Weirton Steel's Steubenville plant.

Weir had refused at first to submit to arbitration, but the National Labor Board, led by Senator Robert Wagner, gave the Weirton Steel workers a public hearing, and helped obtain an agreement that allowed the workers to return to their jobs and elect representatives. Striking workers also ended a long strike without explicit recognition of their union. Weir found a way around the established unions by forming the Weirton Independent Union. For many years, Weirton Steel paid the salaries of that union's officials.

In 1936 T.E. Millsop, who had been with Weirton Steel since 1926, was named president upon Williams's death, continuing a tradition of promoting from within. In fact, throughout the many decades that National Steel controlled Weirton Steel, Weirton Steel employees were generally chosen to lead the company.

In 1938 Weirton turned over its idle Clarksburg plant to the local chamber of commerce. Weir's original tin-plate plant had become obsolete because of increased freight charges, outdated machinery, and expansion of the Weirton and Steubenville plants. That same year, in an attempt to modernize further, Weirton Steel built a quality-control laboratory opposite the company's main office.

During World War II, the steel industry adapted to help the nation's war effort. In 1942 the War Production Board appealed to the steel industry to devise plans to increase and tailor output for army use. In March of that year, Weirton Steel became the first member of the steel industry to respond, establishing a special plant committee, and soliciting suggestions from employees. When the War Production Board ordered a reduction in tin-plate operations, Weir, now chairman of National Steel Corporation, shut down Weirton Steel's Steubenville plant in October 1942. Partly because of the rush to meet the war effort, Weirton Steel made new records in 1942, twice establishing world records for steel ingot production, and producing an average of 5,080 net tons of ingot steel a day. In 1945 Weirton was fined after the company pleaded no contest to a charge of obtaining critical materials in order to build an emergency hospital but instead using the items for air conditioning at a company-owned country club.

The economy and the steel industry shifted gears after World War II. President Harry S. Truman called on the steel industry to expand its capacity, produce more steel, and lower prices, but industry officials resisted. Still, the 1950s and 1960s brought almost continuous growth and expansion for Weirton Steel. New blast furnaces, products, and production methods were developed. In 1960 Weirton continued its commitment to research by beginning construction on a steel research center. Concerns about pollution inspired new measures, such as the institution of open hearth smoke controls in 1963 and studies on the environmental effects of steel production.

Declining Fortunes for the Steel Industry

By the time Ernest Weir died in 1957, there were signs of bad times ahead for the steel industry. Throughout the 1950s, for example, total U.S. steel exports remained static, and the nation's share of the world steel trade dropped from 53.6 percent in 1947 to 6.9 percent in 1960. Most of this decline was the result of postwar reconstruction in Japan and Europe and these countries' reintegration into the world economy, and not to a decline in steel use. Instead of relying on domestic steel producers, U.S. industrial firms imported increasing quantities of steel from abroad. In fact, between 1950 and 1965, total U.S. imports of steel grew from 1,077 tons to 10,383 tons.

The rise in imports, coupled with mounting labor costs, crippled the U.S. steel industry. Debates raged between the industry and the government over the imposition of price controls and the enactment of protectionist measures. In 1969 the federal government finally imposed import quotas for foreign steel.

Throughout the 1960s, Weirton Steel developed new products and production methods. In 1967 the company began making basic oxygen steel. In 1968, Weirton Steel inaugurated its continuous casting process, which represented a fundamental change in production technique. A new four-strand slab caster boosted production, efficiency, and quality at the main plant. In 1973 a coke plant, which provided coke for the Weirton plants, went into operation.

National and Weirton's Diverging Interests

During the 1970s the interests of Weirton Steel and its parent company, National Steel, increasingly diverged. Throughout the 1960s and 1970s, National Steel, then America's third largest steelmaker, used its earnings to diversify—buying interests in savings and loans, and investing in the production of aluminum—rather than investing in its current facilities. Eventually, National Steel began to plan for a future that did not include Weirton and its 13,000 employees.

When National Steel began to consider closing the Weirton plant for three weeks in 1977, it was an ominous foreshadowing of events to come. The slipping economy aggravated Weirton Steel's situation. With the inflation of the late 1970s, and the recession of the 1980s, Weirton's fortunes took a turn for the worse. Between 1978 and 1982, net sales decreased from $1.09 billion to $904 million, while operating expenses soared from $79 million to $103 million. Pretax earnings plunged from $16 million in 1978 to a loss of $104 million in 1982.

At the same time, shipment of products declined from 2.94 million tons in 1978 to 1.68 million tons in 1982. At this point, tin-plate accounted for about half of Weirton's shipments, with galvanized steel accounting for about one-fifth, and cold-roll steel and hot rolled bands representing about one tenth of shipments each.

The slowdowns took their toll. In 1981, Weirton Steel experienced the first major layoffs in its history. By the end of the year, more than 3,000 workers had lost their jobs. As the town's economy ground to a halt, workers were forced onto public aid, peripheral businesses began to decline, and Weirton's young began to leave in increasing numbers. The company's coke plant closed in 1982, and 275 more workers were laid off.

In 1982 National Steel further shocked Weirton's 24,000 residents by announcing that the aging mill complex would be largely shut down, but National Steel offered an alternative. Employees could buy the plant with borrowed money and try to run it on their own.

Employee Takeover

In November 1982 Weirton Steel Corporation was organized to acquire the assets of National Steel's Weirton Steel division. An agreement for the corporation was reached in April 1983. Under the terms of the agreement, employee-owned Weirton Steel Corporation bought the Weirton Steel division from National Steel for $194.2 million in cash and debt. The workers accepted a 20 percent pay cut and a six-year wage freeze in exchange for a stake in the factories. Under this employee stock ownership plan (ESOP) the company would henceforth be owned by the employees and directed by seven outside directors. The same year, Robert L. Loughhead, previously president of Copperweld Steel Company, joined the firm as president. Also in 1983, National Steel Corporation reorganized, and changed its name to National Intergroup, Inc.

Weirton Steel instantly became the nation's largest employee-owned company. It would soon become the nation's most successful. While many steelmakers were losing money, Weirton posted earnings of $48.3 million on sales of $845.5 million in the first nine months of 1984. That year, however, Weirton Steel was forced to lay off 250 more workers.

In 1985 sales increased by 9.1 percent over 1984, as income rose about 1.5 percent. The following year, an increase in orders led Weirton Steel to start a third blast furnace, and the company recalled about 60 laid-off workers. The same year, Weirton

Steel exercised its option to buy the Steubenville mill plant, which had been closed since 1981, from National Intergroup.

Weirton Steel enjoyed 16 consecutive profitable quarters after the transition, which proved a boon to employees. Under the terms of the ESOP, employees would receive a share of corporate profits. In 1987 alone, some 8,400 Weirton Steel workers received average profit-sharing checks of $4,500, the highest of any steel firm. This payout came after profits in 1987 of $80 million, a dramatic increase from the 1986 figure of $30 million. Sales increased to $1.3 billion in 1987 from $1.17 billion in 1986, and production rose from 2.8 million tons in 1986 to 3.3 million tons in 1987, placing Weirton Steel seventh among U.S. steel producers.

Weirton Steel displayed a new commitment to improving its facilities. In 1984, for example, Weirton hired the Mellon Institute, a division of Carnegie-Mellon University, to conduct metallurgical studies on surface quality. In 1986 the Department of Energy (DOE) provided $65 million for the construction of the first Kohle-reduction iron process plant in the United States, to be built in Weirton. The plant was to be part of a DOE program to implement environmentally clean coal technology but was aborted when Weirton decided to invest elsewhere.

In 1987 Loughhead stepped down, and director Herbert Elish was appointed to the post of chairman, president, and chief executive officer. Under Elish, Weirton Steel had suffered some setbacks, although the company also moved forward with large-scale modernization, most notably the construction of a state-of-the-art continuous caster and rebuilt hot mill. Between 1987 and 1989 production actually declined from 3.2 million tons to 2.9 million tons. Between 1988 and 1989 sales decreased only slightly but shipments were down by about 8.4 percent, and the profit-sharing provision dropped from $75 million in 1988 to $21.9 million in 1989. This figure reflected both a decline in income and a decrease in the percentage of profits paid to employees, from 50 percent to 33 percent.

The decline in profit-sharing was due to another Weirton financing innovation. In search of the means to avoid an ESOP stock repurchase liability and to permit a five-year, $500 million investment in modernization, Weirton decided to go public in 1989. It offered four million shares—about 23 percent of its stock—at $14.50 per share on the New York Stock Exchange.

1990s Difficulties

The economic downturn of the early 1990s, increased competition, and delays in the modernization program all led Weirton Steel to post its first losses as an employee-owned company. In 1992 the company lost $32 million on sales of $1.07 billion. Reflecting increasingly acrimonious relations with management, in August of that year a group of workers filed a shareholder suit accusing officers and directors of mismanagement in relation to renovation cost overruns. The directors responded by gaining approval—with only 51 percent shareholder support—of a new bylaw protecting the board from such charges.

Workers were further angered by Elish's announcement in July 1992 of a plan to cut the company's workforce by 25 percent over a three- to five-year period. At the same time, the modernization program had increased the company's long-term debt to an unwieldy $495 million by 1993, leading the board to propose a public offering of an additional 60 million Weirton shares. Workers balked at a move that would severely dilute their voting power. They eventually agreed to a revised plan, calling for a 20 million share offering, with five million shares reserved for employee purchases. The offering took place in October 1994, leaving workers in control of about 49 percent of the common stock.

In early 1996, upon Elish's retirement, Richard K. Riederer was named president and CEO of Weirton Steel, while Richard R. Burt was named chairman. The company had operated in the black during 1994 and 1995, but Weirton posted a loss of $49.9 million during the new management team's first year in charge. In order to contain costs, Weirton reduced its workforce by 500 in 1996, including the elimination of 200 of its 1,000 management workers. The company also restructured about $100 million in debt during 1996, giving itself more time to pay the debt off and more financial flexibility. Weirton Steel began to see the benefits of these moves in 1997, when it cut its losses to $17.7 million for the year.

With the company seemingly on the rebound as the eighth largest integrated steel producer in the United States, Riederer and Burt began seeking out joint ventures for international expansion and in pursuit of higher-value steel product production. In September 1997 Weirton Steel announced the formation of a venture with Balli Group plc, known as WeBco International LLC, whose purpose was to market and sell Weirton steel products overseas. The following month the company joined with Koninklijke Hoogovens NV of the Netherlands to form GALVSTAR, L.P., which would construct a 300,000-ton-per-year steel galvanizing mill in Jeffersonville, Indiana, that was to be operational in the summer of 1999. Weirton and ATAS International of Allentown, Pennsylvania, formed W&A Manufacturing Co., LLC in April 1998, with the aim of producing residential steel roofing shingles with a 40-year lifespan. Finally, after finding success selling its products via the company web site, Weirton Steel joined with LTV Steel and Steel Dynamics, Inc. to create an independent company called MetalExchange offering a secure web-based marketplace for the online purchase of metal products from various suppliers.

Principal Subsidiaries

Weirton Receivables, Inc.; Weirton Venture Holdings Corp.

Further Reading

Angrist, Stanley W., "Class Consciousness Raising," *Forbes,* November 30, 1987, p. 77.

Baker, Stephen, and Keith L. Alexander, "The Owners Vs. the Boss at Weirton Steel," *Business Week,* November 15, 1993, p. 38.

"A Bicentennial Year Look at Weirton and Its Heritage of Steel," *Weirton Employee Bulletin,* 1976.

Cotter, Wes, "Weirton's Stock Hurt by Earnings, Rolling Mill Glitch," *Pittsburgh Business Times,* July 29, 1991, p. 1.

Kelton, Peter, "Weirton's Passion: Making Better Steel," *American Metal Market,* September 13, 1995, p. 13A.

Lieber, James B., *Friendly Takeover: How an Employee Buyout Saved a Steel Town,* New York: Viking, 1995.

"Making Money—and History—at Weirton," *Business Week,* November 12, 1984.

Mallory, Maria, " 'How Can We Be Laid Off If We Own the Company?'," *Business Week,* September 9, 1991, p. 66.

McManus, George J., "Weirton Steel Begins to Pick Itself Up," *Chilton's Iron Age,* November 7, 1983.

Milbank, Dana, "Weirton Steel's Managers Face Possible Fight," *Wall Street Journal,* November 24, 1992, p. A4.

Rose, Robert L., and Erle Norton, "UAL Worker-Owners May Face Bumpy Ride If the Past Is a Guide," *Wall Street Journal,* December 23, 1993, pp. A1, A6.

"Town Bids to Save Itself," *Fortune,* April 18, 1983.

—Daniel Gross
—updated by David E. Salamie

Werner Enterprises, Inc.

14507 Frontier Road
Omaha, Nebraska 68145-0308
U.S.A.
(402) 895-6640
(800) 228-2240
Fax: (402) 894-3927
Web site: http://www.werner.com

Public Company
Incorporated: 1956
Employees: 7,521
Operating Revenues: $772.09 million (1997)
Stock Exchanges: NASDAQ
Ticker Symbol: WERN
SICs: 4213 Trucking Except Local

Werner Enterprises, Inc., headquartered in Omaha, Nebraska, is the fourth largest trucking company in the United States. Founded by Clarence L. Werner in 1956, it is a publicly traded company led by the Werner family, which retains 40 percent ownership. Werner's fleet of 5,500 trucks and 15,000 trailers serves the United States and Canada, and the company operates trailer service in Mexico. Werner offers a variety of transportation services, and transports a range of goods that includes beverages and foodstuffs, containers and paper products, lumber and building materials, plastic and metal products, and retail merchandise. In the 1990s, Werner Enterprises had increasingly moved into specialty trucking, including dedicated fleet services. Innovations such as the company's paperless log system have helped put Werner at the forefront of growth in the trucking industry, and its stock has been a consistently strong performer; however, like other trucking companies, it suffers from a dearth of available drivers.

Beginnings with Just One Truck

The vast Werner Enterprises fleet grew from just one truck. In 1956, 19-year-old Clarence ("C. L.") Werner sold his car to purchase a truck, which he used to launch his business. Many years later, in 1993, a *Fortune* magazine write-up on Werner Enterprises noted Clarence Werner's recollections of the early days and hard times of the trucking company he founded. Werner, the president and CEO of Werner Enterprises in 1993, told *Fortune*'s John Labate with a chuckle, "There's a lot of water under the bridge, and I generally was in it."

Starting in Council Bluffs, Iowa, near the geographical center of the 48 contiguous states, Werner Enterprises was well-suited to become a leader in the long-haul sector of the trucking industry. By 1965, the company had ten trucks, and it grew steadily throughout the 1970s. But a giant barrier stood between Werner—or, for that matter, most trucking companies—and significant growth: government regulation.

The federal government held control over the operating rights for trucking service between major cities, and it usually accorded such rights to large companies. Thus, when the administration of President Jimmy Carter deregulated trucking in 1980, it was a boon to Werner and others—just as deregulation of the telephone industry later in the decade would provide a boost to MCI and other challengers to the supremacy of AT&T. With the end of regulation, a small carrier such as Werner Enterprises could compete on a level playing field, and its customer base began to grow rapidly.

A Key Player in the Truckload Segment

In 1977, Werner Enterprises had moved its headquarters across the Missouri River from Council Bluffs, to Omaha, Nebraska. In April 1986, when it completed its initial public offering, Werner had a fleet of some 630 trucks. By that time, the company had begun to develop the business philosophy that would propel it to enormous growth in the decade that followed. Its philosophy, as later stated in its 1997 annual report, was "to provide superior on-time service to its customers at a low cost." To accomplish this objective, the company used premium-class, state-of-the-art tractors and trailers which were less likely to break down, and which assisted it in attracting and retaining qualified drivers.

Werner operated in the truckload segment of the trucking industry, providing its customers with specialized services including van, flatbed, and temperature-controlled trucks. It serviced regional routes, or medium to long-haul routes throughout the lower 48 states, and also provided dedicated fleets—that is, fleets in which all of the company's trucks were Werner-operated. Werner offered customized service over a broad geographic field, and held impressive claims about the quality of its equipment. In 1993, the company reported that the average age of a Werner tractor was 1.3 years, while the average trailer was only 2.8 years old.

Using its reliable equipment, Werner focused on shippers who valued the broad geographic coverage, equipment capacity, and customized services that were available from a large, financially stable carrier such as Werner. Among its principal customers were the department stores Sears and Target, and food companies such as Kellogg and Frito-Lay. Even with such big-name clients, however, Werner's customer base remained diversified. In 1997, for example, its 25 largest customers comprised a mere 40 percent of the company's income, and no one client accounted for more than seven percent of revenues.

Fast Growth with a Cautious Attitude in the 1990s

In 1992, Werner Enterprises greatly broadened its service offerings by expanding into the temperature-controlled, regional short-haul and dedicated-fleet segments of the trucking industry. Also in 1992, the company made strides in improving its technology. In 1993 it was reported that all of the company's trucks had on-board computers which connected truckers to headquarters via satellite, thus providing both the trucker and the home office with real-time information.

Such technology was the result of a September 1992 agreement with QUALCOMM, maker of advanced communication systems. Under the terms of the $12 million deal, QUALCOMM would provide its OmniTRACS mobile communications system for Werner's use. According to Jake Wood, Werner's president at the time of the deal, "After completing a comprehensive cost analysis and field evaluation of the systems available, QUALCOMM emerged as a winner. Our operating strategy is simple—everything we do must help ensure [that] our customers receive the highest level of service possible."

In spite of fast-paced growth in 1994, Werner was cautious about the company's future, according to a May 1995 *Omaha World-Herald* report on its annual meeting. Though Werner had topped its revenues and earnings record for eight years running, stock prices were down from $29 in early 1994, to $21.25 the following year. Vice-President and Chief Operating Officer Robert Synowicki stated that the downturn could be related to a general slowing in the economy, a nationwide condition which

Matt Kelley of the *Omaha World-Herald* wrote "may be making investors nervous about trucking companies in general." Nonetheless, Werner's executives expressed optimism about the company's long-term prospects, particularly in light of its low debt, high equity, and modern equipment.

During a question-and-answer session following the presentation of the 1995 company annual report, Kelley wrote, "One attendee generated the most interest by asking whether the trucking industry was taking steps to counter a recent spate of negative publicity about the industry and overworked drivers." As Kelley explained, during the previous month, a news magazine program presented on a major television network had featured an exposé on overworked and fatigued truck drivers who created a hazard for others on the highway. In answering the question, Werner executives explained the satellite reporting system, which helps the company to prevent drivers from working beyond the maximum number of hours permissible without a rest. With regard to the negative publicity itself, Clarence Werner said, "We can't do much about the national news when they go out and pick some screwball driver and do a story." The important thing, he suggested, was to focus on ways to prevent situations in which fatigued drivers were on the road.

In line with its cautious approach to business, in 1997 Werner Enterprises built a "disaster recovery site" near 72nd and Q streets in Omaha. In light of the many natural disasters which had begun striking the United States with regularity in the 1990s, the company was preparing a second headquarters to use in the event of fire, tornado, or other forms of emergency. "If there were some sort of disaster," Synowicki told Chris Olson of the *Omaha World-Herald,* "like a fire or chemical spill on the highway... we could transfer most of the business to the disaster recovery site and continue operating." The building, which Olson described as a one-story L-shaped structure of precast concrete with 30-foot ceilings, would be used for record storage; but, Synowicki noted, "If the headquarters were damaged, the stored items would be moved out and the building would be used as offices."

Issues of Growth Near the Turn of the Century

In addition to the construction of the 66,000-square-foot disaster recovery building, in 1997 Werner Enterprises was also building a 140,000-square-foot office building. The latter, on the east side of Nebraska Highway 50, would augment the existing headquarters building of 110,000 square feet on the west side of the highway. "The new building will more than double our headquarters office space," Synowicki told the *Omaha World-Herald.* "It should hold us for another five years."

With a goal having been set to grow its business by 15 percent yearly, Werner's facilities were expanding quickly as well. "We had about five acres when we first moved to this headquarters site," Synowicki stated. "Now we have more than 200 acres and are still growing." Its growth had an increasing effect on that of Omaha itself: as Steve Jordon of the *Omaha World-Herald* reported in June 1997, the expansion "would be a key to opening a new industrial development area south of Interstate 80 and east of Nebraska Highway 50." In 1998 or soon thereafter, according to Werner Enterprises Executive Vice-President and General Counsel Richard S. Reiser, the company's trailer shop and later its body shop would move to the east side of the highway, leaving room for the headquarters building to expand into what was a parking area.

With so much growth taking place, one of the problems faced by both Werner Enterprises and its competitors was finding enough capable drivers. In February 1997, John Taylor of the *Omaha World-Herald* reported that Green Bay, Wisconsin's Schneider National, Inc., the number-one trucking company in the nation, had come to Werner Enterprises' backyard to recruit 125 drivers. Officials at Werner refused to comment on the Omaha recruitment effort by its competitor, but they did say that the company had been forced to turn down business due to lack of drivers. "Some trucking industry analysts," Taylor reported, "have said there is no shortage of people qualified to drive trucks; instead, they say, potential drivers don't seek work because they don't like the wages, hours, working conditions and the fact that they have to be away from home." For this reason, "Trucking companies like Werner have boosted pay in recent years." Although Taylor did not provide figures for Werner, he reported that at Schneider, new drivers could expect to earn as much as $36,000 a year, while drivers with three years' experience could earn up to $50,000.

In line with its continued growth as a company, in 1993 Werner Enterprises had moved into intermodal transportation, which combines trucking and rail transport. In April 1997, it signed an agreement with Hub Group, the largest intermodal marketing company in the United States, to market each other's services to customers. It had also created a division to handle logistics in 1995.

One of Werner Enterprises' most significant customers in the late 1990s was retailer Dollar General, for whom it began providing dedicated trucking services in 1996. In September 1997, Werner began handling a number of services for Dollar General distribution centers in Oklahoma, Virginia, Kentucky, and Georgia. In February 1998, Werner signed an agreement with Dollar General whereby it would handle all trucking operations at the four distribution centers. Thus, the Dollar General dedicated fleet soon grew from 150 to 400 trucks.

In December 1997, Werner Enterprises announced a plan to buy back as many as two million shares of its common stock, presumably to drive up the value of what its leadership believed were undervalued certificates. In the following month, January 1998, the company reported record earnings for 1997. Revenues for the fourth quarter, for instance, had increased to $206 million, marking a 22 percent increase over fourth quarter revenues in 1996. Furthermore, profits grew by 23 percent, to almost $14.2 million for the quarter.

At that point, Werner Enterprises was solidly in fourth place among trucking companies in the United States. Schneider, with $2.5 billion, was still far ahead of the pack, with J.B. Hunt and Landstar also ahead of Werner as billion-dollar corporations. Werner reported that it expected to hit the $1 billion mark in 1999. These four companies—along with Swift Transportation, completing the "Big Five"—each experienced 15 to 20 percent growth every year. Moreover, the big were only going to get bigger, because consolidation was increasingly becoming the rule in trucking just as in other types of business.

In June 1998, Werner Enterprises—which had long emphasized information technology and the use of the latest advancements in communication—got a jump on its competitors when it introduced a "paperless log system." According to a company press release, Federal Highway Administrator Kenneth Wykle had come to Omaha to sign an agreement with Clarence Werner whereby Werner Enterprises would be the first national trucking company to make use of satellite logging technology rather than paper logbooks to follow truck movement and truckers' work hours. Drivers' hours and activities would automatically be recorded throughout the day on a computer keyboard unit located in their trucks, which would then transfer the information to Werner's computer system in Omaha. According to Clarence Werner, Werner Enterprises had worked three years to create the paperless log system, but "the long-term benefits for our customers, the general public, and Werner Enterprises far outweighs the significant investment of resources." And thus, the company moved into the end of the century much the same way it had been operating for years—successfully integrating new technologies and ideas into its daily operations for the good of its customers and its own growth.

Principal Subsidiaries

Werner Leasing, Inc.; Werner Aire, Inc.; Drivers Management, Inc.; Fleet Truck Sales, Inc.; Werner Transportation, Inc.

Further Reading

"Hub, Werner in Working Relationship," *Traffic World,* April 28, 1997, p. 32.

Jordon, Steve, "Werner May Spur Sarpy Industrial Expansion," *Omaha World-Herald,* June 7, 1997, p. 40.

Kelley, Matt, "Werner Sees Caution Lights in Economy," *Omaha World-Herald,* May 3, 1995, p. 18.

Labate, John, "Companies to Watch," *Fortune,* November 29, 1993, p. 105.

Olson, Chris, "Werner's Contingency Plans Geared for Growth, Disaster," *Omaha World-Herald,* October 10, 1997, p. 22.

Schulz, John D., "Bigger 'Dollar' Bill," *Traffic World,* March 2, 1998, p. 18.

——, "Big Getting Bigger," *Traffic World,* March 9, 1998, p. 15.

Taylor, John, "Trucking Firms Seeking Drivers," *Omaha World-Herald,* February 13, 1997, p. B16.

—Judson Knight

The Wolfgang Puck Food Company, Inc.

1333 Second St.
Santa Monica, California 90401
U.S.A.
(310) 319-1350
Fax: (310) 451-5595
Web site: http://www.wolfgangpuck.com

Private Company
Incorporated: 1983
Employees: 1,700
Sales: $80 million (1998 est.)
SICs: 2000 Food & Kindred Products; 5810 Retail-Eating
& Drinking Places

The Wolfgang Puck Food Company, Inc. brings the trademark cuisine of one of America's most celebrated chefs to an audience far beyond the white tablecloths of Los Angeles's renowned Spago. Since arriving in the United States in the 1970s, Wolfgang Puck has become one of the wealthiest and possibly the most famous chef in history, thanks in part to regular television appearances on ABC's "Good Morning America" and other national network programs. Observers have described him as the first chef ever to successfully start and run his own chain of restaurants and the Food Company has been successful in capitalizing on his name in both mid-range restaurant chains, frozen foods, and the home meal replacement category.

Puck's wife, Barbara Lazaroff, has been instrumental in his success; she focuses on management details and designing the restaurant's unique interiors. Puck and Lazaroff's interests in their seven fine dining restaurants, each separate partnerships with other investors, were held under Puck Lazaroff Inc. These produced approximately $60 million of revenue in 1997. Puck and Lazaroff owned 30 percent of the Food Company in 1998, which operated 21 casual restaurants (the full-service Wolfgang Puck Cafés and Oba-Chine, and the counter-service Wolfgang Puck Express) and Wolfgang Puck Packaged Foods.

Birth of a Legend

Wolfgang Puck was born in St. Veit-Glan, Austria. His mother was an accomplished chef at a posh resort, and Puck began his culinary training at the age of 14. He apprenticed at L'Oustau de Baumaiere in Provence at 19, and later worked in several top Parisian restaurants such as Maxim's as well as the Hotel de Paris in Monaco. He reportedly dreamed of owning his own restaurant and becoming rich doing it.

In 1973, at the age of 24, Puck emigrated to Indianapolis, working at La Tour. A year and a half later found him as co-owner of Hollywood's illustrious Ma Maison, where the celebrity of its clients seemed contagious and Puck became renowned for his skill and creativity. Puck prided himself on using the freshest and finest ingredients, and also displayed a flair for showmanship.

In 1979, Puck met Barbara Lazaroff, a Bronx native who was studying biochemistry. An outspoken contrast to the somewhat reticent Puck, Lazaroff quickly became his champion, urging him first to ask for a raise at Ma Maison and then guiding him into the limelight of television cooking shows. Puck's own cookbook *Modern French Cooking for the American Kitchen* (1982) soon followed.

With the help of a few investors, in January 1982 Puck fulfilled a lifelong dream by opening his own restaurant, Sunset Boulevard's illustrious Spago. Lazaroff was responsible for the striking design of the $512,000 restaurant, which featured an open kitchen illuminated like a stage; she reported taking up to four years, from concept to completion, to develop the eatery. At Spago, Puck perfected his trademark of topping pizzas with exotic gourmet ingredients such as duck sausage or smoked salmon.

A second, Asian-California fusion restaurant, Chinois on Main, was established in Santa Monica in 1983. This was opened as a buffer against the inconstant fashions of the food business, but it provided what many feel to be Puck's most creative outlet: mixing Asian and French cuisine with the assistance of chef Richard Krause. Lazaroff again designed the restaurant's interior, which also featured an open kitchen.

Birth of the Food Company

The Wolfgang Puck Food Company began as the brainchild of Robert Koblin, a Beverly Hills heart specialist. Koblin's original concept was to offer healthful frozen dinners designed by a number of prominent chefs. Eventually the health aspect was minimized and Koblin settled on Puck alone as the chef.

The company's first products were frozen desserts, created by Spago's pastry chef Nancy Silverton. However, the quality of ingredients seemed to price the company out of the market. In 1987 the company then tried frozen pizza but the company still quickly ran through its $3 million of start-up capital. Koblin's bankers subsequently replaced him as leader of the company with Selwyn Joffe.

According to the *New Yorker*, Joffe saw Puck as "the Armani of the food business," and imagined a range of lines for different budgets to parallel the eminent couturier's empire. Lower-priced restaurants and frozen foods would cash in on Puck's stature in the world of fine dining, where his star continued to shine. In 1989, Puck ventured outside of southern California with the opening of the Postrio in San Francisco. However, opening the high-overhead Eureka in West Los Angeles in 1990 proved disastrous. Puck lacked control of the brewery to which the sausage house was attached and subsequently his restaurant shared its failure, losing $5 million. Puck himself owned ten percent of the venture. Granita, an elaborate, $3 million Mediterranean-themed restaurant that opened in 1991, struggled to break even in its seasonal Malibu home.

Greener pastures were just around the bend. Though initially reluctant, Wolfgang Puck became one of the first eminent chefs to try his luck in Las Vegas with the opening of the Spago there in 1992. The most successful of the high-end restaurants, it eventually achieved $12 million in annual sales. Eventually a Café and an upscale Chinois restaurant followed.

Food Company Expands in the 1990s

In 1991, the company opened its first, limited-menu, self-service Wolfgang Puck Express inside Macy's in San Francisco's Union Square. In 1993, the Wolfgang Puck Café, a less ambitious counterpart to Spago, opened in Universal Studio's Universal City. The Café featured table service and a larger menu than the Express. The Express and Café were originally designed to promote frozen foods, but they quickly became profit centers for the Food Company, thanks to their immediate appeal and high profit margins. The full-service cafés annually generated between $2 and $4.5 million each. By 1995, there were 10 cafés in existence, half of them express units.

Puck boasted of having more great chefs among his 1,400 employees than any other chain, and executives described the Cafés as more "chef-driven" than other chain restaurants. Menus were somewhat customized at each one, and the chefs cooked from scratch. The dining areas were individualized as well: seating at various Cafés ranged from 88 to 200. The company capitalized upon the success of Puck's Asian fusion creations by starting another chain in 1996. The first ObaChine opened in Beverly Hills; restaurants in Seattle and Phoenix soon followed.

Frozen foods, where the company squared off against giants such as Kraft, proved a much more difficult market to penetrate. Nevertheless, the Food Company claimed growth exceeding 50 percent a year in the mid-1990s. The scale of operations prompted the partners to choose Frank Guidara as the company's chief executive in September 1996. Unlike Joffe, Guidara possessed extensive experience in food service management, gained at steakhouse chains and fine dining restaurants. He soon induced new levels of consistency across the Food Company. Guidara's concept of the Wolfgang Puck brand included merchandising. A Florida entrepreneur licensed the right to make Wolfgang Puck cookware, but the Food Company itself offered a range of souvenir items from glasses to T-shirts.

The Food Company's packaged foods, managed by former Procter and Gamble executive Tom Warner, garnered sales of approximately $17 million in 1997. Under Warner, the company's expensive frozen products became more competitively priced. The costs of ingredients were trimmed to match consumer reality. From 1997 to 1998, the number of packaged items offered by the Food Company grew from 23 to 43. Besides ten different types of pizza, Puck's lasagna, ravioli, tortellini, and cannelloni were also available in the freezer.

Completing the Empire in the Late 1990s

Puck and Lazaroff topped off their fine dining empire with a few new openings in 1996 and 1997. They licensed Spago branches in Tokyo and Mexico City. The third US Spago opened in the River North section of Chicago in 1996. It adjoined a new Café. *Nation's Restaurant News* reported the new restaurant received 3,000 reservation requests per day. A new Chinois opened in Las Vegas in January 1997 as did a Spago in Palo Alto, California.

The Food Company opened a Grand Café, an expanded branch of the Wolfgang Puck Café, at Disney World in Orlando, Florida, in the summer of 1997. It also included a sushi bar known as B's Bar. The $8 million Disney World Café and Express were expected to earn at least $15 million in sales per year.

At the end of 1997, Puck and Lazaroff owned majority shares in several fine dining restaurants which had grossed $56 million in 1996. These interests were kept separate from the Wolfgang Puck Food Company, however, of which they owned just over a third. It collected revenues of $70 million in 1996. Revenues for 1997 were reported at $60 million for the Food Company, while the upscale restaurants grossed $56 million. A series of INS (Immigration and Naturalization Services) raids in late 1997 in southern California provided some inconvenience for company executives, however.

About a dozen Wolfgang Puck Food Company restaurants were planned to open before the end of the century, including Grand Cafés in Auburn Hills, Michigan, and Atlanta, Georgia. Conceived spinoffs of the Wolfgang Puck brand included salad dressing and pasta sauce.

Further Reading

Barrier, M., "The Chef As Famous As His Customers," *Nation's Business,* July 1991.

Butler, Charles, "Recipe for Success," *Sales and Marketing Management,* August 1998.

Cohen, Richard L., "Wolfgang Puck Invades Supermarkets," *Pizza and Pasta,* February 1996, p. 24.

Cuthbert, Lauren, "Convenience and Taste Boost Frozen Sales," *Natural Food Merchandiser,* March 1998.

Elam, Shade, "Wolfgang Puck May Open Three Restaurants Here," *Atlanta Business Chronicle,* May 18, 1998.

Gellene, Denise, "Breaking Bread: Puck Deal Indicative of American Express' Renewed Efforts," *Los Angeles Times,* May 8, 1996.

Howard, Theresa, "Wolfgang Puck," *Nation's Restaurant News,* February 1, 1996, p. 124.

Kessler, John, "Coming Soon: Celebrity Chef Wolfgang Puck's Dining Empire," *Atlanta Journal and Constitution,* May 29, 1998.

Lempert, Phil, "America's Top Chefs Find Success in Retail Market," *Chicago Tribune,* October 8, 1997, Detroit Free Press, *freep/fun/ food,* http://www.freep.com/fun/food/qmarket8.htm.

Lubow, Martin, "Puck's Peak," *New Yorker,* December 1, 1997, pp. 46–53.

Martin, Patricia, "Redefining Dining," *Las Vegas Business Press,* January 26, 1998.

Martin, Richard, "Frank Guidara," *Nation's Restaurant News,* January 1997, pp. 80–81.

——, "Wolfgang Puck Café," *Nation's Restaurant News,* May 22, 1995.

——, "Wolfgang Puck: Chef, Restaurateur, Celebrity, Los Angeles," *Nation's Restaurant News,* January 1995, pp. 159–60.

Morris, Kathleen, "Add a Dash of Show Biz and Stir," *Business Week,* May 19, 1997.

"NRN Names Puck, Lazaroff 1997 Innovator of the Year Recipients," *Nation's Restaurant News,* June 2, 1997, pp. 1, 4.

Puck, Wolfgang, *Adventures in the Kitchen with Wolfgang Puck,* New York: Random House, 1991.

——, *Modern French Cooking for the American Kitchen,* New York: Random House, 1982.

——, *The Wolfgang Puck Cookbook: Recipes from Spago, Chinois and Points East and West,* New York: Random House, 1986.

Reckard, E. Scott, "Fifty-Eight More Workers Suspected by INS in Eatery Raids," *Los Angeles Times,* September 11, 1997, p. D1.

——, "INS Raids Shut Puck Café, Fellow OC Mall Eatery," *Los Angeles Times,* September 10, 1997, p. D1.

Specht, Jeff, "Live, Love, Eat," *Business Geography,* July/August 1996.

Swetlow, Frank, "A Casual Interview with the King and Queen of Fine Dining in Los Angeles," *Los Angeles Business Journal,* October 27, 1997.

Walkup, Carolyn, "Spago Chicago Premiers As Puck Dining Portfolio Grows, Diversifies," *Nation's Restaurant News,* December 9, 1996.

"What's Cooking at the Wolfgang Puck Food Company," *California Centers,* Spring 1996, pp. 8–12.

—Frederick C. Ingram

W.W. Grainger, Inc.

455 Knightsbridge Pkwy.
Lincolnshire, Illinois 60069-3620
U.S.A.
(847) 793-9030
Fax: (847) 647-5669
Web site: http://www.grainger.com

Public Company
Incorporated: 1928
Employees: 12,180
Sales: $4.14 billion (1997)
Stock Exchanges: New York Midwest
Ticker Symbol: GWW
SICs: 5063 Electrical Apparatus & Equipment; 5075
Warm Air Heating & Air Conditioning; 5084
Industrial Machinery

W.W. Grainger, Inc. is the largest distributor of maintenance, repair, and operating supplies to the commercial, industrial, contractor, and institutional markets in North America. As of 1998, the company had increased sales and earnings nearly every year since 1927. It has accomplished its steady growth not primarily through diversification but by expansion of its core business in terms of geographic scope and volume of its product line. Privately held until March 1967, the company finances most growth internally. The company has traditionally served small industrial contractors and institutions but expanded in the 1980s and 1990s to serve specialty markets for general industrial, replacement parts, and safety and sanitary products, and to supply large corporations with multiple locations.

Early History

In the late 1920s, William W. Grainger—motor designer, salesman, and electrical engineer—sought to tap a segment of the market for wholesale electrical equipment sales. He set up an office in Chicago in 1927 and incorporated his business one year later. The company sold goods primarily through *Mo-torBook*, an eight-page catalog, which would become the backbone of the company's name recognition. It contained electrical motors that Grainger himself, his sister Margaret, and two employees would ship. In 1991 Grainger published two editions of its general catalog—the successor to *MotorBook*—offering more than 35,000 items. The catalog also included extensive technical and application data.

The market for electric motors was so expansive in the late 1920s and 1930s that many companies developed with it. In 1926 two of the ten largest U.S. corporations were electrical companies. City utilities made the switch from direct current (DC) to alternating current (AC) for nearly every apparatus driven by electricity. Manufacturers moved away from uniform, DC-driven assembly lines and toward separate work stations, each with individually driven AC motors. This development created a vast market, and distributors like Grainger could reach segments untapped by volume-minded manufacturers.

Grainger established its first branch in Philadelphia in 1933. Atlanta, Dallas, and San Francisco branches opened in 1934. Sales in 1932 fell below the previous year's, to $163,000—the first of only four years where sales would not increase. In 1937 Grainger had 16 branches and sales of more than $1 million.

The complexity of the industry allowed Grainger to decentralize marketing efforts and strengthen its regional presence by adding an outside sales force in 1939, but the company limited it to one sales representative for every branch for the first ten years. Branches opened around the country at a brisk pace, with 24 operating by 1942.

Yet Grainger did not expand solely through the number of outlets. In 1937 it began merchandising selected products under the Dayton trademark, Grainger's first private label. In order to stimulate summer business, a line of air circulators and ventilating fans was designed, assembled, and offered for sale by the company in 1938. Assembly operations continued to be performed by the company until it got out of manufacturing in the 1980s.

Grainger acted as a distributor of electric motors for government use during World War II. With its normal market disrupted, Grainger offered furniture, toys, and watches through

MotorBook for a brief period. Grainger continued expansion during the war as sales grew from 1941's $2.6 million to $7.8 million in 1948, and earnings increased almost tenfold to $240,000 in 1948.

Post-World War II Growth

The rapid growth continued immediately after the war. Sales more than doubled from 1948 to 1952, calling for organizational adjustments. A single sales representative could no longer serve an entire branch, and in 1948 Grainger expanded the sales force for the first time. The postwar transition also required renewed efficiency, and in 1949 Grainger had a branch office built to its own specifications for the first time. Most new branches since have also been built specifically for Grainger.

Beginning in 1953 the company created a regional warehousing system that replenished branch stock and filled larger orders. Called regional distribution centers, they were eventually located in Chicago; Atlanta; Oakland, California; Ft. Worth, Texas; Memphis, Tennessee; and Cranford, New Jersey. This system operated until the mid-1970s.

As alternating current became standard in the United States, Grainger's market changed. No longer processing large orders, the company intensified its focus on the secondary market that existed throughout the country—small manufacturers, servicers, and dealers who purchased with high frequency but low volume. Grainger could anticipate the needs of this market and purchase from manufacturers in high volume. Grainger's distribution system, warehousing, and accounting allowed manufacturers to produce at low cost for Grainger's customers. These customers were otherwise difficult for manufacturers to reach.

Most of the increases in sales volume after World War II were due to large-scale geographic expansion. This expansion continued through the 1950s and 1960s at a consistent pace. By 1967 Grainger operated 92 branches. Branches built after 1949 were automated to keep administrative and personnel costs low. In 1962 sales were $43.5 million. In 1966 sales nearly doubled to $80.2 million. Automation helped build the company's reputation as a reliable supplier and brought in accounts with bigger clients. Average branch sales grew from $596,000 in 1962 to more than $2.1 million in 1974.

In 1966 Grainger acquired those shares of Dayton Electric Manufacturing Company that it did not already own. Also in the 1960s, Grainger acquired a producer of home accessories, which was divested in the 1970s. In 1967 the company went public.

In 1969 the company purchased Doerr Electric Corporation, a manufacturer of electric motors, and three Doerr affiliates. Two thirds of Doerr's sales volume was already to Grainger. In 1972 Grainger acquired McMillan Manufacturing, another maker of electric motors. By 1974—seven years since the company had gone public—sales had more than tripled.

Continued Expansion in the 1970s and 1980s

Brands exclusive to Grainger—Dayton, Teel, Demco, Dem-Kote, and Speedaire—accounted for about 65 percent of the company's 1975 sales. As Grainger's branches became larger, the need for a centralized stock diminished. The company eliminated the regional distribution centers by the mid-1970s. It discontinued its McMillan Manufacturing operations in 1975.

Grainger's prominence allowed it to count on sales increases due to population growth. In addition, the replacement market for small motors exceeded that of the repair market. Slimmed-down operations and reduced long-term debt, however, poised the company for more aggressive growth through the 1980s.

Unlike the 1960s, the company saw no need to diversify during the 1980s, recognizing that the electrical industry itself could provide enough opportunity for growth. The transition from electromechanical equipment to electronics provided long-term growth during boom and bust periods—comparable to the motor market upgrades of the 1920s and 1930s. Growth in domestic business activity led to broad-scale upgrades and system replacements—resulting in increased orders for Grainger and more disposable cash for its own expansion. In 1986 the company sold Doerr to Emerson Electric Company for $24.3 million.

A study showed that while Grainger sold products in every county in the United States, it held less than a two percent share of a $70 billion to $90 billion industry. The study also indicated that most Grainger customers had fewer than 100 employees and valued immediacy over breadth of product line or price. In response, Grainger accelerated its decades-old expansion rate of six branches a year. It opened more than 100 new branches between 1987 and 1989, trying to bring a branch to within 20 minutes of every customer.

Investment in computer automation allowed Grainger to resurrect its centrally managed regional distribution centers. In 1983 the company opened a heavily automated distribution center in Kansas City, Missouri, and in 1989 opened a third such operation in Greenville County, South Carolina.

During the 1980s Grainger returned to its origins, trying to reach larger institutional customers. Although essentially the same business since its inception, Grainger expanded the scope of its services. Starting in 1986, through acquisition and internal development, the company began building specialty distribution businesses that were intended to complement the market position held by Grainger. These businesses included replacement parts, general industrial products, safety products, and sanitary supplies. Parts distribution continued to expand under the Parts Company of America (PCA) name. PCA provided parts service for more than 550 equipment manufacturers and offered 80,000 parts.

Acquisitions and Reorganization in the 1990s

General industrial distribution expanded in the late 1980s and early 1990s through a series of acquisitions. In 1989 Grainger purchased Vonnegut Industrial Products. The following year, the company acquired Bossert Industrial Supply, Inc. Bossert, positioned in the Midwestern market, provided manufacturing and repair operations products, cutting tools and abrasives, and other supplies used in manufacturing processes. Also in 1990, the company entered into the safety-products distribution business through the acquisition of Allied Safety, Inc. The new safety products line included such items as respiratory systems, protective clothing, and other equipment used by individuals in the workplace and in environmental clean-up operations. Grainger added to the line in 1992 by purchasing Lab Safety Supply.

JANI-SERV Supply was created in 1990 to service the sanitary supply market. It offered more than 1,200 items, representing a full range of sanitary products. The subsidiary was expanded in 1991 with the purchase of Ball Industries, Inc., a distributor of sanitary and janitorial supplies based in California.

In 1993 Grainger began a three-year reorganization of the company and its subsidiaries with the goal of streamlining its sales force and eliminating redundant inventories. Grainger began by dismantling JANI-SERV Supply 1993 and incorporating its product line into its core business. The following year it began the same process with Allied Safety, the company's safety products subsidiary, and Bossert, finishing the integration in 1995. In addition to this streamlining, Grainger opened zone distribution centers in Dallas and Atlanta in 1994.

Costs related to the reorganization and upgrades to information systems contributed to lower gross margins in the mid-1990s. A more important factor in these lower margins was Grainger's decision to lower prices on some products to attract new customers and expand existing accounts. As part of the company's effort to return to national accounts and larger industrial customers, the strategic pricing helped expand Grainger's customer base. Although the stock price fell in response to the lower margins, this effect was temporary.

Leadership of the company left the hands of a Grainger for the first time when David Grainger, son of the founder, retired as chief executive officer in 1995. He remained as chair of the board and was succeeded as CEO by Richard Keyser. In another change from the status quo, the company moved its headquarters to Lincolnshire, Illinois, the same year.

In the late 1990s, Grainger established operations outside the United States for the first time. In 1996 the company opened a branch in Monterrey, Mexico. The same year, Grainger purchased a division of Acklands, Ltd., a Canadian manufacturer of industrial safety and automotive aftermarket products.

The company made great strides in adding large national accounts in the mid- and late 1990s. In 1996 it signed supply agreements with several large companies, including Lockheed Martin, Procter & Gamble, and American Airlines. In 1998 it announced a materials management outsourcing agreement with Compaq Computer Corporation. With the addition of new accounts and new products, sales at Grainger almost quadrupled in a decade, growing from $1.3 billion in 1987 to $4.1 billion in 1997.

Principal Subsidiaries

Lab Safety Supply, Inc.

Principal Divisions

Grainger; Parts Company of America.

Further Reading

Cohen, Andy, ''Practice Makes Profits: Sales Training Spurs Double-Digit Increases Every Year for W.W. Grainger,'' *Sales and Marketing Management,* July 1995, pp. 24–25.

''Compaq Signs Outsourcing Agreement with Grainger Integrated Supply,'' *PR Newswire,* July 28, 1998.

''Grainger: The Positive View,'' *Forbes,* November 21, 1994, pp. 248–49.

''How the Big Get Bigger,'' *Industrial Distribution*, February 1988.

60 Years of Growth, Skokie, Ill., W.W. Grainger, Inc., 1987.

''W.W. Grainger, Inc., 2-for-1 Stock Split Declared,'' *PR Newswire,* April 29, 1998.

—Ray Walsh
—updated by Susan Windisch Brown

XEIKON

Xeikon NV

Vredebaan 72
2640 Mortsel
Belgium
(32) 3 443 1311
Fax: (32) 3 443 1309
Web site: http://www.xeikon.be

Public Company
Incorporated: 1988
Employees: 340
Sales: BF 2.95 billion (US$81.7 million) (1997)
Stock Exchanges: NASDAQ
Ticker Symbol: XEIKY
SICs: 3555 Printing Trades Machinery

Xeikon NV is one of the pioneers of color digital printing technology for the professional printing market. Based near Antwerp, Belgium, Xeikon manufactures a line of digital color presses sold through a worldwide network of distributors. The company also functions as an OEM (original equipment manufacturer) for providing the digital press cores of industry giants' products such as Xerox's DocuColor 70, IBM's InfoColor 70, Agfa-Gevaert's Agfa Chromapress, and Nilpeter's digital presses.

Xeikon's product line centers around three digital color presses, the second-generation DCP/32D and DCP/32S, and, introduced in 1998, the DCP/50D. Both the DCP/32D and the DCP/32S print to the A4 (European) or A3 (North American) paper formats. The DCP/32D is a duplex (double-sided press) capable of printing up to 4,200 full-color, double-sided A4 pages per hour. The DCP/32D is capable of printing to a variety of paper stock; the use of Xeikon's Variable Data System defines a page into data segments, which permit the changing of the images of individual elements for each printed page at high speeds. The DCP/32S extends the DCP/32D's range of materials. Developed as a simplex (single-sided) digital color press, the DCP/32S prints to a variety of materials, including plastics and other substrates, tapes, and films, making it an ideal companion to the label printing market. Both the DCP/32D and

the DCP/32S can print continuous rolls up to 307 mm wide and 11 meters long.

The DCP/50D, introduced in 1998, represents the world's first digital color printer providing eight-page-plus duplex printing in the B2 size standard. Two versions of the DCP/50D offer printing capacity to either the paperboard or the flexible packaging printing markets. In 1998 the company also introduced a fifth color unit and opaque white print toner, which could be adapted to the company's DCP/32 and DCP/50 series printers, extending the color range from four-color to five-color systems. Opaque white toner also extends Xeikon's print possibilities to the transparent materials market. Also introduced in 1998 was the DCP/50S, a simplex B2 printer for the packaging industry.

Publicly held Xeikon posted revenues of US$87 million in 1997. The company, traded on the NASDAQ stock exchange, is led by President and CEO Alfons Buts, and by Chairman and company founder Lucien De Schamphelaere. The company's primary competitor is Israel's Indigo N.V., another digital printing pioneer.

Founded in the 1980s

Considered by many printing industry analysts to be nearly as groundbreaking as the creation of the printing press, the arrival of digital technology in the printing industry in the early 1990s began to revolutionize not only the printing industry, but the marketing, packaging, and publishing industries as well. Traditional offset printing involved a series of steps to prepare an image to be printed. While offering high-quality print images, offset printing nonetheless demanded high turnaround times. In addition, the cost of the setup process for an offset run prohibited offset printing from being cost-effective for short-run print orders.

Digital printing technology provided a solution for the high turnaround times of offset printing. Instead of the multiple steps needed to produce an offset-ready print run, digital presses eliminated the make-ready time, while offering greater flexibility for proofing and other typically time-consuming processes. With digital printing, a print run could be prepared entirely as data, which in turn could be easily manipulated, changed, or

540

Company Perspectives:

Xeikon's mission is to develop, produce and market digital color printing systems and related consumables specifically designed to meet the quality, speed, liability, cost, variable content and on-demand requirements for the digital color printing market.

even interrupted and replaced by a different print run. In addition, digital presses offered new printing opportunities, especially the ability to print a different image for each page in a print run. Print orders could now be personalized, without becoming economically unfeasible. Although offset printing continued to be more cost-effective for large print runs, digital printing began to challenge the traditional method for short print runs. During the 1990s, continued refinements in digital printing technology enabled digital presses to compete with offset presses for medium print runs as well.

One of the pioneers of the digital printing revolution was Lucien De Schamphelaere. Born in Flemish Belgium in 1931, De Schamphelaere built a 40-year career with Agfa-Gevaert. Among De Schamphelaere's achievements with Agfa was the leadership in creating and implementing a process control system for the production of the company's film products. From there, De Schamphelaere was instrumental in forming the company's Electronic Imaging System Department, which introduced the world's first LED-based, 400 dpi Postscript printer, the Agfa P400, at the start of the 1980s.

Where most people began to look forward to retirement, De Schamphelaere instead looked toward beginning a new career. De Schamphelaere had become convinced that digital technology could be adapted to professional quality color printing. In August 1988 De Schamphelaere left Agfa to set up Xeikon NV, in Mortsel, near Antwerp. De Schamphelaere was aided by strong investor support from Agfa; by the beginning of 1989 he had succeeded in rounding out Xeikon's investor base. Starting with just five employees, Xeikon began to build up its team, reaching some 15 employees over the following year. Another sign of Xeikon's closeness to Agfa was the company's location on an Agfa-owned site.

Xeikon would remain, in large part, a research and development house for its initial years, as the company sought to transform De Schamphelaere's concept for a digital color press into reality. De Schamphelaere's team continued to enjoy strong support from Agfa and its investors. Xeikon was not alone, however, in seeking a color digital printing solution. Whereas the giants in the printing and document reproduction industry also were seeking to develop digital color technology, Xeikon's chief competition would come especially from Israel's Indigo, which was developing a parallel technology based around the company's patented liquid ink. Indigo would announce its first digital color press for 1993.

Xeikon was able to maintain its competitor's pace, however. In June 1993 the company unveiled the first prototype of the DCP-1, the digital color press that would provide the basis for the company's full-scale product line. By August 1993 the company was ready to begin beta testing of the machine, setting up a number of beta sites with eventual customers around the world. The following month, the DCP-1 was unveiled at the annual IPEX convention in Birmingham, England, where Xeikon and its digital color press was discovered by the worldwide printing and graphics industries.

Until then, Xeikon had existed as a research house. The development of the DCP-1, and the strong industry response for the press, would encourage Xeikon to develop its commercial arm. By April 1994, when Xeikon first began shipping its machine, it already had booked a strong portfolio of orders for the DCP-1. By the end of that year, the company's orders had risen to more than 100 presses. The move into full-scale manufacturing and commercial sales prompted a steady expansion of the company's payroll. By 1995 the company listed more than 160 employees; by the end of 1997 the number of employees had grown to more than 300.

The young company's revenues for its first year of commercial operations were encouraging, as the company closed 1994 with sales of more than US$20 million. Although Xeikon continued to post operating and net losses into 1994, the industry's acceptance of the DCP-1 had only just begun to build. Orders for the DCP-1 remained strong throughout 1995, averaging some 60 machines each quarter. By the end of 1995 Xeikon's revenues had climbed to US$81 million. The company also had turned a profit, of some US$700,000.

Digital Color Printing in the 1990s

Industry acceptance of digital color printing, although slow at the outset, nevertheless held great promise for Xeikon's future growth. In the United States alone, estimates approached some US$50 billion for Xeikon's targeted short-run (less than 5,000 copies) market. With Europe offering an equal potential for growth, and fast-developing markets in other areas of the world, Xeikon's leadership in the digital color press segment placed it in a strong position to capitalize on the building market momentum. The company recognized that, while building its commercial business, its competitive edge would come from its emphasis on research and development. Even as the company's growth brought it more and more into the commercial and manufacturing sphere, Xeikon's research and development staff would continue to form some 25 percent of the entire company payroll.

Aiding Xeikon's early development had been its close relationship with Agfa, which incorporated Xeikon technology into its Chromapress line of digital color presses. Xeikon also worked on developing other OEM agreements, including a mutual agreement with Barco, which had acquired nearly five percent of Xeikon in 1994, to incorporate the DCP-1 into Barco's pre-press and RIP systems. Meanwhile, Xeikon had continued to expand its technology. In November 1994 the company introduced its Variable Data System, which allowed single-pass personalizing of individual pages. The DCP-1 also was extended for support of flexible printing substrates. The next development in the DCP-1 would occur in March 1995, when Xeikon revealed its DCP-1/F2, offering dual-channel printing and in-line finishing, with compatibility with a variety of industry data formats.

Xeikon already was working on its second-generation presses. To fuel this development, as well as its manufacturing and commercial expansion, Xeikon went public in March 1996, listing on the NASDAQ stock exchange and becoming only the second Flemish company to do so. Less than six months later the company's new investors were rewarded with the launch of the Xeikon DCP/32D digital color press. The move into public status also enabled Xeikon to expand its range of OEM partnerships. The company's presses quickly began finding new names under the IBM, Nilpeter, and other brands.

The DCP/32D, a duplex press capable of printing to some 300 types of substrates, was joined by its companion system, the DCP/32S, a simplex press directed especially toward the packaging and label printing industries. The introduction of the Xeikon second generation was greeted enthusiastically, and the company saw its net profits rise to more than US$1.8 million.

At the end of 1996 Xeikon also made the determination to expand its distribution activities by creating a network of VADs (value-added distributors). Although the company continued its own direct-sales activities, the VAD network provided the company with more extensive coverage, in particular on the international scene, while the individual distributors picked up support and service activities. By the end of 1997 Xeikon had successfully built its VAD network to some 40 members, including the United States' PrimeSource and other printing supplies heavyweights. In a move to deepen its North American penetration, Xeikon also set up a U.S. subsidiary in Chicago.

The 1997 year proved significant in other ways. After adding Xerox as an OEM partner for Xeikon press technology, Xeikon introduced a new press. The DCP/50D debuted in September 1997, representing an industry breakthrough as the first digital color press capable of printing to the B2 size. The DCP/50D would be joined by a single-sided version in early 1998, ex-panding the press's range to the packaging industry. In 1997, in addition, Xeikon purchased a research and development unit from Agfa.

Xeikon was beginning to outgrow its original quarters, and the company began looking for a new larger location in the Antwerp area. The company, which had grown to some 340 employees, also marked an important milestone in early 1998: the sale of its 1,000th digital color press. In September 1998 the company introduced a fifth color unit for its presses, as well as an opaque white toner expected to be of interest in particular to the packaging industry.

In the ten years since Xeikon's founding, the company had made an impressive leap from think tank to full commercial organization. But in the late 1990s the market for professional-grade digital color printing that Xeikon had helped to create had only just begun to develop. Xeikon's extensive emphasis on research and development placed it in a confident position to maintain its market leadership.

Principal Subsidiaries

Xeikon America, Inc.

Further Reading

Van den Broek, Guy, "Xeikon zoekt nieuwe vestingsplaats rond Antwerpen," *De Financieel-Economische Tijd,* May 16, 1998, p. 9.

Ward, Gareth, "1000th Digital Press in Xeikon's Sights," *Printing World,* November 3, 1997, p. 4.

"Xeikon Develops New Product Initiatives," *Paperboard Packaging,* June 1998, p. 80.

"Xeikon Tempts the Digital Taste Buds," *Printing World,* May 18, 1998, p. 22.

"Xeikon verbetert records," *De Financieel-Economische Tijd,* February 19, 1998, p. 7.

—M. L. Cohen

Xerox Corporation

800 Long Ridge Road
Stamford, Connecticut 06904
U.S.A.
(203) 968-3000
(800) 828-6396
Fax: (203) 968-4312
Web site: http://www.xerox.com

Public Company
Incorporated: 1906 as The Haloid Company
Employees: 91,400
Sales: $18.17 billion (1997)
Stock Exchanges: New York Midwest Boston Cincinnati
Pacific Philadelphia London Basel Berne Geneva
Lausanne Zürich
Ticker Symbol: XRX
SICs: 3577 Computer Peripheral Equipment, Not
Elsewhere Classified; 3579 Office Machines, Not
Elsewhere Classified; 5044 Office Equipment; 7374
Computer Processing & Processing & Data
Preparation Services; 7375 Information Retrieval
Services; 7379 Computer Related Services, Not
Elsewhere Classified

Xerox Corporation, virtually synonymous with photocopying, now touts itself as The Document Company. In addition to its flagship copiers, Xerox also makes production publishers, electronic printers, fax machines, scanners, networks, software, and supplies. The company is also a market leader in the area of document outsourcing services. Xerox markets its products in more than 130 countries. Its Xerox Limited subsidiary (formerly Rank Xerox, a joint venture with the Rank Organisation Plc of the United Kingdom) distributes Xerox products in Europe, Africa, the Middle East, and parts of Asia (including Hong Kong, India, and China). Xerox Co., Limited—a joint venture with Photo Film Company Limited —develops, manufactures, and distributes document processing products in Japan and the Pacific Rim (including Australia, New Zealand, Singapore, and Malaysia).

Origins As The Haloid Company in 1906

Xerox can trace its roots to 1906, when a photography-paper business named the Haloid Company was established in Rochester, New York. Its neighbor, Kodak, ignored the company, and Haloid managed to build a business on the fringe of the photography market. In 1912 control of the company was sold for $50,000 to Rochester businessman Gilbert E. Mosher, who became president but left the day-to-day running of the company to its founders.

Mosher kept Haloid profitable and opened sales offices in Chicago, Boston, and New York City. To broaden the company's market share, Haloid's board decided to develop a better paper. It took several years, but when Haloid Record finally came out in 1933 it was so successful that it saved the company from the worst of the Great Depression. By 1934 Haloid's sales were approaching $1 million. In 1935 Joseph R. Wilson, the son of one of the founders, decided that Haloid should buy the Rectigraph Company, a photocopying machine manufacturer that used Haloid's paper. Haloid went public to raise the money, and selling Rectigraphs became an important part of Haloid's business.

In 1936 Haloid's 120 employees went on strike for benefits and higher wages. When Mosher proved intransigent, Wilson stepped in and offered concessions. Tension and resentment between labor and management persisted until World War II. During the war the Armed Forces needed high-quality photographic paper for reconnaissance, and business boomed. When the war ended Haloid faced stiff competition from new paper manufacturers.

Amidst this, Haloid needed to come up with new products, particularly following a showdown between Mosher, who wanted to sell Haloid off, and Wilson, who did not. Wilson won, and in 1947 Haloid entered into an agreement with Battelle Memorial Institute, a nonprofit research organization in Columbus, Ohio, to produce a machine based on a new process called xerography.

Xerography, a word derived from the Greek words for "dry" and "writing," was the invention of Chester Carlson. Carlson was born in Seattle, Washington, in 1906 and became a patent lawyer employed by a New York electronics firm. Frustrated by the difficulty and expense of copying documents, Carlson in 1938 invented a method of transferring images from one piece of paper to another using static electricity. In 1944 Battelle signed a royalty-sharing agreement with Carlson and began to develop commercial applications for xerography.

The XeroX Copier Debuts in 1949

In 1949, two years after Haloid signed its agreement with Battelle, Haloid introduced the XeroX Copier, initially spelled with a capital X at the end. The machine, which required much of the processing to be done manually, was difficult and messy to use and made errors frequently. Many in the financial community thought that Haloid's large investment in xerography was a big mistake, but Battelle engineers discovered that the XeroX made excellent masters for offset printing—an unforeseen quality that sold many machines. Haloid invested earnings from these sales in research on a second-generation xerographic copier.

In 1950 Battelle made Haloid the sole licensing agency for all patents based on xerography, but Battelle owned the basic patents until 1955. Haloid licensed the patents liberally to spread the usage of xerography to such corporations as RCA, IBM, and General Electric. In 1950 Haloid sold its first commercial contract for a xerographic copier to the State of Michigan. Meanwhile, Haloid's other products were again highly profitable, with paper sales increasing and several successful new office photocopying machines selling well.

In 1953 Carlson received the Edward Longstreth Medal of Merit for the invention of xerography from the Franklin Institute. In 1955 Haloid revamped its 18 regional offices into showrooms for its Xerox machines instead of photo-paper warehouses, hired 200 sales and service people, began building the first Xerox factory in Webster, New York, and introduced three new types of photography paper. Haloid also introduced the Copyflo, Haloid's semiautomatic copying machine. In 1956 Haloid president Joe Wilson, Joseph R. Wilson's son, formed an overseas affiliate called Rank Xerox with the Rank Organisation, a British film company seeking to diversify. This arrangement paved the way for Xerox factories in Great Britain and a sales and distribution system that brought Xerox machines to the European market.

1960: The Xerox 914 Copier Becomes an Instant Hit

In 1958 Haloid changed its name to Haloid Xerox, reflecting its belief that the company's future lay with xerography, although photography products were still more profitable. That balance quickly changed with the success of the Xerox 914 copier. Introduced in 1960, it was the first automatic Xerox copier, and the first marketable plain-paper copier. The company could not afford a blanket advertising campaign, so it placed ads in magazines and on television programs where it hoped business owners would see them. The company also offered the machines for monthly lease to make xerography affordable for smaller businesses.

Demand for the 650-pound 914 model exceeded Haloid-Xerox's most optimistic projections, despite its large size. *Fortune* later called the copier "the most successful product ever marketed in America." Sales and rental of xerographic products doubled in 1961 and kept growing. In 1961 the company was listed on the New York Stock Exchange and changed its name to the Xerox Corporation; photography operations were placed under the newly created Haloid photo division. In 1962 Xerox formed Xerox in Japan with Photo Film Company. Also during the 1960s Xerox opened subsidiaries in Australia, Mexico, and continental Europe. The company had sunk $12.5 million into developing the 914 copier, more than Haloid's total earnings from 1950 to 1959, and the 914 had led the company to more than $1 billion in sales by 1968. In 1963 Xerox introduced a desktop version of the 914; although this machine sold well, it was not very profitable, and Xerox depended on its larger machines thereafter.

With its suddenly large profits, Xerox began a string of acquisitions, purchasing University Microfilms in 1962 and Electro-Optical Systems in 1963. The market for copiers continued to expand at such a rate that they remained Xerox's chief source of revenue. The 1960s were a tremendously successful time for Xerox, which became one of the 100 largest corporations in the United States and, in 1969, moved its headquarters to Stamford, Connecticut.

In the late 1960s Xerox began to focus its efforts on the concept of an electronic office that would not use paper. With this end in mind the corporation bought a computer company, Scientific Data Systems, in 1969, for nearly $1 billion in stock, only to have it fail and close down in 1975. Xerox also formed Xerox Computer Services in 1970, bought several small computer firms in the next few years, and opened the Xerox Palo Alto Research Center (PARC) in California.

Scientists at PARC invented what may have been the world's first personal computer. So innovative was the work of the PARC scientists that many features they invented later appeared on Apple Macintosh computers. In fact, in December 1989 Xerox would sue Apple Computer for $150 million, alleging that Apple had stolen the technology that helped make its computers so successful. Apple cofounder Steven Jobs, who later hired some researchers from PARC, claimed that his company had refined Xerox's work, and thus made it original.

PARC's innovations were largely overlooked by Xerox; the computer division and the copier division competed for resources and failed to communicate. Products were released by the office products division in Dallas, Texas, that PARC had never seen before. Disagreements broke out at Xerox headquarters at the suggestion of change, which further stifled innovation.

Struggling Through the 1970s and 1980s

In April 1970 IBM introduced an office copying machine, giving Xerox its first real competition. IBM's machine was not as fast or as sophisticated as the Xerox copiers, but it was well built and was backed by IBM's reputation. Xerox responded with a suit charging IBM with patent infringement. The dispute was settled in 1978 when IBM paid Xerox $25 million. Meanwhile, Xerox itself became a defendant in several antitrust violation investigations, including a lawsuit by the Federal Trade Commission. Distracted from its market by legal battles, Xerox lost its lead in the industry when Kodak came out with a more sophisticated copier. IBM and Kodak followed a strategy similar to that of Xerox, leasing their machines and attracting many large accounts on which Xerox depended.

According to most critics, Xerox had become inefficient during this time, as its executives had concentrated too heavily on growth during the 1960s. Xerox had spent hundreds of millions of dollars on product development but introduced few new products. Engineers and designers were divided into small groups that fought over details as they missed deadlines. While the company sought to perfect the copying machine, it failed to challenge the new products on the market, and Xerox's market share dropped.

By 1985 Xerox's worldwide plain-paper copier share had dropped to 40 percent, from 85 percent in 1974. Yet Xerox's revenues grew from $1.6 billion in 1970 to $8 billion in 1980, partially because Xerox began to sell the machines it had been renting, thus depleting its lease base.

Beginning in the mid-1970s, Japanese products emerged as an even more dangerous threat. Xerox machines were big and complex and averaged three breakdowns per month. The Japanese company Ricoh, however, introduced a less expensive, smaller machine that broke down less often. The Japanese strategy was to capture the low end of the market and move up. By 1980 another Japanese competitor, Canon, was challenging Xerox's market share in higher-end machines.

In the late 1970s Xerox began reorganizing, making market share its goal and learning some lessons about quality control and low-end copiers from its Japanese subsidiary. The company also cut manufacturing costs drastically. Xerox regained copier market share but intense price competition kept copier revenues around $8 billion for most of the 1980s.

In 1981 Xerox finally began releasing new products, beginning with the Memorywriter typewriter. This typewriter soon outsold IBM's and captured over 20 percent of the electric typewriter market. By January 1983 Xerox had unveiled a Memorywriter that could store large amounts of data internally. In 1982 the 10-Series copiers, the first truly new line since the 1960s, was introduced. These machines used microprocessors to regulate internal functions and were able to perform a variety of complicated tasks on different types of paper. They were also smaller and far less likely to break down than earlier Xerox copiers. The 10-Series machines used technology developed at PARC, which was becoming more integrated with the company. Xerox began gaining market share for the first time in years, and morale improved.

Xerox also released computer workstations and software and built a $1 billion business in laser printers. The workstations proved an expensive flop, however, and by 1989 the company planned to close its workstation hardware business. Xerox also moved to protect its 50 percent share of the high-end market in the United States with machines that made 70 or more copies per minute. The major high-end competition was Kodak, but the Japanese—led by Ricoh—were again launching a drive for this market.

During the 1970s Xerox had also diversified into financial services. In 1983 it bought Crum and Forster, a property casualty insurer, and in 1984 it formed Xerox Financial Services (XFS), which bought two investment-banking firms in the next few years. By 1988 XFS supplied nearly 50 percent of Xerox's income—$315 million of the $632 million total. XFS performed well, able to raise funds at a low cost because it was backed by the Xerox "A" credit rating.

Xerox spent more than $3 billion on research and development in the 1980s looking for new technologies, such as those for digital and color copying, to promote growth. Xerox was a leader in developing technologies, but often had trouble creating and marketing products based on them, particularly computers.

A Late 1980s Comeback

In 1988 Xerox underwent a $275 million restructuring, cutting 2,000 jobs, shrinking its electronic typewriter output, dropping its medical systems business, and creating a new marketing organization, Integrated Systems Operations, to get new technologies into the marketplace more effectively. Xerox's comeback was so impressive that in 1989 its Business Products & Systems unit won Congress's Malcolm Baldrige National Quality Award for regaining its lead in copier quality. Xerox had demonstrated its ability to change in the late 1970s when it responded to the first wave of Japanese competition.

In 1990 when David T. Kearns, CEO since 1932, retired to become U.S. Deputy Secretary of Education, and Paul A. Allaire, a career Xerox man, was named to replace him, industry analysts speculated that Allaire would have to repeat the feats of the 1970s if Xerox was to survive as an independent corporation. A restructuring of company management occurred almost immediately. The office of the president was transformed into a document processing corporate office led by Allaire and including executive vice-presidents A. Barry Rand and Vittorio Cassoni, and senior vice-presidents Mark B. Myers and Allan E. Dugan. Two years later, Xerox announced plans to restructure the company as well. Three customer service operations units were created in Connecticut, New York, and England. In addition, nine document processing business units were established, each of which was headed by a president responsible for the profitability of the unit.

During the seven-month period from September 1990 to March 1991, Xerox introduced five new types of computer printers: the Xerox 4350, Xerox 4197, Xerox 4135, Xerox

4235, and Xerox 4213. These printers were designed to handle a wide variety of office needs from two-color printing to desktop laser printing. In October 1990 the Docu-Tech Production Publisher signaled Xerox's intent to take advantage of what the company foresaw as an industry move from offset printing to electronic printing and copying.

The introduction of the Xerox 5775 Digital Color Copier was met with great fanfare and was expected to rejuvenate sales. Xerox also continued to update and improve its facsimile machines by developing a personal-sized model that could be used as a copier as well as a telephone, and by developing thermal, recyclable fax paper. In May 1992 Xerox introduced Paperworks, software making it possible to send documents to a fax machine directly from a PC.

Despite these new products, financial and legal woes continued to plague Xerox in the early 1990s as American economic conditions worsened. After earnings of $235 million in the fourth quarter of 1990, Xerox reported only $91 million in profits for the same period the following year. Earlier in 1990, just four months after the creation of the X-Soft division, which was to develop and market the company's software products, Xerox announced that it would lay off ten percent of X-Soft's employees. In February 1992 the company offered severance pay to 6,000 of its American employees in an attempt to reduce the workforce by 2,500 by July.

By the end of 1991, Xerox was announcing the sale of three of its insurance wholesalers. Crum and Forster sold Floyd West & Co. and Floyd West of Louisiana to Burns & Wilcox Ltd. London Brokers Ltd. was sold to Crump E & S. Moreover, several lawsuits resulted in losses for Xerox during this time. In February 1992 Xerox was ordered to pay Gradco Systems, Inc. $2.5 million to settle a patent dispute; and a suit settled in favor of Monsanto a month later was expected to cost Xerox $142 million to clean up a hazardous waste dump site.

The Document Company Emerges in the Mid-1990s

With its core office products businesses on the upswing, Xerox announced in January 1993 that it intended to exit from insurance and its other financial services businesses. Later that year Crum and Forster was renamed Talegen Holdings Inc. and was restructured into seven stand-alone operating groups in order to facilitate their piecemeal sale. This exit took several years, however, and was delayed when a 1996 deal to sell several units to Kohlberg Kravis Roberts & Company for $2.36 billion collapsed. During 1995 two of the groups were sold for a total of $524 million in cash. In 1997 three more were sold for a total of $890 million in cash and the assumption of $154 million in debt. Then in January 1998 Xerox completed the sale of Westchester Specialty Group, Inc. to Bermuda-based ACE Limited for $338 million, less $70 million in transaction-related costs. Finally, Xerox in August 1998 sold its last remaining insurance unit, Crum & Forster Holdings, Inc., to Fairfax Financial Holdings Limited of Toronto for $680 million.

As it was exiting from financial services, Xerox was also beginning to shed its image as a copier company. In 1994 Xerox began calling itself The Document Company to emphasize the wide range of document processing products it produced. A new logo included a red "X" that was partially digitized, representing the company's shift from analog technologies to digital ones. A number of new digital products were developed over the next several years, including digital copiers that also served as printers, fax machines, and scanners (so-called multifunction devices). From 1995 to 1997 revenue from analog copiers was virtually stagnant, even falling slightly, whereas revenue from digital products enjoyed double-digit growth, increasing to $6.7 billion by 1997.

Xerox also shifted focus from black-and-white to highly sought-after color machines, with revenues from color copying and printing increasing 46 percent to $1.5 billion in 1997. The most notable introduction here was the DocuColor 40, launched in 1996, which captured more than 50 percent of the high-speed color copier market based on its ability to print 40 full-color pages per minute. Revitalized new product development at Xerox resulted in the introduction of 80 new products in 1997 alone, the most in company history and twice the number of the previous year. More Xerox products were being developed for the small office/home office market, with prices low enough that the company increasingly marketed its products via such retailers as CompUSA, Office Depot, OfficeMax, and Staples.

However, the new Xerox was about more than just office products. The company introduced DocuShare document-management software in 1997, providing a system for users to post, manage, and share information on company intranets. Xerox also gained the leading market share position in the burgeoning document outsourcing services sector through the 1997-created Document Services Group. This group offered such services as the creation of digital libraries, the design of electronic-commerce systems for Internet-based transactions, as well as professional document consulting services. In May 1998 Xerox bolstered its Document Services Group through the $413 million acquisition of XLConnect Solutions Inc. (renamed Xerox Connect) and its parent Intelligent Electronics, Inc. XLConnect specialized in the design, building, and support of networks for companywide document solutions.

The mid-1990s also saw Xerox launch a restructuring in 1994, leading to 10,000 job cuts over a three-year period. In February 1995 the company paid The Rank Organisation about $972 million to increase its stake in Rank Xerox to 80 percent. Then in June 1997 Xerox spent an additional $1.5 billion to buy Rank out entirely. With full control of the unit, Xerox renamed it Xerox Limited. That same month G. Richard Thoman, who had been senior vice-president and chief financial officer at IBM, was named president and chief operating officer of Xerox, with Allaire remaining chairman and CEO.

In April 1998 Xerox announced yet another major restructuring, as its shift to the digital world led it to spend more on overhead than its competitors. The company planned to eliminate 9,000 jobs over two years, taking a $1.11 billion after-tax charge in 1998's second quarter in the process. The cuts came at a time when Xerox was enjoying record sales and earnings as well as a surging stock price, so the company was clearly proactive in maintaining the momentum it had gained through its impressive 1990s resurgence.

Principal Subsidiaries

Xerox Financial Services, Inc.; Xerox Credit Corporation; Xerox Realty Corporation; Xerox (UK) Limited; Fuji Xerox Co., Ltd. (Japan; 50%); Xerox Canada Inc. The company also lists some 275 additional subsidiaries in the United States, United Kingdom, Canada, Japan, Peru, Venezuela, Colombia, Netherlands Antilles, Panama, Brazil, Barbados, Chile, Mexico, Dominican Republic, Hong Kong, China, Egypt, Singapore, Australia, New Zealand, Taiwan, Belgium, Russia, Germany, Sweden, Switzerland, Denmark, Norway, Austria, Spain, Poland, Finland, Portugal, Italy, France, and elsewhere.

Further Reading

Alexander, Robert C., and Douglas K. Smith, *Fumbling the Future: How Xerox Invented, Then Ignored, the First Personal Computer,* New York: William Morrow, 1988, 274 p.

Dessauer, John H., *My Years with Xerox,* Garden City, N.Y.: Doubleday, 1971.

Deutsch, Claudia H., "Original Thinking for a Digital Xerox," *New York Times,* April 15, 1997, pp. D1, D6.

Driscoll, Lisa, "The New, New Thinking at Xerox," *Business Week,* June 22, 1992, pp. 120+.

Hamilton, David P., "United It Stands: Xerox Is a Rarity in World Business: A Joint Venture That Works," *Wall Street Journal,* September 26, 1996, p. R19.

Jacobson, Gary, and John Hillkirk, *Xerox: American Samurai,* New York: Macmillan Publishing, 1986, 338 p.

Kearns, David T., and David A. Nadler, *Prophets in the Dark: How Xerox Reinvented Itself and Beat Back the Japanese,* New York: Harper Business, 1992, 334 p.

Narisetti, Raju, "Pounded by Printers, Xerox Copiers Go Digital," *Wall Street Journal,* May 12, 1998, pp. B1, B6.

——, "Xerox Aims to Imprint High-Tech Image," *Wall Street Journal,* October 6, 1998, p. B8.

——, "Xerox to Cut 9,000 Jobs Over Two Years," *Wall Street Journal,* April 8, 1998, pp. A3, A6.

——, "Xerox to Sell Crum & Forster for $565 Million," *Wall Street Journal,* March 12, 1998, p. B6.

——, "Xerox to Sell Resolution Group for $612 Million in Cash, Securities," *Wall Street Journal,* September 10, 1997, p. B4.

Sheridan, John H., "A CEO's Perspective on Innovation," *Industry Week,* December 19, 1994, pp. 11–12, 14.

Smart, Tim, and Peter Burrows, "Out to Make Xerox Print More Money," *Business Week,* August 11, 1997, pp. 81+.

Smart, Tim, "Can Xerox Duplicate Its Glory Days?," *Business Week,* October 4, 1993, pp. 56, 58.

——, "So Much for Diversification," *Business Week,* February 1, 1993, p. 31.

The Story of Xerography, Stamford, Conn.: Xerox Corporation, n.d.

Weber, Thomas E., "Xerox to Pay $1.5 Billion to Buy Rank's Stake in Copier Venture," *Wall Street Journal,* June 9, 1997, p. B4.

Ziegler, Bart, "Success at IBM Gives Thoman Edge at Xerox," *Wall Street Journal,* June 13, 1997, pp. B1, B8.

Ziegler, Bart, and Leslie Scism, "Xerox Shares Fall 5.6% After Collapse of the Sale of Insurance Units to KKR," *Wall Street Journal,* September 13, 1996, pp. A2, A4.

—Scott M. Lewis and Mary McNulty
—updated by David E. Salamie

YES! Entertainment Corporation

3875 Hopyard Rd., Ste. 375
Pleasanton, California 94588
U.S.A.
(925) 847-9444
Fax: (925) 734-0997
Web site: http://www.yesent.com

Public Company
Incorporated: 1992
Employees: 123
Sales: $50.9 million (1997)
Stock Exchanges: NASDAQ
Ticker Symbol: YESS
SICs: 3944 Games, Toys, & Children's Vehicles; 3942
    Dolls & Stuffed Toys

YES! Entertainment Corporation (YES!) develops, manufactures, and markets toys and other children's products domestically and internationally. YES! products frequently incorporate popular characters licensed from companies including the Walt Disney Company, in addition to characters created by YES! designers such as the world's bestselling animated talking toy, Teddy Ruxpin. The company's products are designed with the dual purpose of combining a learning experience for children (focusing on children between the ages of two and 12), which generally appeals to the educational concerns of parents, while providing fun and pleasure for the child. YES! Interactive Books, Princess of the Flowers, Travel Traxx, Where Is It?, Sound Mixers, Sound Doodles, Pop 'N Hear, Listen to This, Zoundies, Play-Along Stories, Comes to Life Books, Yak Bak, Yak Bak 2, and Yak Bak 3 are trademarks of the company. The North American market for these and other related products is estimated to be in the range of 44 million consumers. Company employees are headquartered in Pleasanton, California; Carson, Nevada; and in Hong Kong.

1992: Former Atari Executive Incorporates YES!

YES! was founded by Donald Kingsborough in 1992, at which time the company began producing toys and other chil-dren's entertainment products, including a variety of interactive items. Prior to his involvement at YES!, Kingsborough gained valuable experience in the toy production business while at Nintendo, where Kingsborough was credited with much of the initial success of the hugely popular Nintendo software games. He also worked as an executive at the consumer division of Atari, but by the mid-1980s Atari's game products were falling out of favor with young consumers and Kingsborough moved on in 1985 to found a publicly owned company, Worlds of Wonder, Inc. That company—for a time ranking as the fastest-growing toy company in the nation, quickly expanding to sales of more than $300 million—failed after its flagship Teddy Ruxpin dolls dazzled, then fizzled. Then in 1989 Kingsborough became the CEO of Intelligy Corporation, a creator of educational and child development products. He next decided to make another attempt at directing his own company and formed YES! His idea was to steer the company towards adapting innovative technology in product designs, in new ways that could enhance enjoyment as well as natural creativity in children. Kingsborough explained in a press release that ''The products we are introducing in 1993 combine the success of such children's classics as teddy bears and storybooks with new, easy-to-use technology,'' adding ''the new products, designed to encourage family activity and early childhood skill development, are both educational and fun.'' The company patented their technology, incorporated in their TV Teddy, a toy that interacted with specially encoded children's videotapes and TV broadcast programs, talking, laughing, and asking questions related to numbers, the alphabet, and about popular characters. The company also developed and patented *Comes to Life Books*, a system that allows the book's characters to read stories aloud to children in their own voices, accompanied by realistic sound effects and music. *Comes to Life Books* featured a DiscPlayer placed on Story Discs throughout the book, enabling children to hear the stories and follow along with the text and illustrations. Following a licensing agreement with Disney Publishing, YES! developed a newer version of *Comes to Life StoryPlayer* package that included the StoryPlayer unit and a Mickey Mouse storybook. YES! also added a Winnie the Pooh storybook made available separately from the StoryPlayer package. Other products introduced during this period included the Princess of the Flowers mini-dolls, YES! Interactive Books, *Nickelodeon* electronic games, and Yak Bak instant playback recording devices. YES!

Company Perspectives:

Our mission is to apply existing technologies to develop brands of products that are fun, interactive, and which emphasize creativity. These brands may emerge in existing industry categories or create new categories. Most importantly, the Company expects these will be brands that represent a significant point of difference from the competition and represent value to the consumer. We will employ a brand strategy in an attempt to develop product lines that are extendible for multiple years. This emphasizes a focus on products that generate logical product extensions at separate and distinct retail price points. To be successful, we must apply this brand discipline to rebuild and grow our existing core brands such as Yak Bak, Power Penz, and Air Vectors, as well as in our development of new core brands.

relied primarily on major national chains to market their products. The company's ten largest customers accounted for approximately 80 percent of gross sales in 1994, with Wal-Mart Stores, Inc. and Toys "R" Us, Inc. each accounting for approximately 25 percent of gross sales.

1995: Public Financing into Play

In 1994, revenues had reached $36.3 million but the company's operating losses hit $21.9 million, and by early 1995 the company had incurred operating losses that had accumulated to a deficit of $45 million. In June YES! made its initial public offering, raising $10.9 million. At the time, auditors Ernst & Young characterized the offering as "risky and questioned whether the new money would be enough to sustain the company through the year," according to Mara Der Hovanesian of *Knight-Ridder/Tribune Business News*. A toy industry analyst with Standard & Poor's also quoted by Hovanesian stated: "I think Don (Kingsborough) has shown an uncanny understanding for product development and marketing, but his downfall (previously) was a profound lack of financial controls." Hovanesian noted that YES! was offering shares at 42 percent below the previous price paid by insider investors, an unusual strategy for a growing company.

The company's subsidiary in Hong Kong, Entertainment Products Limited, had been established to facilitate the purchase of YES! products, a significant portion of which were manufactured in the People's Republic of China, and to distribute shipments internationally as well as to the parent company. Entertainment Products Ltd. also coordinated the manufacturing process with the company's vendors. According to the SEC filings, YES! recorded the transactions of the subsidiary in its accounting records through the use of intercompany accounts, but was unable to reconcile those accounts, resulting in over $7.6 million in charges for the unaccountable balance. The company blamed poor tracking of operations at the foreign subsidiary and made plans for improving accounting and control procedures in Hong Kong. Executives felt that the company's rapid growth contributed to many of the problems they were experiencing, straining management, financial, and other resources.

In an industry where consumer preferences are constantly changing and unpredictable, the company determined to lengthen the life cycle of its successful minirecorder products. YES! introduced four new Yak Bak products for 1996 following encouraging sales of its 1995 line of minirecorders. Pricing on many of the company's micro-chip-based products had dropped into a more affordable range for consumers. Retail priced at $19.99 and geared to the six-year-old consumer, Yak Backwards records the user's voice via microchip and plays it back, backwards. The toy also featured a "YALP" button ("play" backwards) that recorded users voices speaking words in reverse that would "YALP" it back to normal. Yak Back was incorporated into a special watch design with LCD time display and alarm features, capable of recording personal memos. The watch was designed to appeal to girls and boys of eight and older. Designed for six-year-olds and older, Yak Guard was a motion-triggered device capable of guarding rooms and belongings, or to "pull gags on friends and family members," as suggested in company advertisements. A personally recorded "alarm" could be placed on door knobs or drawers, for example, alerting the owner of trespass. The company also introduced a colorful ballpoint pen that housed the Yak Write SFX, with "say," "play," and "warp" features, in addition to four unique sound effects.

On another front, YES! launched a line of food activity products, notably Mrs. Fields Baking Factory, a toy cookie oven that used mixes developed along with the Mrs. Fields Development Corporation. Kingsborough told Douglas Robson of the *San Francisco Business Times* that "Our goal is to license brands that kids ask for and that parents and grandparents would be familiar with." YES! also introduced a kid-sized ice-cream/yogurt machine carrying the Baskin Robbins moniker.

Although YES! normally targeted children aged two to 12, the company experimented with the development of V-Link, geared to youth from the ages of ten through 17. The V-Link devices were developed as a private communications product including voicemail and messaging capabilities, allowing teens to communicate with each other at school, in malls, or anywhere within a 1,000-foot radius without toll or monthly charges. Unfortunately, the devices were shipped to retailers without the required FCC approval due to the low-power transmitters. Ongoing shipment delays meant that the devices were not in stores until very late in the Christmas selling season. Compounding the company's woes, consumers who did buy the V-Links were disappointed in product performance. It was generally thought that the V-Links were an overpriced version of the walkie-talkie, but with less operating range. Another product, the PowerPenz "phone" device with a built-in infrared transmitter and receiver, was also delayed when the company withheld shipments and reported disappointments with "initial quality." In the product design department an effort was underway to attract more young female customers, since most of YES!'s electronic gadgets appealed primarily to boy. The company entered the doll market when it signed licensing agreements with England-based Vivid Imagination, producers of Tweeny Weeny Families. YES! secured the rights to market the line of miniature animal toys in the United States and Canada, planning to feature the Hoppit family of eight rabbits. Vivid Imagination had experienced a remarkable success with the toys in Europe, claiming European sales in excess of $68 million.

Toy Sales Tumbled in 1996

Reporting in *Forbes*, Caroline Waxler stated that the company was probably trying to offer too much. She argued that the company was overreaching when it showed seven different toys at the New York toy fair, in addition to pushing their established Yak Bak toys and V-Link products. Sales had dropped in the fourth quarter of 1996, tumbling 30 percent. The company reported a loss of $12.7 million for the year. YES! stock that had risen to a price of $16.87 the previous summer plummeted to $3.50 by May 1997. Two class-action lawsuits were initially filed by unhappy investors, charging that company officials overstated earnings and sales potential deliberately to inflate the stock price. According to Greg Smiley of *Knight-Ridder/Tribune Business News*, one of the suits, filed in 1997, alleged that Kingsborough and retired CFO Sol Kershner overstated company profits to allow venture capitalists comprising a majority of the company's board of directors to recoup some of the $40 million they had invested in YES! between 1993 and 1995. Five additional lawsuits were filed in the ensuing seven months.

Struggling to turn the company around, YES! hired Mark Shepherd to the executive management team. Shepherd, formerly the chief financial officer of the much larger toy company, Lewis Galoob, and a senior vice-president of finance for Einstein/Noah Bagel Corporation took over duties as COO and CFO at YES! The company reported that Kingsborough would henceforth concentrate on strategic relationships, marketing, and product direction. Other changes included the hiring of Leonard Ciciretto as executive vice-president of sales. By this time YES! had technically breached the terms of its BNY Financial Corp. credit line by losing so much money in a very short time, but the lender agreed to waive action and allowed YES! another year in which to become profitable. YES! gave 831,000 shares of stock to persuade six vendors to forgive debts totaling $3.1 million, and sold several of their toy lines, including assets of its food and Girls Activity business units, to Wham-O for $9.8 million plus potential royalties, in capital-raising moves that left the company heavily dependent on two of its most popular lines, Yak Bak and Power Penz. COO Shepherd explained that "the current financial foundation of the company, which includes approximately $10 million of capital raised by the sale of product lines, better positions YES! to move forward," adding, "we have made progress toward lowering our break-even point and our goal is to improve margins throughout the remainder of 1998."

In June 1998, YES! retained Gruntal & Co., LLC, a New York investment banking firm established in 1880, to advise the company in pursuing opportunities to maximize shareholder value. In July, YES! announced that it signed an agreement to settle all securities class-action lawsuits that were pending, although company officials maintained that the lawsuits were without merit. The $2.25 million was funded under the company's insurance policies. A month later, the company announced that it had signed a letter of intent with Infinity Investors Limited, Infinity Emerging Opportunities Limited, and Glacier Capital Limited, the investors that held a majority of the company's convertible preferred stock and five percent convertible debentures, to resolve issues between investors and YES! Terms of the letter of intent, involving a $3 million loan and a $10 million working capital line, allowed the company to replace The Bank of New York revolving credit agreement. Two of the Investor designees joined the YES! board of directors, and conditions of the preferred stock and debentures were modified.

The major market leaders competing with YES! included Mattel, Inc., Hasbro, Inc., Tyco Toys, Inc., Tiger Electronics, and Video Technology, all companies with substantial resources. Given Yes! Entertainment's restricted working capital, heavy debt, and poor financial results into 1998, the company ran the risk of becoming "no" entertainment—at least of the desirable kind—for its shareholders.

Principal Subsidiaries

Entertainment Products, Ltd. (Hong Kong); Familywise, Inc.; YES! Entertainment International (Cayman Islands).

Further Reading

Hovanesian, Mara Der, "Interactive Toy Maker's Stock Dives 17 Percent," *Knight-Ridder/Tribune Business News*, February 7, 1997, p. 207B1169.
——, "Most Shareholders Are Sanguine About Long-Term Outlook for YES!," *Knight-Ridder/Tribune Business News*, May 21, 1997, p. 521B0916.
——, "Pleasanton, Calif.-Based Toymaker YES! Entertainment to Go Public," *Knight-Ridder/Tribune Business News*, April 26, 1995, p. 4260033.
"In Wake of FCC Inquiry," *Television Digest*, June 9, 1997, p. 19.
Liedtke, Michael, "Pleasanton, Calif. Toy Maker Posts Loss," *Knight-Ridder/Tribune Business News*, November 12, 1997, p. 1112B0940.
——, "Pleasanton, Calif. Toy Maker YES! Gains U.S. Rights to Dolls," *Knight-Ridder/Tribune Business News*, June 13, 1997, p. 613B0944.
Robson, Douglas, "Turning Tech into Toys Is Child's Play," *San Francisco Business Times*, January 31, 1997, p. 6A.
Waxler, Caroline, "Just Say No," *Forbes*, March 24, 1997, p. 188.

—Terri Mozzone

INDEX TO COMPANIES

Index to Companies

Listings in this index are arranged in alphabetical order under the company name. Company names beginning with a letter or proper name such as Eli Lilly & Co. will be found under the first letter of the company name. Definite articles (The, Le, La) are ignored for alphabetical purposes as are forms of incorporation that precede the company name (AB, NV). Company names printed in bold type have full, historical essays on the page numbers appearing in bold. Updates to entries that appeared in earlier volumes are signified by the notation (**upd.**). Company names in light type are references within an essay to that company, not full historical essays. This index is cumulative with volume numbers printed in bold type.

California Portland Cement Co., **III** 718; **19** 69

California Pro Sports Inc., **24** 404

California Steel Industries, **IV** 125

California Telephone and Light, **II** 490

California Test Bureau, **IV** 636

California Texas Oil Co., **III** 672

California Tile, **III** 673

California Woodfiber Corp., **IV** 266

California-Western States Life Insurance Co., **III** 193–94

Caligen, **9** 92

Call-Chronicle Newspapers, Inc., **IV** 678

Callaghan & Company, **8** 526

Callard and Bowser, **II** 594

Callaway Golf Company, 15 77–79; 16 109; **19** 430, 432; **23** 267, 474

Callaway Wines, **I** 264

Callebaut, **II** 520–21

Callender's Cable and Construction Co. Ltd., **III** 433–34

Calloway's Nursery Inc., **12** 200

Calma, **II** 30; **12** 196

Calmar Co., **12** 127

CalMat Co., III 718; **19 69–72**

Calmic Ltd., **I** 715

Calor Group, **IV** 383

Caloric Corp., **II** 86

Calpine Corp., **IV** 84

Calsil Ltd., **III** 674

Caltex Petroleum Corporation, II 53; **III** 672; **IV** 397, 434, 440–41, 479, 484, 492, 519, 527, 536, 545–46, 552, 560, 562, 718; **7** 483; **19 73–75**; **21** 204; **25** 471

Calumatic Group, **25** 82

Calumet & Arizona Mining Co., **IV** 177

Calumet Electric Company, **6** 532

Calvert & Co., **I** 293

Calvert Insurance Co. *See* Gryphon Holdings, Inc.

Calvin Bullock Ltd., **I** 472

Calvin Klein, Inc., 9 203; **22 121–24**; **25** 258

Camargo Foods, **12** 531

Camber Corporation, **25** 405

Cambex, **12** 147–48

Cambrex Corporation, 16 67–69

Cambria Steel Company, **IV** 35; **7** 48

Cambridge Applied Nutrition Toxicology and Biosciences Ltd., **10** 105

Cambridge Biotech Corp., **13** 241

Cambridge Electric Co., **14** 124, 126

Cambridge Gas Co., **14** 124

Cambridge Interactive Systems Ltd., **10** 241

Cambridge Steam Corp., **14** 124

Camco Inc., **IV** 658

Camden Wire Co., Inc., **7** 408

CAMECO, **IV** 436

Camelot Barthropp Ltd., **26** 62

Camelot Music, Inc., 26 52–54

Cameron & Barkley Co., **13** 79

Cameron Ashley Inc., **19** 57

Cameron Iron Works, **II** 17

Cameron Oil Co., **IV** 365

Cameron-Brown Company, **10** 298

CAMI Automotive, **III** 581

Camintonn, **9** 41–42

Camp Manufacturing Co., **IV** 345; **8** 102

Campbell Box & Tag Co., **IV** 333

Campbell Cereal Company. *See* Malt-O-Meal Company.

Campbell, Cowperthwait & Co., **17** 498

Campbell Hausfeld. *See* Scott Fetzer Company.

Campbell Industries, Inc., **11** 534

Campbell Soup Company, I 21, 26, 31, 599, 601; **II 479–81**, 508, 684; **7 66–69 (upd.)**, 340; **10** 382; **11** 172; **18** 58; **25** 516; **26 55–59 (upd.)**

Campbell Taggart, Inc., **I** 219; **19** 135–36, 191

Campbell-Ewald Co., **I** 16–17

Campbell-Mithun-Esty, Inc., 13 516; **16 70–72**

Campeau Corporation, IV 721; **V 25–28**; **9** 209, 211, 391; **12** 36–37; **13** 43; **15** 94; **17** 560; **22** 110; **23** 60

Campo Electronics, Appliances & Computers, Inc., 16 73–75

Campo Lindo, **25** 85

Campofrio Alimentacion, S.A., **18** 247

CAMPSA. *See* Compañia Arrendataria del Monopolio de Petróleos Sociedad Anónima.

Campus Services, Inc., **12** 173

Canada & Dominion Sugar Co., **II** 581

Canada Cable & Wire Company, **9** 11

Canada Cement, **III** 704–05

Canada Cup, **IV** 290

Canada Development Corp., **IV** 252; **17** 29

Canada Dry, **I** 281

Canada, Limited, **24** 143

Canada Packers Inc., II 482–85

Canada Safeway Ltd., **II** 650, 654

Canada Surety Co., **26** 486

Canada Trust. *See* CT Financial Services Inc.

Canada Tungsten Mining Corp., Ltd., **IV** 18

Canada Wire & Cable Company, Ltd., **IV** 164–65; **7** 397–99

Canadair, Inc., I 58; **7** 205; **13** 358; **16 76–78**

Canadian Ad-Check Services Inc., **26** 270

Canadian Airlines International Ltd., **6** 61–62, 101; **12** 192; **23** 10; **24** 400

Canadian Bank of Commerce, **II** 244–45

Canadian British Aluminum, **IV** 11

Canadian Cellucotton Products Ltd., **III** 40; **16** 302

Canadian Copper, **IV** 110

Canadian Copper Refiners, Ltd., **IV** 164

Canadian Dominion Steel and Coal Corp., **III** 508

Canadian Eastern Finance, **IV** 693

Canadian Fina Oil, **IV** 498

Canadian Football League, **12** 457

Canadian Forest Products, **IV** 270

Canadian Fuel Marketers, **IV** 566

Canadian General Electric Co., **8** 544–45

Canadian Government Merchant Marine, **6** 360–61

Canadian Gridoil Ltd., **IV** 373

Canadian Imperial Bank of Commerce, II 244–46; **IV** 693; **7** 26–28; **10** 8

Canadian Industrial Alcohol Company Limited, **14** 141

Canadian International Paper Co., **IV** 286–87; **15** 228

Canadian Keyes Fibre Company, Limited of Nova Scotia, **9** 305

Canadian National Railway System, I 284; **6 359–62**; **12** 278–79; **22** 444; **23** 10

Canadian Odeon Theatres, **6** 161; **23** 123

Canadian Overseas Telecommunications Corporation, **25** 100

Canadian Pacific Enterprises, **III** 611

Canadian Pacific Limited, V 429–31; **8** 544–46

Canadian Pacific Railway, **I** 573; **II** 210, 220, 344; **III** 260; **IV** 272, 308, 437; **6** 359–60; **25** 230

Canadian Packing Co. Ltd., **II** 482

Canadian Petrofina, **IV** 498

Canadian Radio-Television and Telecommunications Commission, **6** 309

Canadian Telephones and Supplies, **6** 310

Canadian Tire Corporation, Limited, **25** 144

Canadian Transport Co., **IV** 308

Canadian Utilities Limited, 13 130–32

Canadian Vickers, **16** 76

Canal Bank, **11** 105

Canal Electric Co., **14** 125–26

Canal Plus, III 48; **7** 392; **10 195–97**, 345, 347; **23** 476

CanAmera Foods, **7** 82

Canandaigua Wine Company, Inc., 13 133–35

Cananwill, **III** 344

Candle Corporation of America. *See* Blyth Industries, Inc.

Candy SpA, **22** 350

Canfor Corp., **IV** 321; **17** 540

Cannell Communications, **25** 418

Cannon Assurance Ltd., **III** 276

Cannon Mills, Co., **9** 214–16

Cannondale Corporation, 16 494; **21 88–90**; **26** 183, 412

Canon Inc., I 494; **II** 103, 292; **III 120–21**, 143, 172, 575, 583–84; **6** 238, 289; **9** 251; **10** 23; **13** 482; **15** 150; **18 92–95 (upd.)**, 186, 341–42, 383, 386–87; **24** 324; **26** 213

Canpet Exploration Ltd., **IV** 566

Canpotex Ltd., **18** 432

Cans Inc., **I** 607

Canstar Sports Inc., 15 396–97; **16 79–81**

Canteen Corp., **I** 127; **II** 679–80; **12** 489; **13** 321

Cantel Corp., **11** 184; **18** 32; **20** 76

Canton Chemical, **I** 323; **8** 147

Canton Railway Corp., **IV** 718

Cantor Fitzgerald Securities Corporation, **10** 276–78

Cap Rock Electric Cooperative, **6** 580

CAPCO. *See* Central Area Power Coordination Group *or* Custom Academic Publishing Company.

Capcom Co., **7** 396

Cape and Vineyard Electric Co., **14** 124–25

Cape Cod-Cricket Lane, Inc., **8** 289

Cape Horn Methanol, **III** 512

Cape May Light and Power Company, **6** 449

Cape PLC, **22** 49

Cape Wine and Distillers, **I** 289

Capehart-Farnsworth, **I** 463; **11** 197

Capex, **6** 224

AB Capital & Investment Corporation, **6** 108; **23** 381

Capital Advisors, Inc., **22** 4

Capital Airlines, **I** 128; **III** 102; **6** 128

Capital and Counties Bank, **II** 307; **IV** 91

Capital Bank N.A., **16** 162

Shared Medical Systems Corporation, 14 432–34

Shared Technologies Inc., **12** 71

Shared Use Network Systems, Inc., **8** 311

Sharon Steel Corp., **I** 497; **7** 360–61; **8** 536; **13** 158, 249

Sharon Tank Car Corporation, **6** 394; **25** 169

Sharp & Dohme, Incorporated, **I** 650; **11** 289, 494

Sharp Corporation, **I** 476; **II 95–96**; **III** 14, 428, 455, 480; **6** 217, 231; **11** 45; **12** 447–49 (upd.); **13** 481; **16** 83; **21** 123; **22** 197

The Sharper Image Corporation, 10 486–88; **23** 210; **26** 439

Sharples Co., **I** 383

Sharples Separator Co., **III** 418–20

Shasta Beverages. *See* National Beverage Corp.

Shaw Communications Inc., **26** 274

Shaw Industries, 9 465–67; **19** 274, 276; **25** 320

Shaw's Supermarkets, Inc., **II** 658–59; **23** 169

Shawell Precast Products, **14** 248

Shawinigan Water and Power Company, **6** 501–02

Shawmut National Corporation, **II** 207; **12** 31; **13 464–68**

Shea's Winnipeg Brewery Ltd., **I** 268; **25** 280

Sheaffer Group, **23** 54, 57

Shearson Hammill & Company, **22** 405–06

Shearson Lehman Brothers Holdings Inc., **I** 202; **II** 398–99, 450, 478; **III** 319; **8** 118; **9 468–70 (upd.)**; **10** 62–63; **11** 418; **12** 459; **15** 124, 463–64

Shearson Lehman Hutton Holdings Inc., **II** 339, 445, **450–52**; **III** 119; **9** 125; **10** 59, 63; **17** 38–39

Shedd's Food Products Company, **9** 318

Sheepbridge Engineering, **III** 495

Sheffield Banking Co., **II** 333

Sheffield Motor Co., **I** 158; **10** 292

Sheffield Twist Drill & Steel Co., **III** 624

Shekou Container Terminals, **16** 481

Shelby Insurance Company, **10** 44–45

Shelby Steel Tube Co., **IV** 572; **7** 550

Shelby Williams Industries, Inc., 14 435–37

Shelco, **22** 146

Sheldahl Inc., 23 432–35

Shelf Life Inc. *See* King Kullen Grocery Co., Inc.

Shell. *See* Shell Transport and Trading Company p.l.c. *and* Shell Oil Company.

Shell Australia Ltd., **III** 728

Shell BV, **IV** 518

Shell Chemical Corporation, **IV** 410, 481, 531–32, 540; **8** 415; **24** 151

Shell Coal International, **IV** 532

Shell Forestry, **21** 546

Shell France, **12** 153

Shell Nederland BV, **V** 658–59

Shell Oil Company, **I** 20, 26, 569; **III** 559; **IV** 392, 400, 531, **540–41**; **6** 382, 457; **8** 261–62; **11** 522; **14** 25, **438–40 (upd.)**; **17** 417; **19** 175–76; **21** 546; **22** 274; **24** 520; **25** 96, 232, 469; **26** 496

Shell Transport and Trading Company p.l.c., **I** 605; **II** 436, 459; **III** 522, 735; **IV** 363, 378–79, 381–82, 403, 412, 423, 425, 429, 440, 454, 466, 470, 472, 474,

484–86, 491, 505, 508, **530–32**, 564. *See also* Royal Dutch Petroleum Company *and* Royal Dutch/Shell.

Shell Western E & P, **7** 323

Shell Winning, **IV** 413–14

Sheller-Globe Corporation, I 201–02; **17** 182

Shelly Brothers, Inc., **15** 65

Shenley Laboratories, **I** 699

Shepard Warner Elevator Co., **III** 467

Shepard's Citations, Inc., **IV** 636–37

Shepherd Hardware Products Ltd., **16** 357

Shepherd Plating and Finishing Company, **13** 233

Shepler Equipment Co., **9** 512

Sheraton Corp. of America, **I** 463–64, 487; **III** 98–99; **11** 198; **13** 362–63; **21** 91

Sherborne Group Inc./NH Holding Inc., **17** 20

Sherbrooke Paper Products Ltd., **17** 281

Sheridan Bakery, **II** 633

Sheridan Catheter & Instrument Corp., **III** 443

Sherix Chemical, **I** 682

Sherr-Gold, **23** 40

Sherritt Gordon Mines, **7** 386–87; **12** 260

The Sherwin-Williams Company, **III** 744–46; **8** 222, 224; **11** 384; **12** 7; **13** 469–71 (upd.); **19** 180; **24** 323

Sherwood Medical Group, **I** 624; **III** 443–44; **10** 70

SHI Resort Development Co., **III** 635

ShianFu Optical Fiber, **III** 491

Shibaura Seisakusho Works, **I** 533; **12** 483

Shieh Chi Industrial Co., **19** 508

Shields & Co., **9** 118

Shikoku Drinks Co., **IV** 297

Shikoku Electric Power Company, Inc., V 718–20

Shikoku Machinery Co., **III** 634

Shimotsuke Electric Railway Company, **6** 431

Shimura Kako, **IV** 63

Shin Nippon Machine Manufacturing, **III** 634

Shin-Nihon Glass Co., **I** 221

Shinano Bank, **II** 291

Shinko Electric Co., Ltd., **IV** 129

Shinko Rayon Ltd., **I** 363; **V** 369–70

Shinriken Kogyo, **IV** 63

Shintech, **11** 159–60

Shinwa Tsushinki Co., **III** 593

Shiomi Casting, **III** 551

Shionogi & Co., Ltd., **I** 646, 651; **III** 60–61; **11** 90, 290; **17** 435–37 (upd.)

Ship 'n Shore, **II** 503; **9** 156–57; **10** 324

Shipley Co. Inc., **26** 425

Shipowners and Merchants Tugboat Company, **6** 382

Shipper Group, **16** 344

Shipstad & Johnson's Ice Follies, **25** 313

Shiro Co., Ltd., **V** 96

Shirokiya Co., Ltd., **V** 199

Shiseido Company, Limited, **II** 273–74, 436; **III** 46, 48, **62–64**; **8** 341, 343; **22** 485–88 (upd.)

Shockley Electronics, **20** 174

Shoe Carnival Inc., 14 441–43

Shoe Corp., **I** 289

Shoe Supply, Inc., **22** 213

Shoe Works Inc., **18** 415

Shoe-Town Inc., **23** 310

Shohin Kaihatsu Kenkyusho, **III** 595

Shoman Milk Co., **II** 538

Shonac Corp., **14** 427

Shonco, Inc., **18** 438

Shoney's, Inc., **7** 474–76; **14** 453; **19** 286; **23** 436–39 (upd.)

Shop & Go, **II** 620

Shop 'n Bag, **II** 624

Shop 'n Save, **II** 669, 682; **12** 220–21

Shop Rite Foods Inc., **II** 672–74; **7** 105; **19** 479. *See also* Big V Supermarkets, Inc.

ShopKo Stores Inc., **II** 669–70; **18** 505–07; **21 457–59**

Shoppers Food Warehouse Corporation, **16** 159, 161

Shoppers World Stores, Inc. *See* LOT$OFF Corporation.

ShopRite, **24** 528

Shopwell/Food Emporium, **II** 638; **16** 247, 249

Shore Manufacturing, **13** 165

Short Aircraft Co., **I** 50, 55, 92

Short Brothers, **24** 85

Shoseido Co., **17** 110

Shoshi-Gaisha, **IV** 320

Shotton Paper Co. Ltd., **IV** 350

Showa Aircraft Industry Co., **I** 507–08

Showa Aluminum Corporation, **8** 374

Showa Bank, **II** 291–92

Showa Bearing Manufacturing Co., **III** 595

Showa Cotton Co., Ltd., **IV** 442

Showa Denko, **I** 493–94; **II** 292; **IV** 61; **24** 324–25

Showa Marutsutsu Co. Ltd., **8** 477

Showa Paper Co., **IV** 268

Showa Photo Industry, **III** 548

Showa Products Company, **8** 476

Showa Shell Sekiyu K.K., **II** 459; **IV** 542–43

ShowBiz Pizza Time, Inc., **12** 123; **13** 472–74; **15** 73; **16** 447

Showboat, Inc., 19 400–02

Showcase of Fine Fabrics, **16** 197

Showerings, **I** 215

Showtime, **II** 173; **7** 222–23; **9** 74; **23** 274–75, 391, 503; **25** 329–30

Shredded Wheat Co., **II** 543; **7** 366

Shreve and Company, **12** 312

Shreveport Refrigeration, **16** 74

Shrewsbury and Welshpool Old Bank, **II** 307

Shu Uemura, **III** 43

Shubert Organization Inc., 24 437–39

Shubrooks International Ltd., **11** 65

Shueisha, **IV** 598

Shuford Mills, Inc., **14** 430

Shugart Associates, **6** 230; **8** 466; **22** 189

Shull Lumber & Shingle Co., **IV** 306

Shun Fung Ironworks, **IV** 717

Shunan Shigyo Co., Ltd., **IV** 160

Shurgard Storage Centers of Seattle, **21** 476

Shuttleworth Brothers Company. *See* Mohawk Industries, Inc.

Shuwa Corp., **22** 101

SHV Holdings N.V., **IV** 383; **14** 156

SI Holdings Inc., **10** 481

SIAS, **19** 192

SIAS-MPA, **I** 281

SIATA S.p.A., **26** 363

Sibco Universal, S.A., **14** 429

Siboney Shoe Corp., **22** 213

SIBV/MS Holdings, **IV** 295; **19** 226

Sicard Inc., **I** 185

SICC. *See* Univision Communications Inc.

INDEX TO INDUSTRIES

Index to Industries

Boc Group PLC, I
BOC Group plc, 25 (upd.)
Brenntag AG, 8; 23 (upd.)
Cabot Corporation, 8
Cambrex Corporation, 16
Celanese Corporation, I
Chemcentral Corporation, 8
Chemi-Trol Chemical Co., 16
Ciba-Geigy Ltd., I; 8 (upd.)
The Clorox Company, 22 (upd.)
Crompton & Knowles, 9
DeKalb Genetics Corporation, 17
The Dexter Corporation, I; 12 (upd.)
The Dow Chemical Company, I; 8 (upd.)
DSM, N.V, I
E.I. Du Pont de Nemours & Company, I; 8
   (upd.); 26 (upd.)
Eastman Chemical Company, 14
Ecolab, Inc., I; 13 (upd.)
English China Clays plc, 15 (upd.)
ERLY Industries Inc., 17
Ethyl Corporation, I; 10 (upd.)
Ferro Corporation, 8
First Mississippi Corporation, 8
Formosa Plastics Corporation, 14
Fort James Corporation, 22 (upd.)
G.A.F., I
Georgia Gulf Corporation, 9
Great Lakes Chemical Corporation, I; 14
   (upd.)
Hawkins Chemical, Inc., 16
Hercules Inc., I; 22 (upd.)
Hoechst A.G., I; 18 (upd.)
Hoechst Celanese Corporation, 13
Huls A.G., I
Huntsman Chemical Corporation, 8
IMC Fertilizer Group, Inc., 8
Imperial Chemical Industries PLC, I
International Flavors & Fragrances Inc., 9
Koppers Industries, Inc., I; 26 (upd.)
L'air Liquide, I
Lawter International Inc., 14
LeaRonal, Inc., 23
Lubrizol Corporation, I
M.A. Hanna Company, 8
Mallinckrodt Group Inc., 19
Mitsubishi Chemical Industries, Ltd., I
Mitsui Petrochemical Industries, Ltd., 9
Monsanto Company, I; 9 (upd.)
Morton International Inc., 9 (upd.)
Morton Thiokol, Inc., I
Nagase & Company, Ltd., 8
Nalco Chemical Corporation, I; 12 (upd.)
National Distillers and Chemical
   Corporation, I
National Sanitary Supply Co., 16
NCH Corporation, 8
NL Industries, Inc., 10
Nobel Industries AB, 9
Novacor Chemicals Ltd., 12
NutraSweet Company, 8
Olin Corporation, I; 13 (upd.)
OM Group, Inc., 17
Pennwalt Corporation, I
Perstorp A.B., I
Petrolite Corporation, 15
Praxair, Inc., 11
Quantum Chemical Corporation, 8
Reichhold Chemicals, Inc., 10
Rhône-Poulenc S.A., I; 10 (upd.)
Rohm and Haas Company, I; 26 (upd.)
Roussel Uclaf, I; 8 (upd.)
The Scotts Company, 22
Sequa Corp., 13
Shanghai Petrochemical Co., Ltd., 18
Solvay & Cie S.A., I; 21 (upd.)
Sterling Chemicals, Inc., 16

Sumitomo Chemical Company Ltd., I
Terra Industries, Inc., 13
Teva Pharmaceutical Industries Ltd., 22
TOTAL S.A., 24 (upd.)
Union Carbide Corporation, I; 9 (upd.)
Univar Corporation, 9
Vista Chemical Company, I
Witco Corporation, I; 16 (upd.)
Zeneca Group PLC, 21

CONGLOMERATES

Accor SA, 10
AEG A.G., I
Alcatel Alsthom Compagnie Générale
   d'Electricité, 9
Alco Standard Corporation, I
Alfa, S.A. de C.V., 19
Allied-Signal Inc., I
AMFAC Inc., I
Aramark Corporation, 13
Archer-Daniels-Midland Company, I; 11
   (upd.)
Arkansas Best Corporation, 16
Barlow Rand Ltd., I
Bat Industries PLC, I
Bond Corporation Holdings Limited, 10
BTR PLC, I
C. Itoh & Company Ltd., I
Cargill Inc., 13 (upd.)
CBI Industries, Inc., 7
Chemed Corporation, 13
Chesebrough-Pond's USA, Inc., 8
CITIC Pacific Ltd., 18
Colt Industries Inc., I
Daewoo Group, 18 (upd.)
Deere & Company, 21 (upd.)
Delaware North Companies Incorporated, 7
Desc, S.A. de C.V., 23
The Dial Corp., 8
El Corte Inglés Group, 26 (upd.)
Elders IXL Ltd., I
Engelhard Corporation, 21 (upd.)
Farley Northwest Industries, Inc., I
First Pacific Company Limited, 18
Fisher Companies, Inc., 15
Fletcher Challenge Ltd., 19 (upd.)
FMC Corporation, I; 11 (upd.)
Fuqua Industries, Inc., I
GIB Group, 26 (upd.)
Gillett Holdings, Inc., 7
Grand Metropolitan PLC, 14 (upd.)
Great American Management and
   Investment, Inc., 8
Greyhound Corporation, I
Grupo Carso, S.A. de C.V., 21
Grupo Industrial Bimbo, 19
Gulf & Western Inc., I
Hankyu Corporation, 23 (upd.)
Hanson PLC, III; 7 (upd.)
Hitachi Ltd., I; 12 (upd.)
Hutchison Whampoa Ltd., 18
IC Industries, Inc., I
Inchcape plc, 16 (upd.)
Ingram Industries, Inc., 11
Instituto Nacional de Industria, I
International Controls Corporation, 10
International Telephone & Telegraph
   Corporation, I; 11 (upd.)
Istituto per la Ricostruzione Industriale, I
Jardine Matheson Holdings Limited, I; 20
   (upd.)
Jason Incorporated, 23
Jefferson Smurfit Group plc, 19 (upd.)
Justin Industries, Inc., 19
Kanematsu Corporation, 24 (upd.)
Kao Corporation, 20 (upd.)
Katy Industries, Inc., I

Kesko Ltd (Kesko Oy), 8
Kidde, Inc., I
KOC Holding A.S., I
Koninklijke Nedlloyd N.V., 26 (upd.)
Koor Industries Ltd., 25 (upd.)
K2 Inc., 16
The L.L. Knickerbocker Co., Inc., 25
Lancaster Colony Corporation, 8
Lear Siegler, Inc., I
Lefrak Organization Inc., 26
Leucadia National Corporation, 11
Litton Industries, Inc., I; 11 (upd.)
Loews Corporation, I; 12 (upd.)
Loral Corporation, 8
LTV Corporation, I
Marubeni Corporation, 24 (upd.)
Marubeni K.K., I
MAXXAM Inc., 8
McKesson Corporation, I
Menasha Corporation, 8
Metallgesellschaft AG, 16 (upd.)
Metromedia Co., 7
Minnesota Mining & Manufacturing
   Company (3M), I; 8 (upd.); 26 (upd.)
Mitsubishi Corporation, I; 12 (upd.)
Mitsui Bussan K.K., I
The Molson Companies Limited, I; 26
   (upd.)
Montedison S.p.A., 24 (upd.)
NACCO Industries, Inc., 7
National Service Industries, Inc., 11
Nichimen Corporation, 24 (upd.)
Nissho Iwai K.K., I
Norsk Hydro A.S., 10
Ogden Corporation, I
Onex Corporation, 16
Orkla A/S, 18
Park-Ohio Industries Inc., 17
Pentair, Inc., 7
Preussag AG, 17
Pubco Corporation, 17
Pulsar Internacional S.A., 21
The Rank Organisation Plc, 14 (upd.)
Red Apple Group, Inc., 23
Rubbermaid Incorporated, 20 (upd.)
Samsung Group, I
San Miguel Corporation, 15
Sara Lee Corporation, 15 (upd.)
ServiceMaster Inc., 23 (upd.)
Sime Darby Berhad, 14
Standex International Corporation, 17
Stinnes AG, 23 (upd.)
Sudbury Inc., 16
Sumitomo Corporation, I; 11 (upd.)
Swire Pacific Ltd., I; 16 (upd.)
Talley Industries, Inc., 16
Teledyne, Inc., I; 10 (upd.)
Tenneco Inc., I; 10 (upd.)
Textron Inc., I
Thomas H. Lee Co., 24
Thorn Emi PLC, I
Thorn plc, 24
TI Group plc, 17
Time Warner Inc., IV; 7 (upd.)
Tomen Corporation, 24 (upd.)
Tomkins plc, 11
Toshiba Corporation, I; 12 (upd.)
Tractebel S.A., 20
Transamerica Corporation, I; 13 (upd.)
The Tranzonic Cos., 15
Triarc Companies, Inc., 8
TRW Inc., I; 11 (upd.)
Unilever PLC, II; 7 (upd.)
Valhi, Inc., 19
Valores Industriales S.A., 19
Veba A.G., I; 15 (upd.)
Viacom Inc., 23 (upd.)
Virgin Group PLC, 12

ENGINEERING & MANAGEMENT SERVICES

ENTERTAINMENT & LEISURE

FINANCIAL SERVICES: BANKS

FOOD SERVICES & RETAILERS

HEALTH & PERSONAL CARE PRODUCTS

HEALTH CARE SERVICES

Watts Industries, Inc., 19
WD-40 Company, 18
Welbilt Corp., 19
Wellman, Inc., 8
Weru Aktiengesellschaft, 18
West Bend Co., 14
Western Digital Corp., 25
Whirlpool Corporation, III; 12 (upd.)
White Consolidated Industries Inc., 13
Wilson Sporting Goods Company, 24
Windmere Corporation, 16
WinsLoew Furniture, Inc., 21
WMS Industries, Inc., 15
Wolverine Tube Inc., 23
Wood-Mode, Inc., 23
Woodward Governor Co., 13
Wyman-Gordon Company, 14
Yamaha Corporation, III; 16 (upd.)
York International Corp., 13
Zero Corporation, 17
Zippo Manufacturing Company, 18

MATERIALS

AK Steel Holding Corporation, 19
American Biltrite Inc., 16
American Colloid Co., 13
American Standard Inc., III
Ameriwood Industries International Corp., 17
Apogee Enterprises, Inc., 8
Asahi Glass Company, Limited, III
Blessings Corp., 19
Blue Circle Industries PLC, III
Boral Limited, III
British Vita PLC, 9
Carborundum Company, 15
Carlisle Companies Incorporated, 8
Cemex SA de CV, 20
Chargeurs International, 21 (upd.)
Compagnie de Saint-Gobain S.A., III; 16 (upd.)
Cookson Group plc, III
Corning Incorporated, III
CSR Limited, III
Dal-Tile International Inc., 22
The David J. Joseph Company, 14
The Dexter Corporation, 12 (upd.)
ECC Group plc, III
84 Lumber Company, 9
English China Clays plc, 15 (upd.)
Envirodyne Industries, Inc., 17
Feldmuhle Nobel A.G., III
Fibreboard Corporation, 16
Foamex International Inc., 17
Formica Corporation, 13
GAF Corporation, 22 (upd.)
The Geon Company, 11
Giant Cement Holding, Inc., 23
Granite Rock Company, 26
Groupe Sidel S.A., 21
Harbison-Walker Refractories Company, 24
Harrisons & Crosfield plc, III
"Holderbank" Financière Glaris Ltd., III
Howmet Corp., 12
Ibstock plc, 14
Joseph T. Ryerson & Son, Inc., 15
Lafarge Coppée S.A., III
Lehigh Portland Cement Company, 23
Manville Corporation, III; 7 (upd.)
Matsushita Electric Works, Ltd., III; 7 (upd.)
Medusa Corporation, 24
Mitsubishi Materials Corporation, III
Nippon Sheet Glass Company, Limited, III
OmniSource Corporation, 14
Onoda Cement Co., Ltd., III
Owens-Corning Fiberglass Corporation, III

Pilkington plc, III
Pioneer International Limited, III
PPG Industries, Inc., III
Redland plc, III
RMC Group p.l.c., III
Schuff Steel Company, 26
Sekisui Chemical Co., Ltd., III
Shaw Industries, 9
The Sherwin-Williams Company, III; 13 (upd.)
Simplex Technologies Inc., 21
Sommer-Allibert S.A., 19
Southdown, Inc., 14
Spartech Corporation, 19
Ssangyong Cement Industrial Co., Ltd., III
Sun Distributors L.P., 12
Tarmac PLC, III
Toto, Ltd., III
Toyo Sash Co., Ltd., III
Ube Industries, Ltd., III
USG Corporation, III; 26 (upd.)
Vulcan Materials Company, 7
Walter Industries, Inc., III
Waxman Industries, Inc., 9

MINING & METALS

A.M. Castle & Co., 25
Alcan Aluminium Limited, IV
Alleghany Corporation, 10
Allegheny Ludlum Corporation, 8
Aluminum Company of America, IV; 20 (upd.)
AMAX Inc., IV
Amsted Industries Incorporated, 7
Anglo American Corporation of South Africa Limited, IV; 16 (upd.)
ARBED S.A., IV, 22 (upd.)
Arch Mineral Corporation, 7
Armco Inc., IV
ASARCO Incorporated, IV
Battle Mountain Gold Company, 23
Bethlehem Steel Corporation, IV; 7 (upd.)
Birmingham Steel Corporation, 13
Boart Longyear Company, 26
British Coal Corporation, IV
British Steel plc, IV; 19 (upd.)
Broken Hill Proprietary Company Ltd., IV, 22 (upd.)
Brush Wellman Inc., 14
Carpenter Technology Corporation, 13
Chaparral Steel Co., 13
Christensen Boyles Corporation, 26
Cleveland-Cliffs Inc., 13
Coal India Limited, IV
Cockerill Sambre Group, IV; 26 (upd.)
Coeur d'Alene Mines Corporation, 20
Cold Spring Granite Company, 16
Commercial Metals Company, 15
Companhia Vale do Rio Duce, IV
CRA Limited, IV
Cyprus Amax Minerals Company, 21
Cyprus Minerals Company, 7
Daido Steel Co., Ltd., IV
De Beers Consolidated Mines Limited/De Beers Centenary AG, IV; 7 (upd.)
Degussa Group, IV
Dofasco Inc., IV; 24 (upd.)
Echo Bay Mines Ltd., IV
Engelhard Corporation, IV
Fansteel Inc., 19
Freeport-McMoRan Inc., IV; 7 (upd.)
Fried. Krupp GmbH, IV
Gencor Ltd., IV, 22 (upd.)
Geneva Steel, 7
Gold Fields of South Africa Ltd., IV
Handy & Harman, 23
Hecla Mining Company, 20

Hemlo Gold Mines Inc., 9
Heraeus Holding GmbH, IV
Hitachi Metals, Ltd., IV
Hoesch AG, IV
Homestake Mining Company, 12
The Hudson Bay Mining and Smelting Company, Limited, 12
Imetal S.A., IV
Inco Limited, IV
Industrias Penoles, S.A. de C.V., 22
Inland Steel Industries, Inc., IV; 19 (upd.)
Johnson Matthey PLC, IV; 16 (upd.)
Kaiser Aluminum & Chemical Corporation, IV
Kawasaki Steel Corporation, IV
Kennecott Corporation, 7
Kerr-McGee Corporation, 22 (upd.)
Klockner-Werke AG, IV
Kobe Steel, Ltd., IV; 19 (upd.)
Koninklijke Nederlandsche Hoogovens en Staalfabrieken NV, IV
Laclede Steel Company, 15
Layne Christensen Company, 19
Lonrho Plc, 21
The LTV Corporation, 24 (upd.)
Lukens Inc., 14
Magma Copper Company, 7
The Marmon Group, IV; 16 (upd.)
MAXXAM Inc., 8
Metaleurop S.A., 21
Metallgesellschaft AG, IV
Minerals and Metals Trading Corporation of India Ltd., IV
Minerals Technologies Inc., 11
Mitsui Mining & Smelting Co., Ltd., IV
Mitsui Mining Company, Limited, IV
National Steel Corporation, 12
NERCO, Inc., 7
Newmont Mining Corporation, 7
Nichimen Corporation, IV
Nippon Light Metal Company, Ltd., IV
Nippon Steel Corporation, IV; 17 (upd.)
Nisshin Steel Co., Ltd., IV
NKK Corporation, IV
Noranda Inc., IV; 7 (upd.)
North Star Steel Company, 18
Nucor Corporation, 7; 21 (upd.)
Oglebay Norton Company, 17
Okura & Co., Ltd., IV
Oregon Metallurgical Corporation, 20
Oregon Steel Mills, Inc., 14
Park Corp., 22
Peabody Coal Company, 10
Peabody Holding Company, Inc., IV
Pechiney, IV
Peter Kiewit Sons' Inc., 8
Phelps Dodge Corporation, IV
The Pittston Company, IV; 19 (upd.)
Placer Dome Inc., 20
Pohang Iron and Steel Company Ltd., IV
Potash Corporation of Saskatchewan Inc., 18
Quanex Corporation, 13
Reliance Steel & Aluminum Co., 19
Republic Engineered Steels, Inc., 7; 26 (upd.)
Reynolds Metals Company, IV
Rio Tinto plc, 19 (upd.)
Rouge Steel Company, 8
The RTZ Corporation PLC, IV
Ruhrkohle AG, IV
Saarberg-Konzern, IV
Salzgitter AG, IV
Sandvik AB, IV
Schnitzer Steel Industries, Inc., 19
Southwire Company, Inc., 8; 23 (upd.)
Steel Authority of India Ltd., IV
Stelco Inc., IV

PUBLISHING & PRINTING

REAL ESTATE

RETAIL & WHOLESALE

RUBBER & TIRE

NOTES ON CONTRIBUTORS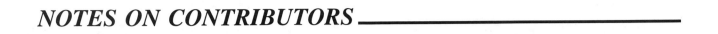

Notes on Contributors

BENBOW-PFALZGRAF, Taryn. Freelance editor, writer, and consultant in the Chicago area.

BIANCO, David. Freelance writer.

BROWN, Susan Windisch. Freelance writer and editor.

COHEN, M. L. Novelist and freelance writer living in Paris.

COVELL, Jeffrey L. Freelance writer and corporate history contractor.

DERDAK, Thomas. Freelance writer and adjunct professor of philosophy at Loyola University of Chicago.

DORGAN, Charity Anne. Detroit-based freelance writer.

FROMM, J. D. Educator and author of teaching and planning resources.

HALASZ, Robert. Former editor in chief of *World Progress* and *Funk & Wagnalls New Encyclopedia Yearbook*; author, *The U.S. Marines* (Millbrook Press, 1993).

INGRAM, Frederick C. South Carolina-based business writer who has contributed to *GSA Business, Appalachian Trailway News*, the *Encyclopedia of Business*, the *Encyclopedia of Global Industries*, the *Encyclopedia of Consumer Brands*, and other regional and trade publications.

KNIGHT, Judson. Freelance writer.

LEMIEUX, Gloria A. Freelance writer and editor living in Nashua, New Hampshire.

MALLETT, Daryl F. Freelance writer and editor; actor; contributing editor and series editor at The Borgo Press;

series editor of SFRA Press's *Studies in Science Fiction, Fantasy and Horror*; associate editor of Gryphon Publications and for *Other Worlds Magazine*; founder and owner of Angel Enterprises, Jacob's Ladder Books, and Dustbunny Productions.

MOZZONE, Terri. Minneapolis-based freelance writer specializing in corporate profiles.

PASSAGE, Robert Alan. Freelance writer.

PEIPPO, Kathleen. Minneapolis-based freelance writer.

ROTHBURD, Carrie. Freelance technical writer and editor, specializing in corporate profiles, academic texts, and academic journal articles.

SALAMIE, David E. Part-owner of InfoWorks Development Group, a reference publication development and editorial services company.

UHLE, Frank. Ann Arbor-based freelance writer; movie projectionist, disc jockey, and staff member of *Psychotronic Video* magazine.

WALDEN, David M. Freelance writer and historian in Salt Lake City; adjunct history instructor at Salt Lake City Community College.

WERNICK, Ellen D. Freelance writer and editor.

WEST, Melissa. Freelance writer.

WHITELEY, Laura E. Freelance writer based in Germantown, Tennessee.

WOODWARD, A. Freelance writer.